ICCA
CONGRESS SERIES NO. 20

INTERNATIONAL ARBITRATION CONGRESS
SYDNEY, 15-18 APRIL 2018

Wolters Kluwer

INTERNATIONAL COUNCIL
FOR COMMERCIAL ARBITRATION

EVOLUTION AND ADAPTATION: THE FUTURE OF INTERNATIONAL ARBITRATION

GENERAL EDITORS:
JEAN KALICKI AND MOHAMED ABDEL RAOUF

with the assistance of the
Permanent Court of Arbitration
Peace Palace, The Hague

Published by:
Kluwer Law International B.V.
PO Box 316
2400 AH Alphen aan den Rijn
The Netherlands
Website: lrus.wolterskluwer.com

Sold and distributed in North, Central and South America by:
Wolters Kluwer Legal & Regulatory U.S.
7201 McKinney Circle
Frederick, MD 21704
United States of America
Email: customer.service@wolterskluwer.com

Sold and distributed in all other countries by:
Air Business Subscriptions
Rockwood House
Haywards Heath
West Sussex
RH16 3DH
United Kingdom
Email: international-customerservice@wolterskluwer.com

Printed on acid-free paper.

ISBN 978-94-035-2041-4

e-Book: ISBN 978-94-035-2043-8
web-PDF: ISBN 978-94-035-2044-5

Printed in the United Kingdom.

Preface

ICCA Congress Series no. 20 comprises the proceedings of the XXIV ICCA Congress, held in Sydney, Australia, on 15-18 April 2018. We thank the ICCA Sydney Host Committee for their hard work and gracious hospitality, which created such a well-organized and welcoming setting for the substantive work of the Congress participants.

The theme of the Congress, "Evolution and Adaptation: The Future of International Arbitration", was chosen with great care. We wished to highlight arbitration as a "living organism" which has adapted in the past to various substantive and practical challenges, and that today – under attack from various quarters – might need to demonstrate its adaptability again. Under this theme, the Programme Committee developed a range of plenary and parallel sessions to address the evolving needs of users, the impact of the rapidly changing face of technology, the expectations of the public, and the convergence and divergence of different aspects of legal traditions and cultures.

As Jean Kalicki explained in her opening remarks on the first day of the Congress, a 1996 book entitled *Dealing in Virtue: International Commercial Arbitration and the Construction of a Transnational Legal Order*[1] had described a great transition in the field of arbitration. The authors' thesis was that what had begun as an informal, settlement-oriented system, once dominated by European academics whom they called the "grand old men", had shifted to a more formalized and litigious practice, dominated by US or multinational law firms and what the authors called the "arbitration technocrats". The authors wondered about the future, particularly whether it might see the growth of regional arbitration centers. But there were other changes on the horizon that the authors did not foresee in 1996. The index to the book contained only a single reference to bilateral investment treaties – and also only a single reference to the topic of women in arbitration. Each of those solitary listings led to a single footnote reference, not even a discussion in the body of the book itself.

Yet if someone today were to write a new book about the few decades of arbitration since *Dealing in Virtue* was published, it would tell a very different story – including about change in the subject matter of disputes and diversity in the composition of counsel teams and arbitrators. One need only look at today's headlines, not only in the specialized arbitration press but also in the mainstream media, to see how investor-State dispute settlement has come to dominate a good portion of the public debate about arbitration. And one need only look at the delegates to the XXIV ICCA Congress, who hailed from some sixty-two different countries, to understand the globalization of arbitration practice. Thanks both to generational change, and to the concerted efforts of arbitral institutions and community leaders, the field also has made major strides in gender diversification.

But the story of evolution will not end today either, because arbitration is an adaptive and not a static mechanism. If another book on our community is published a few decades from now, the tale it will tell will be different again from whatever story we might tell today. What that future story will look like will depend in large part on how

---

1. Yves DEZALAY and Bryant G. GARTH, *Dealing in Virtue: International Commercial Arbitration and the Construction of a Transnational Legal Order* (University of Chicago Press 1996).

the members of our community, and the next generation of thought leaders, manage to address some of the major challenges and opportunities that are coming to the fore today.

So what is it about our field that makes it so open to evolution and adaptation? What are the main pressure points today, and the unmet needs of stakeholders? What are the opportunities for expansion to new sectors and new audiences? What are the drivers for change, what are the obstacles, and what are the risks? And equally important, what are the core principles that should never be lost? These were the topics of the XXIV ICCA Congress, and of the sixteen separate panels that were developed by our dedicated Programme Committee.

There was a method to our organization of the individual panels, which is reflected also in the Chapters of this Congress Book. First, after the opening keynote address on 16 April 2018 organized by the Host Committee, we set the stage for the Congress theme with an initial plenary session examining the underlying notion of lawmaking in arbitration. How much authority do various actors – tribunals, arbitral institutions, professional organizations, national legislators, courts, and international organizations like ICCA – have to create or to change the rules by which disputes are resolved? Where does that authority come from, and what is the source of its legitimacy? These plenary questions led naturally into a lunchtime program at which four leading arbitrators shared their personal reflections on evolution and adaptation, discussing the past, present and future of their own careers, and of arbitration itself.

The next day and a half featured six time slots offering concurrent programming, allowing delegates to sample from among a twelve-course "arbitration smorgasbord". On the first afternoon, we started with two parallel panels on reform ideas for investment treaties and for commercial arbitration respectively, and moved to parallel programs on rethinking party autonomy in choosing decision-makers and on the important issue of "equality of arms", which requires special attention in light of the increasing expense of arbitration proceedings. The following morning, 17 April 2018, in one room we offered consecutive panels discussing two different aspects of the increasingly public nature of arbitrations: the role of public entities even in commercial disputes, and the questions of confidentiality, transparency and public participation. Meanwhile, in the other room we focused on practical suggestions for building better proceedings, first with a panel on rethinking conventional wisdom in organizing proceedings, and second with one asking what lessons might be learned from others, particularly commercial courts and specialized arbitration regimes. That afternoon, in one room we focused on the changing impact of technology, first with some show-and-tell on new tools that might facilitate arbitration, and then with the question of technological disruption, including the increasingly vital issue of cybersecurity. In the other room, we offered an ICCA "rapid response" panel tackling some of the hottest topics of the last few months, informed by recent headlines and by suggestions from delegates themselves. That panel was followed by the first ever ICCA "New Voices" panel, with substantive presentations from four next-generation scholars and practitioners chosen through a public competition based on short abstracts. Their topics included arbitration of disputes in conflict and post-conflict zones, inter-generational blame and praise in investment arbitration, the emergence of sovereign wealth funds as arbitration participants, and fresh approaches to briefing damages in investment cases.

Finally, we closed the Congress on 18 April 2018 with a two-part plenary on "new frontiers in arbitration". Our panelists offered an ICCA "mission to the future", asking – for both new types of claims and new types of stakeholders – whether arbitration might venture before long into strange and exciting worlds, where no arbitrator has gone before.

As Co-Chairs of the Programme Committee, we recognize that none of this dynamic programme would have been possible without the concerted and sustained efforts of many people. The ideas began at the XXIII ICCA Congress in Mauritius, where we sat down with ICCA President Donald Donovan and Vice President Meg Kinnear to begin discussing possible themes for the XXIV Congress in Sydney. Thereafter, we were the beneficiaries of a very active and thoughtful Programme Committee consisting of Chiann Bao, Ndanga Kamau, Makhdoom Ali Khan, Brandon Malone, Wendy Miles, Ina Popova, Stephan Schill, James Spigelman, Monty Taylor, Byung-Choi (B.C.) Yoon, and Eduardo Zuleta. Some of these Programme Committee members later served as moderators or session chairs for the panels they helped develop,[2] but we wish to thank particularly our additional moderators and session chairs (Lisa Bingham, Stavros Brekoulakis, Paul Cohen, Stephen Drymer, Susan Franck, Gabrielle Kaufmann-Kohler, Mark Kantor, Meg Kinnear, Carolyn Lamm, and Dietmar Prager), as well as the rapporteurs who greatly supported their efforts (Marina Kofman, Mallory Silberman, and Laura Sinisterra). We also extend a special word of thanks to the members of the ICCA Bureau (Lise Bosman, Lisa Bingham, Lucy Burns, and Lauren Voges), without whom this Congress simply could not have been possible.

In addition, we wish to acknowledge the contributions of the Young ICCA co-chairs who served on the review committee to select the "New Voices" panelists (Gardar Gunnarsson, Sylvia Tonova, Nhu-Hoang Tran Trang and Tolu Obamuroh). In general, one of the innovations of the XXIV ICCA Congress was that selection of panelists drew significantly on two public calls for expressions of interest, one specifically for the New Voices panel but the other for the Congress sessions as a whole. We received hundreds of well-developed ideas from around the globe, and we could have filled many Congresses over with the talent and enthusiasm we received. We worked hard to make sure the final composition featured a good balance of experience and new faces, and that it also reflected ICCA's broad constituency. We are proud to report that our final list of speakers included nationals of thirty-five different countries, which says a lot about the globalization of arbitration and of ICCA itself. We were also particularly pleased that 45 percent of our speakers were women, which was a record for ICCA and perhaps for a major arbitration conference more generally. We did not try to calculate the average age of our speakers – which would have required asking some delicate questions! – but we believe the Congress featured more younger faces than in the past. This was important to us, as any program about evolution and adaptation must feature the voices of tomorrow, and not just the ones of yesterday and today.

Lastly, one of the things that make ICCA Congresses different from all others is the emphasis on scholarship. With the exception of a few panels, ICCA speakers are expected to prepare publication-ready papers before the Congress in order to make a

2. The moderators, session chairs, panelists and rapporteurs for each individual panel are listed in the Table of Contents of this Congress Book.

serious contribution to the field. Our panelists took that responsibility very seriously, as you will see from the final papers published in this Congress Book. We also had the invaluable support of the Editorial Staff of ICCA Publications, in particular the tireless efforts of Ms. Alice Siegel (Assistant Managing Editor), in preparing this volume for publication. We are grateful to the Permanent Court of Arbitration and its Secretary-General, H.E. Hugo Hans Siblesz, for hosting the ICCA Staff at the headquarters of its International Bureau at the Peace Palace. The continued support of the entire administrative and technical staff of the PCA is much appreciated as well.

Looking ahead, we are excited for the next ICCA Congress, which will take place in Edinburgh, Scotland, from 10-13 May 2020, and feature the theme, "Arbitration's Age of Enlightenment?". Information on the XXV ICCA Congress will be posted on the ICCA website, <www.arbitration-icca.org>, as well as at <http://icca2020.scot>.

Jean Kalicki and Mohamed Abdel Raouf
October 2019

XXV ICCA CONGRESS

10 - 13 May 2020

Edinburgh, Scotland

"Arbitration's Age of Enlightenment?"

For program and registration information:

http://icca2020.scot
www.arbitration-icca.org

For the Young ICCA Event:
www.arbitration-icca.org/YoungICCA/Home.html

TABLE OF CONTENTS

Luncheon Panel: Personal Reflections of Leading Arbitrators

Arbitration Challenged Part I

Reforming Substantive Obligations in Investment Treaties and Conditions of Access to Investment Arbitration

Reforming Commercial Arbitration in Response to Legitimacy Concerns

Arbitration Involving Public Bodies and Public Interests: Salient Issues

Part I:
The Increasing Participation of Public Entities in International Arbitration

Moderator: *Stavros Brekoulakis*
Speakers: *Adriana Braghetta, Paolo Di Rosa, Reza Mohtashami QC and Marie Talašová*

Part II:
Confidentiality, Transparency and Public Participation: Too Far or Not Far Enough?

Moderator: *Byung–Chol (B.C.) Yoon*
Speakers: *Stanimir A. Alexandrov, Chester Brown, Constantine Partasides QC and Patrick W. Pearsall*

Building Better Arbitration Proceedings: Practical Suggestions

Part I:
Revisiting Conventional Wisdom in the Organization of Arbitral Proceedings

Moderator: *Chiann Bao*
Speakers: *Funke Adekoya, SAN, Fuyong Chen, Nayla Comair-Obeid, Klaus Reichert SC*

Part II:
Efficiency and the Lessons to Be Learned from Other Dispute Resolution Frameworks

Moderator: *Stephen L. Drymer*
Session Chair: *Lisa Bingham*
Speakers: *Henry C. Alvarez, The Honourable P.A. Bergin SC, Flip Petillion and Shen Hongyu*

The Moving Face of Technology

Part I:
Technology as Facilitation

Moderator: *Paul H. Cohen*
Speakers: *Hugh Carlson, Gabrielle Nater-Bass and Rashda Rana*

Part II:
Technology as Disruption

Moderator: *Brandon Malone*
Speakers: *Hagit Muriel Elul, Matthew Kuperholz, Alana Maurushat, Sophie Nappert, Carsten van de Sande and Edna Sussman*

Hot Topics and New Voices

Part I: Hot Topics

Moderator: *Mark Kantor*
Speakers: *Joongi Kim, Judith Levine and Natalie L. Reid*
Rapporteur: *Marina Kofman*

Part II: New Voices

Moderator: *Monty Taylor*
Speakers: *Jawad Ahmad, Lucas Bastin, Solomon Ebere, Samantha Lord Hill*

Plenary: New Frontiers in International Arbitration

Part I: Potential of Arbitration Involving New Types of Claims

Moderator: *Wendy Miles*
Speakers: *Massimo V. Benedettelli, Annette Magnusson, Ana Stanič and S.I. Strong*

Opening Keynote Address

Commercial and Investor-State Arbitration: The Importance of Recognizing Their Differences

James L.B. Allsop AO[*]

TABLE OF CONTENTS PAGE

Much has been written and said in recent years about perceived problems in international arbitration. The very theme of this important Congress is the reassessment of, and introspection about, basal conceptions and structures of the process of arbitration. Concerns about investor-state dispute settlement (ISDS) provisions in international investment treaties have been an area of particular focus, and the debate about investment arbitration has become prominent both within the arbitration community, and in government, the academy and the press. These issues, by and large, are focused on national sovereignty and public accountability issues, and are arising at a time of increased fragmentation of, and scepticism toward, globalized trade. International commercial arbitration has also been the subject of criticism and hard evaluation. Many of the concerns in relation to international commercial arbitration are expressed in language similar to concerns about ISDS arbitration, but that superficial similarity should not be allowed to disguise the important differences between the two types of dispute resolution, and the quite different issues involved.

Let me begin by saying something of ISDS.

I. CONCERNS REGARDING INVESTOR-STATE DISPUTE SETTLEMENT

The perceived problems with investment arbitration have been summarized in numerous works by judges, scholars and bodies such as the European Union.[1] These include: a

* Chief Justice of the Federal Court of Australia.

1. See, e.g., Stephen M. SCHWEBEL, "Keynote Address: In Defence of Bilateral Investment Treaties" in *International Arbitration – Legitimacy: Myths, Realities and Challenges*, ICCA Congress Series no. 18 (Kluwer 2012) at p. 6; Jeswald W. SALACUSE, "The Emerging Global Regime for Investment", 51 Harvard International Law Journal (2010) p. 428 at pp. 469-470; Robert FRENCH AC, "Investor-State Dispute Settlement – A Cut Above the Courts?" (Paper presented to the Supreme and Federal Courts Judges' Conference, Darwin, 9 July 2014) at pp. 3-4, 7-9 (henceforth FRENCH 2014); Robert FRENCH AC, "ISDS – Litigating the Judiciary", 81

perception of illegitimacy of ISDS in its impacts on national sovereignty, due to the lack of public accountability; the affectation of the capacity of states to legislate on issues of public policy; perceived bias or unsuitability of arbitrators of private commercial background adjudicating public disputes involving public policy; so-called "issue conflict" as arbitrators accept repeated appointments, or continue to act as counsel, and deal with the same issue more than once; issues of consistency and predictability and the lack of a developed system of precedent; the process of the appointment of arbitrators; the limited ability to review the substance of awards; and the costs of investment arbitration.

In an illustration of the tone of some of the coverage that ISDS has attracted in the press, *The Economist* went so far in 2014 to describe ISDS as "a special right to apply to a secretive tribunal of highly paid corporate lawyers for compensation whenever a government passes law…". It cited as concerns "the secretive nature of the arbitration process [and the fact that] the lack of any requirement to consider precedent allows plenty of scope for creative adjudications".[2]

The Hon Robert French AC, when Chief Justice of the High Court of Australia, expressed what, to my mind, is the fundamental issue of concern about investment arbitration:[3] the implications of ISDS arbitration for "national sovereignty, democratic governance and the rule of law within domestic legal systems".[4] Such concerns led the Council of Chief Justices of Australia (of which, I should say, I was and am a member) to write to the Commonwealth Attorney-General requesting that Australia:[5]

> "have regard to the possibility that, absent suitable qualifications, arbitral processes might be invoked to call into question the decisions of domestic courts either by submissions that such decisions are breaches of an investment treaty or alternatively seeking findings based upon propositions inconsistent with such decisions".

As the former Chief Justice said:[6]

> "The public interest dimensions of arbitral decisions arising out of [investment treaties], particularly where they involve State regulatory action or a judicial decision, means that the public policy debate will continue and continue to focus upon questions of national sovereignty, the privileging of foreign investors and the democratic legitimacy of the arbitral process."

Arbitration (2015) p. 288 (henceforth FRENCH 2015); Sir Vivian RAMSEY, "The Challenges to International Arbitration", Asian Dispute Review (2017) p. 54; UNCITRAL, "Possible Reform of Investor-State Dispute Settlement (ISDS) Submission from the European Union" (12 December 2017) UN Doc A/CN.9/WG.III/WP.145 at 12.

2. The Economist, "The Arbitration Game: Investor-State Dispute Settlement" (11 October 2014) <http://www.economist.com/news/finance-and-economics/2163756-governments-are-souring-treaties-protect-foreign-investors-arbitration>.
3. See FRENCH, 2014, *op. cit.*, fn. 1; FRENCH, 2015, *op. cit.*, fn. 1.
4. FRENCH, 2014, *op. cit.*, fn. 1 at pp. 3-4.
5. FRENCH, 2015, *op. cit.*, fn. 1 at p. 3.
6. FRENCH, 2015, *op. cit.*, fn. 1 at p. 9.

Such rule of law concerns have also been noted by Lord Neuberger, the former President of the Supreme Court of the United Kingdom, as based on the fact that ISDS can have the outcome of an arbitral tribunal being able to review public policy or domestic law that has already been adjudicated upon by the court of a sovereign state.[7]

It should be noted at this point (as explicitly recognized in the letter from the Council of Chief Justices) that many of the concerns can be addressed at the point of treaty negotiation.

Well-known examples of ISDS claims have been used to justify these concerns. One example is the arbitral claim that was brought by Chevron against Ecuador, and the tribunal's interim award requiring Ecuador to suspend enforcement or recognition of a US$ 9 billion judgment against Chevron.[8] Another is the International Centre for Settlement of Investment Disputes (ICSID) claim by Eli Lilly against Canada that contended that a decision by the Supreme Court of Canada interpreting the validity provisions of the Canadian Patent Act violated provisions of the North American Free Trade Agreement (NAFTA).[9] It should be noted, however, that case was decided in favour of Canada and an award in its favour was issued on 17 March 2017.[10] A third was the claim brought by Philip Morris Asia under Australia's investment treaty with Hong Kong in 2011 seeking compensation of more than one billion dollars for expropriation of trade marks caused by the enactment of the Australian Government's plain packaging tobacco legislation.[11] Philip Morris, together with a number of other tobacco companies, lost a constitutional challenge to the legislation in the High Court of Australia in 2012.[12] The legislation was found not to be expropriatory. The arbitral claim constituted a challenge to an Australian public policy that had been declared lawful and not confiscatory by the highest court in Australia. The arbitration occurred under the United Nations Commission on International Trade Law (UNCITRAL) Rules and under the auspices of the Permanent Court of Arbitration. Then Chief Justice French's concerns about ISDS were expressed in the context of that claim being on foot. That claim was ultimately rejected on jurisdictional grounds by the arbitral tribunal in December 2015.[13] In a redacted version of the award published in 2016, the tribunal found that the claim constituted an abuse of rights, finding that Philip Morris had engaged in corporate restructuring when it was foreseeable that the government would introduce plain packaging legislation and that the "principal, if not sole, purpose of the restructuring was

7. Lord NEUBERGER, "Keynote Speech" 81 Arbitration (2015) p. 427 at pp. 430-431.
8. See FRENCH, 2015, *op. cit.*, fn. 1 at pp. 7-8; NEUBERGER, *op. cit.*, fn. 7 at pp. 430-431.
9. International Centre for Settlement of Investment Disputes, *Eli Lilly and Company v. Canada* (ICSID Case No. UNCTT/14/2) <https://icsid.worldbank.org/en/Pages/cases/casedetail.aspx?CaseNo=UNCT/14/2>; Global Affairs Canada, "Cases Filed Against the Government of Canada – *Eli Lilly and Company v. Government of Canada*" <https://www.international.gc.ca/trade-agreements-accords-commerciaux/topics-domaines/disp-diff/eli.aspx?lang=eng>; Amokura KAWHARU and Luke NOTTAGE, "Renouncing Investor-State Dispute Settlement in Australia, then New Zealand: Déjà vu" (University of Sydney Law School, Legal Studies Research Paper Series No 18/03, February 2018) at pp. 18, 31; NEUBERGER, *op. cit.*, fn. 7 at pp. 430-431; FRENCH, 2015, *op. cit.*, fn. 1 at p. 16.
10. Global Affairs Canada, *op. cit.*, fn. 9.
11. Tobacco Plain Packaging Act 2011 (Cth).
12. *JT International SA v. Commonwealth* [2012] HCA 43; 250 CLR 1.
13. See the discussion by KAWHARU and NOTTAGE, *op. cit.*, fn. 9 at pp. 25-26.

to gain protection under the Treaty in respect of the very measures that form[ed] the subject matter of the present arbitration".[14]

The claim brought by Philip Morris was brought during the process of negotiation for the proposed Transpacific Partnership (TPP), which was proposed to include ISDS.[15] The argument over the TPP was part of a broader zeitgeist against globalization that in some ways has grown even more aggressive in recent years. Following the *Philip Morris* case, the Australian Government that was then in office withdrew its support for ISDS in trade negotiations,[16] and the New Zealand government has now also adopted that position.[17] In the negotiations for the Comprehensive and Progressive Agreement for Trans-Pacific Partnership (CPTPP), the successor to the TPP (after it was abandoned by the Trump Administration) that was concluded on 8 March 2018,[18] New Zealand also attempted in negotiations to exclude ISDS from the agreement though such a position was rejected by the other parties.[19] It is not appropriate for me to make any comment on those policy positions, but I suggest it shows the prominence of the debate and the level, perhaps, of concern about ISDS.

The implications of ISDS for public policy and national sovereignty have driven arguments about the need for transparency in investment arbitration, on the basis that the public nature of these disputes means that there should be a capacity for, at least, public awareness and potentially public involvement.[20] Four principles of transparency have been proposed: publication of documents, public hearings, the capacity for other State parties to an investment treaty such as an investor's home state to participate, and the ability of non-State parties to participate as amici curiae.[21]

---

14. *Philip Morris Asia Limited v. Commonwealth of Australia* (PCA Case No 2012-12), Award on Jurisdiction and Admissibility (17 December 2015) <https://www.pcacases.com/web/sendAttach/1711> at [585]-[590].
15. KAWHARU and NOTTAGE, *op. cit.*, fn. 9 at p. 3. They also discuss ISDS claims that have been brought by Australian corporations against other nations, including Indonesia and Thailand: KAWHARU and NOTTAGE, *op. cit.*, fn. 9 at pp. 34-38.
16. KAWHARU and NOTTAGE, *op. cit.*, fn. 9 at p. 40.
17. KAWHARU and NOTTAGE, *op. cit.*, fn. 9 at p. 40.
18. For the text of the CPTPP, see Australian Department of Foreign Affairs and Trade, "TPP-11 Text and Associated Documents" (21 February 2018) <http://dfat.gov.au/trade/ agreements/not-yet-in-force/tpp/official-documents/Pages/official-documents.aspx>.
19. New Zealand Ministry of Foreign Affairs and Trade, "Comprehensive and Progressive Agreement for Trans-Pacific Partnership: National Interest Analysis" <https://www.mfat.govt.nz/assets/CPTPP/Comprehensive-and-Progressive-Agreement-for-Trans-Pacific-Partnership-CPTPP-National-Interest-Analysis.pdf> at pp. 38-39. See also the detailed analysis by KAWHARU and NOTTAGE, *op. cit.*, fn. 9 at pp. 6-13.
20. See Taida Begic SARKINOVIC, "Investor-State Arbitration: Between Private and Public Interests", 12 Manchester Journal of International Economic Law (2016) p. 250 at pp. 253-254; James D. FRY and Odysseas G. REPOUSIS, "Towards a New World for Investor-State Arbitration Through Transparency", 48 NYU Journal of International Law and Politics (2016) p. 795 at pp. 804-808. It should be noted that there are also transparency debates in international commercial arbitration, though with different motivations: see Catherine A. ROGERS, "Transparency in International Commercial Arbitration", 54 Kansas Law Review (2006) pp. 1301.
21. FRY and REPOUSSIS, *op. cit.*, fn. 20 at pp. 808-811. See also a slightly different formulation in Matthew CARMODY, "Overturning the Presumption of Confidentiality: Should the UNCITRAL Rules on Transparency Be Applied to International Commercial Arbitration?", 19 International

There have been several developments toward greater transparency in investment arbitrations. They include the publication by UNCITRAL in 2014 of the UNCITRAL Rules on Transparency in Treaty-based Investor-State Arbitration that apply to investment treaties concluded after 1 April 2014 and where arbitrations are conducted under UNCITRAL rules. UNCITRAL has subsequently developed its Rules on Transparency into the United Nations Convention on Transparency in Treaty-based Investor-State Arbitration (the Mauritius Convention) which was opened for signature on 17 March 2015 and entered into force on 18 October 2017.[22] The Mauritius Convention applies the UNCITRAL Rules on Transparency to investment treaties concluded before 1 April 2014.[23] The preamble of the Convention speaks of "recognizing the need for provisions on transparency in the settlement of treaty-based investor-State disputes to take account of the public interest involved in such arbitrations". The UNCITRAL Rules provide for: publication to the public of information at the commencement of arbitral proceedings as to the parties, the economic sector involved and the treaty under which the claim is brought;[24] the publication of documents to the public such as the notice of arbitration, the response, statement of claim, statement of defence, written submissions, exhibit and witness lists;[25] submissions by third persons;[26] submissions by non-disputing parties to the treaty;[27] public hearings for oral argument (with provision for *in camera* arrangements for parts of hearings where necessary);[28] a regime for exceptions to transparency in the context of confidential or protected information or to protect the integrity of the arbitration.[29]

Nevertheless, despite these steps the debates about ISDS, and international arbitration, have, if anything, accelerated, most recently by the contribution of the European Court of Justice.[30]

Trade and Business Law Review (2016) p. 96 at pp. 103-104: "the publication of information about arbitral proceedings; access to various documents from the arbitration; the involvement of third parties in the conduct of proceedings; and access to hearings".

22. See UNCITRAL, "Status – United Nations Convention on Transparency in Treaty-based Investor-State Arbitration (New York, 2014) <http://www.uncitral.org/uncitral/en/uncitral_%20texts/arbitration/2014Transparency_Convention_status.html>. While the treaty has entered into force, as at 6 April 2018 there are only three State parties that have ratified it: Mauritius, Canada and Switzerland. Twenty-two State parties have signed the Mauritius Convention, including Australia, the United States, the United Kingdom, France, Germany, and Italy.
23. Mauritius Convention, Arts. 1(1), 2.
24. Mauritius Convention, Art. 2.
25. Mauritius Convention, Art. 3.
26. Mauritius Convention, Art. 4.
27. Mauritius Convention, Art. 5.
28. Mauritius Convention, Art. 6.
29. Mauritius Convention, Art. 7.
30. *Slovak Republic v. Achmea BV* (Court of Justice of the European Union, Case C-284/16, 6 March 2018).

II. THE ISDS LANDSCAPE

As at 2017, there were estimated to be over 3,300 investment treaties in existence.[31] As this audience will be well aware, since the first bilateral investment treaty in 1959, these treaties have been developed in order to encourage foreign investment and to provide an enforceable mechanism for protecting these foreign investments, in the form of investment arbitration.[32] The rationale for its introduction involved a critical issue in world power relationships. In his insightful opening address at the 2012 ICCA Congress in Miami, Judge Schwebel described the context in which investment arbitration developed, in the wake of the expropriation of Anglo-Iranian Oil by the Mossadegh government in 1951 in Persia and debates about permanent sovereignty over natural resources in the United Nations in the 1960s and 1970s. Judge Schwebel pointed out that investment arbitration was designed to prevent "gunboat diplomacy" and characterized the "entitlement to international arbitration as one of the most progressive developments in the procedure of international law of the last fifty years".[33]

The development of ISDS included the conclusion of the Convention on the Settlement of Investment Disputes between States and Nationals of Other States (the ICSID Convention) in 1965, under which the majority of investment arbitrations are undertaken. The conclusion of ICSID and the numerous bilateral treaties that utilize ICSID for dispute resolution superseded the indirect remedy of diplomatic protection and completed the progression from the gunboat diplomacy of the late nineteenth and early twentieth century to the now well-established system of direct private rights of enforcement against sovereign states by way of investment arbitration, a remarkable flowering of the protection by the rule of law of commercial rights. In the criticisms of ISDS this history should be recalled.

Statistics collected by the United Nations Conference on Trade and Development (UNCTAD) reveal the growth in, and characteristics of, investor-state arbitrations.[34] They reveal that there have been 817 known investor-state cases. During the period of January to July 2017, there were at least 35 new cases brought, against 32 different countries. A total of 69 new cases were brought in 2016. Eighty per cent of the investment arbitrations commenced in 2017 were brought under bilateral investment treaties, while the remaining 20 percent were under treaties with investment provisions such as the Energy Charter Treaty and NAFTA.

---

31. Jeswald W. SALACUSE, "Of Handcuffs and Signals: Investment Treaties and Capital Flows to Developing Countries", 58 Harvard International Law Journal (2017) p. 127 at p. 127.
32. See Jeswald W. SALACUSE, "The Emerging Global Regime for Investment", 51 Harvard International Law Journal (2010) p. 428; SCHWEBEL, *op. cit.*, fn. 1; SALACUSE, 2017, *op. cit.*, fn. 31 at pp. 130-131; Gordon SMITH, "An Introduction to Investor-State Arbitrations", 13 International Trade and Business Law Review (2010) p. 3 at p. 3.
33. SCHWEBEL, *op. cit.*, fn. 1 at p. 5. See also, for a general discussion of the development of investment treaties and ISDS: Gus VAN HARTEN, "Investment Treaty Arbitration and Public Law" (Oxford University Press 2007) at pp. 12-44.
34. United Nations Conference on Trade and Development (UNCTAD), Special Update on Investor-State Dispute Settlement: Facts and Figures (November 2017) <https://unctad.org/en/PublicationsLibrary/diaepcb2017d7_en.pdf>.

Out of the 530 cases decided as at 31 July 2017, approximately one third were decided in favour of states and a quarter in favour of investors. The others settled or were discontinued. The most frequent domicile of claimants is the United States (152 cases) and the most frequent respondent is Argentina, reflecting the economic turmoil in that nation in the early 2000s (60 cases). Over the 30-year period from 1987 to 2017, 61 percent of all known cases were conducted under ICSID, with 31% conducted under UNCITRAL arbitration rules. Eighty per cent of awards over this period were unanimous, and approximately 500 different individuals have been involved as arbitrators in investment arbitrations, with UNCTAD noting a "small number" of individuals being involved in more than 30 arbitrations each.[35]

These statistics give one a picture of the overall investment arbitration landscape, and of the prevalence and characteristics of investment arbitrations. Nevertheless, despite the noble goals of ISDS, and perhaps because of the prevalence of investment arbitration, concerns about ISDS and investment arbitration have continued to increase in prominence.

III. DISTINGUISHING INTERNATIONAL COMMERCIAL ARBITRATION FROM INVESTMENT ARBITRATION

While debates about the legitimacy of investment arbitration have been occurring, and to a certain extent arising out of them, there has been a broader critique of international arbitration as a dispute resolution system.

The difficulty with this broader criticism is that far too often the two different types of international arbitration – commercial arbitration and investment arbitration – have been elided in the discussion of problems with international arbitration generally. Some of the concerns do overlap, but commercial arbitration and investment arbitration are fundamentally different, as are the reasons for the most prominent criticisms of each.

Although they share procedures, especially since a number of investment arbitrations occur under UNCITRAL rules and employ much of the same infrastructure, they address different matters. Investment arbitration involves a dispute between an investor and a sovereign state. It generally arises under the terms of an investment treaty and often may involve a challenge or assessment of the consequences of government policy. The dispute is one fundamentally involving a state in its sovereign capacity. In contrast, commercial arbitration involves a dispute between parties acting in their private capacity and arises out of a commercial transaction.[36] This is so even if one of the parties is governmental in character.

Though ISDS awards may, at the enforcement stage, make use of the structures of international commercial arbitrations,[37] the award arises through a process initiated

35. UNCTAD, *op. cit.*, fn. 34.

36. A distinction that is also adopted by commentators: see, e.g., CARMODY, *op. cit.*, fn. 21 at p. 100. SARKONOVIC, *op. cit.*, fn. 20 at p. 250, has identified that that the nature of investment disputes "as between a private party ... and a sovereign State raise a number of issues not present in traditional commercial arbitration".

37. See, e.g., International Arbitration Act 1974 (Cth) Pt IV, for enforcement of awards made under ICSID, and Pt II for enforcement of awards made under UNCITRAL rules.

under the relevant investment treaty that has been created in public international law to which the claimant is not a party. By contrast, in a commercial arbitration the arbitrator's power to decide is a solely contractual one conferred by the decision of the parties to submit the relevant dispute to arbitration.[38]

It is important, however, to remember, in the context of ISDS, that such disputes do not solely involve matters of public international law and treaty interpretation, or the effect of government policy on private business operations, but also require an understanding of the proper behaviour of government decision-making processes and the attendant principles of public law. ISDS is not solely a dispute about the interpretation of the bare text of an international treaty without regard to considerations of proper governance and the proper realm and extent of legitimate public policy. Thus an understanding of or familiarity with principles that attend the validity and invalidity of government decisions is essential for the proper conduct of ISDS dispute resolution.

While there may be debates to be had about the legitimacy of ISDS – and I express no view other than identifying some aspects of them – we should not transmogrify concerns about ISDS into concerns about international commercial arbitration. The sovereignty and rule of law issues associated with ISDS, due to its inherent "public" nature, make it distinct from international commercial arbitration.[39] These considerations do not impinge upon commercial arbitration, and so criticisms concerning international commercial arbitration need to be considered from its own perspective, and with an appreciation of the proper nature of commercial arbitration as opposed to investment arbitration.

Lord Neuberger has identified nine reasons for why commercial parties have a preference for arbitration over litigation: the greater number of disputes demanding international arbitration; the high professional standards of arbitrators; the fact that arbitrators can be selected for their particular expertise; distrust of national courts in the context of international disputes; the enforceability of arbitral awards; greater speed; less expense; confidentiality; and finality.[40] The reality of some of those advantages can be debated. To them, however, can be added, a sense of control of the dispute, in particular with the absence of one or two levels of appeal.

---

38. See generally *Hancock Prospecting Pty Ltd v. Rinehart* [2017] FCAFC 170 at [397]; *TCL Airconditioner (Zhongshan) Co Ltd v. Judges of the Federal Court of Australia* [2013] HCA 5; 251 CLR 533. See also James ALLSOP and Clyde CROFT, "The Role of the Courts in Australia's Arbitration Regime" (Paper delivered at the Commercial CPD Seminar Series, Melbourne, 11 November 2015).
39. Though it has been suggested that, despite its "public" nature, the "still dominant conceptualisation of investor-state dispute settlement [is] as a form of commercial arbitration and private justice": Stephan W. SCHILL, "Editorial: The Mauritius Convention on Transparency", 16 Journal of World Investment & Trade (2015) p. 201 at p. 203.
40. NEUBERGER, *op. cit.*, fn. 7 at p. 429. Cf. recent data that indicates cost and delay as some of the "worst characteristics of international arbitration": Queen Mary University of London, White & Case 2015 International Arbitration Survey: Improvements and Innovations in International Arbitration <http://www.arbitration.qmul.ac.uk/media/arbitration/docs/2015_International_Arbitration_Survey.pdf> at 7.

IV. CHALLENGES FOR INTERNATIONAL COMMERCIAL ARBITRATION

The questioning of international commercial arbitration can be seen in four broad categories that overlap and relate to each other: first, confidentiality as a feature asserted to undermine legitimacy; secondly, the asserted negative influence on the development of the law by the lack of precedent; thirdly, concern over the characteristics and practice of arbitrators; and fourthly, unacceptable cost and delay.

One immediately sees a superficial similarity with legitimacy concerns of ISDS: the need for transparency and precedent, hence, the Mauritius Convention; and the complaint as to private commercial arbitrators dealing with public policy issues. But the problems and solutions for commercial arbitration reveal the very different nature of the subject and the very different nature of the problem.

The public nature of ISDS has been put forward as a justification for the movement toward transparency and disclosure in investment arbitration. There are also public policy concerns attending confidentiality in commercial arbitration. The Australian High Court's decision in *Plowman* suggests that information pertaining to a commercial arbitration that was in the "public interest" ought to be disclosed.[41] Lord Neuberger has spoken of the role international commercial arbitration plays in support of the rule of law internationally and that, having regard to this, there is an argument that arbitration should not always be confidential.[42] Some commentators have even gone so far as to suggest that the UNCITRAL Rules on Transparency should be applied to international commercial arbitration on an "opt out basis", as this would "increase the legitimacy of the system".[43] One cannot avoid, however, the reality that confidentiality in many cases is a critical demand of the parties and a feature of commercial arbitration that is a significant attraction. Insistence upon "transparency" (whatever that may mean in any given circumstance) in commercial arbitration in furtherance of some (not fully articulated) public policy may only drive parties to settle their differences outside arbitration and reduce the contribution of arbitration to the rule of law.

The assertion that the prevalence of international commercial arbitration has had a negative impact upon the law has been espoused most prominently by Lord Thomas.[44] He described arbitration as a "serious impediment to the development of the common law".[45] This view can perhaps be seen to be premised on the view that only courts make law and that arbitrators do not make any contribution to its development.

Lord Thomas was instrumental in establishing the Standing International Forum of Commercial Courts which met for the first time in London in May 2017. It is a gathering of heads of jurisdiction and experienced commercial judges from commercial courts all over the world. It aims to revitalize and strengthen the effective resolution of commercial disputes in commercial courts. I should add that the Federal Court of Australia is one of the courts in the Forum and I am on the Steering Committee. It aims

41. *Esso Australia Resources Ltd v. Plowman* [1995] HCA 19; 183 CLR 10 at 31, 35, 48.
42. NEUBERGER, *op. cit.*, fn. 7 at [26].
43. CARMODY, *op. cit.*, fn. 21 at pp. 168-178. See also ROGERS, *op. cit.*, fn. 20.
44. Lord THOMAS, "Developing Commercial Law Through the Courts: Rebalancing the relationship between the courts arbitration" (Paper presented as the BAILII Lecture, 9 March 2016) at [6], [22]-[23].
45. Lord THOMAS, *op. cit.*, fn. 44 at [6].

to draw together the experience of commercial courts all around the world to enhance on a global level the skill of commercial courts. From its meetings there will develop an exchange of ideas about techniques and procedures to improve curial resolutions of commercial disputes.

I will say a little more on the question of arbitrators making law in a moment. It suffices to say at this point that the publication of redacted reasons of arbitral awards of importance on legal questions would go a long way to solving Lord Thomas' expressed concern without impinging necessarily upon the rights of privacy and confidentiality of the parties to their dispute. It may also burnish the reputation of the arbitral process, of the arbitrator and of the institution connected with the arbitration.

As has been pointed out by others, arbitrators can be seen to make law.[46] Publication of arbitral awards occurs, for instance, under the auspices of some arbitral institutions, such as the International Chamber of Commerce (ICC) and the London Court of International Arbitration (LCIA).[47] Also, in the field of maritime arbitration, there would be little doubt that arbitrators make a contribution to the development of maritime law. Reports of arbitrations conducted under London Maritime Arbitrators Association (LMAA) rules are reported in the *Lloyd's Maritime Law Newsletter* and used as precedents in arbitrations and in court. Similarly, the Society of Maritime Arbitrators in New York publishes the full text of its arbitral awards on LexisNexis.[48] The issue, thus, is one of practice and expectation. ICCA's own publication of case law and its educational work are further examples of public dissemination of arbitral law.[49]

This question, however, raises the topic of the nature of the law in arbitration. This is a topic in itself: What is the place of law in arbitration? It is not a silly question. With the removal of any review on a question of law in the UNCITRAL Model Law, the freedom of arbitrators to adjudicate even upon nominated systems of law is real. The legitimacy of the parties choosing non-national law, such as principles of international commercial law,[50] makes the nature of law in commercial arbitration a subject that is not self-evident. The ability of arbitrators of skill and experience to recognize and apply primary rules of law, fundamental international principles as well as secondary specific rules laid down by national statute and precedent means that if their decisions are public arbitrators can contribute to the rule of law just as judges do and the academy does.

Law is not merely the declared rules of a sovereign state. Law involves primary rules, principles and values that are timeless and not constrained by political or geographic boundaries. Commercial law is founded upon honesty, good faith and fair dealing, the requisite degree of relevant trust, a rejection of abuse of power and unconscionability, and faithfulness to the bargain freely and properly entered. That law can be non-national

---

46. Doug JONES AO, "Arbitrators as Law-Makers", 6 Indian Journal of Arbitration Law (2018) p. 19.
47. JONES, *op. cit.*, fn. 46 at pp. 24-27.
48. See information at Society of Maritime Arbitrators, "Find the SMA on Lexis-Nexis" (10 April 2018) <http://www.smany.org/lexis-nexis-find.html>.
49. See International Council for Commercial Arbitration, "Publications" (2018) <https://www.arbitration-icca.org/publications.html>.
50. See, e.g., *Channel Tunnel Group Ltd v. Balfour Beatty Construction Ltd* [1992] 1 QB 656 and [1993] AC 334.

and non-binding was most eloquently expressed by Justice Jackson in *Lauritzen v. Larsen*, reflecting upon the real existence of international maritime law, where he said:[51]

> "... courts of this and other commercial nations have generally deferred to a non-national or international maritime law of impressive maturity and universality. It has the force of law not from extraterritorial reach of national laws, nor from abdication of its sovereign powers by any nation, but from acceptance by common consent of civilized communities of rules designed to foster amicable and workable commercial relations."

Turning to the arbitrators themselves, there have been a suite of concerns raised about arbitrators. These include concerns about the repeated appointments by the same parties of the same arbitrators, the prospect of so-called "issue conflict" presented by arbitrators acting in subsequent arbitrations where the same issues arise and issues about the lack of recourse to courts available after the rendering of an award. The concerns also include the inability of popular arbitrators to be available on a timely basis to hear arbitrations with sufficient promptness desired by commercial parties. This extends the timeline of disposition, and, axiomatically therefore, the costs.

The same issues appear to arise in respect of investment arbitration, where they are arguably more significant. In the Queen Mary University of London White & Case 2015 International Arbitration Survey respondents were asked whether, in the context of both international commercial arbitration and investment arbitration, there should be greater regulation of the appointment of arbitrators where an arbitrator had previously taken a view on an issue in the arbitration, had been repeatedly nominated as an arbitrator in multiple arbitrations by the parties, or had been repeatedly nominated in multiple arbitrations by counsel. The percentage of respondents answering "yes" was higher for investment arbitrations, though not substantially so in respect of the latter two issues.[52]

It is worth making at least three points about these concerns. First, they would be diminished if there were regular publication of redacted reasons. Secondly, so-called issue conflict may be a concern to parties, but it is not necessarily apprehended bias. A judge and an arbitrator are not prevented from hearing a case because they have decided some legal aspect on a prior occasion. The relevant apprehension is not that one might lose, but that one will not have the dispute heard with an open mind. That said, if one does not know that one has a mind to change one may not appreciate the task before that particular arbitrator. Once again, publication of redacted reasons might alleviate this difficulty. Thirdly, the arbitration community has taken steps to address issues such as this, through measures including the International Bar Association's Guidelines on Conflicts of Interest in International Arbitration[53] adopted in 2014. (I pause momentarily to make a plea about the misuse of the phrase "conflicts of interest". There is no such thing. One's interests never conflict. Interest can conflict with duty. Duty can conflict with duty. Questions of apprehended bias may arise. Documents such as the IBA's

51. *Lauritzen v. Larsen* 345 US 571 (1953) at 581-582.
52. Queen Mary University of London, *op. cit.*, fn. 40 at pp. 39-40.
53. International Bar Association, IBA Guidelines on Conflicts of Interest in International Arbitration (23 October 2014).

Guidelines on Conflicts reflect, I think, the development of common principles attending apprehended bias rather than the questions of duty and interest or duty and duty conflicting. There is a danger in muddled language.)

There are significant challenges for international commercial arbitration in relation to dealing with cost, expense and delay. I have referred to this on previous occasions as the increasing "industrialization" of arbitral procedure and practice.[54] I adopted this term in preference to that of what I saw as the somewhat offensive term of "judicialization" used by some commentators.[55] The reason I did so, and why I took some offence, is because there is nothing inherently more costly or inefficient about litigation in a commercial court compared to arbitration. Good commercial courts can be swift and highly efficient. The real problem is a cultural one that leads to the generation of unnecessary process-driven costs.[56] The nature of the complaint is that arbitration has developed the same process-driven costs that accompany poorly managed litigation.[57] This complaint is borne out by the results of the 2015 International Arbitration survey which identified cost, "lack of insight into arbitrators' efficiency" and lack of speed as three of the most significant criticisms of international arbitration.[58]

The problem of industrialization needs to be resolved in both arbitration and litigation. It is a cancer in the body of both. It may be an exaggeration to describe industrialization as an existential threat to arbitration, but the fact is that if arbitration cannot exist as an efficient and cost-effective means of dispute resolution then it will simply not find favour with commercial parties.

The essential problem (in both litigation and arbitration) is that parties and their advisors have often ceased to view litigation and arbitration as a species of problem solving. I will return to this momentarily.

The issues facing international commercial arbitration are shared with investment arbitration. To a large extent, what the debate about the legitimacy of ISDS has done is reveal a shortcoming with the process of arbitration itself – investment and commercial – that members of the arbitration community should address.

Public interest is a common feature of ISDS and international commercial arbitration. But the public interest in international commercial arbitration is not sovereignty and public policy. Rather, it is the deep importance of international commercial arbitration in assisting to provide a global, cross-border dispute resolution system that operates in conjunction with, supported and supervised by, the dispute resolution mechanisms

---

54. See James ALLSOP, "National Courts and Arbitration: Collaboration or Competition?", 81 Arbitration (2015) p. 434 at p. 437 (henceforth ALLSOP 2015); James ALLSOP, "International Arbitration and Conformity with International Standards of Due Process and the Rule of Law" (Paper presented at the ICCA Congress, Mauritius, 2016, published in *International Arbitration and the Rule of Law: Contribution and Conformity*, ICCA Congress Series no. 19 (Kluwer 2017) at p. 792 (henceforth ALLSOP 2016).
55. See, e.g., T.J. STIPANOVICH, "Arbitration: The 'New Litigation', University of Illinois Law Review (2010) p. 1.
56. See ALLSOP, 2015, *op. cit.*, fn. 54 at p. 437; ALLSOP, 2016, *op. cit.*, fn. 54 at p. 792.
57. ALLSOP, 2016, *op. cit.*, fn. 54 at p. 792, citing STIPANOVICH, *op. cit.*, fn. 55.
58. Queen Mary University of London, *op. cit.*, fn. 40 at p. 2. See also the discussion of this issue in RAMSEY, *op. cit.*, fn. 1 at pp. 1-2.

provided by commercial courts.[59] This public role for international commercial arbitration is what Lord Neuberger was referring to when he spoke of the function of arbitration in maintaining the rule of law over international commerce and, therefore, of the need for skilled arbitrators and sophisticated arbitral processes.[60] The public interest in maintaining skill and confidence in that system is what should drive any reassessment in relation to international commercial arbitration, not the public interest and sovereignty considerations that attend ISDS.

V. SOME POTENTIAL SOLUTIONS TO THE CRITICISMS OF INTERNATIONAL COMMERCIAL ARBITRATION

An appreciation of the differences between commercial arbitration and investment arbitration to which I have referred can contribute to a discussion of solutions to criticisms of commercial arbitration.

Confidentiality is undoubtedly an important reason why commercial parties opt for arbitration in relation to many of their commercial disputes. Given that international commercial arbitration does not attract the same sovereignty and public legitimacy issues as investment arbitrations, I would suggest that there is no principled basis to require the implementation of transparency standards such as are contained in the Mauritius Convention into international commercial arbitration.[61] That instrument provides for the public disclosure of documents pertaining to the arbitration, the openness of hearings to the public and the ability of third parties to intervene. The public aspect of commercial arbitration should be focused upon supporting its efficiency and the public's, including the commercial community's, confidence in its fair and just operation. That fundamentally important public policy consideration does not, it seems to me, demand transparency of the kind reflected in the Mauritius Convention.

However, to the extent that the absence of reasons for award can be seen to potentially undermine the confidence in individual arbitrators and prevent the development of publicly available jurisprudence that degree of confidentiality may be seen to undermine the legitimacy of the worldwide arbitral process. This is not to be met by measures akin to the Mauritius Convention. Rather it should be met by a widespread acceptance of the publishing of redacted reasons for award. The reality is that, given the qualifications and experience of a number of international commercial arbitrators, the awards they would publish would provide a significant contribution to international commercial law. They will also provide enhanced confidence in those arbitrators and in the institutions that publish the awards.

As Professor Jones has argued, the publication of redacted arbitral awards would provide access to the "rich source of law to be found in the decisions of international

59. ALLSOP, 2016, *op. cit.*, fn. 54 at pp. 765-766. A similar point is made by Susan L. KARAMANIAM, "Courts and Arbitration: Reconciling the Public with the Private", 9 Arbitration Law Review (2017) p. 1 at p. 8.
60. Lord NEUBERGER, *op. cit.*, fn. 7 at [14]-[15].
61. Cf. CARMODY, *op. cit.*, fn. 21.

commercial arbitrators".[62] Such is obvious from some of the great minds that regularly act as arbitrators. The more widespread publication of awards, in some form, would better enable the development of substantive commercial law for the benefit of international commercial law. In addition, it may go some way to resolve issues about inconsistency between different arbitral awards and the reasoning employed by some arbitrators, if awards are available for analysis, debate and use. Such a practice is being adopted by a number of arbitral institutions. These include the ICC's time delayed issuing of redacted awards and the LCIA's publishing of summaries of challenges to arbitrators.[63] I have already discussed the practice of the LMAA and Society of Maritime Arbitrators in publishing details of awards in respect of maritime arbitrations conducted in London and New York.

In the context of international commercial arbitration, I see all of these steps as means of enhancing arbitration as a sought-after dispute resolution mechanism and as part of a system of cross-border dispute resolution.

The question of whether commercial arbitration is stifling the development of commercial law contains an at least implicit allegation that international commercial arbitration is usurping the role of national courts. There are several observations I wish to make about this. First, the publication of redacted awards may also assist with resolving this concern as there would be a body of arbitral law that could be explored and, if necessary, critiqued by the courts in appropriate cases. Secondly, it is important to remember that international commercial arbitration remains subject to the supervision of the domestic court of the seat. A nuanced and principled body of law has been developed by commercial courts to supervise arbitrations, review arbitral awards and, ultimately, enforce arbitral awards. In many jurisdictions, the framework for this supervision is provided by the UNCITRAL Model Law on International Commercial Arbitration and its international adoption means there has been a development of a harmonized approach to the supervision of arbitrations.[64] This approach gives authority to the arbitrator, but does not prevent review of certain matters such as jurisdiction by a national court, with that court also able to supervise and provide support to the arbitral process.[65] The continued involvement of the courts in supervising arbitrators reflects the public role of international commercial arbitration as part of the cross-border civil justice system. Thirdly, the relationship between national commercial courts and arbitration is not a static one. It is dynamic. The attraction of either method of dispute resolution depends upon many factors but chief among them are skill and capacity of commercial judges and arbitrators; the speed with which a reliable decision can be reached by them; the vulnerability to challenge whether by appellate review or by judicial supervision; and, most importantly, enforcement. The astonishing success of the 1958 New York Convention is too well-known to require any discussion here. Over the

62. JONES, *op. cit.*, fn. 46 at p. 24.

63. JONES, *op. cit.*, fn. 46 at p. 26; ROGERS, *op. cit.*, fn. 20 at p. 1315.

64. For a discussion of Australia's approach to the supervision of international commercial arbitration by the Courts see, e.g., ALLSOP and CROFT, *op. cit.*, fn. 38; Patrick KEANE AC, "Courts and International Arbitration: A reappraisal of roles" in John MCKENNA, *Queensland Legal Yearbook 2016* (Supreme Court of Queensland Library 2018) at p. 360.

65. For an example of this approach based on the UNCITRAL Model Law, albeit in a domestic arbitration context, see *Hancock Prospecting Pty Ltd v. Rinehart* [2017] FCAFC 170.

coming years, as the adherence to the Hague Convention on Choice of Courts increases, national commercial courts will begin to have the same regime of enforcement as does arbitration for its awards. Fourthly, in recent years a number of jurisdictions have sought to develop bespoke international commercial courts characterized by excellence and dispatch. These include the Singapore International Commercial Court, the Dubai International Financial Centre Courts, Abu Dhabi Global Market Courts and the Qatar International Court.[66] These seek to rival the dominance in the English-speaking world of the London Commercial Court. These exist together with the numerous international arbitration centres in London, Singapore, Hong Kong, New York, Paris, Geneva, here in Sydney and also in Melbourne. These courts are not replacements for international commercial arbitration. Rather, they represent the development of a mature transnational commercial dispute resolution system. Commercial courts and commercial arbitration complement each other,[67] though they are competitive with each other. I have previously described the relationship as one of "competitive collaboration".[68] Competition between courts and arbitrators for disputes is healthy, particularly in parts of the world which are supportive both of skilled arbitrators and focused and innovative commercial courts. Such competition promotes efficiency and, for arbitrators, it may present an impetus for resolving some of the matters discussed today.[69]

In the context of investment arbitration, there is presently a push toward the establishment of a multilateral investment court to replace ISDS-based arbitration. The European Union has emerged as an advocate for this proposal and has made submissions to UNCITRAL. This is based upon what it describes as "systemic" issues with ISDS, coupled with a recognition of the "public" nature of investment arbitration and its impact upon "the sovereign capacity of states to regulate".[70] The EU proposal for a multilateral investment court is predicated on a recognition of the fundamental public issues implicated in investment arbitration and which I have indicated above. Its concerns about ISDS arise in that context, as does its proposal for a multilateral investment court. Those arguments, thus, have a different motivation than those complaints about international commercial arbitration that are in favour of the development of international commercial courts.

66. See the discussion, in particular of the Singapore International Commercial Court, by Marilyn WARREN AC and Clyde CROFT, "An International Commercial Court for Australia – Looking Beyond the New York Convention" (Paper presented at the Commercial CPD Seminar Series, 13 April 2016). I have expressed the view on an earlier occasion that, but for the decision *in Re Wakim* [1999] HCA 27; 198 CLR 511, Australia would have an International Commercial Court in operation today: James ALLSOP, "The Role and Future of the Federal Court Within the Australian Judicial System" (Paper presented at the ANU 40th Anniversary of the Federal Court of Australia Conference, 9 September 2017) at p. 9.

67. RAMSEY, *op. cit.*, fn. 1 at 2-3; ALLSOP, 2015, *op. cit.*, fn. 54 at pp. 434.

68. ALLSOP, 2015, *op. cit.*, fn. 54 at p. 434.

69. Chief Justice Menon of Singapore has suggested that some of these issues may, indeed, be a reason for parties to take their disputes to an international commercial court: Sundaresh MENON, "International Commercial Courts: Towards a Transnational System of Dispute Resolution" (Paper presented as the Opening Lecture for the Dubai International Financial Centre Courts Lecture Series 2015, Dubai, 2015) at [14]-[15].

70. See UNCITRAL, *op. cit.*, fn. 1.

The 2015 International Arbitration Survey asked respondents how a potential appeal mechanism in both international commercial arbitration and investment arbitration should be structured. Fifty-one percent of respondents responded in favour of an international court in respect of investment arbitration. Only 20 percent did so in respect of international commercial arbitration, just in front of a domestic court at 19 percent. The most favoured option for international commercial arbitration was an appeal to another arbitral tribunal or the arbitral institution (26 percent each).[71] Commercial parties often will provide in an arbitration agreement for a right of appeal, if it is desired by the parties.

These responses do reveal an appreciation of the differences between investment and commercial arbitration. For international commercial arbitration, there is no equivalent market demand nor is there any compelling policy reason to add some appellate structure. The parties after all have it within their power, the power of contract, to create such an appeal structure. Given the nature of international commercial dispute resolution and the present unstructured system that promotes competition between so-called international commercial courts and domestic commercial courts there are not attendant sovereignty and legitimate issues that might be said to require a supranational body.

The most significant issue for international commercial arbitration is, in my view, its increasing cost. It can be described as the cancer of industrialization which also invades the body of court litigation. This is not per se an issue of competence (although it may reflect a lack thereof) or legitimacy but it is a topic of concern amongst commercial parties and members of the arbitration community.[72] The problem is contributed to by parties, counsel and arbitrators. Respondents to the 2015 International Arbitration Survey indicated that counsel could do better to narrow issues, limit document production, encourage settlement, not over-lawyer, consider joint expert reports and generally act more efficiently.[73] The problem of "industrialization", and the consequent incurring of large, process-driven costs, is one shared with court litigation. Commercial arbitration, along with commercial litigation, needs to be recognized as a process for efficient resolution of a mutual problem; it should not be seen as a means of fee generation. To adapt what was said by Harvey CJ in Eq of the Supreme Court of New South Wales in *Read v. Chown*[74] back in 1929 in a judgment dealing with costs of an originating summons in Equity:[75]

> "The primary duty of solicitors is of course to their clients, and it is the duty of solicitors to give their clients such advice as will reduce the costs [of the litigation]. Human nature is human nature. Of course, solicitors have to live, and it is not unnatural they should look to the chance of appearing in a [matter] of this sort for the purpose of making legitimate fees from it, but I wish to point out to solicitors that it is their duty ... to attempt to reduce the costs."

71. Queen Mary University of London, *op. cit.*, fn. 40 at p. 9.
72. Queen Mary University of London, *op. cit.*, fn. 40 at p. 2.
73. Queen Mary University of London, *op. cit.*, fn. 40 at p. 30.
74. (1929) 46 NSWWN 154
75. 46 NSWWN at 155-156.

The concerns raised about "industrialization" are not so lacking in nuance as to be a mere criticism of the cost of arbitration or of the legitimate charging of professional fees by skilled lawyers, counsel and arbitrators for the work that needs to be done. Rather, it is a complaint about the creation of process-driven costs, incurred merely because such costs are seen to be usually required, or have become common practice. It is a complaint against unoriginality, and a lack of lateral thinking in how to run a proceeding. It is also a criticism of the habit of thought that proceedings exist to create such processes or costs for their own sake, rather than for resolving the dispute between the parties. There is no complaint against the legitimate earning of fees for work well done. These ideas are captured, if I may say so, by Chief Judge Harvey's statement.

Thus, I would suggest that the greatest challenge for the continued popularity and indeed legitimacy of international commercial arbitration is developing greater efficiencies and adopting a more problem-solving focused approach to arbitral procedure. On a previous occasion I suggested that greater use of early and proactive case management within arbitration may be a means of resolving these problems around industrialization.[76] Arbitration culture, indeed dispute resolution culture, needs to recognize that issues of cost and a lack of efficiency must be addressed.

Competition between courts and arbitration is an important way for both dispute resolution processes to improve their processes and reduce costs, as it provides an incentive for both judges and arbitrators to experiment and innovate.[77]

Those involved in arbitration must examine for themselves how they are working. However, just as court litigation can learn from arbitration, so arbitration may be able to learn from court litigation. With increasing frequency, courts are rejecting standardized one-size-fits-all cookie-cutter approaches to litigation. Commercial judges in Australia will generally not tolerate the linear progression of interlocutory procedure like some critical path building programme for the construction of a skyscraper. Discovery has either been curtailed or replaced by more flexible solutions. Examples are the restriction of discovery in a limited way after, not before, the exchange of evidence; the use of referees to replace the need for competing expert evidence; the replacement of discovery in the traditional way by giving a party a right to place a prospective expert within the business of the other party and simply call for documents. This last example can be most effective in cases such as business interruption claims on industrial special risk (ISR) policies where the potential for discovery is overwhelmingly burdensome. The provision of an office, a computer and a photocopying machine to an investigating accountant who calls for documents which are provided in a recorded and indexed fashion does away with the need for armies of blindfolded automatons preparing and then examining meaningless lists of millions of documents. None of these solutions are a panacea to costs but each of them in its proper context can be a nuanced and intelligent substitute for mindless and often useless pre-trial procedure.

The problem is also related to arbitrators. They must be readily available to hear cases as soon as possible. The longer a proceeding lasts, the more it costs. They must also exert control over the expenditure of time and money on less than central issues.

---

76. ALLSOP, 2016, *op. cit.*, fn. 54 at p. 752.
77. ALLSOP, 2015, *op. cit.*, fn. 54 at p. 437.

What must be emphasized is the need to consider the individual characteristics of each matter. This is not detracting from predictability of outcome. It is the recognition that every piece of litigation is unique and the most effective and cost-effective resolution of any particular problem will call upon the parties and their representatives for goodwill, a shared understanding of the need to solve a problem, skill and diligence, and a recognition of what Chief Judge Harvey said, that those who act for commercial parties have a duty to those parties to solve their problems at the least possible cost. I do not consider that these are dreamings of a simpler past. I have been involved in dispute resolution for nearly forty years. I have seen dispute resolution ranging from the appalling to the excellent. It is not a matter of it having been done better in the past. It was often done far worse in the past. But the only dispute resolution that I have seen that exhibits the public good of an efficient justice system had at its heart a shared understanding that the process was attempting to resolve as quickly and as cost effectively as possible a mutual problem for the clients concerned. Sometimes this came from the representatives themselves. Sometimes it came from the uncompromising demands of the commercial court in question. It is not a question of speed alone. It is not a question of a magic formula. It is a question of culture and a recognition that for clients to be served honestly and effectively the practitioner had to do his or her best to extricate the client from the problem whether by settling or winning the dispute in the most efficient manner.

The development and widespread use of international commercial arbitration around the globe has been one of the most significant features of international commercial law that developed over the course of the twentieth century. It has produced a cross-border dispute resolution system that is supported by and interacts with, but is independent from, national courts and which operates in parallel with international commercial courts. This has been a major step in the application of the rule of law to global commercial transactions. It is important that, in this age of reactionary policy-making, we do not allow concern about certain aspects of investor-state dispute settlement – itself a remarkable triumph of law over war – to weaken the system of international commercial arbitration that has been established, for reasons that are not relevant to commercial arbitrations. Ensuring that international commercial arbitration remains efficient, effective and innovative will go a long way toward ensuring that this does not occur. The kind of thoughtful introspection reflected in the programme for this week that picks up many of the threads of what I have been discussing will no doubt advance that position. There is no perfect model of dispute resolution. As soon as you think you have found it and try to write it down you begin to ossify it and create a framework for more procedural costs. Critical is the recognition that costs and delay are often, indeed usually, a product of bad litigation culture. There are countless tools and innovative approaches in the management of commercial dispute resolution. A cultural approach that focuses upon mutual problem solving, effectively, innovatively and cost effectively, will generally help to illuminate the best way to run and manage a piece of litigation. That best way will rarely, if ever, be manifested in the serried ranks of litigation troops ready to die of exhaustion at 3:00 a.m. reviewing documents on discovery. If one is awake, 3:00 a.m. is the time to contemplate the heart, not conduct litigation.

I hope that the discussions to follow as part of this Congress might go some way to developing proposals for the resolution of some of the matters I have identified, and that my remarks resonate to a degree with you in this room.

Plenary Session

Lawmaking in International Arbitration: What Legitimacy Challenges Lie Ahead?

Legitimacy Pragmatism in International Arbitration: A Framework for Analysis

Thomas Schultz[*]

TABLE OF CONTENTS PAGE

I. INTRODUCTION

This paper concerns itself with a 30,000-foot view of the legitimacy of lawmaking in international arbitration – where "lawmaking" is understood broadly as all the effects of a given arbitration regime.

But why should we care about legitimacy? What is the point of thinking about it? To be sure, legitimacy studies are fashionable on all matters international law. In some countries it appears to be truly de rigueur to debate the legitimacy of this or that area of international legal studies. Yet beyond that, seriously, why do we care about legitimacy?

The question isn't cynical. My claim is quite to the contrary. I think the question cuts to the heart of the conceptual equipment we use to conduct these debates. Indeed, what does legitimacy mean anyway? It actually depends on why we care about legitimacy, on what we want to get done with legitimacy discussions. So why we care about legitimacy is the sort of question that we should not only not be ashamed of asking, but that we actually should really ask.

I argue that one useful purpose of legitimacy preoccupations is that they help us understand the stability of a regime; its likelihood of change; the direction, velocity, extent, drivers of that change; its implications too. The simple point at the core of this paper is that a regime which is not legitimate to the actors who can change it is unlikely not to change, to be stable. Change and stability, in turn, are of interest to all of us, in the arbitration industry and beyond.

This particular purpose of legitimacy preoccupations calls for a certain understanding of the concept of legitimacy. The first part of this paper discusses this understanding. It considers it in the context of a broader reflection on how the purposes of concepts, their

---

* Professor of Law, King's College London; Professor of International Arbitration, University of Geneva; Of Counsel, Penvern & Corniglion. Particular thanks go to Fuad Zarbiyev for a treasure trove of references and ideas. Many thanks also to Andrea Bianchi and Stephan Schill for comments on earlier drafts. This paper builds on earlier and ongoing work with Cédric Dupont and Jason Yackee.

"cash-value" as some people put it, should in many situations frame the concepts as we use them, and not some quest for a universally valid, logically coherent, conceptually clean definition, some sort of conceptual truth. Thinking about legitimacy is worthwhile if it helps us understand or do something. And so the goal of understanding or doing should determine how we define the concept. If the goal is to understand a regime's stability and anticipate its changes – there are, of course, other goals – then an appropriate definition of legitimacy is one that takes into account reasons that would push certain actors to provoke change. It is, as we will see, a deliberately interest-based, output-oriented, and relative notion of legitimacy – relative in the sense that it depends on the perspective of a given actor, may vary from one actor to another, is only relative to the particular perspective of a particular actor. With this notion of legitimacy, nothing is per se legitimate or not; there are no universal standards of legitimacy.

The second part of the paper then addresses the question of the actors from whose perspective legitimacy matters – the overall point, of course, remains to determine a given regime's stability. I address that question from a general, theoretical perspective; not from the perspective of a particular, concrete regime. The point is to offer a framework or model to help us think about which actors can input what change, with what consequences, based on the reasons for change identified by the legitimacy considerations conducted in the earlier parts of the paper. That model, building on prior and ongoing work with colleagues,[1] is inspired by the concept of "political system" suggested by political scientist David Easton.

A simply take-away point of the model is that legitimacy issues in the sense used in this paper will likely lead to reactions in the form of input into the regime by actors to whom the regime is not legitimate (at least from a rational perspective, which admittedly has its limitations, which I will address later). These reactions are likely to continue until some equilibrium among the input-actors is reached, taking the regime through several probable iterations. For instance, if we apply this to the case of investment arbitration, taken as a regime, as a lawmaking system, we might expect it to go through several iterations, several rounds of change, until an equilibrium is found among states, the different powerful constituencies within states, investors, arbitrators, arbitration institutions, and possibly NGOs and other civil society representatives.

Perhaps that conclusion will sound forgone. Then again, the discussion helps clarify a useful area within the overall debate about the legitimacy crisis or legitimacy deficit of investment arbitration and other forms of international arbitration.

Clarification, I think, is needed. The legitimacy debate is occasionally somewhat wooly. It tends to echo the lament expressed from perspectives as different as James Crawford's and Martti Koskenniemi's: in Crawford's words, "In recent discourse there has been very little attempt to use [legitimacy] in a discriminating way"; and in Koskenniemi's: "legitimacy" [is a] mediate word[], rhetorically successful only so long as

1. Cédric DUPONT, Thomas SCHULTZ and Jason YACKEE, "Investment Arbitration and Political Systems Theory" in Thomas SCHULTZ and Federico ORTINO, eds., *Oxford Hanbook of International Arbitration* (OUP forthcoming 2019); Cédric DUPONT and Thomas SCHULTZ, "Towards a New Heuristic Model: Investment Arbitration as a Political System", 7 JIDS (2016) p. 3.

[it] cannot be pinned down either to formal rules or moral principles".[2] "Legitimacy", from their perspective, would just muddle rather than clarify. This tends to have the regrettable consequence, expressed by Crawford, that we lawyers can dispense with and actually shouldn't engage with legitimacy preoccupations at all: "Of legitimacy it is for others to judge."[3]

"Go home", in effect, would be Crawford and Koskenniemi's welcome to scholars and practitioners gathering to discuss legitimacy problems in arbitration.

It surely is an interesting thought – this idea that if it is unclear what we are talking about we should not be talking about it. That if there is no authoritative or generally accepted definition of "legitimacy", it is an unhelpful concept. But I don't think we should leave the question behind, not on that ground. Then again, we cannot simply take any definition of legitimacy and run with it. We should rather take Crawford and Koskenniemi's argument as an invitation to think for a moment about what's involved here: What are concepts meant to do? How do we define them? Can we define legitimacy in a constructive way, so that it isn't marked as unhelpful and quickly put away? I think this apparent detour on the way to debating legitimacy is not a detour at all, but is rather essential in giving meaning to the discussion. So this is where the paper will start.

The paper overall moves in five parts. The first three deal with the concept of legitimacy: the first discusses the purposes, or "jobs", of concepts generally; the second reviews possible jobs for the concept of legitimacy, what it might help us do; the third gives a particular job to the concept of legitimacy and defines it according to that job. The fourth part then suggests a political systems model to mark those actors whose legitimacy views matter, based on their capacity to provide input in international arbitration lawmaking regimes. The fifth part starts a discussion about how this paper's point might be used to anticipate backlashes and overreactions to legitimacy issues.

A caveat must be entered before we begin, although it is probably self-evident by now: much of this paper relies on theories which don't have their usual habitat in arbitration – pragmatic philosophy, the legitimacy literature in international law, and political science theories. The paper's approach, then, may be unusual for an arbitration publication. It may appear to have been written in a slightly foreign language. In some form of dialect of the arbitration discourse. But I think there are several important general points that come from thinking about arbitration from that particular approach, in that particular dialect. Then again, the hurried reader not too excited about polyglottism and in need of going straight to the point may jump ahead to Part V, ideally after a brief look at the chart at the end of Part IV. The other parts are for those who don't quite buy my point and want to know here it comes from; for those who want to understand why legitimacy in this discussion has nothing to do with morality or political ideals; and for those who would find either comfort or halt in the idea that what most people think most of the time about the legitimacy of arbitration is actually quite irrelevant.

---

2. Martti KOSKENNIEMI, "Miserable Comforters: International Relations as New Natural Law", 15 EJIR (2009) p. 395, p. 409.
3. James CRAWFORD, "The Problems of Legitimacy-Speak", 98 ASIL Proceedings (2004) p. 271, p. 273.

II. THE JOB OF CONCEPTS

To understand what meaning we should give to the concept of legitimacy, let us first take a step back and consider the question generically: how do we generally give meaning to concepts? What is the purpose of concepts anyway? What is their job in our cognitive economy?

Most philosophers, in particular analytic philosophers, consider that a given concept has a given meaning. One concept, one meaning. Our job then, as thinkers of all varieties, is to figure out what that meaning is, what the *proper* meaning of the concept is, to find certainty in the identification of its meaning. Once we who think analytically about the concept have agreed on a meaning, that meaning becomes authoritative, and that's that; everyone can move on to something else. The great advantages of such janitorial work for concepts are cleanliness, possibly logical coherence between concepts, and clarity in communication among thinkers – we know what we one another mean because we use the same concept with the same meaning. Fair enough.

And yet.... If we think about it, as Wittgenstein did, the problem with this approach is that it might separate analytic thinking from reality. Or, in the same direction but less far, it doesn't get much done. If I tell you "stay roughly here", accompanied by a vague pointing gesture, you know what I mean, even though "roughly here" is, well, only roughly defined.[4] There is not much point in defining it analytically, not much purpose in making it a "rigorously scientific" concept.[5] And if nevertheless we were to define it analytically, the definition likely wouldn't change anything for anybody, would not achieve anything. It might even evolve, congress after conference after workshop on "roughly here-ness", in a direction that takes it ever further from the way it actually is used in practice by actual people. "Legitimacy" might face the same fate.

As Wittgenstein put it, "My father was a businessman, and I am a businessman; I want my philosophy to be business-like, to get something done."[6] From that perspective, the definition of a concept doesn't start from a pursuit of analytic cleanliness, but from a pursuit of what a concept can get done. The purpose and utility of a concept, its "cash-value", are the starting point of its definition. ("Cash-value": a term introduced by the philosopher and psychologist William James in 1898 in his advocacy of pragmatic doctrines, expressing the idea that philosophical conceptions really should try to make practical differences to individuals.[7] Unexpectedly this still both annoys and unnerves many philosophers.) The central argument for the validity of a concept's definition is not where it sits in the field among other concepts or whether it agrees with an authoritative understanding by a school of thought. It rather is its practical explanatory purchase, what explanation it can concretely "buy", what it helps us do. "Let them, the pundits, solemnly pontificate; and we, let's get something done," the pragmatic philosopher would say.

4. Ludwig WITTGENSTEIN, *Philosophical Investigations* (Macmillan 1953), §71,
5. Toril MOI, *Revolution of the Ordinary (*University of Chicago Press 2017) p. 76.
6. Reported by Maurice O'Connor DRURY, "Conversations with Wittgenstein" in Rush RHEES, ed., *Recollections of Wittgenstein* (OUP 1984) p. 110.
7. William JAMES, "Philosophical Conceptions and Practical Results", paper presented at the 1898 Berkeley Philosophical Union, reported and discussed in George COTKIN, "William James and the Cash-Value Metaphor", Et Cetera (1985) p. 37.

Concepts, indeed, are instruments. They serve a purpose. The purpose may vary. It may vary from one concept to another, in the sense that different concepts may play different roles in our cognitive economy.

Some concepts help us simplify, some help us distinguish. Some help us understand, some help us argue. Some evoke, some lull. Some help us justify, some help us resist and object. Some help us assess, some help us decide.[8] Some provide camouflage for things we need to hide. Some stop the discussion, the inquiry, the argument, and thus place constraints on objectivity – constraints which often are indispensable, as Richard Rorty puts it, "because some particular social practice needs to block the road of inquiry, halt the progress of interpretations, in order to get something done".[9]

Or, to offer a different typology from a different perspective, we might say that the purposes of concepts, their functions in our cognitive economy, their different possible cash-values, can at least be the following: To help us understand something; then their job is to explain; and explaining can be done in at least two ways: by simplifying knowledge and by complexifying it (achieved by introducing further distinctions). To help us decide; then their job is to act as proxys, to stop inquiries. To help us win arguments; then their job is to stop discussions, to act as rhetorical devices. To help us communicate; then their job is to generalize ideas so that it takes less nominal information to transmit them.

One way to put all this is that concepts have idiosyncratic functions – different functions are proper to different concepts. Now, better concepts serve their purpose, their function better. A concept is well defined if it serves its function well.

Consider a parallel to make the point clearer: the parallel is between concepts and genres of legal thought. Here's how Pierre Schlag puts it for legal thought: "it seems evident that what is required of the various genres of legal thought (knowledge, understanding, interpretation, edification, etc.) differs somewhat across the genres."[10] Different types of legal scholarship have different purposes. What marks them as good scholarship varies across types and thus across purposes. The same is true of concepts: what marks them as good, well-defined concepts varies across functions.

This implies that to different functions correspond different defining principles. A concept meant to evoke is not well defined according to the same principles as a concept meant to distinguish is well defined: the former must, for example, connect to the contingent social and cultural symbolism of its audience (notice the concepts used in political statements); the latter must, for instance, be precise (notice the concepts used

8. This quasi-typology conspicuously eschews the question of the purpose of knowledge. Let me explain: arguably, the purpose of every concept is to do something with knowledge. Then the question might be posed of what the purpose of knowledge is: Is it to understand? Is it to decide? One might recall Foucault's insistence on the view that "knowledge is not made for understanding; it is made for cutting [in the sense of deciding, from the original in French "*trancher*"]": Michel FOUCAULT, "Nietzsche, Genealogy, History" in *Essential Works of Foucault, 1954-1984 (Aesthetics, Method, and Epistemology)* (The New Press 1998) p. 380. But can one really be so categorical? Is there really no evolutionary or psychological drive to understand for the sake of understanding?
9. Richard RORTY, *Consequences of Pragmatism* (University of Minnesota Press 1982) p. xli.
10. Pierre SCHLAG, "The Knowledge Bubble—Something Amiss in Expertopia" in Justin DESAUTELS-STEIN and Christopher TOMLINS, eds., *In Search of Contemporary Legal Thought* (CUP 2017) p. 428, at p, 445.

by engineers). A concept whose primary role in our cognitive economy is to simplify knowledge should, for example, be defined in a way that maximizes its capacity to explain as many things as possible, as accurately as possible, and as eloquently as possible (think of the concept of law, for instance).[11] A concept whose primary role is to help us decide should, by contrast, rather be defined in a way that maximizes its straightforwardness, its manageability, its "black-box-ness", its accord with the core values we hold (think of the concept of comity, for example).[12]

Then of course the purpose of concepts does not only vary from one concept to another as they play different roles in our cognitive economy. A single given concept may also play different roles in different cognitive economies: the same concept may have different purposes depending on what it is used for.

Consider this simple example: When we say to ourselves "this is a just decision", "justice" is meant to help us decide, to help us stop thinking, to help us cope with the fact that, as Jacques Derrida put it, the just decision "cannot furnish itself with infinite information and the unlimited knowledge of conditions, rules or hypothetical imperatives that could justify it".[13] When we need to make a decision, we need to stop thinking at some stage, even if more thinking could be done, and the purpose of "justice" is to allow us to do just that. Then again, the same concept of justice, in a different context, can be used to do a very different job: when we say to others "oh but this is unjust!", the reference to "justice" is meant to gear us into thinking, into arguing, into finding knowledge.[14]

In the hope of making the point clearer by taking it into territory more familiar to lawyers, let us briefly consider how it applies to legal doctrines. Schlag again explains the point intelligibly, even though it might make us double back before we actually quite accept it: "the [legal] academic will present his or her work as faithfully devoted to the analysis of some unitary object of inquiry – as if the invocation, for instance, of a legal doctrine meant the same thing in a law review article, in a lawyer's conference call to the client, in a judicial opinion, in a legislative committee hearing, in a press conference.

---

11. Karl POPPER, "A Note on Verisimilitude", 27 British Journal of the Philosophy of Science (1976) p. 147; François OST, "*Science du droit*" in André-Jean ARNAUD, ed., *Dictionnaire encyclopédique de sociologie et de théorie du droit* (1993) p. 540; Jean LADRIERE, "*Les sciences humaines et le problème de la scientificité*" in Patrick de NEUTER and Jean FLORENCE, eds., *Sciences et Psychanalyse* (1985). For an application to the concept of law, see Thomas SCHULTZ, "Non-Analytical Obstacles to Stateless Law", 43 North Carolina Journal of International Law (2018) p. 182.
12. Thomas SCHULTZ, Jason MITCHENSON and Niccolò RIDI, *The Principle of Comity in Public and Private International Law* (CUP, forthcoming 2019); Thomas SCHULTZ and Niccolò RIDI, "Comity and International Courts and Tribunals", 50 Cornell International Law Journal (2017) p. 577; Thomas SCHULTZ and Jason MITCHENSON, "Navigating Sovereignty and Transnational Commercial Law: The Use of Comity by Australian Courts", 12 Journal of Private International Law (2016) p. 344.
13. Jacques DERRIDA, "*Force de loi: le fondement mystique de l'autorité*", 11 Cardozo Law Review (1989) p. 920, p. 967.
14. One could of course argue that concepts that are nominally the same are functionally different – same name for a concept, different use – and should thus really be considered different concepts, so that we remain with the idea that one concept has one purpose. But this is just a semantic debate.

In all likelihood, the "same doctrine" will be invoked to mean different things in all those speech acts even if the speakers (incorrectly?) presume that it means the same thing."[15]

To make it yet brutally simpler, which should really not be taken as an accurate representation of the argument because it is meant to illustrate the argument and not enunciate it, take the concept or doctrine of good faith: it means different things in different legal systems; within a given legal system it tends to mean different things for different branches of the law; within a given branch of the law, it tends to mean different things for different uses, in different situations.

Legitimacy is a concept that falls within this category of concepts with multiple purposes. And quite squarely so. When Jutta Brunnée and Stephen Toope argue that "'legitimacy' can have a specific, legal meaning" (which they pin on Lon Fuller's eight principles of inner morality),[16] they go in the right direction, but not far enough. The plural would have helped: legitimacy can and does have several specific meanings for lawyers. The different meanings of legitimacy correspond to its different uses and purposes, across disciplines but also within law, even within international law.

Let me restate the argument so far without the jargon, from a slightly different perspective and a lighter approach. Some concepts are fixed; they have a uniform meaning within a field, or even across fields. The point of departure for the use of such concepts should then be that meaning, be it only for the sake of clarity of statements made using the concept – that I don't mean something else than you when we use the same concept. But that doesn't work with legitimacy. Legitimacy is a concept that has a great variety of meanings, even within the comparatively narrow confines of the international law literature – at least one study, by Chris Thomas, has mapped that array of meanings well enough.[17] Put differently, legitimacy is characterized by clear and significant conceptual pluralism.

For its definition there is, then, no fixed starting point. Its starting point should rather be floating, relative. It should be its purpose, its use: the purpose or use of the concept of legitimacy. The questions we should start from should be: What is the purpose of the concept of legitimacy? What are we trying to do with the concept? What is it meant to capture? And then, how should we define legitimacy so that it serves that purpose as well as possible?

The starting point should not be, against much of the current practice, the definition of legitimacy offered by some well-known author because the author is well known. This would be inappropriate, even wrong argumentatively (it would be an argument by authority). To get an idea of how these discussions often go, consider this: Some people say that legitimacy is "the right to rule" and refer to Allen Buchanan and Robert Keohane's authoritative, "classic" statement of this definition.[18] No, no, no, other people respond, this is quite wrong. The correct definition of legitimacy is necessarily one that

15. SCHLAG, "The Knowledge Bubble", p. 433.
16. Jutta BRUNNÉE and Stephen J. TOOPE, *Legitimacy and Legality in International Law* (CUP 2010) p. 34.
17. Christopher A. THOMAS, "The Uses and Abuses of Legitimacy in International Law", 34 Oxford Journal of Legal Studies (2014) p. 729.
18. Allen BUCHANAN and Robert O. KEOHANE, "The Legitimacy of Global Governance Institutions", 20 Ethics & International Affairs (2006) p. 405.

marks a distinction between political normativity and applied morality, as Matt Sleat[19] and Bernard Williams[20] authoritatively pointed out. No, no, no, yet others respond: the definition of legitimacy must entail some combination of sociological elements and moral elements, they argue, and quickly enlist Jürgen Habermas's good name for help.[21]

What discussions like these don't seem to acknowledge is that these different authors wanted to achieve different things with legitimacy, which call for different definitions. It is like asking which of an airplane, a motorbike, and a snowboard is the better transportation mode: you don't usually use them for quite the same purposes; their fitness for the purpose in question is what makes them better. That nuance is of course easily lost if the only reference point for a definition is its author and the author's authority in a field.

As the example also suggests, a search for *the* purpose of legitimacy would be misguided. It would lead us into a totalizing account of the concept, which is neither helpful nor required and would need to operate at such a level of generality that nothing useful remains.[22] In the end, the simple point is that the concept of legitimacy has several purposes, some firmly established, some we could find out and add.

Perhaps you find this trite. That would be good, in fact. But others won't like it. Indeed my story so far has been, to borrow from Schlag once again, "dissonant with the pretence to certainty of the juridical style that remains so dominant in academic legal writing".[23] My story would be more popular if it came with reassuring certainty. But I think Crawford and Koskenniemi were right: many of the discussions of legitimacy don't seem to be going anywhere much. Embracing the uncertainty of the meaning of legitimacy while trying to tie it to a concrete job might be one way to go somewhere.

19. Matt SLEAT, "Legitimacy in Realist Thought: Between Moralism and Realpolitik", 42 Political Theory (2014) p. 314.
20. Bernard WILLIAMS, *In the Beginning Was the Deed: Realism and Moralism in Political Argument* (Princeton University Press 2005).
21. Jürgen HABERMAS, *Legitimation Crisis* (Polity Press 1988); Jürgen HABERMAS, *Between Facts and Norms: Contribution to a Discourse Theory of Law and Democracy* (MIT Press 1996).
22. For an example of such a (nearly) totalizing account: Terry MACDONALD, "Political Legitimacy in International Border Governance Institutions", 14 European Journal of Political Theory p. 409, at p. 418, who offers this definition: "The legitimacy of an institutionalised subject S tracks reasons R for agents A to engage in conduct C in relation to S." The definition is based on this (remarkable) argument: "*all analysis* of legitimacy is concerned with evaluating an institutionalised subject (such as a state, law or international governance regime) to determine whether there are sufficient reasons (understood as considerations that count in favour of an action, in the sense of either motivating or justifying it) for particular agents within the institutional scheme (such as citizens, legal subjects or states) to engage in particular forms of conduct (such as political participation, legal compliance or cooperative engagement) towards the subject of the legitimacy evaluation." (Emphasis added.)
23. SCHLAG, "The Knowledge Bubble", p. 449.

III. THE JOBS OF THE CONCEPT OF LEGITIMACY

What are the purpose and utility, as I said, of the concept of legitimacy in the context of our discussion? What are we trying to achieve when we talk about the legitimacy of lawmaking in international arbitration?

You may still not buy my story about the variegatedness of the concept of legitimacy, despite my repetitions. You may still think that legitimacy means legitimacy and that my job should have been to simply find out what that meaning is. That with a little effort surely we can find an apodeictic definition of legitimacy (one that is undisputed, on which we can safely build). Granted, my story isn't an easy sell. It brings Humpty Dumpty to mind ("'When I use a word,' Humpty Dumpty said in rather a scornful tone, 'it means just what I choose it to mean — neither more nor less.' 'The question is,' said Alice, 'whether you can make words mean so many different things.'") And that might not be entirely heartening.

So let me show you. By the end of the discussion, I will convince you that we can and must *choose* between different meanings, and that this choice should depend on the job we want to give to the concept of legitimacy. I hope you will agree with the choice I eventually make.

Let us first look at what is around it, what it connects to. So: in the conceptual neighbourhood of legitimacy there live authority, fairness, justice, allegiance, conscientious adhesion, values, ethics, morality, but also crisis, opposition, resistance, and change. Legitimacy connects to all these neighbouring concepts. All these neighbouring concepts may help us see what legitimacy can be used for.

By way of illustration, for Max Weber the purpose of legitimacy is to explain authority, and the purpose of both (legitimacy and authority) is to explain social regularities: why people obey norms, perceived or real. Legitimacy and authority are here very close, to the point that Fuad Zarbiyev states that "the phrase "legitimate authority" denotes a redundancy."[24] Legitimacy helps define authority; authority helps define legitimacy. While the two concepts are discrete (in the sense that their meanings do not fully overlap, even if some overlap is possible), they are connected, at least from this particular perspective: thinking about authority may then help understand what the concept of legitimacy can be used for.

To take another example, legal validity arguably depends on one of three types of factors, or a combination of these factors: formalism in the positivistic tradition, effectiveness in the legal realist tradition, and indeed legitimacy in the natural law tradition.[25] Brutally simplified, the idea of the natural law tradition (which in truth very much permeates the way we practice law) is to bring to light the role of people's allegiance to rules, people, institutions, psychologically inevitable preoccupations with ethics when we declare rules and decisions valid or invalid, attempts to morally justify our actions when we draw the boundaries of what is lawful and what isn't. From that perspective, legitimacy is the conceptual device we use to anchor our law-related

24. Fuad ZARBIYEV, "Saying Credibly What the Law Is: On Marks of Authority in International Law", 9 JIDS (2018) p. 291.

25. François OST and Michel van de KERCHOVE, *De la pyramide au réseau?* (Publ FUSL 2002) pp. 361-363.

activities in our humanity. Deep down, our conscious and unconscious considerations of humanity, of the human condition, of the values we derive from it, they all contribute to making us take legal positions; legitimacy is the concept we tend to use to make these decisions or camouflage the reasoning leading there.

And a third example of how legitimacy connects to neighbouring concepts which in turn give purpose to the concept of legitimacy: as Chris Thomas puts it, "The language of legitimacy and the language of crisis have long been associated with each other, standing as they both do at the borders of order and chaos." He goes on to cite a string of publications which speak of "legitimacy crisis".[26] What does this tell us? First that systems, regimes, structures in which law is made are "in crisis" because of legitimacy problems; legitimacy is used to explain, possibly justify, why a regime changes or need to change. Too often, sadly, and to echo Crawford's and Koskenniemi's laments reported at the outset of this paper, the concept of legitimacy is often left under-defined, under-theorized in these publications – many essentially say that "something is wrong" with the regime, that it shows dysfunctions, which cause instability and urgent crisis-type change. If the purpose of "legitimacy" is to make us understand something about the neighbouring principle of "crisis", how then should we best define legitimacy?

Beyond the somewhat fuzzy conceptual neighbourhood of legitimacy, can we draw a more informed, a crisper typology of the uses and purposes of the concept of legitimacy? I suggest the following, which is strictly not meant to be exhaustive; it isn't a totalizing account, to use the words from above, of the uses and purposes of legitimacy.

1. *Job One: Justification*

The concept of legitimacy is often used for justificatory purposes. Notice that one of the definitions of legitimacy offered by the Oxford English language dictionary is this: the "ability to be defended with logic or *justification*" (emphasis added – somehow the authors of the Dictionary didn't consider that logic is a form of justification).

In this category, perhaps the most common example of something justified on the ground that it is "legitimate" is coercive power. A given regime coerces certain actors into doing something, but that is okay, justified, the regime is worthy of compliance by its actors and of non-interference by external forces, because it is a legitimate situation; the regime and its sway are legitimate. The concept of "legitimacy" is used to justify that coercive power.

26. Christine GRAY, "A Crisis of Legitimacy for the UN Collective Security System", 56 ICLQ (2007) p. 157; Manfred ELSIG, "The World Trade Organization's Legitimacy Crisis: What Does the Beast Look Like?", 41 JWT (2007) p. 75; Jason WIENER, "The World Trade Organization's Identity Crisis: Institutional Legitimacy and Growth Potential in the Developing World", 2 MJIEL (2005) p. 54; Susan D. FRANCK, "The Legitimacy Crisis in Investment Treaty Arbitration: Privatizing Public International Law Through Inconsistent Decisions", 73 Fordham L Rev (2005) p. 1521; Ari AFILALO, "Towards a Common Law of International Investment: How NAFTA Chapter 11 Panels Should Solve Their Legitimacy Crisis", 17 Geo Int'l Envtl L Rev (2004) p. 51; Robert KAGAN, "America's Crisis of Legitimacy", 83 Foreign Affairs (2004) p. 65; A. Claire CUTLER, "Critical Reflections on the Westphalian Assumptions of International Law and Organization: A Crisis of Legitimacy", 27 Rev Int'l Stud (2001) p. 133.

Of course, the same reasoning applies to exercises of power not based on coercion, on force. Any regime, any power, anything that exercises normative effects can find justification for its existence and impact in arguments that it is legitimate.

Legitimacy refers here to the "right to rule", broadly taken.[27] It serves to justify the power of one actor over another and the exercise of that power. As Chris Thomas puts it, "Questions about legitimacy may be understood as questions about the *justificatory frameworks* behind the expansion, contraction, formation, transformation, maintenance and dissolution of legal orders."[28]

For instance, we could justify the power of arbitrators over the parties – from the issuance of procedural orders, to the creation of new rules for the case at hand and/or future cases – on the ground that it is legitimate. (Notice that, from this perspective, the question whether this power is legitimate would be the question whether arbitrators *should indeed have* this power.) Used in that sense, legitimacy might call for a standard found in party autonomy: the parties consented to arbitration, therefore it is legitimate that the arbitrators ... and so on.

A good definition of legitimacy, if it is used for that purpose, is one that resonates with the moral orientation of the particular audience to which one tries to justify something, a definition that is attuned to its rhetorical sensitivities. It could for instance be a definition of legitimacy that uses standards which tend to evoke values of order, obedience, peace, stability, anxiety of "the other", anxiety of change, security, predictability, certainty.

The justificatory purposes of the concept of legitimacy also extend, beyond power and normative effects, to someone's social position. As Zarbiyev puts it: "measured by sociological criteria, legitimacy is a matter of 'social credibility and acceptability' of a social position."[29]

And legitimacy can of course also be used to justify an action. Thomas suggests the example of "Goldstone report's memorable verdict that the NATO military intervention in Kosovo was 'illegal but legitimate'."[30]

2. *Job Two: Objection*

The concept of legitimacy may also be used to contest, to resist. To oppose, to object. To revolt. In many ways this is simply the flip side of justification: what is legitimate is justified, what is not should be contested, resisted. Zarbiyev summarizes some of the arguments on this use of legitimacy in the following way: "In another attempt to show that authority and legitimacy cannot be equated with each other, it is sometimes

27. BUCHANAN and KEOHANE, "The Legitimacy of Global Governance Institutions".
28. THOMAS, "The Uses and Abuses of Legitimacy in International Law", pp. 757-758.
29. ZARBIYEV, "Saying Credibly What the Law Is", citing Julia BLACK, "'Says Who?' Liquid Authority and Interpretive Control in Transnational Regulatory Regimes", 9 International Theory (2017) p. 292. See also Michael BARNETT and Martha FINNEMORE, *Rules for the World. International Organizations in Global Politics* (Cornell University Press 2004) p. 20.
30. THOMAS, "The Uses and Abuses of Legitimacy in International Law", p. 732.

suggested that resistance to, and contestation of, authority cannot be properly accounted for without keeping authority and legitimacy separate."[31]

This use of legitimacy is central to the natural law tradition, when it makes the point that one does not have a moral obligation to obey the law if the law is not legitimate.[32]

This use of legitimacy is also central to civil disobedience discourses, from Henry David Thoreau (illegitimate state), to the student revolts of the 1960s and 70s (illegitimate establishment), to the alter-globalization movements (illegitimate economic system), to the rhetoric of resistance to investment arbitration as a component of the global economic straightjacket (illegitimate geopolitical function). To take just one quick example, Muthucumaraswamy Sornarajah refers to "legitimacy" on roughly 10 percent of all the pages of his latest book – a significant building block of his overall argument.[33]

A good definition of legitimacy, if it is used for the purpose of resistance or opposition, is certainly one that, once again, resonates with the moral orientation of the particular audience one tries to stir into action, a definition that captures the general sense that injustice must not be condoned. It would be a definition that uses standards which tend to evoke values of freedom and independence and liberation, enough-is-enough-ness, unfairness, injustice, self-interest, inequity aversion, a sense of the possibility of change, joy in what is new, progress, hope. A good definition of legitimacy for the purposes of resistance or opposition would tend not to admit of degrees (something is legitimate or, indeed, illegitimate, not more or less legitimate) so that an attack on one piece of the architecture of an institution, or regime, or rule makes the entire construction collapse. A good definition for these purposes is probably also one that is quite blurry, which the audience can infuse with its own individual preferences, while being categorical.

Sornarajah, for example, considers that investment arbitration is illegitimate because of (a) the "democratic deficit that is involved in a law made by ad hoc tribunals" in the sense that "[a]rbitrators have no mandate to make the profound changes they have on the basis of hazy provisions in investment treaties" and (b) "There is also an absence of ethical values in the type of decisions that have been made. The legitimacy of an international norm must be based on fairness criteria."[34] One might be tempted to ask in response what exactly democracy would entail in such a situation and why, and whether hazy abandonment of decision control by states necessarily is undemocratic. One might also be tempted to point out that ethical values and fairness criteria do permeate investment arbitration decisions and investment rules; they are simply not those values that Sornarajah seems to have in mind.

But who would get excited by such tedious responses? They would require tiresome discussions of the definition of legitimacy. And these don't quite trigger the same knockout oomph as does a well-turned call for freedom and justice.

---

31. ZARBIYEV, "Saying Credibly What the Law Is", citing Michael ZÜRN, Martin BINDER and Matthias ECKER-EHRHARDT, "International Authority and its Politicization", 4 International Theory (2012) p. 83; Birgit PETERS and Johan Karlsson SCHAFFER, "The Turn to Authority Beyond States", 4 Transnational Legal Theory (2013) p. 334.
32. John FINNIS, *Natural Law and Natural Rights* (2nd edn, Oxford University Press 2011), pp. 25-29.
33. Muthucumaraswamy SORNARAJAH, *Resistance and Change in the International Law on Foreign Investment* (CUP 2015).
34. *Ibid.*, p. 390.

So it seems easier to point out a thing or two that investment arbitration obviously does not do well and call it illegitimate, to resist it, than to carefully review all its effects and call it on the whole legitimate, to positively justify its existence and overall functioning. To risk a brutal parallel, Trumpism and Brexitism face a much lower definitional duty in their arguments that the established order is illegitimate (contestation) than the opposite arguments that it is legitimate (justification).

Again, different uses of the concept of legitimacy simply call for different definitions if the point of the concept of legitimacy is to get something done. A definition of legitimacy that gets the thing better done, whatever the thing is, is a better definition.

3. *Job Three: Explanation*

The concept of legitimacy is also often used neither to justify something nor to contest and resist, which are both evaluative-normative claims ("it *should* stay as it is", "it *should* change"), but rather to explain something.

Perhaps the most obvious thing that legitimacy is used to explain is authority: someone or something has authority, which means that it will tend to be obeyed even in the absence of coercive power, self-interest, habit, and error, if it is considered legitimate. In that sense, the concept of legitimacy is almost an empty container, a placeholder for whatever the individuals who are obeying happen to value and respect. As Julia Black puts it: "the relevant criteria ... are not those which an external observer (including a commentating academic) would see to be normatively valid or valuable; the relevant criteria are those being used by those who are interacting with the actor in order for them to accept ... its authority."[35]

A good definition of legitimacy, in this context, is one that clearly keeps out coercion, self-interest, habit, and error (or any other reasons-for-action depending on the typology at hand), in order to isolate legitimacy as an independent reason-for-action.[36] Legitimacy and authority then largely overlap.[37] Simply put, the purpose of the concept of legitimacy here is to explain why people obey certain rules or orders even if they are not forced to, gain nothing from it, don't simply do it routinely, and are not mistaken about any of this.

For instance, one might wonder why parties comply with law made in international arbitration – from precedents to procedural orders – if they are not coerced to do so, if it is not in their interest to do so, if they don't do it out of habit, and if they didn't misunderstand something: the answer would be because they find the relevant norms or orders legitimate, and thus grant them authority. This use of the concept of legitimacy would for instance point the way to studies on why exactly and under which conditions the parties do that.

35. Julia BLACK, "'Says Who?' Liquid Authority and Interpretive Control in Transnational Regulatory Regimes", 9 International Theory (2017) p. 293.

36. See, e.g., THOMAS, "Uses and Abuses of Legitimacy in International Law", p. 753: "it is important to clearly distinguish between legitimacy as a reason for action and alternative reasons for compliance, including coercion, self-interest and habit." The addition of "error" is my own.

37. ZARBIYEV, "Saying Credibly What the Law Is".

A variant of this use of legitimacy is the simpler distinction between coercion and other reasons-for-action: if I am not coerced to do something but nevertheless do it, I do it because I think it is "legitimate". The point of the concept of legitimacy here is to get a general picture of how people, or any other subjects of any rule, regime, etc., likely exercise their freedom, where "freedom" simply means non-coerced space, generically. From that perspective one can indeed say, as Daniel Bodansky does, that "one of the reasons why states might agree to subject themselves to the authority of an international institution, and consider its authority legitimate, is that they think such institutions are in their self-interest".[38] What I think is in my interest I would tend to find legitimate. Whether this is a better or worse definition than the preceding definition (which opposes legitimacy not only to coercion but also to self-interest, habit, and error) depends entirely on what the purpose of the concept of legitimacy is in the analysis at hand, what it seeks to explain, to get done.

4. *Other Jobs: Assessment, Acceptable Expression of Emotions, Thinking*

Legitimacy can also do a number of other jobs, which I can but mention in passing.

Legitimacy can be used to assess. To assess the morally cherishable character of something. For example to assess if the something satisfies Kantian criteria, or Habermasian criteria, or rule of law criteria if rule of law is taken as a moral-political ideal. Or if it promotes liberal values, communitarian aspirations, global justice ideals, a neoliberal agenda, … – you get the point. In such cases, the purpose of the concept of legitimacy is often to lull the critical sense of the audience, to prevent the discussion from going into a certain direction – namely the direction of a proper comparison, in political philosophy, of the respective moral-political advantages of liberalism vs communitarianism vs neoliberalism, etc. (Think "lawmaking in international arbitration is illegitimate because it promotes a neoliberal agenda", which says nothing about the undesirability in this particular case or even in general of the pursuit of such a neoliberal agenda.)

It can be used to assess our own work also. As Chris Thomas puts it: "as international lawyers, global actors and human beings, we have a responsibility to reflect on the motivations for our actions and to take responsibility for our role in propagating particular constellations of power and subjugation".[39] Is what we do legitimate? Which should lead us to ask: What are the effects of what we do (assuming it has any, of course)? Are we quite content with the structures of power we propagate as we fulfil the functions assigned to us by "the system"?

Then legitimacy can also be used as a socially accepted way of banging on the table: if I think something really has to stop I can use "This is not legitimate!" to express that emotion.

38. Daniel BODANSKY, "The Concept of Legitimacy in International Law" in Rüdiger WOLFRUM and Volker RÖBEN, eds., *Legitimacy in International Law* (Springer 2008) p. 309, p. 312, citing Robert KEOHANE, "Discussion Following Presentations by Rüdiger Wolfrum, Robert Keohane, Alain Pellet and Anthony D'Amato" in Rüdiger WOLFRUM and Volker RÖBEN, eds., *Legitimacy in International Law* (Springer 2008) p. 93, p. 104.

39. THOMAS, "Uses and Abuses of Legitimacy in International Law", p. 732.

Legitimacy can further be used to free lawyers from the narrow confines of mechanical black letter law thinking, by unlocking human questioning beyond legality and lawfulness: it is legal but is it quite legitimate? It is illegal but is it nevertheless legitimate?

The list could go on. But I think the point has been reached where it is clear enough that the concept of legitimacy can be given one of a number of different possible jobs.

IV. ONE UNDERSTANDING OF LEGITIMACY AND ITS IMPLICATIONS

So we are quite free in defining the concept of legitimacy; what matters is to decide what we want to use it for, what we want to get done with the concept, and then define it accordingly. (Clearly, I repeat but the point is important, this paper forgoes conceptual truth, and on this particular question of legitimacy, it posits that actually *there is no* conceptual truth.)

As I said at the outset of this paper, my purpose in using legitimacy is to help us understand and assess the stability of structures of lawmaking (regimes, systems, orders, spaces, etc.) in international arbitration, when and how these structures are likely to change, where the impetus may come from, etc.

To be very clear, my purpose in using legitimacy is not to justify any regime; not to resist it; not to oppose it; not to assess its moral laudability; not to say what political agenda it does, should or shouldn't promote; not to make us ponder our responsibility in propagating the power structure it implies; not to bang on any table. I'm not arguing that these aren't important questions or valuable endeavours. I'm not claiming either that the question I am asking is more important than any of these other questions. But again the one thing we have to be wary about is the temptation to offer a totalizing account, an account that would try to capture all of these aspects of legitimacy, all of the purposes of the concept. To say the least, an article-length treatment of legitimacy cannot encompass all these variants of legitimacy. And it must not try. It is, then, patently a choice to focus on this use of legitimacy in this particular paper, a choice determined by altogether contingent factors – which like all contingent factors come into being and pass out of being.

Now, what does this imply for our understanding of legitimacy? The first point is hackneyed and obvious, but important: a regime is easier to sustain, more stable, if it reflects the self-interests of its addressees. For the chosen use of the concept of legitimacy, anchoring it in self-interest is then apt. To be clear, I'm talking about self-interest not as a reason to comply with a regime but as a reason to input or not input change.

This further means that the perspective is relative: for that particular use of legitimacy, there is no universal standard, it all depends on the relative perspective of the actors concerned. A given regime may be legitimate from the perspective of a given actor, because it advances its self-interests, and illegitimate from the perspective of another actor because it doesn't advance its interest as it thinks it should. To paraphrase Ian Hurd, the idea is that actors make decisions on whether to input change or not based on "an instrumental and calculated assessment of the net benefits of [change] versus [stability], with an instrumental attitude toward social structures and other people".[40] Julia Black uses the idea of "legitimacy communities" to make a different point in a different context (the exercise of interpretive control) but which echoes this reliance on relativism. She first says this: "whilst regulatory actors can compete for legitimacy, whether they are accepted, and by whom, depends on whether their legitimacy communities will endow them with the legitimacy and authority they seek". And then she draws this consequence: regulatory actors "can adopt various strategies to 'solidify' their position by gaining legitimacy from different legitimacy communities. Legitimacy in turn affects their ability to exercise authority, and their ability to function."[41] From these perspectives – Hurd's, Black's, and the perspective advanced here – the legitimacy of a given normative structure is always only relative to a given addressee, varies from one "ruled" to another.

To be clear, we as observers have plainly no judgment to pass on this. It is beside the point whether we think that it is ethically or morally or historically or legally right or wrong that the interests of this or that actor are furthered – the chosen use of the concept of legitimacy excludes the relevance of such judgments. Put technically, the perspective is axiologically agnostic.

If the perspective is relative and depends on the actors' perspective, which actors are relevant? Recall: we are interested in stability, so the relevant actors are those who can change the regime in question. Think of political realism à la Henry Kissinger: as he put it, "An international order, the basic arrangements of which are accepted *by all the major Powers*, may be called 'legitimate'."[42] The international order is stable if the major players consider it legitimate – the *major* players, the others we don't care about. A given instance of arbitral lawmaking is stable if the major actors consider it legitimate – "major" in the sense of those that have the power to change it.

Eventually it might rejoice us lawyers: if asked whether a given arbitral regime is legitimate, the answer would have to be "it depends". It depends on the different actors' perspective. Certain types of parties might find that a given regime is not legitimate, others will; arbitrators in turn might find it legitimate; perhaps states won't find it legitimate; and so on. Why are these different actors' perspectives relevant? Because they can change the regime, because they can affect its stability: if the regime is not legitimate to them, they might try to alter it, which is what we want to know.

Once more on this idea of relativism: among the many things that legitimacy is *not* used for in this paper is the search for any form of "absolute" assessment of political morality, where "absolute" means that the view is meant to exclude the validity of other views. Such a view would be, for instance, that a given instance of international arbitration lawmaking is legitimate, in the sense of morally justified, not from any actor's point of view, but from the point of view of an observer, according to some

40. Ian HURD, *After Anarchy: Legitimacy and Power in the United Nations Security Council* (Princeton University Press 2007) p. 37. In Hurd's original version, the words "input" and "stability" read "compliance" and "non-compliance".

41. BLACK, "'Says Who?'", p. 306.

42. Henry KISSINGER, "Reflections on American Diplomacy", 35 Foreign Affairs (1956) p. 37, p. 43 (emphasis added). See further Vanessa LISHINGMAN, "Henry Kissinger's Contribution to the Conception of International Relations Legitimacy, Consensus and Order: the Foreign Policy of Moderation", 1 Glendon Journal of International Studies (2000).

metaphysically determined standard. Party autonomy and consent, for instance, form one such metaphysical standard of legitimacy: arbitration's lawmaking is legitimate because the parties have consented to it; the effects of BITs as applied by arbitrators are legitimate because states have agreed to them: these are notions of legitimacy that are based on an "absolute", metaphysical standard. Standards such as these belong into an entirely different discussion than the one I'm offering here. Indeed party autonomy and consent, which figure prominently in many debates on legitimacy in international arbitration, have per se no place in the current discussion: party autonomy and consent are not determinants of stability. (I recognize that *indirectly* they may have a role to play, for instance through sunset clauses, which have an impact on regime stability, but this is a different matter.)

To situate it in the literature, the understanding of legitimacy used in this paper is, then, different from the usual three understandings Thomas identifies in his extensive compilation of the literature on legitimacy in international law. It is not legal legitimacy, because it doesn't concern itself with whether lawmaking by international arbitration is lawful, whether the parties to international arbitrations, or anyone else, have a legal obligation to submit to the relevant international arbitration regime. It is not moral legitimacy because it doesn't concern itself with universal, metaphysical assessments; it doesn't concern itself with the question whether the parties to international arbitrations, or anyone else, have a moral obligation to submit to the relevant international arbitration regime. It is not social legitimacy, although it comes close to it, because it doesn't concern itself with actors' beliefs that a regime is legally or morally legitimate; it doesn't quite try, as social legitimacy tends to do, to "account for legitimacy's capacity to motivate obedience even for those who are consistently disadvantaged by the system".[43] To the contrary, the point is rather to ask how the actors are likely to react when they understand whether they are advantaged or disadvantaged by the system, assuming that they react rationally. It thus concerns itself with the interests the different actors of the systems actually have, regardless whether they currently happen to perceive and understand these interests.

If the understanding of legitimacy used in this paper required a label specifying its basis, to situate it more precisely in the literature, it would be called interest-based or outcome-based or output legitimacy.[44] It might then be compared in the literature to Ernst Haas's approach, when he writes that "[o]rganizational legitimacy exists when the membership values the organization and generally implements collective decisions because they are seen to implement the members' values".[45] It might also be likened to output legitimacy in Sharpf's classification of "the functions of input-oriented and output-oriented legitimating arguments in liberal democracies".[46] Output legitimacy, in Sharpf's classification, refers to "government *for* the people"[47] – in the language of this

43. THOMAS, "Uses and Abuses of Legitimacy in International Law", p. 741.

44. FRANCK, *The Power of Legitimacy Among Nations*, pp. 17-18 (process-based, procedural-substantive and outcome-based legitimacy).

45. Ernst HAAS, *When Knowledge Is Power: Three Models of Change in International Organizations* (University of California Press 1990) p. 87.

46. Fritz SHARPF, "Problem-Solving Effectiveness and Democratic Accountability in the EU", MPIfG Working Paper 03/1, February 2003.

47. *Ibid.*

paper, we would say "lawmaking *for* the actors of the regime". It understands legitimacy as the capacity to "generally represent effective solutions to common problems of the governed"[48] – in the language of this paper, we would say "advance the interests of the addressees of the regime", more precisely those addressees who are also actors of the regime, who can effectively change it. A failure of output legitimacy is a failure to satisfy the self-interests of the regime's actors; it will usually trigger attempts to alter the system's workings.

V. MODELLING ACTOR INPUT IN INTERNATIONAL ARBITRATION LAWMAKING

The chosen purpose of the use of legitimacy, as explained abundantly in the preceding sections, is to help us elaborate a framework that will allow us to better assess the stability and better predict the evolution of different instances of international arbitration lawmaking, different arbitral regimes broadly speaking. Brutally simplified, if a given arbitral regime is good to a given actor, it will be understood as legitimate from that actor's perspective, and that actor is unlikely to input much change; conversely, if the regime is not legitimate to an actor who can change it, it likely will try to alter it. If the regime is not legitimate to an actor who cannot change it, probably nothing much will happen.

Can we, then, model this simple idea, provide a model that can be applied to analyze discrete actual instances of international arbitration lawmaking? I argue, based on prior and ongoing work with Cédric Dupont and Jason Yackee,[49] that David Easton's model of a political system is a good starting point.[50]

Easton developed a model of political systems based on Harold Laswell's straightforward idea that politics is the question of "who gets what, when, how"[51] – in other words whose self-interests are furthered, when, and how. In the model, actors influence a system through so-called "inputs".

Inputs are attempts to make the system do the bidding of the actors providing the input, to make it maximize their self-interests. The system then aggregates these inputs and transforms them into so-called "outputs".

Outputs are effectively determinations of who gets what, when, and how; they are determinations of whose self-interests are advanced when and how; they are authoritative allocations of values, as Easton puts it; they are normative outcomes in the sense that they say what things ought to be, in principle with some power to make things be that way.

Once the cards have thus been dealt, some actors will of course be unhappy because their self-interests are not as maximized as they wanted or because their self-interests have been harmed by the input of another actor. These disgruntled actors then adapt

---

48. *Ibid.*
49. See below, from notes 52 onwards.
50. David EASTON, *A Systems Analysis of Political Life* (Wiley 1965); David EASTON, *The Political System: An Inquiry into the State of Political Science (*Knopf 1953).
51. Harold D. LASSWELL, *Politics: Who Gets What, When, How* (P. Smith 1950 [1936]).

their input or provide new input. This reaction Easton calls feedback loops from output to input.

The result is a constant competition among the actors to influence the system. Such a political system is thus dynamic, constantly evolving through reactions to its own outputs.

To put this technically, political systems in Easton's sense are organic collective mechanisms of steps in value-allocation decision-making, transforming certain types of input into certain types of output, thereby furthering certain goals by effectively allocating values. The output in turn feeds back to the actors providing the input, leading them to adapt that input in order to continuously seek the maximization of their own interests.

To put this in the language used earlier in this paper, a political system is a regime which produces normative outcomes (lawmaking, regulation, for instance). The regime's actors are those who have the power to influence it, to shape it. Each actor influences, tries to shape the regime in such a way that the regime is as legitimate as possible to the actor in question, which means that it advances its self-interests as much as possible. If the regime doesn't advance the interests of a given actor, or doesn't advance it enough, that actor tries to change the regime, it adapts the way in which it influences it, how it tries to shape it. Each influence successfully exercised on the regime alters the normative outcomes it produces, modifies the interests it advances, therefore at least possibly harming one actor's self-interests while better advancing another actor's self-interests. This reallocation of interests will thus make the regime less legitimate for one actor, who is likely to push back and try to vary the regime, back to its original position or onwards to a new position, so that it again maximizes its self-interests. These iterations stop if an equilibrium is reached in which each actor's self-interests are maximized to an extent that corresponds to their power to influence the regime. The regime is then in a situation of stability lasting until an actor discovers what self-interests it could make the regime maximize or until the power play changes.

The model, of course, assumes purely rational utilitarian behaviour on the part of the actors and tends to assume that we are in a situation of finite resources where one's gain is another's loss. Clearly none of these assumptions is systematically true in the real world. But I take it to be reasonably representative of the purpose of the entire analysis, which, as explained above, is to assess the stability of a regime. A more complete, and ultimately more accurate model would factor in the respective weights of altruistic and self-serving pursuits, as well as other behavioural distortions of rationality, such as cognitive biases, in each actor's attempts to shape the regime into what it would like it to be. Such a more complete, behavioural model, however, would most likely become unwieldy to the point of being unusable, as the proportion of altruistic/self-serving pursuits is highly variable from one individual or institution to another, as are cognitive biases.

Easton himself applied his model to national, typically parliamentary politics, and to international political systems such as NATO, the UN, and the Southeast Asia Treaty Organization (SEATO). But his model can in fact be applied to everything that aggregates input and allocates who gets what: from international organizations, to "the" international system, to companies, law firms, university departments, families, all manner of regimes, policy spaces, groups, institutions.

Importantly, what the model is applied to – the "system" – does not have to be an actual, real, naturally demarcated, independently existing system per se, in the sense that the human body is, for example. It doesn't have to be a truly discrete system because the purpose of Easton's model, its heuristic value as it were, is not to make us see the separateness of the "system", that it has a specific, distinct identity. It lies instead in encouraging us to focus on identifying the main actors who can modify the system by shaping and influencing the rules it produces and thus the values it allocates. It also helps us see the overall incentive structure in which they operate, which combines both rule creation and experiencing the consequences of these rules.

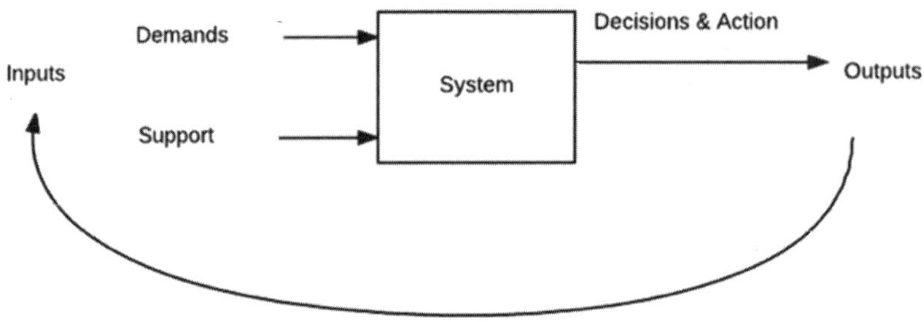

Figure 1. David Easton's model of a political system - Dupont, Schultz & Yackee, "Investment Arbitration and Political Systems Theory", Oxford Handbook of International Arbitration, forthcoming.

Easton's model can be represented as shown in Figure 1.[52]

With Dupont and Yackee we have applied the model to investment arbitration.[53] There it means that states, investors, arbitrators, and arbitration institutions all constantly, to the best of their bounded rationality, attempt to push the regime in a given direction so that it best produces their own investment-law demands. The cumulative result of these influences is the existing, evolving investment arbitration case law. We used the chart in Figure 2 to represent this.[54]

52. DUPONT, SCHULTZ and YACKEE, "Investment Arbitration and Political Systems Theory".
53. *Ibid.*, and DUPONT and SCHULTZ "Towards a New Heuristic Model".
54. DUPONT and SCHULTZ "Towards a New Heuristic Model".

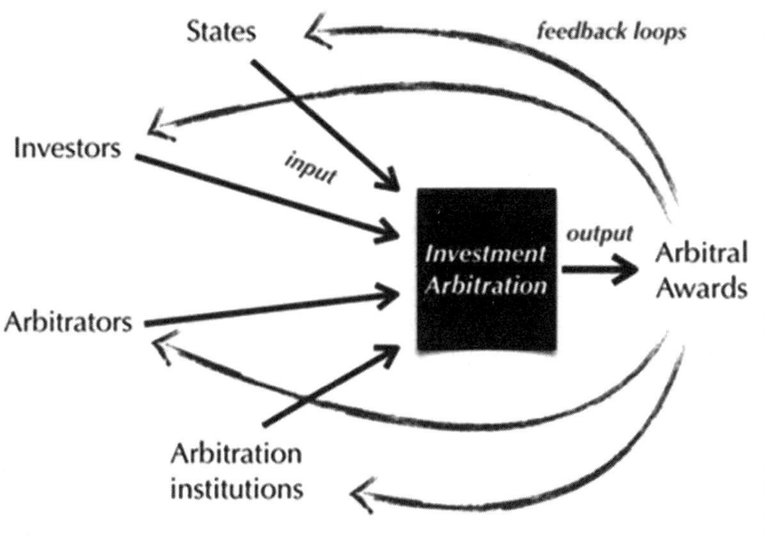

Figure 2. Investment arbitration as a political system, showing only actors able to make changes directly in the system - Dupont & Schultz, Towards a New Heuristic Model, JIDS 2016.

All the actors providing input on the charts are represented there because they have the power to change the regime. As I said above, what makes them actors is precisely the fact that they can modify the regime.

The "input" arrows on the charts represent attempts, real or likely, to make the regime advance their self-interests, to make it legitimate from their perspective.

A quick and partial example, which we've used elsewhere:[55] a state may consider that international investment law is legitimate if it reflects an understanding of the fair and equitable treatment (FET) standard in line with the *Neer* decision, which assumably serves the state's self-interest. The state provides an input into the system by arguing to an arbitral tribunal that its decision should articulate that particular understanding, as an authoritative statement and application of the law. The decision of the tribunal to articulate a certain understanding of FET is the "output" of the system. The system itself can be viewed as the place of interactions between the system's various actors; it consists of the processes through which their various inputs are aggregated into the system's outputs.

The states' input is their consent to investment arbitration, the ways in which they express that consent, their treaty-making activity, their contractual practices with

55. DUPONT, SCHULTZ and YACKEE, "Investment Arbitration and Political Systems Theory".

foreign investors, and their domestic legislative actions (when a national "investment code" contains an offer to arbitrate addressed to foreign investors). Another type of states' input relates to their behaviour during and in relation to arbitration procedures. Yet another is their role in choosing arbitrators for institutional lists.

The investors' input is the claims they file or threaten to file, the conditions under which they do so, against which states, the procedural rules or institution they use, what they seek to obtain in doing so, how they frame their claims, and so on. Another type of investors' input relates, here too, to their behaviour during arbitration procedures.

The arbitrators' input is their choices, conscious or not, in framing and determining the awards and orders they render.

The arbitration institutions' input is their drafting of their own procedural rules and their residual capacity in appointing arbitrators.

The system's output is the arbitral awards, taken in the aggregate, including all their variegated effects, from the determination of rights, to their precedential value, to their actual financial implications for all actors involved, to their impact on the reputation of all actors involved, and including all forms of legal, economic, social, and political dimensions.

The awards, either individually or in the aggregate, feed back into the system as they have effects on the actors, who react to it by, for example, changing the content or intensity of their level of support, by changing their input.

Then of course there are also indirect actors: actors who cannot directly change the system, cannot provide direct input into it, but who can influence the actors who can change it directly. We have referred to them elsewhere as "the public".[56] Luke Nottage calls them "society at large".[57] They include NGOs, academia, various institutionalized forms of expression of civil society, various forms of expression of various industries (including of course the arbitration industry and ICCA, one of its expressions), occasionally particularly motivated individuals, the media.

Moreover, the different actors tend to try to influence one another, with the ultimate purpose of shaping the investment regime.

With this additional layer of complexity, the model looks as shown in Figure 3.

56. DUPONT, SCHULTZ and YACKEE, "Investment Arbitration and Political Systems Theory".
57. Luke R. NOTTAGE, "International Arbitration and Society at Large" in Andrea BJORKLUND, Franco FERRARI, and Stefan KROELL, eds., *Cambridge Compendium of International Commercial and Investment Arbitration* (CUP forthcoming).

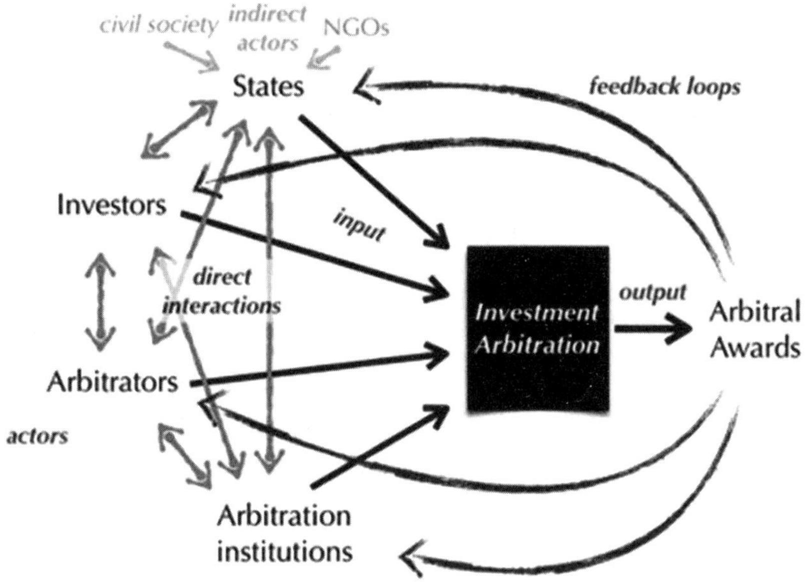

Figure 3. Investment arbitration as a political system, showing both actors able to make changes directly in the system and indirect actors - Dupont & Schultz, Towards a New Heuristic Model, JIDS 2016.

Of course this still remains quite schematic. That is the point. It keeps the model simple. Then again, when concretely applied, the model might call for some disaggregation. Most obviously, and this tends to be a pervasive problem in international relations, attributing an intention to a state is not much better than attributing an intention to "women" or to "men", collectively. States, obviously, are collectivities made up of constituent units with different interests, and different pathways and powers to express that interest. For instance, a state's foreign ministry or trade ministry may have very different ideas about what investment arbitration should do than the ministry whose actions are being challenged. Likewise, the output of the system may be disaggregated into customary international law, arbitral case law, treaty interpretation. Moreover, one might debate whether other key actors should enter the picture: amicus curiae, for instance, may be considered to provide direct input into the system.[58] But again, one of the purposes of the model is to simplify the complications of reality in order to see a more general picture.

The legitimacy question, in this situation, would be this: to what extent do states, investors, arbitrators, arbitration institutions consider that investment arbitration, as a

58. This is discussed at some length in DUPONT, SCHULTZ and YACKEE, "Investment Arbitration and Political Systems Theory" and DUPONT and SCHULTZ "Towards a New Heuristic Model".

regime of international arbitration lawmaking, is legitimate for them, to what extent does it advance their self-interests? From that perspective – I repeat the point but it is important – the question of the legitimacy of investment arbitration has nothing to do with the fact that states consented to it, or did not consent to some of it; it has also nothing to do either with the fact that the regime promotes a neoliberal agenda (if indeed it does). The fact that the system of investment arbitration exhibits inconsistencies, to the extent it does, is not an argument relevant to its legitimacy either – not per se, it would be relevant if it were demonstrated that the sort of inconsistency we are talking about here harms the interests of one of the regime's actors.

If we now asked whether the current investment arbitration regime is stable, on the grounds that it is legitimate from the perspective of its actors, the answer would likely be some shade of grey: it might be that it isn't legitimate to many states but it might well be to many investors, to arbitrators, and to arbitration institutions. The resultant of these different forces, of these different attempts to make the regime legitimate for its respective actors, might well be small, not terribly far from nil, which would mean that the regime is indeed stable, unlikely to move.

As I said above, this entire approach is grounded in realism, not in any form of normativism such as morality or historical intent or even legal objectives. So the argument that investment arbitration was never meant to promote the self-interests of arbitrators is irrelevant, beside the point. It uses a different understanding of legitimacy which would itself serve a different purpose. It doesn't answer the question posed, which concerns stability. Whether investment arbitration should or should not promote the interests of arbitrators to the expense of, say, states is simply not this perspective's concern.[59]

Applied to international arbitration lawmaking generically (not all arbitration lawmaking as a whole, but generically to all individual instances of arbitration lawmaking), the model would look as represented in Figure 4.

In this chart, states, parties, transnational soft-law producers, arbitrators, and arbitration institutions are all input-actors, as I called them at the outset of this paper. Here I alternatively label them "change-empowered actors", in the sense that they are empowered to procure change: they are the actors who can change the international arbitral regime by providing direct input, by doing something that will have an immediate effect in the regime. "Society at large", to use Nottage's terminology, is an array of indirect actors, who cannot directly change the international arbitral regime in question but can exercise various forms of influence on the change-empowered actors.

One might note similarities between the change-empowered actors vs. indirect actors dichotomy and Emmanuel Gaillard's "service providers" vs. "value providers" distinction. While there are overlaps, the fault line falls at a quite different place. "Service providers" are those actors who "do" arbitration, in the sense of practicing it,

59. To be clear, I do not argue that arbitrators only seek to promote their self-interest in their decision-making; as I've argued elsewhere, arbitrators are like any other individual: they promote in part the interests of others and in part their own interests, this is only human: Thomas SCHULTZ, "Arbitral Decision-Making: Legal Realism and Law & Economics", 6 JIDS (2015) p. 231.

while "value providers" are those actors who say how it should be done.[60] In these terms, change-empowered actors are those who "make" arbitration – make it be, make it what it is – while indirect actors are those who inform and influence the makers. All of the actors in my suggested distinction try, do, or could influence the normative structure of international arbitration – the "law" produced for and through international arbitration. The fault line marks the difference in their power to do it.

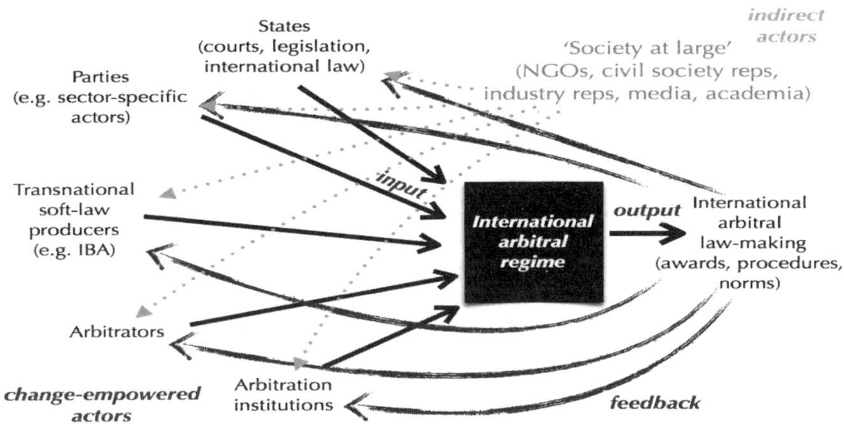

Figure 4. International arbitration lawmaking modelled as a political system

VI. ANTICIPATING BACKLASHES AND OVERREACTIONS TO LEGITIMACY ISSUES

Let us go back to the initial question this paper asked: Why do we care about the legitimacy of international arbitration lawmaking?

Surely we all have an interest in occupying ourselves with what we find morally right or wrong, because we naturally do tend to want the world to be a morally better place. But let us put these lofty aspirations aside. As I suggested above, such questioning would

60. Emmanuel GAILLARD, "Sociology of International Arbitration", 31 Arbitration International (2015, no. 1) p. 4, p. 5, p. 7: in Gaillard's words, service providers are the "social groups who dedicate their activity exclusively, or almost exclusively, to international arbitration" and value providers those who "provide guidance as to the way international arbitration should develop and arbitral social actors should behave"; he adds a third category of "essential actors", who are "the actors without which international arbitration would not exist [namely] the parties and the arbitrators".

require that we engage seriously with moral or political philosophy, which would be a very different discussion than what I've offered in this paper. To be clear, I'm not arguing that this is a more important discussion, or a less important one; my point is simply that separate discussions should be kept separate. Discussions too should better not be totalizing.

One pragmatic reason to care about the legitimacy of international arbitration lawmaking, as I have suggested above, is that a given regime of arbitration lawmaking that is not considered legitimate by an actor that has the capacity to change the regime is unlikely to remain unchanged in the longer run. A typical, but of course not exclusive, reason for an actor to think a regime illegitimate is its failure to serve the actors' self-interests. Hence my hinging of legitimacy on self-interest.

Then again, if different actors, all of which can change the regime, have different views on its legitimacy, and are thus all likely at some stage to try to pull it in a different direction, its likelihood and direction of change will depend on the cumulative effects of these different pulls. Hence the model of a political system I've suggested.

What, now, does that mean for us? If we care about arbitration, for whatever reason (egotistic, altruistic, academic), we probably should care about its stability, about how it might evolve. We should then, first, identify the relevant actors who can change international arbitration (international arbitration in general or a specific regime of international arbitration). Who can make it be something different, for better or worse. Who can affect its stability. And understand how exactly they can change it. Second, we should clarify what exactly the effects of arbitral regimes are on its different actors, which would tend to call for empirical research, ideally conducted by individuals with as little self-interest in the system as possible. Obviously, the findings of such research should then be communicated to the relevant actors. This should be done even if the findings are negative, even if they are disappointing about what international arbitration effectively does for these actors: only this can avoid that these actors overreact to wrong appreciations of these effects, that they overreact to wrongly perceived legitimacy issues.

Brutally simplified, to illustrate the idea with just one example: some states are currently probably overreacting to what they (mis)understand to be the effects of investment arbitration on them, thinking it is not a legitimate system for them. Others are probably under-reacting. Yet others are probably reacting in a way that is beside the point, that doesn't address the problem. None of this is good. I said "probably": there is not yet quite enough empirical research on the complex question of the socio-economic effects of investment arbitration to really say that the reactions are adequate or not.

It is tempting to paraphrase Stavros Brekoulakis's words of caution. As he put it, "Arbitration lawyers often seem to have been under the self-reassuring delusion that arbitration's contribution to the public is somehow axiomatic, namely that arbitration is there to serve the business community, and by extension it serves the interests of the public too. However, the prevailing perception of arbitration by a critical mass of the public is often quite different."[61] Paraphrased in the language of this paper, it would be: "Those who are centrally occupied with international arbitration often seem to have been

61. Stavros BREKOULAKIS, "Introduction: The Evolution and Future of International Arbitration" in Stavros BREKOULAKIS, Julian LEW and Loukas MISTELIS, eds., *The Evolution of International Arbitration* (Kluwer 2016) p. 13.

under the self-reassuring delusion that arbitration's contribution to those actors who can change it is somehow axiomatic, namely that arbitration either serves the interests of a given actor, or the actor is unable to do any harm, to change the regime. However, the prevailing perception of arbitration by a critical mass of change-empowered actors is often quite different, namely that arbitration is not legitimate from their perspective."

Possibly many if not most of these perceptions are not grounded in fact. But do we really know? It certainly seems unwise to respond, off the cuff, that there are no problems, without evidence to back up such statements. It also seems unwise to respond to such concerns by arguing that states, or other parties, consented to the regime so it is their problem: that might be morally and legally true, but it is beside the point if the preoccupation is stability. It relies on a different concept of legitimacy which belongs in a different discussion.

Lawmaking by Arbitrators

Lucy Reed[*]

TABLE OF CONTENTS PAGE

I. INTRODUCTION

This panel is tasked with examining "lawmaking" in international arbitration and the attendant "legitimacy" issues. The panellists have had the good fortune of guidance from our moderator that in:

> "covering the different aspects and actors relevant for lawmaking in international arbitration (we should use a loose notion of lawmaking here, encompassing not only binding norms, but *any material* that influences the normative expectations of parties or that is *useful in making decisions* relating to international arbitration) and its legitimacy (another vague notion, which we could circumscribe as encompassing some level of social acceptance short of coercion because those who accept it have normative reasons for doing so)". (Emphasis added.)

This guidance is particularly welcome for the assigned topic of this paper – lawmaking by arbitrators – because arbitrators are neither legislators nor judges with police power behind them. Arbitrators make rulings binding only on the parties before them (subject to national court enforcement), there being no system of binding precedent in international arbitration. Perhaps the most direct influence international arbitrators have in making law is through input in United Nations Commission on International Trade Law (UNCITRAL) sessions on the Model Law and model conventions.

However, if one examines whether international arbitrators produce "any material … useful in making decisions", then it is readily apparent that arbitrators can and do make law – in certain situations.[1] In the author's view, the main situations fall into three

---

* Professor of Law and Director, Centre for International Law, National University of Singapore; ICCA Governing Board Member. The author thanks Sophie Ryan, a New Colombo Plan Scholarship exchange student at the NUS Law Faculty, for her invaluable assistance with this paper.

1. See D. Brian KING and Rahim MOLOO, "International Arbitrators as Lawmakers", 46 New York University Journal of International Law and Politics (2014, no. 3) p. 875 at pp. 878-879. The author recommends this often-cited article to readers seeking an incisive overview of the topic. Messrs. King and Moloo were colleagues of the author at Freshfields Bruckhaus Deringer.

categories: (1) arbitrators in international commercial arbitration are not meant to, and rarely do make law; (2) arbitrators in standing and specialized *ad hoc* international tribunals are meant to, and do make law; and (3) the latest guests at the table – arbitrators sitting on *ad hoc* investor-state arbitration (*ISA*) tribunals – were not necessarily meant to, but now do make law, sometimes in denial and sometimes necessarily inconsistently.

Lest these categories seem too stark, some introductory description is warranted.

First, commercial arbitration tribunals rarely make law for the obvious reason that the disputes generally are transaction-specific and confidential. To the extent commercial arbitration awards are published in redacted form by institutions or emerge through setting-aside and enforcement litigation in national courts, the outside world benefits from the guidance provided, but not in the sense of having precedents to cite.

Second, the rare standing arbitration tribunals – foremost, the Iran-United States Claims Tribunal in its early chapters – deal with a universe of similar cases and publish their awards. They are constituted as standing tribunals precisely so they can develop consistent rulings on recurring procedural and substantive issues. The same is true of tribunals set up under specialized sector regimes that publish decisions, the best known of which are the Court of Arbitration for Sport and the World Intellectual Property Organization.

Third, in related vein because their awards now are almost always public, investment treaty tribunals default to the role of *de facto* lawmakers. This function is most acceptable when the arbitrators provide thoughtful reasoning in applying international law (and any other applicable law) to the facts before them and, when citing to prior awards, engage transparently with the legal analysis in those awards. This function is suspect, and hence least legitimate, when arbitrators set out to develop the law outside of the context and purpose of the case before them.

It is this third category – lawmaking by ISA tribunals – that garners the most attention. The attention comes in the form of recent books, articles and blogs on individual cases and perceived trends, thoughtful legal theory (along the lines of the questions in Professor Thomas Schulz' paper for this panel), and far less thoughtful attacks in academia and the media.[2] On the ethics front, the attention falls not just on the phenomena of "double-hatting" and issue conflict, but also on the very idea of private

2. To cite only some of the leading commentary: Andreas FOLLESDAL and Geir ULFSTEIN, *The Judicialization of International Law* (Oxford University Press 2018); Dolores BENTOLILA, *Arbitrators as Lawmakers* (Wolters Kluwer 2017); W. Michael REISMAN, "'Case Specific Mandates' versus 'Systemic Implications': How Should Investment Tribunals Decide?", 29 Arbitration International (2013) p. 131; Irene M. TEN CATE, "The Costs of Consistency: Precedent in Investment Treaty Arbitration", 51 Columbia Journal of Transnational Law (2013) p. 418; Stephan W. SCHILL, "International Arbitrators as System Builders", 106 *Proceedings of the Annual Meeting (American Society of International Law)* (2012) p. 295; Stephan W. SCHILL, "System Building in Investment Treaty Arbitration and Lawmaking", 12 German Law Journal (2011) p. 1083; W. Mark C. WEIDEMAIER, "Toward a Theory of Precedent in Investment Treaty Arbitration", 51 William and Mary Law Review (2010) p. 1901; Jeffrey P. COMMISSION, "Precedent in Investment Treaty Arbitration: A Citation Analysis of a Developing Jurisprudence", 24 Journal of International Arbitration (2007) p. 129; Susan D. FRANCK, "The Legitimacy Crisis in Investment Treaty Arbitration: Privatizing Public International Law Through Inconsistent Decisions", 73 Fordham Law Review (2005) p. 1521.

arbitrators judging and influencing public policy. Even the criticism that is well-deserved tends to be at best general and at worst sensational.

This third category of arbitrator lawmaking is therefore the richest for discussion at this ICCA Congress. Hence, ISA will be the main focus of this paper, and in particular – because there is so little new to offer on the topic – the contributions of new empirical research on the realities and impact of arbitrator lawmaking.

II. INTERNATIONAL COMMERCIAL ARBITRATION

The historic purpose of international commercial arbitration is to resolve cross-border business disputes via independent *ad hoc* tribunals rather than national courts. The process may be more or less expeditious and expensive than court litigation, depending on the nature and magnitude of the dispute and the proclivities of the parties. But the arbitration is always connected to a transactional relationship, which has generated a dispute that must be resolved if the parties are to move forward together or separately. The parties rely on a one-off tribunal to resolve the dispute, typically not wanting or expecting – or paying for – the arbitrators to draft a reasoned award aimed at any person or any issue outside their case. This ring-fence is protected by the rigorous practice (if not requirement) of confidentiality for the proceedings, the deliberations and the award itself.[3]

The fence necessarily comes down if and when a party goes to court to set aside or enforce the award. Only at that point will outsiders have the benefit of reading the arbitrators' dispositive (and other) reasoning and learning how the tribunal managed the case. This operates, in effect, as a windfall for the broader commercial community, allowing lawyers to learn how tribunals – and sometimes individual arbitrators – apply institutional procedural rules, interpret common contractual provisions, structure compensation and award interest. The value of such practical knowledge is what motivates many arbitral institutions to publish redacted awards. The redacted compilations are helpful in illuminating institution-specific procedural practice, but only rarely offer insight into legal analysis useful beyond the case at hand because the analysis generally is transaction focused and fact specific.

That being said, those rare insights can be useful indeed. There is a case to be made – and being made – for greater access to international commercial arbitration awards, or at least weighty ones. To the extent companies and individuals are increasingly choosing arbitration over the courts, and arbitrators are writing incisive awards on recurring commercial legal issues, the secrecy of those awards is a loss overall. Private justice takes its toll on public national court justice. Professor Mark Feldman, noting the "compelling and multifaceted nature of the public interest in the availability of awards – particularly with respect to the development of international law", argues for mandatory publication of awards, or publication of the legal reasoning of awards or, at very least, publication of

3. In her seminal 2007 article, Professor Gabrielle Kaufmann-Kohler found that only 15 percent of the 190 ICC awards in her dataset cited to prior awards, and that was in the context of common issues such as jurisdiction and non-signatories. Gabrielle KAUFMANN-KOHLER, "Arbitral Precedent: Dream, Necessity or Excuse?", 23 Arbitration International (2007) p. 357.

redacted awards.[4] Sir Bernard Rix has written that commercial law goes "underground" when parties submit "the basic feedstock of our commercial law" to arbitrators, and suggests that publication of anonymized awards should be the default.[5] Ben Juratowitch QC goes farther, advocating for the default that any commercial arbitration award be made public in unredacted form unless the tribunal, after hearing the parties, decides otherwise.[6] This reflects Juratowitch's views, based on experience, that "there are a number of high quality arbitral awards dealing with matters of general interest that very few people have the benefit of reading", and:

> "For better or worse, international commercial arbitration is now a major forum for the resolution of disputes that impact on those other than the parties to them. It is a forum in which claims of corruption of public officials and of breaches of competition law are made and decided, in which States and State-owned entities are routinely parties, and in which large swathes of commercial law, including standard form commercial contracts, are applied and developed. There are therefore compelling reasons for people to be increasingly concerned about the fact that it is to a substantial degree happening in secret."[7]

The author's view, also based on experience (including as a Vice President of the ICC Court of Arbitration involved in award scrutiny), is that only a small percentage of international commercial arbitration awards – as well reasoned as they may be – would move the law forward if published, anonymized or not. Even for that small percentage, it is the rare commercial client that would volunteer to share its good or bad fortune in arbitration with its competitors and the world at large. And even if, as Juratowitch observes, "[s]ecrecy is a habit, not a need", commercial parties show little sign of wanting to cure themselves of this habit.

What are the implications, from a lawmaking perspective, for the legitimacy of international commercial arbitration awards? In the author's view, the key test of legitimacy is the view – and the actions – of the owners, or key stakeholders, of arbitration. As the late Lord Mustill wrote, "commercial arbitration exists for one purpose only: to serve the commercial man".[8] It could be that the commercial man – now better said, commercial person – will one day want greater transparency of the

---

4. M. FELDMAN, "International Arbitration and Transparency", Working Draft 25 September 2006 available at <https://ssrn.com/aabstract-2843140> (last accessed on 26 March 2018) (cited with permission of the author).
5. Rt. Ho. Sir Bernard RIX, "Confidentiality in International Arbitration: Virtue or Vice", Jones Day Professorship in Commercial Law Lecture, Singapore Management University, 12 March 2015, pp. 19-21.
6. Ben JURATOWITCH QC, "Departing from Confidentiality in International Dispute Resolution", BIICL Seminar on Difficult Issues in Commercial, Investor-State, and State-State Dispute Resolution: Differences and Commonalities, 8 June 2017 at <www.biicl.org/documents/1676_2017.pdf?showdocument=1> (last accessed 23 March 2018). Mr. Juratowitch was the author's colleague at Freshfields Bruckhaus Deringer.
7. B. JURATOWITCH, "Departing from Confidentiality in International Dispute Resolution", pp. 8-10.
8. Lord Michael MUSTILL QC, "The New Lex Mercatoria: The First Five Years", 4 Arbitration International (1988) p. 86.

awards resolving his or her disputes, and thereby maximize lawmaking by *ad hoc* arbitrators, but that day apparently has not yet come.

In sum, the private nature of most commercial arbitration awards does not undermine the legitimacy of the system. Nonetheless, it is interesting to contemplate whether and how arbitrators would write their awards differently, if they were selected and empowered – to recall Sir Bernard's words – to "unbury" their legal reasoning and affirmatively make international commercial law.

III. SPECIALIZED TRIBUNALS

There are standing or specialized international arbitral tribunals that fall between *ad hoc* commercial arbitration tribunals and investment treaty tribunals in terms of arbitrator lawmaking.

1. *The Iran-United States Claims Tribunal*

The prime example may be the Iran-United States Claims Tribunal, in its early stages. The Tribunal was established under the Claims Settlement Declaration of the post-hostage crisis Algiers Accords, with jurisdiction (on the commercial side) to resolve contract breach and expropriation claims between nationals of the United States or Iran and the opposite government. The Tribunal consisted of (and still consists of) nine judges: three from the United States, three from Iran, and three from third states. Remarkably, the United States and Iran agreed that all Tribunal awards would be published.

Working with this circumscribed jurisdiction and the certainty of publication, the original Tribunal members – all full-time arbitrators – proceeded to develop a specialized jurisprudence of general principles of international contract and expropriation law.[9] In the course of finalizing almost 4,000 commercial cases by award, decision or order by 2003, the Tribunal issued over 350 reasoned awards in "large claims" with a value of US$ 250,000 and above.[10] Interestingly, and of relevance here, the government Agents (of which the author was one for the United States) played a significant role in facilitating the consistency of Tribunal process. It was the Agents who

9. Among other works on the jurisprudence of the Iran-United States Claims Tribunal: Lucy F. REED, "Mixed Private and Public International Solutions to International Crises", Chapter II, *Recueil des cours*, Vol. 306 (2003); David D. CARON and John R. CROOK, eds., *The Iran-United States Claims Tribunal and the Process of International Claims Resolution* (Transnational Publishers 2000); Charles N. BROWER and Jason D. BRUESCHKE, *The Iran-United States Claims Tribunal* (Kluwer Law International 1998); Richard B. LILLICH and Daniel B. MAGRAW, eds., *The Iran-United States Claims Tribunal: Its Contribution to the Law of State Responsibility* (Brill 1998); George ALDRICH, *The Jurisprudence of the Iran-United States Claims Tribunal: An Analysis of the Decisions of the Tribunal* (Clarendon Press 1996); Allahyar MOURI, *The International Law of Expropriation as Reflected in the Work of the Iran-U.S. Claims Tribunal*, (Martinus Nijhoff 1994); John A. WESTBERG, *International Transactions and Claims Involving Government Parties: Case Law of the Iran-United States Claims Tribunal* (International Law Institute 1991); Charles N. BROWER, "The Iran-United States Claims Tribunal", *Recueil des cours*, Vol. 224 (1990).
10. D. CARON and J. CROOK, *Iran-United States Claims Tribunal,* fn. 9 above, p. 140.

could alert counsel for the private claimants, most of whom had only one case before the Tribunal, to relevant prior awards before general publication. The Agents also attended all commercial claim hearings, and often noted and flagged inconsistencies in procedure.

The Iran-United States Claims Tribunal awards later became a primary substantive resource for parties in North American Free Trade Agreement (NAFTA) and bilateral investment treaty arbitration, especially on international legal principles for expropriation, state contract breach and dual nationality.[11] While ISA has largely moved on to its own universe of "precedents", Tribunal awards remain a rich resource of guidance on practice with the UNCITRAL Arbitration Rules. The UNCITRAL Rules were new when the United States and Iran selected them (subject to necessary amendments) for the fledging Tribunal in 1981, allowing the Tribunal – with publicity from commentators – in effect to make UNCITRAL Rule procedural law.[12]

In sum, albeit at the risk of overstatement, the United States and Iran (through the Algiers Accords) created and specifically tasked the Iran-United States Claims Tribunal with making and following international contract and expropriation law. The Tribunal did so. One may agree or disagree with the legal principles that emerged, but there is no question as to the basic legitimacy of the lawmaking done by Tribunal arbitrators.

2. *Specialized Sector Tribunals*

There need not be a standing court like the Iran-United States Claims Tribunal to promote consistency in substantive and procedural arbitral outcome. Specialized sector tribunals can fulfil this function by mission and publication of awards.

The leading example is the Court of Arbitration for Sport (*CAS*). CAS conducts arbitrations by *ad hoc* panels drawn from over 200 CAS arbitrators, who are appointed for four-year terms. There is both an Ordinary Arbitration Division and an Appeals Arbitration Division.

The mission of CAS is to develop a coherent body of sports law, to be applied in fact-specific individual cases and set out in published decisions.[13] The lawmaking role of CAS arbitrators is open and unmistakable. The CAS website, for example, reports that the Code of Sports-related Arbitration, which has governed the organization and procedures of the institution since 1994, was revised in 2003 "in order to incorporate certain *long-established principles of CAS case law or practices consistently followed by the arbitrators* and the Court Office" (emphasis added).[14] The website includes a public database of CAS

11. See, e.g., Christopher S. GIBSON, "Iran-United States Claims Tribunal Precedent in Investor-State Arbitration", 23 Journal of International Arbitration (2009) p. 521.
12. Howard M. HOLTZMANN, "Drafting the Rules of the Tribunal" in D. CARON and J. CROOK, fn. 9 above, p. 75; Stewart A. BAKER and Mark D. DAVIS, *The UNCITRAL Arbitration Rules in Practice: The Experience of the Iran-United States Claims Tribunal* (Kluwer Law and Taxation 1992); Jacomijn J. VAN HOF, *Commentary on the UNCITRAL Arbitration Rules: The Application by the Iran-U.S. Claims Tribunal* (Kluwer Law and Taxation 1991).
13. D.B. KING and R. MOLOO, "International Arbitrators as Lawmakers", pp. 878-879.
14. CAS website, <www.tas-cas.org/en/general/information/history-of-the-cas.html> (last accessed 14 March 2018).

awards, which "regroups all the non-confidential *CAS jurisprudence* from 1986, the year of the first arbitration procedure" (emphasis added),[15] and summaries of recent decisions.[16]

CAS panels proceed accordingly. The panel in *Andrea Anderson et al v. IOC* stated plainly that prior rulings by other panels:

> "form a *valuable body of case law* and can *contribute to strengthen legal predictability* in international sports law. Therefore, although not binding, previous CAS decisions can, and should, be taken into attentive consideration by subsequent CAS panels, in order to help developing legitimate expectations among sports bodies and athletes. ... Although a CAS panel in principle might end up deciding differently from a previous panel, it must accord to previous CAS awards a *substantial precedential value* and it is up to the party advocating a jurisprudential change to submit persuasive argument and evidence to that effect."[17] (Emphasis added.)

With the same goal of developing case law to "contribute to strengthen legal predictability" in another specialized sector, the World Intellectual Property Organization (WIPO) administers panel arbitrations to resolve domain name disputes and publishes the awards. The Internet Corporation for Assigned Names and Numbers (ICANN), which allows parties to submit cybersquatting and other domain name disputes to courts or to approved arbitration providers, mandates public decisions in its Uniform Domain-Name Dispute-Resolution Policy:

> "All decisions under this Policy will be published in full over the internet, except when an Administrative Panel determines in an exceptional case to redact portions of its decision."[18]

Again, like the Iran-United States Claims Tribunal, the institutions behind the specialized CAS and WIPO domain name tribunals specifically tasked them to make law in their respective sectors. The tribunals do so. And again, one may accept or challenge the legal principles that emerge, but there is no question as to the basic legitimacy of the arbitrator lawmaking involved.

IV. INVESTMENT TREATY TRIBUNALS

We now come to the less straightforward *genus* of investor-state arbitration tribunals.

For better or worse, when states began entering into bilateral investment treaties (*BITs*) in earnest in the 1990s, they chose to entrust resolution of disputes between

15. CAS website, <www.tas-cas.org/en/jurisprudence/archive.html> (last accessed 14 March 2018).
16. CAS website, <www.tas-cas.org/en/jurisprudence/recent-decisions.html> (last accessed 14 March 2018).
17. *Anderson v. Int'l Olympic Comm.*, CAS 2008/A/1545, paras. 53-55 (16 July 2010) (Coccia, Fortier, Nater, arbitrators) (citing CAS 97/176, para. 40 (1998)).
18. ICANN website: <www.icann.org/resources/pages/policy-2012-02-25-en> (last accessed 15 March 2018).

qualifying investors and host states to purely *ad hoc* arbitration tribunals. There are various theories as to how this came about, more or less supported by the available *travaux*, one of the best of which (in the author's view) was the desire of many states to sidestep requests by their nationals for diplomatic protection in foreign investment disputes. Much of the heated debate on the legitimacy of this *ad hoc* ISA regime seems to ignore that participating states chose this path – for themselves and, under international law, for their nationals – and it is only states that can step off the path.

The primary task of the arbitrators on an *ad hoc* tribunal resolving an investor-state dispute, whether at the jurisdictional or merits phase, is to apply the relevant treaty (or investment legislation) to the facts of the specific dispute before them. The menu of treaty protections is limited, even in the broadest iterations: promotion of investment, fair and equitable treatment (*FET*), full protection and security (*FPS*), direct and indirect expropriation. It is true that states have refined both jurisdictional requirements (i.e., disallowance of "post-box" foreign investors) and substantive protections (i.e., the minimum standard for FET) over time, often in response to being named respondent in multiple cases. But the reality remains that the core provisions in the hundreds and hundreds of BITs now in effect are similar, and are subject to interpretation over and over again. And while it was once correct to distinguish ICSID arbitrations from those proceeding under the UNCITRAL Rules (or other rules) on the basis that the existence of ICSID arbitrations and ICSID awards were public, while other cases could stay underground, today virtually all cases become known and all awards become public via social media and the legal trade press.

The equation now is: common investment treaty provision + public awards + *ad hoc* tribunals = unavoidable lawmaking by arbitrators. In terms of sequence, a tribunal in BIT case "A v. B" is tasked (by the relevant treaty states) with interpreting treaty provisions that other tribunals have already interpreted and will interpret in future cases, and the tribunals in those future cases in turn are tasked with interpreting language interpreted in the "A v. B" Award. Putting aside for now the questions of whether and how much the "A v. B" tribunal *will be* and *should be* influenced by history and posterity, it is naïve for the "A v. B" arbitrators to think they somehow stand alone.

It could be that the "persistent objectors" – those arbitrators who insist their task is to decide only the dispute before them, with no eye to past or future interpretations of similar treaty language – were justified in taking this position in the early days of BIT arbitration. It could be that, without a body of prior decisions to be cited by the parties for tribunal review, the tribunals followed the practice of international commercial arbitration in staying within the four corners of the dispute before them, as if a treaty FET article were akin to a contract performance clause or a commercial civil code provision. Many tribunals were emphatic about the limits on their role. In the words of the *Methanex v. United States* tribunal in 2001, ISA tribunals "can set no legal precedent, in general or at all".[19] While these protests seem to have waned as the BIT "case law" has waxed, they are still heard. A classic example can be found in the 2009 Award in *Romak v. Uzbekistan*:

19. *Methanex Corp. v. United States* (UNCITRAL), Decision of the Tribunal on Petitions from Third Persons to Intervene as "Amici Curiae" (15 January 2001) para. 51.

> "Ultimately, the Arbitral Tribunal has not been entrusted, by the Parties or otherwise, with a mission to ensure the coherence or development of 'arbitral jurisprudence.' The Arbitral Tribunal's mission is more mundane, but no less important: to resolve the present dispute between the Parties in a reasoned and persuasive manner, irrespective of the unintended consequences that this Arbitral Tribunal's analysis might have on future disputes in general. It is for the legal doctrine as reflected in articles and books, and not for arbitrators in their awards, to set forth, promote or criticize general views regarding trends in, and the desired evolution of, investment law."[20]

At the other end of the spectrum lie tribunals that label lawmaking to be their positive obligation. For example, according to the tribunal in the 2007 Decision on Jurisdiction in *Saipem v. Bangladesh*: "subject to compelling contrary grounds", it is the arbitrators' "duty to adopt solutions established in a series of consistent cases"[21] and to "contribute to the harmonious development of investment law".[22]

There is a middle ground in cases such as *Glamis Gold v. United States*, where the NAFTA tribunal explained in its 2009 Final Award that it had "addressed the particular case before it" while being "aware of the larger context in which it operates" by exhibiting a "modicum of awareness of each of these tribunals for each other and the system as a whole".[23]

Assuming a robust "modicum of awareness", this middle ground seems a realistic and responsible approach. As any individual tribunal is only one among many that are interpreting the same or similar treaty language, the members should perform that task modestly, cautiously and with eyes open, knowing that they may have something to learn from those who have come before them and they may influence those who come after them. As King and Moloo conclude, "whether they like it or not, arbitrators do in fact 'make law' in the sense of rendering decisions that are likely to influence the behavior of both future tribunals and economic actors".[24]

This brings us to the questions of whether, in practice, ISA awards *do* influence the behavior of future tribunals and, if so, how? Still holding the legitimacy-laden question of whether such influence is desirable or not, what ISA lawmaking actually takes place?

There is compelling new empirical research on ISA lawmaking, led by social scientist and law professor Alec Stone Sweet.[25] To minimize suspense, the research first confirms

20. *Romak S.A. v. Republic of Uzbekistan* (UNCITRAL, PCA Case No. AA280), Award (26 November 2009) para. 171.
21. *Saipem S.p.A. v. People's Republic of Bangladesh* (ICSID Case No. ARB/05/7), Decision on Jurisdiction and Recommendation of Provisional Measures (21 March 2007) para. 67.
22. *Ibid.*
23. *Glamis Gold Ltd v. United States* (UNCITRAL), Award (8 June 2009) paras. 4-5. For approval of the *Glamis* Award, see I.M. TEN CATE, "The Costs of Consistency", pp. 476-477; for criticism of the Award, see W.M. REISMAN, "'Case Specific Mandates' versus 'Systemic Implications'", pp. 135-138.
24. D.B. KING and R. MOLOO, "International Arbitrators as Lawmakers", p. 877.
25. Professor Alec Stone Sweet, formerly at Yale Law School, is the author's colleague on the Law Faculty of the National University of Singapore.

that investment treaty arbitrators do indeed make law – markedly increasingly – and then illuminates the lawmaking process, with legitimacy implications.

1. *New Empirical Research on Arbitral Lawmaking*

In their recent article entitled "Arbitral Lawmaking and State Power: An Empirical Analysis of Investor-State Arbitration", Stone Sweet and co-authors Michael Yunsuck Chung and Adam Saltzman define "lawmaking" as occurring when an ISA award "supplements the corpus of normative materials that counsel and tribunals will take into account in future proceedings".[26] Anyone who writes or reads investment treaty arbitration submissions and awards knows instinctively, if only from the ever-longer citation chains in footnotes, that we practice with a "de facto doctrine of precedent"[27] that "can only be denied by those determined to close their eyes".[28]

There has been solid research on citation data, as the best objective indicator of the influence of prior awards on arbitral lawmakers. Most notable are the early studies by Jeffrey Commission in 2007 and Ole Kristian Fauchald in 2008, both of whom published data available through 2006.[29] The number of citations to previous awards can never be the full picture, of course, because the scope and content of a tribunal discussion of an earlier award carries more weight than a bare citation. As noted by King and Moloo, arbitrators no doubt are also influenced by cases raised by the parties or known to them independently, but not cited in their award.[30] Beyond citation data, commentary has tended to focus on specific case studies and the evolution of specific standards in investor-state treaty arbitration.[31]

We now have substantial new material. In addition to the referenced article, Stone Sweet studied the phenomenon of arbitrator lawmaking with fellow social scientist Florian Grisel in their recent book, *The Evolution of International Arbitration: Judicialization,*

---

26. Alec STONE SWEET, Michael Yunsuck CHUNG and Adam SALTZMAN, "Arbitral Lawmaking and State Power: An Empirical Analysis of Investor-State Arbitration", Journal of International Dispute Settlement (2017) p. 1 at pp. 4-5; see also Alec STONE SWEET and Florian GRISEL, *The Evolution of International Arbitration: Judicialization, Governance, Legitimacy* (OUP 2017).
27. Domenico DI PIETRO, "The Use of Precedents in ICSID Arbitration: Regularity or Certainty?", 3 International Arbitration Law Review (2007) p. 96.
28. Jan PAULSSON, "International Arbitration and the Generation of Legal Norms: Treaty Arbitration and International Law" in *International Arbitration 2006: Back to Basics?*, (ICCA Congress Series no. 13 (2007) p. 886.
29. J.P. COMMISSION, "Precedent in Investment Treaty Arbitration", p. 129, especially pp. 148-153; Ole Kristian FAUCHALD, "The Legal Reasoning of ICSID Tribunal – An Empirical Analysis", 19 European Journal of International Law (2008) p. 301. Professor Kaufmann-Kohler also notes the increase in citation to prior awards. G. KAUFMANN-KOHLER, "Arbitral Precedent: Dream, Necessity or Excuse?", pp. 358-371.
30. D.B. KING and R. MOLOO, "International Arbitrators as Lawmakers", p. 885; see also M.C. WEIDEMAIER, "Toward a Theory of Precedent in Investment Treaty Arbitration", p. 1901.
31. E.g. G. KAUFMANN-KOHLER, "Arbitral Precedent: Dream, Necessity or Excuse?", pp. 368-373; Christoph SCHREUER and Matthew WEINIGER, "Conversations Across Cases – Is there a Doctrine of Precedent in Investment Arbitration" in Peter MUCHLINSKI, Federico ORTINO, Christoph SCHREUER, eds., *The Oxford Handbook on International Investment Law* (Oxford University Press 2008).

Governance, Legitimacy. Stone Sweet and Grisel delve deeply into the textual discussion of "*de facto* precedent" in ISA awards dating from 1977 through 2014, and use the Argentina economic crisis ICSID cases to illustrate arbitrator lawmaking in action.[32]

a. Research methodology

Stone Sweet and Grisel (and an army of Yale Law School students) employed a research methodology aimed at rendering the resulting dataset "a robust, relatively direct, indicator of the influence of precedent on decision-making".[33] They assess the evolution of precedent in ISA by compiling "comprehensive information on citation to prior awards and judicial decisions in all final ISA awards on the merits".[34] Rather than pure counting, this compilation consists of "every instance in which a tribunal had cited to decisions on which it *positively relied*, on which it *expressly disagreed*, and on which it *engaged* in order to distinguish the present case from a prior case" (emphasis added).[35] Citations in the summaries of counsel submissions in the awards were included in the dataset only if the tribunal "later addressed the relevant arguments *in its own assessment*" (emphasis added).[36] Where it was unclear whether a cited case informed the tribunal's interpretation of the relevant law, it was excluded from the dataset. Where one case was cited multiple times within the same award for the same proposition, it was counted only once. The authors did include multiple citations to the same award where the tribunal relied upon that award for multiple discrete propositions.

b. Salient findings

Several of the primary findings discernible from Stone Sweet and Grisel's dataset are illuminating in the context of ISA lawmaking. These are set out below, with representative charts and tables.

First, while investment treaty tribunals regularly have cited prior awards, the average number of citations per decision has *more than doubled* since 2000. (Figure 4.1 below)

32. A. STONE SWEET and F. GRISEL, *The Evolution of International Arbitration*, fn. 26 above; A. STONE SWEET, M.Y. CHUNG and A. SALTZMAN, "Arbitral Lawmaking and State Power", pp. 1-31.
33. A. STONE SWEET and F. GRISEL, *The Evolution of International Arbitration*, fn. 26 above, p. 152.
34. *Ibid.*, p. 151.
35. *Ibid.*
36. *Ibid.*

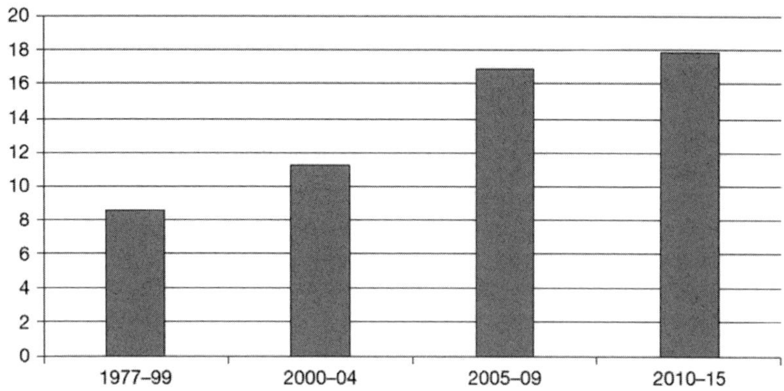

Figure 4.1 Average Number of Citations Per Award and by Period

Source: Yale Law School Data Sets on Investor-State Arbitration, compiled by Alec Stone Sweet, Sheng Li, Meng-Jia Yang, Michael Chung, Moeun Cha, and Tara Zivkovich.

Second, citation by ISA tribunals of prior awards has grown *exponentially* as available awards have accumulated. Per the authors, 97% of all citations added to the investor-state arbitration system between 1977 and 2014 have been produced since 2000; 84% since 2005; and 45% in the 2010 to 2014 period alone.[37] (Figure 4.2 below)

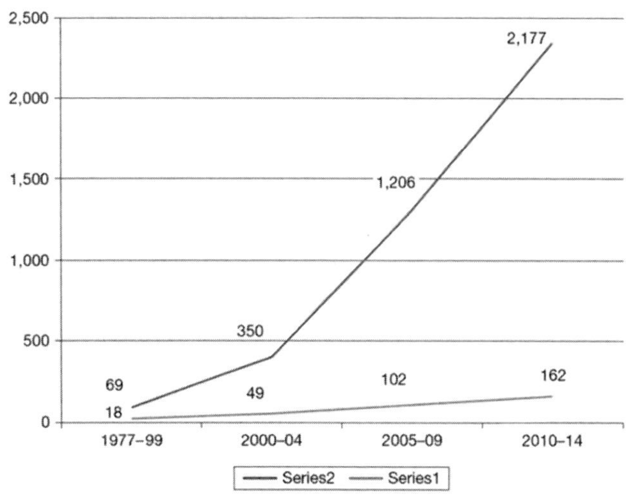

Figure 4.2 Cumulative Number of Awards and Cases Cited, by Period

Source: Yale Law School Data Sets on Investor-State Arbitration, compiled by Alec Stone Sweet, Sheng Li, Meng-Jia Yang, Michael Chung, Moeun Cha, and Tara Zivkovich.

37. *Ibid.*

Third, the trend is for investment treaty tribunals to cite more awards from within the investor-state arbitration system than from outside that system (i.e., International Court of Justice decisions).[38] Since 2005, approximately 90% of all ISA awards have cited to prior ISA awards, and in particular to ICSID cases.[39] Tribunals routinely cite across treaty instruments; for example, ICSID tribunals cite to NAFTA tribunals operating under UNCITRAL rules and vice versa.[40] (Figure 4.3 below)

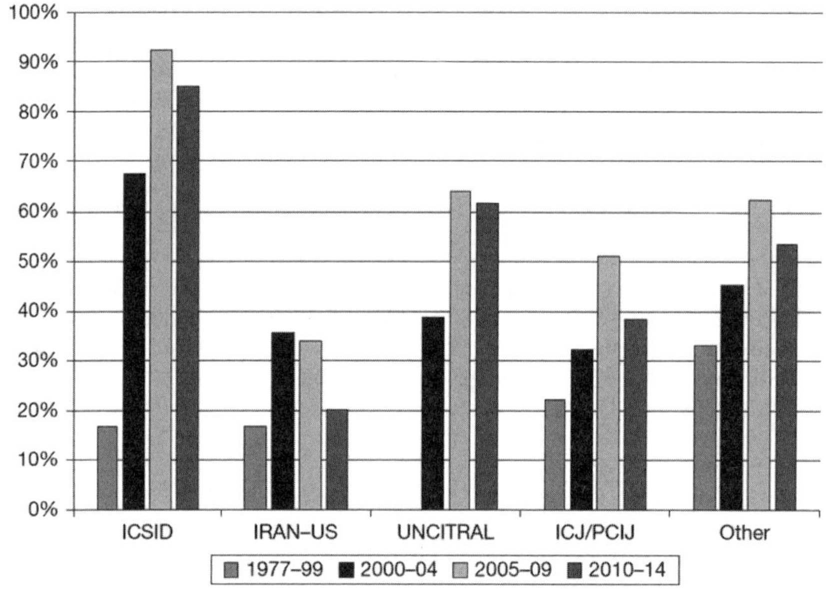

Figure 4.3 Percentage of Awards Citing to Case Law, by Source and Period

Source: Yale Law School Data Sets on Investor-State Arbitration, compiled by Alec Stone Sweet, Sheng Li, Meng-Jia Yang, Michael Chung, Moeun Cha, and Tara Zivkovich.

Fourth, per the authors, "legal domains have been steadily brought into closer relationship to one another as the case law has evolved, creating a system of interdependent norms".[41] Upon examining tribunal approaches to recurrent questions (for example, arbitrary or discriminatory treatment, FPS, denial of justice, umbrella clause), Stone Sweet and Grisel found that questions have "tended either (a) to converge around a leading case, or line of consistent precedents, or (b) to diverge, generating two or more lines of case law".[42] They found important trends towards convergence or, in

38. *Ibid.*
39. *Ibid.*
40. *Ibid.*, pp. 152, 154.
41. *Ibid*, p. 154.
42. *Ibid.*

other areas, that a single award served to generate a high degree of consistency where there had been none previously. The latter phenomenon is illustrated, for example, in the convergence in approach toward awarding compound interest rather than simple interest following the *Santa Elena v. Costa Rica* award.[43] Similarly, tribunals now widely use the *Salini* approach in determining what assets held by an investor are protected as an "investment".[44] Per the authors, "the drive toward jurisprudential coherence is facilitated by the fact that at least one member of a relatively small group of elite arbitrators is usually present on any investor-state tribunal, and repeat arbitrators that specialize in chairing tribunals dominate the production of awards".[45] (Table 4.1 below)

Table 4.1 Citation to Case Law by Legal Domain

Domain	Citations	% of All Citations Per Domain	Awards Citing to Case Law Per Domain	% of Awards Citing to Case Law Per Domain
Fair and Equitable Treatment	640	28.5%	87	51.8%
Expropriation	453	20.1%	83	49.4%
Damages	273	12.1%	55	32.7%
Protection and Security	136	6.1%	27	16.1%
Interest Assessment	91	4.1%	16	9.5%
MFN or National Treatment	89	4.0%	21	12.5%
Investment	86	3.8%	21	12.5%
Arbitrary or Discriminatory Treatment	62	2.8%	22	13.1%
Denial of Justice	60	2.7%	15	8.9%
Umbrella Clause	59	2.6%	14	8.3%
Necessity	48	2.1%	11	6.6%
Cost/Fees	44	2.0%	10	6.0%
Other	135	9.2%		
Total	2,249	100.1%		

Source: *Yale Law School Data Sets on Investor-State Arbitration*, compiled by Alec Stone Sweet, Sheng Li, Meng-Jia Yang, Michael Chung, Moeun Cha, and Tara Zivkovich.

43. *Ibid.* 155; *Santa Elena v. Costa Rica* (ICSID Case No ARB/96/1), Award (17 February 2000), paras. 97-105; Florian GRISEL, « *L'octroi d'intérêts composés par les tribunaux arbitraux d'investissement* » 3 *Journal du Droit International* (2011) p. 545.
44. *Salini Costruttori SpA and Italstrade SpA v. Kingdom of Morocco* (ICSID Case No ARB/05/22), Decision on Jurisdiction (31 July 2001).
45. A. STONE SWEET and F. GRISEL, *The Evolution of International Arbitration*, fn. 26 above, p. 155.

Fifth, investment treaty tribunals do not look only to other investment treaty tribunals for "precedent" but rely heavily, if indirectly, on other sources of international law.[46] The dataset illustrates that in 78 different awards (38% of the total), tribunals cited to international courts 204 times.[47]

However, say Stone Sweet and Grisel, this count is an inadequate representation of the impact of international case law, because "[s]ome of the most highly cited ISA awards have been those that invoke the authority of international courts when making major doctrinal moves".[48] The primary example is the 2003 Award in *Tecmed v. Mexico*,[49] which relied on the jurisprudence of the European Court of Human Rights (*ECtHR*) to incorporate the doctrine of "legitimate expectations" into FET.[50] Interestingly, *Tecmed* was the most highly cited ISA award in the database, having been cited 87 times overall and 48 times regarding FET. Cases such as *Saluka v. Czech Republic* (the 2006 Partial Award being cited 57 times, 31 times in the FET domain),[51] which hold that the investor's "legitimate expectations" are to be balanced against the state's "legitimate regulatory interests" cite heavily to *Tecmed* and other ISA awards, but *not* back to the European Court of Human Rights or other international courts.[52]

Representative examples of repeat citations given to international court decisions include, not surprisingly: the Permanent Court of International Justice (*PCIJ*) *Chorzow Factory* decision for the principle of full reparation of losses suffered by the aggrieved through compensation;[53] the ICJ *ELSI* decision for the definition of arbitrariness as an action that "shocks, or at least surprises, a sense of judicial propriety";[54] Judge Higgins' separate opinion in the ICJ *Oil Platforms* case for equation of the FET standard with "legal terms of art well known in the field of overseas investment protection";[55] the *Korea-Beef* decision of the WTO Appellate Body regarding the definition of "necessity";[56] the ECtHR *Mellacher v. Austria* decision for the definition of expropriation;[57] and the PCIJ

46. *Ibid.*, pp. 155-157.
47. *Ibid.*, p. 155.
48. *Ibid.*
49. *Técnicas Medioambientales Tecmed SA v. United Mexican States* (ICSID Case No. ARB(AF)/00/2), Award (29 May 2003).
50. A. STONE SWEET and F. GRISEL, *The Evolution of International Arbitration*, fn. 26 above, p. 155 fn. 156.
51. *Saluka Investments BV v. Czech Republic* (UNCITRAL), Partial Award (17 March 2006).
52. A. STONE SWEET and F. GRISEL, *The Evolution of International Arbitration*, fn. 26 above, p. 156.
53. See *Enron Corporation, Ponderosa Assets, L.P. v. Argentina* (ICSID Case No ARB/01/3), Award (22 May 2007) para. 359; *Metalclad Corporation v. Mexico* (ICSID Case No ARB(AF)/97/1), Award (30 August 2000) para. 122; *National Grid PLC v. Argentina* (UNCITRAL), Award (3 November 2008) para.270.
54. See *Técnicas Medioambientales Tecmed SA v. United Mexican States*, fn. 49, para. 154; *Total SA v. Argentina* (ICSID Case No ARB/04/1), Decision on Liability (27 December 2010) para. 110.
55. See *Total SA v. Argentina*, fn. 54 above, para. 108; *Unglaube v. Costa Rica* (ICSID Case Nos, ARB/08/1 and ARB/09/20), Award (16 May 2012) para. 247.
56. *Continental Casualty Company v. Argentina* (ICSID Case No ARB/03/9), Award (5 September 2008) para. 193.
57. *Ronald S Lauder v. Czech Republic* (UNCITRAL), Award (3 September 2001) para. 202; *Técnicas Medioambientales Tecmed SA v. United Mexican States*, fn. 49 above, para. 122.

Oscar Chinn decision for the proposition that potential profits are not protected rights under international law.[58] (Figure 4.4 below)

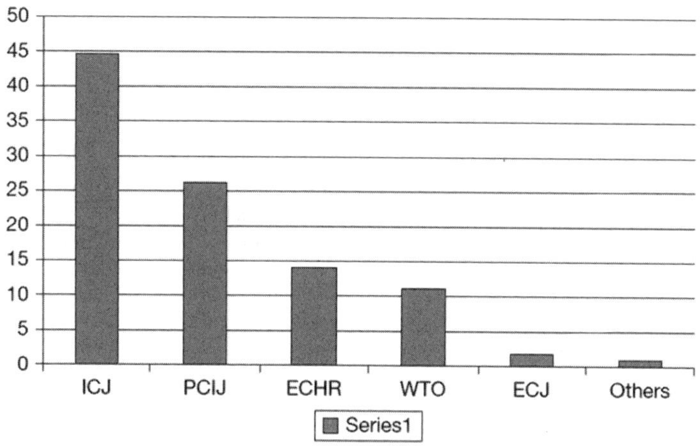

Figure 4.4 Awards Citing to International Courts: Percentage by Jurisdiction

Source: Yale Law School Data Sets on Investor-State Arbitration, compiled by Alec Stone Sweet, Sheng Li, Meng-Jia Yang, Michael Chung, Moeun Cha, and Tara Zivkovich.

c. *The Argentina cases*

Moving from data to actual ISA awards, Stone Sweet and Grisel and others use the suite of BIT cases generated by the Argentine financial crisis to illustrate how tribunals in practice rely on previous awards, even as they decry any doctrine of precedent in international law. Two chapters of the Argentina story are useful for these purposes: first, Argentina's persistence in raising jurisdictional defenses despite consistent losses;[59] and second, Argentina's systematic pleading of the "necessity defense" against US investors, to mixed results.[60]

i. Jurisdictional objections

Argentina repeatedly objected to jurisdiction in cases brought by indirect and/or minority shareholders as qualified investors. Argentina failed in each and every instance.

58. *Merrill & Ring Forestry LP v. Canada* (UNCITRAL), Award (31 March 2010) para. 215; *El Paso Energy International Company v. Argentina* (ICSID Case No ARB/03/15), Award (31 October 2011) para. 366.
59. C. SCHREUER and M. WEINIGER, "Conversations Across Precedents", p. 1192.
60. A. STONE SWEET and F. GRISEL, *The Evolution of International Arbitration*, fn. 26 above, pp. 155-157; I.M. TEN CATE, "The Costs of Consistency", pp. 427-435; Gilbert GUILLAUME, "The Use of Precedent by International Judges and Arbitrators", 2 Journal of International Dispute Settlement (2011) p. 5 at p. 17.

The way in which different tribunals handled the repeat scenario reveals a certain diffidence, if not schizophrenia, in arbitrator lawmaking.

In *Vivendi v. Argentina*, the tribunal unapologetically rejected Argentina's jurisdictional objection, adding an appendix to its jurisdiction decision listing eighteen previous decisions rejecting the same argument. Making explicit that it accorded these decisions authority, the tribunal said:

> "Finally, numerous arbitral tribunals have rejected this very same jurisdictional objection as shown by the 18 cases referred to in Appendix 1 to this Decision. In each of those eighteen cases the tribunals upheld the right of shareholders to pursue such claims. In 11 cases, the Argentine Republic was respondent and asserted, and lost, this same objection. In the last one of these cases, the Tribunal observed that the very objection which Argentina raises in this case 'has been made numerous times, never, so far as the Tribunal has been aware, with success' [citing *Gas Natural v. Argentina*]".[61]

In *Enron v. Argentina*, the tribunal rejected the jurisdictional objection, while cautiously explaining that it was citing earlier decisions rejecting a similar objection because it agreed with those decisions:

> "The Tribunal is of course mindful that decisions of ICSID or other arbitral tribunals are not a primary source of rules. The citations of and references to those decisions respond to the fact that the Tribunal in examining the claim and arguments of this case under international law, believes that in essence the conclusions and reasons of those decisions are correct."[62]

Later in the decision, the tribunal again emphasized the targeted scope of its mandate by stating its agreement "with the view expressed by the Argentine Republic in the hearing on jurisdiction held in respect of this dispute, to the effect that the decisions of ICSID tribunals are not binding precedents and that every case must be examined in light of its own circumstances".[63]

In *AES Corp v. Argentina*, perhaps the high-water mark for explanation of the "*de facto* precedent" approach, the tribunal described and attempted to align the competing considerations.[64] The tribunal faced extreme positions: the claimant challenged

---

61. *Compañía de Aguas del Aconquija, SA & Vivendi Universal (formerly Compagnie Générale des Eaux) v. Argentine Republic* (ICSID Case No. ARB/97/3), Decision on Jurisdiction (14 November 2005) para. 94.
62. *Enron Corporation, Ponderosa Assets, L.P. v. Argentine Republic* (ICSID Case No. ARB/01/3), Decision on Jurisdiction (14 January 2004) para. 40.
63. *Enron v. Argentina*, Decision on Jurisdiction, fn. 62 above, para. 25.
64. *AES Corporation v. The Argentine Republic* (ICSID Case No. ARB/02/17), Decision on Jurisdiction (26 April 2005). Commentators Abdulqawi Ahmed Yusuf and Guled Yusuf consider the *AES* award to contain the most extensive consideration of the role of precedent. Abdulqawi Ahmed YUSUF and Guled YUSUF, "Precedent & Jurisprudence Constante: *AES v. Argentina*, ICSID Case No. ARB/02/17" in Meg KINNEAR, Geraldine R. FISCHER, Jara Minguez ALMEIDA, Luisa

Argentina's jurisdictional objections as "moot if not even useless" given their similarity to the objections always raised and always rejected in previous arbitrations,[65] and Argentina replied that for the tribunal to follow the earlier decisions "without making factual and legal distinctions" was tantamount to "an excess of power and may affect the integrity of the international system for the protection of investments".[66] The Tribunal offered the following series of observations:[67]

(a) "There is so far no rule of precedent in general international law; nor is there any within the specific ICSID system for the settlement of disputes between one State party to the Convention and the National of another State Party";
(b) "Each tribunal remains sovereign and may retain, as it is confirmed by ICSID practice, a different solution for resolving the same problem";
(c) "[E]ach decision or award delivered by an ICSID Tribunal is only binding on the parties to the dispute settled by this decision or award";
and, with a silent "but";
(d) It is an "excessive assertion" to contend that "absolutely no consideration might be given to other decisions on jurisdiction or awards delivered by other tribunals in similar cases";
(e) "[D]ecisions on jurisdiction dealing with the same or very similar issues may at least indicate some lines of reasoning of real interest."

It is fair to interpret this line of observations as the tribunal saying "we are not obliged to consider or give any weight to prior decisions, but we can if we want to and if we agree with them". Thus, while defending its own independence and Argentina's right to repeat losing objections, the *AES* tribunal proceeded systematically to describe and rely upon previous decisions by other tribunals rejecting Argentina's jurisdictional objections.[68]

ii. The necessity defense

Once through the jurisdiction phase, several US claimants faced Argentina's necessity defense under Art. XI of the 1991 US-Argentina BIT. Irene M. Ten Cate provides a succinct summary of the basic factual and legal scenario:

> "The operative facts in the five cases are substantially similar. The claimants invested in Argentine companies as part of Argentina's privatization program in the early 1990s. In these investment transactions, Argentina made commitments aimed at stabilizing the tariff structure in case of fluctuation of the peso. During the unprecedented economic meltdown approximately ten years later, the Argentine government effectively abrogated the stabilization measures. The

---

Fernanda TORRES and Mairée Uran BIDEGAIN, eds., *Building International Investment Law: The First 50 Years of ICSID* (Wolters Kluwer 2016) pp. 71, 73.

65. *Enron v. Argentina*, Decision on Jurisdiction, fn. 62 above, para. 25.

66. *AES v. Argentina*, Decision on Jurisdiction, fn. 64 above, para. 22.

67. *Ibid.*, paras. 26-30.

68. *Ibid.*, paras. 51-59, 70, 73, 86, 89, 95-97.

> investors who filed claims with ICSID claimed that Argentina's actions violated several obligations under the BIT, including the obligations to accord fair and equitable treatment to investments and to honor commitments made to investors. The disagreements among the adjudicators in these cases center on Argentina's argument that it was not liable under the necessity defense under customary international law and the BIT's emergency clauses, chiefly Article XI. In *CMS*, *Enron* and *Sempra*, the tribunals held that Argentina did not meet the standards for either defense. The *LG&E* and *Continental* tribunals, on the other hand, held that Argentina had successfully established the emergency defense under the BIT."[69]

At the end of the day, there were six final ICSID awards and five associated annulment decisions addressing the necessity defense, which Stone Sweet and Grisel describe as offering insight into the evolution and enforcement of *de facto* precedent. The relevant final awards are: *CMS* (May 2005),[70] *LG&E* (October 2006),[71] *Enron* (May 2007),[72] *Sempra* (September 2007),[73] *Continental Casualty* (September 2008),[74] and *El Paso* (October 2011).[75] Taken together, the awards and annulment decisions open a window into arbitrators' conflicting views as to their status as lawmakers.

The *CMS*, *Enron* and *Sempra* tribunals – all presided by Professor Francisco Orrego Vicuña – found that Argentina had violated its FET obligations, rejected Argentina's necessity defense under Art. XI of the United States-Argentina BIT, and issued Awards in favor of the claimants. Each tribunal took the same approach to Art. XI, with *CMS* coming first and subsequent awards reproducing holdings verbatim from *CMS* and following awards.

Each tribunal looked to customary international law to find that Art. XI is not an autonomous source of law but is rather subsumed by the doctrine of necessity under customary international law as expressed through Art. 25 of the ILC's 2001 Articles on the Responsibility of States for Internationally Wrongful Acts (*ASR*). In brief, under the rubric of necessity articulated in ASR Art. 25, each of the *CMS, Enron* and *Sempra* tribunals rejected Argentina's defense on three bases: (1) the economic crisis did not involve an "essential interest of the State" because it did not undermine the "very existence of the State and its independence";[76] (2) the means chosen by Argentina to manage its economic crisis could not qualify as the "only means" under Art. 25, because

69. I.M. TEN CATE, "The Costs of Consistency", pp. 428-429.

70. *CMS Gas Transmission Company v. The Republic of Argentina* (ICSID Case No. ARB/01/8), Decision of the *Ad Hoc* Committee on the Application for Annulment of the Argentine Republic (25 September 2007). The author represented the claimant in the *CMS* case while a partner with Freshfields Bruckhaus Deringer.

71. *LG&E Energy Corp., LG&E Capital Corp. and LG&E International Inc. v. The Argentine Republic* (ICSID Case No. ARB/02/1), Decision on Liability (3 October 2006).

72. *Enron v. Argentina*, Decision on Jurisdiction, fn. 62 above.

73. *Sempra Energy International v. The Argentine Republic* (ICSID Case No. ARB/02/16), Award (28 September 2007).

74. *Continental Casualty Company v. Argentina*, Award, fn. 56 above.

75. *El Paso Energy v. Argentina*, Award, fn. 58 above.

76. *CMS Gas Transmission Company v. The Republic of Argentina* (ICSID Case No. ARB/01/8, Award (12 May 2005) paras. 354-356; *Enron v. Argentina*, Award, fn. 53 above, para. 306; *Sempra v. Argentina,* Award, fn. 73 above, para. 348.

experts disagreed on available measures;[77] and (3) Argentina's efforts exacerbated rather than mitigated the crisis.[78]

The *LG&E* tribunal, which issued its Award between the Awards of the *CMS* and *Enron* tribunals, also found FET violations by Argentina, but *accepted* Argentina's necessity defense under both Art. XI of the BIT and ASR Art. 25 as discrete bases.

At the annulment stage, the *CMS* Annulment Committee did not annul the Award, but nonetheless soundly criticized the tribunal's legal analysis of the necessity defense. In the Annulment Decision, the Committee recited its lack of authority under the ICSID Convention to act in an appellate capacity and then proceeded to a detailed analysis of the tribunal's "manifest" errors of treaty interpretation, in failing to examine necessity under Art. XI of the BIT and ASR Art. 25 separately.[79] The Committee explained its view that the codified customary international law in ASR Art. 25 arises to preclude the wrongfulness of a breach only after breach has been admitted or found, while the plea of necessity under Art. XI, in contrast, precludes the finding of breach. The Committee added:

> "errors made by the Tribunal could have had a decisive impact on the operative part of the Award.... In fact, it did not examine whether the conditions laid down by Article XI were fulfilled and whether, as a consequence, the measures taken by Argentina were capable of constituting, even prima facie, a breach of the BIT. If the Committee was acting as a court of appeal, it would have to reconsider the Award on this ground."[80]

In the *Sempra* case, the Annulment Committee annulled the Award on terms seemingly inspired by the *CMS* Annulment Decision. The *Sempra* Committee acknowledged the relevance of customary international law in interpreting a BIT, but stated that "[i]t does not follow, however, that customary international law (*in casu*, Article 25 of the ILC Articles) establishes a 'peremptory definition of necessity and the conditions for its operations'".[81] The Committee found that the tribunal's failure to apply Art. XI of the United States-Argentina BIT separately, and its application of ASR Art. 25 as if the latter "trumped" Art. XI,[82] constituted failure to apply the relevant law amounting to a "manifest excess of powers" sufficient to justify annulment of the Award.[83]

The back-and-forth of arbitrator and Annulment Committee lawmaking continued in the later *Continental Casualty* and *El Paso* cases.

---

77. *CMS v. Argentina*, Award, fn. 76 above, para. 323; *Enron v. Argentina,* Award, fn. 53 above, para. 305; *Sempra v. Argentina*, Award, fn. 73 above, para. 347.
78. *CMS v. Argentina,* Award, fin. 76 above, paras. 328-329; *Enron v. Argentina*, Award, fn. 53 above, paras. 311-312; *Sempra v. Argentina*, Award, fn. 73 above, paras. 353-354.
79. *CMS v. Argentina*, Decision on Annulment, fn. 70 above, para. 130.
80. *Ibid.,* para. 135.
81. *Sempra Energy International v. The Argentine Republic* (ICSID Case No. ARB/02/16), Decision on the Argentine Republic's Application for Annulment of the Award (29 June 2010) para. 197.
82. *Ibid.*, para. 208.
83. *Ibid.*, paras. 213-214.

In *Continental Casualty*, the tribunal cited the *CMS* Annulment Decision in its assessment of Argentina's necessity defense under Art. XI of the BIT.[84] Applying a proportionality approach, the tribunal found that the Argentine economic crisis fell within the criteria of Art. IX both as to "maintenance of public order" and "essential security interests" and hence accepted Argentina's necessity defense.

Continental Casualty was unsuccessful in annulment proceedings. The *Continental Casualty* Annulment Committee cited and endorsed the reasoning of the *CMS* Annulment Committee on the need to separate the legal analysis of necessity under Art. XI of the BIT and ASR Art. 25.[85]

In *El Paso*, the last case in the series, the tribunal relied heavily on the legal analysis in the *Continental Casualty* Award and on the *CMS* Annulment Decision in focusing, first, on Art. XI of the BIT as primary law and only then, if Art. XI did not apply, on ASR Art. 25 as secondary law.[86] The tribunal, however, reached an outcome in its Award opposite to that in *Continental Casualty* and *LG&E*. The tribunal rejected Argentina's necessity defense, on the basis that Argentine Government measures had contributed to the economic crisis.[87]

2. *Evolution of Investment Law Standards by "De Facto Precedent"*

Viewed in the "evolution of ISA" perspective offered by Stone Sweet and Grisel, it is readily evident that the necessity defense analyses of the early ICSID Argentina tribunals had an impact on the later tribunals and, even more starkly, that the *dicta* in the *CMS* Annulment Decision had an impact on the arbitration and annulment proceedings to follow. It is equally evident that the later arbitrators were not merely stringing citations or relying blindly on the earlier Awards and Annulment Decision, but *engaging* with the legal reasoning of the arbitrators who had written before them.

McNair observed that "[i]t is only by taking a backward glance that we can realize the importance of the accumulation of case law".[88] Stone Sweet and Grisel's "*de facto* precedent" research necessarily is backwards-facing: the research posits that ISA tribunals are making law, whether they intend to or not, because later tribunals do not merely cite prior awards, but *engage with and rely on* the reasoning in those awards, with which those later arbitrators (one hopes) agree, as the basis for their own decisions in (one hopes) similar cases.

This evolutionary approach raises the further question of exactly *what law* arbitrators are making. Now that hundreds of investor-state awards are available, what law have arbitrators bequeathed to us?

A brief answer must suffice for this paper: with the proliferation of awards, investment treaty standards have increasingly taken on substance and shape. Whether

84. *Continental Casualty v. Argentina*, Award, fn. 56 above, para 187.

85. *Continental Casualty Company v. The Argentine Republic* (ICSID Case No ARB/03/9), Decision on the Application for Partial Annulment of Continental Casualty Company and the Application for Partial Annulment of the Argentine Republic (16 September 2011) para 127.

86. *El Paso v. Argentina*, Award, fn. 58 above, paras. 552-555, 649.

87. *Ibid.*, para. 665.

88. Sir Arnold Duncan McNAIR, *The Development of International Justice* (New York University Press 1954) p. 15, cited in J.P. COMMISSION, "Precedent in Investment Treaty Arbitration", p. 154.

one uses (or abuses) the common law label of "precedent" or civil law label of *jurisprudence constante*, ISA tribunal awards have steadily added paint to the canvas. Again instinctively, we appreciate that this process had to be somewhat unruly with the originally bare FET and FPS canvases provided by early BIT states, and more satisfactory as states have elaborated the standards in later treaties.

We now have the benefit of substantial literature on the evolution of investment treaty standards, both substantive and procedural.[89] As one example, Professor Kaufmann-Kohler provides an overview of evolutionary trends in her 2007 study on arbitral precedent.[90] Kaufmann-Kohler's general conclusion is that "there is a progressive emergence of rules through lines of consistent cases on certain issues, though there are still contradictory outcomes on others".[91] The umbrella clause is at one end of the spectrum: "the tribunals are divided when it comes to the umbrella clause, and no clear rule has emerged".[92] The most-favored-nation clause falls somewhere in the middle: "arbitral practice appears to be evolving towards a consistent rule".[93] At the other end of the spectrum is FET: "sufficiently established" standards have emerged to "influence future tribunals".[94] In the words of Stone Sweet, Chung and Saltzmann, in relation to tribunal development of FET language:

89. See, e.g., A. STONE SWEET, M.Y. CHUNG and A. SALTZMAN, "Arbitral Lawmaking and State Power", pp. 1-31; Rudolph DOLZER, "Fair and Equitable Treatment: Today's Contours", 12 *Santa Clara Journal of International Law* (2013) p. 7; Roland KRÄGER, *Fair and Equitable Treatment in International Investment Law* (Cambridge University Press 2011) pp. 308-316.

90. G. KAUFFMAN-KOHLER, "Arbitral Precedent: Dream, Necessity or Excuse?", p. 357.

91. *Ibid.*, p. 373.

92. *Ibid.*, p. 369. The restrictive approach – that an umbrella clause cannot transform a contract claim into a treaty claim – can be found in *Salini v. Jordan* (ICSID Case No. ARB/02/13), Decision on Jurisdiction (9 November 2004) and Award (31 January 2006), *Joy Mining v. Egypt* (ICSID Case No. ARB/03/11), Award on Jurisdiction (6 August 2004), *El Paso v. Argentina* (ICSID Case No. ARB/03/15), Decision on Jurisdiction (27 April 2006) and Award (31 October 2011), and *Pan American v. Argentina* (ICSID Case No. ARB/03/13), Decision on Preliminary Objections (27 July 2006). The liberal approach – that an umbrella clause can operate to transform municipal law obligations into obligations directly recognizable in international law – can be found in *Eureko v. Poland* (UNCITRAL), Partial Award (19 August 2005), *Noble Ventures Inc. v. Romania* (ICSID Case No. ARB/01/11), Award (12 October 2005), and *Siemens v. Argentina* (ICSID Case No. ARB/02/8), Award (17 January 2007).

93. G. KAUFMANN-KOHLER, "Arbitral Precedent: Dream, Necessity or Excuse?", p. 371. The two seemingly conflicting schools of thought – represented by *Maffezini* and *Plama* – can be combined to produce the rule that "MFN clauses *can* be used to overcome waiting periods and similar admissibility requirements, but *not* to replace, in whole or in part, the dispute resolution mechanism provided in the treaty upon which jurisdiction is based". *Emilio Augustín Maffezini v. Kingdom of Spain*, ICSID Case ARB/97/7, Decision on Jurisdiction, (25 January 2000); *Plama Consortium Ltd v. Republic of Bulgaria*, ICSID Case ARB/03/24, Decision on Jurisdiction, (8 February 2005).

94. G. KAUFMANN-KOHLER, "Arbitral Precedent: Dream, Necessity or Excuse?", p. 373. Starting with the 1926 *Neer* case, to circa-2007 cases including *Siemens v. Argentina* and *PSEG v. Turkey* (ICSID Case No. ARB/02/5), Decision on Jurisdiction (4 June 2004) and Award (19 June 2007), tribunals focus on the wording and purpose of the relevant treaty, as well as the facts, and emphasize the need for stability of legal and business frameworks as 'an emerging standard of fair and equitable treatment in international law'. Tribunals have abandoned the requirement of bad faith and increasingly focus on legitimate expectations of the investor. *LG&E v. Argentina*, Decision

"They did not camouflage their lawmaking but, instead adopted the mantle of a judge of general principles."[95]

It is fair to say that some degree of inconsistency in treaty interpretation is inevitable in *ad hoc* ISA. Indeed, some inconsistency can have positive benefits, given the risks of arbitrators following the interpretation of, say, an FET clause in a prior award without critically scrutinizing the original reasoning or, if they find the reasoning sound, without critically applying that reasoning to the relevant facts in their case. Professor Mark Feldman, in the context of ISA appellate mechanisms, reminds those calling for more consistency in investment treaty interpretation of the dangers posed by consistent – but *wrong* – earlier interpretations:

"For policymakers exploring appellate mechanism options, analysis should include consideration of the risk of a standing, permanent appellate body developing a consistent, but *inaccurate*, line of case law on certain issues".[96] (Emphasis added.)

The practical challenge for arbitrator lawmakers is to find the proper place and balance for consistency. One task is to assess the proper precedential value of prior awards, for which King and Moloo identify possible guidelines.[97] In addition to comparing the relevant treaty texts in the later arbitrator's case and a prior award, King and Moloo suggest that the later arbitrator consider: (1) the factual matrix at issue; (2) the quality of the reasoning in the precedent; and (3) the reputation and experience of the arbitrators rendering the prior award. Cognizant that the second and third factors raise issues of elitism, they remind that Art. 38(1)(d) of the ICJ Statute identifies "teachings of the most qualified publicists of the various nations" as a subsidiary source of international law.

In addition to such guidelines, it is – in the view of the author – increasingly clear that investment treaty tribunals should advise the parties against citing each and every possibly relevant prior award in their submissions and, to underscore that advice, refrain from addressing in their own awards each and every prior award cited by the parties. It is sufficient – and indeed it would seem to be more responsible lawmaking – for tribunals to *engage* with the analysis in what they assess to be the best reasoned awards, as relevant to the legal issues before them on the facts before them, and explain why they find that reasoning relevant and compelling. Conversely, tribunals should feel no compunction to distinguish each and every award cited tangentially by the parties. In the more elegant

on Liability, fn. 71 above, para. 125; *Azurix Corp. v. Argentine Republic* (ICSID Case RB/01/12), Award (14 July 2006) para. 372.

95. A. STONE SWEET, M.Y. CHUNG and A. SALTZMAN, "Arbitral Lawmaking and State Power", p. 17.

96. Mark FELDMAN, "Investment Arbitration Appellate Mechanism Options: Consistency, Accuracy, and Balance of Power", 32 ICSID Review – Foreign Investment Law Journal (2017) pp. 528, 530. Ten Cate takes a similar position. I.M. TEN CATE, "The Costs of Consistency", pp. 456-471. See also William W. PARK, "Arbitrators and Accuracy", 1 Journal of International Dispute Resolution (2010) p. 25.

97. D.B. KING and R. MOLOO, "International Arbitrators as Lawmakers", pp. 897-909.

words of Professor Michael Reisman, what is merited is "thoughtful consideration of previous awards that are on-point".[98]

In sum, the blessing and the curse of *ad hoc* investment treaty arbitration is that arbitrators have the responsibility to make law by interpreting common treaty provisions as best they can, with due – not slavish – regard to interpretations made in prior awards in similar circumstances, but also anchored to the facts and circumstances of the unique case before them.

V. LEGITIMACY OF INVESTMENT TREATY ARBITRATOR LAWMAKING: STATE RESPONSES

With the reality of arbitrator lawmaking through investor-state arbitration awards firmly established, the question of legitimacy of that reality arises.

King and Moloo, as active practitioners in the field of international arbitration, not surprisingly defend the legitimacy of arbitrator lawmaking, in the investment treaty tribunal context and more broadly. They base their position on four features unique to international arbitration: (1) the selection of arbitrators by the parties, with the result that "different views and approaches to the law are typically going to be represented on the arbitral panel"; (2) the adversarial process, which "allows an arbitral tribunal the benefit of testing the merits and demerits of the various positions being advanced by the parties"; (3) the generally unanimous decisions by tribunals, "informed by the rigorous submissions of the parties and the arbitrators' own prior experiences"; and (4) the availability and use of post-award review of awards, providing "the opportunity for judicial 'blessing' (or 'cursing') of awards".[99] They concede that the process is not perfect, and flag the risks of arbitrators using their platform to offer legal opinions not necessary to decide the issues before them. But, overall, King and Moloo vote for the legitimacy of arbitrator lawmaking:

> "Paradoxically, the practical consequence of this analysis [the authors' four factors] is that arbitral awards can often be viewed as a legitimate articulation of the law precisely *because* arbitrators understand their primary task as resolving the dispute before them. Three individuals with potentially diverse views come together to decide, typically unanimously, factual and legal arguments tested in the fire of the adversarial process, in an award that may be further tested in the national courts or some other review procedure. What emerges, we suggest, is a decision that can, in many instances, legitimately be considered as a valid articulation of the law. On the other hand, and for the same reasons, basing a decision on considerations not before the tribunal, such as how the law ought to evolve, would undermine the legitimacy of the resulting award."[100] (Emphasis in original.)

98. W.M. REISMAN, "'Case Specific Mandates' versus 'Systemic Implications'", p. 132.
99. D.B. KING and R. MOLOO, "International Arbitrators as Lawmakers", pp. 891-895.
100. D.B. KING and R. MOLOO, "International Arbitrators as Lawmakers", p. 897 (footnote omitted).

Noting again that King and Moloo are practitioners, there is good reason to seek additional appraisers of the legitimacy of arbitrator lawmaking. Just as one looks to the ultimate stakeholders in international commercial arbitration – the commercial players themselves – to see if there is demand for greater publication of awards (and one sees little), one should look to the ultimate stakeholders in investment treaty arbitration as a barometer of legitimacy – the states themselves.

In the author's view, the most objective way to assess legitimacy in ISA is to examine how states react to the arbitrator lawmaking process. From the viewpoint of delegation theory, it is states – as the principals – that confer authority on *ad hoc* arbitrators – as their agents – to resolve disputes by interpreting the states' treaties.[101] Through treaties, it is states – and states alone – that have the power to, in the words of Stone Sweet and Grisel, "consolidate the main lines of arbitral case law", "codify certain arbitral approaches to liability", "presumptively reduce the parameters of choice available to future tribunals" and even, should they so choose, "destroy influential lines of case law, or to block future developments".[102] Treaty content can show the "revealed preference of states".[103] The actions that states take in drafting, amending and terminating treaties – or not – is the best evidence of their views on arbitrator lawmaking.

In examining such state action, we again have the benefit of new empirical research.

1. *Introducing the Empirical Studies*

There are two recent empirical studies of state treaty-making practice and the implications for arbitral lawmaking. The first, again, comes from Stone Sweet and Grisel in *The Evolution of International Arbitration: Judicialization, Governance, Legitimacy*, where they analyze a dataset of 398 "New BITs" (signed from 2002 through 2015) and available in English (*Stone Sweet Study*).[104] The second is the forthcoming study by Tomer Broude, Yoram Z. Haftel and Alexander Thompson, who analyze "renegotiated BITs" – defined as "a signed and ratified treaty that replaces an existing mutually ratified BIT or a signed (and where relevant, ratified) amendment to an existing mutually ratified BIT"– entered into between 1986 and 2010 (Broude *et al* Study)[105]. Broude and colleagues identified a total of 196 renegotiated BITs, of which both texts were found for 170 BITs in various languages, leading to a final dataset for the Broude *et al* Study of 160 treaty pairs in English, French, Spanish, Arabic and Russian.

The two empirical studies are complementary. The Stone Sweet Study dataset includes all New BITs signed from 2002 through 2015, while the Broude *et al* Study, by

---

101. See A. STONE SWEET and F. GRISEL, *The Evolution of International Arbitration*, fn. 26 above, pp. 22-33.

102. *Ibid.*, p. 212.

103. Tomer BROUDE, Yoram Z. HAFTEL and Alexander THOMPSON, "Who Cares About Regulatory Space in BITs? A Comparative International Law Approach" in Anthea ROBERTS, Pierre-Hugues VERDIER, Mila VERSTEEG and Paul B. STEPHAN, eds., *Comparative International Law* (Oxford University Press 2018) p. 7.

104. A. STONE SWEET and F. GRISEL, *The Evolution of International Arbitration*, fn. 26 above. The UNCTAD database provides a further 137 BITs that are not available in English and hence not included in the Stone Sweet-Grisel study.

105. T. BROUDE, Y. HAFTEL and A. THOMPSON, fn. 103 above.

including only pairs of renegotiated BITs, offers insight into how states may have changed their position on arbitration in the wake of ISA awards. The Broude *et al* Study spans 24 years as compared to 13 years for the Stone Sweet Study, thereby offering a longer historic view on state practice. The Stone Sweet Study, however, contains the most recent data and is therefore more useful in charting current state practice. Both studies analyze substantive BIT provisions, with the Stone Sweet Study containing deeper analysis of distinct investment law standards, specifically FET and indirect expropriation and FET.

2. *The Big Picture: No Apparent Backlash Against Arbitrator Lawmaking*

Although states possess the power through treaty-making to "reform, exit or even destroy the system" of international investment law and arbitration,[106] neither the Stone Sweet Study nor the Broude *et al* Study finds evidence of systemic backlash from states. To the contrary, the Stone Sweet Study reports that:

> "(a) states continue to negotiate and sign investment treaties; (b) the mix of treaty protections on offer has remained remarkably stable; and (c) what states have mostly done is to consolidate the system in line with how arbitrators have, in fact, developed it in their awards on liability".[107]

The Broude *et al* Study echoes these conclusions: "the revised BITs reflect much stronger ISDS and, by implication, much lower flexibility for host governments".[108] According to the Broude *et al* Study: "[t]his simple observation contradicts the idea of a 'backlash' against and a 'legitimacy crisis' of the global investment regime".[109]

3. *Salient Findings of the Stone Sweet Study*

The Stone Sweet Study analyzes the 398 New BIT dataset (2002 to 2015) against the backdrop of possible state reactions to arbitrator lawmaking. These reactions include a state's:

(a) exiting the system, by denouncing BITs and/or the ICSID Convention;
(b) limiting protections for indirect expropriation and/or FET;
(c) entering into new treaties with carve-outs;
(d) expressly constraining arbitral discretion or otherwise limiting the arbitral process, including with interpretive guidelines; and
(e) replacing *ad hoc* tribunals with a court.[110]

106. A. STONE SWEET, M.Y. CHUNG and A. SALTZMAN, "Arbitral Lawmaking and State Power", p. 24.
107. A. STONE SWEET and F. GRISEL, *The Evolution of International Arbitration*, fn. 26 above, p. 212.
108. T. BROUDE, Y. HAFTEL and A. THOMPSON, fn. 103 above, p. 11.
109. *Ibid.*
110. A. STONE SWEET and F. GRISEL, *The Evolution of International Arbitration*, fn. 26 above, p. 211.

Overall, Stone Sweet and Grisel conclude that "States have broadly acquiesced to arbitral lawmaking when it comes to indirect expropriation and the FET" and have actually "done more to consolidate major strands of arbitral case law than they have to block the extension of that jurisprudence by future tribunals".[111]

In terms of the specific state reactions studied:

a. Exiting the system

Only a small number of states have taken the extreme step of exiting the system altogether. These include Ecuador's termination of nine BITs in 2008; Venezuela's termination of one BIT in 2009; Indonesia's termination of 14 BITs since 2014; Bolivia's denunciation of the ICSID Convention in 2007, Ecuador's in 2009 and Venezuela's in 2012; and South Africa's initiation of withdrawal from certain BITs.[112]

b. Limiting protections

Only 46 of the New BITs include substantive criteria for determining indirect expropriation.[113] Of interest here, all of the 46 BITs adopt the standard formula developed by arbitrators through awards (i.e., indirect expropriation having an equivalent effect to direct expropriation without formal transfer of title or outright seizure).[114]

Stone Sweet observes "states working to consolidate the FET as a framework for the development of general principles, while doing virtually nothing to dismantle it".[115] The study documents the following state responses:[116]

(i) Only 7 of the 398 New BITs have no FET provision. Five of these (only 1 post-dating 2005) contain no provision at all relating to host state treatment of investors, and 2 require the international law "minimal standard of treatment".

(ii) Of the BITs containing an FET provision, 40 contain interpretative guidelines. Of those, 34 reference the guidelines used by the NAFTA Art. 2001 Free Trade Commission stating: (1) "The concepts of 'FET' and 'full protection and security' do not require treatment in addition to ... that which is required by the CIL minimum standard of treatment of aliens"; and (2) "A determination that there has been a breach of ... a separate international agreement, does not establish that there has been a breach of [FET]."

(iii) No New BIT removed the arbitrator-developed test of "legitimate expectations" of investors from FET considerations.

111. *Ibid.*, p. 217. The Study notes that only four awards in the data set involve treaties signed after 1999, with the latest involving a 2003 BIT, and there can be no assessment of the impact of new treaties on awards until there are new awards interpreting the new generation of treaties. *Ibid.*, p. 212.

112. A. STONE SWEET and F. GRISEL, *The Evolution of International Arbitration*, fn. 26 above, pp. 212-213.

113. *Ibid.*, p. 211.

114. *Ibid.*, p. 213.

115. *Ibid.*, p. 216.

116. *Ibid.*, pp. 215-216.

Certain of the 40 New BITs adding substantive criteria expressly codify elements of FET arbitrator-developed case law, for example, inclusion of the need for explicit promises made by host states to investors, the prohibition of denial of justice, obligations of due process, and transparency.

c. Carve-outs

The "clearest example of treaty-making seeking to hinder the development of an approach to liability found in an arbitral award" is found in the carve-outs for public interest that followed the 2000 *Santa Elena v. Costa Rica* case, where the tribunal found:

> "The purpose of protecting the environment for which the Property was taken does not alter the legal character of the taking for which adequate compensation must be paid. The international source of the obligation to protect the environment makes no difference. Expropriatory environmental measures – no matter how laudable and beneficial to society as a whole – are, in this respect, similar to any other expropriatory measures that a state may take in order to implement its policies: where property is expropriated, even for environmental purposes, whether domestic or international, the state's obligation to pay compensation remains."[117]

Forty-two of the New BITs provide that general measures taken for purposes of "health, safety and environmental protection" do not in and of themselves, constitute expropriation.[118] This provision conforms to the position taken in *Saluka v. Czech Republic*, one of the most-cited awards, that "a State does not commit an expropriation and is thus not liable to pay compensation to a dispossessed alien investor when it adopts general regulations that are 'commonly accepted as within the police power of the States'".[119] Stone Sweet notes that few "arbitrators would consider [this limitation on indirect expropriation] a reining-in of their powers".[120]

Carve-outs also include derogation clauses in the form of non-precluded measures provisions. For example, Canada's New BITs carve out measures "necessary to protect human, animal or plant life or health" and also "for the conservation of living or non-living exhaustible natural resources", on the condition that measures are not "applied in a manner that constitutes arbitrary or unjustifiable discrimination between investments or between investors' or constitute 'a disguised restriction on international trade or investment'".

d. Constraining tribunals – interpretive guidelines

The research reflects that state usage of interpretive guidelines is growing only slowly. This is illustrated at the macro level in Figure 5.1 below, which graphs the 398 New BITs against those BITs that contain substantive interpretative guidelines for either

117. *Compañia del Desarrollo de Santa Elena SA v. Republic of Costa Rica* (ICSID Case No ARB/96/1), Award (17 February 2000), paras. 71-72.

118. A. STONE SWEET and F. GRISEL, *The Evolution of International Arbitration*, fn. 26 above, p. 214.

119. *Saluka Investments BV v. Czech Republic* (UNCITRAL), Partial Award (17 March 2006), para. 262.

120. A. STONE SWEET and F. GRISEL, *The Evolution of International Arbitration*, fn. 26 above, p. 214.

indirect expropriation or FET. The second group started at nil in 2002 and grew to 46 and 40 for substantive interpretive language for indirect expropriation and FET, respectively, in 2015.

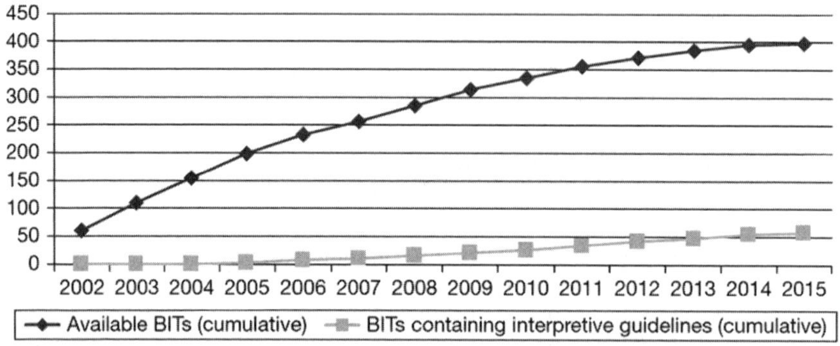

Figure 5.1 Cumulative Number of New BITs and New BITs Containing Interpretive Guidelines for Indirect Expropriation and the FET, 2002–2015

Source: 'Data Set of New BITs Signed since 2002', *Yale Law School Data Sets on Investor-State Arbitration*, compiled by Michael Chung.

e. Courts

As of the publication of the Stone Sweet Study in 2017, no investment treaty contained a provision substituting a standing court for *ad hoc* arbitration. Developments in the European Union, mentioned below, may soon change this status quo.

4. Salient Findings of the Broude et al Study

The Broude *et al* Study, as stated above, identifies 160 pairs of original and renegotiated treaties entered into between 1986 and 2010. The Study notes that the "trend" of treaty negotiation is considered "rather new" yet is "becoming more significant over time",[121] as illustrated by Figure 1 below:

121. T. BROUDE, Y. HAFTEL and A. THOMPSON, fn. 103 above, p. 6.

Figure 1: The Annual Number of Renegotiated BITs, 1986-2010

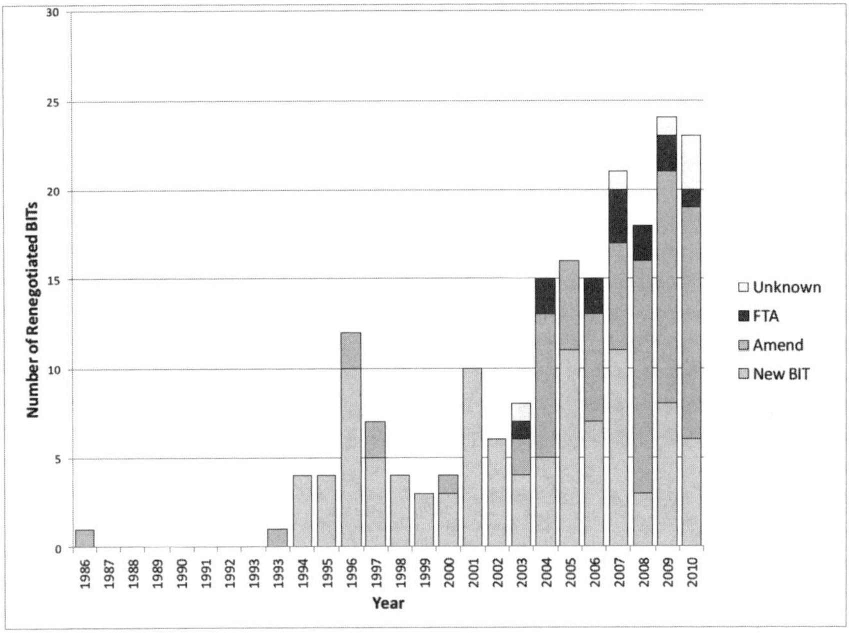

The first renegotiation was in the mid-1980s, leading to amendment of the France-Egypt BIT in 1986. Renegotiation became more frequent in the mid-1990s and, overall, 86 states from all 5 continents have undertaken BIT renegotiation. Some states – for example, Mexico and the Philippines – have renegotiated only one treaty. Other states have renegotiated so often that only 15 states account for half of the 160 paired treaties in the Broude *et al* Study.[122]

As reflected in Figure 2 below, the leaders in renegotiation are Romania with 38 renegotiations and the Czech Republic with 23 renegotiations (this despite the fact that the dataset did not include BITs available only in Romanian). Next in line are Germany and China, which each renegotiated at least 15 BITs. The lead renegotiators come from many geographical regions, including Europe, the Middle East and East Asia.[123] Interestingly, given reports of regional investment treaty discontent, Latin American and sub-Saharan African states renegotiated no more than 3 BITs each.

122. *Ibid.*, p. 6.
123. *Ibid.*, pp. 6-7.

Figure 2: Number of Renegotiated BITs for the Top Fifteen Renegotiating Countries

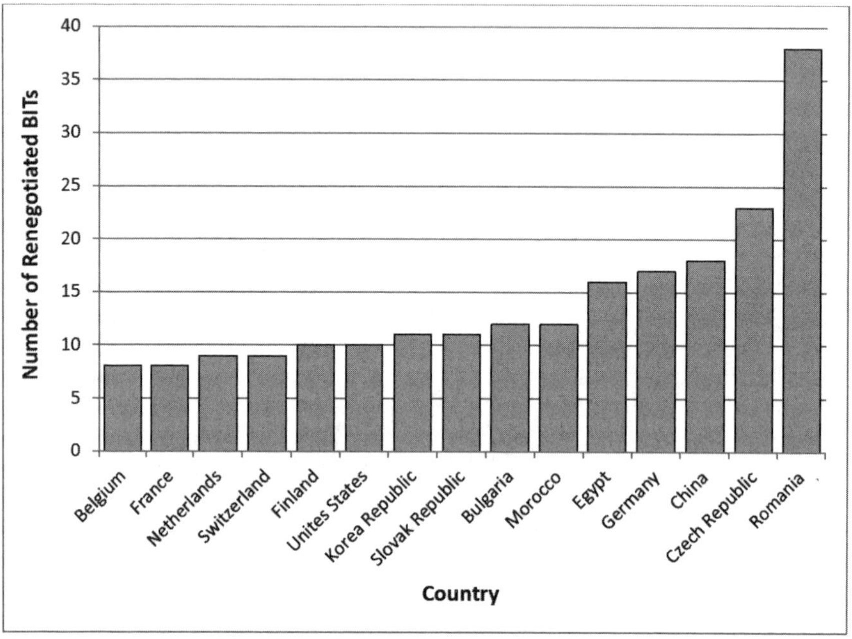

Overall, looking at the geographic spread and total numbers of renegotiations, the Broude *et al* Study posits that "the preference for renegotiation over outright termination positively indicates that the overall function of BITs, writ large, is not considered illegitimate or entirely undesirable, in contrast with particular substantive and procedural legal attributes of BITs (including ISDS), which may be understood as requiring change and reform".[124]

a. BIT renegotiation in relation to "State Regulatory Space"

The Broude *et al* Study gauges the extent to which states are concerned with the impact of ISA on their regulatory autonomy through the concept of "State Regulatory Space" (***SRS***). They define the SRS concept as referring "to the extent of the ability of governments to freely legislate and implement regulations in given public policy domains",[125] with "regulation" referring to "rules issued for the purpose of controlling the manner in which private and public enterprises conduct their operations".[126] SRS is presented as a "continuum": at one end, the state has great flexibility to pursue policies, insulated from external pressure or attempts to influence; at the other end, the state is

124. *Ibid.*, p. 2.
125. *Ibid.*, p. 8.
126. Giandomenico MAJONE, *Regulating Europe* (Psychology Press 1996) p. 9 cited in T. BROUDE, Y. HAFTEL and A. THOMPSON, fn. 103 above, p. 8.

subject to high constraint by foreign investors' abilities to challenge their policies under BITs.[127]

The Broude *et al* Study measures the extent to which BITs have implications for SRS by building upon UNCTAD's BIT text coding scheme.[128] Without going into technical detail here, the authors classify ISA provisions into nine SRS-related categories, including: available alternatives to arbitration; limitations on BIT protections subject to ISA; exclusion of policy areas from ISA; the extent of party input into treaty interpretation; and transparency.

The authors observe that:

> "most (but not all) states have *not* made a systematic effort over the years to recalibrate their BITs for the purpose of preserving more SRS so far as [ISA] is concerned. In fact, *many updated BITs either leave* [ISA] *provisions unchanged or render them more 'investor-friendly'*, in terms of litigation. Without investigating the parallel changes in the substance of investment protection rules, this may only reflect comparatively robust support for ISDS, not a lack of concern for SRS." (Emphasis added.)[129]

In sum, until the late 2000s, "most renegotiated ISA provisions reflect less, rather than more, regulatory space".[130]

b. Global and regional trends

Looking at global trends, the Broude *et al* Study observes that revised BITs reflect "much stronger [ISA] and, by implication, much lower flexibility for host governments".[131] The Study's observations regarding regional developments are particularly interesting, looking through the lens of tribunal lawmaking legitimacy:

(i) The decline in SRS is significantly more pronounced in North-South BITs than in South-South BITs.
(ii) It is Western European countries that "play a key role in the move towards greater investor protection at the ostensible expense of SRS".[132]
(iii) While former socialist countries, such as Russia, China and Romania, concluded many BITs in the 1980s allowing ISA only with respect to compensation, the change in their economic orientation in the 1990s coincides with their negotiation and renegotiation of BITs with broader ISA provisions.
(iv) As for Central and Eastern European countries, their renegotiation of BITs in the 2000s led to almost no change from a low SRS in the original treaties.

127. T. BROUDE, Y. HAFTEL and A. THOMPSON, fn. 103 above, p. 8.
128. *Ibid.*, pp. 9-11.
129. *Ibid.*, p. 3.
130. *Ibid.*
131. *Ibid.*, p. 11.
132. *Ibid.*, p. 12.

(v) In comparison, the Americas moved to a higher SRS: per the authors, "[i]t appears, then, that the Americas are spearheading the turn to more nuanced and less sweeping [ISA] provisions in investment and trade agreements".[133]

5. *A Turning Point?*

One cannot help but wonder whether the relatively rosy observations of the Stone Sweet and Broude *et al* Studies – that states are for the most part content with arbitrator lawmaking through ISA – will stand up in the currently unsettled ISA environment. Two recent developments bear particular note.

First, the European Court of Justice (*ECJ*) ruled on 6 March 2018 that the investor-state arbitration clause in the Netherlands-Slovakia BIT is not compatible with EU law, in that it "established a mechanism for settling disputes between an investor and a Member State which could prevent those disputes from being resolved in a manner that ensures the full effectiveness of EU law, even though they might concern the interpretation or application of that law".[134] The ECJ ruling has serious implications for over 150 intra-EU treaties, scores of arbitrations pending under those treaties, and perhaps even the enforceability of existing awards – and, in turn, for all the arbitrator lawmakers involved in those arbitrations and awards. This likely brightens the prospects for the EU investment treaty court regime, a complex topic in itself that is beyond the scope of this paper.

Second, the ECJ ruling was followed two days later, on 8 March 2018, by signature of the Comprehensive and Progressive Agreement for Trans-Pacific Partnership (*CPATPP*). The CPATPP is, in essence, the Trans-Pacific Partnership Agreement (*TPPA*) without the United States as a twelfth participant.[135] Overall, the content of the CPATPP does not stray far from the TPPA, but a number of original TPPA provisions will be suspended from the date of entry into force of the CPATPP (expected by late 2018 or 2019) unless and until reinstated by agreement of all eleven CPATPP Member States.

As relevant here, the Member States have *not* turned their backs – at least 180 degrees – on arbitrator lawmaking, which they could have done by excluding investor-state arbitration provisions. Chapter 9, the Investment Chapter, retains the basic menu of investor-state arbitration options for disputes arising under the Agreement, including the choice of ICSID, ICSID Additional Facility, UNCITRAL or other party-agreed arbitration rules. However, as set out in Annexes to Chapter 9, several Member States have entered into side agreements limiting recourse to arbitration, for example, in respect of foreign investment decisions by relevant agencies of Australia, Canada,

---

133. *Ibid.*, p. 13.

134. *Slovak Republic v. Achmea BV*, Case C-284/16, Judgment of the Court (Grand Chamber, March 2018, Request for a preliminary ruling under Art. 267 TFEU from the Bundesgerichtshof (Federal Court of Justice, Germany), made by decision of 3 March 2016, received at the Court on 23 May 2016, at <http://curia.europa.eu/juris/document.jst> (last accessed on 16 March 2018).

135. Comprehensive and Progressive Agreement for Trans-Pacific Partnership (CPATPP), text at <www.mfat.govt.nz/en/trade/free-trade-agreements-concluded-but-not-in-force/cptpp> (last accessed on 16 March 2018).

Mexico and New Zealand.[136] Further, the CPATPP provides for establishment of a Ministerial/senior official level Commission similar to the NAFTA Art. 2001 Free Trade Commission, which will have authority to issue interpretations of CPATPP. CPATPP Art. 9.25(3) – under the telling heading of "Governing Law" – provides as follows:

> "A decision of the Commission on the interpretation of a provision of this Agreement ... shall be binding on a tribunal and any decision or award issued by a tribunal must be consistent with that decision."

This obviously may set a brake on arbitrator lawmaking under the CPATPP.

The bigger question is whether the CPATPP opt-outs and Commission advisory role, in conjunction with the ECJ ruling, mark a turning point in the role of arbitrators as investment treaty lawmakers. This question is ripe for discussion at the ICCA Congress.

VI. CONCLUSION

To construct a conclusion, it is worth repeating the categories and roles of arbitrator lawmakers set out in the Introduction: (1) arbitrators in international commercial arbitration are not meant to, and rarely do make law; (2) arbitrators in standing and specialized *ad hoc* tribunals are meant to, and do make law; and (3) and arbitrators in *ad hoc* investment treaty arbitration were not necessarily meant to, but now do make law, sometimes in denial and sometimes necessarily inconsistently. The third category has raised, and will continue to raise, the most challenging legitimacy questions because of the inherently unstable intersection – one chosen by states, it must be remembered – between private judges and public international law and policy. The newest empirical research, canvassed above, confirms the embedded role of investment treaty tribunals as lawmakers and the continuing blessing from most states – so far – of that role.

Perhaps one way to make sense of arbitrator lawmaking is to borrow the International Bar Association "traffic light" approach. Arbitrators in standing courts and specialized sector tribunals – and in investment treaty courts likely to come – have a green light to make law, being expressly responsible for consistent and correct application of common standards. Commercial arbitrators, in general, have a red light against making law, being appointed to resolve a dispute anchored in a specific transaction in confidential proceedings. Arbitrators on *ad hoc* investment treaty tribunals face an orange or (in United States vocabulary) yellow light, signalling the need for caution. As they cannot realistically avoid making law in the course of interpreting common treaty provisions, they should look carefully in all directions, consider and reference the prior awards – and only those awards – they find most well-reasoned and relevant to the unique case before them, avoid the temptation of abusing their power for abstract lawmaking or with an eye otherwise to posterity, and then proceed to issue the best reasoned award possible to resolve the dispute entrusted to them.

136. CPATPP, fn. 135 above, Annex 9-H.

Arbitral Institutions and Professional Organizations as Lawmakers

Alexis Mourre[*]

TABLE OF CONTENTS

I. INTRODUCTORY REMARKS

The topic I have to address is the rule-making role of arbitration institutions and organizations.

By arbitration institutions and professional organizations, I refer to entities whose scope is either to promote the practice of arbitration or to administer arbitration proceedings. These entities might be private or have a public or semi-public status, as is often the case of chambers of commerce. I will not include in my analysis, however, States, regulators, and other actors acting in the public's interest that may, in pursuing their general goals, adopt rules applying to arbitration. This presentation will also not consider the role of professional Bars, which are vested with the goal of enforcing ethical rules applying to the law profession in a given jurisdiction. Finally, the role of the United Nations Commission on International Trade Law (UNCITRAL) is the topic of another presentation. Nor will I consider in the article the work of the Hague Conference on Private International Law, which is an intergovernmental organization established by treaty.

In addressing this topic, I will focus on the making of rules of a procedural nature, whether or not of a binding or quasi-binding nature. Many non-arbitral private bodies in fact play an important role in making rules of a substantive nature in international relations. It suffices to think of the UNIDROIT Principles, or of the role of the International Chamber of Commerce (ICC) in promulgating rules such as the Incoterms. Many private bodies are also active in creating model contracts, which in turn also contribute to what Klaus-Peter Berger once called the "creeping codification of the lex mercatoria".[1] Addressing the role of these private bodies in creating such substantive rules would push this presentation way beyond its boundaries.

At the core of this presentation is the relationship and interaction between the autonomous nature of international arbitration, its increasingly competitive and complex environment, and the growing codification of its procedures. At first blush, these two realities could seem contradictory. Common wisdom would suggest that free markets go hand-in-hand with lesser and lighter rules. Precisely because arbitration is an

---

* Independent Arbitrator; President of the ICC International Court of Arbitration.

1. Klaus Peter BERGER, *The Creeping Codification of the Lex Mercatoria* (Kluwer 1999).

autonomous system of justice that is based on party consent, should it not be loosely regulated, or entirely unregulated? Historically, however, free markets have never emerged as some autonomous domain of freedom, independent of, and opposed to, State authorities. Quite to the contrary, free markets have generally arisen as a consequence of government policy. Antitrust is a good example: the free hand of the market tends to create monopolies, which in turn are an obstacle to open markets. It is therefore necessary, for a free and open market to exist, that there is regulation against cartels and anticompetitive behaviors. Likewise, autonomous arbitration is a product of government policy, expressed first by the States' endorsement of the 1958 New York Convention, and then by the convergence of virtuous legislations aimed at limiting judicial interference in the arbitration and ensuring the enforcement of awards. This hands-off and pro-arbitration policy, however, does not stand in a vacuum. It can only be maintained if arbitration is perceived as a fair and legitimate means of resolving disputes, which in turn implies that the system is capable of generating rules that ensure its transparency, predictability, and that abuses are sanctioned.

An interesting comparison can in this regard be made with the financial and banking sectors. When financial markets were liberalized and disintermediated in the 1980s and 1990s, the level of rules and norms applying to them did not diminish significantly. State norms were simply replaced by sectorial and professional regulation. This has led an academic to conclude in a somewhat paradoxical manner that "any market reform, any government initiative intended to reduce red tape and promote market forces will have the ultimate effect of increasing the total number of regulations, the total amount of paperwork, and the total number of bureaucrats the government employs".[2] While it is fair to say that such a phenomenon has not been observed in arbitration, in particular as far as bureaucracy is concerned, the general rule according to which liberalization goes hand in hand with regulation is certainly topical. There is no doubt that maintaining the autonomy of arbitration requires the development of a certain level of self-regulation. States would otherwise no longer accept waiving their right to control the process at all stages of the procedure.

1. *Arbitral Soft Law and the Epistemic Arbitration Community*

From that perspective, the development of procedural soft law can be seen as a fundamental condition for establishing trust in arbitration.[3] International arbitration cannot stand in a vacuum, and if it is to be autonomous from State legal orders, it needs to have rules of its own. The multiplication of guidelines, rules and codes, which has been described and harshly criticized by some authors as a pathology,[4] is therefore, to the contrary, a measure of the maturity of an activity the role of which in the global economy is of fundamental importance. Seen as a measure of the autonomy of

2. David GRAEBER, *The Utopia of Rules: On Technology, Stupidity, and the Secrets Joys of Bureaucracy*, (Melville House 2015) p. 9.
3. Alexis MOURRE, "Soft Law as a Condition for the Development of Trust in International Arbitration", 13 Revista Brasileira de Arbitragem, p. 82.
4. Pierre LALIVE, "*De la Fureur réglementaire*", 12 ASA Bulletin (Kluwer Law International 1994, issue 2) pp. 213-219; Serge LAZAREFF, "*Avant-propos: Le bloc-notes de Serge Lazareff*", 124 Gazette du Palais: Cahiers de l'Arbitrage 3 (No. 338/339, 3 and 4 Dec. 2004).

arbitration and of its ability to self-regulate, the development of a comprehensive and generally accepted body of arbitral soft law is a healthy phenomenon, for it marks an evolution towards more predictability and more consistency of arbitration as a – albeit imperfect – global system of justice. It is also an element of objectification that is such as to increase the confidence in, and the acceptability of, the arbitral process.

The development of soft normativity in arbitration is also the expression of the strength of what Gabrielle Kaufmann-Kohler defined as the epistemic arbitration community, a community of practitioners, academics and institutions sharing the same interests and expertise.[5] The epistemic community has a number of peculiar characteristics that make it unique. It is multifaceted. It is at the same time very homogeneous – for it shares the same goals and is made of players all involved in the same area of practice – and extremely diverse, due to the national and cultural diversity of its members. It is fundamentally international in nature, and it evolves rapidly. Its dynamism is fostered by the fact that the members of the community compete against each other. All this contributes to the creativity of the group as far as rule-making is concerned. As Gabrielle Kaufmann-Kohler puts it: "through a process of intellectual cross-fertilization, these actors play a dominant role in shaping the transnational consensus on arbitration law and practice".[6]

This rule-making process greatly benefits from this cross-fertilization between the various components of the arbitral community by combining the compilation of existing practices and innovation by the elaboration of new rules. Its dynamism is also increased, for better or worse, by the fact that participating in a rule-making exercise is seen by practitioners as an important contribution to their own prestige and careers. Likewise, for an institution, authoring rules that will in turn be adopted by the community at large reinforces its prestige. The Arbitration Committee of the International Bar Association (IBA) is a perfect example of an institution having gained a central role in the arbitration community by its ability to create high-quality rules that have become widely used in practice. There is, in other words, a marketing versant of the rule-making exercise that may contribute to an undesired proliferation of rules.

The affirmation of soft law however supposes that there is convergence in the content of the rules and guidelines emanating from the arbitration community. In other words, it requires a sufficient level of consensus on a certain number of international standards of practice. If, to the contrary, the arbitration community fragments regionally or adopts inconsistent views on important procedural matters, there can be no emergence of a global soft procedural law. This question will be further addressed in subsequent sections of this presentation.

2. *Arbitral Institutions*

Arbitral institutions and professional organizations are the backbone of the epistemic arbitration community. It is a diverse group of entities, composed on the one hand of institutions whose main scope is to provide administrative services in support of

5. Gabrielle KAUFFMAN-KOHLER, "Soft Law in International Arbitration: Codification and Normativity", Journal of International Dispute Settlement (2010) p. 1, at p. 13.
6. *Ibid.*, p. 13.

arbitration proceedings, and on the other of bodies having the primary role of promoting the practice of arbitration and defending the interests of arbitration practitioners. Still, this institutional community is much more diverse than what this *summa divisio* would seem to suggest. In addition, arbitral institutions see themselves as important promoters of the practice of arbitration and some arbitral bodies whose scope is to promote arbitration in a given jurisdiction sometimes also maintain arbitration rules.

Arbitral institutions are those whose main scope is to administer arbitral proceedings. They can be divided in several categories. Some institutions are local and focus on their domestic markets, with at times very large domestic caseloads and more limited international exposure. China alone has more than 200 arbitral commissions. Some of these local institutions, however, have embarked on ambitious programs of internationalization, as shown by the change of name, in January 2018, of the Kuala Lumpur Regional Centre for Arbitration to become the Asia International Arbitration Centre. Others, as the ICC, essentially deal with international cases and are global in nature. Some are full service institutions, such as the ICC, Singapore International Arbitration Centre (SIAC), Hong Kong International Arbitration Centre (HKIAC), International Centre for Dispute Resolution (ICDR), London Court of International Arbitration (LCIA) or Arbitration Institute of the Stockholm Chamber of Commerce (SCC), while others specialize in a particular field of practice, such as the International Centre for Settlement of Investment Disputes (ICSID) for investment arbitration, the World Intellectual Property Organization (WIPO) for intellectual property (IP) disputes, the Court of Arbitration for Sport in Lausanne (CAS), the London Maritime Arbitrators Association (LMAA), or certain institutions specialized in insurance, such as the Insurance and Reinsurance Arbitration Society (ARIAS, London). Finally, some arbitral institutions are active in particular industries, such as the Independent Film and Television Alliance (IFTA), formerly known as American Film Market Association (AFMA), or in commodity arbitrations, such as the Grain and Feed Trade Organization (GAFTA), the Federation of Oils, Seeds and Fats Associations, or the Refined Sugar Association in London.

All in all, it is a diverse and uneven net of players, which nevertheless plays a fundamental role in establishing arbitration as a global system of justice. The 2015 Queen Mary Survey noted in this regard that 79 percent of the respondents' arbitrations over the past five years were institutional rather than *ad hoc*. There are therefore strong indicia showing that international arbitration is nowadays predominantly administered, which gives to institutions a particular responsibility in maintaining the legitimacy of the system. Jan Paulsson, in his now famous article on moral hazard in international arbitration,[7] noted in this regard that:

> "Only a few arbitral institutions can make credible claims to legitimacy. Many arbitration institutions are empty edifices waiting for someone to bother to dismantle them. Others cannot get away from features of cronyism which were their *raison d'être* in the first place. When such defects are uncovered, it also becomes more difficult for well-established and punctilious institutions to seek

7. Jan PAULSSON, "Moral Hazard in International Dispute Resolution", 25 ICSID Review–Foreign Investment Law Journal (1 October 2010, issue 2) p. 339.

> credence. So, how do we enhance and protect the legitimacy of decent arbitral institutions?"

These are strong words which, however, undoubtedly describe a reality. In contrast to arbitral practice, which has generated its own self-regulation, the creation and operation of arbitral institutions remain largely unregulated. There are no rules applicable to the creation of an institution, and very little regulation applying to their functioning and governance, which arguably poses a systemic risk for arbitration. A good example of how the defects of a flawed arbitral institution can affect the legitimacy of the arbitration system as a whole was given in 2014 in Romania, when the president of the Arbitral Chamber of the Romanian Chamber of Commerce was indicted for taking bribes in exchange for appointments that would favor one of the parties. He was consequently sentenced in 2015 to five years in prison, with several cases for related crimes – such as embezzlement and signature forgery – still pending.[8] Another example is the proliferation in Russia of the so-called "pocket arbitral institutions" and the reaction that such situation prompted on the part of the Russian government.

The lack of a regulatory regime applicable to arbitral institutions also has the consequence that there are very significant differences as to their structures and governance. The ICC International Court of Arbitration, for example, has no legal personality; it is part of the International Chamber of Commerce, which is itself a French association created under the 1901 law, a liberal statute allowing virtually anyone, with no control and very few formalities, to create a non-profit organization. The LCIA is a private not-for-profit company, limited by guarantee. The HKIAC has been established as an independent company limited by guarantee and a non-profit organization under Hong Kong law, much like SIAC, which was incorporated as a public company limited by guarantee. Some institutions exist under the umbrella of chambers of commerce, such as the Milan or the Vienna centers, and have as such para-public status, and others not, such as the ICDR. Some institutions have international law status, such as the Permanent Court of Arbitration (PCA) or ICSID. Some were created upon the initiative of States. The Asian-African Legal Consultative Organization (AALCO), a body comprising forty-seven member States from Asia and Africa, was for example instrumental in creating the former Kuala Lumpur Regional Centre for Arbitration, as well as the Cairo Regional Centre for International Commercial Arbitration and arbitration institutions in Nigeria, Kenya and Iran.[9] Others are purely private organizations.

Because arbitral institutions evolve in an open and largely unregulated and competitive marketplace, they may split, consolidate or merge to better serve the needs of their users, a phenomenon that also affects their rule-making activity. For example, the creation in 2007 of the Swiss Chambers Association for Arbitration, as a joint

8. <www1.agerpres.ro/english/2015/06/18/former-chamber-of-commerce-head-mihail-vlasov-to-serve-five-years-in-prison-14-40-08> (Romanian national news agency), <www.romaniajournal.ro/former-chamber-of-commerce-head-mihail-vlasov-sentenced-to-five-years-in-prison/> (Romanian online-newspaper).
9. Regional Centre for International Commercial Arbitration – Lagos (RCICAL), Nigeria; Tehran Regional Arbitration Centre (TRAC), Islamic Republic of Iran; Nairobi Centre for International Arbitration (NCIA), Republic of Kenya; <www.aalco.int/scripts/view-posting.asp?recordid=10> (homepage of AALCO).

initiative of the Basel, Bern, Geneva, Neuchatel, Ticino, Vaud and Zurich chambers of commerce, which all previously had their own arbitration institute, resulted in the creation of the Swiss Rules of International Arbitration and of a common Arbitration Court dedicated to international arbitration. In December of 2017, the three main arbitral institutions in Spain, the Corte Española de Arbitraje, the Cámara Arbitral de Madrid and the Corte Civil y Mercantil de Arbitraje (CIMA), entered into an agreement to merge, which will result in the creation of one single international arbitration chamber. Another example of arbitral institutions having joined forces is the merger at the end of 2017 of the Shenzhen Court of International Arbitration with the Shenzhen Arbitration Commission.[10] In contrast, CIETAC has in 2012 split in three separate institutions, which now compete one against the other.[11] Likewise, the Indonesia National Board of Arbitration (BANI) has in 2016 split into two competing institutions, each of which claiming to be the legitimate successor of the pre-existing body.[12]

States have realized that significant economic interests go with the presence on their soil of major arbitral institutions, and with the development of internationally recognized seats where parties can safely locate their arbitrations. For example, when the ICC considered in 2010-2011 the possibility of relocating from France to another country, the institution representing the French arbitration community, Paris Place d'Arbitrage, authored a report quantifying in € 200 million the yearly revenues generated by the presence in Paris of large numbers of arbitration practitioners, experts, interpreters, court reporters, etc.[13] And this study was in turn one of the factors leading to the decision by the French government to grant certain incentives to the ICC in order for it to maintain its headquarters in France.[14] Likewise, the creation in 1991 of the Singapore International Arbitration Centre was part of an ambitious plan by the government to create an international arbitration hub on its soil.[15] Another example is the plan recently adopted by NITI Aayog, the former planning commission of the Government of India, to develop an institutional framework for the development of administered arbitration, including the creation of a national arbitral institution.[16] There is now global competition between arbitral marketplaces, one of the effects of which is to encourage the creation of local arbitration institutions in order to enhance the profile and attractiveness of each country. And to a certain extent, this proliferation of arbitral centers also results in more rule-making, because the creation of rules is a marker of prestige and a tool of communication.

---

10. <www.sccietac.org/web/news/detail/1722.html> (Merger Announcement).
11. Justin D'AGOSTINO, Jessica BOOTH and Tracy WU, "The Aftermath of the CIETAC Split", Kluwer Arbitration Blog, 2 May 2014.
12. Togi PANGARIBUAN, "Reconciling the Conciliators: The BANI Split in Indonesia", Kluwer Arbitration Blog, 2 February 2018.
13. DURAND-BARTHEZ, KLEIMAN, BOIVIN, "*Enquête relative à la localisation de la CCI et au rôle de Paris comme place d'arbitrage*", 24 November 2010.
14. Michel PRADA, "*Rapport sur certains facteurs de renforcement de la compétivité juridique de la place de Paris*", March 2011.
15. <https://globalarbitrationreview.com/insight/guide-to-regional-arbitration-volume-5-2017/1070152/white-list-asia-pacific>.
16. <https://thewire.in/law/india-global-arbitration-hub-modi-government> (Indian web publication).

3. *Professional Organizations*

The other institutional versant of the arbitral community is composed of professional organizations and bodies whose role is not primarily to administer arbitrations, but essentially to promote the practice of arbitration, develop best practices, provide training services, or organize conferences and other events aimed at disseminating the culture of arbitration at the local or global level. Some of these institutions, however, have a dual role, by at the same time aiming at representing the arbitration community in a given jurisdiction and maintaining arbitration rules. Such is the case of the Russian Arbitration Association.

As for arbitral institutions, the landscape of these "non-institutional" bodies has remarkably evolved with the process of globalization and diversification that has marked the evolution of the international arbitration community in the past thirty years. The number of local arbitration associations has flourished, as a tool for local arbitration groups to structure their communities and to develop exchanges with more established arbitral jurisdictions. The Associazione Italiana per l'Arbitrato, the Association Suisse d'Arbitrage, the Comité Français de l'Arbitrage, the Club Español de Arbitraje, the Swedish Arbitration Association are only examples of that phenomenon. Some of these bodies have been created at the regional level, such as the Asociación Latinoamericana de Arbitraje, the Asia Pacific Regional Arbitration Group (APRAG) or the Association pour la Promotion de l'Arbitrage en Afrique. ICC National Committees also play an important role in the promotion of arbitration in their jurisdictions. Some of these bodies were created as a result of contacts established between practitioners of different jurisdictions, such as the Comitê Brasileiro de Arbitragem (CBAr) in Brazil, after long-established contacts between the Comité Français de l'arbitrage and the Brazilian arbitration community.[17] Again, a distinction can be made between national arbitration associations and those having a more international constituency, even though membership in most domestic associations is not restricted to nationals of their home jurisdictions.

Amongst the main international associations are the IBA Arbitration Committee, arguably the world's largest arbitration group with over 4,500 members, and ICCA. The two institutions, which both focus on academic activities, training and rule-making, are however different in nature. The IBA, which was established in 1947, has a membership of both individual lawyers and bar associations, and it is managed by a Board essentially composed of representatives of over 80,000 individual lawyers and 190 professional bar associations spanning more than 170 countries. In contrast, ICCA was created in 1961 as a private club upon the initiative of a limited group of academics, amongst whom, as we know, were professors Jean Robert and Roberto Minoli.

In this context, it is also relevant to mention the work of the International Law Association (ILA), a non-profit organization based in London that promotes the study, unification and furtherance of international law. The ILA has an arbitration committee which every two years produces a report that is relevant to the practice of arbitration, including recommendations. These recommendations encompass recognized principles and best practices, and are therefore a hybrid product sharing some of the characteristics

17. Bertrand MOREAU, "*Editorial, La lettre de l'AFA*", March 2016, N 19.

of normative rules and those of a practice note. Recent reports dealt with *Lis Pendens* and Res Judicata in Arbitration, the Inherent and Implied Powers of Arbitrators, Public Policy as a Ground for Non-recognition or the Means for Ascertaining the Content of the Applicable Law in Arbitration.[18]

Some associations focus on the making of rules in specialist areas of practice, such as FIDIC – the International Federation of Consulting Engineers – for construction, the National Grain and Feed Association for commodities, the European Federation of Energy Traders (EFET) for energy or the Association of International Petroleum Negotiators (AIPN) in the petroleum industry. The rules promulgated by these bodies, such as the FIDIC rules, may have a direct impact on the practice of arbitration, as they determine the applicable arbitral rules in case of a dispute, as well as the conditions in which pre-arbitral steps (such as Dispute Board determinations) may enter into play.

Other associations focus on particular aspects of the arbitral practice. Young practitioners groups, such as the ICC Young Arbitrators Forum (YAF) or Young ICCA, aim at training activities and at helping young arbitrators and counsel gain visibility on the arbitration marketplace. Others, such as Arbitral Women, aim at promoting gender parity in arbitration, in particular through instruments such as the Pledge,[19] which can be seen as having para-normative value in that they seek to encourage institutions to adopt rules consistent with the goal that they promote.

4. *Institutional Exchanges and Peer Review*

One of the most notable characteristics of this net of institutions and associations is the constant exchange of views and experiences between them through formal and informal networks. Their representatives meet at conferences, they often sit together in institutional boards and councils, and they know each other well for having participated in the same cases as counsel or arbitrators. Part of the role of a good arbitral institution officer is to get constantly apprised of the thinking and initiatives of its competitors as indicia of the evolution of practice and expectations of the users. Rules are sometimes promulgated by several institutions joining forces, such as the recent ICCA-Queen Mary proposed Principles and Best Practices on Third Party Funding[20] or the ICCA/International Institute for Conflict Prevention and Resolution (CPR)/New York City Bar Association Draft Cybersecurity Protocol for International Arbitration.[21]

Interestingly, these inter-institutional exchanges have themselves been institutionalized with the creation in 1985 of the International Federation of Commercial Arbitration Institutions (IFCAI), regrouping today fifty-two member organizations. The creation of IFCAI is an indication of the awareness of the importance of inter-

18. Recommendations on Lis Pendens and Res Judicata and Arbitration, Resolution No. 1/2006; other mentionable reports include Recommendations on Inherent and Implied Powers of International Arbitral Tribunals, Resolution No.4/2016, Recommendations on the Application of Public Policy as a Ground for Refusing Recognition or Enforcement of International Arbitral Awards, Resolution No. 2/2002; Recommendations on Ascertaining the Contents of the Applicable Law in International Commercial Arbitration, Resolution No. 6/2008.
19. <www.arbitrationpledge.com/>.
20. <https://www.arbitration-icca.org/projects/Third_Party_Funding.html>.
21. <https://www.arbitration-icca.org/projects/Cybersecurity-in-International-Arbitration.html>.

institutional dialogue. It is evidence of the fact that most arbitral institutions see themselves as part of a structured community sharing identical goals and values. Many institutions have also signed bilateral cooperation agreements, whereby each offers access to services offered by its counterpart, such as hearing facilities.

An important part of this fertile cross-institutional cooperation is, as we shall see, the consultations that are organized on occasion of the adoption of new institutional rules, guidelines or other sets of soft law rules, as well as the peer review of their implementation.

5. *A Decentralized and Horizontal Rule-Making Process*

We therefore see the emergence of a flexible, dynamic and decentralized system of rule-making, where there is no hierarchy between rule-makers that are in fact competing one against the other, and where rules are constantly amended to incorporate innovations introduced elsewhere.

An interesting and somewhat counterintuitive characteristic of this institutional sociology is that the multiplication of potential rule-makers results neither in an inflation of rules nor in divergence as to their content. Rather, there is growing convergence between the rules promulgated by various players, conducive to greater harmonization of arbitral practices that were previously determined to a larger extent by local judicial culture and domestic procedural rules. Where the pyramidal process of lawmaking that characterizes States conduces on the international scene to conflicts of norms because of the persistent differences between national traditions, the production of norms in the context of a horizontal network leads to fewer conflicts of norms and more harmonization.[22] The norms adopted in this network are also simpler and easier to access than the procedural rules that are adopted by States to apply to Court proceedings. The three more widely used sets of non-binding arbitration procedural rules, which arguably are the IBA Rules on Evidence, the Guidelines on Conflicts of Interest in International Arbitration (the Guidelines on Conflicts of Interest) and Guidelines on Party Representation, for example represent, if put together, fewer than seventy pages, while any national code of civil proceedings runs hundreds if not thousands of pages. The comparison of course has only limited value, for domestic codes would cover a much broader range of questions, but it is nonetheless a good indication of the fact that, consistent with the inherent flexibility of arbitral proceedings, the rules emanating from the arbitral community have remained simple and easy to understand.

One of the reasons why this process of rule-making does not result in greater complexity may also be the utilitarian nature of these rules and their low normativity. Those who participate in the making of these rules are also those who will use and apply them and, in contrast to governments or legislators, they are not directly bound to take into account considerations of general interest. Unlike legislators, who have to respect the general coherence and goals of the national system of law that they represent, arbitral bodies engaged in rule-making only serve the special interest of the arbitral

22. On the emergence of a horizontal mode of production of norms in modern systems of law, F. OST and M. VAN DE KERCHOVE, "*De la pyramide au réseau, pour une théorie dialectique du droit*" (Saint-Louis, Brussells 2002).

community. This makes considerations of legitimacy of the rule-making process all the more significant to their acceptability by States.

An interesting example of that interaction can be drawn from an episode that occurred in France, where the preparation of witnesses is not allowed before courts. In an international arbitration seated in France in which both counsel were registered French lawyers, one of them sued the other before the Paris Bar precisely for having had contacts with a fact witness before the arbitration hearing. The French arbitral community at that point made a submission before the Bar, explaining that this was normal practice in international arbitration.[23] Shortly thereafter, the IBA adopted its Guidelines on Party Representation, dealing with that same matter. Based on that submission made by French arbitration practitioners, the Paris Bar adopted a resolution applying specifically to arbitration and derogating from the general rule applicable in courts.[24] In such a context, the existence of a norm such as the IBA Guidelines on Conflicts of Interest is a significant element leading to the acceptance by the State of a practice that would otherwise be at odds with domestic law.

Having described who the institutional rule-makers are and how they interact, it is now necessary to address the typology of norms that are produced by institutions (II), their legitimacy (III) and normativity (IV).

II. TYPOLOGY OF NORMS

It is submitted that the norms made by arbitral institutions and bodies can be classified in four broad categories: soft law (*1*), best practices (*2*), institutional rules and practice notes (*3*), and governance rules (*4*).

1. *Soft Law*

The concept of soft law has been widely discussed[25] and it is not the topic of this paper to address it in detail. A soft law rule is a norm which has no direct binding character but, because of its wide acceptance, has acceded to soft normativity, which is to say that a large number of practitioners feel compelled to apply it or to draw inspiration from it.

The wide acceptance of the norm can derive from a consensus on its content, from the legitimacy and wide recognition of the rule-maker, or from a combination of both factors. An indication that a given norm has acceded to soft normativity may be the fact that it is referred to by domestic courts in their decisions dealing with the topic

23. *Le Bulletin du barreau de Paris*. No. 9, 4.3.2008, 45.

24. Ian MEREDITH, Hussain KHAN, "Witness Preparation in International Arbitration – A Cross Cultural Minefield", 26 Mealey's International Arbitration Report (September 2011, no. 9) p. 3.

25. Lawrence NEWMAN and Michael RADINE, eds., *Soft Law in International Arbitration* (JurisNet, LLC 2014); Gabrielle KAUFMANN-KOHLER, "Soft Law in International Arbitration: Codification and Normativity", 1 Journal of International Dispute Settlement (2010, no. 2), pp. 283-299; Alexis MOURRE, "Soft Law as a Condition for the Development of Trust in International Arbitration" 13 Revista Brasileira de Arbitragem, (2016, issue 51) pp. 82-98; for a critical view, Daniele FAVALLI, ed., *The Sense and Non-Sense of Guidelines, Rules, and Other Para-Regulatory Texts In International Arbitration,* ASA Special Series No. 37 (2015).

addressed by the norm. Such was the case of a 2008 decision of the Swiss Federal Tribunal, referring to the IBA Guidelines on Conflicts of Interest.[26] Similarly, the High Court of Justice of Madrid in a decision in 2015[27] and the Austrian Supreme Court in 2016[28] stressed that IBA guidelines may serve as a point of reference for whether an arbitrator has to disclose certain circumstances. In this context it is also interesting to note that the Singapore High Court has stated that the IBA Rules on the Taking of Evidence in International Commercial Arbitration (the IBA Rules on Evidence) constituted guidance that could be adopted by the arbitral tribunal under the SIAC Rules.[29]

In the view of the author, only two sets of arbitral norms can claim to have acceded to the status of soft normativity: the IBA Rules on Evidence and the IBA Guidelines on Conflicts of Interests. The different labeling of these two sets of norms is of little relevance: whether they are called rules or guidelines does not change the fact that they are not directly binding, nor does it affect their capacity to acquire soft normativity. The use of the term "guidelines" rather than "rules" is probably more reflective of a caution of the drafters of the conflicts guidelines, which at the time of their adoption in 2003 felt that there was less consensus on their content than was the case in 1999 for the Rules on Evidence. The same caution prevailed in 2013 at the time of the adoption of the Guidelines on Party Representation in International Arbitration (the Guidelines on Party Representation). What matters in order to assess whether a given set of norms has acquired soft normativity is not the title that was given to it but its level of acceptance amongst users.

The wide acceptance that these two sets of rules have gained has been the subject matter of a large number of studies.[30] A recent study made by a Sub-Committee of the IBA[31] is in this regard particularly enlightening.

---

26. 26 ASA Bull., pp. 565-579.
27. High Court of Justice of Madrid, Resolution No. 13/2015, 28.1.2015, ECLI: ES:TSJM:2015:1286.
28. OGH, 19.04.2016, 18 ONc 3/15h, ECLI:AT:OGH0002:2016:018ONC00003.15H.0419.000.
29. *Dongwoo Mann+Hummel Co Ltd v. Mann+Hummel GmbH* [2008] 3 SLR(R) 871.
30. André ABBUD, Rafael ALVES, Victor RUIZ, "Taking Evidence in Latin America: Some Observations on Local Practices and Use of the IBA Rules", 23 ICC International Court of Arbitration Bulletin (2012) pp 13-21; Margaret MOSES, "The Role of the IBA Guidelines on Conflicts of Interest in Arbitrator Challenges", Kluwer Arbitration Blog, 23 November 2017, Queen Mary Study 2012, p. 11; Queen Mary Study 2015, p. 33; Queen Mary Study 2018, p. 36; Survey by Berwin Leighton Paisner 2012, p. 12; Elina MEREMINSKAYA, "Results of the Survey on the Use of Soft Law Instruments in International Arbitration", Kluwer Arbitration Blog, 6 June 2014; Judith GILL, "2010 Revisions to the IBA Rules on Taking of Evidence", Les Cahiers de l'Arbitrage (2011-1), Matthias SCHERER, "The IBA Guidelines on Conflicts of Interest in International Arbitration: The First Five Years 2004-2009", 4 Dispute Resolution International (May 2010) p. 5.
31. The IBA Arbitration Guidelines and Rules Subcommittee, Report on the Reception of the IBA Arbitration Soft Law Products, September 2016.

a. IBA Rules on Evidence

As to the Rules on evidence, the Sub-Committee noted that:

> "in approximately 80% of those arbitrations in which reference was made to the Rules on Evidence, the arbitral tribunal consulted them on the basis that they represented non-binding guidelines. In the remaining 20% of instances, the Rules on Evidence were considered binding. Yet, even in those arbitrations in which the tribunal consulted the Rules on Evidence as guidelines only, it overwhelmingly followed them (in more than 90% of the cases). There appears to be a general consensus that the use of the Rules on Evidence ... will grow."[32]

This is a clear indication that, on the one hand, the Rules on Evidence have gained general acceptance and, on the other hand, that most arbitrators feel compelled to apply them, even if they do not consider them to be mandatory. The Sub-Committee also noted that "North American, Asia-Pacific, and European Respondents and Reporters have noted instances in which domestic courts have referred to the Rules on Evidence",[33] which is also a clear indication that the Rules have acceded to soft normativity.

This general acceptance can be explained by the fact that the Rules on Evidence have achieved a balanced synthesis between the civil law and common law traditions. As to written evidence, the Rules lean more to the civil law tradition by limiting the scope of documents disclosure and requiring that requests to produce refer to identified documents or to narrow and specific categories of documents. Concerning oral evidence, however, the Rules are more inspired by the Anglo-Saxon tradition by allowing wide categories of individuals to testify, permitting the preparation of witnesses and relying on cross-examination conducted by counsel.[34] Even if imperfect, this synthesis has allowed arbitration to move away from local procedural rules and permitted the emergence of a transnational arbitral procedural law. As such, the Rules have been a powerful driver for the unification of practice and the establishment of arbitration as an autonomous system of justice.

It should be noted, however, that there seems to be, in certain jurisdictions, a trend to a return to more local procedural traditions for the conduct of arbitral procedures. A group of practitioners has recently launched an initiative called the Prague Inquisitorial Rules,[35] openly as an attempt to find an alternative to the IBA Rules. The draft Prague Rules question the usefulness of allowing document production requests in the form allowed by the IBA Rules, and they express reservations as to the examination of witnesses and the use of party-appointed experts. The initiators of these new rules propose to develop an inquisitorial model essentially based on a more active role of the

32. Paras. 16-17.
33. Para. 63.
34. Yves DERAINS, "*Le professionnalisme des arbitres*" in Cahiers de Droit de l'Entreprise no. 4 (Lexis-Nexis, July-August 2012); Gisele STEPHENS-CHU and Julie SPINELLI, "The Gathering and Taking of Evidence Under the IBA Guidelines on Party Representation in International Arbitration: Civil and Common Law Perspectives", 8 Dispute Resolution International (2014) p. 37.
35. The Prague Inquisitorial Rules, Draft of 26 March 2018, <http://praguerules.com/upload/medialibrary/697/697f654d36c0275b310cb3ccc1e0e9f3.pdf>.

arbitral tribunal, on a model that is more inspired by the procedures followed in court in civil law countries. In particular, the tribunal would under these rules have the duty to establish the facts and the law, the *jura novit curia* principle would be applicable as a matter of principle, and there would be a priority given to documents over testimony.[36] The initiative has already been endorsed by some institutions, such as the Russian Arbitration Association. This initiative, would it gain traction in civil law jurisdictions, could be such as to fragment the existing consensus around the IBA Rules, therefore putting into question the very idea that an arbitral soft procedural law has emerged.

b. IBA Guidelines on Conflicts of Interest

Concerning the Guidelines on Conflicts of Interest, the IBA Sub-Committee reported that:

> "the Guidelines have gained broad acceptance and are used often by the international arbitration community. Of the three IBA instruments surveyed, the Conflicts of Interest Guidelines are the most commonly referenced. By way of example, in the 3201 arbitrations known to respondents over the past five years in which issues of conflicts of interest arose, the Guidelines were referenced in 57% of them.
>
> .... [C]ounsel make use of the Guidelines when appointing arbitrators in 67% of all reported cases. Arbitrators also appear to make frequent use of the Guidelines across all regions.
>
> The survey also confirms that the Guidelines often have been referenced by the relevant Decision-maker (arbitral institutions, tribunals, or courts) in reaching a pronouncement on the existence of a conflict of interest. At a global level, the Guidelines were referenced in 67% of decisions resolving issues of conflicts of interest. Perhaps more importantly, in 69% of the decisions that referenced the Guidelines in solving a conflicts of interest issue, the Decision-maker chose to follow the Guidelines."[37]

Here again, this is a clear indication that the Guidelines have gained a certain soft normativity. There is general consensus amongst counsel, arbitrators, institutions and courts that these rules are appropriate and strike a proper balance, as far as disclosures are concerned, between the need to preserve the integrity of the process and that of avoiding the disclosure of entirely irrelevant circumstances.

---

36. "However, from a civil law perspective, the IBA Rules are still closer to the common law traditions.... In addition to that many arbitrators are reluctant to actively manage arbitration proceedings, including earlier determination of issues in dispute and the disposal of such issues, to avoid the risk of a challenge. These factors contribute greatly to the costs of arbitration, while their efficiency is sometimes rather questionable.... In light of all of this, the drafters of the Prague Rules believe that developing the rules on taking evidence, which are based primarily on the inquisitorial model of procedure and would enhance more active role of the tribunals, would contribute to increasing efficiency in international arbitration. By adopting a more inquisitorial approach, the new rules will help the parties and tribunals to reduce the time and costs of arbitrations", Introduction to the Prague Inquisitorial Rules, p. 2.
37. "Report on the Reception of the IBA Arbitration Soft Law Products" (2016) paras. 101-103.

It should be noted, however, that certain courts, in deciding whether a challenge should be accepted, have departed from the Guidelines. Such is the case of the English High Court in a case involving the IBA Guidelines Non-Waivable Red List.[38] In that case, an arbitrator had not disclosed that his law firm had advised an affiliate of one of the parties and that substantial income for the firm had derived from this representation. Such a fact is included in the IBA Non-Waivable Red List, thus necessarily disqualifying the arbitrator. The arbitrator however responded that this representation had not been revealed by his internal conflict check, that he was working as a sole practitioner within the firm that had represented the affiliate, and that he had not received any income from it. Had he known the situation, he would have disclosed it, but the representation was not on his mind at all. The court, as a preliminary matter, held that the IBA Guidelines are not binding, but can still be of assistance for the decision. Nevertheless, given that the case was of an international nature, it felt the need to examine the IBA Guidelines. The court took the case as an opportunity to criticize the Guidelines by stressing that in the circumstances of the case, a conflict did not "necessarily" exist. Rather, the court concluded that a fair-minded and informed observer, having considered the facts, would not consider that there was a real possibility that the arbitrator was biased or lacked independence or impartiality. The court therefore departed from the IBA Guidelines and rejected the challenge.

It is also noteworthy that most major arbitral institutions have been careful not to bind themselves to the Guidelines. Some of them have even adopted guidance of their own. For example, the ICC has on 12 February 2016 decided to adopt in its guidance note[39] a set of rules of its own dealing with the disclosure obligations of ICC arbitrators. Although these rules are largely inspired by, and consistent with, the IBA Guidelines on Conflicts of Interest, they depart from them in certain instances.

The ICC decision to adopt guidance on conflicts disclosures was made out of various considerations. First, although the Court regularly referred to the IBA Guidelines when deciding challenges, it had never wanted to say so in a transparent manner, out of fear that it would otherwise be bound by them; as a result, in absence of guidance, there was a lack of transparency as to the rules that would be applied in its decision-making. Second, the Court felt that although reflecting general accepted practice, there was the need to encourage disclosures beyond what would in certain cases be mandated by the Orange List, for example in case of multiple appointments by the same counsel or party more than three years before a given appointment.[40]

This is a good example of the difference in nature between the role of a body such as the IBA and that of an arbitral institution as far as the making of rules is concerned. While an arbitral institution, as we shall see, is not primarily concerned with reflecting consensus and is only driven by promoting its own policies, a body such as the IBA has to set the basis for a consensus within the arbitral community, and therefore aims at

38. *W Limited v. M SDN BHD*, [2016] EWHC 422 (Comm), 2.3.2016.

39. Note to Parties and Arbitral Tribunals on the Conduct of the Arbitration Under the ICC Rules of Arbitration, version of 30 October 2017.

40. Alexis MOURRE, "Message from the President", ICC Dispute Resolution Bulletin (2016, issue 1) pp. 3, 4.

elaborating rules that will be acceptable across the board, in institutional as well as *ad hoc* arbitrations and in all parts of the world.

c. *IBA Guidelines on Party Representation*

Another set of rules that may claim to soft normativity is the IBA Guidelines on Party Representation. The Guidelines on Party Representation are the most recent set of rules adopted by the IBA, and also the more controversial. On their adoption in 2013, the Guidelines were harshly criticized by a number of practitioners, in particular in Switzerland, to the point that the Swiss Arbitration Association launched an initiative to discourage their use.[41] It is still today difficult to understand the violence of this reaction, which can in part be attributed to the fear that arbitrators would unduly interfere with the attorney-client relationship, in part to the idea that the Guidelines would create artificial grounds for unnecessary skirmishes, and in part to the perception that the Guidelines are an import of Anglo-Saxon procedural devices into arbitration. The scope of this paper is not to address such criticisms, which I have done in several other articles.[42] It is noteworthy, however, that the Swiss Arbitration Association has subsequently changed its position, by advocating in 2015 the creation of an international arbitration ethics council,[43] which role would have been precisely to address issues of counsel conduct in arbitration, thereby acknowledging the need for transnational rules to address these issues. Faced with multiple oppositions to the idea, the Swiss Arbitration Association then decided, in 2016, not to push this project further.[44]

The IBA Sub-Committee noted that "the Party Representation Guidelines are the least frequently used of the three IBA Rules and Guidelines, with references to the party Representation Guidelines being made in less than 20% of arbitrations involving issues of counsel conduct". The Sub-Committee also noted that the Guidelines "appear to be more frequently used in common law jurisdictions than in civil law jurisdictions".[45]

The Guidelines on Party Representation, however, seem to be progressively gaining acceptance.[46] We should not forget, in this regard, that the IBA Guidelines on Conflicts

41. ASA Board Position on IBA Guidelines on Party Representation, 4 April 2014 ("the ASA Board has serious reservations about the Guidelines. These reservations relate not just to some of the provisions of the Guidelines but more generally arise from the approach adopted for dealing with these differences.").
42. Alexis MOURRE and Eduardo ZULETA JARAMILLO, "The IBA Guidelines on Party Representation in International Arbitration" in Nassib G. ZIADÉ, et al., eds., *Festschrift Ahmed Sadek El-Kosheri* (Kluwer 2015) pp. 109-120; Alexis MOURRE, "Soft Law as a Condition for the Development of Trust in International Arbitration", XIII Revista Brasileira de Arbitragem (2016, issue 51) pp. 82-98; Alexis MOURRE, "Chapter 25: About Procedural Soft Law, the IBA Guidelines on Party Representation and the Future of Arbitration" in Patricia SHAUGHNESSY and Sherlin TUNG, eds., *The Powers and Duties of an Arbitrator: Liber Amicorum Pierre A. Karrer*, (Kluwer 2017) pp. 239-250.
43. Anne-Carole CREMADES, "The Creation of a Global Arbitration Ethics Council: A Truly Global Solution to a Global Problem", Kluwer Arbitration Blog, 24 November 2015.
44. <www.arbitration-ch.org/en/asa/asa-news/details/993.asa-working-group-on-counsel-ethics-releases-latest-findings.html>.
45. Para. 203.
46. Queen Mary Study 2015, p. 35; Queen Mary Study 2018, p. 36.

were also criticized upon their publication in 2003[47] and are still criticized today,[48] but have nevertheless ultimately gained universal success. It should also be noted that the Guidelines are gaining some ground amongst institutions, with their adoption in 2016 by the Australian Centre for International Commercial Arbitration (ACICA),[49] and their endorsement in 2016 by the ICC.[50] It can nevertheless be concluded that the Guidelines on Party Representation have not yet acceded to the same level of soft normativity as the two other sets of IBA rules and guidelines.

d. The ICCA-Queen Mary Principles on Third-Party Funding

Another interesting example of a set of rules that may gain general acceptance is the recent ICCA-Queen Mary Report on Third-Party Funding.[51] This report and the recommendations it entails, adopted at the 2018 ICCA Congress, were drafted by a joint task force established in 2013 by ICCA and Queen Mary University of London, composed of a diverse group of leading experts from a wide range of professional backgrounds, including arbitrators, in-house counsel, attorneys, representatives from arbitral institutions, states, academics, and a range of third-party funders and brokers. The Principles address a wide range of issues, some of which are still unsettled in arbitral practice, such as disclosures, privilege, and security for costs, and they clearly have the potential to accede to some level of soft normativity if they become endorsed by parties, funders and practitioners. This, however, still remains to be seen, as at least one major funder has strongly rejected them.[52]

There are of course many other sets of guidelines that could claim to a certain degree of normativity, such as the Chartered Institute of Arbitrators' (CIArb) Guidelines on

---

47. Markham BALL, "Probably Deconstructed – How Helpful, Really, Are the New International Bar Association Guidelines on Conflicts of Interest in International Arbitration?", 15 World Arbitration and Mediation Report (2004, no. 11) p. 333; Hilmar RAESCHKE-KESSLER, "The Production of Documents in International Arbitration – A Commentary on Article 3 of the New IBA Rules of Evidence", 18 Arbitration International (Kluwer Law International 2002, issue 4) p. 411; John TOWNSEND, "Clash and Convergence on Ethical Issues in International Arbitration", 36 U Miami Inter-American Law Review (2004, issues 1-2) p. 1; Carlos Alberto CARMONA, "Considerations on the IBA Guidelines on Party Representation in International Arbitration: A Brazilian point of view", Les Cahiers de l'Arbitrage (2014, no. 1) p. 29; the same is also the point of view of Nathan O'MALLEY, "An Annotated Commentary on the 2010 Revised IBA Rules of Evidence for International Arbitration", 27 International Construction Law Review (2010) p. 464.
48. Mark R. JOELSON, "A Critique of the 2014 International Bar Association Guidelines on Conflicts of Interest in International Arbitration", 26 American Review of International Arbitration (2015, no. 3); Gary B. BORN, *International Commercial Arbitration*, 2nd ed. (Kluwer 2014) p. 1853.
49. In the ACICA Arbitration Rules 2016, see also <https://acica.org.au/iba-guidelines/> (may serve as an important resource for practitioners and arbitrators).
50. Note to parties and arbitral tribunals on the conduct of the arbitration under the ICC rules of arbitration (30 October 2017), para. 33 ("Parties and arbitral tribunals are encouraged to draw inspiration from and, where appropriate, to adopt the IBA Guidelines on Party Representation in International Arbitration").
51. Report of the ICCA-Queen Mary Task Force on Third-Party Funding in International Arbitration, April 2018, can be accessed under <https://www.arbitration-icca.org/publications/Third-Party-Funding-Report.html>.
52. <https://www.burfordcapital.com/blog/icca-queen-mary-task-force-report-flaws/>.

Jurisdictional Challenges,[53] the Club Español de Arbitraje's code of good arbitration practices,[54] or the JAMS' Arbitrators Ethics Guidelines.[55] But these texts are unlikely to gain a level of acceptance such as to elevate them to the level of soft law. There may be several reasons for that. The first is that some of these texts were authored by a local association, and are therefore directed to a local community. Such is the case, for example, of the rules and guidelines adopted by the Club Español de Arbitraje.[56] Even though they may have gained acceptance locally, they are by definition not reflective of an international consensus and their scope also overlaps in some respect with that of the IBA Rules and Guidelines.[57] Some of these texts may also express a particular legal tradition and would therefore not be perceived as an international standard. Such may be the case of certain rules emanating from the Chartered Institute of Arbitrators.[58] Finally, some rules may address questions in respect of which there is no consensus on the need for regulation.[59]

It is of course notable that the only sets of norms that may claim to the status of soft normativity were authored by the IBA and ICCA. This, as we shall see later in this presentation, is in direct correlation with the unique characteristics of these organizations, both because of their global nature, the legitimacy conferred upon them by their broad membership and the transparency and inclusiveness of the process having led to the adoption and revisions of norms such as the Rules on Evidence and Conflicts Guidelines. This has allowed the bridging of the gap between different legal traditions and finding a synthesis that has in turn gained general recognition. Of particular relevance, as far as the IBA is concerned, is also the participation of professional Bars.

Conceivably, the IBA Rules and Guidelines, with rules such as the ICCA-Queen Mary Task Force Principles on Third-Party Funding, could be seen as forming the core of a truly global and transnational arbitral procedural law. This idea is, however, subject to potential tensions. As we have seen, the IBA Rules on Evidence are challenged by civil law practitioners believing that in certain cases arbitrations may be better conducted under inquisitorial rules. As to the Guidelines on Conflicts, although they are widely referred to, certain courts and even arbitral institutions have departed from them or have adopted standards of their own. The ICCA-Queen Mary Task Force Principles have yet to gain acceptance and are already challenged.

---

53. Jurisdictional Challenges, last revised on 29 November 2016, <https://www.ciarb.org/docs/default-source/ciarbdocuments/guidance-and-ethics/practice-guidelines-protocols-and-rules/international-arbitration-guidelines-2015/2015jurisdictionchallenges.pdf?sfvrsn=26>.
54. *Código des Buenas Prácticas Arbitrales*, December 2005, <https://www.clubarbitraje.com/sites/default/files/090216_buenas_practicas_arbitrales_castellano_1.pdf>.
55. Arbitrators Ethics Guidelines, <www.jamsadr.com/arbitrators-ethics/>.
56. *Código de Buenas Prácticas Arbitrales*, September 2013.
57. Gonzalo JIMÉNEZ-BLANCO and Lucas OSORIO ITURMENDI, "*Los Llamados 'Árbitros de Parte'*", Revista del Club Español del Arbitraje (2013, issue 18) pp. 63-122.
58. Tim HARDY and Elina ZLATANSKA, "CIArb Arbitration Practice Guidelines: An Overview", 83 The International Journal of Arbitration, Mediation and Dispute Management (August 2017, issue 3) p. 310.
59. Hans VAN HOUTTE, "Arbitration Guidelines: Straitjacket or Compass?" in K. HOBÉR et al., *Between East and West: Essays in Honour of Ulf Franke* (Juris 2010) p 528.

2. *Best Practices*

Certain institutions have adopted rules and practice notes whose aim is to express the state of the art in certain areas of arbitral procedure. Best practices are desirable techniques that are believed to be widely followed and to be beneficial to users. A topical example is the UNCITRAL Notes on Organizing Arbitral Proceedings, which have been revised in 2016.[60] The UNCITRAL Notes go to the efficient organization of arbitral proceedings.

The CIArb has adopted guidelines on the interview of prospective arbitrators[61] or guidelines on the conduct of proceedings dealing with particular aspects of the arbitration, such as e-discovery,[62] documents-only decisions[63] or party non-participation.[64]

Recommended best practices may relate to the drafting of an arbitration agreement, such as the 2010 IBA Guidelines for Drafting Arbitration Clauses.[65] Certain of these guidelines go to the needs of a given industry. For example, the Association of International Petroleum Negotiators (AIPN) has established several model clauses that are adapted to oil and gas disputes.[66] Similarly, the WIPO proposes arbitration agreements that are specifically tailored to disputes concerning intellectual property.[67] Also the proposed arbitration agreement of the Insurance and Reinsurance Arbitration Society provides for specific requirements in its model arbitration agreement.[68]

---

60. UNCITRAL Notes on Organizing Arbitral Proceedings, United Nations Commission on International Trade Law 2016 ("UNCITRAL finalized a second edition of the Notes at its forty-ninth session, in 2016").
61. Chartered Institute of Arbitrators, Interviews for Prospective Arbitrators (30 August 2016), can be accessed at <https://www.ciarb.org/docs/default-source/ciarbdocuments/guidance-and-ethics/practice-guidelines-protocols-and-rules/international-arbitration-guidelines-2015/guideline-on-interviews-for-prospective-arbitrators.pdf?sfvrsn=16>.
62. Chartered Institute of Arbitrators, Protocol for E-Disclosure in International Arbitration (no date indicated), can be accessed at <https://www.ciarb.org/docs/default-source/ciarbdocuments/guidance-and-ethics/practice-guidelines-protocols-and-rules/international-arbitration-protocols/e-iscolusureinarbitration.pdf?sfvrsn=10>.
63. Chartered Institute of Arbitrators, Documents-Only Arbitration Procedures (30 August 2016), can be accessed at <https://www.ciarb.org/docs/default-source/ciarbdocuments/guidance-and-ethics/practice-guidelines-protocols-and-rules/international-arbitration-guidelines-2015/2015guideline-on-documents-only-arbitration-proceedings.pdf?sfvrsn=12>.
64. Chartered Institute of Arbitrators, Party Non-Participation (22 November 2016), can be accessed at <https://www.ciarb.org/docs/default-source/ciarbdocuments/guidance-and-ethics/practice-guidelines-protocols-and-rules/international-arbitration-guidelines-2015/2011partynonparticipation.pdf?sfvrsn=28>.
65. IBA Guidelines for Drafting International Arbitration Clauses, 7 July 2010, <https://www.ibanet.org/Document/Default.aspx?DocumentUid=D94438EB-2ED5-4CEA-9722-7A0C9281F2F2>.
66. AIPN, International Dispute Resolution Agreement, 2017.
67. WIPO, Future Disputes: WIPO Arbitration Clause, accessible under <https://www.wipo.int/amc/en/clauses/arbitration/>.
68. ARIAS Arbitration Clause, accessible under <http://arias.org.uk/arbitration-rules-and-clauses/>.

Recommended best practices may also go to substantive matters, at times in a prospective way. There have been several attempts, for example, to reach consensus on how best to arbitrate matters of corruption,[69] antitrust,[70] or even questions of human rights[71] and climate change.[72]

These best practices may not rise to soft normativity, because they address questions that do not need to be legally settled, such as how to best draft an arbitral agreement or organize the arbitration procedure; because they address a narrow area of practice from a local or regional perspective; or because they impinge on substantive matters on which there is no general consensus.

3. *Institutional Rules and Practice Notes*

Institutional rules are of an entirely different nature, because they are contractual instruments that become binding by way of the parties' choice to elect a given arbitral institution to administer the arbitration. The same applies to non-institutional arbitration rules, such as the UNCITRAL Rules. These rules do not and cannot have the status of soft law. They are rules that are followed because they are contractually binding upon the parties, not out of a sense of moral obligation.

The practice notes issued by arbitral institutions have a status akin to that of the institutional rules themselves, even though their adoption process may be more flexible. Their legitimacy does not depend on any consensus in the arbitration community, as they reflect the policies implemented by a given institution for the arbitrations submitted to its rules, and are as such binding upon the parties and the arbitrators. Good examples of such practice notes are the ICC Note to Parties and Arbitral Tribunals on the Conduct of the Arbitration, the HKIAC Practice Notes[73] or the LCIA Guidance Notes.[74] Their scope

---

69. ICC Rules on Combating Corruption, 2011, <https://iccwbo.org/publication/icc-rules-on-combating-corruption/>; see also in general OECD Good Practice Guidance on Internal Controls, Ethics, and Compliance, 18 February 2010, <www.oecd.org/investment/anti-bribery/anti-briberyconvention/oecdantibriberyrecommendation2009.htm>; Council of Europe, Committee of Ministers, Resolution (97) 24 on the twenty guiding principles for the fight against corruption, 6 June 1997 <https://rm.coe.int/16806cc17c>.
70. European Commission, Guidelines on Vertical Restraints, 2010, SEC (2010) 411; ASEAN Regional Guidelines on Competition Policy, August 2010.
71. There are currently guidelines in this regard underway, see Claes CRONSTEDT, Jan EIJSBOUTS and Robert C. THOMPSON "Report on International Business and Human Rights Arbitration", 13 February 2017; see also "Questions and Answers", 17 August 2017, <https://www.ihrb.org/other/remedy/international-arbitration-answers-to-key-questions>.
72. See for example the Report by the IBA, Achieving Justice and Human Rights in an Era of Climate Disruption, July 2014, <http://www.ibanet.org/PresidentialTaskForceCCJHR2014.aspx>; the PCA has also established specialized rules in that regard, see Optional Rules for Arbitration of Disputes Relating to Natural Resources and/or the Environment, <https://pca-cpa.org/en/services/arbitration-services/environmental-dispute-resolution/>.
73. HKIAC has published various practice notes regarding specific situations, such as the Practice Note on the Challenge of an Arbitrator, 31 October 2014, accessible under <https://www.hkiac.org/sites/default/files/ck_filebrowser/PDF/arbitration/4_Practice%20Note_2014_0.pdf>; or the Practice Note on Arbitral Tribunal's Fees, Expenses, Terms and Conditions, 1 November 2013, accessible under <https://www.hkiac.org/sites/default/files/ck_filebrowser/PDF/arbitration/5.g.ii_.%20Practice%20Note%20-%20Schedule%202.pdf>.

is twofold. On the one hand, they provide guidance to the parties as to how institutional rules should be applied. On the other, they may supplement institutional rules in a way that is reflective of the established practice of the institution. The ICC practice note, for example, includes rules relating to questions that are not directly dealt with in the Rules themselves, such as the time limit to submit draft awards to the Court and the consequences of a delay in doing so, dispositive motions, or the use of sealed offers. In principle, the adoption of practice notes is not subject to the same requirements as for the arbitration rules themselves. For example, pursuant to Art. 7 of Appendix I of the Rules, changes to the ICC Rules of Arbitration need to be adopted by the ICC Executive Board after having been laid down before the ICC Commission on Arbitration and ADR. In contrast, the ICC Practice Note can be amended by the Bureau of the Court in a speedier and more flexible way, with no need of an approval by the ICC Board. As long as these supplemental rules are not inconsistent with the Rules themselves, the Court's power to amend its Practice Note is based on its general power to interpret and apply the Rules. In this regard, Art. 1(1) of Appendix I to the Rules provides that the Court has "all the necessary powers" for the purpose of ensuring the application of the Rules.

4. *Governance Rules*

Governance rules relate to the integrity of the internal processes of a given institution. These rules are therefore endogenous. For bodies having promotional or educational scopes, they essentially apply to the election of their leadership and the accountability of their officers to the membership. Ensuring the integrity of these processes is critical to the legitimacy of any institution and is a fundamental condition for the acceptance of the rules and guidelines that it promulgates.

Governance rules are even more important for institutions having the role of administering arbitrations, because of the need to prevent the conflicts of interest that may arise for their officers.

Governance rules emanating from arbitral institutions can be divided in several categories. The first sub-category is common to other arbitral bodies and concerns the processes for the selection of the leadership of the organization. Arbitral institutions, however, do not all have similar structures, and the constitution of their governing bodies therefore differs greatly from one to the other. The ICC International Court of Arbitration, for example, has no legal personality and therefore no Board of its own, as a consequence of which decisions pertaining to the finances of the Court are made by the ICC Executive Board, which has a sub-committee called Governing Body for Dispute Resolution Services, which is involved in strategic thinking and planning. The LCIA is, in contrast, a private not-for-profit company limited by guarantee, with a Board of its own. The HKIAC has been established as an independent company limited by guarantee and a non-profit organization under Hong Kong law, and is governed by a Council. SIAC was incorporated as a public company limited by guarantee under Singapore law, and is governed by a Board of Directors.

74. LCIA Notes for Parties, 18 August 2017, or the Notes for Arbitrators, 26 October 2017, all accessible under <https://www.lcia.org/adr-services/guidance-notes.aspx>.

The second sub-category of governance rules applies specifically to those arbitral institutions that have been created under the umbrella of a Chamber of Commerce, such as the ICC International Court of Arbitration, the Milan or the Vienna centers. It is then necessary to ensure that decisions relating to the administration of cases are made in complete independence from the host chamber. Any perception that industry interests of other influence groups may, through the host chamber or other body to which the institution is related, exercise any influence on the administration of cases, must be completely eliminated. In an article on the governance of arbitral institutions,[75] Urs Weber-Stecher notes for example that the independence of the Court of Arbitration for Sport from the International Olympic Committee was discussed before the Swiss Federal Tribunal, which confirmed that CAS decisions could be given the same standing as court decisions.[76] Appendix I of the ICC Rules of Arbitration provides, to that effect, that the Court is "an autonomous body" carrying out its functions "in complete independence from the ICC and its organs". Appendix II to the Rules also provides that ICC Court members are independent from the ICC National Committee having proposed them for appointment. Finally, because ICC National Committees and Groups may, according to the ICC Rules, have a role to play in proposing arbitrators to the Court for their appointment, the Court has established a detailed note establishing strict procedures to preserve the integrity and independence of the nomination process within each of them, as well as to prevent the existence of conflicts of interest that may affect the independence and impartiality of any individual taking part in the selection process.[77]

While most well-established arbitral institutions have put in place proper Chinese walls between themselves and their host bodies, there have been instances of corrupt procedures leading to undue influence by interest groups in the administrative work of the institution.[78]

The third sub-category of governance rules relates to the selection of the members and officers of the arbitration court and other bodies entrusted with the administration of cases. Because there is very little regulation applying to the activity of arbitral institutions, the situation in this regard is rather uneven. ICC Court members are appointed by the ICC World Council, the highest body within the organization, upon the nomination of the relevant National Committee, or of the President of the Court for alternate Court members, the President also having the power to nominate, for their appointment by the World Council, the Vice-Presidents of the Court as well as Court members in countries where there is no National Committee. As to the President of the Court, he or she is elected by the ICC World Council upon the recommendation of the Executive Board. However, in order to ensure the integrity of the process and the acceptance of the choice within the arbitration community, a transparent selection process is established before an independent selection body composed of members of the ICC leadership and recognized arbitration practitioners, which choice is then submitted

75. Urs WEBER-STECHER, "Principles of Good Governance and Organisation of Arbitral Institutions" in *Arbitral Institutions under Scrutiny*, ASA Special Series No. 40 (2013) pp. 37-54.

76. BGE 129 III 445.

77. ICC, Note to national committees and groups of the ICC on the proposal of arbitrators, 10 May 2016.

78. WEBER-STECHER, fn. 75 above, p. 41, about the National Arbitration Forum (NAF).

to the Executive Board for its recommendation. The same process applies to the top management of the Secretariat, which employment, however, is not subject to approval by the Executive Board.

The fourth sub-category of rules relates to the internal disclosure of conflicts of interest by individuals involved in the administration of cases and the exclusion of said individuals from the decision-making process. Clause 5 of the Constitution of the LCIA Court, for example, provides that "No member of the Court who has a connection with an arbitration in relation to which the LCIA exercises any functions of any kind may participate in or influence any decision of the Court relating to such arbitration". Arts. 2-5 of Appendix II to the ICC Rules contain similar provisions, adding that the individuals involved have a duty to disclose any involvement in the cases administered by the Court. Most well-established international arbitral institutions also contain rules dealing with internal conflicts of interest.

Finally, institutions establish rules and procedures aimed at ensuring the confidentiality of the work of the Court. To that effect, Art. 1 of Appendix I to the ICC Rules of Arbitration establishes the confidential character of the work of the Court. The ICC also requires its Court members, as well as any individual involved in the selection process of arbitrators at the level of National Committees, to sign a Non-Disclosure Agreement. Internal confidentiality rules can also be found in the 2012 Swiss Rules and in the Rules of the Vienna International Arbitral Centre (VIAC).

III. LEGITIMACY

Any rule needs to be perceived, to one degree or another, as legitimate by those to whom it will apply. This requirement of legitimacy is of course even stronger for soft law rules, which are not directly binding but will be applied out of a sense of moral obligation. Because arbitral soft law is meant to apply to a global community of practitioners, it needs in order to be endorsed to reflect the shared values of the community. The legitimacy requirement can be analyzed from two perspectives: representativeness and reflexivity.

1. *Representativeness*

Representativeness means that the institution or body having authored a given set of rules be perceived as legitimate for doing so. This condition of legitimacy is objective and subjective.

Objectively, the institution needs to have a scope that is general enough to allow it to legislate on questions of a general nature. For example, an institution whose scope would be limited to promoting arbitration in family and divorce matters would not be accepted as a legitimate source for promulgating procedural rules for international commercial disputes generally. Membership in the institution also needs to reflect the diversity and internationality of the arbitral community. Diversity implies that membership includes sufficient representation from different regions of the world, and that such membership includes representation from different legal cultures. It is of particular importance that it includes a balance between members originating from common law and civil law jurisdictions. For a given set of rules to gain acceptance, it is in fact necessary that it is not perceived as an import from a legal culture against another. The success of the IBA Rules on Evidence, for example, rests in large part on the fact that the IBA managed to strike the proper balance between the civil and common law approaches on the taking of evidence, which it was in a better position to do because its membership covers both civil and common law jurisdictions. Generational and gender diversity are also important conditions. An arbitral body excluding women or young practitioners from its membership would certainly not be accepted as a legitimate rule-maker.

Subjectively, the institution needs to be perceived as a body whose authority is acceptable to anyone in the arbitral community. According to Max Weber, political rule-making rests on three different possible sources of authority: the legal authority that is given by a system of rules that is applied administratively and judicially according to known principles; tradition, which is the fact for an authority to have been long established; and charisma, which is given by the unique personal qualities of a leader.[79] As far as arbitral institutions and bodies are concerned, the first source of power only applies to arbitral rules having a contractually binding nature and being enforced as such by the relevant States' legal systems. The authority of other non-binding rules rests on the two other factors.

Tradition is certainly an important tenet of the legitimacy of an arbitral rule-maker. It includes factors such as experience (for one would assume that history goes with experience and acquired knowledge) and reputation (as a condition for the ability of an institution to maintain its operations for a long period of time). The IBA, founded in 1947, and ICCA, founded in 1963, surely have historical credentials such as to give them traditional authority. Amongst arbitral institutions, the ICC Court (established in 1923), the LCIA (having its roots in 1883) and the SCC (established in 1917), amongst others, can also claim traditional legitimacy.

Charisma would point to another direction. When applied to an arbitral institution or body, the charismatic basis of authority implies both the recognized personal qualities of its leadership and the existence of legitimate internal processes for the access to membership, the selection of officers, and governance. These procedures need at the same time to enable an institution to acquire as leaders the most prestigious arbitration practitioners, to ensure the inclusiveness of its membership, and to establish a transparent and predictable system of governance. Democratic governance, though, is not a necessary condition for the legitimacy of an arbitral institution or body as rule-maker. While some institutions, such as the Swiss Arbitration Association, rest on democratic processes for the election of their officers and adoption of projects, with annual assemblies where officers are elected by their members and important projects discussed, that is not the case in others. Members of the IBA or of ICCA, for example, are not called to elect the officers of these organizations, which are rather selected based on a top-down process. Nonetheless, these organizations dispose of transparent selection processes, with nominating committees choosing officers for limited and generally non-renewable mandates.

79. "The Three Types of Legitimate Rule", 4 The Berkeley Publications in Society and Institutions (1958, no. 1) pp. 1-11.

2. *Reflexivity*

Reflexivity refers to the inclusiveness of the rule-making process itself. The necessity of a transparent exercise of consultation of the arbitral community is of particular importance because no arbitral institution can claim to represent the arbitral community in its entirety, and because most of these institutions do not adopt democratic procedures for the selection of their leadership. It is therefore all the more necessary that rules and guidelines be adopted after a process allowing consultation of the broader arbitration community. In absence of such procedures, the argument would be made that arbitral soft law is hijacked by what Toby Landau once called the new clergy of arbitration[80] and elaborated behind closed doors by people who have no legitimacy to elevate themselves as legislators for the entire arbitration community.

This idea of a lack of legitimacy of soft law has been presented in a rather violent and polemic form by Felix Dasser in an article against the Guidelines on Party Representation.[81] The author, in describing the process of discussion and adoption of the IBA Guidelines within the IBA, writes that "the opinion of the IBA Arbitration Committee members at large was not really welcome", and that "many, if not most, members of the Arbitration Committee at large realized what was cooking only after the IBA Guidelines had been published in their name", and concludes that "the IBA Guidelines were drafted by a small circle within the IBA with the membership at large having no real say in the drafting".[82] Mr. Dasser's description, however, stands in contrast with the consultation process that was put in place by the IBA, including two public consultations opened to the general public as well as individual consultation of all arbitral institutions, further to which the text was unanimously approved by the 190 professional Bars spanning 160 different jurisdictions composing the IBA Council.

Most prominent arbitral institutions and bodies engaging in a rule-making exercise will essentially aim at a three-step deliberation process. First, a draft would be elaborated by a task force or a working party as diverse and representative as possible, with observers delegated by other institutions and stakeholders. Second, the draft will be submitted to public consultation, with feedback from the public being digested by the drafting group. Third, some institutions will engage in periodic review and update of their rules. The IBA practice is for example to revise its Rules and Guidelines ten years after their adoption, this revision process being subject to the same drafting exercise by a large and diverse working group followed by a public consultation.

---

80. Lecture by Toby LANDAU at the opening of the MIDS session in September 2014 (which can be accessed at: <https://vimeo.com/107493952>).

81. Felix DASSER, "A Critical Analysis of the Guidelines on Party Representation" in *The Sense and Non-Sense of Guidelines, Rules and Other Para-Regulatory Texts in International Arbitration*, ASA Special Series No. 37 (2015) pp. 33-62.

82. *Ibid.*, p. 35.

IV. NORMATIVITY

The foregoing shows that the rules and norms emanating from arbitration institutions and bodies fall in very distinct categories. The normativity of institutional rules and practice notes derives from their contractual nature. By agreeing to submit to the arbitration rules of a given institution, the parties accept to be bound by said rules, and by the decisions made by the institution in the exercise of its administrative role, including the practice notes adopted in that context.

The question of soft normativity therefore only arises for non-binding norms. Soft law norms are those that cannot be enforced through public force. They can nevertheless be perceived as norms that should be applied out of a sense of moral obligation. The question therefore becomes how to identify the factors that generate that sense of moral obligation.

In a March 2008 decision, the Swiss Federal Tribunal referred to the IBA Guidelines on Conflicts of Interest as "a valuable tool capable of contributing to the harmonization and unification of the standards applied in the field of international arbitration".[83] The Swiss Federal Court therefore referred to the harmonization and unification roles of the Guidelines. Gabrielle Kauffmann-Kohler has shown, in this regard, that this harmonization and unification implies an exercise of both codification and innovation.[84]

In order to accede to the level of soft normativity, non-binding rules need to satisfy the need for a positive solution to a controversial question. For example, to say that any person may act as a witness[85] is a legal rule that may accede to soft normativity. To say that parties should submit lists of exhibits with a hyperlink is a mere point of practice which may find its way in a guidance note, but which does not elevate to the level of a rule having soft normativity.

It is in any case necessary, for a norm to accede to the level of soft law, that there is sufficient consensus amongst the arbitral community on its acceptability and appropriateness. As we have seen, the existence of such a consensus depends on the cohesion of the community and the fact that practitioners around the globe perceive themselves as part of a global group sharing common values and the same vision of arbitration as an autonomous global system of justice.

The other condition is that of the legitimacy of both the institution having adopted the rules and of the process adopted for rule-making. Legitimacy implies that the institution is sufficiently representative of the arbitration community. Its membership must be diverse, the institution must not be perceived as expressing a particular legal culture, and its experience and prestige must be recognized. Legitimacy also lies in the transparency and inclusiveness of the decision-making process having led to the adoption of a particular set of rules.

83. 26 ASA Bull, pp. 565-579.

84. G. KAUFMANN-KOHLER, "Soft Law in International Arbitration: Codification and Normativity", 1 Journal of International Dispute Settlement (2010, no. 2) pp. 283-299.

85. IBA Rules on the Taking of Evidence in International Arbitration, 29 May 2010, Art. 4 Sect 2.

The process of codification of rules by institutions such as the IBA contributes to their stabilization, their dissemination, and ultimately to their widespread acceptance, thereby creating a body of transnational procedural soft law rules that is indispensable to maintaining the autonomy of arbitration as a global system of justice detached from States.

The Influence of Public Actors on Lawmaking in International Arbitration: Domestic Legislatures, Domestic Courts and International Organizations

Sundaresh Menon[*]

TABLE OF CONTENTS PAGE

I. INTRODUCTION

At the twenty-first session of this Congress some six years ago, I shared my thoughts about the coming of a new age of international arbitration and the concomitant challenges and opportunities which this presents. Among other things, I spoke about how arbitration seemed increasingly beset with problems of legitimacy from both within and without. From within, the problems of the lack of consistent standards or efforts to tackle issues of moral hazard, ethics, and conflicts of interest were threatening the legitimacy of the industry.[1] From without, the use of arbitration as a means of resolving questions of a public law character (particularly in the context of investor-state arbitrations) was increasingly being questioned, given that the arbitral process contains none of the traditional safeguards present in administrative law which have developed to handle sensitive questions relating to the relationship between a state and its subjects.[2] I was not alone in expressing these concerns, as can be seen from the fact that the entirety of the 2014 session of this Congress was devoted to a discussion of these issues.[3]

* Chief Justice of the Supreme Court of Singapore; ICCA Governing Board Member. I am grateful to my colleague, Assistant Registrar Scott Tan, and my law clerk, Ashley Ong, who discussed the ideas which are contained here, and assisted me greatly with the research for and preparation of this paper.

1. Sundaresh MENON, "International Arbitration: The Coming of a New Age for Asia (and Elsewhere)", Keynote Address for the ICCA Congress 2012, para. 43, available online at <https://www.arbitration-icca.org/media/0/13398435632250/ags_opening_speech_icca_congress_%202012.pdf>.
2. *Ibid.*, paras. 32-33.
3. Stephan W. SCHILL, "Developing a Framework for the Legitimacy of International Arbitration" in *Legitimacy: Myths, Realities, Challenges,* ICCA Congress Series no. 18 (Kluwer 2015) at p. 789 and the articles cited at fn. 1.

The issue of legitimacy is central to arbitration because arbitration has become an integral pillar of the rule of law. For centuries, businesses and states have relied on arbitration to resolve their disputes;[4] but in recent times, it has become the primary justice system for the global economy.[5] Arbitration is no longer, if it ever was, just about the private settlement of individual disputes. Rather, it has become, in the words of Prof. Schill, "a system of transnational governance that has an impact on society at large" that "contributes significantly to ordering social relations *ex ante* [not only] between the disputing parties but also beyond".[6] In the context of commercial arbitration, it strives to guarantee predictability, certainty, fairness, and enforceability in the enforcement of commercial transactions. In the context of inter-state arbitration, it provides a mechanism for the peaceful resolution of disputes between states or between investors and states. Because of its pervasive role in the regulation of rights and liabilities, it has become a channel through which power is exercised over persons – at times even persons who might not be parties to the arbitration agreement.[7] This necessarily gives rise to the question: under what conditions is the exercise of this power, which is mediated through the laws of international arbitration, rightful? And to what extent is it appropriate for certain actors to have a role in shaping the rules by which such power is acquired and exercised? This, in broad terms, is the problem of legitimacy in arbitration.

This paper will consider a particular aspect of this problem by considering some of the myriad ways in which public actors create, or influence the development of, transnational norms, rules and principles in international arbitration, and the legitimacy concerns that underlie their participation in such lawmaking. It will be divided into four parts. First, it will define the terms which are central to the discussion in this paper. Second, it will describe the different roles played by public actors in the development of the law of international arbitration. Third, it will consider the legitimacy concerns that arise out of their participation. Finally, it will peek into the future of lawmaking by public actors in the sphere of international arbitration.

4. See David W. RIVKIN, "The Impact of International Arbitration on the Rule of Law", 29 Arbitration International (2013, no. 3) p. 327.
5. S. MENON, "International Arbitration: The Coming of a New Age for Asia (and Elsewhere)", fn. 1 above, para. 31.
6. *Ibid.*, pp. 793-795.
7. This takes place in a variety of different ways. For instance, arbitration has contributed to the making of substantive transnational rules in areas which are governed almost exclusively by arbitration, such as sport: see, for example, Lorenzo CASINI, "The Making of a *Lex Sportiva* by the Court of Arbitration for Sport", 12 German Law Journal (2011) p. 1317 at pp. 1325-1334. However, its effects are perhaps most acutely felt in arbitrations concerning states, where arbitral tribunals develop the law through treaty interpretation. The outcome of their decisions can sometimes have dramatic effects on the nationals in the affected states: see, generally, Sundaresh MENON, "International Investment Arbitration in Asia: The Road Ahead", Keynote Address for the 4th Annual Singapore International Investment Arbitration Conference (3 December 2013), available at <https://www.supremecourt.gov.sg/docs/default-source/default-document-library/sjc/international-investment-arbitration-in-asia---the-road-ahead-on-3-december-2013-(final-031213---clean).pdf> (last accessed 15 May 2018).

II. DEFINING THE KEY CONCEPTS

Two key concepts lie at the heart of this paper. The first is the "law" of international arbitration. The second is the concept of "legitimacy".

1. *The "Law" of International Arbitration*

The first of these, the "law" of international arbitration, may usefully be discussed by considering two pairs of distinctions. The first is that between the law governing the arbitration (or *lex arbitri*) on the one hand, and its substantive law on the other; the second is the distinction between "hard law" and "soft law".

a. *Lex arbitri vs. substantive law*

As the learned authors of *Redfern and Hunter on International Arbitration* (*Redfern and Hunter*) explain, the difference between the lex arbitri and the law governing the substance of a dispute was part of the Continental tradition, but it has come to be widely accepted in international commercial arbitration.[8] Although the lex arbitri is sometimes also referred to as the "procedural law" of an arbitration, this expression is perhaps somewhat a misnomer, because it is not concerned only with the conduct of an arbitration (such as the scheduling of hearings or the appointment and composition of a tribunal), but also what happens afterwards, such as the recognition and enforcement or, in some situations, the setting aside of an arbitral award. As Steyn J (as His Lordship then was) explained in *Paul Smith Ltd v. H & S International Holding Inc.*:[9]

> "What then, is the law governing the arbitration? It is ... a body of rules which sets a standard external to the arbitration agreement, and the wishes of the parties, for the conduct of the arbitration. The law governing the arbitration comprises the rules governing interim measures (eg Court orders for the preservation or storage of goods), the rules empowering the exercise by the Court of supportive measures to assist an arbitration which has run into difficulties (eg filling a vacancy in the composition of the arbitral tribunal if there is no other mechanism) and the rules providing for the exercise by the Court of its supervisory jurisdiction over arbitrations (eg removing an arbitrator for misconduct)."

In short, the lex arbitri is shorthand for the entire legal framework that governs international arbitration.[10] It typically regulates at least three sets of matters: (a) the internal conduct of the arbitration, such as the appointment of the tribunal and the requirements for the rendering of an award; (b) the external relationship between the

8. Nigel BLACKABY and Constantine PARTASIDES with Alan REDFERN and Martin HUNTER, *Redfern and Hunter on International Arbitration*, 6th edn. (Oxford University Press 2015) at para. 3.38.
9. [1991] 2 Lloyd's Rep 127 at 130.
10. Simon GREENBERG, Christopher KEE and J. Romesh WEERAMANTRY, *International Commercial Arbitration: An Asia-Pacific Perspective* (Cambridge University Press 2011) at para. 2.14.

arbitration and the domestic courts, including the extent to which the courts may assist the conduct of the arbitration through, among other things, the grant of interim relief; and (c) the relationship between the arbitration and the domestic legal order more generally (e.g., the law governing the arbitrability of disputes).[11] This is what Prof. Jan Paulsson refers to as "the law applicable *to* arbitration",[12] and it has accounted for almost all of the key legal developments to date. This paper will focus on the ways that public actors, particularly international organizations, have influenced the shape of its development.

By contrast, the *lex causae*, or the law of the substance of the dispute governs the rights and liabilities of the parties as it relates to the dispute at hand. This is what Prof. Paulsson refers to as the "law applicable *in* arbitration".[13] This is still very much a matter that is regulated by domestic law and the choice of the parties. As things stand, there is yet no free-standing substantive law of international arbitration, at least not in the sense envisioned by Lord Wilberforce during the second reading of the United Kingdom's 1996 Arbitration Bill in the House of Lords,[14] where His Lordship spoke about the development of a transnational lex mercatoria. Despite the strides that have been taken in recent years, the goal of developing an autonomous law of international trade founded on universally accepted standards of business conduct that applies without regard for national borders remains a distant dream. Progress is perhaps more encouraging in the field of investment arbitration, where certain core principles (such as "fair and equitable treatment") have been the subject of multiple decisions, and a body of international case law has been developing. But inconsistencies still exist and this has meant that often, there is no common understanding of the obligations which states – even those bound by identically worded treaty obligations – might owe each other.

b. Hard vs. soft law

The second pair of distinctions is that between "hard law" and "soft law". Even though the term "soft law" has been with us for some time, there is no clear academic consensus on what it means. The orthodox definition is that hard law is "binding" whereas "soft law" refers to obligations which are hortatory rather than binding.[15] Some have argued that because of its non-binding character, soft law is not "law" in any meaningful sense of the word.[16]

---

11. Alastair HENDERSON, "*Lex Arbitri*, Procedural Law and the Seat of Arbitration", 26 Singapore Academy of Law Journal (2014) p. 886 at para. 5.
12. A. HENDERSON, "*Lex Arbitri*, Procedural Law and the Seat of Arbitration", fn. 11 above, para. 3, citing Jan PAULSSON, "Arbitration in Three Dimensions", 60 International and Comparative Law Quarterly (2011, no. 2) p. 291 at p. 306.
13. *Ibid.*
14. Second reading of the 1996 Arbitration Bill in the House of Lords, Hansard (HL Debates), 18 January 1996 at col. 778. This was later quoted by Lord Steyn in *Lesotho Highlands Development Authority v. Impregilo SpA and others* [2006] 1 AC 221 at 230-231.
15. Gregory C. SHAFFER and Mark A. POLLACK, "Hard vs. Soft Law: Alternatives, Complements, and Antagonists in International Governance", 94 Minnesota Law Review (2010) p. 706 at p. 712 and the authorities cited therein.
16. Jan KLABBERS, "The Redundancy of Soft Law", 65 Nordic Journal of International Law (1996) p. 167 at p. 170.

It is beyond the scope of this paper to consider this conceptual quagmire save to say that for present purposes "soft law" will be treated as falling within the ambit of "law". This is an important point because the norms of the procedural law of arbitration run the gamut from treaty obligations to model legislation, rules and codes of conduct, and finally, to purely political commitments generated by a convergence in international behaviour.[17] Thus, instead of relying on a single binary distinction between "binding" and "non-binding" norms, laws can usefully be compared along three axes: normativity,[18] precision, and enforceability.[19] What is critical is that parties consider that the norms in question have normative force and apply equally to everyone without distinction – this is perhaps the dividing line between law and the absence of legal obligation.[20]

2. *"Legitimacy" in International Arbitration*

The second concept that requires definition for the purposes of this paper is the meaning of "legitimacy". Legitimacy is a protean concept. To social scientists and political philosophers, "legitimacy" is understood as a quality of *persons* and refers to the "right" of a political actor to exercise political power. In his influential essay on the subject, Max Weber explained legitimacy in descriptive terms. Thus, a political regime is legitimate if the participants believe or have faith in the right of that actor or system to exercise power.[21] Others, such as the philosopher John Rawls, have preferred to understand legitimacy in normative terms. To him, a political actor or system is legitimate if it is *justified* in exercising power over its subjects.[22] To lawyers, however, legitimacy is not merely a quality of persons, but also a quality of *norms*, and it refers to the (political) conditions that need to be in place for enacted laws to bind those who are subject to them.[23]

This provides a useful conceptual platform, but it still does not explain *what* legitimacy is. The difficulty arises, in part at least, because legitimacy, like concepts such as "good" or "beauty", is "simple" and irreducible.[24] In a helpful paper presented at the 2014 ICCA Congress, Prof. Schill wrote that legitimacy "constitutes a multidimensional

17. Andrew T. GUZMAN and Timothy L. MEYER, "International Soft Law", 2 Journal of Legal Analysis (2010) p. 171 at p. 173.
18. See, generally, Prosper WEIL, "Towards Relative Normativity in International Law", 77 American Journal of International Law (1983) p. 413. Although this article was written about norms in public international law, the analysis of "normativity" is a useful one in this context.
19. *Ibid.*
20. See Gabrielle KAUFMANN-KOHLER, "Soft Law in International Arbitration: Codification and Normativity", Journal of International Dispute Settlement (2010) p. 283 at p. 284.
21. Donald H. J. HERMANN, "Max Weber and the Concept of Legitimacy in Contemporary Jurisprudence", 33 DePaul Law Review (1983, no. 1) Article 1 at p. 10, citing Max WEBER, *Economy and Society: An Outline of Interpretive Sociology* (University of California Press 1978) at pp. 31-32.
22. John RAWLS, *Political Liberalism*, 2nd edn. (Columbia University Press 2005) at p. 137.
23. Dan PRIEL, "The Place of Legitimacy in Legal Theory", 57 McGill Law Journal (2011, no. 1) p. 1 at p. 6.
24. This is a stream of thought that is popular in moral philosophy and is perhaps most closely associated with the work of G. E. Moore: see G. E. MOORE, *Principia Ethica* (Cambridge University Press 1903) at p. 8.

concept that plays different roles in relation to different actors and social constituencies in a transnational legal space".[25] He presented four perspectives from which legitimacy might be understood:

(a) First, there is party legitimacy, which views the issue of legitimacy from the perspective of the disputing parties. Prof. Schill explained that in order for arbitration to be accepted as legitimate by the parties, it has to be carried out by a process which they have accepted, and "the resolution of the dispute has to be performed by an independent tribunal that treats the parties equally and, despite the significant power it has over the parties ... justifies its decision on the basis of pre-determined legal standards."[26]
(b) Second, there is community legitimacy, which approaches the issue from the viewpoint of the wider arbitration community. Here, the focus is not so much on the individual outcomes of arbitrations, but on the extent to which the process coheres with "the entrenched practices in international arbitration that are accepted by the user community", such as standards relating to arbitral procedure, arbitrator independence, and party equality.[27]
(c) Third, there is national legitimacy, which takes the viewpoint of specific countries and societies. In this context, legitimacy is largely a function of coherence with the standards prescribed in the country's arbitration statutes and the practice of its supervising courts.[28] This is where concerns of public policy come to the fore, particularly as regards sensitive areas such as creditor protection in insolvency laws, environmental protection regulations, and sensitive socio-political subjects such as affirmative action programmes.
(d) Finally, there is global legitimacy, which focuses on the interests of the global society, including the interests of persons who do not use arbitration. The focus in this context is with the implications of arbitration as a "system of governance that affects not only how private parties interact ... but also how private rights and public interests more generally are (re-)balanced in international arbitration."[29] An example which Prof. Schill gave was the growing influence of arbitral institutions in issuing guidelines on such matters as party representation, the taking of evidence, and managing conflicts of interest, where they have a powerful impact on shaping international due process standards.

The indices of legitimacy which emerge from these various perspectives are (a) consent (that is, the autonomous acceptance of a party to be bound by certain legal standards); (b) coherence (with prevailing arbitral standards such as minimal curial intervention); (c)

25. S. SCHILL, "Developing a Framework for the Legitimacy of International Arbitration", fn. 3 above, p. 803.
26. S. SCHILL, "Developing a Framework for the Legitimacy of International Arbitration", fn. 3 above, p. 811.
27. S. SCHILL, "Developing a Framework for the Legitimacy of International Arbitration", fn. 3 above, pp. 812-813.
28. S. SCHILL, "Developing a Framework for the Legitimacy of International Arbitration", fn. 3 above, pp. 813-814.
29. S. SCHILL, "Developing a Framework for the Legitimacy of International Arbitration", fn. 3 above, p. 815.

the rule of law (which imports notions such as the principle of legality, procedural fairness, a right to representation, and legal precision in the laws); (d) proportionality and reasonableness (particularly when there are competing interests to be balanced, as there often are, where sensitive public policy issues are concerned); and (e) democratic participation (both nationally and supra-nationally). What unites all of these is the ultimate goal to which they point – the establishment of a fair, stable, and predictable framework that stakeholders can accept and have confidence in.[30] This entails achieving the appropriate balance among the interests of the various stakeholders (such as those of the arbitrating parties, states and the broader arbitration community) which are at play.

III. LAWMAKING BY PUBLIC ACTORS

In that light, it is apt to turn to the lawmaking role of public actors, but as a starting point it may be asked: Why do public actors even have a role in international arbitration? On one view, the involvement of states in international arbitration is incongruous, even suspect, because it affects the ability of litigants to avail themselves of a binding dispute resolution mechanism that exists outside the framework of state-administered courts. Proponents of this view might argue that arbitration exists as an autonomous and private system of justice based on freedom of contract in which states do not – nor should – have any role. This paper will examine two aspects of this issue. The first is the extent to which public actors are presently involved in lawmaking in international arbitration. The second is whether public actors *should* be so involved and the possible legitimacy challenges that may arise from their involvement.

1. *International Organizations*

In the 1920s, there was a push at the inter-state level to establish a common framework for international commercial arbitration. This led to the passage of the Geneva Protocol on Arbitration Clauses in 1923 (the Geneva Protocol)[31] and the Geneva Convention on the Execution of Foreign Arbitral Awards of 1927 (the Geneva Convention),[32] both of which were concluded under the auspices of the League of Nations. The scope and reach of these early treaties were limited. The contracting states were mostly European,[33] and the treaties contained very little in the way of meaningful guidance. The Geneva Protocol, for example, only had four articles that might properly be described as setting out substantive obligations that bound its contracting states.

30. See Alexis MOURRE, "Arbitral Institutions and Professional Organizations as Lawmakers", this volume, pp. 86-111 at p. 87.

31. Geneva Protocol on Arbitration Clauses (24 September 1923) 27 League of Nations Treaty Series 157 (1924).

32. Geneva Convention on the Execution of Foreign Arbitral Awards (26 September 1927) 92 League of Nations Treaty Series 301 (1928).

33. Samuel PISAR, "The United Nations Convention on Foreign Arbitral Awards", 33 Southern California Law Review (1959-1960) p. 14 at p. 14.

a. The high-water mark: The New York Convention and the Model Law

In 1958, the New York Convention on the Recognition and Enforcement of Foreign Arbitral Awards (the New York Convention) was adopted.[34] Two of the central tenets of the Convention are, first, that member states should give full effect to agreements by parties to arbitrate their disputes; and second, that foreign arbitral awards should generally be capable of being enforced in the same way as domestic awards.[35] Today, these two principles are considered so integral and fundamental to the law and practice of international arbitration that it is difficult to imagine international commercial arbitration without them. Structurally, the genius in the design of the New York Convention lay in the way it obviated the need for a central reviewing and enforcing authority by enlisting domestic courts to recognize and enforce arbitral awards on the basis of a uniform set of rules.[36] Starting with 24 signatories, the New York Convention today has 159 state parties.[37] The widespread adoption of the treaty and, more significantly, the broad consensus over the general understanding and application of the norms contained therein is nothing short of remarkable.

In 1966, the United Nations (UN) General Assembly established the UN Commission on International Trade Law (UNCITRAL) "to promote the progressive harmonization and unification of international trade law".[38] UNCITRAL is composed of sixty member states from various geographical regions and different economic and legal systems, elected by the UN General Assembly for six-year terms. Much of its work is done in working groups, which have a broad remit to consider issues relating to international trade such as investor-state dispute settlement, electronic commerce, and cross-border insolvency law.[39] UNCITRAL has achieved much, but the preparation and adoption of the 1985 Model Law on International Commercial Arbitration (the Model Law)[40] probably stands as its greatest achievement to date.[41]

The Model Law is consistent with the core tenets of the New York Convention in that it proceeds from the premise of the presumptive validity of the arbitral award, but it goes much further in prescribing a suite of rules that "[cover] all stages of the arbitral process from the arbitration agreement to the recognition and enforcement of the

34. Convention on the Recognition and Enforcement of Foreign Arbitral Awards (10 June 1958) 330 UNTS 3.
35. *Ibid.*, Introduction, p. 1.
36. Sundaresh MENON, "An Overview of Arbitration" in Sundaresh MENON and Denis BROCK, *Arbitration in Singapore: A Practical Guide* (Sweet & Maxwell 2014) at paras. 1.020-1.021 and 1.030.
37. UNCITRAL, "Status of the Convention on the Recognition and Enforcement of Foreign Arbitral Awards (New York, 1958)", available at <www.uncitral.org/uncitral/en/uncitral_texts/arbitration/NYConvention_status.html> (last accessed 13 May 2018).
38. UN General Assembly Resolution 2205(XXI) of 17 December 1966.
39. UNCITRAL, "Origin, Mandate and Composition of UNCITRAL" (27 June 2016), available at <https://www.uncitral.org/uncitral/en/about/origin.html> (last accessed 13 May 2018).
40. UNCITRAL, UNCITRAL Model Law on International Commercial Arbitration (1985).
41. That is not to say that UNCITRAL has rested on its laurels. In 1976, it published a set of model rules for ad hoc arbitrations, which was intended for use in a broad range of disputes such as arbitrations not involving any particular arbitral institution. These Arbitration Rules were revised in 2010, and most recently in 2013 to introduce a new paragraph incorporating the UNCITRAL Rules on Transparency in Treaty-based Investor-State Arbitration.

arbitral award".[42] By way of Resolution 40/72, the General Assembly recommended that all states give due consideration to the Model Law when drafting their domestic legislation statutes, "in view of the desirability of uniformity of the law of arbitral procedures and the specific needs of international commercial arbitration practice".[43] Since then, seventy-six states have adopted legislation based on the Model Law. While the Model Law is not mandatory, in that states are free to depart from its provisions in the enactment of their domestic statutes, its influence is such that, as Prof. Pieter Sanders put it, "no State, modernizing its arbitration law will do so without taking it … into account".[44] Even the United Kingdom, which was initially sceptical of the Model Law, ended up adopting many of its articles when it passed the 1996 Arbitration Act (the UK Arbitration Act),[45] including the provisions allowing a tribunal to rule on its own jurisdiction and appoint experts,[46] all of which represented changes to English law.[47]

The New York Convention and the Model Law represent the high-water mark of what international organizations have achieved in the field of international arbitration. Together, they have created a system in which national courts have been recruited into a connected global network that reviews and enforces arbitral awards in a reasonably effective manner, despite the absence of any supranational organizing authority.[48] Yet there have also been other successes. Outside the UN, there are regional organizations which have concluded regional instruments of their own. One example is the Organization of American States, whose members concluded the Inter-American Convention on International Commercial Arbitration (the Panama Convention) in 1975.[49] Another is the UN Economic Commission for Europe, which promoted the conclusion of the European Convention on International Commercial Arbitration of 1961 (the European Convention).[50]

Mention should also be made of the work of other intergovernmental organizations like the International Law Commission (ILC) as well as the International Institute for the Unification of Private Law or "UNIDROIT". In 1958, the year the New York Convention was passed, the ILC adopted the Model Rules on Arbitral Procedure[51] and submitted them to the UN General Assembly, which in turn brought them to the

42. UNCITRAL Secretariat, "UNCITRAL Model Law on International Commercial Arbitration" (A/CN9/309) at para. 2.
43. UN General Assembly Resolution 40/72 of 11 December 1985.
44. Pieter SANDERS, "Unity and Diversity in the Adoption of the Model Law", 11 Arbitration International (1995, no. 1) p. 1.
45. Arbitration Act 1996 (c. 23) (United Kingdom).
46. *Ibid.*, ss. 30 and 37.
47. Richard GARNETT, "International Arbitration Law: Progress Towards Harmonisation" 30 Melbourne Journal of International Law (2002, no. 2) p. 400 at 408.
48. S. MENON and D. BROCK, *Arbitration in Singapore*, fn. 36 above, para. 1.030.
49. Inter-American Convention on International Commercial Arbitration (30 January 1975) Organization of American States Treaty Series No. 42.
50. European Convention on International Commercial Arbitration of 1961 (17 December 1962), 484 UNTS 364 at Arts. VI(2) and VIII-X. Both the Panama Convention and the European Convention are similar, although the latter goes further in certain respects such as covering matters in relation to the arbitrability of disputes, the giving of reasons for awards, and the setting aside of awards.
51. UNCITRAL Model Rules on Arbitral Procedure (1958) (the Model Rules on Arbitral Procedure).

attention of member states for their consideration and use.[52] While these Model Rules were intended to apply only to arbitrations between states, the Commission noted that some of the articles were capable of being used in the context of arbitrations between states and foreign private corporations.[53] UNIDROIT has contributed significantly to the convergence of substantive commercial laws through the development of uniform legal instruments such as the Principles of International Commercial Contracts,[54] which has been recognized as containing useful guidelines on the law of contracts.[55]

b. General principles articulated in key international legal instruments

As noted at the start of this section, the signal achievement of international organizations in this area has been the creation of broad consensus on a number of key principles that undergird the modern international arbitration framework.

One is party autonomy, which today is recognized as the foundation of the international arbitration regime. The widespread acceptance of this principle owes much to the work of international organizations. As Alastair Henderson has observed, "[t]he Model Law-influenced respect for party autonomy is reflected in most modern arbitration laws by the absence of prescriptive detail regarding the internal procedures of the arbitration, and by the considerable latitude afforded to parties to supplement, vary or exclude provisions of the law of the seat either directly or by the adoption of institutional rules."[56] *Redfern and Hunter* describes party autonomy as "a principle that is endorsed not only in national laws, but also by international arbitral institutions worldwide, as well as by international instruments such as the New York Convention and the Model Law".[57]

Another principle is that of minimal curial intervention. The Model Law takes the approach that the courts should, as a general rule, refrain from being involved: Art. 5 provides that "[i]n matters governed by this Law, no court shall intervene except where so provided in this Law". The influence of this is such that deference towards arbitration represents the mainstream philosophy of courts all around the world today.[58]

Apart from these two well-established precepts, there is a host of other general principles and norms that have developed and broadly achieved consensus as a result of international legal instruments like the Model Law and the New York Convention. Examples include:

52. UN General Assembly Resolution 1262(XXIII) of 14 November 1958; UN, "Summaries of the Work of the International Law Commission", 15 July 2015, available at <http://legal.un.org/ilc/summaries/10_1.shtml> (last accessed 13 May 2018).
53. *Yearbook of the International Law Commission* (1958) vol. II, doc. A/3859 at fn. 16.
54. See the UNIDROIT Principles of International Commercial Contracts, UNIDROIT Principles 2016, Art. 1.6(2).
55. Hans VAN HOUTTE, "The UNIDROIT Principles of International Contracts", 11 Arbitration International (1 December 1995, no. 4) p. 373 at p. 373.
56. A. HENDERSON, "*Lex Arbitri*, Procedural Law and the Seat of Arbitration", fn. 11 above, para. 27.
57. N. BLACKABY, C. PARTASIDES, A. REDFERN and M. HUNTER, fn. 8 above, para. 6.07.
58. S. MENON, "International Arbitration: The Coming of a New Age for Asia (and Elsewhere)", fn. 1 above, paras. 4-5.

(a) the twin doctrines of separability and *Kompetenz-Kompetenz*;[59]
(b) the rule that there is no specific requirement as to the form of an arbitration agreement save only that it must be in writing;[60]
(c) the presumptive validity of arbitration agreements;[61]
(d) the obligation of the courts to refer parties to arbitration where an arbitration agreement applies, barring certain narrow exceptions;[62]
(e) the sanctity of certain fundamental notions of procedural fairness, such as those relating to the equal treatment of parties,[63] and due process;[64]
(f) specific and limited grounds for the setting aside of awards which parallel those for refusing recognition and enforcement;[65]
(g) the principle that questions of public policy remain within the province of the domestic courts;[66] and
(h) the uniform treatment of all arbitral awards irrespective of their country of origin.[67]

These norms and principles, which have laid the foundation for the success of international arbitration today, span all stages of the arbitral process and their widespread acceptance is testament to the influence that international organizations have had in the development of norms. In addition, other more specific norms have coalesced around these broad principles – for example, the requirement in Sect. 70(2) of the United Kingdom's Arbitration Act 1996 that all available arbitral processes of appeal and review must be exhausted before any challenge against the arbitral award may be brought in court has been found to be consistent with the principle of minimal curial intervention.[68]

2. *Domestic Legislatures*

Domestic public actors are no less important. As Julian Lew QC's analogy goes, international arbitration can be seen as a giant squid which stretches its tentacles down into national legal systems "to forage for legitimacy, support, recognition, and effectiveness".[69] The debate between adherents of territorialism and delocalization has gone on for several decades, with no resolution in sight. It is beyond the scope of this

59. Model Law, Art. 16; Model Rules on Arbitral Procedure, Art. 23(1).
60. Model Law, Art. 7 (Option 1); New York Convention, Art. II(2).
61. This has been in existence since the 1923 Geneva Protocol, where it was set out at Art. I. Today, it can be found in, among other places, Art. II(1) of the New York Convention.
62. Model Law, Art. 8(1).
63. Model Law, Art.18; Model Rules on Arbitral Procedure, Art. 17(1).
64. New York Convention, Art. V(1)(*b*); European Convention, Art. IX(1)(*b*).
65. Model Law, Art. 34(2), cf. New York Convention, Art. V(1).
66. Model Law, Art. 34(2)(*b*); New York Convention, Art. V(2).
67. See Explanatory Note by the UNCITRAL Secretariat on the 1985 Model Law on International Commercial Arbitration as amended in 2006, para. 49.
68. See *BLC and others v. BLB and another* [2014] 4 SLR 79 at para. 113.
69. Julian D. M. LEW QC, "Does National Court Involvement Undermine the International Arbitration Processes?", 24 American University International Law Review (2009, no. 3), p. 489 at pp. 493 and 535.

paper to traverse this ground[70] and all that will be said is that even the most ardent supporters of delocalization will admit that the law of the seat performs several vital functions. Among other things, it supplements the procedural rules chosen by the parties where these are incomplete, it supports the arbitral process with the coercive powers of the state, and it regulates the four corners of the arbitration by setting the parameters of what is arbitrable and by specifying when an award may be set aside. To use the language of *Dicey, Morris and Collins*, these may respectively be termed the "directory", "mandatory", and "supportive" functions of the domestic legislature.[71]

a. Directory: Setting the basic framework for arbitration and the general attitude towards arbitration

In general, the arbitration statutes of different jurisdictions prescribe only the rudiments of procedural regulation which will apply in the absence of more specific prescription by the parties. These prescriptions, which are often contained in the international arbitration statute of the jurisdiction in question, commonly deal with such matters as the appointment and challenge of arbitrators, the authentication and delivery of an award, as well as whether arbitrators can compel the attendance of witnesses and the production of documents.[72]

Apart from the *formal* regulation of the relationship between the tribunals and courts that is achieved through the provisions of written law, domestic legislatures can exert a tremendous, albeit *indirect*, influence on the procedural law of arbitration by articulating the general attitude of the jurisdiction towards arbitration as a method of dispute resolution. In a section of his speech in the decision of the House of Lords in *Lesotho Highlands Development Authority v. Impregilo SpA and others*[73] entitled "the Ethos of the 1996 Act", Lord Steyn said:[74]

70. I have shared my thoughts on this subject in past speeches I have delivered: see Sundaresh MENON, Keynote Address for the Chartered Institute of Arbitrators (CIArb) International Arbitration Conference 2013, paras. 51-67; Sundaresh MENON, Keynote Address for the Nani Palkhivala Arbitration Centre Annual International Conference 2018: "The Role of the National Courts of the Seat in International Arbitration" (17 February 2018).
71. This three-fold classification is taken from Lord COLLINS of Mapesbury et al., *Dicey, Morris & Collins on the Conflict of Laws*, vol. 2, 15th edn. (Sweet & Maxwell 2012) at paras. 16-031 and 16-034.
72. See, for example, UK Arbitration Act, Sects. 16 (appointment of arbitrators), 52 (form of award), and 38(5) (power of the arbitral tribunal to direct examination of witnesses); International Arbitration Act (Cap. 143A, 2002 Rev. Ed.) (Singapore) (International Arbitration Act (Singapore)), Sects. 12 (powers of the arbitral tribunal including the ordering of discovery) and 13 (court may issue *subpoena* to compel attendance of a witness).
73. [2006] 1 AC 221.
74. *Ibid.* at 230-231, quoting the preface to Lord Mustill's and Stewart Boyd QC's Commentary on the 1996 Act (Sir Michael J. MUSTILL and Stewart C. BOYD, *Commercial Arbitration: 2001 Companion Volume to the Second Edition* (Butterworth, 2001), preface) and Lord WILBERFORCE's comments during the Second Reading in the House of Lords of the 1996 Arbitration Bill (Hansard (HL Debates), 18 January 1996, col. 778).

"*XI. The Ethos of the 1996 Act*
17. It is important to take into account the radical nature of the changes brought about by the Arbitration Act 1996. Lord Mustill and Stewart Boyd QC (*Commercial Arbitration: 2001 Companion Volume to the Second Edition, preface*) stated:

'The Act has however given English arbitration law an entirely new face, a new policy, and new foundations. The English judicial authorities ... have been replaced by the statute as the principal source of law. The influence of foreign and international methods and concepts is apparent in the text and structure of the Act, and has been openly acknowledged as such. Finally, the Act embodies a new balancing of the relationships between parties, advocates, arbitrators and courts which is not only designed to achieve a policy proclaimed within Parliament and outside, but may also have changed their juristic nature.'

These general propositions are correct but do not fully explain the important changes which are relevant to the present case.
18. Lord Wilberforce played a large role in securing the enactment of the Arbitration Bill. During the second reading of the Bill in the House of Lords he explained the essence of the new philosophy enshrined in it: Hansard (HL Debates), 18 January 1996, col. 778. He said:

'I would like to dwell for a moment on one point to which I personally attach some importance. That is the relation between arbitration and the courts. I have never taken the view that arbitration is a kind of annex, appendix or poor relation to court proceedings. *I have always wished to see arbitration, as far as possible, and subject to statutory guidelines no doubt, regarded as a freestanding system, free to settle its own procedure and free to develop its own substantive law – yes, its substantive law*. I have always hoped to see arbitration law moving in that direction. That is not the position generally which has been taken by English law, which adopts a broadly supervisory attitude, giving substantial powers to the court of correction and otherwise, and not really defining with any exactitude the relative positions of the arbitrators and the courts.

Other countries adopt a different attitude and so does the UNCITRAL model law. The difference between our system and that of others has been and is, I believe, quite a substantial deterrent to people to sending arbitrations here. ...

How then does this Bill stand in that respect? After reading the debates and the various drafts that have been moving from one point to another, I find that on the whole, although not going quite as far as I should personally like, it has moved very substantially in this direction. It has given to the court only those essential powers which I believe the court should have; that is, rendering assistance when the arbitrators cannot act in the way of enforcement or procedural steps, or, alternatively, in the direction of correcting very fundamental errors.'

(My emphasis)

> Characteristically, Lord Wilberforce did not express his understanding of the new Arbitration Bill in absolute terms. But the general tendency of his observations, and what Parliament was being asked to sanction, is clear. It reflects the ethos of the 1996 Act."

In like manner, in the case of *Tjong Very Sumito and others v. Antig Investments Pte Ltd*, the Singapore Court of Appeal – after citing a lengthy extract from the second reading of the International Arbitration Bill in Parliament – said the following about the modern judicial policy towards arbitration:[75]

> "There was a time when arbitration was viewed disdainfully as an inferior process of justice. Those days are now well behind us. An unequivocal judicial policy of facilitating and promoting arbitration has firmly taken root in Singapore. It is now openly acknowledged that arbitration, and other forms of alternative dispute resolution such as mediation, help to effectively unclog the arteries of judicial administration as well as offer parties realistic choices on how they want to resolve their disputes at a pace they are comfortable with. More fundamentally, the need to respect party autonomy (manifested by their contractual bargain) in deciding both the method of dispute resolution (and the procedural rules to be applied) as well as the substantive law to govern the contract, has been accepted as the cornerstone underlying judicial non-intervention in arbitration. In essence, a court ought to give effect to the parties' contractual choice as to the manner of dispute resolution unless it offends the law."

What is clear from this is that the influence of the principal arbitration statute extends beyond the alphabet of its particular prescriptions. Not just the text, but also the structure and the legislative progress of the bill speak eloquently of the legislative attitude towards arbitration, which in turn shapes judicial policy and leaves an indelible mark on the state's arbitration jurisprudence. I will comment more about this in the next section on the role of domestic courts.

b. Mandatory: Equality, arbitrability, and the relationship between arbitration and the courts

Despite the very free rein bestowed upon arbitration by the modern consensus on party autonomy, this liberty is ultimately bounded by those provisions of the law of the seat which are of mandatory application. As *Redfern and Hunter* put it, "[i]t may well be that the *lex arbitri* will govern with a very free rein, but it will govern nonetheless."[76] For instance, Art. 18 of the Model Law, which provides that the parties must be treated equally, is considered a mandatory norm from which no derogation is permitted.[77] This principle is enshrined in the national arbitration statutes of many jurisdictions.[78] Another

75. [2009] 4 SLR(R) 732 at para. 28.
76. N. BLACKABY, C. PARTASIDES, A. REDFERN and M. HUNTER, fn. 8 above, para. 3.50.
77. Model Law, Art. 18; see Michael PRYLES, "Limits to Party Autonomy in Arbitral Procedure", 24 Journal of International Arbitration (2007, no. 3) p. 327 at p. 329.
78. See Georgios PETROCHILOS, *Procedural Law in International Arbitration* (Oxford University Press 2004) at para. 3.78.

example is arbitrability. In common law jurisdictions, it is usually the function of the courts to determine what matters are arbitrable, and what are not.[79] However, there are jurisdictions which have elected to regulate this in statute. For example, Art. 3 of the Chinese arbitration law expressly carves out certain administrative and family law disputes as those which may not be submitted to arbitration.[80]

Critically, domestic legislatures also regulate the relationship between the courts and arbitration. They have an enormous hand in shaping the contours of the relationship between arbitral tribunals and the courts by providing for such matters as: (a) the jurisdiction of the courts in ruling over questions relating to the validity of arbitration agreements or to issues of public interest, and (b) the ability of parties to enforce, challenge, or even appeal decisions of arbitral tribunals. For instance, the United Kingdom provides for a limited right of appeal in respect of questions of law.[81] By contrast, federal circuit courts in the United States remain divided – in the absence of express statutory guidance on this point – on whether "manifest disregard of the law" can be a basis upon which an arbitral award is challenged.[82] Parties who have a preference regarding whether to leave open the possibility of review for errors of law by the arbitral tribunal will have to consider practical questions such as whether the seat of arbitration allows for this, whether there is a need to contract out of a right to appeal, and whether to provide for the possibility of setting up an arbitration appeal panel.[83] By varying the degree of curial intervention permitted in their domestic statutes, domestic legislatures can have immense influence over the conduct of arbitrations.[84]

Sometimes, legislatures intervene directly in more dramatic ways, by passing laws to amplify, minimize, negate, or otherwise change the effects of judicial decisions and interpretations. For example, a few years ago, the Indian Parliament amended the 1996 Arbitration and Conciliation Act (the Indian Arbitration Act) to introduce a new Sect. 34(2A) to clarify that Indian courts do not have the jurisdiction to set aside awards

---

79. See, for example, the Australian case of *Larkden Pty Ltd v. Lloyd Energy Systems Pty Ltd* (2011) 279 ALR 772; the English case of *Fulham Football Club (1987) Ltd v. Richards and another* [2012] Ch 333, 343; and the Singaporean case of *Tomolugen Holdings Ltd and another v. Silica Investors Ltd and other appeals* [2016] 1 SLR 373.

80. Robert FRENCH AC, 2016 Goff Lecture: "Arbitration and Public Policy" (18 April 2016) at pp. 17-18.

81. UK Arbitration Act, Sect. 69.

82. Jason P. STEED, "Appealing Arbitration Awards and the Circuit Split over 'Manifest Disregard of the Law'", (10 May 2016), available at <http://apps.americanbar.org/litigation/committees/appellate/articles/spring2016-0516-appealing-arbitration-awards-circuit-split-manifest-disregard-law.html> (last accessed 13 May 2018), citing *Affymax, Inc. v. Ortho-McNeil-Janssen Pharm., Inc.*, 660 F.3d 281 (7th Cir. 2011) at 284-285, *Stolt-Nielsen SA v. AnimalFeeds Int'l Corp.*, 548 F.3d 85 (2d Cir. 2008) at 95.

83. See Bruce G. PAULSEN and Jeffrey M. DINE, "Manifest disregard of the law after Hall Street Associates: considerations in the enforcement of international arbitration awards rendered in the United States", 15 International Bar Association Arbitration News (March 2010, no. 1) p. 206 at p. 208.

84. For a particular current debate on the proper ambit of s. 69 of the UK Arbitration Act, see Lord THOMAS of Cwmgiedd, "Developing commercial law through the courts: rebalancing the relationship between the courts and arbitration", The BAILII Lecture 2016, 9 March 2016, paras. 32-34.

rendered in foreign-seated arbitrations.[85] This section is essentially a codification of the holding in *Bahrat Aluminium Co and others v. Kaiser Aluminium Technical Inc and others*,[86] in which the Indian Supreme Court overruled its earlier decision in *Venture Global Engineering v. Satyam Computer Services Ltd and another* (*Venture Global*)[87] and held that Sect. 34 of the Indian Arbitration Act did not permit the Indian courts to set aside foreign-seated awards.[88] Another example is when the Singapore Parliament amended the International Arbitration Act in 2009 to vest the courts with the power to grant interim relief in aid of foreign arbitrations.[89] This overruled *Swift-Fortune Ltd v. Magnifica Marine SA*,[90] in which the Singapore Court of Appeal had held that such a power could only be exercised in aid of domestic arbitrations.[91]

c. *Supportive: Ancillary procedures and curial support*

The arbitration statute of a jurisdiction will often provide for the ways in which the courts may lend support to an arbitration. For instance, national courts may validate interim measures granted by the arbitral tribunal, make orders to compel the attendance of witnesses at the hearing of the arbitration, compel third parties (that is, parties who are not bound by the arbitration agreement and therefore not subject to the jurisdiction of the arbitral tribunal) to disclose documents, grant injunctions to preserve property pending the conclusion of the arbitration, and order a stay of pending court proceedings in favour of arbitration.[92] These are secondary aspects of the law of arbitration which might not be governed by the Model Law but nonetheless have considerable practical implications on the conduct of the proceedings.

Relevantly, domestic legislatures will often control matters such as funding and representation which, while not part of the law of international arbitration *per se*, nevertheless have an important impact on the way that arbitrations take place. A good example is the law on third-party funding. Recently, both Hong Kong and Singapore amended their laws to allow third-party funding in international arbitration.[93] Following the introduction of third-party funding frameworks, the Singapore International Arbitration Centre (SIAC) responded by putting additional rules in place to empower investment arbitration tribunals to order the disclosure of the existence and details of

85. Arbitration and Conciliation (Amendment) Act 2015 (No. 3 of 2016) (India).
86. (2012) 9 SCC 552.
87. AIR 2010 SC 3371.
88. Another noteworthy amendment is the addition of an explanation to Sect. 34 to clarify that "the test as to whether there is a contravention with the fundamental policy of Indian law shall not entail a review on the merits of the dispute". This amendment appears to have been directed at reversing the holding in *Oil & Natural Gas Corp v. Saw Pipes Ltd* (2003) 5 SCC 705 where the court had decided that awards which were contrary to substantive provisions of Indian law or against the terms of the contract could be set aside for being contrary to Indian public policy.
89. International Arbitration Act (Singapore), Sect. 12A.
90. [2007] 1 SLR(R) 629.
91. Steven CHONG SC, "The Past, Present and Future of International Arbitration in Singapore" at the 5th Asia Pacific Alternative Dispute Resolution Conference (12 October 2016) at para. 15.
92. See, generally, N. BLACKABY, C. PARTASIDES, A. REDFERN and M. HUNTER, fn. 8 above, paras. 7.13-7.62.
93. Arbitration and Mediation Legislation (Third Party Funding) Amendment Ordinance 2017 (Ord. No. 6 of 2017) (Hong Kong); Civil Law (Amendment) Act 2017 (No. 2 of 2017) (Singapore).

any third-party funding arrangements in place.[94] In this way, domestic legislatures have a direct and tangible impact on the conduct of arbitrations through the laws they pass, and arbitral institutions in turn may be called on to respond by changing their procedures to suit such changes. The relationship of influence that states have with their respective arbitral institutions flows both ways. For instance, the emergency arbitrator procedure incorporated into the SIAC's rules[95] prompted the Singapore Parliament to legislate in order to clarify the enforceability of interim measures ordered by emergency arbitrators.[96]

The impact of a domestic legislature is undoubtedly greatest within its own jurisdiction, but it also extends beyond its borders to influence the actions and decisions of other stakeholders in the international community. The aforementioned example of third-party funding will illustrate this point. The law against third-party funding in Singapore traces its origins to the common law's longstanding suspicion of champertous interference with lawsuits. In considering whether the law ought to be changed, the Singapore Government surveyed the experience of other legal regimes in other major arbitration jurisdictions such as France, Switzerland and the United Kingdom and concluded that third-party funding could in some cases further rather than impede the cause of justice.[97] This is reminiscent of the way that Singapore amended its Legal Profession Act to permit foreign-qualified lawyers to appear in arbitration proceedings in Singapore, mirroring global trends.[98]

3. *Domestic Courts*

In the words of then Chief Justice Robert French AC of Australia, "[a]rbitration cannot be quarantined from the judicial system".[99] Under the structure created by the combined effect of the New York Convention and the Model Law, domestic courts not only play an important gatekeeping role when it comes to the recognition and enforcement of arbitral awards, but also contribute significantly to the development of transnational norms and principles in at least three ways.

a. *Interpreting international legal instruments*

First, they play a vital role in the interpretation of international legal instruments. Although the New York Convention and the Model Law have been instrumental in

94. Investment Arbitration Rules of the Singapore International Arbitration Centre, 1st edn. (1 January 2017), Rule 24(l).

95. Arbitration Rules of the SIAC, 6th edn. (1 August 2016), Schedule 1.

96. International Arbitration (Amendment) Act 2012 (No. 12 of 2012) (Singapore); see Julian WALLACE and Glen ROSEN, "Recent Amendments to the International Arbitration Act and their Influence on the Insurance Industry", available at <http://www.siac.org.sg/2013-09-18-01-57-20/2013-09-22-00-27-02/articles/199-recent-amendments-to-the-international-arbitration-act-and-their-influence-on-the-insurance-industry> (last accessed 13 May 2018).

97. Ministry of Law Singapore, "Press Release: Legislative Changes to Enhance Singapore as an International Hub for Commercial Dispute Resolution" (7 November 2016).

98. *Singapore Parliamentary Debates, Official Report* (15 June 2004) vol. 78 at cols. 96-97; Legal Profession (Amendment) Act 2004 (No. 23 of 2004).

99. R. FRENCH AC, "Arbitration and Public Policy", fn. 80 above, p. 12.

forging consensus on many key principles in the law of arbitration, principles alone do not determine the outcome of cases. Instead, the success of international arbitration has always rested on the consistent implementation of these core principles by domestic courts which have been called on to interpret and, in some cases, extend these principles. Nowhere is this clearer than in the area of the recognition and enforcement of arbitral awards.

Under the New York Convention, the recognition and enforcement of an arbitral award "may" be refused on one of seven grounds, of which the first five relate broadly to procedural irregularities in the commencement or carriage of the arbitration while the remaining two relate to the issues of arbitrability and public policy.[100] As is the nature of these matters, the wording of these provisions has been the subject of extensive litigation in the past few decades. Over time, the international body of case law which these disputes have generated has coalesced into a form of "international common law"[101] that has provided an important gloss on some of these provisions. In this regard, a key difference between courts and arbitral tribunals is that court decisions, unlike arbitral decisions, are routinely published. This was alluded to by Lord Thomas in his 2016 BAILII lecture where he spoke of the way that the confidential nature of arbitral awards "denudes the ability of individuals, and lawyers apart from the few who are instructed in arbitrations, to access the law, to understand how it has been interpreted and applied".[102] Judicial decisions, by contrast, serve as a publicly accessible resource on the interpretation of such instruments and they foster debate about the interpretation of these provisions and potential lacunae in the law.

Of course, the reality is that courts do not always speak with one voice when it comes to the interpretation of international legal instruments. A commonly cited example is Art. V(1) of the New York Convention, which sets out the grounds upon which "[r]ecognition and enforcement of the award *may* be refused" (emphasis added). This has been read by some courts to mean that the enforcement court has a residual discretionary power to grant enforcement even when a ground for refusal of enforcement is present.[103] In contrast, the interpretation placed by the French courts on Art. V(1) is that recognition and enforcement *must* be refused if any of the grounds enumerated therein are satisfied. It has been suggested that this difference in interpretation arises from inherent ambiguity in the French text of Art. V(1), the literal wording of which may be read to mean that recognition and enforcement *will* be refused, and only if the stated grounds are met.[104] Such examples do not, however, detract from

100. The grounds for refusing to recognize or enforce an award under Art. V(1)(*a*)-(*d*) and (2)(*a*) and (*b*) of the New York Convention mirror the grounds for setting aside an arbitral award under Art. 34 of the Model Law.

101. See, generally, A. GUZMAN and T. MEYER, "International Soft Law", fn. 17 above, pp. 201-221. Although the article focuses on public international law, and the examples given related to the decisions of supranational tribunals like the International Court of Justice, the same concept of "international common law" is a useful analytical tool that can be employed here.

102. Lord THOMAS, The BAILII Lecture 2016, fn. 84 above, para. 23.

103. ICCA *Yearbook Commercial Arbitration* (henceforth *Yearbook*) XXVIII (2003) p. 186.

104. Jean-Louis DELVOLVÉ, Jean ROUCHE and Gerald H. POINTON, *French Arbitration Law and Practice: A Dynamic Civil Law Approach to International Arbitration*, 2nd edn. (Kluwer Law International 2009) at p. 214.

the point that domestic courts are a vital source of law when it comes to the interpretation of the provisions in international legal instruments.

b. Filling in gaps in the lex arbitri

Second, domestic courts have contributed to the law of arbitration by developing principles to address areas that are not exhaustively governed by international agreement or by domestic arbitration statutes. It is of course impossible for any law to cover every possible scenario. For various reasons – inadvertence, a lack of resources, or simply the lack of collective will – the provisions in a governing treaty or statute might underdetermine the outcome of a dispute, and it is in such cases that domestic courts may step into the breach, as they often do in the domestic legal order, to supply the legislature's omission.

A good example concerns the effect to be given in subsequent enforcement proceedings to an order of a foreign court refusing to enforce the award under Art. V of the New York Convention. In *Diag Human SE v. The Czech Republic*,[105] a dispute between Diag and the Czech Republic was referred to arbitration. The Czech tribunal rendered an award in favour of Diag, which then attempted to enforce the award in France, Luxembourg, the United States, and Austria. The Supreme Court of Austria held that the award was not binding within the meaning of Art. V(1)(*e*) of the New York Convention and therefore not enforceable. Diag tried to enforce the award in England, and the question before the English High Court was whether the earlier Austrian judgment gave rise to an issue estoppel such that the award should likewise be held to be not binding in the English enforcement proceedings. After a careful review of the case law on the subject, the court answered the question in the affirmative.[106]

What is notable about *Diag* is that Bernard Eder J appears to have drawn a distinction between one of the so-called "international" grounds set out in Art. V(1)(*a*)-(*e*) of the New York Convention and the more "domestic" ones set out at Art. V(2)(*a*) and (*b*). He opined that a decision on the former might give rise to an estoppel whereas one decided on a "domestic" ground might not. The development and application of the doctrine of issue estoppel in this area has arisen in part because courts have had to reach for tools within their judicial arsenal in order to come up with a principled approach towards an issue to which there was then no clear answer provided within the relevant legal instruments.

c. Case management: Shaping the relationships with domestic curial proceedings, foreign curial proceedings, and arbitral tribunals

The third area in which domestic courts play an important role in the development of the law of arbitration is in the field of case management. Matters concerning the interface between domestic and foreign litigation and arbitration will arise for

105. [2014] EWHC 1639 (Comm).

106. See *Owens Bank v. Bracco* [1992] 2 AC 443 at 470-F–472E and *House of Spring Gardens Ltd v. Waite* [1991] QB 241. The Federal Court of Australia applied the concept of issue estoppel in the context of enforcement proceedings in *Coeclerici Asia (Pte) Ltd v. Gujarat NRE Coke Limited* [2013] FCA 882. When this matter was appealed to the Full Court, it was held that it was unnecessary to decide this issue, but the first instance decision was upheld: see *Gujarat NRE Coke Limited v. Coeclerici Asia (Pte) Ltd* [2013] FCAFC 109.

determination by the courts with increasing frequency. For instance, courts are regularly called on to grant a stay of court proceedings in favour of arbitration;[107] Art. II(3) of the New York Convention requires domestic courts to refer the parties to arbitration where an arbitration agreement exists, but leaves the determination of issues such as the validity and scope of the agreement within the courts' purview. Anti-suit injunctions are also sometimes granted by courts – primarily those from the common law tradition from which this concept originated[108] – to restrain the bringing of proceedings both domestically as well as overseas.[109]

One particularly fraught area concerns the subject of what is to be done when there are curial proceedings involving some matters which are arbitrable and some of which are not; and where only some, but not all, of the parties are bound by an agreement to submit some of their disputes to arbitration. In a decision handed down by the Singapore Court of Appeal in 2015, this was described as a "case management quandary".[110] The question of whether the courts should be permitted in such a case to grant a "case management stay" – that is, a stay of those parts of a dispute not covered by an arbitration agreement in order that those which are so covered may be arbitrated and decided first – is one which has divided the common law world.[111] Whichever view one takes of that question, the broader point is that the precise contours of the proper relationship between the courts and arbitral tribunals is a deeply important domain of arbitration law, and it is one which has largely been developed through judge-made law.[112]

To summarize, public actors play integral, and largely complementary, roles in the development of arbitration law. At some risk of oversimplification, international organizations provide an effective platform for attaining consensus and harmonization on key issues of principle, while domestic legislatures and courts put the flesh on these bones by making sense of and applying the law in international legal instruments. In so doing, they further harmonize initiatives, highlight gaps in the law, and encourage reform and innovation in the industry.

This also addresses the second of the two aspects of this issue that was raised at the start of this section, namely whether public actors *should* have a lawmaking role in international arbitration.[113] As I remarked at the 2012 session of this Congress, arbitration is in its golden age. In a 2015 survey, arbitration was named by corporate counsel as the preferred dispute resolution mechanism for cross-border disputes, with

107. See, for example, *Channel Tunnel Group Ltd v. Balfour Beatty Construction Ltd and others* [1993] AC 334 at 367-368; *Tomolugen*, fn. 79 above.

108. Emmanuel GAILLARD, "Reflections on the Use of Anti-Suit Injunctions in International Arbitration" in Loukas A. MISTELIS and Julian D. M. LEW, *Pervasive Problems in International Arbitration* (Kluwer Law International 2006) p. 201 at p. 201.

109. See *Ust-Kamenogorsk Hydropower Plant JSC v. AES Ust-Kamenogorsk Hydropower Plant LLP* [2013] UKSC 35 at para. 60; *Paramedics Electromedicina Comercial Ltda. V. GE Medical Systems Information Technologies* 369 F.3d 645 (2d Cir. 2004).

110. *Tomolugen*, fn. 79 above, para. 140.

111. *Ibid.*, paras. 143-185.

112. In *Tomolugen*, the Singapore Court of Appeal expressed the view that it was the domestic court which, "as the final arbiter", should "take the lead in ensuring the efficient and fair resolution of the dispute as a whole": *ibid.*, para. 186.

113. See p. 118 above.

almost two-thirds lauding the widespread enforceability of arbitral awards – the legacy of the New York Convention and the Model Law – as its most desirable feature.[114] There is no question that the present success of international arbitration would have been impossible to achieve in the absence of the involvement of public actors, who have played (and continue to play) a vital role in providing a stable and reliable framework for arbitration today.

IV. LEGITIMACY CHALLENGES

This next part of the paper concerns the legitimacy challenges presented by the influence of public actors in lawmaking in international arbitration. As a starting point, it is important to recall *why* legitimacy is important to international arbitration in the first place. In broad terms, the answer which Prof. Thomas Schultz gives, with which I agree, is that legitimacy brings about stability.[115] If the users of arbitration have no belief in the legitimacy of its norms they will either agitate for change or abandon the system entirely, threatening the future of the profession. This is why legitimacy is crucial for the long-term viability of international arbitration.

In the remainder of this part, five legitimacy challenges will be examined, although it should be clarified that this is not an exhaustive list. The first three relate to the concerns that arbitration users might have over the *authority* of the lawmakers who have created the norms or the lawmaking process through which these norms are created. These are matters which touch on, to borrow an expression from the political science literature, issues of *input* legitimacy.[116] The next two challenges concern dissatisfaction with the nature and quality of the laws which are produced by public actors.[117] These relate to issues of *output* legitimacy.

1. *The Problem of Sovereignty*

The first challenge is the problem of sovereignty, or the lack of it. Given that all states are sovereign, no state can or should be subjected to laws which it did not freely consent to be bound by. But having regard to the diversity in legal traditions and the differing interests of states, it is unsurprising that true consensus is elusive. For instance, while the Explanatory Note to the Model Law states that the work "reflects a worldwide consensus on the principles and important issues of international arbitration practice",[118]

114. White & Case and Queen Mary University of London School of International Arbitration, "2015 International Arbitration Survey: Improvements and Innovations in International Arbitration", available at <http://www.arbitration.qmul.ac.uk/media/arbitration/docs/2015_International_Arbitration_Survey.pdf> (last accessed 13 May 2018).

115. Thomas SCHULTZ, "Legitimacy Pragmatism in International Arbitration: A Framework for Analysis", this volume, pp. 25-51.

116. See Fritz W. SCHARPF, *Governing in Europe, Effective and Democratic?* (Oxford University Press 1999) at p. 6.

117. Donald H. J. HERMANN, "Max Weber and the Concept of Legitimacy in Contemporary Jurisprudence", 33 DePaul Law Review (1983, no. 1) Art. 1 at p. 10.

118. Explanatory Note to the Model Law, fn. 67 above, para. 2.

commentators have long questioned the extent to which this claim of "a worldwide consensus" is true. Marc Blessing and Katherine Lynch suggest that the provisions of the Model Law "reflect the hegemonic view of Western developed states embracing liberal free trade theory" and that developing states felt that they were not equal participants in the drafting process and that their concerns were not adequately reflected in the finished product.[119] For instance, Prof. M. Sornarajah notes that the Model Law provides for a wide definition of "commercial" agreements and expressly lists "exploitation agreements and concessions" as examples. However, the arbitrability of such disputes may come into conflict with the doctrine of permanent sovereignty over natural resources, which is enshrined in the constitutions of many developing countries.[120]

It has also been observed that the difficulties faced by developing countries in participating in international arbitration stem from the "perception that they have neither participated in the creation of international law to be applied by [arbitral tribunals], nor recognized or endorsed them".[121] One example is the norm that the consent of all parties is not a prerequisite to arbitral proceedings progressing once the arbitral tribunal is seised of the case, which traces its origins to the principles of the presumptive validity of arbitration agreements and the recognition of arbitral awards in the Geneva Protocol. This is now such an entrenched part of the international arbitration system that it is almost incapable of being questioned. While one can understand the doctrinal soundness of this position, this has contributed to the view of some African states that arbitration is an involuntary process under which an award can be enforced against the respondents in a foreign country whether they contest the proceedings or not.[122]

This is a problem which persists today. The longstanding practice in UNCITRAL has been to reach decisions by consensus. In 2007, however, France sought clarifications as to what this really meant, noting that "there cannot be consensus without the consent of all delegates" and that there had never been a vote at UNCITRAL.[123] Australia similarly registered its concern in 2008 that "on occasion in certain Working Groups, consensus has been deemed to have been reached when the room was clearly divided on the decision in question".[124] UNCITRAL responded to these observations in its 2010 Report

119. Katherine LYNCH, *The Forces of Economic Globalization – Challenges to the Regime of International Commercial Arbitration* (Kluwer Law International 2003) at pp. 224-225, citing Marc BLESSING, "Globalization (and Harmonization) of Arbitration", 9 Journal of International Arbitration (1992, no. 1) p. 79 at pp. 82-88.

120. M. SORNARAJAH, *The UNCITRAL Model Law: A Third World Viewpoint*, 6 Journal of International Arbitration (1989, no. 4) p. 7 at p. 16.

121. Samuel K. B. ASANTE, "The Perspectives of African Countries on International Commercial Arbitration", 6 Leiden Journal of International Law (1993, no. 2) p. 331 at p. 334, quoting *The Permanent Court of Arbitration – New Directions*, Report by the Working Group on Improving the Functioning of the Court (13 May 1991) at p. 9.

122. S. ASANTE, "The Perspectives of African Countries on International Commercial Arbitration", fn. 121 above, p. 345.

123. Claire R. KELLY, "The Politics of Legitimacy in the UNCITRAL Working Methods" in Tomer BROUDE, Marc. L. BUSCH and Amelia PORGES, *The Politics of International Economic Law* (Cambridge University Press 2011) at pp. 113-114; note that the UNCITRAL Report to the UN General Assembly, A/65/17 (2010) at Annex III, para. 4, states that there has been one vote at UNCITRAL, which was on a procedural matter.

124. UN Doc. No. A/CN.9/660 (28 May 2008).

to the UN General Assembly by clarifying that the practice was to reach consensus as far as possible, and to engage the "exceptional procedure" of voting (in accordance with the General Assembly's rules of procedure) in the absence of such consensus.[125] These formal clarifications, however, do not actually resolve the nub of the concern, which is that decisions are being taken in working groups and passed off as the product of a "consensus", notwithstanding dissenting voices in the room.[126] Anecdotally, others will have seen that impasses at these discussions are sometimes resolved by a strategic adjournment "for consultation", which typically involves a handful of the most forceful (although it may be granted that they might also be the best-informed) voices meeting in caucus to find common ground, which is then presented as a solution to the group as a whole. A delegation from a country that might have been struggling to follow the debate can at times feel quite lost, even as it is presented as having contributed to the "consensus". These illustrations raise the concern of whether the idea of "democratic participation", which was identified earlier at Part II(2) as one of the indices to legitimacy, is satisfied.

The consequences of settling for an illusory consensus inevitably manifest themselves further down the line. International arbitration as it exists today cannot function without the cooperation of national courts, which are the gateways through which arbitral awards enter the domestic legal order via the recognition and enforcement of arbitral awards.[127] This is the system of "core uniformity coupled with devolved application",[128] but it works only if the consensus holds, and the individual national courts all subscribe to the same core tenets. Without a true consensus, the centre cannot hold, and the consequence may be a sudden and dramatic rip in the fabric of international arbitration, as happened recently in *Slovak Republic v. Achmea BV* (*Achmea*).

In *Achmea*, the Grand Chamber of the European Court of Justice (ECJ) held that investor-state arbitration clauses in intra-European Union (EU) bilateral investment treaties (BITs) were incompatible with fundamental treaty provisions of EU law.[129] The effect of this ruling is still being studied but it appears to be the case that investors will have to submit any dispute previously protected by an intra-EU BIT to the jurisdiction of the host state, and can no longer arbitrate their disputes.[130] Admittedly, the circumstances are different, but this calls to mind the somewhat wider retreat from investor-state arbitration that has been noted.[131] In recent years, Bolivia, Venezuela, and

125. C. KELLY, "The Politics of Legitimacy in the UNCITRAL Working Methods", fn. 123 above, p. 114.
126. UN, "Uniform Commercial Law in the Twenty-First Century", Proceedings of the Congress of UNCITRAL (18-22 May 1992) at p. 15.
127. See Albert Jan VAN DEN BERG, *New York Arbitration Convention of 1958: Towards a Uniform Judicial Interpretation* (Kluwer Law International 1981) at p. 5.
128. See S. MENON and D. BROCK, *Arbitration in Singapore*, fn. 36 above, para. 1.021.
129. *Slovak Republic v. Achmea BV*, Case C-284/16 (6 March 2018).
130. Sebastian PERRY, "ECJ rules against intra-EU BITs" (6 March 2018) in Global Arbitration Review, available at <https://globalarbitrationreview.com/article/1166355/ecj-rules-against-intra-eu-bits> (last accessed 15 May 2018).
131. See Clint PEINHARDT and Rachel L. WELLHAUSEN, "Withdrawing from Investment Treaties but Protecting Investment" (20 April 2016), available at <http://www.rwellhausen.com/uploads/6/9/0/0/6900193/peinhardt_wellhausen_bitwithdrawal.pdf> (last accessed 15 May 2018) at pp. 4-5.

Ecuador have withdrawn from the ICSID Convention,[132] and four other States – South Africa, Indonesia, Italy, and Russia – have unilaterally withdrawn from certain investment treaties.[133] Even Australia, which is an established part of the global north, turned its back on investor-state arbitration a few years ago under the Gillard administration in the wake of the plain packaging arbitration and has not fully reconciled itself to its use of these mechanisms since.[134] While two recent studies cited in Prof. Lucy Reed's paper have shown that there has not been that wholesale flight from treaty arbitration that some have feared, the growing popularity (albeit gradual) of interpretive guidelines in BITs and the pronounced shift towards the use of narrower treaty clauses in the Americas – reveal a degree of dissatisfaction with the current regime and an appetite for further reform.[135]

If there is truth in the perception that states are becoming increasingly guarded about investor-state arbitration, then there can be no real doubt that questions of politics are driving such a trend. This was pointedly noted by Advocate General Wathelet in his opinion in the *Achmea* case, where he observed that all of the states that had intervened in on behalf of the petitioner (Slovakia) had been respondents in a number of arbitral proceedings relating to intra-EU investments while all the states which intervened on behalf of the respondent-investor were states of origin for investors and had rarely, if ever, been respondents in such proceedings. Strikingly, he also noted that it was curious that the European Commission had intervened on behalf of the investor, because for a long time, the argument of all EU institutions had been that – far from being incompatible with EU law – BITs of this nature were in fact necessary to prepare Central and Eastern European states for accession to the union.[136] It may be observed at the same time that the People's Republic of China (PRC) has moved in the opposite direction. It has, in relative terms, morphed from being less of an investment host state towards being more of an investor state,[137] and this shift has been accompanied by a more positive stance towards investor-state dispute settlement mechanisms.[138]

---

132. More formally, the Convention on the Settlement of Investment Disputes between States and Nationals of Other States (14 October 1966) 575 UNTS 159.
133. C. PEINHARDT and R. WELLHAUSEN, "Withdrawing from Investment Treaties but Protecting Investment", fn. 131 above, pp. 4-5; See FU Chenyuan, "China's Prospective Strategy in Employing Investor-State Dispute Resolution Mechanism for the Best Interest of Its Outward Oil Investment", Peking University Transnational Law Review (2014) p. 266 at pp. 290-291.
134. Luke NOTTAGE, "Investor-State Arbitration Policy and Practice in Australia", Investor-State Arbitration Series, Paper No. 6 (June 2016) at pp. 1-2. The tribunal eventually issued a unanimous decision agreeing with Australia that it had no jurisdiction to hear the claim: see Australian Government Attorney-General's Department, "Tobacco plain packaging – investor-state arbitration", available at <https://www.ag.gov.au/Internationalrelations/International Law/Pages/Tobaccoplainpack aging.aspx> (last accessed 15 May 2018).
135. Lucy REED, "Lawmaking by Arbitrators", this volume, pp. 52-85, at pp. 79-80 and 84 under (v).
136. *Achmea*, Opinion of Advocate General Wathelet (19 September 2017) at paras. 34-41.
137. For statistics on China's foreign direct investment flow, see The World Bank, "Foreign direct investment, net outflows (BoP, current US$)", available at <http://data.worldbank.org/indicator/BM.KLT.DINV.CD.WD> (last accessed 15 May 2018).
138. See FU C., "China's Prospective Strategy in Employing Investor-State Dispute Resolution Mechanism", fn. 133 above, pp. 285-287 and Dilini PATHIRANA, "A look into China's slowly increasing appearance in ISDS cases", International Institute for Sustainable Development:

However, politics aside, there is no question that sincere concerns over matters of sovereignty and legitimacy underlie the growing disenchantment with investment arbitration. South Africa, for instance, declared in 2010 that 2twenty-three of its investment treaties "pose risks and limitations on the ability of the Government to pursue its Constitutional-based transformation agenda" because they had repeatedly been used by investors to challenge the Black Economic Empowerment programmes it had passed.[139] Likewise, Ecuador has long couched its opposition to investment arbitration in the language of sovereignty. In 2008, it amended its constitution to prohibit agreements under which Ecuador "would have to cede sovereign jurisdiction to international arbitral tribunals in contractual or commercial matters between the State and individuals or corporations". This provision was later relied on when Ecuador terminated its investment treaties with eight other Central American countries.[140] Equally, there is no question in *Achmea* that the ECJ was sincerely convinced (however rightly or wrongly) that the fact that questions of EU law might be decided by arbitral tribunals that were not part of the EU's judicial structure, violated the principle of the autonomy and supremacy of EU law.[141]

These cases present themselves as sobering reminders that if legitimacy concerns are left unaddressed for too long, there will inevitably be a pushback. This can already be seen from the current confusion and dissatisfaction in the aftermath of the *Achmea* decision, as investors in the EU (especially those who have obtained but not enforced arbitral awards, and those in the midst of ongoing arbitrations) struggle with the sudden loss of recourse to the international arbitration system, which has long been recognized as "the most essential element of the BITs" and "an indispensable guarantee that encourages and promotes investments".[142]

2. *The Problem of the Lack of Accountability*

The second legitimacy concern relates to the absence of true accountability and participation. In a democratic state, accountability is a necessary precondition for the legitimate exercise of power. However, while domestic public actors are accountable within their respective constitutional and administrative law frameworks to their local constituencies, there are no equivalent relationships of formal accountability in international arbitration. Public actors need not answer to the international community at large which may be affected by their actions. This includes the parties who may come

---

Investment Treaty News (26 September 2017), available at <https://www.iisd.org/itn/2017/09/26/a-look-into-chinas-slowly-increasing-appearance-in-isds-cases-dilini-pathirana> (last accessed 15 May 2018).

139. Republic of South Africa Department of Trade and Industry, "Newsroom: Minister Davies Launched UNCTAD Investment Policy Framework", available at <https://dti.gov.za/delegationspeechdetail.jsp?id=2465> (last accessed 16 May 2018).

140. C. PEINHARDT and R. WELLHAUSEN, "Withdrawing from Investment Treaties but Protecting Investment", fn. 131 above, p. 573; see Constitution of the Republic of Ecuador (20 October 2008), Art. 422.

141. *Achmea*, fn. 129 above, paras. 32-34.

142. *Achmea*, Opinion of Advocate General Wathelet (19 September 2017) at para. 77.

into their jurisdiction for arbitrations as well as the international community for whom these domestic public actors may be creating laws, whether directly or indirectly.

At first blush, it may seem odd that this poses a legitimacy challenge at all. After all, the position would appear to be that states are free to regulate all activities taking place within their jurisdiction as they see fit, and all persons who find themselves within their jurisdiction (including persons who elect to seat their arbitrations there) must take the law as they find it. The problem with this argument, however, is that even if it were accepted that the parties have freely chosen to abide by *all* the laws of the seat state (which is a contestable proposition),[143] this only settles the matter through the lenses of the disputing parties and the seat state (the "party" and "national" perspectives), and does not consider the matter from the viewpoints of the wider arbitration community (the "community" and global" perspectives").[144] From the perspective of the wider arbitration community, a law is only legitimate if it coheres with settled normative expectations of the way that the system of international arbitration should function (this is the so-called "coherence" standard of legitimacy: see Part II(2) above). The absence of an effective check and balance has meant that domestic actors have sometimes acted in the furtherance of their national interests in a manner that ignores basic notions of fairness with seeming impunity. Two examples will serve to illustrate this point.

In the *Yukos* arbitration, the Russian seat court set aside an arbitral award that Yukos had obtained against Rosneft, a Russian state-owned entity, in circumstances which were widely criticized as being the product of a partial judicial process.[145] In *Salini Costruttori S.p.A. v. Ethiopia* (*Salini*), the Ethiopian courts ordered the suspension of the arbitration proceedings despite the International Court of Arbitration's rejection of a challenge against the arbitral tribunal for bias.[146] The tribunal however decided not to give effect to the Ethiopian courts' orders and continued with the arbitral proceedings, simply stating that it did not consider itself bound by the injunctions issued by the Ethiopian courts and "that, in the particular circumstances of the case, it [was] under a duty to proceed with the arbitration".[147]

Quite apart from issues of bias and partiality, there is also the problem that domestic courts may be insufficiently sensitive to the needs of the wider international arbitration

143. As argued in Georgios PETROCHILOS, *Procedural Law in International Arbitration*, fn. 78 above, when parties elect to submit their dispute to arbitration, what they have "chosen" is to submit themselves to an adjudicative dispute resolution mechanism attended by certain due process safeguards that secure for the arbitration the character of a binding determination of rights and liabilities. However, this does not mean that they "choose", in any meaningful sense, the full panoply of laws that constitute the lex arbitri of that jurisdiction (at para. 1.25).

144. See pp. 116-117 above.

145. However, there was perhaps a happy ending to this tale, for Yukos was nonetheless able to enforce the vacated award in both the Netherlands and the United Kingdom: see *Yukos Capital SARL v. OAO Rosneft,* Gerechtshof Amsterdam (2009) *Yearbook* XXXIV p. 703 (*Yukos* (Netherlands)) and *Yukos Capital S.a.r.L. v. OJSC Oil Company Rosneft* [2014] EWHC 2188 (Comm) (*Yukos* (UK)).

146. See Giulia CARBONE, "Interference of the Court of the Seat with International Arbitration, The Symposium", 2012 Journal of Dispute Resolution (2012, no. 1) p. 217 at p. 227 and generally.

147. *Salini Costruttori S.p.A. v. The Federal Democratic Republic of Ethiopia, Addis Ababa Water and Sewerage Authority*, Award regarding the Suspension of the Proceedings and Jurisdiction dated 7 December 2001, 20(3) Mealey's IAR A1 (2005) at para. 124.

community. The *Dallah* cases[148] are a case in point. The key question in those cases was whether the Government of Pakistan was bound by an arbitration agreement contained in a contract between the Awami Hajj Trust, a separate legal entity set up by the Government of Pakistan, and Dallah Real Estate. A tribunal seated in Paris thought so, and an award was handed down in Dallah's favour, which was sought to be enforced in both the United Kingdom and in France. In November 2010, the UK Supreme Court held that there was insufficient evidence of a "common intention" for Pakistan to be a party to the arbitration agreement and refused to enforce the award. At the time the enforcement proceedings were taking place in the United Kingdom, setting aside proceedings were taking place simultaneously in France. The UK Supreme Court was invited to, but refused, to stay the proceedings pending the decision of the French court. As it happened, the *Cour d'appel de Paris* reached the opposite conclusion three months later, and found that the parties had intended for Pakistan to be party to the arbitration agreement and refused to set aside the award. As Prof. Gary Born argues, *Dallah* was a good example of a case where the UK Supreme Court might have adjourned its decision on enforcement pending the French court's decision on the setting aside application, given that the matter involved issues of French law that were best adjudicated by the French courts. The outcome was unsatisfactory, at least from the perspective of the parties, and it could have been different if national courts were encouraged to be aware of the accountability concerns of the users of arbitration and so to be more attuned to the interests and expectations of the international community.

3. *The Problem of Overreach*

The third, and closely related, legitimacy challenge relates to overreach. In arbitration, as in other fields of law, there are competing interests that must be resolved, and a balance must be struck between the interests of arbitration users and those of the state. Where this balance is struck in a manner which appears unreasonable or disproportionate, legitimacy concerns may arise. This can happen, for example, when public actors include excessive restrictions on the arbitrability of disputes, provide for an unprecedented expansion of the grounds of curial intervention by allowing merits-based reviews of arbitral awards, or impose additional grounds for a court to refuse the enforcement of arbitral awards (for example by adopting an expansive reading of public policy).

This was the case in a trilogy of decisions of the Indian Supreme Court. In 2002, the court in *Bhatia International v. Bulk Trading SA and another* (*Bhatia*) held that Part 1 of the Indian Arbitration Act, which confers power on the court to grant interim measures, would also apply to foreign-seated arbitrations unless specifically excluded by the parties.[149] This decision, worrying in and of itself, became more of a concern because in 2003, the court held – in the *Oil & Natural Gas Corp v. Saw Pipes* case (*Saw Pipes*) – that an award may be set aside on grounds of public policy if it was patently illegal, which it

148. *Dallah Real Estate and Tourism Holding Co v. Ministry of Religious Affairs of the Government of Pakistan* [2011] 1 AC 763; *Gouvernement du Pakistan – Ministère des Affaires Religieuses v. Société Dallah Real Estate and Tourism Holding Company* C.A. Paris, 17 February 2011 (Case No. 09/28533).

149. (2002) 4 SCC 105.

would be if it was wrong in law.[150] The logical corollary of this, as the court confirmed in its 2008 *Venture Global* decision, was that *foreign-seated* awards could be set aside for being wrong in law.[151] These cases have since been legislatively overruled,[152] but they illustrate the dangers of overreach. The intention in these cases might have been benign, and even laudable (for instance, the court in *Bhatia* was probably motivated by a desire not to leave parties to international arbitrations outside India but who had assets in India without the prospect of interim relief) but they plainly went too far.[153]

These decisions may be contrasted with what happened in *Sanum Investments Ltd v. Laos* (*Sanum*). That case concerned a dispute between a Macanese investor and the Government of Laos which was submitted to arbitration pursuant to a bilateral investment treaty (BIT).[154] The wrinkle was that the BIT in question was concluded between the PRC and the Laos People's Democratic Republic *before* sovereignty over Macau was transferred from Portugal to China. The Singapore Court of Appeal eventually decided, contrary to the positions of *both* the PRC and the Government of Laos (as revealed in two *notes verbale* which were sent only after the dispute arose), that the BIT did extend to Macau.[155]

The reasoning of the court is involved, but the only point which bears on the present discussion is the way in which the court strove to uphold the rule of law without encroaching upon the sovereignty of the states involved. On the one hand, the court showed itself alive to its obligations to the parties where it clarified (contrary to the submissions of the investor in the court below that the issue was non-justiciable) that not only was it competent to consider the issue, but obliged to do so, having been designated as the court of the seat by the parties.[156] On the other hand, it took pains to clarify that its decision was confined to the facts surrounding the specific BIT which was before the court, and did not extend to other treaties concluded between the parties or with other states.[157]

As organs of their respective states, domestic actors naturally view matters through a national prism. However, the challenge – when their actions take on transnational

150. (2003) 5 SCC 705.
151. (2010) AIR 2010 SC 3371.
152. See pp. 126-127 above.
153. See, generally, Sameer SATTAR, "Enforcement of Arbitral Awards and Public Policy: Same Concept, Different Approach?" (2011), available at <www.employmentlawalliance.com/Templates/media/files/Misc%20Documents/Enforcement-of-Arbitral-Awards-Public-Policy.pdf> (last accessed 15 May 2018).
154. *Sanum Investments Ltd v. Government of the Lao People's Democratic Republic* [2016] 5 SLR 536 (*Sanum*).
155. The decision of the court was criticized by the government of the PRC: see People's Republic of China Ministry of Foreign Affairs, "Foreign Ministry Spokesperson Hua Chunying's Regular Press Conference on October 21, 2016", available at <http://www.fmprc.gov.cn/mfa_eng/xwfw_665399/s2510_665401/t1407743.shtml> (last accessed 16 May 2018).
156. *Sanum*, para. 38.
157. *Ibid.*, para. 45; see also Gary B. BORN, Jonathan W. LIM and Dharshini PRASAD, "Sanum v. Laos (Part II): The Singapore Court of Appeal Affirms Tribunal's Jurisdiction under the PRC-Laos BIT" (11 November 2016), available at <http://arbitrationblog.kluwerarbitration.com/2016/11/11/sanum-v-laos-the-singapore-court-of-appeal-affirms-tribunals-jurisdiction-under-the-prc-laos-bit-part-ii> (last accessed 15 May 2018).

significance – is for a balance to be struck between national interests and the broader interests of the disputing parties (including their expectations and choices made in the exercise of their autonomy), the arbitration community, and the wider international community. Jurisdictions whose domestic public actors fail to strike an appropriate balance will naturally be avoided by arbitration users when selecting an arbitral seat. In the 1988 decision of *Turner (East Asia) Pte Ltd v. Builders Federal (Hong Kong) Ltd* (*Turner*), the Singapore High Court read its domestic Legal Profession Act to preclude foreign lawyers from representing parties in Singapore-seated arbitrations.[158] It was roundly criticized by the international community for espousing an unacceptably parochial attitude towards protecting the local Bar while ignoring commercial realities and party autonomy.[159] This affected Singapore's attractiveness as an arbitral seat, but it has managed to redirect its course in the years hence, when it legislatively overruled *Turner* and liberalized its rules on the appearance of foreign counsel in arbitrations. Likewise, the Indian legislature's post-*Venture Global* reform efforts are similarly laudable. But these cases and the criticisms that followed do illustrate the need for public actors to be judicious in the exercise of their domestic lawmaking powers. Described in terms of the indices of legitimacy set out in Part II(2) above, the issue here is one of the "reasonableness" and "proportionality" of their lawmaking efforts.

4. *The Problem of Fragmentation and Inconsistency*

The fourth legitimacy challenge relates to the problem of fragmentation and inconsistency. The foregoing discussion would have highlighted that there is, not infrequently, a lack of consistency in the norms and principles determined by public actors. It is unsurprising that without a supranational legislature, starkly differing rules and standards will develop across different jurisdictions. The need for a common framework and a core set of shared principles and canons provided the impetus for the creation of the Model Law, which deals with many aspects of arbitration procedure. But there remain many unresolved areas of controversy, including the significant matter of the precise role of the seat court and the effect of its decisions. Further, the development and harmonization of norms through such international agreements is slow, ad hoc, and episodic. It is a process that has been punctuated by landmark events such as the introduction of the New York Convention, followed by decades-long lulls of somnambulant silence.

The risks of inconsistency are greatest when domestic public actors "make law" in international arbitration. Domestic public actors apply different rules in different frameworks and different legal cultures and traditions, in the pursuit of different objectives. With the potential for conflicting rules and norms to emerge from different sources of law, concerns about clarity will undoubtedly be in the minds of arbitration practitioners, users and other stakeholders alike. I return here to the well-known debate over the effect of an order by the seat court setting aside an arbitral award in subsequent enforcement proceedings. On the so-called "delocalized" view – which is taken by the

158. [1988] 1 SLR(R) 281.

159. S. CHONG, "The Past, Present and Future of International Arbitration in Singapore", fn. 91 above, para. 6.

French courts and is best expressed in cases such as *Société OTV v. Société Hilmarton*[160] (*Hilmarton*) and *Société PT Putrabali Adyamulia v. Société Rena Holdings et Société Moguntia Est Epices*[161] (*Putrabali*) – an international arbitral award is not anchored in any national legal order and may therefore remain in existence even after it has been set aside by the seat court.[162] This may mean that the same issues and arguments may be revisited in multiple jurisdictions, with possibly conflicting results.

The problem of fragmentation and inconsistency also presents itself in the area of professional ethics, where standards and expectations of counsel and arbitrator conduct diverge dramatically across different legal traditions.[163] Take the example of the preparation of witnesses. Civil law jurisdictions generally have strict prohibitions against this, and speaking to a witness before he takes the stand may be a ground for professional censure. In the United States, a common law jurisdiction, a lawyer who fails to prepare a witness might be thought to have breached his ethical duty to advance his client's best case.[164] I will return to this area of professional ethics in the next section on the lack of legal precision.

The challenge here is that the persons to whom arbitration laws apply must be able to know how to conform to them – it is an essential tenet of the rule of law that norms must be certain, predictable and therefore capable of providing effective guidance.[165] This cannot be achieved if the laws are not only variegated in content, but also uncertain in application.

---

160. *Société OTV v. Société Hilmarton*, Cour de Cassation, First Civil Chamber, 92-15137, 23 March 1994, 1994 Rev. Arb. 327.

161. *Société PT Putrabali Adyamulia v. Société Rena Holding et Société Moguntia Est Epices*, Cour de Cassation, 05-18053, 29 June 2007, 2007 Rev. Arb. 50.

162. Jean-Louis DELVOLVÉ, Jean ROUCHE and Gerald H. POINTON, *French Arbitration Law and Practice: A Dynamic Civil Law Approach to International Arbitration*, 2nd edn. (Kluwer Law International 2009) at p. 214; see, for example, *TermoRio S.A. E.s.p. and Leaseco Group, Llc v. Electranta S.P. et al*, 487 F.3d 928 (D.C. Cir. 2007) at 930 and *Malicorp Ltd v. Government of the Arab Republic of Egypt and others* [2015] EWHC 361 (Comm) at para. 14(2). See also Sundaresh MENON, Patron's Address, CIArb London Centenary Conference (2 July 2015) at paras. 53-57).

163. See, eg, Niklas ELOFSSON, "Ex Parte Interviews of Party-Appointed Arbitrator Candidates: A study based on the views of counsel and arbitrators in Sweden and the United States", 30 Journal of International Arbitration (2013, no. 4) p. 381.

164. Sundaresh MENON, "Adjudicator, Advocate, or Something In Between?: Coming to terms with the role of the party-appointed arbitrator", presented at the 2016 Herbert Smith Freehills - Singapore Management University Asian Arbitration Lecture (24 November 2016) at para. 22 citing Catherine A. ROGERS, "Fit and Function in Legal Ethics: Developing a Code of Conduct for International Arbitration", 23 Michigan Journal of International Law p. 341 at p. 344; Catherine A. ROGERS, "Ethics & Conflicts in International Arbitration", presented at the Singapore International Arbitration Academy (3 December 2011) at p. 15, available at <https://cil.nus.edu.sg/wp-content/uploads/2012/11/CATHERINE-ROGERS-SIAA-Counsel-Ethics-Session-Mon-3-Dec.pdf> (last accessed 15 May 2014).

165. Joseph RAZ, *The Authority of Law: Essays on Law and Morality*, 2nd edn. (Oxford University Press 2009) at p. 221; Jeffrey JOWELL, "The Rule of Law and its Underlying Values" in Jeffrey JOWELL, Dawn OLIVER and Colm O'CINNEIDE, *The Changing Constitution*, 8th edn. (Oxford University Press 2015) at p. 19.

5. *The Problem of the Lack of Legal Precision*

This brings me to the fifth and final challenge that I address in this paper, which is that of the lack of legal precision. As a starting point, it is important to recall that the efficacy of arbitration relies on voluntary compliance. Parties overwhelmingly comply with the majority of directions made by arbitral tribunals – not because they are backed by the threat of sanction – but because they are *seen* to be the authoritative pronouncements of a dispute resolution mechanism with the authority and legitimacy to make them.[166] Thus, congruence with fundamental precepts of the rule of law is essential to the viability of arbitration as a method of dispute resolution.[167] However, it is not clear if the laws made by international organizations are precise enough to offer practical guidance.[168] This is a problem that affects the work of international organizations most acutely. In order to broker a compromise between differing schools of thoughts and state interests, principles laid down by international organizations often end up being framed in broad and open-textured terms.

This problem is perhaps most acute in investment arbitration, where the use of vague boilerplate clauses was much more common than it perhaps is today. In the *SGS* arbitrations, ICSID tribunals convened under the Switzerland-Pakistan BIT and the Switzerland-Philippines BIT reached different conclusions on whether an identical umbrella clause[169] had the effect of elevating contractual claims to treaty claims.[170] In the field of international commercial arbitration, the disagreement over whether and to what extent a court may recognize and enforce a foreign award even though a Convention ground has been established (or, conversely, the extent to which it may *refuse* recognition and enforcement even though the validity of a foreign award has been upheld in an overseas jurisdiction) is a good example of how excessive generality in the wording of broad treaty provisions has produced difficulties in practice.[171] Viewing all of this, it may be asked whether international organizations, constrained as they are by the institutional limitations within which they operate, are able to make laws that possess the necessary legal precision to legitimately be regarded as law.[172] It appears that the arbitration community is alive to at least some of these concerns, for it has been observed that more

166. Stavros L. BREKOULAKIS, "International Arbitration Scholarship and the Concept of Arbitration Law", 36 Fordham International Law Journal (2013) p. 745 at p. 784.

167. *Ibid.*, p. 785.

168. See George A. BERMANN, "Recognition and Enforcement of Foreign Arbitral Awards: The Interpretation and Application of the New York Convention by National Courts" in *Ius Comparatum – Global Studies in Comparative Law* 23 (Springer 2017) at para. 4.1.1.

169. The clause read "[each Sovereign] shall constantly guarantee the observance of the commitments it has entered into with respect to the investments of the Investors [from the other Sovereign]": cited in *SGS Société Générale de Surveillance SA v. Islamic Republic of Pakistan*, ICSID Case No. ARB/01/13 (Decision on Jurisdiction) (2004) at para. 163.

170. *Ibid.*, cf. *SGS Société Générale de Surveillance SA v. Republic of the Philippines*, ICSID Case No. ARB/02/6 (Decision on Objections to Jurisdiction) (2003) para. 115.

171. For a general survey of the positions of various jurisdictions on this point, see G. BERMANN, "Recognition and Enforcement of Foreign Arbitral Awards", fn. 168 above, para. 4.1.1 and fn. 97.

172. An essential desideratum of law is that it must be capable of providing effective guidance: see pp. 32-33.

recent BITs have been drafted with greater specificity.[173] More will be said on this later.[174]

The problem of lack of legal precision also brings with it the concomitant danger that the end-users of international arbitration will operate under the misapprehension that they are entering an ordered space when in fact the terrain is uneven and unregulated. An area of particular concern in this regard is that of professional ethics.[175] International organizations have not gone much further in this area than the current provisions in the Model Law relating to a general requirement to treat parties equally,[176] and for an arbitrator to disclose grounds which might "give rise to justifiable doubts as to his impartiality or independence",[177] and a broad reference to "public policy" which has been clarified in several states' national arbitration statutes to encompass principles of natural justice.[178] The generality and vagueness of the language in existing international instruments provides scant guidance in terms of the standards of professional ethics applicable to arbitrators and counsel in international arbitration and, perhaps more dangerously, they obscure what Prof. Catherine Rogers has described as the "many unresolved and largely unacknowledged ethical quandaries [which] lurk below the surface".[179] These include the abovementioned tensions across jurisdictions and legal traditions on the rules relating to the propriety of witness preparation, as well as pre-appointment interviews and other ex parte communication with party-appointed arbitrator candidates – matters which are likely to arise for a closer look by parties and counsel only when difficulties really present themselves. The existence of these potential pitfalls beneath the veneer of regulation calls into question whether the rules and principles currently in place are too vague to properly guide conduct, and as such cannot be said to satisfy the requirements of the rule of law.

173. Kathryn GORDON and Joachim POHL, "Investment Treaties over Time – Treaty Practice and Interpretation in a Changing World", OECD Working Papers on International Investment 2015/02, available at <http://www.oecd.org/investment/investment-policy/WP-2015-02.pdf> (last accessed 15 May 2018) at p. 25.

174. See pp. 146-147 below.

175. See p. 141 above.

176. Model Law, Art. 18 provides: "The parties shall be treated with equality and each party shall be given a full opportunity of presenting his case."

177. Model Law, Art. 12(1) provides:

> "When a person is approached in connection with his possible appointment as an arbitrator, he shall disclose any circumstances likely to give rise to justifiable doubts as to his impartiality or independence. An arbitrator, from the time of his appointment and throughout the arbitral proceedings, shall without delay disclose any such circumstances to the parties unless they have already been informed of them by him."

178. Australia's International Arbitration Act 1974, Sect. 8(7A) provides that "To avoid doubt ... enforcement of a foreign award would be contrary to public policy if ... (b) a breach of the rules of natural justice occurred in connection with the making of the award."; also see International Arbitration Act (Singapore), Sect. 24(*b*) and the UK Arbitration Act, Sect. 68(2) for similar provisions.

179. Catherine A. ROGERS, *Ethics in International Arbitration* (Oxford University Press 2014), Abstract.

V. THE FUTURE OF LAWMAKING BY PUBLIC BODIES

In order to address some of the issues that have been outlined, Prof. Schill has rightly noted that what is needed is the development of a "constitutional legal mindset in thinking about the functioning and legitimacy of international arbitration".[180] If arbitration is to continue to be the "primary justice system for the global economy",[181] users must share the view – which arbitration has long held of itself – that it *is* a critical enabler of the rule of law. In this regard, there is no need to fear or even resent the influence of public actors. The challenge, instead, is to consider how best to promote the legitimacy of their lawmaking efforts in the light of the foundational precepts of international arbitration. This will take time, but to start with, these are some specific ways in which each of the legitimacy challenges identified in this paper might be addressed.

The first problem of sovereignty is naturally a difficult one to grapple with, but one meaningful way to improve the quality and diversity of participation in the creation of arbitration norms is to invest in capacity building efforts, especially for developing countries where sentiments of a lack of real consensus and participation are likely to be most acutely felt. The aim of this is to enable a real conversation and exchange of ideas which enriches the global dialogue. States which are smaller and less developed will thereby be given a real opportunity to participate in the process of lawmaking. And, on the other hand, States which have historically played a prominent role in the process will not only gain the opportunity to reconsider and adjust their perspectives based on the input from these newer voices, but also have the chance to win over states which fall outside the mainstream in order to forge a true consensus. To be fair, the number of voices has increased significantly in the last fifteen years, and this trend will hopefully continue apace as commendable initiatives such as the ICCA Judiciary Committee's "New York Convention Roadshow",[182] and the Singapore International Arbitration Academy's programme on investment arbitration continue to run.[183] Over time, this will improve the diversity of the arbitration community and equip more states with the tools necessary for them to participate meaningfully in the lawmaking process.

The second problem of accountability is particularly difficult in the arbitration context, because there is no linear or hierarchical reporting relationship. This does not,

180. S. SCHILL, "Developing a Framework for the Legitimacy of International Arbitration", fn. 3 above, p. 826.

181. Catherine A. ROGERS, "The Vocation of the International Arbitrator", 20 American University International Law Review (2005) p. 957.

182. The Roadshow is a series of judicial colloquia and workshops on the critical role of national court judges in the application of the New York Convention, and in 2017 alone, ran successful judicial dialogue events in Ecuador, Brazil, and Egypt: see ICCA, "New York Convention Roadshow", available at <http://www.arbitration-icca.org/NY_Convention_Roadshow.html> (last accessed 15 May 2018).

183. The Singapore International Arbitration Academy was launched in 2012 by the Centre for International Law at the National University of Singapore, and it has organized programmes on investment treaty arbitration targeted at government officials, private practitioners and academics from the Asia-Pacific region: see Centre for International Law, "Singapore International Arbitration Academy", available at <https://cil.nus.edu.sg/research/international-dispute-resolution/topics/singapore-international-arbitration-academy> (last accessed 15 May 2018).

however, mean that the concept of accountability does not exist in the arbitration context. Instead of a vertical relationship between supervisor and supervisee, accountability in the arbitration context emerges out of a complex system of interlocking feedback loops as illustrated in Prof. Schultz's model.[184] For example, arbitrators who misbehave are accountable to arbitral institutions (among others) who might sanction them for misconduct or refuse to admit them to their panels, while arbitral institutions are accountable to arbitration users in the way that every commercial provider is accountable to her customers, who can make their displeasure known by refusing to engage their services. Public actors are, in turn, accountable to users of arbitration, who might refuse to seat their arbitrations in the jurisdiction, and also to their fellow state actors in the global community through a system of honest "peer review".

The *Yukos* cases are a powerful example of this paradigm of peer review at work. The Amsterdam Court of Appeal remarked that the Russian judgment in Rosneft's favour was "the result of a judicial process that must be qualified as partial and dependent".[185] In like manner, the English Court of Appeal commented that the Russian setting-aside decision "offended against basic principles of honesty [and] natural justice".[186] In so doing, they effectively held the Russian courts accountable on behalf of the international community. To be fair, the *Yukos* decision is perhaps the exception that proves the rule, and in the vast majority of cases the principle of judicial comity will prevent courts from being openly critical about the decisions of other courts; but at least it does offer a failsafe against particularly egregious breaches. In the absence of any vertical supranational judicial structure, the only bodies which evaluate the decisions of domestic courts are other domestic courts which should not, in the appropriate case, shy away from doing what they think to be right. In this regard, one should also note the proposal for the establishment of a permanent international investment court, potentially with its own appellate structure. It is not yet clear if the international consensus necessary for such an initiative can be found, but if such a court is set up, it will rapidly and dramatically transform the landscape of investment arbitration by providing for a system of direct accountability through vertical review and central oversight.[187]

The third problem of overreach generally results from the failure of public actors to respect or abide by the appropriate balance between party autonomy and the domestic interests of the state. In one sense, there is little to be done if public actors overreach – states have the sovereign right to decide how they wish to govern their affairs, and can even choose not to adopt or accede to treaties such as the New York Convention.

184. T. SCHULTZ, "Legitimacy Pragmatism and Political Systems in International Arbitration Lawmaking", this volume, pp. 25-54.

185. *Yukos (Netherlands)*, para. 3.10.

186. *Yukos (UK)*, para. 20.

187. See European Commission, "Investment in TTIP and beyond – the path for reform: Enhancing the right to regulate and moving from current *ad hoc* arbitration towards an Investment Court" (5 May 2015), available at <http://trade.ec.europa.eu/doclib/docs/2015/may/tradoc_153408.PDF> (last accessed 15 May 2018); UK Law Societies' Joint Brussels Office, "The Multilateral Investment Court: a plausible attempt at reform, or cosmetic changes only?" (21 September 2017), available at <http://www.lawsocieties.eu/news/the-multilateral-investment-court-a-plausible-attempt-at-reform-or-cosmetic-changes-only/5062902.fullarticle> (last accessed 15 May 2018).

However, there are two potential countervailing forces which might address this. At the "macro" level, overreach will naturally be corrected by the market when users choose not to arbitrate in such jurisdiction. Through education, discourse and an appreciation of one's enlightened self-interest, outlier states can be encouraged to fall in line, as has happened in major jurisdictions such as China and India,[188] which today no longer view arbitration with the same level of distrust and suspicion as they once did.[189] At the "micro" level, arbitrators and counsel must have the courage of their convictions to adhere to established legal principles in the face of plain instances of overreach by public actors in particular cases. A good illustration of this would be the decision of the arbitral tribunal in *Salini* to continue with the arbitral proceedings despite the injunctions issued by the Ethiopian courts. But of course, this is something which applies only in extreme cases. Ultimately, the goal is to build a constellation of effective and efficient arbitral seats which are steeped in the core precepts of arbitration and can act as the leading lights of the industry in a more or less consistent way. To extend an analogy I used in a 2015 speech,[190] like the spokes of a wheel, seat courts need not be perfectly aligned, but they must all take reference from the hub and none of them can protrude or extend much beyond their remit if the wheel is to run true.

This leads to the fourth problem of fragmentation and inconsistency. Again, this problem will be a challenging one to resolve, considering that the divisions on issues such as the delocalization debate are very deep. But the tools we can use to address some of these divisions are already on hand, in the form of international organizations, arbitral institutions, and professional bodies that can provide platforms for serious discussions on core issues of concern such as the effect of decisions of seat courts and the issue of ethics. There are also other areas in which public actors – especially international organizations – may be able to play a prominent role in the future. One such area is the development of a substantive body of international commercial law. The favourable response to UNIDROIT's Principles of International Commercial Contracts[191] suggests that there may be reasonable prospects for the eventual establishment and widespread acceptance of a substantive legal framework that regulates this area. Needless to say however, there will be considerable hurdles, and a fuller discussion of this subject will doubtless have to be the subject of a separate paper.

Finally, on the last problem of the lack of legal precision, I stress that in order for something to have the quality of law, it must be capable of giving precise guidance to those who have to abide by its strictures. Investment treaty law as created by states appears to be headed in the right direction, considering the trend that has been observed of states parties drafting investment treaties with greater specificity and interpretive

188. India's legislative changes following *Venture Global* are described at Part III(*2*)(*b*) above, while the Supreme Court of China has in recent years published "judicial instructions" that in effect conform a pro-arbitration stance towards the enforceability of arbitral awards: see Keith BRANDT and Michael KAN, "China" in *The International Arbitration Review Edition* 7, available at <http://www.lawsocieties.eu/news/the-multilateral-investment-court-a-plausible-attempt-at-reform-or-cosmetic-changes-only/5062902.fullarticle> (last accessed 15 May 2018).

189. This may have been due to these states' perceptions of arbitration as a concept developed and dominated by Western states and thinkers.

190. S. MENON, CIArb Patron's Address, fn. 162 above, paras. 71, 72 and 76.

191. See para. 15 above.

guidance on how certain key concepts such as "fair and equitable treatment" should be interpreted.[192] In the field of international commercial arbitration, one area that is in particularly urgent need for reform is professional ethics. The lack of clear standards on arbitrator and counsel conduct threatens real and serious harms, and it is troubling that greater progress has not been achieved to date. Much has been written about the need for a clear code of ethics to be developed to provide guidance, at least, on what cannot be done.[193] This is a difficult undertaking, because it concerns an area in which there exists a multiplicity of views, all of which are deeply and sincerely held. Caution must therefore be exercised. While consensus is valuable, it is not to be achieved at all costs. There is a real danger that a search for common ground will result in the adoption of the lowest common denominator whenever a serious divergence of views exists, but such an outcome will hardly inspire confidence in the fairness of arbitration.

It cannot be emphasized enough that the scale of the challenges that lie ahead should not be underestimated, and the points made in this section are offered as nothing more than the first broad strokes on the canvas to begin the discussion. What is needed moving forward is for there to be a concerted effort by the various stakeholders in the arbitration community – practitioners, academics, judges, lawmakers – to colour within the lines by developing a set of core principles – a charter, if you will – to articulate the proper relationship between public actors and international arbitration. The development of a coherent set of principles will be the labour of many hands, and I have no illusions that this will be achieved soon, but I suggest that the following four criteria of legitimacy – "4 Ps" – may be used as a starting point for the development of these principles:

First, the laws established by public actors must be *precise*. A system cannot be stable if its laws are excessively general and incapable of providing effective guidance.

Second, the reach of these laws must be *proportionate* to the legitimate interests of the public actor creating them. The process of balancing competing interests is one which domestic legislatures are already used to doing (the perennial debate between development and conservation, for instance, is a good example), while domestic courts should remain cognizant of the interests of the wider global community when adjudicating.

Thirdly, there must be adequate *participation* in the lawmaking process. This is particularly important for international organizations, for there must be adequate representation and participation in the lawmaking process in order for the product to be considered legitimate. As suggested above, capacity building initiatives can play a critical role in this area.

Last, it must uphold the value of *personal autonomy*. At its core, arbitration is founded on personal freedom, which entails that persons should be free to contract to resolve their disputes in a manner of their choosing. As a corollary of this, several cognate principles may be derived, including: (i) freedom of contract and party consent – no

192. K. GORDON and J. POHL, "Investment Treaties over Time", fn. 173 above, p. 25.

193. See, generally, C. ROGERS, *Ethics in International Arbitration*, fn. 179 above; S. MENON, "Adjudicator, Advocate, or Something In Between?", fn. 164 above; Doak BISHOP and Margrete STEVENS, "The Compelling Need for a Code of Ethics in International Arbitration: Transparency, Integrity and Legitimacy" in *Arbitration Advocacy in Changing Times*, ICCA Congress Series no. 15 (Kluwer 2011) pp. 391-407.

person may be compelled to arbitrate if he/she has not agreed to do so; (ii) party autonomy in the selection of the manner and form of arbitration; and (iii) process autonomy – in the sense that arbitrations should be minimally regulated.

VI. CONCLUSION

The successes that have been achieved in the field of international arbitration to date would be unimaginable if not for the involvement of public actors in arbitration lawmaking. It was states who, through an enormous collective effort of will, designed the basic programme of international arbitration that was embodied in the New York Convention. It was again states who, through the auspices of UNCITRAL, wrote the basic doctrinal syllabus of international arbitration when they agreed on the Model Law. And today, it continues to be domestic legislatures and courts that toil away at the coal face by passing laws to ensure conformity with basic precepts of international arbitration and do the basic work of supporting, recognizing, and enforcing arbitral awards. As long as we live in this world of nation-states, the answer to the question of whether public actors do and should have a role to play in international arbitration is plain: yes, of course they must. Without the cooperation and active participation of public actors, the lex arbitri would be in a state of flux, and awards cannot effectively be enforced.

Having accepted this, the concern lies in identifying the potential challenges to the legitimacy of such a lawmaking power. The problem of legitimacy is, at its core, the call to justify the exercise of power. This call should be met, first and foremost, by a proper appreciation for arbitration's role as a pillar of the international rule of law and as a mechanism for global governance. Viewed in this light, the challenge is for public actors, as they make law in international arbitration, to broaden their legislative horizons to consider not only the interests of the particular constituencies which they serve, but the global community of which they are part and whose interests they must protect. In this globalized age, nobody can stand alone in a state of regulatory autarky. It was in recognition of this that the Standing International Forum of Commercial Courts was set up last May to enhance judicial dispute resolution through the sharing of best practices.[194]

Arbitration is well into its golden age and yet – *Et in Arcadia Ego*.[195] Already there are some signs of disenchantment with its promises, and signals of a cautious retreat from its use as a dispute resolution mechanism. Left unchecked, these problems could well prove to be the thin end of the wedge that will grow in number and intensity, threatening the future of the industry. Perhaps we are at arbitration's inflexion point. If care is not taken, disquiet might give way to active retreat and then to flight; and *Achmea* might in

194. See Supreme Court of Singapore, Media release: "Standing International Forum of Commercial Courts", available at <https://www.supremecourt.gov.sg/docs/default-source/default-document-library/standing-international-forum-of-commercial-courtsae763033f22f6eceb9b0ff0000fcc945.pdf> (last accessed 15 May 2018).

195. S. MENON, "International Arbitration: The Coming of a New Age for Asia (and Elsewhere)", fn. 1 above, paras. 1-2.

time come to be seen as arbitration's reverse *Scott v. Avery* moment.[196] It is therefore vital that the challenge of legitimacy is taken seriously, and steps are taken to address these problems in order that the future of arbitration might be secured for generations to come.

196. *Alexander Scott v. George Avery* (1856) 5 HL Cas 811, in which the UK House of Lords first held that an arbitration agreement was not contrary to public policy, and observed that such agreements could yield "great advantage" (at 853 *per* Lord Campbell). This is widely seen as a landmark in the history of arbitration for it marked a shift in judicial attitude, and paved the way for its widespread adoption and use.

Luncheon Panel:

Personal Reflections of Leading Arbitrators

Personal Reflections from Leading Arbitrators: Transcript of Luncheon Panelists' Remarks*

TABLE OF CONTENTS

I. INTRODUCTION – REMARKS BY CAROLYN B. LAMM[1]

Today's program is an innovative program for ICCA, and I am delighted to be here to host with our fabulous arbitrators. For the past two decades, maybe more, we certainly have witnessed a transformation in business, in law, in life and in dispute resolution as a result of globalization and technology. This entire week we are examining the impact of that evolution and the adaptation of our international arbitral systems. Despite the dramatic changes we have witnessed, the one constant that all can agree on, really, is that parties and counsel very much want impartial, independent, objective arbitrators. It is the arbitrators who are truly the guardians of our system of international arbitration.

Despite much change, it is the arbitrators who still are required to assure that parties have due process, to assure that their cases are understood and fairly decided, and to apply the rule of law carefully with judgment in a fair and balanced way. And that is of fundamental importance no matter what the changes.

Today, another thing that is certain is that we have four of our best arbitrators here to talk with us about their approaches and observations reflecting on how they became who they are as arbitrators, what their decision-making processes are, where they see arbitration now, and where it is going on the basis of their experiences. We really hope you enjoy each of their presentations.

The format is that each of them will discuss all of the questions for a ten-minute segment, and at the end of their remarks we will consider your questions, if you have any. We will begin first with Julian Lew. Then we will proceed in alphabetical order to Loretta Malintoppi, Brigitte Stern, and Claus von Wobeser. Each will do a very interesting presentation, so enjoy it.

---

* The General Editors would like to thank Rapporteurs Mallory Silberman, Partner, Arnold & Porter LLP, and Laura Sinisterra, Associate and member of the International Dispute Resolution Group, Debevoise & Plimpton LLC, for preparing the transcript of the Personal Reflections from Leading Arbitrators Luncheon Panel.

1. Partner, White & Case LLP; Co-Chair, Distinguished Faculty Chair, White & Case International Arbitration LL.M. and Adjunct Faculty, International Arbitration Institute, University of Miami School of Law; ICCA Governing Board Member.

II. REMARKS BY JULIAN LEW QC[2]

Good afternoon, ladies and gentlemen. This is a novel setting. The organizers have found something new. Hopefully it will work. I'm going to deal briefly with three issues: (1) how I became involved with international arbitration; (2) what I see as the main changes that have taken place in recent years; and (3) where I think that things will go in the future.

I got involved in arbitration in a strange way. I was registering for a PhD at the Université Catholique de Louvain in Belgium. My main interest was private international law. I went to see the professor who was to supervise my research. He asked me what subject I was interested in researching. I said I didn't know. After a moment of reflection, he suggested "*le choix de la loi applicable en matière d'arbitrage commercial international*" – the choice of applicable law in international commercial arbitration. I asked, "What is '*arbitrage*'?" He told me to look it up. That was in 1970. The rest is history.

In 1974, I went to India to attend my first ICCA Conference in New Delhi. I don't know if many people here were at that conference. I came into a session room, and I sat down next to two individuals. Some of them you may remember – Howard Holtzmann, an American, and Professor Sergei Lebedev from the Soviet Union. These two men were experts and had a great influence in international arbitration; they were greatly influential in developing the US-Soviet agreement to accept Stockholm as a neutral arbitration venue. At the podium in that session was Professor Pieter Sanders, introducing the draft UNCITRAL Arbitration Rules. Professor Sanders was one of the luminaries of international arbitration.

From there, I developed my interest and practice on the basis of my academic background. I then started to practice in the area of international arbitration, going into practice – first as counsel, and later as an arbitrator.

Arbitration was very different then. I think it was recognized as a dispute resolution system to resolve difficult international commercial disputes. Today it is also used as a commercial tactic in the context of negotiating or achieving a better settlement or result than otherwise.

There was one fundamental at that stage in addition to party autonomy: the New York Convention. At the time, there weren't that many countries that had ratified the Convention; about forty-five. Now, there are over 150. At that stage, even my own country, the United Kingdom, had not ratified the New York Convention; it did so in 1975. With the changing political world then, there was a need for neutral arbitration rules. It was in that background that the UNCITRAL Arbitration Rules were developed. Controversial at the time, they were focused specifically on *ad hoc* arbitration. The UNCITRAL Rules, now in an updated edition, have proved their merits and are now widely used. At that time, the mid-1970s, there was only one major international

---

2. Full-time Arbitrator at Twenty Essex; Professor and Head of the School of International Arbitration, Centre for Commercial Law Studies, at Queen Mary University of London;. involved with international arbitration for more than forty years as an academic, counsel and arbitrator; before 2005, partner and, for some years, the head of the international arbitration practice group of (what is now) Herbert Smith Freehills LLP.

arbitration institution – the ICC – which only had one office, in Paris, although they did international work.

What has happened since then? Over the last forty-plus years, a plethora of arbitration institutions have started offering arbitration services. There are now several thousand international arbitrations every year, either administered by the various arbitration institutions or *ad hoc* arbitrations. Also, and perhaps as a result of these developments, many major law firms have developed specialized international arbitration departments. In the past decade or so, we have seen more and more arbitrations being undertaken in other regions around the world, and in particular in the Asian region.

New seats have also been accepted. I remember when arbitrations were in Switzerland and in France in the 1970s. In London, we didn't have a great deal of international arbitration (other than the specialist areas of shipping, insurance, and commodities). It was only after the restructuring of the LCIA (London Court of International Arbitration) and the 1996 Arbitration Act that arbitrations began to come to England as a favored jurisdiction.

In the 1980s, after the success of the UNCITRAL Arbitration Rules, UNCITRAL developed its Model Law on International Commercial Arbitration. This too has had a remarkable acceptance around the world. Now adopted in over sixty jurisdictions, it has majorly affected the regulation and practice of international arbitration. The adoption of the Model Law in many Asian jurisdictions may well be one of the reasons why there has been an increase in arbitration in the Asian region. It should be noted that the so-called major arbitration jurisdictions, i.e., the United Kingdom, France, Sweden, Switzerland, and the United States, have not adopted the Model Law.

Finally, I must, and you would expect me to, mention that in the early 1980s, we created the School of International Arbitration at Queen Mary University of London. So we have been going now for thirty-three years. At the time, many argued that arbitration was not a subject for academic study. It was a matter of procedure to be governed by the law of the venue of the arbitration; whose private international law rules should apply to any conflict of law issues. Well, we proved that wrong. There are now arbitration institutions teaching arbitration all over the world, including in Switzerland, in France, in Sweden, in the United States, and in China. Arbitration is now seen as sufficient of a specialty to have dedicated teaching at undergraduate and postgraduate levels.

I turn now to the last topic: the future for international arbitration. One of the issues is technology. I'm not going to address that; others will do so. However, the progress of transcripts, video links with parties, examination of witnesses and experts in different places, has made enormous changes to the acceptability and efficiency of the arbitration process. In principle, computerization has made research and the recording of information easier and more efficient; on the other hand, parties' submissions have become ever more complicated and lengthy.

I do think we run a risk of (and there was some discussion of this in the last panel before lunch), of an increasing (backward-looking) interference in arbitration from outside bodies – courts, institutions, governments, NGOs, and others, wanting to know what's going on in the arbitration process, and to control the organization and structure of arbitration. This would be a throwback to thirty-forty years ago. Judges and national jurisdictions sometimes still consider they should manage what, if anything, the parties should refer to arbitration, and to review the decisions arbitrators reach. I hope the arbitration institutions in particular will work to resist these interferences.

Other issues being experienced in practice, are the increase in aggression in international arbitration – in the way that cases are fought, the amount of paper that is presented, the increasing length of time involved, the level of fees which are being incurred. Who can control these – the parties. Will they do so?

Exactly where arbitration will go, time alone will tell. I believe that arbitration will continue to prosper. The principal reason why it will prosper is because of party autonomy; the parties who wish to refer their disputes to arbitration and to resolve matters privately and without recourse to national courts. It is for the lawyers, the parties and arbitrators to make the system work.

It is a question that remains on all these issues and reminds us that the only reason arbitration exists, certainly commercial arbitration, is due to party autonomy.

III. REMARKS BY LORETTA MALINTOPPI[3]

When I started out in international arbitration in Europe in the late 1980s, the world of international law and international arbitration was a very different place. I'm Italian. I'm from Rome, and Rome was really not an option to practice arbitration. I remember when I went to interview for the first time in a law firm in Rome, I had two questions from the senior partner. The first was, "Are you engaged to be married?" and the second was, "This is not a profession for women, is it?" Now, needless to say, I did not go to work with that law firm and I did not go to work in Rome. As I said, Rome was not an option. The capitals of Europe that really were leading in international arbitration and international law were Paris, London, and Geneva. And so, I went to Paris.

But even at the time, there were no dedicated international arbitration teams, and even fewer public international law teams. I saw that Jeremy Carver is here today. He was one of the few people practicing State-to-State litigation and arbitration in those days, because otherwise it was a handful of practitioners, mainly senior silks or professors of international law – counsel who were frequently former legal advisors of the UK Foreign Office.

There were no women at all, I don't think. Not even Brigitte Stern, at that time. It was a really selective club, and things have changed since then. You know, investment arbitration hardly existed at all. But I was lucky enough to start in the profession in the heyday of international arbitration and when State-to-State disputes were on the rise, with the law firm Frere Cholmeley (which later became Eversheds), which was the leading firm in public international Law. The Permanent Court of Arbitration (PCA) was starting to really appear on the scene with a number of big cases between States, and the International Court of Justice's (ICJ's) docket was busier and busier.

But has arbitration today taken the path that I would have predicted? Well, there are a few things that, of course, I could have seen even then. For instance, the potential for growth in the international arbitration field after the adoption of the UNCITRAL Model

3. Independent arbitrator with 39 Essex Chambers, based in Singapore; ICCA Governing Board Member.

Law in 1985 and the PCA Optional Rules for Arbitrating Disputes between Two States (1992) and between Two Parties of Which Only One Is a State (1993). But I do not think anybody could have seriously predicted the incredible growth of international arbitration and its impact on the business community or the proliferation of international courts and tribunals that fundamentally changed the landscape of international adjudication.

Some of what has happened perhaps was predictable, but certain developments, not quite as much. A few come to mind. The first, particularly for me, having started out as a public international law specialist, is the mingling of private lawyers — corporate, commercial lawyers – and public international law lawyers in the field of investment arbitration. The establishment of large, dedicated public international law and international arbitration teams was perhaps not entirely predictable.

And then there is the fact that we have raised the bar of our work and our specialties higher and higher. We are now international lawyers living all over the world, based everywhere and nowhere, leading, as Toby Landau says, disjointed lives. We wear so many different hats – scholar, practitioner, (private) adjudicator, and even lawmakers in investment arbitration, as Lucy Reed mentioned earlier today. And there has also been a growing harmonization of procedural practices through the construction of the soft, moral edifices of codes of conduct, guidelines, and best practices that we have built for ourselves.

I also can mention a collegial group of women and a growing number of women practitioners and leading figures in the world of international law and arbitration. But I think that gender diversity still needs some fixing. Similarly, there is much more that can be done to increase racial, cultural and geographic diversity, all of which are extremely important. We all have to work collectively towards doing a better job at that.

Another thing that strikes me is the sudden media attention and the creation of all these specialized arbitration reviews and journals. Incidentally, recently, arbitration media has ventured a far-fetched comparison between Hollywood and international arbitration in connection with the *#MeToo* scandal. Now, aside from the fact that there is nothing further removed from the glitz and glamour of Hollywood than the solitary job of an arbitrator, I think that such a comparison is not only misguided – it is also potentially quite dangerous. Equating arbitrators and arbitration practitioners to movie stars helps feed the image of a wealthy and rarefied environment that is detached from the realities of international business and provides further ammunition to the detractors of the system.

Another point that I cannot fail to mention is arbitrator challenges, which I think, at least looking at the most recent SIAC [Singapore International Arbitration Centre] statistic, seems to be at a phase of decline at the moment. But it has certainly led a number of us practicing mainly as arbitrators to leave international law firms and set up our own practices or join barristers' chambers, as I did.

I also have witnessed a growing horizontal dialogue between international courts and tribunals, from which everybody is benefiting, and a change in the role of arbitral institutions. Arbitral institutions today are also educational centers. They pay more attention to the users. They are more transparent. They publish better statistics. But will those institutions take a step forward and accept the proposal that was made by the SIAC to consolidate related arbitral proceedings across different institutions and subject to different arbitration rules? Now, I do not know the answer to that, but the ICC Court's President, Alexis Mourre, does not appear to agree with the proposal. So, we do not know yet how far this initiative will go. But to me, it is witness of the fact that institutions are working together more and they are collaborating more, or *trying* to collaborate more, in a world that is increasingly competitive.

What do I see for the future? I think that Artificial Intelligence and Big Data will play a role in how we conduct arbitral proceedings. That said, I suspect we are not about to see automated arbitrators or to witness hot-tubbing of robots. But programs can render proceedings much more efficient and reduce arbitrators' and counsels' time, ultimately diminishing costs. Maxwell Chambers in Singapore is gearing up to become the first smart, fully automated hearing center in the world. They have an app that one can download to reserve hearing facilities and program secretaries and so on. And they even have a little robot that looks like R2-D2 and is aptly named Max who delivers food and files to the hearing rooms.

Will arbitration be supplanted by permanent courts? That is clearly a danger when it comes to investment arbitration, but perhaps not quite yet. A related question is whether the appointment process will be gradually taken off the hands of the disputing parties. Whether it is by institutions or a permanent sitting court, it looks like parties will have less control over the constitution of tribunals.

Another interesting development is the creation of specialized courts in a number of jurisdictions: Singapore, Paris, Amsterdam and Brussels. Foreign judges sit on the Singapore International Commercial Court, and the same happens in Hong Kong. Now in Paris, a national court will be hearing complex cross-border disputes in English, which is in itself an amazing feat, and applying foreign laws. Imagine how modern the French have become! But what will be the impact of that on international arbitration? Will national jurisdictions become a threat, a competitor to international arbitration? We shall see.

I cannot help but to say something about the criticism of the investor-State system, and I will not join that particular chorus. I think the reality is actually quite different. I will just mention the fact that last month the US Trade Representative, Robert Lighthizer, gave public testimony before the House Committee on Ways and Means of the United States. He said, very openly, that the United States is thinking about opting out of investor-State arbitration in NAFTA. But he also added that American investors making investments abroad would still have the potential for their disputes with Canada or Mexico to be adjudicated under Chapter 20 of NAFTA. Now, of course, Chapter 20 concerns State-to-State disputes. Therefore, this could be an interesting step backwards to the past practice of espousal of claims and diplomatic protection. It is like "Back to the Future". But at the same time, we are hearing that lawyers of the US President are starting a consultation process against Panama under the US-Panama BIT in a dispute regarding his hotel in Panama. So, we are getting mixed signals. We are not quite sure what the United States is prepared to do for the time being.

A safe prediction for the future is that, with the growing number of multilateral international conventions addressing matters relating to the environment, health, science, and technology, the future will see a growth of new topics for international dispute resolution.

I am thinking in particular of issues which may encompass trans-border phenomena, such as climate change and other environmental issues, natural resource exploitation, the Internet, privacy and data encryption, cybersecurity and crime, maritime border issues (including deep sea-bed mining and extensions of the continental shelf beyond 200 nm), access to fresh water and international watercourse law. It is to be expected that disputes will arise from these issues in the future that will need to be settled by international courts and tribunals.

I shall close on a positive note. I do not see the future of arbitration as being bleak – the contrary actually. As long as there are conflicts, and God knows that there is no lack of them in today's world, there will be a need for the peaceful resolution of those conflicts. The methods and mechanics may change, but as Stephen Hawking once said: "Intelligence is the ability to adjust to change."

IV. REMARKS BY BRIGITTE STERN[4]

As you might have seen on the program, we were asked to speak about the past, the present, and the future of our careers, and of arbitration itself. This immediately caused me to see the famous painting by Paul Gauguin, which appeared before my eyes: *D'où venons-nous ? Que sommes-nous ? Où allons-nous ?* "Where do we come from? Who are we? Where are we going?" These are the three questions that I will try to answer now, during this lunch.

Where do I come from? Well, clearly from the university where I have been teaching in France for many years, as well as at the Graduate Institute in Geneva, where I have been a professor for more than ten years. In fact, my last teaching assignment was at MIDS, whose director is Gabrielle Kaufmann-Kohler, and it's a great pleasure to see that she will soon be leading ICCA. My second career, if I may say so, as an international arbitrator, only started in the year 2000. So, less than twenty years ago; believe it or not, I'm a sort of young arbitrator.

If you were to ask me if I have any regrets, I would say that what I regret is that my career as an arbitrator did not start earlier, because I think it's fascinating. As a matter of fact, France put me on the ICSID [International Centre for settlement of Investment Disputes] list far back in 1990. Wow. But, for ten years, I did not receive any nominations. So, for those of you who want to become international arbitrators, just be patient! In those medieval times, there was not as much of a proactive approach as there is now – like how ICSID, for example, tries to promote diversification, and bring new faces to the forefront. So, for ten years, I was just an obscure French professor who happened to be on a confidential international list of potential arbitrators.

Then, in 2000, there was a change of century, and two events happened. First, I was elected by the General Assembly as a member of the United Nations Administrative Tribunal, to resolve employment disputes for UN employees. This triggered my career as an arbitrator, because I was transformed – like Cinderella – from a mere French professor into a person with some international visibility. The second event happened

4. International arbitrator; Professor Emeritus, University of Paris - I Panthéon-Sorbonne; Member and Vice-President of the United Nations Administrative Tribunal (2000-2009).

the same year, probably as a result; I don't know. One of my colleagues nominated me in an ICSID arbitration, and then I had another nomination by an investor and the State accepted me as a sole arbitrator. This was my second arbitration. I was very scared because I had no experience at all, but both cases settled, so all was fine.

After that, the wheels started to turn easily by themselves, and I had nomination after nomination. Now I'm sitting amongst you – well standing amongst you – with quite a few cases waiting on my desk in Paris.

Who are we? Well, I think that the arbitration community present here is an extremely rich and lively community. I always immensely enjoy working with my co-arbitrators, almost all are really sharp lawyers. But what I really enjoy – admire – is those who are capable of listening and truly understanding a point of view which is different from their own. When all three members have this approach, it's very challenging to discuss the cases and to come with the best result. Of course, there are some impossible arbitrators. I won't give any names – you probably all have your list: people with whom it's barely possible to enter into a dialogue. But this is a very, very small minority.

So, as I said, it's a rich community of arbitrators who come from different backgrounds. They come from civil law. They come from common law. They come from commercial law. They come from international law. Some are or were judges, professors, diplomats, or counsel. I think it's a very interesting community.

As an academic, I have a tendency to try always to set the theoretical framework. I know that some of my co-arbitrators want to go directly to the solution, but I think that I prefer to set the scenery. I think that it gives more predictability to the rule of law. This might explain why I have written, as you all (or at least some of you) probably know, some dissents: because I'm very eager to have a common approach to the fundamental principles. I know that there are two schools of thought on this. Some consider that they will always go with the majority, as a democratic gesture; others are prepared to issue dissenting opinions and sometimes do. I think that the first school of thought is respectable, but I personally could not always accept the majority position without a critical eye. So, when needed, I'm ready to dissent on a question of principle, but not on minor points.

Besides the usual work on cases and hearings, we have sometimes very frustrating experiences, and sometimes very exciting experiences. Among the frustrating experiences, I can mention the cancellation of a hearing when I arrived in Singapore after twenty-five hours of travelling, so that's a frustration, of course. Among the exciting experiences, one of the most interesting I can mention was a site visit to the Amazonian rainforest where all of the tribunal members had anti-mosquito outfits from head to feet, and where the lawyers were pleading in jeans and boots in the forest. This really helped us to understand what the surroundings were; it was very important, as the legal rules were dependent on whether we were in an industrial surrounding, in a residential surrounding, in an agriculture surrounding, or in a sensitive ecosystem.

Where are we going? That's the most difficult question. It has been some years now that everybody has been speaking of a crisis in international investment arbitration. In 2008 – that is, ten years ago – in a conference at Columbia University, I said that the so-called crisis of the international investment law and policy system is only a "*crise de croissance*", a teenager's crisis. In fact, today, I think that investment arbitration has not overcome what I thought was only a teenager's crisis, and that the crisis runs much deeper. There are, of course, some procedural problems which can very easily be solved. There are a few aspects of investment arbitration that, as you probably all know, have become a little bit out of control. I can mention document production, and I think that lawyers should control themselves; when we have 300 pages of document production requests, I'm not sure if that is efficient, and it takes up too much paper. This is starting to improve, but I would like for my grandchildren to still have some forests left. Nowadays, many arbitrators, myself included, will accept everything in USB drives. But of course, you know, we have the passwords, and it's sometimes a little difficult to deal with. The next step, I think, would be to rise to the level of cloud arbitration, and to get rid of the USB sticks.

But what is of greater concern are the attacks, coming from all parts, against investment arbitration. Attacks come from NGOs [non-governmental organizations], from States (first the developing States, and now the United States and the European Commission), from academics and even from arbitrators, and probably I have forgotten some. I think that the role of NGOs is crucial in the current attacks towards investor-State arbitration, because they see this as a result of the globalization against which they are fighting.

I will give you a really interesting example of the systematic criticism of investor-State arbitration by NGOs, which is totally disconnected from objective reality. I will read to you some abstracts of an article published by an NGO after the release of an arbitral award by a tribunal on which I was sitting. And I quote, "Regardless of the outcome, the arbitration has had a chilling effect on the development and the human rights to water. What we have now is a clear example of what is wrong with investor-State dispute settlement." Now, if I were to ask you who won, you would probably say that it was the investor. But that's wrong; it was the State. I wonder what the NGO would have written if the decision would have been different. What I would like to convey with this example is that, quite often, criticism against investment arbitration is not rooted in reality, but in rhetoric and ideology.

In spite of this, States have more or less adopted the same discourse, without sufficiently analyzing the objective situation.

Not to mention of course, the fierce fight against investor-State arbitration in intra-EU BITs, launched by the European Commission some years ago, and which culminated with the *Achmea* Judgment by the European Court on 6 March 2018. If you expect me to discuss the case, you will be disappointed, as I have to deal with the decision in a few cases.

In spite of this, some are optimistic, like Meg Kinnear. I don't know if she is here. Where is she? Well, hello if she is here. She said at the conference last month at the American Society of International Law: "Much of the discussion I read is peppered with dramatic language, such as backlash, crisis, or abandonment of the system, but I have trouble reconciling this narrative with what I see on the ground every day."

Some suggest solutions, among them the creation of a standing court for investment arbitration. I am not sure that it will solve all the problems, but let's see.

Some see no solution as there is a really deep-rooted crisis, but still have hope. After a crisis there is a major improvement of the law. Every cloud has a silver lining, so let's hope for a brilliant future and drink to arbitration.

V. REMARKS BY CLAUS VON WOBESER[5]

The first question that I will address is: what would you have done differently knowing what you know now? In general, I am sure that all members of the arbitration community are in favor of arbitration and I strongly believe that it is the most adequate mechanism of dispute resolution for international business.

In the past thirty-five–forty years, the arbitration community has been busy improving the system. Arbitration institutions have worked hard and have done a great job of adapting and improving their arbitral rules. Arbitration practitioners have participated actively in this process through discussions at conferences and congresses. UNCITRAL, for its part, has developed a successful Model Law, with eighty States having adopted legislation based on it. Further, the IBA [International Bar Association] instruments, such as the IBA Rules on the Taking of Evidence in International Arbitration and the Guidelines on Conflicts, have been very useful as soft law tools and are widely accepted today. Similarly, ICCA has done a fantastic job of promoting the 1958 New York Convention in many countries and educating judges all over the world in its application.

Having said that, what we have largely missed during the past forty years is dialogue with the users of arbitration. We, as the arbitration community, have not made sufficient efforts to talk to industry associations, chambers of commerce, and other users of arbitration as a dispute resolution mechanism. I believe that this lack of broader dialogue has been a failure and something I would have done differently, had I known what I know now, when I started my career. The legal community needs to be more engaged with the other stakeholders, especially the critics of arbitration.

The second question that I will try to answer is: what are the biggest challenges facing arbitration? In the past few years, we have received abundant criticism of investor-State arbitration. Today, bureaucrats from different governments, including, notably, the European Union, are trying to fix the perceived problems of investment arbitration and, in doing so, have come up with the idea of a permanent multinational investment court. As you know, for example, the EU-Canada Comprehensive Economic and Trade Agreement (CETA) already includes the new investment court system. I believe this system will fail. I do not think that a permanent court system will resolve the perceived problems of investor-State arbitration. Similarly, going back to diplomatic protection or to inter-State resolution of investment disputes is certainly not a desirable solution.

As to the challenges facing international commercial arbitration, the main concern today is the perception of excessive duration and cost. However, in my view, these concerns are not hugely significant in practice. When parties and companies are faced with arbitration, they are usually ready to incur the necessary costs and take the required time to win their cases. Parties want to win. Although in-house counsel often raise the issue of excessive cost and duration in conferences, when their companies are faced with a dispute, cost and duration are usually not a problem. Therefore, I think the excessive cost and duration of commercial arbitration is more of a perceived problem than a real problem.

Third, is arbitration taking the path that you would have predicted? In this regard, I would like to mention two developments that we did not predict. *First*, thirty-five years

5. Managing Partner and head of the Dispute Resolution practice of Von Wobeser y Sierra, S.C.

ago, we did not predict the volume of expansion of foreign trade and investment that the world has seen. Some twenty-two years ago, when NAFTA was negotiated, few would have imagined that the NAFTA region would become the world's most important trade bloc together with the European Union. Similarly, nobody would have thought that the European Union, which had nine member-States forty years ago, would enlarge to include twenty-eight members within a single market.

Another development that we did not foresee is the technological revolution and its impact on all aspects of life, including arbitration practice. Thirty-five years ago, we used typewriters, and everything was done by hand. There was no email or computers. Similarly, we had no DHL, no Federal Express. We transmitted documents through regular mail and, as you can imagine, the dynamics of the work were completely different. Technological advances and the digitalization of arbitral procedures can undoubtedly improve the system. Unfortunately, technology has not always been used to that end. In the old days, memorials used to be twenty-forty pages long and included a maximum of ten-twenty exhibits. In contrast, today, the use of computers and software has resulted in longer briefs that can easily include hundreds of exhibits. In practice, however, arbitral tribunals often request core bundles of exhibits, which usually have only around twenty documents. At the hearing, it is those twenty documents that are mostly used. Still, the record for the case may include thousands of documents and while it is possible that some of those additional thousands of exhibits will be useful in deciding the case, the reality is that, often, they are not. Therefore, in my view, practitioners should use technology to make the system more efficient, without abusing the new tools. For instance, I would advise against abusing the facility of copy-pasting between documents. Before, to copy-paste, we actually had to cut the pages and adapt them to the brief, so it was done far less frequently.

Finally, how will arbitration look in ten or twenty years to come? I am absolutely certain that arbitration is the best method to resolve international disputes – both in the commercial field and in the investor-State field. I believe that, ultimately, arbitration will prevail. In fact, I believe that in the next ten or twenty years, arbitration will multiply by perhaps 500 percent, as it has done in the past. If we compare the number of cases that we had thirty-five years ago with those of today, the numbers have increased by 1,000 percent. I believe this trend will continue. Free trade and free flow of investments will continue, as it is the only means to create wealth in a world that keeps growing. In that context, arbitration will continue to be the best method to resolve international disputes and, thus, arbitration will continue to prevail.

Arbitration Challenged Part I

Arbitration Challenged Part I

Reforming Substantive Obligations in Investment Treaties and Conditions of Access to Investment Arbitration

The Definition of "Investment": Recent Developments and Lingering Issues

Wenhua Shan[*] *and Lu Wang*[**]

TABLE OF CONTENTS

I. INTRODUCTION

The term "investment" plays a fundamental role in the entire international investment regime. On the one hand, the definition of "investment" determines the subject matter coverage of investment treaties. Only "covered" investments enjoy protections granted by investment treaties, such as non-discriminatory treatment, fair and equitable treatment and compensation for expropriation. On the other hand, the definition of "investment" determines a fundamental jurisdictional basis, namely the ratione materiae, for dispute resolution under the Convention on the Settlement of Investment Disputes between States and Nationals of Other States (the ICSID Convention) and/or other investment treaties.

Earlier investment treaties tend to use a broad open-ended definition of "investment",[1] which may help to attract foreign investments, but may also expose States to undesired obligations and risks, as demonstrated by arbitration practices. The ICSID Convention stipulates that "[t]he jurisdiction of the Centre shall extend to any legal dispute arising directly out of an *investment*",[2] without defining what constitute an "investment". While many arbitral tribunals have held that the concept of "investment"

---

* Ministry of Education Yangtze River Chair Professor of International Economic Law and Dean of Law School, Xi'an Jiaotong University; Vice President, Judicial Case Academy, Supreme People's Court, PR China.

** Lecturer, Faculty of Law, UNSW Sydney, Australia

1. See, e.g., Art. 8(1) of the Germany-Pakistan BIT (1959), which provided that:

"(a) The term 'investment' shall comprise capital brought into the territory of the other Party for investment in various forms in the shape of assets such as foreign exchange, goods, property rights, patents and technical knowledge. The term 'investment' shall also include the returns derived from and ploughed back into such 'investment'.
(b) Any partnerships, companies or assets of similar kind, created by the utilisation of the above mentioned assets shall be regarded as 'investment'."

2. Art. 25(1) of the ICSID Convention.

under the ICSID Convention should be understood as connotating certain objective requirements, others insist on a party autonomy approach of treaty interpretation rejecting such objective criteria. Consequently, interpretations of the concept of "investment" remain widely divided and deeply controversial. In response, newer investment treaties have employed techniques for narrowing down the scope of protected investments and limiting the access to investor-State dispute settlement (ISDS) mechanisms.

This article attempts to examine and assess the evolution of the definition of "investment" in international investment law, by reference to recent developments in both investment treaty-making and arbitration practices. Part II reviews the different definitions of "investment" in investment treaties, including the traditional and newer definitions. Part III focuses on the interpretations of the concept of "investment" in arbitral practice including in ICSID and non-ICSID cases. Part IV discusses the key lingering issues, namely, the relationship between Art. 25 of the ICSID Convention and the definition of "investment" clause in the governing substantive investment treaty; the "ordinary meaning" of "investment" and its constitutive elements; and the applicability of such "ordinary meaning" in non-ICSID arbitration. It concludes that whilst the recent treaty practice has generally responded to the need of clarification on the definition of "investment" particularly by adding the "characteristics of investment" requirement, some treaties might have gone too far to become overly restrictive. Further, it is submitted that the "ordinary meaning" of the term "investment", strictly confined to the minimum hard core of the concept, should apply in ICSID arbitrations given that the term is undefined under the ICSID Convention. Such "ordinary meaning" should also apply to non-ICSID arbitration unless the governing substantive investment treaty contains a clear definition of "investment" establishing a "special meaning" of the concept under Art. 31(4) of the Vienna Convention on the Law of Treaties (VCLT).[3]

II. DEFINITIONS OF "INVESTMENT" IN INVESTMENT TREATIES

1. *Asset-Based or Enterprise-Based Definitions*

Almost all investment treaties have contained a definition of "investment", but the specific wordings of the definition differ. Most investment treaties provide that "investment" means "every kind of assets", suggesting that the term embraces everything of economic value, virtually without any limitation.[4] For example, Art. 1 of the UK-Singapore Bilateral Investment Treaty (BIT) (1975) provides that:

> "(a) 'investment' means *every kind of asset* and in particular, *though not exclusively*, includes:

3. Art. 31(4) of the Vienna Convention provides that "[a] special meaning shall be given to a term if it is established that the parties so intended".
4. UNCTAD, *Scope and Definition: UNCTAD Series on Issues in International Investment Agreement II* (UN 2011) p. 24.

> (i) movable and inmovable property and any other property rights such as mortgages, liens or pledges;
> (ii) shares, stock and debentures of companies or interests in the property of such companies;
> (iii) claims to money or to any performance under contract having a financial value;
> (iv) intellectual property rights and goodwill;
> (v) business concessions conferred by law or under contract, including concessions to search for, cultivate, extract or exploit natural resources;".[5] (Emphasis added.)

Accordingly, the definition of "investment" is broadly worded covering all kinds of assets. Such an asset-based definition of investment is often followed by a non-exhaustive list of assets to be protected. Typically, these categories include movable and immovable property, interests in companies, contractual rights, intellectual property rights, and business concessions.[6]

Some treaties include fewer or more categories of assets as protected investments. The China-Poland BIT (1988), for instance, includes only four categories: (i) movable and immovable property and other rights in rem; (ii) shares in companies or other form of interest in such companies; (iii) a claim to money or to any performance having an economic value; (iv) copyrights, industrial property rights, know-how and technical process.[7] By contrast, the Energy Charter Treaty (ECT) provides six illustrative categories of "investment" as follows:

> "(6) 'Investment' means every kind of asset, owned or controlled directly or indirectly by an Investor and includes:
> (a) tangible and intangible, and movable and immovable, property, and any property rights such as leases, mortgages, liens, and pledges;
> (b) a company or business enterprise, or shares, stock, or other forms of equity participation in a company or business enterprise, and bonds and other debt of a company or business enterprise;
> (c) claims to money and claims to performance pursuant to contract having an economic value and associated with an Investment;
> (d) Intellectual Property;
> (e) Returns;
> (f) any right conferred by law or contract or by virtue of any licences and permits granted pursuant to law to undertake any Economic Activity in the Energy Sector."[8]

---

5. Art. 1(a) of the UK-Singapore BIT (1975).
6. See Campbell MCLACHLAN, *International Investment Arbitration: Substantive Principles* (OUP 2007) p. 171; Norah GALLAGHER and Wenhua SHAN, *Chinese Investment Treaties: Policies and Practice* (OUP 2009) p. 59; Kenneth J. VANDEVELDE, *Bilateral Investment Treaties: History, Policy, and Interpretation* (OUP 2010) pp. 126-128.
7. Art. 1(a) of the China-Poland BIT (1988).
8. Art. 1(b) of the ECT.

The 2012 U.S. Model BIT provides an open asset-based definition with eight categories listed as investments, including:

> "(a) an enterprise;
> (b) shares, stock, and other forms of equity participation in an enterprise;
> (c) bonds, debentures, other debt instruments, and loans;[1]
> (d) futures, options, and other derivatives;
> (e) turnkey, construction, management, production, concession, revenue-sharing, and other similar contracts;
> (f) intellectual property rights;
> (g) licenses, authorizations, permits, and similar rights conferred pursuant to domestic law;[2, 3] and
> (h) other tangible or intangible, movable or immovable property, and related property rights, such as leases, mortgages, liens, and pledges.[9]
>
> [[1] Some forms of debt, such as bonds, debentures, and long-term notes, are more likely to have the characteristics of an investment, while other forms of debt, such as claims to payment that are immediately due and result from the sale of goods or services, are less likely to have such characteristics.
> [2] Whether a particular type of license, authorization, permit, or similar instrument (including a concession, to the extent that it has the nature of such an instrument) has the characteristics of an investment depends on such factors as the nature and extent of the rights that the holder has under the law of the Party. Among the licenses, authorizations, permits, and similar instruments that do not have the characteristics of an investment are those that do not create any rights protected under domestic law. For greater certainty, the foregoing is without prejudice to whether any asset associated with the license, authorization, permit, or similar instrument has the characteristics of an investment.
> [3] The term 'investment' does not include an order or judgment entered in a judicial or administrative action.]"

It should be noted that categories of investment are provided only as examples to clarify the content of protected assets.[10] Therefore, an asset or interest in question falling out of the listed categories may still be considered as a covered "investment" since assets of "every kind" are included.

Whereas the broad asset-based definition is present in the vast majority of investment treaties and has been subject to extensive arbitral interpretations, some treaties use an enterprise-based definition of "investment". For example, the North American Free Trade Agreement (NAFTA) Art. 1139 provides that:

> "investment means:
> (a) an enterprise;
> (b) an equity security of an enterprise;
> (c) a debt security of an enterprise
> (i) where the enterprise is an affiliate of the investor, or

9. Art.1 of the 2012 U.S. Model BIT.
10. K. J. VANDEVELD, *Bilateral Investment Treaties*, fn. 6 above.

(ii) where the original maturity of the debt security is at least three years, but does not include a debt security, regardless of original maturity, of a state enterprise;
(d) a loan to an enterprise
(i) where the enterprise is an affiliate of the investor, or
(ii) where the original maturity of the loan is at least three years, but does not include a loan, regardless of original maturity, to a state enterprise;
(e) an interest in an enterprise that entitles the owner to share in income or profits of the enterprise;
(f) an interest in an enterprise that entitles the owner to share in the assets of that enterprise on dissolution, other than a debt security or a loan excluded from subparagraph (c) or (d);
(g) real estate or other property, tangible or intangible, acquired in the expectation or used for the purpose of economic benefit or other business purposes; and
(h) interests arising from the commitment of capital or other resources in the territory of a Party to economic activity in such territory, such as under
(i) contracts involving the presence of an investor's property in the territory of the Party, including turnkey or construction contracts, or concessions, or
(ii) contracts where remuneration depends substantially on the production, revenues or profits of an enterprise;
but investment does not mean,
(i) claims to money that arise solely from
(i) commercial contracts for the sale of goods or services by a national or enterprise in the territory of a Party to an enterprise in the territory of another Party, or
(ii) the extension of credit in connection with a commercial transaction, such as trade financing, other than a loan covered by subparagraph (d); or
(j) any other claims to money, that do not involve the kinds of interests set out in subparagraphs (a) through (h);".[11]

Similarly, the 2004 Canada Model BIT also provides an enterprise-based definition of investment.[12] The enterprise-based definition provides a narrower scope of investment

---

11. Art. 1139 of the NAFTA.
12. Art. 1 of the 2004 Canada Model BIT provides that:

"investment means:
(I) an enterprise;
(II) an equity security of an enterprise;
(III) a debt security of an enterprise
(i) where the enterprise is an affiliate of the investor, or
(ii) where the original maturity of the debt security is at least three years,
but does not include a debt security, regardless of original maturity, of a state enterprise;
(IV) a loan to an enterprise
(i) where the enterprise is an affiliate of the investor, or
(ii) where the original maturity of the loan is at least three years,
but does not include a loan, regardless of original maturity, to a state enterprise;

compared with the asset-based definition, since the former is limited to assets and interests related to an "enterprise". An enterprise-based definition of investment also has some practical implications: First, the affiliation or subsidiary of an enterprise is an independent investment; Second, the subsidiary enterprise as an investment should normally be established in accordance with the host State's law; Third, treaties with enterprise-based approach often expressly enable a foreign investor to bring claims not only on its own behalf but also on behalf of its enterprise.[13]

2. *Newer Definitions of "Investment"*

As demonstrated in the following part, the conventional definitions, particularly the open-ended asset-based definition of "investment", have caused many controversies and criticisms. As a result, an increasing number of States have adopted newer definitions of "investment" in their BITs and multilateral investment treaties (MITs) with a view to clarifying and limiting the scope of the definition. Typical techniques include imposing the "characteristics of investment" requirement, excluding specific assets from the

---

(V) (i) notwithstanding subparagraph (III) and (IV) above, a loan to or debt security issued by a financial institution is an investment only where the loan or debt security is treated as regulatory capital by the Party in whose territory the financial institution is located, and
(ii) a loan granted by or debt security owned by a financial institution, other than a loan to or debt security of a financial institution referred to in (i), is not an investment;
for greater certainty:
(iii) a loan to, or debt security issued by, a Party or a state enterprise thereof is not an investment; and
(iv) a loan granted by or debt security owned by a cross-border financial service provider, other than a loan to or debt security issued by a financial institution, is an investment if such loan or debt security meets the criteria for investments set out elsewhere in this Article;
(VI) an interest in an enterprise that entitles the owner to share in income or profits of the enterprise;
(VII) an interest in an enterprise that entitles the owner to share in the assets of that enterprise on dissolution, other than a debt security or a loan excluded from subparagraphs (III) (IV) or (V);
(VIII) real estate or other property, tangible or intangible, acquired in the expectation or used for the purpose of economic benefit or other business purposes; and
(IX) interests arising from the commitment of capital or other resources in the territory of a Party to economic activity in such territory, such as under
(i) contracts involving the presence of an investor's property in the territory of the Party, including turnkey or construction contracts, or concessions, or
(ii) contracts where remuneration depends substantially on the production, revenues or profits of an enterprise;
but investment does not mean,
(X) claims to money that arise solely from
(i) commercial contracts for the sale of goods or services by a national or enterprise in the territory of a Party to an enterprise in the territory of the other Party, or
(ii) the extension of credit in connection with a commercial transaction, such as trade financing, other than a loan covered by subparagraphs (IV) or (V); and
(XI) any other claims to money,
that do not involve the kinds of interests set out in subparagraphs (I) through (IX);".

13. UNCTAD, *Scope and Definition*, fn. 4 above, pp. 22-23.

definition, adding a legality requirement or adopting a narrower enterprise-based definition, as detailed below.

a. Requiring investment to fulfill specific characteristics

The U.S. BITs typically provide that "investment" means assets that carry certain "characteristics of investment".[14] For example, both the 2004 and the 2012 U.S. Model BITs define "investment" as "every asset that an investor owns or controls, directly or indirectly, that has the characteristics of an investment, including such characteristics as the commitment of capital or other resources, the expectation of gain or profit, or the assumption of risk".[15]

In recent years, an increasing number of treaties expressly require that the covered investment must contain characteristics of an investment. For instance, the Comprehensive and Progressive Agreement for Trans-Pacific Partnership (CPTPP) stipulates that "investment means every asset that an investor owns or controls, directly or indirectly, that has the characteristics of an investment, including such characteristics as the commitment of capital or other resources, the expectation of gain or profit, or the assumption of risk".[16] The China-Australia Free Trade Agreement (FTA) also provides that the characteristics of an investment include "the commitment of capital or other resources, the expectation of gain or profit, or the assumption of risk".[17] A similar definition was adopted in the 2016 amendments to the Singapore-Australia FTA.[18]

Some recent investment treaties, however, require four criteria for having the characteristics of investment, which add an element of "duration". For example, the EU-Canada Comprehensive Economic and Trade Agreement (CETA) provides "investment" as "every kind of asset that an investor owns or controls, directly or indirectly, that has the characteristics of an investment, which includes a certain duration and other characteristics such as the commitment of capital or other resources, the expectation of gain or profit, or the assumption of risk".[19] The latest model BIT draft of Netherlands of 2018 followed this approach and also included the four characteristics.[20] Likewise, the Morocco-Nigeria BIT provides that "investment" must have the characteristics of an

14. K. J. VANDEVELD, *Bilateral Investment Treaties*, fn. 6 above, p. 129. Notably, earlier treaties of the United States did not specify the "characteristics of investment" but provided that "investment" means "every kind of investment", See, e.g., Art. I(d) of the Panama-U.S. BIT (1982). See also Kenneth VANDEVELDE, *U.S. International Investment Agreements* (OUP 2009) p. 114.
15. See Art. 1 of the 2004 and the 2012 U.S. Model BITs.
16. See 9.1 of the TPP (2016). The CPTPP incorporates, by reference, the provisions of the TPP with the exception of a small number of technical articles.
17. Art. 9.1(d) of the China-Australia FTA (2015).
18. Art. 8.1(k) of the Agreement to Amend the Singapore-Australia FTA (SAFTA). The SAFTA entered into force on 28 July 2003, and the 2016 Agreement to Amend SAFTA entered into force on 1 December 2017.
19. Art. 8.1 of the CETA (2016).
20. Art. 1(a) of the draft model BIT of the Netherlands (2018) stipulates: "'[i]nvestment' means every kind of asset that has the characteristics of an investment, which includes a certain duration, the commitment of capital or other resources, the expectation of gain or profit, and the assumption of risk".

investment involving "a commitment of capital or other similar resources, pending profit, risk-taking and certain duration".[21]

Notably, the Morocco-Nigeria BIT also requires that the investment has to be made "in good faith", in accordance with local law and make contribution to the sustainable development of the host State: Art. 1 provides that "[i]nvestment means an enterprise within the territory of one State established, acquired, expanded or operated, in good faith, by an investor of the other State in accordance with law of the Party in whose territory the investment is made taken together with the asset of the enterprise which *contribute sustainable development* of that Party"; Art. 24 further provides that "investors and their investments should strive to make the *maximum feasible contributions to the sustainable development of the Host State and local community* through high levels of socially responsible practices." (Emphasis added.)[22] Likewise, the Egypt-Mauritius BIT and the 2015 Indian Model BIT also contain the contribution to (sustainable) development as a characteristic of investment.[23] In February 2016, India proposed a "Joint Interpretative Statement for Indian Bilateral Investment Treaties" to twenty-five countries with which it has BITs whose initial period of validity had not expired.[24] Paragraph 4.3 of the Statement lays out that "the minimum characteristics of an 'investments' are (a) the lasting contribution of capital or other resources; (b) the expectation of gain or profit; (c) the assumption of risk by the investor; and (d) significance for development of the Contracting Party receiving the investment".[25]

b. Excluding specific assets from the definition of "investment"

The broad asset-based definition of investment typically includes both direct investments and portfolio investments without any limitations to the types of assets. However, some recent treaties expressly exclude certain assets from the scope of "investment", including portfolio investments, sovereign debt, ordinary commercial transaction, etc. For example, the Colombia-Turkey BIT (2014) provides that:

> "[T]he term 'investment' does not include:
> (a) investments which are in the nature of acquisition of shares or voting power amounting to, or representing of less than (10) percent of a company through stock exchange;
> (b) public debt operations;
> (c) claims to money arising solely from:

21. Art. 1 of the Morocco-Nigeria BIT (2016).
22. Art. 1 and Art. 24 of the Morocco-Nigeria BIT (2016).
23. See Art. 1(1) of the Egypt-Mauritius BIT (2014), and Art. 1.4 of the 2015 Indian Model BIT, available at <http://indiainbusiness.nic.in/newdesign/upload/Model_BIT.pdf> (last accessed 6 February 2018).
24. See India's Consolidated Interpretive Statements (dated 8 February 2016), available at <http://indiainbusiness.nic.in/newdesign/upload/Consolidated_Interpretive-Statement.pdf> (last accessed 6 February 2018). These countries are Bahrain, Bangladesh, Bosnia and Herzegovina, Brunei, China, Colombia, Finland, Iceland, Jordan, Kuwait, Laos, Latvia, Libya, Lithuania, Macedonia, Mexico, Mozambique, Myanmar, Saudi Arabia, Senegal, Serbia, Sudan, Syria, Trinidad and Tobago, and Turkey.
25. Para. 4.3 of the India's Consolidated Interpretive Statements.

> (i) commercial contracts for the sale of goods and services by a national or legal entity in the territory of a Contracting Party to a national or a legal entity in the territory of the other Contracting Party; or
> (ii) credits granted in relation with a commercial transaction."[26]

The 2015 Brazilian Model BIT provides:

> "Investment means a direct investment of an investor of one Party, established or acquired in accordance with the laws and regulations of the other Party, that, directly or indirectly, allows the investor to exert control or significant degree of influence over the management of the production of goods or provision of services in the territory of the other Party, including but not limited to:
> ....
> For the purposes of this Agreement and for greater certainty, 'Investment' does not include:
> (i) an order or judgment issued as a result of a lawsuit or an administrative process;
> (ii) debt securities issued by a Party or loans granted from a Party to the other Party, bonds, debentures, loans or other debt instruments of a State-owned enterprise of a Party that is considered to be public debt under the legislation of that Party;
> (ii) [sic] portfolio investments, i.e., those that do not allow the investor to exert a significant degree of influence in the management of the company; and
> (iii) claims to money that arise solely from commercial contracts for the sale of goods or services by an investor in the territory of a Party to a national or an enterprise in the territory of another Party, or the extension of credit in connection with a commercial transaction, or any other claims to money that do not involve the kind of interests set out in sub-paragraphs (a)-(e) above."[27]

Similarly, the Brazil-Malawi BIT (2015) provides that "investment" does not include: (a) debt securities issued by a government or loans to a government; (b) portfolio investments; and (c) claims to money that arise solely from commercial contracts.[28] The Morocco-Nigeria BIT (2016) further excludes "letters of bank credits" and "claims to money with maturities less than three years" from the definition of "investment".[29] By contrast, India's 2015 Model BIT additionally excludes "pre-operational expenditure

26. Art. 1.1.2 of the Colombia-Turkey BIT (2014).
27. Art. 3.1.3 of the 2015 Brazilian Model BIT, available at <http://investmentpolicyhub.unctad.org/Download/TreatyFile/4786> (last accessed 6 February 2018). This article provides that "investment" includes but is not limited to: (a) an enterprise; (b) shares, stocks, participations and other equity types in an enterprise; (c) movable or immovable property and other property rights such as mortgages, liens, pledges, encumbrances or similar rights and obligations; (d) concession, license or authorization granted by the Host State to the investor of the other Party; (e) loans and debt instruments to a company; (f) intellectual property rights as defined or referenced to in the TRIPS.
28. Art. 2.1 of the Brazil-Malawi BIT (2015).
29. Art. 1 of the Morocco-Nigeria BIT (2016).

relating to admission, establishment, acquisition or expansion of the enterprise", "goodwill, brand value, market share or similar intangible rights" and "order or judgment" from the definition of "investment".[30] According to the Iran-Slovakia BIT of 2016, the term "investment" shall not include:

> "(a) goodwill or market share;
> (b) portfolio investment, which is 10% or less shareholding;
> (c) claims to money deriving solely from commercial contracts for the sale of goods or services to or from the territory of a Contracting Party to the territory of another country, or to a State enterprise;
> (d) futures, swaps, forwards, options, and other derivatives;
> (e) assets used for non-business purposes, other than assets of research and development of non-profit organizations;
> (f) funds;
> (g) the following loans and debt securities:
> i. debt securities and loans with the original maturity of less than three years;
> ii. a loan to or debt security issued by a financial institution, which is not treated as regulatory capital by the Contracting Party in whose territory the financial institution is located;
> iii. the extension of credit in connection with a commercial transaction, such as trade financing".[31]

Some recent treaties have used footnotes to exclude certain assets from the definition of "investment". The 2012 U.S. Model BIT, for instance, provides that "an order or judgment entered in a judicial or administrative action" should not be included in the scope of investment in footnote 3.[32]

Likewise, the above-mentioned India's "Joint Interpretative Statement" in 2016 contains extensive limitations on the scope of protected investment.[33] Paragraph 4.1 clarifies that "investment" does not cover "pre-establishment or pre-investment activities". Moreover, certain interests or assets that do not typically possess the characteristics of "investments" are expressly excluded, including portfolio investments, claims to payment resulting from a sale of goods or services by an individual or entity in one Contracting Party to an individual or entity in the other, or an order or judgment sought or entered in a judicial, administrative, or arbitral action.[34] In addition, an investor of one Contracting Party must make its investments "in the territory of" the other Contracting Party.[35] Hence, claims to money arising solely from cross-border commercial contracts for the sale of goods or services, or the extension of trade financing in connection with a cross-border commercial transaction, or other

---

30. Art. 1.4 of the 2015 Indian Model BIT.
31. Art. 1.2 of the Slovak Republic-the Islamic Republic of Iran BIT (2016).
32. Art. 1 of the U.S. 2012 Model BIT, footnote 3.
33. India's Consolidated Interpretative Statements (8 February 2016), available at <http://indiainbusiness.nic.in/newdesign/upload/Consolidated_Interpretive-Statement.pdf> (last accessed 6 February 2018).
34. Para. 4.3 of India's Consolidated Interpretative Statements, footnote 2.
35. Para. 4.4 of India's Consolidated Interpretative Statements.

relationships or instruments not involving an investor's actual investment project in the territory of the other Contracting Party, do not constitute covered investments.[36] Furthermore, an investment that merely "benefits" the Contracting Party is not sufficient to establish an investment made "in territory of" that Contracting Party.[37]

c. Adopting a narrower enterprise-based definition

As mentioned above, the 2015 Indian Model BIT defines "investment" as "an enterprise constituted, organised and operated in good faith by an investor in accordance with the law of the Party ... taken together with the assets of the enterprise, has the characteristics of an investment...".[38] Accordingly, only enterprises owned and controlled by investors and the assets of the enterprises are covered investments, i.e., no other types of assets are included in the definition of "investment".

In August 2016, members of the Southern African Development Community (SADC) amended Annex 1 of the SADC Finance and Investment Protocol, which narrowed the definition of "investment" to include only enterprises and their assets of an SADC member State investing in another member State. The specific amendment read as follows:

> "'[I]nvestment' means an enterprise within the territory of one State Party established, acquired or expanded by an investor of the other State Party, including through the constitution, maintenance or acquisition of a juridical person or the acquisition of shares, debentures or other ownership instruments of such an enterprise, provided that the enterprise is established or acquired in accordance with the laws of the Host State and registered in accordance with the legal requirements of the Host State...."[39]

d. Including a legality requirement

Some treaties include a legality requirement of protected investments, with a reference to "in accordance with laws and regulations". Most Chinese BITs, for instance, typically include the legality requirement in their definitions of "investment".[40] Nonetheless, most Chinese BITs do not further explain this qualification. However, an interesting explanation is found in the amendment to the China-Cuba BIT, which statesthat:

36. *Ibid.*
37. *Ibid.*
38. Art. 1.4 of the Indian 2015 Model BIT, available at <http://indiainbusiness.nic.in/new design/upload/Model_BIT.pdf> (last accessed 6 February 2018).
39. Art. 1(2) of the Agreement Amending Annex 1 (Co-operation on Investment of the Protocol on Finance and Investment) (2016), available at <http://investmentpolicyhub.unctad.org/Down load/TreatyFile/5527> (last accessed 6 February 2018). The original definition of "investment" provided in Art. 1(2) of Annex 1 of the SADC Protocol on Finance and Investment read that, "'investment' means the purchase, acquisition or establishment of productive and portfolio investment assets ...", available at <http://investmentpolicyhub.unctad.org/Download/ TreatyFile/2730> (last accessed 6 February 2018).
40. N. GALLAGHER and W. SHAN, *Chinese Investment Treaties*, fn. 6 above, p. 55.

> "ONE: In reference to Article 1, Paragraph 1, the expression 'pursuant to the latter's laws and regulations'[41] shall mean that for any kind of invested asset to be considered as investment protected in this Agreement, it shall be in accordance with any of the foreign investment modalities defined by the legislation of the Contracting Party receiving the investment and registered as such in the correspondent registry."[42]

Many recent investment treaties also include the "in accordance with the laws and regulations of the other Contracting Party" requirement in the definition of "investment", such as the Argentina-Qatar BIT,[43] the Egypt-Mauritius BIT,[44] the Algeria-Serbia BIT,[45] etc.

Clearly, it can be seen that a new trend has emerged to clarify and limit the scope of covered "investment" in the definition provisions of recent investment treaties. Such practice is evident in both developed states (such as the United States and the EU) and developing states (such as India and Brazil), though the measures taken by the latter tend to be more dramatic and restrictive than the former. Such changes have been prompted by a range of domestic and international events, one of which has been the rapid increase of treaty-based investment arbitration cases, partly owing to the "open-end" definitions of "investment" adopted in the vast majority of BITs worldwide.

III. DEFINITIONS OF "INVESTMENT" IN ARBITRATION PRACTICE

As mentioned above, Art. 25(1) of the ICSID Convention stipulates that the Centre's jurisdiction "shall extend to any legal dispute arising directly out of an investment, between a Contracting State ... and a national of another Contracting State, which the

41. The wording used in the original English version is actually "in accordance with the laws and regulations", see Art. 1(1) of the China-Cuba BIT (1995).
42. N. GALLAGHER and W. SHAN, *Chinese Investment Treaties*, fn. 6 above, at para. 55. Amendment protocol of the China-Cuba BIT (2007).
43. Art. 1(2) of the Argentina-Qatar BIT (2016) read that: "The term 'investment' means any kind of asset invested by an investor of one Contracting Party in the territory of the other Contracting Party in accordance with the laws and regulations of the latter Contracting Party, which involves commitment of resources into the territory of the host Contracting Party," available at <http://investmentpolicyhub.unctad.org/Download/TreatyFile/5383> (last accessed 6 February 2018).
44. Art. 1(1) of the Egypt-Mauritius BIT (2014) provides that "investment" means assets "established or acquired by an investor of one Contracting Party in the territory of the other Contracting Party in accordance with the laws and regulations of the latter Contracting Party", available at <http://investmentpolicyhub.unctad.org/Download/TreatyFile/3285> (last accessed 6 February 2018).
45. Art. 1(1) of the Algeria-Serbia BIT (2012) provides that the term "investment" shall mean "every kind of assets established or acquired by an investor of one Contracting Party in the territory of the other Contracting Party in accordance with the laws and regulations of the latter", available at <http://investmentpolicyhub.unctad.org/Download/TreatyFile/3168> (last accessed 6 February 2018).

Parties to the dispute consent in writing to submit to the Centre".[46] However, the ICSID Convention ultimately does not give any explanation of what constitutes an "investment".

It is against the fact of no-definition of "investment" under the ICSID Convention that efforts of searching for and applying the ordinary, or "objective"/ "inherent" meaning of the term have been made by numerous arbitral tribunals and commentators, in order to prevent investors from abusing the ICSID system.[47] At times, however, the issue has also arisen in non-ICSID arbitration cases, as it has been argued and accepted by some tribunals that such objective or inherent meaning of "investment" shall equally apply to investment treaties that provide for consent to investment treaty arbitrations.

1. *From Fedax Decision to Salini Test*

The *Fedax v. Venezuela* case was the first case in which a challenge to jurisdiction was made on the ground that the underlying transaction did not quality as an "investment" under the ICSID Convention.[48] The question at stake was whether the purchase of promissory notes issued by the government could be considered as an "investment". The tribunal eventually decided that they were protected investments as they met the five "basic features" of an investment, which included "a certain duration, a certain regularity of profit and return, assumption of risk, a substantial commitment and a significance for the host State's development".[49] In identifying the features, the tribunal relied on earlier writing by Schreuer, which read as follows:

> "It would not be realistic to attempt yet another definition of 'investment' on the basis of ICSID's experience. But it seems possible to identify certain features that are typical to most of the operations in question: the first such feature is that the projects have a certain *duration*. Even though some break down at an early stage, the expectation of a longer-term relationship is clearly there. The second feature is a certain *regularity of profit and return*. A one-time lump-sum agreement, while not impossible, would be untypical. Even where no profits are ever made, the expectation of return is present. The third feature is the assumption of *risk* usually by both sides. Risk is in part a function of duration and expectation of profit. The fourth typical feature is that the commitment is *substantial*. This aspect was very much on the drafters' minds although it did not find entry into the Convention. A contract with an individual consultant would be untypical. The fifth feature is the

46. Art. 25(1) of the ICSID Convention.

47. See, e.g., *Salini Costruttori S.p.A. and Italstrade S.p.A. v. Kingdom of Morocco* (ICSID Case No. ARB/00/4), Decision on Jurisdiction (23 July 2001) para. 52, published at 42 International Legal Materials 621 (2003) 622. See also C. LAMM, "The Jurisdiction of the International Centre for Settlement of Investment Disputes", 6 ICSID Review (1991) p. 462 at p. 474; N. RUBINS, "The Notion of 'Investment' in International Investment Arbitration" in Norbert HORN, ed., *Arbitrating Foreign Investment Disputes: Procedural and Substantive Legal Aspects* (Kluwer Law International 2004) p. 283 at p. 289.

48. *Fedax N.V. v. The Republic of Venezuela* (ICSID Case No. ARB/96/3), Decision on Jurisdiction (11 July 1997) para. 25, published at 37 International Legal Materials 1387 (1998) p. 1383.

49. *Ibid.*, para. 43 at p. 1387.

> operation's significance for the host State's *development*. This is not necessarily characteristic of investments in general. But the wording of the Preamble and the Executive Directors' Report suggest that development is part of the Convention's object and purpose. These features should not necessarily be understood as jurisdictional requirements but merely as typical characteristics of investments under the Convention."[50]

Starting with *Fedax*, tribunals appear to have adopted these criteria, subject to variations, to determine the existence of an investment for jurisdictional purposes.[51]

The *Salini v. Morocco* case, which produced the "*Salini* test", was a landmark case particularly in the jurisprudence on the definition of "investment" in investment treaty arbitration history. One of the core issues that the tribunal had to decide was whether the underlying transaction (i.e., a highway construction contract) qualified as an "investment" under applicable treaties. Following the *Fedax* and other decisions, this tribunal first opined that its jurisdiction depended on "the existence of an investment within the meaning of both the Bilateral Treaty as well as that of the Convention", i.e., a "dual test".[52] This approach reveals that although claimants may have access to investor-State arbitration if the dispute falls within the scope of the consent to arbitration by parties in investment treaties, the requirements ratione materiae in the ICSID Convention must also be satisfied in order to obtain ICSID jurisdiction. Hence, Art. 25 of the ICSID Convention sets out the "outer limits" of ICSID jurisdiction whereas parties retain discretion to determine the scope of disputes to investor-State arbitration, including through the definition of "investment" in a specific investment treaty.[53] The tribunal then set out five "elements" of investment, which later became the famous "*Salini* test":

50. *Ibid.*, citing Christoph SCHREUER, "Commentary on the ICSID Convention", 11 ICSID Review–Foreign Investment Law Journal (1996, no. 2) para. 122 at pp. 372-373. This paragraph is substantively identical with C. H. SCHREUER, et al., *The ICSID Convention: A Commentary*, 2nd edn. (CUP 2009) para. 153 at p. 128.
51. See C. H. SCHREUER, et al., *The ICSID Convention: A Commentary*, fn. 50 above, pp. 129-133; N. RUBINS, "The Notion of 'Investment' in International Investment Arbitration", fn. 47 above, pp. 297-300.
52. *Salini v. Morocco* (ICSID Case No. ARB/00/4), Decision on Jurisdiction (23 July 2001) para. 44, published in 42 International Legal Materials 621 (2003) p. 620. See also Rudolf DOLZER, Christoph SCHREUER, *Principles of International Investment Law*, 2nd ed. (OUP 2012) p. 61. This dual test has at times been referred to as the "double keyhole" approach or the "double barreled" test, See, e.g., *Aguas del Tunari, S.A. v. Republic of Bolivia* (ICSID Case No. ARB/02/3), Decision on Jurisdiction (21 October 2005) para. 278; *Malaysian Historical Salvors, SDN, BHD v. The Government of Malaysia* (ICSID Case No. ARB/05/10), Award on Jurisdiction (17 May 2007) para. 55.
53. See, e.g., Aron BROCHES, "The Convention on the Settlement of Investment Disputes Between States and Nationals of Other States", 136 RC 331 (1972) pp. 360-361. Nonetheless, the definition of investment in investment treaties is decisive in jurisdiction ratione materiae if the parties' consent to arbitration permits arbitration under other rules such as the UNCITRAL and ICC. See N. RUBINS, "The Notion of 'Investment' in International Investment Arbitration", fn. 47 above, p. 290.

> "The doctrine generally considers that investment infers: contributions, a certain duration of performance of the contract and a participation in the risks of the transaction (*cf. ... commentary by E. Gaillard...*). In reading the Convention's preamble, one may add the contribution to the economic development of the host State of the investment as an additional condition.
>
> In reality, these various elements may be interdependent. Thus, the risks of the transaction may depend on the contributions and the duration of performance of the contract. As a result, these various criteria should be assessed globally even if, for the sake of reasoning, the Tribunal considers them individually here."[54]

It then assessed the case against the five elements one by one, and like *Fedax*, arrived at a conclusion confirming its jurisdiction.[55]

The *Salini* approach was followed by a series of subsequent decisions, and at one point was thought to have been firmly accepted,[56] until it was challenged by the *Biwater* and the *MHS Annulment* decisions.[57]

Among the cases that followed the *Salini* approach, the *MHS v. Malaysia* award stood out as it drew a distinction between a "Typical Characteristics Approach" and a "Jurisdictional Approach" in the application of the defining elements (or "hallmarks"), using the Sole Arbitrator's language: the former approach used the elements merely as "typical characteristics", whilst the latter used them as "jurisdictional requirements":

> "The differences between the Typical Characteristics Approach and the Jurisdictional Approach may only be the expression of the conclusion formed by a tribunal on the strength of the particular facts of a case on the issue of 'investment.' While the Jurisdictional Approach, strictly defined, requires that all the established hallmarks of 'investment' must be present before a contract can even be considered as an 'investment,' the Typical Characteristics Approach does not necessarily mean that a tribunal would find that there is an 'investment,' even if one or more of the established hallmarks of 'investment' were missing. Where the evidence in support of one or more of the hallmarks of 'investment' is weak, a tribunal may approach the issue from a holistic perspective and determine whether there is other evidence in support of the other hallmarks of 'investment' which is so strong as to off-set the weakness in the other hallmarks of

54. *Salini v. Morocco*, Decision on Jurisdiction, para. 52 at p. 622.
55. *Ibid.*, paras. 53-58.
56. See, e.g., *Joy Mining Machinery Limited v. Arab Republic of Egypt* (ICSID Case No. ARB/03/11), Award on Jurisdiction (6 August 2004) para. 53; *SGS Société Générale de Surveillance S.A. v. Islamic Republic of Pakistan* (ICSID Case No. ARB/01/13), Decision on Jurisdiction (6 August 2003) para.133, footnote 153: *Bayindir Insaat Turizm Ticaret Ve Sanayi A.S. v. Islamic Republic of Pakistan* (ICSID Case No. ARB/03/29), Decision on Jurisdiction (14 November 2005) para. 130; *Jan de Nul N.V. and Dredging International N.V. v. Arab Republic of Egypt* (ICSID Case No. ARB/04/13), Decision on Jurisdiction (16 June 2006) paras. 91-96; *Saipem S.p.A. v. The People's Republic of Bangladesh* (ICSID Case No. ARB/05/07), Decision on Jurisdiction (21 March 2007) paras. 99-111; *Malaysian Historical Salvors, SDN, BHD v. The Government of Malaysia* (ICSID Case No. ARB/05/10), Award on Jurisdiction (17 May 2007) paras. 108-145.
57. R. DOLZER, C. SCHREUER, *Principles of International Investment Law*, fn. 52 above, p. 67.

'investment.' However, even under the Typical Characteristics Approach, it would probably be exceptional for a tribunal to conclude that there was an 'investment' where one or more of the hallmarks of 'investment' were completely missing."[58]

Although the Sole Arbitrator conceded that "the differences between the two approaches are likely to be academic" and might not "make any significant difference to the ultimate finding of the tribunal" in practice,[59] the distinction proved to be important as the following attacks to the so-called "*Salini* approach" were precisely directed at the "jurisdictional requirement" approach, rather than the "typical characteristics" approach.

2. The Biwater and the MHS Annulment Challenges

The most serious attack came with the *Biwater Gauff v. Tanzania* and the *MHS v. Malaysia Annulment* decisions. The *Biwater* tribunal pointed out that:

> "[T]here is no basis for a rote, or overly strict, application of the five *Salini* criteria in every case. These criteria are not fixed or mandatory as a matter of law. They do not appear in the ICSID Convention. On the contrary, it is clear from the *travaux préparatoires* of the Convention that several attempts to incorporate a definition of 'investment' were made, but ultimately did not succeed. In the end, the term was left intentionally undefined, with the expectation (inter alia) that a definition could be the subject of agreement as between Contracting States....
>
> Given that the Convention was not drafted with a strict, objective, definition of 'investment', it is doubtful that arbitral tribunals sitting in individual cases should impose one such definition which would be applicable in all cases and for all purposes....
>
> Further, the *Salini Test* itself is problematic if, as some tribunals have found, the 'typical characteristics' of an investment as identified in that decision are elevated into a fixed and inflexible test, and if transactions are to be presumed excluded from the ICSID Convention unless each of the five criteria are satisfied. This risks the arbitrary exclusion of certain types of transaction from the scope of the Convention. It also leads to a definition that may contradict individual agreements (as here), as well as a developing consensus in parts of the world as to the meaning of 'investment' (as expressed, e.g., in bilateral investment treaties)."[60]

In the end, the tribunal concluded that "a more flexible and pragmatic approach to the meaning of 'investment' is appropriate, which takes into account the features identified in *Salini*, but along with all the circumstances of the case, including the nature of the instrument containing the relevant consent to ICSID".[61]

58. *MHS v. Malaysia*, Award on Jurisdiction (17 May 2007) para. 70.
59. *Ibid.*, para. 105.
60. *Biwater Gauff (Tanzania) Ltd. v. United Republic of Tanzania* (ICSID Case No. ARB/05/22), Award (24 July 2008) paras. 312-314.
61. *Ibid.*, para. 316.

The *Biwater* reasoning was accepted and relied on by the *MHS v. Malaysia* Annulment Decision which adopted a more critical position on the *Salini* approach. The *ad hoc* committee first noted that "[t]he 'ordinary meaning' of the term 'investment' is the commitment of money or other assets for the purpose of providing a return".[62] Nonetheless, it pointed out that the meaning of the term "investment" in the ICSID Convention might be regarded as "ambiguous or obscure" under Art. 32 of the Vienna Convention and hence justifying resort to the preparatory work of the Convention "to determine the meaning".[63] After examining the applicable BIT provisions, the *ad hoc* committee then analyzed the meaning of investment under Art. 25 of the ICSID Convention, by detailing the preparatory history of the Convention,[64] and stated that:

> "However it is important to note that the *travaux préparatoires* do not support the imposition of 'outer limits' such as those imposed by the Sole Arbitrator in this case. Little more about the nature of outer limits is indicated in the *travaux* than is contained in Article 25(1), namely that, '[t]he jurisdiction of the Centre shall extend to any legal dispute arising directly out of an investment....' It appears to have been assumed by the Convention's drafters that use of the term 'investment' excluded a simple sale and like transient commercial transactions from the jurisdiction of the Centre. Judicial or arbitral construction going further in interpretation of the meaning of 'investment' by the establishment of criteria or hallmarks may or may not be regarded as plausible, but the intentions of the draftsmen of the ICSID Convention, as the *travaux* show them to have been, lend those criteria (and still less, conditions) scant support."[65]

The committee also highlighted the importance of the 2,800 investment treaties signed after the adoption of the ICSID Convention and criticized that: "[i]t is those bilateral and multilateral treaties which today are the engine of ICSID's effective jurisdiction. To ignore or depreciate the importance of the jurisdiction they bestow upon ICSID, and rather to embroider upon questionable interpretations of the term 'investment' as found in Article 25(1) of the Convention, risks crippling the institution".[66]

Since the above two decisions, the jurisprudence on the definition of "investment" under the ICSID Convention became unsettled, as some tribunals started to follow this "party autonomy" approach of interpretation, whilst others continued to rely on the *Salini* approach, albeit in modified form, mostly without mentioning *Biwater* and the *MHS Annulment* decisions.[67]

The *Pantechniki v. Albania* and the *Inmaris v. Ukraine* decisions are good examples of earlier decisions supporting the "party autonomy" approach to identifying what constitutes an "investment". In the first case, the tribunal considered that the *Salini* criteria were not found in the Convention so that they introduced elements of subjective

62. *MHS v. Malaysia*, Decision on Annulment (16 April 2009) para. 57.
63. *Ibid.*
64. *Ibid.*, paras. 58-74.
65. *Ibid.*, para 69.
66. *Ibid.*, para. 73.
67. R. DOLZER, C. SCHREUER, *Principles of International Investment Law*, fn. 52 above, p. 69.

judgment and led to unpredictability.[68] It submitted that "[f]or ICSID arbitral tribunals to reject an express definition desired by two States-party to a treaty seems a step not to be taken without the certainty that the Convention compels it".[69]

In *Inmaris v. Ukraine*, the tribunal pointed out:

> "[I]n most cases – including, in the Tribunal's view, this one – it will be appropriate to defer to the State parties' articulation in the instrument of consent (e.g. the BIT) of what constitutes an investment. The State parties to a BIT agree to protect certain kinds of economic activity, and when they provide that disputes between investors and States relating to that activity may be resolved through, *inter alia*, ICSID arbitration, that means that they believe that that activity constitutes an 'investment' within the meaning of the ICSID Convention as well. That judgment, by States that are both Parties to the BIT and Contracting States to the ICSID Convention, should be given considerable weight and deference. A tribunal would have to have compelling reasons to disregard such a mutually agreed definition of investment."[70]

Among the tribunals that generally follow the *Salini* approach after the *Biwater* and *MHS* rulings, most have modified the original concept by abandoning the "contribution to the host State's development" requirement.[71] Examples of such cases include *Société Générale v. Dominican Republic*,[72] *Saba Fakes v. Turkey*,[73] *Alpha Projektholding v. Ukraine*,[74] *Phoenix v. Czech Republic*.[75]

An interesting decision was rendered by the *Romak v. Uzbekistan* tribunal sitting under the rules of UNCITRAL (not ICSID), which for the first time considered that the word "investment" in a BIT must also have an inherent meaning of its own that should be applied to the definition of "investment" under the applicable BIT.[76] Resorting to the Black's Law Dictionary, the tribunal identified the "ordinary meaning" of the term "investments" to be "the commitment of funds or other assets with the purpose to receive a profit, or 'return', from that commitment of capital".[77] The tribunal then

68. *Pantechniki S.A. Contractors & Engineers (Greece) v. The Republic of Albania* (ICSID Case No. ARB/07/21), Award (30 July 2009) para. 43.
69. *Ibid.*, para. 42.
70. *Inmaris Perestroika Sailing Maritime Services GmbH and Others v. Ukraine* (ICSID Case No. ARB/08/8), Decision on Jurisdiction (8 March 2010) para. 130.
71. R. DOLZER, C. SCHREUER, *Principles of International Investment Law*, fn. 52 above, pp. 70-72.
72. *Société Générale in respect of DR Energy Holdings Limited and Empresa Distribuidora de Electricidad del Este, S.A. v. The Dominican Republic* (LCIA Case No. UN 7927), Award on Preliminary Objections to Jurisdiction (19 September 2008) paras. 32-36.
73. *Saba Fakes v. Republic of Turkey* (ICSID Case No. ARB/07/20), Award (14 July 2010) para. 111.
74. *Alpha Projektholding GmbH v. Ukraine* (ICSID Case No. ARB/07/16), Award (8 November 2010) para. 312.
75. *Phoenix Action Ltd v. Czech Republic* (ICSID Case No. ARB/06/5), Award (15 April 2009) para. 85.
76. *Romak S.A. v. The Republic of Uzbekistan* (PCA Case No. AA280), Award (26 November 2009) para. 176.
77. *Ibid.*, para. 177, footnote 152.

rejected the literal interpretation approach held by the claimant and insisted that the "inherent meaning" of the term must be applied.[78] The tribunal stated as follows:

> "Indeed, as already mentioned, the categories of investments enumerated in Article 1(2) of the BIT are not exhaustive, and do not constitute an all-encompassing definition of 'investment.' Both Parties agree that this is the case. Therefore, there may well exist categories different from those mentioned in the list which, nevertheless, could properly be considered investments protected under the BIT. Accordingly, there must be a benchmark against which to assess those non-listed assets or categories of assets in order to determine whether they constitute an 'investment' within the meaning of Article 1(2). The term 'investment' has a meaning in itself that cannot be ignored when considering the list contained in Article 1(2) of the BIT."[79]

The tribunal thus considered that the term "investments" under the BIT also has an inherent meaning – irrespective of whether the investor resorted to ICSID or UNCITRAL arbitral proceedings – entailing "a contribution that extends over a certain period of time and that involves some risk".[80] In the tribunal's view, asset types enumerated in the BIT's non-exhaustive list might, by their nature, exhibit the inherent meaning of "investment".[81] But, if an asset did not correspond to the inherent definition of "investment", the fact that it fell within one of the categories listed in Art. 1 of the BIT did not transform it into an "investment".[82]

3. *More Recent Decisions*

The divergence in approaches in the appreciation and application of the ordinary meaning of the concept of "investment" carried on in more recent decisions. In *GEA v. Ukraine*, the tribunal highlighted the controversy about the relevant definition of "investment" for purposes of Art. 25 of the ICSID Convention, noting the contrast between an "objective" meaning and a "subjective" definition.[83] The tribunal avoided taking sides by noting that whatever test was applied, each leads to the same conclusions[84] and concluded, inter alia, that a previous ICC Award could not be deemed a protected investment as "the fact that the Award rules upon rights and obligations arising out of an investment does not equate the Award with the investment itself".[85]

The *SGS v. Paraguay* tribunal suggested that "it would go too far to suggest that *any* definition of investment agreed by states in a BIT (or by a state and an investor in a

78. *Ibid.*, paras. 180-183.
79. *Ibid.*, para. 180.
80. *Ibid.*, para. 207.
81. *Ibid.*
82. *Ibid.*
83. *GEA Group Aktiengesellschaft v. Ukraine* (ICSID Case No. ARB/08/16), Award (31 March 2011) paras. 141-142.
84. *Ibid.*, para. 143.
85. *Ibid.*, para. 162.

contract) must constitute an 'investment' for purpose of Article 25(1)".[86] However, the tribunal ultimately adopted the approach of the *BIVAC* tribunal by defining the relevant question as whether "the definition [of investment] in the BIT exceed[s] what is permissible under the Convention".[87]

In *Quiborax v. Bolivia*, the respondent objected that the claimants did not make an "investment" in Bolivia within the meaning the Art. 25(1) of the ICSID Convention. The tribunal concluded that the ICSID Convention contained an objective definition of "investment", which must be met regardless of whether that same test is also inherent to the term "investment" used in the BIT or whether it is additional to the BIT definition.[88] In the tribunal's view, the drafting history of the Convention, i.e., "no attempt was made to define the term 'investment'", means that "the Contracting States to the ICSID Convention intended to give to the term 'investment' an 'ordinary meaning' as opposed to a 'special meaning'" and the ordinary meaning is an objective one supported in the *Saba Fakes* award.[89] The tribunal acknowledged that investor-State cases indeed give substance and content to an objective meaning of "investment".[90] It thus concluded that "[w]hether the objective test under the ICSID Convention is independent from and additional to the definition found in the BIT, or whether the same objective test is inherent to the term investment used in the BIT, the Tribunal must in any event review the elements of the objective definition to ascertain the existence of an investment".[91]

In *Phillip Morris v. Uruguay*, the tribunal considered that the concept of "investment" is "central to the Centre's jurisdiction and the Tribunal's competence '*ratione materiae*'".[92] It then pointed out that the consent of the Contracting Parties under the BIT to the scope of "investment" is of relevance when establishing the meaning of the term under Art. 25(1) of the ICSID Convention, though such Parties do not have an unfettered discretion to go beyond what have been called the "outer limits" set by the ICSID Convention, the

86. *SGS Société Générale de Surveillance S.A. v. Republic of Paraguay* (ICSID Case No. ARB/07/29), Decision on Jurisdiction (12 February 2010) para. 93.
87. *Ibid.*, para. 94, citing *Bureau Veritas, Inspection, Valuation, Assesment and Control, BIVAC B.V. v. Republic of Paraguay* (ICSID Case No. ARB/07/9), Decision on Jurisdiction (29 May 2009) para. 94.
88. *Quiborax S.A. and Non-Metallic Minerals S.A. v. Plurinational State of Bolivia* (ICSID Case No. ARB/06/2), Decision on Jurisdiction (27 December 2012) para. 211.
89. *Ibid.*, para. 212.
90. *Ibid.*, para. 214: for example, the *Global Trading* tribunal held that "it is now beyond argument that there are two independent parameters that must both be satisfied [to establish that there is an investment]", see *Global Trading Resource Corp. and Globex International, Inc. v. Ukraine* (ICSID Case No. ARB/09/11), Award (1 December 2010) para. 43; the *GEA* tribunal considered that the objective meaning was inherent regardless of whether it is mentioned in the ICSID Convention or in the BIT, see *GEA Group Aktiengesellschaft v. Ukraine* (ICSID Case No. ARB/08/16), Award (31 March 2011) para. 141; the *Romak* tribunal conducted arbitration under the UNCITRAL Rules also held that "the term 'investment' under the BIT has an inherent meaning entailing a contribution that extends over a certain period of time and that involves some risk...", see *Romak S.A. (Switzerland) v . The Republic of Uzbekistan* (UNCITRAL, PCA Case No. AA280) Award (26 November 2009) para. 207.
91. *Quiborax v. Bolivia*, Decision on Jurisdiction, para. 217.
92. *Philip Morris Brands Sàrl, Philip Morris Products S.A. and Abal Hermanos S.A. v. Oriental Republic of Uruguay* (ICSID Case No. ARB/10/7), Decision on Jurisdiction (2 July 2013) para. 193.

establishment of which must be based on "the ordinary meaning to be given to the terms of the treaty in their context and in the light of its object and purpose".[93]

Regarding the relevance of the *Salini* test, the tribunal pointed out that:

> "Whether the so-called *Salini* test relied upon by the Respondent has any relevance in the interpretation of the concept of 'investment' under Article 25(1) of the ICSID Convention is very doubtful.... Assuming arbitral decisions and awards are 'judicial decisions' within the meaning of Article 38(d) of the Statute of the ICJ, which is far from being commonly accepted, this would be on condition that they have attained a sufficient degree of publicity and are part of a '*jurisprudence constante*'. As shown hereafter, there is no such a '*jurisprudence constante*' with respect to acceptance of the *Salini* test.
>
> (....)
>
> The *Salini* test has received varied applications by investment treaty tribunals and doctrinal writings. In the tribunal's view, the four constitutive elements of the *Salini* list do not constitute jurisdictional requirements to the effect that the absence of one or the other of these elements would imply a lack of jurisdiction. They are typical features of investments under the ICSID Convention, not 'a set of mandatory legal requirements'. As such, they may assist in identifying or excluding in extreme cases the presence of an investment but they cannot defeat the broad and flexible concept of investment under the ICSID Convention to the extent it is not limited by the relevant treaty, as in the present case."[94]

In contrast, the *KT Asia v. Kazakhstan* decision made in the same year firmly upheld the *Salini* and *Romak* approaches, deciding that an objective meaning not only existed under Art. 25 of the ICSID Convention, but also within the definition of "investment" under the applicable BIT. The tribunal stated that:

> "... The absence of a definition of 'investment' under the ICSID Convention implies that the Contracting States intended to give to the term its ordinary meaning under Article 31(1) of the VCLT as opposed to a special meaning under Article 31(4) of the same treaty.[95] This ordinary meaning is an objective one, as was confirmed inter alia in *Saba Fakes* and *Quiborax*. It is inherent to the word 'investment', irrespective of the application of the ICSID Convention....
>
> As stated by the *Romak* tribunal, the inherent meaning of investment is also present in the BIT. The assets listed in Article 1(1)(a) of the BIT are the result of the act of investing. They presuppose an investment in the sense of a commitment

---

93. *Ibid.*, paras. 199-200.
94. *Ibid.*, paras. 204 and 206.
95. Art. 31 of the VCLT provides as follows:

> "1. A treaty shall be interpreted in good faith in accordance with the ordinary meaning to be given to the terms of the treaty in their context and in the light of its object and purpose.
>
> ...
>
> 4. A special meaning shall be given to a term if it is it established that the parties so intended."

> of resources. Without such a commitment of resources, the asset belonging to the claimant cannot constitute an investment within the meaning of the ICSID Convention and the BIT. Since the BIT does not add further requirements to the inherent meaning of investment as it arises from the objective definition, the decisive test for the existence of an investment is the same under the BIT and the ICSID Convention."[96]

The tribunal agreed that "a contribution of money or assets (that is, a commitment of resources), duration and risk" formed part of the objective definition of the term "investment", while "the expectation of a commercial return" was sometimes viewed as a separate component. This tribunal was rather of the opinion that "such expectation is part of the risk element".[97]

Following recent cases, the tribunal rejected the "contribution to host State's development" element[98] and eventually concluded that "the objective definition of investment under the ICSID Convention and the BIT comprises the elements of a contribution or allocation of resources, duration, and risk, which includes the expectation (albeit not necessarily fulfilled) of a commercial return".[99]

In *OIEG v. Venezuela,* both parties accepted that the shares that the OI group held are contemplated in the non-exhaustive list of assets in the broad notion of "investment" in the BIT. The tribunal held that "[n]ot all assets, based on the simple fact that they are included in the non-exhaustive list of examples, constitute an investment. Such assets must be a true investment in order to meet the objective and inherent characteristics of all investments".[100] Hence, the tribunal held that:

> "States enjoy wide discretion to define which investments they wish to protect through a BIT and that Article 25(1) of the ICSID Convention should not be subject to a restrictive interpretation. If two States have included a certain asset within a list of investments, a tribunal should only exclude it if it fails to meet the requirements of the objective and inherent concept of investment, if there is a compelling reason to do so."[101]

---

96. *KT Asia Investment Group B.V. v. Republic of Kazakhstan* (ICSID Case No. ARB/09/8), Award (17 October 2013) paras. 165-166.
97. *Ibid.*, para. 170.
98. *Ibid.*, paras. 171-172. In the tribunal's view, "such a contribution may well be the consequence of a successful investment"; however, "if the investment fails, and thus makes no contribution at all to the host State's economy, that cannot mean that there has been no investment". Similar conclusions see *Phoenix Action, Ltd. v. Czech Republic*, Award, para. 85; *Saba Fakes v. Republic of Turkey*, Award, paras. 110-111; *Quiborax v. Bolivia*, Decision on Jurisdiction, paras. 223-224.
99. *Ibid.*, para. 173.
100. *OI European Group B.V. v. Bolivarian Republic of Venezuela* (ICSID Case No. ARB/11/25), Award (10 March 2015), para. 218. This conclusion is commonly accepted by case law, see *KT Asia v. Kazakhstan*, Award, para. 165; *Quiboraz* v. *Bolivia*, Decision on Jurisdiction, para. 214.
101. *Ibid.*, para. 219. See also *Ambiente Ufficio S.p.A. and others v. Argentine Republic* (ICSID Case No. ARB/08/9), Decision on Jurisdiction and Admissibility (8 February 2013) para. 470; *Inmaris Perestroika Sailing Maritime Services GmbH and others v. Ukraine* (ICSID Case No. ARB/08/8), Decision on Jurisdiction (8 March 2010) para. 130.

The *Garanti v. Turkmenistan* tribunal determined that claimant made an investment under the BIT in Turkmenistan, as "[n]either the nature of the Claimant's investment itself nor the definition of 'investment' in the BIT 'exceed[s] what is permissible under the Convention'[102] or is 'absurd or patently incompatible with [the] object and purpose'[103] of the ICSID Convention".[104]

In *Vestey v. Venezuela*, the majority of the tribunal generally followed the *Salini* approach and held that "the term 'investment' in Article 25 of the ICSID Convention has an independent meaning ... [and] comprises three components: a commitment or allocation of resources, risk and duration".[105]

The *Borissov and others v. Uzbekistan* tribunal held that to establish jurisdiction, "the claim must pass both through the institutional jurisdictional keyhole set forth in Article 25 as well as the specific jurisdictional keyhole defined in the BIT"; the requirements of the ICSID Convention "were cognizant that the parties to a particular BIT may construct a more specific jurisdictional keyhole in their instrument".[106] Also, the tribunal disagreed that there was a restrictive test to be applied to the broad definition of "investment" in the BIT.[107] In the tribunal's view, "the BIT itself contains no such restrictions [i.e., 'must involve substantial contribution and risk'] when read in accordance with [Article 31 of] the VCLT. The definition of 'investment' is broad, as is not uncommon in such treaties, so as to encompass a wide range of business and financial activities in Host States."[108]

In *Orascom v. Algeria*, the tribunal considered that the meaning of "investment" under the ICSID Convention was an objective one, which included elements of (i) a contribution or allocation of resources; (ii) a duration; and (iii) risk, which included the expectation (albeit not necessary fulfilled) of a commercial return.[109] The tribunal agreed with the *Saba Fakes* award that these requirements "are both necessary and sufficient to define an investment" under the ICSID Convention.[110] Further, the tribunal quoted the *KT Asia* case, considering that this "objective" or "inherent" meaning was also present in a bilateral investment treaty's definition of "investment".[111] It stated that:

102. See also *SGS Société Générale de Surveillance S.A. v. Republic of Paraguay* (ICSID Case No. ARB/07/29), Decision on Jurisdiction (12 February 2010) para. 94.
103. See also *Enron Corporation and Ponderosa Assets, L.P. v. Argentine Republic* (ICSID Case No. ARB/01/3), Decision on Jurisdiction (2 August 2004) para. 42.
104. *Garanti Koza LLP v. Turkmenistan* (ICSID Case No. ARB/11/20), Award (19 December 2016) para. 241.
105. *Vestey Group Ltd v. Bolivarian Republic of Venezuela* (ICSID Case No. ARB/06/4), Award (15 April 2016) para. 187, see also *LESI, S.p.A. and Astaldi, S.p.A. v. People's Democratic Republic of Algeria* (ICSID Case No. ARB/05/3), Decision on Jurisdiction (12 July 2006) para. 72; *Saba Fakes v. Turkey*, Award, para. 102.
106. *Pavel Borissov, Aibar Burkitbayev, Almas Chukin and others v. Republic of Uzbekistan* (ICSID Case No. ARB/13/6), Decision on Jurisdiction (8 March 2017) para. 242.
107. *Ibid.*, para. 325.
108. *Ibid.*, paras. 323 and 326-327.
109. *Orascom TMT Investments S.à r.l. v. People's Democratic Republic of Algeria* (ICSID Case No. ARB/12/35), Final Award (31May 2017) para. 370.
110. *Ibid.*, quoting *Saba Fakes v. Turkey*, Award, para. 110.
111. *Ibid.*, quoting *KT Asia v. Kazakhstan*, Award, paras. 165-166.

> "The listed items normally exhibit the hallmarks of an 'investment' in the objective sense seen above. But, if any of these items does not correspond to the inherent definition of 'investment', the fact that it falls within one of the categories listed in Article 1(2) does not transform it into an 'investment'. In other words, the use of the term 'investment' in both the ICSID Convention and the BIT imports the same basic economic attributes of an investment derived from the ordinary meaning of that term, which comprises a contribution or allocation of resources, duration, and risk."[112]

Whilst it is clear that the investment arbitration community remains widely divided on the appreciation and application of the definition of "investment", three points of consensus seem to have emerged. First, the "double test", or "double keyhole" theory, has been generally accepted in case of ICSID arbitrations, requiring the "investment" at issue to meet both the requirements under Art. 25 of the ICSID Convention and the definition of "investment" under applicable investment treaties. Second, all tribunals have agreed that Art. 31(1) of the VCLT should be the governing rule for the interpretation of relevant provisions. And under this rule, third, the "ordinary meaning" of the term "investment" should be sought and applied particularly in case the term is not specifically defined in the relevant treaties, as in the case of the ICSID Convention.

Regarding the key features, or elements, or "hallmarks" of the concept of "investment", it seems that elements such as contribution, duration, risk and return expectation have been now generally accepted, whilst the "contribution to the development of the host State" aspect seems to have been generally abandoned.

IV. LINGERING ISSUES

The central debate surrounding the definition of "investment" appears to remain focused on the question of the legal function of the aforementioned features or elements of "investment" known as the "*Salini* test": jurisdictional requirement or merely characteristics (*indicia*)? No tribunal seems to have denied that the aforementioned elements can provide guidelines for the ascertainment or exclusion of certain extreme transactions from the concept of "investment". Schreuer also considered that these criteria were typical features of investments under the ICSID Convention, rather than "a set of mandatory legal requirements".[113] Therefore, they might assist in "identifying or excluding in extreme cases the presence of an investment", but could not "defeat the broad and flexible concept of investment under the ICSID Convention to the extent it is not limited by the relevant treaty".[114] What many tribunals have rejected seems to be a rigid application as jurisdictional requirements of a set of loosely defined criteria, some of which have gone beyond the ordinary, objective or inherent meaning of the term.

Indeed, the constitutive elements of the "investment" need to be clarified and concentrated on the ones that constitute the inherent hardcore aspects of the term, such

---

112. *Ibid.*, para. 372.
113. C. H. SCHREUER, et al., *The ICSID Convention: A Commentary*, fn. 50 above, para. 171 at p. 133.
114. *Philip Morris v. Uruguay*, Decision on Jurisdiction, para. 206.

as contribution, duration, risk and return expectation, as identified above, but without further qualifications on such aspects in forms such as "substantial contribution" or "regular return" or imposition of any extra-textual requirements such as legality, good faith or contribution to the host State's development. This conforms to the "plain" or "ordinary" meaning of the term "investment" as for example defined in the Oxford English Dictionary (OED). In the OED, the term "investment" is defined as "the act of investing money in something", and "invest" is defined as "to buy property, shares in a company, etc., in the hope of making a profit". Clearly, the most fundamental elements involved under the OED definition of "investment" are "contribution" (i.e., money or other resources "to buy property, shares in company etc.") and "return expectation" (i.e., "hope of making a profit"). And from the "return expectation" (i.e., "hope of making a profit"), the "risk" and "duration" elements can also deduced. It is important to note that the "plain" or "ordinary" meaning of "investment", as illustrated in the definition under OED, does not require the contribution to be "substantial", or the expected profit or return to be "regular", let alone any reference to extra-textual aspects such as legality, good faith or (significant) contribution to the host State's (sustainable) development. The success of the "*Salini* test" lies in the fact that it "substantiated" the "ordinary meaning" of the term "investment" under Art. 25(1) of the ICSID Convention by identifying certain constitutive elements. But its failure to receive wider acceptance was precisely due to the imposition of an extra-textual element, namely, the contribution to the host State's development element, into the list of the constitutive elements.

If the constitutive elements of the "investment" were so clarified to include only the minimum, inherent core aspects of the term, there should be little hesitance for tribunals to apply such "ordinary meaning" and its constitutive elements as jurisdictional requirements, as there should be little difference in the result adopting either of the "jurisdictional requirement" or "characteristics/indicia" approach. The ordinary meaning constitutes implied terms of the relevant treaties, which shall apply unless it has been overridden by explicit treaty provisions conferring it another "special meaning", as stipulated under Art. 31(4) of the VCLT.

In this connection, it helps to recall two most relevant paragraphs of the Report of the Bank's Executive Directors on the ICSID Convention:

> "While consent of the parties is an essential prerequisite for the jurisdiction of the Centre, consent alone will not suffice to bring a dispute within its jurisdiction. In keeping with the purpose of the Convention, the jurisdiction of the Centre is further limited by reference to the nature of the dispute and the parties thereto. (....)
>
> No attempt was made to define the term 'investment' given the essential requirement of consent by the parties, and the mechanism through which Contracting States can make known in advance, if they so desire, the classes of disputes which they would or would not consider submitting to the Centre."[115]

115. International Bank for Reconstruction and Development, *Report of the Executive Directors on the Convention on the Settlement of Investment Disputes Between States and Nationals of Other States*, 18 March 1965 ("Report of the Executive Directors"), paras. 25 and 27.

The first paragraph was significant in that it demonstrates that the jurisdictional requirements under the ICSID Convention are independent from the jurisdictional requirements under the applicable substantive investment treaty providing the consent to ICSID arbitration. Although such consent is essential for ICSID arbitrations, it alone does not necessarily fulfil jurisdictional conditions for ICSID arbitrations, as certain "further limitations" are imposed by the Convention. It is on this basis that the "double test" or "double keyhole" theory rests and is accepted.

However, a "double door" analogy might be more accurate, as the claim has to pass two "doors" of jurisdictional test: First, the claim has to pass the jurisdictional threshold (the first door) set by the applicable substantive investment treaty to access various dispute settlement channels. Second, if ICSID arbitration is the chosen remedy, the claim then has to pass the second door, namely, the jurisdictional threshold set by Art. 25 of the ICSID Convention. The difference between this analogy and the "double test" or "double keyhole" theory is that this analogy demonstrates the independence of the two jurisdictional tests from each other, whilst the latter two, particularly the "double keyhole" theory, suggest that the two tests are integrated as a united mechanism (a key to ICSID jurisdiction). Thus, Art. 25 should be read and applied independently from the definition under the applicable substantive investment treaty. This has been confirmed by numerous investment arbitration decisions as well as rejections by the ICSID Secretary-General to register certain disputes (such as pure commercial sales disputes) for ICSID arbitrations. According to Art. 31(1) of the VCLT, the undefined "investment" under Art. 25(1) of the ICSID Convention should be interpreted in accordance with its "ordinary meaning" and cannot be deemed as "everything" or "anything". Indeed as noted above, even tribunals that rejected the "*Salini* approach" had accepted that the "*Salini* test" could assist in including or excluding certain extreme transactions.

Regarding the second paragraph, many tribunals and commentators have noted it and have considered that it exhibits a balance achieved between capital-exporting and -importing States in the process of negotiating the Convention, as the former succeeded in securing a "no definition" of "investment" in the Convention imposing no extra qualifications on the term (such as a minimum amount of asset invested, or a debt of at least a certain number of years as originally proposed), whilst the latter were satisfied by the possibility of excluding classes of disputes that they would not want to be submitted to the Centre.[116] However, it was not really a "balance", since whilst the former's success was substantial and substantiated as demonstrated in numerous arbitration cases, the latter's satisfaction was illusionary, as the said declarations turned out to be of merely declaratory value and could not amount to jurisdictional exclusions.[117] As developing States were representing capital-importing States in international investment activities, such factual imbalance can be read as an enhancement to the justification for the application of the "ordinary meaning" of "investment" (including its inherent constitutive elements) as a jurisdictional requirement for ICSID arbitrations.

116. See, e.g., *MHS Annulment,* fn. 62 above, paras. 63-68.

117. See, e.g., R. DOLZER, C. SCHREUER, *Principles of International Investment Law*, fn. 52 above, p. 78.

Whether or not the same "ordinary meaning" and accordingly its constitutive elements apply to substantive investment treaties (such as BITs, within or beyond ICSID arbitrations) is another question of debate particularly in recent cases. According to the aforementioned principle, the answer should depend on the wording of the relevant provisions. If the governing treaty has clearly "defined" the term "investment" to the extent that a "special meaning" under Art. 31(4) of the VCLT can be established as having been conferred on the term, e.g., in the formula of "investment means...", it would be inappropriate to impose the said "ordinary meaning" and elements to qualify such clear, explicit treaty definition, even if the treaty definition manifestly deviates from the "ordinary meaning".[118] However, if the governing treaty does not actually "define" the term "investment" or otherwise confer a "special meaning" onto "investment", but merely provides some illustrations (or *indicia*) of what should or should not be included under the term (even if it is placed in the "definition" provision), it would be appropriate and indeed necessary to import and apply the "ordinary meaning" and its constitutive elements to help out in treaty interpretation.

V. CONCLUSIONS

The definition of "investment" is one of the fundamental and most controversial issues in investor-State arbitration. The vast majority of investment treaties existing today adopt an open-end asset-based definition, whilst other treaties employed an enterprise-based definition. The open-end asset-based definition in particular, has caused many difficulties and controversies in ISDS practice, as arbitral tribunals have been struggling to find a balance between respecting the party autonomy as spelt out in the substantive treaties and preventing abuse of the ISDS system by claimants for transactions that do not fall within the ordinary meaning of "investment". The issue became more complicated in cases of ICSID arbitrations as the jurisdiction of the ICSID requires disputes to qualify as "investment" disputes under both the ICSID Convention and applicable substantive investment treaties and as the ICSID Convention is silent on the definition of "investment".

118. This view seems to have been supported by a most recent decision by the French *Cour de Cassation* that quashed a 2016 decision of the Paris Court of Appeal. The Court of Appeal decision had ruled the acquisition of a right of claim (originated in a delivery of electricity contract) could not constitute, in the absence of contribution, an "investment" within the meaning of the ECT. In the French *Cour de Cassation*'s view, the provisions of the ECT did not specify the criteria characterizing an investment, but listed only, without limitation, assets considered as "investments". According to the French *Cour de Cassation*, if host States want to set a limit in the ratione materiae application of investment treaties, they have to define the notion of "investment" rather than using non-exhaustive lists. For the 2016 Paris Court of Appeal ruling, see *Energoalians SARL (Komstroy) v. Moldova - Cour d'Appel de Paris* - Pôle 1 - Chambre 1Numéro d'inscription au répertoire général: 13/22531 - Arret du 12 avril 2016, available at <https://www.transnational-dispute-management.com/legal-and-regulatory-detail.asp?key=20201> (last accessed 10 March 2018); for the 2018 decision of the *Cour de Cassation*, see *Energoalians SARL (Komstroy) v. Moldova - Cour de Cassation* - Chambre civile 1 No de pourvoi: 16-16568 - 28 March 2018 <https://www.transnational-dispute-management.com/legal-and-regulatory-detail.asp?key=20202> (last accessed 10 March 2018).

The silence on the definition of "investment" under the ICSID Convention has given rise to divided interpretations: earlier decisions started with *Fedax* and *Salini* where tribunals adhered to an "objective" approach insisting that the ordinary, objective or inherent meaning of the term "investment" should apply to establish ICSID jurisdiction. In so doing, they have identified several constitutive elements of "investment" (such as resources commitment, certain duration, assumption of risk, and contribution to the development of the host State) to be applied to ascertain whether an investment existed in a given case. This approach, which was later known as "*Salini* test", was generally and consistently followed by a number of subsequent decisions as established practice until it was seriously attacked by the *Biwater* and the *MHS* Annulment Decisions. These two decisions advocated a "subjective" or "party autonomy" approach of treaty interpretation insisting that the absence of a definition of "investment" in the ICSID Convention was meant to leave the definition to the discretion of the Contracting Parties, which was implemented when they entered into bilateral or other substantive investment treaties granting consent to ICSID arbitration.

Since the *Biwater* and the *MHS* Annulment Decisions the arbitration jurisprudence on the issue became divided, as some tribunals followed the new "subjective" or "party autonomy" line of treaty interpretation, whilst others continued the "*Salini* approach". Some "*Salini* approach" tribunals have gone further to require that the same "*Salini* test" be applied in non-ICSID arbitrations, which was rejected by other tribunals.

As a response to the controversies generated by the open-end asset-based definition of the "investment", many States have adopted newer definitions of "investment" in more recent investment treaties. A most common practice is the inclusion of certain "characteristics of investment", such as resource contribution, expectation of return, and assumption of risk, in the definition of "investment". More and more treaties also explicitly exclude certain categories of asset from the investment treaty protection, such as claims to money deriving solely out of commercial transactions, short term loans, an order or judgement, or portfolio investments. Some States have gone further to opt for a narrower enterprise-based definition of "investment", and other States have attached a series of further requirements such as legality, good faith, and significant contribution to the development of host States, for investments to be protected under their BITs.

It is difficult to assess the propriety of the newer definitions, given that each State has its own conditions and priorities. In general terms, inclusion of the "characteristics of investment" in the investment definition should be regarded as a welcome development considering controversies generated by the expansive open-end asset-based definition, but adding extra-textual elements such as "contribution to the development of host States" to the list of "characteristics of investment", and excluding portfolio investments altogether from treaty protection, seem to be a step too far.

Regarding ISDS interpretations of the concept of "investment", a "double door" theory may better describe the relationship between Art. 25 under the ICSID Convention and the definition of "investment" clause under governing substantive treaties. Given that the Convention requires a dispute to be "arising out of an investment" without defining the term, it is appropriate and indeed necessary to apply the objective and inherent ordinary meaning of the term "investment" in ICSID arbitrations, though it is essential to ensure that the applied "ordinary meaning" should only be the minimum hard core of the concept. The same ordinary meaning may also be applied in non-ICSID arbitrations in case an applicable investment treaty does not clearly define "investment". It seems to be too far-fetched to apply it in investment treaties where "investment" is clearly (even if expansively) defined to establish a "special meaning" under Art. 31(4) of the VCLT.

Fair and Equitable Treatment – Ten Years On

Christophe Bondy[*]

TABLE OF CONTENTS PAGE

I. INTRODUCTION

About a decade ago, as a newly hired counsel in Canada's Trade Law Bureau, I was asked to speak about the obligation of fair and equitable treatment (FET), at an international investment treaty conference in Washington. Several investment treaty decisions recently had been released that espoused an expansive view of the contents of FET.[1] The buzzword at the time was arbitral precedent. Gabrielle Kaufmann-Kohler in a speech the year before had asserted that arbitrators had a duty to follow arbitral precedent, to promote investor certainty about the contents of international investment law.[2]

The thrust of my remarks at the time was to raise the issue of the potential State responses to arbitral decision-making concerning the content of investment treaty rules in general, and of FET in particular.[3] If States disagreed with current arbitral interpretations, I suggested, there likely would be an eventual response in new treaties. This response already had occurred in the context of the North American Free Trade Agreement (NAFTA), with the 2001 Note of Interpretation. That Note clarified that the reference to FET in Art. 1105(1) of NAFTA meant a reference to the Minimum Standard of Treatment (MST) at customary international law.[4] The substance of that

* Special Counsel in the Public International Law Group, Cooley, LLP, London.

1. Among others, *Técnicas Medioambientales Tecmed SA v. Mexico* (ICSID Case No. ARB (AF)/00/2), Award (29 May 2003) (*Tecmed*); *CMS Gas Transmission Company v. The Republic of Argentina* (ICSID Case No. ARB/01/8), Award (12 May 2005); *LG&E Energy Corp., LG&E Capital Corp., and LG&E International, Inc .v. Argentine Republic* (ICSID Case No. ARB/02/1), Award (3 October 2006)
2. Gabrielle KAUFMANN-KOHLER, "Arbitral Precedent: Dream, Necessity or Excuse?", 23 Arbitration International (2007) at pp. 357-377.
3. My remarks ultimately were published as "Fair and Equitable Treatment, Arbitral Jurisprudence, and the Implications of State Treaty Practice" in Ian A. LAIRD and Todd WEILER, eds., *Investment Treaty Arbitration and International Law*, Vol. 2 (Juris Publications, New York 2009) pp. 233-251.
4. NAFTA Free Trade Commission, *Notes of Interpretation of Certain Chapter Eleven Provisions*, 31 July 2001, at B.

Note had then been translated into the new Model Bilateral Investment Treaties (BITs) of both Canada and the United States. Assuming such State restatements were to occur more broadly, what would be the status going forward of arbitral jurisprudence developed before these new treaties emerged, notably regarding the content of the FET standard?

Ten years on, and the biggest sea change in international investment law arguably has been "the return of the State". In their new treaties, in new model BITs and in public statements about their respective investment treaty programmes, States around the world have signalled a desire to reassert control both over the substance of investment treaty standards, and over the process of investor-State dispute resolution. One of the key turning points of this evolution arguably was the change in the European approach to investment treaties, notably through the Canada-European Union Comprehensive Trade and Investment Agreement (CETA). Before that, Western Europe had been a bastion of liberalism vis-à-vis investment treaty obligations. One of the biggest targets in this new wave of treaty-making has been to reign in the FET standard.

Meanwhile, through a steady stream of decisions the FET jurisprudence has grown exponentially.

All of which returns to the question I asked ten years ago, with a new urgency: what will be the impact of these new treaties on the direction of travel for investor-State obligations, and notably for FET? How will the clash of norms between existing FET jurisprudence and its treatment in new treaties be resolved?

This article seeks to provide an encapsulated history of the FET standard, providing a backdrop to these questions. I first will reference early recognition of the need to provide an objective minimum standard of treatment for investors, and the expression of that standard in early model treaties (II). I then will evoke the split that occurred in investment treaty jurisprudence, between FET understood as a reference to the minimum standard of treatment (MST) at customary international law and FET as a treaty standard open to the interpretations of investment tribunals (III). I then will describe the content tribunals have ascribed to FET as a bare treaty standard (IV), before considering the parallel content of FET as the customary international MST (V). This overview will serve as a backdrop for considering recent State attempts at resetting the dial on FET – responses ranging from eliminating all reference to FET, to expressly limiting FET to MST, to ascribing specific content to FET (VI). Finally, I will consider potential responses to next-generation treaties by current and future arbitral tribunals (VII).

II. TOWARDS AN INTERNATIONAL BASELINE

Legal theorists have been promoting an international standard of treatment of foreigners since at least the eighteenth century.[5] Through the nineteenth century, States asserting

5. E. DE VATTEL, *Droit des Gens*, Vol. II Chap. VIII (Duties owed to Foreigners), e.g. at para. 104: "The sovereign ought not to grant an entrance into his state for the purpose of drawing foreigners into a snare: as soon as he admits them, he engages to protect them as his own subjects, and to afford them perfect security, as far as depends on him." For this section, see generally the historical

arbitral claims on behalf of their national investors abroad in effect were asserting the existence of international standard of treatment. In the early twentieth century former US Secretary of State Elihu Root famously asserted that

> "There is a standard of justice, very simple, very fundamental and of such general acceptance by all civilized countries as to form a part of the international law of the world. The condition upon which any country is entitled to measure the justice due from it to an alien by the justice which it accords to its own citizens is that its system of law and administration shall conform to this general standard. If any country's system of law and administration does not conform to that standard, although the people of the country may be content or compelled to live under it no other country can be compelled to accept it as furnishing a satisfactory means of treatment to its citizens." [6]

As Elihu Root's encapsulation confirms, the key characteristic of such theories was their focus on protecting foreigners against the most egregious forms of treatment by States – treatment that any international observer would view as unacceptable, regardless of the standard of treatment accorded by that State to its own citizens. The theory of an international "minimum standard" stood as a counterpart to the competing Calvo doctrine protecting national sovereignty, which held that foreigners could expect no better treatment in a host State than that State offered its own citizens.[7] The core elements of customary international MST were protection against expropriation without compensation; protection of the physical integrity of foreign nationals; and the provision of basic due process – i.e., protection against "denial of justice" in judicial proceedings. The standard thus expressed placed limited but nonetheless real boundaries on the absolute sovereignty of States. The standard was articulated in various claims in the early twentieth century – the most often cited is *Neer (USA) v. United Mexican States*, where the Mexican US General Claims Commission held that "the treatment of an alien, in order to constitute an international delinquency should amount to an outrage, to bad faith, to wilful neglect of duty, or to an insufficiency of governmental action so far short of international standards that every reasonable and impartial man would readily acknowledge its insufficiency".[8]

---

overview in Martins PAPARINSKIS, *The International Minimum Standard and Fair and Equitable Treatment* (OUP 2013), Part I, "Development of the International Minimum Standard". For an earlier historical overview, see OECD, *Fair and Equitable Treatment Standard in International Investment Law, in International Investment Law: A Changing Landscape: A Companion Volume to International Investment Perspectives* (OECD Publishing 2006) p. 118.

6. Elihu ROOT, "The Basis of Protection to Citizens Residing Abroad", 4 Am. J. Int'l Law (1910) pp. 517, 512-522.
7. Carlos Calvo set out the classical expression of this competing doctrine in his *Derecho internacional teórico y práctico de Europa y América* (Paris, 1868).
8. *LFH Neer and Pauline Neer (USA v. United Mexican States)* (1926) 4 RIAA 60, 61-62. This decision's status as reflective of a customary international law minimum standard of treatment of aliens owes much to subsequent reliance by States on its formulation as reflective of custom regarding the treatment of foreign investors and of their investments.

As of at least the 1950s, the United States began expressing this basic protection of foreigners as an obligation of "fair and equitable treatment" (FET) in its treaties of friendship, commerce and navigation (FCN). FET shared with the MST the notion that States should offer foreign investors a baseline level of treatment.[9] FCN treaties did not provide a direct right of action for foreign investors, requiring State espousal of a claim. In the absence of such claims, the content of FET and its relation to MST remained unexplored.

The 1960s saw new impetus for the development of international investment rules, to assist in the promotion of developing economies emerging from colonialism. This notably included the negotiation of the Convention on the Settlement of Investment Disputes between States and Nationals of Other States (ICSID Convention): a Convention that set out a procedural framework for disputes, and guarantees of the enforceability of the resulting judgments, while deliberately avoiding substantive standards. Indeed, the drafters of the ICSID Convention assumed that most investor-State disputes would arise out of investment contracts, rather than investment treaties.[10]

On the substantive side, leading proponents of international investment protection sought to generate a model investment protection treaty, notably the Abs-Shawcross draft of the early 1960s, whose obligations included the requirement to provide "fair and equitable treatment".[11] Picking up on the language from US treaties of Friendship, Commerce and Navigation, the draft 1967 model investment treaty of the Organisation for Economic Co-operation and Development (OECD) also included an obligation of FET. The explanatory notes to the OECD draft treaty confirmed that reference to FET was understood to be a reference to MST.[12] By that time, the wave of anti-colonial and Cold War sentiment prompted hostility to the notion of a (Western-generated) customary international standard, which in any event had generated controversy over the

9. See R. DOLZER and CH. Schreuer, *Principles of International Investment Law* (Oxford University Press 2008) p. 120, for references to 1950s US FCN treaties. The Havana Charter for an International Trade Organization (1948) (UN Doc E/CONF.2/78, 3) also contained reference to the phrase. As Judge Higgins noted in *Oil Platforms (Iran v. US)* (Preliminary Objections) [1996] ICJ Rep 803, Separate Opinion of Judge HIGGINS 847, FET at that point in time (the mid-1990s) was a legal term of art well known in the field of overseas investment protection.

10. See Andreas F. LOWENFELD, "The ICSID Convention: Origins and Transformation", 38 Ga. J. Int'l & Comp. L. (2009) p. 47.

11. E.g., the Abs-Shawcross Draft Convention on Investment Abroad (1960) 9 J Public L 116.

12. OECD, Draft Convention on the Protection of Foreign Property (1968) 7 ILM 117, Notes and Comments to Art. 1, para. 4(a):

> "The phrase 'fair and equitable treatment', customary in relevant bilateral agreements, indicates the standard set by international law for the treatment due by each State with regard to the property of foreign nationals. The standard requires that – subject to essential security interests – protection afforded under the Convention shall be that generally accorded by the Party concerned to its own nationals, but, being set by international law, the standard may be more exacting where rules of national law or national administrative practices fall short of the requirements of international law. *The standard required conforms in effect to the 'minimum standard' which forms part of international law.*" (Emphasis added.)

course of the century.[13] In the OECD Model, FET thus became a stand-in for the expression of the customary MST.[14] Meanwhile one of the original elements of MST, protection against expropriation, was set out in a distinct article, as was the obligation to provide full protection and security.

The 1970s and 1980s saw virtually no investment treaty cases, addressing FET or otherwise.[15] One exception was the *ELSI* case that exceptionally went before the International Court of Justice (ICJ) in the late 1970s. The case concerned the application of the US-Italy Treaty of Friendship, Commerce and Navigation, and turned on that treaty's express protection against "arbitrary" treatment. The Court famously noted that "[a]rbitrariness is not so much something opposed to a rule of law, as opposed to the rule of law... It is wilful disregard of due process of law, an act which shocks, or at least surprises, a sense of judicial propriety."[16] The ICJ was interpreting a treaty-based protection against arbitrary treatment, and not FET itself. Despite this, the decision would go on to inform arbitral tribunals' interpretations of FET in later investment treaty decisions.[17]

In the 1980s and 1990s the number of investment treaties expanded exponentially, as capital-importing States (moving on from anti-colonial sentiment in the 1960s and 1970s) accepted the need to signal respect for international standards, in particular acceptance of prompt and effective compensation for expropriation, as a counterpoint to attracting additional investment.[18] Again, during this phase actual disputes arising under investment treaties were rare. The drafters involved were international lawyers and

13. See discussion in Stephen SCHWEBEL, "The Influence of Bilateral Investment Treaties on Customary International Law", *Proceedings of the 98th Annual Meeting of the American Society of International Law, 31 March – 3 April 2004*, pp. 27-30.

14. As noted by Judge Nikken, "... the question of why there is no mention in the BITs of the international minimum standard cannot be answered properly if the historical controversy on the concept of minimum standard is completely ignored....", Judge NIKKEN, Separate Opinion in *AWG v. Argentina* (UNCITRAL), Decision on Liability (30 July 2010) paras. 11-12. See also OECD, "Fair and Equitable Treatment Standard in International Investment Law", OECD Working Papers on International Investment (2003/2004) p. 8, n. 33.

15. The UNCTAD database of decided cases only lists arbitrations initiated as of 1987, and from that year until 1993 only two cases, with a further two in 1994 and 1995. As for 1996, the rhythm of cases initiated accelerates: see <http://investmentpolicyhub.unctad.org/ISDS/FilterByYear>. Of course, earlier cases may not have been disclosed.

16. *Elettronica Sicula S.p.A. (ELSI) Case (United States of America v. Italy)*, [1989] ICJ Rep. p. 15, at para. 128. Treaty of Friendship, Commerce and Navigation between the United States and Italy, signed 2 February 1948, entered into force 26 July 1949 [79 UNTS 171].

17. As a recent OECD analysis notes, the United States expressly has rejected reliance on *ELSI* as support for a customary international rule against arbitrary treatment given that the ICJ was interpreting a specific treaty provision, not commenting on customary international law: see David GAUKRODGER, "Addressing the Balance of Interests in Investment Treaties: The Limitation of Fair and Equitable Treatment Provisions to the Minimum Standard of Treatment Under Customary International Law", OECD Working Papers on International Investment 2017/03, p. 48, citing the US Counter-Memorial in *Glamis Gold, Ltd v. United States of America*, 19 September 2006, p. 228.

18. Stephen SCHWEBEL, "The Influence of Bilateral Investment Treaties on Customary International Law", *Proceedings of the 98th Annual Meeting of the American Society of International Law, 31 March – 3 April 2004*, pp. 27-30.

diplomats from State departments of foreign affairs. They were familiar with public international law treaties, and with State-to-State disputes. Such disputes tend to be pursued with a view to the systemic implications of particular interpretative positions. Using the OECD Model Treaty as a basis, reference to an obligation of "fair and equitable treatment" became commonplace in treaties entered into during this phase. The treaties linked FET to an international standard in varying ways: under the express heading of "Minimum Standard of Treatment"; by reference to FET "in accordance with international law"; making reference to FET in conjunction with other standards, such as protection against arbitrariness; and finally, by a "bare" reference to FET.[19]

As of the 1980s, the majority of international lawyers continued to recognize the link between a reference to FET and the customary MST. A minority view was expressed by UK international lawyer F.A. Mann. In an oft-cited publication, he asserted that

> "the terms 'fair and equitable treatment' envisage conduct which goes far beyond the minimum standard and afford protection to a greater extent and according to a much more objective standard than any previously employed form of words. A tribunal would not be concerned with a minimum, maximum or average standard. It will have to decide whether in all the circumstances the conduct at issue is fair and equitable or unfair and inequitable. No standard defined by other words is likely to be material. The terms are to be understood and applied independently and autonomously."[20]

Less often-cited is Mann's follow-up comment in a paper published the following year, where he noted that

> "In some cases, it is true, treaties merely repeat, perhaps in slightly different language, what in essence is a duty imposed by customary international law; the foremost example is the familiar provision whereby states undertake to accord fair and equitable treatment to each other's nationals and which in law is unlikely to amount to more than a confirmation of the obligation to act in good faith, or to refrain from abuse or arbitrariness."[21]

Reflecting the international development origins of investment treaty protections, the vast majority of treaties entered into during this period were between developed and developing countries. One exception was the NAFTA, which bound together the United States, Canada and Mexico. Its predecessor, the Canada-United States Free Trade Agreement, contained an investment protection chapter, but only State-to-State dispute

19. See overview in United Nations Conference on Trade and Development, "'Fair and Equitable Treatment': UNCTAD Series on Issues in International Investment Agreements II" (United Nations, New York and Geneva 2012) pp. xiiv-xiv.
20. F.A. MANN, *The Legal Aspects of Money*, 4th ed. (Clarendon Press, Oxford 1982) p. 510. See related discussion in J.C. THOMAS, "Reflection on Article 1105 of NAFTA: History, State Practice and the Influence of Commentators", 17 ICSID Review – Foreign Investment Law Journal (2002, no. 1) pp. 21-101, p. 58.
21. As quoted by J.C. THOMAS, "Reflection on Article 1105 of NAFTA: History, State Practice and the Influence of Commentators", p.58.

resolution, and no reference either to FET or to protection of a customary MST.[22] Given the long and troubled experience of US investors in Mexico (the *Neer* claim, for example, related to a US national in Mexico), when the NAFTA was negotiated the United States proposed the inclusion of investor-State dispute settlement, including an update of the statement of obligations. Canada agreed. The obligations addressed (non-discrimination, protection against expropriation with compensation, respect for an international MST) were all consistent with basic standards of good governance, which Canada fully respected. NAFTA therefore guaranteed investors among other things "treatment in accordance with international law, including fair and equitable treatment and full protection and security", under the heading Minimum Standard of Treatment.[23]

III. FET AND MST PART WAYS

By the mid-1990s, lawyers began to recognize the potential power of investment treaties, which for the first time in public international law allowed investors to initiate arbitrations directly against States for alleged violations of international obligations.[24] They began launching what was to become a wave of claims over the next twenty years. In these claims, the scope of FET and its relation to the MST at customary international law soon became an issue.[25]

A key interpretative shift occurred when arbitrators began deciding that FET in investment treaties was a pure treaty standard, not tied the contents of any international minimum standard arising in customary international law.[26] In many treaties, FET had expressly been tied neither to customary international law, nor to a MST. Arbitrators accordingly reasoned that FET was a freestanding treaty standard.[27]

22. Canada–United States Free Trade Agreement, entered into force 1 January 1989: <http://www.international.gc.ca/trade-commerce/assets/pdfs/agreements-accords/cusfta-e.pdf>.
23. NAFTA Art. 1105(1).
24. Jan PAULSSON, "Arbitration Without Privity", 10 ICSID Review – Foreign Investment Law Journal, (1 October 1995, issue 2) pp. 232-257.
25. The 2004 OECD survey of FET in investment cases suggested that up to that date at least, the earliest investment tribunals had not sought to interpret FET as a "bare" treaty standard: OECD, "Fair and Equitable Treatment Standard in International Investment Law", OECD Working Papers on International Investment Law (2004/03). The exception to this would be early cases under NAFTA Chapter Eleven, notably *Metalclad* and *Pope & Talbot*. As set out in what follows, these initial decisions were in effect overturned by the 2001 NAFTA Free Trade Commission Note of Interpretation.
26. Apparently the first tribunal to apply the FET standard as a "bare" treaty standard was *Emilio Augustin Maffezini v. The Kingdom of Spain* (ICSID Case No. ARB/97/7), Award (13 November 2000), 5 ICSID Rep. 274 (2010). However, the OECD's 2004 analysis of FET found that, to that date, no tribunal had yet interpreted FET as a "bare" treaty obligation. This appears to have excluded the award in *Tecmed*, dating from 2003. See OECD, "Fair and Equitable Treatment Standard in International Investment Law", OECD Working Papers on International Investment (2004/03).
27. One such case was *Azurix v. Argentina* (ICSID Case No. ARB/01/12), Award (14 July 2006), where the tribunal interpreted a clause that said investments shall be provided FET and "in no case be accorded treatment less than required by international law". They found that reference to

This crucial interpretative shift left the expression "fair and equitable treatment" open to be interpreted in accordance with the Vienna Convention on the Law of Treaties (VCLT). According to Art. 31 of the VCLT, treaty language is to be given its ordinary meaning, in its context and in light of its object and purpose.[28]

Given the breadth of the expression "fair and equitable treatment" and its relative indeterminacy, reference to an obligation of FET understood as a bare treaty obligation (rather than an obligation disciplined by the evidentiary requirements of customary international law) quickly became the site for a broad range of arbitral interpretations. Indeed, arbitrators frequently have asserted that the content of FET can only be assessed *in concreto*, in light of specific fact scenarios.[29]

This interpretative shift arguably first manifested itself in the context of NAFTA Chapter Eleven claims. Early NAFTA cases recognized the typical public international law rule that State sovereignty may be limited only by clear rules.[30] Yet early tribunals

---

international law "set a floor, not a ceiling" and thus "permits to interpret fair and equitable treatment... as [a] higher [standard] than that required by international law" (para. 361).

28. Vienna Convention on the Law of Treaties, Art. 31(1): "A treaty shall be interpreted in good faith in accordance with the ordinary meaning to be given to the terms of the treaty in their context and in light of its object and purpose".

29. NAFTA Chapter Eleven tribunals have sought to retain the same margin for manoeuvre in applying FET as the customary international minimum standard, holding that it "cannot be reached in the abstract; it must depend on the facts of the particular case" (*Mondev International Ltd. v. United States of America* (ICSID Case No. ARB(AF)/99/2), Award (11 October 2002) para. 118; *Chemtura Corporation v. Government of Canada, (formerly Crompton Corporation v. Government of Canada)* (UNCITRAL), Award (2 August 2009) p. 123:

"In assessing whether the treatment afforded to the Claimant's investment was in accordance with the international minimum standard, the Tribunal must take into account all the circumstances, including the fact that certain agencies manage highly specialized domains involving scientific and public policy determinations. This is not an abstract assessment circumscribed by a legal doctrine about the margin of appreciation of specialized regulatory agencies. It is an assessment that must be conducted *in concreto*. The Tribunal will proceed to such assessment *in concreto* when reviewing the specific measures challenged by the Claimant."

30. *Case of the S.S. Lotus (France v. Turkey),* Permanent Court of Int'l Justice, P.C.I.J. (ser. A) No. 10 (1927); *Robert Azinian, Kenneth Davitian, & Ellen Baca v. The United Mexican States* (ICSID Case No. ARB (AF)/97/2), Award (1 November 1999):

"Arbitral jurisdiction under Section B is limited not only as to the persons who may invoke it (they must be nationals of a State signatory to NAFTA), but also as to subject matter: claims may not be submitted to investor-state arbitration under Chapter Eleven unless they are founded upon the violation of an obligation established in Section A.

To put it another way, a foreign investor entitled in principle to protection under NAFTA may enter into contractual relations with a public authority, and may suffer a breach by that authority, and *still not be in a position to state a claim under NAFTA*. It is a fact of life everywhere that individuals may be disappointed in their dealings with public authorities, and disappointed yet again when national courts reject their complaints. It may safely be assumed that many *Mexican* parties can be found who had business dealings with governmental entities which were not to their satisfaction; Mexico is unlikely to be different from other countries in this respect. NAFTA was not intended to provide foreign investors with blanket protection from this kind of disappointment, and nothing in its terms so provides." (Emphasis in original.)

quickly began to push the boundaries of FET. The *Myers* tribunal asserted that the breach of another standard under NAFTA – in this case, the obligation to provide national treatment – automatically would amount to a breach of FET, despite the lack of any grounding for a protection against discrimination in purely customary international law.[31] The *Metalclad* tribunal appeared to apply FET without any evaluation of customary international law, adding to the standard an obligation of "transparency".[32] Soon, the *Pope & Talbot* tribunal expressly asserted that reference to FET in Art. 1105(1), despite appearing under the heading "Minimum Standard of Treatment", in effect was additive to the MST – in other words, that investors were to be afforded customary international law MST, *plus* new "fairness" elements derived from FET.[33]

The decision of the *Pope & Talbot* tribunal elicited a swift reaction from the three NAFTA Parties. By 2001, the NAFTA Free Trade Commission (FTC) released what to date has been the only binding interpretative statement issued by the Parties under Chapter Eleven of NAFTA. The main thrust of the Note was to state plainly that reference to FET in NAFTA Art. 1105(1) was not meant to and did not bring into the scope of Chapter Eleven obligations beyond those provided by the customary international law minimum standard of treatment of investors.[34] Thus, the Note expressly ruled out the possibility of tribunals treating the reference to FET as a pure treaty standard, open to their own interpretations under the VCLT. Moreover, the Note confirmed that a breach of any other part of the NAFTA, or of some other international standard, did not amount to a breach of FET.

It is noteworthy that this State intervention took place in the context of the only investor-State dispute settlement procedure applicable at the time between developed States (with the exception of the Energy Charter Treaty). Tribunals interpreting FET outside of the NAFTA context, in treaties between capital exporting and largely capital importing States, apparently did not face the same level of policy pushback to broad interpretations of FET, at least from both treaty partners. Notably, the United States did not seek to intervene in the numerous cases arising out of the Argentinian economic crisis of the early 2000s, to argue that the reference to FET in its investment treaty with Argentina was limited to customary international law.[35] As many of the broader

---

31. *S.D. Myers, Inc. v. Government of Canada* (UNCITRAL), Partial Award (13 November 2000), para. 266.
32. *Metalclad Corporation v. United Mexican States* (ICSID Case No. ARB(AF)97/1), Award (30 August 2000). The decision was set aside in part by the British Columbia Supreme Court for excess of jurisdiction, precisely because the Tribunal had not established that transparency formed part of the applicable customary international law standard: *Mexico v. Metalclad, Supreme Court of British Columbia* (2001). Despite this, tribunals outside of the NAFTA context continued to rely on *Metalclad* to find that FET as a bare treaty standard includes an obligation of "transparency".
33. *Pope & Talbot v. Government of Canada* (UNCITRAL), Award on the Merits of Phase 2 (10 April 2001) para. 110.
34. NAFTA Free Trade Commission, *Notes of Interpretation of Certain Chapter Eleven Provisions* (31 July 2001).
35. Treaty between the United States of America and the Republic of Argentina Concerning the Encouragement and Reciprocal Protection of Investment (adopted 14 November 1991; entered into force 20 October 1994) 1992 (3) ILM 124 Art. II(2)(a): "Investment shall at all times be

interpretations of FET were developed in cases arising out of the Argentinian economic crises, and heard under the US-Argentinian BIT, the United States' silence on this issue outside of the NAFTA context arguably was crucial to FET emerging as a stand-alone treaty standard, outside of the NAFTA context.[36]

Indeed, while the 2001 FTC Note of Interpretation laid down a marker for the interpretation of FET under NAFTA Art. 1105(1), effectively tying it to customary international law, an increasing cleavage emerged between two expressions of the FET standard.[37] According to the first line of interpretation, and consistent with its historical use, FET refers to the MST of investors at customary international law. This was a standard that could expand and change only to the extent custom itself evolved.[38] According to the second line of interpretation, FET is a pure treaty standard, open to arbitral interpretation in light of the rules set out in the VCLT.[39] Unsurprisingly, since the first half of the 2000s the "bare" FET treaty standard has become the focal point of most investment treaty claims, and its alleged content has far outstripped the protections offered under customary international law FET.

IV. ARBITRAL INTERPRETATIONS OF FET AS A "BARE" TREATY OBLIGATION

What amounts to "fair and equitable" can depend very much on one's point of view. When interpreting an FET clause as a bare treaty obligation, arbitrators formally are bound by the rules of the VCLT. Within the confines of the VCLT, however, arbitrators have ascribed a broad array of substantive content to the phrase.

The breadth of such interpretations has been encouraged by at least three features of international investment arbitration.

First, in early treaties (drafted before any claims had been launched) State treaty drafters tended to use preambular language exclusively emphasizing their intended role to protect and to promote investors. Since the preamble of a treaty has formal status as

---

accorded fair and equitable treatment, shall enjoy full protection and security and shall in no case be accorded treatment less than that required by international law."

36. The Vienna Convention on the Law of Treaties provides at Art. 31(3)(a) that a subsequent agreement of the States Parties to a treaty regarding its interpretation or application "shall be taken into account" in interpreting that treaty.

37. This cleavage recently was explored in the OECD study by David GAUKRODGER, "Addressing the Balance of Interests in Investment Treaties", supra fn. 17.

38. MST is typically seen as comprising two main elements: FET, and Full Protection and Security (FPS). As with FET, there has been a debate in arbitral jurisprudence as to the scope of the FPS obligation, with some tribunals finding it a bare treaty standard, open to expansive interpretations (including protection of "legal stability"). As with FET, there has been a State reaction against such interpretations in more recent treaty drafting such as CETA, with States confirming that FPS addresses only the physical protection of investors and their investments.

39. See for example *Azurix Corp. v. The Argentine Republic* (ICSID Case No. ARB/01/12), Award (14 July 2006), where the tribunal interpreted a clause providing that investments shall be provided FET and "in no case be accorded treatment less than required by international law". Reminiscent of *Pope & Talbot v. Canada*, the tribunal found that the reference to international law "set a floor, not a ceiling" and thus "permits to interpret fair and equitable treatment ... as [a] higher [standard] than that required by international law" (para. 361).

"context" for purposes of the VCLT, arbitrators turning to this source as guidance for interpreting FET took direction from the expansive language.[40]

Second, unlike traditional public international law dispute resolution, which was State to State, investment treaties grant investors the right to bring claims directly against a State. Investors' interests are bound to the outcome of their particular claim. In practice, this has promoted creative and arguably expansive readings of FET, promoting a higher level of recovery.

Third, arbitrators have tended to use FET as a fallback obligation, where State conduct fails to rise to the level of express discrimination, or does not amount to a substantial taking of the investment (a requirement for indirect expropriation). While arbitrators may hesitate to sanction State regulation as a "taking", they arguably have found it easier to sanction the manner of its implementation as unfair to an investor.[41]

The development of FET as a bare treaty standard also has been encouraged by the notion of arbitral precedent. While investment treaties expressly rule out a formal doctrine of *stare decisis*, arbitrators nonetheless in practice pay close attention to decisions of previous tribunals (where available). Indeed, as noted in the introduction to this article, arbitrators have expressed respect for arbitral precedent as a formal duty on the part of arbitrators, to promote certainty.[42] The result has been the rapid development over the span of a decade of multiple repeating and expanding heads of content for FET.

Reliance on rapidly concretized initial readings of investment treaties has begged the question whether such interpretations reflected State policy or State intentions when entering into the treaty. The known contents of State submissions in investment treaty claims suggest to the contrary.[43] This has generated an inherent tension between FET jurisprudence and State policy intentions, arguably eliciting current State responses.

---

40. E.g., *CMS Gas Transmission Co. v. Argentine Republic* (ICSID Case No. ARB/01/8), Award (14 July 2006) at paras. 274 and 280, relying on the Preamble to the Treaty between the United States of America and the Argentine Republic concerning the reciprocal encouragement and protection of investment, which provided that "fair and equitable treatment of investment is desirable in order to maintain a stable framework for investment".
41. *PSEG Global Inc. v. Republic of Turkey* (ICSID Case No. ARB/02/5), Award (19 Jan. 2007) para. 238:

    "The standard of fair and equitable treatment has acquired prominence in investment arbitration as a consequence of the fact that other standards traditionally provided by international law might not in the circumstances of each case be entirely appropriate. This is particularly the case when the facts of the dispute do not clearly support the claim for direct expropriation, but when there are notwithstanding events that need to be assessed under a different standard to provide redress in the event that the rights of the investor have been breached."

42. Gabrielle KAUFMANN-KOHLER, "Arbitral Precedent: Dream, Necessity or Excuse?", 23 Arbitration International (2007) at pp. 357-377.
43. David GAUKRODGER, in "Addressing the Balance of Interest in Investment Treaties", supra fn. 17, surveys the stark distinction between the content of FET as articulated by the NAFTA Parties in their submissions in claims, compared with the expansive readings of FET offered by tribunals who do not consider themselves bound to cleave to customary international law in interpreting FET. Given the longstanding failure of many States to take steps in favour of transparency of investment treaty proceedings, the submissions of States in particular disputes outside of the NAFTA context are only sporadically available. This hopefully will be increasingly

It is beyond the scope of this paper to conduct a definitive survey of the range of meaning arbitrators have ascribed to FET interpreted as a pure treaty standard. The following instead is a survey of some of the main lines of jurisprudence.[44]

1. *Legitimate Expectations*

No treaty iteration of the FET clause expressly affirms a right to protection of investors' expectations. Nonetheless, protection of investors' "legitimate expectations" has become a central feature of FET jurisprudence, when interpreting the clause as a "bare" treaty standard. To a greater or lesser degree, the doctrine interprets FET as giving force of law to the expectations of investors with regard to the operation and conduct of their investment. State measures upsetting such expectations can give rise to a right to compensation. The relative starkness of application of this doctrine arguably has evolved, from early cases affirming a right to expectations in the "stability of the legal and regulatory environment", to more current expressions, which set out stricter requirements for legitimate reliance and acknowledge that investors cannot expect the regulatory environment to remain frozen. Nonetheless, protection of investor "expectations" marks a wide berth from a customary standard focussed on the minimum levels of State protection.

The earliest expression of the doctrine was in *TecMed*, which (1) interpreted FET as an obligation separate from MST under customary international law, and (2) grounded enforcement of "legitimate expectations" of investors under FET upon the general principle of good faith.[45]

The doctrine continued to gain prominence in investment treaty jurisprudence as arbitrators considered claims relating to alleged dramatic changes to the legal and regulatory environment of investments made in Argentina, flowing from the economic crisis of the early 2000s. In that context, following the direction of the VCLT to interpret language in light of its "context", arbitrators interpreted the guarantee of FET in light of preambular language asserting among the purposes of the treaty, the creation of a stable and predictable environment for the investor. This led to early decisions affirming that to provide FET, States had to respect investors' reasonable expectations in a "stable regulatory and legal environment".[46]

---

remedied over time by the adherence of most States to the United Nations Convention on Transparency in Treaty-based Investor-State Arbitration (New York, 2014) (the Mauritius Convention on Transparency).

44. Proposed content for FET as a stand-alone treaty standard includes protection against denial of justice and in favour of administrative due process, protection against coercion and harassment of investors, requirements of stability, predictability, consistency and legality, protection of legitimate expectations, protection against arbitrariness and discrimination, transparency, and a requirement of reasonableness and proportionality See Stephan SCHILL, "Fair and Equitable Treatment, the Rule of Law, and Comparative Public Law" in Stephan W. Schill, *International Investment Law and Comparative Public Law* (OUP, Oxford and New York 2010) Chapter 5.

45. *Tecmed, s*upra fn. 1, para. 154; *Saluka Investments BV v. Czech Republic* (UNCITRAL), Partial Award (17 March 2006) para. 307.

46. See *CMS* supra.

The challenge with this doctrine was that it risked imposing a standstill requirement on States. Indeed, even within the four corners of VCLT interpretation, the approach adopted in relation to investor expectations has tended to soften over time. Few arbitrators would ascribe the extreme view that investment treaties protect the "subjective" expectations of investors.[47] More typically, arbitrators find that to be enforceable under FET expectations must be objectively reasonable, evidenced by a commitment made directly to the investor prior to the making of the investment, upon which the investor in effect relied when making the investment, and upon which it would be reasonable to rely.[48]

Indeed, the determination of what constitutes a "reasonable" expectation has been the locus for working out a more tempered view of the obligation.

For example, tribunals early on rejected the notion that investors could expect the regulatory environment for their investment to be frozen in time.[49] To the contrary, tribunals now more typically assert that reasonable expectations must be that the regulatory environment will evolve. This is all the more reasonable where an investment is conducted in a highly regulated environment, in which State policy is in continual evolution in light of expanding knowledge and shifting public tolerance for risk. For example, some tribunals have considered the range of factors of which an investor ought to have known at the time its alleged expectation was formed, based upon reasonable due diligence . To the extent an investor's alleged expectations failed to account for such known factors, they have been found unreasonable.[50]

Despite these tempering factors, and despite current centrality to FET analysis, the enforcement of "legitimate expectations" is arguably the most controversial doctrine arising out of arbitral interpretations of FET, and one that States regularly resist in their submissions to tribunals. As the NAFTA Parties have noted, under general international law it is widely accepted that violation of a contract entered into by a State with an

47. See *Eastern Sugar B.V. (Netherlands) v. The Czech Republic* (SCC Case No. 088/2004), Partial Dissenting Opinion of Robert Volterra (12 April 2007) para. 27: "The fair and equitable treatment obligation in Art. 3.1 of the BIT protects the Claimant's legitimate *subjective* expectations" (my emphasis), relying on *Tecmed.*

48. *Duke Energy Electroquil v. Republic of Ecuador* (ICSID Case No. ARB/04/19), Award (18 August 2008) para. 340 – protection of objective expectations based upon representations made to investors.

49. *Saluka v. Czech Republic* (UNCITRAL Rules), Partial Award, (17 Mar 2006), para. 304 – legitimate expectations in order to be protected must rise to the level of legitimacy and reasonableness in light of the circumstances.... No investor may reasonably expect that the circumstances prevailing at the time the investment is made remain totally unchanged. In order to determine whether frustration of the foreign investor's expectations was justified and reasonable, the host State's legitimate right subsequently to regulate domestic matters in the public interest must be taken into consideration as well ... the determination of a breach of Article 3.1 by the Czech Republic therefore requires a weighing of the Claimant's legitimate and reasonable expectations on the one hand and the Respondent's legitimate regulatory interests on the other."

50. See, e.g., in *Eli Lilly v. Canada* treatment of Eli Lilly's apparent failure to engage in any due diligence into the then-current state of Canadian patent law vs. Canada's demonstration that the legal doctrine that took them by "surprise" had in fact been widely discussed in contemporary commentary by leading patent scholars: *Eli Lilly and Company v. Government of Canada* (UNCITRAL, ICSID Case No. UNCT/14/2), Final Award (16 March 2017) paras. 383-384.

investor of another State is not, by itself, a violation of international law.[51] In these circumstances, they argue, it is illogical and unwarranted to elevate disappointed expectations to a breach of an international rule. Moreover, to the extent legitimate expectations are grounded in a notion of quasi-contract, the NAFTA Parties note that such a reading of FET would render the "umbrella clause" provision of investment treaties redundant, in violation of the interpretive rule of *effet utile*.[52] Other critiques have focussed on the disconnect between the doctrine and its alleged foundations on general principles of law or the requirement of good faith.[53] Scholars have noted the limited extent to which such expectations would give rise to obligations at domestic law, *contra* the attempt of some tribunals to ground the doctrine through an exercise of comparative law.[54] The stark contrast between the elevation of expectations of foreign investors to legal obligations and typical domestic remedies has fed into public perceptions that investment treaties – and notably the FET obligation –grant investors special rights unavailable in domestic law.

2. Transparency

Investment tribunals also have asserted that FET includes a State obligation to act transparently vis-à-vis investors. *Metalclad v. Mexico* was the first case under NAFTA Chapter Eleven to suggest that Art. 1105(1) of NAFTA included an obligation of "transparency" by reference to the provision in favour of transparency elsewhere in the agreement (Art. 102(1)). The award was set aside in part by the British Columbia Supreme Court on the grounds that the obligation of "transparency" had not been demonstrated to form part of the applicable standard under Art. 1105(1), i.e. customary

51. See *SGS Société Générale de Surveillance S.A. v. Pakistan* (ICSID Case No. ARB/01/13), Decision on Jurisdiction (6 August 2003) para. 167; International Law Commission, 53rd Session (2001), "Of course the breach by a State of a contract does not as such entail a breach of international law"); see other sources cited in *Glamis v. United States of America*, US Rejoinder, p. 179 and note 703. See also *Parkerings-Compagniet AS v. Lithuania* (ICSID Case No. ARB/05/8), Award (11 September 2007); *Hamester v. Ghana* (ICSID Case No. ARB/07/24), Award (18 June 2010).
52. Umbrella clauses typically provide that a State shall respect all undertakings to an investor. Canada has never included umbrella clauses in its treaties, precisely since they potentially elevate purely contractual disputes to the level of a breach of public international law.
53. See Josef OSTRANSKY, "An Exercise in Equivocation: A Critique of Legitimate Expectations as a General Principle of Law under the Fair and Equitable Treatment Standard" in A. GATTINI; A. TANZI, F. FONTANELLI, eds., *General Principles of Law and International Investment Arbitration* (Brill 2018); Jonathan BONNITCHA, "The Problem of Moral Hazard and Its Implications for the Protection of 'Legitimate Expectations' Under the Fair and Equitable Treatment Standard", International Institute for Sustainable Development, Investment Treaty News (7 April 2011); Christopher CAMPBELL, "House of Cards: The Relevance of Legitimate Expectations Under Fair and Equitable Treatment Provisions in Investment Treaty Law", 30 Journal of International Arbitration (Kluwer Law International 2013, Issue 4) pp. 361-379.
54. See Josef OSTRANSKY, "An Exercise in Equivocation: A Critique of Legitimate Expectations as a General Principle of Law Under the Fair and Equitable Treatment Standard" in A. GATTINI, A. TANZI, F. FONTANELLI, eds., *General Principles of Law and International Investment Arbitration* (Brill 2018); compare with survey in *Total S.A. v. The Argentine Republic* (ICSID Case No. ARB/04/01), Decision on Liability (27 Dec 2010).

international law.[55] Nonetheless, *Metalclad* has continued to be cited in support of this proposed element of FET, understood as a "bare" treaty standard. The transparency requirement famously was restated in the *TecMed* case, in which the tribunal set out an ideal view of how States should act vis-à-vis investors (comments that were in effect *obiter*, as they did not form the basis of the tribunal's actual finding of liability).[56] *Tecmed* quickly became the wellspring for framing FET as the driver of international administrative law reform. Rather than guaranteeing certain basic standards including protection against denial of justice, reference to FET for some became seen as an invitation to engage in prescriptive behaviour towards States in support of a broad range of good governance principles.[57]

The challenge with such approaches to FET, from a State perspective, is the democratic gap inherent in an *ad hoc* tribunal purporting to engage in a prescriptive exercise of good governance, relying to a greater or lesser degree on academic commentators' theories of international administrative best practice, derived through an undoubtedly learned but inevitably personal review of domestic practices collected from jurisdictions around the world. In actual practice the circumstances in which FET violations have been found on the basis of "lack of transparency" have tended to be egregious, suggesting that attempts to fine-tune domestic administrative practice via investment law may be overrated. However, from a State policy perspective concern about overreach through such interpretations remains.

As with legitimate expectations, the ability to impose damages for perceived failings in administrative practice highlights another gap between available remedies under FET (understood as a "bare" treaty standard), and remedies available for equivalent breaches in domestic administrative law. Administrative law rarely, for example, provides for an award of damages in cases of breach.[58]

55. *Metalclad Corporation v. The United Mexican States* (ICSID Case No. ARB(AF)/97/1), Award (30 August 2000).
56. *Tecmed,* supra fn. 1, para. 154:

> "*El Tribunal Arbitral considera que esta disposición del Acuerdo, a la luz de los imperativos de buena fé requeridos por el derecho interncional, exige de las Partes Contratantes del Acuerdo brindar un tratamiento a la inversión extranjera que no desvirtúe las expectativas básicas en razón de las cuales el inversor extranjero decidió realizar su inversión. Como parte de tales expectativas, aquél cuenta con que el Estado receptor de la inversión se conducirá de manera coherente, desprovista de ambigüedades y transparente en sus relaciones con el inversor extranjero, de manera que éste pueda conocer de manera anticipada, para. planificar sus actividades y ajustar su conducta, no sólo las normas o reglamentaciones que regirán tales actividades, sino también las políticas perseguidas por tal normativa y las prácticas o directivas administrativas que les son relevantes....*"

The reference to transparency has been incorrectly translated in the English version, into a requirement to act "totally transparently".

57. See, for example, Stephan SCHILL, "Fair and Equitable Treatment as an Embodiment of the Rule of Law" in R. HOFMANN and C. TAMS, eds., *The International Convention on the Settlement of Investment Disputes (ICSID): Taking Stock after 40 Years* (Nomos 2007).
58. See comments to this effect in OECD Working Papers on International Investment 2012/3, *Investor-State dispute settlement: A scoping paper for the investment policy community*.

3. *Reasonableness, Proportionality and the "Balancing" Exercise*

On its face, the right to FET is an absolute right, reinforced by its status as a non-contingent standard not dependent on the treatment offered by a State to its own citizens. Perhaps inspired by this understanding of FET, arbitral tribunals and commentators on investment law have fallen into the habit of referring to investors "rights", without defining their scope. Yet under classical international law, State sovereignty can be limited only to the extent of express undertakings to this effect. Rather than acknowledge this formal legal requirement, tribunals and commentators have instead evoked a need to "balance" investors' rights (including to FET) against corresponding rights of the State, notably the right to regulate.[59]

The challenge with this discourse is the lack of determinacy of FET understood as a bare treaty norm: the analysis begs the question of the content of the "right" against which one is "balancing" the State's right to regulate.

In practice, the approach has led to doctrinal formulations that arguably leave tribunals significant leeway to second-guess and to sanction State regulatory decisions: notably, the notion that States should be allowed to exercise "reasonable" regulatory powers, or subjecting the actions of States affecting investors to a test of "proportionality".

Thus, the tribunal in *Philip Morris v. Uruguay*, while stressing the right to regulate of the State, and (in a majority) finding no violation of the FET obligation, nonetheless noted in its reasoning that State regulation had to be "reasonable" to avoid sanction. This and other tribunals have expressed the notion of reasonableness as "proportionality", i.e. that the State's means must be proportionate to the end pursued, and that no one investor may be particularly singled out through the application of the measure.[60]

The potential breadth of limiting State regulatory action on the basis of potential idiosyncratic notions of what constitutes "reasonable" regulation ora "proportionate" response continues to generate controversy around FET as a treaty standard. Again, to the extent State submissions in investment treaties are available, they suggest that States vigorously contest the correctness of employing FET to second-guess good faith State policy decisions that are not tainted by failure to respect the customary MST.[61]

V. FET AS THE CUSTOMARY INTERNATIONAL LAW MINIMUM STANDARD OF TREATMENT

In parallel to the development of a jurisprudence interpreting FET as a treaty standard, arbitrators (primarily but not exclusively under the NAFTA) have been prompted to

59. C. MCLACHLAN, L. SHORE and M. WEINIGER, *International Investment Arbitration* (OUP) p. 206.

60. *Philip Morris Brands Sàrl, Philip Morris Products S.A. and Abal Hermanos S.A. v. Oriental Republic of Uruguay* (ICSID Case No. ARB/10/7), Award (9 July 2016).

61. See survey of NAFTA Party submissions in D. GAUKRODGER, "Addressing the Balance of Interests in Investment Treaties: The Limitation of Fair and Equitable Treatment Provisions to the Minimum Standard of Treatment under Customary International Law", supra fn. 17.

consider and to apply FET as the customary international law minimum standard of treatment, on the understanding that reference to FET is a shorthand for that standard.

In this customary international law context, arbitral tribunals' interpretative role in relation to FET formally is more constrained. In accordance with standard rules of public international law, the content of customary international law must be determined in light of consistent State practice, guided by a sense that such practice reflects a legal obligation.[62] In practice, this means that any attempt to add to the recognized content of a customary international law standard, or to lower the threshold for a breach of a recognized element of the standard, must be based upon evidence of consistent State practice and *opinio juris*. Proving advances to existing customary norms is difficult. This has put a natural breaking effect on the expansion of the FET standard, understood as a customary minimum norm.

The result has been a standard that includes a more limited range of obligations than FET as a treaty standard open to arbitral interpretation, and one with a relatively higher threshold for breach.[63] Notably, under their interpretation of FET understood as the customary minimum standard of treatment of investors, NAFTA Parties exclude:

– legitimate expectations;
– discrimination on a national treatment basis;
– transparency; or
– the broad "fairness, equity and reasonableness" standard articulated by the tribunal in *Merrill*.

To the contrary, core obligations recognized by NAFTA Parties under FET as a customary standard include the prevention of denial of justice (including avoidance of gross procedural unfairness in judicial decision-making), as well as direct targeting and harassment of investors. Some NAFTA States also acknowledge that the MST precludes State decision-making on manifestly arbitrary grounds.[64]

In this context, the notion of "balancing" investor rights against those of the State has been far more mitigated, for the simple reason that the standard places fewer constraints on State policy space in the first place.

Nonetheless, the standard continues to experience interpretive pressure.

First, claimants have relied upon decisions of arbitral tribunals interpreting FET as a stand-alone treaty standard, to assert novel content for FET as a customary standard. Tribunals typically have rejected such attempts, on the understanding that arbitral tribunals' decisions do not count as State practice.[65]

62. The *North Sea Continental Shelf Cases (Germany/Denmark; Germany/Netherlands)*, ICJ (1969).
63. As recently reviewed in D. GAUKRODGER, "Addressing the Balance of Interests in Investment Treaties: The Limitation of Fair and Equitable Treatment Provisions to the Minimum Standard of Treatment Under Customary International Law", supra fn. 17.
64. For example, the United States recently acknowledged as such in its Non-Disputing Party Submission in *Mesa v. Canada*, para. 9.
65. This has also been the consistent position of the NAFTA parties: "the Claimant cannot turn to the decisions of international tribunals as evidence of State practice that the protection of an investor's expectations is required by the customary international law minimum standard of treatment." *Mesa* v. *Canada*, Canada's Response to Non-Disputing Party Submissions, para. 12. "Arbitral decisions

Formally, there is no contradiction in referring to decisions of arbitral tribunals articulating the contents of a customary rule, so long as these decisions themselves refer back to consistent State practice and to *opinio juris*. Indeed, arbitral decisions often can be a convenient shorthand when they summarize the contents of an existing rule. Where arbitral tribunals simply hark back to a recognized articulation of the standard, their statements arguably will be less scrutinized for evidence of State practice and *opinio juris*. However, arbitral assertions necessarily will be subjected to greater scrutiny as statements of customary international law when they assert novel content for the customary standard, or suggest a lower threshold for a breach.

Indeed, State endorsement of a particular articulation of an international rule by an arbitral tribunal is itself evidence of State practice and of *opinio juris*. By endorsing an arbitrator's articulation of what the State considers a customary rule, the State gives weight (although not necessarily definitive weight) to the rules' standing as part of customary international law. A basic challenge to establishing State practice on the basis of their investment case submissions is the failure of most States to publish their submissions. Their endorsement of this practice, as of 2001, has given NAFTA Parties' submissions substantial prominence in the analysis of international investment law. It is to be hoped that States increasingly will adopt the same policy, by adopting the United Nations Convention on Transparency in Treaty-based Investor-State Arbitration (the Mauritius Convention on Transparency). Currently, these submissions can only be determined at second hand, as rehearsed by tribunals in awards.

Second, claimants and commentators have sought to ground an expanded notion of FET in general principles of law.[66] They note that reference in investment treaties to a guarantee of FET "in accordance with international law" formally does not restrict the contents of "international law" purely to customary international law. According to the Statutes of the International Court of Justice, the primary sources of international law are treaties, custom, and general principles of law.[67] Harking to these "general principles of law", claimants have argued a general duty of good faith in dealings, through which they seek (inter alia) to introduce respect for legitimate expectations amongst the obligations of even customary FET.

The challenge with this second approach is that the contents of recognized general principles of law are relatively limited. The duty of "good faith" or related requirement that *pacta sunt servanda* are stated in general terms, rather than as specific obligations owed by a State to an investor. Commentators have questioned expanding the content of FET as a minimum standard in specific ways (such as respect for "legitimate expectations"), by reference to such general obligations.[68] In any event, to the extent

interpreting 'autonomous' fair and equitable treatment and full protection and security provisions in other treaties, outside of the context of customary international law, do not constitute evidence of the content of the customary international law standard required by Article 1105." *Mesa v. Canada*, US Non-Disputing Party Submission, para. 6.

66. See C. MCLACHLAN, L. SHORE and M. WEINIGER, *International Investment Arbitration* (OUP) p. 205, p. 259.

67. Art. 38(1) of the Statutes of the ICJ.

68. Martins PAPARINSKIS, "Good Faith and Equitable Treatment in International Investment Law" in A. MITCHELL, M. SORNARAJAH and T. VOON, eds., *Good Faith and International Economic Law* (Oxford University Press, Oxford 2015) recalls the standard understanding at international law

FET is understood at a customary minimal norm, in formal terms this is distinct from general principles.

Third, several tribunals have suggested that the content of FET as the customary minimum standard of treatment has been expanded by the widespread reference to an obligation of FET in the over 3,000 bilateral investment treaties signed over the past forty years. This is put forward as evidence of consistent State practice, confirming that customary international law has moved on, at least from the standard expressed in *Neer*. Tribunals suggesting that MST has evolved through the introduction of thousands of additional treaties providing for FET have been noticeably silent as to the precise new content added to the customary standard through this mechanism.[69]

Commentators and States take issue with the above argument, on several grounds. As recognized by the International Law Commission (ILC) in its commentary on the development of customary international law, reference to an obligation in a treaty does not necessarily signal an intention to make that obligation binding, other than as a treaty standard.[70] Indeed, it arguably signals the reverse. Beyond this, there is no confirmation that States when referencing FET in treaties meant anything other than the minimum standard of treatment, as classically understood. Finally, there is an inherent circularity to arguments that States in referencing FET intended to expand the recognized content of the minimum standard. The jurisprudence interpreting FET clauses as a bare treaty standard post-dates the wave of entry into force of most BITs. One can hardly ascribe to States an intention to adhere to specific content for FET that was unknown at the time States began inserting a requirement of "FET" into their investment treaties. The doctrine of legitimate expectations, entirely arbitrator-made, is a good example. Indeed, as we shall see below, the recent wave of treaties entered into by States suggests the reverse of any intention to develop customary international law in the direction ascribed in FET jurisprudence.

---

that good faith is a tool for interpreting existing obligations, not a means of creating new ones : "... legitimate expectations may be a particularly prominent element of good faith, and might provide a useful perspective for thinking about treaty interpretation or customary law-making, but one still needs to satisfy the usual law-making criteria to conclude that a primary obligation of respect of legitimate expectations is imposed". (p. 34).

69. See *Mondev International Ltd v. United States of America* (ICSID Case No. ARB (AF) 99/2), Award (11 Oct. 2002) paras. 110-117; *Pope & Talbot v. Canada*, Award in respect of damages, paras. 52-66; *CMS Gas Transmission Co v. Argentina*, Award, para. 284; Stephen SCHWEBEL, "The Influence of Bilateral Investment Treaties on Customary International Law", *Proceedings of the 98th Annual Meeting of the American Society of International Law, 31 March – 3 April 2004*, pp. 27-30. For a contrary view, see Patrick DUMBERRY, "The Practice of States as Evidence of Custom: An Analysis of Fair and Equitable Treatment Standard Clauses in States' Foreign Investment Laws", 2 McGill J. Disp. Resol. (2015-2016) p. 66, finding explicit reference to the FET standard in only a small number of State laws protecting foreign investments. See also Patrick DUMBERRY, "Are BITs Representing the 'New' Customary International Law in International Investment Law?", 28 Penn State International Law Review (2010, no. 4) at pp. 675-701.

70. "[t]here is no presumption that a succession of similar treaty provisions gives rise to a new customary rule with the same content." – Principle No. 25 adopted by the International Law Association Statement of Principles Applicable to the Formation of General Customary International Law, Final Report 8 (2000) at p. 47. Work at the ILC on this topic is ongoing.

Yet the inherent disciplines on FET as a customary standard have not entirely forestalled attempts to expand the content of the standard.

In one approach, investment tribunals have waived away differences between FET interpreted as a bare treaty standard and FET as a reference to the customary minimum standard of treatment.[71] This typically arises where a claimant asserts that FET is a (more expansive) treaty standard, and the responding State argues that reference to FET is to the customary minimum standard. Some tribunals have resolved this difference by finding that there is (or is not) a violation of the standard irrespective of which standard applies, asserting (without any analysis or evidence) that the two expressions are essentially the same thing, or have converged.

In another approach, tribunals have asserted that they are applying the customary minimum standard of treatment, while going on to apply that standard in a manner implying a substantial (and undemonstrated) expansion of its scope.

For example, in the *Bilcon v. Canada* case the tribunal recognized that the applicable standard was FET as the customary MST.[72] Nonetheless, the Tribunal went on to find Canada in violation of Art. 1105(1) of NAFTA (Minimum Standard of Treatment) because it disagreed with the application of Canadian law by a domestic administrative tribunal. This was in circumstances in which the Claimants had not sought judicial review of the decision forming the "measure" at issue in the arbitration. It is difficult to square this interpretation with MST, one of the core standards of which is protection against denial of justice. It is trite law to note that in considering alleged State breaches of an international standard, State behaviour must be taken as a whole. In the context of a claim based upon an administrative review decision with which the claimant disagreed, this necessarily must take into consideration the investor's ability to seek review of the impugned decision through impartial courts. Where tribunals ignore this, as in *Bilcon*, they are in effect dramatically expanding the scope of the FET obligation.

Other tribunals have purported to give novel content to the MST standard by referring spontaneously to the results of their own investigation into State practice and *opinio juris*. One example of this was the decision of the Tribunal in *Merrill & Ring v. Canada*.[73] The Tribunal found no violation of Art. 1105(1) in that case. However, this did not constrain the Tribunal from engaging in a lengthy excursion into alleged developments of public international law since the 1960s. Curiously for a decision considering inter alia obligations of due process, the Tribunal in that matter saw no need to consult with the disputing parties for their views on the materials the Tribunal had relied upon *sua sponte* to set out an elaborate new statement of FET as a customary norm.

71. In *CMS v. Argentina*, the Tribunal stated (without the aid of reference to state practice, *opinio juris*, other cases, or academic commentary) that its interpretation of FET was "not different from the international law minimum standard of treatment and its evaluation under customary international law". (para. 284). *Occidental Exploration & Production Co v. Ecuador* (LCIA Case UN 3467), Final Award (1 Jul. 2004) at paras. 190 and 196, followed a similar reasoning.
72. *Bilcon of Delaware et al. v. Government of Canada* (UNCITRAL Case No. 2009-04), Award (2 May 2018).
73. *Merrill and Ring Forestry L.P. v. Canada* (ICSID Case No. UNCT/07/1), Award (31 March 2010).

Still other tribunals have looked to the decision-making of tribunals not purporting to apply the customary minimum standard, to expand the scope of custom. The award in *Railroad Development Corp v. Guatemala* (RDC) is an example of this approach.[74]

States have continued to push back on the contents of FET as the customary MST in their submissions in ongoing cases. For example, in the *Mesa v. Canada* matter, the tribunal invited the disputing parties to provide their views on the significance of the *Bilcon* decision. In that context, the United States in a non-disputing party submission set out a starkly restrictive view of the contents of the Minimum Standard.[75]

Overall, tying FET to the customary MST has had a mitigating effect on the strength of the obligation. Nonetheless, the absence of universally recognized content for the customary international law standard has led claimants, tribunals and commentators to seek through a variety of means to expand the contents of the standard. While States regularly have pushed back, the dynamic arguably has led to a climate of uncertainty. Given mounting opposition of some members of civil society to investor-State dispute resolution – or at least, mounting questions – continued reliance on an undefined standard, especially one designated as the "core" protection, may seem unsatisfactory at best.

VI. STATE ATTEMPTS AT REDRAFTING THE STANDARD

In light of the uncertainties surrounding the use of FET in investment treaties, States around the world in recent years have pushed back by altering their treaty practice, in at least three ways.

The most radical approach has been to remove reference to the FET obligation altogether (*1*). The second approach has been to follow the practice of the NAFTA Parties, by clarifying that FET provides no more than the MST at customary international law (*2*). The third has been to ascribe specific content to the FET standard, while confirming that only States may expand the scope of this content (*3*). However, there is also evidence of a failure on the part of some States to react, and to pursue older approaches to treaty-drafting – suggesting the emergence of a "split" in State practice (*4*).

Overall, the direction of travel is a challenge to existing arbitral jurisprudence interpreting FET as a bare treaty standard. The end result of these efforts remains to be seen.

74. Matthew C. PORTERFIELD, "A Distinction Without a Difference? The Interpretation of Fair and Equitable Treatment Under Customary International Law by Investment Tribunals", International Institute for Sustainable Development, blog, (22 March 2013: <https://www.iisd.org/>).
See also *Windstream Energy LLC v. Canada* (UNCITRAL), Award (27 September 2016) (finding breach of MST-FET without identifying supporting state practice or *opinio juris* despite concordant interpretations from the three NAFTA Parties insisting on those sources as the basis for an asserted customary international law rules).

75. United States Non-Disputing Party Submission in *Mesa v. Canada,* comment on the Award in *Bilcon v. Canada*.

1. Eliminating FET Altogether

Faced with the perceived intolerable impact of FET on their policy space, some States have responded to recent jurisprudence by eliminating the FET obligation altogether from their investment treaties.

For some States, this has been accomplished as part of a broader effort to eliminate the perceived restrictions of international investment agreements. States such as Venezuela, Ecuador and Bolivia have pursued this policy, in parallel with denouncing the ICSID Convention. While this arguably radical approach on its face does not specifically target FET, concerns about the potential scope of this obligation (as applied to these States) have been front and centre.

Ironically, this approach may be adopted by the United States in the new version of NAFTA currently being renegotiated. According to current media reports, the United States has accepted a policy proposal from Canada to remove the investment chapter from NAFTA altogether. From a Canadian point of view, this may be seen as less of a radical policy move, given that Canada in any event maintains investment protection vis-à-vis Mexico through the parallel Trans-Pacific Partnership (TPP) treaty. Canadian investors in the United States have met little success in NAFTA Chapter Eleven claims. Canada by contrast has repeatedly been at the receiving end of claims brought by litigious US investors. From a US perspective elimination of investment protection in NAFTA would amount to a radical policy shift. To recall, the United States initially was *demandeur* of investor-State dispute resolution in the original version of the Treaty. Failure to maintain investment protection in what is arguably the United States' marquee free trade agreement may make it more difficult to claim investment protection as a necessary feature of US relations with non-NAFTA States, going forward.[76]

The approach of some other States has been to retain commitment to investment protection, while eliminating FET from the scope of new treaties. This has been the approach proposed by India in its new model bilateral investment treaty.[77] In the place of even mentioning FET, India instead provides a list of protections that otherwise have been proposed as elements of the standard:

> "No Party shall subject investments made by investors of the other Party to measures which constitute a violation of customary international law through: (i) Denial of justice in any judicial or administrative proceedings; or (ii) fundamental breach of due process; or (iii) targeted discrimination on manifestly unjustified grounds, such as gender, race or religious belief; or (iv) manifestly abusive treatment, such as coercion, duress and harassment."

The challenges with this approach are twofold. In the first place, eliminating investment treaties altogether may be perceived as reducing the attractiveness of the countries in

76. The United States did not include investor-State dispute resolution in its free trade agreement with Australia, but this was prompted by Australia's policy opposition to investment treaty protections at that time. Moreover, the US-Australia FTA is an example of an FTA solely between two developed States, where concerns about appeal to local courts presumably were mitigated.
77. 2016 Model Indian Bilateral Investment Treaty.

question as FDI destinations, given their apparent refusal to endorse international-level protections in any form. Secondly, this outcome has the corresponding negative impact on a State's own investors abroad, by removing any international protections they would otherwise have enjoyed under the State's previous treaties (subject to sunset clauses). This might not be a consideration for States that exclusively import capital. But increasingly, Southern States and "emerging market" States are both capital exporters as well as capital importers – particularly amongst countries in their region. This sort of reasoning applies a fortiori for developed countries. Thus, this approach is arguably unlikely to be adopted by most States.

As for the approach of eliminating FET while retaining other protections, this approach continues to raise some of the issues arising with the elimination of investment treaties. The challenge is that it sends a signal to investors that a State is unwilling to ascribe even to a minimum threshold of treatment of investors.

In any event, this approach clearly signals the rejection by the States involved of modern iterations of FET interpreted either as a bare treaty standard, or as a customary international law norm (whether "minimum" or something more).

2. *Confirming That FET Refers to the MST at Customary International Law*

The alternative approach – one that arguably has gained the highest level of adherence over the past ten years – has been for other States to follow the NAFTA Free Trade Commission in expressly linking reference to FET in any new treaties to the customary international law MST.[78] This connection frequently has been included in new draft treaties prefaced by the words "for greater certainty". In other words, States entering into these treaties are formally signalling, not only that FET should be limited to a customary international minimum norm, but that this has always been their intention. Given the language of the explanatory note of the 1967 OECD Model Treaty, there is some historical support for this contention. In any event, in terms of the *lege lata*, these new treaties clearly distance State parties from obligations deemed to arise under FET interpreted as a bare treaty obligation. This means that as in the NAFTA context, State parties to such treaties likely will reject any attempt to interpret the FET standard along the lines of recent arbitral jurisprudence.

Linking FET to the customary minimum standard of treatment naturally has been adopted by States entering into international investment agreements with NAFTA Parties. But the approach has also spread beyond negotiations involving NAFTA Parties.[79] The approach also has been multilateralized through its use in the recently concluded renewed TPP agreement. Given this, it seems an approach likely to gain more State adherents in the future.

78. See, for example, the ASEAN-Korea Investment Agreement, Art. 5; ASEAN-India Investment Agreement, Art. 7; China-Korea Free Trade Agreement, Art. 12.5 and Annex A; Singapore-US FTA, Art. 15(5); Australia-Korea FTA, Art. 14.5; Canada-China BIT, Art. 4; Japan-Mongolia EPA, Art. 10.5; Korea-US FTA, Art. 11(5) and Annex 11-A; Japan-Philippines EPA, Art. 91 (cited in D. GAUKRODGER, supra fn. 17, at p. 18).

79. As demonstrated by the list in the preceding note.

The challenge with continued reliance on FET as an expression of the MST at customary international law, as reviewed above, is the relative indeterminacy of this standard. As described above, in the NAFTA context linking FET to the customary minimum standard no doubt constrained FET's scope, marking a substantial difference with FET understood as a bare treaty option. Regardless, it has also prompted consistent attempts to expand the standard beyond traditionally recognized categories, and to lower the threshold for breach of the standard. Thus, while linking FET to MST arguably is the most common approach to reform at the current juncture, it may not finally resolve longstanding uncertainty about the content of the FET standard.

3. *Setting Out a Clearly Delineated Definition of FET in the Treaty*

A third State response to uncertainty about the scope FET clauses has been to seek to define with more precision FET as a treaty standard, and expressly to preclude tribunals' ability to move beyond that tight definition.

The best-known example of this approach is in the investment chapter of the Canada-European Union Comprehensive Economic and Trade Agreement (CETA).[80] Under the heading of "treatment of investors", the CETA offers FET to investors, but then immediately imposes a constraining definition on the content of FET:

> "*Article 8.10 Treatment of investors and of covered investments*
> 1. Each Party shall accord in its territory to covered investments of the other Party and to investors with respect to their covered investments fair and equitable treatment and full protection and security in accordance with paragraphs 2 through 7.
> 2. A Party breaches the obligation of fair and equitable treatment referenced in paragraph 1 if a measure or series of measures constitutes:
> (a) denial of justice in criminal, civil or administrative proceedings;
> (b) fundamental breach of due process, including a fundamental breach of transparency, in judicial and administrative proceedings;
> (c) manifest arbitrariness;
> (d) targeted discrimination on manifestly wrongful grounds, such as gender, race or religious belief;
> (e) abusive treatment of investors, such as coercion, duress and harassment; or
> (f) a breach of any further elements of the fair and equitable treatment obligation adopted by the Parties in accordance with paragraph 3 of this Article."

The CETA then goes on to confirm that this interpretative list can be expanded only by the agreement of the CETA Joint Commission (i.e. by the State Parties to the agreement):

80. Another approach, adopted, e.g., in the ASEAN-Australia-New Zealand Free Trade Agreement (AANZFTA), is to link FET to customary international law, but then also expressly to link FET with denial of justice. The ASEAN-China Investment Agreement takes this a step further, in effect expressly limiting FET to denial of justice.

> "3. The Parties shall regularly, or upon request of a Party, review the content of the obligation to provide fair and equitable treatment. The Committee on Services and Investment, established under Article 26.2.1(b) (Specialised committees), may develop recommendations in this regard and submit them to the CETA Joint Committee for decision."

The list of obligations set out in Art. 8.10.2 of the CETA as the fixed content of FET is notable in several respects.

First, the list clearly sets out a high threshold for breach of FET. Overall, the list clearly focusses on situations of substantially abusive and unfair behaviour of States vis-à-vis investors. This is reflected both in the main content of the list, and in the accompanying qualifiers ("manifest" arbitrariness, "fundamental" breach, "manifestly" wrongful grounds). There is no reference to any ability to judge the reasonableness or proportionality of State decision-making. There is no reference in this main list giving legal effect to investor expectations.

Second, the list aligns with the kinds of behaviour that investment tribunals applying Art. 1105(1) of NAFTA have found in violation of the MST under customary international law.

Third, there is no reference in the passage to customary international law, nor indeed to international law simpliciter, contrary to Canada's typical practice of expressly linking FET to the customary minimum standard. Thus, one might *a contrario* consider that the list refers to a purely treaty-based standard. This would mean that the standards set out in the list would themselves be subject to interpretation in light of the requirements of the VCLT. This might arguably lead to a recurrence of interpretative issues arising under "bare" treaty versions of FET. The difference is that here, that power is substantially circumscribed by the defined list.

Fourth, it is also notable that the FET article in CETA does not exclude reference to legitimate expectations. However, the treaty makes it clear that breach of such an expectation does not in and of itself amount to a breach of the standard. Instead, State failure to respect an expectation arising in tightly defined circumstances is something that may be "taken into account" by tribunals, in connection with established elements of the list:

> "4. When applying the above fair and equitable treatment obligation, the Tribunal may take into account whether a Party made a specific representation to an investor to induce a covered investment, that created a legitimate expectation, and upon which the investor relied in deciding to make or maintain the covered investment, but that the Party subsequently frustrated."

The place of investor expectations in the analysis is further mitigated by the Article's express affirmation of State right to regulate:

> "*Article 8.9 Investment and regulatory measures*
> 1. For the purpose of this Chapter, the Parties reaffirm their right to regulate within their territories to achieve legitimate policy objectives, such as the

protection of public health, safety, the environment or public morals, social or consumer protection or the promotion and protection of cultural diversity.
2. For greater certainty, *the mere fact that a Party regulates, including through a modification to its laws, in a manner which negatively affects an investment or interferes with an investor's expectations, including its expectations of profits, does not amount to a breach of an obligation under this Section*." (Emphasis added.)

CETA also restates the basic public international law principle that a breach of domestic law absent something more does not amount to a breach of international law.

The CETA approach to FET is part of arguably the biggest policy change in international investment law since the 1960s. Rejecting the typical liberal approach of Western European BITs, in the CETA the EU has moved to investment protection that is much more tightly defined and much more clearly upholds the right of the State to regulate. And the centrepiece of that effort arguably is its approach to FET.

The circumstances of this shift bear some consideration.

The first and likely driving circumstance has been the potential expansion of the EU's existing treaty network (as developed by EU Member States) beyond treaties with developing States, towards treaties with developed States. This trend began with EU negotiations with Canada and Singapore. It accelerated when the EU began considering entering into the TransAtlantic Trade and Investment Partnership (TTIP) with the United States.

The second circumstance was the shift of investment treaty negotiation competency away from EU Member States towards the EU Commission, through the 2009 Treaty of Lisbon. This accelerated the EU policy shift by handing responsibility to a new set of officials, answerable among others to the European Parliament. Members of the European Parliament, alarmed by the prospect of investment protection in the CETA or (worse) TTIP, pushed the EU Commission to reconsider and rebalance the traditional EU Member State approach.

Ironically, this meant that while benefitting from arguably the densest network of investment treaties in the world, Europe suddenly became one of the most vocal critics of the system.

The EU policy shift is all the more significant in that, at least up to 2010-2011, EU Member States resisted the "North Americanization" of investment treaties, i.e. the approach that sought to give more definition to substantive standards, and more clarity to dispute resolution procedures. The EU's shift took place in the context of discussions with Canada relating to CETA investment protections. The ultimate consequences of this shift will be worked out for years to come.

4. *An Alternative Approach: The Status Quo*

While reform to FET in investment treaties is widespread, one must also acknowledge that the direction of travel for State treaty drafters is not all one way. Despite all of the concerns expressed by States and by civil society about the contents of investment treaties – and about interpretations of FET in particular – some States continue to enter into bilateral investment treaties relatively unchanged from models current in the 1970s.

These States include, somewhat surprisingly, Argentina – if anything, the poster child for States affected by tribunal's interpretations of "bare" FET clauses.

Interpreting this countercurrent of State practice presents challenges. It is difficult to judge State intentions linked to this treaty-making practice in the current context. Does it reflect an express intent to maintain liberally-defined investor obligations, with a view to encouraging foreign investment? A conscious determination that adopting new language comports as many risks as sticking to familiar texts? Or simply a lack of will and capacity on the part of some States to adopt new treaty practices, with a view to mitigating risk?

In any event, the continued adopting of "first generation" style BITs by some States suggests another parting of the ways in investment treaty practice: between a range of States seeking to reform the system and "reset the dial" on obligations, notably on FET; and some other States sticking to existing treaty practice. This in turn has implications for the potential development of any further customary rules of international investment protection.

VII. IMPLICATIONS FOR EXISTING TREATIES?

The above historical overview and review of current treaty practice brings us back to our starting-point: what will be the implications of new State treaty practice on the interpretation and application of existing BITs? More specifically, how will new treaty practice affect existing interpretations of "bare" FET clauses in old treaties? Will it disrupt the tendency of tribunals to rely upon existing jurisprudence, generated before States sought to clarify their intentions?

At very least, from a formal point of view new treaties constitute evidence of State practice and *opinio juris* regarding the emergence of standards of investment protection. Among other things, in light of such evidence it is difficult to sustain the thesis of "convergence" between FET interpreted as a bare treaty obligation, and the customary international law minimum standard of treatment of investors. Beyond this, the specific list of content of FET in CETA might be viewed by some as setting a new bar for the contents of a customary MST standard.

As for the retroactive implications of new treaty practice for the interpretation of first-generation "bare" FET clauses, tribunals may take different approaches.

Some may decide simply to ignore the new practice. Formally, each treaty is to be interpreted on its own terms. The decision of States to adopt a different approach in subsequent treaties might be viewed as irrelevant to the interpretation of a separate, earlier instrument.

Others may look to the new treaties – in particular, language stating "for greater certainty" that FET is intended to mean no more than MST at customary international law – to revisit the interpretation of "bare" FET clauses in older treaties. The challenge in this regard are the formal rules of interpretation under the VCLT: subsidiary rules of interpretation under VCLT Art. 31, based upon State practice, depend upon concurrent practice of the *same* parties to a treaty, not practice of one of the parties alone. This dynamic would of course change if *both* parties indeed agreed to a joint statement regarding the interpretation of the FET clause. More challenging would be circumstances where each of the State Parties to Treaty A (containing a "bare" FET clause) individually entered into separate treaties with B and C but with different State counterparts, each of which held that "for greater certainty, the obligation to provide FET is limited to the level of protection provided under the customary international law minimum standard of treatment". Would such different treaties interpreting the same language become "relevant rules of international law applicable in the relations between the parties", under VCLT Art. 31.3(c)?

Ultimately, the most efficient way States might collectively resolve any uncertainty arising out of their new treaty practice would be to enter into a Mauritius-Convention type fix, retroactively clarifying their intentions (whatever these may be) regarding the interpretation of existing treaties, notably with regard to the content of FET. Given existing divergences in State treaty practice, it remains to be seen whether there is sufficient consensus at the international level to achieve such an instrument. As the drafters of the ICSID Convention determined over fifty years ago, it is much easier to seek agreement on process than on substance. Notably, drivers of the current UNCITRAL Third Committee investment treaty reform process have studiously avoided addressing issues of substance.

VIII. CONCLUSIONS

The modern expression of international investment law is in its infancy. Yet arbitrators, counsel and commentators function in individual time. States function much more naturally in the "*longue durée*" of international law. They are slow to rouse. They are slow to respond. But in the long run they do react. And at the end of the day, despite the rise of other actors, States remain the ultimate masters of the contents of public international law – for reasons ultimately rooted in democracy. The analogy is to domestic legislation: if a court has in the State's view misinterpreted a law, or the law requires clarification, Parliament can reconsider the law.

The abundant international investment law jurisprudence generated over the past twenty years provides rich grounds for arbitrators, commentators and State officials to consider what international investment law *might* provide. There will be no lack of people proposing what it *ought* to provide.

In a sense, academics and arbitrators have been the victims of their own success – through their work, they have revealed to States the potential interpretative consequences of FET language. The responding direction of travel of States largely reflects concerns about the indeterminacy of the FET standard, and the limitations FET potentially may place on State's right to regulate.

This article is not concerned with *de lege ferenda*. It is concerned *de lege lata*. And on the basis of current evidence, for FET at least, the tectonics plates of international law appear to be shifting.

The Evolution of the Expropriation Obligation in Investment Arbitration and Its Adaptation in Treaties to Reflect State Rights

*Mélida Hodgson** *and Patricia Cruz Trabanino***

TABLE OF CONTENTS | PAGE

I. INTRODUCTION

As recognized by an international tribunal in the early twentieth century, "the right of a State ... to appropriate private property for public use is unquestioned".[1] The State's right to expropriate has long been considered an essential component of sovereignty – a fact that plays into foreign investors' decisions as to where, how much, and in what form, to invest in other States. Foreign investment requires the movement of the investor's assets into the jurisdiction of the host State, where they may be subject to State acts that cause severe interference with the investor's property rights. Unsurprisingly, a foreign investor's preeminent concern is the risk that the host State may seize its assets.

The sovereign right to expropriate, however, is not unqualified. Customary international law has long offered foreign investors certain protections in the realm of expropriation. More recently, international investment agreements (IIAs) have crystallized these customary protections into treaty obligations and have expanded the scope of protection. These treaty provisions, however, have varied in their drafting and interpretation, leading to longstanding debates in the jurisprudence about how to appropriately balance investor protection and State sovereignty. More recently, States and several of their constituencies have pushed back against perceived encroachment of expropriation provisions on States' right to regulate in the public interest or welfare.

* Partner in the International Litigation and Arbitration Department of Foley Hoag LLP.

** Associate in the International Litigation and Arbitration Department of Foley Hoag LLP.
The views expressed in this chapter are solely of the authors.

1. *Upton Case* (United States-Venezuela Mixed Claims Commission), 9 UNRIAA 234, Award (17 February 1903), at p. 236 (henceforth *Upton Case*).

Expropriation provisions have accordingly been increasingly restricted over the last decade – raising complaints that they are being gutted.

This paper provides an overview of the major issues relating to the protection against expropriation by tracing the historical development of States' obligations on expropriation by reference to customary international law, treaty provisions, arbitral decisions and other legal materials. Part II will discuss the sovereign right to expropriate under customary international law. Part III will examine how the customary norms were incorporated into IIAs and the different ways in which States' obligations in regard to expropriation have been articulated in bilateral and multilateral agreements. Part IV examines the concept of indirect expropriation, and discusses tribunals' attempt to distinguish this form of taking from non-compensable State regulation. Part V discusses the difference between lawful and unlawful expropriation, as well as the consequences of illegality. Finally, Part VI concludes by discussing open issues relating to expropriation, including recent State efforts to balance their right to regulate with investor protection.

II. THE SOVEREIGN RIGHT TO EXPROPRIATE UNDER CUSTOMARY INTERNATIONAL LAW

International law has always recognized States' power to seize property in certain circumstances. This right to expropriate derives from the concept of territorial sovereignty: a State has sovereignty over all things within its boundaries.[2] This power is so fundamental, that a State cannot validly bind itself not to exercise it at all, because its "fundamental purpose is to safeguard the public interest of its citizens and, if such interest will be properly safeguarded by nationalization, the state must be free to pursue that course of action".[3]

The State's right to expropriate foreign property, however, is not absolute. As stated in the 1928 *Goldenberg* case, "[r]espect for private property and the vested rights of foreigners is without question part of the general principles accepted by the law of nations".[4] For this reason, it is understood that "up to a certain point, the interest of the State in being able to protect its nationals and their property must carry more weight than respect for territorial sovereignty, even in the absence of conventional obligations".[5] Customary international law imposes certain limitations on the taking of foreign investors' assets in order to balance the protection of property and territorial sovereignty.

Early twentieth century jurisprudence explored the customary limitations on the power to expropriate foreign property. One such limitation is that the taking of foreign property must be for a public purpose. This requirement was discussed in the 1929

2. Jeswald W. SALACUSE, *The Law of Investment Treaties*, 2nd edn. (Oxford 2015) p. 64.
3. *Ibid.*
4. *Goldenberg Case (Romania v. Germany)*, 2 UNRIAA 901 (27 September 1928), at p. 909 (original text in French: "*Le respect de la propriété privée et des droits acquis des étrangers fait sans conteste partie des principes généraux admis par le droit des gens.*").
5. *British Claims in the Spanish Zone of Morocco (Spain v. Great Britain)*, 2 UNRIAA 615 (1 May 1925), at p. 641 (original text in French: "*à un certain point l'intérêt d'un État de pouvoir protéger ses ressortissants et leurs biens, doit primer le respect de la souveraineté territoriale, et cela même en l'absence d'obligations conventionnelles*").

Walter Fletcher Smith case, in which an American citizen's property in Cuba was "seized [and] turned over immediately to the defendant company, ostensibly for public purposes, but, in fact, to be used by the defendant for purposes of amusement and private profit".[6] Accordingly, the arbitrator found the expropriation of an American citizen's property in Cuba to be in violation of international law.[7]

Customary international law repudiates the discriminatory treatment of foreign-owned property, as was repeatedly explained in the jurisprudence of the Permanent Court of International Justice (PCIJ). For example, in the *Oscar Chinn* case, the Court held that "discrimination based upon nationality and involving differential treatment by reason of their nationality as between persons belonging to different national groups" is "forbidden".[8] The dispossession of property for racially discriminatory reasons has also been deemed to contravene international law.[9] To comply with this standard of non-discrimination, the taking cannot merely be formally neutral; rather, it must also be non-discriminatory as a matter of fact. As explained by the PCIJ, in the context of the treatment of Polish nationals in Danzig, "the prohibition against discrimination, in order to be effective, must ensure the absence of discrimination in fact as well as in law. A measure which in terms is of general application, but in fact is directed against Polish nationals and other persons of Polish origin or speech, constitutes a violation of the prohibition".[10]

Customary international law also requires that an expropriation be effected against payment of compensation. The U.S.-Venezuela Mixed Claims Commission highlighted this requirement in the *Upton Case*, when it reasoned that "the right of the State ... to appropriate private property for public use is unquestioned, but always with the corresponding obligation to make just compensation to the owner thereof".[11] In the *Chorzów Factory* case, the PCIJ echoed this view when it stated that "not having paid ... the just price of what was expropriated" would constitute a "wrongful act".[12] This rule is also embodied in the Hull Doctrine, which prohibits expropriation without "prompt, adequate, and effective compensation".[13]

---

6. *Walter Fletcher Smith Claim (Cuba/U.S.A.)*, 2 UNRIAA 913, at pp. 917-918 (henceforth *Walter Fletcher Smith Claim*).
7. *Ibid.*, p. 918.
8. *Oscar Chinn (U.K. v. Belg.)*, Judgment, 1934 P.C.I.J. (ser. A/B) No. 63 (12 December 1934), at p. 87.
9. Muthucumaraswamy SORNARAJAH, *The International Law on Foreign Investment*, 3rd edn. (Cambridge 2010) p. 409 (citing the takings of Jewish property in Nazi Germany and the expropriation of property of Indians in Uganda during the Idi Amin regime).
10. *Treatment of Polish Nationals and Other Persons of Polish Origin or Speech in Danzig Territory*, Advisory Opinion, 1932 P.C.I.J. (ser. A/B) No. 44 (4 February 1932), at p. 28.
11. *Upton Case*, fn. 1 above, p. 236.
12. *Factory at Chorzów (Germ. v. Pol.), Judgment*, 1928 P.C.I.J. (ser. A) No. 17 (13 September 1928), at p. 47 (henceforth *Factory at Chorzów*); see also *Marguerite de Joly de SABLA (United States) v. Panama* (United States-Panama Claims Commission), 6 UNRIAA 358, Award (29 June 1933), at p. 366 ("It is axiomatic that acts of a government in depriving an alien of his property without compensation impose international responsibility.").
13. Letter from the Secretary of State of the United States Cordell HULL to the Mexican Ambassador Francisco CASTILLO NAJERA (22 August 1938), available at <https://history.state.gov/historicaldocuments/frus1938v05/d665> (last accessed 2 February 2018) ("The Government of

The Restatement (Third) of the Foreign Relations Law of the United States summarizes these customary international law limitations as follows:

> "A state is responsible under international law for injury resulting from:
> (1) a taking by the state of the property of a national of another state that
> (a) is not for a public purpose, or
> (b) is discriminatory, or
> (c) is not accompanied by provision for just compensation."[14]

As shown by the jurisprudence, already in the early twentieth century these three elements – public purpose, non-discrimination, and compensation – were generally recognized as limitations on the sovereign power to expropriate.[15] It is thus no surprise that in the latter half of the twentieth century these protections were incorporated into IIAs as part of the provisions dealing with the conditions and consequences of expropriations.

III. STANDARD OF PROTECTION AGAINST EXPROPRIATION IN IIAS

While customary international law continues to be applicable to the treatment of foreign nationals and their property, in the present day any discussion about expropriation turns, to a large extent, on the provisions in IIAs, and bilateral investment treaties (BITs) in particular. The first BIT was signed by Germany and Pakistan in 1959.[16] There are almost 3,000 BITs in existence today and over 300 treaties with investment provisions.[17] The vast majority of them contain protections against expropriation.

---

the United States merely adverts to a self-evident fact when it notes that the applicable precedents and recognized authorities on international law support its declaration that, under every rule of law and equity, no government is entitled to expropriate private property, for whatever purpose, without provision for prompt, adequate, and effective payment therefor.").

14. Restatement (Third) of the Foreign Relations Law of the United States, § 712 (Am. Law Inst., 1987).
15. While already generally recognized in the early twentieth century, these limitations on the sovereign power to expropriate were not entirely uncontested. For example, as of 1959, the International Law Commission still considered that the topic of the international responsibility that States may incur as a result of acts of expropriation "require[d] more thorough study". "Fourth report on State Responsibility by Mr. F.V. Garcia-Amador, Special Rapporteur" (26 February 1959), International Law Commission, UN Doc. A/CN.4/119 p. 2. Accordingly, the Special Rapporteur studied "the new doctrinal and practical trends which have made their appearance mostly since the last World War", including the three topics of public purpose, non-discrimination and compensation in the context of expropriation. See *ibid.* pp. 2, 13-24.
16. Treaty Between the Federal Republic of Germany and Pakistan for the Promotion and Protection of Investments, 25 November 1959, BGBl. II at 793, at <http://investmentpolicyhub.unctad.org/Download/TreatyFile/1387> (last accessed 6 February 2018) (henceforth Germany-Pakistan BIT).
17. UNCTAD Investment Policy Hub, "International Investment Agreements Navigator", at <http://investmentpolicyhub.unctad.org/IIA> (last accessed 6 February 2018) (indicating that there are 2,952 BITs and 374 treaties with investment provisions in existence as of 6 February 2018).

The 1959 Germany-Pakistan BIT included the customary international law protections of public purpose, non-discrimination, and payment of compensation. Art. 2 of the BIT enshrined the prohibition of discriminatory treatment (including in relation to expropriation) as follows:

> "*Neither Party shall subject to discriminatory treatment* any activities carried on in connection with investments including the effective management, use or enjoyment of such investments by the nationals or companies of either Party in the territory of the other Party unless specific stipulations are made in the documents of admission of an investment." (Emphasis added.)[18]

The Germany-Pakistan BIT also included provisions specific to expropriation:

> "Nationals or companies of either Party shall not be subjected to expropriation of their investments in the territory of the other Party *except for public benefit against compensation*, which shall represent the equivalent of the investments affected. Such compensation shall be actually realizable and freely transferable in the currency of the other Party without undue delay. Adequate provision shall be made at or prior to the time of expropriation for the determination and the grant of such compensation. The legality of any such expropriation and the amount of compensation shall be subject to review by due process of law."[19] (Emphasis added.)

In addition to requiring that any expropriation be effected for a public purpose and against compensation, the Germany-Pakistan BIT expanded the generally accepted scope of protection by specifying how compensation is to be determined and carried out, as well as by requiring that the expropriation be carried out in accordance with due process.[20]

More recent BITs retain similar language enshrining these customary protections. For example, the 2010 United Kingdom-Colombia BIT states that

18. Germany-Pakistan BIT, fn. 16 above, Art. 2.
19. *Ibid.* at Art. 3(2).
20. While Sect. 712 of the Restatement (Third) of the Foreign Relations Law of the United States, fn. 14 above, does not refer to due process, many BITs and treaties with investment provisions do. See, e.g., "2012 U.S. Model Bilateral Investment Treaty", at <https://www.state.gov/documents/organization/188371.pdf> (last accessed 6 February 2018), Art. 6(1)(d) (henceforth United States Model BIT). According to some commentators, "[d]ue process is an expression of the minimum standard under customary international law and of the requirement of fair and equitable treatment. Therefore, it is not clear whether such a clause, in the context of the rule on expropriation, adds an independent requirement for the legality of the expropriation". Rudolf DOLZER and Christoph SCHREUER, *Principles of International Investment Law*, 2nd edn. (Oxford 2012) p. 100.

> "Investments of investors of a Contracting Party in the territory of the other Contracting Party shall not be the subject of nationalisation, direct or indirect expropriation, or any measure having similar effects (hereinafter 'expropriation') *except for reasons of public purpose or social interest* (which shall have a meaning compatible with that of 'public purpose'), in accordance with due process of law, *in a non-discriminatory manner*, in good faith and *accompanied by prompt, adequate and effective compensation*."[21] (Emphasis added.)

These formulas are not limited to BITs. Agreements with investment provisions, such as free trade agreements, also explicitly refer to the customary international law standard. The investment chapter of the North American Free Trade Agreement (NAFTA), for example, prohibits expropriation "except: (a) for a public purpose; (b) on a non-discriminatory basis; (c) in accordance with due process of law...; and (d) on payment of compensation...".[22] Similarly, the Energy Charter Treaty permits expropriation only "where such Expropriation is: (a) for a purpose which is in the public interest; (b) not discriminatory; (c) carried out under due process of law; and (d) accompanied by the payment of prompt, adequate and effective compensation".[23]

While there are commonalities in the language used by different States at different points in time, it has been noted that BITs include "a range of 'boilerplate' expropriation sections that manifest ... differences in diction", but that the "fluctuation in terminology over time defies easy identification of any trends. Perhaps the only safe conclusion that can be drawn from such a review is that States generally seek to incorporate in their BITs the 'customary international law standards for expropriation'."[24]

Treaties drafted in recent decades are noteworthy in that they initially distinguished between different kinds of expropriation creating a perception of an expansion of rights, but soon after narrowed the scope of the expropriation protection. NAFTA commands that "[n]o Party may directly or indirectly nationalize or expropriate an investment ... or take a measure tantamount" to expropriation.[25] Similar formulations abound: "measures having an effect equivalent to nationalization or expropriation";[26] "measure having a

21. Bilateral Agreement for the Promotion and Protection of Investments between the Government of the United Kingdom of Great Britain and Northern Ireland and Republic of Colombia, 17 March 2010, Gr. Brit. T.S. No. 24 (2014), Cm. 8973 (henceforth U.K.-Colombia BIT), Art. VI(1), at <http://investmentpolicyhub.unctad.org/Download/TreatyFile/3253> (last accessed 6 February 2018).
22. North American Free Trade Agreement between the Government of the United States of America, the Government of Canada and the Government of the United Mexican States, 17 December 1992, 32 I.L.M. 289 (henceforth NAFTA), Art. 1110(1).
23. Energy Charter Treaty, 17 December 1994, 2080 U.N.T.S. 95, Art. 13(1) (henceforth Energy Charter Treaty).
24. Campbell MCLACHLAN, Laurence SHORE, and Matthew WEINIGER, *International Investment Arbitration: Substantive Principles*, 1st edn. (Oxford 2007) p. 275.
25. NAFTA, fn. 22 above, Art. 1110(1).
26. Agreement between the Government of Canada and the Government of the Republic of Costa Rica for the Promotion and Protection of Investments, 18 March 1998, 1999 Can. T.S. 43, Art. VIII(1), at <http://investmentpolicyhub.unctad.org/Download/TreatyFile/601> (last accessed 6 February 2018) (henceforth Canada-Costa Rica BIT).

similar effect";[27] "measures having the same effect";[28] "any other similar measures having an effect equivalent to nationalization or expropriation".[29] The United Kingdom-Colombia BIT, for example, refers to "direct" and "indirect" expropriation, as well as "measure[s] having similar effects".[30] As discussed next, the meaning of these terms has been debated in countless arbitral awards and academic works. While some of the debate has settled, the scope of indirect expropriation, measures equivalent to expropriation, and similar terms, remains the subject of discussion.

IV. INDIRECT EXPROPRIATION: BLURRED DEMARCATION LINES

1. *Direct vs. Indirect Expropriation*

Indirect expropriation is, or should be, understood by comparison to direct expropriation. Direct expropriation occurs when State authorities take ownership or control of the investor's assets, often tangible property such as a mine or a factory. In a direct expropriation, title over the property may be transferred to the State or to a third party. Some international tribunals that have provided definitions for the term "expropriation" have done so in terms consistent with the traditional understanding of direct expropriation. For example, the Iran-U.S. Claims Tribunal defined expropriation as "a compulsory transfer of property rights",[31] while the tribunal in the NAFTA case *S.D. Myers v. Canada* explained that "the term 'expropriation' carries with it the connotation of a 'taking' by a governmental-type authority of a person's 'property' with a view to transferring ownership of that property to another person, usually the authority that exercised its *de jure* or *de facto* power to do the 'taking'".[32]

---

27. Agreement between the Government of the Republic of France and the Government of the United Mexican States on the Reciprocal Promotion and Protection of Investments, 12 November 1998, Art. 5(1), at <http://investmentpolicyhub.unctad.org/Download/TreatyFile/1253> (last accessed 6 February 2018) (henceforth France-Mexico BIT).
28. Agreement between the Government of the Republic of Kenya and the Government of the State of Qatar for Reciprocal Promotion and Protection of Investments, 13 April 2014, Art. 5(1), at <http://investmentpolicyhub.unctad.org/Download/TreatyFile/5542> (last accessed 6 February 2018).
29. Agreement on the Promotion and Protection of Investments Between the Government of the Republic of Korea and the Government of the Arab Republic of Egypt, 18 March 1996, Art. 5(1), at <http://investmentpolicyhub.unctad.org/Download/TreatyFile/1087> (last accessed 6 February 2018).
30. U.K.-Colombia BIT, fn. 21 above, Art. VI(1).
31. Peter MUCHLINSKI, Federico ORTINO and Christoph SCHREUER, eds., *The Oxford Handbook of International Investment Law* (Oxford 2008) p. 414 (citing *Amoco International Finance Corporation v. The Government of the Islamic Republic of Iran, National Iranian Oil Company, National Petrochemical Company and Kharg Chemical Company Limited* (15 Iran-U.S. C.T.R. 189), 14 July 1987, para. 191.).
32. *S.D. Myers, Inc. v. Government of Canada* (UNCITRAL), Partial Award of 13 November 2000, para. 280, at <www.italaw.com/sites/default/files/case-documents/ita0747.pdf> (last accessed 6 February 2018) (henceforth *S.D. Myers v. Canada*).

Despite those definitions, it is generally accepted that an expropriation can take place even where the State action leaves the investor's title unaffected. In an indirect expropriation, the investor may formally retain title over the property, but may still find that the State's action has severely impaired his ability to use the investment in any meaningful way, or has caused a significant depreciation in the value of the investment.[33] While the jurisprudence on expropriation in the early twentieth century focused largely on direct expropriation,[34] it also recognized that the concept of expropriation extended beyond the direct taking of tangible property.

One example is the 1922 *Norwegian Shipowners' Claims* case. The case arose in 1917 when, upon the United States' entry into World War I, the United States requisitioned all ships over 2,500 tons, including those that were in the process of being constructed for a group of Norwegian nationals who had put in their orders before the United States' requisition action.[35] The order "expressly requisitioned not only the ships and the material, but also the contracts, the plans, detailed specifications and payments made, and it even commandeered the yards (depriving them of their right to accept any further contracts)".[36] The United States disputed that the order extended to contractual rights,[37] such as those held by the Norwegian nationals, but the tribunal was not persuaded that the United States' actions did not amount to a taking. The tribunal found that the Fleet Corporation (an entity of the United States government) "took over the legal rights and duties of the shipowners towards the shipbuilders", "insert[ing] itself between the builders and the shipowners by an exercise of what is called, in the United States Law and Jurisprudence, the power of eminent domain".[38] Consequently, it held that "the United States took, both in fact and in law, the contracts under which the ships in question were being or were to be constructed".[39]

33. See, e.g., *Middle East Cement Shipping and Handling Co. S.A. v. Arab Republic of Egypt* (ICSID Case No. ARB/99/6), Award (12 April 2002), para. 107 (henceforth *Middle East Cement v. Egypt*) ("When measures are taken by a State the effect of which is to deprive the investor of the use and benefit of his investment even though he may retain nominal ownership of the respective rights being the investment, the measures are often referred to as a 'creeping' or 'indirect' expropriation or, as in the BIT, as measures 'the effect of which is tantamount to expropriation'."). Commentators have noted that there is no single generally accepted definition of an indirect expropriation, and that "investment treaties rarely try to define indirect expropriations". P. MUCHLINSKI, F. ORTINO and C. SCHREUER, *Oxford Handbook*, fn. 31 above, p. 422.
34. See, e.g., *Factory at Chorzow*, fn. 12 above (involving the seizure of a nitrate factory); *Upton Case*, fn. 1 above (dealing with the seizure and destruction of ships); *Walter Fletcher Smith Claim*, fn. 6 above (in which the State condemned two parcels of land and demolished the property on those parcels).
35. *Norwegian Shipowners' Claims (Norway v. USA)* (Permanent Court of Arbitration), 1 UNRIAA 307, Award (13 October 1922), at p. 323 (henceforth *Norwegian Shipowners' Claims*).
36. *Ibid.*, at p. 318.
37. *Ibid.*, at p. 318 ("the United States have contended that there was no requisition, except of 'physical property' and have strongly maintained that the word 'contract' in the letter of 3rd August only referred to commitments for material".).
38. *Ibid.*, at p. 323.
39. *Ibid.*, at p. 325.

The case is an important precedent in the jurisprudence of indirect expropriation for two reasons. First, the tribunal's holding expressly referenced a de facto taking, i.e., one that need not require a formal transfer of title, but one where merely the effect of fully depriving a foreign national of its property is sufficient to trigger international responsibility.[40] Whether the United States' order was intended to seize title or only control of the ships under construction was not specified.[41] The United States did claim to hold title to the Norwegian property, but the tribunal deemed it unnecessary to decide whether it could validly hold such title.[42] Instead, the tribunal considered it "sufficient to state that the United States, in fact, did take and hold the title, the property of the claimants; that they had the 'de facto' possession, enjoyment and use, and that they acted as owners of the claimants' property after the formal taking".[43] Thus it concluded that a taking had been effected, and that compensation was due.[44]

Second, and more broadly, the *Norwegian Shipowners* case is noteworthy because of its contribution to the jurisprudence expanding the traditional notion of the kinds of property that could be expropriated. In the early twentieth century, expropriation claims usually involved the taking of physical property, as was the case, for example, of the nationalization of petroleum reserves, facilities and oil companies in Mexico in 1938.[45] At the time, many still held the view that only physical property could be expropriated, as the United States argued in the *Norwegian Shipowners* case.[46] The tribunal in that case, however, expressly held that intangible property, such as contractual rights, could be subject to expropriation (and by extension the protections against it).[47] This principle is of key importance for the concept of indirect expropriation, given that State action can interfere with the use and enjoyment of all kinds of property, not only tangible assets. Subsequent jurisprudence continued to reinforce the validity of this principle.[48] It is now well established that intangible property can also be the subject of an expropriation.[49]

---

40. *Ibid.*, at p. 325 (holding that an expropriation had taken place both in law and in fact).
41. *Ibid.*, at p. 323. The United States, however, kept the Norwegian claimants' ships after the war, even though it had returned other ships back to their owners once they were no longer needed for the war effort. *Ibid.*, at pp. 329-330.
42. *Ibid.*, at p. 329.
43. *Ibid.*, at p. 329.
44. *Ibid.*, at p. 340 ("Just compensation should have been paid to the Claimants or arranged with them on the basis of the net value of the property taken.").
45. See, e.g., Office of the Historian of the Department of State of the United States of America, "Mexican Expropriation of Foreign Oil", at <https://history.state.gov/milestones/1937-1945/mexican-oil> (last accessed 7 February 2018).
46. *Norwegian Shipowners' Claims*, fn. 35 above, p. 318 ("the United States have contended that there was no requisition, except of 'physical property'".).
47. The *Norwegian Shipowners* case, however, was certainly not the first with such a holding. The 1903 *Rudloff* case, for example, articulated the same principle when it held that "[t]he taking away or destruction of rights acquired, transmitted, and defined by a contract is as much a wrong, entitling the sufferer to redress, as the taking away or destruction of tangible property". *Rudloff Case* (United States-Venezuela Mixed Claims Commission), 9 UNRIAA 244, Interlocutory Decision (1903), at p. 250.
48. See, e.g., *Starrett Housing Corp. v. Iran*, 4 Iran-US CTR 122, Interlocutory Award (19 December 1983), 1983 WL 233292 at *27 (noting that claimants relied on "precedents in international law in which cases measures of expropriation or taking, primarily aimed at physical property, have

In the present day, expropriation is most often effected indirectly. This is due, in part, to the rise of the global economy and States' resulting desire to foster a more welcoming environment for foreign investment. Put simply, States are less willing to bear the reputational cost of seizing property outright. In addition, the prevalence of indirect expropriation is also due to States' increased regulatory activity in areas like the environment, public health, and natural resources that can interfere with and cause a diminution in the value of a foreign national's property. The prevalence of indirect expropriation does not mean, however, that direct takings are a thing of the distant past.[50]

2. *One or More Kinds of Indirect Expropriation?*

Indirect expropriation is now a well-established concept that has been explicitly referenced in most IIAs in force today.[51] In addition to the use of the term "indirect", IIAs often refer to measures "tantamount",[52] "equivalent"[53] or "similar"[54] to expropriation. The variation in terminology has raised the question of whether there are types of expropriation beyond the direct/indirect distinction. The jurisprudence and the academic commentary suggest that there are not.

In the NAFTA case *Metalclad v. Mexico*, the claimant, a United States waste disposal company, argued that the Mexican government's refusal to permit its subsidiary to open and operate a hazardous waste facility constituted an expropriation of its investment. Art. 1110(1), the relevant NAFTA chapter, provides that:

---

been deemed to comprise also rights of a contractual nature closely related to the physical property".); *Amoco Finance Corp. v. Iran*, 15 Iran-US CTR 189, Partial Award (14 July 1987), para. 108, 1987 WL 503881 at *23 (stating, more broadly, that "[e]xpropriation, which can be defined as a compulsory transfer of property rights, may extend to any right which can be the object of a commercial transaction".) (henceforth *Amoco v. Iran*).

49. See *Wena Hotels Limited v. Arab Republic of Egypt* (ICSID Case No. Arb/98/4), Award (8 December 2000), para. 98 ("It is also well-established that an expropriation is not limited to tangible property rights."). Most IIAs include contractual and other intangible rights within the scope of their protection. See, e.g., NAFTA, fn. 22 above, Art. 1139 (protecting "real estate or other property, tangible or intangible"); Germany Federal Ministry for Economics and Technology, "German Model Treaty – 2008", Art. 1(c), at <http://investmentpolicyhub.unctad.org/Download/TreatyFile/2865> (last accessed 7 February 2018) (protecting "claims to any performance having an economic value"); Free Trade Agreement between the Government of the United States of America and the Government of the Republic of Chile, 6 June 2003, 42 I.L.M. 1026, Annex 10-D (protecting any "tangible or intangible property right or property interest in an investment".).

50. For example, the expropriation of American nationals' property in Iran after the Iranian Revolution took place only forty years ago. And more recently, Zimbabwe expropriated Dutch nationals' farmland as part of a land redistribution program. See *Funnekotter v. Zimbabwe* (ICSID Case No. ARB/05/6), Award (22 April 2009).

51. See, e.g., NAFTA, fn. 22 above, Art. 1110(1); Energy Charter Treaty, fn. 23 above, Art. 13(1); U.K.-Colombia BIT, fn. 21 above, Art. VI(1).

52. See, e.g., NAFTA, fn. 22 above, Art. 1110(1).

53. See, e.g., Canada-Costa Rica BIT, fn. 26 above, Art. VIII(1).

54. See, e.g., France-Mexico BIT, fn. 27 above, Art. 5(1).

> "No Party may directly or indirectly nationalize or expropriate an investment of an investor of another Party in its territory or take a measure tantamount to nationalization or expropriation of such an investment ('expropriation'), except: (a) for a public purpose; (b) on a non-discriminatory basis; (c) in accordance with due process of law and Article 1105(1); and (d) on payment of compensation in accordance with paragraphs 2 through 6."[55]

NAFTA's reference to indirect expropriations and measures "tantamount" to expropriation raised the question of whether two (or three) different kinds of expropriation were envisioned by this article. The United States, one of the NAFTA drafting parties, submitted a non-disputing party submission in which it explained that the terms were equivalent. According to the tribunal, the United States' position articulated in its submission was that

> "the NAFTA, Article 1110, term 'tantamount to expropriation' addressed both measures that directly expropriate and measures tantamount to expropriation that thereby indirectly expropriate investments. *The United States rejected the suggestion that the term 'tantamount to expropriation' was intended to create a new category of expropriation* not previously recognized in customary international law."[56] (Emphasis added.)

Ultimately, the tribunal decided that Mexico's actions constituted an indirect expropriation and acts tantamount to expropriation, with both terms being used synonymously.[57] Other tribunals interpreting the same provision agreed with the *Metalclad* tribunal's interpretation of these terms. For example, in the *Feldman v. Mexico* case, the tribunal held that "Article 1110 deals not only with direct takings, but indirect expropriation and measures 'tantamount to expropriation,' which potentially encompass a variety of government regulatory activity that may significantly interfere with an investor's property rights. *The Tribunal deems the scope of both expressions to be functionally equivalent* (emphasis added)."[58]

There have been some dissenters, however. The tribunal in *Waste Management v. Mexico*, for example, reasoned that the terms must have different meanings as the terms could not be superfluous. It distinguished the terms as follows:

> "Article 1110(1) distinguishes between direct or indirect expropriation on the one hand and measures tantamount to an expropriation on the other. An indirect expropriation is still a taking of property. By contrast where a measure tantamount to an expropriation is alleged, there may have been no actual transfer, taking or loss of property by any person or entity, but rather an effect on property

55. NAFTA, fn. 22 above, Art. 1110(1).
56. *Metalclad Corporation v. The United Mexican States* (ICSID Case No. ARB(AF)/97/1), Award (30 August 2000), para. 27 (henceforth *Metalclad v. Mexico*).
57. See *Metalclad v. Mexico,* fn. 56 above, paras. 111-112.
58. *Marvin Feldman v. Mexico* (ICSID Case No. ARB(AF)/99/1), Award (16 December 2002), para. 100 (henceforth *Feldman v. Mexico*).

> which makes formal distinctions of ownership irrelevant.... Evidently the phrase 'take a measure tantamount to nationalization or expropriation of such an investment' in Article 1110(1) was intended to add to the meaning of the prohibition, over and above the reference to indirect expropriation. Indeed there is some indication that it was intended to have a broad meaning, otherwise it is difficult to see why Article 1110(8) was necessary."[59]

Decisions like *Waste Management* are outliers. The majority opinion is that "[i]n practice, the distinction between indirect expropriations and measures equivalent to expropriations does not appear to be a meaningful one. No case has yet identified a measure that was tantamount to an indirect expropriation but not itself an indirect expropriation."[60] For practical purposes, terms like "tantamount", "equivalent", and "similar" to expropriation can be understood to be interchangeable with "indirect expropriation".

There is, however, at least one subcategory of indirect expropriation. An indirect expropriation need not be accomplished through a single act of the State. When the expropriation results from a series of State actions, it is referred to as a "creeping expropriation". The tribunal in *Generation Ukraine* defined a creeping expropriation as "a form of indirect expropriation with a distinctive temporal quality in the sense that it encapsulates the situation whereby a series of acts attributable to the State over a period of time culminate in the expropriatory taking of such property" (emphasis removed).[61] The *Pope & Talbot* tribunal described it more succinctly as "a process that has the effect of taking property through staged measures".[62] The concept of creeping expropriation arose as a way to prevent States from circumventing the protections against expropriation by realizing a taking in a series of cumulative steps that individually do not rise to the level of expropriation, but in conjunction do have an expropriatory effect.[63]

3. *Indirect Expropriation and Non-compensable Regulation*

Perhaps the most significant unresolved question regarding indirect expropriation is where to draw the line between indirect expropriation and a regulation that triggers no international responsibility. The distinction is critical: an expropriation requires compensation, while good-faith regulation pursuant to the police powers of the State

59. *Waste Management, Inc. v. United Mexican States* (ICSID Case No. ARB(AF)/00/3), Award (30 April 2004), paras. 143-144.
60. SALACUSE, *Law of Investment Treaties*, fn. 2 above, p. 328.
61. *Generation Ukraine, Inc. v. Ukraine* (ICSID Case No. ARB/00/9), Award (16 September 2003), para. 20.22 (henceforth *Generation Ukraine v. Ukraine*).
62. *Pope & Talbot Inc. v. The Government of Canada* (UNCITRAL), Interim Award (26 June 2000), para. 83 (henceforth *Pope & Talbot*).
63. See *Tradex Hellas S.A. v. Republic of Albania* (ICSID Case No. ARB/94/2), Award (29 April 1999), para. 191 ("While the above examination in Sections b) to l) of this Award has come to the conclusion that none of the single decisions and events alleged by Tradex to constitute an expropriation can indeed be qualified by the Tribunal as expropriation, it might still be possible that, and the Tribunal, therefore, has to examine and evaluate hereafter whether the combination of the decisions and events can be qualified as expropriation of Tradex' foreign investment in a long, step-by-step process by Albania.").

does not.[64] While the notion of "police powers" has been long recognized in the doctrine and by the courts, the discussion on this issue has been lively, particularly in the arbitral jurisprudence.

a. Factors considered by arbitral tribunals

Arbitral tribunals have been at the front lines of the battle to delimitate the concepts of indirect expropriation and non-compensable regulation. In deciding the cases before them, tribunals have weighed a variety of factors in order to determine whether an expropriation took place.

i. The nature of the measure

The nature of the regulatory measures that are claimed to have effected an expropriation are a factor in tribunals' analysis. The *Saluka* tribunal expressed the view that when the measures are "within the police power of States" the State is not liable to pay compensation to the foreign investor.[65] This was echoed in the *Feldman v. Mexico* award, which stated that:

> "governments must be free to act in the broader public interest through protection of the environment, new or modified tax regimes, the granting or withdrawal of government subsidies, reductions or increases in tariff levels, imposition of zoning restrictions and the like. Reasonable governmental regulation of this type cannot be achieved if any business that is adversely affected may seek compensation, and it is safe to say that customary international law recognizes this."[66]

For example, taxation measures, as a general rule, are not considered to constitute an expropriation. In the words of the *EnCana* tribunal: "In itself such a law [imposing a tax] is not a taking of property; if it were, a universal State prerogative would be denied by a guarantee against expropriation, which cannot be the case".[67] The tribunal went on to enumerate the exceptional circumstances under which a tax law would rise to the level of an expropriation: "Only if a tax law is extraordinary, punitive in amount or arbitrary in its incidence would issues of indirect expropriation be raised."[68] The *RosInvest* case

64. See Restatement (Third) of the Foreign Relations Law of the United States, fn. 14 above, §712, Comment (g) ("A state is not responsible for loss of property or for other economic disadvantage resulting from bona fide general taxation, regulation, forfeiture for crime, or other action of the kind that is commonly accepted as within the police power of states, if it is not discriminatory."). But see *Metalclad v. Mexico,* fn. 56 above, para. 103 (endorsing the "sole effects" doctrine, which posits that the effect of the State measure alone can determine whether an expropriation has taken place, meaning that the regulatory purpose of the State measure is irrelevant. The "sole effects" doctrine is a minority position.).

65. *Saluka Investments B.V. v. The Czech Republic* (UNCITRAL), Partial Award (17 March 2006), para. 262 (henceforth *Saluka v. Czech Republic*).

66. *Feldman v. Mexico*, fn. 58 above, para. 103.

67. *EnCana Corporation v. Republic of Ecuador* (LCIA Case No. UN3481, UNCITRAL), Award (3 February 2006), para. 177.

68. *Ibid.*

echoed this view, stating that abusive tax law enforcement can constitute an expropriation.[69]

In addition to taxation, other kinds of measures that generally are not categorized as compensable takings include the imposition of criminal penalties or export controls.[70] In fact, as will be discussed, some recent treaties even specify that certain kinds of non-discriminatory regulatory actions do not constitute expropriations, except in rare circumstances. The United States and Canada Model BITs, for instance, specifically carve out measures "designed and applied to protect legitimate public welfare objectives, such as public health, safety, and the environment" from the meaning of expropriation.[71] This kind of language – codifying customary international law on police powers – may have been added to treaties as a response to some tribunals' expansive view of the kinds of measures that can be expropriatory. The tribunal in *Santa Elena v. Costa Rica*, for example, rejected the argument that environmental measures were somehow exempted:

> "Expropriatory environmental measures – no matter how laudable and beneficial to society as a whole – are, in this respect, similar to any other expropriatory measures that a state may take in order to implement its policies: where property is expropriated, even for environmental purposes, whether domestic or international, the state's obligation to pay compensation remains."[72]

ii. The level of deprivation

A recurring factor in tribunals' determination of whether regulation amounts to expropriation has been the level of deprivation caused by the State measure. While there seems to be consensus that this is a relevant factor in the analysis, there is disagreement as to the level of deprivation that is required for a finding of expropriation. Some tribunals have expressed the view that a total deprivation is required. For example, the *Goetz v. Burundi* tribunal's finding of expropriation was based on the fact that the State action caused "*all* activity" of the enterprise to stop and deprived the investments of "*all* utility" (emphasis added).[73] The *Grand River* tribunal expressed the same view in stronger terms:

---

69. *RosInvestCo UK Ltd. v. The Russian Federation* (SCC Case No. V079/2005), Final Award (12 September 2010), para. 628 ("it is generally accepted that the mere fact that measures by a host state are taken in the form of application and enforcement of its tax law, does not prevent a tribunal from examining whether this conduct of the host state must be considered, under the applicable BIT or other international treaties on investment protection, as an abuse of tax law to in fact enact an expropriation.").

70. M. SORNARAJAH, *Foreign Investment*, fn. 9 above, p. 374.

71. United States Model BIT, fn. 20 above, Annex B; Agreement between Canada and _____ for the Promotion and Protection of Investments (2004), at <https://www.italaw.com/documents/Canadian2004-FIPA-model-en.pdf> (last accessed 7 February 2018), Annex B.13(1) (henceforth Canada Model BIT).

72. *Compañía del Desarrollo de Santa Elena, S.A. v. The Republic of Costa Rica* (ICSID Case No. ARB/96/1), Award (17 February 2000), para. 72. Note that in the *Santa Elena* case, the fact of expropriation was not in dispute. Costa Rica had directly expropriated the claimant's property by decree. Rather, the arbitral tribunal's task was to determine the amount of compensation due.

73. *Antoine Goetz et consorts v. Republic of Burundi* (ICSID Case No. ARB/95/3, Award (10 February 1999), para. 124.

> "The starting point must be the language of Article 1110(1), providing that '[n]o Party may directly or indirectly nationalize or expropriate an investment of an investor of another Party in its territory,' unless certain conditions are met.... The text speaks of 'an investment,' not 'an investment or some portion thereof.' *The most natural reading of the language is that any act of expropriation will affect the totality of an investment.*"[74] (Some emphasis added; some emphasis omitted.)

The reasoning in *Goetz* and *Grand River* may provide strong incentives to investors to "slice and dice" their investment in order to be able to claim that the level of deprivation is total. An example of this "slicing and dicing" took place in the *Eli Lilly v. Canada* case, where the Claimant argued that the State measure expropriated the totality of its interest in two patents, even though its full investment in Canada was far greater than those two patents.[75]

The *Goetz* and *Grand River* cases, however, express a minority view.[76] Most tribunals have been willing to find an expropriation where there has been significant, but not total, deprivation. In *Biwater Gauff*, the tribunal explained that an indirect expropriation occurs where there is a "substantial deprivation of rights, for at least a meaningful period of time".[77] Other tribunals have applied the same test,[78] but few have provided detailed guidance on how to conduct this analysis. The *Telenor* tribunal, for example, merely indicated that one must consider the "intensity and duration of the economic deprivation suffered by the investor".[79]

The *Tokios Tokelés* tribunal went further, suggesting a sliding scale approach for determining whether the deprivation is substantial. While recognizing that this determination was fact-specific, it argued that "a diminution of 5% of the investment's value will not be enough for a finding of expropriation, while a diminution of 95% would likely be sufficient".[80]

---

74. *Grand River Enterprises Six Nations, Ltd., et al. v. United States of America* (UNCITRAL), Award (12 January 2011), para. 147.
75. See *Eli Lilly and Company v. Government of Canada* (ICSID Case No. UNCT/14/2), Final Award (16 March 2017), para. 5 (henceforth *Eli Lilly v. Canada*).
76. Other tribunals have imposed a very high standard of deprivation in order to find that there has been an expropriation, but the standard is not as absolute as the one applied in *Grand River*. For example, the *CMS* tribunal stated that "[t]he essential question is therefore to establish whether the enjoyment of the property has been effectively neutralized", but then accepted the "substantial deprivation" test as applicable. *CMS Gas Transmission Company v. The Republic of Argentina* (ICSID Case No. ARB/01/8), Award (12 May 2005), para. 262. Similarly, the *Pope & Talbot* tribunal stated that for interference to rise to the level of expropriation, it must prevent an investor from using, enjoying, or disposing of his property. *Pope & Talbot*, fn. 62 above, para. 102.
77. *Biwater Gauff (Tanzania) Ltd. v. United Republic of Tanzania* (ICSID Case No. ARB/05/22), Award (24 July 2008), para. 463 (henceforth *Biwater Gauff v. Tanzania*).
78. See e.g., *Suez, Sociedad General de Aguas de Barcelona S.A. and Vivendi Universal S.A. v. The Argentine Republic* (ICSID Case No. ARB/03/19), Decision on Liability (30 July 2010), para. 134 (explaining that the relevant test was whether the State measures effected "a substantial, permanent deprivation of the Claimant's investments or the enjoyment of those investments' economic benefits".).
79. *Telenor Mobile Communications A.S. v. The Republic of Hungary* (ICSID Case No. ARB/04/15), Award (13 September 2006), para. 70.
80. *Tokios Tokelés v. Ukraine* (ICSID Case No. ARB/02/18), Award (26 July 2007), para. 120.

Other tribunals have conducted a qualitative, rather than quantitative, analysis of the level of deprivation. One such example was the *Azurix* case, in which the tribunal found that no expropriation had taken place where, though there was a financial impact on the investment, the State measures were not sufficient to strip Azurix of the attributes of ownership:

> "Therefore, the Tribunal finds that the impact on the investment attributable to the Province's actions was not to the extent required to find that, in the aggregate, these actions amounted to an expropriation; Azurix did not lose the attributes of ownership, at all times continued to control ABA and its ownership of 90% of the shares was unaffected. No doubt the management of ABA was affected by the Province's actions, but not sufficiently for the Tribunal to find that Azurix's investment was expropriated."[81]

The jurisprudence contains a wide range of formulations defining the level of deprivation that is required for a finding of expropriation. Commentators have summarized these formulations in this way:

> "In sum, in order to be considered an expropriation, the effect of a regulatory measure on property rights – that is, the required level of interference with such rights – has been variously described as: (1) unreasonable; (2) an interference that renders rights so useless that they must be deemed to have been expropriated; (3) an interference that deprives the investor of fundamental rights of ownership; (4) an interference that makes rights practically useless; (5) an interference sufficiently restrictive to warrant a conclusion that the property has been 'taken'; (6) an interference that deprives, in whole or in significant part, the use or reasonably-to-be-expected economic benefit of the property; (7) an interference that radically deprives the economical use and enjoyment of an investment, as if the rights related thereto had ceased to exist; (8) an interference that makes any form of exploitation of the property disappear (i.e., it destroys or neutralizes the economic value of the use, enjoyment or disposition of the assets or rights affected); and (9) an interference such that the property can no longer be put to reasonable use."[82] (Emphasis removed.)

While the specific language may vary from treaty to treaty and from award to award, it is generally accepted that the deprivation need not be absolute, but must at least be substantial.

---

81. *Azurix Corp. v. The Argentine Republic* (ICSID Case No. ARB/01/12), Award (14 July 2006), para. 322. But see *LG&E Energy Corp., LG&E Capital Corp., and LG&E International Inc. v. Argentine Republic* (ICSID Case No. ARB/02/1), Decision on Liability (3 October 2006) (henceforth *LG&E v. Argentina*), in which the tribunal found no expropriation where Argentina's measures reduced the value of the claimants' investment by over 90 percent, because the investors retained control over and the right to enjoy the investment.
82. L. Yves FORTIER and Stephen L. DRYMER, "Indirect Expropriation in the Law of International Investment: I Know It When I See It, or *Caveat Investor*", 19 ICSID Review–FILJ (2004, no. 2) p. 293 at p. 305.

iii. Duration

In addition to the level of deprivation experienced by the investor, tribunals also consider the duration of the deprivation in determining whether there has been an indirect expropriation. The tribunal in *LG&E* held that its analysis must consider not only the effects of the measure on the use, enjoyment, and value of the investment, but also "the duration of the measure as it relates to the degree of interference with the investor's ownership rights".[83] And as mentioned previously, the *Biwater Gauff* formula looked not only at deprivation suffered by the investor, but also at its duration, which must be "at least a meaningful period of time".[84]

There is agreement that where the effect of the state measures is "irreversible and permanent", the duration requirement is met and the regulation is expropriatory.[85] Permanence is not required, however. Even temporary measures may rise to the level of expropriation if their effect is "lasting".[86] But once again, this is a fact-specific inquiry for which no hard and fast rules can be discerned.

iv. The investor's legitimate expectations

The concept of the investor's legitimate expectations, most often discussed in the context of fair and equitable treatment, has increasingly been considered by tribunals as a relevant factor in the determination of indirect expropriation.[87] When foreign nationals invest in a host State, they have expectations for the economic benefit to be derived from their investment. States may create expectations by making assurances to investors

83. *LG&E v. Argentina*, fn. 81 above, para 193.
84. *Biwater Gauff v. Tanzania*, fn. 77 above, para. 463.
85. *Técnicas Medioambientales Tecmed S.A. v. The United Mexican States* (ICSID Case No. ARB (AF)/00/2), Award (29 May 2003), para. 116 ("it is understood that the measures adopted by a State, whether regulatory or not, are an indirect *de facto* expropriation if they are irreversible and permanent and if ... the economic value of the use, enjoyment or disposition of the assets or rights affected by the administrative action or decision have been neutralized or destroyed".) (henceforth *Tecmed v. Mexico*). See also *Generation Ukraine v. Ukraine,* fn. 61 above, para. 20.32 (holding that a regulation is expropriatory where its effects are "persistent or irreparable".).
86. *S.D. Myers v. Canada*, fn. 32 above, para. 283.
87. The analysis of the investor's legitimate expectations may also consider whether the investor should have expected the level of regulation it experienced. For example, the reasonable expectation of an investor in the tobacco industry is that the sector will be regulated increasingly restrictively because of the well-known health effects of tobacco use. In the fair and equitable treatment context, see *Philip Morris Brands Sàrl, Philip Morris Products S.A. and Abal Hermanos S.A. v. Oriental Republic of Uruguay* (ICSID Case No. ARB/10/7), Award (8 July 2016), paras. 429-430 (henceforth *Philip Morris*) ("Manufacturers and distributors of harmful products such as cigarettes can have no expectation that new and more onerous regulations will not be imposed.... On the contrary, in light of widely accepted articulations of international concern for the harmful effect of tobacco, the expectation could only have been of progressively more stringent regulation of the sale and use of tobacco products."). The reasoning is that investors in highly regulated sectors should have expected that the State would exercise its police powers in these sectors. The *Philip Morris* tribunal resolved that there was no expropriation on the basis of Uruguay's exercise of police powers, but did not appear to specifically address the investor's expectation. See paras. 300, 305-307. Given that the direction to tribunals to make this analysis in a regulatory context is almost exclusively found in post-2000s treaties, a similar analysis in the expropriation context has yet to materialize.

about, for example, the issuance of licenses and permits or the stability of the existing regulatory regime. If the State fails to honor these assurances and thereby affects the use, enjoyment or value of the investment, an indirect expropriation may be found. The *Metalclad* tribunal, for example, explained that the concept of expropriation envisioned by NAFTA includes "covert or incidental interference with the use of property which has the effect of depriving the owner, in whole or in significant part, of the use or *reasonably-to-be-expected economic benefit* of property" (emphasis added).[88] Accordingly, the tribunal took into account "the representations of the Mexican federal government, on which Metalclad relied" as a factor in finding that the State measures amounted to an expropriation.[89] Other tribunals have also considered the investor's legitimate expectations in their expropriation analysis.[90]

In recent years, some States have pushed back and contextualized the concept of reasonable investment-backed expectations in their treaties when determining if an indirect expropriation has occurred. The 2012 United States Model BIT, for example, states that the article on expropriation is to be interpreted in accordance with Annex B.[91] Annex B, in turn, instructs that

> "The determination of whether an action or series of actions by a Party, in a specific fact situation, constitutes an indirect expropriation, requires a case-by-case, fact-based inquiry that considers, among other factors: ... *the extent to which the government action interferes with distinct, reasonable investment-backed expectations....*"[92] (Emphasis added.)

Many newer United States treaties include this instruction,[93] as do Canadian[94] and Indian[95] treaties. The drafting of treaties containing this kind of provision reinforces the

88. *Metalclad v. Mexico*, fn. 56 above, para. 103.
89. *Ibid.* at para. 107.
90. See, e.g., *Tecmed v. Mexico*, fn. 85 above, paras. 149-150.
91. United States Model BIT, fn. 20 above, footnote 10.
92. *Ibid.* at Annex B (4)(a). This provision in the 2012 U.S. Model BIT had been introduced earlier by the 2004 U.S. Model BIT, which codified the concept of reasonable investment-backed expectations articulated in the U.S. Supreme Court case *Penn Central Transportation Co. v. New York City*, 438 U.S. 104, 124 (1978).
93. See, e.g., Treaty Between the United States of America and the Oriental Republic of Uruguay Concerning the Encouragement and Reciprocal Protection of Investment, 4 November 2005, T.I.A.S. 06-1101, Annex B 4(a)(ii) (henceforth United States-Uruguay BIT); Free Trade Agreement between the United States and the Republic of Korea, 30 June 2007, Annex 11-B(3)(a)(ii), at <https://ustr.gov/trade-agreements/free-trade-agreements/korus-fta/final-text> (last accessed 9 February 2018); The Dominican Republic – Central America – United States Free Trade Agreement, 5 August 2004, Annex 10-C(4)(a)(ii).
94. See, e.g., Agreement Between the Government of Canada and the Government of the Republic of Benin for the Promotion and Reciprocal Protection of Investments, 9 January 2013, 2014 Can. T.S. No. 13, Annex I(b)(2); Agreement Between the Government of Canada and the Government of the People's Republic of China for the Promotion and Reciprocal Protection of Investments, 9 September 2012, 2014 Can. T.S. No. 26, Annex B.10(2)(b).
95. See, e.g., Agreement Between the Government of India and the Government of Nepal for the Reciprocal Promotion and Protection of Investments, 21 October 2011, Art. 5(2)(iii), at <http://investmentpolicyhub.unctad.org/Download/TreatyFile/1583> (last accessed

increasingly recognized trend of directing tribunals to find direct expropriation only where the investor is able to demonstrate that it had reasonable expectations that went unmet due to the State's action. In essence, State parties are signaling to tribunals that in making investments in highly regulated sectors, investors can only have limited expectations regarding negative effects of regulation.

v. Proportionality

Another factor taken into consideration when determining whether a State measure is expropriatory is whether the measure is proportional to the end it seeks to achieve. Citing *Tecmed*, the *LG&E* tribunal explained the role of proportionality in differentiating between expropriation and regulation:

> "With respect to the power of the State to adopt its policies, it can generally be said that the State has the right to adopt measures having a social or general welfare purpose. In such a case, the measure must be accepted without any imposition of liability, *except in cases where the State's action is obviously disproportionate to the need being addressed*. The proportionality to be used when making use of this right was recognized in *Tecmed*, which observed that 'whether such actions or measures are proportional to the public interest presumably protected thereby and the protection legally granted to investments, taking into account that the significance of such impact, has a key role upon deciding the proportionality'."[96] (Emphasis added.)

Subsequent tribunals have reaffirmed the importance of proportionality. The tribunal in *Deutsche Bank v. Sri Lanka* rejected the respondent State's argument that it had "extremely broad discretion to interfere with investments" so long as it did so in the exercise of "legitimate regulatory authority".[97] Rather, the tribunal reasoned that the State's measures had to be proportionate to the public welfare purpose sought. It explained that the proportionality requirement "prevents the States from taking measures which severely impact an investor unless such measures are justified by a substantial public interest".[98]

Other States have imposed a less rigorous proportionality test for expropriation that allows for a greater range of regulatory action and raises the legal standard for a finding of expropriation. The Canadian Model Foreign Investment Promotion and Protection Agreement, for example, states that non-discriminatory State measures to protect public

---

9 February 2018); Agreement Between the Government of the Republic of India and the Government of the Republic of Lithuania for the Promotion and Protection of Investments, 31 March 2011, Annex (2)(iii), at <http://investmentpolicyhub.unctad.org/Download/TreatyFile/1574> (last accessed 9 February 2018); Agreement for the Promotion and Protection of Investments Between the Republic of Colombia and the Republic of India, 10 November 2009, Art. 6(2)(b)(iii), at <http://investmentpolicyhub.unctad.org/Download/TreatyFile/796> (last accessed 9 February 2018).

96. *LG&E v. Argentina*, fn. 81 above, paras. 194-195, citing *Tecmed v. Mexico*, fn. 85 above, para. 122.

97. *Deutsche Bank AG v. Democratic Socialist Republic of Sri Lanka* (ICSID Case No. ARB/09/2), Award (31 October 2012), para. 522.

98. *Ibid.*

welfare objectives do not constitute indirect expropriation "[e]xcept in rare circumstances, such as when a measure or series of measures are so severe in the light of their purpose that they cannot be reasonably viewed as having been adopted and applied in good faith".[99] In other words, the measure must be so disproportionate to the end sought that one is led to the conclusion that the measure was not adopted in good faith.

b. Treaty guidance on the distinction between regulation and taking

Recently drafted treaties seek to draw a clear distinction between indirect expropriation and non-compensable regulation, and provide guidance to assist adjudicators in determining whether compensation is required by the facts before them. For example, the United States 2012 Model BIT acknowledges that this exercise is fact-dependent and requires a weighing of various factors (though it does not provide an exhaustive list of factors to consider nor does it comment on the relative weight that should be given to each enumerated factor). Specifically, its Annex B provides that:

> "The determination of whether an action or series of actions by a Party, in a specific fact situation, constitutes an indirect expropriation, *requires a case-by-case, fact-based inquiry* that considers, among other factors: (i) the economic impact of the government action, although the fact that an action or series of actions by a Party has an adverse effect on the economic value of an investment, standing alone, does not establish that an indirect expropriation has occurred; (ii) the extent to which the government action interferes with distinct, reasonable investment-backed expectations; and (iii) the character of the government action. (b) Except in rare circumstances, non-discriminatory regulatory actions by a Party that are designed and applied to protect legitimate public welfare objectives, such as public health, safety, and the environment, do not constitute indirect expropriations."[100] (Emphasis added.)

Despite the additional guidance in these treaties, the debate about the delimitation of indirect expropriation is likely to continue. As tribunals have noted, the determination of whether a State measure constitutes an indirect expropriation is fact-specific. Thus, even if the applicable treaty lays out the specifics of the test to be applied by a tribunal, including the factors to take into account, the tribunal will still have discretion to weigh factors as it deems appropriate, including factors beyond those included in newer treaties' non-exhaustive lists.[101] And disputes will continue to arise under treaties that do not have this level of specificity as to the definition of indirect expropriation. As the *Saluka* tribunal commented:

99. Canada Model BIT (2004), fn. 71 above, Annex B.13(1)(c).
100. United States Model BIT, fn. 20 above, Annex B. The Canada Model BIT contains very similar language. See Canada Model BIT (2004), fn. 71 above, Annex B.13(1).
101. For some, this very fact is unacceptable and leads to calls to remove expropriation protections from IIAs or to remove the access of investors to dispute settlement on the grounds of a violation of indirect expropriation. These issues will be discussed in greater detail later.

> "international law has yet to identify in a comprehensive and definitive fashion precisely what regulations are considered 'permissible' and 'commonly accepted' as falling within the police or regulatory power of States and, thus, noncompensable. In other words, it has yet to draw a bright and easily distinguishable line between non-compensable regulations on the one hand and, on the other, measures that have the effect of depriving foreign investors of their investment and are thus unlawful and compensable in international law."[102]

The *Saluka* case arose under the Netherlands-Czech Republic BIT signed in 1991. As mentioned earlier, in more modern treaties, particularly those drafted in the 2000s, States have set clearer limits on the kinds of State measures that can constitute an indirect expropriation.

To date, there have been relatively few arbitral awards examining these limits. One such case is *Berkowitz v. Costa Rica*, which arose under the Dominican Republic-Central America Free Trade Agreement (CAFTA).[103] CAFTA's Expropriation Annex, Annex 10-C, establishes a non-exhaustive list of factors to be considered in the determination of whether State measures have effected an indirect expropriation. The enumerated factors are the economic impact of the government action, the extent to which the government action interferes with distinct, reasonable investment-backed expectations, and the character of the government action.[104] These factors clearly express a rejection of the sole effects doctrine and a requirement that explicit consideration be given to the nature of the State measure. For additional clarity, the Annex goes on to specify that measures intended to protect public welfare do not constitute indirect expropriation.[105] It states:

> "Except in rare circumstances, nondiscriminatory regulatory actions by a Party that are designed and applied to protect legitimate public welfare objectives, such as public health, safety, and the environment, do not constitute indirect expropriations."[106]

While the *Berkowitz* tribunal's award was focused on jurisdictional questions, the tribunal nonetheless commented on CAFTA's Annex 10-C. It acknowledged that the Annex imposes a high bar for a finding of indirect expropriation, and found that the claimants in the case had not satisfied this burden:

> "While the present enquiry is focused on issues of jurisdiction, the Tribunal notes the exacting requirements in respect of claims of indirect expropriation set out in paragraph 4 of Annex 10-C of the CAFTA, including that the fact of an adverse effect on the economic value of an investment, standing alone, does not establish

102. *Saluka v. Czech Republic*, fn. 65 above, para. 263.
103. *Aaron C. Berkowitz, Brett E. Berkowitz and Trevor B. Berkowitz* (formerly *Spence International Investments and others) v. Republic of Costa Rica* (ICSID Case No. UNCT/13/2), Interim Award of the Tribunal (Corrected) (30 May 2017) (henceforth *Berkowitz v. Costa Rica*).
104. Dominican Republic-Central America-United States Free Trade Agreement, 5 August 2004, 43 I.L.M. 514 (henceforth CAFTA), Annex 10-C (4)(a).
105. CAFTA, fn. 104 above, Annex 10-C (4)(b).
106. *Ibid.*

that an indirect expropriation has occurred. The Tribunal does not consider that the Claimants have satisfied the burden upon them in respect of these claims."[107]

As more tribunals engage with these new-generation treaty provisions on expropriation, it will be possible to identify trends on whether States have provided sufficient clarity on – and whether tribunals have recognized – the distinction between non-compensable regulation and indirect expropriation.

V. LEGALITY OF THE EXPROPRIATION AND ITS CONSEQUENCES

As discussed in Part III, under most treaties, the requirements for a lawful expropriation are a public purpose, non-discrimination, due process and the payment of prompt, adequate and effective compensation. These four elements have been examined by arbitral tribunals tasked with determining the legality of an expropriation.

1. *Public Purpose*

The concept of public purpose is both nebulous and broad. The Iran-U.S. Claims Tribunal has stated that "[a] precise definition of the 'public purpose' for which an expropriation may be lawfully decided has neither been agreed upon in international law nor even suggested.... [T]his term is broadly interpreted, and ... States, in practice, are granted extensive discretion."[108] Because of the broad discretion afforded to States,[109] the public purpose requirement is not challenged often. Even when the public purpose prong is challenged, Tribunals often decline to decide the question, because the illegality has already been demonstrated by a finding of discrimination, lack of due process, and/or inadequate compensation.[110] However, there have been some instances in which tribunals explored the limits of the public purpose requirement.

Though the State is entitled to broad deference in this regard, public purpose requirement for a lawful expropriation is not met when the State fails to provide "convincing facts or legal reasoning" substantiating its claim that its measures were motivated by a legitimate public purpose (emphasis removed).[111] It is not sufficient that the State declares it acted in the public interest; the standard is not self-judging. This is because, as the *ADC* tribunal explained, "[i]f mere reference to 'public interest' can magically put such interest into existence and therefore satisfy this requirement, then this requirement would be rendered meaningless".[112] Some arbitral awards found States'

107. *Berkowitz v. Costa Rica*, fn. 103 above, para. 271.
108. *Amoco v. Iran*, fn. 48 above, para. 145.
109. See also Restatement (Third) of the Foreign Relations Law of the United States, fn. 14 above, § 712 Comment (e) ("the concept of public purpose is broad and not subject to effective reexamination by other states".).
110. See, e.g., *Quiborax S.A. and Non Metallic Minerals S.A. v. Plurinational State of Bolivia* (ICSID Case No. ARB/06/2), Award (16 September 2015), para. 245 (henceforth *Quiborax v. Bolivia*).
111. *ADC Affiliate Limited and ADC &ADMC Management Limited v. The Republic of Hungary* (ICSID Case No. ARB/03/16), Award (2 October 2006), paras. 429-433 (henceforth *ADC v. Hungary*).
112. *Ibid.*, at para. 432.

claims of public interest not credible. In *British Caribbean Bank*, for example, the tribunal found that the expropriation had been carried out of personal animus towards a particular individual, rather than for its stated purpose of providing reliable telecommunications services to the public.[113] In *Yukos*, the tribunal found it "profoundly questionable" that "the destruction of Russia's leading oil company and largest taxpayer was in the public interest".[114]

Tribunals have also found that the State's claim that it acted for a public purpose is questionable when the nexus between the measure and its stated purpose is unclear. In *Vestey*, the tribunal questioned (but did not decide) the validity of Venezuela's claim that it had seized the investor's farmland for the purpose of increasing domestic availability of and access to food. While the Tribunal agreed that this was a legitimate purpose, the government's post-expropriation conduct (i.e., the failure to increase domestic food security) suggested the expropriation had been carried out for purposes other than expanding access to food.[115]

2. *Non-discrimination*

To determine whether an expropriation was discriminatory, tribunals often apply the three-pronged test formulated in *Saluka* (or a version of it), which posits that "State conduct is discriminatory, if (i) similar cases are (ii) treated differently (iii) and without reasonable justification".[116] The Restatement (Third) of Foreign Relations further explains that "a program of taking that singles out aliens generally, or aliens of a particular nationality, or particular aliens, would violate international law".[117] Foreign nationality, of any kind, is therefore an illegitimate reason to treat an investor differently. In *Quiborax*, the tribunal determined that Quiborax's subsidiary was targeted because of Quiborax's Chilean nationality, thus making the expropriation of its concessions unlawful.[118] Similarly, the expropriation in *Eureko v. Poland* was held to be discriminatory, because the State measures were pursued in order to "keep PZU under majority Polish control and to exclude foreign control such as that of Eureko".[119]

Evaluating whether different treatment is justified, however, can be challenging. The Restatement warns that "[d]iscrimination may be difficult to determine where there is no comparable enterprise owned by local nationals or by nationals of other countries, or where nationals of the taking state are treated equally with aliens but by discrete actions

113. *British Caribbean Bank Ltd. v. Government of Belize* (PCA Case No. 2010-18), Award (19 December 2014), paras. 239-240.
114. *Yukos Universal Limited (Isle of Man) v. The Russian Federation* (PCA Case No. AA 227), Final Award (18 July 2014), para. 1581 (henceforth *Yukos v. Russia*).
115. *Vestey Group Ltd v. Bolivarian Republic of Venezuela* (ICSID Case No. ARB/06/4), Award (15 April 2016), paras. 293-300.
116. See *Saluka v. Czech Republic*, fn. 65 above, para. 313. See also *Quiborax v. Bolivia*, fn. 110 above, at fn. 272 (listing cases in which the test was applied).
117. Restatement (Third) of the Foreign Relations Law of the United States, fn. 14 above, § 712 Comment (f).
118. *Quiborax v. Bolivia*, fn. 110 above, paras. 247-248.
119. *Eureko B.V. v. Republic of Poland*, Partial Award (19 August 2005), para. 242.

separated in time".[120] This was the case in *ADC v. Hungary*.[121] Hungary argued that ADC could not have been treated in a discriminatory manner because the State's measure affected all airport operators, and it was merely incidental that the only airport operator was ADC. There could therefore be no different treatment for different parties – there was only one party to begin with. The tribunal rejected Hungary's argument and found that there had been discrimination. Unfortunately, the tribunal provided little reasoning for its holding, making it difficult to derive further conclusions of general applicability.

3. *Due Process*

Many treaties require compliance with due process for an expropriation to be lawful.[122] The *ADC* tribunal explained the requirement as follows:

> "'due process of law', in the expropriation context, demands an actual and substantive legal procedure for a foreign investor to raise its claims against the depriving actions already taken or about to be taken against it. Some basic legal mechanisms, such as *reasonable advance notice, a fair hearing and an unbiased and impartial adjudicator to assess the actions in dispute, are expected to be readily available and accessible to the investor* to make such legal procedure meaningful. In general, the legal procedure must be of a nature to grant an affected investor a reasonable chance within a reasonable time to claim its legitimate rights and have its claims heard. If no legal procedure of such nature exists at all, the argument that 'the actions are taken under due process of law' rings hollow. And that is exactly what the Tribunal finds in the present case."[123]

In *Yukos,* the tribunal found that the expropriation had been effected without regard to due process. In that case, the Russian courts were not "unbiased and impartial" as required by the *ADC* standard, but rather "bent to the will of Russian executive authorities to bankrupt Yukos, assign its assets to a State-controlled company, and incarcerate a man who gave signs of becoming a political competitor".[124] The *Bear Creek* tribunal also found an unlawful expropriation where the expropriation was effected by a decree that was hastily drafted and issued – i.e., between the hours of 9:00 pm and 1:30 am, on the basis of documents that the ministers did not review (and that respondent claimed to have lost and therefore could not produce in the arbitration), and without giving *Bear Creek* the opportunity to comment.[125]

120. Restatement (Third) of the Foreign Relations Law of the United States, fn. 14 above, § 712 Comment (f).
121. See *ADC v. Hungary*, fn. 111 above, paras. 441-443.
122. See, e.g., United States-Uruguay BIT, fn. 93 above, Art. 6(1)(d).
123. *ADC v. Hungary*, fn. 111, ¶ 435. The same test was applied in *Kardassopoulos v. Georgia*, where the tribunal also found that the expropriation was not effected in accordance with due process. *Ioannis Kardassopoulos v. Georgia* (ICSID Case No. ARB/05/18), Award (3 March 2010), paras. 395-408.
124. *Yukos v. Russia*, fn. 114 above, para. 1583.
125. *Bear Creek Mining Corporation v. Republic of Peru* (ICSID Case No. ARB/14/21), Award (30 November 2017), paras. 445-447.

There remains debate, however, on whether customary international law requires an expropriation to be in accordance with due process to be lawful. In cases where the applicable treaty does not include due process as a requirement for legality, tribunals have reached disparate results on whether there is a general international law rule that would require compliance with due process.[126]

4. *Compensation*

The requirement to provide prompt, adequate and effective compensation is perhaps the most controversial.[127] The consensus appears to be that this requirement is met when the fair market value of the investment is paid without delay and in a convertible currency.

Some argue, however, that the mere fact that compensation has not been paid does not necessarily render an expropriation unlawful. The tribunal in *Venezuela Holdings* explained that this is the case where the respondent State has made a fair offer that was not accepted by the claimant:

> "An offer of compensation may have been made to the investor and, in such a case, the legality of the expropriation will depend on the terms of that offer. In order to decide whether an expropriation is lawful or not in the absence of payment of compensation, a tribunal must consider the facts of the case.
> (....)
> It is not disputed that negotiations too [*sic*] place, and it has been established that Venezuela made proposals during those negotiations. It seems likely that there were discussions at the time on the method of valuation of the expropriated interests, on the relevance of the cap provisions referred to by Venezuela and on the exact amount of the compensation payable to the Claimants. The Tribunal finds that the evidence submitted does not demonstrate that the proposals made by Venezuela were incompatible with the requirement of 'just' compensation of

126. Compare *AIG Capital Partners Inc. and CJSC Tema Real Estate Company v. Republic of Kazakhstan* (ICSID Case No. ARB/01/6), Award (7 October 2003), para. 10.5.1. ("Expropriation of alien property is not itself contrary to international law provided certain conditions are met, and perhaps the most clearly established condition is that expropriation must not be arbitrary (i.e., must not be contrary to 'the due process of law').") with *Guaracachi America, Inc. and Rurelec PLC v. Plurinational State of Bolivia* (PCA Case No. 2011-17), Award (31 January 2014), para. 439 ("the Tribunal also does not consider it possible to derive ... the existence of a rule of customary international law obliging expropriating States to grant to the expropriated national or company a right to participate in such valuation process".).

127. It is generally understood that for compensation to be appropriate it must be prompt, adequate and effective. See "Guidelines on the Treatment of Foreign Direct Investment" in World Bank, *Legal Framework for the Treatment of Foreign Investment: Report to the Development Committee and Guidelines on the Treatment of Foreign Direct Investment*, volume II (World Bank 1992), Guideline IV (2) ("Compensation for a specific investment taken by the State will, according to the details provided below, be deemed 'appropriate' if it is adequate, effective and prompt.").

> Article 6(c) of the BIT. Accordingly, the Claimants have not established the unlawfulness of the expropriation on that ground."[128]

What made the offer of compensation meaningful in *Venezuela Holdings* appeared to be not just the existence of negotiations, but also the detailed discussion of the method by which the assets would be valued and the determination of a precise amount of compensation due.

5. *Consequences of an Unlawful Expropriation*

What is the effect of a finding of illegality with regard to an expropriation? Tribunals have consistently held that where the applicable treaty does not contain a standard of compensation specifically applicable to unlawful expropriation, the customary international law standard is applicable.[129] That is to say, an unlawful expropriation should entail full reparation, rather than the payment of fair market value of the investment at the time of the taking.

Full reparation must "as far as possible, wipe out all the consequences of the illegal act and reestablish the situation which would, in all probability, have existed if that act had not been committed".[130] This was the standard applied by the *Burlington* tribunal, which considered that the United States-Ecuador BIT's prescription that expropriation could only be effected upon "payment of prompt, adequate and effective compensation" was inapplicable in the case of an unlawful expropriation. It stated:

> "Article III(1) only describes the conditions under which an expropriation is considered lawful; it does not set out the standard of compensation for expropriations resulting from breaches of the Treaty. This conclusion has been reaffirmed in a number of cases where the treaty in question had similar language."[131]

One of the main differences between full restitution and payment of compensation is that the former permits the recovery of lost profits.[132] The reasoning is that "damages in the case of an illegal nationalisation ... will include both present and future loss, whereas in the case of a legal nationalisation there is compensation which is payable by the state. Future loss has no role to play in the assessment of the compensation, as the state has a present right to terminate the venture."[133]

---

128. *Venezuela Holdings, B.V., et al. (case formerly known as Mobil Corporation, Venezuela Holdings, B.V., et al.) v. The Bolivarian Republic of Venezuela* (ICSID Case No. ARB/07/27), Award (9 October 2014), paras. 301-305.
129. See, e.g., *ADC v. Hungary*, fn. 111 above, para. 483.
130. *Factory at Chorzów*, fn. 12 above, p. 47.
131. *Burlington Resources Inc. v. Republic of Ecuador (formerly Burlington Resources Inc. and others v. Republic of Ecuador and Empresa Estatal Petróleos del Ecuador (PetroEcuador))* (ICSID Case No. ARB/08/5), Decision on Reconsideration and Award (7 February 2017), para. 160.
132. *Tecmed v. Mexico*, fn. 85 above, para. 195.
133. M. SORNARAJAH, *Foreign Investment*, fn. 9 above, p. 447.

An additional difference is the ability to recover for the increase in value that the investment may have experienced between the date of the expropriation and the date of the award.[134]

VI. THE ROAD AHEAD: OPEN ISSUES AND THE FUTURE OF STANDARD

While much of the discussion about expropriation in recent years has focused on the general contours of indirect expropriation and the requirements for the legality of expropriation, there are other important issues that have not been the subject of as much discussion but whose impact on the understanding of expropriation could be quite significant. These topics include the question of whether judicial acts can have an expropriatory effect and whether a new generation of treaties will successfully protect States' regulatory space in the public health and environmental arenas by more clearly demarcating the boundary between regulation and expropriation.

1. *Expropriation by Judicial Act*

Expropriation most often results from action by the State's executive or legislative branch. Nationalizations, for example, are often achieved through the passing of laws or decrees. Meanwhile, indirect expropriations are often the result of the State's regulation of activities in the areas of public health, environment, and essential services, such as water, electrical power, and telecommunications. While less common, expropriation can also be effected by a judicial act. The Draft Articles on State Responsibility recognize that the judiciary can also trigger international responsibility:

> "Article 4. Conduct of organs of a State
> 1. The conduct of any State organ shall be considered an act of that State under international law, *whether the organ exercises legislative, executive, judicial or any other functions*, whatever position it holds in the organization of the State, and whatever its character as an organ of the central Government or of a territorial unit of the State."[135] (Emphasis added.)

This principle has been recognized by international tribunals since at least the 1950s.[136] Discussion of judicial takings, however, has been virtually nonexistent until recently.

The *Eli Lilly* tribunal provided the hypothetical example of a "judicial act (or omission) [that] may engage questions of expropriation under NAFTA Article 1110, such as,

134. *Joseph Houben v. Republic of Burundi* (ICSID Case No. ARB/13/7), Award (12 January 2016), para. 226; *ADC v. Hungary,* fn. 111 above, paras. 496, 499.

135. International Law Commission, "Draft Articles on Responsibility of States for Internationally Wrongful Acts, with commentaries" (2001), Art. 4(1), at <http://legal.un.org/ilc/texts/instruments/english/commentaries/9_6_2001.pdf> (last accessed 9 February 2018).

136. See *Rumeli Telekom A.S. and Telsim Mobil Telekomunikasyon Hizmetleri A.S. v. Republic of Kazakhstan* (ICSID Case No. ARB/05/16), Award (29 July 2008), para. 702 (citing the 1986 *Oil Field of Texas Inc. v. The Government of the Islamic Republic of Iran* case, which in turn cited a 1952 decision by the French-Italian Commission) (henceforth *Rumeli v. Kazakhstan*).

perhaps, in circumstances in which a judicial decision crystallizes a taking alleged to be contrary to NAFTA Article 1110".[137] Other tribunals have provided more detailed examples. In *Rumeli,* the tribunal found that the claimant's investment, composed of shares in a telecommunications company, had been taken via a creeping expropriation in which the Kazakh courts participated with the intent of forcing the redemption of the claimant's shares:[138]

> "The Tribunal is left in no doubt, however, that the court process which resulted in the expropriation of Claimants' shares was brought about through improper collusion between the State, acting through the Investment Committee, and Telcom Invest. The fact that the result may not have been intended by the Investment Committee is not decisive of the issue of expropriation. Moreover, it is beyond doubt that expropriation *was* the intended consequence of the court orders for compulsory redemption of Claimants' shares."[139] (Emphasis in original.)

The *Rumeli* case is an example of the scenario envisioned by the *Eli Lilly* tribunal, in which the courts play a deliberate role in crystallizing a taking.

Another example is the *Saipem* case. Saipem contracted with Petrobangla, a Bangladeshi government entity, to construct a pipeline. The contract had a dispute resolution clause that provided for arbitration under the ICC rules, and when a dispute arose, Saipem sought recourse before an ICC arbitral tribunal. Petrobangla petitioned Bangladeshi courts to revoke the arbitral tribunal's authority, and its request was granted. Saipem eventually received an ICC award in its favor, but it was unenforceable in Bangladesh because of the court's decision. Saipem initiated a separate arbitration, this time before ICSID, where it argued that Bangladesh had expropriated its residual contractual rights, i.e., the right to pursue ICC arbitration and to derive the benefit of the ICC award.[140] The ICSID tribunal agreed that an expropriation had been effected by the judicial decision. The tribunal held that

> "Such actions [of the Bangladeshi courts] resulted in substantially depriving Saipem of the benefit of the ICC Award. This is plain in light of the decision of the Bangladeshi Supreme Court that the ICC Award is 'a nullity'. Such a ruling is tantamount to a taking of the residual contractual rights arising from the investments as crystallised in the ICC Award. As such, it amounts to an expropriation within the meaning of Article 5 of the BIT."[141]

Some tribunals have been careful to note that a "seizure of property by a court as the result of normal domestic legal process does not amount to an expropriation under

137. *Eli Lilly v. Canada*, fn. 75 above, para. 221.
138. *Rumeli v. Kazakhstan*, fn. 136 above, paras. 705-707.
139. *Rumeli v. Kazakhstan*, fn. 136 above, para. 707.
140. It is worth noting that the treaty under which the ICSID arbitration was initiated did not contain a protection against denial of justice.
141. *Saipem S.p.A. v. People's Republic of Bangladesh* (ICSID Case No. ARB/05/07), Award (30 June 2009), para. 129.

international law unless there was an element of serious and fundamental impropriety about the legal process".[142] Accordingly, an action by a state court to terminate a contract, for instance, generally would not amount to an expropriation.[143]

2. *Drafting Treaties to Protect Regulatory Space in the Health and Environmental Arenas*

Public health and the environment are two areas where States have especially sought to protect their regulatory space. These are areas of great concern to increasingly vocal citizenry and, accordingly, areas in which States wish to enforce regulations without the threat of international liability looming over their heads. The increase in awards finding indirect expropriation over the past two decades has led some States to add language to their IIAs to protect their ability to regulate in the public interest, particularly in areas like public health and the environment. The 2012 United States Model BIT, for instance, provides that

> "Except in rare circumstances, non-discriminatory regulatory actions by a Party that are designed and applied to protect legitimate public welfare objectives, such as public health, safety, and the environment, do not constitute indirect expropriations."[144]

The Comprehensive Economic and Trade Agreement (CETA) between Canada and the European Union contains language intended to achieve a similar effect. The preamble states that the provisions of the CETA are intended to protect investments and investors, but "without undermining the right of the Parties to regulate in the public interest within their territories".[145] In addition, the CETA contains an annex that, like the U.S. Model BIT, codifies a police powers exception. The CETA, however, provides more detail than the U.S. Model BIT as to what the "rare circumstances" are in which non-discriminatory State measures with a public welfare objective become expropriatory. The CETA's Annex clarifies that "rare circumstance" is when the measures are grossly disproportionate:

142. *Garanti Koza LLP v. Turkmenistan* (ICSID Case No. ARB/11/20), Award (19 December 2016), para. 365 (henceforth *Garanti Koza v. Turkmenistan*). See also *Middle East Cement v. Egypt*, fn. 33 above, para. 139 ("though, normally, a seizure and auction ordered by the national courts do not qualify as a taking, they can be a 'measure the effects of which would be tantamount to expropriation' if they are not taken 'under due process of law'".). But see *Sistem Muhendislik Insaat Sanayi ve Ticaret A.S. v. Kyrgyz Republic* (ICSID Case No. ARB(AF)/06/1), Award (9 September 2009), paras. 118, 128 ("That abrogation [of ownership rights in a hotel] was effected by an organ of the Kyrgyz State.... The Court decision deprived the Claimant of its property rights in the hotel just as surely as if the State had expropriated it by decree.... Any chance of the restoration of that interest was removed by the decision of the Kyrgyz Supreme Court.")

143. *Garanti Koza v. Turkmenistan*, fn. 142 above, para. 365.

144. United States Model BIT, fn. 20 above, Annex B(4)(b).

145. Comprehensive Trade and Economic Agreement between Canada and the European Union, 30 October 2016, Preamble, at <www.international.gc.ca/trade-commerce/trade-agreements accords-commerciaux/agr-acc/ceta-aecg/text-texte/PRE.aspx?lang=eng> (last accessed 9 February 2018) (henceforth CETA).

> "except in the rare circumstance when the impact of a measure or series of measures is so severe in light of its purpose that it appears manifestly excessive, non-discriminatory measures of a Party that are designed and applied to protect legitimate public welfare objectives, such as health, safety and the environment, do not constitute indirect expropriations".[146]

The Trans-Pacific Partnership, now Comprehensive and Progressive Agreement for the Trans-Pacific Partnership (CP-TPP) after the withdrawal of the United States, provides even more specificity. In addition to stating that as a general rule "[n]on-discriminatory regulatory actions by a Party that are designed and applied to protect legitimate public welfare objectives, such as public health, safety and the environment" do not constitute indirect expropriations, it further provides a non-exhaustive list of areas that are within the scope of the term "public health": pharmaceuticals, diagnostics, vaccines, and medical devices, among others.[147]

Notably, CP-TPP includes a "carve-out" that permits member countries to block the use of investor-state dispute settlement to seek compensation for tobacco control measures.[148] This carve-out is unique – to the authors' knowledge, no other international investment agreement excludes a specific product or industry from the scope of the investment protection provisions. It remains to be seen whether this controversial use of "carve-outs" is replicated in future agreements.

Perhaps the most recent indication that this trend will continue is the recently released Netherlands Draft Model BIT, which in Art. 12 - Expropriation essentially adopts CETA, and additionally notes the protection of consumer protection and the promotion and protection of cultural diversity as "legitimate public interests".[149]

It remains to be seen whether tribunals will be more likely to find that a State regulation was lawful and non-compensable where the applicable treaty contains the kind of language exemplified by the CETA, TPP, and U.S. Model BIT's provisions quoted above. There are still too few awards to clearly identify trends. The jurisprudence that

---

146. CETA, fn. 145 above, Annex 8-A(3), at <https://www.international.gc.ca/trade-commerce/trade-agreements-accords-commerciaux/agr-acc/ceta-aecg/text-texte/08-A.aspx?lang=eng#a> (last accessed 9 February 2018).
147. Trans-Pacific Partnership, 4 February 2016, Annex 9-B, 3(b) and footnote 37, at <https://www.mfat.govt.nz/assets/Trans-Pacific-Partnership/Text/9.-Investment-Chapter.pdf> (last accessed 9 February 2018) (henceforth CP-TPP). The quoted Trans-Pacific Partnership's provisions track the words of the tribunal in the 2010 case *Chemtura v. Canada*, which arose out of the termination of the claimant's licenses for pesticides containing the chemical lindane due to health concerns. In that context, the *Chemtura* tribunal stated that there had been no indirect expropriation because the State measures were taken "in a non-discriminatory manner, motivated by the increasing awareness of the dangers presented by lindane for human health and the environment. A measure adopted under such circumstances is a valid exercise of the State's police powers and, as a result, does not constitute an expropriation." *Chemtura Corporation v. Government of Canada* (UNCITRAL), Award (2 August 2010), para. 266.
148. TPP, fn. 147 above, Art. 29.5.
149. The draft model BIT also contains various other provisions protecting the right to regulate for legitimate public policy objectives (and in Art. 2 this is even if such regulation "negatively affects" investors' expectations). Netherlands draft model BIT, 16 May 2018, at <https://www.internetconsultatie.nl/investeringsakkooden> (last accessed 1 June 2018).

comes out of the next few years will signal to States whether their concerns about their regulatory range of action have been addressed or whether further recalibration is necessary in future treaties.

These open issues – expropriation by judicial act and the continued demarcation of State's regulatory space in the health and environmental arenas – will continue to evolve in the near future, as the relevant actors continue voicing their interests and concerns: States, drafting treaty provisions that enable them to serve the public interest without fear of international liability; investors, lobbying for increased or at least, not eroding, protections for their investments abroad; and tribunals, tasked with resolving disputes in accordance with ever-evolving treaties.

VII. CONCLUSION

So we have seen the protection against expropriation expand from a narrow physical protection involving a direct taking in the twentieth century to protect against intangible expropriation. But as the twenty-first century dawned we have experienced a recalibrating by States concerned about protecting their policy space. Will tribunals follow?

Reforming Substantive Obligations in Investment Treaties: Most Favoured Nation Clauses

Max Bonnell[*]

TABLE OF CONTENTS PAGE

I. INTRODUCTION

"Reform" is a concept loaded with connotations. It implies the existence of an unsatisfactory practice, and the potential for change to improve that practice. It also suggests the existence of some power capable of effecting desirable change. Any consideration of the potential for reform of substantive obligations in investment treaties first requires an examination of the current practice, in order to identify what aspects of it might be amenable to constructive change, and then leads to the question, if change is desirable, by whom can it be made?

II. ROOTS AND PURPOSE OF MFN

Most favoured nation (MFN) status is conferred when one state agrees to treat another state (or its nationals) in a manner that is at least as favourable as the treatment it accords to other states (or their nationals). MFN treatment is not a requirement of customary international law, so that any state that seeks to obtain MFN treatment from another must do so by way of treaty.

MFN clauses have been included in trade treaties for hundreds of years, and were frequently found in early agreements concerning customs and tariffs. A well-known early example is the treaty of 1642 between Great Britain and Portugal, while the first treaty entered into by the United States of America (with France, in 1778) included an

* Partner, White & Case, LLP; Adjunct Professor of Law, University of Sydney. Research assistance was provided by Marina Kofman, Associate, Norton Rose Fulbright. While all responsibility for the contents of this paper is taken by the author, valuable comments on an earlier draft, from Christophe Bondy and Professor Chester Brown, are acknowledged with thanks.

MFN clause. By the Jay Treaty of 1794, Great Britain and the United States exchanged mutual promises to the effect that imported "Goods and Merchandize shall be subject to no higher or other Duties than would be payable by His Majesty's Subjects on the Importation of the same from Europe". A more significant modern example is Art. 1.1 of the General Agreement on Tariffs and Trade (GATT), which provided, in 1947, that in relation to the subject matter of the treaty, "any advantage, favour, privilege or immunity granted by any contracting party to any product originating in or destined for any other country shall be accorded immediately and unconditionally to the like product originating in or destined for the territories of all other contracting parties". Its inclusion in GATT helped to entrench the MFN concept in modern international trade law.

MFN clauses have been included in most bilateral investment treaties (BITs). One estimate is that MFN clauses are found in more than 90 percent of investment treaties.[1] Their purpose is to secure, for nationals of each party, treatment in the host state that is at least as favourable as the treatment accorded to investors of other states.

A reasonably typical MFN clause is Art. 3 of the 1986 BIT between the United Kingdom and China, which provides:

> "(1) Neither Contracting Party shall in its territory subject investments or returns of nationals or companies of the other Contracting Party to treatment less favourable than that which it accords to investments or returns of nationals or companies of any third State.
> (2) Neither Contracting Party shall in its territory subject nationals or companies of the other Contracting Party as regards their management, use, enjoyment or disposal of their investments, to treatment less favourable than that which it accords to nationals or companies of any third State."

Arts. 3(1) and 3(2) (versions of which are to be found in the Model BITs of many states) are qualified by Art. 3(4), which provides that they do not require either Party to extend to the other's nationals or companies any treatment that results from "any existing or future customs union or similar international agreement or agreement for facilitating frontier trade" or from "any international agreement or arrangement relating wholly or mainly to taxation or any domestic legislation relating wholly or mainly to taxation". Similar qualifications are, again, commonly found in investment treaties (they appear, for example, in the German Model BIT).

In spite of these qualifications, the striking thing about most MFN clauses is their unconditional and general language. One commentator has observed that "MFN clauses in BITs ... are of a particularly voracious variety", and "overwhelmingly ... are generalized promises of MFN treatment with respect to all areas addressed by the BIT".[2] It is this apparent breadth of scope that has generated so many disputes about the true extent of the protection offered by MFN clauses.

1. Jonathan BONNITCH, Lauge N. Skovgaard POULSEN and Michael WAIBEL, *The Political Economy of the Investment Treaty Regime* (Oxford University Press 2017) p. 93.
2. Tony COLE, *The Boundaries of Most Favored Nation Treatment in International Investment Law*, 33 Michigan Journal of International Law (2012) p. 537

III. SUBSTANTIVE MFN TREATMENT

Until recently, it has been relatively uncontroversial that "an MFN rule grants a claimant the right to benefit from substantive guarantees contained in third treaties".[3] The earliest investment treaty award in which the question was considered was *Asian Agricultural Products Ltd v. Sri Lanka*,[4] which dealt with a claim under the UK-Sri Lanka BIT. That BIT offered full protection and security to investments made by investors of each party, but included exemptions for war and civil disturbance. The claimant argued that the MFN clause in that BIT allowed it to rely upon the equivalent provision in the BIT between Sri Lanka and Switzerland, which did not contain the same exemptions. The tribunal appears to have assumed that the MFN clause could operate to allow the obligation in one BIT to be incorporated into another, although on the facts it found that it was "not proven that the Sri Lanka/Switzerland Treaty contains rules more favourable than those provided for under the Sri Lanka/U.K. Treaty, and hence, Article 3 of the latter Treaty cannot be justifiably invoked in the present case".[5]

Lawyers who practice in the field of investment treaty disputes lack neither ingenuity nor imagination in their formulation of claims. It is perhaps surprising, therefore, that there have not been more cases in which MFN clauses have been invoked by claimants seeking to attract more favourable substantive protections. A large number of the cases in which this has occurred concern the application of variations of the fair and equitable treatment standard of treatment.

1. *Fair and Equitable Treatment*

Several tribunals[6] have ruled that the "fair and equitable treatment" standard, or some variant of it, may be imported into a BIT by means of an MFN clause. In *MTD v. Chile*,[7] the claimants commenced the arbitration under the provisions of the 1992 BIT between Malaysia and Chile. Art. 3(1) of that BIT provided that "Investments made by investors of either Contracting Party in the territory of the other Contracting Party shall receive treatment which is fair and equitable, and not less favourable than that accorded to investments made by investors of any third State." The Malaysian investor (which was undertaking a large construction project) relied upon that Article to invoke broader protections that were not present in the BIT between Chile and Malaysia but were found in Chile's BITs with Denmark and Croatia.

3. Rudolf DOLZER and Christoph SCHREUER, *Principles of International Investment Law* (Oxford University Press 2008) p. 191
4. ICSID Case No. ARB/87/3, Award of 27 June 1990 (Dr.Dr. Ahmed Sadek El-Kosheri, Professor Berthold Goldman, Dr. Samuel K.B. Asante).
5. At [54].
6. See, for example, *ADF Group Inc v. United States of America*, ICSID Case No. ARB(AF)/00/1, Award of 9 January 2003; *ATA Construction, Industrial and Trading Co v. Jordan*, ICSID Case No. ARB/08/2, Award of 18 May 2010; and *Sergei Paushok, CJSC Golden East Company, CJSC Vostokneftgaz Company v. Mongolia*, (UNCITRAL Rules) Award of 28 April 2011.
7. *MTD Equity Sdn. Bhd. and MTD Chile S.A. v. Republic of Chile*, ICSID Case No. ARB/01/7, Award of 25 May 2004 (Andres Rigo Sureda, Marc Lalonde and Rodrigo Oreamuno Blanco).

The claim in *Bayindir v. Pakistan*[8] was made under the BIT between Turkey and Pakistan, which contained an MFN clause but no provision promising fair and equitable treatment. The tribunal determined that the MFN clause operated to provide Turkish investors in Pakistan with the same promise of fair and equitable treatment contained in the Pakistan-Switzerland BIT. By 2008, this approach had become so commonplace that in *Rumeli Telekom v. Kazakhstan*, the respondent state did not even trouble to dispute the claim that

> "in view of the MFN clause contained in the BIT, Respondent's international obligations assumed in other bilateral treaties, and in particular the United Kingdom-Kazakhstan BIT, are applicable to this case, such obligations including:
>
> – the obligation to ensure the fair and equitable treatment of the investments of investors of the other Contracting Party;
> – the duty not to deny justice;
> – the obligation to accord full protection and security to such investments; and
> – the obligation not to impair by unreasonable, arbitrary, or discriminatory measures the management, maintenance, use, enjoyment, or disposal of such investments".[9]

2. *Umbrella Clauses*

An umbrella clause, in the context of an international investment treaty, obliges the host state to observe specific contractual obligations it has made to covered investors. MFN clauses have been used to make the benefit of umbrella clauses available to investors.

In *EDF v. Argentina*,[10] the claimants relied upon Art. 4 of the BIT between France and Argentina, by which each state promised the investors of the other "a treatment no less favourable than that accorded to ... investors of the most favoured Nation". The claimants argued that the effect of this provision was that they were "entitled to any substantive protections in third-party investment treaties which might be considered more favourable than those contained in the Argentina-France BIT" and, in particular, they sought to invoke the umbrella clauses set out in Art. 10(2) of the Argentina-Luxembourg BIT and Art. 7(2) of the Argentina-Germany BIT. Argentina disputed this: it contended that umbrella clauses provide a distinctive form of protection that must be specifically negotiated. The tribunal agreed with the claimants, pointing out that "To ignore the MFN clause in this case would permit more favourable treatment to investors

8. *Bayindir Insaat Turizm Ticaret Ve Sanayi AS v. Islamic Republic of Pakistan*, ICSID Case No. ARB/03/29, Award dated 27 August 2009 (Professor Gabrielle Kaufmann-Kohler, Sir Franklin Berman and Professor Karl-Heinz Böckstiegel).
9. *Rumeli Telekom A.S. and Telsim Mobil Telekomikasyon Hizmetleri A.S. v. Republic of Kazakhstan*, ICSID Case No. ARB/05/16, Award dated 29 July 2008 (Bernard Hanotiau, Marc Lalonde, Stewart Boyd) at pp.152-153.
10. *EDF International SA, Saur International SA and Leon Participiones Argentinas SA v. Argentine Republic*, ICSID Case No. ARB/03/23, Award of 11 June 2012 (William W. Park, Gabrielle Kaufmann-Kohler and Jesus Remon).

protected under third countries, which is exactly what the MFN Clause is intended to prevent."

Similarly, in *Franck Charles Arif v. Moldova*,[11] both parties agreed that the MFN clause in the France-Moldova treaty could be used to import substantive protections from other treaties, and the tribunal held that an umbrella clause was substantive in nature. There have been at least two cases, however, in which tribunals were invited to apply umbrella clauses from other treaties and refused to do so, on the basis that they did not consider that those clauses would have any impact on the instant case.[12]

3. *Measure of Compensation*

In *CME v. Czech Republic*,[13] the Dutch claimant sought relief under the BIT between the Netherlands and the Czech Republic, claiming (amongst other things) that the Czech Republic had deprived it of its investment in certain television broadcasting licences. The Czech-Netherlands BIT provided that when an expropriation occurred, the investor was entitled to "just compensation" that reflected the "genuine value of the investment". CME argued that the appropriate measure of compensation was "fair market value", and the tribunal agreed, finding that:

> "The determination of compensation under the Treaty between the Netherlands and the Czech Republic on basis of the 'fair market value' finds further support in the 'most favored nation' provision of Art. 3(5) of the Treaty. That paragraph specifies that if the obligations under national law of either party in addition to the present Treaty contain rules, whether general or specific, entitling investments by investors of the other party to a treatment more favourable than provided by the present Treaty, 'such rules to the extent that they are more favourable prevail over the present Agreement.' The bilateral investment treaty between the United States of America and the Czech Republic provides that compensation shall be equivalent to the fair market value of the expropriated investment immediately before the expropriatory action was taken.... The Czech Republic therefore is obligated to provide no less than 'fair market value' to Claimant in respect of its investment, should (in contrast to this Tribunal's opinion) 'just compensation' representing the 'genuine value' be interpreted to be less than 'fair market value'."[14]

11. ICSID Case No. ARB/11/23, Award of 11 June 2012.
12. *Waguih Elie George Siag and Clorinda Vecchi v. Egypt*, ICSID Case No. ARB/05/15, Award of 1 June 2009 (David Williams QC, Professor Michael Pryles, Professor Francisco Orrego Vicuña) at [461]-[464]; *Abaclat and others v. Argentine Republic*, ICSID Case No. ARB/07/5, Decision on Jurisdiction and Admissibility, 4 August 2011 (Professor Pierre Tercier, Professor Georges Abi-Saab, Professor Albert Jan van den Berg) at [332].
13. Final Award, 14 March 2003 (UNCITRAL Rules) (Dr Wolfgang Kuhn, Judge Stephen M. Schwebel and Mr Ian Brownlie QC).
14. At [500].

4. *But What Is "Treatment"?*

The term "treatment", in the present context, has usually been understood to operate in the manner set out in the commentary to the ILC's Draft Articles on most-favoured-nation clauses of 1978. That commentary states that an *obligation* contained in a treaty may be considered "treatment" *as such* for the purposes of an MFN clause:

> "[T]he fact of favourable treatment may consist also in the conclusion or existence of an agreement between the granting State and the third State by which the latter is entitled to certain benefits. The beneficiary State, on the strength of the clause, may also demand the same benefits as were extended by the agreement in question to the third State. The mere fact that the third State has not availed itself of the benefits which are due to it under the agreement concluded with the granting State cannot absolve the granting State from its obligation under the clause…."[15]

This was also the position taken in the decision of the International Court of Justice in the *Rights of Nationals of the USA in Morocco*, which found that but for the fact that more favourable rights accorded by Morocco to France and Great Britain had ceased to apply at the relevant time, the rights enshrined in Morocco's treaties with those States would otherwise have sufficed for the purpose of establishing more favourable treatment.[16] Thus, the existence of obligations in a third treaty is enough to demonstrate de jure discrimination by reference to a hypothetical investor in like circumstances who is, as a matter of law, entitled to the more favourable treatment. This is enough for a person in a determined relationship with the beneficiary state to claim an entitlement to the promised treatment through the operation of an MFN clause.[17]

Consequently, in international investment law, MFN clauses have functioned primarily to enable the importation of more favourable provisions, subject to the *ejusdem generis* rule, from a third treaty into the basic treaty.

This position has not been universally accepted. In NAFTA cases, Canada has frequently expressed the view that Art. 1103 of NAFTA cannot "be invoked to import a *standard* provided for in a different treaty that may potentially or theoretically result in a more favourable treatment of an investor from another Party or of a non-Party. The provision is concerned with '*treatment*' accorded to investors."[18]

In recent times, some respondents have followed the position taken by Canada, and the other NAFTA States, and have challenged the notion that an MFN clause automatically allows claimants the benefit of substantive provisions contained in other

15. ILC Draft Articles on Most Favoured Nation Clauses 1978, comment 6 to draft article 5, p. 23.

16 Campbell MCLACHLAN, Laurence SHORE and Matthew WEINIGER, *International Investment Arbitration: Substantive Principles,* 2nd ed. (Oxford University Press 2017) p. 345 citing Rights of Nationals of the United States of America in Morocco (France v. United States of America) ('Morocco') [1952] ICJ Rep 176, 190–7.

17. Jonathan BONNITCHA, Lauge N. Skovgaard POULSEN and Michael WAIBEL, *The Political Economy of the Investment Treaty Regime* (Oxford University Press 2017) p. 97.

18. *Chemtura Corporation v. Government of Canada*, UNCITRAL arbitration, Canada's Rejoinder dated 10 July 2009.

treaties. In 2016, the respondent in *İçkale İnşaat Limited Şirketi v. Turkmenistan* (discussed in further detail below) succeeded in arguing that (at least under the terms of the Turkey-Turkmenistan BIT), the mere making of a promise to investors of a third country did not amount to "treatment". It's reasonable to expect that, in future cases, there will be a more searching test of the conventional proposition that MFN clauses permit a claimant to benefit from mere promises contained in other treaties.

It may be, if the *İçkale* award finds favour with future tribunals, that claimants will no longer be able to assume complacently that the mere existence of a promise in another treaty constitutes more favourable treatment.

IV. MFN TREATMENT AND PROCEDURAL QUESTIONS

1. *What Is an "Investment"?*

Claimants in several cases have sought to expand the definition of "investment" by invoking MFN clauses but, so far, without success.

Vannessa Ventures v. Venezuela[19] was a claim made under the Canada-Venezuela BIT, which required that investments be made "in accordance with the ... laws" of the host state. The claimant argued that it was entitled to invoke the MFN clause to import into the principal treaty a broader definition of "investment" from the BIT between Venezuela and the United Kingdom. The tribunal decided

> "that the MFN treatment under the Canada-Venezuela BIT is promised to investments as defined in Article I of the BIT. The benefit of the MFN provision in Article III of the Canada-Venezuela BIT can only be asserted in respect of investments that are within the scope of Article I(f) of the Canada-Venezuela BIT to begin with. The MFN clause cannot be used to expand the category of investments to which the Canada-Venezuela BIT applies."[20]

Similarly, the tribunal in *Metal-Tech Ltd v. Uzbekistan*[21] rejected the claimant's contention that the MFN clause in the BIT between Israel and Uzbekistan could be used to avoid the requirement in that treaty that investments be "implemented in accordance with the laws and regulations of the Contracting Party in whose territory the investment is made". The tribunal explained that "one must fall within the scope of the treaty, which is in particular circumscribed by the definition of investment and investors, to be entitled to invoke the treaty protections, of which MFN treatment forms part. Or, in fewer words, one must be under the treaty to claim through the treaty."[22] Much the same

19. *Vannessa Ventures Ltd v. The Bolivarian Republic of Venezuela*, ICSID Case No. ARB(AF)/04/6, Award of 16 January 2013 (Professor Vaughan Lowe QC, Hon. Charles N Brower, Professor Brigitte Stern).
20. At [133].
21. *Metal-Tech Ltd v. The Republic of Uzbekistan*, ICSID Case No. ARB/10/3, Award of 4 October 2013 (Professor Gabrielle Kaufmann-Kohler, John M Townsend, Claus von Wobeser).
22. At [145].

reasoning prevented the claimant in *Rafat Ali Rizvi v. Indonesia*[23] from avoiding the restrictive definition of "investment" in the BIT between the United Kingdom and Indonesia.

2. *Who Is an Investor?*

Nor have claimants succeeded in using MFN clauses to broaden the definition of the term "investor". Such an argument was attempted in *HICEE v. Slovakia*,[24] in which the tribunal ruled that since the "clear purpose" of the MFN clause was "to broaden the scope of the substantive protection granted to the eligible investments of eligible investors", it could not "legitimately be used to broaden the definition of the investors or the investments themselves".[25]

3. *Dispute Resolution Provisions*

A more controversial question – indeed, in this area, the *most* controversial question – is whether an MFN clause may be invoked in relation to matters of procedure, especially dispute resolution procedure. The broad drafting of most MFN clauses allows room for argument but, among academics and commentators, it remains the orthodox view that an "MFN clause will not apply to investment treaties' dispute settlement provisions, save where States expressly so provide".[26]

This position has a cogent theoretical basis. The jurisdiction of any arbitral tribunal, even one constituted under the terms of a treaty, is derived from the consent of the parties. In a treaty arbitration, one finds that consent in the terms of the treaty: the conventional analysis is that the treaty sets out a standing offer to arbitrate, extended by each state to the investors of the other, which may be accepted by an investor by commencing an arbitration. It is undesirable for a state's consent to arbitration to be given in ambiguous or uncertain terms. Yet MFN clauses are contingent in nature; they have meaning only to the extent that more favourable treatment has in fact been afforded to another state (or its nationals). It is therefore undesirable for a tribunal, purportedly appointed under the terms of one treaty, to search for the basis of its jurisdiction in a different instrument (under which the claimant would have no standing to bring a claim). And it is especially undesirable for this to occur when (as happens in many cases), the principal treaty sets out the parties' consent to a very specific form of dispute resolution. Not only that, but an MFN clause is a promise of protection; ordinarily, before a party can claim the benefit of that promise in an arbitration, it must first establish jurisdiction and it is, at best, extremely circular to find the basis of jurisdiction in a promise that cannot be enforced unless jurisdiction exists.

---

23. *Rafat Ali Rizvi v. Republic of Indonesia*, ICSID Case No. ARB/11/13, Award on Jurisdiction, 16 July 2013 (Dr. Gavan Griffith QC, Judge Joan Donoghue, Professor Muthucumaraswamy Sornarajah).
24. *HICEE B.V. v. The Slovak Republic*, PCA Case No. 2009-11, Partial Award, 23 May 2011 (Sir Franklin Berman KCMG QC, Judge Charles N. Brower, Judge Peter Tomka).
25. At [149].
26. Campbell MCLACHLAN QC, Laurence SHORE and Matthew WEINIGER, *International Investment Arbitration* (Oxford University Press 2007) p. 257 (henceforth McLachlan, Shore and Weiniger).

So much for orthodoxy. There are, however, enough tribunal decisions to the contrary to create a high degree of uncertainty in this area.

Oxygen was provided to the contrary position by the decision in *Maffezini v. Spain.*[27] In that case, the BIT between Argentina and Spain provided that no arbitration could be commenced by an investor until the host state's domestic courts had been provided with an opportunity to resolve the dispute within eighteen months. The Argentine claimant avoided the Spanish courts. Instead it relied upon Art. IV of the BIT between Argentina and Spain, which relevantly provided that "In all matters subject to this Agreement, this treatment shall not be less favourable than that extended by each Party to the investments made in its territory by investors of a third country", and invited the tribunal to apply the dispute resolution provisions found in the BIT between Chile and Spain (which allowed for arbitration after a six-month negotiation period). The tribunal agreed with the claimant, finding that "the most favoured nation clause included in the Argentine-Spain BIT embraces the dispute settlement provisions of this treaty". More generally, it thought that "if a third party treaty contains provisions for the settlement of disputes that are more favorable to the protection of the investor's rights and interests than those in the basic treaty, such provisions may be extended to the beneficiary of the most favored nation clause as they are fully compatible with the *ejusdem generis* principle".

Maffezini v. Spain has been followed in cases such as *Tecmed v. Mexico*[28] and *Siemens v. Argentina.*[29] But some commentators have called it "heretical"[30] (another refers simply to "an error made by the Tribunal"),[31] and prefer the approach adopted by the tribunal in *Salini v. Jordan*[32] and *Plama v. Bulgaria.*[33]

The question that arose in *Salini v. Jordan* was whether the BIT between Italy and Jordan allowed an investor to commence an ICSID arbitration against the host state. The claimant urged the tribunal to follow the decision in *Maffezini* and employ the BIT's MFN clause to establish jurisdiction. But the tribunal observed that the MFN clause "does not include any provision extending its scope of application to dispute settlement. It does not envisage 'all rights or all matters covered by the agreement'. Furthermore, the Claimants have submitted nothing from which it *might* be established that the common intention of the Parties was to have the most favored-nation clause apply to dispute settlement." (Emphasis in original.) It concluded that the MFN clause "does not

---

27. *Emilio Agustin Maffezini v. Kingdom of Spain*, ICSID Case No. ARB/97/7, Decision of the Tribunal on Objections to Jurisdiction, 25 January 2000 (Professor Francisco Orrego Vicuña, Judge Thomas Buergenthal and Maurice Wolf).
28. *Tecnicas Medioambientales Tecmed SA v. United Mexican States*, ICSID Case No. ARB/00/2, Award of 29 May 2003 (Horacio A Grgigera Naon, Professor Jose Carlos Fernandez Rozas and Carlos Bernal Verea).
29. *Siemens AG v. Argentine Republic*, ICSID Case No. ARB/02/8, Decision on Jurisdiction, 3 August 2004 (Dr Andres Rigo Sureda, Judge Charles N. Brower and Professor Domingo Bello Janeiro).
30. McLachlan, Shore and Weiniger, p. 254
31. Zachary DOUGLAS, "The MFN Clause in Investment Arbitration: Treaty Interpretation Off the Rails", 2 Journal of International Dispute Settlement (February 2011, Issue 1) p. 102
32. *Salini Costruttori S.p.A. and Italstrade S.p.A. v. The Hashemite Kingdom of Jordan*, ICSID Case No. ARB/02/13, Decision on Jurisdiction, November 2004 (Judge Gilbert Guillaume, Bernardo Cremades, Sir Ian Sinclair).
33. *Plama Consortium Limited v. Republic of Bulgaria*, ICSID Case No. ARB/03/24, Decision on Jurisdiction, 8 February 2005 (Albert Jan van den Berg, VV Veeder and Carl F. Salans).

apply insofar as dispute settlement clauses are concerned", reflecting that it "shares the concerns that have been expressed in numerous quarters with regard to the solution adopted in the *Maffezini* case. Its fear is that the precautions taken by authors of the award may in practice prove difficult to apply, thereby adding more uncertainties to the risk of 'treaty shopping'."[34]

Plama was a Cypriot company which had purchased almost all of the shares in a Bulgarian corporation that owned an oil refinery in Bulgaria. It complained that the Bulgarian government had impaired the value of its investment in a manner that breached its obligations under both the Cyprus-Bulgaria BIT and the Energy Charter Treaty (ECT). Plama asserted that an ICSID tribunal had jurisdiction to hear the case, both under the ECT and by application of the MFN clause in the Cyprus-Bulgaria BIT. The Cyprus-Bulgaria BIT provided only for disputes concerning expropriation to be settled by reference to an *ad hoc* tribunal applying UNCITRAL Rules. But Plama argued that the MFN clause "must be construed as extending to more favourable dispute settlement mechanisms than those in the Bulgaria-Cyprus BIT which are contained in other investment treaties concluded by Bulgaria" – such as a clause in the Bulgaria-Finland BIT which referred disputes to ICSID arbitration.

The tribunal accepted that it had, under the ECT, jurisdiction to deal with any claims made by Plama that fell within the scope of the ECT's dispute resolution provisions (that is, claims for breaches of Part III of the ECT). But it also determined that

> "The most favored nation provision of the Bulgaria-Cyprus BIT, read with other BITs to which Bulgaria is a Contracting Party (in particular the Bulgaria-Finland BIT), cannot be interpreted as providing the Respondent's consent to submit the dispute with the Claimant under the Bulgaria-Cyprus BIT to ICSID arbitration or entitling the Claimant to rely in the present case on dispute settlement provisions contained in these other BITs."

Central to the tribunal's reasoning was its belief in

> "the basic prerequisite for arbitration: an agreement of the parties to arbitrate. It is a well-established principle, both in domestic and international law, that such an agreement should be clear and unambiguous. In the framework of a BIT, the agreement to arbitrate is arrived at by the consent to arbitration that a state gives in advance in respect of investment disputes falling under the BIT, and the acceptance thereof by an investor if the latter so desires."

Accordingly, the tribunal considered that any "intention to incorporate dispute settlement provisions must be clearly and unambiguously expressed". Incorporating a dispute resolution provision by way of an MFN clause did not, in its view, satisfy that criterion. There might be, for example, no clarity about which method of dispute settlement was "more favourable". The tribunal observed that

34. At [115].

> "It is also not evident that when parties have agreed in a particular BIT on a specific dispute resolution mechanism, as is the case with the Bulgaria-Cyprus BIT (*ad hoc* arbitration), their agreement to most-favored nation treatment means that they intended that, by operation of the MFN clause, their specific agreement on such a dispute settlement mechanism could be replaced by a totally different dispute resolution mechanism (ICSID arbitration). It is one thing to add to the treatment provided in one treaty more favorable treatment provided elsewhere. It is quite another thing to replace a procedure specifically negotiated by parties with an entirely different mechanism."

Understandably, the claimant urged the tribunal to follow the approach adopted in *Maffezini v. Spain*. Having dealt dismissively with the reasoning in that case, the tribunal concluded that:

> "The decision in *Maffezini* is perhaps understandable. The case concerned a curious requirement that during the first 18 months the dispute be tried in the local courts. The present Tribunal sympathizes with a tribunal that attempts to neutralize such a provision that is nonsensical from a practical point of view. However, such exceptional circumstances should not be treated as a statement of general principle guiding future tribunals in other cases where exceptional circumstances are not present."

Plama was soon followed by *Berschader v. Russia*,[35] in which the tribunal insisted that

> "the fundamental issue in determining whether or not an MFN clause encompasses the dispute resolution provisions of other treaties must always be an assessment of the intention of the contracting parties upon the conclusion of each individual treaty. In each case, the question must be asked as to whether the contracting parties to the treaty intended the MFN provision to incorporate by reference the dispute settlement provisions of other treaties. Ultimately, that question can only be answered by a detailed analysis of the text and, where available, the negotiating history of the relevant treaty, as well as other relevant facts."[36]

The *Berschader* tribunal was not persuaded by the claimants' argument that the question was settled by the fact that the MFN clause was expressed to apply to "all matters covered by the present Treaty". It stated that

> "not even seemingly clear language like this can be considered to have an unambiguous meaning in the context of an MFN clause. As emphasised by the *Maffezini* tribunal, with regard to treaties which in their MFN clauses speak of 'all rights' or 'all matters' subject to the treaty in question, but which do not provide *expressly* (our emphasis) that dispute settlement as such is covered by the clause, 'it

35. *Vladimir Berschader and Moise Berschader v. The Russian Federation*, SCC Case No. 080/2004, Award of 21 April 2006 (Bengt Sjovall, Sergei Lebedev, Professor Todd Weiler).
36. At [175].

must be established whether the omission was intended by the parties or can reasonably be inferred from the practice followed by the parties in their treatment of foreign investors and their own investors'."[37]

The tribunal accepted that

> "the ordinary meaning of the words 'all matters covered by the present Treaty' is clear. However, such expression must be seen in its context, particularly in relation to the concept with which it is intertwined in the text of the Treaty, i.e. 'the most favoured nation clause'. The Treaty itself contains no definition of the expression 'the most favoured nation clause'. However, the Protocol to the Treaty provides that the Soviet Union will accord, in its territory, to Belgian investors treatment at least equivalent to that accorded to investors from countries that are members of the OECD on the date when the Protocol was signed. This suggests that what the Contracting Parties had in mind was a fairly standard form of MFN-clause, according to which each Contracting Party accords, in its territory, to investors from the other Contracting Party, treatment at least equivalent to that accorded to investors from third countries. The use of the expressions 'treatment' and 'in its territory' should be noted. This language appears to indicate that what the Contracting Parties had in view was the material rights accorded to investors within the territory of the Contracting States."[38]

The tribunal decided that the words "'all matters covered by the present Treaty'... certainly cannot be understood literally"[39] and refused to extend their application to dispute resolution procedures. Even commentators who agree with the result reached by this tribunal might not be entirely comfortable with the route by which that result was achieved, which was to deny the words used in the BIT their ordinary meaning.

Many commentators expressed satisfaction that awards such as *Salini*, *Plama* and *Berschader* had resolved the uncertainty created by *Maffezini*. McLachlan, Shore and Weiniger, for example, wrote that

> "The result, if, as is suggested, the approach in *Plama* is preferred, will be that the MFN clause will not apply to investment treaties' dispute settlement provisions, save where the States expressly so provide. Its domain of application will be as to the substantive rights vouchsafed to investors from third States to which special preferences have been granted."[40]

lf. As it happened, the illusion of certainty was fleeting, and was soon dispelled by such cases as the decision on jurisdiction in *Garanti Koza v. Turkmenistan*.[41] That case, and

37. At [184].
38. At [185].
39. At [192].
40. McLachlan, Shore and Weiniger, p. 257.
41. *Garanti Koza LLP v. Turkmenistan*, ICSID Case No. ARB/11/20, Decision on the Objection to Jurisdiction for Lack of Consent, 3 July 2013 (John M. Townsend, George Constantine Lambrou and Laurence Boisson de Chazournes).

others that followed it, illustrated the difficulty of identifying whether States had expressly consented to MFN provisions being applied to dispute clauses.

Garanti Koza was a United Kingdom company which complained that it had suffered loss and damage as a result of state interference in its contract to construct twenty-eight highway bridges and overpasses in Turkmenistan. Art. 8 of the UK-Turkmenistan BIT relevantly provided that

> "(2) Where the dispute is referred to international arbitration, the national or company and the Contracting Party concerned in the dispute may agree to refer the dispute either to:
> (a) the International Centre for the Settlement of Investment Disputes ... ; or
> (b) the Court of Arbitration in the International Chamber of Commerce; or
> (c) an international arbitrator or ad hoc arbitration tribunal to be appointed by a special agreement or established under the Arbitration Rules of the United Nations Commission on International Trade Law.
> If after a period of four months from written notification of the claim there is no agreement to one of the above alternative procedures, the dispute shall at the request in writing of the national or company concerned be submitted to arbitration under the Arbitration Rules of the United Nations Commission on International Trade Law as then in force. The parties to the dispute may agree in writing to modify these Rules."

Art. 3 of the UK-Turkmenistan BIT contained an MFN clause in a familiar form, but significantly Art. 3(3) stated that "For the avoidance of doubt it is confirmed that the treatment provided for in paragraphs (1) and (2) above shall apply to the provisions of Article 1 to 11 of this Agreement" – which included the dispute resolution provisions. For that reason, Garanti Koza contended that it was able to rely upon the MFN clause to import ICSID dispute resolution provisions from the BIT between Switzerland and Turkmenistan.

The majority of the tribunal accepted both that it was a fundamental requirement that the State party must consent to jurisdiction, and that consent could not be presumed but must be established by an express declaration or actions that demonstrate consent. But at that point, the majority parted from the reasoning in *Plama v. Bulgaria*:

> "Some arbitration tribunals have followed *Plama v. Bulgaria* in grafting onto the requirement that the State must consent to arbitration the corollary that the State's consent must be 'clear and unambiguous.' This Tribunal finds no basis in the Vienna Convention for imposing such a standard onto the interpretation of the terms of a treaty. Rather, this Tribunal agrees with the tribunal in *Suez and Interagua v. Argentina* 'that dispute resolution provisions are subject to interpretation like any other provisions of a treaty, neither more restrictive nor more liberal.'"

The majority found that the effect of Art. 8 of the UK-Turkmenistan BIT was that "Turkmenistan has consented to international arbitration with UK investors, but not to ICSID Arbitration. Turkmenistan has simply expressed its willingness to consider ICSID arbitration as one of three options, and only on a case by case basis." The tribunal then entered the "fiercely contested no-man's land in international law" to consider "whether the MFN clause of a BIT may be used to vary the terms of the investor-state arbitration article of the same BIT".

The tribunal was guided by the Concurring and Dissenting Opinion of Professor Brigitte Stern in *Impregilo v. Argentina*,[42] in which Professor Stern explained "why, in principle, an MFN clause cannot import, in part or *in toto*, a dispute settlement mechanism from a third party BIT into the BIT which is the basic treaty applicable to the dispute". She added, however, that

> "Naturally, an important caveat has to be presented here. The interpretation of the MFN clause is only necessary when the intention of the parties concerning its applicability or inapplicability to the dispute settlement mechanism is not expressly stated or clearly ascertained. It is quite evident that if there is an MFN clause expressly including the dispute settlement procedures or expressly excluding them, there is no need for an interpretation. There are indeed cases where the parties expressly state that the MFN clause applies to the dispute settlement mechanism. This has been done, for example, by the drafters of the UK Model BIT, who have provided in Article 3(3) that 'for avoidance of doubt' MFN treatment shall apply to certain specified provisions of the BIT including the dispute settlement provision."

It followed, on Garanti Koza's argument, that the MFN clause in the UK-Turkmenistan BIT clearly applied to the dispute settlement provisions of that BIT, and Garanti Koza invoked several other BITs entered into by Turkmenistan that included submissions to ICSID arbitration. Taking those documents together, Garanti Koza asserted, the tribunal would find the evidence of Turkmenistan's consent to jurisdiction. Specifically, Garanti Koza argued that the dispute settlement provisions of the Switzerland-Turkmenistan BIT were "more favourable" because they provided investors with a choice between ICSID arbitration and UNCITRAL arbitration.

The majority of the tribunal found that "the essential consent of the State – the consent to resolve disputes with UK investors by means of international arbitration – does not in this case need to be imported by operation of the MFN clause, because that consent is contained in Art. 8(1) of the BIT". The majority rejected Turkmenistan's submission that "a specific agreement" was necessary for ICSID arbitration, concluding that the effect of the MFN clause was that "there is no reason why Turkmenistan's consent to ICSID arbitration in its BIT with Switzerland may not be relied upon by a UK investor, if the provision for ICSID arbitration or an unrestricted choice between ICSID Arbitration and UNCITRAL Arbitration provides treatment more favourable to the investor than the treatment provided by the base treaty". And the majority found that the treatment offered by Turkmenistan to Swiss investors was more favourable than the treatment offered to UK investors, primarily because Swiss investors were given "the option of selecting, as between two different systems of arbitration, the one that appears

42. *Impregilo S.p.A. v. Argentine Republic*, ICSID Case No. ARB/07/17.

to that investor most favourable to the presentation of the particular claim that investor wishes to pursue with regard to an investment protected by the BIT".

Similar considerations arose in *Venezuela US v. Venezuela*.[43] The claim was made under the BIT between Barbados and Venezuela, Art. 8 of which set out the following dispute resolution mechanism:

> "(1) Disputes between one Contracting Party and a national or company of the other Contracting Party concerning an obligation of the former under this Agreement in relation to an investment of the latter shall, at the request of the national concerned, be submitted to the International Centre for Settlement of Investment Disputes for settlement by arbitration or conciliation under the Convention on the Settlement of Investment Disputes between States and Nationals of other States, opened for signature at Washington on March 18, 1965.
> (2) As long as the Republic of Venezuela has not become a Contracting State of the Convention as mentioned in paragraph 1 of this Article, disputes as referred to in that paragraph shall be submitted to the International Centre for Settlement of Investment disputes under the Rules Governing the Additional Facility for the Administration of Proceedings by the Secretariat of the Centre (Additional Facility Rules). If for any reason the Additional Facility is not available the investor shall have the right to submit the dispute to arbitration under the rules of the United Nations Commission on International Trade Law (UNCITRAL).
> (3) The arbitral award shall be limited to determining whether there is a breach by the Contracting Party concerned of its obligations under this Agreement, whether such breach of obligations has caused damages to the national concerned, and if such is the case, the amount of compensation.
> (4) Each Contracting Party hereby gives its unconditional consent to the submission of disputes as referred to in paragraph 1 of this Article to international arbitration in accordance with the provisions of this Article."

Venezuela had become a Contracting State to the Washington Convention, but denounced the Convention with effect from 25 July 2012. The Claimant therefore commenced its arbitration (in 2013) under the UNCITRAL Rules. Venezuela contested jurisdiction on the ground that its consent to UNCITRAL arbitration set out in Art. 8(2) was extended only to cover the interim period between the execution of the BIT on 15 July 1994 and the date (1 June 1995) upon which Venezuela became a Contracting State. The tribunal agreed with Venezuela's argument, but the majority considered that the "Tribunal's analysis ... cannot stop here, as the Claimant also relies on Article 3" – the MFN clause.[44] The Claimant asserted that it could rely upon the MFN clause to import provisions of other Venezuelan BITS which were "more favourable because they provide investors with a choice of dispute resolution fora".[45]

43. *Venezuela US, S.R.L v. The Bolivarian Republic of Venezuela*, PCA Case No. 2013-34, Interim Award on Jurisdiction, 26 July 2016 (Judge Peter Tomka, The Honorable Yves Fortier QC, Professor Marcelo Kohen).
44. At [89]-[90].
45. At [91].

The reasoning of the majority was founded upon the language of Art. 3(3), which provided that the MFN clause "shall apply to the provisions of Article 1 to 11 of this Agreement". The dispute settlement clause, clause 8, "thus features among the Articles to the provisions of which the MFN treatment *shall* apply".[46] (Emphasis added.) The majority insisted that it was unnecessary for it to "pronounce itself on the applicability of MFN clauses to arbitration clauses or dispute settlement provisions in general", but said that "it must give bona fide effect to the provisions agreed by the Parties in their BIT, and not ... empty Article 3(3) of its meaning, thereby rendering it inapplicable to Article 8".[47] The majority accepted that "the MFN clause cannot serve the purpose of importing consent to arbitration where none exists under the BIT between Barbados and Venezuela", but found that consent in the language of Art. 8(4). For these reasons, the majority found that the Claimant was able to invoke the dispute resolution provisions of the BIT between Venezuela and Ecuador, and commence an UNCITRAL arbitration on the same conditions as would apply to investors from Ecuador.

The award in *Venezuela US v. Venezuela* was accompanied by a strongly worded dissenting opinion by Professor Kohen, who did not accept that the MFN clause applied to Art. 8, notwithstanding the provisions of Art. 3(3). Professor Kohen contended that the broad language of Art. 3(3) could not be read literally. He also observed that the MFN provisions of Arts. 3(1) and 3(2) referred to treatment by a Contracting Party "in its territory" and argued that "[b]y definition, international arbitration does not occur in the territory of the Contracting State".[48] Professor Kohen acknowledged that in principle, MFN clauses might be applied to dispute settlement provisions, but insisted that this should be done only with great caution, and could not be done in the present case – in which, he asserted, "the majority decision is the one that has gone the farthest in the use of an MFN clause in order to establish jurisdiction".[49] Professor Kohen may take some comfort in the fact that precisely his reasoning has been adopted subsequently by the tribunal in *Beijing Urban Construction v. Yemen*.[50] There the tribunal, faced with a similar provision and a similar argument, accepted that "[f]ull meaning must be given to the words 'in the territory'" and found that international arbitration was not an activity linked to the territory of the host state.[51]

Three further cases involving Argentina have offered additional encouragement to claimants seeking to extend MFN clauses to include dispute resolution procedures. In *Siemens v. Argentina*,[52] the claimant had been awarded a contract to establish a system for migration control and personal identification. That contract was suspended, and later terminated, following a change of government in Argentina. Siemens pursued some administrative remedies in Argentina, without success, and then commenced an

46. At [100].
47. At [102].
48. *Venezuela US, S.R.L v. The Bolivarian Republic of Venezuela*, PCA Case No. 2013-34, Dissenting Opinion of Professor Marcelo G. Kohen, 26 July 2016, at [19].
49. At [6].
50. *Beijing Urban Construction Group Co. Ltd v. Republic of Yemen*, ICSID Case No. ARB/14/30, Decision on Jurisdiction, 31 May 2017 (Ian Binnie QC, Zachary Douglas QC, John M. Townsend).
51. At [116]-[121].
52. *Siemens AG v. The Argentine Republic*, ICSID Case No. ARB/02/8, Decision on Jurisdiction, 3 August 2004 (Dr. Andres Rigo Sureda, Judge Charles N. Brower, Professor Domingo Bello Janeiro).

arbitration under the BIT between Germany and Argentina. That BIT prevented a claimant from commencing an arbitration before it had spent eighteen months seeking to resolve the dispute in the courts of Argentina. Siemens invoked the MFN clause in the BIT, and sought to rely upon the provisions of the BIT between Argentina and Chile, which did not require any prior submission to local courts.

Argentina argued that the word "treatment" in the MFN clause should be taken to refer only to substantive treatment. In its reasoning, however, the tribunal emphasized the very general terms in which the MFN clause was cast:

> "The first two clauses of Article 3 refer simply to a 'not less favorable treatment' – '*trato no menos favorable*' in the Spanish version. 'Treatment' in its ordinary meaning refers to behavior in respect of an entity or a person. The term 'treatment' is neither qualified nor described except by the expression 'not less favorable'. The term 'activities' is equally general. The need for exceptions confirms the generality of the meaning of treatment or activities rather than setting limits beyond what is said in the exceptions. In clarifying in the Protocol the term 'activities' used in Article 3(2), the drafters were careful to qualify twice that the clarification is special but not exclusive. This is a clear indication that the clarifications do not limit the meaning of the term 'activities'. They simply emphasize matters of particular concern to the parties. When the parties meant to provide an outright limitation by way of an exception they have done so in paragraphs (3) and (4) of Article 3 and in the Protocol in relation to security measures or taxation privileges of nationals or national companies. If it were the intention to limit the content of Article 3 beyond the limits of those exceptions, then the terms 'treatment' or 'activities' would have been qualified. The fact that this is not the case is an indication of their intended wide scope. Treatment in Article 3 refers to treatment under the Treaty in general and not only under that article."[53]

The tribunal, endorsing the decision in *Maffezini*, concluded that "the term 'treatment' and the phrase 'activities related to the investments' are sufficiently wide to include settlement of disputes".[54]

That approach was also adopted by the tribunal in *Impregilo S.p.A. v. Argentina*.[55] There the tribunal lamented the fact that

> "these issues remain controversial and that the predominating jurisprudence which has developed is in no way universally accepted. Nevertheless, the Arbitral Tribunal finds it unfortunate if the assessment of these issues would in each case be dependent on the personal opinions of individual arbitrators. The best way to avoid such a result is to make the determination on the basis of case law whenever a clear case law can be discerned. It is true that, as stated above, the jurisprudence

53. At [85].
54. At [104].
55. ICSID Case No. ARB/07/17, Award of 21 June 2011 (Judge Hans Danelius, Judge Charles N. Brower, Professor Brigitte Stern).

> regarding the application of MFN clauses to settlement of disputes provisions is not fully consistent. Nevertheless, in cases where the MFN clause has referred to 'all matters' or 'any matter' regulated in the BIT, there has been near-unanimity in finding that the clause covered the dispute settlement rules. On this basis, the majority of the Tribunal reaches the conclusion that Impregilo is entitled to rely, in this respect, on the dispute settlement rules in the Argentina-US BIT and that the case cannot be dismissed for non-observance of the requirements in Article 8(2) and (3) of the Argentina-Italy BIT."[56]

The claimant was equally successful in *Hochtief v. Argentina*.[57] Hochtief had been awarded a twenty-five-year concession to construct, maintain and operate a toll road between Rosario and Victoria. It claimed that it had suffered loss as a result of actions of the Argentine government that breached the BIT between Germany and Argentina. In an echo of the *Siemens* case, Hochtief argued that the MFN clause in that BIT allowed it to rely upon the dispute resolution procedures set out in the BIT between Argentina and Chile. Predictably, Argentina opposed this, arguing that the MFN clause applied only to substantive provisions. The tribunal insisted that it was

> "conscious of the advantages of consistency in the approaches of different tribunals to similar questions. It is also aware of the significance that other tribunals have attached to differences between the formulations of MFN provisions in various treaties. That said, it is the responsibility of this Tribunal to interpret to the best of its ability the specific provisions of the particular treaties that are applicable in this case, and not to choose between broad doctrines or schools of thought, or to conduct a head-count of arbitral awards taking various positions and to fall in behind the numerical majority."[58]

The tribunal went on to find that

> "The BIT is an agreement both for the promotion and for the reciprocal protection of investments. It is an agreement between two States, which no doubt is intended to operate to the benefit of both States but which plainly confers benefits directly upon investors. The Tribunal considers that the provisions of Article 10, which on any interpretation confer upon investors the possibility of recourse to arbitration in addition to the right to have recourse to national courts, are a form of protection that is enjoyed within the scope of 'the management, utilization, use and enjoyment of an investment'. Unlike the inter-State dispute settlement provisions in Article 9, which safeguard the interests of the States parties in the event of a dispute regarding the interpretation or application of the

---

56. At [107]-[108]. In her Concurring and Dissenting Opinion, Professor Stern explained that she remained "very strongly convinced that MFN clauses should not apply to dispute settlement mechanisms".

57. *Hochtief AG v. The Argentine Republic*, ICSID Case No. ARB/07/31, Decision on Jurisdiction, 24 October 2011 (Professor Vaughan Lowe QC, Judge Charles N. Brower, Christopher Thomas QC).

58. At [58].

BIT, Article 10 is a benefit conferred on investors and designed to protect their interests and the interests of a State Party in its capacity as a host State party to a dispute with an investor: it is a protective right that sits alongside the guarantees against arbitrary and discriminatory measures, expropriation, and so on."[59]

On that basis, the tribunal concluded that "the MFN provision is in principle applicable to the pursuit of dispute settlement procedures".[60]

If an MFN clause may be used to import from another treaty a basis for the tribunal's jurisdiction, then it can circumvent the (presumably deliberate) use of very narrow language by the parties to a treaty. This was demonstrated in *RosInvest v. Russia*,[61] a claim made under the UK-USSR BIT. By Art. 8 of that BIT, each state agreed to submit to arbitration any dispute concerning "the amount or payment of compensation" due for an expropriation, or "concerning any other matter consequential upon an act of expropriation in accordance with Article 5 of this Agreement". The tribunal concluded that this language did not confer jurisdiction upon a tribunal to determine whether an expropriation had actually occurred and, if so, whether it was lawful. But that did not end the matter, because the claimant argued that it was entitled to rely upon the much broader dispute settlement provisions in the Denmark-Russia BIT. The tribunal took the view that

> "While indeed the application of the MFN clause of Article 3 widens the scope of Article 8 and thus is in conflict to its limitation, this is a normal result of the application of MFN clauses, the very character and intention of which is that protection not accepted in one treaty is widened by transferring the protection accorded in another treaty. If this effect is generally accepted in the context of substantive protection, the Tribunal sees no reason not to accept it in the context of procedural clauses such as arbitration clauses. Quite the contrary, it could be argued that, if it applies to substantive protection, then it should apply even more to 'only' procedural protection. However, the Tribunal feels that this latter argument cannot be considered as decisive, but that rather, as argued further above, an arbitration clause, at least in the context of expropriation, is of the same protective value as any substantive protection afforded by applicable provisions such as Article 5 of the BIT."[62]

As a result, the tribunal concluded that it had "jurisdiction beyond that granted" by the BIT under which it had been constituted. This was directly contrary to the decision of the tribunal in *Telenor v. Hungary*,[63] in which the tribunal was invited to expand a restrictive dispute settlement provision in the Norway-Hungary BIT by use of its MFN clause. Refusing to do so, the tribunal insisted that

59. At [68].
60. At [72].
61. *RosInvestCo UK Ltd v. Russia*, SCC Case No. Arb V079/2005, Award on Jurisdiction, October 2007 (Prof. Dr. Böckstiegel, Lord Steyn, Sir Franklin Berman KCMG, QC).
62. At [131]-[132].
63. *Telenor Mobile Communications AS v. Republic of Hungary*, ICSID Case No. ARB/04/15, Award of 13 September 2006 (Professor Sir Roy Goode, CBE, QC, Nicholas W Allard, Arthur Marriott QC).

> "In the absence of language or context to suggest the contrary, the ordinary meaning of 'investments shall be accorded treatment no less favourable than that accorded to investments made by investors of any third State' is that the investor's substantive rights in respect of the investments are to be treated no less favourably than under a BIT between the host State and a third State, and there is no warrant for construing the above phrase as importing procedural rights as well. It is one thing to stipulate that the investor is to have the benefit of MFN investment treatment but quite another to use an MFN clause in a BIT to bypass a limitation in the very same BIT when the parties have not chosen language in the MFN clause showing an intention to do this, as has been done in some BITs."[64]

It may be possible for some highly gymnastic intellect to reconcile these disparate decisions by finding, for example, subtle nuances of meaning in the language used in various treaties. And, to some extent, it's true that superficial inconsistencies between decisions can be explained by reference to differences in the wording of various treaties. But we cannot escape the fact that different tribunals have reached diametrically opposed results when dealing with precisely the same wording. The fact is that some tribunals have considered that, as a matter of principle, MFN clauses do not apply to dispute resolution procedures, while others have taken the opposite view.

On one point, the thinking of tribunals has been, so far, consistent. The various decisions which have applied MFN provisions to dispute resolution provisions have allowed investors to expand or add content to the standards of treatment already contained in a BIT or allowed investors to overcome unfavourable provisions in the BIT. But there is as yet no decision where an investor has successfully been able to import an investor-State arbitration clause where there was none before. The only publicly available decision in which such an argument was rejected is *Menzies Middle East and Africa SA v. Senegal*,[65] where the investor optimistically sought to invoke the MFN provision in the General Agreement on Trade in Services (GATS) to rely on an investor-State arbitration provision from a different (or two different) BITs. The investor failed. Reportedly, there is a similar attempt currently underway against Australia, which seeks to import dispute resolution procedures into the Australia-US FTA.

International investment law occupies a curious no-man's land, in which there is a general consensus that tribunals ought to seek to achieve consistency in their application of important principles, but those tribunals are not bound by any strict doctrine of precedent. It is difficult to find many academic writers who endorse the decision in *Maffezini*;[66] but, even so, since that award was rendered, the tribunals who have been asked to apply MFN clauses to dispute resolution provisions have been more or less evenly divided on the point, so it cannot be said that anything resembling a *jurisprudence constante* has yet developed. Of course, each case will depend upon its specific facts and

64. At [92].

65. *Menzies Middle East and Africa SA and Aviation Handling Services International Ltd v. Republic of Senegal*, ICSID Case No. ARB/15/21, Award of 5 August 2016 (Professor Bernard Hanotiau, Hamid Gharavi and Professor Pierre Mayer).

66. One exception is Stephan SCHILL: see *Multilateralization of International Investment Law*, (Cambridge University Press 2009) at pp. 152-163.

the language of the specific treaty in issue, so it is natural that there is scope for different approaches. Yet we have reached a point at which the manner in which an MFN clause will be applied, in this context at least, depends less upon any clear and settled principles of international law, and more upon the composition of the specific tribunal. There are arbitrators who have owed their appointments primarily to the fact that their views on this question are known to tend in one direction or another. That is not a circumstance that encourages confidence in the existing system of investor-state dispute settlement.[67]

This is the single area of the law and practice of investment arbitration concerning MFN clauses that is most in need of desirable change. That is not to suggest, for a moment, that the outcome of each case should be identical, because not every treaty is identical to all others. But it would be beneficial to investors and states alike to know with greater certainty the *principles* that a tribunal will apply to the question of whether jurisdiction can be established through an MFN clause.

It is easier to identify this problem than to solve it. To speak of "reform" implies the existence of an authority capable of imposing change, yet there is no central authority capable of imposing consistency upon the decisions of diverse tribunals, appointed under different treaties and, often, conducting arbitrations under different rules. In a process that began more than fifty years ago, the International Law Commission set out to formulate what eventually became its 1978 Draft Article on Most Favored Nation Clauses; but attempts to embody those clauses in a multilateral treaty were never successful. In 2015, the International Law Commission adopted a Final Report of the Study Group on the Most-Favoured-Nation clause, but its conclusion on the question of dispute settlement provisions amounted to little more than a frank confession of impotence:

> "The Study Group decided not to attempt to decide between the conflicting views of investment tribunals over the application of MFN clauses to dispute settlement provisions. The Commission does not have an authoritative role in relation to the decisions of investment tribunals, and to conclude that one tribunal was right and another wrong would simply insert the Commission as just another voice in an ongoing debate."[68]

On one point there is general, if not unanimous, agreement, and that is that tribunals ought to interpret treaties so as to give effect to the intentions of the parties. Tribunals repeatedly invoke Art. 31 of the Vienna Convention on the Law of Treaties, which sets out the unarguable principle that a "treaty shall be interpreted in good faith in accordance with the ordinary meaning to be given to the terms of the treaty in their

67. The problem is illustrated by the case of *Astrida Benita Carrizosa v. Republic of Colombia*, ICSID Case No. ARB/18/5, in which the claimant has sought to use an MFN clause to import into the US-Colombia Free Trade Agreement more favourable dispute resolution provisions found in other Colombian treaties. The respondent state appointed as arbitrator Zachary Douglas QC, the author of articles unsympathetic to this use of MFN clauses. The claimant promptly raised a challenge to Douglas, the result of which is unknown at the time of writing.
68. International Law Commission, *Final Report of the Study Group on the Most-Favored-Nation Clause* (2015) at [8].

context and in the light of its object and purpose".[69] It follows that the most efficient way to improve certainty in this area is for parties – the contracting States – to express their objects and purpose in clearer language. In the United Kingdom's current model BIT, for example, para. (3) of the MFN clause states that "For the avoidance of doubt it is confirmed that the treatment provided for in paragraphs (1) and (2) above shall apply to the provisions of Articles 1 to 12 of this Agreement." Since this encompasses the dispute settlement provisions, it seems tolerably clear that dispute resolution mechanisms fall within the scope of the MFN clause. Yet Professor Kohen, in his dissenting opinion in *Venezuela US v. Venezuela*, did not think so, and certainly there is scope for the parties' intentions to be expressed with even greater specificity. States negotiating investment agreements ought now to be well aware of this issue, and there is no reason why they ought not to address it squarely.

One can hope (not unreasonably) for greater clarity to be found in new treaties; that does not assist in the interpretation of the thousands of existing treaties. In a few cases, parties to a treaty have sought to clarify their attention by means of an addendum: the Protocol appended to the Colombia-Switzerland BIT, for example, makes it plain that "the most favourable treatment referred to in the" BIT "does not encompass mechanisms for the settlement of investment disputes provided for in other international agreements related to investments concluded by the Party concerned".

Other states have exchanged diplomatic notes setting out their positions. In *National Grid v. Argentina*,[70] the tribunal observed that "after the decision on jurisdiction in *Siemens*, the Argentine Republic and Panama exchanged diplomatic notes with an 'interpretative declaration' of the MFN clause in their 1996 investment treaty to the effect that, the MFN clause does not extend to dispute resolution clauses, and that this has always been their intention".[71]

A slightly different approach was adopted in the Dominican Republic-Central American Free Trade Agreement, a draft of which included a footnote, intended to form part of the *travaux préparatoires* of the agreement, stating:

> "The Parties agree that the following footnote is to be included in the negotiating history as a reflection of the Parties' shared understanding of the Most-Favored-Nation Treatment Article and the *Maffezini* case. This footnote would be deleted in the final text of the Agreement. The Parties note the recent decision of the arbitral tribunal in *Maffezini (Arg.) v. Kingdom of Spain*, which found an unusually broad most-favored-nation clause in an Argentina-Spain agreement to encompass international dispute resolution procedures. See Decision on Jurisdiction ¶¶ 38-64 (Jan. 25, 2000), reprinted in 16 ICSID Rev. – F.I.L.J. 212 (2002). By contrast, the Most-Favored-Nation Treatment Article of this Agreement is expressly limited in its scope to matters 'with respect to the establishment, acquisition, expansion, management, conduct, operation, and sale or other

69. The tribunal in *Venezuela US, S.R.L v. Venezuela* (at [49]) went so far as to find that Arts. 31 and 32 of the Vienna Convention "reflect customary international law".

70. *National Grid plc v. The Argentine Republic* (UNCITRAL Rules), Decision on Jurisdiction, 20 June 2006 (Dr. Andres Rigo Sureda, E. Whitney Debevoise, Professor Alejandro Garro).

71. At [85].

disposition of investments.' The Parties share the understanding and intent that this clause does not encompass international dispute resolution mechanisms such as those contained in Section C of this Chapter, and therefore could not reasonably lead to a conclusion similar to that of the *Maffezini* case."

V. WHAT IS TREATMENT IN LIKE CIRCUMSTANCES?

An MFN clause is subject to the *ejusdem generis* principle, so it may be invoked only in relation to matters of the same kind as those contemplated by the clause. As the International Law Commission explained in the commentary to its Draft Articles on most-favoured-nation clauses:

> "No writer would deny the validity of the *ejusdem generis* rule which, for the purposes of the most-favoured-nation clause, derives from its very nature. It is generally admitted that a clause conferring most-favoured-nation rights in respect of a certain matter, or class of matter, can attract the rights conferred by other treaties (or unilateral acts) only in regard to the same matter or class of matter."[72]

The effect of the *ejusdem generis* principle becomes especially important when a claimant seeks to use an MFN clause to invoke the dispute resolution provisions of another treaty. In *Maffezini*, Spain argued that application of the principle of *ejusdem generis* meant that the reference to "all matters" in Art. IV (2) of the Argentine-Spain BIT should be read to mean only "substantial matters or material aspects of the treatment granted to investors and not to procedural or jurisdictional questions".

The tribunal did not accept that argument. It ruled that: "if a third-party treaty contains provisions for the settlement of disputes that are more favourable to the protection of the investor's rights and interests than those in the basic treaty, such provisions may be extended to the beneficiary of the most favoured nation clause as they are fully compatible with the *ejusdem generis* principle".

Conversely, if the protections covered by the MFN clause are more confined, the impact of the clause may not apply to dispute resolution provisions. This was the tribunal's approach in *Renta4 v. Russia*,[73] a claim made under the Spain-Russia BIT. Art. 5 of that BIT relevantly provided that

> "(1) Each Party shall guarantee fair and equitable treatment within its territory for the investments made by investors of the other Party.

---

72. International Law Commission, *Draft Articles on most-favoured nation clauses, with commentaries*, 1978, Commentary (10) to Arts. 9 and 10.

73. *Renta4 S.V.S.A. Ahorro Corporacion Emergentes F.I., Ahorro Corporacion Eurofondo F.I., Rovime Inversiones SICAV S.A., GBI 9000 SICAV S.A. v. The Russian Federation* (SCC Arbitration 24/2007), Award on Preliminary Objections, 20 March 2009 (Jan Paulsson, Judge Charles N. Brower, Toby T. Landau).

> (2) The treatment referred to in paragraph 1 above shall be no less favourable than that accorded by either Party in respect of investments made within its territory by investors of any third State."

The majority of the tribunal accepted Russia's argument that

> "The MFN promise affects only matters within the scope of Article 5(2) of the Spanish BIT which in turn covers only 'treatment referred to in paragraph 1 above'. The treatment in question is 'fair and equitable treatment' ('FET'). FET is a substantive standard of treatment. Russia insists that access to international arbitration is not an inherent part of FET. This is confirmed by the existence of BITs guaranteeing FET without any recourse to international arbitration whatever. A promise to match the level of FET extended to third-party nationals therefore cannot in Russia's submission widen the scope of arbitral jurisdiction."[74]

Essentially, an application of the *ejusdem generis* principle in *Renta4* limited the scope of the MFN clause to fair and equitable treatment.

But it would be wrong to assume that this question arises only in cases concerning questions of procedure. There may be many circumstances in which it will be relevant to consider whether the treatment offered to nationals of a third state is actually treatment of the kind envisaged in the MFN clause. The obvious difficulty with the *ejusdem generis* principle is that while it is capable of a broad application, it can also be interpreted very narrowly. On the broadest view, any substantive treatment afforded to investors by a host state might be taken to fall within the subject matter contemplated by an investment treaty. Tribunals taking a more narrow view, however, might seek a closer similarity between the treatment promised in the primary treaty and the additional protections claimed through the operation of an MFN clause.

The narrower approach was illustrated in *Accession Mezzanine Capital L.P. and Danubius Kereskedöház Vagyonkezelö v. Hungary*,[75] in which the claimants (under the UK-Hungary BIT) argued that an MFN Clause could be used to import into that BIT more favourable expropriation clauses from other Hungarian treaties. The tribunal agreed, but cautiously, stating that

> "Claimants maintain that the Respondent's expropriation measures permit Claimants to utilize the BIT Articles 3 and 11 to bring in most-favored-nation treatment with respect to expropriation. Care has to be taken in this context. MFN clauses are not and should not be interpreted or applied to create new causes of action beyond those to which consent to arbitrate has been given by the Parties. In view of the relief sought at pages 31-32 of the Revised Amended Request for Arbitration, it is the Tribunal's understanding that Claimants are not now claiming that the MFN provisions allow more than Articles 3 and 11 would properly permit, that is, the Tribunal jurisdiction over customary international

74. At [103].

75. ICSID Case No. ARB/12/3, Decision on Respondent's Objection under Arbitration Rule 41(5), 16 January 2013 (Arthur W. Rovine, Marc Lalonde, Donald M. McRae).

> law insofar as that law is relevant to the Parties' rights and obligations pursuant to Articles 6 of the BIT. The Tribunal is of the view that an investor may properly rely only on rights set forth in the basic treaty, meaning the BIT to which the investor's home state and the host state of the investment are directly parties, but not more than that. The question should be whether the rights and benefits sought by virtue of the MFN clause are included within the arbitrable scope of the basic treaty. In the instant case, the arbitrable scope of the basic treaty is expropriation, including fact and law questions related thereto. In that light, Claimants are entitled to rely on the MFN provisions of the BIT, but only insofar as such provisions relate to expropriation."[76]

An equally restrictive approach appears to have been adopted in *MTD v. Chile* (although it was not necessary, in that case, for the tribunal to decide whether the MFN clause might apply more broadly). The MFN clause in the BIT between Malaysia and Chile provided (relevantly) that "Investments made by investors of either Contracting Party in the territory of the other Contracting Party shall receive treatment which is fair and equitable, and not less favourable than that accorded to investments made by investors of any third State." The tribunal found that "matters that can be construed to be part of the fair and equitable treatment of investors would be covered by the clause".[77]

It's difficult, if not impossible, to reconcile this narrow approach with the decisions in such cases as *White Industries v. India* or *EDF v. Argentina*, in each of which the tribunal permitted the claimant to use an MFN clause to import into the principal treaty a protection that had no obvious equivalent in that treaty.

The tribunal in *İçkale İnşaat Limited Şirketi v. Turkmenistan*[78] readily accepted that "the legal effect" of Art. II(2) of the BIT between Turkey and Turkmenistan was "to prohibit discriminatory treatment of investments of investors of a State party (the home State) in the territory of the other State (the host State) when compared with the treatment accorded by the host State to investments of investors of any third State". But that was not the end of the tribunal's deliberations, because Art. II(2) contained an express statement that the MFN obligation applied to "treatment no less favourable than that accorded in similar situations to investments of its investors or to investments of investors of any third country". The tribunal interpreted this language as imposing a significant restriction upon the MFN undertaking, stating that

> "this obligation exists only insofar as the investments of the investors of the home State and those of the investors of the third State can be said to be in 'a similar situation.' Conversely, the MFN treatment obligation does not exist if and when an investment of an investor of the home State is not in a 'similar situation' to that of the investments of investors of third States; in such a situation, there is de facto no discrimination."[79]

---

76. At [73-74].
77. At [104].
78. ICSID Case No. ARB/10/24, Award dated 8 March 2016 (Dr. Veijo Heiskanen, Carolyn B. Lamm and Professor Philippe Sands QC).
79. At [328].

What was required, in this tribunal's view, was "a comparison of the factual situation of the investments of the investors of the home State and that of the investments of the investors of third States, for the purpose of determining whether the treatment accorded to investors of the home State can be said to be less favorable than that accorded to investments of the investors of any third State".

The tribunal concluded that

> "given the limitation of the scope of application of the MFN clause to 'similar situations,' it cannot be read, in good faith, to refer to standards of investment protection included in other investment treaties between a State party and a third State. The standards of protection included in other investment treaties create legal rights for the investors concerned, which may be more favorable in the sense of being additional to the standards included in the basic treaty, but such differences between applicable legal standards cannot be said to amount to 'treatment accorded in similar situations,' without effectively denying any meaning to the terms "similar situations." Investors cannot be said to be in a 'similar situation' merely because they have invested in a particular State; indeed, if the terms 'in similar situations' were to be read to coincide with the territorial scope of application of the treaty, they would not be given any meaning and would effectively become redundant as there would be no difference between the clause 'treatment no less favourable than that accorded in similar situations ... to investments of investors of any third country' and 'treatment no less favourable than that accorded [...] to investments of investors of any third country.' Such a reading would not be consistent with the generally accepted rules of treaty interpretation, including the principle of effectiveness, or *effet utile*, which requires that each term of a treaty provision should be given a meaning and effect."[80]

As there was no evidence before the tribunal that other investors in a similar position to the claimant had actually received superior treatment from the respondent, the tribunal refused to allow the claimant simply to import other treatment standards into the BIT by means of the MFN clause.

The award in *İçkale İnşaat Limited Şirketi v. Turkmenistan* is relatively recent, and it remains to be seen what impact it will have. Perhaps the decision will be seen as confined to its own facts, turning on the very specific language of the MFN clause in the Turkey-Turkmenistan BIT. But, at the very least, the award opens up scope for argument that the language of that BIT only enunciates the widely accepted *ejusdem generis* rule. It may be that, in future, tribunals will no longer automatically assume that the promise of a standard of treatment in a treaty itself constitutes "treatment", without a closer consideration of the underlying facts. Already, treaties are appearing (such as CETA and JEEPA, discussed below), which make it explicit that a mere promise contained in another treaty cannot be regarded as "treatment".

80. At [329].

VI. UNCTAD PROPOSALS FOR REFORM

Late in 2017, the United Nations Conference on Trade and Development (UNCTAD) published a policy document entitled Reform Package for the International Investment Regime, which posited that the relevant "question is not about whether to reform, but about the substance of such reform (the what), as well as the process and mechanisms of reform (the how)".[81] The UNCTAD group responsible for the Reform Package considered MFN clauses to be ripe for reform. The "challenges" that it identified included the tendency of investors to invoke "the MFN clause to access more 'investor-friendly' provisions in IIAs concluded by the host State with third countries";[82] the use of "the MFN clause to avoid dispute resolution requirements imposed by the applicable IIA";[83] and the practice of

> "investors 'cherry picking' the most advantageous clauses from different treaties concluded by the host State, thereby potentially undermining individual treaty bargains and sidelining the base treaty. For example, treaty commitments may clash, or hard-won concessions in a negotiation (e.g. on flexibility in performance requirements) may be undone through the application of a broadly worded MFN clause, as interpreted by arbitral tribunals. This concern is particularly heightened given countries' current efforts to reform their IIA regimes, which implies a refinement and rebalancing of treaty standards. Clearly, States will need and want to be careful that the desired effects of newly crafted treaty provisions are not obviated by the application of a broadly worded MFN clause."[84]

MFN clauses, the UNCTAD authors conclude, present a "particularly pronounced"[85] challenge to the reform of international investment agreements. They offer several options by which this challenge may be addressed. One is simply "to omit the MFN clause altogether", which "preserves a maximum of flexibility and can facilitate IIA reform"[86] – but which is also reminiscent of the doctor whose cure for a pain in the leg is amputation. The other options are:

– "to specify that the MFN clause does not allow for the importation of substantive or ISDS-related elements contained in older treaties";

81. United Nations Conference on Trade and Development, "UNCTAD's Reform Package for the International Investment Regime" (2017) p. 7.
82. United Nations Conference on Trade and Development, "UNCTAD's Reform Package for the International Investment Regime" (2017) p. 29.
83. United Nations Conference on Trade and Development, "UNCTAD's Reform Package for the International Investment Regime" (2017) p. 30.
84. United Nations Conference on Trade and Development, "UNCTAD's Reform Package for the International Investment Regime" (2017) p. 30
85. United Nations Conference on Trade and Development, "UNCTAD's Reform Package for the International Investment Regime" (2017) p. 79.
86. United Nations Conference on Trade and Development, "UNCTAD's Reform Package for the International Investment Regime" (2017) p. 31.

– "to specify that MFN treatment does not apply to ISDS provisions found in other IIAs, existing or future";
– "to specify that the MFN clause does not apply to substantive obligations undertaken in (existing or future) IIAs";
– "carving out from the MFN obligation certain sectors or industries or certain policy measures through a general carve-out (applicable to both parties) or through country-specific reservations"; and
– clarifying "that the MFN obligation requires comparison of investors/investments that are 'in like circumstances'".[87]

These five "options" are, in fact, five expressions of the same basic principle, which is that if two or more States wish their agreement to include an MFN clause that is limited in its scope, it is sensible to express that wish in suitably precise terms. If this appears to be a statement of the obvious, then it bears repeating that the overwhelming majority of MFN clauses in investment agreements are neither narrow nor specific in their scope.

VII. TREATY RESPONSES TO MFN DECISIONS: INDIA, JOINT INTERPRETATIVE STATEMENTS, CETA, TPP, JEEPA

In recent years, states have become increasingly aware of the potential impact of MFN clauses, and BITs concluded in the twenty-first century are much more likely to display greater clarity in their wording than treaties entered into in the second half of the previous century.

Several recent BITs address specifically the question of whether MFN clauses may apply to dispute settlement provisions. The positions adopted vary: the 2006 BIT between Colombia and Switzerland, for example, specifically provides that the MFN clause "does not encompass mechanisms for the settlement of investment disputes provided for in other international agreements related to investments concluded by the Party concerned". The 2004 Economic Partnership Agreement between Japan and Mexico includes a note confirming that "Each Party shall in its Area accord to investors of the other Party treatment no less favorable than the treatment which it accords, in like circumstances, to its own investors or investors of a non-Party with respect to access to the courts of justice and administrative tribunals and agencies in all degrees of jurisdiction, both in pursuit and in defense of such investor's rights." Whether dispute settlement provisions are included or excluded, the trend towards greater clarity is both overdue and welcome.

Some states have come to regard MFN clauses as a threat, and have responded by attempting to remove or restrict their exposure to claims. None has taken more emphatic action than India.

87. United Nations Conference on Trade and Development, "UNCTAD's Reform Package for the International Investment Regime" (2017) p. 31.

1. India

The case of *White Industries v. India* developed from an ICC award rendered in Paris in May 2002. An Australian company, White Industries, the successful claimant, sought to enforce its modest award against Coal India, an Indian government corporation, in the High Court of Mumbai. Almost simultaneously, Coal India applied to the High Court of New Delhi to set aside the award. The enforcement proceedings were stayed in 2006 so that the annulment proceedings could be determined first. But the annulment proceedings did not progress, partly because of the inefficiencies of the Indian court system, and partly because of judicial indecision as to which Indian legislation ought to apply to the case.

White Industries lost confidence in its ability to enforce its award in India, and in 2010 it commenced a claim against India under the BIT between Australia and India (Australia-India BIT). White Industries advanced most of the usual claims that are made in investment arbitration (expropriation, denial of fair and equitable treatment), but without success. Significantly, it also relied upon Art. 4(2) of the Australia-India BIT, which provided that "A Contracting Party shall at all times treat investments in its own territory on a basis no less favourable than that accorded to investments or investors of any third country". White Industries argued that the effect of Art. 4(2) was that India undertook to Australian investors an obligation equivalent to the one found in Art. 4(5) of the Agreement between the Republic of India and the State of Kuwait for the Encouragement and Reciprocal Protection of Investments of 2001. That Article relevantly provided that "Each Contracting State shall maintain a favourable environment for investments in its territory by investors of the other Contracting State. Each Contracting State shall, in accordance with its applicable laws and regulations, provide effective means of asserting claims and enforcing rights with respect to investments...." The tribunal accepted that the MFN clause imported the "effective means" standard into the Australia-India BIT, and found that India had breached Art. 4(2) by failing to provide "effective means of asserting claims and enforcing rights".

The quantum of the *White Industries* award was, by the standards of investment treaty claims, tiny. But its impact in India was immense. One Indian commentator observed that the "award opened a Pandora's box, and since then 17 investors have issued notices of arbitration against India.... As a reaction to the White Industries case and the various subsequent notices of arbitration, the government published a Draft Model proposing to renegotiate the BITs it had already entered into in line with the draft."[88]

In 2015, the Indian government produced a new Model Bilateral Investment Treaty, which included a limited "national treatment" provision, but no MFN clause at all. Within India, this was widely regarded as a direct consequence of the *White Industries* decision; there had been an MFN clause in the previous Indian Model Bilateral Investment Treaty, drafted in 1993. But, as the Law Commission of India commented,

> "The Indian government has not provided any detailed explanation for its absence. It appears that the purpose behind not having an MFN provision is to ensure that foreign investors are not able to borrow beneficial provisions from other Indian

88. Anirudh KRISHNAN, "A bit for the state, a bit for the investor", *The Hindu* (8 September 2015).

> BITs (Treaty Shopping). India's major concern with the MFN is the use of this provision by foreign investors to borrow beneficial substantive and procedural provisions from third-country BITs. The absence of an MFN provision will surely prevent the foreign investor from indulging in such borrowing."[89]

In July 2016, the Modi government announced its intention to terminate India's fifty-eight BITs then in force in order to negotiate their replacement with new agreements based on the new Model Bilateral Investment Treaty. Since that time, India has unilaterally terminated at least thirteen of its BITs.[90] It has not, to date, replaced any of these with new agreements, although a treaty based on the new Model was signed with Cambodia in 2016, and there have been reports that India and Brazil were negotiating a BIT that included neither an MFN clause nor any provision for investor-state arbitration.

Any state entering into a BIT needs to weigh the potential benefits of increased inbound investment and increased protection for its investors abroad against the risk of exposure to claims by foreign investors. The Indian Model BIT now prioritizes reducing the risk of claims against the state (partly, but not only, through the omission of an MFN clause); it remains to be seen whether other states will find this approach palatable.

2. *Joint Interpretative Statements*

Art. 31(3)(a) of the Vienna Convention on the Law of Treaties provides that an interpretation of a treaty may take account of "any subsequent agreement between the parties regarding the interpretation of the treaty or the application of its provisions". There is scope, therefore, for States who have become concerned that the scope of their MFN clauses has surpassed what was intended, to clarify the position in a joint interpretative statement. India has already issued at least one such joint statement in connection with a BIT.[91]

In February 2016, India proposed a "Joint Interpretative Statement" to twenty-five countries with which it has investment agreements whose initial period of validity had not expired, which included India's interpretation of terms including MFN clauses. No such statement can, of course, carry any weight while it remains unilateral.

The issuing of joint interpretative statements is potentially a useful mechanism for addressing the problem of broad MFN clauses being given wider meaning than the parties intended. Some newer treaties have established joint bodies with a mandate to issue binding interpretations.[92]

---

89. Law Commission of India, Report No. 260, "Analysis of the 2015 Draft Model Indian Bilateral Investment Treaty", August 2015.
90. Between September 2016 and May 2017, India terminated its BITs with Australia, Austria, Croatia, Czech Republic, Denmark, Germany, Hungary, Italy, Malaysia, the Netherlands, Oman, Spain and Switzerland.
91. For example, the recent Joint Interpretative Declaration between India and Colombia regarding the Agreement for the Promotion and Protection of Investments signed on 10 November 2009 <http://pib.nic.in/PressReleseDetail.aspx?PRID=1508988> last accessed 13 February 2018.
92. UNCTAD Reform Package, p. 81 citing CETA (2016); Morocco-Nigeria BIT (2016); Chile-Hong Kong BIT (2016).

3. *Trans-Pacific Partnership*

The text of the Trans-Pacific Partnership (TPP) (between Australia, Brunei, Canada, Chile, Japan, Malaysia, Mexico, New Zealand, Peru, Singapore and the United States) was finalized on 5 October 2015 and the treaty was formally signed on 4 February 2016. The treaty was to come into force if it was ratified within two years either by all signatories or by at least six signatories who between them represent at least 85 per cent of the combined GDP of the signatory states. The decision of the administration of the United States not to ratify the TPP made it improbable that the treaty would ever come into force.[93] However, the remaining eleven states resumed negotiations, which resulted, in November 2017, in a further partial agreement, now known as the Comprehensive and Progressive Agreement for Trans-Pacific Partnership or TPP-11. This agreement was signed in Santiago on 8 March 2018. Late in January 2018, the President of the United States stated, in an interview, that he would consider re-entering the TPP if it were "substantially better" for the United States, but without indicating what a "substantially better" deal might look like. At about the same time, the United Kingdom announced an interest in joining the agreement, as it prepared to sever its trading links with its more geographically apposite neighbours.

The TPP remains an interesting example of a multilateral treaty that contains investor protections but has been crafted with a view to limiting the vulnerability of states to investor claims.

Chapter 9 of the TPP, which deals with investments, does contain an MFN clause (Art. 9.5). Its first two paragraphs provide:

> "1. Each Party shall accord to investors of another Party treatment no less favourable than that it accords, in like circumstances, to investors of any other Party or of any non-Party with respect to the establishment, acquisition, expansion, management, conduct, operation, and sale or other disposition of investments in its territory.
> 2. Each Party shall accord to covered investments treatment no less favourable than that it accords, in like circumstances, to investments in its territory of investors of any other Party or of any non-Party with respect to the establishment, acquisition, expansion, management, conduct, operation, and sale or other disposition of investments."

These are followed, however, by a third paragraph, which expressly excludes the dispute resolution provisions from the scope of the MFN clause: "For greater certainty, the treatment referred to in this Article does not encompass international dispute resolution procedures or mechanisms, such as those included in Section B (Investor-State Dispute Settlement)." It is a reasonable expectation that clauses of this nature will become increasingly common in new investment treaties, as states seek to confine their disputes with investors to the procedures expressly identified in their specific treaty.

93. At the time of writing, however, the stated position of the United States appeared to change frequently and erratically.

In addition, the signatories to the TPP chose to impose further limits on the application of the MFN clause, although they did so in a rather circuitous fashion. Australia's Schedule to Annex II to the treaty contains numerous very specific reservations to the MFN clause, and one broad reservation which makes it clear that the MFN clause is to have prospective effect only: "Australia reserves the right to adopt or maintain any measure that accords more favourable treatment to any service supplier or investor under any bilateral or multilateral international agreement in force or signed prior to the date of entry into force of this Agreement." And every other signatory has made a reservation in substantially similar terms. Canada, for example, in its Schedule to Annex II, stated that it: "reserves the right to adopt or maintain a measure that accords differential treatment to countries under any bilateral or multilateral international agreement in force or signed prior to the date of entry into force of this Agreement". Only those who were responsible for negotiating the treaty can explain why every party to the TPP had the same attitude towards the TPP, but expressed that consensus through reservations rather than the body of the treaty. Even so, the trend that emerges here is a reluctance on behalf of states to enter into MFN clauses with broad application.

Every state made further reservations to the MFN clause. Some were very specific, others extremely broad. Japan, for instance, reserved "the right to adopt or maintain any measure relating to investments or the supply of services in public law enforcement and correctional services, and in social services established or maintained for a public purpose: income security or insurance, social security or insurance, social welfare, public training, health, child care and public housing".

Another important limitation upon the scope of the MFN clause is that states may elect to exclude from the dispute resolution provisions claims that they had "breached an investment authorisation by enforcing conditions or requirements under which the investment authorisation was granted". These reservations, which are set out in Annex 9-H, were made by Australia, Canada, Mexico and New Zealand. Effectively, this mechanism excludes claims alleging that the investment policy of a state has been operated in such a manner as to breach the MFN clause.

4. CETA

Canada and the European Union signed the Comprehensive Economic and Trade Agreement (CETA) on 30 October 2016.

Chapter 8 of CETA deals with investment protection and includes, at Art. 8.7, a most-favoured-nation clause. Paragraph 1 of Art. 8.7 is unremarkable:

> "Each Party shall accord to an investor of the other Party and to a covered instrument treatment no less favourable than the treatment it accords in like situations, to investors of a third country and to their investments with respect to the establishment, acquisition, expansion, conduct, operation, management, maintenance, use, enjoyment and sale or disposal of their investments in its territory."

That obligation is, however, qualified in three interesting ways. Paragraph 2 deals with a complication arising from the federal nature of both the European Union and Canada's system of government. It is well established that the acts of a state or provincial government within a federation may give rise to a breach of the obligations undertaken by a federal government in a treaty. "For greater certainty, the treatment accorded by a Party under paragraph 1 means, with respect to a government in Canada other than at federal level, or, with respect to a government of or in a Member State of the European Union, treatment accorded, in like situations, by that government to investors in its territory, and to investments of such investors, of a third country." This provision is designed to reduce the risk of an investor seeking the benefit of an arrangement between third-country investors and a state or province other than the one in which its investment is located.

Paragraph 3 of Art. 8.7 is a curiously specific exclusion applying to arrangements with any third country "that recognises the accreditation of testing and analysis services and service suppliers, the accreditation of repair and maintenance services and service suppliers, as well as the certification of the qualifications of or of the results of work done by those accredited services and service suppliers".

Significantly, para. 4 expressly excludes the application of the MFN clause to dispute resolution processes. It provides that "The 'treatment' referred to in paragraphs 1 and 2 does not include procedures for the resolution of investment disputes between investors and states provided for in other international investment treaties and other trade agreements." But para. 4 also attempts to limit the application of the MFN clause to substantive matters, stating that "Substantive obligations in other international treaties and other trade agreements do not in themselves constitute 'treatment', and thus cannot give rise to a breach of this Article, absent measures adopted or maintained by a Party pursuant to those obligations." This provision creates some curious conceptual difficulties. As we have already seen, in most cases concerning MFN clauses, it has usually been assumed that the promise that an investment or investor would be treated in a certain way is sufficient to constitute "treatment". It has generally been thought that an "MFN clause allows a claimant investor to invoke certain more favourable provisions of investment treaties that the host state had concluded with third states"[94] – that is, that the mere making of the promise amounted to "treatment" offered to investors of a third state.

But the intention of this language of para. 4 appears to be to enable a State to rely on its breach of an obligation in one treaty to circumvent that obligation being imported into CETA through Art. 8.7. This places a substantial additional hurdle in the way of a claiming investor, who must now demonstrate that the state has not only made a promise to the third-state investor, but has actually *honoured* its obligation. The effect of this is that Art. 8.7(4) appears to allow a state to invoke its own breach of one treaty as a defence to a claim brought under CETA. By way of example, had a similar clause existed in the Australia-India BIT, India could have defended the claim in *White Industries* by arguing that the provision in the Kuwait-India BIT promising "effective means of asserting claims and enforcing rights" could not be invoked through an MFN clause because Kuwaiti investors in India had never actually been provided with any such benefit.

94. Richard HAPP and Noah RUBINS, *Digest of ICSID Awards and Decisions, 2003-2007* (Oxford University Press 2009) p. 364.

Any claims made under CETA that call in aid the MFN provisions of Art. 8.7(1) will now involve an extra degree of complexity, because it will no longer be sufficient for the claimant to point to the existence of a promise in another treaty. The evidentiary burden of proving that investors of a third country have in fact received preferable treatment could, in some cases, be very substantial indeed.

5. *JEEPA*

Chapter 8 Art. 4 of the EU-Japan Economic Partnership Agreement (2017, but as of this writing not yet in force) (JEEPA) specifically excludes ISDS from its promise of MFN treatment. Chapter 8, Section G, Art. X1 contains wide-ranging general exceptions to the protections afforded in the investment liberalization chapter of the agreement, including for measures taken in relation to inter alia health, public order and privacy of individuals in relation to personal data. At first blush, JEEPA seems to follow CETA in respect of defining what constitutes "treatment" for MFN purposes. Art. 4(5) of JEEPA provides:

> "Substantive provisions in other international agreements concluded by a Party with a non-Party do not in themselves constitute 'treatment' under this Article. For greater certainty, actions or inactions of a Party in relation to such provisions can constitute treatment and thus can give rise to establishing a breach of this Article to the extent that the breach is not established solely based on the said provisions."

This position is to some extent modified by Note 4 to Art. 4, which clarifies that "For greater certainty, the entrepreneurs of the other Party or their covered enterprises would be entitled to receive such treatment even in the absence of enterprises established by entrepreneurs of the non-Party at the time when the comparison is made."

Compared to CETA, therefore, JEEPA departs less dramatically from the generally accepted position in international law.

VIII. CONCLUSION

It is ultimately for contracting States to determine whether there is any need to change the manner in which the MFN standard is articulated in their treaties. In doing so, each State needs first to consider whether its MFN clauses are achieving their intended purpose of attracting foreign investors by creating a desirable climate for investment, and whether that benefit outweighs the risk to the State of broader investor claims. If there is a discernible trend, it is towards a tightening of the application of MFN clauses – but that is by no means universal. The most desirable trend is towards increasing specificity in the content of MFN clauses, which will help to remove uncertainty as to their application.

The primary concerns of lawyers and arbitrators are different. They are less concerned with the benefits of MFN clauses for the host economy, and for them, change is desirable if it makes the principles applied in investment cases more consistent and predictable. Prospectively, this aim can be pursued through more careful drafting of new clauses. There are still, however, many hundreds of older, existing broad MFN clauses in operation, and for almost every tribunal decision in which a controversy has been resolved in one particular way, it remains possible to find another that reaches the opposite result. This position will not change quickly. For the foreseeable future, we should expect that arbitrators will continue to be appointed by parties who expect, from a careful study of their awards and other writings, that they will resolve a particular controversy in a certain way.

Sustainable Development Obligations and Access to Treaty Remedies in Contemporary Investment Treaties and Models

Won Kidane[*]

TABLE OF CONTENTS

I. INTRODUCTION

Traditionally, investment treaties impose external substantive standards on the host state, and outsource dispute settlement to non-governmental international tribunals. The external substantive standards[1] and the accompanying access to treaty remedies[2] that investment treaties grant have, by structural design,[3] exclusively benefited foreign

* Associate Professor of Law, Seattle University School of Law.

1. See VATTEL, *The Law of Nations*, Vol. II, pp. 8, 104, cited in M. SORNARAJAH, *The International Law on Foreign Investment*, 3rd ed. (2010) p. 19 ("[This view] was motivated by the concern that the standards of treatment provided to nationals in a host state may be low and therefore unacceptable.") A modern articulation of the philosophical predicate is contained in Elihu Root's 1910 statement, which reads in part:

   "The condition upon which any country is entitled to measure the justice due from it to an alien by the justice it accords to its own citizens is that its system of law and administration shall conform to that standard. If any country's system of law and administration does not conform to that standard, although the people of that country may be content or compelled to live under it, no other country can be compelled to accept it as furnishing a satisfactory measure of treatment to its citizens."

   Quoted in Rudolf DOLZER and Christoph SCHREUER, *Principles of International Investment Law*, 2nd ed. (Oxford 2012) p. 2.
2. By "treaty remedies" I mean both the procedural access to international dispute settlement and the availability of treaty-based substantive rights.
3. The lack of reciprocity is by no means a design flaw. It is rooted in what Kate Miles describes as the "process of applying these [the original Eurocentric] standards to non-European states that became inextricably linked with colonialism, oppressive protection of commercial interests, and military intervention". Kate MILES, *The Origins of International Investment Law: Empire, Environment and the Safeguards of Capital* (Cambridge 2013) p. 28 citing Charles LIPSON, *Standing Guard: Protecting Foreign Capital in the Nineteenth and Twentieth Centuries* (University of California Press 1985) pp. 11-12. Joost Pauwelyn offers a slightly different perspective i.e., "abuses occurred on both sides", which means that

investors without imposing meaningful reciprocal obligations on them.[4] The lack of corresponding substantive treaty obligations on the investor, the unilateral investor access to investor-state dispute settlement (ISDS) coupled with the perceived deficiencies and excesses of ISDS[5] have in recent years prompted a significant rise in proposals for the inclusion in contemporary investment treaties and models of provisions imposing certain substantive obligations on investors,[6] and the reform of the ISDS[7]

"[h]ost states abused their territorial power against aliens, discriminating, expropriating, or expelling them. Home states even more so, used their power to expand their territory, through conquest or colonialism, imposing their laws and courts for the benefit of nationals abroad (e.g., the British capitulation regime in China) and protected those nationals and their assets by use or threat of force including invasions, gunboat attacks, and blockades."

Joost PAUWELYN, "Rational Design or Accidental Evolution? The Emergence of International Investment Law" in Zachary DOUGLAS, Joost PAUWELYN and Jorge E. VINUALES, *The Foundations of International Investment Law: Bringing Theory into Practice* (Oxford 2014) p. 19. In any case, the design was a part of what Dezalay and Garth call the "gradual legalization" of North-South relations. See Yves DEZALAY and Bryant GARTH, *Dealing in Virtue: International Commercial Arbitration and the Construction of a Transnational Legal Order* (University of Chicago Press 1996) p. 64.

4. Investors as third-party beneficiaries to investment treaties owe no duties to the host state under the investment treaty and are largely immune from treaty claims against them. The addition of substantive obligations in recent treaties introduces a new concept but does not resolve the access dilemma. This will be discussed in Sect. III infra.
5. The most notable of such efforts is spearheaded by the European Union Commission. Both the diagnostics and reform proposals are very well captured in the Commission's 2015 Concept Paper. See European Union Commission Concept Paper, *Investment in TTIP and Beyond – the Path for Reform, Enhancing the Right to Regulate and Moving from Current Ad Hoc Arbitration Towards an Investment Court* (2015) at p. 1; available at <http://trade.ec.europa.eu/doclib/docs/2015/may/tradoc_153408.PDF>. On the question of the perceived deficiencies of ISDS, the Concept Paper states:

   "Currently, arbitrators on ISDS tribunals are chosen by the disputing parties (i.e. the investor and the defending state) on a case-by-case basis. The current system does not preclude the same individuals from acting as lawyers (e.g. preparing the investor's claims) in other ISDS cases. This situation can give rise to conflicts of interest – real or perceived – and thus concerns that these individuals are not acting with full impartiality when acting as arbitrators. The ad hoc nature of their appointment is perceived by the public as interfering in their ability to act independently and to properly balance investment protection against the right to regulate. It has also led to perceptions that this provides financial incentives to arbitrators to multiply ISDS cases."

   Id. at pp. 6-7.
6. Such efforts are reflected in recent Bilateral Investment Treaties (BITs) and models (including the new Indian Model) as well as investment chapters in many newly negotiated and pending regional trade agreements including the Transpacific, Trans-Atlantic Partnerships, and EU-Canada and EU-Vietnam. Some of these are cited and discussed in Sect. III.*2* infra.
7. The most radical of these efforts seeks to replace it with a standing court system altogether. The European Union Commission is at the forefront of this effort. Indeed, the EU-Canada and EU-Vietnam Treaties already have effected this transformation. The opposition to a radical reform is also equally vocal and vigorous. See e.g., Speech by Stephan M. SCHWEBEL (17 May 2016, Washington DC)

system.[8] Correspondingly, it also sparked academic discussions about the very essence of the structural design of the ISDS from an access vantage point.[9]

Whereas the proposals for the equalization of access to international arbitration and the related academic discourse currently remain at experimental stages, a growing number of contemporary investment treaties and models now contain some provisions on substantive obligations designed to widen the host state's policy space and impose corresponding obligations on investors. These contemporary substantive obligations often focus on four broad areas in varying formulations and frequency: (1) the environment, (2) labor standards, (3) anti-corruption, and (4) human rights.[10]

A 2014 OECD statistical study[11] surveyed 2,107 investment treaties and 1,113 investment treaty based cases and arrived at the following useful conclusions: although only 12 percent of the entire stock of investment treaties in effect contained provisions relative to sustainable development, more than three-quarters of treaties concluded between 2008 and 2013 contain provisions relating to at least one of the above four sustainable development areas.[12] Moreover, the OECD Study has also established that nearly all treaties concluded in 2012 and 2013 covered at least one of the four areas designed to help sustainable development.[13]

The nearly complete lack of attention to sustainable development issues in the older treaties and the greater attention paid to the same issues in the more contemporary treaties is now well documented. With that as a background, this article intends to accomplish three objectives: (1) survey the sustainable development related provisions of selected recent models and treaties, (2) identify and critically analyze the structures and

---

"A paramount question is, should ICSID in particular really be left to wither and expire after having successfully administered a very large number of cases, not because the criticism mounted against it and investor/State arbitration more broadly is valid but because uninformed or misinformed critics have made so much uninformed and misinformed noise that the EU has been moved to appease the views of those critics?"

Full speech available at <http://isdsblog.com/wp-content/uploads/sites/2/2016/05/THEPROPOSALSOFTHEEUROPEANCOMMISSION.pdf>.

A working group set up by United Nations Commission on International Trade Law (UNCITRAL) is also currently looking into the matter. Materials relating to the works of the working group including audio recordings of some sessions is available at <http://www.uncitral.org/pdf/english/workinggroups/wg_3/WGIII-34th-session/930_for_ the_website.pdf>.

7. EU Commission Concept Paper, supra fn. 5, at p. 7.
8. Whether it is a system or not is a subject of academic debate but it is used here loosely without getting into such debate. For a discussion of the various schools on whether it is a system or a framework, see Won KIDANE, *The Culture of International Arbitration* (OUP 2017) pp. 64-89.
9. The most recent addition to the literature that directly addresses the access issue is Jose Daniel AMADO, Jackson Shaw KERN and Martin DOE RODRIGUEZ, *Arbitrating the Conduct of International Investors* (Cambridge 2018).
10. See Kathryn GORDON, Joachim POHL and Marie BOUCHARD, *Investment Treaty Law, Sustainable Development and Responsible Business Conduct: A Fact Finding Survey*, OECD Working Papers on International Investment Law, 2014/01, (OECD Publishing 2014) Available at <www.oecd.org/investment/investment-policy/WP-2014_01.pdf> (OECD Study).
11. *Id.*
12. See *id.* at p. 5.
13. *Id.*

substantive formulations of these provisions, and finally, (3) evaluate the mechanisms of their enforcement against the investor including the challenges of the host states' and host communities' access to ISDS or other treaty remedies.

It is divided into three parts mirroring the above listing with Part II offering the results of the survey, and Parts III and IV dealing with the substantive formulations and procedural access issues respectively.

II. SUSTAINABLE DEVELOPMENT OBLIGATIONS IN CONTEMPORARY TREATIES AND MODELS

For purposes of this study, a defined set of representative treaties and models are selected. These are: (*1*) Trans-Pacific Partnership (TPP)[14] (*2*) Transatlantic Trade and Investment Partnership (TTIP),[15] (*3*) the EU-Canada Comprehensive Economic Trade Agreement (CETA),[16] (*4*) India's new Model BIT,[17] (*5*) the Draft Pan-African Investment Code (PAIC), and (*6*) sixteen BITs concluded in 2016 and 2017.[18]

1. Trans-Pacific Partnership (TPP)[19]

The TPP, before the United States withdrew, was to be the largest economic and trade partnership of the United Sates and eleven Pacific Rim states representing about 40 percent of the world's GDP.[20] Although it was supposed to be a part of the most

---

14. Text of the investment chapter is available at <https://ustr.gov/sites/default/files/TPP-Final-Text-Investment.pdf>.
15. The text is available at <http://trade.ec.europa.eu/doclib/docs/2015/september/tradoc_153807.pdf>.
16. The text is available at <http://trade.ec.europa.eu/doclib/docs/2014/september/tradoc_152806.pdf>.
17. The Model Text is available at <http://finmin.nic.in/reports/ModelTextIndia_BIT.pdf> (December 2015).
18. Sixteen of the forty-nine most recent BITs as of this writing have been selected mainly because of the accessibility of the texts but are fairly representative of recent trends. These are Israel-Japan (2017), Morocco-Nigeria (2017), Chile-China/Hong Kong (2017), Argentina-Qatar (2016), Nigeria-Singapore (2016), Rwanda-Turkey (2016), Rwanda-Morocco (2016), Canada-Mongolia (2016), Japan-Kenya (2016), Austria-Kyrgyzstan (2016), Argentina-US (2016), Canada-China/Hong Kong (2016), Japan-Iran (2016), UAE-Mexico (2016), Iran-Slovakia (2016), Nigeria-UAE (2016). The texts of all the sixteen treaties discussed below are available at <http://investmentpolicyhub.unctad.org/IIA/MostRecentTreaties#iiaInnerMenu>.
19. The text of the investment chapter is available at <https://ustr.gov/sites/default/files/TPP-Final-Text-Investment.pdf>.
20. See Peter BAKER, "Trump Abandons Trans-Pacific Partnership; Obama's Signature Deal" (23 January 2017) available at <www.nytimes.com/2017/01/23/us/politics/tpp-trump-trade-nafta.html>; Thomas L. FRIEDMAN, "Trump Is a Chinese Agent", NY Times, 29 March 2017 at 1; available at <www.nytimes.com/2017/03/29/opinion/trump-is-a-chinese-agent.html?mabReward=ACTM4&recp=5&action=click&pgtype=Homepage&region=CColumn&module=Recommendation&src=rechp&WT.nav=RecEngine&_r=0>. Efforts are now underway to revitalize TPP without the United States. See Daniel MOSS, "Revived TPP Shows Trade Will Go on Without U.S.: A pact without the U.S. proves that American leadership is not essential to the

contemporary models, the reforms that it sought to introduce to both investor obligations and access to international arbitration were very modest.

Two provisions address the state's policy space and corporate social responsibility matters but neither is extraordinary by any means. With respect to policy space, Art. 9.16 provides:

> "*Investment and Environmental, Health and other Regulatory Objectives*
> Nothing in this Chapter shall be construed to prevent a Party from adopting, maintaining or enforcing any measure *otherwise consistent* with this Chapter that it considers appropriate to ensure that investment activity in its territory is undertaken in a manner sensitive to environmental, health or other regulatory objectives." (Emphasis added.)

Any policy measures that a state party might take for the protection of the environment or health are subordinated to the treaty's investment protection provisions. This particular approach is more akin to the traditional BITs than the recent treaties. Even the 2012 US BIT envisions a more robust regulatory space for environmental and labor matters than this TPP provision.[21]

With respect to Corporate Social Responsibility (CSR), Art. 9.17 of the TPP simply states:

> "*Article 9.17. Corporate Social Responsibility*
> The Parties reaffirm the importance of each Party encouraging enterprises operating within its territory or subject to its jurisdiction to voluntarily incorporate into their internal policies those internationally recognised standards, guidelines and principles of corporate social responsibility that have been endorsed or are supported by that Party."

This basically sets up a voluntary compliance regime. In both the policy and CSR respect, the TPP does not indicate a progressive trend. This fact is more important for its indication of the position that the United State seems to have taken in the reform effort than the substance of this particular model.

march of progress" (8 March 2018) available at <www.bloomberg.com/view/articles/2018-03-08/revived-trans-pacific-partnership-shows-trade-will-go-on-without-u-s>.

21. See, e.g., US BIT Model (2012) at Art. 12(3). ("The Parties recognize that each Party retains the right to exercise discretion with respect to regulatory, compliance, investigatory, and prosecutorial matters, and to make decisions regarding the allocation of resources to enforcement with respect to other environmental matters determined to have higher priorities. Accordingly, the Parties understand that a Party is in compliance with paragraph 2 where a course of action or inaction reflects a reasonable exercise of such discretion, or results from a *bona fide* decision regarding the allocation of resources.") The text of the Model BIT is available at <www.state.gov/documents/organization/188371.pdf>.

2. *Transatlantic Trade and Investment Partnership (TTIP)*[22]

The TTIP is the EU's most contemporary initiative and perhaps one of the most elaborate. The reforms it introduces appear both fundamental and progressive. With respect to substantive investor obligations, it adopts a non-interventionist approach.

> "1. The provisions of this section shall not affect the right of the Parties to regulate within their territories through measures necessary to achieve legitimate policy objectives, such as the protection of public health, safety, environment or public morals, social or consumer protection or promotion and protection of cultural diversity.
> 2. For greater certainty, the provisions of this section shall not be interpreted as a commitment from a Party that it will not change the legal and regulatory framework, including in a manner that may negatively affect the operation of covered investments or the investor's expectations of profits."

With the exception of a modest check "the necessity test" might impose, this essentially gets rid of external standards that investment treaties impose on signatories and leaves domestic regulatory space largely unconstrained in the areas of the environment, health and other legitimate domestic concerns. Indeed, it specifically exempts such domestic regulations from external scrutiny.[23] The chosen approach is thus not to prescribe external substantive sustainable development standards but to leave the domestic regulatory space unaffected by treaty standards. In fact, it goes as far as expressly eliminating any semblance of a stabilization clause.[24]

3. *EU-Canada Comprehensive Economic and Trade Agreement (CETA)*

The EU-Canada Comprehensive Economic and Trade Agreement (ECTA) is the first fully in force contemporary investment regime. In terms of investor obligations, just like TTIP, it takes a non-interventionist domestic regulatory approach. It does not prescribe external standards but almost completely preserves domestic policy space in the areas of environment, health, safety and morals.[25] This would mean that to the extent the states

---

22. The text and comprehensive information relative to the TTIP is available at <http://ec.europa.eu/trade/policy/in-focus/ttip/documents-and-events/index_en.htm#eu-position>.
23. TTIP, Art. 2(1): "The provisions of this section shall not affect the right of the Parties to regulate within their territories through measures necessary to achieve legitimate policy objectives, such as the protection of public health, safety, environment or public morals, social or consumer protection or promotion and protection of cultural diversity."
24. TTIP, Art. 2(2) ("For greater certainty, the provisions of this section shall not be interpreted as a commitment from a Party that it will not change the legal and regulatory framework, including in a manner that may negatively affect the operation of covered investments or the investor's expectations of profits.").
25. CETA, Art. 8.9. (Investment and regulatory measures)

    "1. For the purpose of this Chapter, the Parties reaffirm their right to regulate within their territories to achieve legitimate policy objectives, such as the protection of public health, safety,

parties wish to impose certain obligations on the investors, they may do so in their domestic laws, which will be exempt from any internationally agreed external standards.

4. *Indian BIT Model*

Profusely disappointed by its abysmal track record in ISDS, as of 2015, India sought to renounce its existing BITs and replace them with a new model.[26] It unveiled a draft in March 2015 for comment.[27] The comments overwhelmingly suggested that India might have overcorrected to the perceived inequities of the existing mechanism. India issued a final version, which moderated the initial changes.[28] Although the initially proposed changes are put to rest for now as far as India is concerned, the changes they sought to introduce will continue to have theoretical significance in shaping future policy directions. As such, they are relevant to note here.

Sustainable development was front and center in the Indian Draft BIT Model, which deemphasized protection:

> "Reaffirming the right of Parties to regulate Investments in their territory in accordance with their Law and policy objectives including the right to change the conditions applicable to such Investments; and

---

the environment or public morals, social or consumer protection or the promotion and protection of cultural diversity.
2. For greater certainty, the mere fact that a Party regulates, including through a modification to its laws, in a manner which negatively affects an investment or interferes with an investor's expectations, including its expectations of profits, does not amount to a breach of an obligation under this Section.
3. For greater certainty, a Party's decision not to issue, renew or maintain a subsidy:
(a) in the absence of any specific commitment under law or contract to issue, renew, or maintain that subsidy; or
(b) in accordance with any terms or conditions attached to the issuance, renewal or maintenance of the subsidy,
does not constitute a breach of the provisions of this Section.
4. For greater certainty, nothing in this Section shall be construed as preventing a Party from discontinuing the granting of a subsidy, or requesting its reimbursement where such measure is necessary in order to comply with international obligations between the Parties or has been ordered by a competent court, administrative tribunal or other competent authority, or requiring that Party to compensate the investor therefor."

(Footnotes omitted.)

26. For a discussion of India's new model, see Won KIDANE, "China's and India's Investment Treaty Approaches and Implications for Africa", 49 Loyola Chicago Law Journal (2018) pp. 406, 445-461.
27. The Draft Model BIT was released for comment in March 2015. A copy of the Draft is available at <www.mygov.in/sites/default/files/master_image/Model%20Text%20for%20the%20Indian%20Bilateral%20Investment%20Treaty.pdf>.
28. The official approved and signed final Model BIT Text is Referenced F. No. 26/5/2013-iC, Government of India Ministry of Finance Department of Economic Affairs (Investment Division), Northern Block, New Delhi, Dated 28 December 2015. The Model Text is available on the Website of the Indian Ministry of Finance at <http://investmentpolicyhub.unctad.org/Download/TreatyFile/3560> (last accessed 11 September 2018).

> Seeking to align the objectives of Investment with sustainable development and inclusive growth of the Parties[.]"[29]

With respect to investor obligation and sustainable development, the Indian Draft BIT did something quite remarkable. Not only did it prescribe elaborate investor obligation rules on labor, environmental protection, finance and corruption, it also sanctioned their violations by nullifying the investor's treaty protections. It sought to effect this as follows.

The investor obligations the Draft sets forth include compliance with anti-corruption laws,[30] disclosure of information about the investor and its investments including the sources of its finances,[31] compliance with labor and employment laws[32] as well as environmental, human rights and tax laws.[33] Under the Draft,

> "'Investment' means an Enterprise in the Host State, constituted, organised and operated in compliance with the Law of the Host State and owned or controlled in good faith by an Investor:
> (i) in accordance with this Treaty; and
> (ii) that is at all times in compliance with the obligations in Articles 9, 10, 11 and 12 of Chapter III of this Treaty."[34]

Entitlement to treaty protection thus depends on holding the investment in good faith and compliance to domestic laws relating to sustainable development. For example, Art. 9 imposes an obligation not to engage in corrupt activities and sets forth detailed rules on what is prohibited, including lobbying. Technically, therefore, the violation of the anti-corruption provision would deny the protection of the treaty to the investor because the investment would not be a covered investment under the definition. The violations of Arts. 10 (failure to disclose required information), 11 (failure to comply with tax obligations), and 12 (failure to comply with host state laws including minimum wage requirements) have a similar effect of the denial of protection. Consider the application of Art. 12 for example.

---

29. Draft Indian BIT Text, Preamble. The final Model Text states:

> "Desiring to promote bilateral cooperation between the Parties with respect to foreign investments; and
> Recognizing that the promotion and the protection of investments of investors of one Party in the territory of the other Party will be conducive to the stimulation of mutually beneficial business activity, to the development of economic cooperation between them and to the promotion of sustainable development,
> Reaffirming the right of Parties to regulate investments in their territory in accordance with their law and policy objectives."

Final Model Text, at Preamble.

30. See Draft BIT Text, Art. 9.
31. See Draft BIT Text, Art. 10.
32. See Draft BIT Text, Art. 12.
33. See Draft BIT Text, Arts. 11 and 12.
34. Draft BIT Text, at Art. 1.6.

> "12.1 Investors and their Investments shall be subject to and comply with the Law of the Host State. This includes, but is not limited to, the following:
> (i) Law concerning payment of wages and minimum wages, employment of contract labour, prohibition on child labour, special conditions of work, social security and benefit and insurance schemes applicable to employees;
> (ii) information sharing requirements of the Host State concerning the Investment in question and the corporate history and practices of the Investment or Investor, for purposes of decision making in relation to that Investment or for other purposes;
> (iii) environmental Law applicable to the Investment and its business operations;
> (iv) Law relating to conservation of natural resources;
> (v) Law relating to human rights;
> (vi) Law of consumer protection and fair competition; and
> (vii) relevant national and internationally accepted standards of corporate governance and accounting practices."

Read in conjunction with the Draft Text's definition of investment, any violation of this provision would deny protection by excluding whatever capital invested from the definition of investment. That would mean any failure to meet "Law relating to human rights" or "relevant national and internationally accepted standards of corporate governance and accounting practices". In practical terms, this would mean that any alleged violations of any one of these provisions would have to be litigated to determine whether there is a protected investment in the first place.[35]

The Final Model BIT kept only a considerably weakened and permissive provision on corporate social responsibility. It reads in simple terms:

> "Investors and their enterprises operating within its territory of each Party shall endeavour to voluntarily incorporate internationally recognized standards of corporate social responsibility in their practices and internal policies, such as statements of principle that have been endorsed or are supported by the Parties. These principles may address issues such as labour, the environment, human rights, community relations and anti-corruption."[36]

35. The final text defines "investment" simply as:

> "an enterprise constituted, organised and operated in good faith by an investor in accordance with the law of the Party in whose territory the investment is made, taken together with the assets of the enterprise, has the characteristics of an investment such as the commitment of capital or other resources, certain duration, the expectation of gain or profit, the assumption of risk and a significance for the development of the Party in whose territory the investment is made".

Indian Final BIT Model Text, at Art. 1.4.

36. Model BIT Text, Art. 12.

5. *The Draft Pan-African Investment Code*

The Draft Pan-African Investment Code ("PAIC" or the "Code")[37] is also a part of the most contemporary trend. It is remarkable for both the breadth and depth of the sustainable development related provisions. The Code's objectives are stated in the following terms: "[]to promote, facilitate and protect investments that foster the sustainable development of each Member State, and in particular, the Member State where the investment is located".[38] It also aims at achieving "an overall balance of the rights and obligations among Member States and the investors under this Code".[39] Moreover, it recognizes "the crucial role played by women and youth in the development of Africa".[40] It uniquely adds a note on the free movement of persons as a "fundamental pillar of African integration". [41]

PAIC also contains perhaps the most elaborate investor obligations rules. For example, it requires investments to comply with "nationally and internationally accepted standards of corporate governance",[42] and "[e]nsure the equitable treatment of all shareholders, in accordance with national laws".[43] The Code also obligates investors to undertake "socio-political obligations" and refrain from political interference and respect "socio-cultural values".[44]

PAIC's other notable provisions include anti-bribery,[45] corporate social responsibility, the obligation to contribute to the achievement of "sustainable development of the host state",[46] business ethics, and human rights. The human rights provision requires member states to "support and respect the protection of internationally recognized human rights", and more importantly, "[e]nsure equitable sharing of wealth incurred from investments".[47] PAIC goes further to uniquely provide that: "Member States may adopt policies on cultural and linguistic diversity in promotion of investments."[48] Relatedly, PAIC omits the fair and equitable treatment and full protection and security provisions

---

37. The text of the Pan-African Investment Code is available at <https://au.int/sites/default/files/documents/32844-doc-draft_pan-african_investment_code_december_2016_en.pdf>. It is important to note this draft is under review and may change substantially. Structurally, if the PAIC were to be adopted, it would have the potential of replacing intra-Africa investment treaties over time. See PAIC, Art. 3(2) ("Notwithstanding Paragraph 1, Member States may agree that this Code could be reviewed to become a binding instrument and to replace the intra-African bilateral investment treaties (BITs) or investment chapters in intra-African trade agreements after a period of time determined by the Member States or after the termination period as set in the existing BITs and investment chapters in the trade agreements.").
38. PAIC, Art. 1.
39. PAIC, Preamble.
40. PAIC, Preamble.
41. PAIC, Preamble.
42. PAIC, Art. 19(1).
43. PAIC, Art. 19(3)(a).
44. PAIC, Art. 20.
45. See PAIC, Art. 21.
46. PAIC, Art. 22(3).
47. PAIC, Art. 24(a) and (e).
48. PAIC, Art. 38.

that most traditional investment treaties contain. In this regard, the balance that the PAIC attempts to strike appears to tilt towards sustainability than investment protection.

6. *BITs Concluded in 2016 and 2017*

There are at least forty-nine known BITs concluded in the years 2016 and 2017.[49] The texts of sixteen of the forty-nine are publicly available in English.[50] This section surveys the sustainable development provisions of these BITs.

A close review of the sustainable development related provisions of the sixteen BITs concluded in 2016 and 2017 shows that all but four contain some reference to sustainable development in varying details.[51] All of the twelve BITs that make express reference to sustainable development goals do so in their preambles and a few provisions often focusing on the environment, labor, corporate social responsibility, human rights, and anti-corruption. All of these provisions, with one exception discussed below, seek to regulate state behavior and are formulated in permissive terms. They do not seek to impose direct sustainable development obligations on the investor. The most common formulation is the following:

> "*Article 15 Health, Safety and Environmental Measures*
> The Parties recognize that it is inappropriate to encourage investment by relaxing their health, safety or environmental measures. Accordingly, a Party should not waive or otherwise derogate from, or offer to waive or otherwise derogate from, those measures to encourage the establishment, acquisition, expansion or retention in its area of an investment of an investor. If a Party considers that the other Party has offered such an encouragement, it may request consultations with the other Party and the two Parties shall consult with a view to avoiding the encouragement."[52]

The one exception mentioned above is the treaty between Iran and Slovakia. It slightly departs from common formulation by seeking to impose certain affirmative obligations in the following terms:

> *Article 10. Environmental and labor rights and other standards*
> 1. The Contracting Parties recognize that it is inappropriate to encourage investment by relaxing labor, public health, safety or environmental measures. They shall not waive or otherwise derogate from, or offer to waive or otherwise derogate from, such measures as an encouragement for the establishment, acquisition, expansion or retention in their territories, of an investment.

49. See Recent IITs tab at <http://investmentpolicyhub.unctad.org/IIA/MostRecentTreaties#iiaInnerMenu>.
50. See *id.*
51. The four that do not contain any express reference to any sustainable development related provisions are Rwanda-Morocco; Japan-Kenya; UAE-Mexico, UAE-Nigeria.
52. Canada-Hong Kong /China, BIT, at Art. 15.

> 2. Recognizing the right of each Contracting Party to establish its own level of environmental protection and its own sustainable development policies and priorities, and to adopt or modify its environmental laws and regulations, each Contracting Party shall ensure that its laws and regulations provide for appropriate levels of environmental protection and shall strive to continue to improve those laws and regulations.
> 3. *Investors and investments should apply national, and internationally accepted, standards of corporate governance for the sector involved, in particular for transparency and accounting practices. Investors and their investments should strive to make the maximum feasible contributions to the sustainable development of the Host State and local community through appropriate levels of socially responsible practices.*"[53] (Emphasis added.)

Even this provision is ostensibly permissive as the terminology employed is "should strive" rather than a clear-cut mandatory rule. Overall, it is fair to conclude that there is no robust movement towards using BITs for the purpose of imposing any meaningful substantive obligations on investors. Although there appears to be an increase in the number of references to sustainable development, the provisions are almost invariably designed to preserve the state's policy space than to impose external obligations on the investor. As such, to the extent the newer treaties depart from tradition, they purport do so only inasmuch as they shrink the scope of the protection of investment under the treaties' protection provisions.

Moreover, in terms of the substantive obligations, no South-South or North-South patterns could be discerned. An example of the most elaborate one is the Morocco-Nigeria BIT. Reference to sustainable development runs through the text beginning from the preamble[54] and definition of investment,[55] and continues to address the

---

53. Iran-Slovakia BIT, at Art. 10.

54. "RECOGNIZING the important contribution investment can make to the sustainable development of the state parties, including the reduction of poverty, increase of productive capacity, economic growth, the transfer of technology, and the furtherance of human rights and human development;
SEEKING to promote, encourage and increase investment opportunities that enhance sustainable development within the territories of the state parties;
UNDERSTANDING that sustainable development requires the fulfillment of the economic, social and environmental pillars that are embedded within the concept;
REAFFIRMING the right of the State Parties to regulate and to introduce new measures relating to investments in their territories in order to meet national policy objectives and taking into account any asymmetries with respect to the measures in place, the particular need of developing countries to exercise this right;
SEEKING an overall balance of the rights and obligations among the State Parties, the investors, and the investments under this Agreement;".

55. Art. 1(3): "'*Investment*' Investment means an enterprise within the territory of one State established, acquired, expanded or operated, in good faith, by an investor of the other State in accordance with law of the Party in whose territory the investment is made taken together with the asset of the enterprise which contribute sustainable development of that Party and has the characteristics of an investment involving a commitment of capital or other similar resources, pending profit, risk-taking and certain duration."

environment,[56] labor standards and human rights,[57] as well as corruption[58] in great detail. On the opposite side of the spectrum are Rwanda-Morocco, Japan-Kenya, UAE-Mexico,

---

56. "*Article 13. Investment and Environment*
(1) The Parties recognize that their respective environmental laws policies and multilateral environmental agreements to which they are both party, play an important role in protecting the environment.
(2) The Parties recognize that each Party retains the right to exercise discretion with respect to regulatory, compliance, investigatory, and prosecutorial matters and to make decisions regarding the allocation of resources to enforcement with respect to other environmental matters determined to have higher priorities.
(3) The Parties recognize that each Party undertakes to respect and observe the social responsibility owed to the other Party.
(4) Nothing in this Agreement shall be constructed to prevent a Party from adopting maintaining, or enforcing, in a non-discriminatory manner, any measure otherwise consistent with this Agreement that it considers appropriate to ensure that investment activity in its territory is undertaken in a manner sensitive to environmental and social concerns."

57. "*Article 15. Investment, Labour and Human Rights Protection*
(1) The Parties reaffirm their respective obligations as members of the International Labour Organization (ILO) and their commitments under the ILO Declaration on Fundamental Principles and Rights at Work and its Follow-up.
(2) The parties recognize that it is inappropriate to encourage investment by weakening or reducing the protection accorded in domestic labour laws. Accordingly, each Party shall ensure that it does not waive or otherwise derogate from or offer to waive or otherwise derogate from its labour laws where the waiver or derogation would be inconsistent with the labour rights conferred by domestic laws and international labour instruments in which both are parties are signatories, or fail to effectively enforce its labour laws through a sustained or recurring course of action or inaction.
(3) The Parties recognize that it is inappropriate to encourage investment by relaxing domestic labour, public health or safety. They shall not waive or otherwise derogate from, or offer to waive or otherwise derogate from, such measures as an encouragement for the establishment, acquisition, expansion, or retention in their territories, of an investment.
(5) Each Party shall ensure that its laws and regulations provide for high levels of labour and human rights protection appropriate to its economic and social situation, and shall strive to continue to improve these law and regulations.
(6) All parties shall ensure that their laws, policies and actions are consistent with the international human rights agreements to which they are a Party."

58. "*Article 17. Anti-Corruption*
(1) Each Contracting Party shall ensure that measures and efforts are undertaken to prevent and combat corruption regarding matters covered by this Agreement in accordance with its laws and regulations.
(2) Investors and their Investments shall not, prior to the establishment of an Investment or afterwards, offer, promise or give any undue pecuniary or other advantage, whether directly or through intermediaries, to a public official of the Host State, or a member of an official's family or business associate or other person in close proximity to an official, for that official or for a third party, in order that the official or third party act or refrain from acting in relation to the performance of official duties, in order to achieve any favour in relation to a proposed investment or any licenses, permits, contracts or other rights in relations to an investment.

and UAE-Nigeria. These BITs contain no reference to sustainable development at all. The only possible conclusion is that the treaty-making process in this field remains remarkably *ad hoc* with no impressive movement towards the elaboration and harmonization of the substantive rules.

III. ACCESS TO INTERNATIONAL ARBITRATION IN CONTEMPORARY TREATIES AND MODELS

From the very beginning, ISDS is understood to be a profound aberration in the rules of *locus standi* under international law. It is unclear whether the designers planned a one-way street or it is just how it evolved. Be that as it may, this section begins with a brief theoretical perspective on access and surveys how contemporary models are attempting to redefine it.

1. *Access Issues in Perspective*

There is certainly some credible evidence suggesting either that the ICSID designers never sought to purposefully exclude the possibility of a treaty-based claim against the investor (whether in the form of counterclaims or direct claims) or that they never purposefully intended to shield the investor from answering treaty-based claims against it on an international arbitral platform. In their recently released book, *Arbitrating the Conduct of International Investors*, Amado, Kern and Doe Rodriguez plausibly argue that the designers did indeed anticipate the possibility, and, in fact, the prospect of proceedings against the investor on the same arbitral platform either in the form of counterclaims or direct claims.[59] They note in particular a forgotten provision that

---

(3) Investors and their Investments shall not be complicit in any act described in Paragraph 1 above, including incitement, aiding and abetting, and conspiracy to commit or authorization of such acts.
(4) A breach of this article by an investor or an investment is deemed to constitute a breach of the domestic law of the Host State Party concerning the establishment and operation of an investment.
(5) The States Parties to this Agreement, consistent with their applicable law, shall prosecute and where convicted penalize persons that have breached the applicable law implementing this obligation."

59. See AMADO et al., *Arbitrating the Conduct of International Arbitrators*, supra fn. 9. Quoting from "Report of the Executive Directors of the International Bank for Reconstruction and Development on the Convention on the Settlement of Investment Disputes between States and Nationals of Other States", para. 13, available at: <http://icsidfiles.worldbank.org/icsid/ICSID/StaticFiles/basicdoc/partB-section03.htm> ("'The Convention [on the Settlement of Investment Disputes between States and Nationals of Other States of 1965, sometimes known as the Washington Convention or, more universally, the ICSID Convention] permits the institution of proceedings by host States as well as by investors and the Executive Directors have constantly had in mind that the provisions of the Convention should be equally adapted to the requirements of both cases.'").
Finding further support for the proposition that the ICSID design did not preclude claims against the investor from commentary offered by none other than the former general counsel of the World Bank, Ibrahim Shihata, who wrote: "The 'balance' which pervades the provisions of the [ICSID Convention] is only natural; the system provides conciliation and arbitration facilities to

featured within an early Netherlands-Indonesia economic treaty, to the effect that a foreign investor "shall comply with any request of the [host State], to submit, for conciliation or arbitration, to [ICSID] any dispute that may arise in connection with the investment".[60] However, this language "quickly disappeared from the provision",[61] and whether by design or evolution, ISDS has remained a one-way street. As Amado, Kern and Doe Rodriguez aptly describe: "Fifty years later, we do not believe it controversial to observe that this aspiration often falls short of reality: there has been a departure from this reciprocal vision of the founders."[62]

There are two barriers to access: the first one is legalistic and mechanical; the second is a quintessential policy dilemma. Whereas the frequently discussed mechanical access problem is more or less symbolic with an engineering solution, the policy dilemma goes to the genetic core of the ISDS design, and as such does not lend itself to a simple solution. Each one is briefly discussed below.

The mechanical access problem revolves around two apparent complications: (1) obtaining the investor's assent to the jurisdiction of the treaty tribunal, and (2) the absence of substantive obligations on the investor in traditional investment treaties.[63] The assent difficulty inheres in the nature of investment treaties. Reciprocal only to the contracting states in the sense of granting each other's investors certain rights by law, the beneficiaries are technically non-parties to the instrument that bestows the benefits on them.[64] Where the political will exists, however, imposing somewhat corresponding

host States and foreign investors alike, and the proceedings may be initiated by either party," *id.* quoting from. I. F. I. SHIHATA, *The World Bank in a Changing World: Selected Essays and Lectures* (M. Nijhoff Publishers 1995) p. 426.

60. *Id.*, p. 13, citing Art. 11 of the Netherlands-Indonesia Agreement on Economic Cooperation (with Protocol and Exchanges of Letters dated 17 June 1968), signed on 7 July 1968 (entered into force on 17 July 1971), 799 UNTS 13.

61. *Id.* p. 13, quoting K. VANDEVELDE, *Bilateral Investment Treaties: History, Policy and Interpretation* (Oxford University Press 2010) p. 458.

62. AMADO et al, *Arbitrating the Conduct of International Investors*, supra fn. 9, at p. 1.

63. See *id.* at pp. 14-16. ("In the case of treaty-born investor-State arbitration, the scope of a tribunal's jurisdiction is more heavily circumscribed still. As with contractual rights and obligations falling within the scope of a contractual arbitration agreement, the scope of a treaty-born tribunal's jurisdiction is often limited to the adjudication of those rights and obligations enumerated within the treaty instrument itself. Further, in sharp contrast to a typical bilateral or synallagmatic contract, there is a failure of mutuality or reciprocity in the treaty model. Where the disputant parties in an arbitration are not the States party to the treaty, but rather one of those States and an investor-national of another, the substantive rights typically flow in a singular direction. The treaty gives rise to obligations in the host State alone, with corresponding rights arising in the foreign investor. Insofar as any 'obligations' might fall upon the investor, these are typically addressed via rules of admissibility or jurisdiction. In other words, an investor may face the need to satisfy certain conditions in order to avail his right to enforce the treaty's substantive guarantees, to gain access to the arbitration mechanism, but there is no justiciable obligation imposed upon the investor. The forum often operates as a one-way street. There is thus little prospect under the text of present investment treaties for host State claims, or indeed even a host State counterclaim once an investor has elected to launch his own. In the case of a host State counterclaim lodged in response to an investor's claim which is founded upon the respondent State's treaty obligations alone, there often prevails a vacuum of justiciable obligations of the investor. Prospects of any claim by a host State national are smaller still.")

64. *Id.*

duties and designing mechanisms of their enforcement through the arbitral process are limited only by imagination. Indeed, Amado, Kern and Doe Rodriguez chart out possible solutions to the assent question in some detail.[65]

Unlike the mechanical problems that lend themselves to engineering solutions, the political economy presents a more profound dilemma. Canada's dilemma in its recent NAFTA negotiations demonstrates this aspect of the problem very well. Its dilemma is rooted in its dual objectives of protecting its own policy space while at the same time ensuring the maximum possible protection and access to its investors in less developed markets. As a matter of fact, thirty-nine of all eighty-four known NAFTA cases were against Canada. It has so far reportedly paid at least CAD 215 million in compensation to satisfy these claims. On the other hand, however, Canada is a party to forty-three BITs and its enterprises have initiated at least forty-four investor-state claims seeking billions in damages.[66] The political economy does thus require a choice between these competing interests and values. With this background, this section observes trends in both the mechanics and political economy of investor obligations and access.

2. *Counterclaims and Direct Claims Against Investors in Contemporary Treaties and Models*

Although it does not directly introduce any notable substantive investor obligations, the TPP allows the submission by the host state of counterclaims.[67] The counterclaims

65. See *id.* at Chapter 3, Jurisdiction *Ratione Personae*: The Foreign Investor; See also Chapter 2, The Four Models. The authors envision the possibility of granting access to host states and their nationals or communities via various treaty, contractual, or municipal legislative instruments with a caution that this might require the exploration of non-ICSID venues, as a claim by a host state national against the investor would not involve "a Contracting State" for purposes of ICSID jurisdiction. Two remedies they propose are to either make the home state a guarantor of the investor's obligations, or to have the host state espouse the claims of its nationals, as in the old saying "whoever ill-treats a citizen indirectly injures the State". *Id.* at pp. 23-24, 42-55. In their words, "[w]here a foreign investor becomes bound by obligations owing to a host State national, where such host State national sufficiently assigns a corresponding claim to the host State, and where the host State then initiates arbitration as opposable to the investor, there is a dispute between a State and a national of another State". *Id.* at pp. 54-55. For more nuanced models they propose, see *id.* at pp. 55-66 (what they have labeled the *Qui Tam* Model, in which a host state national prosecutes the state's claim as its appointed representative, even in an extreme case where the state might ultimately oppose the action – this they suggest could be achieved through domestic rules) and pp. 66-67 (what they have called the Hybrid Model, where the host state national first assigns his claim to his state (as under the Espousal Model), and the state thereafter appoints this national as its representative for the prosecution of the claim (as under the *Qui Tam* Model)). For a tabular overview of the models, including cross-references to graphical illustrations, see *id.* at p. 69, Table 2.1.
66. See Riyaz DATTU, Sonja PAVIC, "Canada Seeks to Reform NAFTA Investor-State Dispute Settlement Chapter" (23 August 2017). Available at <www.lexology.com/library/detail.aspx?g=35def3e7-276a-4e78-9b31-e209151a927f> (last accessed 26 December 2017).
67. See TPP Investment Chapter, Art. 9.19. ("2. When the claimant submits a claim pursuant to paragraph 1(a)(i)(B), 1(a)(i)(C), 1(b)(i)(B) or 1(b)(i)(C), the respondent may make a counterclaim in connection with the factual and legal basis of the claim or rely on a claim for the purpose of a set off against the claimant.")

presumably arise out of what the text refers to as "investment authorization"[68] or "investment agreement".[69] These instruments would naturally contain certain reciprocal obligations and a choice of law that governs such obligations.[70] The counterclaims would thus assert breach of the investor's obligations under these instruments and the domestic laws that they select in addition to principals of international law referred to in the treaty.[71]

The TPP does not create any mechanism for direct treaty claim by the host state against the investor. It appears then that the only mechanism for direct claims against the investor would be limited to those contained in the investment agreements, which in many cases would have some type of non-treaty contract-based international arbitration option.

Under the TPP, there is no direct or indirect reference to host communities' access to international arbitration against the investor. The counterclaims provisions do, however, anticipate that causes of action arising out of investment agreements could be brought to international arbitration at least in the form of counterclaims by the host state. Since the treaty effectively integrates the investment agreement, it is not inconceivable that where the investment agreement provides for host community rights and imposes corresponding substantive obligations on the investor for the benefit of such communities, the communities would have standing to present counterclaims against the investor. The mechanics of how these community counterclaims could be presented would be determined by the exact prescriptions in the investment agreement and the arbitration rules that apply in the treaty claim.

TTIP does not anticipate treaty-based sustainable development related counterclaims before the treaty-based international investment court that it seeks to establish.[72] This is

---

68. See TPP, definition of terms ("investment authorisation means an authorisation that the foreign investment authority of a Party grants to a covered investment or an investor of another Party").
69. See TPP, definition of terms: ("investment agreement means a written agreement that is concluded and takes effect after the date of entry into force of this Agreement between an authority at the central level of government of a Party and a covered investment or an investor of another Party and that creates an exchange of rights and obligations, binding on both parties under the law applicable under Article 9.25.2 (Governing Law), on which the covered investment or the investor relies in establishing or acquiring a covered investment other than the written agreement itself, and that grants rights to the covered investment or investor…").
70. See TPP, Art. 9.25.
71. See TPP, Art. 9.25(2) ("2. Subject to paragraph 3 and the other provisions of this Section, when a claim is submitted under Article 9.19.1(a)(i)(B) (Submission of a Claim to Arbitration), Article 9.19.1(a)(i)(C), Article 9.19.1(b)(i)(B) or Article 9.19.1(b)(i)(C), the tribunal shall apply: (a) the rules of law applicable to the pertinent investment authorisation or specified in the pertinent investment authorisation or investment agreement, or as the disputing parties may agree otherwise; or (b) if, in the pertinent investment agreement the rules of law have not been specified or otherwise agreed: (i) the law of the respondent, including its rules on the conflict of laws; and (ii) such rules of international law as may be applicable.")
72. As it is common knowledge by now, TTIP seeks to establish a court of first instance (TTIP, Art. 9) and an appeals court (TTIP, Art. 10) to replace the existing ISDS mechanism. This is an area of current debate but the aspect that is most related to the topic counterclaims is the identification of the parties. The definitional and other relevant sections recognize only three possible parties: the Claimant, the Respondent, a third party called non-disputing Party, which is always the home state of the investor. No other party is anticipated. See TTIP, at definition of terms: ("'disputing

consistent with its non-interventions complete domestic policy-space approach.[73] By eliminating external substantive standards on certain narrowly defined areas of regulation such as health and the environment, the TTIP effectively renders the provision of access to international arbitration for the host state in the form of counterclaims both improbable and unnecessary. It essentially presumes that the state would have domestic remedies at its disposal and the treaty does not attempt to moderate it.

For the highly advanced economies represented in the TTIP, the elimination of access to international decision-making may not have serious consequences but as emerging literature would suggest, for developing host countries, an arbitral award against an offending investor may at times have a greater chance of enforcement abroad than their domestic court judgments.[74] As such, access in some cases remains essential. Some of the other models discussed below would seem to have taken this into account.

Similarly, the TTIP dispute settlement design does not anticipate treaty claims by the host state against the investor mainly because the remedy that it anticipates for matters of sustainability is almost exclusively domestic.

The CETA establishes the Investment Court System (ICS) with an appellate mechanism[75] but it does nothing to modify the existing ISDS rules of *locus standi*. Taking a similar domestic approach as the TTIP, the CETA does not anticipate treaty-based counterclaims. Barring some creative lawyering, which cannot be ruled out, counterclaims before the CETA court thus generally appear improbable not only because the substantive treaty rules impose no direct investor obligations but also because unlike the TPP, domestic contractual documents such as the investment agreement, which

---

parties' means the claimant and the respondent; 'claimant' means an investor of a Party, as defined in Article 1 of Chapter X (General Provisions), which seeks to submit or has submitted a claim pursuant to this section, either (a) acting on its own behalf; or (b) acting on behalf of a locally established company which it owns or controls. The locally established company shall be treated as a national of another Contracting State for the purposes of Article 25(2)(b) of the Convention on the Settlement of Investment Disputes between States and Nationals of Other States of 18 March 1965 (ICSID-Convention). 'Non-disputing Party' means either the United States, when the respondent is the European Union or a Member State of the European Union; or the European Union, when the United States is the respondent. 'Respondent' means either the United States; or in the case of the European Union, either the European Union or the Member State of the European Union concerned as notified pursuant to Article 5.").

73. TTIP, Art. 2 ("1. The provisions of this section shall not affect the right of the Parties to regulate within their territories through measures necessary to achieve legitimate policy objectives, such as the protection of public health, safety, environment or public morals, social or consumer protection or promotion and protection of cultural diversity. 2. For greater certainty, the provisions of this section shall not be interpreted as a commitment from a Party that it will not change the legal and regulatory framework, including in a manner that may negatively affect the operation of covered investments or the investor's expectations of profits.").

74. See AMADO et al, *Arbitrating the Conduct of International Investors*, supra fn. 9, at Chapter 1, The Legal Landscape.

75. See CETA, Arts. 8.27 and 8.28. Canada is also reportedly advocating for a similar ICS approach in the ongoing NAFTA negotiations. See Riyaz DATTU, Sonja PAVIC, "Canada Seeks to Reform NAFTA Investor-State Dispute Settlement Chapter" (23 August 2017). Available at <www.lexology.com/library/detail.aspx?g=35def3e7-276a-4e78-9b31-e209151a927f>.

presumably contain contractual investor obligations, are not recognizably integrated. Direct claims against investors is also not a part of the CETA investor court design.

The TTIP does not anticipate the possibility of host communities accessing international decision-making because of its almost exclusive domestic remedies approach. Similarly, there are no traces of host community standing under the CETA investment court system. This is an issue left for domestic legal processes. In the United States and Canada, the various Keystone pipeline cases demonstrate how local communities on both sides of the border could hold the host state or the investor liable in domestic court processes.[76] CETA seems to have left host community concerns to these kinds of domestic legal processes.

Although the Indian Draft Text permits counterclaims by the respondent state for violations of investor responsibilities,[77] the Final Model BIT Text maintains most of the provisions of the Draft Text on dispute settlement including exhaustion requirements, but it eliminates the counterclaims provision that would have allowed the host state to proceed against the investor for violations of the investor's responsibilities in such areas as corruption, taxation, disclosure, and generally compliance with the laws of the host state.[78] In terms of access, the Indian Draft BIT had also done something unique: it sought access to the home state's judicial process to hold the investor accountable for actions and omissions in the home state presumably with effect in the host state.[79]

---

76. See Ethan LOU, "TransCanada's $ 15 billion U.S. Keystone XL NAFTA Suit Suspended" (28 Feb. 2017) available at <www.reuters.com/article/us-canada-pipeline-lawsuit/transcanadas-15-billion-u-s-keystone-xl-nafta-suit-suspended-idUSKBN1671W1> ("TransCanada Corp (TRP.TO) has suspended a $ 15 billion NAFTA suit filed against the United States over the Keystone XL pipeline, the company said on Tuesday, after US President Donald Trump approved the project last month.") See also Valerie VOLCOVICI, "Environmental Groups Sue Trump Administration for Approving Keystone Pipeline" (30 March 2017). Available at <www.reuters.com/article/us-usa-pipeline-keystone-lawsuit/environmental-groups-sue-trump-administration-for-approving-keystone-pipeline-idUSKBN1712DZ> ("In two separate filings to a federal court in Montana, environmental groups argued that the U.S. State Department, which granted the permit needed for the pipeline to cross the Canadian border, relied on an 'outdated and incomplete environmental impact statement' when making its decision earlier this month.") An American subsidiary of the Canadian Company, TransCanada Keystone Pipeline had also initiated its own lawsuit against the Obama administration challenging the President's authority to stop the project on environmental grounds. See *TransCanada Keystone Pipeline, LP and TC Oil Pipeline Operations Inc. Plaintiffs, v. John F. Kerry*, complaint available at <www.chamberlitigation.com/sites/default/files/cases/files/16161616/Complaint%20--%20Transcanada%20Keystone% 20Pipeline%20LP%20v.%20Kerry%20%28USDC%20-%20Southern%20District%20of%20Te xas%29.pdf> (last accessed on 26 December 2017).
77. See Draft BIT Text, Art. 14.11. The matters that give rise for counterclaims are violations of Art. 9 (obligations against corruption), Art. 10 (disclosure), Art. 11 (taxation), and Art. 12 (compliance with laws of host state).
78. See Draft BIT Text, Art. 14.11.
79. See Draft BIT Text, Art. 13:

"13.1 Without prejudice to the jurisdiction of the Courts located in the Host State, Investors and its Investments shall be subject to civil actions for liability in the judicial process of their Home State for the acts, decisions or omissions made in the Home State in relation to the Investment where such acts, decisions or omissions lead to significant damage, personal injuries or loss of life in the Host State.

The Pan-African Investment Code contains an independent provision on counterclaims against the investor. It provides in full as follows:

> "*Counterclaims by Member States*
> 1. Where an investor or its investment is alleged by a Member State party in a dispute settlement proceeding under this Code to have failed to comply with its obligations under this Code or other relevant rules and principles of domestic and international law, the competent body hearing such a dispute shall consider whether this breach, if proven, is materially relevant to the issues before it, and if so, what mitigating or off-setting effects this may have on the merits of a claim or on any damages awarded in the event of such award.
> 2. A Member State may initiate a counterclaim against the investor before any competent body dealing with a dispute under this Code for damages or other relief resulting from an alleged breach of the Code."[80]

The intention here is clear that if the investor initiates a claim, the host state may submit its own counterclaims for purposes of set-off or even independent damages. It anticipates that the counterclaims could arise not only out of the Code but also "other relevant rules and principles of domestic and international law". Mechanical access issues such as obtaining investor consent notwithstanding, it appears more expansive than almost all the other models and treaties that make rules for possible counterclaims because almost all reviewed for purposes of this article limit counterclaims to those arising out of the particular substantive obligations contained in the particular treaty itself. In any case, the Code has not taken the extra step of permitting host communities to proceed directly against the investor in international arbitration or other international fora. Their claims would presumably have to be espoused by the host state.[81]

The access provisions of the newer BITs do not show a great departure from the traditional BITs with one exception profiled later. None of the sixteen most recent BITs reviewed expressly permit counterclaims much less direct claims against the investor by the state or its nationals or communities. Indeed most of these BITs do not refer to counterclaims at all. Wherever counterclaims are referred to, it is often to prohibit, not to permit. For example, a relevant provision in the Israel-Japan BIT says:

13.2 The Home State shall ensure that their legal systems and rules allow for, or do not prevent or unduly restrict, the bringing of court actions on their merits before their domestic courts relating to the civil liability of Investors and Investments for damages resulting from alleged acts, decisions or omissions made by Investments or Investors in relation to their Investments in the territory of the Host State."

80. PAIC, Art. 43. But note that under Art. 41, PAIC itself does not extend a standing offer of arbitration to the investor. Presumably, some other instrument would express the state's consent. ("1. Member States may, in line with their domestic policies, agree to utilize the Investor-State dispute settlement mechanism. In the event that the Investor-State dispute settlement mechanism is agreed upon, the process below shall apply....")

81. See AMADO et al, *Arbitrating the Conduct of International Investors*, supra fn. 9, at pp. 42-55 (The Espousal Model).

> "*Article 24*
> 12. In an arbitration under this Article, the respondent shall not assert, as a defense, counterclaim, right of setoff or otherwise, that the claimant has received or will receive indemnification or other compensation for all or part of the alleged damages pursuant to an insurance or guarantee contract." (The only reference to counterclaims.)[82]

In terms of investor liability and access, the Nigerian model concluded with Morocco appears to depart in a significant way albeit in the context of domestic legal process than in international arbitration. It states in relevant part:

> "*Article 20. Investor Liablity*
> Investors shall be subject to civil actions for liability in the judicial process of their home state for the acts or decisions made in relation to the investment where such acts or decisions lead to significant damage, personal injuries or loss of life in the host state."[83]

The most interesting access provision is in the Iran-Slovakia BIT. It is the only exception mentioned above. It reads in relevant part:

> "*General provisions*
> 2. For avoidance of doubt, an investor may not submit a claim under this Agreement where the investor or the investment has violated the Host State law. The Tribunal shall dismiss such claim, if such violation is sufficiently serious or material. For avoidance of any doubt, the following violations shall always be considered sufficiently serious or material to require dismissal of the claim:
> (a) Fraud;
> (b) Tax evasion;
> (c) Corruption and bribery; or
> (d) Investment has been made through fraudulent misrepresentation, concealment, corruption, or conduct amounting to an abuse of process.
> 3. The respondent may assert as a defense, counterclaim, right of set off or other similar claim that the claimant has not fulfilled its obligations under this Agreement to comply with the Host State law or that it has not taken all reasonable steps to mitigate possible damages. For avoidance of any doubt, if the tribunal does not dismiss the claim under paragraph 2 above, it shall take such violations into account when assessing the claim if raised as a defense, counterclaim, right of set off or other similar claim by the respondent." [84]

---

82. Israel-Japan BIT, Art. 24(12).
83. Nigeria-Morocco, Art. 20. Note that the other two Nigerian BITs (with Singapore and UAE) concluded within months of the Nigeria-Morocco BIT do not contain this particular access to the home state's judicial process provision. See generally, Nigeria-Singapore, and Nigeria-UAE BITs.
84. Iran-Slovakia BIT, Art. 14.The remainder of this provision reads:

> "4. The UNCITRAL rules on transparency in treaty-based investor-State arbitration shall apply to any international arbitration proceedings initiated against the Slovak Republic pursuant to this

This provision burdens the investor with two serious consequences if it violates the host state's domestic laws by engaging in fraud, corruption, tax evasion and the like. The first consequence is the loss of investment protection. In essence, it appears to shield the host state from liability by serving as an affirmative defense. In other words, a state that has violated the investor's rights by denying protection otherwise conferred by the treaty, could escape liability by pleading the investor's violations of its domestic laws as a substantive defense.[85] Secondly, the same provision seems to envision the possibility of host state counterclaims for the purpose of mitigation of damages or set-off.

In practice, it is unclear how the tribunal would arrive at the second stage if it is required to dismiss the case upon finding the said investor violation. In any case, even then, however, the purpose of this provision seems to be limited to counterclaims only if the investor initiates the claim first. It does not seem to anticipate a stand-alone or direct claim against the investor in a situation where the investor has not chosen to initiate a claim in the first place. Needless to say, however, that the state or its nationals may avail themselves of domestic judicial remedies against the investor for violations of the aforementioned state laws pertaining to fraud, corruption, and taxation. As mentioned in Sect. III.*1* above, access to international arbitration against the investor may at times be preferable to domestic legal processes against the investor as, at the very least, it would mean access to a more advanced international enforcement regime.[86] Although most interesting by all means, even the Iran-Slovakia formulation does not herald a revolutionary approach to resolving the access dilemma.

IV. CONCLUSION

Designed principally for the purpose of encouragement and protection of investment, traditional international investment treaties neither typically impose any meaningful substantive obligations on the investor nor grant the host state or its nationals and local communities access to international arbitration. Addressing the increasing concerns over the imbalance, some contemporary treaties and models now appear to impose varying degrees of substantive obligations on the investor. A close examination of the various contemporary models and treaties shows that they do so mainly through reference to domestic instruments, not through the addition of corresponding external standards.

The obligations are mostly crafted in the form of broadening the state's policy space in the areas of labor, the environment, corporate social responsibility, anti-corruption,

---

Agreement. The Islamic Republic of Iran shall duly consider the application of the UNCITRAL rules on transparency in treaty-based investor-State arbitration to any international arbitration proceedings initiated against the Islamic Republic of Iran pursuant to this Agreement. Nothing in this Agreement or the applicable arbitration rules shall prevent the exchange of information relating to a dispute between the European Union and the Slovak Republic or vice versa."

85. Given the first sentence of this provision, it could also be viewed as a jurisdictional defense. ("2. For avoidance of doubt, an investor may not submit a claim under this Agreement where the investor or the investment has violated the Host State law.")

86. See AMADO et al, *Arbitrating the Conduct of International Investors*, supra fn. 9, at Chapter 1, The Legal Landscape.

and to a lesser extent, human rights. Indeed, with few exceptions these recent treaties and models do not seek to impose direct obligations on the investor. Ultimately, however, what most additions succeed in doing is constraining the rules designed for purposes of investor and investment protection rather than adding independent investor obligations.

The contemporary models are even less successful in reformulating rules of standing relative to access to international arbitration. The treaties and models surveyed, with few exceptions, do not attempt to create a pathway to international arbitration for the host state or its nationals and communities. This appears to be more a function of policy choice or perhaps simple failure to give considered attention to the abundant range of opportunities, rather than the mechanical – and thus eminently surmountable – barriers to standing discussed in Sect. III above.

Finally, where there is the political will, there are credible engineering solutions to the mechanical access barriers, but states, both developed and developing, may have chosen to continue to believe that international investment law and ISDS should remain true to what has become understood to be its original design of a one-way street. The dilemma thus appears to be one of balancing economic priorities and values rather than the absence of technical craftsmanship. At the more general level, as the North-South dichotomy diminishes and the nationality of capital increasingly loses its meaning[87] and many states simultaneously become recipients and senders of significant capital at the same time, they seem to have left international investment treaties in a state of profound doctrinal uncertainty.

87. See, e.g., Mukhisa KITUYA, Secretary-General of the UNCTAD, "Key Messages in World Investment Report 2016: Investor Nationality: Policy Challenges", at p. xiii. Available at <http://unctad.org/en/PublicationsLibrary/wir2016_en.pdf> ("The blurring of investor nationality has made the application of rules and regulations on foreign ownership more challenging.... About one third of ISDS claims are filed by claimant entities that are ultimately owned by a parent in a third country (not party to the treaty on which the claim is based.").

Arbitration Challenged Part I

Reforming Commercial Arbitration in Response to Legitimacy Concerns

Private and Public Interest in International Commercial Arbitration

Andrés Jana L.[*]

TABLE OF CONTENTS PAGE

I. INTRODUCTION

The topic of this Panel is whether there is a need to reform international commercial arbitration in response to legitimacy concerns that have arisen. That requires addressing what are those legitimacy concerns, and whether a reform is required to address them. As was discussed in the Plenary Session on what legitimacy challenges lie ahead for international arbitration,[1] legitimacy concerns in investment arbitration have received significant attention. The voices that have raised these legitimacy concerns have focused on what they perceive as an inappropriate structure of the current system to properly address the strong presence of public interest in such disputes. Emphasis is put on the fact that investment arbitration constitutes a form of adjudication of public international law.

In the case of international commercial arbitration, criticism comes mostly from the user, as explained in Laura Abrahamson's article,[2] in particular with respect to matters of cost, efficiency and information. In contrast to investment arbitration, the presence of public interests so far has not created major issues as to its legitimacy. Private interests are considered to be predominant in commercial arbitration, whereas public interests appear to be rather exceptional.

This distinction between public and private interests is the standard traditionally used in legal systems to decide whether a matter belongs to the realm of public or private law. In this context, (international) commercial arbitration is seen as an exercise of freedom of contract where private interests prevail: two parties freely agree to resolve their legal dispute before a tribunal formed by private citizens, excluding the jurisdiction of domestic courts. As a result, party autonomy is the basic principle on which arbitration is based. With very few exceptions, parties are free to decide, among other things, how

* Partner at Bofill Mir & Álvarez Jana Abogados (Santiago, Chile); Professor of Law Universidad de Chile. This article was prepared with the collaboration of Catalina Fernández Carter, associate at Bofill Mir & Álvarez Jana Abogados.

1. See this volume, pp. 23-149.

2. Laura ABRAHAMSON, "Costs, Delay and Transparency – A Comment on Continued Legitimacy Concerns from the User's Perspective", this volume, pp. 354-360.

arbitrators will be selected, the rules of arbitration, the seat of arbitration and the law that will govern the dispute.

Nonetheless, international commercial arbitration also engages with concurring public interests, which may lead to tension with its predominantly private nature: for instance, the definition of what is considered arbitrable; what limitations public interest may impose on the parties in the exercise of their private autonomy; the extent to which courts are allowed to intervene in arbitral proceedings, and how much deference courts should give to the decisions of arbitral tribunals. These are all questions that arise in the context of commercial arbitration, and that arbitral tribunals and courts are struggling to answer, both domestically and internationally.

Even though the tension between private and public interests has always been part of commercial arbitration, various factors are pressing for an increased recognition of public interests. The enhanced importance of transparency in modern society; the widespread participation of state entities in commercial arbitration; the blurred distinction between purely private and public interests; the possibility for arbitrators to decide in matters of public interest, among others, are all factors that are making it more difficult to maintain the traditional view pursuant to which international commercial arbitration belongs to the private sphere of the parties and hence is controlled mostly by their interests.

This paper aims to explore the central question of this panel – how could or should commercial arbitration adapt in light of these legitimacy concerns? – from the perspective of the public and private interests concerned in commercial arbitration and how such interests may enter into tension: in particular, how this tension may have an impact on the understanding of arbitration and its traditional features.

For this purpose, it will first address some of the traditional sources of tension between public and private interests: in particular, the determination of arbitrability and public order. Later, it will deal with some of the new challenges that have arisen as a consequence of the presence of public interest, to determine if such challenges demand that international commercial arbitration needs to adapt aspects of its traditional private character.

II. TRADITIONAL SOURCES OF TENSION BETWEEN PUBLIC AND PRIVATE INTERESTS IN ARBITRATION

1. *Traditional Categories of Tension*

Law has always had to deal with a tension between private and public interests. Notwithstanding the classification of an area of law as private, law has an inherently public nature, as it is aimed at maintaining peace and facilitating collaboration.[3] Accordingly, the tension between public and private interests is present in almost every field of law, although in different degrees, and subject to different solutions. For instance, contract law has to deal with the protection of consumers, establishing

3. Enrique BARROS, "*Lo público y lo privado en el derecho*", 81 Estudios Públicos (summer 2001) p. 7.

solutions to address abusive clauses and offering remedies for breaches which differ from its traditional approach.[4]

International commercial arbitration is rooted in the logic of private law: party autonomy is the main principle, reinforced by the principle of limited intervention of courts.[5] Throughout the evolution of arbitration, some states have imposed several restrictions on arbitration agreements,[6] and arbitrators and parties alike experienced judicial and legislative hostility towards arbitration.[7] Such hostility lasted – in general terms – until the twentieth century, when states started adopting conventions on arbitration,[8] while also establishing procedures and an institutional framework to facilitate arbitration.[9]

Although a positive evolution of a state's disposition towards arbitration can be easily identified, it remains true that almost all states have maintained some restrictions, excluding certain matters from the competence of arbitral tribunals. Such restrictions are usually aimed at protecting the public interest, in the understanding that such interest cannot be subject to private dispute mechanisms.

Additionally, even in the most liberal and pro-arbitration states, arbitration still requires, and remains dependent on, the acquiescence of such state. The general framework and organization provided by a particular state to recognize and give effect to arbitration may be categorized as public.[10] States need to give deference to arbitral awards, and most importantly, allow individuals the possibility to submit their disputes to private arbitration.[11] Additionally, international commercial arbitration – either if

4. Notwithstanding this tension, authors recognize that the protection of consumers is still within the realm of contract (and thus, private) law. See Enrique BARROS, *Tratado de Responsabilidad Extracontractual* (Editorial Jurídica, Santiago 2007) p. 244. See also *AT&T v. Concepcion*, 563 US 333 (2011), a divided US Supreme Court decision on whether the Federal Arbitration Act prohibited States from conditioning the enforceability of certain arbitration agreements on the availability of class wide arbitration procedures.
5. The principle of party autonomy is, for instance, recognized in Art. 19 of the UNCITRAL Model Law on International Commercial Arbitration (1985, as amended in 2006), while the limited intervention of courts is established in Art. 5.
6. Gary B. BORN, *International Commercial Arbitration*, Vol. I (Kluwer Law International 2009) p. 38.
7. *Ibid.*, p. 40.
8. See for instance: Hague Convention of 1899 on Pacific Settlement of Dispute; Hague Convention of 1907 on Pacific Settlement of International Disputes; Geneva Protocol of 1923, Geneva Convention of 1927; New York Convention on the Recognition and Enforcement of Foreign Arbitral Awards (1958); European Convention on International Commercial Arbitration (1961); ICSID Convention (1966), Inter-American Convention on International Commercial Arbitration (1975); Inter-American Convention on Extraterritorial Validity of Foreign Judgements and Arbitral Awards (1979), and several bilateral investment treaties (BITs).
9. UNCITRAL Model Law on International Commercial Arbitration (1985), with amendments as adopted in 2006. As of this writing, 80 states have adopted the Model Law, constituting a total of 111 jurisdictions. See <www.uncitral.org/uncitral/en/uncitral_texts/arbitration/1985Model_arbitration_status.html>.
10. Enrique BARROS, "*Lo público y lo privado en el derecho*",. 81 Estudios Públicos (summer 2001) p. 8.
11. Indeed, as has been recognized, "[s]hould they so desire, states can simply legislate to contract the boundaries of arbitrability, or deny it altogether". See Andrew BARRACLOUGH and Jeff WAINCYMER, "Mandatory Rules of Law in International Commercial Arbitration", 6 Melbourne Journal of International Law (2005, no. 2).

rooted under national legal systems or in a transnational legal order[12] – constitutes a system belonging to a public sphere.

Two traditional categories of tension between public and private interests are the determination of what is arbitrable and the compatibility of the arbitral award with public order. These two categories are useful for identifying basic concerns regarding public interest and international commercial arbitration.

The first step in the analysis of arbitration is the determination of what is arbitrable, as some matters are considered to be incapable of resolution by arbitration.[13] This concerns the doctrine of non-arbitrability.

Traditionally, the definition of arbitrability was associated with public interest: it was considered that a dispute was non-arbitrable if it went beyond the individual interests of the parties and concerned public interests (e.g., disputes requiring the application of competition laws, disputes connected with criminal conduct, disputes related to insolvency proceedings, among others).[14] Arbitrability was allowed in matters which were considered to be subject to the parties' freedom of contract.[15]

Consequently, the non-arbitrability doctrine was based on the idea that some matters involving public rights or interests of third parties required resolution by the judicial hierarchy of the state, so that agreements to resolve such disputes by "private arbitration" should not be given effect.[16] In other words, this notion of non-arbitrability was grounded upon the old notion that some categories of disputes, if not subjected to the control of the state itself, may go against sovereign dignity[17] or public interest.[18]

A variation of the non-arbitrability doctrine went even further, stating that the damage that private arbitration may cause constitutes a ground to dismantle arbitration altogether, for the protection of the public interest.[19]

12. Emmanuel GAILLARD, "Transcending National Legal Orders for International Arbitration" in *International Arbitration: The Coming of a New Age?*, ICCA Congress Series no. 17 (2013) p. 371
13. Gary B. BORN, *op. cit.*, fn. 6, p. 767.
14. Klára DRLIČKOVÁ, "Arbitrability and Public Interest in International Commercial Arbitration", 17 International and Comparative Law Review (2017, no. 2) p. 58.
15. See, for instance, in Spain, Art. 2 of Law 60 of 23 December 2003; in Peru, Art. 2 of Legislative Decree 1071 of 1 September 2008, and in Costa Rica, Art. 37 of Law 8937 of 27 April 2011.
16. Gary B. BORN, *op. cit.*, fn. 6, p. 768.
17. Loukas A. MISTELIS, and Stavros L. BREKOULAKIS, *Arbitrability: International & Comparative Perspectives* (Kluwer Law International 2009) p. 6.
18. Accordingly, Courts often argued that "public law issues are too complicated for arbitrators; that arbitration proceedings are too informal; or that arbitrators are like foxes guarding the chicken coop, with a pro-business bias that will lead to under-enforcement of laws designed to protect the public". See William W. PARK, "National Law and Commercial Justice: Safeguarding Procedural Integrity in International Arbitration", 63 Tulane Law Review (1989) p. 647.
19. See Heinrich KRONSTEIN, "Arbitration is Power", 38 New York University Law Review (1963) pp. 699-700:

"Arbitration is power, and courts are forbidden to look behind it. The protection of awards against judicial interference, and, under that umbrella, of the development of organized arbitration as a rule-maker have established 'judicial powers' other than those provided by federal and state constitutions. It is not possible to maintain any legally established policy or order in domestic and international trade, whether it is an order of free competition protected by antitrust legislation or any other type of economic order provided by law, if courts abdicate their power in favor of

In more recent years, the scope of the non-arbitrability doctrine has changed.[20] National courts have increasingly abandoned their traditional distrust of arbitral proceedings and have reaffirmed the vital role of private autonomy, especially when it comes to international commercial matters.[21] Pursuant to this new trend, public interest and non-arbitrability are no longer synonyms: if a certain dispute concerns public interest or requires the application of public law rules, it does not automatically mean that it is non-arbitrable.[22] Further, the presumption in respect of arbitration has radically changed: it is generally recognized that non-arbitrability is an exception to the general rule of arbitrability.

The lack of substantial correlation between arbitrability and public interest is to be noted. The restrictions of arbitrability that are more relevant today do not deal with public interest, but are more related to the origin of arbitration: due to its contractual nature, arbitration cannot affect third parties that are outside the scope of the arbitration agreement.[23] In this sense, the limitation on arbitrability in insolvency disputes is justified by the fact that the resolution of this type of claim can be more efficiently achieved by collective litigation proceedings, where the parties may appear before the same court, thereby eliminating the risk of contradictory awards.[24]

Despite the existence of some limitations, the scope of what can be considered arbitrable is notably more comprehensive today than it was before. Therefore, disputes arising from economic activities involving public interest may be resolved by arbitral tribunals, including private-law enforcement of competition rules, claims related to illegal actions, disagreements concerning intellectual property rights, among others.[25] In this sense, the scope of arbitration has expanded to include new topics that may involve matters of public interest.

Another traditional source of tension between private and public interests in arbitration is related to the possibility of arbitrators to rule on matters of public order.[26] This general category encompasses matters that are mandatory, and that accordingly, are not to be disposed or modified by the parties' agreement.

As a preliminary matter – and as has been anticipated – it should be noted that authors currently differentiate between arbitrability and public order. The fact that a certain

private tribunals serving private interests. American courts are presently confronted with a conflict with such private courts. In the face of the current trends in our society, the central concept of a social regime whose exclusive ordering is the totality of legislative and judicial mandates, has been weakened by the cession of the law to organized arbitration."

20. See Stephan SCHILL, "Developing a Framework for the Legitimacy of International Arbitration", Amsterdam Law School Legal Studies Research Paper No. 2017-23, p. 8.
21. Gary B. BORN, *op. cit.*, fn. 6, p. 837.
22. Alexis MOURRE, "Arbitration and Criminal Law: Jurisdiction, Arbitrability and Duties of the Arbitral Tribunal" in Loukas A. MISTELIS and Stavros L.BREKOULAKIS, *op. cit.*, fn. 17, p. 216.
23. Loukas A. MISTELIS and Stavros L.BREKOULAKIS, *op. cit.*, fn. 17, p 32.
24. *Ibid.*, p. 33.
25. Klára DRLIČKOVÁ, *op. cit.*, fn. 14, p. 69.
26. Although authors have discussed the differences between both, this article will use the concepts of public order to refer to matters traditionally treated both under public order (from civil law, under the doctrine of *ordre public* or *orden público*) and public policy (from common law).

matter is arbitrable does not necessarily mean that it does not involve matters of public order. Arbitrability and public order cover two different aspects.[27]

Public order constitutes a clear manifestation of the tension between private and public interest in arbitration. While international commercial arbitration is fundamentally based on the parties' autonomy, public order provides mandatory rules that restrict such autonomy.

That explains why some authors considered that matters of public order were actually excluded from arbitration.[28] However, nowadays, most scholars agree that the arbitrator may make determinations on mandatory laws, and such determinations should not be subject to revision by state courts.[29] As put forward by Paulsson, "if arbitrators were powerless to make such decisions, any respondent could readily defeat any attempt to arbitrate by raising a spurious defense said to involve public policy".[30]

Other authors have adopted a position that further protects private interest – even surpassing public interest, arguing that if the parties intended on a mandatory rule to be excluded, the arbitrator should respect that will, as the parties could have easily chosen a different law which did not contain such provision.[31] In that sense, the only limitation to the parties' autonomy would be transnational public order – which may not be excluded by any choice of law provision, and which would encompass basic ethical standards and the enduring moral consensus of the international business community.[32]

2. *Mechanisms for Addressing the Traditional Tension*

As stated previously, the traditional tension between public and private interest has been generally resolved in favor of arbitration. That explains why matters excluded from arbitrability have been reduced, expanding the scope of arbitration, while at the same time, allowing arbitral tribunals to decide on matters of public order.

This deference that states have shown towards arbitration is also reflected in the limited grounds under which an arbitral award can be annulled, and in a similar manner, the also limited grounds for denial of recognition and enforcement of such awards.

27. This distinction is, for instance, expressed in the 1958 New York Convention on the Recognition and Enforcement of Foreign Arbitral Awards. Indeed, Art. V(2) of the New York Convention differentiates between awards in which "the subject matter of the difference is not capable of settlement by arbitration under the law of that country" (dealing thus, with arbitrability), and awards whose recognition "would be contrary to the public policy of that country". In turn, the UNCITRAL Model Law on International Commercial Arbitration (1985, as amended in 2006) also makes such a distinction. Art. 34(2)(b), regarding the application for setting aside, distinguishes between cases in which "the subject matter of the dispute is not capable of settlement by arbitration under the law of this State", and cases in which "the award is in conflict with the public policy of this state". Such a distinction is also recognized in Art. 36 (b) of the Model Law, regarding the possibility of enforcement.
28. Klára DRLIČKOVÁ, *op. cit.*, fn. 14, p. 58.
29. Jan PAULSSON, *The Idea of Arbitration* (Oxford University Press 2013) p. 129.
30. *Ibid.*
31. Yves DERAINS, "*L'ordre public et le droit applicable au fond du litige dans l'arbitrage international*", Revue de l'Arbitrage (1986).
32. Andrew BARRACLOUGH and Jeff WAINCYMER, *op. cit.*, fn. 11.

The United Nations Commission on International Trade Law Model Law on International Commercial Arbitration (UNCITRAL Model Law) and the 1958 New York Convention, the two main pillars of the normative architecture of international commercial arbitration,[33] recognize such exceptionality.[34] These basic principles of both texts confirm the view of their drafters that international commercial arbitration is mostly governed by and intended to serve private interests.[35]

However, at the same time, the fact that both the New York Convention and the UNCITRAL Model Law recognize non-arbitrability and public order as grounds (either for the application to set aside or to deny enforceability), confirms that the drafters understood the need to protect public interest in arbitration, even if such protection may be applied only when the tribunal is dealing with "serious departures from fundamental notions of procedural justice".[36] It is in this sense that public order has been invoked – and accepted by tribunals – only in cases of clear violations of fundamental and mandatory legal rules.[37]

---

33. Michael W. REISMAN and Brian RICHARDSON, "The Present: Commercial Arbitration as a Transnational System of Justice: Tribunals and Courts: An Interpretation of the Architecture of International Commercial Arbitration" in *Arbitration: The Next Fifty Years*, ICCA Congress Series no. 16 (Kluwer Law International 2012) pp. 17-65.
34. Indeed, for instance, the UNCITRAL Model Law establishes the application to set aside as the only available recourse against arbitral awards, which will be available in limited cases and provides for exceptional grounds for refusing recognition or enforcement. Indeed, regarding the grounds that may be invoked (and proved) by the party that makes the application for setting aside, Art. 34 of the UNCITRAL Model Law on International Commercial Arbitration (1985, as amended in 2006) includes the incapacity of one of the parties to the arbitration agreement; the invalidity of the arbitration agreement; the lack of proper notice to the party making the application of the appointment of arbitrator or lack of possibility to present its case; the dispute not contemplated or not falling within the terms of the submission to arbitration, or containing decisions on matters beyond the scope of the submission to arbitration; and the composition of the arbitral tribunal or the arbitral procedure in violation of the agreement of the parties. As for the grounds that may be identified by the Court, the UNCITRAL Model Law includes: the subject matter of the dispute is not capable of settlement by arbitration under the law of this state; or the award is in conflict with the public policy of this state. The list is almost identical to the one contained in the New York Convention (See Art. V of the 1958 New York Convention on the Recognition and Enforcement of Foreign Arbitral Awards), and was prepared in an attempt to harmonize international arbitration legislation and to restrict the possibility for state tribunals to intervene. See Explanatory Note by the UNCITRAL Secretariat on the Model Law on International Commercial Arbitration, p. 35:

   "Some outdated laws on arbitration, by establishing parallel regimes for recourse against arbitral awards or against court decisions, provide various types of recourses, various (and often long) time periods for exercising the recourse, and extensive list of grounds on which recourse may be based. The situation (of considerable concern to those involved in international commercial arbitration) is greatly improved by the Model Law, which provides uniform grounds upon which (and clear time periods within which) recourse against an arbitral award may be made."

35. In a similar sense, explaining the view that sees arbitration as a "private normative order", see Stephan SCHILL, *op. cit.*, fn. 20, pp. 17-19.
36. *Ibid.*, p. 35.
37. In other words, "not in cases of judicial disagreement with a tribunal's substantive decisions or procedural rulings". Gary B. BORN, *op. cit.*, fn. 6, p. 2625.

Under the influence of this "normative architecture", national courts around the world have upheld such basic principles. Latin America is a good example, having changed its attitude towards arbitration, from hostility to acceptance.

Indeed, after the extensive application of the Calvo Doctrine during the nineteenth and twentieth century, pursuant to which foreign investors could only make claims before the national courts of the state where the investment was made, Latin American states have shifted their traditional hostility towards arbitration, mostly since 1990.[38] Several Latin American states have adopted the UNCITRAL Model Law,[39] expanding arbitration to areas of public interest,[40] and the general trend nowadays is that national courts may not use an application to set aside an award as an excuse to reopen the case and evaluate the merits of the decision.[41]

However, the tension between private and public interests in commercial arbitration becomes apparent by the fact that when courts depart from this framework, they justify their intervention based on the presence of public interest. This shows that, notwithstanding that this framework theoretically represents the worldwide consensus as to the standards of international commercial arbitration, public interest constitutes a permanent source of risk for unjustified judicial intervention.

Again, Latin America serves as an example. The use of domestic constitutional claims – *Amparos* – against arbitral decisions[42] contravenes the special framework of arbitration that provides for a single recourse against arbitral awards: the request for setting aside. Such use is also problematic, considering that the application to set aside already includes a ground that deals with public interest, which is precisely the reference to public order. In this sense, using constitutional claims to allege transgressions of due process may jeopardize the appropriate balance between public and private interests envisaged in such framework, by granting state courts an excessive power to review arbitral awards.[43]

---

38. Andrés JANA, "International Commercial Arbitration in Latin America: Myths and Realities", 32 Journal of International Arbitration (2015, no. 4) p. 421.
39. Chile, Costa Rica, Dominican Republic, Guatemala, Honduras, Jamaica, Mexico, Nicaragua, Paraguay, Peru and Venezuela. See <www.uncitral.org/uncitral/en/uncitral_texts/arbitration/1985Model_arbitration_status.html> for an updated list. Additionally, for a list of the relevant legislation adopted by Latin American countries, see: Mario CASTILLO, et al., "*El arbitraje en la experiencia latinoamericana*", Revista de la Facultad de Derecho de la Pontificia Universidad Católica del Perú (2008, no. 61).
40. For instance, Colombia has incorporated arbitration agreements in several contracts celebrated by the state. The only limitation is that the arbitrator must decide according to the law, and not ex aequo et bono. In the same sense, in 2004 Brazil adopted Law 11.079 which allowed public entities to participate in arbitrations, and on 2005 adopted Law 11.196 which also permitted arbitration for disputes regarding public concessions. For further details, see Marjorie CÁRDENAS, "*El arbitraje en las concesiones de obras públicas: ¿Fortalecimiento de la posición del Estado en el sistema de solución de controversias?*". Master of Laws thesis , Pontificia Universidad Católica de Chile (2013) pp. 104-110.
41. Andrés JANA, *op. cit.*, fn. 38, p. 427.
42. *Ibid.*, pp. 428-432.
43. This phenomenon of presenting constitutional challenges against arbitration – and therefore the risk it envisages – has also developed in other countries. See Stephan SCHILL, *op. cit.*, fn. 20, pp. 14-16.

III. NEW SOURCES OF TENSION BETWEEN PUBLIC AND PRIVATE INTERESTS IN ARBITRATION

1. *New Sources of Tension*

Against this general framework, new sources of tension have arisen. The concerns of civil society, the internationalization of economic relations, the private presence in matters of public interest, the worldwide demands for transparency, and the increasingly blurred line between what is private and what is public, create an increased pressure for addressing public concerns in areas traditionally considered of the exclusive interest of private parties. This has been the case with law in general, and is also the case with commercial arbitration where new forms of tension are present.

These changes in society, the expansion of arbitrability well beyond the traditional contractual dispute that concerns only the two parties involved, and the participation of state entities in commercial arbitration are sources of new tensions. Accordingly, in the present day, arbitral tribunals deal with an extensive list of matters in which the public interest involved is direct.[44]

Professor Stephan Schill mentions five main factors that explain the significant development and large-scale social significance of commercial arbitration: (i) the reorientation from *ad hoc* to institutional arbitration; (ii) the broadening of the subject matter of disputes that are resolved through arbitration; (iii) the territorial expansion of arbitration, now, of global reach; (iv) the participation of specialized law firms and experienced actors and the proliferation of arbitration as a mechanism for settlement of disputes; and, (v) a convergence of how arbitration is practiced worldwide.[45] All these factors have affected arbitration and have given rise to new sources of tension between private and public interests.

Expressions like *transnational legal order* or the *universal character of arbitration*[46] point to the fact that arbitration needs to have a broader view of the interests at stake. In the words of Professor Schill, this broader social impact has brought to the fore challenges to international arbitration giving rise to a question of international arbitration's legitimacy.[47]

Another effect of the expansion of arbitration as a dispute resolution mechanism is that the participation of state entities now constitutes a common feature of international commercial arbitration.[48] This has forced arbitrators, accustomed to dealing with private parties, to address public interests that are relevant to the dispute. Statistics published by the International Chamber of Commerce (ICC) show that 15.4 percent of the arbitral

44. These matters even include disputes arising out of the state's exercise of regulatory powers. See Stavros BREKOULAKIS, "The Protection of the Public Interest in Public Private Arbitrations", Kluwer Arbitration Blog (8 May 2017) <http://arbitrationblog.kluwerarbitration.com/2017/05/08/the-protection-of-the-publicinterest-in-public-private-arbitrations/>.
45. Stephan SCHILL, *op. cit.*, fn. 20, pp. 8-9.
46. Jan PAULSSON, 2012 Alexander Lecture at the Chartered Institute of Arbitrators <www.ciarb.org/conferences/alexander-lecture-1/>.
47. Stephan SCHILL, *op. cit.*, fn. 20, pp. 8-9.
48. Bernardo M. CREMADES, "*La participación de los estados en el Arbitraje Internacional*", Revista Internacional de Arbitraje (2011).

proceedings initiated in 2017 involved a state or state entity as party.[49] In the past years, the ICC commissioned a Task Force on Arbitration Involving States and State Entities to consider the need to amend its rules to reflect this new reality, and finally prepared a Report,[50] acknowledging that states – and state entities – have certain peculiarities when it comes to arbitration, and that arbitration mechanisms must adapt to address them. Nevertheless, as the result of the ICC Task Force shows, the perceived required changes to the rules in the presence of a state or state entities were few, with none of the changes altering any fundamental aspect of the ICC Rules.[51] This outcome shows an interesting feature of the participation of states or state entities in commercial arbitration, which is that such entities, by choosing to enter into international commercial arbitration agreements, to a large extent, adapt their public interest to the predominant private-interest nature of commercial arbitration.

Other cases, without the involvement of state entities, may also reflect an increased presence of public interests, although in an indirect manner. This is the case in disputes relating to natural resources or public works, or even consumer[52] or labor disputes.[53]

Additionally, the development of arbitration as a global system to resolve disputes that requires predictability and certainty may also bring the issue of a broader interest involved in the disputes that may go beyond the individual interest of the parties: an interest that concerns the arbitration system as a whole. In other words, the notable success of commercial arbitration as a means for resolving disputes has led authors to characterize it as a transnational legal order:[54] an order that goes beyond individual states and to some extent beyond individual disputes.

---

49. The International Chamber of Commerce has reported a total of 810 new cases in 2017, which would mean that arbitrations involving states or state entities would correspond to around 124 cases. Only four of them correspond to arbitration on the basis of a BIT. See <https://iccwbo.org/media-wall/news-speeches/icc-announces-2017-figures-confirming-global-reach-leading-position-complex-high-value-disputes/>.
50. See "ICC Commission Report: States, State Entities and ICC Arbitration" (2017). Available at: <https://iccwbo.org/publication/arbitration-involving-states-state-entities-icc-rules-arbitration-report-icc-commission-arbitration-adr/>.
51. Indeed, the result of the Task Force was the introduction of minor amendment of certain provisions of the ICC Rules, for instance: Art. 1, which used to refer to "business disputes" and was changed to "disputes"; Art. 6 concerning possible objections to the extension of an arbitration agreement; Art. 13 regarding the appointment of arbitrators; the incorporation of the term "impartiality" in Arts. 11 and 14; among others. Other amended rules referred exclusively to investment arbitration.
52. See Stephan SCHILL, *op. cit.*, fn. 20, p. 14. See also Julia A. SCARPINO, "Mandatory Arbitration of Consumer Disputes: A Proposal to Ease the Financial Burden on Low-Income Consumers", American University Journal of Gender Social Policy and Law (2002, no. 3).
53. Stephan SCHILL, *op. cit.*, fn. 20, p. 14, regarding the widespread practice of using arbitration as a mechanism for settling disputes in labor matters. In contrast, Chilean law only recognizes an arbitration proceeding in the Labor Code (Arts. 385-398), in the context of collective bargaining with the employers, but not as a mechanism to solve disputes between the employer and the employee.
54. See Emmanuel GAILLARD, *op. cit.*, fn. 12, p. 373. Authors who support this position state that arbitration transcends legal orders, constituting a different system (the "arbitral legal order"). This does not mean that national legal systems are excluded, but that "the arbitral process no longer hinges on the particularities of the national order of the seat of the arbitration or elsewhere".

The question then is does this increased presence of public interest justify the adoption of reforms in commercial arbitration, or are the current features of the system well suited to absorb them?

As has been mentioned, the public interest is more direct and specific in cases where the state or state entities are a party to a contract that goes to commercial arbitration, as is the case with public works, concessions for public services, government procurement or contracts for the exploitation of natural resources. Taking the findings of the ICC Task Force, only a few changes were required. Interestingly, the Task Force did not consider that transparency was an area where change was required due to the presence of a public entity.[55]

This brings me to the particular area where a discussion for a need of reform in commercial arbitration has taken place: the need for increased transparency in commercial arbitration.[56]

This discussion is not specific to commercial arbitrations where a state or state entity is a party, but is relevant for commercial arbitration as a whole. In particular the debate has been focused on confidentiality and the publication of awards: specifically, the tension between the private interest of the parties in having the dispute resolved with secrecy and the public interest in having access to the result of such arbitration. In the words of Ben Juratowitch "... international commercial arbitration is now a major forum for the resolution of disputes that impact on those other than the parties to them.... There are therefore compelling reasons for people to be increasingly concerned about the fact that it is to a substantial degree happening in secret."[57]

To address this debate, it is useful to refer first to transparency in investment arbitration, and then turn to the issue of confidentiality. During the discussion in UNCITRAL about the adoption of transparency rules for investment arbitration, the justification for adopting such rules was that in investment arbitration there was a public interest that went beyond the interest of the parties involved in the dispute. It was also repeatedly stated that this was a feature that distinguished investment arbitration from commercial arbitration, where such interest was not present in the same form. Such argument does not seem very convincing. As a general matter, it is true that all arbitration investment cases have a direct public interest and that in commercial arbitration such an interest does not always exists. But cases where a state entity is involved may have a similar if not bigger public interest. It will not be long before similar demands for transparency will be made with respect to commercial arbitration where states or state entities are involved. This does not constitute the so-called spill-over effect of investment arbitration on commercial arbitration, but the necessary acknowledgment of the same strong public interest in both types of cases.

---

55. See "ICC Commission Report: States, State Entities and ICC Arbitration" (2017). The Report included minimum references to transparency, maintaining a rule of confidentiality but referring to the possibility for the parties to agree on transparency. It was also established that the ICC Rules were capable of accommodating to eventual demands for transparency.
56. See Ben JURATOWITCH, "Departing from Confidentiality in International Dispute Resolution", Seminar on 8 June 2017 in London on Difficult Issues in Commercial, Investor-State, and State-State Dispute Resolution: Differences and Commonalities, p. 8.
57. *Id.*, pp. 9-10.

In this regard, it is interesting to note that certain countries that have accepted arbitration as a mechanism to resolve contract disputes between state entities and private parties, have established certain requirements of publicity to the arbitration. This is the case, for example, of a recent reform to Arbitration Law in Brazil that made arbitrations that involve public administration subject to the principle of publicity.[58]

Confidentiality is generally considered to be one of the most important features of commercial arbitration.[59] A survey conducted in 2015 by Queen Mary University of London shows that 33 percent of those consulted considered "confidentiality and privacy" as one of the three most valuable characteristics of international arbitration.[60] Another survey conducted in 2016, specific to technology, media and telecommunications disputes, shows that 60 percent of those consulted consider that confidentiality is a "*very important*" feature of international arbitration.[61] Indeed, it is common ground to mention confidentiality as one of the benefits of arbitration,[62] useful for parties that wish to avoid their conflict being in the public domain or accessible to the media, competitors or third parties in general.[63]

There is no single solution to this matter, but in most places commercial arbitrations are mostly confidential most of the time. Countries like the United Kingdom and France recognize an "implied" duty of confidentiality in arbitration.[64] In turn, Australia has not recognized such presumption: In a notorious case – *Esso Australia* – the High Court of Australia found that confidentiality should not be considered an essential attribute of private arbitration.[65] In turn, Brazilian law establishes that public-private arbitration

58. Brazilian Law No 13.129 of 26 May 2015. Art. 2, Third Paragraph. Also the Peruvian Arbitration Act in its Art. 51 orders the publication of arbitral awards in the arbitrations where the Peruvian State intervenes.
59. Gary. B. BORN, *op. cit.*, fn. 6, p. 87. In a similar sense, Stephen Bond, a former ICC Secretary General, stated:

> "It became apparent to me very soon after taking up my responsibility at the ICC that the users of international commercial arbitration ... place the highest value upon confidentiality as a fundamental characteristic of international commercial arbitration ... the fact that these proceedings and the resulting award would not enter into the public domain was almost invariably mentioned."

See Stephen BOND, "Expert Report in *Esso/BHP v. Plowman*", 11 Arbitration International (1995, issue 3).
60. Queen Mary University of London and White & Case, "2015 International Arbitration Survey: Improvements and Innovations in International Arbitration".
61. Queen Mary University of London, International Dispute Resolution Survey "Pre-empting and Resolving Technology, Media and Telecoms Disputes" (2016).
62. Bernardo CREMADES and Rodrigo CORTÉS, "The Principle of Confidentiality in Arbitration: A Necessary Crisis", 23 Journal of Arbitration Studies (2013, no. 3), pp. 25-38.
63. Avinash POOROOYE,and Ronán FEEHILY, "Confidentiality and Transparency in International Commercial Arbitration: Finding the Right Balance", 22 Harvard Negotiation Law Review (spring 2017) p. 275 at p. 278.
64. *Ibid.*, p. 279.
65. See *Esso Australia Resources Ltd v. Plowman* [1995] HCA, 19. In a similar sense, in *Commonwealth v. Cockatoo Dockyard Pty Ltd*, the Court of Appeal of New South Wales established that there could not

would be subject to a principle of publicity.[66] In a more radical provision, Chilean arbitrators are obliged, under an old provision of the Organic Code of Tribunals – to submit a copy of their entire case file to the Judicial Archive.[67] As for international instruments, the UNCITRAL Model Law makes no reference to confidentiality or transparency, while Art. 22 of the ICC Rules on Arbitration provides the possibility for the tribunal to make orders concerning confidentiality – without establishing a general rule; Art. 34 of the UNCITRAL Arbitration Rules (as revised in 2010) refers to the possibility to publish awards with the consent of the parties;[68] and Art. 30 of the London Court of International Arbitration Rules (of 2014) imposes a general duty of confidentiality of the entire arbitration.

Notwithstanding these different approaches, in most places commercial arbitrations are mainly confidential most of the time. In spite of this lack of uniformity, as was mentioned, the prevailing view is that confidentiality is a core element of commercial arbitration

However, considering the development of arbitration, and particularly the increased participation of state entities, several authors recognize that a "public interest" exception may apply in international commercial arbitration, which would serve to mitigate the rule of confidentiality,[69] and have even gone further, to support a default rule of publicity of awards.[70] Other authors have emphasized the importance of confidentiality in arbitration, but still have recognized that the duty of confidentiality is subject to qualifications or exceptions.[71] Additionally, authors recognize that the principle of confidentiality in commercial arbitration "could not stand in the way of a statutory duty to publish the relevant information".[72]

The underlying question is how to find the right balance. It is clear that there is a requirement for more information, in particular for the benefit of the users as Laura Abrahamson's paper shows,[73] which explains why the ICC has adopted certain

---

be accepted that private agreement may exclude, from the public domain, matters of legitimate public concern. *Commonwealth v. Cockatoo Dockyard Pty Ltd* [2007], HCA.

66. See Brazilian Law No 13.129 of 26 May 2015. Art. 2, Third Paragraph of the law establishes that "Arbitration that involves public administration will always be at law and be subject to the principle of publicity".
67. See Art. 455 of the Chilean Organic Code of Tribunals.
68. It is interesting to note that Costa Rica adopted the UNCITRAL Model Law almost verbatim, with a few departures from its original text. One of these changes is the requirement that arbitral awards shall be made public. See Arbitration Law of Costa Rica Law No. 8937 of 27 May 2011, Art. 38.
69. Yves FORTIER, "Arbitrating in the Age of Investment Treaty Disputes", 31 The University of Southern Wales Law Journal (2008, no. 1) p. 8. See also Patrick NEILL, "Confidentiality in Arbitration", 12 Arbitration International (1996, no. 3) p. 312.
70. See Ben JURATOWITCH, *op. cit.*, fn. 56, p. 8.
71. See Patrick NEILL, *op. cit.*, fn. 69, p. 290: consent, compulsion of law, disclosure by leave of the court and disclosure necessary for the purposes of protecting the legitimate interest of an arbitrating party. Seminar on 8 June 2017 in London on Difficult Issues in Commercial, Investor-State, and State-State Dispute Resolution: Differences and Commonalities.
72. *Ibid.*, p. 312.
73. Laura ABRAHAMSON, *op. cit.*, fn. 1.

measures, such as the publication of the composition of the arbitral tribunals.[74] When state entities are involved, the answer in some of the cases is simpler, considering the existence of statutory duties of transparency of such entities.[75] But the more difficult question is whether duties of transparency may be imposed on commercial arbitration, for the benefit of the potential users but also in light of a public interest present in the arbitration. This is especially relevant when the public interest may be indirect – for instance, arbitrations in which the state is not directly involved, but which concern activities developed with public funds, or with a public purpose.

More generally, as Ben Juratowitch argues:

> "[I]nternational commercial arbitration .... is a forum in which claims of corruption of public officials and of breaches of competition law are made and decided, in which States and State-owned entities are routinely parties, and in which large swathes of commercial law, including concerning standard form commercial contracts, are applied...."[76]

It is not questionable that transparency may provide benefits, which are not novel to arbitration: accountability, protection of due process, higher degree of trust and acceptance of arbitration.[77] Transparency may also help to develop arbitral jurisprudence.[78] The question is whether transparency will come as an unacceptable cost for the parties. It seems compelling that the developments in arbitration require acknowledging that arbitration has evolved into a widespread forum for the resolution of disputes that have relevance not only for the parties involved. That being the case, a balance needs to be found: the precise balance between transparency and confidentiality, between private and public interests.

2. *Have These New Sources of Tension Affected the Traditional Features of Arbitration?*

The new demands for transparency may be seen as clashing with the parties' interest in confidentiality, which as explained, is a traditional feature of arbitration. In this matter, it is worth mentioning that in 2014, UNCITRAL adopted Rules on Transparency for Treaty-based Investor-State Arbitration. As its name confirms, such rules are not applicable to international commercial arbitration. The question then is whether the rationale – or part of it – that justified its adoption in investment arbitration may also be present in commercial arbitration. Are there grounds to extend some of these rules to international commercial arbitration, especially taking into consideration the increased participation of state entities? This is relevant, as the main justification to impose these duties of transparency was the fact that, in investment arbitration, public interests were involved. There are several instances in international commercial arbitration where that

74. See <https://iccwbo.org/media-wall/news-speeches/icc-begins-publishing-arbitrator-information-in-drive-for-improved-transparency>.
75. *Ibid.*, p. 62.
76. See Ben JURATOWITCH, *op. cit.*, fn. 56, p. 9.
77. Avinash POOROOYE and Ronán FEEHILY, *op. cit.*, fn. 63, p. 285.
78. *Ibid.*, p. 303.

assertion is also applicable. But in that case, what should be the scope of transparency?[79] Most of the voices favoring transparency in commercial arbitration have focused on the publication of the final awards.

Can this tension between public and private interests affect arbitration's legitimacy as has been the case with investment arbitration? Arbitration is a mechanism of dispute settlement that competes with national courts; therefore the worldwide success of arbitration and its expansion make competition a matter that raises serious potential issues,[80] especially when national courts are also making efforts to become more attractive to resolve commercial disputes.[81]

A system of adjudication of disputes must be concerned with the perception of its users in terms of legitimacy, but also before the overall framework in which it operates. To that end, international commercial arbitration needs to find a way not only to properly resolve the private interest of the parties but also to strike a balance with the public interest present in the dispute. As the question of confidentiality vs. transparency portrays, this poses a challenge to our traditional understanding of arbitration and its function.

To this date, it is not clear how this tension between the traditional features of arbitration and the new pressures coming from the appearance of public interests should be dealt with. A change in the paradigm of commercial arbitration as a system of disputes based on the autonomy of the parties is not required. Arbitration can incorporate these new manifestations of public interest while maintaining its inherently private nature. Moreover, the inherent flexibility of arbitration derived from the parties' autonomy allows for the inclusion of specific arrangements by participants in arbitrations where the public interest has a stronger presence, as is the case when a state or state entity decides to enter into an arbitration agreement. On the other hand, commercial arbitration has to recognize its public dimension, and that the increased relevance of such a public dimension requires due attention to its legitimacy as a global mechanism for resolving disputes.

IV. CONCLUSION

The question for the panel is whether international commercial arbitration should be reformed to respond to legitimacy concerns. This paper proposes that such a question should be addressed by analyzing the traditional tension between public and private interests in international commercial arbitration.

So far, commercial arbitration has been successful in dealing with this public interest with its traditional tools of arbitrability and public order.

79. For instance, the UNCITRAL Rules on Transparency in Treaty-based Investor-State Arbitration establish, in Art. 3, that certain documents will be made available to the public in certain cases.
80. Some authors have referred to international commercial arbitration as a "system of governance", and state that such system raises questions of legitimacy, especially considering the exercise of functions that affect third-parties that are not involved in the arbitration, impacting social expectations. See Stephan SCHILL, *op. cit.*, fn. 20, p. 11.
81. See the Jill Pool Memorial Lecture, "Keeping Commercial Law Up to Date" by Lord Chief Justice of England and Wales, the Lord Thomas of Cwmgiedd. Aston University (8 March 2017).

International commercial arbitration is now facing new challenges. Some of them are coming from external sources such as the legitimacy allegations against investment arbitration, and others are, in a certain manner, a consequence of the incredible success of international commercial arbitration and its expansion to new areas that demand actors to take into consideration public interest, in both, a strict sense – when state entities are directly involved– but also in a broad one – when the dispute between private parties may have impact on others.

Considering its extraordinary expansion, international arbitration needs to address possible concerns that the increased presence of public interests raised, both in specific cases but also in its function as a worldwide system of dispute resolution.

It was suggested at the ICCA 2014 Congress in Miami that the more universal arbitration becomes the more customized it will be for responding to the concerns of specific users. This makes sense: arbitration should not function as a Procrustean bed. As has been mentioned, the ICC's concern for developing special rules for arbitration involving States or state entities is also reflected in arbitration legislation of countries such as Brazil or Peru.

The new developments in international arbitration demand finding a balance between the respect of what is considered to be fundamental and constitutive of arbitration, and the acceptance of the changes that are required to consider the presence of public interests in the dispute.

The debate about the need for increased transparency in commercial arbitration is a good example of the new forms of tensions that commercial arbitration is facing and the need to address them.

As was said, commercial arbitration, as a system of adjudication of disputes requires an ongoing assessment of any possible legitimacy concerns from its users and more broadly from those who have control over the normative structure that permits its functioning.

Commercial Arbitration and the Development of Common Law

Noradèle Radjai[*]

TABLE OF CONTENTS PAGE

I. OVERVIEW

Recent years have seen concerns raised about the increasing use of arbitration and its potential hindrance on the development of common law. The criticism across the common law world is essentially that the growth of arbitration and the subsequent ebbing of court decisions are freezing doctrinal development.[1]

Some critics have gone so far as declaring arbitration responsible for "the end of law".[2] Most recently, the Lord Chief Justice of England and Wales, Lord Thomas, fueled the debate with a controversial speech which called for an urgent rebalancing of the relationship between courts and arbitration, accusing arbitration of turning the common law into "an ossuary".[3] Another critic has lamented that: "Arbitration is retreating into its lair, dragging with it into the darkness the very cases that should be used to develop the common law as it applies to modern commerce".[4]

---

* Partner in the international arbitration team at LALIVE, specializing in commercial and investment arbitration in the energy, telecommunications and construction sectors; member of the Steering Committee of the International Bar Association Arbitration 40 Subcommittee (IBA Arb 40) as well as a member of several other professional associations, namely the London Court of International Arbitration (LCIA), the Chartered Institute of Arbitrators (CIArb), the British Institute of International and Comparative Law (BIICL), the American Bar Association and Arbitral Women.
The author would like to thank Nicole Chalikopoulou for her assistance with this paper.

1. Lord Chief Justice THOMAS, "Developing Commercial Law Through the Courts: Rebalancing the Relationship Between the Courts and Arbitration", The BAILII Lecture 2016 (9 March 2016) p. 10. Available at: <https://www.judiciary.uk/wp-content/uploads/2016/03/lcj-speech-bailli-lecture-20160309.pdf> (last accessed 7 June 2018).
2. Myriam GILLES, "The Day Doctrine Died: Private Arbitration and the End Of Law", 2016 U. Ill. L. Rev. (2016) p. 371 at p. 376.
3. Lord Chief Justice THOMAS, "Developing Commercial Law Through the Courts: Rebalancing the Relationship Between the Courts and Arbitration", The BAILII Lecture 2016 (9 March 2016) p. 10. Available at: <https://www.judiciary.uk/wp-content/uploads/2016/03/lcj-speech-bailli-lecture-20160309.pdf> (last accessed 7 June 2018).
4. Harris BOR, "Comments on Lord Chief Justice Thomas' 2016 BAILII Lecture which promotes a greater role for the courts in international arbitration", Kluwer Arbitration Blog, 11 April 2016,

This paper will explore these criticisms of the legitimacy or reach of commercial arbitration and assess how commercial arbitration should adapt in light of these legitimacy concerns, by exploring the following questions:

(1) Does commercial arbitration hinder the development of common law?
(2) If so, does this hindrance render commercial arbitration any less legitimate?
(3) If so, how should commercial arbitration adapt?

II. DOES COMMERCIAL ARBITRATION HINDER THE DEVELOPMENT OF COMMON LAW?

It is broadly accepted that arbitration is today the most common means of resolving international commercial disputes. In particular, international arbitration has become the method of choice for dispute resolution in certain industries when operating in a cross-border context, such as major construction projects, insurance and reinsurance, and the oil and gas industry.[5] Because arbitration proceedings are often confidential,[6] it is difficult to cite numbers to support these assertions. A renowned German international arbitration scholar, has stated that 90 percent of international economic contracts have an arbitration clause.[7] Even if this may be an exaggeration,[8] data from the major international arbitration institutions show a steady growth in the number of disputes they administer.[9] In the survey conducted by the Queen Mary University of London and White & Case in 2015, 90 percent of the respondents stated arbitration to be the

available online at <http://arbitrationblog.kluwerarbitration.com/2016/04/11/comments-on-lord-chief-justice-thomas-2016-bailii-lecture-which-promotes-a-greater-role-for-the-courts-in-international-arbitration/> (last accessed 26 March 2019).

5. Ank SANTENS and Romain ZAMOUR, "Dreaded Dearth of Precedent in the Wake of International Arbitration – Could the Cause Also Bring the Cure?", 7 Y.B. Arb. & Mediation (2015) p. 73 at p. 75.
6. Alan REDFERN and Martin HUNTER with Nigel BLACKABY and Constantine PARTASIDES, *Redfern and Hunter on International Arbitration*, 5th ed. (Oxford University Press 2009) p. 136 at para. 2.145; Ank SANTENS and Romain ZAMOUR, "Dreaded Dearth of Precedent in the Wake of International Arbitration – Could the Cause Also Bring the Cure?", 7 Y.B. Arb. & Mediation (2015) p. 73 at p. 75.
7. Klaus Peter BERGER, *International Economic Arbitration* (Kluwer Law and Taxation Publishers 1993) p. 8 at n. 62 ("About ninety percent of international economic contracts contain an arbitration clause."); Ank SANTENS and Romain ZAMOUR, "Dreaded Dearth of Precedent in the Wake of International Arbitration – Could the Cause Also Bring the Cure?", 7 Y.B. Arb. & Mediation (2015) p. 73 at p. 75.
8. See, e.g., Gary BORN, *International Commercial Arbitration*, 2nd ed. (Kluwer Law International 2014) p. 97 ("This figure lacks empirical support and is almost certainly inflated: in reality, significant numbers of international commercial transactions – certainly much more than 10% of all contracts – contain either forum selection clauses or no dispute resolution provision at all."); Ank SANTENS and Romain ZAMOUR, "Dreaded Dearth of Precedent in the Wake of International Arbitration – Could the Cause Also Bring the Cure?", 7 Y.B. Arb. & Mediation (2015) p. 73 at p. 75.
9. Christopher R. DRAHOZAL and Richard W. NAIMARK, eds., *Towards a Science of International Arbitration: Collected Empirical Research*", (Kluwer Law International 2005) p. 1, at p. 341; see also BORN, supra fn. 8, at p. 94.

preferred dispute settlement method for cross-border commercial disputes.[10] Therefore, it cannot be denied that arbitration is the primary means of resolving disputes.[11] It follows that this has led, in turn, to a diversion of commercial disputes away from commercial courts.

This diversion of disputes away from the courts is further compounded by the broadening scope of arbitrability, for instance over consumer and employment disputes.[12]

Many of these disputes that are being channelled away from commercial courts are governed by common law. On the latest available statistics from the International Chamber of Commerce (ICC), it would appear that English law and New York alone are the most frequent choices of law.[13] In 2014 English law as a choice of law was in first place with 14.1 percent, followed by US law.[14] It follows therefore that these cases, were they not being diverted to arbitration, would be heard before the courts of the common law jurisdictions. So, it seems logical to conclude that the increase of arbitrations is removing from the state courts cases that might otherwise contribute to the development of common law.

In England, the most recent and vocal proponent of this criticism, Lord Chief Justice Thomas, argues that by taking place behind closed doors, arbitration undermines the "means through which much of the common law's strength – its 'excellence' was developed…". It also "retards public understanding of the law" and "public debate over its application".[15]

In the United States, arbitration, mainly domestic, has been under attack for being "confidential affairs shielded from public view and decided by arbitrators who do not

---

10. *2015 International Arbitration Survey: Improvements and Innovations in International Arbitration*, conducted by Queen Mary University of London and White & Case, p. 2. Available at: <https://www.whitecase.com/publications/insight/2015-international-arbitration-survey-improvements-and-innovations> (last accessed 7 June 2018).
11. Ank SANTENS and Romain ZAMOUR, "Dreaded Dearth of Precedent in the Wake of International Arbitration – Could the Cause Also Bring the Cure?", 7 Y.B. Arb. & Mediation (2015) p. 73 at p. 76.
12. Stavros L. BREKOULAKIS, "Chapter 14: Systemic Bias and the Institution of International Arbitration: A New Approach to Arbitral Decision-Making" in Tony Cole, ed., *The Roles of Psychology in International Arbitration* (Kluwer Law International 2017) p. 339 at p. 339.
13. 2016 ICC Dispute Resolution Statistics published in ICC Dispute Resolution Bulletin (2017, no. 2). Available at: <http://library.iccwbo.org/content/dr/STATISTICAL_REPORTS/SR_0039.htm?l1=Statistical+Reports&AUTH=9b9ace50-7103-4bf8-9c7f-7c3a255074b4&Timeframe=lFpRLm7D9VnsUTYnT4ea734tgV1WUYujvRvjpq6rJov2b2KavSnQg==> (last accessed 7 June 2018).
14. 2014 ICC Dispute Resolution Statistics published in ICC Dispute Resolution Bulletin (2015, no. 1). Available at: <http://library.iccwbo.org/content/dr/STATISTICAL_REPORTS/SR_0037.htm?l1=Statistical+Reports&AUTH=9b9ace50-7103-4bf8-9c7f-7c3a255074b4&Timeframe=lFpRLm7D9VnsUTYnT4ea734tgV1WUYujvRvjpq6rJov2b2KavSnQg==> (last accessed 7 June 2018).
15. Lord Chief Justice THOMAS, "Developing Commercial Law Through the Courts: Rebalancing the Relationship Between the Courts and Arbitration", The BAILII Lecture 2016 (9 March 2016) p. 4. Available at: <https://www.judiciary.uk/wp-content/uploads/2016/03/lcj-speech-bailli-lecture-20160309.pdf> (last accessed 7 June 2018).

write precedential decisions".[16] The lack of *stare decisis* in arbitration has been the reason to suggest that arbitration does not generate law, and by stripping the courts from the caseload consequently leads to the "end of law".[17] The prohibition of class action after the judgments of *AT&T Mobility v. Concepcion*[18] and *American Express Company v. Italian Colors Restaurant,*[19] has resulted in assertions that "entire classes of claims" are evicted from the public justice system, and that "arbitration ... fundamentally precludes the common law development".[20] Even arbitration practitioners refer to the "dearth of precedent".[21]

In Australia, similar problems have been reported about fewer cases reaching the courts, which "has the effect of stunting the development of the common law" in certain legal fields, such as construction, where arbitration is preferred.[22]

Thus, the criticism that arbitration is stunting the development of common law is, to varying degrees, shared across the common law world.

Many have protested against the criticism at this juncture, by referring to the fact that there are still many cases before the courts that contribute to the development of common law.[23] Indeed, 25.7 percent of the cases commenced in 2015 before the Commercial Court were arbitration-related claims.[24] Furthermore, statistics from the Ministry of Justice indicate that over 1,100 cases per year are heard by the commercial

16. Myriam GILLES, "The Day Doctrine Died: Private Arbitration and The End of Law", University of Illinois Review (2016) p. 376.
17. *Id.*
18. *AT&T Mobility v. Concepcion,* 131 S.Ct. 1740 (2011).
19. *American Express Company v. Italian Colors Restaurant,* 133 S.Ct. 2304 (2013).
20. Myriam GILLES, "The Day Doctrine Died: Private Arbitration and the End of Law", University of Illinois Review (2016) p. 409.
21. See A. SANTENS & R. ZAMOUR, "Dreaded Dearth of Precedent in the Wake of International Arbitration – Could the Cause Also Bring the Cure?", (2015) 73(7) Yearbook of Arbitration & Mediation.
22. A. STEPHENSON and A. ANDERSSON, "Arbitration: Can It Assist in the Development of the Common Law – An Australian Point of View", 33 International Construction Review (2016, no. 4) p. 413 (Sect. 5).
23. Sir Bernard EDER, "Does Arbitration Stifle Development of the Law? Should s.69 Be Revitalised?", AGM Keynote Address for the Chartered Institute of Arbitrators (28 April 2016) p. 4. Available at <https://www.londonarbitrators.org/sites/londonarbitrators.org/files/CIArb%20_%20EDER%20AGM%20Keynote%20Address%2028%20April%202016%20AMND.pdf> (last accessed 7 June 2018); J. William ROWLEY QC, "Rowley: London Arbitration Under Attack", GAR Arbitration Review (16 May 2016). Available at: <https://globalarbitrationreview.com/article/1036328/rowley-london-arbitration-under-attack> (last accessed 7 June 2018); Justice BLAIR, "Commercial Dispute Resolution – Current Developments in the Commercial Court", 2016 Commercial Litigation and Arbitration Forum (3 November 2016) p. 7.
24. Justice BLAIR, "Commercial Dispute Resolution – Current Developments in the Commercial Court", 2016 Commercial Litigation and Arbitration Forum (3 November 2016) p. 7.

courts.[25] In 2015 the Ministry of Justice indicated that the caseload of the commercial courts was on the rise.[26]

It is not only arbitration practitioners and scholars that have rallied against these criticisms,[27] but also other judges. Sir Bernard Eder states that "the common law continues to develop at a pace with a constant stream – indeed flood – of cases over a wide area of jurisprudence".[28] Lord Woolf has also been reported to say that the courts retain a sufficient workload to develop the common law in commercial matters.[29] As noted by Griffiths QC: "The Courts have had enough time to develop the common law and still do so with plenty of opportunity to further refine the principles of common law which have been there for centuries."[30]

One could also argue that the rise of popularity of arbitration in England, Singapore, Australia, etc. brings with it a tide of popularity for these jurisdictions including for their state courts – the notion that increased competition brings with it increased business.

Ultimately, however, the weight of these arguments will always be questionable, against the undeniable fact of the diminishing caseload of commercial courts relative to arbitrations. Also undeniable is that new case law is required for common law to be able to adapt to and respond to developments in markets, trade and commerce, including those associated with globalization and new technologies.[31] Common law relies on precedent developed over generations and prides itself on its ability to adapt its principles to changes in trade, commerce and the markets.[32] As per the analogy drawn by

25. J. William ROWLEY QC, "Rowley: London Arbitration Under Attack", GAR Arbitration Review (16 May 2016). Available at: <https://globalarbitrationreview.com/article/1036328/rowley-london-arbitration-under-attack> (last accessed 7 June 2018).
26. J. William ROWLEY QC, "Rowley: London Arbitration Under Attack", GAR Arbitration Review (16 May 2016). Available at: <https://globalarbitrationreview.com/article/1036328/rowley-london-arbitration-under-attack> (last accessed 7 June 2018).
27. J. William ROWLEY QC, "Rowley: London Arbitration Under Attack", GAR Arbitration Review (16 May 2016). Available at: <https://globalarbitrationreview.com/article/1036328/rowley-london-arbitration-under-attack> (last accessed 7 June 2018); Rachel Tan XI'EN, "Essay on Lord Chief Justice Thomas' 2016 BAILII Lecture", Singapore Academy of Law (2017) (unpublished). Available at: <https://www.sal.org.sg/Portals/0/Documents/Christopher%20Bathurst%20Prize%20submission/Tan%20Xi%E2%80%99en%20Rachel.pdf?ver=2017-09-21-181339-383> (last accessed 7 June 2018).
28. Sir Bernard EDER, "Does Arbitration Stifle Development of the Law? Should s.69 Be Revitalised?", AGM Keynote Address for the Chartered Institute of Arbitrators (28 April 2016) p. 4. Available at <https://www.londonarbitrators.org/sites/londonarbitrators.org/files/CIArb%20_%20EDER%20AGM%20Keynote%20Address%2028%20April%202016%20AMND.pdf> (last accessed 7 June 2018).
29. Robert GRIFFITHS QC, "Litigation v Arbitration", 2016 Speech during the British American Group of Lawyers (BAGOL) Conference (11 May 2016) para. 27.
30. Robert GRIFFITHS QC, "Litigation v Arbitration", 2016 Speech during the British American Group of Lawyers (BAGOL) Conference (11 May 2016) para. 25.
31. A. STEPHENSON and A. ANDERSSON, "Arbitration: Can It Assist in the Development of the Common Law – An Australian Point of View", 33 International Construction Review (2016, no. 4) p. 413 (Sect. 5).
32. Lord Chief Justice Thomas, "Developing Commercial Law Through the Courts: Rebalancing the Relationship Between the Courts and Arbitration", The BAILII Lecture 2016 (9 March 2016) p. 2. Available at: <https://www.judiciary.uk/wp-content/uploads/2016/03/lcj-speech-bailli-

Justice McLachlin, Chief Justice of Canada, common law is akin to a living tree: "All areas of law ... are living, constantly evolving trees. Some branches sprout and grow; others crack and need trimming. Thus, the law develops and remains responsive to changes in society."[33]

There are numerous examples, across the common law world, of recent cases which have marked important developments of law.[34] The relatively reduced caseload of commercial courts must necessarily limit these developments. As put by the Right Honourable Beverley McLachlin, Chief Justice of Canada in the context of construction case law: "the tree looks different than it used to. It may not be dead, but new branches are not appearing as often as they once did. And old branches that need pruning are often neglected."[35]

It seems safer to conclude, therefore, that commercial arbitration probably *does* hinder the development of common law and that the debate cannot end at this first question.

More importantly, to curtail the debate at this juncture would be a missed opportunity – a missed opportunity for a candid dialogue with the critics and a missed opportunity at a potential solution. So rather than deny that arbitration is taking away cases from the courts and therefore from the development of common law as we know it, it is preferable to tackle the issue at the more crucial juncture: what does this hindrance of the common law mean for the legitimacy of commercial arbitration and should we do anything about it?

III. DOES THE HINDRANCE OF COMMON LAW DEVELOPMENT MAKE COMMERCIAL ARBITRATION ANY LESS LEGITIMATE?

The outcome of any debate about legitimacy will be influenced by how broadly or narrowly the concept is defined. An analysis of the concept of legitimacy falls outside the scope of this paper and has already been explored by many before me, including at the

lecture-20160309.pdf> (last accessed 7 June 2018); Harris BOR, "Comments on Lord Chief Justice Thomas' 2016 BAILII Lecture which Promotes a Greater Role for the Courts in International Arbitration", Kluwer Arbitration Blog (11 April 2016). Available at: <http://arbitrationblog.kluwerarbitration.com/2016/04/11/comments-on-lord-chief-justice-thomas-2016-bailii-lecture-which-promotes-a-greater-role-for-the-courts-in-international-arbitration/> (last accessed 7 June 2018).

33. The Right Honourable Beverly MCLACHLIN, "Judging the 'Vanishing Trial' in the Construction Industry", 5 Construction Law International (2010, no. 2) p. 9 at p. 10.
34. Andrew STEPHENSON and Astrid ANDERSSON, "Arbitration: Can It Assist in the Development of the Common Law – An Australian Point of View", 33 International Construction Review (2016, no. 4) p. 413; Myriam GILLES, "The Day Doctrine Died: Private Arbitration and the End of Law", U. Ill. L. Rev. (2016) p. 371 at p. 375 et seq.; Lord Chief Justice THOMAS, "Developing Commercial Law Through the Courts: Rebalancing the Relationship Between the Courts and Arbitration", The BAILII Lecture 2016 (9 March 2016) p. 5 et seq. Available at: <https://www.judiciary.uk/wp-content/uploads/2016/03/lcj-speech-bailli-lecture-20160309.pdf> (last accessed 7 June 2018).
35. Justice Beverley MCLACHLIN PC, "Judging the 'Vanishing Trial' in the Construction Industry", 5 Construction Law International (2010, no. 2) p. 10.

ICCA 2014 Congress.[36] This paper will therefore build on the commendable work on this subject that has already been done.

The dominant perception of arbitration is that it constitutes a jurisprudential system that provides the "legal infrastructure" for the settlement of private disputes.[37] This is of course undeniable. What is, however, the nature of this quasi-judicial system? Depending on the answer, the standard of its legitimacy changes.

If, for instance, arbitration is understood as an entirely private normative order, whose existence derives solely from the will of its users,[38] then its legitimacy is also inferred by the party autonomy of the disputing parties only, since their acceptance of the system is what creates it.

However, such a perspective fails to take into consideration "the effects of international arbitration on non-users".[39]

Over recent years, arbitration has undergone a transformation from a purely private mechanism of dispute resolution into an institution of governance, through a multitude of factors. This phenomenon began in the field of investment arbitration but is by no means limited to it.

It is by now indisputable that investment disputes involve issues that pertain to public interests.[40] As explained by Professor Schill, the normative effects of arbitration "go beyond the realm of the disputing parties and have important repercussions on recalibrating social relations, and the rights connected to them, both private and public".[41]

The same can be argued, albeit to a lesser extent, in the context of commercial arbitration where certain developments have contributed to its transformation into an institution of governance. The first factor is the role of a state in its commercial capacity

---

36. See, e.g., Stephan W. SCHILL, "Developing a Framework for the Legitimacy of International Arbitration" in *Legitimacy: Myths, Realities, Challenges*, ICCA Congress Series no. 18 (Kluwer 2015) (henceforth *ICCA Congress Series no. 18*) p. 789.

37. Stephan W. SCHILL, "Conceptions of Legitimacy of International Arbitration" in David D. CARON, Stephan W. SCHILL, Abby C. SMUTNY and Epaminontas E. TRIANTAFILOU, eds., *Practising Virtue: Inside International Arbitration* (Oxford 2015) p. 106; Amsterdam Law School Research Paper No. 2017-17; Amsterdam Center for International Law No. 2017-14, p. 13. Available at SSRN <https://ssrn.com/abstract=2932147> (last accessed 6 June 2018).

38. See, e.g., Jan PAULSSON, *The Idea of Arbitration* (Oxford University Press 2013); Jan PAULSSON, "Arbitration Unbound: Award Detached from the Law of Its Country of Origin", 30 Int'l & Comp LQ (1981) p. 358; Jan PAULSSON "Delocalisation of International Commercial Arbitration: When and Why It Matters", 32 Int'l & Comp LQ (1983) p. 53.

39. Stephan W. SCHILL, "Conceptions of Legitimacy of International Arbitration" in David D. CARON, Stephan W. SCHILL, Abby C. SMUTNY and Epaminontas E. TRIANTAFILOU, eds., *Practising Virtue: Inside International Arbitration* (Oxford 2015) p. 106; Amsterdam Law School Research Paper No. 2017-17; Amsterdam Center for International Law No. 2017-14, p. 13. Available at SSRN <https://ssrn.com/abstract=2932147> (last accessed 6 June 2018).

40. Michael WAIBEL, Asha KAUSHAL with Kyo-Hwa CHUNG, Claire BALCHIN, eds., *The Backlash Against Investment Arbitration: Perceptions and Reality* (Kluwer Law International 2010) p. xxxvii – li, p. xxxvii.

41. Stephan W. SCHILL, "Developing a Framework for the Legitimacy of International Arbitration" in *ICCA Congress Series no. 18*, pp. 794-795.

as *jure gestionis*.[42] When a state participates in a commercial contract, it does so in its private capacity.[43] However, even where the party to the contract is a state-owned entity, it is still plausible that government officials signed the contract.[44] Moreover, a state-owned entity is possibly exercising governmental authority, such that it deals with matters closely linked to the public interests, especially in the fields of energy, construction or telecommunications; an arbitral tribunal, in turn, will potentially have to deal with matters arising out of the state's exercise of regulatory powers.[45] Consequently, the effect of the contract, and disputes resolved under it, will not be confined to the contracting parties.[46]

For instance, if a state-owned company that is in charge of energy-related policies in the country enters into a contract with a foreign company for the installation of photovoltaic panels, the two companies will not be the only affected parties. The population of the state will also be affected, because they will have access to new sources of renewable power; but also this project may be funded through their taxes, and if the project fails they will also have to bear the consequences indirectly. Through this simple example, we see that even with commercial arbitration, the pool of persons affected can be wider than just the users or stakeholders.

The ever-increasing scope of arbitrability, noted above, also broadens the group of people directly or indirectly affected by arbitral decisions.[47] The authority of arbitral tribunals has expanded greatly, resulting in a wide range of cases being adjudicated by them, cases which in the past belonged in the realm of public law and courts.[48] Most recently, for example, the US Supreme Court decision in *Epic Systems v. Lewis* upheld mandatory individual labor arbitration agreements.[49] A commentator observes that "the scope of rights amenable to arbitration has grown to such an extent that, the concept of arbitrability (or its mirror image, inarbitrability) as central as it may be to arbitration theory, has virtually died in real arbitral life".[50]

42. See, e.g., Veijo HEISKANEN; "State as a Private: The Participation of States in International Commercial Arbitration", 1 TDM (2010) p. 2. Available at <www.transnational-dispute-management.com/article.asp?key=1525> (last accessed 6 June 2018).
43. Veijo HEISKANEN; "State as a Private: The Participation of States in International Commercial Arbitration", 1 TDM (2010) p. 2. Available at: <www.transnational-dispute-management.com/article.asp?key=1525> (last accessed 6 June 2018).
44. Veijo HEISKANEN; "State as a Private: The Participation of States in International Commercial Arbitration", 1 TDM (2010) p. 7. Available at: <www.transnational-dispute-management.com/article.asp?key=1525> (last accessed 6 June 2018).
45. Andrés JANA, "Private and Public Interest in International Commercial Arbitration", this volume, p. 317 at p. 325.
46. Cindy G. BUYS, "The Tensions Between Confidentiality and Transparency in International Arbitration", 14 The American Review of International Arbitration (2003) p. 121 at p. 135.
47. See, e.g., Karim Abou YOUSSEF, "Part I: Fundamental Observations and Applicable Law, Chapter 3 – The Death of Inarbitrability" in Loukas A. MISTELIS and Stavros L. BREKOULAKIS, eds., *Arbitrability: International and Comparative Perspectives* (Kluwer Law International 2009) p. 47.
48. Stavros L. BREKOULAKIS, "Chapter 14: Systemic Bias and the Institution of International Arbitration: A New Approach to Arbitral Decision-Making" in Tony Cole, ed., *The Roles of Psychology in International Arbitration* (Kluwer Law International 2017) p. 339 at p. 339.
49. *Epic Systems Corporation v. Jacob Lewis*, 584 U. S. (2018) p. 25.
50. Karim Abou YOUSSEF, "Part I: Fundamental Observations and Applicable Law, Chapter 3 — The Death of Inarbitrability" in Loukas A. MISTELIS and Stavros L. BREKOULAKIS, eds.,

Such a development, it goes without saying, has had crucial implications for other actors, outside the margins of commercial arbitration. Commercial tribunals, through dealing with such issues, have an impact on other parties, unrelated to the specific dispute. Therefore, it becomes apparent that international commercial arbitration is no longer confined within the margin of the parties' autonomy, but has an increased social impact transcending the disputing parties.

Furthermore, the increase of institutional arbitrations has led to a standardization and consolidation of the arbitral procedure, with institutions and associations organizing conferences, trainings and seminars for the promotion of arbitration.[51]

This function of arbitration, of developing rules and an arbitration culture, reflects the transformation of arbitration from a dyadic mechanism of dispute settlement to a system of global governance.

As such, arbitration is no longer a plain mechanism of private dispute settlement, where party autonomy remains the single concern, but arbitration has grown to become a means of decision-making, a system that provides transnational norms that affect many more than just the disputing parties.[52]

Such a concept of arbitration, though, leads to the conclusion that the parties to the disputes are not the only actors in arbitration, and their perspective is not the only one to consider. The interests involved in the disputes go beyond the individual interest of the parties, to "an interest that concerns the arbitration system as a whole".[53] The standard of legitimacy for arbitration must therefore evolve, also in the commercial realm, for the simple reason that arbitration has evolved into a system of governance impacting on social spheres beyond the disputing parties, and for this reason its legitimacy cannot derive solely from the consent of the latter.

That assessment may not be shared by all, however, and for the purpose of this discussion, the answer to the question before us – namely whether the hindrance of common law gives rise to a legitimacy concern for commercial arbitration – may be the same regardless of the standard of legitimacy adopted.

Generally speaking, we can consider a focused notion of legitimacy, looking at the interests of the stakeholders, usually the parties themselves, or what Professor Schill referred to in his seminal paper, as party or community legitimacy.[54] Or we can consider legitimacy from the perspective of a broader population – per Professor Schill's categories, this would be national or global legitimacy.[55]

Arbitrability: International and Comparative Perspectives (Kluwer Law International 2009) p. 47 at p. 47.

51. Stephan W. SCHILL, "Developing a Framework for the Legitimacy of International Arbitration" in *ICCA Congress Series no. 18*, p. 796.
52. Stephan W. SCHILL, "Developing a Framework for the Legitimacy of International Arbitration" in *ICCA Congress Series no. 18*, p. 803.
53. Andrés JANA, "Private and Public Interest in International Commercial Arbitration", this volume, at p. 326.
54. Stephan W. SCHILL, "Developing a Framework for the Legitimacy of International Arbitration" in *ICCA Congress Series no. 18*, pp. 812-813.
55. Stephan W. SCHILL, "Developing a Framework for the Legitimacy of International Arbitration" in *ICCA Congress Series no. 18*, pp. 813-817.

Taking first the broader notions of legitimacy: from a national interest perspective, the hindrance of the development of common law in any particular jurisdiction must be viewed as contrary to those interests. This is true whether we view the issue from the perspective of state courts whose mandate is to develop the law, from the perspective of parties to commercial court cases who will have expectations of how common law develops, or from the perspective of the public at large whose interest is to be governed by a law that evolves and adapts in line with its programmed path.

From a global perspective, we could argue that the stifling of the evolution of common law is not inconsistent with the interests of the population at large, since they may refer to other legal systems to govern their relationships. However, few people would disagree that the stifling – or death, taken to its extreme – of an entire system of law, is not a desirable outcome, not least a system which forms the basis of almost one third of the world's 320 legal jurisdictions.[56] As Lord Thomas puts it, this hindrance undermines the very means through which much of the common law's strength was developed.[57]

Even the civil law world is not unaffected by this stifling. While more poignant in common law systems which base their development on binding precedent, civil law systems also develop by reference to cases, even if these are not binding precedent.[58] Even the reliance by civil law courts on doctrine and scholarly articles is necessarily curtailed by the limited access to cases also for the purpose of commentary. Seen from this light, there can be little doubt that legitimacy issues arise from the global and national perspectives.

Taking a more focused notion of legitimacy, which examines the issue from the perspective of the parties or the arbitration community, one could argue that the courts and law are there to serve the public, not the other way around.[59] Stakeholders of commercial arbitration, the parties, care about one thing: their own commercial advantage. Few commercial parties will be interested in acting altruistically in the interest of the wider industry or the development of the common law as a whole.[60] If parties choose to resolve their disputes in arbitration rather than before commercial

56. J. William ROWLEY QC, "Rowley: London Arbitration Under Attack", GAR Arbitration Review (16 May 2016). Available at: <https://globalarbitrationreview.com/article/1036328/rowley-london-arbitration-under-attack> (last accessed 7 June 2018).

57. Lord Chief Justice THOMAS, "Developing Commercial Law Through the Courts: Rebalancing the Relationship Between the Courts and Arbitration", The BAILII Lecture 2016 (9 March 2016) p. 4. Available at: <https://www.judiciary.uk/wp-content/uploads/2016/03/lcj-speech-bailli-lecture-20160309.pdf> (last accessed 7 June 2018).

58. Guy I. SEIDMAN, "Comparative Civil Procedure" in Colin B. PICKER and Guy I. SEIDMAN, eds., *The Dynamism of Civil Procedure – Global Trends and Developments* (Springer 2015) p. 15.

59. Derek AUCHIE, "A Response to Judicial Comments on the Arbitration-Litigation Debate", University of Aberdeen BlogSpot (5 May 2016). Available at: <https://www.abdn.ac. uk/law/blog/a-response-to-judicial-comments-on-the-arbitrationlitigation-debate/> (last accessed 7 June 2018).

60. Harris BOR, "Comments on Lord Chief Justice Thomas' 2016 BAILII Lecture which Promotes a Greater Role for the Courts in International Arbitration", Kluwer Arbitration Blog (11 April 2016). Available at: <http://arbitrationblog.kluwerarbitration.com/2016/04/11/comments-on-lord-chief-justice-thomas-2016-bailii-lecture-which-promotes-a-greater-role-for-the-courts-in-international-arbitration/> (last accessed 7 June 2018).

courts, and as a result the law is less developed, that is the parties' choice. In terms of legitimacy, one could argue that there is thus no incoherence between the parties' choices and the outcome. However, this is perhaps overly simplistic: when parties choose English or another system of common law to govern their contracts, they do so with certain notions of what that system of law represents. At the very least those notions must include an assumption that the parties are referring to a system of law which evolves and adapts with jurisprudence over time. If this aspect of common law is being limited by commercial arbitration, then the legitimacy question must at least arise, even when seen from the perspective of users, the principal stakeholders.

So, whichever concept of legitimacy is adopted, there is a more or less strong argument to be made against commercial arbitration's legitimacy by virtue of its impact on the development of law.

Moreover, whether we put on them the label of legitimacy or not, these concerns are certainly enough to require us to consider the third and final question – how should commercial arbitration adapt to these concerns?

IV. HOW COULD OR SHOULD COMMERCIAL ARBITRATION ADAPT TO THESE CONCERNS?

1. *The Proposal to Limit the Scope of Arbitration*

Let us first examine the solution presented by the critics: their proposed solution is to revise arbitration legislation to restrict the scope of arbitration and increase the scope of court's jurisdiction over commercial disputes.[61] Lord Chief Justice Thomas contemplates a revision of the English Arbitration Act 1996 to allow for more appeals from arbitration to the courts, or to encourage a greater use of Sect. 45 of the Arbitration Act to enable the courts to make judgments on points of law that arise during the arbitral proceedings (before the award is rendered).[62] Essentially, the proposed solution is to force parties to return to litigation to ensure the continued development of law.

But a solution that seeks to override party autonomy strikes at the heart of legitimacy. Parties surely do not opt for arbitration, only to be returned to the state courts.[63] The development of the law is not of primary concern to parties; if it were, they could elect to go to the courts directly. On the contrary, the limitation of the referral to courts from arbitration cases has evidently increased the number of cases going to arbitration. By electing arbitration as their method of dispute resolution, the parties have agreed to accept the decision of their chosen tribunal instead of that of the court. What an English

61. Lord Chief Justice THOMAS, "Developing Commercial Law Through the Courts: Rebalancing the Relationship Between the Courts and Arbitration", The BAILII Lecture 2016 (9 March 2016) p. 13. Available at: <https://www.judiciary.uk/wp-content/uploads/2016/03/lcj-speech-bailli-lecture-20160309.pdf> (last accessed 7 June 2018).
62. *Id.*
63. Dorothy MURRAY, "Are Arbitration Clauses Killing Development of Domestic Law?", Commercial Dispute Resolution Blog (28 November 2016). Available at: <https://www.cdr-news.com/categories/arbitration-and-adr/6887-are-arbitration-clauses-killing-development-of-domestic-law> (last accessed 7 June 2018).

(or other national) court would have decided is of no concern to these parties.[64] Parties use arbitration to resolve their disputes, not to add to the body of common law. And it is undeniable that the courts should serve the public, not the other way around.[65]

The absurdity of the proposed approach is aptly illustrated by the response of Lord Devlin, when confronted with the opposers of the initial curtailing of the right of appeal under the 1979 English Arbitration Act: "The next step would, I suppose, be a prohibition placed on the settlement of cases concerning interesting points of law."[66]

There is no legitimate reason why international (or English) parties should be put to the expense and delay occasioned by appeals to the courts in the name of the development of common law.[67] Indeed, while the critics accuse arbitration of not living up to its billing when it comes to time and costs,[68] a topic covered by the paper of Laura Abrahamson at this ICCA Congress,[69] the proposal to increase the scope of the courts' intervention in arbitration cases would only compound those concerns.[70]

The proposed solution would moreover not serve its purpose: if parties are actively choosing arbitration over courts, then a system that sends them back to the common law courts will only likely alienate them also from arbitration in common law jurisdictions, further compounding the problem of the dearth of precedent in the common law. As it

---

64. Mark SAVILLE, "Reforms Will Threaten London's Place as a World Arbitration Centre", The Times (28 April 2016). Available at: <https://www.thetimes.co.uk/article/reforms-will-threaten-londons-place-as-a-world-arbitration-centre-02t50mgrd> (last accessed 7 June 2018).
65. Derek AUCHIE, "A Response to Judicial Comments on the Arbitration-Litigation Debate", University of Aberdeen BlogSpot (5 May 2016). Available at: <https://www.abdn.ac.uk/law/blog/a-response-to-judicial-comments-on-the-arbitrationlitigation-debate/> (last accessed 7 June 2018).
66. Mark SAVILLE, "Reforms Will Threaten London's Place as a World Arbitration Centre", The Times (28 April 2016). Available at: <https://www.thetimes.co.uk/article/reforms-will-threaten-londons-place-as-a-world-arbitration-centre-02t50mgrd> (last accessed 7 June 2018).
67. As Lord Saville, who chaired the committee that formed the Arbitration Act 1996, has argued "[p]eople use arbitration to resolve their disputes, not to add to the body of English commercial law.... Why, in other words, should they be obliged to finance the development of English commercial law?" Mark SAVILLE, "Reforms Will Threaten London's Place as a World Arbitration Centre", The Times (28 April 2016). Available at: <https://www.thetimes.co.uk/article/reforms-will-threaten-londons-place-as-a-world-arbitration-centre-02t50mgrd> (last accessed 7 June 2018); see also Rachel Tan XI'EN, "Essay on Lord Chief Justice Thomas' 2016 BAILII Lecture", Singapore Academy of Law (2017) (unpublished) p. 5. Available at: <https://www.sal.org.sg/Portals/0/Documents/Christopher%20Bathurst%20Prize%20submission/Tan%20Xi%E2%80%99en%20Rachel.pdf?ver=2017-09-21-181339-383> (last accessed 7 June 2018).
68. Lord Chief Justice THOMAS, "Developing Commercial Law Through the Courts: Rebalancing the Relationship Between the Courts and Arbitration", The BAILII Lecture 2016 (9 March 2016), p. 16. Available at: <https://www.judiciary.uk/wp-content/uploads/2016/03/lcj-speech-bailli-lecture-20160309.pdf> (last accessed 7 June 2018).
69. Laura ABRAHAMSON, "Costs, Delay and Transparency – A Comment on Continued Legitimacy Concerns from the User's Perspective" this volume, pp. 354-360.
70. Sir Bernard EDER, "Does Arbitration Stifle Development of the Law? Should s.69 Be Revitalised?", AGM Keynote Address for the Chartered Institute of Arbitrators (28 April 2016) p. 7-8. Available at <https://www.londonarbitrators.org/sites/londonarbitrators.org/files/CIArb%20_%20EDER%20AGM%20Keynote%20Address%2028%20April%202016%20AMND.pdf> (last accessed 7 June 2018).

is, the English Arbitration Act is in the minority in that it upholds the appeals mechanism, a provision that does not exist in most other arbitration jurisdictions. Even common law judges accept that the critics' proposed approach would "[set] the clock back almost 40 years".[71]

The development of the common law before courts cannot depend on, or call for, the regression of arbitration. Instead a solution must be found which recognizes courts and tribunals as "mutually supportive parts of what is a developing system of international commercial dispute resolution",[72] and which builds upon the place that arbitration holds today – while enabling the courts to perform a mandate which in a strict sense can be performed by them and them only.[73]

2. *A Solution Based on Greater Interaction Between Courts and Tribunals*

It is a fact that many parties today refer their large international disputes to arbitration. If arbitration is hindering the development of common law, or even national law generally, to the detriment of its legitimacy, then we must develop a solution which taps into the lawmaking potential of arbitration.

a. *Body of decisions produced by arbitral tribunals (or "lawmaking" for the bold)*

It cannot credibly be denied that a body of law is developing through arbitral awards, even if there may continue to be – in the words of Lucy Reed – "persistent objectors".[74]

Indeed, there was a time when even English judges tried to pretend that they did not make new law – they merely declared it.[75] As Lord Reid put it in 1972, the "fairy tale"

71. Sir Bernard EDER, "Does Arbitration Stifle Development of the Law? Should s.69 Be Revitalised?", AGM Keynote Address for the Chartered Institute of Arbitrators (28 April 2016) p. 10. Available at <https://www.londonarbitrators.org/sites/londonarbitrators.org/files/CIArb%20_%20EDER%20AGM%20Keynote%20Address%2028%20April%202016%20AMND.pdf> (last accessed 7 June 2018).

72. Justice BLAIR, "Commercial Dispute Resolution – Current Developments in the Commercial Court", 2016 Commercial Litigation and Arbitration Forum (3 November 2016) p. 7.

73. Justice Beverley MCLACHLIN PC, "Judging the 'Vanishing Trial' in the Construction Industry", 5 Construction Law International (2010, no. 2) p. 321; Ank SANTENS and Romain ZAMOUR, "Dreaded Dearth of Precedent in the Wake of International Arbitration – Could the Cause Also Bring the Cure?", 7 Y.B. Arb. & Mediation (2015) p. 73 at p. 83.

74. Lucy REED, "Lawmaking in International Arbitration: What Legitimacy Challenges Lie Ahead?", this volume, p. 52 at p. 59. The "persistent objectors" still insist that their role as arbitrators is to decide the dispute alone without any regard to future interpretation of similar treaty provisions. An illustrative example is the finding of the *Romak* tribunal that "the Arbitral Tribunal has not been entrusted, by the Parties or otherwise, with a mission to ensure the coherence or development of 'arbitral jurisprudence.' The Arbitral Tribunal's mission is more mundane, but no less important: to resolve the present dispute between the Parties in a reasoned and persuasive manner, irrespective of the unintended consequences that this Arbitral Tribunal's analysis might have on future disputes in general," *Romak S.A. v. Republic* of *Uzbekistan* (UNCITRAL, PCA Case No. AA280) Award (26 November 2009) para. 171.

75. Joshua ROZENBERG, "Is English Common Law at Risk of Becoming Out of Date?", BBC News (31 March 2016). Available at: < https://www.bbc.com/news/uk-35883590> (last accessed 7 June 2018).

was that common law was hidden in an Aladdin's cave and judges were given the magic password on appointment.[76]

In the investment arbitration world, a "de facto doctrine of precedent" is by now a given, which, as Professor Paulsson puts it, "can only be denied by those determined to close their eyes".[77]

In the realm of commercial arbitration, the expected development of "a formation of a free-standing body of law responsive to the needs of international commerce"[78] has been somewhat slower by virtue of the limited publication of awards.[79] Nonetheless, arbitrators can and do perform a lawmaking function.[80] It is accepted that between tribunals, awards, while not being binding precedent, may constitute persuasive precedent: "past solutions have some impact on the thinking of arbitrators having to resolve future cases".[81] The arbitrators develop normative rules that may not be binding but they influence future awards.

In other words, international arbitrators strive, as they must,[82] to be consistent with past decisions of other tribunals so as to meet commercial parties' legitimate expectations for their disputes to be resolved in a consistent fashion. These propositions are echoed by the Chief Justice of Singapore Sundaresh Menon, who recognized that the international commercial arbitration framework has begun a process leading towards a formation of a "free-standing body of law responsive to the needs of international commerce".[83]

---

76. Joshua ROZENBERG, "Is English Common Law at Risk of Becoming Out of Date?", BBC News (31 March 2016). Available at: <https://www.bbc.com/news/uk-35883590> (last accessed 7 June 2018).
77. Jan PAULSSON, "International Arbitration and the Generation of Legal Norms: Treaty Arbitration and International Law" in *International Arbitration 2006: Back to Basics?*, ICCA Congress Series no. 13 (2007) p. 886.
78. Sundaresh MENON, "International Commercial Courts: Towards A Transnational System of Dispute Resolution", Opening Lecture for the DIFC Courts Lecture Series (2015) p. 6. Available at: <https://www.supremecourt.gov.sg/docs/default-source/default-document-library/media-room/opening-lecture---difc-lecture-series-2015.pdf> (last accessed 7 June 2018).
79. D. Brian KING and Rahim MOLOO, "International Arbitrators as Lawmakers", 46 N.Y.U. Journal International Law & Politics (2014) p. 875 at p. 886, noting that the publication of awards is one of the critical prerequisites to arbitrators as lawmakers.
80. D. Brian KING, and Rahim MOLOO, "International Arbitrators as Lawmakers", 46 N.Y.U. Journal International Law & Politics (2014) p. 875 at p. 882; Alexis MOURRE, "Precedent and Confidentiality in International Commercial Arbitration: The Case for the Publication of Arbitral Awards" in Emmanuel GAILLARD and Yas BANIFATEMI, eds., *Precedent in International Arbitration* (Juris 2008) p. 39 at p. 41 et seq.
81. Alexis MOURRE, "Precedent and Confidentiality in International Commercial Arbitration: The Case for the Publication of Arbitral Awards" in Emmanuel GAILLARD and Yas BANIFATEMI, eds., *Precedent in International Arbitration* (Juris 2008) p. 39 at p. 43.
82. Gabrielle KAUFMANN-KOHLER, "Arbitral Precedent: Dream, Necessity or Excuse?", The 2006 Freshfields Lecture, 23 Arbitration International (2007, no. 3) p. 357 at p. 374, noting that "when making law, decision makers have a moral obligation to strive for consistency and predictability, and thus to follow precedents. It may be debatable whether arbitrators have a legal obligation to follow precedents – probably not – but it seems well settled that they have a moral obligation to follow precedents so as to foster a normative environment that is predictable."
83. Chief Justice Sundaresh MENON, "International Commercial Courts: Towards a Transnational System of Dispute Resolution", Opening Lecture for the DIFC Courts Lecture Series (2015) p. 6.

In practice we can see this in the formation of a body of law in certain industries, for instance a so-called lex petrolea in oil and gas industry and lex sportiva in sports. These laws have been developed though the development of a group of principles that are considered standard practices in the respective industries, and hence widely accepted by them.[84] It may be true that arbitral decisions only rarely refer back to previous decisions.[85] But in a context where a limited pool of players are involved, whether as counsel or arbitrator, it is inevitable that prior decisions influence subsequent ones, whether they are expressly referred to or not[86] – thus leading to an emergence of a certain approach to certain issues. Indeed, when a party appoints any given arbitrator on the basis of her prior expertise, that party accepts and even expects that the arbitrator will take into account that prior experience and expertise in rendering her decision. As summarized by one English law commentator:[87]

> "For better or worse, international commercial arbitration is now a major forum for the resolution of disputes that impact on those other than the parties to them. It is a forum in which claims of corruption of public officials and of breaches of competition law are made and decided, in which States and State-owned entities are routinely parties, and in which large swathes of commercial law, including standard form commercial contracts, are applied and developed."

Thus, if we define lawmaking as being when an award "supplements the corpus of normative materials that counsel and tribunals will take into account in future proceedings",[88] certain commercial arbitration decisions are already making law today.

Moreover, regardless of whether commercial arbitration decisions could be said to create a body of law, these decisions are being rendered, in the hundreds, each year and

---

Available at: <https://www.supremecourt.gov.sg/docs/default-source/default-document-library/media-room/opening-lecture---difc-lecture-series-2015.pdf> (last accessed 7 June 2018).

84. Ank SANTENS and Romain ZAMOUR, "Dreaded Dearth of Precedent in the Wake of International Arbitration – Could the Cause Also Bring the Cure?", 7 Y.B. Arb. & Mediation (2015) p. 73 at p. 90.
85. Gabrielle KAUFMANN-KOHLER, "Arbitral Precedent: Dream, Necessity or Excuse?", The 2006 Freshfields Lecture, 23 Arbitration International (2007, no. 3) p. 357. A 2006 survey of International Chamber of Commerce awards showed that out of the 190 awards reviewed, about 15 percent cited other arbitral decisions in matters of jurisdiction and procedure, the powers of the tribunal to order provisional measures, and in connection with the determination of the law governing the merits.
86. "[M]ost of the time it is difficult to analyse the exact role that reference to the past played in the arbitral tribunal's reasoning." Alexis MOURRE, "Precedent and Confidentiality in International Commercial Arbitration: The Case for the Publication of Arbitral Awards" in Emmanuel GAILLARD and Yas BANIFATEMI, eds., *Precedent in International Arbitration* (Juris 2008) p. 39 at p. 44.
87. Ben JURATOWITCH QC, "Departing from Confidentiality in International Dispute Resolution", BIICL Seminar on Difficult Issues in Commercial, Investor-State, and State-State Dispute Resolution: Differences and Commonalities (8 June 2017) p. 9.
88. Alec S. SWEET, Michael Y. CHUNG and Adam SALTZMAN, "Arbitral Lawmaking and State Power: An Empirical Analysis of Investor-State Arbitration", 1 Journal of International Dispute Settlement (2017) pp. 4-5. Available at SSRN: <https://ssrn.com/abstract=2919723> (last accessed 6 June 2018).

access to those decisions could – directly or indirectly depending on the jurisdiction – assist with the development of law. However we label these decisions, whether lawmaking or not, they constitute an important source for state courts that could then in turn develop the law in the strict sense. The debate on lawmaking by tribunals has largely focused on lawmaking for the reference of parties and tribunals in future arbitrations. There is no reason why tribunals cannot contribute to lawmaking in a broader sense of the word for national systems of law as well.[89]

There is even precedent for this development, at least as far as issues of procedure are concerned, where solutions adopted in past arbitration awards have not only been considered as precedent by arbitrators but also by national courts.[90] There is no reason why awards cannot form persuasive precedent also on matters of national law; as explained by Alexis Mourre: "The assumption that reference to arbitral precedents would not be conceivable with respect to substantive issues in presence of choice of law clause is therefore incorrect."[91]

b. More systematic publication of arbitral decisions

The only way to enable this valuable interaction between arbitral tribunals and the courts, for the furtherance of the law, is to engage in a more systematic publication of commercial arbitral awards. Publication would enable parties to refer to such decisions in support of their arguments before courts, which would then be free to allocate the appropriate weight to such decisions. The awards would not have precedential value in a strict sense but can be just as persuasive as other non-precedential material that is used by common law courts – such as academic articles and court decisions from other jurisdictions.[92] Even for the civil law realm, greater transparency of arbitral awards would also enable scholars and practitioners to debate certain issues, which could indirectly also influence the development of law by national courts.

It may be true that arbitral awards rarely offer insight into legal analysis useful beyond the case at hand because the analysis is transaction-focused and fact-specific.[93] But arbitrators are rarely presented with contracts that have no governing law and it cannot

89. Stefan PISLEVIK, "*Precedent and Development of Law: Is It Time for Greater Transparency in International Commercial Arbitration?*" (Oxford University Press 2018) p. 10.
90. Alexis MOURRE, "Precedent and Confidentiality in International Commercial Arbitration: The Case for the Publication of Arbitral Awards" in Emmanuel GAILLARD and Yas BANIFATEMI, eds., *Precedent in International Arbitration* (Juris 2008) p. 39 at p. 44, referring to the *Dow Chemical* Award (ICC Case No. 4131, *Dow Chemical France v. Isover Saint Gobain*, Interim Award, 23 September 1982), which has been adopted by national courts in relation to the issue of procedural jurisdiction over a group of companies. See also Francois PERRET, "Is There a Need for Consistency in International Commercial Arbitration?" in Emmanuel GAILLARD and Yas BANIFATEMI, eds., *Precedent in International Arbitration* (Juris 2008) p. 37.
91. Alexis MOURRE, "Precedent and Confidentiality in International Commercial Arbitration: The Case for the Publication of Arbitral Awards" in Emmanuel GAILLARD and Yas BANIFATEMI, eds., *Precedent in International Arbitration* (Juris 2008) p. 39 at p. 47.
92. Andrew STEPHENSON and Astrid ANDERSSON, "Arbitration: Can It Assist in the Development of the Common Law – An Australian Point of View", 33 International Construction Review (2016, no. 4) p. 413 at Sect. 6.
93. Gabrielle KAUFMANN-KOHLER, "Arbitral Precedent: Dream, Necessity or Excuse?", The 2006 Freshfields Lecture, 23 Arbitration International (2007, no. 3) p. 357 at p. 376.

be excluded that some make decisions which are founded on their application of that law. Moreover, and this is hinted at by Lucy Reed in her paper for this Congress,[94] if there were more systematic publication, the way awards are written and motivated may adapt in order to provide the allegedly missing analysis.

Most importantly, the law would no longer be "underground".[95] To the extent companies are increasingly choosing arbitration over courts, and arbitrators are writing awards on recurring commercial legal issues, the secrecy of those awards is a loss overall. It is this consideration that has led to a broader call for publication of commercial arbitral awards, with some suggesting that the publication of anonymized awards should be the norm.[96] Others propose that publication should be automatic unless the tribunal decides otherwise.[97]

In view of the lawmaking potential of commercial arbitration, a more systematic publication of arbitral awards is also imperative from a legitimacy perspective. As highlighted by one commentator:[98]

> "As more and more international commercial cases go to arbitration rather than the courts, we are more and more losing sight of the basic feedstock of our commercial law. In such circumstances, it is in my opinion inevitable that the public interest is being and will increasingly be damaged as more and more decisions on areas of commercial law become inaccessible to the public arena."

Indeed, this problem has been identified also by reference to the visibility of law from within the arbitration community. In the field of construction, an illustrative example is the observations Christopher Seppälä has made in relation to FIDIC – International Federation of Consulting Engineers – contracts. After collecting arbitration awards rendered in arbitration under FIDIC contracts he found only forty awards. Considering that this type of contract has been in use for over fifty years, forty awards is only a small

94. Lucy REED, "Lawmaking in International Arbitration: What Legitimacy Challenges Lie Ahead?", this volume, pp. 52-85.
95. Sir Bernard RIX, "Confidentiality in International Arbitration: Virtue or Vice", Jones Day Professorship in Commercial Law Lecture, Singapore Management University in Singapore (12 March 2015) p. 18. Available at: <https://law.smu.edu.sg/sites/default/files/law/CEBCLA/Notes_Confidentiality_in_International_Arbitration.pdf> (last accessed 7 June 2018).
96. Sir Bernard RIX, "Confidentiality in International Arbitration: Virtue or Vice", Jones Day Professorship in Commercial Law Lecture, Singapore Management University in Singapore (12 March 2015) p. 19-20. Available at: <https://law.smu.edu.sg/sites/default/files/law/CEBCLA/Notes_Confidentiality_in_International_Arbitration.pdf> (last accessed 7 June 2018).
97. Ben JURATOWITCH QC, "Departing from Confidentiality in International Dispute Resolution", BIICL Seminar on Difficult Issues in Commercial, Investor-State, and State-State Dispute Resolution: Differences and Commonalities (8 June 2017) p. 8.
98. Sir Bernard RIX, "Confidentiality in International Arbitration: Virtue or Vice", Jones Day Professorship in Commercial Law Lecture, Singapore Management University in Singapore (12 March 2015) p. 18-19. Available at: <https://law.smu.edu.sg/sites/default/files/law/CEBCLA/Notes_Confidentiality_in_International_Arbitration.pdf> (last accessed 7 June 2018).

sample.[99] In the same vein, in relation to oil and gas disputes, it has not been possible for the courts, especially in the United States, to develop any new precedent. The absence of it is so stark that the Second Circuit certified questions of contract interpretation for oil and gas leases to the New York Court of Appeals.[100] Finally, the same can be said for the excess insurance disputes, especially under the "Bermuda Form", which calls for the resolution of disputes by *ad hoc* arbitration in London, such that that there are almost no reported decisions on the issue.[101]

A legitimacy concern therefore arises not only with regard to the arrested development of national laws but also with regard to the exclusion of the public at large from the development of law that is undoubtedly taking place before tribunals. In certain fields, such as construction and energy, it is already the case that a practice is developing as to the way certain matters are being argued before tribunals, which only a small group of practitioners are privy to. As summarized by Ben Juratowitch QC: "there are a number of high quality arbitral awards dealing with matters of general interest that very few people have the benefit of reading", and that: "There are therefore compelling reasons for people to be increasingly concerned about the fact that it is to a substantial degree happening in secret."[102]

Finally, greater publication of awards is widely expected to enhance not only the development of arbitral case law but also the quality of arbitration,[103] by resulting in "greater certainty".[104] It is broadly accepted by all practitioners and scholars that have treated this topic, that increased publication will lead to awards being referred to more often.[105] And an eminent law professor and arbitrator has stated that the legitimacy of

99. Christopher SEPPÄLÄ, "The Development of a Case Law in Construction Disputes Relating to FIDIC Contracts" in Emmanuel GAILLARD and Yas BANIFATEMI, eds., *Precedent in International Arbitration* (Juris 2008) p. 67 at p. 69.

100. Ank SANTENS and Romain ZAMOUR, "Dreaded Dearth of Precedent in the Wake of International Arbitration – Could the Cause Also Bring the Cure?", 7 Y.B. Arb. & Mediation (2015) p. 73 at p. 81.

101. Ank SANTENS and Romain ZAMOUR, "Dreaded Dearth of Precedent in the Wake of International Arbitration – Could the Cause Also Bring the Cure?", 7 Y.B. Arb. & Mediation (2015) p. 73 at pp. 79-80.

102. Ben JURATOWITCH, "Departing from Confidentiality in International Dispute Resolution", BIICL Seminar on Difficult Issues in Commercial, Investor-State, and State-State Dispute Resolution: Differences and Commonalities (8 June 2017) pp. 8-10.

103. Alexis MOURRE, "Precedent and Confidentiality in International Commercial Arbitration: The Case for the Publication of Arbitral Awards" in Emmanuel GAILLARD and Yas BANIFATEMI, eds., *Precedent in International Arbitration* (Juris 2008) p. 39.

104. Jean-Michel JACQUET, "*Avons-nous besoin d'une jurisprudence arbitrale?*", 3 Revue de l'arbitrage (2010) p. 445 at p. 445.

105. Alexis MOURRE, "Precedent and Confidentiality in International Commercial Arbitration: The Case for the Publication of Arbitral Awards" in Emmanuel GAILLARD and Yas BANIFATEMI, eds., *Precedent in International Arbitration* (Juris 2008) p. 39 at p. 53; Gabrielle KAUFMANN-KOHLER, "Arbitral Precedent: Dream, Necessity or Excuse?", The 2006 Freshfields Lecture, 23 Arbitration International (2007, no. 3) p. 357 at p. 376; Stefan PISLEVIK, *Precedent and Development of Law: Is It Time for Greater Transparency in International Commercial Arbitration?* (Oxford University Press 2018) p. 8; Catherine A. ROGERS, "Transparency in International Commercial Arbitration", 54 University of Kansas Law Review (2006) p. 1301 at pp. 1319-1320.

commercial arbitration *depends* on the coherence of published decisions.[106] More widespread publication of awards would allow broader access to this body of decisions, thus enhancing commercial arbitration's legitimacy.

c. *On issues of confidentiality*

Of course, the manner and system we adopt for this broader publication of awards would have to be carefully assessed, also in view of confidentiality concerns. But these are not insurmountable.

First, there has already begun a shift away from confidentiality in arbitration in recent years, and not only in the investment realm. The new edition of the ICC Rules, for example, does not have a default provision on confidentiality.[107] In addition, in recent years, several national courts have made findings that the country's arbitration law does not include an express or implied duty of confidentiality.[108] Indeed, there is no unanimity on the issue of confidentiality across different legal systems.[109] Even in systems which do integrate notions of confidentiality, parties who arbitrate necessarily accept that the details of an award may become public due to challenges to courts or through its enforcement.[110] One notes also that in the investment realm, the increased transparency has not by and large posed a hindrance to parties. On the contrary, awareness of public scrutiny may have a positive effect on how the proceedings are conducted and awards drafted.

106. Pierre TERCIER, "*La légitimité de l'arbitrage*", 3 Revue de l'arbitrage (2011) p. 653 at p. 667; Ank SANTENS and Romain ZAMOUR, "Dreaded Dearth of Precedent in the Wake of International Arbitration – Could the Cause Also Bring the Cure?", 7 Y.B. Arb. & Mediation (2015) p. 73 at p. 83.

107. See ICC Arbitration Rules, Art. 22(3) (2017); Jason FRY, Simon GREENBERG and Francesca MAZZA, *The Secretariat's Guide to ICC Arbitration* (International Chamber of Commerce 2012) p. 235 at paras. 3-807: "The Rules do not provide that the arbitration proceedings are confidential. Rather than creating a general rule requiring the proceedings to be kept confidential and then attempting to define the exceptions that will inevitably arise, the Rules take a more flexible and tailor-made approach, leaving the matter for the parties or the arbitral tribunal to address in light of the specific circumstances of the case."

108. See, e.g., *Esso Australia Res. Ltd v. Plowman*, ICCA Yearbook Commercial Arbitration XXI (1996) (henceforth *Yearbook*) pp. 137, 151 (Australian High Ct. 1995); Judgment of 27 October 2000, *Bulgarian Foreign Trade Bank Ltd v. A.I. Trade Fin. Inc.*, *Yearbook* XXVI (2001) pp. 291, 298 (Swedish S.Ct.).

109. Sir Bernard RIX, "Confidentiality in International Arbitration: Virtue or Vice", Jones Day Professorship in Commercial Law Lecture, Singapore Management University in Singapore (12 March 2015) p. 6. Available at: <https://law.smu.edu.sg/sites/default/files/law/CEBCLA/Notes_Confidentiality_in_International_Arbitration.pdf> (last accessed 7 June 2018); Samuel MAYANK, "Confidentiality in International Commercial Arbitration", Kluwer Arbitration Blog (2017). Available at: <http://arbitrationblog.kluwerarbitration.com/2017/02/21/confidentiality-international-commercial-arbitration-bedrock-window-dressing/> (last accessed 7 June 2018).

110. Constantine PARTASIDES, "What Has Been The 'Spillover' Effect of The Transparency Debate on Commercial Arbitrations?", this volume, p. 699 at p. 706, referring also to the fact that the obligation of confidentiality is not implied by the agreement of the parties, but is a matter of law, meaning that it can change.

Second, certain arbitral institutions and associations already publish excerpts of awards in a redacted form, including the ICC Bulletin, the ICCA *Yearbook Commercial Arbitration* and the American Arbitration Association.[111] Indeed, arbitration rules of several institutions expressly allow the publication of awards under certain conditions. For instance, the Rules of the American Arbitration Association-International Centre for Dispute Resolution (AAA-ICDR) allow for the publication of selected awards that became public in the course of enforcement,[112] while the Rules of the Vienna International Arbitral Centre (VIAC), which have been revised in 2018, provide for the publication of anonymized summaries or extracts of awards.[113] According to the Rules of the Swiss Chambers' Arbitration Institution (SCAI) an award may be published if no party objects to it.[114] The International Bar Association (IBA) Arbitration Committee has also formed a subcommittee led by Professor Pierre Mayer with the aim of compiling and analyzing international commercial arbitration decisions dealing with matters of contract interpretation.[115] In the field of academia, scholars are also compiling arbitral awards for the purpose of identifying an evolution in contract law as applied by tribunals.[116]

The publication of awards can also be done in a manner that preserves the confidentiality of the parties and their business secrets, through a variety of means. Commentators have suggested, for example, publication of the award only after a certain period has elapsed;[117] publication limited to only the tribunal's reasoning;[118] and the possibility of tribunals to exclude publication of certain parts of awards upon hearing the parties.[119] For instance, the default rule of the applicable arbitration rules could be the publication of awards in an anonymized version, from which the parties could opt out.[120]

111. See, e.g., 25 ICC International Court of Arbitration Bulletin (2015, no.2) for ICC Oil and Gas Cases, or 25 ICC International Court of Arbitration Bulleting (2015, no.1) for the first ICC cases dealing with Emergency Arbitrator procedures.

112. AAA-ICDR Arbitration Rules, Art. 30(3).

113. VIAC Rules of Arbitration, Art. 41.

114. SCAI Rules of International Arbitration, Art. 44(3).

115. The link to the Subcommittee's page is the following: <https://www.ibanet.org/LPD/Dispute_Resolution_Section/Arbitration/Default.aspx>.

116. See, e.g., Joshua D. H. KARTON, *The Culture of International Arbitration and the Evolution of Contract Law* (Oxford University Press 2013).

117. Sir Bernard RIX, "Confidentiality in International Arbitration: Virtue or Vice", Jones Day Professorship in Commercial Law Lecture, Singapore Management University in Singapore (12 March 2015) p. 21. Available at: <https://law.smu.edu.sg/sites/default/files/law/CEBCLA/Notes_Confidentiality_in_International_Arbitration.pdf> (last accessed 7 June 2018).

118. Mark FELDMAN, "International Arbitration and Transparency", Peking University School of Transnational Law Research Paper No. 16-12 (25 September 2016) p. 21. Available at SSRN: <https://ssrn.com/abstract=2843140 or http://dx.doi.org/10.2139/ssrn.2843140> (last accessed 7 June 2018).

119. Ben JURATOWITCH, "Departing from Confidentiality in International Dispute Resolution", BIICL Seminar on Difficult Issues in Commercial, Investor-State, and State-State Dispute Resolution: Differences and Commonalities (8 June 2017) p. 8.

120. Sir Bernard RIX, "Confidentiality in International Arbitration: Virtue or Vice", Jones Day Professorship in Commercial Law Lecture, Singapore Management University in Singapore (12 March 2015) p. 21. Available at: <https://law.smu.edu.sg/sites/default/files/law/CEBCLA/Notes_Confidentiality_in_International_Arbitration.pdf> (last accessed 7 June 2018);

There are therefore possible solutions for the publication of arbitral awards which can be applied in a manner that respects the confidentiality expectations and interests of arbitrations users. And while confidentiality remains an important element, even users have expressed a growing appetite for the publication of awards.[121]

V. CONCLUSION

The legitimacy of commercial arbitration is undoubtedly under fire for a variety of reasons. As to the criticism regarding the development of common law, commercial arbitration probably does have an impact and it is only with the more systematic publication of awards that we can effectively respond. These latest calls for publication from the common law world may thus be the cue to finally take this long-heralded next step in the journey of commercial arbitration – a step which may also address some of the broader legitimacy challenges being faced by arbitration today.

Constantine PARTASIDES, "What Has Been The 'Spillover' Effect of The Transparency Debate on Commercial Arbitrations?", this volume, pp. 699-710.

121. When asked about what institutions could do to improve international arbitration, 64 percent of the respondents to the Queen Mary University of London survey mentioned the publication of awards in a redacted form and/or summaries. 2015 International Arbitration Survey: Improvements and Innovations in International Arbitration, conducted by the Queen Mary University of London and White & Case, p. 23. Available at: <https://www.whitecase.com/publications/insight/2015-international-arbitration-survey-improvements-and-innovations> (last accessed 7 June 2018).

Costs, Delay and Transparency – A Comment on Continued Legitimacy Concerns from the User's Perspective

Laura C. Abrahamson[*]

TABLE OF CONTENTS

I. THE CONCERNS: COSTS, DELAY AND LACK OF TRANSPARENCY

International commercial arbitration, like any type of arbitration, is of course a creature of contract – it is only possible with the consent of the parties. Corporate users of arbitration have in recent years become more vocal about their concerns about the costs of arbitration, the delay between filing and award, and the transparency of the arbitral process in getting to an award.[1] If those concerns are not adequately addressed, they could ultimately pose an existential threat to the continued legitimacy of international commercial arbitrations.[2] Almost every major arbitral institution has paid lip service to concerns about costs, delays and transparency in the last few years,[3] but are they doing

---

* Senior Vice President, Deputy General Counsel and Global Head of Litigation at AECOM.

1. See, e.g., Queen Mary University of London and White & Case, *2015 International Arbitration Survey: Improvements and Innovations in International Arbitration* (2015) p. 7 (showing 68% of respondents cite "cost" among the worst characteristics or arbitration, 39% cite "lack of insight into arbitrators' efficiency", 36% cite "lack of speed" and 12% cite "lack of insight into institutions' efficiency") (henceforth 2015 QMUL Survey); Queen Mary University of London and PriceWaterhouseCoopers, *Corporate Choices in International Arbitration: Industry Perspectives* (2013) p. 5 ("For respondents who considered arbitration not to be well suited to their industry, costs and delay were cited as the main reasons more than any other factors.") (henceforth 2013 QMUL Survey).
2. Notably, in the 2013 QMUL Survey, across all sectors, respondents referred equal percentages of disputes to arbitration as they did to litigation. 2013 QMUL Survey, supra fn. 1, at p. 7. In the 2010 survey, of the 68% of corporate respondents who had a dispute resolution policy, only 10% had a mandatory policy to choose arbitration over state court. Queen Mary University of London and White & Case, *2010 International Arbitration Survey: Choices in International Arbitration* (2010) p. 6 (henceforth 2010 QMUL Survey). A full 50% of the corporate respondents either left the choice of arbitration vs. state courts to the judgment of the negotiators, or it was not a feature of their corporate policy. *Id.*
3. See, e.g., International Chamber of Commerce, "ICC Court Announces New Policies to Foster Transparency and Ensure Greater Efficiency", News and Releases (1 May 2016) ("Users are concerned by the time and costs of international arbitrations, and rightly so. The expeditious resolution of disputes is one of our top priorities.... By releasing this new note, we send a clear signal to tribunals that unjustified delays will not be tolerated, and we provide transparency on the consequences that the Court will draw from such situations.").

enough about it? From the perspective of corporate end users, will it be too little, too late?

Historically, corporate decision makers have been motivated to select international arbitration as their contractual dispute mechanism because it offered a faster, more effective way to decide disputes, in addition to providing comfort on enforceability, and avoiding some specific legal systems/national courts.[4] But as it is becoming increasingly common for large commercial international arbitrations to take months to constitute a panel, and years to reach an award, the goal of a faster, more cost efficient process seems to be a mirage – and corporate counsel may start to seriously look at courts in some countries as a viable, and perhaps preferred solution.[5]

Although international arbitral institutions appear to have taken some steps forward, their actions are not robust enough to allay corporate users concerns. In 2015, the London Court of International Arbitration (LCIA) became the first major institution to provide actual average cost and duration figures,[6] followed by the Stockholm Chamber of Commerce (SCC).[7] In 2016, the Singapore International Arbitration Centre (SIAC) and Hong Kong International Arbitration Centre (HKIAC) provided more limited data about the mean and median duration of their arbitrations.[8] The latest statistical reports

4. See 2013 QMUL Survey, supra fn. 1, at p. 8.

5. Although the 2015 QMUL Survey reported a strong preference for international arbitration as a dispute resolution mechanism, that result is hardly surprising given the population surveyed. The 2015 QMUL Survey, unlike the 2013 QMUL Survey, cast a much broader net and included responses from private practitioners, arbitrators, academics, experts, institutional staff and third-party funders in addition to corporations' in-house counsel. In fact, in-house counsel only comprised 8% of the respondents. 2015 QMUL Survey, supra fn. 1, at p. 51. It is notable that, even with the wider pool, in the 2015 survey only 2% of respondents indicated cost was the most valuable characteristic of international arbitration, and only 10% indicated speed was the most valuable. *Id.*

6. Prompted by the 2015 QMUL Survey, in the fall of 2015 the LCIA first provided users with its analysis of average costs and duration of LCIA arbitration. The LCIA's 2015 publication and its recent 2017 updated publication are the most forthcoming disclosures of all arbitral institutions, but still fall far short of survey respondents' requests. See generally London Court of International Arbitration, *Facts and Figures – Costs and Duration: 2013-2016* (2017) p. 3; London Court of International Arbitration, *Tools to Facilitate Smart and Informed Choices* (2015). The most recent publication shows that 70% of cases with an amount in dispute under US$ 1 million are resolved in twelve months. London Court of International Arbitration, *Facts and Figures – Costs and Duration: 2013-2016* (2017) p. 3. However, since the average duration of all cases is 16 months, it appears that large matters are still taking two to three years to get to award. *Id.*

7. The SCC reports shorter durations – only 16% of SCC matters take two years or more to award. Celeste E. Salinas QUERO (Legal Counsel to SCC), *Costs of Arbitration and Apportionment of Costs Under the SCC Rules* (February 2016) p. 9. It does not provide a breakdown by amount in dispute. However, since almost half of SCC cases have an amount in dispute of under € 500,000, compared to only 17.5% of the SCC docket are cases involving € 5 million or more, the SCC report similarly suggests that large cases can take two to three years or more to get to award. *Id.*

8. In the fall of 2016, SIAC and HKIAC also provided more basic cost and duration of proceedings information for the first time. SIAC reported a mean duration of 15.3 months for three-member tribunals and an average duration of 11.3 months, but did not provide a further breakdown based on the size of its matters. Singapore International Arbitration Centre, "SIAC Releases Cost and Duration Study" (10 October 2016) p. 1. The HKIAC study, based on 62 matters, reported a median duration of 14.3 months and a mean duration of 16.3 months. Hong Kong International

issued by the International Chamber of Commerce (ICC) and the International Center for Dispute Resolution (ICDR) still do not provide any information about the average, median or any other measure of the duration of their proceedings, leaving corporate users frustratingly in the dark about the time and cost it can be expected to take to arbitrate a matter under their auspices.

The gap between what international commercial arbitral institutions are currently providing and what users want in terms of data is massive. The 2015 Queen Mary University of London/White & Case survey: "*Improvements and Innovations in International Arbitration*" reported that respondents felt arbitral institutions could improve international arbitration by publishing data not only on the average length of their cases, but also on the time taken by individual arbitrators to issue awards.[9] In fact, 65% of respondents want institutions to publicize the average length of time their arbitrations take, and almost 50% want institutions to disclose the time individual arbitrators took from appointment to award in previous cases.[10] None of the international commercial arbitral institutions appears to have made any attempt to respond to this latter suggestion,[11] nor do any of them appear to be taking steps to respond to respondents' desires to publish awards, either in full, in a redacted form, or in summary.[12]

In 2016, the ICC did announce that it would publish names of arbitrators sitting in ICC cases, but that information alone is of limited utility to corporate arbitration users.[13] At the same time, the ICC announced a new policy that established ICC tribunals are expected to submit draft awards within three months after the last substantive hearing or last substantive written submissions,[14] with cost consequences for "unjustified" delays beyond that time frame. This was touted as a "groundbreaking move", but was it? It is

---

Arbitration Centre, "Costs and Duration" (2017), available at <www.hkiac.org/content/costs-duration>. It did not provide any further breakdown by size, but did acknowledge that ten of those matters were decided under its expedited procedures. The mean duration of expedited arbitrations was reported as 8.1 months. *Id.*

9. 2015 QMUL Survey, supra fn. 1, at p. 2.
10. A full 64% of respondents also would like to see arbitral institutions publish arbitration awards, in redacted form or in summary, 50% would like to see decisions on challenges to arbitrators published, and almost 20% suggest arbitral institutions should publish full awards. *Id.* at p. 23.
11. ICSID is publishing data from which one can derive the time it takes arbitrators to render awards in individual cases. But since the average time between registration and award was reportedly averaged 1,381 days, that will hardly help to allay corporate concerns. Global Arbitration Review, "How Long Is Too Long to Wait for an Award?", Arbitration News (18 February 2016), available at <https://globalarbitrationreview.com/article/1035249/how-long-is-too-long-to-wait-for-an-award>.
12. 2015 QMUL Survey, supra fn. 1, at p. 23.
13. Unfortunately from a corporate user's perspective, the information on the ICC website is provided in a table that is not searchable by name. See International Chamber of Commerce, *ICC Arbitral Tribunals* (2018), available at <https://iccwbo.org/dispute-resolution-services/arbitration/icc-arbitral-tribunals/>. As of 19 February 2018, there were 1,200 entries, as the table includes both pending and closed matters. One can only imagine that as time goes by, attempting to use the data as it is presently published to determine how many active cases a prospective arbitrator is sitting on will be increasingly time consuming and inefficient.
14. This excludes written cost submissions and is two months in matters with a single arbitrator. International Chamber of Commerce, "Note to Parties and Arbitral Tribunals on the Conduct of the Arbitration Under the ICC Rules of Arbitration", para. 92 (Revised 30 October 2017).

difficult to assess without transparency as to what the typical time to award in ICC proceedings was before the policy was adopted.[15] Although the ICC President acknowledged that users are rightly "concerned by the time and costs of international arbitrations", and declared "[t]he expeditious resolution of disputes is one of our top priorities", corporate users are left wondering whether that is true, or if the ICC does not understand that it is often the time and cost it takes to get to that last substantive hearing that drives corporate concerns. While one would be hard-pressed not to agree it is important for tribunals to deliver awards within two to three months of the last substantive hearing or briefing, when larger cases appear to be taking two to three years on average to get to award, that alone doesn't get at the crux of the problem with delays and costs. If the ICC and other arbitral institutions are to really make the expeditious (and cost-effective) resolution of disputes a top priority, then they need to enact policies to shorten the time between filing a request for arbitration and getting to that last substantive hearing.

Recognizing that in any individual matter multiple factors may influence the time it takes to get from filing to the substantive hearing, from a corporate perspective there seem to be two particular factors which predominantly contribute to the lengthy (and costly) time lapse of up to twelve to eighteen months or more between filing and the last substantive hearing: (1) arbitrator availability and schedules; and (2) the "due process paranoia" identified in the 2015 Queen Mary University/White & Case survey – a concern that respondents described as a "reluctance by tribunals to act decisively in certain situations for fear of the arbitral award being challenged on the basis of a party not having had the chance to present its case fully".[16] Without transparently tackling these issues, it is difficult to see how international commercial arbitration will continue to be the default preferred dispute resolution procedure.[17] Unfortunately for users, none of the arbitral institutions appear to be ready to do so.

15. The LCIA reported median "time to award" is three months across all cases except those under US$ one million; if the ICC experience was similar, this might not have much impact on the total time to award. Users may also question whether the "consequences" lack teeth: the new policy suggest the ICC court will reduce by 5% to 10% the fees it otherwise would have "considered fixing" for unjustified delays in submitting awards up to four months late (seven months after the last substantive hearing or submissions), reducing by 10% to 20% for draft awards submitted up to seven months late, and reducing by 20% or more if awards are submitted more than seven months late.

16. Particularly interesting is the report that both arbitrators and participants agreed that this is a prevalent problem contributing to delays. Not only did interviewees complain about situations where deadlines were repeatedly extended, fresh evidence submitted late in the process and disruptive behavior was permitted due to a perceived concern by tribunals that otherwise their award would be vulnerable to challenge, but arbitrators confirmed that concern had influenced their decisions. 2015 QMUL Survey, supra fn. 1, at p. 10.

17. *Id.*

II. POSSIBLE SOLUTIONS

So what *is* needed? Here are some suggested steps, from a corporate client's perspective, to minimize the length, cost and increase transparency in international commercial arbitration:

First, from our corporate clients' perspective, *arbitral institutions across the board need to share much more data with their potential customers*. Preserving the confidentiality of arbitrations is often cited as the insurmountable obstacle to publishing data, but it need not be. Protecting corporations' confidentiality and privacy concerns and publishing the types of data arbitral stakeholders are looking for to provide greater transparency are not mutually exclusive.[18] Even if publishing redacted awards is a step too far,[19] arbitral institutions have a significant amount of data corporate users could use to better inform their decision makers both in drafting arbitration clauses and in selecting arbitrators that can be shared without compromising the privacy or disclosing the identity of the parties to an arbitration. In particular, the date of filing, the names of arbitrators, the names of counsel, the date of substantive hearings, whether a matter is pending, and date of award could all be published without violating the confidentiality of the parties. This information would go a long way to providing corporations with the data they need to enable them to assess how busy potential arbitrators are *before* they consider nominating them. It would be even more helpful if institutions would publish this data in a format that allows potential customers to search by potential arbitrators' names to pull up the list of matters an individual arbitrator has been appointed in.

Second, *arbitral institutions need to adopt rules or policies to reduce the length of time between when a case is filed and the last substantive hearing date*. These could include:

(a) Obtaining a commitment in advance from prospective arbitrators – before they are appointed – that they have sufficient time in their diaries to hold all necessary substantive hearings in a matter within the following twelve months (or six months for smaller matters);
(b) Obtaining a commitment in advance from prospective arbitrators – before they are appointed – that they will not take on additional appointments during the duration of a matter that would reduce the arbitrator's ability to conduct the case efficiently;[20]
(c) Requiring arbitrators to set an early procedural conference (within the first two months of filing) and then encouraging tribunals to make use of that early procedural

18. See Avinash POOROOYE and Ronan FEEHILY, "Confidentiality and Transparency in International Commercial Arbitration: Finding the Right Balance", 22 Harvard Neg. L. Rev. (2017) p. 275.
19. There is significant demand among users for publication of awards, whether in full, in redacted form, or in summary. 2015 QMUL Survey, supra fn. 1, at p. 23. Publication of awards, even in a redacted or summary form, would be a huge step towards transparency and would provide corporate clients a much greater ability to assess potential arbitrators' performance and reasoning. A. POOROOYE and R. FEEHILY, supra fn. 18, at p. 305.
20. See Debevoise & Plimpton LLP, *Protocol to Promote Efficiency in International Arbitration* (2010, revised in 2018).

conference to set a definitive schedule for all substantive hearings, as well as for deliberations.

Arbitrators who cannot commit that they have the time to sit for hearings within the next year, or who aren't willing to commit the time necessary to conduct an arbitration in the most efficient, expeditious manner – by not taking on additional work that would interfere – could contribute to, if not cause, significant delays that might be seen as disqualifying from a corporate perspective. At the least, corporate clients will take comfort knowing that if they choose a certain arbitral institution, that institution's procedures for appointing arbitrators are designed so that the appointed panel can and will devote sufficient time to their matter. Similarly, a tribunal's focus at the outset on completing the substantive hearings at the earliest possible date could significantly improve the time to award. Knowing that the arbitral institution directs its tribunals to focus on this will provide reassurance to potential customers that the arbitral process is designed to be as efficient as possible.

Third, *arbitral institutions need to adopt rules or policies to reduce "due process paranoia"*. The fact reported in the 2015 Queen Mary University of London/White & Case survey that "many" arbitrators revealed in interviews that their decisions were influenced by concerns their awards would be vulnerable to challenge if they did not allow parties to "fully" present their cases[21] is troubling – and arbitral institutions need to respond. Arbitral tribunals can and should be encouraged to use their experience and discretion to appropriately limit submissions – before, during and after the hearings. Adopting explicit rules or policies that encourage this could counter concerns about challenges. Similarly, arbitral institutions can encourage arbitral tribunals to utilize available sanctions to deal with dilatory or abusive parties or counsel. Corporate users want arbitral tribunals to be proactive in managing their matters:[22] overly cautious, permissive panels that are unwilling to set limits or impose sanctions drive up costs and delay resolution.

Corporations today have many choices when drafting dispute resolution clauses. If they want to continue to provide for international arbitration, there are an increasing number of arbitral institutions, and updated rules, to choose from.[23] As of the 2015 Queen Mary University of London/White & Case survey, the ICC, LCIA, HKIAC, SIAC, SCC, ICSID and ICDR were still the preferred institutions.[24] It will be interesting to see if any of them, in an effort to satisfy the needs of corporate clients, continue to attract new users and/or increase their market share in the future, start providing the types of enhanced reporting and data corporate clients are clamoring for, or if some of the other international arbitral institutions, like the Australian Centre for International

21. 2015 QMUL Survey, supra fn. 1, at p. 10.
22. 2015 QMUL Survey, supra fn. 2, at p. 25.
23. Almost every major international arbitration institution seems to have updated its rules at least once in the last five years: Vienna International Arbitration Centre (VIAC) and Dubai International Arbitration Centre (DIAC) in 2018, ICC and SCC in 2017, SIAC and the Australia Centre for International Commercial Arbitration (ACICA) in 2016, LCIA and ICDR in 2014, HKIAC and UNCITRAL in 2013. MARC (the alternative dispute resolution arm of the Mauritius Chamber of Commerce and Industry) is proposing new amendments in 2018 to their 2014 rules.
24. 2015 QMUL Survey, supra fn. 1, at p. 17.

Commercial Arbitration (ACICA), the Dubai International Arbitration Centre (DIAC), the Swiss Chambers Arbitration Institution (SCIA), or the Vienna International Arbitration Centre (VIAC) step up to fill the void and successfully capitalize on the desire for more information.

Allocation of Competence Between a National Court and an Arbitral Tribunal: Striking a Balance Between Efficiency and Legitimacy of Arbitration – Asian Perspectives

Yoshimi Ohara[*] *and John Lane*[**]

TABLE OF CONTENTS

I. OVERVIEW

This article considers how best to allocate the "competence" between an arbitral tribunal and a national court in order to strike a balance between efficiency and legitimacy in arbitration. Arbitral proceedings will only be legitimate if they are based on a valid and effective arbitration agreement. A national court's power to review the jurisdiction of an arbitral tribunal is therefore essential to ensure the legitimacy of arbitration. However, excessive judicial intervention in arbitration undermines both party autonomy and the efficiency of arbitration and can cause unwarranted procedural delay. Indeed, it is not uncommon that a court's jurisdiction is invoked by a party as a dilatory tactic.

One recent high profile dispute, between a Malaysian media group (Astro), and its former JV partner, a group company of the Indonesian conglomerate Lippo Group (PT First Media TBK (First Media)), illustrates how jurisdictional disputes can make arbitration inefficient. This matter, which has been going on for more than a decade, offers an opportunity to pause and revisit the fundamental principle of *competence-competence* to see how different approaches have been adopted in Asia by comparing Singapore, Hong Kong, Japan and China, and to consider as a policy matter the optimal

* Partner in Nagashima Ohno & Tsunematsu; serves as both counsel and arbitrator in international arbitration in various seats under the rules of major arbitration institutions and the UNCITRAL; currently serves as a Vice-President of the ICC International Court of Arbitration (ICC), a Board Member of the Japan Association of Arbitrators (JAA) and the Swiss Arbitration Association (ASA); former Vice President of the London Court of International Arbitration (LCIA); ICCA Governing Board Member. The author would like to thank Claire Chong and Mo Yan for their valuable assistance.

** Registered Foreign Lawyer (England & Wales) in Nagashima Ohno & Tsunematsu's disputes and global investigations practice; contributed Sect. III of this article.

balance between the powers of an arbitral tribunal and those of a national court when questions of jurisdiction arise.

II. COMPETENT AND COMPETENCE

"Competence-competence" is one of the basic doctrines in modern international arbitration. It is taken for granted that an arbitral tribunal has the power to determine its own jurisdiction (i.e., it is "competent" to determine its own "competency", hence "competence-competence"). Such power includes the tribunal's ability to rule on the existence, validity, legality and scope of the parties' arbitration agreement.[1] It derives from the notion of party autonomy and ensures an efficient and viable alternative dispute resolution mechanism. Otherwise a dissatisfied party could always go to a court to derail arbitration proceedings.

This principle of competence-competence was incorporated by the Convention on the Recognition and Enforcement of Foreign Arbitral Awards 1958 (New York Convention)[2] and further developed in the UNCITRAL Model Law on International Commercial Arbitration 1985 (Model Law).

Whilst the principle of competence-competence is widely recognized, its implementation varies by jurisdiction. The variation between jurisdictions includes areas such as the priority of review between an arbitral tribunal and a national court and the standard and timing of judicial review and its finality.[3]

1. New York Convention

Art. II of the New York Convention provides for so-called "negative competence", requiring a national court whose jurisdiction has been invoked in relation to an arbitration agreement to refer parties to arbitration *unless* the court finds that the purported agreement is "null and void, inoperative or incapable of being performed".[4]

Later, at the enforcement stage, the New York Convention contemplates that a national court may refuse to recognize and grant leave to enforce an award in circumstances where, inter alia, the arbitral tribunal has made the award in excess of its jurisdiction.[5]

Under the New York Convention, it is clear that both arbitral tribunals and national courts have the power to consider and decide jurisdictional disputes. However, the

1. Gary BORN, *International Commercial Arbitration*, 2nd ed. (Kluwer 2014).
2. New York Convention, Art. II(3).
3. Supra. Simon GREENBERG, "Chapter 4 – Direct Review of Arbitral Jurisdiction Under the UNCITRAL Model Law on International Commercial Arbitration: An Assessment of Article 16(3)" in F. BACHAND and F. GÉLINAS, eds., *The UNCITRAL Model Law After Twenty-Five Years: Global Perspectives on International Commercial Arbitration* (Juris 2013). Nadja ERK-KUBAT, Julian D.M. LEW, *Parallel Proceedings in International Arbitration: A Comparative European Perspective* (Kluwer 2014). George A. BERMANN "The Role of National Courts in the Threshold of Arbitration", 28 American Review of International Arbitration (2017, no. 3).
4. Model Law, Art. 8.
5. New York Convention, Art. V.

timing, scope and standard of review by national courts on the issue of the arbitral tribunal's jurisdiction is less clear.

2. *UNCITRAL Model Law*

The Model Law defines, and limits, the appropriate intervention by a national court in international arbitration in favour of arbitration. In addition to negative competence, which is prescribed in the New York Convention,[6] the Model Law provides for an arbitral tribunal's "positive competence", i.e. the ability to rule on its own jurisdiction.[7] Such a ruling can be made either: (a) "as a preliminary question"; or (b) "in an award on the merits". In response to the former, a party may request the court to review the arbitral tribunal's positive jurisdictional ruling.[8] Such national court's decision on jurisdiction is subject to no appeal.[9] In response to the latter, a court review of the arbitral tribunal's ruling on jurisdiction has to wait until setting-aside proceedings.[10]

3. *Unsettled Answers in the UNCITRAL Model Law*

The Model Law unequivocally prescribes an arbitral tribunal's competence, but it also provides for judicial review of a tribunal's competence potentially four times without: (a) providing clear guidance as to how those opportunities for judicial review relate to each other; or (b) specifying review standards for a national court.

First, when a party submits a dispute in breach of an arbitration agreement to a national court, the court must refer the parties to arbitration unless a court finds that the arbitration agreement is null, void, inoperable or incapable of being performed (the First Stage).[11]

Second, when a tribunal makes a determination on its jurisdiction as a preliminary question, a dissatisfied party may apply to a national court for its review (the Second Stage).[12]

Third, once an award is issued, a dissatisfied party may apply to a national court of the seat of arbitration to have the award set aside based on a jurisdictional objection (the Third Stage).[13]

Fourth, at the time of enforcement, a dissatisfied party may resist the enforcement of an award on a jurisdictional objection at a national court in the place of enforcement (the Fourth Stage).[14]

It is not clear from the Model Law whether a national court's review standard in each of the above four occasions is the same, how each judicial review interrelates to the other or the consequence of failure to apply for judicial review at any one of those stages.

6. Model Law, Art. 8.
7. Model Law, Art. 16(1).
8. Model Law, Art. 16(3).
9. Model Law, Art. 16(3).
10. Model Law, Art. 34(2).
11. Model Law, Art. 8.
12. Model Law, Art. 16(3).
13. Model Law, Art. 34.
14. Model Law, Art. 35.

Since the Model Law does not give a clear answer to these questions, national arbitration acts (even among the countries that have adopted the Model Law) and national courts have taken divergent approaches.[15] The battle between Astro and First Media in the courts of Singapore and Hong Kong, which lasted more than eight years, centered on the question of whether First Media could successfully argue – at the Fourth Stage in both jurisdictions – that the courts should decline to enforce the awards because the arbitral tribunal lacked jurisdiction in circumstances where First Media deliberately chose not to challenge the arbitral tribunal's jurisdiction at the Second and Third Stages.

III. JUDICIAL REVIEW OF AN ARBITRAL TRIBUNAL'S JURISDICTIONAL DECISION – THE DISPUTE BETWEEN ASTRO AND FIRST MEDIA

1. Facts

First Media entered into a joint venture with a number of companies from the Astro group for the provision of multi-media and television services in Indonesia. The JV vehicle was called 'PT Direct Vision' (DV), and the terms of the JV were set forth in a subscription and shareholders' agreement dated 11 March 2005 (SSA). The SSA contained a clause stating that the parties would submit any disputes to arbitration under Singapore International Arbitration Centre (SIAC) rules.

By mid-2007 it had become apparent that certain conditions precedent contained in the SSA would not be met. As a result, the JV deal never closed. However, before it became clear that the deal would not work out as envisaged, DV had already launched its satellite television service in Indonesia and a number of Astro group companies had been providing substantial funding to DV since about December 2005. However, the Astro group companies that had been providing the majority of the funding to the DV[16] were not parties to the SSA (the Additional Parties).

2. Arbitration Procedural History

First Media commenced litigation against the Additional Parties in the Indonesian courts in September 2008, seeking the continued funding of DV. As would ultimately become clear, commencing litigation rather than arbitration against the Additional Parties was the proper course of action. However, in response, Astro commenced arbitration proceedings in Singapore in October 2008. At the same time, Astro made an application to the arbitral tribunal (the Tribunal) to join the Additional Parties to the arbitration (the Application).

Having considered the Application at a hearing in February 2009, the Tribunal issued an award in May 2009 finding that it *did* have jurisdiction to add the Additional Parties to the arbitration (erroneously, as it would turn out) and deciding to exercise that jurisdiction (the Joinder Award). At this point, First Media could have appealed the

15. Supra.
16. These companies were: "Astro All Asia Networks Plc"; "Measat Broadcast Network"; and "All Asia Multimedia Network FZ-LLC".

Joinder Award to the Singapore High Court,[17] but it chose not to. Instead, First Media simply reserved its position.[18]

The Tribunal proceeded to hear the substance of the dispute and rendered four awards in favour of Astro in excess of US$ 130 million between October 2009 and August 2010 (the Awards). The vast majority of that sum was in relation to claims advanced by the Additional Parties.

3. *Singapore Proceedings*

a. *Singapore enforcement*

First Media took no action to set aside the Award. Astro sought to enforce the Awards in Singapore and received leave to enforce on 5 August and 3 September 2010 (the Singapore Enforcement Orders). The Singapore Enforcement Orders were then served on First Media in Indonesia. On 24 March 2011, Astro had judgments entered against First Media in Singapore. First Media then applied to set aside the judgments on 3 May 2011.

On 22 August 2011, an Assistant Registrar set aside the judgments and granted First Media leave to set aside the Enforcement Orders. Astro appealed, but the Registrar's decision was upheld by a judge. First Media then made an application on 12 September 2011 to set aside the Singapore Enforcement Orders. This application was dismissed by a judge in chambers. First Media appealed to the High Court.

b. *Singapore High Court decision*

First Media argued, amongst other things, that there was never an arbitration agreement between it and the Additional Parties, but in a decision handed down on 22 October 2012,[19] the High Court essentially held that it was too late for First Media to rely on this argument.

The High Court found that First Media could have challenged the Joinder Award under the International Arbitration Act 2002 (Singapore) (IAA), read with Art. 16(3) of the Model Law, when the Joinder Award was made. However, it had chosen not to. The High Court held that this meant First Media had, as a result, lost its "sole and exclusive opportunity to raise its jurisdiction objection before the Singapore courts".[20] First Media appealed to the Singapore Court of Appeal.

c. *Singapore Court of Appeal decision*

The issue before the Court of Appeal was whether a party to an international arbitration under the IAA can resist enforcement of an award against it in Singapore on the grounds of an alleged lack of jurisdiction of the arbitral tribunal in circumstances where that party

---

17. Under Sect. 10 International Arbitration Act 2002 (Singapore), First Media had the right to appeal this decision.
18. *PT First Media TBK (fka PT Broadband Multimedia TBK) v. Astro Nusantara International BV and ors* [2014] 1 SLR 372, [223].
19. *Astro Nusantara International BV and ors v. PT Ayunda Prima Mitra and ors* [2013] 1 SLR 636.
20. *PT First Media TBK (fka PT Broadband Multimedia TBK) v. Astro Nusantara International BV and ors* [2014] 1 SLR 372, [21].

did not challenge the lack of jurisdiction at an earlier stage despite having had an opportunity to do so.[21]

In a thoroughly reasoned judgment delivered by the Chief Justice, Sundaresh Menon, the Court of Appeal answered that question affirmatively and unanimously allowed the appeal. The Court of Appeal held that the enforcement of international arbitration awards in Singapore is governed by Sect. 19 IAA and this section, which contains the power to refuse enforcement, is to be interpreted in conjunction with the "underlying philosophy" of the Model Law,[22] which provides for the principle of a "choice of remedies", namely choice between an active remedy to set aside an award and a passive remedy to contest the enforcement of an award.[23] This principle however is not explicit in the Model Law, so the Court of Appeal undertook a forensic analysis of the Model Law *travaux préparatoires*.

Having reviewed the *travaux préparatoires* of the Model Law Working Group, the Court of Appeal held that a "choice of remedies" is "fundamental to the design of the Model Law",[24] and that this applied both to domestic international arbitration awards and foreign international arbitration awards.[25]

Given that one of the purposes of the IAA is to incorporate the Model Law in Singapore legislation, the Court of Appeal held that First Media may resist enforcement of the award under Sect. 19 of the IAA on the same grounds for resisting enforcement under Art. 36(1) of the Model Law.[26] It then refused to enforce the award because it found that the Tribunal had exceeded its jurisdiction by joining the Additional Parties to the arbitration.

The Singapore Court of Appeal handed down its decision on 31 October 2013, four years and five months after the Tribunal's Joinder Award.

---

21. *PT First Media TBK (fka PT Broadband Multimedia TBK) v. Astro Nusantara International BV and ors* [2014] 1 SLR 372, [1].
22. The Court of Appeal undertook a detailed analysis of the legislative history of Sect. 19 IAA. Sect. 19 can be traced back to Sect. 26 Arbitration Act 1950 (United Kingdom) via Sect. 20 Arbitration Act 1985 (Singapore) and Sect. 20 Arbitration Act 1953 (Singapore). By the 1970s, at the latest, it was settled law in the United Kingdom that a "choice of remedies" was available to a party that wanted to challenge an arbitral tribunal's jurisdiction. This was likely the position in Singapore until the IAA because both the Arbitration Act 1953 and the Arbitration Act 1985 closely followed the wording of the UK Act. The question was whether the position changed when the IAA was promulgated because the IAA was informed not only by the previous Arbitration Acts in Singapore, and, ultimately, the UK Act, but also by the Model Law. The Court of Appeal held that it had not changed, see *PT First Media TBK (fka PT Broadband Multimedia TBK) v. Astro Nusantara International BV and ors* [2014] 1 SLR 372, [34]-[35], [40], [44] and [55].
23. *PT First Media TBK (fka PT Broadband Multimedia TBK) v. Astro Nusantara International BV and ors* [2014] 1 SLR 372, [26] and [71].
24. *PT First Media TBK (fka PT Broadband Multimedia TBK) v Astro Nusantara International BV and ors* [2014] 1 SLR 372, [65]-[68], [71] and [143].
25. *PT First Media TBK (fka PT Broadband Multimedia TBK) v. Astro Nusantara International BV and ors* [2014] 1 SLR 372, [71].
26. *PT First Media TBK (fka PT Broadband Multimedia TBK) v. Astro Nusantara International BV and ors* [2014] 1 SLR 372, [143].

4. *Hong Kong Proceedings*

a. *Hong Kong enforcement*

Astro also sought to enforce the awards in Hong Kong and a number of enforcement orders were made against First Media between August 2010 and October 2013. Originally, First Media did not apply to set aside any of the enforcement orders because it believed that it did not have assets in Hong Kong. It later transpired that First Media *did* have assets in the jurisdiction and it made an application to have the enforcement orders set aside, fourteen months late after the expiry of the time limit.

b. *Hong Kong Court of First Instance*

The issues before the Court of First Instance were whether: (i) First Media would be granted leave to appeal out of time to resist enforcement; and (ii) if the answer to the first question was "yes", whether First Media could bring itself within one of the recognized grounds in Hong Kong for refusing enforcement of an international arbitral award under Sect. 44(2)(b) Arbitration Ordinance (Cap 341) (AO).[27]

In a decision handed down on 17 February 2015, the Court of First Instance upheld the enforcement orders and rejected First Media's application for leave to apply out of time to set them aside on the ground that they had been made without jurisdiction.

The judge, Chow J, answered the second question first. He found that, prima facie, First Media *had* brought itself within Sect. 44(2)(b) because the Singapore Court of Appeal had held that the Tribunal lacked jurisdiction to join the Additional Parties, and that it was not now open to Astro to dispute this.[28] However, Chow J stated that the Singapore Court of Appeal's finding was not "definitive", and that the question of enforcement of arbitral awards is governed by Hong Kong law and that refusal of enforcement of an award in another jurisdiction is not a proper ground for refusal in Hong Kong.

Chow J refused First Media leave to set aside the enforcement orders on two grounds: (i) the "good faith" principle; and (ii) a refusal of an extension of time of the fourteen-day period stipulated under the AO to have the enforcement orders set aside.[29]

In relation to the latter, Chow J held First Media could not rely on Sect. 44(2) because it had not acted in good faith. As a result, he exercised his residual discretion to permit enforcement, even though Sect. 44(2) otherwise applied.[30]

Chow J refused to grant leave out of time because: (a) the delay of fourteen months was very significant; (b) First Media's original decision not to challenge the enforcement of the Awards in Hong Kong was deliberate; and (c) the Awards had not actually been

27. "Enforcement of a [New York] Convention award may be refused if the person against whom it is invoked proves ... (b) that the arbitration agreement was not valid under the law to which the parties subjected it or, failing any indication thereon, under the law of the country where the award was made."

28. *Astro Nusantara International BV and ors v. PT First Media TBK (fka PT Broadband Multimedia TBK) and ors* HCCT 45/2010 (17 February 2015), [95].

29. *Astro Nusantara International BV and ors v. PT First Media TBK (fka PT Broadband Multimedia TBK) and ors* HCCT 45/2010 (17 February 2015).

30. *Astro Nusantara International BV and ors v. PT First Media TBK (fka PT Broadband Multimedia TBK) and ors* [2018] HKCFA 12, [24]-[32].

set aside in Singapore.[31] First Media appealed to the Hong Kong Court of Appeal (HKCA).

c. Hong Kong Court of Appeal

The HKCA heard First Media's appeal in November 2016 and gave its judgment on 5 December 2016.[32] The Court of Appeal overturned Chow J's decision on the good faith principle, but upheld his decision refusing an extension of time.[33] First Media then appealed to the Hong Kong Court of Final Appeal.

d. Hong Kong Court of Final Appeal

The issue for the Court of Final Appeal (HKCFA) was whether Chow J's reliance at first instance on the fact that the Awards had not been set aside at the seat of the arbitration was a proper factor to consider when refusing the extension of time. The HKCFA held that it was not a proper factor and unanimously allowed the appeal.

The HKCFA held that the choice of remedies principle is subsumed within Sect. 44(2) of the AO and, therefore, a party may resist enforcement of an arbitral award in Hong Kong, even if the award was not challenged in the courts of the supervisory jurisdiction.

The HKCFA handed down its decision on 11 April 2018, nearly nine years after the Tribunal's Joinder Award.

IV. COMPARATIVE ANALYSIS

The choice of remedies recognized by the courts in Singapore and Hong Kong allowed First Media to continue to challenge the Awards nearly a decade after the Tribunal's preliminary jurisdictional decision. Would the outcome have been the same in civil law jurisdictions in Asia, such as Japan and China – i.e. do these jurisdictions also recognize the choice of remedies? Also what is the standard of judicial review – a full review or deference to an arbitral tribunal's decision absent manifest error?

This Section compares remedies available in Singapore, Hong Kong, Japan and China at each stage of the four stages in circumstances where it has been alleged that the arbitral tribunal lacks jurisdiction.

---

31. *Astro Nusantara International BV and ors v. PT First Media TBK (fka PT Broadband Multimedia TBK) and ors* HCCT 45/2010 (17 February 2015) [129].

32. *PT First Media TBK (fka PT Broadband Multimedia TBK) and ors v. Astro Nusantara International BV and ors* CACV 272/2015 (5 December 2016).

33. The Hong Kong Court of Final Appeal summarized the Court of Appeal's reasons for not interfering with the exercise of Chow J's discretion to refuse an extension of time: "The Court of Appeal declined to interfere with Chow J's exercise of discretion and endorsed his reliance on the three factors mentioned above, namely, (i) the length of the delay, (ii) the fact that deliberate decision was taken not to apply to set aside within the time prescribed and (iii) the fact that the awards had not been set aside at the seat of the arbitration." See *Astro Nusantara International BV and ors v. PT First Media TBK (fka PT Broadband Multimedia TBK) and ors* [2018] HKCFA 12, [46].

1. *Singapore*

Singapore, which is a signatory to the New York Convention, has adopted the Model Law. It incorporated nearly all the Model Law's provisions in Sect. 3 IAA, thereby recognizing both positive and negative competence.[34]

The law in Singapore appears to be settled in relation to the standard of judicial review of an arbitral tribunal's jurisdiction. At the First Stage, if a party submits a dispute to a national court in breach of an arbitration agreement, the court must stay its proceedings and refer the matter to arbitration so long as the court, having conducted a prima facie review, finds the arbitration agreement to be valid.

Judicial review at the outset of the proceedings is made on a prima facie basis as a full review could "significantly hollow [out]" the competence-competence principle since a party could strategically manoeuvre away from arbitration merely by bringing its claim in court if the court were to conduct a full review.[35]

On the other hand, once the arbitral tribunal has determined its own jurisdiction, regardless of whether it does or does not find it has jurisdiction, the court may review the arbitral tribunal's jurisdictional decision de novo[36] at the Second, Third and Fourth Stages. The de novo review ensures a court's ability to verify whether a party has truly forgone its right of access to a court.

A party that wishes to challenge the High Court's judgment on its review of the arbitral tribunal's jurisdictional ruling at the Second Stage may appeal to the Court of Appeal, provided that leave to appeal is granted by the High Court.[37] The Court of Appeal is the highest court in Singapore, so any decision by the Court of Appeal is final and binding. This is different to the Model Law, which does not provide for a right of appeal to the judicial review at the High Court at the Second Stage.

In *Astro v. First Media*, the High Court held that if a party fails to appeal a tribunal's preliminary ruling on jurisdiction, such ruling will be treated as final between the parties and a party is then precluded from challenging the tribunal's jurisdiction in a subsequent annulment action.[38] As this particular issue ultimately did not arise on appeal, the Court of Appeal observed obiter that a party which fails to avail itself of the active remedy in the Second Stage would be precluded from doing so in the Third Stage.[39] Thus, pending a ruling by the apex court of Singapore on a future occasion, the current position appears to be that Singapore courts are unlikely to afford a choice of the active remedies between the Second and Third Stage.

What if a party did not participate at all in the arbitral proceedings and therefore failed to make known its challenge to the tribunal's ruling on jurisdiction? In *Rakna Arakshaka Lanka Ltd v. Avant Garde Maritime Services (Private) Limited*,[40] the High Court dismissed an application filed by a non-participating party to set aside an award on

34. Model Law, Arts. 8 and 16.
35. *Tomolugen Holdings Ltd and anor v. Silica Investors Ltd and ors* [2015] SGCA 57.
36. *Insigma Tech. Co. v. Alstom Tech. Ltd.* [2008] SGHC 134.
37. Sect. 10(4) and (5) IAA.
38. *Astro Nusantara Int'l BV v. PT Ayunda Prima Mitra*, [2012] SGHC 212, para. 151.
39. *PT First Media TBK (fka PT Broadband Multimedia TBK) v. Astro Nusantara International BV and ors* [2014] 1 SLR 372, [130].
40. [2018] SGHC 78 (Quentin Loh J).

jurisdictional grounds on the basis that the non-participating party had failed to challenge the tribunal's preliminary ruling on its own jurisdiction within the time prescribed in Sect. 10(3) IAA.

The High Court stated:

> "Art 16(3) of the Model Law was intended as an early avenue for parties to promptly and finally resolve jurisdictional disputes so as to save costs and time, and it would defeat these purposes to allow a party to reserve jurisdictional challenges to the award on the merits [...] It was therefore intended that a failure to raise a plea on jurisdiction within the 30-day limit should have a preclusive effect on subsequent setting aside proceedings at the seat."[41]

The Court of Appeal recently overturned the decision of the High Court and upheld the application by the non-participating party to set aside the final award on jurisdictional grounds.[42] Departing from the emphasis placed by the High Court on the need to reduce delays and wastage of costs, the Court of Appeal ruled that a respondent which believes that the tribunal has no jurisdiction (as the non-participating party in question did) can legitimately refuse to participate in arbitral proceedings.

The Court of Appeal stated:

> "The established rule is that a party to a contract which contains an arbitration clause is legally obliged to resolve disputes arising under that contract by arbitration. This principle is enshrined in the IAA via s 6 which directs the court to stay any court proceedings that have been instituted in breach of an agreement to arbitrate. While a claimant in this situation is obliged to arbitrate however, there is no such duty on the respondent. The law does not compel a respondent against whom arbitration proceedings have been started to take part in those proceedings and defend his position. If the respondent believes that the arbitration tribunal has no jurisdiction, for one reason or another, he is perfectly entitled to sit by and do nothing in the belief that either the proceedings will not result in a final award against him or that if an award is made, he will have valid grounds to resist enforcement. Such a respondent may therefore let the opportunity to challenge the tribunal's jurisdiction afforded to him by Art 16 go unutilised. This might be a risky course of action to pursue but it is one that lies within the prerogative of every respondent. If the respondent is mistaken in his belief, then the arbitration which proceeds without his participation will end in an award which will be enforceable against him and no challenge to jurisdiction that he seeks to mount thereafter will be successful. If in fact he does not have a valid objection, then even if Art 16(3) does not have preclusive effect, whatever he does would not affect the ultimate result or the justice of the case."[43]

41. *Rakna Arakshaka Lanka Ltd v. Avant Garde Maritime Services (Private) Limited* [2018] SGHC 78, 61-62.
42. *Rakna Arakshaka Lanka Ltd v. Avant Garde Maritime Services (Private) Limited* [2019] SGCA 33.
43. *Rakna Arakshaka Lanka Ltd v. Avant Garde Maritime Services* (Private) Limited [2019] SGCA 33, [73].

In terms of the relationship amongst the four opportunities for judicial review, the Court of Appeal clarified in its judgment in *First Media v. Astro* that a party has a choice between an "active remedy" and a "passive remedy" under the IAA. Provided that a party has made its jurisdictional objection known in the arbitration proceedings in a timely manner, it is not obliged to seek a judicial review of the arbitral tribunal's jurisdictional decision at the Second Stage or at the Third Stage by seeking to set aside the award on the merits. Rather, it may wait until enforcement is attempted – i.e. the Fourth Stage – to "passively" resist.

The High Court in *Rakna* also noted in reliance on the decision of the Singapore Court of Appeal in *First Media v. Astro* that a defaulting party who fails to challenge the tribunal's preliminary decision on jurisdiction does not lose its right to passively resist enforcement of the award.

The Singapore courts apply different standards of judicial review depending on the stage of the arbitration proceedings and thereby encourage the arbitral tribunal to rule on its own jurisdiction first, subject to a full judicial review in the later stages. Among remedies at the four different stages, while the court recognizes a choice between active remedies (at the Second and Third Stages) and a passive remedy (at the Fourth Stage), the court by denying a choice between two active remedies, at least partly incentivizes a party to make an immediate appeal to the tribunal's jurisdictional decision which permits prompt resolution of jurisdictional disputes.

2. *Hong Kong*

China acceded to the NY Convention in 1987 and the Convention therefore applies in Hong Kong due to its status as a Special Administrative Region of China.

The AO (see above) came into force in 2011 and governs both international and domestic arbitration. The AO is substantially modelled on the 2006 version of the Model Law and recognizes both positive and negative competence.

As in Singapore, the position in Hong Kong is that arbitral tribunals are encouraged to rule on their own jurisdiction first.

At the First Stage, unless it is a clear that an arbitration agreement is "null and void, inoperative or incapable of being performed",[44] the court should stay its proceedings in favour of arbitration. It will then be for the arbitral tribunal to determine whether there is a valid arbitration agreement.[45]

The arbitral tribunal's preliminary ruling on its jurisdiction is provisionally binding, but it is subject to challenge in the Hong Kong Court of First Instance,[46] which has authority to make a final decision in relation to the question of a tribunal's jurisdiction. Unlike in Singapore, there is no right of appeal against the Court of First Instance's decision.[47]

44. Model Law, Art. 8.
45. *Chimbusco International Petroleum (Singapore) Pte ltd v. Fully Best Trading Ltd* HCA No. 2416 of 2014, 2 December 2015 (Mimmie Chan J) at [19].
46. Sect. 34(1) and (5) AO.
47. Sect. 34(4) and (5) AO.

In terms of the relationship amongst the four opportunities for judicial review, as in Singapore if a party fails to appeal an award on jurisdiction, the award will be treated as final between the parties and a party is precluded from challenging the tribunal's jurisdiction in a subsequent annulment action under Art. 34 of the Model Law.[48] Thus, the Hong Kong court does not afford a choice of remedies between the Second and Third Stage.

It is now clear following the HKCFA's judgment in *Astro v. First Media* that a choice of remedies (i.e., between an active remedy whereby an award is set aside, and a passive remedy whereby enforcement of an award is resisted) is also available in Hong Kong.

It is worth noting that in Hong Kong it may be acting in bad faith for a party who wishes to subsequently raise a jurisdictional challenge to keep silent about some procedural or jurisdictional irregularity in the course of arbitration proceedings.[49] On this point the HKCA made the following *obiter* observation in its judgment in *First Media v. Astro*:

> "The principle of 'good faith' and the 'choice of remedies' principle are not mutually exclusive but complementary. Applying the principle of 'good faith' too rigorously whenever there is a failure to pursue active remedies might bring this into conflict with the 'choice of remedies' principle."[50]

In what circumstances a choice of remedies may be affected by a lack of good faith requires further consideration by the courts in Hong Kong.

3. *Japan*

Japan, which is a signatory to the New York Convention, enacted its Arbitration Act (AA) in 2003. The AA is substantially based on the 1986 version of the Model Law and it recognizes both positive and negative competence-competence.[51]

Unlike courts in Singapore and Hong Kong, courts in Japan will conduct a full review of an arbitration agreement if a party submits a dispute to the court in breach of an arbitration agreement. For instance, in a case in which a subcontractor brought court proceedings seeking payment of its fees under a contract – which included a provision in general terms that in the event a party considered that it would be unlikely that a dispute could be resolved by mediation, the parties shall refer the matter to arbitration *upon their agreement* – the Tokyo High Court denied the contractor's application to dismiss the proceedings based on the existence of an arbitration agreement. The court reasoned that because an agreement to arbitrate precludes a party's right of access to the court, the court should carefully construe the meaning of any purported agreement to arbitrate.[52]

48. Gary BORN, *International Commercial Arbitration*, 2nd ed. (Kluwer 2014) Chapter 7.
49. Anselmo REYES, *The Practice of International Commercial Arbitration* (Informa Law from Routledge 2018) p. 173.
50. *PT First Media TBK (fka PT Broadband Multimedia TBK) and ors v. Astro Nusantara International BV and ors* CACV 272/2015 (5 December 2016) [69].
51. Arts. 14 and 23 AA.
52. Tokyo High Court decision, 10 July 2013, 2013 (Ne) 2899.

Courts in Japan will also conduct a full review of the arbitral tribunal's jurisdiction at the Second, Third and Fourth Stages. However, the drafters of the AA considered that the court's decision at the Second Stage in relation to the arbitral tribunal's preliminary ruling on its jurisdiction would not carry a res judicata effect despite the court having conducted a full review.[53] This is because the AA provides for abridged judicial proceedings at the Second Stage without any guarantee of a full hearing, and subject to no appeal, while the AA stipulates that proceedings at the Third and Fourth Stage include a full hearing and a right to appeal.[54] However, it is possible that a losing party may be estopped at the Third and Fourth Stages from raising the same argument raised at the Second Stage if that argument was dismissed by the court at the Second Stage.[55]

Since the AA provides for abridged judicial proceedings at the Second Stage, the drafters considered that a party contesting the arbitral tribunal's jurisdiction has a choice of remedies between the Second and Third Stages.[56] This means that, provided a party has filed a jurisdictional plea with the arbitral tribunal within time limits, a party who failed to appeal the arbitral tribunal's preliminary ruling on its jurisdiction to the court will not be precluded from challenging an award on the merits at the Third Stage on a jurisdictional ground. This is different to the current position in Singapore and Hong Kong but it has not been tested before the courts in Japan.

The drafters also interpreted the Model Law to afford a party a choice of remedies between the Third and Fourth Stages and the AA is drafted in a way which recognizes this.[57] Again, although this choice of remedies has not been tested by courts in Japan, it seems likely that a court will recognize a choice of remedies at the Second, Third and Fourth Stages considering both the plain meaning of the AA (which does not explicitly preclude such choice of remedies) and the drafters' intent.

4. *China*

China, which is a signatory to the New York Convention, enacted its Arbitration Law in 1994 (AL) and it came into force in 1995. The AL governs both domestic and international arbitration. The Supreme People's Court plays a quasi-legislative role in China and from time to time issues judicial interpretations of laws related to arbitration.[58] While the AL incorporates some Model Law principles there is also

53. Koichi MIKI and Kazuhiko YAMAMOTO *Theory and Practice Under New Arbitration Act* (2006) p. 189 (in Japanese).
54. Art. 44(5)(8) AA.
55. MIKI, supra, p. 190.
56. MIKI, supra, p. 191.
57. MIKI, supra, p. 381.
58. Some of the interpretation relevant to arbitration issued by the Supreme Court of China is as follows: Interpretation of the Supreme People's Court on Certain Issues Relating to Application of the Arbitration Law of the PRC; Notice of the Supreme People's Court on Handling by People's Courts of Relevant Issues Pertaining to Foreign-related Arbitration and Foreign Arbitration; Notice of the Supreme People's Court on Matters Relating to Setting Aside of Foreign-related Arbitral Awards by the People's Courts; and Notice of the Supreme People's Court on Implementing the Convention on the Recognition and Enforcement of Foreign Arbitral Awards, to which this State Has Acceded.

significant divergence, including arbitral tribunals' lack of positive competence-competence.[59]

A party that wishes to challenge the validity of an arbitration agreement may request an 'Arbitration Commission', which is considered to be an arbitral institution (as opposed to an arbitral tribunal), to make a decision or request that the People's Court makes a ruling. If one party requests an Arbitration Commission to make a decision and the other party requests a ruling from the People's Court, the People's Court shall rule on the validity of an arbitration agreement.[60] However, once an Arbitration Commission has determined the question of the validity of an arbitration agreement, a party may not appeal to the People's Court for a review of this decision.[61] In this sense there is no judicial review of a jurisdictional decision by an Arbitration Commission at the Second Stage in China.[62]

A party must raise any challenge to the validity of an arbitration agreement prior to the first hearing. Failure to do so precludes a party from challenging the arbitral tribunal's jurisdiction in the People's Court at the Third or Fourth Stage.[63]

If a jurisdictional challenge is submitted to the People's Court before the Arbitration Commission rules on its jurisdiction, the arbitral tribunal suspends its proceedings pending the People's Court's review. The People's Court conducts a full review and its decision binds the arbitral tribunal. Whether the rulings on a jurisdictional issue by the People's Court bind the court at the Third or Fourth Stage may vary depending on jurisdictions.

While the AL does not recognize positive competence, the AL does provide for negative competence. If court proceedings are brought in China in relation to a dispute governed by a valid arbitration agreement, the People's Court must dismiss the proceedings, save for instances where the court finds that the arbitration agreement is void (provided that evidence of the arbitration agreement has been submitted prior to the first court hearing).[64]

In China, a party contesting jurisdiction has a choice of remedies between the Third and Fourth Stage provided that the party has submitted a jurisdictional plea to the arbitral tribunal within the time limits for doing so, i.e. a failure to apply to set aside the award on the merits will not preclude a party from resisting the enforcement of the award.

---

59. Some Arbitration Commissions occasionally delegate their power to make decisions on jurisdictional challenges to arbitral tribunals. Art. 6.1, of the Chia International Eeconomic and Trade Arbitration Commission (CIETAC) Rules, Art. 6.4, the Beijing Arbitration Commission (BAC) Rules.
60. Art. 20 AL. Art. 20 provides for the power of an "Arbitration Commission" to decide the validity of an arbitration agreement. Lu SONG, "National Report China" in ICCA *International Handbook on Commercial Arbitration* (2018).
61. Art. 13, Interpretation of the Supreme People's Court.
62. The People's Court may decide on a jurisdictional issue after the Arbitration Commission decides its jurisdiction so long as a jurisdictional question arises from so-called splits between the CIETAC and its former sub-commissions of Shanghai and Shenzhen.
63. Art. 20, AL, Art. 13, Interpretation of the Supreme People's Court. Some institutional rules require that the jurisdictional objection be raised before the submission of the first substantive defense (Art. 6.2, the CIETAC Rules).
64. Art. 26 AL.

At the Third and Fourth Stages the court will review the validity of an arbitration agreement de novo. However, once a party raises a jurisdictional objection at the Third Stage (setting aside) such party is precluded from resisting an award on the same grounds at the Fourth Stage.[65]

V. CONCLUSION

As international arbitration has played an increasingly essential role in resolving disputes, not only between private parties but also disputes involving public interests, it would not be surprising if judicial scrutiny became even more robust. With that backdrop it is important to revisit the basic principle of competence-competence, and the timing and extent of judicial intervention, in arbitration to consider how best to streamline the judicial review process of international arbitration.

The Model Law laid the foundation for the recent tremendous growth of international arbitration in the globalized economy by limiting court intervention into arbitration proceedings and by promoting efficiency and harmonization of arbitration practices in many different jurisdictions.

It is therefore lamentable that a choice of remedies, which courts in two prominent jurisdictions in Asia have found to be a fundamental part of the architecture of the Model Law, has caused tremendous delay in resolving the dispute between Astro and First Media. After more than eight years from the date of the tribunal's preliminary ruling on jurisdiction First Media was still able to challenge the Tribunal's jurisdiction in the Hong Kong court.

There are at least two areas of prevailing practices in judicial review that are worth revising to better strike the balance between efficiency and legitimacy of arbitration: (i) the standard of judicial review; and (ii) the consequence of a failure to seek remedies at certain stages.

First, the standard of juridical review. In all four jurisdictions (Singapore, Hong Kong, Japan and China) a court will conduct a full review of an arbitral tribunal's jurisdiction except at the First Stage in Singapore and Hong Kong.

In terms of a judicial review at the First Stage the approach of a prima facie review adopted by the court in Singapore and Hong Kong is highly recommended. Such approach serves efficiency of arbitration by encouraging the arbitral tribunal to rule on its jurisdiction first and deters dilatory tactics to bring a claim to the court in contravention of an arbitral agreement.

In terms of a judicial review at the Second, Third and Fourth Stages, it may make more sense for a court to determine the standard of judicial review (either a de novo review or a deferential approach) depending on the nature of jurisdictional disputes, rather than to apply a full judicial review in a blanket manner. For instance it has been suggested that admissibility issues, such as issues of whether preconditions to arbitrate have been met, are more adequately dealt with by an arbitral tribunal and therefore a court should be more deferential to an arbitral tribunal's determination.[66] Some

65. Art. 26, Interpretation of the Supreme People's Court.
66. GREENBERG, supra, p. 88; BERMANN, supra, p. 46; REYES, supra, p. 168.

jurisdictions, such as Canada, in principle have gone as far as to apply deference to the arbitral tribunal's decisions.[67]

When a jurisdictional decision inextricably relates to disputes on the merits, a court should take a more deferential approach. For instance, when the parties dispute whether a certain claim arises out of or in connection with underlying contracts and thereby falls within an arbitration agreement it is inevitable for the tribunal and the court to analyze the nature and substance of the claim to rule on the tribunal's jurisdiction. Once the tribunal has interpreted the underlying contracts and analyzed the claims in full it makes more sense for the court to defer to such tribunal's findings in the same way as the court refrains from stepping into the tribunal's ruling on the merits of the case at the Third and Fourth Stages. This will discourage a party from having two (or more) bites at the cherry by re-running the same, or similar, arguments in the jurisdictional context.

Second, final resolution of jurisdictional disputes at the early stage of the arbitration proceedings will bolster both the efficiency and legitimacy of arbitration. To that end, certain consequences should follow the failure to seek a judicial review in order to encourage early determination of jurisdictional disputes.

For instance, assuming the Second Stage affords a full judicial review of the tribunal's jurisdictional determination, the failure to seek a judicial review at the Second Stage should prevent a dissatisfied party from seeking to set aside an award on a jurisdictional ground unless there is a justifiable reason for its failure to do so or evolution of the case warrants a full judicial review. When a party disputing jurisdiction of the arbitral tribunal has fully participated in the arbitration proceedings such party may bear the consequences of its failure to seek a judicial review at the Third Stage (active remedy) without any reasonable reason. The Model Law attaches weight to "freedom of a party to decide on how to raise its objections."[68] From the perspectives of early determination of jurisdictional disputes, however, a choice of remedies afforded under the Model Law is worth revisiting. The final resolution of a jurisdictional issue at the court of the seat, rather than the same being left at hands of the courts of the place of enforcement serves not only efficiency but also consistency of the resolution of jurisdictional disputes.

Competition among arbitral institutions and seats of arbitration in different jurisdictions has been increasing and it has become government policy in some states to actively promote arbitration in the hope of turning their jurisdiction into an arbitration hub. It is time for each country to revisit its own system to see if any reforms to streamline judicial review of jurisdictional challenges in international arbitration can be made. The Model Law should not impede each country's continued efforts to improve efficiency and legitimacy of arbitration.

67. GREENBERG, supra, p. 86.

68. Report of the UNCITRAL Working Group on International Contract Practices on the Work of its Seventh Session (A/CN.9/246, 6-17 February 1984) at para. 154.

Arbitration Challenged Part II

Arbitration Challenged Part II

Party Autonomy in Choosing Decision-Makers: Advantages and Drawbacks – Should It Be Revisited?

A Special Role of Party-Appointed Arbitrators?

Alfonso Gómez-Acebo[*]

TABLE OF CONTENTS PAGE

I. INTRODUCTION

One of the questions addressed at the ICCA Sydney 2018 Congress is "Party Autonomy in Choosing Decision-Makers: Advantages and Drawbacks – Should it be Revisited?". This question raises the issue of whether or not it is worth keeping the system of unilateral appointments in international arbitration as the default method for the constitution of multiple-member tribunals, or keeping it at all.

The main advantage of unilateral nominations is the possibility for each party to influence the composition of the arbitral tribunal by alone deciding the identity of some of its members, a possibility that is valued by many arbitration users.[1] Unilateral appointments enable each party to appoint someone with the combination of qualities that, in the eyes of that party, must be present in the arbitral tribunal (e.g., education, professional experience or expertise in a given field, personal integrity, knowledge of the rules applicable to the merits of the dispute, arbitration practice, gravitas, academic background, availability, cultural awareness, communicative or language skills, etc.). This allows each party to directly manage the risk of a bad arbitral award, something that is important because human beings are fallible, judging can be a difficult task, justice is also in the eye of the beholder and, last but not least, the parties rarely have any legal remedy against a bad arbitral award. Furthermore, the possibility for each party to make a unilateral appointment may also allow each party to feel more reassured that the dispute will be settled in a fair process.

On the downside, the main drawback of unilateral nominations is the widespread perception that party-appointed arbitrators are not truly impartial and independent, at least on appearance. First, right from the outset, party-appointed arbitrators offer one less objective reason than presiding arbitrators to believe in their impartiality and independence, as they lack a neutral appointor. Party-appointed arbitrators who are under the duty of impartiality and independence must be willing and able to act without

---

* Lawyer, Doctor in Law, Partner at Cuatrecasas and author of the book *Party-Appointed Arbitrators in International Commercial Arbitration* (Kluwer 2016), on which this paper is partly based.

1. According to the 2012 International Arbitration Survey conducted by the School of International Arbitration, Queen Mary University of London, on *Current and Preferred Practices in the Arbitral Process*, 71 percent of in-house counsel considered unilateral party appointments as the preferred method of selecting co-arbitrators in a three-member tribunal.

favouritism or bias towards any of the disputing parties, but their appointment is the result of each party's natural tendency to choose someone who is believed to be better (closer or less hostile) to the appointor's case than other possible candidates – *better* therefore meaning in this context, as arbitration is normally a zero-sum game (what is gained by one party is lost by the other), *worse* for the non-appointing party. Second, most arbitrators like to be appointed and nowadays virtually all of them receive fees for their services. Party-appointed arbitrators may have a natural feeling of thankfulness towards the appointing party for the intangible and tangible satisfaction that the unilateral choice of that party will bring them. Each party may legitimately wonder if the arbitrator appointed by the other party will be unwilling or unable, perhaps even unconsciously, not to reward the sense of professional achievement that the appointment as an arbitrator procures him[2] with bias in favour of the appointing party, without it being possible to know or prove – at least in most cases – if such bias exists. Third, it is a fact of life that, more often than not, each party-appointed arbitrator finds more strengths in the appointing party's case than the arbitrator appointed by the other party, again without it being possible to know or prove – at least in most cases – if there is an ethical problem or rather the arbitrator genuinely sees certain propositions of law or circumstances of fact in the same way as the party who appointed him. And fourth, even when one can reasonably suspect that there is an ethical problem, the ethical analysis may not always be an easy one because some party-appointed arbitrators are cynically disingenuous about their duty to be impartial at all times[3] while others breach that duty in the understanding that it is a legitimate defense against a prior breach of fair play by the other. All this creates a pervasive problem of ethical tension that is unsolvable.

There has been an interesting debate for and against unilateral appointments in arbitration for quite some time. This debate has been particularly lively in recent years, since Paulsson lit the fuse in 2010. It has been argued that the system of impartial and independent party-appointed arbitrators is not worth keeping in international arbitration, with some critics suggesting that it would be better not to require the duty of impartiality and independence from party-appointed arbitrators[4] and others deeming it preferable to do away with unilateral nominations completely or, at least, as the default solution for the constitution of multiple-member tribunals.[5] Many others, including myself, consider that the system is worth keeping.[6]

2. All generic references to the masculine obviously include the masculine and feminine.
3. The "truly independent arbitrators", the way a witty and very fine lawyer humorously used to call the party-appointed arbitrators who will always agree with the position of the appointing party *independently* of the case.
4. Elihu LAUTERPACHT, *Aspects of the Administration of International Justice* (Grotius Publications, Cambridge 1991) pp. 79-81 and fn. 9; Robert COULSON, "An American Critique of the IBA's Ethics for International Arbitrators", 4 J. Int'l Arb. (1987, no. 2) pp. 107-109.
5. Lucius R. EASTMAN, "The Independence of Commercial Arbitration Tribunals", 2 Arb. J. (1938) p. 9; Tom ARNOLD, "The Unacceptable Common Partiality of 'Neutral' Party Appointed Arbitrators" in G.M.BERESFORD HARTWELL, ed., *The Commercial Way to Justice – The 1996 International Conference of the Chartered Institute of Arbitrators* (Kluwer Law International 1997) pp. 162 and 152; Hans SMIT, book review of *Quo Vadis Arbitration? Sixty Years of Arbitration Practice, by Pieter Sanders*, 11 Am. Rev. Int'l Arb. (2000) pp. 430-431; Jan PAULSSON, "Moral Hazard in International Dispute Resolution", 25 ICSID Review –Foreign Investment Law Journal (2010, issue 2) pp. 348 and 352 (a shorter version of this text was presented as Inaugural Lecture as Holder of

It is not my intention here to revisit that debate but rather to simply focus on the role of party-appointed arbitrators, role meaning their mission or job description, what they have to do to earn their fees. I think that any possible reflection on whether unilateral nominations are worth keeping depends, to a certain extent, on such role. Whatever one's preference in relation to unilateral appointments, all progress towards a common international understanding of what the role of party-appointed arbitrators is, should or could be, would benefit us all.

In this paper, I attempt to achieve two objectives. They may seem contradictory at first glance, although actually they are not. First, I would like to create more awareness of the present unsatisfactory situation of the role of party-appointed arbitrators, with written rules suggesting that all arbitrators have the same mission and non-written rules

---

the Michael R. Klein Distinguished Scholar Chair at the University of Miami School of Law on 29 April 2010); Hans SMIT, "The Pernicious Institution of the Party-Appointed Arbitrator", Columbia FDI Perspectives, No. 33 (14 December 2010); Juan FERNÁNDEZ-ARMESTO, "Salient Issues of International Arbitration", 27 American University International Law Review (2012, no. 4) p. 726; Joseph P. KLOCK, Dissenting Opinion of 18 January 2017 in *Supervisión y Control S.A. v. Costa Rica* (ICSID Case No. ARB/12/4); Jan PAULSSON, "Shall We Have an Adult Conversation About Legitimacy?", a summary of his keynote address on 2 March 2017 at the Annual Meeting of the CPR Institute at the Biltmore Hotel, Coral Gables, available at <https://blog.cpradr.org/2017/03/15/shall-we-have-an-adult-conversation-about-legitimacy/> (last accessed 12 February 2018).

6. Frédéric EISEMANN, "*L'arbitre-partie*" in Pieter SANDERS, ed., *International Arbitration: Liber Amicorum for Martin Domke* (Martinus Nijhoff, The Hague 1967) pp. 84-85; Jean ROBERT, "Conclusion" in *Qualification de l'arbitre international – Symposium du 20 novembre 1970*, Rev. arb., (1970, no. 4 special) p. 260; René DAVID, *Arbitration in International Trade* (Kluwer Law and Taxation Publishers 1985) p. 254; Joseph M. MATTHEWS, "Difficult Transitions Do Not Always Require Major Adjustment – It's Not Time to Abandon Party-Nominated Arbitrators in Investment Arbitration", 25 ICSID Review – Foreign Investment Law Journal (2010, issue 2) p. 366; Alexis MOURRE, "Are Unilateral Appointments Defensible? On Jan Paulsson's Moral Hazard in International Arbitration" in Stefan M. KRÖLL, Loukas A. MISTELIS, Pilar PERALES and Vikki ROGERS, eds., *International Arbitration and International Commercial Law: Synergy, Convergence and Evolution, Liber Amicorum Eric Bergsten* (Kluwer Law International 2011) pp. 381-386 (first published on Kluwer Arbitration Blog on 5 October 2010); Giorgio SACERDOTI, "Is the Party-Appointed Arbitrator a 'Pernicious Institution'? A Reply to Professor Hans Smit", Columbia FDI Perspectives, No. 35 (15 April 2011); Michael E. SCHNEIDER, "Forbidding Unilateral Appointments of Arbitrators – A Case of Vicarious Hypochondria?", President's Message, 29 ASA Bull. (2011, no. 2) pp. 273-276; Charles N. BROWER and Charles B. ROSENBERG, "The Death of the Two-Headed Nightingale: Why the Paulsson – Van den Berg Presumption that Party-Appointed Arbitrators Are Untrustworthy Is Wrongheaded", 29 Arb. Int'l (2013, no. 1) pp. 7-44; V. V. VEEDER, "The Historical Keystone to International Arbitration: The Party-Appointed Arbitrator – From Miami to Geneva" (Inaugural Charles N. Brower Lecture on International Dispute Resolution), 107 ASIL Proceedings (2013) pp. 401-403; Alfonso GÓMEZ-ACEBO, *Party-Appointed Arbitrators in International Commercial Arbitration*, International Arbitration Law Library, Vol. 34 (Kluwer Law International 2016) paras. 3.66-3.78 (against doing away with unilateral nominations) and 4.41-4.57 (in favour of requiring the duty of impartiality and independence by default from party-appointed arbitrators); Manuel CONTHE, "Paulsson's Nirvana Fallacy", Spain Arbitration Review (2017, issue 29) pp. 58-60; Siegfried H. ELSING and Alexander SHCHAVELEV, "Chapter 8: The Role of Party-Appointed Arbitrators" in Patricia SHAUGHNESSY and Sherlin TUNG, eds., *The Powers and Duties of an Arbitrator: Liber Amicorum Pierre A. Karrer* (Kluwer Law International 2017) p. 77.

suggesting that party-appointed arbitrators have a so-called special role to perform in relation to the appointing party's case. In this respect it is also a call for clarity, in the hope that arbitral institutions, soft law producers and arbitration practitioners may contribute to building trust and value for international arbitration by reducing the ambiguity and confusion about the role of party-appointed arbitrators. It would be desirable to reach a common international understanding that, unless otherwise agreed by the parties, party-appointed arbitrators who are under the duty of impartiality and independence do not have a duty to do anything special in relation to the appointing party's case. And second, I would like to share some thoughts on how the role of party-appointed arbitrators may evolve in the future and, in particular, why a special role of party-appointed arbitrators combining arbitration and mediation, if clearly and openly agreed upon by the parties, could bring added value to international arbitration. In my opinion, a meaningful evolution of party-appointed arbitrators would be for them to be impartial and independent arbitrators that are nevertheless required to act as mediators who support their respective appointing parties for the sole purpose of exploring zones of possible agreement in one or more mediation periods within the arbitration process.

II. A CALL FOR CLARITY

1. *The Long Journey Made to Avoid Confusion About the Role of Party-Appointed Arbitrators*

In private arbitration in ancient Greece, all arbitrators had the two-tier role of mediating between the parties and, if mediation failed, to adjudicate the dispute. Close links between unilateral appointors and appointees were common, the appointment often being based on the existence of family relationships or friendship.[7] Party-appointed arbitrators were expected to support their respective appointing parties while trying to mediate between them. However, if mediation failed, they were expected to reach a decision based only on what they regarded as just, under oath.[8] As explained by Roebuck:

> "Mediation was expected to come first. Private arbitration could be by a single arbitrator but it was more common for each side to appoint one, or sometimes two. These were considered to be 'friends' or 'supporters' of the parties appointing them, which was not inappropriate because their first responsibility was to help them reach a settlement. They might take an oath to do so. If mediation failed, they would usually go on to adjudicate, even if reluctantly, and

7. The Attic orator Lysias, in his speech "Against Archebiades", refers to the party-appointed arbitrators, from the parties' perspectives, as "my friends and yours" (*Lysias, The Oratory of Classical Greece*, Vol. 2, translated by S. C. Todd (University of Texas Press, 2000) p. 362). Another Attic orator, Isaeus, notes in his speech "On the Estate of Dicaeogenes" that one of the party-appointed arbitrators was the brother-in-law of the party appointing him (*Isaeus*, translated by Edward Seymour Forster, (The Loeb Classical Library 1943) para. 33, p. 183).
8. *Ibid.*, para. 32, p. 183: "The arbitrators said that if they could effect a compromise without putting themselves under an oath, they would do so; otherwise they would themselves also take an oath and declare what they regarded as just."

would then take the oath appropriate for anyone sitting in judgment, as *dikasts* did."[9]

The oath that *dikasts* (ordinary judges or jurors) had to take was:

> "I shall vote according to the laws and the decrees of the Athenian people and the Council of the Five Hundred, but concerning things about which there are no laws, I shall decide to the best of my judgment, neither with favor nor enmity. I shall judge concerning those things which are at issue and shall listen impartially to both the accusation and the defense. I swear these things by Zeus, by Apollo, by Demeter. May there be many blessings on me if I keep my oath, but if I break it may there be destruction on me and my family."[10]

In the Middle Ages, the role of party-appointed arbitrators became more ambivalent. Party-appointed arbitrators were often expected to support their respective appointing parties while seeking conciliation and an amicable settlement before proceeding to judge.[11] This two-fold role resembles the two-tier role of party-appointed arbitrators in ancient Greece, although without the clean separation in ancient Greece between the time to conciliate and the time to adjudicate. Yet, similarly to ancient Greece, the two-fold role of party-appointed arbitrators in the Middle Ages seems to be related to the broad powers that arbitrators were frequently given, as 'peace-makers' or *amiables compositeurs.*[12].

This ambivalence remained during the early Modern era, when arbitrators were generally appointed as arbitrators and *amiables compositeurs* as far as it could be useful.[13] As noted by Ralston: "before the Eighteenth Century it was often very difficult, sometimes impossible, to clearly separate cases of mediation and of arbitration, either because the terminology was not yet very well defined, or because the expressions employed were equivocal, or that the difference was not clearly in the thought of the negotiators".[14]

---

9. Derek ROEBUCK, *Ancient Greek Arbitration* (Holo Books, The Arbitration Press 2001) p. 205.
10. James Farley CRONIN, *The Athenian Juror and his Oath* (University of Chicago 1936) p. 18, citing FRANKEL's *Der Attische Heliasteneid*.
11. Jackson Harvey RALSTON, *International Arbitration from Athens to Locarno* (Garland Pub, New York 1929) p. 179, citing NOVACOVITCH; Derek ROEBUCK, "Odds or Evens: How Many Arbitrators?", 80 Arbitration (2014, issue 1) p. 15.
12. In England, the role of arbitrators, irrespective of the method of their appointment, could normally be seen as that of restoring peace between the parties as "peace-makers" (Derek ROEBUCK, "*L'arbitrage en droit anglais avant 1558*", Rev. arb. (2002, no. 3) pp. 551-552). In the French, Italian and Swiss cases, it was common for the arbitrators to be appointed as "arbiters, arbitrators and *amiable compositeurs*" (Yves JEANCLOS, "*La pratique de l'arbitrage du XIIe au XVe siècle: éléments d'analyse*", Rev. arb. (1999, no. 3) p. 439; Fabrizio MARRELLA, "*L'arbitrage à Venise (XIIe-XVIe siècles)*", Rev. arb. (2002, no. 2) p. 286; Jean-François POUDRET, "*Deux aspects de l'arbitrage dans les pays romands au moyen âge: l'arbitrabilité et le juge-arbitre*", Rev. arb. (1999, no. 1) p. 6).
13. Jean HILAIRE, "*L'arbitrage dans la période moderne (XVIe-XVIIIe siècle)*", Rev. arb. (2000, no. 2) p. 199.
14. J. H. RALSTON, fn. 11 above, p. 179, citing MÉRIGNHAC.

Historical sources show that, from the seventeenth century onwards, there was criticism in Europe and the United States of party-appointed arbitrators who acted more like advocates than judges, both in arbitration between private parties and in interstate arbitration. Domat complained in the seventeenth century that each party often expected the arbitrator it appointed to defend its interests and urged party-appointed arbitrators not to allow the intentions of the parties to prevent them from indeed being arbitrators obliged to determine the rights of both parties.[15] Russell contended in 1849 that it was in general much better for the parties to agree on a single arbitrator because of the frequent confusion of roles incurred by both party-appointed and non-party-appointed arbitrators. In his view, "notwithstanding the objectionable nature of such a course, the arbitrators named by the parties often seem to think that they are to represent their respective nominors, and act rather as advocates than judges, while the third arbitrator frequently supposes that he is an umpire, and that his active interference is not to commence until the others have differed finally".[16] The main case referred to by Russell in support of his view, which ended with the arbitral award being set aside, contains strong criticism of the judiciary against such confusion:

> "I am, therefore, upon the whole, brought to the conclusion that the objection is made out, and that the miscarriage arose from the arbitrators mistaking the duty they had to perform. Holt seems to have thought that his active interference was not to commence till Keyton and Buxton differed finally, and Keyton and Buxton that they were to represent their respective nominors, and act as advocates instead of judges. Courts of law will always construe awards, and hear motions respecting them with a desire to sustain the judgment of the tribunal which the parties have selected, and which in so many instances act most beneficially for them; but I must say that I the less regret the conclusion I am now brought to, because references of this kind, which are frequently resorted to, are, in my opinion, senseless and mischievous, founded on a totally wrong principle, expensive in their operation, and constantly ending in failure and disappointment."[17]

Signs of disappointment with the confusion as to the role of party-appointed arbitrators, when they were obliged to be impartial, were also visible in treaty-based arbitration in the nineteenth century. A good example of this is provided by Mr. William Henry Wadsworth, the arbitrator unilaterally appointed by the United States in *J.G.A. McKenny v. Mexico*, when he complained of what he saw as "a total misconception of the nature and character" of his office as a party-appointed arbitrator. *J.G.A. McKenny v. Mexico* was one of the cases between Mexico and the United States that were settled under a Convention between both countries of 1868.[18] This Convention provided for an

15. Jean DOMAT (1625-1695), *Les loix civiles dans leur ordre naturel, le droit public, et legum delectus*, revised edition (Nicolas Gosselin, Paris 1713) p. 189.
16. Francis RUSSELL, *A Treatise on the Power and Duty of an Arbitrator and the Law of Submissions and Awards* (Benning, London 1849) p. 207.
17. *Templeman and Reed*, 1841, A. Dowling, Vol. IX, p. 966.
18. Convention for the arbitration of all pending claims of the citizens of either state against the government of the other, signed in Washington on 4 July 1868. The arbitration provisions of this Convention are available, for instance, at William Ray MANNING, *Arbitration Treaties Among the*

arbitral body comprised of two commissioners, one appointed by each party, and a third person to act as an umpire when the first two differed in opinion. It also stated that the party-appointed commissioners "shall, before proceeding to business, make and subscribe a solemn declaration that they will impartially and carefully examine and decide, to the best of their judgment, and according to public law, justice, and equity, without fear, favor, or affection to their own country", in all the claims that were brought before them. The umpire, once subsequently appointed, had to make a solemn declaration similar to the one made by the other two arbitrators.

In *J.G.A. McKenny v. Mexico* the claimant sought compensation for the destruction of property by allegedly Mexican authorities in 1859, while Mexico contended that it was not liable for such acts because the persons that had destroyed Mr. McKenny's property were not Mexican authorities, but members of the revolutionary movement which, led by Félix Zuloaga, had rebelled against the constitutional authorities at the end of 1857. Mr. Wadsworth, while reasoning his view that there was no liability on the part of Mexico, rejected the argument raised by the claimant that he, as the commissioner appointed by the United States, was bound by the recognition of the Zuloaga government which had been made by a minister of the United States in January of 1858. In Mr. Wadsworth's opinion, his authority was derived from both the United States and Mexico, he was not more bound to represent the interests of one party as opposed to the other and he was obliged to act impartially for the benefit of both countries.

> "[I]t is argued by counsel that the act of the United States Government in recognizing Zuloaga is conclusive upon Mr. Commissioner Wadsworth, because he is the 'judicial representative of the United States in this commission,' and that for this reason he is precluded from even inquiring into the propriety of the recognition by the United States of the government of Zuloaga. It is scarcely necessary to remark that this view is founded upon a total misconception of the nature and character of the office of a commissioner under the convention between the United States and Mexico. Mr. Commissioner Wadsworth is not a 'judicial representative of the United States in this commission,' nor 'a judicial officer' of that government. The authority which he possesses he derives from both the United States and Mexico, and is obliged to exercise it impartially for the benefit of both. He would possess neither office nor authority without the consent and concurrence of both nations, and is not more bound by the official acts or municipal regulations of the United States than by those of Mexico. He derives his appointment to a place on the board – a place created by the action of both governments – from the Government of the United States, indeed, but is no more bound by this appointment to represent the interests of the United States than those of Mexico, and no more bound by the acts of that government than his colleague on the board, or their umpire. He is an impartial arbiter selected by the

American Nations: To the Close of the Year 1910 (Oxford University Press, Publications of the Carnegie Endowment for International Peace 1924) pp. 72-76.

> United States, but deriving all his powers from the United States and Mexico, nor more the officer of the former than of the latter."[19]

In the twentieth century there was a long doctrinal discussion as to whether party-appointed arbitrators should be required to be impartial and independent. The need for them to have such qualities was probably obvious for many legal minds. National legislators around mid-century, for instance, usually provided that arbitrators could be challenged for the same reasons as judges. However, and perhaps paradoxically, some of the same legal minds preferred not to require the duty of impartiality or independence from party-appointed arbitrators for the sake of consistency with what they often observed in practice. The UNIDROIT draft of a uniform law on arbitration of 1954, for example, allowed the challenge of an arbitrator "if any circumstances exist capable of casting doubt on his impartiality or independence", but excluded these grounds of challenge in the case of party-appointed arbitrators. The reason then given for this exclusion was that party-appointed arbitrators should not be subject to challenge due to their lack of impartiality or independence when practice often showed that they did not possess such qualities. As the UNIDROIT Committee put it at the time:

> "it did not seem desirable to the members of the Committee to confine themselves to a theoretical point of view and it was not possible to ignore the unsatisfactory practice, according to which arbitrators nominated by the parties too often tend to conduct themselves as advocates for the parties which have nominated them, the only really judicial function being then, in truth, reserved for the third arbitrator".[20]

Eventually UNIDROIT changed its mind. The UNIDROIT draft of a uniform law on arbitration of 1957, which was prepared with the participation of the Council of Europe, allowed the challenge of any arbitrator on the grounds of a lack of impartiality or independence.[21] Most of the following steps also abandoned the idea of making any distinction between party-appointed and non-party-appointed arbitrators. The 1966 Rules of the United Nations Economic Commission for Europe (UNECE) and the 1966 Rules of the United Nations Economic Commission for Asia and the Far East (UNECAFE) allowed the challenge of arbitrators on the grounds of a lack of impartiality or independence irrespective of the method of appointment of the arbitrator and this same approach was the same one later adopted by the United Nations Commission on International Trade Law (UNCITRAL).[22]

---

19. Vincent COUSSIRAT-COUSTERE and Pierre Michel EISEMANN, *Répertoire de la jurisprudence arbitrale internationale – Repertory of International Arbitral Jurisprudence, Vol. I (1794-1918)*, (Martinus Nijhoff Publishers 1989) p. 395.
20. "Draft of a Uniform Law on Arbitration in Respect of International Relations of Private Law and Explanatory Report", UNIDROIT, U.P.L. 1954, Draft III (3), Art. 12, second paragraph, p. 15, and Explanatory Report, p. 43.
21. "Draft Uniform Law on Arbitration in Respect of International Relations of Private Law", UNIDROIT Y.B. 1957, Art. 12, second and third paragraphs.
22. UNECE Rules (1966), Art. 6; UNECAFE Rules (1966), Art. III.1; UNCITRAL Arbitration Rules (1976), Art. 10.1; UNCITRAL Model Law (1985), Art. 12.2.

When the drafters of the UNCITRAL Arbitration Rules discussed the question of whether or not the duty of impartiality and independence should be required from party-appointed arbitrators, those who considered that the answer to the question should be affirmative – as it eventually was – contended that the institution of arbitration would gain greater respect if the arbitrators acted with independence and impartiality; that the obligation was in accordance with the arbitration law of many countries, it would be widely acceptable and it would not come into conflict with the law governing the arbitration; and that the parties, eventually, were free to waive this requirement by agreement.[23] In the same line Kopelmanas, commenting on the end of the long doctrinal discussion, noted that to consider party-appointed arbitrators as independent and not as party representatives was a solution that could perhaps not correspond entirely with "the reality of our days" ("*la réalité de nos jours*") but would contribute to the good administration of justice in arbitration.[24]

Nowadays the impartiality and independence of arbitrators, however appointed, is clearly an international standard. Virtually all arbitration rules and national laws require the impartiality and independence of all arbitrators, without making any distinction between party-appointed and non-party-appointed arbitrators. This is also the standard set by the most well-known guidelines on arbitrator conduct, such as the International Bar Association (IBA) Rules of Ethics for International Arbitrators, the IBA Guidelines on Conflicts of Interest in International Arbitration and the American Arbitration Association/American Bar Association (AAA/ABA) Code of Ethics for Arbitrators in Commercial Disputes. The last Code explains that the term "neutral" is used equivalently to "independent and impartial" and specifically states that in three-member tribunals with two party-appointed arbitrators "all three arbitrators are presumed to be neutral and are expected to observe the same standards as the third arbitrator", further noting that "[t]his expectation generally is essential in arbitrations where the parties, the nature of the dispute, or the enforcement of any resulting award may have international aspects".[25]

The twentieth century was also witness from its very outset to the interest in separating arbitration from other systems of dispute resolution, following a trend particularly visible in interstate arbitration during the nineteenth century. The clear distinction between mediation and arbitration received a strong boost by the Hague

23. "Report of the United Nations Commission on International Trade Law on the work of its eighth session" (Geneva, 1-17 April 1975), UN Doc. A/10017, UNCITRAL Y.B. 1975, Vol. VI, Annex I ("Preliminary draft set of Arbitration Rules for optional use in *ad hoc* arbitration relating to international trade: Summary of discussion by the United Nations Commission on International Trade Law"), p. 32, para. 68.

24. Lazare KOPELMANAS, "*Le role des règlements d'arbitrage dans le développement des procédures arbitrales applicables au règlement de litiges commerciaux a caractère international (a propos de quelques règlements et projets de règlements d'arbitrage récents)*", XXI Annuaire Français de Droit International (1975) pp. 301-302.

25. IBA Rules of Ethics for International Arbitrators (1987), Rule 1 ("Fundamental Rule"); IBA Guidelines on Conflicts of Interest in International Arbitration (2014), Part I(1), General Principle and Explanation to General Standard 1; ABA/AAA Code of Ethics for Arbitrators in Commercial Disputes (2004), Canon IX(A) and Note on Neutrality.

Conventions of 1899 and 1907.[26] These Conventions promoted the use of different methods to resolve international disputes between states: good offices and mediation, international commissions of inquiry and international arbitration. While the role of the mediator consisted in trying to reconcile the parties only by way of advice,[27] and the role of the international commissions of inquiry was to issue a report limited to a statement of facts, leaving the parties free to determine the effects of the statement,[28] the role of the international arbitrator was to settle disputes on the basis of the respect for law[29] and by means of a binding arbitral award.[30]

The clear distinction between arbitration and mediation is common ground nowadays. Furthermore, an increasing number of rules, laws and guidelines make it expressly clear that arbitrators are not allowed to act as mediators in the same dispute unless otherwise agreed by the parties.[31]

Alongside the interest to separate arbitration from other alternative dispute resolution (ADR) mechanisms, there was a movement in the twentieth century to make the rule of law prevail in arbitration over other forms of adjudicating disputes (e.g., "peace-making" and *amiable composition*). The power of the arbitrator to decide ex aequo et bono or as an *amiable compositeur*, which used to be the fall-back rule for centuries, became the exception. The international standard today is that arbitrators can only assume such power if the parties have expressly agreed to grant it to them.[32]

26. Conventions for the Pacific Settlement of International Disputes of 29 July 1899 and 18 October 1907, adopted at the first and the second Hague Peace Conferences, respectively.
27. Hague Convention of 1899, Art. 4: "The part of the mediator consists in reconciling the opposing claims and appeasing the feelings of resentment which may have arisen between the States at variance"; Art. 6: "Good offices and mediation, either at the request of the parties at variance, or on the initiative of Powers strangers to the dispute, have exclusively the character of advice, and never have binding force."
28. Hague Convention of 1899, Arts. 9 and 14.
29. Hague Convention of 1899, Art. 15: "International arbitration has for its object the settlement of disputes between States by judges of their own choice and on the basis of respect for law". In equal terms, Hague Convention of 1907, Art. 37.
30. Hague Convention of 1899, Arts. 18 and 56. According to the former: "The Arbitration Convention implies the engagement to submit loyally to the Award." In similar terms, replacing "loyally" with "in good faith", Hague Convention of 1907, Art. 37.
31. See, e.g., IBA Rules of Ethics for International Arbitrators (1987), Rule 8; IBA Guidelines on Conflicts on Interest in International Arbitration (2014), General Standard 4(d); ICC Mediation Rules (2014), Art. 10(3); Spanish Arbitration Act, Art. 17(4); ABA/AAA Code of Ethics for Arbitrators in Commercial Disputes (2004), Canon IV(F); Singapore International Arbitration Act, Sect. 17; International Institute for Conflict Prevention and Resolution (CPR) International Mediation Procedure (2017), Art. 3(k); UNCITRAL Model Law on International Commercial Conciliation (2002), Art. 12.
32. See, e.g., UNCITRAL Model Law, Art. 28(3); UNCITRAL Arbitration Rules (1976), Art. 33(2) [Art. 35(2) in the 2010 version]; ICC Arbitration Rules (2017), Art. 21(3); ICSID Convention (1965), Art. 42(3); Hong Kong International Arbitration Centre (HKIAC) Administered Arbitration Rules (2013), Art. 35(2); China International Economic and Trade Arbitration Commission (CIETAC) Arbitration Rules (2015), Art. 47.

2. *Present Ambiguity and Confusion About the Role of Party-Appointed Arbitrators*

One would expect that, after the long journey to achieve international consensus on the impartiality and independence of all arbitrators, the clean separation between arbitration and mediation and the arbitrators' duty to decide the dispute by default under the rule of law, these achievements would have brought the ambiguity and confusion about the role of party-appointed arbitrators to an end. Of course, there would still be people that do not honour fair play, which is something we cannot change. But at least the standards would be clearly set (the role of party-appointed arbitrators as supporters, mediators or peace-makers for their respective appointing parties cannot be presumed to exist) and these standards would allow arbitration users to expect all arbitrators to perform the same fundamental role that anyone would expect from a judge: to decide the case on the sole basis of the applicable procedural and substantive rules, without leaning or favouritism towards any party.

However, if we look outside the written rules, what we see makes us doubt whether the international arbitration community is currently in a position to provide a clear answer to the question of whether party-appointed arbitrators who are under the duty of impartiality and independence have the same mission as the presiding arbitrator. And I cannot help thinking with unease about something the famous anthropologist Margaret Mead once said, "If one cannot state a matter clearly enough so that even an intelligent twelve-year-old can understand it, one should remain within the cloistered walls of the university and laboratory until one gets a better grasp of one's subject matter," because some seemingly non-written rules make me unable to find an answer to that question that is clear enough to pass Mead's twelve-year-old test.

A significant number of members of the arbitration community have suggested that party-appointed arbitrators have a so-called special role to perform which is compatible with their impartiality and independence. It is a presumed special role because arbitration rules and laws do not provide for any such thing as a different arbitrator role depending on the method used for appointment. This special role is usually formulated in terms of a specific behaviour that each party-appointed arbitrator may deploy in relation to the appointing party's case. In particular, many authors consider that party-appointed arbitrators have the special role of ensuring that the appointor's case is properly understood by the other members of the arbitral tribunal. Promoters of such a special role normally justify it by suggesting that it is implicitly accepted by the parties and good for the arbitration process – a sort of reasonable unwritten rule of the game.

Explanations of this so-called special role are found since the early 1970s up to the present day. For De Vries, "[t]he party-appointed arbitrator must be truly impartial yet ensure that in the course of the tribunal's deliberations full understanding is attained by the entire tribunal of the presentation of facts and law advanced by his nominator".[33] For Blessing, the impartiality that is expected from the party-appointed arbitrator "does not prevent the arbitrator from examining the arguments advanced by 'his party' with particular care, seeing to it that they are carefully examined and weighed within the

33. Henry P. DE VRIES, "Practical Aspects of International Litigation-Arbitration", 64 American Journal of International Law (no. 4) *The United Nations: Appraisal at 25 Years* (September 1970) p. 253.

framework of the deliberations".[34] Werner conceived the role of a party-appointed arbitrator as someone "who must be independent enough to award against the party who appointed him should the merits of the case warrant it, but who will ensure that all the arguments of his party get a thorough and fair hearing".[35] In Bond's view the party-appointed arbitrator should be someone who "will endeavor to see that this party's position [the appointing party's position] is clearly understood by the arbitral tribunal".[36] Lowenfeld noted that a party-appointed arbitrator has a special role consisting in giving confidence to the appointing party in that he will carefully consider its case, and also serving as a cultural translator:

> "While the same legal and ethical duties in principle apply equally to party-appointed arbitrators, it is nevertheless recognized that they have a special role to perform. In particular, the party-appointed arbitrator must give confidence to the party who appointed him, in that he will listen carefully to that party's presentation and will study any supporting documents with care. In this way, the two party-appointed arbitrators attempt to offer, if not ensure a fair hearing and sound decision where all evidence and arguments are considered. Second, the arbitrator serves as a translator, not of language only, but rather of legal and business culture between lawyers from different countries."[37]

This author also notes that one role that is proper for a party-appointed arbitrator is to ensure that the appointing party's case is adequately heard.[38]

Blackaby and Partasides, sharing the vision of Redfern and Hunter, note that party-appointed arbitrators should be able to ensure that the case presented by the party that appointed them is properly understood by all members of the arbitral tribunal:

> "An arbitrator nominated by a party will be able to make sure that the arbitral tribunal properly understands the case of the appointing party. In particular, such an arbitrator should be able to ensure that any misunderstandings that may arise during the deliberations of the arbitral tribunal (for example because of differences of legal practice, culture, or language) are resolved before they lead to injustice. In this way, a party-nominated arbitrator can fulfil a useful role in

34. Marc BLESSING, "The New International Arbitration Law in Switzerland", 5 J. Int'l Arb. (1988, no. 2) p. 39.
35. Jacques WERNER, "Editorial – The Independence of Party-Appointed Arbitrators: For a Rule of Reason", 7 J. Int'l Arb. (1990, no. 2) p. 5.
36. Stephen BOND, "The International Arbitrator: From the Perspective of the ICC International Court of Arbitration", 12 Northwestern Journal of International Law and Business (1991) p. 7.
37. Andreas F. LOWENFELD, "The Party-Appointed Arbitrator in International Controversies: Some Reflections", 30 Texas International Law Journal (1995) p. 86.
38. A. F. LOWENFELD, "The Party-Appointed Arbitrator: Further Reflections" in *Lowenfeld on International Arbitration – Collected Essays over Three Decades* (Juris Publishing 2005) p. 104 (previously published in *The Leading Arbitrators' Guide to International Arbitration* (Juris Publishing 2003)).

ensuring due process for the party that nominated him or her, without stepping outside the bounds of independence and impartiality."[39]

Bishop and Reed note that the party-appointed arbitrator may "serve" the appointed party in the limited sense of ensuring that the party's case is understood and carefully considered by the tribunal:

> "It is also generally recognized that the party-appointed arbitrators may 'serve' the appointing party in the limited sense – consistent with deciding the case impartially – of ensuring that the presiding arbitrator selected will not be inimical to the party's case, ensuring that the party's case is understood and carefully considered by the panel, 'translating' the party's legal and cultural system (and occasionally the language) for the benefit and understanding of the other arbitrators, and ensuring that the procedure adopted by the panel will not unfairly disadvantage the appointing party."[40]

For Lew, Mistelis and Kröll, "[b]y working as a cultural interpreter the party appointed arbitrator can and should help to ensure that the arguments [of the party that appointed him] will be properly appreciated and considered during the tribunal's deliberations".[41] Also putting a special emphasis on the cross-cultural encounters that take place in international arbitration, De Fina suggests that party-appointed arbitrators, while they cannot be an advocate or a servant of the appointing party, can and should fulfil the role of ensuring that the contentions and arguments of the appointing party are fully understood and appreciated.[42]

For Seppälä, "[t]he duty of any party-nominated arbitrator should be to ensure that all of the arguments made by the party who nominates him or her are fully considered, properly weighed and taken into account by the tribunal in making its decisions".[43] For Júdice and Calado, party-appointed arbitrators, notwithstanding their duty of impartiality and independence, have the function of ensuring that the position of the appointing party is duly known, taken into account and understood by the other

39. Nigel BLACKABY and Constantine PARTASIDES with Alan REDFERN and Martin HUNTER, *Redfern and Hunter on International Arbitration*, 6th ed. (Oxford University Press 2015) para. 4.30, in the same vein as A. REDFERN and M. HUNTER, *Law and Practice of International Commercial Arbitration*, 3rd ed. (Thomson – Sweet & Maxwell 1999) p. 193.
40. Doak BISHOP and Lucy REED, "Practical Guidelines for Interviewing, Selecting and Challenging Party-Appointed Arbitrators in International Arbitration", 14 Arb. Int'l (1998, no. 4) p. 405 and fn. 56. The authors added: "It might be questioned whether the last point should be listed since it is the duty of all arbitrators to ensure that the procedure used does not unfairly prejudice either party."
41. Julian D. M. LEW, Loukas A. MISTELIS and Stefan M. KRÖLL, *Comparative International Commercial Arbitration* (Kluwer Law International 2003) para. 11.48.
42. Antonino A. DE FINA, "The Party Appointed Arbitrator in International Arbitration – Role and Selection", 15 Arb. Int'l (1999, no. 4) p. 382.
43. Christopher R. SEPPÄLÄ, "Obtaining the Right International Arbitral Tribunal: A Practitioner's View", 25 International Construction Law Review, Part 2 (April 2008) p. 212.

members of the tribunal.[44] Draetta criticizes party-appointed arbitrators who assume the role of an extra advocate for his appointing party by "uncritically defending the party's arguments with a pleading stance" while also suggesting that party-appointed arbitrators must ensure that the arguments of the appointing party are taken into account and given due consideration.[45]

Rogers has gone a step further by suggesting that party-appointed arbitrators can perform the function of acting as a devil's advocate that challenges, within the tribunal, the positions that are harmful to the appointing party's position.[46] Conthe, Elsing and Shchavelev concur with this vision.[47]

I understand all the above-mentioned opinions that support a special role of party-appointed arbitrators in relation to the appointing party's case. However, I find it difficult, with great respect, to agree with the suggestion that a special role of party-appointed arbitrators should be presumed to exist. My disagreement does not lie with the idea itself that a special role may exist but rather with the outright presumption of its existence. This presumption carries the risk of bringing ambiguity and confusion to the arbitral process because it condones the party-appointed arbitrator's conduct of doing something special in relation to the appointing party's case irrespective of whether or not such conduct is expressly provided for or allowed under the rules governing the arbitration.

The presumption of a special role of party-appointed arbitrators that is conceived only in terms of cultural assistance is not of great concern and may even be considered reasonable, although it seems unnecessary to me. When the party-appointed arbitrators share a common cultural background with their respective appointing parties, as is often the case, each party-appointed arbitrator is probably the member of the tribunal who is exposed to fewer risks of a cultural misunderstanding affecting the party who appointed him; and in such capacity, if the risk of such a misunderstanding ever arises and he can clarify it, he must help the other members of the tribunal to get out of the dark. Attentively considered, a party-appointed arbitrator who is in a position to perform this special role when necessary must do so because, otherwise, he would be acting with bias. Hence, it would not be necessary to call this cultural assistance a special role, all the more so when such cultural assistance should take place regardless of whether it benefits the appointing party's case or not.

However, the presumption of a special role of party-appointed arbitrators that goes beyond a mere cultural translation, such as that of paying particular attention or care to the appointing party's case in some respect, faces more relevant difficulties. In particular, the special role consisting of each party-appointed arbitrator ensuring that the appointor's case is properly understood by the other members of the arbitral tribunal

---

44. José Miguel JÚDICE and Diogo CALADO, "*Independencia e imparcialidad del árbitro: algunos aspectos polémicos, mediante una visión ibérica*", VIII Arbitraje: Revista de arbitraje comercial y de inversiones, (2015, no. 3) p. 762.
45. Ugo DRAETTA, "Cooperation Among Arbitrators in International Arbitration", V Indian Journal of Arbitration Law (2016-2017, issue 1) pp. 132-133.
46. Catherine A. ROGERS, *Ethics in International Arbitration* (Oxford University Press 2014) paras. 8.57-8.76.
47. M. CONTHE, "Paulsson's Nirvana Fallacy", fn. 6 above, pp. 55-56; S. H. ELSING and A. SHCHAVELEV, "The Role of Party-Appointed Arbitrators", fn. 6 above, p. 75.

poses three problems: it can cause confusion as to its compatibility with the impartiality and independence of the arbitrator, it can cause an imbalance in the arbitral procedure and it introduces a bias into the arbitration in the form of an advantage for the party appointing the best arbitrator.

First, the presumption of a special role consisting of making sure that the appointor's case is properly understood by the other members of the arbitral tribunal can cause confusion as to its compatibility with the arbitrator's impartiality and independence. Does such a special role not resemble what non-neutral party-appointed arbitrators have always done? The point was fairly made by Branson when he noted that the special role of party-appointed arbitrators is sometimes formulated in the field of international arbitration not only in terms of paying particular attention to the appointing party's case, but also in terms of being "sympathetic" to the appointing party. This observation led him to wonder whether the "sympathetic" reference in international arbitration does not really amount to advocacy inasmuch as such term is used as encompassing some kind of special action by the party-appointed arbitrator in relation to the appointing party's case.[48] Along the same lines, Rau observed the tension between "an official rhetoric of independence" and "a tolerated latent sympathy", and warned against the ambiguities of the system of impartial and independent party-appointed arbitrators.[49]

Against these concerns it could be said that the formulation of "being sympathetic" has normally been used in the context of unilateral nominations in international arbitration to express how the appointing party pictures the arbitrator in its mind, not how the arbitrator actually sees the case.[50] There is indeed a common international understanding that a party's attempt to appoint someone "in sympathy" with its case does not allow that party, nor anyone acting on its behalf, to ask the prospective candidates for appointment as arbitrators about their views on the substantive and procedural issues that are expected to arise in the case.[51] Furthermore, none of the authors who accept that party-

48. David BRANSON, "American Party-Appointed Arbitrators – Not the Three Monkeys", 30 University of Dayton Law Review (2004, no. 1) p. 46. By the same author, more recently, "Sympathetic Party-Appointed Arbitrators: Sophisticated Strangers and Governments Demand Them", 25 ICSID Review – Foreign Investment Law Journal (2010, issue 2) pp. 367-392.

49. Alan Scott RAU, "The Culture of American Arbitration and the Lessons of ADR", 40 Texas International Law Journal (2004-2005) pp. 459-461. By the same author, previously, "On Integrity in Private Judging", 14 Arb. Int'l (1998, no. 2) pp. 129-131.

50. See, e.g., Martin HUNTER and Jan PAULSSON, "A Code of Ethics for Arbitrators in International Commercial Arbitration?", 13 International Business Lawyer (April 1985, no. 4) p. 153: "Naturally, when the arbitration agreement calls for party-appointed arbitrators, the parties will wish to choose persons who are in a very general sense likely (in their view) to be sympathetic to their respective cases. No one would expect a government which has undertaken an act of nationalisation to nominate as its arbitrator a banker with a life-long career history of defending the inviolability of foreign investments. This is obvious, and it is perfectly proper."

51. See, e.g., N. BLACKABY, C. PARTASIDES, A. REDFERN and M. HUNTER, *Redfern and Hunter*, fn. 39 above, paras 4.72 and 4.76, rejecting any attempt to ascertain the prospective arbitrator's views on the substantive or procedural issues that are expected to arise in the case but considering good policy "to appoint a person who may, by reason of culture or background, be broadly in sympathy with the case theory to be put forward, but who will be strictly impartial when it comes to assessing the facts and evaluating the arguments on fact and law".

See also, setting limits in pre-appointment interviews: AAA International Arbitration Rules (2014), Art. 13.6; CPR Rules for Administered Arbitration of International Disputes (2014), Rule

appointed arbitrators have a special duty of care with regard to the appointing party's case suggest in the slightest way that party-appointed arbitrators may be allowed to favour their respective appointing parties by giving support for or recommendation of their respective causes.[52]

However, the foregoing remarks do not remove the risk of confusion, as the boundaries of what is appropriate to ask a prospective arbitrator during a pre-appointment interview are blurry and there is not even an international consensus on the inappropriateness of certain topics of discussion, such as the specific facts related to the dispute or prior views expressed on a particular legal issue.[53] So when it is said, as Shani notes, that party-appointed arbitrators "are often nominated because of their presumed dispositions",[54] we do not know what is presumed and what is not. We actually do not know if different arbitration users would understand the following remarks by Draetta in the same way: "The system according to which, in a three-member arbitration panel, each party appoints an arbitrator and the two so appointed nominate the President is precisely aimed at ensuring that each party-appointed arbitrator, though remaining independent and impartial, has views on legal, commercial and cultural issues which make him/her particularly responsive to his/her nominating party."[55] This uncertainty creates a risk of double yardsticks that can undermine the parties' trust in the ability of the system to serve as a fair dispute resolution system.

Second, the presumption of a special role consisting in making sure that the appointor's case is properly understood by the other members of the arbitral tribunal can cause an imbalance in the arbitral process. Given that the rules governing the arbitration do not normally provide for any such thing as a duty of each party-appointed arbitrator to inspire particular confidence in the appointing party or pay particular attention to the appointing party's case, the situation may arise in which one of the party-appointed arbitrators works on the assumption that he has such a special role to perform whereas the other works as if his role were the same as the presiding arbitrator. This imbalance can produce injustice and should be avoided. The status of party-appointed arbitrators

---

7.4; London Court of International Arbitration (LCIA) Arbitration Rules (2014), Art. 13.5; World Intellectual Property Organization (WIPO) Arbitration Rules (2014), Art. 21; HKIAC Administered Arbitration Rules (2013), Art. 11.5; Singapore International Arbitration Centre (SIAC) Arbitration Rules (2016), Rule 13.6.

52. Some of these authors have been particularly adamant in making it clear. See, e.g., D. BISHOP and L. REED, "Practical Guidelines", fn. 40 above, p. 405: "[I]t bears repeated emphasis that party-appointed and presiding arbitrators alike are expected to maintain an impartial demeanour and to decide the case in favour of the party with the better factual and legal position."

53. Niklas ELOFSSON, "Ex Parte Interviews of Party-Appointed Arbitrator Candidates: A Study Based on the Views of Counsel and Arbitrators in Sweden and the United States", 30 J. Int'l Arb. (2013, no. 4) p. 396. As I developed elsewhere, this lack of consensus and other reasons question the presumption that unilateral pre-appointment interviews and post-appointment discussions on the choice of the presiding arbitrator are appropriate even if the rules governing the arbitration do not expressly allow them. A. GÓMEZ-ACEBO, *Party-Appointed Arbitrators*, fn. 6 above, paras 5.29-5.41.

54. Yuval SHANI, "Squaring the Circle? Independence and Impartiality of Party-Appointed Adjudicators in International Legal Proceedings", 30 Loyola of Los Angeles International and Comparative Law Review (2008) p. 488.

55. U. DRAETTA, "Cooperation among Arbitrators", fn. 45 above, p. 142.

must not be defined on the basis of assumptions of what the parties' expectations are, given that these presumed expectations may actually be expectations of none of the parties or of only some of them.

The risk of an imbalance might not disappear even if all the parties think that a special role of party-appointed arbitrators exists, as they could still see in different ways what specific behaviour this special role allows. Diverging approaches on the understanding of what party-appointed arbitrators are allowed to do differently from the presiding arbitrator are likely to bring confusion to the arbitration and jeopardize a level playing field, a process in which the disputing parties can legitimately expect to be required to follow the same rules and be given equal opportunity to present their case. Where should we draw the line between a party-appointed arbitrator's acceptable behaviour and misbehaviour when performing his supposedly existing special role? Should we draw the line applying the vision of a special role of party-appointed arbitrators consisting in them acting only as cultural interpreters? Should we apply the broader vision of a special role consisting in ensuring that the position of the appointing party is properly understood by the other members of the arbitral tribunal? Should we draw the line applying the even broader view that suggests that the party-appointed arbitrator can go as far as acting as a devil's advocate that challenges, within the tribunal, the positions that are harmful to the appointing party's position? Or should we apply Minoli's old vision that the parties' agreement to have unilaterally appointed arbitrators on the tribunal encompasses in most cases a common understanding that each party may expect the arbitrator appointed by it to give special consideration to the aspects of the case that are favourable to that party's position ("*envisage spécialement les aspects du cas traité qui lui sont favorables*") and, at the same time, accept that the arbitrator appointed by the other party will do likewise in the opposite direction ("*dans le sens contraire*")?[56] There is again a risk of double yardsticks that may jeopardize the parties' trust in the ability of the system to serve as a fair dispute resolution system.

Third, the presumption of a special role consisting in making sure that the appointor's case is properly understood by the other members of the arbitral tribunal introduces a bias into the arbitration in the form of an advantage for the party appointing the best arbitrator. The presumption of a special duty of care on the part of each party-appointed arbitrator with regard to the appointing party's case implies that the smarter or more hard-working a party-appointed arbitrator, as compared to the other party-appointed arbitrator, the better the position of the appointing party in comparison to the other party. A special role that carries such a risk, in my opinion, should not be presumed.

This risk is a subtle one. An impartial and independent party-appointed arbitrator who believes that he must perform the special role of making sure that the other members of the tribunal properly understand the case of the party who appointed him may reasonably wish to first make sure that he thoroughly understands that case; and, given that a day has twenty-four hours for everyone, this may easily lead him to devote more time and attention to the "case" of the party who appointed him than to that of the other party. While both party-appointed arbitrators may genuinely be impartial and see such a special role just as an allocation of tasks within the arbitral tribunal, the

56. Eugenio MINOLI, "*Relations entre partie et arbitre*", in *Qualification de l'arbitre international – Symposium du 20 novembre 1970*, Rev. arb. (1970, no. 4 (special)) p. 223.

differences between both party-appointed arbitrators may introduce a bias into the arbitral process, a kind of consequential bias, in the form of an advantage for the party who chooses the most intelligent, diligent or zealous arbitrator. Ironically enough, the same sort of advantage that results from the parties' choice of counsel.

In short, as I have expressed elsewhere, I believe that the presumption of a special role of party-appointed arbitrators consisting in a special duty of care by them with respect to the appointing party's case is not good for international arbitration and should be rejected.[57] I agree with Menon when he says that "to the extent it is suggested that a party-appointed arbitrator should see himself as having a special duty to *one* of the parties, I remain fundamentally uncomfortable with such a view".[58] Arbitration users and observers may raise their eyebrows in distrust when they read in so many places – none of which are within the rules governing the arbitration proceedings – that party-appointed arbitrators have the same obligation of impartiality and independence as the presiding arbitrator but, unlike the latter, they have an unwritten special duty of care towards their respective appointing parties' cases. This theoretical construction is confusing and unnecessary. Unless the arbitration agreement or the arbitration rules provide otherwise, the only acceptable presumption is that impartial and independent party-appointed arbitrators must attempt to give equal confidence to all parties in that they will carefully listen to and study their case, and must also attempt to ensure that all the parties' cases are properly understood by all the members of the arbitral tribunal.

Here comes a call for clarity. Given the circumstances, it is probably not enough for arbitration rules and laws to require a duty of impartiality and independence from all arbitrators, no matter how they are appointed, nor is it probably even enough to include in the rules governing the arbitration proceedings that party-appointed arbitrators must not act as advocates for appointing parties nor advise them on the merits or outcome of the dispute, as some rules and laws already do.[59] I think that we need an active change to make it clear to arbitration users that, unless otherwise agreed by the parties, the role or mission of party-appointed arbitrators is the same as that of the presiding arbitrator.[60]

This active change could be made by leading arbitral institutions and organizations such as UNCITRAL given their important role in defining and refining the rules governing international arbitration proceedings. Whatever their view may be on the

57. A. GÓMEZ-ACEBO, *Party-Appointed Arbitrators*, fn. 6 above, paras. 5.14-5.28.

58. Sundaresh MENON, "Adjudicator, Advocate, or Something in Between? Coming to Terms with the Role of the Party-Appointed Arbitrator", 34 J. Int'l Arb. (2017, issue 3) (a version of this article was first presented as the 2016 Herbert Smith Freehills – Singapore Management University Asian Arbitration Lecture on 24 November 2016) p. 364.

59. See, e.g.: LCIA Arbitration Rules (2014), Art. 5.3: "All arbitrators shall be and remain at all times impartial and independent of the parties; and none shall act in the arbitration as advocate for or representative of any party. No arbitrator shall advise any party on the parties' dispute or the outcome of the arbitration"; Hungarian Arbitration Act (1994), Sect. 11: "The arbitrators are independent and impartial, they are not the representatives of the parties"; CIETAC Arbitration Rules (2015), Art. 24: "An arbitrator shall not represent either party, and shall be and remain independent of the parties and treat them equally."

60. Notwithstanding the fact, irrelevant in this respect, that the presiding arbitrator may often be empowered to carry out certain activities of a procedural nature alone and, if no majority is reached, to render the arbitral award alone.

question of whether unilateral appointments should be the default mechanism for the constitution of arbitral tribunals, both those that answer yes (e.g., International Chamber of Commerce (ICC), International Centre for Settlement of Investment Disputes (ICSID), UNCITRAL) and no (e.g., London Court of International Arbitration (LCIA)) could build trust and value for arbitration if they made it clear to arbitration users that, unless otherwise agreed by the parties, (i) the role or mission of party-appointed arbitrators is the same as that of the presiding arbitrator, (ii) a special role of party-appointed arbitrators whereby they are supposed to do something special in relation to the appointing party's case cannot be presumed and is not allowed and (iii) party-appointed arbitrators do not have any more responsibility towards the appointing party than they have towards the non-appointing party.

Soft law producers like the IBA and the Chartered Institute of Arbitrators (CIArb) could also join in on this task of clarification. They could and probably should help to eliminate the ambiguity about the role of party-appointed arbitrators, especially because they have a powerful influence on what may be taken as best international arbitration practice and I feel, with great respect, that they might have partly contributed to that ambiguity. It should be recalled that the IBA Rules of Ethics for International Arbitrators, the IBA Guidelines on Conflicts of Interest in International Arbitration and the IBA Guidelines on Party Representation in International Arbitration, as well as the Chartered Institute of Arbitrators (CIArb) Guidelines on the Interviewing of Prospective Arbitrators, have for years embraced the presumption that party-appointed arbitrators can do certain things relating to the appointing party that the presiding arbitrator cannot (unilateral pre-appointment interviews and post-appointment discussions about the choice of the presiding arbitrator) even though the rules governing the arbitration proceeding do not allow such things, as long as the rules do not prohibit them.[61] Perhaps the IBA and the CIArb could in the future include in their recommendations a statement clarifying the role of party-appointed arbitrators or, at least, a clarification that their acceptance of the presumption of appropriateness of certain unilateral communications between appointors and appointees must not be seen as tacit authorization for party-appointed arbitrators to assume a special role of making sure that the appointing party's case is properly understood by the other members of the arbitral tribunal or, in more general terms, any special role consisting of doing something special in relation to the appointing party's case.

61. IBA Rules of Ethics for International Arbitrators (1987), Rule 5; IBA Guidelines on Conflicts of Interest in International Arbitration (2014), Part II, para. 7 and Green List at para. 4.4.1 [Part II, para. 6 and Green List at para. 4.5.1 in the 2004 version]; IBA Guidelines on Party Representation in International Arbitration (2013), Guidelines 7 and 8; CIArb Guidelines on the Interviewing of Prospective Arbitrators (2016), Arts. 1-3 [Guidelines 9-11 in the 2007 version].

III. A PROPOSAL FOR THE FUTURE

1. *A Special Role of Party-Appointed Arbitrators for the Future?*

I have explained above why, in my view, there should be no presumption of a special role of party-appointed arbitrators and why their role, unless otherwise agreed by the parties, should be the same as that of the presiding arbitrator: to decide the case on the sole basis of the applicable procedural and substantive rules and without leaning or favouritism towards any party.

The question is now a different one and focus on the "unless otherwise agreed by the parties" appearing in the previous paragraph. Still thinking about the future of international arbitration, which is the topic of the 24th ICCA Congress (*Evolution and Adaptation: The Future of International Arbitration*), is it worth exploring possible special roles of party-appointed arbitrators that we may recommend arbitration users to expressly agree on, at least in some cases? And if this effort is worthwhile, what could those special roles be?

The approach to these questions requires a taste for theoretical discussion but also a good dose of healthy pragmatism. For the arbitration users who believe that party-appointed arbitrators should not have the same role as the presiding arbitrator – and these users exist and their number is probably not negligible –, is it worth offering or encouraging them to expressly agree on special party-appointed arbitrator roles that could be useful to better serve their needs? Does this make sense as a way of arbitration adapting itself to the evolving needs of users in both commercial and investor-state arbitration?

There is a wide range of options when thinking about possible special roles of party-appointed arbitrators. One of them, almost always inadvisable, is to agree to have partisan party-appointed arbitrators on the arbitral tribunal. Contrary to oversimplifications that are sometimes made, partisan party-appointed arbitrators have rarely been throughout history mere representatives or advocates of the appointing party, something that indeed makes no sense. In most cases, they have been arbitrators that defended the interests of the appointing party while at the same time being fully or partly entitled to vote against the appointing party without the need for its permission if they considered it appropriate. They have traditionally had their own place in arbitration and they should keep it, as tiny as this place may be in current international arbitration practice. However, partisan party-appointed arbitrators are generally unadvisable, for one reason because of the high degree of uncertainty about what they are allowed to do. "Partisan he may be, but not dishonest," as the Court of Appeals of New York in the *Astoria* case nicely put it.[62] The problem comes later, when defining "partisan" and "dishonest". Even in national contexts like domestic US arbitration, where parties and arbitrators have a common cultural background that may allow all of them to have a similar understanding of what fair partiality may be, there has been confusion and disagreement about the role of "non-neutral" party-appointed arbitrators[63] and they have

62. *Astoria Medical Group v. Health Ins. Plan*, 1962, 11 N.Y.2d at 137.

63. James H. CARTER, "Living with the Party-Appointed Arbitrator: Judicial Confusion, Ethical Codes and Practical Advice", in IUS Arbitrale International – Essays in Honor of Hans Smit, 3 Am.

been criticized as "something of an embarrassment"[64] and a system leading "to all kinds of mischief, including overly contentious proceedings, gamesmanship, additional expense and delay",[65] with the practice of non-neutral party-appointed arbitrators being progressively abandoned.[66] If the parties in a particular case want partisan party-appointed arbitrators on the arbitral tribunal, they may for example give their consent to the non-neutral party-appointed arbitrators allowed under Canon X of the ABA/AAA Code of Ethics for Arbitrators in Commercial Disputes (2004), or adopt the formula suggested elsewhere that each party-appointed arbitrator "is expected to understand and support" the appointing party's position.[67] However, none of this will probably be enough in most cases to deter future deceit. The parties will have to take utmost care to make it clear what the arbitrators can do and where the line between fair and unfair partiality is drawn.

Except in very exceptional circumstances, arbitration agreements providing for biased, partial, partisan or non-neutral party-appointed arbitrators are a step backwards in international arbitration and cannot be wisely recommended to arbitration users who believe that party-appointed arbitrators should not have the same role as the presiding arbitrator. Only impartial party-appointed arbitrators are generally advisable. For good reason, the standard of impartiality and independence of all arbitrators currently reigns by default. The adoption of this standard is the best way to achieve a common international understanding of the rights and obligations of party-appointed arbitrators and thereby to ensure that arbitration is a truly neutral dispute resolution system, because the uncertainty about what a fair biased party-appointed arbitrator may or may not do is too great. Fouchard noted in 1995, speaking of arbitrators in general, that "*[l]e statut de l'arbitre international doit tendre naturellement a l'universalité*".[68] This is particularly desirable in party-appointed arbitrators when the parties have not reached any specific agreement on what they are expected to do. Furthermore, this standard was also

---

Rev. Int'l Arb. (1992, nos 1-4) pp. 153 et seq.; Seth H. LIEBERMAN, "Something's Rotten in the State of Party-Appointed Arbitration: Healing ADR's Black Eye That is Nonneutral Neutrals", 5 Cardozo Journal of Conflict Resolution (2004, no. 2) pp. 233-241.

64. James H. CARTER, "Improving Life with the Party-Appointed Arbitrator: Clearer Conduct Guidelines for 'Nonneutrals'", 11 Am. Rev. Int'l Arb. (2000, no. 3) p. 305.

65. Robert D. TAICHERT, "Why Not Provide for Neutral Party-Appointed Arbitrators?", 57 Dispute Resolution Journal (2002, no. 4) p. 22.

66. Gary BORN, *International Commercial Arbitration*, 2nd ed., Vol. II, (Kluwer Law International 2014) pp. 1797-1801.

67. Mauro RUBINO-SAMMARTANO, "Optional Additions to Standard Arbitration Agreements Issued by the European Court of Arbitration", 30 J. Int'l Arb. (2013, issue 2) p. 163, offering two alternatives with respect to party-appointed arbitrators: "*For Neutral Party Appointed Arbitrators* – The parties formally request the arbitrator, respectively appointed by them as to these proceedings, to be totally neutral, since the combination of the full neutrality of all the party-appointed arbitrators will ensure that the arbitral tribunal will be fully independent"; and for "*Partisan Party Appointed Arbitrators* – The parties formally agree that the arbitrator, whom each of them will appoint in these proceedings, is expected to understand and support their respective position."

68. Philippe FOUCHARD, "*Les rapports entre l'arbitre et les parties et l'institution arbitrale*" in *Le statut de l'arbitre*, ICC Bulletin, Special Supplement (1995, ICC Publ. no. 564) p. 16.

adopted and should serve as a valuable means to protect party-appointed arbitrators against pressure from the appointing party.[69]

Another option, when considering possible special roles of party-appointed arbitrators, is to expressly accept what so often nowadays seems to be an implicit or non-written rule of the game: that party-appointed arbitrators have the special role of ensuring that the appointing party's case is properly understood by the other members of the arbitral tribunal. This could be expressly provided for in the arbitration agreement, the arbitration rules or any other form.[70] However, I do not see much benefit from this possibility, nor from expressly agreeing a special role of party-appointed arbitrators acting as devil's advocates in favour of their respective appointing parties. In my opinion, these special roles are dangerously close to advocating for the appointing party. Their theoretical underpinnings are different from that of advocacy but not their effects. The adjudicative role of an arbitrator requires him to determine the rights and obligations of all the parties. If we wish that each and every member of an arbitral tribunal may be able to properly fulfil this duty, I find it difficult for an arbitrator to form his own judgment about the rights and obligations of all the parties if, at the same time, he also has a special duty to take particular care to ensure the proper understanding of the appointing party's case by all the members of the arbitral tribunal, let alone if he has to play devil's advocate. To make sure that the appointing party's case is properly understood by the other members of the tribunal or to play devil's advocate in favour of the appointing party's case seems to me to be similar to attempting to get as much of what the appointing party claims as possible. Every successful step of the party-appointed arbitrator in performing this special role may be one step closer to improving the outcome of the arbitration for the appointing party.

2. *A Proposal of a Special Role of Party-Appointed Arbitrators Combining Arbitration and Mediation*

a. *Some brief preliminary remarks on concepts and terminology*

The combination of arbitration and mediation has been increasingly researched in recent decades.[71] There are several methods combining arbitration and mediation, often

69. Pierre LALIVE, "*Sur des dimensions culturelles de l'arbitrage international*" in J. MAKARCZYK, ed., *Theory of International Law at the Threshold of the 21st Century – Mélanges Krzysztof Skubiszewski* (Kluwer Law International 1996) p. 779.

70. For instance, Matthews proposes that this could be done in investment treaty arbitration by adding to the oath taken by party-appointed arbitrators an obligation to "ensure that during deliberations with other members of the tribunal the positions asserted on behalf of the party that nominated me are fully understood and considered". J. M. MATTHEWS, "Difficult Transitions", fn. 6 above, p. 365.

71. See, e.g.: David ELLIOT, "Med-Arb: Fraught with Danger or Ripe with Opportunity?", 34 Alberta Law Review (1995, no. 1) pp. 163-179; Michael E. SCHNEIDER, "Combining Arbitration with Conciliation" in *International Dispute Resolution: Towards an International Arbitration Culture*, ICCA Congress Series no. 8 (1996 Kluwer Law International) (henceforth *ICCA Congress Series no. 8*), pp. 57-97; Harold I. ABRAMSON, "Protocols for International Arbitrators Who Dare to Settle Cases", 10 Am. Rev. Int'l Arb. (1999, no. 1) pp. 1-17; Peter TALBOT, "Should an Arbitrator or Adjudicator Act as a Mediator in the Same Dispute?", 67 Arbitration (2001, issue 3) pp. 221-229; Haig OGHIGIAN, "Discussion: On Arbitrators Acting as Mediators", 68 Arbitration

described using a kind of alphabet soup terminology: Med-Arb (M-A, M/A), Arb-Med-Arb (A-M-A, A/M/A, AMA), Co-Med-Arb, etc.[72]

In this paper the terms "mediation" and "conciliation" are used indistinctively to refer to the process whereby one or more persons assist the parties in trying to reach a settlement of their dispute. This broad notion of "conciliation" and "mediation" is the one adopted by the UNCITRAL Model Law on International Commercial Conciliation:

> "For the purposes of this Law, 'conciliation' means a process, whether referred to by the expression conciliation, mediation or an expression of similar import, whereby parties request a third person or persons ('the conciliator') to assist them in their attempt to reach an amicable settlement of their dispute arising out of or relating to a contractual or other legal relationship. The conciliator does not have the authority to impose upon the parties a solution to the dispute".[73]

(2002, issue 1) pp. 42-45; Christian BÜHRING-UHLE, Gabriele SCHERER and Lars KIRCHHOFF, "The Arbitrator as Mediator", 20 J. Int'l Arb. (2003, issue 1) pp. 81-88; Klaus Peter BERGER, "Integration of Mediation Elements into Arbitration – 'Hybrid' Procedures and 'Intuitive' Mediation by International Arbitrators", 19 Arb. Int'l (2003, no. 3) pp. 387-403; Arthur MARRIOTT, "Arbitrators and Settlement", 70 Arbitration (2004, issue 4) pp. 297-307; Andrew BURR, "Med-Arb: A Viable Hybrid Solution?" in José ROSELL, coord., *Les arbitres internationaux* (Centre Français de Droit Comparé, Société de Législation Comparé 2005) pp. 57-76; Hilmar RAESCHKE-KESSLER, "The Arbitrator as Settlement Facilitator", 21 Arb. Int'l (2005, no. 4) pp. 523-536; Christian BÜHRING-UHLE, *Arbitration and Mediation in International Business*, 2nd ed., International Arbitration Law Library, Vol. 13 (Kluwer Law International 2006); Gabrielle KAUFMANN-KOHLER and Víctor BONNÍN, "Arbitrators as Conciliators: A Statistical Study of the Relation Between an Arbitrator's Role and Legal Background", 18 ICC Bulletin (2007, no. 2) pp. 79-90; Gabrielle KAUFMANN-KOHLER and Fan KUN, "Integrating Mediation into Arbitration: Why It Works in China", 25 J. Int'l Arb. (2008, issue 4) pp. 479-492; Gabrielle KAUFMANN-KOHLER, "When Arbitrators Facilitate Settlement: Towards a Transnational Standard", 25 Arb. Int'l (2009, no. 2) pp. 187-205; Harry Kenneth WOOLF, "Mediation in Arbitration in the Pursuit of Justice", 65 Arbitration (2009, issue 2) pp. 169-176; Bernd EHLE, "The Arbitrator as a Settlement Facilitator", in *Walking A Thin Line - What an Arbitrator Can Do, Must Do or Must Not Do, Recent Developments and Trends*, Colloquium CEPANI 40, 29 September 2010 (Bruylant 2010) pp. 77-95; Sophie NAPPERT and Dieter FLADER, "A Psychological Perspective on the Facilitation of Settlement in International Arbitration – Examining the CEDR Rules", 2 Journal of International Dispute Settlement (2011, issue 2) pp. 459-470; Paul Eric MASON, "The Arbitrator as Mediator, and Mediator as Arbitrator", 28 J. Int'l Arb. (2011, Issue 6) pp. 541-551; P. E. MASON, "Follow-Up Note to 'The Arbitrator as Mediator, and Mediator as Arbitrator'", J. Int. Arb. (2011, issue 6) pp. 541 et seq.", 29 J. Int'l Arb. (2012, issue 2) pp. 225-226; Robert RHODES, "Mediation-Arbitration (Med-Arb)", 79 Arbitration (2013, issue 2) pp. 116-119; Kerrod GILES, "Mediation-Arbitration Processes in Queensland: Do They Work?", 81 Arbitration, (2015, issue 2) pp. 150-166; Dilyara NIGMATULLINA, "The Combined Use of Mediation and Arbitration in Commercial Dispute Resolution: Results from an International Study", 33 J. Int'l Arb. (2016, issue 1) pp. 37-82; Stefan Michael KRÖLL, "Chapter 22: Promoting Settlements in Arbitration: The Role of the Arbitrator" in Patricia SHAUGHNESSY and Sherlin TUNG, eds., *The Powers and Duties of an Arbitrator: Liber Amicorum Pierre A. Karrer* (Kluwer Law International 2017) pp. 209-224.

72. For an overview, A. BURR, "Med-Arb: A Viable Hybrid Solution?", fn. 71 above, pp. 57-70.

73. UNCITRAL Model Law on International Commercial Conciliation (2002), Art. 1.3. In the same line, ICC Mediation Guidance Notes (2014) para. 1 ("For the purpose of the ICC Mediation Rules (the 'Rules'), mediation is a flexible settlement technique, conducted privately and confidentially,

Med-Arb is a process in which the parties first attempt to resolve the dispute through mediation and, if mediation fails, it is decided by arbitration, with the same third person assuming both roles of arbitrator and mediator: firstly serving as a mediator to assist the parties in trying to reach a settlement and later, if necessary, changing hats and serving as an arbitrator to resolve the dispute.[74]

Arb-Med-Arb is an arbitration process in which the parties agree to attempt to resolve the dispute through mediation at some point during the course of the arbitration proceedings. If the mediation is successful the parties may request the arbitrator to record their settlement as a consent award and, in any event, the arbitration comes to an end. If mediation fails, the arbitrator resumes the arbitration proceedings and renders an arbitral award. The arbitrator and the mediator in this variant are often different persons[75] although nothing prevents the parties from agreeing otherwise.[76]

Co-Med-Arb is a process in which two different people, one acting as a mediator and the other as an arbitrator, work together but separately to resolve the dispute. They jointly appear before the parties and organize an information exchange between them. If the mediator does his job and is unable to get the parties to reach a settlement, the dispute is decided by the arbitrator.[77]

b. A peculiar form of Arb-Med-Arb: Impartial arbitrators and partial mediators

In my opinion, the special role of party-appointed arbitrators that may in the future be of more practical interest for some arbitration users, those who believe that party-appointed arbitrators should not have the same role as the presiding arbitrator, is a special role combining arbitration and mediation in a peculiar – and presently uncommon – type of Arb-Med-Arb.

In this arbitration process, with a three-member tribunal, the parties would clearly and openly agree to have impartial and independent party-appointed arbitrators that are nevertheless required to act as mediators who support their respective appointing parties

---

in which a mediator acts as a neutral facilitator to help the parties try to arrive at a negotiated settlement of their dispute. The parties have control over both the decision to settle and the terms of any settlement agreement") and fn. 2 ("Internationally, the terms 'conciliation' and 'mediation' are used sometimes to describe processes that are substantively the same and sometimes to describe processes that are similar but have some differences. Where there are substantive differences, there is no uniform understanding of what those differences are. Mediation as referred to in the ICC Mediation Rules and these Mediation Guidance Notes is a concept sufficiently broad to encompass both mediation and conciliation").

74. M. E. SCHNEIDER, "Combining Arbitration with Conciliation" in *ICCA Congress Series no. 8*, p. 70; A. BURR, "Med-Arb: A Viable Hybrid Solution?", fn. 71 above, p. 61.

75. See, e.g., Singapore International Arbitration Centre- Singapore International Mediation Centre (SIAC-SIMC) Arb-Med-Arb Model Clause ("Arb-Med-Arb Clause") and SIAC-SIMC Arb-Med-Arb Protocol.

76. See, e.g., CPR Global Rules for Accelerated Commercial Arbitration (2009), Accelerated Rule 19.4: "With the consent of the parties, the Arbitral Tribunal at any stage of the proceeding may arrange for mediation of the claims asserted in the arbitration by a mediator acceptable to the parties who may be a member of the Arbitral Tribunal."

77. D. ELLIOT, "Med-Arb: Fraught with Danger or Ripe with Opportunity?", fn. 71 above, p. 178, recalling that the variation of Co-Med-Arb was suggested by the Harvard Negotiation Project to address the concern about the impartiality of the arbitrator.

for the sole purpose of exploring zones of possible agreement in one or more mediation periods – mediation windows – within the arbitration process.

A fundamental requirement of the parties' agreement should be the clear separation of roles at different moments in time. The party-appointed arbitrators would have the normal role of an impartial and independent arbitrator during the entire arbitration proceedings except for the mediation periods or windows, in which they would be required to act as mediators supporting their respective appointing parties. The party-appointed arbitrators would not be allowed to perform both roles simultaneously at any single time.

This special role is similar to the normal two-tier role that was performed by party-appointed arbitrators in ancient Greece, where they were expected to support their respective appointing parties while trying to mediate between them but, if mediation failed, they were obliged to reach a decision based only on what they regarded as just, under oath, if they had to make an award. However, unlike the system in ancient Greece, party-appointed arbitrators with this special role would be arbitrators under the duty of impartiality and independence from the commencement of the arbitration, as is standard procedure today. They would only be allowed to act with bias in favour of their respective appointing parties when acting as mediators during the mediation windows. This is advisable to enhance the fact that the party-appointed arbitrators are first and foremost arbitrators with the same duty of impartiality and independence as the presiding arbitrator throughout the entire arbitration proceedings, with the only exception of the mediation periods.

The parties would be free to agree on the manner in which the mediation windows are to be included in the arbitration and what activities within the mediation windows must take place. This could be discussed and agreed in writing by the parties in their arbitration agreement, or later discussed and agreed with the arbitral tribunal at some – preferably early – procedural stage. The Centre for Effective Dispute Resolution (CEDR) Rules for the Facilitation of Settlement in International Arbitration, for example, state that, at the first procedural conference, the arbitral tribunal (i) shall "where appropriate, discuss with the Parties how other dispute resolution processes used to facilitate settlement might be accommodated at an appropriate time within the procedure for the arbitration (for example by way of a Mediation Window)" and (ii) "insert a Mediation Window in the arbitral proceedings when requested to do so by all Parties in order to enable settlement discussions, through mediation or otherwise, to take place".[78] The possibility of including the mediation windows in the arbitration may also be suggested by the arbitral tribunal as one of the various case management techniques that arbitrators may apply in ICC arbitrations.[79]

The exact number, timing and duration of the mediation windows should be determined in each particular case. Whatever the specific arrangement may be, it would be required in all cases to have been clearly determined when each mediation window

78. Centre for Effective Dispute Resolution (CEDR) Rules for the Facilitation of Settlement in International Arbitration (2009), Arts. 4.2.3 and 5.3.1. Available at <https://www.cedr.com/about_us/arbitration_commission/Rules.pdf> (last accessed 2 March 2018).

79. ICC Arbitration Rules (2017), Appendix IV, h(ii); ICC Mediation Guidance Notes (2014), paras. 29-30.

starts and ends. Furthermore, it seems generally advisable to start the first mediation window only after the first round of written submissions, in which the parties have made a full substantive presentation of their positions and evidence. It also seems advisable to agree, when appropriate, that the mediation window periods will not affect other time periods in the arbitration proceeding.

The minimum content of one mediation window would include two things: a meeting between each party-appointed arbitrator and his appointing party and a meeting between the two party-appointed arbitrators.

With respect to the caucusing, the agreement of the parties should provide that each party-appointed arbitrator, when acting as a mediator in the mediation periods or windows: (i) is authorized to conduct separate or ex parte meetings (caucuses) or other types of unilateral communications with the appointing party or its representatives; (ii) is obliged to maintain the confidentiality of all that comes to his knowledge in the course of those meetings or communications, including all information and documentation received from the appointing party or its representatives and all views expressed by the appointing party or its representatives; and (iii) is also obliged to keep confidential all assessments and proposals made and views expressed by him in the course of those meetings or communications.

The mission of the party-appointed arbitrators, while performing their role as a mediator during the caucus, would basically be to assist the appointing party in exploring ways of ending the arbitration with a settlement agreement. They would be required to listen to the appointing party and assist it in exploring zones of possible agreement with the other party. In doing this, the party-appointed arbitrator could take a facilitative role or rather a more proactive evaluative role that may include expressing opinions on the merits of the case, suggesting solutions or making proposals for possible settlements, providing preliminary views on the party's perceptions of the strengths and weaknesses of its case or whatever other activity deemed useful for the purpose of identifying zones of possible agreement.

Whether the mediator should adopt a more facilitative or more evaluative approach would depend to a large extent on the circumstances of each particular case. It would be safer for both party-appointed arbitrators to adopt the same approach, but the parties could agree to allow each party-appointed arbitrator to use the mediation techniques he considered more appropriate in the light of the cultural background of the appointing party or any other factors. The techniques that best help the party to enlarge its zone of possible agreement may be different from one party to another.

In any event, a minimum evaluative role would always appear to be advisable, at least in terms of assessing and letting the party know what the party-appointed arbitrator considers to be clearly unrealistic aspirations in the light of the facts or applicable legal rules. This could also be achieved through a facilitative role by the mediator asking the right – uncomfortable – questions at the right time. A shot of reality, even if only a preliminary and non-binding view of the party-appointed arbitrator, would be most helpful to later face the discussion of the sacrifices that the party may be willing to accept in order to reach a settlement.

After the caucus, the party-appointed arbitrators would meet and explore whether there are any common zones of possible agreement. The party-appointed arbitrators' mission during this meeting would be to attempt to help the parties reach a resolution of the dispute that they all consider acceptable, within the boundaries of their confidentiality obligations.

The third presiding arbitrator would not serve as a mediator nor participate in the mediation activities with the parties or the party-appointed arbitrators at any time during the proceedings. Neither would he be informed of the content of any settlement discussions, offers, proposals or other statements made during the mediation window or windows. Nevertheless, as a member of the arbitral tribunal, he would always keep the role of establishing the instructions to be followed by the parties and the party-appointed arbitrators during the mediation windows and, more in general, of resolving all disputes between the parties on how the mediation activities should be organized or conducted.

If no settlement is reached during the mediation window, the party-appointed members of the arbitral tribunal would retake their role as impartial and independent arbitrators automatically at the very moment the mediation window ends. It is essential for the procedural rules to make it clear that, if mediation fails, the party-appointed arbitrators will have the obligation to decide the case impartially, exactly in the same way as the presiding arbitrator.

Finally, it goes without saying that the party-appointed arbitrators would be obliged to maintain all the deliberations of the arbitral tribunal confidential at all times. In this regard, to have the mediation window or windows scheduled before the substantive deliberations of the arbitral tribunal would appear to be the safest option, not just for avoiding improper conduct but also not to put the party-appointed arbitrators in potentially very uncomfortable situations.

The first peculiarity of the Arb-Med-Arb variant described is the allocation of the mediation functions to the party-appointed arbitrators. Modern formulations of Arb-Med-Arb are not normally articulated to assign the mediation functions to a team comprised of the two party-appointed arbitrators. The more common assumption is that the mediator will be a single person who is not an arbitrator in the case; or, if the same person or persons are going to act as arbitrators and mediators, that the mediation functions in multiple-member tribunals will be assumed either by the whole tribunal or by the presiding arbitrator.[80]

Nonetheless, there are possible combinations of arbitration and mediation in which party-appointed arbitrators form a "settlement team" to perform a conciliatory role without the participation of the presiding arbitrator.[81] It is equally possible, when all the members of the arbitral tribunal take on a role of settlement facilitators, that the allocation of roles between the arbitrators *inter se* in the settlement process may lead the party-appointed arbitrators to have a different role.[82] The possibility for the party-appointed arbitrators to assume a special conciliatory role, with or without the presiding arbitrator assuming conciliatory functions, would also appear to be implied in the ICC

80. See, e.g.: IBA Rules of Ethics for International Arbitrators (1987), Rule 8 ("Involvement in Settlement Proposals"); CEDR Rules for the Facilitation of Settlement in International Arbitration (2009), Art. 5; ICC Mediation Guidance Notes (2014), para. 34.
81. H. I. ABRAMSON, "Protocols", fn. 71 above, pp. 12-13. For an account of a successful example, Ch. BÜHRING-UHLE, Arbitration and Mediation in International Business, fn. 71 above, pp. 255-259 (the *IBM v. Fujitsu* case).
82. S. NAPPERT and D. FLADER, "A Psychological Perspective on the Facilitation of Settlement", fn. 71 above, pp. 466-467.

Mediation Guidance Notes when they make reference to the so-called co-mediation, understood as two or more mediators appointed to work together on the same matter. The same Guidance Notes add that this type of mediation may be used when the parties wish to have the benefit of mediators from different cultural backgrounds or with different expertise and experience.[83]

The second and perhaps most striking peculiarity of this form of Arb-Med-Arb is the partiality of the mediators. Mediation rules usually impose the same obligations of impartiality and independence on mediators that arbitration rules impose on arbitrators. Today's standards require mediators to conduct the mediation in an impartial manner,[84] even in combinations whereby the party-appointed arbitrators perform mediation functions without the participation of the presiding arbitrator.[85] There is little explored nowadays as to the possibility of the conciliation functions of a "settlement team" of party-appointed arbitrators being performed by each of them supporting his respective appointing party. It is likely that the historical movement towards the standard of impartiality and independence of all arbitrators and the desire of the international arbitration community to end improper behaviour by party-appointed arbitrators has, for a good reason, held back any interest in exploring the potential conciliatory functions of party-appointed arbitrators consisting in them supporting howsoever their respective appointing parties.

Be it as it may, there is no fundamental obstacle to requiring party-appointed arbitrators to support or be biased towards their respective appointing parties while acting as mediators during the mediation windows. As a matter of principle, the parties should be free to agree to try to settle their dispute with the assistance of two partial mediators as long as this system is openly agreed upon by the parties and the integrity of the system can therefore be protected.

It is yet unclear whether this form of Arb-Med-Arb might be allowed by some well-known mediation rules. The Singapore International Mediation Centre (SIMC) Mediation Rules (2014) require the mediator to be impartial and independent (Art. 4.5) but give the parties to power to waive any disclosed actual or potential conflict (Art. 4.6). This seems consistent with the possibility that the same rules offer to appoint more than one mediator (Art. 4.4) and the SIMC Request Form (Appendix A of the SIMC Mediation Rules) actually offers the parties the possibility to request the SIMC to appoint one or two mediators. However, in the case of the AAA International Mediation Rules (2014) and the International Institute for Conflict Prevention and Resolution (CPR) International Mediation Procedure (2017), the mediation appears to be only envisioned

83. ICC Mediation Guidance Notes, para. 36.

84. See, e.g.: AAA International Mediation Rules (2014), Art. 5.1; CPR International Mediation Procedure (2017), Art. 3(c); SIMC Mediation Rules (2014), Art. 4.5; UNCITRAL Model Law on International Commercial Conciliation (2002), Art. 5.4.

85. Ch. BÜHRING-UHLE, Arbitration and Mediation in International Business, fn. 71 above, p. 124: "[I]t also occurs that the party-appointed arbitrators act as (co-) mediators. Deliberate mediation attempts where all sides agree that the party-appointed arbitrators serve as mediators and in this function 'officially' confer with their parties are comparatively rare since it creates a potential conflict with the principle that party-appointed arbitrators are supposed to be completely impartial and should, after their appointment, abstain from any contact to 'their party'." In the same vein, H. I. ABRAMSON, "Protocols", fn. 71 above, p. 13.

with one single mediator, whose impartiality and independence should obviously always be required.

c. Potential benefits of this form of Arb-Med-Arb

There are several potential benefits of this specific form of Arb-Med-Arb.

First, the benefits that are typical of mediation: the chance of a faster, cheaper and perhaps substantially better end to the dispute.

Second, the benefits that are typical of Arb-Med-Arb. The way the combination of arbitration and mediation is structured, by means of mediation windows during the course of the arbitration, can make the parties expect that there will be no significant loss of time, money or overall efficiency of the arbitration due to the fact of accepting to create some room for mediation.[86] Furthermore, the room for mediation is created without putting any of the parties in the situation of suggesting mediation only on its own motion, something that in certain cultures is perceived as an uncomfortable move, a sign of weakness or a loss of face.

Third, the likelihood of a successful conciliation may be increased. A settlement agreement needs by hypothesis two previously opposed points of view. When the parties agree to the arbitrators performing a conciliatory role before an adjudicative one, the assignment to each party-appointed arbitrator of the conciliatory role of exploring zones of possible agreement from the appointing party's perspective can make conciliation more effective than if managed by the three members of the tribunal, each assuming an equal conciliatory role. There is always hope of constructive dialogue after a clash of views. To be biased, in this particular context (party-appointed arbitrators acting as biased mediators during the mediation windows), would be a strength rather than a weakness. Two serious party-appointed arbitrators meeting each other in order to confront two opposed positions for conciliation purposes can bring added value to the arbitration.

The idea that bias can be useful in a mediation context with two party-appointed arbitrators is very intuitive and more than 2,000 years old. Some authors have evoked it when considering the possible advantages of biased party-appointed arbitrators. As Bellet put it, biased party-appointed arbitrators can serve the needs of disputing parties who wish to submit their dispute to arbitration but also wish that the arbitration could end with a settlement.[87] Similarly, Coulson considered that biased party-appointed arbitrators can discuss possible settlements with their respective appointing parties and this could produce advantageous settlements.[88] However, as explained above, biased party-appointed arbitrators are generally unadvisable in international arbitration because the dangers outweigh by far the benefits.[89]

Party-appointed arbitrators, according to this proposal, would not be partisan arbitrators but rather impartial and independent arbitrators who would be exceptionally

86. Ch. BÜHRING-UHLE, *Arbitration and Mediation in International Business*, fn. 71 above, pp. 259-260.

87. Pierre BELLET, "*Des arbitres neutres et non neutres*" in Christian DOMINICE, Robert PATRY and Claude REYMOND, eds., *Études de droit international en l'honneur de Pierre Lalive* (Helbing & Lichtenhahn 1993) p. 408.

88. R. COULSON, "An American Critique", fn. 4 above, pp. 107-109.

89. See Sect. III.*1* above.

allowed – and required – during the mediation window or windows to act as mediators who support their respective appointing parties for the sole purpose of exploring zones of possible agreement. The difference between a partial mediator and a partial arbitrator is of critical importance because the bias dynamics change completely from one role to the other. As much as they could and should try to support their respective appointing parties, there would be no point whatsoever in any of the partial mediators considering anything that could not also be satisfactory to the party who did not appoint him. Their bias would not be aimed at making the appointing party prevail in the arbitration but rather at exploring what settlement agreement, if at all possible, could be most beneficial for the appointing party while also being acceptable to the other party.

Fourth, these partial mediators and impartial arbitrators may contribute to the relief of ethical tension in the arbitration. The conceptual underpinning of certain criticism of party-appointed arbitrators is their alleged burden of feeling that they owe something to the appointing party that they do not owe to the other. For example, Smit notes that "[a] party-appointed arbitrator cannot help but realize that counsel who selected him was motivated by the desire that his selection would contribute to the favorable result he seeks and, to some extent, the arbitrator may act upon that realization".[90] In the same vein, Stevenson claims that the principle of independence of arbitrators is "somewhat negated if the parties have the option to select one of the three arbitrators since such arbitrator will feel that he has a certain responsibility to the party selecting him".[91] More recently, in his dissenting opinion in *Supervisión y Control S.A. v. Costa Rica*, Klock noted that "the arrangement whereby two of the panel members are selected by the parties to the agreement creates an uncomfortable aura of conflict which permeates, in my view, the proceedings. It creates a true ethical burden on these other two parties to separate themselves from the interest of those who have selected them to serve."[92]

Bias in the mediation role can contribute to liberating party-appointed arbitrators from this ethical burden. A conciliatory role of party-appointed arbitrators whereby each of them supports his appointing party is consistent with the presumption – which more often than not proves correct – that each party-appointed arbitrator will find more strengths in the appointing party's case than the other party-appointed arbitrator. By each party-appointed arbitrator assuming the biased role as mediator of exploring the limits of what an acceptable solution for the appointing party may be, the parties could achieve a more accurate match between what they expect from party-appointed arbitrators and what they ultimately get. Party-appointed arbitrators would not be worried about their bias towards the appointing party when exploring zones of possible agreement and, thanks to that, they would probably feel relieved from any sense of owing anything to the appointing party after conciliation attempts had failed. And the presiding arbitrator could perhaps be more confident that the party-appointed arbitrators would sit with him, if mediation fails, to simply perform an adjudicative role according

90. H. SMIT, book review of *Quo Vadis Arbitration?*, fn. 5 above, p. 430.
91. John R. STEVENSON, "Regarding Selection of Arbitrators" in Christian DOMINICÉ, Robert PATRY and Claude REYMOND, eds., *Études de droit international en l'honneur de Pierre Lalive*, (Helbing & Lichtenhahn 1993) p. 691.
92. Joseph P. KLOCK, Dissenting Opinion of 18 January 2017 in *Supervisión y Control S.A. v. Costa Rica* (ICSID Case No. ARB/12/4) pp. 13-14.

to the rules applicable to the merits of the dispute. History shows that we have moved from systems in which the parties expected party-appointed arbitrators to first try to persuade each other to the present system, in which many parties simply expect the arbitrator they unilaterally appoint to persuade the presiding arbitrator.[93] One may have opposed feelings about this evolution and wonder whether a time in the arbitral proceedings for party-appointed arbitrators to confront their views with each other, an arbitral feature as old as nowadays neglected, may perhaps help to raise the sense of ethics in international arbitration.

Fifth, and finally, this peculiar form of Arb-Med-Arb mitigates certain risks that are usually associated with the same individual serving as an arbitrator and mediator in the same case.

There is a paradox in the world where arbitration and mediation are combined: some powerful strengths are also powerful weaknesses. On the one hand, there is the perception that the most efficient combination is that in which the same person acts both as an arbitrator and conciliator[94] and the perception that some mediation techniques, like meeting separately with the parties (caucusing)[95] or expressing preliminary views,[96] can be very useful. On the other, there is the perception that the appropriateness for an arbitrator to act as a conciliator is controversial[97] and the perception that the same

93. According to the 2010 International Arbitration Survey conducted by the School of International Arbitration, Queen Mary University of London, on *Choices in International Arbitration*, the seventh most important factor in the choice of co-arbitrators, acknowledged by 47 percent of the respondents, was the likelihood that the co-arbitrator will be able to influence the presiding arbitrator.

94. M. E. SCHNEIDER, "Combining Arbitration with Conciliation" in *ICCA Congress Series no. 8*, p. 77: "In many respects, the most efficient combination of arbitration and conciliation is that in which the same person acts both as arbitrator and conciliator"; A. BURR, "Med-Arb: A Viable Hybrid Solution?", fn. 71 above, p. 63: "The most efficient combination of arbitration and mediation is when the same person acts both as arbitrator and mediator"; G. KAUFMANN-KOHLER, "When Arbitrators Facilitate Settlement", fn. 71 above, p. 197, noting the existence of an added value for three reasons: the arbitrator's knowledge of the case, the arbitrator's ideal position to choose the right timing for settlement purposes and the possibility that the settlement agreement may form part of a consent award enforceable under the New York Convention.

95. See, e.g.: AAA International Mediation Rules (2014), Art. 7.2: "The mediator is authorized to conduct separate or ex parte meetings and other communications with the parties and/or their representatives, before, during, and after any scheduled mediation conference. Such communications may be conducted via telephone, in writing, via email, online, in person, or otherwise"; CPR International Mediation Procedure (2017), Art. 3(d)(i): "The mediator is free to meet and communicate separately with each party and confidentially with each party"; UNCITRAL Model Law on International Commercial Conciliation (2002), Art. 7: "The conciliator may meet or communicate with the parties together or with each of them separately."

96. M. E. SCHNEIDER, "Combining Arbitration with Conciliation" in *ICCA Congress Series no. 8*, p. 75: "The most controversial but perhaps also the most promising form of preparing for settlement is the *indication of preliminary views by the arbitral tribunal itself*."

97. *Ibid.*, p. 77: "The admissibility and appropriateness for an arbitrator to act as conciliator is among the most controversial issues among international arbitration practitioners. The views and practices in this respect differ widely."

techniques that can be useful, such as caucusing[98] and expressing views on the case,[99] are dangerous.

Over the years, it can be observed that there is a growing number of arbitration rules and laws that admit the possibility of the same person assuming both roles in the same dispute as long as it is expressly authorized by the parties.[100] Although this possibility is still not free from controversy, and is seemingly still far from being a preferred choice by those with experience in combining mediation and arbitration,[101] the epicentre of the debate has probably shifted from the possibility itself to how to face the dangers created by the vesting of the two roles in the same person.

The most serious dangers, which may make the arbitral award vulnerable, are related to the impartiality of the arbitrator and to due process. On the one hand, there is a risk relating to the arbitrator's impartiality if he, when acting as a mediator, expresses preliminary views on the merits of the case or makes settlement proposals that lead one party to question the ability of the arbitrator to decide impartially. The risk of prejudgment may also arise from the arbitrator being influenced, consciously or unconsciously, by confidential information received during the mediation. On the other hand, there is a threat to due process that is associated with the practice of caucusing. This threat lies in the possibility that, if mediation fails, the arbitrator's decision may be influenced, consciously or unconsciously, by circumstances that he knew privately from one party and that the other party is unaware of and could never answer or rebut.[102]

In addition to these dangers, there is a problem relating to the parties' reluctance to speak frankly and candidly to the mediator. As noted by Marriot,

> "[t]he main conceptual objection to a combination of roles in one person is that parties will be reluctant to speak freely in private to mediators who will then

---

98. Martin HUNTER, "Ethics of the International Arbitrator", 53 Arbitration, (November 1987, no. 4) p. 224; IBA Rules of Ethics for International Arbitrators (1987), Rule 8 ("Involvement in Settlement Proposals"); D. ELLIOT, "Med-Arb: Fraught with Danger or Ripe with Opportunity?", fn. 71 above, pp. 166-167; M. E. SCHNEIDER, "Combining Arbitration with Conciliation" in *ICCA Congress Series no. 8*, p. 90: "The most controversial question about an arbitrator's activity as conciliator is no doubt that concerning the admissibility for him to meet a party in the absence of the others and discuss the case and a settlement with it"; CEDR Rules for the Facilitation of Settlement in International Arbitration (2009), Art. 5.2: "The Arbitral Tribunal shall not: 2.1. meet any Party without all other Parties being present; or 2.2. obtain information from any Party which is not shared with the other Parties."
99. See fn. 96 above. See also Mercédeh AZEREDO DA SILVEIRA, "Impartiality v. Substantive Neutrality: Is the Mediator Authorized to Provide Legal Advice?" in Sophie NAPPERT, ed., *Arbitrator Bias*, 5 Transnational Dispute Management (July 2008, no. 4).
100. See fn. 31 above.
101. D. NIGMATULLINA, "The Combined Use of Mediation and Arbitration", fn. 71 above, p. 60, showing some specific results of an empirical study carried out by the author in 2014. Participants in the study were asked if the neutral that conducted mediation in the dispute involving the combined use of mediation and arbitration was the sole arbitrator, a member of the arbitral tribunal or a neutral other than the sole arbitrator or a member of the arbitral tribunal. The vast majority of the twenty-six participants who answered this question (84.6 percent) noted that there were different individuals for mediation and arbitration stages.
102. On these dangers, e.g.: G. KAUFMANN-KOHLER, "When Arbitrators Facilitate Settlement", fn. 71 above, pp. 197-200; H. I. ABRAMSON, "Protocols", fn. 71 above, pp. 3-5.

> decide the case if the mediation fails and, the other side of the same coin, that it will be difficult or impossible for arbitrators in deciding the case to forget or ignore what they have been told by the parties privately and confidentially".[103]

It stands to reason that parties may be reluctant to disclose where their true bottom line for settlement lies to the mediator but possible future adjudicator, even in a caucus or separate meeting. The parties may also be reluctant to disclose facts to mediators that may later become arbitrators.[104] Moreover, as Elliot notes, the problem may get worse if the parties pretend to be interested in the mediation when they actually are not:

> "If the parties know that the mediator will become the arbitrator if the dispute is not resolved, it is possible that the parties will use mediation to introduce material and say things strictly with a view to influencing the arbitrator's final decision, rather than with any real intention of reaching a settlement. Of course, if one side sees this happening, they may play the same game, or call the other party on it, but the damage may already be done."[105]

The variation of Arb-Med-Arb proposed mitigates some of the risks that are derived from the fact that the same person or persons act both as arbitrators and mediators in the same dispute. The risk of the parties' reluctance to disclose information to the mediator still exists, but is probably reduced by the fact that the information will only be disclosed to the arbitrator chosen by that party. The risk of the arbitrator being perceived as no longer able to be impartial still exists, but does not affect the whole arbitral tribunal. And the risk to due process disappears, because it is almost impossible for the tribunal to decide on the basis of something that one party disclosed in a caucus and the other party does not know. If mediation fails, each party has to assume that the confidential information that it only shared with the arbitrator it appointed will have no bearing whatsoever in the adjudication phase.

d. Limitations and risks of this form of Arb-Med-Arb

The form of Arb-Med-Arb proposed has limitations relating to its scope of application. Many arbitration users are well acquainted with the pros and cons of arbitration and other ADR methods. They know when and why they want only arbitration, when and why they want mediation and arbitration in separate processes and when and why they want a combination of arbitration and mediation in the same process. As Lalive noted, warning against an excessive enthusiasm for ADR, "there will always be complex and important disputes which simply *cannot* be settled by agreement of the parties – so that ADR methods will prove time-consuming and inadequate, the only remaining way out being a third-party binding decision (by a state judge or arbitrator)".[106] Moreover, some cultures emphasize the value of mediation to a greater extent than others, not all

103. A. MARRIOTT, "Arbitrators and Settlement", fn. 71 above, p. 303.
104. A. BURR, "Med-Arb: A Viable Hybrid Solution?", fn. 71 above, p. 61.
105. D. ELLIOT, "Med-Arb: Fraught with Danger or Ripe with Opportunity?", fn. 71 above, p. 179.
106. Pierre LALIVE, "Towards a Decline of International Arbitration?", 65 Arbitration (1999, no. 4) pp. 253.

arbitration users like the combination of arbitration and mediation and, even if they like it, they may not like or wish party-appointed arbitrators to perform a role different to that of the presiding arbitrator.

In any event, it would be generally advisable in cases with party-appointed arbitrators, both in commercial and investment arbitration, to submit this form of Arb-Med-Arb to the parties at the first procedural conference, for their consideration. The organization of the arbitration procedure with one or more mediation windows would not appear to be particularly difficult. Whatever the decision by the parties, and I assume that in many instances the parties would reject anything different from the arbitrators just performing their adjudicative function, I can only see benefits in making the parties spend some time in thinking and expressing what role they expect from party-appointed arbitrators. At the very least, to ensure a level playing field.

In addition to the above-mentioned limitations, the critical question relating to this specific form of Arb-Med-Arb is, of course, to what extent may party-appointed arbitrators be eventually able to perform their adjudicative role as arbitrators in an impartial manner if mediation fails? Is it realistic to expect that someone who supports one of the disputing parties, even if only for conciliation purposes, can later be able to act impartially? Some may think that his willingness or self-awareness of his capability to act without bias as an arbitrator may possibly have been undermined by the performance of his role as a partial mediator.

It is clear that anyone who assumes the role of settlement facilitator and later that of adjudicator faces the risk of losing his ability to act in an impartial manner in the second stage, and that this risk might increase if the first of those two roles encompasses support for one the parties. Perhaps it would be naive to presume that most party-appointed arbitrators could perform the two-tier biased-unbiased role satisfactorily in practice. The old English system of arbitrator-advocates, for what it is worth as an example of pragmatism, is based on the quite opposite idea that party-appointed arbitrators who try and fail to reach an agreement had better change their role to that of advocates of the parties.[107]

Nevertheless, for the reasons explained above, I believe that the bias of the party-appointed arbitrators when performing their mediation functions during the mediation windows does not necessarily decrease and could even increase their ability to later act impartially, if mediation fails, in the performance of their adjudicative role.

Ultimately, how the limitations and risks of the form of Arb-Med-Arb proposed are viewed also depends on the glasses that one decides to wear when considering party-appointed arbitrators. One may recall Judge Loder, the first president of the Permanent Court of International Justice, when in his inaugural speech at the first session of this Court in 1922 he criticized the power of each party to appoint one of the Court judges as a "*concession faite à la faiblesse humaine*" ("a concession made to human weakness").[108] With these glasses, party-appointed arbitrators will always be inferior to judges or arbitrators

107. Michael J. MUSTILL and Stewart C. BOYD, *Commercial Arbitration*, 2nd ed. (Butterworths 1989) pp. 258-264.

108. "Arbitral Procedure – *Rapport par Georges Scelle, rapporteur spécial*", United Nations International Law Commission, UN Doc. A/CN.4/18 (21 March 1950) 1950 U.N.Y.B. Int'l L. Comm'n, para. 36, p. 126.

appointed by neutral appointors, like a product with an inherent factory flaw. In terms of appearance of impartiality and independence, there is little doubt that party-appointed arbitrators offer fewer guarantees than arbitrators appointed by neutral appointors. If such an appearance is of paramount importance to the parties, they should not agree to unilateral appointments in the first place and, even less, to the form of Arb-Med-Arb herein proposed. However, one can see things through a different prism. As eloquently put by Eisemann, if arbitration is less than judicial systems in the sense that it does not offer the same guarantees as professional permanent judges, it is certainly at the same time much more because of its fundamental orientation towards the appeasement of social and business relationships, an outcome that only the element of trust will ever be able to provide.[109] Furthermore, the main driver of success of international arbitration has never been the same appearance of impartiality and independence in each and every member of an arbitral tribunal (something that is not even required in the judiciary),[110] but rather something much simpler: its usefulness for resolving international disputes.

IV. CONCLUSION

The role of party-appointed arbitrators is nowadays shrouded by ambiguity and confusion. Arbitration rules and laws do not provide for a different arbitrator role depending on the appointment method used. However, there is a widespread presumption that party-appointed arbitrators have a special role to perform in relation to the appointing party's case, irrespective of whether or not such a special role is expressly allowed in the rules governing the arbitration, as long as these rules do not prohibit it. A special role that presiding arbitrators are not allowed to perform and that is still deemed compatible with the duty of arbitrators to be impartial and independent. In this respect, it has been suggested that party-appointed arbitrators have a special role of ensuring that the appointor's case is properly understood by the other members of the arbitral tribunal and even of acting as a devil's advocate that challenges, within the tribunal, the positions that are harmful to the appointing party's position.

In my opinion, we should reject the presumption that party-appointed arbitrators who are under the duty of impartiality and independence have a special role of ensuring that the appointor's case is properly understood by the other members of the arbitral

109. F. EISEMANN, "*L'arbitre-partie*", fn. 6 above, p. 85.

110. The European Court of Human Rights (ECtHR), for example, has on several occasions dealt with tribunals in which some of the members are nominated by appointors that generally represent the interests of groups to which one of the disputing parties belongs or is closely connected, notwithstanding the obligation of all the members of the tribunal to act impartially. In *Langborger v. Sweden* (Judgment 22 June 1989) there was a four-member Housing and Tenancy Court of which two members were nominated by non-neutral appointors, one by an owners' association and one by a tenants' association. In *Ab Kurt Kellermann v. Sweden* (Judgment 26 January 2005) there was a seven-member Labour Court of which four members were nominated by non-neutral appointors, two by employers' associations and two by employees' associations. In both cases, the ECtHR seemed to suggest that tribunals with some members nominated by non-neutral appointors are acceptable as long as there is a balance of interests in the tribunal's composition. The nomination of some members of the tribunal by non-neutral appointors was indeed not even an issue in either of the two cases.

tribunal or, in general, any special role consisting of doing something that the presiding arbitrator cannot, especially if it consists in certain conduct relating to the appointing party's case. This presumption can cause confusion about the arbitrator's duty of impartiality and independence, can cause an imbalance in the arbitral process and introduces a bias into the arbitration in the form of an advantage for the party who chooses the most intelligent, diligent or zealous arbitrator.

Unless otherwise agreed by the parties, the role or mission of party-appointed arbitrators should always be the same as that of the presiding arbitrator: to decide the case on the sole basis of the applicable procedural and substantive rules, without leaning or favouritism towards any party. This would help achieve the desirable goal of making international arbitration a truly neutral dispute resolution system and is also consistent with the international standard of impartiality and independence of all arbitrators. There is no justification for accepting the existence of an unwritten special duty of party-appointed arbitrators who are under the obligation to be impartial and independent, much less so in light of the increasing demands for transparency in international arbitration.

Arbitral institutions, UNCITRAL, soft law producers and practitioners could build trust and value for arbitration if they made it clear to arbitration users that, unless otherwise agreed by the parties, (i) the role or mission of party-appointed arbitrators is the same as that of the presiding arbitrator, (ii) a special role of party-appointed arbitrators whereby they are supposed to do something special in relation to the appointing party's case cannot be presumed and is not allowed and (iii) party-appointed arbitrators do not have any more responsibility towards the appointing party than they have towards the non-appointing party.

Once clarity has been achieved, the next question for the future is if it is worth exploring possible special roles of party-appointed arbitrators that can be useful to better serve the needs of the arbitration users who believe that party-appointed arbitrators should not have the same role as the presiding arbitrator.

I believe this exploration is worth the effort and, in my opinion, the special role of party-appointed arbitrators that may be of more practical interest for such arbitration users is a special role combining arbitration and mediation in a peculiar – and currently uncommon – type of Arb-Med-Arb. In this arbitration process, with a three-member tribunal, the parties would clearly and openly agree to have impartial and independent party-appointed arbitrators that are nevertheless required to act as mediators that support their respective appointing parties for the sole purpose of exploring zones of possible agreement during one or more mediation periods – mediation windows – within the arbitration process.

To a certain extent, this form of Arb-Med-Arb would give back party-appointed arbitrators part of their historical *raison d'être* and value without renouncing the most useful achievement of convergence in the status of international arbitrators: the obligation for all of them, no matter how appointed, to be impartial and independent.

Institutional Appointment of Arbitrators

Ruth Stackpool-Moore[*]

TABLE OF CONTENTS

Arbitration has long been lauded for its flexibility, its ability to adapt to the demands of its users in a way that the rigidity of national legal systems cannot. Another, much praised, feature of arbitration is the opportunity parties have to influence the nature of the decision-maker in their case, to have a say in the appointment of arbitrators to their tribunal. Nevertheless, debate has arisen, mainly amongst practitioners, around the continued desirability of parties retaining the ability to make such appointments. The question has been asked: Is it time to rethink the parties' latitude to shape the tribunal? And, if the answer to this question is "yes", how viable is it to substitute arbitral institutions in the appointment process?

Party appointment having been included in the checklist of advantages of arbitration since many can remember, a reflex response to these questions tends to be (i) party appointment, as an expression of party autonomy, is a keystone of international arbitration, a right guaranteed in the arbitration process; (ii) if party appointment is taken away, arbitration's position as the preferred method of dispute resolution for cross-border disputes will diminish; and (iii) even if it is accepted that something other than party appointment is required, users do not have requisite faith in institutions to make appointments for them, and another alternative must be sought.

It is useful to examine these propositions and consider whether this initial reaction is justified. What arguments exist to support the continued reliance on party appointment? What factors are against it? It is also important to look at what people involved in arbitration say, and then consider in conjunction with that, what they actually do, before concluding one way or another on the best way forward.

* Managing Director of Asia Dispute Funding, Singapore.

I. ARGUMENTS IN FAVOUR OF PARTY APPOINTMENT

The opportunity to choose the decision-maker has long been one of the leading reasons cited for parties to opt for arbitration over litigation. In fact, the ability of parties to choose their own arbitrators has been described as a "well-established right", providing the foundation for the "perceived legitimacy" of arbitration, the restriction of which would "impede the further development of the field".[1] Why?

First and foremost, it engages issues of confidence and control. Psychologically, parties to a dispute are said to gain the former, and at least an illusion of the latter, when they are given the ability to appoint arbitrators and influence the composition of their tribunal, the ultimate decision-maker. This ability to select one of the arbitrators gives a party a sense of control and proximity to the arbitration proceedings which engenders greater confidence in the arbitral process overall.[2] Confidence in the process has a knock-on effect in relation to the perceived legitimacy of the outcome, the final award. For this reason, it is often argued that removal of party appointments will "erode party autonomy and adversely affect party confidence in international arbitration as a desirable method of dispute resolution".[3]

Second, one of the drivers for the selection of arbitration as a means of resolving international disputes stems from the general lack of trust of the other party's "home court". The "I don't feel comfortable in yours, you don't feel comfortable in mine" conundrum is overcome by the ability of each party to select decision-makers with whom they feel at least some degree of comfort. Party appointment is seen as a means for parties to ensure that there is someone on the tribunal who, if desired, shares their own cultural or legal tradition, again increasing the legitimacy of the process from the party's point of view.

Third, parties know their dispute best and are therefore, at least theoretically, in the best position, particularly with the assistance of instructed counsel, to prioritize important characteristics for an arbitrator, in terms of their ability to successfully resolve it.

It is often here that the waters become muddied, in that the priority of these characteristics may be determined not only in relation to suitability to resolve a particular dispute, but also in relation to an estimate of whether or not potential candidates will be "sympathetic" to a particular party's case. It is the acceptable degree of sympathy, both expected and provided, where opinions on the appropriateness of party appointment diverge.

1. Charles N. BROWER and Charles B. ROSENBERG, "The Death of the Two-Headed Nightingale: Why the Paulsson – Van den Berg Presumption that Party-Appointed Arbitrators Are Untrustworthy Is Wrongheaded", 29 Arbitration International (1 March 2013, issue 1) p. 7.
2. Berwin Leighton Paisner's annual International Arbitration Survey "Party Appointed Arbitrators: Does Fortune Favour the Brave?" released on 12 January 2018 (henceforth 2018 BLP Survey) p. 3.
3. 2018 BLP Survey, p. 2.

II. WHAT ARE THE CRITICISMS?

The frequency of challenges for so-called "issue conflicts" or repeat appointments, studies demonstrating the prevalence of dissents by party-appointees in favour of their appointing parties, proposals for standing tribunals and appellate mechanisms, and transparency initiatives, among others, are all recent developments which reflect concerns about the limits and risks of abuse in the party-appointment system.

Such concerns fall along a broad spectrum, for some the practice is undesirable, but in the context of the established status quo regarding its adoption, unlikely to change. For others, party-appointed arbitrators signify a far greater problem, constituting a "moral hazard" which, unless forbidden or rigorously policed, will ultimately destroy the legitimacy of the arbitration process.[4]

The first criticism of party appointment is that it interferes with the impartiality and independence of arbitrators and leads to bias on the tribunal. In the 2018 Berwin Leighton Paisner Survey (BLP Survey), 52% of respondents felt that party appointments increase the risk of partisan arbitrators, while 70% of those who act as counsel said they had been in a situation where they believed a party-appointed arbitrator tried to favour the party that had appointed them and 55% of those who serve as arbitrators said they had encountered a party-appointed arbitrator who had tried to favour the appointing party by some means.

Second, it is suggested that parties select arbitrators they think will help them win, rather than the best arbitrator for the dispute.

Third, it has been said that party appointments may breed distrust and lead to increased challenges.

Finally, party appointments are criticized on the basis that they do not encourage diversity of tribunals, since parties tend to opt for well-known names from a "short list of favourites".

III. WHAT DO RECENT STUDIES TELL US?

The 2012 International Arbitration Survey on current and preferred practices in the arbitral process conducted by White & Case and Queen Mary University of London (2012 Queen Mary Survey) found that a significant majority, 76%, of the 710 respondents, prefer selection of the two co-arbitrators in a three-member tribunal to be made by each party.[5]

Interestingly, although party appointment was the preferred method of arbitrator selection for all categories of respondents, private practitioners voiced a higher degree of support (83%) to in-house counsel (71%),[6] although it is worth noting that respondents

4. Professor Jan PAULSSON, "Moral Hazard in International Dispute Resolution", Inaugural Lecture as Holder of the Michael R. Klein Distinguished Scholar Chair, University of Miami School of Law, 29 April 2010

5. White & Case and Queen Mary University of London's 2012 International Arbitration Survey, *Current and Preferred Practices in the Arbitral Process*, p. 5.

6. *Ibid.*

to the 2012 Queen Mary Survey were primarily private practitioners (53%), with only 10% of respondents being in-house counsel. The remainder were arbitrators (26%); counsel from arbitral institutions; academics and expert witnesses (together, 11%).[7]

On the basis of these figures, the authors of the 2012 Queen Mary Survey concluded that "the arbitration community generally disapproves of the recent proposals calling for an end to unilateral party appointments".[8]

Although based on a smaller sample, the 151 participants in Berwin Leighton Paisner's latest international arbitration survey were specifically asked about the issue of the party appointment of arbitrators. Those taking part included counsel, academics, arbitrators, users of arbitration and staff at arbitral institutions.[9]

Overall, the 2018 BLP Survey found that 66% of participants still consider party appointments to be a desirable practice.[10] As a subset of that, 83% of the respondents who identified themselves as being "parties to arbitration" believed that such appointments were "very desirable". Interestingly, of the survey participants who work at arbitral institutions, the same percentage (83%) also considered the practice to be very desirable, albeit that that category of respondents represented only 4% of the overall number of participants.[11]

Counter to that, 17% of respondents to the BLP Survey said the practice of party appointment is undesirable. Seventeen percent were ambivalent.[12]

And all of this in the context that 52% of the BLP Survey respondents think party appointment increases the risk of partisan arbitrators appearing on a tribunal.[13]

IV. WHERE ARE WE NOW? THE CURRENT FRAMEWORK

A review of four major arbitral institutions' rules – two Asia-based, the Hong Kong International Arbitration Centre (HKIAC) and the Singapore International Arbitration Centre (SIAC) and two from the United Kingdom and Europe, the London Court of International Arbitration (LCIA) and the International Court of Arbitration of the International Chamber of Commerce (ICC), in Paris – demonstrates very clearly that, despite recent amendments (either in force or currently proposed) to each institution's set of rules, party appointment remains a pillar of the modern arbitral framework.

To the extent that parties fail to exploit the opportunities provided to appoint, invariably it is an organ of the relevant institution which is then called upon to exercise this function. How this is done in the case of each of the four surveyed institutions is also set out below.

7. *Op. cit.*, p. 44.
8. *Op. cit.*, p. 2.
9. 2018 BLP Survey.
10. *Op. cit.*, p. 7.
11. *Op. cit.*, p. 8.
12. *Ibid.*
13. 2018 BLP Survey, p. 7.

1. HKIAC

The general framework under the 2013 HKIAC Administered Arbitration Rules[14] is that the parties have the opportunity to agree (on a sole arbitrator) or appoint (their own co-arbitrator) in the first instance (Art. 7; Art. 8) subject to the confirmation of the HKIAC (Art. 9). Likewise, the default position is that the party-appointed arbitrators will choose the Chair (Art. 8). HKIAC will only undertake appointment if the parties (or, in the case of the Chair, the co-arbitrators) fail to do it themselves.

There are only two exceptions to this general framework. First, if there are more than two parties to an arbitration, the dispute is to be referred to three arbitrators and the parties fail to agree that they represent two separate sides for the purposes of designating arbitrators, HKIAC may then appoint all arbitrators without regard to any party's designation (Art. 8.2). Second, if two or more cases are consolidated under Art. 28.6, (i) the parties are deemed to have waived their right to designate an arbitrator, (ii) HKIAC may revoke the appointment of any arbitrators already designated or confirmed and (iii) HKIAC shall appoint the arbitral tribunal in respect of the consolidated proceedings.

In circumstances where HKIAC is required to make appointments, how are these appointments made?

HKIAC maintains both a Panel and a List of Arbitrators. The Panel of Arbitrators comprises members who have demonstrated particular experience acting as arbitrator, and are generally stated to include "senior members of the arbitration community who have been appointed as arbitrator in multiple disputes and have significant experience in award drafting".[15] The List of Arbitrators comprises members who may have some, but not necessarily extensive, experience acting as arbitrator as well as those who may have not yet achieved their first or multiple appointments, but who nevertheless have "significant experience in arbitration to the extent that they would be suitable for appointment as arbitrator in cases either of smaller value or those with less complex issues for decision".[16] Membership is by application only and lasts for a determined duration (three or five years, respectively) with renewal possible only upon proof of continued compliance with membership criteria, including the experience component, and completion of sufficient continued professional development. Notably also, the HKIAC has a designated complaints procedure available in relation to arbitrators on its Panel and List to assist the institution ensure the quality of its members.[17] Unlike other institutions, HKIAC includes full details of members of both the Panel and List of Arbitrators on a fully searchable online database.[18]

Maintenance of the Panel and List of Arbitrators, and the making of arbitrator appointments by HKIAC are conducted by a designated committee, the Appointments Committee, formed by members of the HKIAC's governing body, the HKIAC Council.

---

14. The 2013 HKIAC Administered Arbitration Rules are subject to consultation for amendment. None of the proposed changes relates to the mechanisms for appointment of arbitrators.
15. <http://hkiac.org/arbitration/arbitrators>.
16. <http://hkiac.org/arbitration/arbitrators>.
17. <http://hkiac.org/arbitration/arbitrators/complaints>.
18. <http://hkiac.org/arbitration/arbitrators/panel-and-list-of-arbitrators>.

The names of Members of the Appointments Committee are listed on the HKIAC website.[19]

Despite generally informative content, several salient features of how HKIAC makes arbitrator appointments are either not present or not easily accessible, on HKIAC's website. For example, when HKIAC is called on to make arbitrator appointments, it is not limited to members of its Panel or List of Arbitrators, and may, if circumstances require, appoint a non-listed arbitrator. It does not appear that this is specified on the HKIAC website. Nor is it easy to find out that the HKIAC provides parties with the opportunity to comment on any proposed institutional appointment. It is only in the answer to FAQ no. 19 on the Administered Arbitration Rules, that it is stated that "[i]n any case where HKIAC appoints an arbitrator, the parties will be given the opportunity to comment on the arbitrator proposed".[20] Lastly, although it is known to the author that the HKIAC requests users and arbitrators alike to complete feedback forms, following their conclusion of an HKIAC arbitration, including comment in relation to the performance of arbitrators, this information does not appear to be included on HKIAC's website.

2. *SIAC*

The appointment procedures under the 2016 SIAC Rules are not dissimilar to those under the 2013 HKIAC Administered Arbitration Rules. Initial opportunity for nomination rests with the parties, subject to appointment by the President of the SIAC Court (Art. 10; Art. 11; in conjunction with Art. 9.3). A failure by the parties to utilize this opportunity leads to appointment by the President of the Court. This includes circumstances where multi-party appointments are required (Art. 12). In circumstances where an additional party is joined to the proceedings or where two or more cases have been consolidated into a single arbitration (if the application for consolidation was made prior to any tribunal's constitution), any appointments already made may be revoked by the SIAC Court. However, rather than the institution stepping in at this point (as is the case at the HKIAC), under the SIAC Rules, the parties are given the opportunity to complete the appointment process in accordance with the usual rules again (Arts. 7.6 and 8.6).

In circumstances where SIAC is required to make appointments, how are these appointments made?

SIAC publishes the list of the arbitrators included on their Panel on their website.[21] Although SIAC maintains a Reserve Panel, information regarding its existence is relatively hard to find,[22] and details of members of the reserve panel or circumstances in which they might be appointed do not appear to be made available at all.

---

19. <http://hkiac.org/about-us/council-members-and-committees/appointments-committee>.
20. <http://hkiac.org/arbitration/why-choose-hkiac/hkiac-administered-arbitration-faqs#019>.
21. <http://www.siac.org.sg/our-arbitrators/siac-panel>.
22. The application form for inclusion on the Panel of Arbitrators provides applicants with an option to apply for the Reserve Panel. See <http://siac.org.sg/images/stories/documents/application_form/SIACPanelApplicationForm_Mar2017.pdf>.

To be eligible for inclusion on SIAC's Panel of Arbitrators, arbitrators must demonstrate an appropriate level of expertise and experience in international arbitration and be of good standing and character.[23] A number of minimum qualifications or experience apply, including that arbitrators have (i) a tertiary education; (ii) at least ten years' post-qualification experience; (iii) a fellowship from the Chartered Institute of Arbitrators, Singapore Institute of Arbitrators or any comparable professional arbitration institute; (iv) experience as an arbitrator in five or more cases; (v) completed at least two commercial arbitral awards; and (vi) be aged between thirty and seventy-five years. As with the HKIAC, membership on the Panel is for a fixed term only, although it is not clear from the website or the application form what that term is.

How SIAC makes appointments when it is required to do so is set out in the Practice Note for Administered Cases, PN - 01/14 (2 January 2014), applicable to all cases commenced or submitted for administration on or after 2 January 2014.[24] PN - 01/14 clarifies that the criteria for appointment shall follow the provisions specified in legislation or the contract between the parties, and that in all cases, SIAC's objective is to appoint an arbitrator with the attributes of integrity and competence, who is independent and impartial, and who will be perceived as such by the parties.

In all cases where the President is to make an appointment of an arbitrator, he may, where appropriate, consult two members of the SIAC Court and may seek the assistance of the Secretariat. The Practice Note makes it clear that, in exceptional cases, such as where there are no suitable candidates on the SIAC panel of arbitrators, the President may appoint an arbitrator who is not on the SIAC panel of arbitrators.

3. *LCIA*

The default position under the 2014 LCIA Arbitration Rules differs significantly from that of the HKIAC and SIAC Rules. According to the LCIA Rules, the LCIA will select the members of the tribunal unless the parties have agreed otherwise, whether that be by their arbitration clause or by later agreement.

The LCIA Court is the final authority for the proper application of the LCIA rules, amongst whose principal functions (according to Art. D.1.(a). of its constitution) includes acting as appointing authority under the LCIA Rules.[25] According to those Rules, the LCIA Court alone is empowered to appoint arbitrators, albeit taking into account any written agreement or joint nomination by the parties (Art. 5.7) and with due regard for any particular method or criteria of selection agreed in writing by the parties (Art. 5.9). If the parties have agreed that an arbitrator is to be appointed by one or more of them or by any third person, then a nominee put forward in accordance with that agreement will be appointed by the LCIA Court, subject to the nominee's satisfaction of certain criteria (Art. 7.1). Where the agreed-upon nomination is not made, or not made within time, the LCIA Court shall make the appointment (Art. 7.2). The same is true where multiple parties cannot agree on which "side" they represent for the purpose of agreeing appointment (Art. 8.2).

---

23. <www.siac.org.sg/our-arbitrators/standards-for-admission-to-siac-panel>.
24. <www.siac.org.sg/our-rules/practice-notes/practice-note-for-administered-cases>.
25. <www.lcia.org/LCIA/constitution-of-the-lcia-court.aspx>.

In circumstances where the LCIA is required to make appointments, how are these appointments made?

Under Art. D.2. of the Constitution of the LCIA Court, all appointments of arbitrators shall be made in its name by the President or by a Vice President, whose names are listed on the LCIA's website.[26]

A FAQ listed on the LCIA website asks "[h]ow does the LCIA Court select and appoint arbitrators?"[27] However, unhelpfully, when the link to the answer to this question is clicked, the reader is taken to a page providing a general description of the advantages of LCIA arbitration, mentioning only that the arbitrator appointment process is quick and efficient.[28]

Beyond this, the LCIA states on its website that it has access to "the most eminent and experienced arbitrators ... from many jurisdictions, and with the widest range of expertise".[29] These arbitrators are not included on a panel, similar to those maintained by the HKIAC or SIAC. The LCIA does not maintain such panel. It does, however, maintain a database of neutrals from around ninety jurisdictions, but this database is not publicly available.

Users are told in the FAQ section of the LCIA website that (i) appointments are made "strictly on the basis of the most appropriate qualification for the specific case",[30] and that (ii) if the parties agree, once an arbitration has been commenced, the LCIA will provide both sides with a list of the names of arbitrators who it would be prepared to appoint to determine the dispute, from which the parties may seek to agree the arbitrator(s).

4. *ICC*

As with its Asian counterparts, the default position under the 2017 ICC Arbitration Rules is that parties are initially given the opportunity to appoint sole and co-arbitrators, failing which, the ICC Court will step in (Arts. 12.2 to 12.4). However, unlike under the rules of the HKIAC and SIAC, where the dispute is to be referred to three arbitrators, the default mechanism is that the president of the tribunal shall be appointed by the ICC Court (rather than selected by the party-appointed co-arbitrators), unless the parties have agreed upon another procedure for such appointment (Art. 12.5). Where there are multiple claimants or multiple respondents, or a third party has been joined to the proceedings and parties are unable to agree to a method for the constitution of the tribunal, the ICC Court may appoint each member of the arbitral tribunal and designate one of them to act as President (Art. 12.8).

In circumstances where the ICC is required to make appointments, how are these appointments made?

Where the ICC Court is to appoint an arbitrator, it usually makes that appointment upon the proposal of suitable candidates by an appropriate National Committee or Group of the ICC. If the ICC Court does not accept the proposal, or if the National

26. <www.lcia.org/LCIA/the-lcia-court.aspx>.
27. <www.lcia.org/Frequently_Asked_Questions.aspx#Appoint>.
28. <www.lcia.org/Dispute_Resolution_Services/LCIA_Arbitration.aspx>.
29. <www.lcia.org/LCIA/introduction.aspx>.
30. <www.lcia.org/Frequently_Asked_Questions.aspx#Eligible>.

Committee or Group fails to make the proposal requested, the Court may (i) repeat its request, (ii) request a proposal from another National Committee or Group that it considers to be appropriate, or (iii) appoint directly any person whom it regards as suitable (Art. 13.3).

According to Art. 13.4, the ICC Court may also directly appoint an arbitrator it considers to be suitable to act where:

(a) one or more of the parties is a state or may be considered to be a state entity;
(b) the Court considers that it would be appropriate to appoint an arbitrator from a country or territory where there is no National Committee or Group; or
(c) the President certifies to the Court that circumstances exist which, in the President's opinion, make a direct appointment necessary and appropriate.

The ICC has published a Practice Note entitled "Note to National Committees and Groups of the ICC on the Proposal of Arbitrators" which explains (i) the role of National Committees and Groups of ICC in the appointment process pursuant to the ICC Rules of Arbitration and (ii) the manner in which interaction between the ICC Court and the Secretariat should be conducted with Committees and Groups, in order to enhance the appointment process.[31] In essence, when the ICC Court is to appoint an arbitrator, it will seek proposals of prospective arbitrators from Committee(s) or Group(s) who may then put forward several names for the Court's consideration. The Secretariat will provide the relevant Committee(s) and/or Group(s) with a letter formally requesting the proposal of an arbitrator as well as detailed information concerning the case and specific requests regarding the profile of prospective arbitrators. Committees and Groups have discretion in relation to the process by which they select arbitrators for proposal to the Court; however, the candidates they propose should be those they consider to be best suited to act, taking into account the circumstances of the case and bearing in mind that proposals are to be made in the interest of the parties.

According to the Practice Note, Committees and Groups are encouraged (i) to propose prospective arbitrators having sufficient experience as arbitrators, preferably in ICC cases, when the case is complex or the amount in dispute is high; (ii) to propose prospective arbitrators with experience in arbitration, but not necessarily as arbitrators (such as experience as counsel or as administrative secretary), for simpler cases or cases involving lower amounts in dispute; (iii) to propose new or young arbitrators in relatively simple cases with lower amounts in dispute, as this may help the pool of potential arbitrators in that community to grow; (iv) to favour gender diversity in their proposals; and (v) to propose a prospective arbitrator residing at or near the place of arbitration when the amount in dispute is relatively low, in order to help keep the costs of the arbitration as low as possible.[32]

The ICC Court maintains full discretion as to whether or not to appoint any of the candidate(s) proposed.

---

31. <https://cdn.iccwbo.org/content/uploads/sites/3/2016/06/Note-to-National-Committees-and-Groups-of-the-ICC-on-the-Proposal-of-Arbitrators-ENGLISH.pdf>.
32. Note para. 33 <https://cdn.iccwbo.org/content/uploads/sites/3/2016/06/Note-to-National-Committees-and-Groups-of-the-ICC-on-the-Proposal-of-Arbitrators-ENGLISH.pdf>.

While the ICC website does list the Members of the Court of Arbitration,[33] information, beyond address and contact details, is harder to find in respect of its National Committees, or the nominations commissions they are strongly encouraged to set up for selecting and proposing arbitrators.

Unlike the HKIAC and SIAC, the ICC does not maintain a panel of arbitrators, nor does it keep a centralized database of possible appointees, like the LCIA. Instead, according to the Note on the Proposal of Arbitrators, Committees and Groups may keep unofficial lists of arbitrators for their own internal work, but the Note clearly specifies that such lists should not be published as an official ICC roster.[34]

V. INSTITUTIONAL APPOINTMENT AS AN ALTERNATIVE TO THE CURRENT SYSTEM?

Increased roles for institutions feature heavily in proposed alternatives to the current party appointment model. Suggested approaches fall along a continuum in relation to the degree of residual party input.

One option, the most radical departure from the current system, leaves the appointment of all three arbitrators up to the institution entirely, allowing for no consultation or input form the parties. This approach is generally resisted and rates poorly in surveys of user's preferences. If the institution's appointment were to be made from a pre-existing closed list of candidates, 81% of respondents to the 2018 BLP Survey considered this option undesirable, a figure which reduced to only 34%, if the list of candidates was open.[35]

Another option is for the institution to prepare a short list of candidates for appointment, with input from the parties solicited prior to appointments being made. Variants of this option include giving the parties the opportunity to (i) suggest the arbitrators to be included on the short list, (ii) rank the suitability of the listed arbitrators, leading to those with the highest overall ranking being appointed, or (iii) strike out as well as rank names on the list prepared by the institution that a party considers inappropriate for appointment.

One option tested in the 2018 BLP Survey and ranked as desirable by 62% of respondents, involved the parties suggesting to the institution arbitrators who they would like to see included on the initial short list, before then having the opportunity to rank those candidates for suitability for appointment, with the institution appointing the candidates with the highest overall ranking.[36] Another option, ranked as desirable by 60% of respondents, leaves the composition of the list entirely to the institution, but allows the parties the ability to both rank and strike out candidates on that list.[37]

---

33. <https://iccwbo.org/dispute-resolution-services/icc-international-court-arbitration/court-members/>.
34. Note para. 24 <https://cdn.iccwbo.org/content/uploads/sites/3/2016/06/Note-to-National-Committees-and-Groups-of-the-ICC-on-the-Proposal-of-Arbitrators-ENGLISH.pdf>.
35. 2018 BLP Survey, p. 12.
36. *Ibid.*
37. *Ibid.*

VI. WHAT IS ACTUALLY HAPPENING?

Having examined reported views about party appointment in various surveys, it is important to also look at what is happening in practice. How many appointments are parties making? How many are being handled by institutions?

The HKIAC, whose figures for 2017 are not yet available, reported for 2016 that it made a total of 137 arbitrator appointments,[38] of which the majority, 75, were HKIAC appointments (54.7%) in comparison with 62 confirmations of party nominations (45.3%).[39]

SIAC reports that in 2017 it made a total of 145 individual arbitrator appointments. 114 of those were to sole arbitrator tribunals and 31 to three-member tribunals. This is compared to a reported total of 118 arbitrators nominated and confirmed by SIAC. Therefore, of the 263 appointments made by SIAC in 2017, 44.9% were appointments made by SIAC itself.

In 2016, SIAC made a total of 167 individual arbitrator appointments, 137 to sole arbitrator tribunals and 30 to three-member tribunals. This is compared with a total of 174 arbitrators nominated and confirmed by SIAC. Therefore, of the 341 appointments made by SIAC in 2017, 51% were appointments made by SIAC itself.[40]

Turning to figures for the LCIA, as noted previously, the default position under the LCIA Rules is that the LCIA will select members of the tribunal, unless the parties have agreed otherwise. In the Registrar's Reports for 2015 and prior, the Registrar notes that "[t]he LCIA ... tends to select more candidate arbitrators than many other institutions".[41]

The LCIA reports for 2016 that it made a total of 496 appointments, an increase from 2015 when the LCIA made a total of 449 appointments.

Of the 496 appointments made in 2016:

- 219 (44.2%) were candidates selected by the parties;
- 197 (39.7%) were candidates selected by the LCIA Court; and
- 80 (16.1%) were candidates selected by the co-arbitrators.[42]

This compares to 2015, where, of the 449 appointments:

- 204 (or 45.4%) were of candidates selected by the parties;
- 195 (or 43.5%) were of candidates selected by the LCIA Court;
- 50 (or 11.1%) were of candidates selected by the co-arbitrators.[43]

---

38. HKIAC Annual Report (2016) <http://hkiac.org/sites/default/files/annual_report/annual%20report%202016%20%28low%20resolution%29%20v2.pdf>, p. 10.
39. <http://hkiac.org/about-us/statistics>. A breakdown of the number of total appointments into those made rather than simply confirmed by the HKIAC is not available for 2015 or 2014 for comparative purposes.
40. Figures of the number of arbitrators nominated and confirmed by SIAC are not available for 2014 and 2015 for further comparison.
41. Registrar's Report 2015 p. 4.
42. Facts and Figures – 2016: A Robust Caseload <www.lcia.org//media/download.aspx?MediaId=570>.
43. Registrar's Report 2015, p. 3 <www.lcia.org//media/download.aspx?MediaId=500>.

During the course of 2014, the LCIA made a total of 420 appointment, of which:

- 205 (or 49%) were of candidates selected by the parties;
- 159 (or 38%) were of candidates selected by the LCIA Court;
- 56 (or 13%) were of candidates selected by the co-arbitrators.[44]

Contrary to the Registrar's observation, it actually appears that the percentage of appointments made by the LCIA Court, is lower than comparable figures for its Asian counterparts, the HKIAC and SIAC.

Full statistics for 2017 are not yet available for the ICC, however, those for 2016 are set out below:[45]

	Sole arbitrator	**Co-arbitrator**	**President**	**Total**	**%**
Nominated by parties / confirmed by Court or Secretary General	65	702	27	794	56.3
Nominated by Co-arbitrators, confirmed by Court or Secretary General	N/A	N/A	206	206	14.6
Appointment by Court on proposal from National Committee or Group	145	18	69	232	16.4
Appointment directly by ICC Court	76	42	57	175	12.4
Appointment by an authority other than the ICC Court	0	2	2	4	0.3
Total	286	764	361	1411	100

According to the reported figures, 28.8% of arbitrators were appointed by the ICC Court directly or as a result of a proposal of a National Committee or Group. This represents the lowest percentage of any of the four institutions surveyed.

44. Registrar's Report 2014, p. 3 <www.lcia.org//media/download.aspx?MediaId=499>.
45. ICC Dispute Resolution Bulletin (2017, issue 2) p. 92

VII. WHERE TO FROM HERE?

As much as arbitration practitioners would like to think otherwise, dispute resolution provisions remain a midnight clause. Few want to think about possible deal breakers when expectation and anticipation remain very squarely at the feet of the dealmakers. As a consequence, aside from sophisticated and/or repeat users of arbitration, often little attention is paid to the institution or the rules selected, or, if they are considered, they are often seen as an easy give vis-à-vis other more "important" commercial terms. To the extent that careful thought is given to arbitration issues, it remains rare for consideration of an institution's process and panel for the appointment arbitrators to fall too firmly within the frame.

Contrary to expectations, the four institutions surveyed are already making a significant number of appointments, and, in the case of the HKIAC and SIAC, this number is around, or in some instances even greater than, 50 percent. This number is likely to come as a surprise to many users.

The relative prevalence of institutional appointments in what we still describe as a party-appointment driven system has not caused the end of arbitration as we know it, nor in fact has it generated much concern, or even a great deal of notice. Perhaps the sanctity of party appointment is not as important as general opinion holds, or even as user surveys bear out (after all how people say they will react in response to a hypothetical question is often vastly different to how they actually react when engaged in an actual, concrete dispute).

In this context, should we reassess the importance that we continue to ascribe to the parties' opportunity to choose their decision-maker? Should other values, such as accountability and consistency, be promoted in its stead? Is it time to rethink the parties' latitude to shape the tribunal?

Although starting at the end may be seen as letting the tail wag the dog, surely it is only possible to question the prevalence of party appointment if there is a viable alternative to replace it with.

To have any real legitimacy as the default mechanism, institutional appointment must garner the considered support of users, which can only be achieved if they have confidence in the ability of institutions to appoint good arbitrators.

At the moment, despite the fact that institutions, at least those surveyed, are making significant numbers of appointments, the necessary confidence is lacking. Fifty-nine percent of the 2018 BLP Survey respondents believed that not all institutions can be trusted to maintain an inclusive and qualified list of arbitrators from which all appointments can be made. Sixty-nine percent said "no" when asked if institutions should amend their rules so that all arbitral appointments would be made by them.[46] Distrust of institutions' appointment of arbitrators was also voiced in the 2012 Queen Mary Survey. In particular, respondents were concerned about "the small and static pool from which some institutions pick their arbitrators", and that not all institutions are paying sufficient attention to the availability of arbitrators.[47]

46. 2018 BLP Survey, p. 12.
47. 2012 Queen Mary Survey, p. 5.

A further consideration of the viability of this alternative lies with the institutions themselves. Do they have the appetite to pick up the slack, should party appointments be dispensed with? Arbitral institutions are typically not-for-profit organizations, operating on shoestring budgets in a highly competitive market. Their goal is to facilitate efficiency and administrative ease in the arbitral process and in so doing help to attract future business. Can they stretch to being the default appointers of all arbitrators? And how can this be assessed on a one-size-fits-all basis?

Putting that question aside, assuming institutions have the desire to accept the mandate, in the event that it is given, what can institutions do to better perform the role and foster user confidence?

Although some warn of the risk of increased challenges,[48] transparency will be key. As the ICC concludes in its Note to Parties and Arbitral Tribunals on the Conduct of Arbitration, "[t]ransparency provides greater confidence in the arbitration process, and helps protect arbitration against inaccurate or ill-informed criticism".[49] For users to have the confidence to entrust default decision-making on arbitrator appointment to institutions, they will need to be furnished with clear and complete information about how the process works, in particular, what opportunities, if any, there will be for party input; which candidates will be considered; who within the institution is making the decisions and on what basis.

Parties looking to decide on an institution to administer their arbitration (and potentially appoint their arbitrators) are, if they chose to do any research at all, likely to do a quick search of available (i.e. free) resources, or they may rely on the insight of their lawyers. While lawyers will gain knowledge of appointments processes over time, from the standpoint of transparency and user confidence, this cannot be the principal means that information is shared. Websites have to improve.

Clear, comprehensive and easily accessible information must be available about the appointment process. In particular, details must be provided about who within the institution is responsible for its implementation, and importantly, how those people are selected and for how long they will perform this role. Parties need to know what criteria the institution applies when making appointments. They need to understand if, and at what stages, they may contribute their input. Very important is the quality of individuals from which the institution will choose the arbitrators. Clarity needs to exist about the pool of potential candidates for selection. Is there a panel of arbitrators, what about a secondary list? Are the individuals on it publicly known? How do arbitrators secure inclusion? Further, parties need to understand when an institution will look to its panel, or alternatively, the list, and when it might go beyond listed candidates altogether. It is to be expected that maintained lists will be regularly reviewed and refreshed, both for diversity and quality – is this in fact the case? How is that review conducted? Is there an

48. Juliet BLANCHE, "Appointment and Confirmation of Arbitrators", Chapter 4 in Philipp HABEGGER, Daniel HOCHSTRASSER, Gabrielle NATER-BASS, Urs WEBER-STECHER, eds., *Arbitral Institutions Under Scrutiny, ASA Special Series No. 40* (Juris 2013) p. 72.

49. Note to Parties and Arbitral Tribunals on the Conduct of Arbitration <https://cdn.iccwbo.org/content/uploads/sites/3/2017/03/icc-note-to-parties-and-arbitral-tribunals-on-the-conduct-of-arbitration.pdf>, p. 27.

opportunity for party feedback of both the arbitrators appointed and the appointment process?

Clear and comprehensive information should also be available about the outcomes of the appointment process. How many appointments are being made, in what circumstances, which arbitrators are being appointed, are there breadth and diversity amongst the appointees? At the beginning of 2016, the ICC introduced a policy whereby it publishes on its website the names of the arbitrators sitting in ICC cases, their nationality, as well as whether the appointment was made by the Court or by the parties and which arbitrator is the tribunal chairperson. It is this kind of initiative that will help to foster user confidence in arbitral appointments made by institutions, and perhaps take us to a point where party appointment could be relinquished in their favour.

The T(h)reat of Party Autonomy in ISDS Arbitrator Selection: Any Options for Preservation?

Natalie Y. Morris-Sharma[*]

TABLE OF CONTENTS PAGE

I. INTRODUCTION

Calling for "replacement or radical redesign" of the mechanism of investor-State dispute settlement is the flavour *a la mode*.[1] For better or for worse, rightly or wrongly, the investor-State dispute settlement mechanism is facing a legitimacy crisis. The polemics against investor-State dispute settlement have essentially focussed, in one way or another, on how "arbitral awards erroneously privatise disputes that should only be heard in public forums".[2]

Against this backdrop, this Article will briefly review the advantages and drawbacks that have been perceived in respect of the institution of the party-appointed arbitrator. It will also examine (a) the enhanced role of institutions; and (b) institutionalization, being two of the alternatives to the party-appointed arbitrator that have been put forward as part of suggestions for reform. Questions are posed as points for reflection. Finally, this Article will explore the possibilities for the preservation of party autonomy in choosing decision-makers, to see if there are calibrations of party autonomy in choosing decision-

* Director of the International Legal Division in Singapore's Ministry of Law; negotiated a number of trade and investment agreements, and has represented Singapore at UNCITRAL meetings since 2010; Chairperson of UNCITRAL Working Group II (Dispute Settlement) for its work on mediation; Vice-Chairperson of the 50th UNCITRAL Commission session, and chaired the discussions on UNCITRAL's mandate for investor-State dispute settlement reform. The views expressed herein are the views of the author and do not necessarily represent the views of the Government of Singapore.

1. Charles BROWER and Stephan SCHILL, "Is Arbitration a Threat or a Boon to the Legitimacy of International Investment Law?", 9 Chicago Journal of International Law (2009, no. 2) p. 471 at p. 475.

2. Jose ALVAREZ and Gustavo TOPALIAN, "The Paradoxical Argentina Cases", 6 World Arbitration and Mediation Review (2012) p. 491 at p. 494. Also see Colin BROWN, "A Multilateral Mechanism for the Settlement of Investment Disputes. Some Preliminary Sketches", 32 ICSID Review (2017, issue 3), p. 673 at p. 677; and Daniel BEHN, "Legitimacy, Evolution, and Growth in Investment Treaty Arbitration: Empirically Evaluating the State-of-the-Art", 46 Georgetown Journal of International Law (2015) p. 363 at p. 367.

makers that could be undertaken to strike a balance between the treat and threat of such party autonomy. Specifically, three options are suggested for consideration: agreed appointments, circumscribed appointments, and arbitrator *ad hoc* appointments.

In this way, this Article seeks to contribute to the dialogue on this issue, in the hope that whatever the outcome of bilateral or multilateral negotiations on the issue may be, the eventual system design – whether a multilateral court, rules-based reform, or preserving the status quo[3] – is one that benefits from rigorous and robust deliberations.

II. OVERVIEW OF THE DEBATE

1. *In Support of Party Autonomy in Choosing Decision-Makers*

The linchpin argument in favour of party-appointed arbitrators is the principle of party autonomy in international arbitration. At the very least, the disputing parties' participation in the appointment of their arbitrators would ensure "that the decision-making process is not perceived as something wholly extraneous to the parties", thereby enhancing the legitimacy of the process.[4] This has been said to be "particularly important when states are involved".[5]

The appointment of an arbitrator has been described as "the ultimate form of forum shopping".[6] Apart from the substantive outcome of the case, in the absence of party agreement, the arbitral tribunal can determine critical procedural questions such as those pertaining to the conduct of hearings, the allocation of costs and fees, and issues of evidence.[7] Party appointment of arbitrators therefore offers disputing parties, whether the claimant investor or the respondent State, confidence in their dispute resolution process as a whole.

---

3. The author has previously suggested drawing the distinction between institutional and rules-based reform, rather than the bifurcations that commentators have used as between multilateral or bilateral reform; or between systemic or procedural reform. The bifurcation between institutional and rules-based reform is not intended to suggest that one necessarily precludes the other, but to clarify the suite of options that could be considered. Both institutional reform (for example, a new permanent court or body, so that investor-State dispute settlement is not subject to an *ad hoc* mechanism) and rules-based reform (for example, amendments to or drafting of provisions of rules and procedures of investor-State dispute settlement) can feature as part of a suite of options or as a transitional arrangement, and could be avenues for multilateral reform that introduces systemic solutions.
4. C. BROWER and S. SCHILL, "Is Arbitration a Threat or a Boon", p. 494.
5. C. BROWER and S. SCHILL, "Is Arbitration a Threat or a Boon", p. 494.
6. Catherine ROGERS, "A Window into the Soul of International Arbitration: Arbitrator Selection, Transparency and Stakeholder Interests", 46 Victoria U. Wellington Law Review (2015) p. 1179 at p. 1179. The debate over the party-appointed arbitrator in the context of investment arbitration overlaps significantly with the debate that has taken place in the space of international commercial arbitration. Many of the sources cited in this paper draw from commentary made vis-à-vis international commercial arbitration. Distinctions are drawn where necessary.
7. Catherine ROGERS, "The International Arbitrator Information Project: An Idea Whose Time Has Come", Kluwer Arbitration Blog (9 Aug 2012) at <arbitrationblog.kluwerarbitration.com/2012/08/09/the-international-arbitrator-information-project-an-idea-whose-time-has-come> (last accessed 13 April 2018).

Further, the opportunity to appoint one's arbitrator affords comfort to the disputing party that his case will be properly understood and fairly considered. Proper understanding and fair consideration would involve an understanding of the relevant legal and technical intricacies of the case, as well as cultural factors. As it has been pointed out, "[t]his consideration of sympathy or affinity would seem to be of great importance to many parties in particular in international arbitration where parties and tribunals often are of wide cultural diversity".[8] In a sense, party-appointed arbitrators are an "important structural feature" of arbitral tribunals, as they can "break through groupthink".[9] These elements promote accountability and confidence, and thereby enhance the legitimacy of the arbitral process, in the eyes of its users.

2. *Criticisms of Party Autonomy in Choosing Decision-Makers and Responses Thereto*

a. *The criticisms*

Criticisms of the party appointment of arbitrators have mainly had two facets, both united by the ultimate concern over the undermining of the impartiality and independence of the arbitral process and outcome. The first facet is the ability of the disputing parties, including the private investor, to unilaterally appoint arbitrators to the panel. The second facet is that arbitrators are appointed *ad hoc*, that is, only for a specific dispute and without tenure beyond the dispute.

Where a party to the dispute is able to appoint an arbitrator, arbitrators may be biased or see themselves as party-advocates. This is a concern that was expressed already in the early years when the Convention on the Settlement of Investment Disputes between States and Nationals of Other States (the ICSID Convention) was being negotiated and the modality of party appointment of arbitrators was being considered.[10] In respect of the *ad hoc* nature of arbitration and how arbitrators lack tenure or permanence in their appointments, arbitrators may be perversely incentivized to seek reappointments in future cases by "cater[ing] to the interests of those who will appoint them in the future".[11]

8. Michael SCHNEIDER, "President's Message: Forbidding Unilateral Appointments of Arbitrators – A Case of Vicarious Hypochondria?" 29 ASA Bulletin 2 (June 2011) p. 273 at pp. 274-275.
9. C. ROGERS, "A Window into the Soul", pp. 1184 and 1185. Further, at p. 1186, Rogers highlights that "[i]n the United States and in other systems that have civil law juries, or even in criminal cases, parties very intentionally pick people who are like themselves and are likely to be sensitive to, or reflective of, their concerns in the case. The idea of picking or having some input into the constitution of a tribunal is not as much of an anathema as sometimes suggested in the abstract when people are being critical of arbitration."
10. Christopher THOMAS and Harpreet DHILLON, "The Foundations of Investment Treaty Arbitration: The ICSID Convention, Investment Treaties and the Review of Arbitration Awards", 32 ICSID Review (2017, issue 3) p. 459 at p. 466, citing ICSID, *History of the ICSID Convention: Documents Concerning the Origin and the Formulation of the Convention on the Settlement of Investment Disputes between States and Nationals of Other States*, (ICSID Publication 1968), Vol. II-1 p. 40, that the World Bank's Working Paper (of June 1962) had stated that party-appointed arbitrators might be the "least desirable method [of appointment], because of the danger that each party will look upon the arbitrator to be appointed by it as an advocate".
11. C. BROWER and S. SCHILL, "Is Arbitration a Threat or a Boon", p. 490.

Additionally, the *ad hoc* nature of panel constitution by way of party appointments can have systemic impacts, such as a lack of consistency and coherence in arbitral decisions.[12] Although, on this count, the issue can also be said to be owed to reasons other than party autonomy in the appointment of arbitrators, such as international investment law being a creature formed by an array of unconnected bilateral treaties rather than "agreements that are linked in a comprehensive treaty regime", the lack of Secretariat support, or the possibility for separate and dissenting opinions to be issued.[13]

b. A comment on independence and impartiality

Indeed, impartiality and independence are vital to any legitimate adjudicatory process.[14] The challenge is not in agreeing on the value of these qualities, but in determining whether they have been displayed or compromised. The arbitral tribunal that rejected the proposal to disqualify one of the arbitrators in *Suez v. Argentina* noted that "[i]ndependence and impartiality are states of mind", and nobody is "capable of probing the inner workings of any arbitrator's mind to determine with perfect accuracy whether that person is independent and impartial"; there has to be inference from the conduct of the arbitrator or persons connected with him.[15]

Importantly, one must differentiate between prejudice and predilection, between actual bias and a general favourable disposition. While the former suggests a willingness to decide a case in favour of the appointing party regardless of the merits and would therefore be unacceptable, the latter can be overcome by consideration of the merits and would not be problematic.[16] In a recent case, it was noted that "[n]o arbitrator and, more generally, no human being of a certain age is, in absolute terms, independent and impartial. Simply put, every individual is conveying ideas and opinions based on its moral, cultural, and professional education and experience".[17]

These realities give texture to the debate over whether and how the selection and appointment of arbitrators can or should impact the independence and impartiality of the arbitral process. One wonders if the competing interests have as direct a correlation as some have suggested: the trade-off being between improved confidence and therefore

12. Anna JOUBIN-BRET, "The Growing Diversity and Inconsistency in the IIA System" in Karl SAUVANT, ed., *Appeals Mechanism in International Investment Disputes* (OUP 2008) p. 137 at pp. 137-139.
13. Donald MCRAE, "The WTO Appellate Body: A Model for an ICSID Appeals Facility?", 1 Journal of International Dispute Settlement (2010, issue 2) p. 371 at p. 384.
14. Alfonso GÓMEZ-ACEBO, "A Special Role of Party-Appointed Arbitrators?", this volume, pp. 381-416 at p. 388.
15. *Suez, Sociedad General de Aguas de Barcelona S.A. & InterAguas Servicios Integrales del Agua S.A. v. The Argentine Republic* (ICSID Case No. ARB/03/17), Decision on the Proposal for the Disqualification of a Member of the Arbitral Tribunal (22 October 2007) para. 30.
16. Doak BISHOP and Lucy REED, "Practical Guidelines for Interviewing, Selecting and Challenging Party-Appointed Arbitrators in International Commercial Arbitration", 14 Arbitration International (1998, no. 4) p.395 at p.396.
17. *Urbaser S.A. v. The Argentine Republic* (ICSID Case No. ARB/07/26), Decision on Claimants' Proposal to Disqualify Professor Campbell McLachlan, Arbitrator (12 August 2010) para. 40.

greater inclination to resort to adjudication, on the one hand, and judicial independence and impartiality, on the other hand.[18]

c. Responses to the criticisms: Ensuring impartiality and independence

In response to the question of bias and the possible perverse incentive to pander, investment treaties set out standards that arbitrators are expected to adhere to so as to ensure their impartiality and independence. Some of these standards are more expounded on than others.

For example, in the revised Singapore-Australia Free Trade Agreement (SAFTA) that entered into force on 1 December 2017, a code of conduct for appointed arbitrators was introduced.[19] The code of conduct provides, inter alia, that arbitrators appointed pursuant to the SAFTA "shall avoid impropriety and the appearance of impropriety, shall be independent and impartial, shall avoid direct and indirect conflicts of interests and shall observe high standards of conduct so that the integrity and impartiality of the dispute settlement process are preserved".[20] The code of conduct also sets out disclosure obligations; requires that arbitrators are thorough, expeditious, fair and diligent, in carrying out their duties; and requires that arbitrators are not influenced by factors such as self-interest, outside pressure, or loyalty to a disputing party or non-disputing Party.[21] Violation of the code of conduct may lead to removal of the arbitrator from the panel.[22]

There is also the reputational element that may be factored in. As it has been underlined, "[r]eputation is difficult to build up and is easily destroyed; these characteristics thus work against any incentive to taint one's decision-making in favour of either party in order to secure future appointments."[23]

On the prospect of a party-appointed arbitrator who would serve as a party-advocate, generally speaking, parties and arbitrators in investment arbitrations do understand that unilaterally appointed arbitrators are not party-advocates.[24] Moreover, with two party-appointed arbitrators, some form of balance of perspectives would be achieved. Where there may be a misperception of what the intended role of an arbitrator is, an imbalance may be introduced.[25] However, this can be addressed through a clear articulation or shared understanding of the party-appointed arbitrator's role and function.[26]

---

18. Yuval SHANY, "Squaring the Circle? Independence and Impartiality of Party-Appointed Adjudicators in International Legal Proceedings", 30 Loyola of Los Angeles International and Comparative Law Review (2008) p. 473.
19. Singapore-Australia Free Trade Agreement (SAFTA), Annex 7 (Code of Conduct for Arbitrators appointed under Chapter 8 (Investment) and Chapter 16 (Dispute Settlement)) at <dfat.gov.au/trade/agreements/in-force/safta/Pages/Singapore-australia-fta.aspx> (last accessed 13 April 2018).
20. SAFTA, Annex 7, para. 1.
21. SAFTA, Annex 7, paras. 2, 3, 5 and 12.
22. SAFTA, Annex 7, para. 22.
23. C. BROWER and S. SCHILL, "Is Arbitration a Threat or a Boon", p. 492.
24. C. BROWER and S. SCHILL, "Is Arbitration a Threat or a Boon", p. 491.
25. David BRANSON, "Sympathetic Party-Appointed Arbitrators: Sophisticated Strangers and Governments Demand Them", 25 ICSID Review (2010) p. 367 at p. 368.
26. Sundaresh MENON, "Adjudicator, Advocate, or Something in Between? Coming to Terms with the Role of the Party-Appointed Arbitrator", 34 Journal of International Arbitration (2017, no. 3) p. 347, where Menon expresses support for (i) the publication of clear guidelines on what

As such, there are procedural mechanisms that have been introduced to ensure independence and impartiality on the part of arbitrators in investment arbitration cases, including of party-appointed arbitrators. The question is whether these mechanisms are enough. Can more be done that would make a qualitative difference? If not, may we nevertheless need to look to making a break from the past simply to show that something is being done?

III. SUGGESTIONS FOR REFORM

Against the backdrop of investment arbitration's legitimacy deficit, various suggestions for reform have been proposed. Insofar as it is possible to separate the broader debate on the reform of investor-State dispute settlement from the specific questions on the party appointment of arbitrators, two "solutions" which focus on the latter are of particular interest.

The first is that the role of institutions in the appointment of arbitrators should be enhanced. The second is that there should be the institutionalization of investment arbitration panels, specifically, through the establishment of standing panels or a permanent investment court. The two "solutions" are not necessarily mutually exclusive, particularly in the context of a possible multilateral arrangement.

1. *An Enhanced Role for Institutions in Appointments*

a. *The approaches under ICSID and UNCITRAL*

Currently, both the ICSID Convention and the Arbitration Rules of the United Nations Commission on International Trade Law (UNCITRAL) provide for the possibility of institutional appointment only of the presiding arbitrator of a tribunal. In the establishment of a tribunal of three arbitrators, one arbitrator is to be appointed by each party and the third, presiding arbitrator, is to be appointed either by agreement of the disputing parties (under ICSID) or by agreement of the other two arbitrators appointed (under UNCITRAL).[27]

Where the disputing parties or co-arbitrators cannot agree on the presiding arbitrator, the duty to select a presiding arbitrator falls to the relevant appointing authority. For ICSID cases, the default appointing authority is the Chairman of the Administrative Council (de facto the president of the World Bank). For UNCITRAL cases, unless the

constitutes acceptable conduct in the appointment process; (ii) the institution of a clear rule against unilateral communications following appointment; and (iii) the promulgation of guidelines on conflicts of interest. Also see D. BISHOP and L. REED, "Practical Guidelines", at p. 396; and Alfonso GÓMEZ-ACEBO, "A Special Role of Party-Appointed Arbitrators?", this volume, pp. 381-416 at p. 388.

27. Convention on the Settlement of Investment Disputes between States and Nationals of Other States, Art. 37(2)(b) at <https://icsid.worldbank.org/en/Documents/icsiddocs/ICSID%20Convention%20English.pdf> (last accessed 13 April 2018); UNCITRAL Arbitration Rules (as revised in 2010), Rule 9 at <www.uncitral.org/pdf/english/texts/arbitration/arb-rules-revised/arb-rules-revised-2010-e.pdf> (last accessed 13 April 2018).

disputing parties select the Secretary-General of the Permanent Court of Arbitration as the appointing authority, the Secretary-General would choose the appointing authority.[28]

Beyond the difference in the identity of the appointing authority, varied approaches are taken by appointing authorities in how they go about selecting arbitrators, including how the disputing parties are engaged as part of that process. Under the UNCITRAL Rules, for example, a "veto-rank" procedure is provided for. If this procedure fails, the appointing authority will exercise its discretion to appoint the remaining arbitrator.[29] It has been noted that "these different approaches can produce significantly different selections of sole and presiding arbitrators".[30]

b. *Arguments in favour*

In the absence of an agreement between the disputing parties, appointment of arbitrators by a neutral body or institution was the only mechanism that passed muster in the eyes of Jan Paulsson and in the face of the moral hazard he had identified; "the only decent solution".[31] Alternatively, at least to "reduce contamination", Jan Paulsson has suggested that, even if institutions do not appoint the arbitrators, they could compile a pre-existing list of qualified candidates from which appointments could be made by the disputing parties.

The thinking is that "each potential nominee has been vetted by the institution and is less likely to be beholden to the appointing party".[32] In addition, institutional appointments offer disputing parties the opportunity to leverage on the expertise and experience of the relevant arbitral institution, which would have been built through its exposure to various arbitrators over multiple cases and to how the various arbitrators go about carrying out their duties. To this extent, turning to institutions to appoint arbitrators would offer one way around the information asymmetries between law firms and parties with more experience and tighter informal networks, and those with less experience and looser networks.[33]

c. *Overcoming the challenges constante*

One difficulty that institutions face as appointing authorities is the allegation that they lack neutrality.[34] Where there may be a lack of trust, conferring arbitral institutions with

28. UNCITRAL Arbitration Rules (2010), Rule 6(2) and Rule 9(3).
29. UNCITRAL Arbitration Rules (2010), Rule 8(2) and Rule 9(3).
30. David GAUKRODGER and Kathryn GORDON, "Investor-State Dispute Settlement: A Scoping Paper for the Investment Policy Community", 2012/03 OECD Working Papers on International Investment (2012), Annex 5, at p. 90. Also see Geoffrey DE CLIPPEL, Kfir ELIAZ and Brian KNIGHT, "On the Selection of Arbitrators", 194 The American Economic Review (2014) p. 104.
31. Jan PAULSSON, "Moral Hazard in International Dispute Resolution", Inaugural Lecture as Holder of the Michael R. Klein Distinguished Scholar Chair, University of Miami School of Law (29 April 2010) at https://www.arbitration-icca.org/media/0/12773749999020/paulsson_moral_hazard.pdf (last accessed 13 April 2018) at p. 11.
32. J. PAULSSON, "Moral Hazard", p. 11.
33. C. ROGERS, "A Window into the Soul", p. 1186.
34. Gus VAN HARTEN, Investment Treaty Arbitration and Public Law (OUP 2007) at pp. 169-171. Also see V. V. VEEDER, "Historical Keynote to International Arbitration: The Party-Appointed Arbitrator – from Miami to Geneva", 107 Am. Soc'y Int'l L. Proc. (2013) p. 387 at p. 388, declaring that "most arbitral tribunals cannot be trusted with arbitral appointments".

the duty of arbitrator appointments may shift not only the weight of the responsibility to these institutions but also the scrutiny, without doing much for resolving the underlying concerns. In place of reproaches over the party appointment of arbitrators, we may see suspicion over how arbitral tribunals select arbitrators: their starting points, their guiding principles, the candidates who were considered, the reasons for selection and rejection. Could these be addressed by institutions increasing transparency over various processes by making more information available as appropriate?[35] Or is the ineluctable reality that we will always desire to know "who pulls the strings and who pays the piper"?[36]

Further, "institutional staff ... may prioritise qualities that are helpful from an administrative and institutional perspective".[37] These may be different from the qualities that the disputing parties may hold dear, possibly even the qualities that the non-disputing Parties may seek out. Even the perception of such a misalignment in the prioritization of values could be potentially problematic for building legitimacy in the system amongst its users, even the general public. In order to address this, could the disputing parties be given the opportunity to be consulted? If so, how should they be consulted and to what extent should their input be taken into account?

Above and beyond issues of perception, in the event that an institution seeks out "improvements" in the fielding of investment arbitrators, such as promoting diversity in gender or racial profile or in geographical origin, certain normative questions could arise. For instance, to what extent should this be prioritized over what is desired by the disputing parties, or even the non-disputing Parties, whose interests would be impacted by the choice of persons who would hear their dispute or a dispute arising from a treaty to which they are party? This is also a question that would need to be answered.

2. *Institutionalization and an Investment Court System*

As for institutionalization, the establishment of standing panels of arbitrators has been one of the options for possible reform that has been highlighted. It is useful to recall that the idea of a standing tribunal is a revisiting of an option that was considered when the

35. See Ruth STACKPOOL-MOORE, "Institutional Appointment of Arbitrators", this volume, pp. 417-431. As shared during the ICCA panel session, the author would further note that, first of all, trust and confidence in arbitral institutions as appointing authorities stem from more than just the quality of their appointments. It is important for an arbitral institution to have a generally good reputation all round, such as in terms of its reputation for independence and impartiality, and experience with investor-State dispute settlement. Further, for an arbitral institution to earn trust, it would need to strike the right balance with transparency, both in terms of the types of transparency and the extent. For example, some elements, such as the information pertaining to the identities and nationalities of arbitrators selected, may be important to be made available. Other elements may have a more tenuous link to accountability and may raise other concerns. These include the disclosure of names of arbitrators who were rejected. Usefully, there are now consolidated efforts to promote information and feedback on arbitrators to assist in future arbitration decisions.
36. J. PAULSSON, "Moral Hazard", p. 13.
37. Steven FINIZIO and Claudio SALAS, "It's My Party", CDR News (28 January 2013) at <www.cdr-news.com/categories/arbitration-and-adr/its-my-party> (last accessed 13 April 2018).

ICSID Convention was first being negotiated. At the time, the suggestion to have a standing tribunal was dismissed for being "clearly impractical in the current context", without further elaboration.[38]

Those in favour of reform along the lines of the establishment of standing panels have averred that such a move would "enhance transparency, expedite appointments and promote greater quality and consistency of decisions", and promote global investment governance and institutionalization by creating "a community that would standardise legal norms and practices".[39]

An evaluation of the pros and cons of standing panels is beyond the scope of this Article. That said, from the narrower perspective of the appointment of arbitrators, one can appreciate that there would at least be time and cost savings from a standing panel, arising from dispensing with the need to identify potential arbitrators, as well as subsequent challenges and disqualifications.[40] The question is whether or not, and if so to what extent, this would come at the expense of other costs.

a. The European Union's model

The European Union (EU) has already begun to introduce the seeds for an investment court system in its agreements. This system would envisage, amongst other features, the establishment of a permanent investment court instead of the traditional *ad hoc* arbitration tribunal. This followed the European Parliament's adoption of a resolution which called for "a new system for resolving disputes between investors and states ... by publicly appointed, independent professional judges ...".[41] The intention is to "adopt a court-like solution that adheres to certain key public law principles (for example, independence, impartiality, correctness)".[42]

For example, in the Free Trade Agreement between the EU and the Socialist Republic of Vietnam (EU-Vietnam FTA), a permanent investment tribunal and a permanent appeal tribunal are to be established as of the entry into force of the free trade agreement. The first-instance tribunal will have nine members: three appointed by Vietnam, three appointed by the EU, and three jointly appointed. The appeal tribunal will have six members. Generally speaking, the members of each tribunal are to be appointed for four-year terms, which can be renewed once. Vacancies are to be filled as they arise. The members will hear cases in "divisions", made up of one member from Vietnam, one member from the EU, and one jointly-appointed member who shall chair the "division". The determination of the composition of each "division" will be by the

38. C. THOMAS and H. DHILLON, "The Foundations", p. 465.
39. Leon TRAKMAN and David MUSAYELYAN, "Arguments For and Against Standing Panels of Arbitrators in Investor-State Arbitration: Evidence and Reality" at <https://law.unimelb.edu.au/__data/assets/pdf_file/0004/1954156/Trakman,-ARGUMENTS-FOR-AND-AGAINST-STANDING-PANELS-OF-ARBITRATORS-IN-INVESTOR-STATE-ARBITRATION-EVIDENCE-AND-REALITY.pdf> (last accessed 13 April 2018) at p. 3.
40. C. BROWN, "A Multilateral Mechanism", p. 683.
41. European Parliament, Resolution of 8 July 2015 at <http://www.europarl.europa.eu/doceo/document/TA-8-2015-0252_EN.html?redirect> (last accessed 13 April 2018), containing the European Parliament's recommendations to the European Commission on the negotiations for the Transatlantic Trade and Investment Partnership.
42. C. BROWN, "A Multilateral Mechanism", p. 677.

President of the Tribunal, who is to appoint members "on a rotation basis, ensuring that the composition of the divisions is random and unpredictable, while giving equal opportunity to all Members to serve".[43]

The Comprehensive Economic and Trade Agreement (CETA) between Canada, of the one part, and the EU and its Member States, of the other part is similar in how, in the case of a dispute, all three members of a "division" in the first-instance tribunal would be appointed by the President of the tribunal on the basis of "random and unpredictable" rotation. The first instance tribunal established under the CETA, however, would feature appointments of five nationals of Canada, five nationals of the EU, and five third-country nationals, all of whom would be appointed by the CETA Joint Committee generally for a renewable five-year term (instead of nine members for a four-year term, as with the EU-Vietnam FTA). Further, unlike the EU-Vietnam FTA, the CETA leaves it to the Joint Committee to "promptly" adopt a decision regarding the appointment of members of the appellate tribunal, who will hear cases in divisions of three "randomly appointed" members.[44]

More recently, the Investment Protection Agreement between the EU and its Member States, of the one part, and the Republic of Singapore, of the other part (EU-Singapore IPA), like the EU-Vietnam FTA, features the establishment of both a tribunal of first instance as well as a permanent appeal tribunal. In the case of the EU-Singapore IPA, for both the first instance and appellate tribunals, two nationals of Singapore, two nationals of the EU, and two third-country nationals, would be appointed by the EU-Singapore IPA Committee for an initial eight-year term. Three persons on each tribunal, of the six who are appointed immediately after the entry into force of the EU-Singapore IPA, shall have their terms extended to twelve years. The three persons will be identified by the drawing of lots. Members on each tribunal will be appointed by the President of the relevant tribunal on a rotation basis, ensuring that the composition of each "division" is "random and unpredictable", to hear an individual case. The disputing parties may also agree to have a case heard by a sole Member.[45]

b. Points of departure

In abandoning the ability of the disputing parties to appoint their arbitrators, either unilaterally or by agreement, the EU's agreements with Canada and with Vietnam (and more recently with Singapore) marked a departure from the arbitrator appointment

43. EU-Vietnam FTA: Agreed text as of January 2016, published on 1 February 2016, Sect. 3 (Resolution of Investment Disputes) of Chapter 11 (Investment) of Chapter 8 (Trade in Services, Investment and E-Commerce), Art. 12 (Tribunal) and Art. 13 (Appeal Tribunal) at <trade.ec.europa.eu/doclib/docs/2016/february/tradedoc_154210.pdf> (last accessed 13 April 2018).
44. The revised text of the CETA, made public on 29 February 2016, Chapter 8 (Investment), Art. 8.27 (Constitution of the Tribunal) and Art. 8.28 (Appellate Tribunal) at <trade.ec.europa.eu/doclib/docs/2016/february/tradedoc_154329.pdf> (last accessed 13 April 2018).
45. EU-Singapore IPA (replacing the EUSFTA chapter on investment), made public on 18 April 2018, Chapter 3 (Dispute Settlement), Art. 3.9 (Tribunal of First Instance) and Art. 3.10 (Appeal Tribunal) at <trade.ec.europa.eu/doclib/docs/2018/april/tradedoc_156731.pdf> (last accessed 18 April 2018).

mechanisms in the investment treaties that provided for such mechanisms, either by elaboration of applicable procedures in the text of the investment treaty or by reference to the arbitration rules of UNCITRAL or ICSID or other arbitration institutions.

There is also a conscious change in terminology: "Members of the Tribunal" is used in place of "arbitrator", and "division" in place of "panel". This echoes the nomenclature of the World Trade Organization (WTO) dispute settlement mechanism (although there are critical distinctions between the WTO and investment arbitration contexts that need to be recognized before further parallels can or should be drawn).[46] It has been observed that these "symbolic" adjustments were likely part of the attempt to respond to legitimacy concerns expressed, by stakeholders and other members of the public, about party-appointed arbitrators.[47]

In these respects, the EU's agreements with Canada and with Vietnam (and more recently with Singapore) also marked a departure from their earlier EU position, that was up till then most recently reflected in the CETA text that was made public on 5 August 2014,[48] and the chapter on investment in the free trade agreement that had been negotiated between the EU and the Republic of Singapore (EUSFTA), that was initialled on 22 May 2015.[49] The timing between the previous and subsequent positions hints at the sense of urgency that the EU has had to approach investor-State reform.

c. *Of randomness and unpredictability*

Some questions surrounding randomness and unpredictability immediately arise.

Would the random and unpredictable allocation of arbitrators to hear a dispute, from a list of names pre-established by the treaty Parties, give sufficient comfort to the disputing parties that their case would receive the consideration by arbitrators with the requisite expertise, which may include industry-specific familiarity? Should the pre-established list be enlarged to accommodate a greater diversity of arbitrator profiles, or kept smaller so that the costs of the retainer fees are manageable? Would treaty Parties be able to afford the cost of remunerating the persons on their pre-established lists over an extended period? Should investors bear any of this cost? Further, one does query if there would be problems – real or perceived – that may arise depending on how the President of the Tribunal, who is to appoint members on a random and unpredictable rotation basis, carries out his function as an appointing authority. If comfort is to be had in randomness and unpredictability, should a system of lot drawing be considered, in lieu of the intervention of the President of the Tribunal?

---

46. See generally D. MCRAE, "The WTO Appellate Body", p. 371.
47. Elsa SARDINHA, "The New EU-Led Approach to Investor-State Arbitration: The Investment Tribunal System in the Comprehensive Economic Trade Agreement (CETA) and the EU-Vietnam Free Trade Agreement", 32 ICSID Review (2017, issue 3) p. 625 at p. 633.
48. European Commission, DG Trade, "Note for the Attention of the Trade Policy Committee" (5 August 2014) (appending the 1 August 2014 "consolidated version of all chapters, annexes, declarations, understandings as well as side letters" of CETA) at <www.tagesschau.de/wirtschaft/ceta-dokument-101.pdf> (last accessed 13 April 2018).
49. EUSFTA, Chapter 9 (Investment), Art. 9.18 (Constitution of the Tribunal). The EUSFTA chapter on investment was later superseded by the EU-Singapore IPA, which text was made public on 18 April 2018.

It may be that some of these questions can only be answered through time and experience with the EU model or other similar models. Suffice it to say that the attempt to achieve randomness and unpredictability in arbitrator appointment is not wholly unprecedented. Lot drawing already features in some of the older free trade agreements such as the Agreement between Japan and the Republic of Singapore for a New-Age Economic Partnership (JSEPA). In JSEPA, a procedure of lot drawing is described, whereby the disputing parties would select their presiding arbitrator in the absence of being able to agree on an arbitrator who would be available. In JSEPA, the lots are drawn from ten names, compiled on the basis of two lists of five names prepared and exchanged by the disputing parties (and where there is no name common to both lists).[50] Lot drawing is also a fallback procedure that has been used in the context of State-State dispute settlement mechanisms of free trade agreements.[51]

IV. POSSIBILITIES FOR THE PRESERVATION OF PARTY AUTONOMY IN CHOOSING DECISION-MAKERS

Assuming that we do need to reform the institution of unilateral party appointments, and understanding how party autonomy in the selection of arbitrators for investor-State dispute settlement can be seen by some as a treat and others as a threat, one may ask whether there are conditions under which party autonomy in the selection of arbitrators could be preserved. Three scenarios appear to demonstrate the possibility.

1. *Agreed Appointments: Appointment by Agreement*

First, considering that the invective has been directed at the unilateral appointment of arbitrators, there could be a provision for agreed appointments, thereby preserving some measure of party autonomy in the selection of arbitrators. In other words, disputing parties could be empowered to agree on the constitution of their tribunal, including on the appointment of a sole arbitrator.

In the investor-State dispute settlement mechanisms established by a number of treaties, there is sometimes a provision stating that "*[u]nless the disputing parties otherwise agree*, the tribunal shall comprise three arbitrators, one arbitrator appointed by each of

50. JSEPA, Annex Vc (Investor-to-State Dispute Settlement Special Arbitration Procedure) at <ie.enterprisesg.gov.sg/~/media/IE%20Singapore/Files/FTA/Existing%20FTA/Japan%20Singapore%20EPA/Legal%20Text/Chapter%2021/Annex20VC2020InvestortoState20Dispute20Settlement20Special20Arbitration20Procedure.pdf> (last accessed 13 April 2018).

51. For example, in the event of a dispute under the US-Singapore Free Trade Agreement (USSFTA), if a Party fails to appoint a panellist for the constitution of a dispute settlement panel, or if the Parties are unable to agree on the chair of the panel within a specified period of time, the panellist (or chair) shall be selected by lot from the relevant contingent list established under the Free Trade Agreement. See para. 4(a) of Art. 20.4 (Additional Dispute Settlement Procedures). The text of the USSFTA is available at <ustr.gov/sites/default/files/uploads/agreements/fta/Singapore/asset_upload_file708_4036.pdf> (last accessed 13 April 2018). A similar mechanism is in place in the Free Trade Agreement between Mercosur and the Arab Republic of Egypt. See para. 1 of Art. 14. The text of the FTA is available at <http://www.sice.oas.org/Trade/MER_EGY/English/Text_e.pdf> (last accessed 13 April 2018).

the dispute parties and the third ... appointed by agreement of the dispute parties" (emphasis added).[52] One way of interpreting this provision is as a clause empowering the disputing parties to agree on the composition of their arbitral tribunal. That is, the disputing parties may agree on all of the arbitrators on the arbitral tribunal that is established, whether they may decide to go with one or three or more arbitrators. The EU-Vietnam FTA, CETA, and EU-Singapore IPA, however, do not enable the disputing parties to agree thus.

In the design of their investor-state dispute settlement mechanisms, treaty Parties could consider retaining an option of agreed appointments, howsoever drafted. The concerns over an arbitrator's partiality and a lack of independence would necessarily be resolved by virtue of the disputing parties being able to agree on the arbitrator being appointed to the tribunal. The disputing parties' agreement would speak to their convergence in opinion that the arbitrator could be trusted to hear and decide on the dispute in a fair and impartial manner.

Provision could still be made for a disputing party to resort to an appointing authority, a pre-established list, or other means of composing a tribunal, in case of a need to pre-empt dilatory tactics. Such fallback options (coupled with clear timelines) would be useful to ensure that no disputing party can, by his uncooperativeness, delay the dispute settlement process.

As for whether the freedom and flexibility to agree to the composition of an arbitral tribunal would render the tribunal an instance of "privatized" dispute resolution, one may refer to how the mandate for the appointment and any accompanying circumscriptions would be found in the investment treaty concluded by the States Parties. In this way, unlike commercial arbitrations, "the arbitrators' authority ... is founded in a public office".[53]

Thus far, it is not usual for disputing parties submit investor-State dispute settlement cases to a sole arbitrator. It is also rare that the disputing parties are able to agree on all the arbitrators. However, the signalling effect and upsides of empowering the disputing parties to agree thus, could weigh in favour of providing for such an option in an investment treaty.

2. *Circumscribed Appointments: Choosing from a Pre-established List*

Second, States Parties to an investment treaty could establish and maintain a list or lists of arbitrators, who could be appointed by the disputing parties to form a tribunal in the event of a dispute. The circumscription of options which would form the basis of party appointments would respond to the various criticisms of decision-makers who may lack, or be seen to lack, impartiality and independence.

52. For example, see the ASEAN Comprehensive Investment Agreement, Art. 31 (Selection of Arbitrators) at <cil.nus.edu.sg/wp-content/uploads/formidable/18/2009-ASEAN-Comprehensive-Investment-Agreement.pdf> (last accessed 13 April 2018); and the North American Free Trade Agreement, Chapter Eleven, Art. 1123 (Number of Arbitrators and Method of Appointment) at <www.sice.oas.org/trade/nafta/chap-112.asp> (last accessed 13 April 2018).
53. C. BROWER and S. SCHILL, "Is Arbitration a Threat or a Boon", p. 490.

A key feature of investment arbitration is that the investor is always the claimant, and the State is always the respondent. At the same time, a State Party to an investment treaty does not conclude the treaty only with the perspective of being a respondent State. For every investment arbitration, any State Party to an investment treaty would have an interest in the dispute: if not as a respondent State then either as the home State of the investor, or as a host State of other investors with an interest in how the investment treaty in issue, that it is also party to, is interpreted and applied. States Parties to an investment treaty (or a network of treaties) have a systemic interest in the decision-making undertaken by arbitral tribunals, where investors may not.

As such, States Parties to an investment treaty, especially prior to the crystallization of a dispute, would be effective "gatekeepers" of the investor-State dispute settlement process established by the treaty.[54] When States establish a list or lists of potential arbitrators prior to a dispute, their choices would be internally rationalized. They would be choosing from behind a veil of ignorance of whether they may be a respondent State appearing before any of the shortlisted arbitrators, or a home State of the investor.[55] It would not be the case, for instance, that the interests of investors would be forgotten. Indeed, in investor arbitration as in commercial arbitration, the "appointment" of arbitrators "takes on a different character depending on whether it takes place prior to the dispute arising or subsequent to it".[56] As such, a pre-established list or lists of arbitrators would form a basis for disputing parties to select arbitrators who, *ceteris paribus*, would have been assessed as suitable to be entrusted with conducting an impartial and independent process.

In the case where the Parties to the investment treaty have a pre-established list or lists of arbitrators from which the arbitrators are to be chosen in the event of a dispute, party autonomy in the selection of arbitrators could be preserved.

3. *Arbitrator Ad Hoc Appointments: Arbitrators Ad Hoc on a Permanent Investment Court*

Third, in the event a permanent investment court is established, some measure of party autonomy in the selection of arbitrators could be preserved through having arbitrators *ad hoc* join the members of the permanent court in hearing a particular dispute. This would be an adaptation of the approach in some State-State dispute settlement mechanisms. This could be useful in the context of a multilateralized system in particular, whether a permanent investment body is established at the stage of an initial panel or an appellate panel or at both stages.

It is relevant to examine how party-appointed arbitrators may still be relevant in the context of a multilateral, permanent investment court, because of the efforts underway to establish such a court. For example, looking beyond the EU-Vietnam FTA, CETA, EU-Singapore IPA, and other individual free trade agreements, the EU's objective is the

54. The term "gatekeeper" is borrowed from Charles BROWER and Sadie BLANCHARD, "What's in a Meme? The Truth About Investor-State Arbitration: Why It Need Not, and Must Not, Be Repossessed by States", 52 Columbia Journal of Transnational Law (2014) p. 689 at p. 768.
55. John RAWLS, *A Theory of Justice* (Belknap Press 1971).
56. Daphna KAPELIUK, "Collegial Games: Analyzing the Effect of Panel Composition on Outcome in Investment Arbitration", 31 The Review of Litigation (2012) p. 267 at p. 288.

"creation of one permanent court ... to multi-lateralise the court".[57] In the Joint Interpretative Instrument on the CETA, the EU and Canada have articulated a commitment to "work expeditiously towards the creation of the Multilateral Investment Court. It should be set up once a minimum critical mass of participants is established and immediately replace bilateral systems".[58] The EU is engaging with all of its partners to introduce the investment court system in all of its bilateral agreements, as well as to discuss the possible creation of a multilateral court system.[59] For the EU, and other early adopters who may introduce the system of permanent investment tribunals across a series of their investment agreements, there would potentially be particular cost savings to be had from multilateralization, from the perspective of being able to share the costs of employing fulltime adjudicators.

Multilateral discussions on an investment court are at its nascent stages, and this paper does not have the intention to assess the proposal to have such a court. Nevertheless, the assumption appears to be that there would be a small group of arbitrators who would be selected to be a part of the permanent court. In other words, a multilateral court, whether established as a first instance forum or as an appellate mechanism, would be constituted by a restricted group of judges. Further, the process of selection would be by a diplomatic process, involving States. Necessarily, while one may strive for regional or other forms of representation and diversity, it would not be possible to achieve "full representation" in the composition of a multilateralized institution that is conceptualized as an adjudicatory or quasi-judicial process rather than, for instance, a peer review process.

In State-State dispute settlement, there are adjudicatory bodies that provide for the possibility of having one or two judges *ad hoc* complement a permanent bench of three or more judges. For example, if the bench of the International Court of Justice (ICJ) does not already include a judge of the nationality of a party to the dispute, that party may choose a person to sit as a judge *ad hoc*.[60] A similar provision can be found in the statute of the International Tribunal for the Law of the Sea (ITLOS).[61] The judge *ad hoc* in the context of the ICJ and ITLOS, would have the role of ensuring that "every relevant argument in favour of the party that has appointed him had been fully appreciated in the

57. European Commission, "Investment in TTIP and Beyond – The Path for Reform: Enhancing the Right to Regulate and Moving from Current ad hoc Arbitration Towards an Investment Court", (May 2015) at <trade.ec.europa.eu/doclib/docs/2015/october/tradedoc_153846.pdf> (last accessed 13 April 2018).

58. Joint Interpretative Instrument on the Comprehensive Economic and Trade Agreement (CETA) between Canada and the European Union and its Member States, L 11/3 Official Journal of the European Union (14 January 2017) p. 3.

59. C. BROWN, "A Multilateral Mechanism", p. 682.

60. Statute of the International Court of Justice, Art. 31 at <legal.un.org/avl/pdf/ha/sicj/icj_statute_e.pdf> (last accessed 13 April 2018). Note that the innovation of judges *ad hoc* of the ICJ was not uncontroversial. See generally, Stephen SCHWEBEL, "National Judges and Judges *Ad Hoc* of the International Court of Justice", 48 I.C.L.Q. (1999, no. 4) p. 889.

61. Statute of the International Tribunal for the Law of the Sea, Art. 17 (Nationality of members) at <https://www.itlos.org/fileadmin/itlos/documents/basic_texts/statute_en.pdf> (last accessed 13 April 2018).

course of collegial consideration".[62] That said, this would not bind him to decide in favour of that party. The innovation of judges *ad hoc*, in the experience of State-State dispute settlement, was to ensure States' confidence in submitting their disputes to the relevant adjudicatory body, and in the eventual decision. It was also said to be helpful to States in accounting for the body's eventual decision to their populations.[63]

Similarly, in the investor-State context, even with the establishment of a multilateral investment court, unilateral appointments of arbitrators could be retained for arbitrators *ad hoc*, who would complement the sitting members of the permanent court for a particular dispute. The arbitrators *ad hoc* on a permanent investment tribunal would form only the minority of the bench or tribunal hearing the dispute. As such, the real or perceived concerns over bias or lack of independence would fall away. At the same time, the disputing parties may still take comfort from having an arbitrator familiar with their condition sitting alongside the other decision-makers.

V. CONCLUDING REMARKS

> "*The history of human opinion is scarcely anything more than the history of human errors.*" – *Voltaire*

We are unlikely to ever be able to all fully agree on whether the institution of the party-appointed arbitrator is a boon or bane to investor-State dispute settlement. Diagnoses will be made. Some will disagree with the remedies. Others will question whether the identification of a source ailment is traceable to a case of hypochondria.[64]

If there is to be any change at all to how investor-State dispute settlement is perceived, whether by way of debate to sort out the real problems from the perceived or by way of system reform, what is clear is that, at this stage, truly inclusive multilateral dialogue is needed. Efforts in this regard are already underway at ICSID and UNCITRAL. Some of the dialogue may need to start off with an exchange of views and experiences. In this way, States with less experience are able to appreciate the tensions and trade-offs that may need to be made. But the process cannot be rushed. Consensus cannot be compromised.

In order to tackle the legitimacy crisis that the investor-State dispute settlement mechanism is facing, all options need to be on the table. Middle-of-the-road options, such as the possibilities for calibrating party autonomy in choosing decision-makers, cannot be overlooked or their value underestimated. Such options, including those put forward in this paper, are useful ways to consider how the balance could be struck between giving disputing parties comfort that their case will be properly understood and considered, and assuring others that the arbitrators will not be biased, so that the various stakeholders can have confidence in the system and the outcomes that it generates.

62. Application of the Convention on the Prevention and Punishment of the Crime of Genocide, I.C.J. Rep. (1993), pp. 408-409.
63. S. SCHWEBEL, "National Judges", p. 890.
64. See generally, M. SCHNEIDER, "President's Message".

The Risk of Groupthink in a Multilateral Investment Court

Audley Sheppard QC[*] *and Daphna Kapeliuk*[**]

TABLE OF CONTENTS

I. INTRODUCTION

The current paradigm for investor-State dispute settlement (ISDS), which is arbitration by a three-person *ad hoc* tribunal, with one arbitrator appointed by the investor, the second by the State, and the third (president) being agreed by the parties or selected by the co-arbitrators or by the relevant appointing authority, has been criticized as lacking legitimacy and has resulted in calls for far-reaching structural and systemic reform.

The United Nations Conference on Trade and Development (UNCTAD) has, since 2015, embarked on a programme aimed at reforming the investment treaty regime.[1] The United Nations Commission on International Trade Law (UNCITRAL) is focusing on a review of options for ISDS.[2]

One option being considered for reform is for investment treaty disputes to be resolved by a global permanent and multilateral standing court that would have jurisdiction to resolve disputes under multiple investment treaties (PMIC).

This proposal is already some way to being realized. The European Union has included a standing court on a bilateral basis in its Free Trade Agreements (FTAs) with Canada,[3] Vietnam,[4] and Singapore.[5] The European Commission favours an all-

---

* Partner, Clifford Chance LLP, London; Chairman of LCIA Board.

** Partner, Goldfarb Seligman Law Offices, Tel Aviv.

1. UNCTAD, "World Investment Report 2015: Reforming International Investment Governance", available at: <http://unctad.org/en/PublicationChapters/wir2015ch4_en. pdf>.
2. Working Group III (Investor-State Dispute Settlement Reform) met on 27 November – 1 December 2017 and, since the ICCA 2018 Congress Sydney, has met again on 23 – 27 April 2018, 29 October – 2 November 2018, and 1 – 5 April 2019. It has been mandated: (i) to identify and consider concerns regarding ISDS; (ii) to consider whether reform was desirable in light of any identified concerns; and (iii) if the Working Group were to conclude that reform was desirable, to develop any relevant solutions to be recommended to the Commission.
   See: <http://www.uncitral.org/uncitral/en/commission/working_groups/3Investor_State. html>.
3. Comprehensive Economic and Trade Agreement (CETA), Ch. 29, available at: <http://ec. europa.eu/trade/policy/in-focus/ceta>.

encompassing multilateral version of such court, which it hopes will have jurisdiction with respect to all existing and future bilateral and multilateral trade related agreements to which the EU is party.

The proposed PMIC has obvious similarities to the World Trade Organization (WTO) dispute resolution mechanism,[6] which appears to enjoy widespread legitimacy amongst States (save notably the United States presently). There are several other standing international courts and tribunals to which States appoint semi-permanent judges, such as the International Court of Justice (ICJ) (albeit that the disputing States can appoint one *ad hoc* judge each), the European Court of Human Rights (ECtHR), and the Court of Justice of the European Union (CJEU). A hybrid is the International Tribunal for the Law of the Sea (ITLOS), to which the disputing States appoint some of the adjudicators.

This paper addresses the risk of 'groupthink' amongst the members of a standing court or tribunal, tested by the propensity to issue dissenting opinions. Groupthink is a psychological phenomenon that occurs within a group of people in which the desire for harmony or conformity in the group influences the decision-making outcome. It has also been observed that those in a group who disagree often take a more extreme position.[7]

II. CURRENT SYSTEM

The current system for constituting tribunals is the same in the vast majority of investment treaties and identical to most commercial arbitration agreements, i.e. two party-appointed arbitrators. Whichever procedural rules are prescribed in the treaty (almost invariably the ICSID and UNCITRAL Rules) and selected by the investor, they provide for the claimant-investor to select one arbitrator, the respondent-State to appoint the second, and the parties or the co-arbitrators to agree the third who will be the president of the tribunal, failing which the stipulated appointing authority will make the selection (e.g., the Chairman of the Administrative Council of ICSID under the ICSID Rules, and the Secretary-General of the Permanent Court of Arbitration under the UNCITRAL Rules).

The parties' ability to select their own arbitrator has been considered as one of the most important advantages of commercial arbitration.[8] This opportunity has been described as "the single most determinative step in the arbitration".[9]

---

4. EU-Vietnam Trade and Investment Agreement (EUVFTA), Ch. 15, available at: <http://trade.ec.europa.eu/doclib/press/index.cfm?id=1437>.
5. EU-Singapore Trade and Investment Agreement (EUSFTA), Ch. 14, available at: <http://trade.ec.europa.eu/doclib/press/index.cfm?id=961>.
6. See: <https://www.wto.org/english/tratop_e/dispu_e/disp_settlement_cbt_e/c1s1p1_e.htm>.
7. See, e.g., Cass SUNSTEIN, *Going to Extremes: How Like Minds Unite and Divide* (OUP 2009); also *Conformity* (NYU Press 2019).
8. Daphna KAPELIUK, "Collegial Games – Analyzing the Effect of Panel Composition on Outcome in Investment Arbitration", 31 The Review of Litigation (2012) p. 267; see also Queen Mary University of London – White & Case International Arbitration Survey 2018, p. 7, available at:

However, it is the sense of participation in the arbitration process that has engendered criticism by scholars who have questioned the legitimacy of the selection of arbitrators by the disputing parties.[10] While acknowledging that all arbitrators are required to act independently and impartially,[11] critics have argued that the very concept of party-appointed arbitrator is contrary to traditional notions of judicial impartiality.[12] One author has questioned the ability of party-appointed arbitrators to exercise true independent judgement.[13] This concern stems from the fact that each party selects an arbitrator in the hope that she/he will hold in their favour. This has led one author to question whether "party-appointment leads to 'moral hazard' because those who appoint want to win and those who want to be appointed want the income that appointment brings".[14] This in turn leads one party to be suspicious about the other's appointment.

In investment arbitration, party autonomy in selecting an arbitrator (subject of course to requirements of independence and impartiality) has inevitably led parties, both investors and States, to seek to appoint arbitrators who are considered to be likely to be sympathetic to the presumed opposing mind-sets, namely protecting risk capital from government interference versus permitting governments wide regulatory and sovereign discretion. As a result of more and more published awards and serial appointments, a picture is emerging of how some arbitrators are perceived as falling into one camp or the other, as being investor-friendly or State-friendly. UNCTAD recently observed that "the increasing number of challenges to arbitrators suggests that disputing parties perceive them as biased or predisposed".[15]

Moreover, arbitrators appointed by investors tend to be drawn from lawyers in private practice, rather than being known as academics or former government lawyers (with notable exceptions).[16] This has led to criticism that some arbitrators do not fully appreciate public law and international law issues. There is also a view that investor appointees have a greater influence on tribunals, resulting in procedures more akin to commercial arbitration (which adds to the costs of the State defending claims) and pro-

---

<http://www.arbitration.qmul.ac.uk/media/arbitration/docs/2018-International-Arbitration-Survey---The-Evolution-of-International-Arbitration-(2).PDF>.

9. Yves DEZALAY and Bryant GARTH, *Dealing in Virtue* (University of Chicago Press 1996) p. 8; David BRANSON, "Sympathetic Party-Appointed Arbitrators: Sophisticated Strangers and Governments Demand Them", 25 ICSID Rev. (2010) pp. 367, 381.
10. Detlev F. VAGTS, "Note and Comment: The International Legal Profession: A Need For More Governance?", 90 Am. J. Int'l L (1996) pp. 250, 258.
11. As most major arbitration rules and national laws require.
12. See, e.g., Yuval SHANY, "Squaring the Circle? Independence and Impartiality of Party-Appointed Adjudicators in International Legal Proceedings", 30 Loy. L. A. Int'l & Comp. L. Rev. (2008) p. 473.
13. Jan PAULSSON, "Moral Hazard in International Dispute Resolution", 25 ICSID Rev. (2010) pp. 339, 348. See also Stavros BREKOULAKIS, "Systemic Bias and the Institution of International Arbitration: A New Approach to Arbitral Decision Making", 4 Journal of International Dispute Settlement (2013) p. 553.
14. David BRANSON, supra fn. 9, p. 381.
15. UNCTAD, IIA Issues Note: "Improving Investment Dispute Settlement: UNCTAD Policy Tools" (November 2017) p. 6, available at: <https://unctad.org/en/PublicationsLibrary/diaepcb2017d8_en.pdf>.
16. See statistics at: <https://investmentpolicyhub.unctad.org/ISDS/FilterByArbitrators>.

investor awards. While the evidence does not appear to substantiate that conclusion, the perception remains that investment treaty tribunals favour investors.

There is also disquiet about the apparent lack of consistency in the interpretation and application of key provisions found in similarly worded BITs and the absence of a corrective and harmonising appeal structure.

There is also concern about lack of procedural transparency. This had led to greater voluntary transparency (for example, by the State parties to the North American Free Trade Agreement), and to the adoption in 2014 of the UNCITRAL Rules on Transparency in Treaty-based Investor-State Arbitration.[17]

The EU Commission's proposals and UNCTAD's review are driven by the view that the current *ad hoc* system lacks legitimacy, consistency and transparency.

III. EU COMMISSION PROPOSALS

The European Commission's vision for a PMIC was first articulated most fully in its recommendation in favour of a European Council decision authorizing the opening of negotiations for a convention establishing a multilateral investment court (EUMIC), of 13 September 2017.[18]

The Commission proposes a two-tier court, comprising a court of first instance and an appeal function which has the power to review decisions on the grounds of error of law (including serious procedural shortcomings or "manifest errors in the appreciation of facts"), as well as the ability to remand cases back to the tribunal of first instance.[19]

The adjudicators should be appointed for a fixed period of time on a long and non-renewable mandate. The proposal envisages that they would be subject to "high ethical requirements" and mechanisms should be put in place to ensure their independence and

17. Available at: <http://www.uncitral.org/uncitral/en/uncitral_texts/arbitration/2014Transparency.html>.
18. Recommendation for a Council Decision authorizing the opening of negotiations for a Convention establishing a multilateral court for the settlement of investment disputes, COM (2017) 493 final, together with COM (2017) 493 final 2017/0224(COD), Annex 1, available at: <https://eur-lex.europa.eu/resource.html?uri=cellar:df96826b-985e-11e7-b92d-01aa75 ed71a1.0001.02/DOC_1&format=PDF> and Commission Staff Working Document Impact Assessment, Multilateral Reform of Investment Dispute Resolution (SWD (2017) 302) and Commission Staff Working Document Executive Summary of the Impact Assessment Recommendation for a Council Decision authorising the opening of negotiations for a Convention establishing a multilateral court for the settlement of investment disputes (SWD (2017) 303). Since the ICCA Sydney Congress, the European Commission has confirmed the main features of what is envisaged in a speech on 22 June 2018, by Colin Brown, Deputy Head of Unit, Dispute Settlement and Legal Aspects of Trade Policy, Directorate General for Trade, European Commission (available at <http://trade.ec.europa.eu/doclib/docs/2018/july/tra doc_ 157112.pdf>). The European Commission has also expressed its support for the work of the ISDS Reform Working Group established by UNCITRAL. In a speech on 22 November 2018, the European Commissioner for Trade, Cecilia Malmström, noted that the creation of a PMIC was the only option that effectively addresses concerns with ISDS (available at <http://trade.ec.europa.eu/doclib/press/index.cfm?id=1943)>.
19. Supra fn. 18, COM (2017) 493 final, 2017/0224(COD), Annex 1, para. 8.

impartiality, including random allocation of cases and a certain regime to ensure ethical concerns are upheld. They would "ideally" be appointed by an independent body, or an independent body would have a significant role in the selection process.[20] The proposal further considers that the number of adjudicators would be determined by the court's workload. The EUMIC would rely on a secretariat.

The EU Commission made further proposals in its submission to the UNCITRAL Working Group on ISDS reform in January 2019 in which the EU indicates that: (i) adjudicators should be employed full-time and should not have activities that interfere with their duties to the court (save teaching), (ii) terms of office should be commensurate with other international tribunals (e.g., nine years), and (iii) there should be qualification requirements comparable with other international tribunals (e.g., appointment to the highest judicial office or a jurisconsult of recognized competence in international law). Moreover, the EU proposes that the standing mechanism create its own enforcement regime which does not allow for the review of awards at a domestic level.[21]

These proposals are somewhat different to the court composition that the Commission already has in place in the EU's FTAs with Canada, Vietnam and most recently Singapore.

CETA[22] provides that a joint committee[23] will appoint fifteen members to form a standing tribunal, consisting of five EU nationals, five Canadian nationals and five third-country nationals.[24] The tribunal will hear cases in divisions consisting of three members, comprising one EU national, one Canadian national and one third-country national, with the division chaired by the third-country national.[25] The members of the tribunal are to possess the qualifications required in their respective countries for appointment to judicial office, or be jurists of recognized competence, who have demonstrated expertise in public international law and ideally have expertise in international investment law, international trade law and the resolution of disputes arising under international investment or international trade agreements.[26] The members are also to be independent and not affiliated with any government, but it is stated that the fact that a person receives remuneration from a government does not in itself make that person ineligible.[27] Upon appointment, the members are to refrain from acting as counsel or as party-appointed expert or witness "in any pending or new investment dispute under this or any other

20. Supra fn. 18, SWD (2017) 302, Sect. 6.3, p. 63.

21 Submission of the European Union and its Member States to UNCITRAL Working Group III: Establishing a standing mechanism for the settlement of international investment disputes, 18 January 2019, available at: <http://trade.ec.europa.eu/doclib/docs/2019/january/tradoc_157631.pdf>, paras. 16, 19, 20, and 30-31.

22. Supra fn. 3.

23. CETA, Art. 26.1, comprising representatives of the EU and of Canada and co-chaired by the Minister for International Trade of Canada and the Member of the European Commission responsible for Trade (or their respective designees).

24. CETA, Art. 8.27, para. 2.

25. CETA, Art. 8.27, para. 6. Note that either party may instead propose to appoint up to five members of any nationality, who will be considered to be nationals of the appointing party for these purposes.

26. CETA, Art. 8.27, para. 4.

27. CETA, Art. 8.30, para. 1.

international agreement".[28] The members are appointed for five-year terms with a maximum of two terms.[29] Within ninety days of the submission of a claim, the president of the tribunal will appoint the members comprising a division hearing the case on a rotation basis, ensuring that the composition of the divisions is "random and unpredictable", while giving "equal opportunity" to members to serve.[30] Unlike the EUMIC proposal, Canada and the EU agreed that the disputing parties may agree that a case be heard by a sole member to be appointed at random from the third-country nationals.[31] An appellate tribunal will also be established, appointed by the joint committee and meeting the same requirements as the first instance court. The appellate tribunal has the power to uphold, modify or reverse an award based on (i) errors in the application or interpretation of applicable law; (ii) manifest errors in the appreciation of the facts; and (iii) the grounds set out in Art. 52(1)(a) through (e) of the ICSID Convention.[32] Each division of the appellate tribunal will consist of three randomly appointed members.[33] It is expressly stated that the UNCITRAL Transparency Rules will apply to proceedings and that hearings shall be open to the public.[34]

The ISDS provisions in the EUVFTA[35] and EUSFTA[36] are broadly similar.

None of these FTAs is yet in force. CETA entered provisionally into force on 21 September 2017. The ISDS provisions require ratification by all EU Member States to take full effect;[37] however, the ISDS provisions had been challenged by Belgium, but, in April 2019, the CJEU rendered an opinion that these are compatible with EU law.[38]

28. CETA, Art. 8.30, para. 1.
29. CETA, Art. 8.27, para. 5. Note that the terms of seven of the initial fifteen members appointed immediately after the agreement enters into force will be extended to six years as determined by lot. In addition, if a member is serving on a division when his or her term expires, in principle, he or she may continue to serve until a final award is issued.
30. CETA, Art. 8.27, para.7.
31. CETA, Art. 8.27, para.9.
32. CETA, Art. 8.28, paras. 1-3.
33. CETA, Art. 8.28, para. 5. Note that no specific provisions are made in relation to nationality of the members.
34. CETA, Art. 8.36, para. 5.
35. Supra fn. 4.
36. Supra fn. 5.
37. Following the CJEU ruling on the EU's free trade agreement with Singapore (Commission LI:EU:C:2017:376), of 16 May 2017, which found that ISDS mechanisms are mixed competences, each Member State must ratify said agreements before they can take effect, available at: <http://curia.europa.eu/juris/document/document.jsf?text=&docid=190727&pageIndex=0&doclang=EN&mode=req&dir=&occ=first&part=1&cid=476826>.
38. On 6 September 2017, Belgium requested an opinion from the Court of Justice of the European Union (CJEU) on the compatibility of the investment court system established by CETA with (i) the exclusive competence of the CJEU to provide the definitive interpretation of EU law; (ii) the general principle of equality and the "practical effect" requirement of EU law; (iii) the right of access to the courts; and (iv) the right to an independent and impartial judiciary. The Advocate General in his advisory opinion, dated 29 January 2019, approved the provisions, available at: <http://curia.europa.eu/juris/document/document.jsf?docid=210 244>. The CJEU's Opinion confirmed that the investment court system provided for in CETA is fully compatible with EU law and, specifically, complies with: (i) the principle of autonomy of EU law and the exclusive jurisdiction of the CJEU for the interpretation of EU law; (ii) the principle of equal treatment and of the requirement of effectiveness of EU law; and (iii) the Charter of Fundamental Rights, in

Following that favourable ruling, establishment of the investment court system is a step closer.[39]

IV. KAUFMANN-KOHLER AND POTESTÀ REPORTS

In June 2016, Professor Kaufmann-Kohler and Dr Potestà, from the CIDS-Geneva Center for International Dispute Settlement, wrote a report for UNCITRAL, entitled: "Can the Mauritius Convention Serve as a Model for the Reform of Investor-State Arbitration in Connection with the Introduction of a Permanent Investment Tribunal or an Appeal Mechanism?".[40]

It was supplemented in November 2017 by an extensive report entitled: "The Composition of a Multilateral Investment Court and of an Appeal Mechanism for Investment Award".[41]

In the Supplemental Report, the authors identify the composition of the tribunal as a "critical aspect of the possible reform of the investor-State dispute settlement".[42] The Report examines key structural considerations, including: (i) the number of members and whether there should be "full representation" or "selective representation" (i.e. whether each State will have an adjudicator on a permanent basis);[43] (ii) who should be appointed, taking into account competence (by way of specifying appropriate professional experience and expertise), diversity (including geographical and gender) and independence, the latter encompassing both structural independence (i.e. whether an arbitrator is potentially influenced by selection method, security of tenure, term of office, financial security, adequate resources, incompatibilities, privileges and immunities and case assignment rules) and individual independence and impartiality (i.e. whether an arbitrator is potentially influenced by repeat appointments and issue conflicts, as well as accountability);[44] (iii) the procedure for selection (where the authors submit that the selection process should be multi-layered, open to stakeholders and transparent) and whether there should be screening (and if so, the composition of such an advisory panel, the scope of its mandate and its procedural powers);[45] (iv) the term of office;[46] (v) the assignment of cases (be it by a roster, the disputing parties participating in the constitution of the chamber hearing their case, or by a standing body in which disputing parties play no role) and the number of members in each chamber and their

particular of the right of access to a court and right to an independent and impartial tribunal under the Charter; Opinion 1/17 of the CJEU, 30 April 2019; available at: <https://curia.europa.eu/jcms/upload/docs/application/pdf/ 2019-04/cp190052en.pdf>.

39. European Commission Directorate-General for Trade, "EU-Canada Trade Agreement Enters into Force" (Brussels, 20 September 2017), available at: <http://trade.ec.europa.eu/doclib/press/index.cfm?id=1723>.
40. Available at: <http://www.uncitral.org/pdf/english/CIDS_Research_Paper_Mauritius.pdf>.
41. Available at: <http://www.uncitral.org/pdf/english/workinggroups/wg_3/CIDS_Supplemental_Report.pdf>.
42. *Ibid.*, para. 213.
43. *Ibid.*, paras. 21-27.
44. *Ibid.*, paras. 28-105.
45. *Ibid.*, paras. 106-160.
46. *Ibid.*, paras. 161-165.

nationality.[47] The Supplemental Report concludes that, regardless of the exact manner of composition, there are three elements which are essential to the success of any PMIC: competence, diversity and independence.

The authors recognize that, depending upon the appointment mechanism, a standing court may give rise to acute issues relating to arbitrator neutrality and independence. They state: "appointment on the basis of political considerations rather than competence and merit may undermine the quality of the decisions and ultimately the perception of independence, credibility and legitimacy".[48]

The Supplemental Report points to a number of empirical studies examining the voting patterns of the decision-makers in permanent international courts and tribunals to try to evaluate the potential bias of such decision-makers. Many studies demonstrate that these adjudicators allow their policy preferences and nationalism to influence the outcomes of their cases. Such findings support the view that establishing standing tribunals for investment treaty arbitration cannot necessarily avoid the problem of bias in decision-making.

For instance, Eric Posner and Miguel de Figueiredo found evidence that national bias has significant influence on the judges' decision making in the ICJ. The judges tended to favour the parties from their home States. Whilst the ICJ judges voted for non-home parties about 48 percent of the time, they voted for home State parties around 90 percent of the time. The judges were also more likely to vote for parties from the States that were similar to their home State, in terms of wealth, culture and political regime (e.g., sharing membership of NATO, the EU, OECD or sharing language or religion).[49] Likewise, Erik Voeten found some evidence of national bias amongst the judges in the ECtHR. In particular, the ECtHR judges who had previous careers as diplomats were more likely to favour their national governments and national interest compared to judges who had had other careers.[50]

Michael Waibel and Yanhui Wu in 2017 conducted a study in the context of investment treaty arbitration and reached similar conclusions. The correlation between the legal strength of the case and its arbitral outcome was significantly weaker when personal characteristics and policy preferences of the arbitrator exhibited a strong correlation with the decision outcomes. In particular, the developing status of a country was most prominent amongst the factors of bias.[51] These bias factors were not related to the undesirable incentives attributed to *ad hoc* arbitral tribunals. Therefore, the authors further argue that establishing a standing arbitral tribunal will not necessarily address the bias factors and may even allow arbitrators greater room to influence disputes with their own policy preferences.

---

47. *Ibid.*, paras. 166-204.
48. *Ibid.*, para. 108.
49. Eric A. POSNER and Miguel DE FIGUEIREDO, "Is the International Court of Justice Biased?", John M. Olin Program in Law and Economics Working Paper No. 234 (2004) pp. 18-19 and 28-29; available at: <https://escholarship.org/uc/item/35j504rg>.
50. Erik VOETEN, "The Impartiality of International Judges: Evidence from the European Court of Human Rights", 10 American Political Science Review (2008, no. 4) pp. 428 and 430.
51. Michael WAIBEL and Yanhui WU, "Are Arbitrators Political? Evidence from International Investment Arbitration" (2017) pp. 23-25; available at: <http://www-bcf.usc.edu/~yanhui wu/arbitrator.pdf>.

Scholars such as Susan Franck found no significant statistical relationship between arbitral outcomes, the amount of awards and any characteristics of the parties (e.g., nationality) that match with the arbitrators in investment treaty arbitration.[52]

Ultimately, the empirical research is not conclusive. Catherine Rogers cautions against overstating the implications of any particular study.[53] Instinctively, however, one suspects there is some correlation between party-appointment and decision-making, which has support in research by Albert Jan van den Berg.[54]

V. DISSENTING OPINIONS

We now turn to consider whether, in the international context, the issuing of dissenting opinions distinguishes *ad hoc* party-appointed tribunals and standing courts.[55]

It is said that dissenting opinions are a phenomenon of the common law and not of the civil law. A principal reason given as to why common law jurisdictions permit dissenting opinions is because the courts are making and developing the law, unlike civil law jurisdictions where the law is prescribed in a written code, and therefore it is important that common law appellate courts be allowed to articulate differing opinions.[56] Underpinning the civil law tradition is the principle that the court's decision should appear as the decision of the court as a whole; not the result of a simple mathematical vote in favour of a majority view. Various theories underpin this approach. Richard Mosk and Tom Ginsburg suggest that it "rests on the jurisprudential view of the law as fixed, unchanging and determinate.... Under this theory, courts do not 'make law', but merely find it through the exercise of legal science."[57] Another reason for avoiding dissents in civil law jurisdictions is that they offend against the secrecy of the deliberations, a principle which protects the deliberations process from undue external pressures imposed by the parties or other actors in the proceedings. However, times have changed and civil law countries are now more permissive in their approach to dissents.[58] For example, as at 2012, only seven of the twenty-seven non-UK EU member States (which are generally considered civil law jurisdictions, albeit not homogenous)

52. Susan D. FRANCK, "Development and Outcomes of Investment Treaty Arbitration", 50 Harvard Journal of International Law (2009, no. 2) p. 473.
53. Catherine ROGERS, "The Politics of International Investment Arbitrators", 12 Santa Clara Journal of International Law (2013) p. 223 at p. 262.
54. Albert Jan VAN DEN BERG, "Dissenting Opinions by Party-Appointed Arbitrators in Investment Arbitration" in Mahnoush H. ARSANJANI, Jacob COGAN, Robert SLOANE and Siegfried WIESSNER, eds., *Looking to the Future: Essays on International Law in Honor of W. Michael Reisman* (Brill 2011) p. 822 at p. 824.
55. See Audley SHEPPARD and Daphna KAPELIUK, "Dissents in International Arbitration" in Tony COLE, ed., *The Roles of Psychology in International Arbitration* (Wolters Kluwer 2017).
56. See, e.g., Lord NEUBERGER, "No Judgment – No Justice", First Annual BAILII Lecture (20 November 2012) para. 24, <https://www.supremecourt.uk/docs/speech-121120.pdf>.
57. Richard MOSK and Tom GINSBURG, "Dissenting Opinions in International Arbitration", 4 Mealey's Int'l Arb. Rep (2000) pp. 26, 27.
58. See Rosa RAFFAELI, European Parliament Policy Department C: Citizens' Rights and Constitutional Affairs, Legal and Parliamentary Affairs, "Dissenting Opinions in the Supreme Courts of the Member States" (European Parliament 2012) para. 2.1.2 (EP Report).

expressly prohibited the publication of individual opinions by judges. In the remaining twenty member States, the publication of separate opinions was allowed, although practice varies as to when dissents are most commonly issued.[59]

Undoubtedly, one needs to exercise caution before concluding that the presence of dissenting opinions evidences free and frank debate and the freedom to disagree. Such debate and disagreement may well exist behind the veil of a judgment or award signed by all the judges or arbitrators. Nevertheless, it is an indicia of possible differences (or not) between international *ad hoc* party appointed tribunals and standing courts.

Looking first at ISDS, the UNCITRAL Arbitration Rules 2010 do not expressly refer to dissents. The ICSID Arbitration Rules 2006 provide at Rule 47(3) that: "Any member of the Tribunal may attach his individual opinion to the award, whether he dissents from the majority or not, or a statement of his dissent."[60]

In 2009, Professor Albert Jan van den Berg carried out an extensive review of 150 investment treaty arbitrations (not limited to ICSID) and found that in 34 (or 23 percent) separate opinions were issued (not all of which were dissents).[61] Other commentators have noted that this actually demonstrates a high degree of agreement between arbitrators, as no fewer than 77 percent of the decisions reviewed were unanimous.[62]

Between 2011 to 2014, ICSID authenticated at least seventy publicly known final awards, in respect of which twelve arbitrators issued dissenting opinions, i.e. in approximately 17 percent of cases, which means 83 percent were unanimous.

The following is a small sample of well-known dissents.

In *Tokios Tokeles v. Ukraine*,[63] Professor Prosper Weil dissented. It is one of the rare occasions in which the president of the tribunal has dissented from the decision of the two party-appointed arbitrators. He believed the issue on which he dissented to be a matter of significant legal principle and stated that adopting the majority's view "might jeopardize the future of [ICSID]". Professor Weil also wrote that "I would fail in my duty if I were to conceal my doubts out of friendship for my colleagues".[64]

In *CME v. Czech Republic*, the dissenting opinion of Dr. Jaroslav Hándl, appointed by the Czech Republic, was scathing of his fellow arbitrators, especially with respect to his treatment by them,[65] with his co-arbitrators critical of him.[66] The alleged procedural unfairness of the deliberations formed the basis, amongst others, of a challenge to the

59. EP Report, paras. 2 and 2.2.

60. Rule 47(3) is in identical terms to Art. 48(3) of the ICSID Convention 1965: see, e.g., Christoph SCHREUER, et al., *The ICSID Convention: A Commentary*, 2nd ed. (CUP 2010) paras. 48.92 to 102.

61. A.J. VAN DEN BERG, supra fn. 54, p. 824.

62. Charles BROWER and Charles ROSENBERG, "The Death of the Two-Headed Nightingale: Why the Paulsson-Van den Berg Presumption that Party-Appointed Arbitrators Are Untrustworthy Is Wrongheaded", 29 Arb. Int'l (2013, no. 1) p. 7.

63. ICSID Case No. ARB/02/18, Decision on Jurisdiction (29 April 2004).

64. *Ibid.*, Dissenting opinion of Prosper WEIL (29 April 2004).

65. *CME Czech Republic B.V. v. The Czech Republic*, UNCITRAL Rules, Dissenting opinion of the Arbitrator JUDr Jaroslav HÁNDL against the Partial Arbitration Award (13 September 2001).

66. Partial Award on Liability, para. 625.

award to the Svea Court of Appeal, with the court hearing evidence from all the arbitrators. The challenge was rejected.[67]

Some dissents concern the substantive legal issues. The lengthy dissent of the late Professor Thomas Wälde in *Thunderbird v. Mexico*[68] has become one of the main authorities on the scope of legitimate expectations that forms part of the fair and equitable treatment standard of protection and has contributed to the emerging *de facto* system of precedent.[69]

Some dissents concern procedural issues. In *Impregilo SpA v. Argentina Republic*,[70] Professor Brigitte Stern in her dissenting opinion forcefully warned of the "great dangers" of the majority's view that a conditional right to ICSID could "magically be transformed into an unconditional right by the grace of the [most-favoured nation] clause".[71]

In *RSM Production Corporation v. Saint Lucia*,[72] the tribunal's decision on the State's request for security for costs from the claimant was accompanied by a separate "assenting" opinion by the claimant's appointed arbitrator, Dr Gavan Griffith QC.[73] While agreeing with the orders made by the tribunal, Dr Griffith disagreed as to the basis for making such orders and was unflattering about third-party funding – which generated substantial comment, not least from the third-party funding industry.

Turning now to international standing courts and tribunals, separate opinions and dissents are also fairly commonplace. This may be because public international law derives in part from custom and practice, and because these sources of law are not codified, decision-making is similar to the common law, and consequently the prevalence of dissenting decisions is unsurprising.

The ICJ expressly permits dissents,[74] as did its predecessor, the Permanent Court of International Justice. Dissents are frequent and in only a few cases has the ICJ rendered a judgment to which no separate or dissenting opinion was attached.[75]

---

67. *Czech Republic v. CME Czech Republic BV*, Case No T 8735-01, 87-90 (15 May 2003), 42 ILM 919 (Svea Court of Appeals).
68. *International Thunderbird Gaming Corporation v. United Mexican States*, UNCITRAL, Separate Opinion (1 December 2005) (of 135 pages); Christoph SCHREUER and Ursula KRIEBAUM, "At What Time Must Legitimate Expectations Exist" in Jacques WERNER and Arif Hyder ALI, eds., *A Liber Amicorum Thomas Wälde* (CMP Publishing 2009) p. 265.
69. In *Lemire v. Ukraine* (ICSID Case No. ARB/06/18), the substantive award was 107 pages and awarded the Claimant US$ 8.7 million, but Dr. Jurgen Voss wrote a dissenting opinion of 173 pages: Award (28 March 2011); Dissenting Opinion (1 March 2011).
70. *Impregilo S.p.A. v. Argentine Republic* (ICSID Case No. ARB/07/17), Concurring and Dissenting Opinion of Professor Brigitte STERN (21 June 2011).
71. *Ibid.*, para. 99.
72. *RSM Production Corporation v. Saint Lucia* (ICSID Case No. ARB/12/10), Decision on Saint Lucia's Request for Security for Costs (13 August 2014).
73. *Ibid.*, Assenting reasons of Dr. Gavan GRIFFITH QC, para. 18.
74. Art. 57 of the ICJ Statute provides: "If the judgment does not represent in whole or in part the unanimous opinion of the judges, any judge shall be entitled to deliver a separate opinion" and Art. 95(2) of Rules of Court of the ICJ states: "Any judge may, if he so desires, attach his individual opinion to the judgment, whether he dissents from the majority or not; a judge who wishes to record his concurrence or dissent without stating his reasons may do so in the form of a declaration. The same shall also apply to orders made by the Court." See generally, Ijaz HUSSAIN, *Dissenting and Separate Opinions at the World Court* (Kluwer Academic Publishers, 1984).

Many other international courts or tribunals take the same approach.[76] For example, the rules of the Iran-US Claims Tribunal also expressly provide for dissents.[77]

Similarly, in the ECtHR, any judge can attach a dissenting opinion to a judgment of the Court.[78] There is some evidence that the issue of dissenting opinions depends on judicial temperament and the background of judges prior to their election to the Court.[79] A study of judgments rendered between 1960 and 2006 found that national judges dissented from the majority (in favour of their home State, in judgments finding a violation) in 16 per cent of cases, whereas non-national judges voted against the majority (in favour of the State respondent) in 8 per cent of cases.[80]

The practice of the CJEU stands apart. Although dissents are not prohibited, in practice the CJEU values and protects the secrecy of the deliberations and dissents are not issued.[81] It may be significant that all the founding States of the CJEU, namely Belgium, France, Germany, Italy, Luxembourg and Netherlands, are civil law jurisdictions which predominantly prohibit or at least disfavour dissents.

Similarly, at the WTO, while published dissents are allowed under the rules, they were initially uncommon,[82] but are becoming more frequent.[83]

Thus, at the international level, practice varies, but in general there is a tendency for separate dissenting opinions to be permitted and many are issued.

From this review, it does not appear that there is a great difference between international *ad hoc* party-appointed ISDS tribunals and standing courts in respect of the ability and frequency of dissents.

75. ICJ, *The International Court of Justice: A Handbook* (ICJ 2013) p. 74.
76. See generally, Gleider HERNÁNDEZ, *The International Court of Justice and the Judicial Function* (OUP 2014) p. 112.
77. Rules of Procedure, Art. 32(3) states that "[a]ny arbitrator may request that his dissenting vote or his dissenting vote and the reasons therefore be recorded". Notably, the UNCITRAL Rules which were adopted for the Claims Tribunal did not contain any provision for dissenting opinions and were amended to allow dissenting and concurring opinions.
78. Rule 74 of the Rules of the ECtHR provides that judges are "entitled to annex to the judgment either a separate opinion, concurring with or dissenting from that judgment, or a bare statement of dissent".
79. See Robin WHITE and Iris BOUSSIAKOU, "Separate Opinions in the European Court of Human Rights", 1 Human Rights Law Review (2009, no. 9) pp. 37, 46 citing Fred J. BRUINSMA, "Judicial Identities in the European Court of Human Rights" in A VAN HOEK, ed., *Multilevel Governance in Enforcement and Adjudication* (Intersentia, Antwerp 2006) p. 203; Fred J. BRUINSMA, "The Room at the Top: Separate Opinions in the Grand Chamber of the ECHR (1998-2006)", Ancilla Juris (2008) p. 32; Nina-Louisa AROLD, *The Legal Culture of the European Court of Human Rights* (Brill 2007).
80. EP Report, supra fn. 58, para. 1.2.3 citing E. VOETEN, supra fn. 50 and M. KUIJER, "Voting Behaviour and National Bias in the European Court of Human Rights and the International Court of Justice", 10 Leiden J. of Int'l Law (1997, no. 1) p. 49.
81. EP report, supra fn. 58, pp.33-38.
82. See, e.g., Meredith Kolsky LEWIS, "The Lack of Dissent in WTO Dispute Settlement: Is There a "Unanimity" Problem?", 9 Stanford J. Int'l Econ. (2006) p. 895, available at: <http://law.bepress.com/cgi/viewcontent.cgi?article=6124&context=expresso>.
83. More recently by LEWIS, see her blog at: <https://worldtradelaw.typepad.com/ielpblog/2010/06/a-debate-on-wto-dissents-merediths-opening-post.html>.

VI. COSTS OF DISAGREEING

We now consider the personal ramifications of disagreeing (referred to as the economic cost) and whether this may be different between party-appointed tribunals and standing courts, again viewed from the perspective of dissents.

The analysis of arbitral behaviour from an economic perspective aims at explaining or predicting the behaviour of arbitrators in their decision-making process, based on the assumption that they are rational actors. While it is often the case that economics is associated with money or finances, this economic analysis does not focus on money, but rather on the costs and benefits of the choices that an individual considers. In our discussion here, the analysis focuses on the costs and benefits of an arbitrator's decision whether or not to dissent.

When analyzed from an economic lens, arbitrators and judges incur two types of costs during the decision-making process – internal and external. The internal costs are incurred by all the members of the tribunal/court who have to adopt a collective decision. The external costs are those incurred by an arbitrator/judge who disagrees with the other members of the tribunal/court but finally gives in and agrees with the others. A unanimity rule has the largest internal costs, because the arbitrators/judges must agree on a decision. A majority rule, by contrast, has larger external costs because each arbitrator/judge must decide whether to form a united front or break from it and issue a dissenting opinion. The majority rule may mean that some arbitrators/judges strive less hard to reach a unanimous decision or to persuade the third (or more) arbitrator/judge of their views, safe in the knowledge that a majority is all that is required. However, since dissents are optional, it may well be that the dynamic within the tribunal or the arbitrators' wish to maintain collegiality, causes the majority to moderate the award in order to satisfy the dissenting arbitrator, so that she/he does not write a dissenting opinion.

During the deliberations each arbitrator/judge has to weigh the costs and benefits that her or his decision may engender.[84] From an economic perspective, since writing a dissenting opinion is a cost, an arbitrator who wishes to dissent will do so only if she/he expects the benefits from writing the dissent will offset the costs. However, the costs of a dissent are not imposed on the dissenting arbitrator only. When the dissenting opinion criticizes the majority, the arbitrator who is assigned to write the majority opinion will have to bear the cost of reviewing the minority opinion and addressing the criticism. In addition to the effort and time imposed on the arbitrator/judge assigned to write the majority opinion, there may also be reputational costs, especially when the dissenter criticizes the majority severely.[85] If the costs of dissent for the majority exceed the benefits of ruling only in majority, they may give way.[86]

There are also collegiality costs that may be imposed on the arbitrators/judges. These costs may be different in arbitration tribunals and in standing courts, and between

84. Stephen J. CHOI and G. Mitu GULATI, "Trading Votes for Reasoning: Covering in Judicial Opinions", 81 S. Cal. L. Rev. (2008) pp. 735, 746-747.
85. Lee EPSTEIN, William M. LANDES and Richard A. POSNER, "Why (and When) Judges Dissent: A Theoretical and Empirical Analysis", 3 J. Legal Analysis (2011) pp. 101, 116.
86. Richard A. POSNER, *How Judges Think* (Harv. Univ. Press 2008) p. 33.

established arbitrators and newcomers. Arbitrators are selected by the parties to decide a specific dispute. In investment arbitration, there is a small group of elite arbitrators who are repeatedly appointed, but there are also many newcomers or arbitrators with some but fewer appointments, so it is uncommon for tribunals to be composed of the exact same three arbitrators, albeit it is relatively common for two arbitrators to both be appointed in more than one arbitration. Judges in a standing court are very likely to sit together on several cases. There may be a cost in terms of the relationship between the arbitrators/judges in future cases, and a dissenter may need to take into account the possibility of wanting to persuade the other arbitrators/judges in another case.

The possibility of future appointments may have a conscious or unconscious effect, to the extent that the dissenter may want it known that she/he has a certain view of a particular subject.[87] This may be less of a cost for judges in a standing court, but they too may be thinking of the renewal of their appointment.

VII. CONCLUSION

Widespread criticism of the current system of ISDS is very likely to result in the EU establishing a standing court for its investment treaties, with the potential for UNCTAD/UNCITRAL to recommend a court with global jurisdiction. There is legitimate concern that the judges appointed to such PMIC, following a selection process established by the State parties, will have a homogeneity and predisposition towards the State respondents. This homogeneity may lead to groupthink and an unwillingness publicly to disagree. It is hoped that the individuals appointed will be sufficiently diverse and after constructive debate feel able to publish a dissenting opinion where appropriate, without there being a disadvantageous cost either to the minority or majority. Investment treaties are intended to promote investment and for this to be achieved there must continue to be transparent debate and a balancing of the interests of both investors and States.

87. Daphna KAPELIUK, "The Repeat Appointment Factor: Explaining Decision Patterns of Elite Investment Arbitrators", 96 Cornell L. Rev. (2010) pp. 48, 58.

Arbitration Challenged Part II

The Realities of Arbitration Economics: Who Gets to Play, and What Are the Implications?

Costs in International Arbitration: Navigating Through the Devil's Sea

Mohamed S. Abdel Wahab[*]

TABLE OF CONTENTS PAGE

I. PROLOGUE: DECONSTRUCTING COSTS AND THE ECONOMIC DYNAMICS OF INTERNATIONAL ARBITRATION

It is an undying academic myth of international arbitration that arbitration is an inexpensive mechanism for dispute resolution. This is diametrically opposed to the general positive aspiration regarding costs in international arbitration, as shared by several authors and expressed in court decisions,[1] that is: "the underlying reason many parties choose arbitration is the relative speed, lower cost, and greater efficiency of the process", as stated by the Drafting Committee of the 2000 Revised Uniform Arbitration Act.[2]

More recently, the reality of the high costs of international arbitration led to significant criticism(s) of the system at large.[3] Users of international arbitration often express their concerns about costs and this was affirmed by the Queen Mary University of London (QMUL) 2013 International Arbitration Survey stating that "many corporations continue to express concerns over costs and delays in arbitration proceedings".[4] The said Survey adds that "[f]or respondents who considered arbitration not to be well suited to their industry, costs and delay were cited as the main reasons

---

* Chair of Private International Law and Professor of Dispute Resolution, Cairo University; Founding Partner and head of International Arbitration, Construction and Oil & Gas, Zulficar Law & Partners Law Firm; Vice-President, ICC International Court of Arbitration. The views expressed by the author in this article are his own and are not attributed to any institution with which he is affiliated.

1. See G. BORN, *International Commercial Arbitration* (Kluwer Law International 2014) p. 86, fn. 595.
2. See Prefatory Note on the Revised Uniform Arbitration Act, 2000, p. 2.
3. See, e.g., N. BLACKABY, et al., *Redfern and Hunter on International Arbitration* (Oxford University Press 2015) p. 36; See also G. BORN, *International Commercial Arbitration* (Kluwer Law International 2014); See also M. BÜHLER, "Awarding Costs in International Commercial Arbitration: An Overview", 22 ASA Bull. (2004, issue 2) p. 249.
4. See Queen Mary, University of London, *2013 International Arbitration Survey: Corporate Choices in International Arbitration: Industry Perspectives,* p. 5.

more than any other factors".[5] These concerns were further reiterated in the QMUL 2015 International Arbitration Survey stating that "[w]e also asked respondents what they perceived as the worst characteristics of international arbitration. 'Cost' was by far the most complained of characteristic."[6] Most recently, the QMUL 2018 International Arbitration Survey affirmed that "'cost' is yet again the most selected option, and by a significant margin" and "continues to be seen as arbitration's worst feature".[7]

With the heightened cost-related complaints from the users of the international arbitration system, it appears that the increase in costs is a composite result of two main factors. The *first* being the fact that the parties bear in arbitral proceedings significant costs that they do not normally bear in court proceedings. These costs are mainly the fees and expenses of the arbitrators, the administrative fees of the arbitral institution (in the case of institutional arbitration), the fees and costs of counsel and experts and the costs associated with prosecuting the arbitral proceedings including costs of hearings, tribunal secretaries, transcription and interpretation services, etc. In comparing costs' segments, practitioners and scholars often submitted that tribunal and institutional costs "are usually a drop in the ocean compared with the fees and expenses of the parties' legal advisers and expert witnesses".[8] It is these legal fees and costs that constitute the *second* and most important factor contributing to increased costs in international arbitration. Several scholars and practitioners have alluded to and highlighted the high costs involved in arbitration,[9] and even submitted that such costs are substantial "not only in absolute terms but also compared to the amount in dispute".[10]

Accordingly, it is not unbeknownst to parties that they shall be incurring *substantial* costs in international arbitration. Neil Kaplan affirmed that "[j]oint claims for costs totaling $ 30-50 million are not uncommon",[11] and that he had to deal with costs claims totaling over $ 75 million.[12] This is just an illustration of the prohibitively high costs associated with arbitral proceedings.

5. *Ibid.*
6. See Queen Mary, University London, *2015 International Arbitration Survey: Improvements and Innovations in International Arbitration*, p. 7.
7. See Queen Mary, University London, *2018 International Arbitration Survey: Improvements and Innovations in International Arbitration*, pp. 2, 6 and 7.
8. See N. BLACKABY, et al., *Redfern and Hunter on International Arbitration* (Oxford University Press, 2015) p. 36.
9. See, e.g., *Ibid*; See also J. GOTANDA, "Attorneys' Fees Agonistes: The Implications of Inconsistency in the Awarding of Fees and Costs in International Arbitrations" in Miguel Ángel FERNÁNDEZ-BALLESTEROS and David ARIAS, eds. (Wolters Kluwer España 2010) p. 540; See also M. BÜHLER, "Awarding Costs in International Commercial Arbitration: An Overview", 22 ASA Bull. (2004, issue 2) p. 249.
10. See M. BÜLER, "Awarding Costs in International Commercial Arbitration: An Overview", 22 ASA Bull. (2004, issue 2) p. 249.
11. See N. KAPLAN, "Decision on Costs – A 'Mind Field' for Arbitrators and Uncertainty for Participants", Harbour Lecture (19 October 2016).
12. *Ibid.*

It is this aspect of prohibitively high costs that may deter the parties from agreeing and commencing arbitral proceedings that they may not afford to fund,[13] which, in turn, creates an issue of access to justice.[14]

Conversely, it may be argued that despite the significance of costs, the parties may, nonetheless, accept to bear such costs on the premise that arbitration offers a high quality and "one stop shop" resolution of highly contentious and high-value complex disputes.[15] In other words, even though international arbitration is a costly process, users, when deciding to bear the high costs of arbitral proceedings, take into account the nature of their dispute(s), the desirability of resolving their disputes by individuals of their choice, and the legitimate expectation to have their dispute determined by a well-reasoned and final decision.

However, it is submitted that even if the issue is not as bleak as it sounds, the high costs of international arbitration do ring a bell and serve as a whistle-blower to warn the community of the deterring impact of costs on the future development of international arbitration.

Notwithstanding the view that arbitration users may grudgingly accept the high costs of international arbitration, it is undisputable that they will not be willing to forego the predictability of the decision on costs.[16] In other words, "they often seek advice on how much the arbitration is going to cost them if they lose and whether they will recover their costs if they win. A quick answer to this question may be: "generally, the loser pays", but this statement does little to dispel the *flou artistique* which can sometimes be observed in arbitral practice on costs."[17]

In fact, the added layer of complexity with respect to high costs stems from the fact that arbitral practice reveals that the awarding of costs in international arbitration is "often arbitrary and unpredictable".[18] Thus, the parties would be unable to predict either whether the arbitral tribunal would order a party to incur all or part of costs, or whether and to what extent certain categories of costs would be recoverable.[19]

---

13. See N. KAPLAN, "Decision on Costs – A 'Mind Field' for Arbitrators and Uncertainty for Participants", Harbour Lecture (19 October 2016); See also P. NOWACZYK and K. CZECH, "Rethinking Costs and Costs Awards in International Arbitration: A Call for Less Criticism of Arbitration Costs, But Improvement of Costs Allocation Practices", 33 ASA Bull. (2015, issue 3) (Kluwer Law International 2015) pp. 494-495.
14. *Ibid.*
15. See N. BLACKABY, et al., *Redfern and Hunter on International Arbitration* (Oxford University Press 2015) p. 37.
16. See P. NOWACZYK and K. CZECH, "Rethinking Costs and Costs Awards in International Arbitration: A Call for Less Criticism of Arbitration Costs, but Improvement of Costs Allocation Practices", 33 ASA Bull. (2015, issue 3) p. 496.
17. See M. BÜHLER, "Awarding Costs in International Commercial Arbitration: An Overview", 22 ASA Bull. (2004, issue 2) p. 249.
18. See J. GOTANDA, "Bringing Efficiency to the Awarding of Fees and Costs in International Arbitrations", cited in S. GREENBERG, "Chapter II: The Arbitrator and the Arbitration Procedure, Law Applicable to Costs Claims in International Arbitration: Why Does It Matter?" in Christian KLAUSEGGER, Peter KLEIN, et al., eds., *Austrian Yearbook on International Arbitration, 2015*, p. 176.
19. See M. BÜHLER, "Awarding Costs in International Commercial Arbitration: An Overview", 22 ASA Bull. (2004, issue 2) p. 249.

Thus, the compounded effect of the costs of international arbitration being high and unpredictable as to their allocation by arbitral tribunals creates two major challenges: "First, arbitrary awards undermine the legitimacy of the dispute resolution system. Second, the lack of predictability may hinder parties from being able to settle the dispute and could rob arbitration of its efficiency."[20]

Against this background, the present article aims at providing an overview of certain intricate issues of costs in international arbitration as well as scrutinizing the legal principles and norms governing costs. In light of this, it is important to commence by identifying the categories of costs that may be claimed or recoverable in international arbitration (II). Thereafter, the process of the awarding of and allocating costs in international arbitration should be examined (III). Subsequently, the author shall shed light on the major differences between national jurisdictions regarding the awarding of costs (IV), before considering some solutions to cost-related challenges. The author will then conclude with some recommendations (V).

II. CATEGORIES OF COSTS IN INTERNATIONAL ARBITRATION

In international arbitration, costs are usually classified into two main categories: *Procedural Costs or Costs of the Arbitration* (*1*) and *Costs of the Parties* (*2*).[21] Each category includes different types of costs whose recoverability is controversial as discussed herein.

The issue is that, as shall be discussed further below, whilst arbitral tribunals often hold that the losing party shall pay the costs incurred by the successful party in relation to the arbitral proceedings, it is not anomalous that arbitral tribunals may conversely hold that each party shall bear all its costs and accordingly none of the categories of costs will be recovered, which could be frustrating to the parties and contrary to their legitimate expectations, absent an agreement to that effect.

It is this controversy that affects more the "*Costs of the Parties*" category rather than the "*Procedural Costs*" as will be discussed. It has been submitted that the "*Costs of the Parties*" "make up the bulk (83% on average) of the overall costs of the proceedings" as reported by the 2015 International Chamber of Commerce (ICC) Commission Report on Costs.[22]

20. See J. GOTANDA, "Attorneys' Fees Agonistes: The Implications of Inconsistency in the Awarding of Fees and Costs in International Arbitrations" in Miguel ÁNGEL FERNÁNDEZ-BALLESTEROS and David ARIAS, eds., *Liber Amicorum Bernardo Cremades* (Wolters Kluwer España, 2010) p. 540.
21. See, e.g., N. BLACKABY, et al., *Redfern and Hunter on International Arbitration* (Oxford University Press 2015) pp. 532-533; See also M. BÜHLER, "Awarding Costs in International Commercial Arbitration: An Overview", 22 ASA Bull. (2004, issue 2) p. 250; See also J. LEW, L. MISTELIS, and S. KRÖLL, *Comparative International Commercial Arbitration* (Kluwer Law International 2003) p. 653.
22. See "ICC Commission Report: Decisions on Costs in International Arbitration" (2015) p. 3.

1. *Procedural Costs or Costs of the Arbitration*

The "*Costs of the Arbitration*"[23] – also referred to as the "*Procedural Costs*"[24] – include: (i) the fees of the arbitrators; (ii) the travel and others expenses incurred by the arbitrators;[25] (iii) the administrative fees of the arbitral institution, if any; (iv) the fees and expenses of any tribunal secretary; (v) the fees and expenses of any experts appointed by the arbitrators; and (vi) the expenses of related logistics such as hiring rooms for hearings and meetings, any administrative services related to the arbitration, such as transcription, interpretation and translation.

These costs are, in principle, recoverable in arbitration, unless the arbitral tribunal determines otherwise. The fees and expenses of arbitrators as well as institutional fees are normally fixed according to the applicable arbitration rules in institutional arbitration or set pursuant to an agreement between the parties and the arbitral tribunal in *ad hoc* arbitration.[26] Most legal systems allow the full recovery of these costs,[27] and it is difficult to imagine that the arbitral tribunal would consider the costs paid for tribunal-appointed experts are unreasonable,[28] although the parties may consider, in certain situations, such costs to be unreasonable and undesired, especially if the tribunal exercised its authority according to the applicable procedural rules and appointed experts contrary to the parties' expectations and desire for reasons that the arbitral tribunal considered legitimate and necessary for the proper determination of the dispute.[29]

23. See N. BLACKABY, et al., *Redfern and Hunter on International Arbitration* (Oxford University Press 2015) pp. 532-533; See also J. POWER and C. KONRAD, "Chapter IV: The Award – Costs in International Commercial Arbitration – A Comparative Overview of Civil and Common Law Doctrines" in Christian KLAUSEGGER, Peter KLEIN, et al., eds., *Austrian Arbitration Yearbook 2007*, p. 262; See also J. LEW, L. MISTELIS, and S. KRÖLL, *Comparative International Commercial Arbitration* (Kluwer Law International 2003) p. 653.
24. See M. BÜHLER, "Awarding Costs in International Commercial Arbitration: An Overview", 22 ASA Bull. (2004, issue 2) p. 250.
25. One specific issue that is often unaddressed or overlooked with respect to expenses incurred by the arbitral tribunal is that the parties' and arbitrators' expectations should be aligned regarding the type and class of travel, level of accommodation and any other costs incurred by the arbitrators.
26. See J. WAINCYMER, *Procedure and Evidence in International Arbitration* (Kluwer Law International 2012) pp. 1251-1252.
27. *Ibid.*
28. See J. POWER and C. KONRAD, "Chapter IV: The Award – Costs in International Arbitration – A Comparative Overview of Civil and Common Law Doctrines: Determination of Costs" in Gerold ZEILER, Irene WELSER, et al., eds., *Austrian Arbitration Yearbook 2008*, pp. 407 and 426.
29. An experienced arbitral tribunal should always endeavour to seek and secure the parties' consensus on tribunal-appointed experts and would consult the parties on the necessity of appointing expert(s), their profile, determining their mission and its scope and the likely costs associated with such expertise, prior to rendering its order or decision on appointing the expert(s).

2. *Costs of the Parties*

The *Costs of the Parties* consist of all the costs incurred by the parties in preparing for, prosecuting and presenting their case.[30] Thus, this category of costs is in a constant state of flux and is largely variable with no clear arbitral practice or doctrinal consensus on what type of costs may fall under this category and whether all such types are recoverable or not.

By and large, this category of costs could be classified on the basis of the time/phase in which such costs are incurred or on the basis of the type of costs associated with the parties. If classified temporally, they could fall into three sub-categories: (i) *pre-arbitration costs*; (ii) *in-arbitration costs*; and (iii) *post-award costs for vacatur motions and enforcement*.

If classified on the basis of their type, they could be sub-categorized into: (*a*) *claim(s) preparation and dispute-associated costs incurred prior to the arbitral proceedings*; (*b*) *counsel's fees*; (*c*) *contingency success fees*; (*d*) *parties' own internal costs*; (*e*) *case preparation costs including costs of mock arbitration(s)*; (*f*) *third-party funding or arbitration finance costs*; (*g*) *costs for party-appointed witness(es) and experts, claims consultants and advisors*; (*h*) *costs of contemporaneous and related court proceedings*; and (*i*) *costs incurred in vacatur and/or enforcement proceedings*.

For the purpose of the present contribution, the author submits that the *type-based categorization* of parties' costs offers a better insight and a more detailed sub-classification when compared to the *phased/temporal categorization*. Thus, this section shall address the sub-classification of parties' costs on the basis of the *type-based categorization*.

a. Claim(s) preparation and dispute-associated costs incurred prior to the arbitral proceedings

This category includes all the costs that a party incurs in relation to the dispute for the preparation of its claim(s) before the commencement of the arbitral proceedings. This would include any legal opinions sought, expenses incurred for any pre-arbitration procedures such as negotiations, mediation, litigation, legal notifications, dispute boards, etc.

This first sub-category is quite challenging and the parties should be aware that being awarded such costs in arbitration is difficult for several reasons.

Firstly, absent an agreement to the contrary, arbitral tribunals may refuse to award such costs on the ground that they do not pertain to the arbitral proceedings and are "*premature*".[31]

Secondly, such costs may be considered unforeseen, unreasonable and excessive.[32]

Thirdly, the non-recoverability of the said costs may be a function of the terms of the arbitral rules.[33] For instance, Art. 38 of the 2017 ICC Rules defines the parties' costs as

30. See, e.g., M. BÜHLER, "Awarding Costs in International Commercial Arbitration: An Overview", 22 ASA Bull. (2004, issue 2) p. 250.
31. See J. WAINCYMER, *Procedure and Evidence in International Arbitration* (Kluwer Law International 2012) pp. 1238, 1255; See also M. BÜHLER, "Awarding Costs in International Commercial Arbitration: An Overview", 22 ASA Bull. (2004, issue 2) pp. 268-269.
32. See J. WAINCYMER, *Procedure and Evidence in International Arbitration* (Kluwer Law International 2012) p. 1238.
33. *Ibid.*

"the reasonable legal and other costs incurred by the parties *for the arbitration*". Accordingly, costs which are not directly pertinent for "the arbitration" may not be recoverable.

Finally, since these costs are incurred before the commencement of the arbitral proceedings, there is always an issue of the arbitral tribunal's jurisdiction and powers to consider and award such costs.[34]

By and large, whilst this sub-category is indeed problematic, it is submitted that said sub-category is not barred outright, but must be considered on a case-by-case basis. This sub-category ought to be subject to a three-dimensional test of: (a) *consent and foreseeability*; (b) *direct proximity to the arbitral proceedings*; and (c) *reasonableness*. If collectively fulfilled, such costs may be claimed and awarded.

By way of illustration, if the *parties are in agreement* that such costs can be claimed or said costs are indeed claimed by all parties, this can offer the basic consent to confer on the arbitral tribunal the authority and jurisdiction to consider such costs.

With respect to the *foreseeability and proximity to the arbitration*, it is submitted that in certain cases requisite conditions precedent must be fulfilled prior to resorting to arbitration, such as resorting to mediation, expert determination, negotiations and/or dispute board proceedings, etc. Thus, the failure to fulfill such clear conditions precedent could lead to the inadmissibility of the claims on account of the arbitration proceedings being prematurely commenced. If so, then it is arguable that the costs directly associated with the fulfillment of the conditions precedent to resorting to arbitration would be in direct proximity with, and are objectively foreseeable for the purpose of, the arbitral proceedings.

With respect to reasonableness, this offers an added balancing factor in cases where such pre-arbitration costs fulfill the requirements of consent, foreseeability and proximity. In essence, arbitral tribunals should also consider whether such inseparably associated foreseeable costs are reasonable in *content* and *quantum* before awarding same, noting that not every incurred cost is recoverable. Accordingly, if such costs are exaggerated, inflated or unreasonable in any way, they ought to be disregarded. In considering whether to award or decline to award these costs, arbitral tribunals should consider the pertinent factual matrix, the parties' expectations and the conduct of the parties and the quantitative proximity of the amounts claimed by all parties.

b. Counsel's fees

The counsel's fees constitute the most significant type or part of party-related costs.[35] Despite the importance of such costs, "[i]t is also the category where legal families generally differ the most, some tribunals are more reluctant to award counsel's fees than arbitration fees and expenses".[36] However, as will be discussed further below, the trend in international arbitration is that the counsel's fees are recoverable and this trend is also existent in international investment arbitration.[37] As is the case with all categories of

34. *Ibid.*
35. *Ibid.*, p. 1239.
36. *Ibid.*
37. See infra Sect. III.*3*.

costs, the indispensable requisite is to ascertain that the arbitral tribunal has the jurisdiction and the power to consider, allocate and award costs.

In this specific context, it is important to note that the recoverable counsel's fees should be limited to reasonable fees.[38] In other words, the main limitation to the recovery of counsel's fees is the test of reasonableness which should be objectively applied by the arbitral tribunal as discussed further below.[39]

In applying the test of reasonableness on counsel's fees, arbitral tribunals usually take into account some relevant factors, such as the *complexity of the case*, *the amount in the dispute*,[40] and also *counsel stature and conduct throughout the proceedings*. They may also take into account the awards of costs rendered in similar circumstances.[41]

In the same vein, it is argued that the arbitral tribunal shall reduce counsel's fees to equate the fees of a "hypothetical counsel capable of conducting the particular case".[42] However, it is too difficult to identify what is the normal fee in an international dispute given that "party representation costs may vary widely because of a number of reasons, including the vastly different conditions under which lawyers work around the world and the varying ability of lawyers used to their domestic civil procedure to adapt to the often unfamiliar ways of international commercial arbitration".[43]

In addition, in assessing the reasonableness of counsel's fees, arbitral tribunals may also take into consideration and be guided by the fees and practices in counsel's jurisdiction.[44] This presupposes the existence of comparable counsel within said jurisdiction. In other words, this is not simply a jurisdictional survey, but rather the arbitral tribunal must be able to identify comparable counsel with the requisite stature, expertise, experience, standing and similar fee structures, which is a daunting exercise that may not be easily and readily possible to implement.

In this context, the easier approach that arbitral tribunals usually resort to is to compare the legal costs of each party in order to assess the reasonableness of the claimed legal costs.[45] However, this presupposes that counsel for both parties are of comparable standing. Accordingly, if the legal costs claimed by the successful party are close to those incurred by the losing party, they are in principle held reasonable. Nevertheless, the

---

38. See M. BÜHLER, "Awarding Costs in International Commercial Arbitration: An Overview", 22 ASA Bull. (2004, issue 2) p. 272; See also J. WAINCYMER, *Procedure and Evidence in International Arbitration* (Kluwer Law International 2012) p. 1239.
39. See infra Sect. III.*2.c*.
40. See M. BÜHLER, "Awarding Costs in International Commercial Arbitration: An Overview", 22 ASA Bull. (2004, issue 2) p. 273; See also J. WAINCYMER, *Procedure and Evidence in International Arbitration* (Kluwer Law International 2012) p. 1239.
41. See J. WAINCYMER, *Procedure and Evidence in International Arbitration* (Kluwer Law International 2012) p. 1239.
42. See Michael O'REILLY, "Rethinking Costs in Commercial Arbitration", cited in M. BÜHLER, "Awarding Costs in International Commercial Arbitration: An Overview", 22 ASA Bull. (2004, issue 2) p. 273.
43. See Pierre A. KARRER and Marcus DESAX, "Security for Costs in International Arbitration: Why, When, and What If...", cited in M. BÜHLER, "Awarding Costs in International Commercial Arbitration: An Overview", 22 ASA Bull. (2004, issue 2) p. 273.
44. See M. BÜHLER, "Awarding Costs in International Commercial Arbitration: An Overview", 22 ASA Bull. (2004, issue 2) p. 272.
45. *Ibid.*, p. 273.

legal costs incurred by a party may still be considered reasonable even though they are higher than those incurred by the other party because depending on the circumstances of the particular case a party may be forced to incur more costs.[46]

Notwithstanding the above, nothing prevents arbitral tribunals from holding that the legal costs claimed are unreasonable. In assessing the reasonableness and unreasonableness, a quantitative analysis is usually undertaken since a qualitative one is more difficult to establish and more sensitive to adopt. In certain cases, arbitral tribunals have held that the claimed legal costs are unreasonable based on the fact that the legal costs claimed by the successful party were four times higher than those paid by the losing party.[47] Similarly, in another case, three firms had been involved in favor of the successful party and so the arbitral tribunal reduced the recoverable costs.[48]

c. *Contingency success fees*

At the outset, whilst contingency success fees may form part of counsel legal fees and so should have been addressed as part of counsel fees under sub-section (*b*) above, owing to the intricate legal issues pertaining to contingency fees and the fact that they do not form a standard part of counsel fees, they are addressed herein as a separate type of cost.

Contingency fees are the fees paid by a party to its counsel in case of winning the case, depending on their agreed definition of the winning threshold. The typical agreement of contingency fees is the success fee agreement under which the counsel's fees vary depending on the outcome of the case.

The problem with the recoverability of such fees arises from the fact they are higher than the normally applicable fees. Accordingly, it is controversial whether the losing party should reasonably reimburse the successful party "that kind of a systemic trade-off not agreed to by the loser" even in the case where the "loser-pays" rule is applied.[49]

The first complication that a party claiming the recovery of contingency fees may encounter is the preliminary issue of whether the arbitral tribunal is empowered to award this as part of the costs because such fees are normally unbeknownst to the losing party and are commonly used in jurisdictions which adopt the '*each party bears its costs*' rule.[50]

On a related note, contingency success fee agreements are not globally and uniformly upheld; they are prohibited in certain jurisdictions as being in contravention of public policy or ethical rules. Accordingly, arbitral tribunals must prudently ascertain whether such fees are recoverable under the applicable governing law or not. Arbitral tribunals may refuse to award such fees if there is a credible risk that the award may be annulled or refused to be enforced, especially if the lex loci arbitri or *lex loci executionis* prohibits such fees on account of champerty.

46. *Ibid.*
47. See ICC Case No. 5008 (1992), cited in M. BÜHLER, "Awarding Costs in International Commercial Arbitration: An Overview", 22 ASA Bull. (2004, issue 2) pp. 273-274.
48. See ICC Case No. 5726 (1992), cited in M. BÜHLER, "Awarding Costs in International Commercial Arbitration: An Overview", 22 ASA Bull. (2004, issue 2) p. 274.
49. See J. WAINCYMER, *Procedure and Evidence in International Arbitration* (Kluwer Law International, 2012) pp. 1241-1242.
50. *Ibid.*, p. 1242.

Notwithstanding the above, some practitioners argue that it would be too extreme to refuse the recovery of any contingency fee.[51] From their perspective, it would be illogical and unfair to deprive a party of its right to recover counsel's fees based on the fact that such fees were dependent on the outcome of the case. However, it is worth noting that a number of authors are against the full recovery of contingency fees. If the losing party who paid its counsel on an hourly basis is held liable to pay all the contingency fees paid by the successful party, the entire cost risk of that party's counsel is shifted to the other party.[52]

In any event, if validly recoverable legally and factually, the recoverability of contingency fees should be limited to reasonable fees.[53] In the same vein, some practitioners are of the opinion that the recoverable contingency fees should be limited to "an amount that would have been payable on a time charge basis".[54] This would offer the needed reasonableness and would arguably be foreseeable by the losing party, who is a third party to the contingency fee arrangement between opposing party and its counsel, and so would normally not be bound by it.

d. Parties' own internal costs

The parties' own personnel are usually involved in the preparation of the case and in working closely with external counsel. Moreover, sometimes it is an internal team that represents the party and so, in such case, there is no reason to treat them differently from external counsel.

More specifically, the parties' managers and other staff usually "spend time on instructing their legal representatives, assisting them with regard to factual issues, attending the hearing, etc.".[55] Accordingly, the question whether the parties may request the recovery of the costs for such executive time arises.

As to costs for internal personnel and executive time, arbitral tribunals understandably seem to be reluctant to order the losing party to reimburse such costs. This is based on the "outdated view that before a court, lay parties are 'not allowed anything for their time and trouble, but only for their out-of-pocket expenses'".[56, 57] Moreover, it is argued that costs for executive time are not recoverable since they are "part of the normal costs for running a business enterprise".[58]

---

51. *Ibid.*, p. 1243.
52. See M. BÜHLER, "Awarding Costs in International Commercial Arbitration: An Overview", 22 ASA Bull. (2004, issue 2) fn. 122.
53. See D. WEHRLI, "Contingency Fees/Pactum de Palmario 'Civil Law Approach'", cited in J. WAINCYMER, *Procedure and Evidence in International Arbitration* (Kluwer Law International 2012) p. 1244.
54. See M. O'REILLY, *Costs in Arbitration Proceedings*, cited in J. WAINCYMER, *Procedure and Evidence in International Arbitration* (Kluwer Law International 2012) p. 1243.
55. See M. BÜHLER, "Awarding Costs in International Commercial Arbitration: An Overview", 22 ASA Bull. (2004, issue 2) p. 274.
56. See *Jonathan Alexander Ltd v. Proctor* [1996], cited in M. BÜHLER, "Awarding Costs in International Commercial Arbitration: An Overview", 22 ASA Bull. (2004, issue 2) p. 274.
57. See M. BÜHLER, "Awarding Costs in International Commercial Arbitration: An Overview", 22 ASA Bull. (2004, issue 2) p. 274.
58. See, e.g., J. GOTANDA, *Supplemental Damages in Private International Law* (Kluwer Law International 1998); ICC Case No. 5029 (1991), stating that "arbitrations inevitably take up time

Notwithstanding the above, arbitral tribunals may exceptionally award costs for executive time, if the circumstances so warrant. Amongst the circumstances that may exceptionally warrant awarding costs for executive and internal personnel time are situations where: (a) the judicial practice at the place of the arbitration allows parties to be compensated for such costs in relation to litigation; (b) the parties' consent to the recoverability of such costs; (c) the parties have been put on reasonable notice that such costs will be claimed, are reasonably separable from the usual workplace time and are reasonably quantifiable.

In any event, the principle should remain that personnel's and executives' time form part of the costs for running the business and so is not reimbursable, unless exceptional overwhelming circumstances exist so as to warrant the recoverability of such cost as discussed herein above.

Regarding the costs for in-house counsel, there is also no consensus on the recoverability of such costs.[59] It seems that arbitral tribunals are more likely to allow the recovery of costs for external counsel than internal counsel.[60]

Conversely, a number of notable practitioners are of the opinion that in-house counsel costs should be recoverable.[61] In the same vein, the recovery of in-house counsel costs has been, in principle, accepted in a number of cases.[62] More importantly, in an ICC case, the arbitral tribunal held:

> "'There is no justification to privilege a party in terms of costs for the sole reason that it retained outside rather than in-house counsel. (...) A party must be free in allocating the work between outside counsel and its own services. A party which decides to perform most of the preparatory work for the case by its own legal and

---

of the parties themselves and their staff, but the cost of any such time is (...) not part of the legal costs of the proceedings", cited in M. BÜHLER, "Awarding Costs in International Commercial Arbitration: An Overview", 22 ASA Bull. (2004, issue 2) p. 274.

59. See J. WAINCYMER, *Procedure and Evidence in International Arbitration* (Kluwer Law International 2012) pp. 1246-1247; see also M. BÜHLER, "Awarding Costs in International Commercial Arbitration: An Overview", 22 ASA Bull. (2004, issue 2) pp. 274-275.
60. See ICC Case No.5029 (1991); ICC Case No. 6293 (1990); *Anderson Consulting Business Unit Member Firms v. Arthur Andersen Business Unit Member Firms*, ICC Case No. 9797 (2000): the sole arbitrator dismissed a US$ 15 million claim for internal employee costs with a single sentence: "The Tribunal shall not grant [respondents] their internal costs because their allocation of their employees' time and effort to the present arbitration is a decision dependent entirely on the [respondents'] discretion and therefore, these costs must be assumed by [respondents]," cited in J. WAINCYMER, *Procedure and Evidence in International Arbitration* (Kluwer Law International 2012) p. 1246 and M. BÜHLER, "Awarding Costs in International Commercial Arbitration: An Overview", 22 ASA Bull. (2004, issue 2) p. 275; See also W. CRAIG, W. PARK and J. PAULSSON, *International Chamber of Commerce Arbitration (2002)*, cited in M. BÜHLER, "Awarding Costs in International Commercial Arbitration: An Overview", 22 ASA Bull. (2004, issue 2) pp. 274-275.
61. See J. WAINCYMER, *Procedure and Evidence in International Arbitration* (Kluwer Law International 2012) p. 1247.
62. See, e.g., ICC Case No. 8787 (1997), cited in J. WAINCYMER, *Procedure and Evidence in International Arbitration* (Kluwer Law International 2012) p. 1246

> technical departments should not be placed at a disadvantage compared to one which confers all work to outside counsel and experts.'"[63]

This position has now gained increasing acceptance, both in scholarly writings[64] and in practice.[65] However, even if the recovery of in-house counsel costs is allowed, further challenges exist as to the recovery of such costs.

By contrast to external legal costs which could be easily identified and established, if properly recorded, a party may encounter difficulties in terms of identifying and evidencing in-house counsel costs, especially with respect to the nature of such costs, the persons who incurred them and the type of work performed.[66] That said, a party which is desirous to claim such costs must maintain a proper, reliable and independent record of the work performed by its in-house counsel team in order to be able to claim and recover such costs.

Similarly, the determination of the recoverable portion of such costs is by no means an easy task. On one hand, it has been argued that the principle is that "the costs allowed should not exceed the actual and direct costs suggests using the salary of the in-house lawyer, plus arguably a general overhead, as the basis for the computation".[67] On the other hand, and in light of the complications arising out this computation, it has been suggested that the costs that a party may recover for in-house counsel shall be equal to the normal fees that an external lawyer would have been paid.[68] However, there is an inherent difficulty in ascertaining what would constitute a normal fee, especially if the party resorted to in-house expertise to save costs and expenses that it now seeks to claim in the arbitration.

By and large, the recoverability of in-house counsel costs is far from settled and requires due consideration of the facto-legal circumstances of each case and the applicable legal norms at the place of arbitration and/or place of enforcement, if this matter raises issues of overriding mandatory rules or public policy principles. Nevertheless, it is submitted that the competing interests of saving costs by resorting to in-house expertise and non-discrimination between external and in-house counsel when

---

63. See ICC Case 6564 (1993), cited in M. BÜHLER, "Awarding Costs in International Commercial Arbitration: An Overview", 22 ASA Bull. (2004, issue 2) p. 275.
64. See, e.g., M. WIRTH, Art. 189 PIL and M. BÜHLER and S. Jarvin, *The Arbitration Rules of the International Chamber of Commerce*, cited in M. BÜHLER, "Awarding Costs in International Commercial Arbitration: An Overview", 22 ASA Bull. (2004, issue 2) p. 275.
65. See ICC Case No. 8786 (1997) in which the tribunal allowed the costs for in-house counsels, apparently as a matter of course; see also Yves DERAINS and Eric A. SCHWARTZ, *A Guide to the New ICC Rules of Arbitration* (Kluwer Law International 2005) who state that the allowability of costs for in-house counsel "appears to be increasingly accepted", cited in M. BÜHLER, "Awarding Costs in International Commercial Arbitration: An Overview", 22 ASA Bull. (2004, issue 2) p. 275.
66. See J. WAINCYMER, *Procedure and Evidence in International Arbitration* (Kluwer Law International 2012) p. 1247; See also M. BÜHLER, "Awarding Costs in International Commercial Arbitration: An Overview", 22 ASA Bull. (2004, issue 2) p. 275.
67. See M. BÜHLER, "Awarding Costs in International Commercial Arbitration: An Overview", 22 ASA Bull. (2004, issue 2) p. 276.
68. *Ibid.*

assessing costs must be balanced on a case-by-case basis to discern whether it is sufficiently reasonable to claim such costs or not.

e. Case preparation costs including costs of mock arbitration(s)

It is increasingly becoming common to resort to innovative techniques to best prepare for hearings and maximize the chances for prevailing in the arbitral proceedings. To that extent, parties and counsel resort to the use of technology and innovative techniques when prosecuting arbitral proceedings. This involves using technology and artificial intelligence applications such as predictive coding technology, predictive justice, document production and e-discovery software, as well as mock arbitration techniques.

Whilst it is difficult to provide an all-inclusive account of the diverse case preparation and case prosecution applications and techniques and the possible costs associated therewith, it is important to shed light on a specific type of costs: that is, costs pertaining to mock arbitrations.

Mock arbitrations are arguably a useful tool to prepare for an arbitration case as they help the parties to predict the opinion and reaction of actual arbitrators on the issues at stake.[69] This mock exercise is rooted in US litigation tradition, but its use in arbitration "is likely to grow significantly ... as those in the arbitration community become more familiar with the availability of these tools and their benefits".[70]

Whilst the proliferated use of mock arbitration tools in mega disputes remains rooted across the Atlantic in the United States, it is important to know whether a party may recover the costs of mock arbitration from the losing party. In this regard, some scholars are of the opinion that most tribunals would be reluctant to award costs for mock arbitration.[71] This is because most likely these costs will not pass the reasonableness test as a requisite for entitlement to recovery.

However, it may be argued that the costs that the successful party paid for mock arbitration are reasonable if the losing party itself resorted to mock arbitration and would have claimed same as part of its costs.[72] Nevertheless, in the case where the successful party is the only party who used mock arbitration "and especially if it had deeper pockets", arbitrators will most likely refuse the recovery of the costs incurred in relation to this mock arbitration.[73]

As the practice of recoverability of mock arbitration costs is not yet established, the pertinent question is whether these costs are claimed in full transparency under a clear and specific heading for costs, or whether they are claimed as part of case preparation fees by counsel. In as much as such costs require careful consideration and review as to the legality and reasonableness of claiming them, it is submitted that transparency considerations militate against claiming such costs as part of counsel fees, without

69. See E. SUSSMAN, "Improving Your Arbitration Presentation with a Mock Arbitration", New York Dispute Resolution Lawyer (2012); See also N. KAPLAN and O. BOLTENKO, *A Secret Tool for Winning an Arbitration Case* (Hong Kong International Arbitration Centre 2015) p. 118.
70. See E. SUSSMAN, , "Improving Your Arbitration Presentation with a Mock Arbitration", New York Dispute Resolution Lawyer (2012)
71. See N. KAPLAN and O. BOLTENKO, *A Secret Tool for Winning an Arbitration Case* (Hong Kong International Arbitration Centre 2015) p. 120.
72. *Ibid.*
73. *Ibid.*

expressly indicating that they pertain to mock arbitration. The author submits that the only excused case where such costs could be claimed as part of counsel fees without expressly referring to such costs as mock-arbitration-related is when counsel does not resort to external support and/or does not outsource the process of mock arbitration.

f. Third-party funding or arbitration finance costs

Third-party funding has rocked the world of international arbitration and the implications of arbitration finance extend to all aspects of the arbitration process and costs are no exception.

Whilst the issue of costs in the context of third-party funding arrangements, which are newly branded in practice as '*arbitration finance*' arrangements, are subject to a separate contribution for a different author, it seems in order to briefly shed light on this facet of party costs as a matter of principle.

Over the past few years, third-party funding or arbitration finance has emerged as a new practice in international arbitration. It gained acceptance at an accelerated pace in different jurisdictions, notably in England and in the United States.[74] Other jurisdictions such as Australia, Hong Kong and Singapore, etc. followed. In a nutshell, third-party funding or arbitration finance is "a financing method in which an entity that is not a party to a particular dispute funds another party's legal fees or pays an order, award, or judgment rendered against that party, or both".[75]

The initial selling point for third-party funding arrangements was that they promote access to justice by helping a party to present its claim(s) or defense(s).[76] Basically, a third-party funding agreement offers a party that faces financial distress the necessary funds to access justice. In other words, if a party cannot afford to present its claim or defense because of its limited financial resources, it may resort to a third-party funding agreement in order to overcome this financial status and be able to present its claim or defense.[77]

However, theory and practice have shown that third-party funding and arbitration finance are not limited to impecunious parties; they are frequently used by financially viable parties in order to share the risk and maintain their liquidity.[78]

---

74. See, e.g., Ch. BOGART, "Chapter 4. Overview of Arbitration Finance" in Bernardo M. CREMADES SANZ-PASTOR and Antonias DIMOLITSA, eds., *Third-Party Funding in International Arbitration* (Kluwer International Law 2013) p. 55; See also M. STOYANOV and O. OWCZAREK, "Third-Party Funding in International Arbitration: Is It Time for Some Soft Rules?", 2 BCDR International Arbitration Review (2015, issue 1) pp. 171-199, p. 173.
75. See L.B. NIEUWVELD and V. SHANNON, *Third-Party Funding in International Arbitration* (Kluwer Law International 2017) p. 1.
76. See, e.g., J. VON GOELER, *Third-Party Funding in International Arbitration and Its Impact on Procedure* (Kluwer Law International 2016) p. 82; See also B. CREMADES ROMÁN, *Third Party Litigation Funding: Investing in Arbitration* (Wolters Kluwer España 2012) p.181; See also M. STOYANOV and O. OWCZAREK, "Third-Party Funding in International Arbitration: Is It Time for Some Soft Rules?", 2 BCDR International Arbitration Review (2015, issue 1) p. 172.
77. *Ibid.*
78. See J. VON GOELER, *Third-Party Funding in International Arbitration and Its Impact on Procedure* (Kluwer Law International 2016) p. 83; See also M. STOYANOV and O. OWCZAREK, "Third-Party Funding in International Arbitration: Is It Time for Some Soft Rules?", 2 BCDR International Arbitration Review (2015, issue 1) p. 172.

It is in this context that scholars have argued that the existence of a third-party funding agreement may render the arbitral proceedings more expensive.[79] This is because "defending against a funded claim will turn out more costly than defending against the claim of a financially weak claimant that uses only internal resources".[80] However, this argument is practically refuted by the fact that third-party funders are normally keen on conducting the arbitral proceedings in a cost-effective manner to ensure the best return on their investment.[81]

On the specific issue of recoverability of the third-party funder's costs, the fact remains that the costs had been paid by a third-party funder and this gives rise to the question of whether the funded party may recover these costs. A losing party may argue that the successful party is not entitled to recover the costs which have been paid by a third-party funder and not directly by the funded party.

In reference to the arbitration rules in this regard, many arbitration provisions require that the costs have been "incurred"[82] or "directly incurred"[83] by the party claiming them. While, at first sight, these provisions seem to bar the recovery of the costs paid by a third-party funder, the terms used in these provisions "are broad enough to encompass" the said costs.[84]

Arbitral tribunals have set certain requirements in order to recover costs paid by a third-party funder.[85] For instance, in the *Supplier v. First distributor, Second distributor* case and the *Price Waterhouse SARL and PW Conseil SARL v. Pricewaterhouse Coopers International Limited* case, the arbitral tribunals affirmed that, in order to recover the legal costs incurred by a third-party funder, it is required that the funded party was contractually engaged towards its counsel to pay these costs.[86]

Furthermore, in the *Supplier v. First distributor, Second distributor* case and the *Quasar de Valores v. the Russian Federation* case, the arbitral tribunals affirmed that the funded party should be legally bound to reimburse to the third-party funder the costs claimed.[87]

However, it may be argued that, according to the principle of privity of contractual obligations, the relationship between the funded party and the third-party funder "should not relieve the opposing party from its responsibility to pay costs".[88] Nonetheless, "it can

79. See J. VON GOELER, *Third-Party Funding in International Arbitration and Its Impact on Procedure* (Kluwer Law International 2016) p. 345; See also M. STOYANOV and O. OWCZAREK, "Third-Party Funding in International Arbitration: Is It Time for Some Soft Rules?", 2 BCDR International Arbitration Review (2015, issue 1) p. 191.
80. See J. VON GOELER, *Third-Party Funding in International Arbitration and Its Impact on Procedure* (Kluwer Law International 2016) p. 345.
81. See M. STOYANOV and O. OWCZAREK, "Third-Party Funding in International Arbitration: Is It Time for Some Soft Rules?", 2 BCDR International Arbitration Review (2015, issue 1) p. 191.
82. See, e.g., Art. 38(1) ICC Rules; Art. (40)(2)(e) of UNCITRAL Rules; Art. 50(2) China International Economic and Trade Arbitration Commission (CIETAC) Rules.
83. See, e.g., Art. 44(e) Australian Centre for International Commercial Arbitration (ACICA) Rules.
84. See J. VON GOELER, *Third-Party Funding in International Arbitration and Its Impact on Procedure* (Kluwer Law International 2016) p. 380.
85. *Ibid.*, pp. 380-386.
86. *Ibid.*, p. 383.
87. *Ibid.*, pp. 383-384.
88. *Ibid.*, p. 384.

be asked why the opposing party should still have to pay if the funder decided to give the funded party a 'total free ride' in the arbitration".[89]

Based on the foregoing, even if the above-mentioned decisions are not binding, "[t]he preferable view is that an arbitral tribunal which decides to allocate costs based on the outcome of the case should generally require that the prevailing (funded) party has at least incurred a liability in return for the funding of these costs".[90]

On this specific issue of recoverability, it has been argued that while the funded party may recover the costs that have been paid by the funder, it is debatable whether it may recover the costs payable to the third-party funder as compensation. Accordingly, a distinction should be made between the "*Actual Legal Expenses*" and the "*Funder's Return*".[91]

At the outset, it is worth noting that this funder's return or compensation could take many forms, "such as an additional hourly fee payable to counsel (conditional fee arrangements), a return calculated as a percentage of the recovery payable to a litigation funder or contingency fee lawyer, or a contingent insurance premium (after-the-event insurance)".[92]

While responding to the question of whether the funded party may recover the funder's return, it should be noted that there are two interests at stake: the funded party has a vested interest to recover the success fees payable to the funder according to the full indemnity principle, and the duty of fairness requires to take into consideration the losing party's interest to avoid bearing fees exceeding the reasonable legal costs.[93]

Accordingly, the majority of scholars are of the opinion that the funded party may not recover the funder's return.[94] All the costs that the funded party is obliged to pay only in case of success shall not be recoverable since "a party who knows that it need not pay procedural costs if it loses should also not enjoy the benefit of recovering costs if it wins".[95]

It has also been argued that, in any event, the successful party shall not recover more or less than the costs that have been reasonably incurred in preparing and presenting the case.[96] In this context, it has been said that "[i]f the funder's success portion is deemed recoverable, overcompensation would result".[97]

---

89. *Ibid.*
90. *Ibid.*, p. 385.
91. *Ibid.*, p. 387.
92. *Ibid.*, p. 388.
93. *Ibid.*
94. See authors cited in J. VON GOELER, *Third-Party Funding in International Arbitration and Its Impact on Procedure* (Kluwer Law International 2016) fn. 108 (RONEY and VON DER WEID in *New Developments in International Commercial Arbitration* (2013); WEHRLI, 26 ASA Bull. (2008); O'REILLY, *Costs in Arbitration Proceedings*; HANOTIAU, *Evaluation of Damages*; WAINCYMER, *Procedure and Evidence in International Arbitration*; BÜHLER, 22 ASA Bull. (2004); JÄGER, *Reimbursement for Attorney's Fees*).
95. See J. VON GOELER, *Third-Party Funding in International Arbitration and Its Impact on Procedure* (Kluwer Law International 2016) p. 380.
96. *Ibid.*, p. 393.
97. *Ibid.*

g. Costs for party-appointed witness(es) and experts, claims consultants and advisors

During the arbitral proceedings, the parties may incur fees and expenses of witnesses, experts, consultants and advisors other than counsel. The parties may incur costs to secure the testimony of fact witnesses, pay fees for experts, claim consultants and advisors to help them prepare and present their case legally, technically and logistically.

In principle, a party that incurs such costs in preparing or presenting its case in arbitration may recover them as long as they are reasonable.[98] In assessing the reasonableness of such costs, arbitral tribunals are guided by the complexity of the case, the amount of dispute, the parties' conduct and behavior, and the necessity of averting double recovery.

On the specific issue of averting double recovery, if a party seeks advice and assistance about the strategy and conduct of the arbitral proceedings from individuals other than counsel, this may be seen as an unreasonable cost "as doubling up with the role of counsel and may lead overall to unreasonably high total fees".[99]

h. Costs of contemporaneous and related court proceedings

The parties may incur costs for ancillary and related court proceedings, "such as applications for stays of proceedings, anti-suit injunctions, interim measures, assistance in obtaining evidence or the like".[100]

Technically speaking, the said costs are not arbitration costs per se; they are incurred in separate proceedings beyond the four corners of the arbitration proceedings. As such, they do not technically qualify as arbitration costs, but can arguably be claimed as damages if the applicable law and the circumstances of the case so permit.

However, if the parties are in agreement to claim such costs or have both claimed them in arbitration, the arbitral tribunal may, subject to ascertaining the reasonableness of such costs, consider awarding them in whole or part if they have not been claimed in the parallel, ancillary and/or related proceedings. Alternatively, the said costs may better be claimed and recovered in the relevant court proceedings in which they were incurred.[101] Ideally, the latter alternative would be the best and least problematic option.

i. Costs incurred in vacatur and enforcement proceedings

The costs incurred in relation to the proceedings of challenging or enforcing the award are not considered as arbitration costs in themselves. In fact, they are post-award costs that arbitral tribunals cannot award. At that stage, the arbitral tribunal itself is functus officio and accordingly has no jurisdiction to award any such costs, and the recovery of such costs will be subject to the rules applicable to the vacatur or enforcement proceedings.

However, the question arises when the arbitral tribunal renders partial awards that have been subjected to vacatur motions and/or enforcement proceedings whilst the

98. See J. WAINCYMER, *Procedure and Evidence in International Arbitration* (Kluwer Law International 2012) pp. 1249-1250.

99. *Ibid.*, p.1250.

100. *Ibid.*, p. 1255.

101. B. HANOTIAU, "The Parties' Costs of Arbitration", cited in J. WAINCYMER, *Procedure and Evidence in International Arbitration* (Kluwer Law International 2012) p. 1255.

arbitration proceedings are still pending. It is in such case that the arbitral tribunal is not functus officio, but such costs would be treated as costs of parallel, ancillary and related proceedings as discussed above.

Having discussed the diverse categories of costs in international arbitration, we shall now address the principles and practices governing the awarding of costs.

III. AWARDING COSTS IN INTERNATIONAL ARBITRATION: PRINCIPLES AND PRACTICES

In order for an arbitral tribunal to allocate and award costs in international arbitration cases, it should, in the first place, determine the law(s) governing the awarding of costs and the arbitral tribunal's authority to so award (*1*). Following this, it is important to consider and identify the standards according to which the arbitral tribunal will allocate and award costs (*2*). Nonetheless, in practice, the arbitral tribunals rarely discuss questions of the law applicable to the awarding of costs; instead they prefer to apply general principles (*3*). Also, civil and common law approaches to costs do not offer useful guidance for the arbitral tribunals (*4*).

1. Applicable Law to the Awarding of Costs

In order to determine the applicable law to the awarding of costs, a preliminary question should be answered. This question consists of determining whether the awarding of costs is a procedural or substantive matter (i). The answer to this question reveals that a distinction should be made between the tribunal's power to award costs (ii) and the standards applicable for awarding costs (iii). Additionally, arbitral tribunals should take into consideration the laws that may affect the validity or enforceability of costs award(s) (iv).

a. The characterization of awarding costs: Procedure or substance?

At first sight, awarding costs may come across as a procedural matter. However, the question of characterization of awarding costs is controversial. Some tribunals and authors consider that, in determining whether the awarding of costs is a procedural or substantive matter, a distinction should be made between the question of the tribunal's power to award costs (i) and the question of the standards for awarding costs (ii).

i. The tribunal's power to award costs

The first matter that an arbitral tribunal should consider is whether it enjoys the power to render an award on costs. This question of the tribunal's power to award costs is commonly considered as a procedural matter.[102] This assertion is almost uncontroversial since it is in line with the position followed in regard to the characterization of other

---

102. See, e.g., S. GREENBERG, "Chapter II: The Arbitrator and the Arbitration Procedure, Law Applicable to Costs Claims in International Arbitration: Why Does It Matter?" in Christian KLAUSEGGER, Peter KLEIN, et al., eds., *Austrian Yearbook on International Arbitration, 2015*, p. 171; See also J. WAINCYMER, *Procedure and Evidence in International Arbitration* (Kluwer Law International 2012) p. 1194.

powers granted to arbitral tribunals. For instance, the tribunal's powers to grant interim relief and to order document production are procedural matters.[103]

ii. The standards for awarding costs

Once the arbitral tribunal concludes that it has the power to award costs, it should determine the standards according to which it will award such costs. In this regard, it may be argued that the awarding of costs is a matter which is more closely connected to substantive issues on the ground that the costs incurred in order to prepare and present a claim or a defense are more connected to this claim or defense than to the process of resolving the dispute.[104] The substantive nature of the said issue is similar to the damages approach adopted under substantive laws which consists of compensating an aggrieved party.[105]

b. The law governing the tribunal's power to award costs

Given that there is little doubt that the question of the tribunal's power to award costs is a procedural matter, the applicable law to this issue is the procedural law.[106] Accordingly, the first source that could grant to the arbitral tribunal the power to award costs in international arbitration is the *lex loci arbitri*.

Whilst many national laws include provisions regarding the tribunal's power to award costs, there exist jurisdictions whose arbitration laws do not regulate this issue. If so, arbitral tribunals will need to resort to others sources, notably the arbitration agreement and the applicable institutional arbitration rules, in order to rule on its jurisdiction and power to award costs in an arbitration case.

c. The law governing the standards for awarding costs

Having established that the awarding of costs incurred in the process of preparing and presenting a claim or a defense should be governed by the applicable law to the said claim or defense,[107] being arguably best placed to guide an arbitral tribunal in

103. See G. BORN, *International Commercial Arbitration,* (Kluwer Law International 2014) p. 3100; See also S. GREENBERG, "Chapter II: The Arbitrator and the Arbitration Procedure, Law Applicable to Costs Claims in International Arbitration: Why Does It Matter?" in Christian KLAUSEGGER, Peter KLEIN, et al., eds., *Austrian Yearbook on International Arbitration, 2015*, p. 171.

104. See S. GREENBERG, "Chapter II: The Arbitrator and the Arbitration Procedure, Law Applicable to Costs Claims in International Arbitration: Why Does It Matter?" in Christian KLAUSEGGER, Peter KLEIN, et al., eds., *Austrian Yearbook on International Arbitration, 2015*, p. 175 .

105. See M. BÜHLER, "Awarding Costs in International Commercial Arbitration: An Overview", 22 ASA Bull. (2004, issue 2) p. 251; See also J. WAINCYMER, *Procedure and Evidence in International Arbitration* (Kluwer Law International 2012) p. 1194.

106. See G. BORN, *International Commercial Arbitration* (Kluwer Law International 2014) pp. 3099-3100.

107. See S. GREENBERG, "Chapter II: The Arbitrator and the Arbitration Procedure, Law Applicable to Costs Claims in International Arbitration: Why Does It Matter?" in Christian KLAUSEGGER, Peter KLEIN, et al., eds., *Austrian Yearbook on International Arbitration, 2015*, pp. 175-176; See also G. BORN, *International Commercial Arbitration* (Kluwer Law International 2014) p. 3100.

determining the allocation of those costs,[108] others have argued that the law governing the standards for awarding costs is the *lex loci arbitri*.[109]

It is this controversy over what law governs the standards for awarding costs that has motivated other scholars to argue that it is better to award costs in international arbitration according to international standards and not national laws.[110] The rationale for this suggestion is that international standards established by arbitral tribunals would be more adapted to international disputes than the rules enshrined in national laws.[111]

This suggestion is in line with the approach adopted by the majority of arbitration rules since, indeed, these rules usually provide *general principles* as guidance for the awarding of costs but at the same time they allow the tribunal to depart from these general principles depending on the circumstances of each particular case and its applicable norms.[112] In practice, arbitral tribunals rarely discuss the issue of the applicable law, and prefer to follow the general principles in awarding costs, unless a clear case on other applicable national norms is pleaded and substantiated.

d. Laws potentially affecting the validity or enforcement of awards on costs

In awarding costs, arbitral tribunals should consider the laws that could affect the validity or enforceability of their decisions on costs.[113] These are either the *lex loci arbitri* or the *lex loci executionis*. Arbitral tribunals should be mindful of any overriding mandatory laws or public policy principles prevailing in these jurisdictions.[114]

2. Tribunal's Jurisdiction and Powers over Costs and Determination of Recoverable Costs

The arbitral tribunal should determine whether or not it has the power to award costs (i) and how it should exercise this power (ii). In doing so, the arbitral tribunal should be careful in the event that it lacks jurisdiction to decide on the merits since, in this case, its power is controversial (iii). It should also take into consideration the obstacles which could limit its power (iv).

---

108. See S. GREENBERG, "Chapter II: The Arbitrator and the Arbitration Procedure, Law Applicable to Costs Claims in International Arbitration: Why Does It Matter?" in Christian KLAUSEGGER, Peter KLEIN, et al., eds., *Austrian Yearbook on International Arbitration, 2015*, pp. 175-176.
109. *Ibid.*, p.176.
110. See G. BORN, *International Commercial Arbitration* (Kluwer Law International 2014) pp. 3100-3101.
111. *Ibid.*, p. 3101.
112. *Ibid.*
113. See "ICC Commission Report: Decisions on Costs in International Arbitration" (2015) p. 10; See also S. GREENBERG, "Chapter II: The Arbitrator and the Arbitration Procedure, Law Applicable to Costs Claims in International Arbitration: Why Does It Matter?" in Christian KLAUSEGGER, Peter KLEIN, et al., eds., *Austrian Yearbook on International Arbitration, 2015*, p. 181.
114. See S. GREENBERG, "Chapter II: The Arbitrator and the Arbitration Procedure, Law Applicable to Costs Claims in International Arbitration: Why Does It Matter?" in Christian KLAUSEGGER, Peter KLEIN, et al., eds., *Austrian Yearbook on International Arbitration, 2015*, p. 181.

a. Tribunal's power to award costs

As detailed herein above, and absent an express and valid agreement by the parties, the first source of the tribunal's power to award costs is the procedural law, i.e. *lex loci arbitri*.[115] Some of these national laws explicitly provide that the arbitral tribunal has the power to award costs and others are silent on the issue but they are commonly considered as impliedly empowering the arbitral tribunal to award costs. For instance, Sect. 61 of English Arbitration Act, Sect. 1057 of the German Code of Civil Procedure, Art. 27(1) of Australia's International Arbitration Act 1974 and Sect. 609 of Austria's Arbitration Act explicitly empower the arbitral tribunal to award costs, subject to any contrary arbitration agreement.[116] However, the laws of France and Switzerland, for example, are silent on the issue of awarding costs but it is well established that in these jurisdictions the arbitral tribunal has the power to award costs.[117] The United States Federal Arbitral Act is also silent on the issue, but it is controversial whether or not it allows the awarding of costs. In this context, a number of state laws in the United States provide that arbitral tribunals may only award the costs of the arbitration but the legal costs should be borne by each party.[118] However, a number of US courts have held that the arbitral tribunal has the power to award costs.[119]

Apart from the *lex loci arbitri*, the tribunal's power to award costs may derive from an arbitration agreement that explicitly empowers the arbitral tribunal to allocate costs or refers to institutional arbitration rules which provide that the arbitral tribunal has the power to allocate costs.[120] In fact, most institutional arbitration rules empower the arbitral tribunals to allocate costs.[121] For instance, there are Art. 38 of the 2017 ICC Arbitration Rules, Art. 42 of the 2013 Arbitration Rules of the United Nations Commission on International Trade Law (UNCITRAL), Art. 40(1)-(2) of the 2012 Swiss Arbitration Rules, Art. 28.3 of the 2014 London Court of International Arbitration (LCIA) Rules, Art. 42 of 2011 Cairo Regional Centre for International Commercial Arbitration (CRCICA) Rules and others.[122]

If the *lex loci arbitri*, the arbitration agreement and any applicable institutional arbitration rules are silent on the awarding of costs, some scholars have argued for an

115. See S. GREENBERG, "Chapter II: The Arbitrator and the Arbitration Procedure, Law Applicable to Costs Claims in International Arbitration: Why Does It Matter?" in Christian KLAUSEGGER, Peter KLEIN, et al., eds., *Austrian Yearbook on International Arbitration, 2015*, p. 171.

116. *Ibid.*

117. *Ibid.*

118. *Ibid.*, p. 172.

119. See G. BORN, *International Commercial Arbitration* (Kluwer Law International 2014) p. 3090.

120. *Ibid.*, p. 3093; See also S. GREENBERG, "Chapter II: The Arbitrator and the Arbitration Procedure, Law Applicable to Costs Claims in International Arbitration: Why Does It Matter?" in Christian KLAUSEGGER, Peter KLEIN, et al., eds., *Austrian Yearbook on International Arbitration, 2015*, pp. 173-174.

121. *Ibid.*

122. See, e.g., Art. 34 of the 2018 Hong Kong International Arbitration Centre (HKIAC) Administered Arbitration Rules; See also Art. 33 of the 2018 Deutsche Institution für Schiedsgerichtsbarkeit (German Arbitration Institute – DIS) Arbitration Rules.

inherent and implied power to award costs by arbitral tribunals, and that such inherent and implied power is derived from the general power to decide the dispute.[123]

b. The tribunal's controversial jurisdiction to award costs without jurisdiction to rule on the merits

The arbitral tribunal's power to award costs incurred in preparing and presenting a claim over which the tribunal held that it lacks jurisdiction is controversial.[124] If the arbitral tribunal concluded that there is no valid arbitration agreement concluded between the parties on a given claim, it is questionable whether it could award costs related to this claim, absent any legal basis to do so.[125]

In this context, it is submitted that a provision in the *lex loci arbitri* or the applicable institutional rules empowering the arbitral tribunal to award costs is sufficient to grant the arbitral tribunal the power to allocate costs incurred for a claim over which it lacks jurisdiction.[126] Despite the controversy over this issue, arbitral tribunals have usually awarded costs against a claimant who loses on jurisdiction.[127]

c. Determining and awarding recoverable costs: the reasonableness criterion

In regard to the exercise of the tribunal's power to award costs, most national laws and arbitration rules grant to the arbitral tribunal "the widest"[128] and "unfettered"[129] discretion. As a result, in practice, the arbitral tribunals follow general principles in awarding costs.

On the issue of recoverable costs, this has been detailed herein above when analyzing the categories of costs and the criteria determining the recoverability of them. It is worth noting that certain types of costs can be recoverable according to costs schedules established by the institutional arbitration rules in institutional arbitration and the rules determined by the parties in *ad hoc* arbitration.[130]

---

123. See G. BORN, *International Commercial Arbitration* (Kluwer Law International 2014) p. 3095; See also S. GREENBERG, "Chapter II: The Arbitrator and the Arbitration Procedure, Law Applicable to Costs Claims in International Arbitration: Why Does It Matter?" in Christian KLAUSEGGER, Peter KLEIN, et al., eds., *Austrian Yearbook on International Arbitration, 2015*, p. 174.
124. See, e.g., G. BORN, *International Commercial Arbitration* (Kluwer Law International 2014) p. 3101; See also See M. BÜHLER, "Awarding Costs in International Commercial Arbitration: An Overview", 22 ASA Bull. (2004, issue 2) p. 258.
125. *Ibid.*
126. See M. BÜHLER, "Awarding Costs in International Commercial Arbitration: An Overview", 22 ASA Bull. (2004, issue 2) p. 258; See also G. BORN, *International Commercial Arbitration* (Kluwer Law International 2014) p. 3102.
127. See M. BÜHLER, "Awarding Costs in International Commercial Arbitration: An Overview", 22 ASA Bull. (2004, issue 2) p. 259.
128. *Ibid.*, p. 253.
129. See GREENBERG, "Chapter II: The Arbitrator and the Arbitration Procedure, Law Applicable to Costs Claims in International Arbitration: Why Does It Matter?" in Christian KLAUSEGGER, Peter KLEIN, et al., eds., *Austrian Yearbook on International Arbitration, 2015*, p. 172.
130. See J. POWER and C. KONRAD, "Chapter IV: The Award – Costs in International Arbitration - A Comparative Overview of Civil and Common Law Doctrines: Determination of Costs" in Gerold ZEILER, Irene WELSER, et al., eds., *Austrian Arbitration Yearbook 2008*, pp. 404-407.

In practice, arbitral tribunals usually asses the reasonableness of the claimed costs.[131] Most arbitral tribunals, in assessing the reasonableness of costs claimed, adopt a broad approach which is similar to the approach proposed in a case before the Iran-United States Claims Tribunal.[132] The suggested approach involves answering four questions: (1) "were costs claimed in the arbitration?"; (2) "was it necessary to employ lawyers in the case in question?"; (3) "is the amount of the costs reasonable?"; and (4) "are the circumstances of the particular case such as to make it reasonable to apportion such costs?".[133]

In this context, it is worth noting that the test of reasonableness is not "an invitation to mere subjectivity",[134] but is undertaken "from an objective viewpoint".[135] Typically, in applying this test, arbitral tribunals take into account the time spent as well as the complexity of the case. Accordingly, the time that needs to be spent in order to prepare and present a claim "can be measured by the number of issues involved in a case and the amount of evidence requiring analysis and presentation".[136]

More importantly, in assessing the reasonableness, the reasoning of the arbitral tribunal should be based on an important fact that the party that incurred the costs claimed agreed to pay these costs without knowing whether or not it will be reimbursed for these costs. This fact "is a strong indication that the amount billed was considered reasonable by a reasonable man spending his own money, or the money of the corporation he serves".[137]

d. Limitations on tribunal's power over costs and determination of recoverable costs

Even if the arbitral tribunal is granted a discretionary power to award costs under the *lex loci arbitri*, arbitration agreement, or arbitration rules, this power is not absolute. It can be limited or restrained by certain overriding mandatory rules or principles of public policy under the *lex loci arbitri* or the *lex loci executionis*. For instance, under Sect. 60 of the English Arbitration Act 1996, an arbitral tribunal in awarding costs shall not follow an agreement concluded between the parties on the apportionment of costs *before* the dispute has arisen.[138]

Similarly, a court in the Philippines denied the enforcement of a cost award on the ground that the arbitral tribunal in upholding the "costs follow the event" principle "gravely abused its discretion" since "[i]t is a well-settled public policy of the Philippines

131. See "ICC Commission Report: Decisions on Costs in International Arbitration" (2015) p. 5.
132. See N. BLACKABY, et al., *Redfern and Hunter on International Arbitration* (Oxford University Press 2015) p. 535.
133. *Ibid.*
134. *Ibid.*
135. See M. BÜHLER, "Awarding Costs in International Commercial Arbitration: An Overview", 22 ASA Bull. (2004, issue 2) p. 271.
136. See N. BLACKABY, et al., *Redfern and Hunter on International Arbitration* (Oxford University Press 2015) p. 536.
137. See Separate opinion of Judge HOLTZMANN, reported in 1985 Iranian Assets Litigation Reporter 10860, cited in N. BLACKABY, et al., *Redfern and Hunter on International Arbitration* (Oxford University Press 2015) p. 536, fn. 128.
138. See S. GREENBERG, "Chapter II: The Arbitrator and the Arbitration Procedure, Law Applicable to Costs Claims in International Arbitration: Why Does It Matter?" in Christian KLAUSEGGER, Peter KLEIN, et al., eds., *Austrian Yearbook on International Arbitration, 2015*, p. 181.

that, in the absence of bad faith, a litigant cannot be penalized for the exercise of his right to litigate".[139] Nonetheless, a number of court decisions in other jurisdictions have adopted a more liberal approach and have been reluctant to set aside or refuse to enforce an award on the basis of a public policy principle.[140]

3. *Principles Governing the Awarding of Costs in International Arbitration*

The practice in international arbitration reveals that arbitral tribunals apply one of two main principles in allocating and awarding costs: (i) the "*costs follow the event*"/the "*loser pays*" principle, and (ii) "*each party bears its costs*" principle (the so-called "American rule").[141]

a. *The "costs follow the event"/"loser pays" principle and its variants*

At the outset, the gist of the said principle shall be addressed (i), and then its general application in international commercial arbitration will be considered (ii), before considering its emerging application in international investment arbitration (iii).

i. Overview of the "costs follow the event/loser pays principle"

The "costs follow the event" principle, sometimes referred to as the "loser pays" principle, provides that the losing party shall bear, in addition to its own costs, the costs incurred by the successful party in the arbitral proceedings.[142]

In application of the said principle, arbitral tribunals have followed different approaches. In some cases, arbitral tribunals have adopted a *"winner takes all" approach*".[143] According to this approach, the losing party shall be ordered to bear *all* the costs incurred in the arbitral proceedings. However, in the majority of cases, arbitral tribunals adopted a more varied approach, where the allocation of costs is based on the *relative successes and failures of the claims and defenses pursued by each party* as well as the *conduct of the parties during the arbitral proceedings*. In doing so, arbitral tribunals adopt the "costs follow

139. See Court of Appeals, Manila, *Luzon Hydro Corp. v. Hon. Rommel O. Baybay and Transfield Philippines, Inc.*, 29 November 2006, cited in S. GREENBERG, "Chapter II: The Arbitrator and the Arbitration Procedure, Law Applicable to Costs Claims in International Arbitration: Why Does It Matter?" in Christian KLAUSEGGER, Peter KLEIN, et al., eds., *Austrian Yearbook on International Arbitration, 2015*, p. 182.

140. See S. GREENBERG, "Chapter II: The Arbitrator and the Arbitration Procedure, Law Applicable to Costs Claims in International Arbitration: Why Does It Matter?" in Christian KLAUSEGGER, Peter KLEIN, et al., eds., *Austrian Yearbook on International Arbitration, 2015*, p. 183.

141. See, e.g., M. BÜHLER, "Awarding Costs in International Commercial Arbitration: An Overview", 22 ASA Bull. (2004, issue 2) p. 250; See also "ICC Commission Report: Decisions on Costs in International Arbitration" (2015) p. 3.

142. See, e.g., M. BÜHLER, "Awarding Costs in International Commercial Arbitration: An Overview", 22 ASA Bull. (2004, issue 2) p. 250; See also S. GREENBERG, "Chapter II: The Arbitrator and the Arbitration Procedure, Law Applicable to Costs Claims in International Arbitration: Why Does It Matter?" in Christian KLAUSEGGER, Peter KLEIN, et al., eds., *Austrian Yearbook on International Arbitration, 2015*, p. 178.

143. See S. GREENBERG, "Chapter II: The Arbitrator and the Arbitration Procedure, Law Applicable to Costs Claims in International Arbitration: Why Does It Matter?" in Christian KLAUSEGGER, Peter KLEIN, et al., eds., *Austrian Yearbook on International Arbitration, 2015*, p. 178.

the event" as the starting point and then adjust the principle while taking into account the circumstances of each particular case.

It is worth noting that such principle and its variants discourage arbitration users from raising frivolous claims since the losing party would bear the significant cost-related ramifications of its losses.[144] Accordingly, the application of the "costs follow the event" principle will help ensure that the arbitral proceedings are conducted in an expeditious and cost-efficient manner.

However, the said principle has been criticized by some authors and practitioners,[145] on the premise that

> "[a]rbitrators may consider it too draconian to impose the burden of an opponent's attorney fees on a losing party, and thereby create a system that could chill the assertion of claims unreasonably, without evidence of additional culpability in a particular case. Some claims are deservedly brought, even if they are largely unsuccessful for sound factual or legal reasons that emerge after an airing by adversarial process."[146]

Others have suggested that the risk that a party with a complex case bears all or the substantial part of costs could be avoided by taking into consideration the complexity of issues and facts while awarding costs according to the "costs follow the event" principle.[147]

ii. The "costs follow the event/loser pays" principle is the general principle in international commercial arbitration

The "costs follow the event" principle is widely considered as the general principle followed by arbitral tribunals in international commercial arbitration. This fact was confirmed by several arbitral decisions which held that the losing party shall bear the costs in international arbitration "according to general principles"[148] or "[i]n accordance with basic procedural principles".[149]

In the same vein, several authors have clearly affirmed that the said principle is the "emerging trend"[150] and the "most common approach"[151] followed by arbitral tribunals in international commercial arbitration.

---

144. See S. GREENBERG, "Chapter II: The Arbitrator and the Arbitration Procedure, Law Applicable to Costs Claims in International Arbitration: Why Does It Matter?" in Christian KLAUSEGGER, Peter KLEIN, et al., eds., *Austrian Yearbook on International Arbitration, 2015*, p. 178.
145. See G. BORN, *International Commercial Arbitration* (Kluwer Law International 2014) p. 3097.
146. See CARTER, "A Kiss For Arbitration Costs Allocation", cited in G. BORN, *International Commercial Arbitration* (Kluwer Law International 2014) p. 3098, fn. 528.
147. See SMIT and ROBINSON, "Cost Awards in International Arbitration: Proposed Guidelines for Promoting Time and Cost Efficiency", cited in G. BORN, *International Commercial Arbitration* (Kluwer Law International 2014) p. 3099, fn. 537.
148. See *Manufacturer v. Buyer* (ICC Case No. 8486), Final Award (1996) in ICCA *Yearbook Commercial Arbitration* XXIV (1999) (henceforth *Yearbook*) p. 172.
149. See *Supplier v. Buyer* (ICC Case No. 7645), Interim Award (1995) in *Yearbook* XXVI (2001) p. 152.
150. See J. LEW, L. MISTELIS and S. KRÖLL, *Comparative International Commercial Arbitration* (Kluwer Law International 2003) pp. 654-655.

Furthermore, some arbitration laws[152] and several institutional arbitration rules[153] provide that arbitral tribunals shall in principle adopt the "costs follow the event" principle in awarding costs and accordingly shall order the losing party to bear all or the substantial part of arbitration costs and legal costs.

The ICC Commission Report regarding Decisions on Costs in International Arbitration affirms that "[d]espite the fact that the ICC and at least half of the other major institutional rules contain no presumption in favour of the recovery of costs by the successful party, it appears that the majority of arbitral tribunals broadly adopt that approach as a starting point, thereafter adjusting the allocation of costs as considered appropriate".[154] The Report adds that in the majority of ICC, Hong Kong International Arbitration Centre (HKIAC), International Centre for Dispute Resolution (ICDR), Singapore International Arbitration Centre (SIAC), and Stockholm Chamber of Commerce (SCC) awards (institutions with rules that do not explicitly provide that the costs shall be borne by the losing party), arbitral tribunals have adopted the "costs follow the event" principle.[155]

In light of the foregoing, it is well established that arbitral tribunals in awarding costs in international commercial arbitration generally adopt the "costs follow the event/loser pays" principle with some adjustments in order to take into consideration the circumstances of each particular case.

iii. The "costs follow the event/loser pays" principle as the emerging principle in international investment arbitration

At the outset, it is worth noting that the principle trending in regard to the awarding of costs in international investment arbitration differs from the one trending in international commercial arbitration. More specifically, contrary to the case of international commercial arbitration, arbitral tribunals in investment arbitration proceedings have generally followed the "each party bears its costs" principle. However, in recent years, the "costs follow the event" principle has been adopted by a significant number of arbitration tribunals in investment cases.[156]

151. See S. GREENBERG, "Chapter II: The Arbitrator and the Arbitration Procedure, Law Applicable to Costs Claims in International Arbitration: Why Does It Matter?" in Christian KLAUSEGGER, Peter KLEIN, et al., eds., *Austrian Yearbook on International Arbitration, 2015*, p. 178.

152. See, e.g., Sect. 61(2) of the English Arbitration Act 1996; Sect. 1057(1) German Code of Civil Procedure.

153. See, e.g., Art. 42(2) of the 2013 UNCITRAL Rules; Art. 40(1) of the 2012 Swiss Arbitration Rules; Art. 28.4 of the 2014 LCIA Rules; Art. 46 of the 2011 Cairo Regional Centre for International Commercial Arbitration (CRCICA) Rules; Art. 4(1) of the 2012 Permanent Court of Arbitration (PCA) Arbitration Rules.

154. See "ICC Commission Report: Decisions on Costs in International Arbitration" (2015) p. 5.

155. *Ibid.*

156. See M. HODGSON and E. EVANS, "Chapter 17: Allocation of Costs in ICSID Arbitrations" in Crina BALTAG, ed., *ICSID Convention After 50 Years: Unsettled Issues* (Kluwer Law International 2016) p. 459.

That said, scholars have affirmed that "ICSID tribunals and commentators alike have observed that the loser-pays principle is gaining currency".[157] For instance, in *Telenor Mobile Communications AS v. Republic of Hungary*, the arbitral tribunal adopted the "costs follow the event" principle and ordered the claimant to reimburse to respondent its contributions to the costs of the arbitration and legal costs.[158] In addition, in the *ADC Affiliate Limited v. Hungary* case, the arbitral tribunal ordered respondent to reimburse to the successful claimant the sum of US$ 7,623,693 to cover the claimant's costs and expenses in this arbitration.[159] In doing so, the arbitral tribunal clearly stated that "[i]n the present case, the Tribunal can find no reason to depart from the starting point that the successful party should receive reimbursement from the unsuccessful party". The interesting thing about this decision is that the arbitral tribunal considered the "costs follow the event" principle as the starting point in awarding costs, which "exemplifies the 'growing application to investment arbitration' of 'costs follow the event'".[160] This was further affirmed in many other cases, where arbitral tribunals have upheld the "costs follow the event" principle.[161]

It is worth noting in this regard that when the arbitral tribunals order the unsuccessful party to bear costs in investment arbitration cases, "they do not tend to do so on an all-or-nothing basis".[162] Instead, they usually take into consideration the circumstances of each particular case, including "(i) the degree or extent of a party's success, (ii) the novelty and complexity of the issues raised by the party, and (iii) the conduct of the parties during the proceedings".[163]

Notwithstanding the above, it is difficult to identify a general and uniform principle regarding the awarding of costs in investment arbitration.[164] In the *Waste Management, Inc.*

---

157. See J. POWER, "Chapter V: Investment Arbitration – Determination of Costs in ICSID Arbitration" in Christian KLAUSEGGER, Peter KLEIN, et al., eds., *Austrian Yearbook on International Arbitration, 2010*, p. 343.
158. See *Telenor Mobile Communications v. Republic of Hungary* (ICSID Case No. ARB/04/15), 13 September 2006.
159. See *ADC Affiliate Limited and ADC & ADMC Management Limited v. The Republic of Hungary* (ICSID Case No. ARB/03/16), 2 October 2006.
160. See M. HODGSON and E. EVANS, "Chapter 17: Allocation of Costs in ICSID Arbitrations" in Crina BALTAG, ed., *ICSID Convention After 50 Years: Unsettled Issues* (Kluwer Law International 2016) p. 465.
161. See, e.g., *PSEG Global Inc. and Konya Ilgin Elektrik Üretim ve Ticaret Limited Sirketi v. Republic of Turkey* (ICSID Case No. ARB/02/5), 19 January 2007; See also *Libananco Holdings Co. Limited v. Republic of Turkey* (ICSID Case No. ARB/06/8), 2 September 2011.
162. See Ch. SCHREUER et al., *The ICSID Convention: A Commentary*, Art. 61, cited in J. POWER, "Chapter V: Investment Arbitration – Determination of Costs in ICSID Arbitration" in Christian KLAUSEGGER, Peter KLEIN, et al., eds., *Austrian Yearbook on International Arbitration, 2010*, fn. 34.
163. See J. POWER, "Chapter V: Investment Arbitration – Determination of Costs in ICSID Arbitration" in Christian KLAUSEGGER, Peter KLEIN, et al., eds., *Austrian Yearbook on International Arbitration, 2010*, p. 345.
164. See, e.g., J. GOTANDA, "Attorneys' Fees Agonistes: The Implications of Inconsistency in the Awarding of Fees and Costs in International Arbitrations" in Miguel Ángel FERNÁNDEZ-BÁLLESTEROS and David ARIAS, eds., *Liber Amicorum Bernardo Cremades* (Wolters Kluwer España 2010) pp. 539-540; See also J. POWER, "Chapter V: Investment Arbitration –

v. United Mexican States case, the arbitral tribunal asserted that "[t]here is no rule in international arbitration that costs follow the event. Equally, however, the Tribunal does not accept that there is any practice in investment arbitration (as there may be, at least de facto, in the International Court and in interstate arbitration) that each party should pay its own costs."[165]

Interestingly, the 2018 proposed amendments of the Arbitration Rules of the International Centre for Settlement of Investment Disputes (ICSID) include a new provision (Rule 19) requiring the arbitral tribunals to take into consideration, while allocating costs, all the relevant circumstances, in particular the following four specific factors: (i) the outcome of any part of the proceeding or overall; (ii) the parties' conduct during the proceeding, including the extent to which they acted in an expeditious and cost-effective manner; (iii) the complexity of the issues; and (iv) the reasonableness of the costs claimed.[166] It is submitted that the introduction of this provision to the ICSID Rules will likely make the "costs follow the event/loser pays" principle the default rule in ICSID arbitrations.

b. The "each party bears its costs" principle/the American rule

As is the case with the principle of "loser pays", we shall commence by shedding light on the nature of this principle (i). Subsequently, the commonality of the said principle in international commercial arbitration will be considered (ii), before considering its stature in international investment arbitration (iii).

i. An overview of the "each party bears its costs" principle/the American rule

The principle that "each party bears its costs" in arbitral proceedings is also referred to as the American rule given its prevailing application in US-based arbitration proceedings. The purpose of this American rule is to safeguard the parties' right to access justice and avert being deterred from raising claims or defenses owing to the risk of bearing the costs of the adverse party in the event of losing the case.[167]

Moreover, it has been argued that the application of the American rule will reduce the costs and time spent in arbitral proceedings, since the parties will be exempted from substantiating costs-related claims and the arbitrators will not be required to identify the winning party or ascertain the recoverable costs in content and quantum.[168]

Determination of Costs in ICSID Arbitration" in Christian KLAUSEGGER, Peter KLEIN , et al., eds., *Austrian Yearbook on International Arbitration 2010*, p. 341.

165. See *Waste Management, Inc. v. United Mexican States* ("Number 2") (ICSID Case No. ARB(AF)/00/3), 30 April 2004.

166. See Proposals for Amendment of the ICSID Rules – Synopsis, Volume 1 (August 2018) para. 26; See also Proposals for Amendment of the ICSID Rules – Consolidated Draft Rules, Volume 2 (August 2018) p. 29.

167. See M. HODGSON and E. EVANS, , "Chapter 17: Allocation of Costs in ICSID Arbitrations" in Crina BALTAG, *ICSID Convention After 50 Years: Unsettled Issues* (Kluwer Law International 2016) p. 458.

168. See J. GOTANDA, "Attorneys' Fees Agonistes: The Implications of Inconsistency in the Awarding of Fees and Costs in International Arbitrations" in Miguel Ángel FERNÁNDEZ-BÁLLESTEROS and David Arias, eds., *Liber Amicorum Bernardo Cremades* (Wolters Kluwer España, 2010) p. 545.

ii. The non-prevalence of the American rule in international commercial arbitration

As previously mentioned, in international commercial arbitration, arbitral tribunals commonly adopt the "costs follow the event" principle and its adjusted variants. The alter ego of such practice is the marginalization of the American rule in international commercial arbitration cases.[169] Even in proceedings seated in the United States, where the principle of "each party bears its costs" prevails, it is not uncommon that international arbitral tribunals allocate costs based on the "costs follow the event" principle pursuant to the arbitration agreement or arbitration rules agreed upon by the parties.[170] That is due to the fact that a significant number of arbitration rules permit the allocation of costs based on the "costs follow the event" principle.

This practice emphasizes the fact that "this approach [the American rule] is probably considered as contrary to the preference of parties in most contemporary international commercial arbitrations".[171]

iii. The prevalence of the American rule in international investment arbitration

In contrast to commercial arbitration cases, arbitral tribunals in investment arbitration have long adopted the "each party bears its costs" principle in allocating costs. This distinction between the practice prevailing in commercial arbitration and that which prevails in investment arbitration was expressly underlined by an ICSID decision stating that: "[t]he Tribunal notes that in reference to the allocation of costs, the practice of ICSID investment arbitration differs from commercial arbitration, which tends to award costs to the successful party. Most ICSID tribunals have determined that each party should bear its own costs."[172] Similarly, in *Bayview Irrigation District et al. v. The United Mexican States*, the arbitral tribunal affirmed that the practice of ordering the parties to pay equally the costs of the arbitration and to bear its own legal costs is the "normal practice".[173]

The fact that "each party bears its costs" is the prevailing principle in investment arbitration is not normally deviated from, unless such deviation was justified by special or exceptional circumstances, notably a party's frivolous or bad faith conduct.[174] Nonetheless, in recent years, a decline in the American rule could be traced in

169. See, e.g., S. GREENBERG, "Chapter II: The Arbitrator and the Arbitration Procedure, Law Applicable to Costs Claims in International Arbitration: Why Does It Matter?" in Christian KLAUSEGGER, Peter KLEIN, et al., eds., *Austrian Yearbook on International Arbitration, 2015*, p. 179.

170. *Ibid.*

171. See S. GREENBERG, "Chapter II: The Arbitrator and the Arbitration Procedure, Law Applicable to Costs Claims in International Arbitration: Why Does It Matter?" in Christian KLAUSEGGER, Peter KLEIN, et al., eds., *Austrian Yearbook on International Arbitration, 2015*, p. 180.

172. See *Alasdair Ross Anderson et al v. Republic of Costa Rica* (ICSID Case No. ARB(AF)/07/3), 19 May 2010.

173. See *Bayview Irrigation District et al. v. United Mexican States* (ICSID Case No. ARB(AF)/05/1), 19 June 2007.

174. See J. POWER, "Chapter V: Investment Arbitration – Determination of Costs in ICSID Arbitration" in Christian KLAUSEGGER , Peter KLEIN , et al., eds., *Austrian Yearbook on International Arbitration, 2010*, p. 341; See also M. HODGSON and E. EVANS, "Chapter 17: Allocation of Costs in ICSID Arbitrations" in Crina BALTAG, ed., *ICSID Convention After 50 Years: Unsettled Issues* (Kluwer Law International 2016) p. 464.

investment arbitration. Indeed, "[i]n cases before 2006, some 65% of investment tribunals declined to adjust costs. Since 2006, however, that figure has declined to 51%, as the 'loser pays' and 'relative success' approaches have gained traction."[175]

4. *Civil-Common Law Approaches to Costs: 'No One Size Fits All'*

As detailed herein above, the principles governing costs in international arbitration were generally developed and applied by arbitral tribunals, which are composed of members of diverse legal cultures and systems.

Whilst the world's legal systems are not reduced to civil and common law and there is indeed a broader array of systems, the debate on costs was further considered in the context of the civil-common law dichotomy, noting that the approaches followed by national courts in relation to awarding costs do not constitute "an appropriate guide" for the standards that arbitral tribunals should uphold and endorse when allocating and awarding costs.[176]

At the outset, awarding costs in civil and common law systems is governed by "the most general principles".[177] More specifically, many civil and common law systems adopt the "costs follow the event/losers pays" approach.[178] The notable exception to this general trend is the United States which generally follows the American rule, which seems to have gained endorsement in a few other countries, notably: Japan, Indonesia, China and the Philippines.[179] It is also not uncommon in some Arab countries in the MENA region that arbitrators would be inclined not to award *legal costs* to the prevailing party, especially given that the filing of costs submissions is not fully developed or practiced.

In any event, it is submitted that the debate over costs and the polarized approaches to the "costs follow the event/losers pays" and "each party bears its own costs/American rule" principles are not a function a civil-common law divide. Practice has shown that arbitral tribunals tend to take into consideration the circumstances and peculiarities of each case to mitigate the sharp application of both principles.

Accordingly, arbitral tribunals sitting in jurisdictions generally upholding the "costs follow the event" principle have not hesitated to deviate from the full application of the said principle in certain cases, hence denying the successful party recovery of all or part of its costs. Amongst those cases are: situations where the successful party's conduct

175. See M. HODGSON and E. EVANS, "Chapter 17: Allocation of Costs in ICSID Arbitrations" in Crina BALTAG, ed., *ICSID Convention After 50 Years: Unsettled Issues* (Kluwer Law International 2016) pp. 458-459.

176. See N. BLACKABY, et al., *Redfern and Hunter on International Arbitration* (Oxford University Press 2015) p. 536.

177. See J. POWER and C. KONRAD, "Chapter IV: The Award – Costs in International Arbitration - A Comparative Overview of Civil and Common Law Doctrines: Determination of Costs" in Gerold ZEILER, Irene WELSER, et al., eds., *Austrian Arbitration Yearbook 2008*, p. 402.

178. See, e.g., M. BÜHLER, "Awarding Costs in International Commercial Arbitration: An Overview", 22 ASA Bull. (2004, issue 2) p. 250; See also J. POWER, "Chapter V: Investment Arbitration – Determination of Costs in ICSID Arbitration" in Christian KLAUSEGGER, Peter KLEIN, et al., eds., *Austrian Yearbook on International Arbitration, 2010*, p. 343.

179. See, e.g., M. BÜHLER, "Awarding Costs in International Commercial Arbitration: An Overview", 22 ASA Bull. (2004, issue 2) pp. 250-251.

caused delay to the arbitral proceedings;[180] cases where the party's success was minimal compared to the overall claims;[181] cases where the losing party was cooperative and efficient in presenting its case; and cases where the successful party's costs claim was unreasonably excessive or exaggerated.

Similarly, arbitral tribunals sitting in jurisdictions generally upholding the "each party bears its costs" principle have not hesitated to deviate from the full application of the said principle in certain cases, where full or partial recovery of the costs of the winning party was warranted in light of the specificities and circumstances of the particular case.[182] Amongst those cases are: situations where the losing party's conduct was unreasonable, uncooperative, and this caused the winning party to incur further costs; cases where the party's success was manifest and colossal; and cases where both parties unequivocally claimed full recovery of costs and the successful party's costs claim was reasonable, warranted and substantiated.

On such account, it is submitted that there is no specific model or a sweeping golden standard that governs awarding costs in civil and common law jurisdictions. The overarching principle, absent any specific legal rule or an agreement to the contrary, is that no one size fits all, and that allocating and recovering costs are considered on a case-by-case basis, in due consideration of whether the underlying principle is the "costs follow the event/losers pays" or "each party bears its own costs/American rule".

5. *Claiming, Awarding, Challenging and Enforcing Costs Awards*

Cost-related claims should generally be treated as any other claim in international arbitration, and so arbitral tribunals usually invite the parties to submit their claims and defenses in regard to costs. However, in general, no lengthy submissions on costs are required or expected, and "summary statements of the costs billed by and paid to legal representatives are ordinarily sufficient" except in some cases the tribunal may require extensive submission and evidence.[183]

Thus, there is no specific form or format for costs submissions in international arbitration apart from the fact that arbitral tribunals should grant to the parties the opportunity to present their cost claims or contest the adverse cost claims.[184] Some parties "just submit a total figure followed by a short breakdown of the different cost items" and other parties "submit copies of all invoices and bills".[185]

180. See J. POWER and C. KONRAD, "Chapter IV: The Award – Costs in International Commercial Arbitration – A Comparative Overview of Civil and Common Law Doctrines" in Christian KLAUSEGGER, Peter KLEIN, et al., eds., *Austrian Arbitration Yearbook 2007*, pp. 266, 270 and 271.

181. *Ibid.*, pp. 266 and 271.

182. See J. POWER and C. KONRAD, "Chapter IV: The Award – Costs in International Arbitration – A Comparative Overview of Civil and Common Law Doctrines: Determination of Costs" in Gerold ZEILER, Irene WELSER, et al., eds., *Austrian Arbitration Yearbook 2008*, pp. 402 and 418.

183. See G. BORN, *International Commercial Arbitration* (Kluwer Law International 2014) p. 3097.

184. See, e.g., M. BÜHLER, "Awarding Costs in International Commercial Arbitration: An Overview", 22 ASA Bull. (2004, issue 2) p. 277.

185. See, e.g., *ibid.*

Following the submission of their succinct, yet substantiated, claims and defenses as to costs, the arbitral tribunal will need to consider and rule on the basis of allocating and awarding costs-related claims. In so considering, the arbitral tribunal can either render awards on costs as partial or interim awards,[186] depending on the circumstances, or include its decision on costs in the final award.

Once a final award is rendered, the arbitral tribunal becomes functus officio,[187] yet arbitral tribunals can also deal with issues of costs in an additional award subsequent to the final award,[188] if the circumstances so warrant and if the applicable arbitration rules or laws so permit.

In any event, a decision on costs ordering a party to pay the other party's costs constitutes an award under national arbitration laws, the 1958 New York Convention on the Recognition and Enforcement of Foreign Arbitral Awards, and the UNCITRAL Model Law on International Commercial Arbitration.[189]

Such decision is, therefore, treated as any award in terms of annulment, recognition and enforcement.[190] Accordingly, the decision on costs may be annulled or denied enforcement if it violates the principles of public policy of the *lex loci arbitri* or the *lex loci excutionis* respectively.

However, institutional or arbitral tribunal's decisions on the advance on costs regarding the fees and expenses that the parties should pay to the arbitral tribunal and the arbitral institution do not constitute an award as such,[191] since such decisions do not rule on a claim between the parties, but resolve a procedural issue between the parties and the arbitrators or the arbitral institution.[192] It is the decision allocating costs and enabling recovery of same from either party which qualifies as an award that would normally have a res judicata effect, unless it is an interim award, which the arbitral tribunal may reconsider or revisit throughout the proceedings.

IV. REGIONAL SPECIFICITIES AND COSTS

In as much as a global overview of costs and the analysis of the governing principles are important, it is submitted that national and regional perspectives on costs may prove useful to analyze whether the prevailing international principles uniformly or harmoniously apply across jurisdictions or whether certain regional or national anomalies or variances exist with respect to allocation and recoverability of costs.

That said, this section intends to succinctly test the view that rules and principles applicable to the "allocation of costs" may vary from a jurisdiction to another (*1*), before

---

186. See *ibid*.
187. *Ibid*; See also J. WAINCYMER, *Procedure and Evidence in International Arbitration* (Kluwer Law International 2012) p. 1237.
188. See J. WAINCYMER, *Procedure and Evidence in International Arbitration* (Kluwer Law International 2012) p. 1261.
189. See G. BORN, *International Commercial Arbitration* (Kluwer Law International 2014) p. 3087.
190. *Ibid*.
191. See G. BORN, *International Commercial Arbitration* (Kluwer Law International 2014) p. 3088.
192. *Ibid*.

considering the magnitude of variation with respect to certain issues pertinent to "recoverable costs" (*2*).

1. Regional Specificities on Allocation of Costs

As mentioned herein above, most legal systems generally allocate costs according to the general principle that the loser pays, subject to any needed adjustments based on law, agreement and factual circumstances. According to a global survey on costs in national courts undertaken by the leading firm Hogan Lovells (formerly Lovells), forty-nine of the fifty-six surveyed jurisdictions, representing 87.5 percent, adopt the "loser pays" principle in litigation.[193]

As expected, the notable exception to this trend is the United States where the general rule is that each party shall bear its own legal costs. In addition, the survey demonstrated that in Japan counsel's fees are not recoverable in any event,[194] and in Taiwan, counsel's fees are not recoverable unless counsel has been appointed by the court.[195]

In Europe, the "costs follow the event/loser pays" principle is generally recognized and considered the prevailing applicable practice to the allocation of costs.[196] For instance, this is the case in Austria,[197] Denmark,[198] England,[199] Finland,[200] France,[201] Germany,[202] Greece,[203] Italy,[204] the Netherlands,[205] Portugal,[206] the Russian Federation,[207] Spain[208] and Switzerland.[209]

In contrast, in the United States, whilst national courts generally hold that each party shall bear its legal costs,[210] US courts have held that arbitral tribunals have discretion to

193. See G. HUNTLEY, P. TYLOR, S. BRADSTOCK, eds., *At What Cost? A Lovells Multi Jurisdictional Guide to Litigation Costs* (2010) p. 4
194. *Ibid.*
195. *Ibid.*
196. See J. LEW, L. MISTELIS, and S. KRÖLL, *Comparative International Commercial Arbitration* (Kluwer Law International 2003) p. 655.
197. See W. MELIS, "National Report Austria" (2018) in ICCA *International Handbook on Commercial Arbitration* (Kluwer Law International) (henceforth *Handbook*), p. 32.
198. See O. SPIERMANN, "National Report Denmark" (2009) in *Handbook*, p. 27.
199. See V.V. VEEDER and R. H. DIWAN, "National Report England" (2018) in *Handbook*, pp. 59-60.
200. See G. MÖLLER, "National Report Finland" (2018) in *Handbook*.
201. See Y. DERAINS and L. KIFFER, "National Report France" (2018) in *Handbook*, p. 66.
202. See S.M. KRÖLL, "National Report Germany" (2018) in *Handbook*, p. 50.
203. See I. VASSARDANIS, "National Report Greece" (2018) in *Handbook*, p. 46.
204. See P. BERNARDINI, "National Report Italy" (2007) in *Handbook*, p. 43.
205. See G.J. MEIJER and M.R.P. PAULSSON, "National Report The Netherlands" (2018) in *Handbook*, pp. 52-53.
206. See D.M. VICENTE, "National Report Portugal" (2018) in *Handbook*.
207. See B.R. KARABELNIKOV, "National Report Russian Federation" (2018) in *Handbook*, p. 59.
208. See B. CREMADES and D. CAIRNS, "National Report Spain" (2018) in *Handbook*, 2018, p. 26
209. See P.M. PATOCCHI, "National Report Switzerland" (2018) in *Handbook*, 2018, p. 69.
210. See C.M. AMIRFAR, N.L. REID, et al., "National Report The United States of America" (2018) in *Handbook*, pp. 65-66.

award and allocate costs,[211] which is demonstrative of US courts' disinclination to treat the American rule as an overriding policy principle.

With respect to the MENA region, the majority of legal systems apply the "costs follow the event/loser pays" principle in allocating costs. For instance, in Algeria,[212] Egypt,[213] Qatar,[214] Tunisia[215] and Turkey[216] the prevailing practice is that courts and arbitral tribunals award costs according to the "costs follow the event/loser pays" principle subject to variations in the quantum of the costs awarded.

In contrast, in Saudi Arabia, the prevailing practice seems to be that the legal costs are shared equally by the parties.[217] However, this practice is expected to change given that Art. 42(2) of the Arbitration Regulations requires that the arbitral award states, inter alia, the arbitration costs and how costs should be apportioned between the parties.[218]

More interestingly, whilst the prevailing practice in the United Arab Emirates (UAE) is that "costs follow the event/loser pays", the practice regarding the implementation of the said principle merits a mention. This practice largely depends on whether the arbitration is strictly seated in the so-called "onshore" UAE, is governed by the UAE Federal Code of Civil Procedure (1992) and whether the proceedings involve domestic or international parties, or whether the arbitration takes place in one of the UAE's free zones benefiting from a distinct arbitration regime as is the case of the Dubai International Financial Centre (DIFC) and the Abu Dhabi Global Market (ADGM).[219]

Whilst in non-DIFC and non-ADGM arbitrations, arbitral tribunals are still able to allocate and award costs, the practice is that the parties may need to agree on the arbitral tribunal's authority to award costs, including specifically legal costs. In contrast, in DIFC and ADGM arbitrations, arbitral tribunals, operating under a specific arbitration regime, have more discretion and authority in allocating and awarding costs including legal costs without need for a specific agreement to that effect.

Similarly, in Australia[220] as well as a significant number of Asian and African countries, the "costs follow the event/loser pays" principle is the prevailing approach in a significant number of jurisdictions, such as Hong Kong,[221] Kenya,[222] Malaysia,[223] Nigeria,[224] Pakistan[225] and Singapore.[226] However, as previously mentioned, the American rule found support in some jurisdictions in Asia, mainly in China, Indonesia and Japan.

211. *Ibid.*
212. See "ICC Commission Report: Decisions on Costs in International Arbitration" (2015) p. 46.
213. See K. HAFEZ, "National Report Egypt" (2013) in *Handbook*, p. 31.
214. See "ICC Commission Report: Decisions on Costs in International Arbitration" (2015) p. 46.
215. See A. OUERFELLI, "National Report Tunisia" (2009) in *Handbook*, p. 54.
216. See M.T. BIRSEL, A.YESILIRMAK, et al., "National Report Turkey" (2011) in *Handbook*, p. 30.
217. See J.-B. ZEGERS, "National Report for Saudi Arabia" (2018) in *Handbook*, p. 43.
218. *Ibid.*
219. See S.TANNOUS, S. LORD HILL, et al., "National Report United Arab Emirates" (2018) in *Handbook*, pp. 94-99.
220. See M. PRYLES, "National Report Australia" (2018) in *Handbook*, p. 42.
221. See N. KAPLAN and R. MORGAN, "National Report Hong Kong" (2018) in *Handbook*, pp. 91-92.
222. See E. TORGBOR, "National Report Kenya" (2018) in *Handbook*, pp. 43-44.
223. See T. ABRAHAM, "National Report Malaysia" (2018) in *Handbook*, p. 38.
224. See F. ADEKOYA, "National Report Nigeria" (2018) in *Handbook*, p. 23.
225. See M. KHAN, "National Report Pakistan" (2012) in *Handbook*, p. 31.

In Latin America, the prevailing practice is somewhat divided and less clear. In Argentina,[227] Mexico,[228] Peru,[229] Colombia[230] and Costa Rica,[231] courts and arbitral tribunals normally apply the "costs follow the event/loser pays" principle when allocating costs. In addition, although the general rule in Chile is that the party who loses on all the points shall be ordered to bear all the costs, courts and arbitral tribunals, in practice, are reluctant to make such an order.[232] Furthermore, in Brazil, arbitral tribunals normally order each party to bear its own legal costs but share the costs for the administration of the arbitral proceedings.[233]

In this regard, it is worth reiterating, in virtually all the jurisdictions mentioned above which apply the "costs follow the event/loser pays" principle in allocating costs, courts and arbitral tribunals are allowed to depart from this general principle when the circumstances of a given case so warrant. Thus, in effect, such principle serves as a default presumption that can be displaced or adapted as necessary in light of the factual matrix of the case or as agreed between the parties before or after the commencement of the proceedings.

In specific reference to the parties' agreement on the allocation of costs, it may stipulate that a party will bear all the costs irrespective of the outcome of the dispute. If so, such agreements will generally be upheld and enforced in most jurisdictions, such as Algeria, Austria, Bahrain, British Columbia, Egypt, Finland, Germany, Ghana, Ireland, Italy, Jordan, Lebanon, Mexico, Morocco, the Netherlands, New Zealand, Oman, Qatar, Quebec, Russia, Saudi Arabia, Senegal, Spain, Sweden, Tunisia, the United Arab Emirates and the United States.[234]

In contrast, in the United Kingdom, the enforceability of prior agreements binding a party to bear the costs in any and all cases is questionable. However, subsequent agreements, concluded after a dispute has arisen, raise no issue.[235] In Switzerland, the parties' conclusion of an agreement on costs will not bar the court's discretion in awarding costs.[236] In France, whilst it is permissible, in domestic proceedings, for the parties to agree on allocating counsel's fees, an agreement regarding the allocation of court costs is null and void.[237] However, in arbitration, all types of agreements would generally be upheld in France.[238]

---

226. See M. HWANG, L. BOO, et al., "National Report Singapore" (2019) in *Handbook*, p. 41.
227. See G.S. TAWIL and F. CAMPOLIETI, "National Report Argentina" (2018) in *Handbook*, p. 35.
228. See F.GONZÁLEZ DE COSSÍO, "National Report Mexico" (2018) in *Handbook*, p. 32.
229. See F.C. SALAVERRY, "National Report Peru" (2018) in *Handbook*, p. 28.
230. See E.Z. JARAMILLO, "National Report Colombia" (2018) in *Handbook*.
231. See M.F. ZERR, "National Report Costa Rica" (2018) in *Handbook*, pp. 56-57.
232. See Andrés JANA L., "National Report Chile" (2018) in *Handbook*, 2018 p. 49.
233. See C.N. NETTO, "National Report Brazil" (2018) in *Handbook*, pp. 27-28.
234. See "ICC Commission Report: Decisions on Costs in International Arbitration" (2015) p. 46.
235. *Ibid.*
236. *Ibid.*, p. 47.
237. *Ibid.*
238. *Ibid.*

2. *Regional Specificities Regarding Recoverable Costs*

With respect to recoverability of costs, there remain certain differences between jurisdictions and the *ICC Commission's Report regarding Decisions on Costs in International Arbitration* (the Report) illustrates the differences between jurisdictions on costs-related arrangements as well as third-party funding agreements and the recoverability of costs in the presence of such agreements.[239]

This Report affirms that the fee/costs-related agreements are generally permitted in most jurisdictions, such as Austria, Brazil, British Columbia, Egypt, France, Kuwait, Lebanon, Ontario, Poland, Mexico, Saudi Arabia, the United Arab Emirates and the United States.[240]

However, in others jurisdictions, namely Argentina, British Colombia, Finland, Ghana, New Zealand, Nigeria, Senegal, Spain, Sweden and Tunisia, the fee arrangements are permitted under certain requirements, such as being reasonable and complying with the rules of professional conduct.[241]

On the specific issue of contingency fee agreements, this is quite controversial. Such agreements are considered null and void in Austria, Bahrain, Iraq, Ireland, Morocco, Oman and Qatar. They are also prohibited in French domestic proceedings but permitted in international arbitration. In Germany, such agreements are generally prohibited, but the German Federal Constitutional Court held that the prohibition of such agreements is unconstitutional since it restricts party autonomy and counsel freedom.[242] Nonetheless, contingency fee agreements remain uncommon in arbitration and litigation in Germany. In Russia, the regulation of the contingency fee agreements is also unclear. Although the courts have long refused to enforce contingency fee arrangements, in recent years, they "have become more open to enforcing" said agreements, and arbitral tribunals also allow contingency fees as long as they are reasonable.[243] In contrast, in Argentina and Poland, contingency fee agreements are not taken into account in the calculation of the costs of the arbitration.[244]

As to third-party funding agreements, their impact on the recoverability of costs also varies from one jurisdiction to another due to the jurisdictional perception of third-party funding arrangements. In Argentina, Austria, Ghana, Germany, Ireland, and the United Kingdom, third-party funding agreements do not seem to affect the recoverability of legal costs in court proceedings. Conversely, the costs of third-party funding are not recoverable in Brazil, Finland, Nigeria, Singapore and Sweden.[245]

In the MENA region, the validity of third-party arrangements and recoverability of the third-party-funding-related costs are unclear because such agreements are not yet that common in the region and third-party funders have not yet established notable existence within local markets, especially in the Arab world. This may be due to the

239. See "ICC Commission Report: Decisions on Costs in International Arbitration" (2015) p. 44-46.
240. *Ibid.*
241. *Ibid.*
242. *Ibid.*
243. *Ibid.*
244. *Ibid.*
245. *Ibid.*

skepticism over the validity and/or enforceability of third-party funding arrangements in local markets within some of those jurisdictions.

However, it is submitted that absent any legal constraint on the validity and/or enforceability of third-party funding arrangements, courts and arbitral tribunals would have no ground not to uphold such arrangements. Nevertheless, on the specific issue of recoverability of third-party funding costs, arbitral tribunals and courts would need to consider the specificities and peculiarities of the applicable legal system, taking into consideration the parties' legitimate expectations, the reasonableness of such costs and the factual circumstances of each case. Whilst this does not offer much certainty or predictability, this would be the status quo until such jurisdictions enact regulatory rules that govern all pertinent aspects of third-party funding or arbitration finance.

V. EPILOGUE: TOWARDS PREDICTABILITY AND CERTAINTY

Costs are at the forefront of hot topics in international arbitration. They represent a major concern of law, justice and procedure to all those involved in arbitral proceedings, notably: parties, counsel, arbitrators, arbitral institutions and more recently financiers of arbitral proceedings. The law and economics of cost-related issues remain challenging and problematic amidst the reality of prohibitively high costs and the sea of uncertain practices as to costs in terms of allocation and recoverability.

In addition to the fact that costs are high, the awarding of same remains eventfully unpredictable, owing to the broad discretion granted to arbitral tribunals in this regard. It has been said that matters of costs are left to "the widest discretion of arbitrators",[246] where arbitral tribunals exercise "'their discretionary power' [to award] costs in a diverse and sometimes highly inconsistent manner' which amounts to 'arbitral free styling, devising a formula to apportion costs without relying on any traditional approach'".[247]

Amidst such convoluted realism, the common denominators underlying all the issues of costs in international arbitration, are: (i) the absence of sufficient predictability on microcosmic practices as to costs; (ii) the insufficient attention given to issues of costs by the parties and the arbitral tribunals at the last mile of the proceedings, especially with respect to the characterization of cost issues as matters of procedure or substance, the law that shall govern the awarding of costs and the standards according to which the arbitral tribunals award costs;[248] and (iii) the scarcity of legal studies and comparative analyses on cost-related issues. As correctly stated by some leading practitioners: "There is indeed an arbitral precedent to support nearly any approach a tribunal may wish to

246. See M. BÜHLER, "Awarding Costs in International Commercial Arbitration: An Overview", 22 ASA Bull. (2004, issue 2) p. 253.

247. See E. LITH, Conference speech of 13 February 2014, cited in S. GREENBERG, "Chapter II: The Arbitrator and the Arbitration Procedure, Law Applicable to Costs Claims in International Arbitration: Why Does It Matter?" in Christian KLAUSEGGER, Peter KLEIN, et al., eds., *Austrian Yearbook on International Arbitration, 2015*, p. 177.

248. See S. GREENBERG, "Chapter II: The Arbitrator and the Arbitration Procedure, Law Applicable to Costs Claims in International Arbitration: Why Does It Matter?" in Christian KLAUSEGGER, Peter KLEIN, et al., eds., *Austrian Yearbook on International Arbitration, 2015*, p. 176.

apply to its cost decision. Even cost awards rendered under the same arbitration rules sometimes vary fundamentally without any apparent reason."[249]

Accordingly, there is a dire need for more certainty, predictability and harmonization as to the *standard(s), principles* and *norms* governing all issues of costs in international arbitration and the role of national courts when reviewing awards on issues of costs.

A balance needs to be struck between several issues: (i) the fact that awarding costs is originally intended to compensate the successful party and allow it to recover the costs it has incurred in prosecuting its case; (ii) the consideration that awarding costs can be an effective tool to mitigate the risk of frivolous claims; (iii) the need to sanction inappropriate conduct by counsel or party when prosecuting the arbitral proceedings, which would encourage more cooperation between parties and counsel for efficiency purposes; and (iv) the importance of disambiguating the prevailing principle, and its variants and applications, when allocating and ordering the recoverability of costs.

That said, it is submitted that the departing default rule ought to be the "costs follow the event/loser pays" principle, subject to any warranted adjustments to cater for the specificities of each case, based on reasonably predictable guiding factors. This warrants encouraging arbitral tribunals to ascertain, at the beginning of the proceedings, the criteria and factors which the arbitral tribunal should consider regarding all issues of costs. This would require a detailed process of consultation with the parties, which will facilitate distilling areas of agreement and disagreement on cost-related issues and will enable the arbitral tribunal to chart a proper and transparent course when navigating through the devil's sea of costs.

Taking the above recommendation more globally, it is submitted that the international community is under a duty to consider streamlining and harmonizing international practices and principles governing the awarding of costs, and it is in this context that soft law instruments, treaties and global players such as international arbitral institutions can play a role.

Indeed, costs is an area where international arbitral institutions can showcase the benefits of institutional arbitration when compared to *ad hoc* proceedings. On such account, in recent years, global and institutional efforts to reduce costs and to set clear standards for the awarding of costs are gaining momentum and a growing awareness of the need to address cost-related issues is manifest.

Having recognized the direct relationship and the causation between time and costs and that the longer the proceedings, the more expensive they become, arbitral institutions are taking a leading role to control time and costs.[250] Whilst institutional

249. See M. BÜHLER, "Awarding Costs in International Commercial Arbitration: An Overview", 22 ASA Bull. (2004, issue 2) p. 249.

250. See for example, the "ICC Commission Report: Techniques for Controlling Time and Costs in Arbitration", second ed. The Report suggested some techniques to control costs. Amongst these techniques are: (i) the arbitral tribunal taking into account the extent to which each party has conducted the arbitration in an expeditious and cost-effective manner; (ii) the importance of carefully drafting arbitration agreements in simple and clear terms; (iii) encouraging parties to use expedited or fast-track procedures and most arbitral institutions have issued expedited procedural provisions or rules; (iv) appointing experienced and available counsel as well as arbitrators with strong case management skills; and (v) limiting the parties' written submissions, minimizing the number of witness, experts and hearings and limiting direct examination of

efforts testify to the importance of costs and their related challenges, much remains to be done to ensure proper and informed navigation through the Devil's Sea to guarantee safe arrival at the shores of certainty and predictability and the harbours of justice.

witness, rounds of witness statements, and experts' reports. See also, the most recent "ICC Commission Report: Decisions on Costs in International Arbitration" (2015), which provides a useful overview of awarding costs in different jurisdictions and elaborates on the positive impact of using the techniques for controlling time and costs. This most recent report further underlines the importance of discussing at the outset of the arbitral proceedings or during the proceedings different costs-related issues.

A Thought-Experiment Regarding Access to Justice in International Arbitration

Victoria Shannon Sahani[*]

TABLE OF CONTENTS

I. INTRODUCTION

One reason for the public outcry against third-party funding is the widespread perception that third-party funding is unbalancing our notions of party-driven dispute resolution processes and even-handed tribunals.[1] In the aspirational vision of idyllic dispute resolution, an arbitrator or judge oversees the proper administration of the proverbial "scales of justice" in an orderly manner and "balances" out party power differentials calmly through procedural evenhandedness. Yet, third-party funding indisputably puts a gold-weighted thumb on the scale in favor of funded parties, particularly since funded cases already tend to be calculable winners on the merits, and since third-party funders seeking a profit generally do not fund cases that are demonstrably likely to lose on the merits.[2]

---

* Tenured Associate Professor of Law at Arizona State University's Sandra Day O'Connor College of Law; co-author of *Third-Party Funding in International Arbitration* (with Lisa Bench NIEUWVELD) (2nd ed., Wolters Kluwer, 2017); Member of the ICCA-Queen Mary Task Force on Third-Party Funding, the Executive Council of the American Society of International Law (ASIL), and the Academic Council of the Institute for Transnational Arbitration (ITA); former Deputy Director of Arbitration and ADR in North America in New York, ICC International Court of Arbitration; Bachelor's and law degrees, Harvard University; licensed to practice law in New York and the District of Columbia.

1. See, e.g., Chris HAMBY, *Secrets of a Global Super Court: A BuzzFeed News Investigation*, BuzzFeed.com, (28 Aug. – 12 Oct. 2016) <www.buzzfeed.com/globalsupercourt> (last accessed 2 Feb. 2019) (a six-article series); Rebecca LOWE, "Speculate and Arbitrate to Accumulate", IBA Global Insight (Apr/May 2013); Pia EBERHARDT, "A Response to the Critics of 'Profiting from Injustice'", Kluwer Arbitration Blog, (2 Jan. 2013), <http://arbitrationblog.kluwerarbitration.com/2013/01/02/a-response-to-the-critics-of-profiting-from-injustice/> (last accessed 2 Feb. 2019); Transnational Institute and Corporate Europe Observatory, *Profiting from Injustice* (Brussels/Amsterdam, Nov. 2012), available at <https://corporateeurope.org/sites/default/files/publications/profiting-from-injustice.pdf> (last accessed 23 May 2018).
2. But see Kate BROWN DE VEJAR and Chloe BALDWIN, "The Economics of Access: Systemic Imbalances in ISDS", this volume, p. 520 at p. 541 ("Certainly, third-party funders have no incentive to back a losing claim, and they generally have skilled teams of lawyers who assess the

Thus, we are left with the promising potential for winners to be more likely to win with third-party funding, and the alarming realization that not all parties are offered this same chance to win. For example, traditional for-profit third-party funders only fund cases from which they can make a profit; thus, many merit-based winners whose claims are too expensive to pursue relative to their claim value are turned down. Second, it is likely that longshot-winners – cases too risky even for a third-party funder that are, for example, rightfully arguing for a change in the law or relying on creative theories that require mental and verbal jujitsu to convince the decision-maker (i.e., the stuff of Hollywood films about courageous lawyers and citizens fighting against insurmountable odds) – are less likely to be funded as well. Third, defendant-winners may be less likely to be funded unless those defendants already have hefty funds at their disposal through which to pay the funder either a periodic premium or are willing to pay the funder from their own pockets (rather than from the proceeds of an award) upon winning the case.[3] Fourth, non-financial winners – parties seeking non-financial remedies – are not likely to be funded unless they are willing to pay the funder from their own pockets, since there will be no monetary judgment upon winning the case. Fifth, political-winners are not likely to be funded, as many funders choose not to engage in funding of controversial positions and parties, which may be viewed as courageous or cowardly, depending on the type of party or issue at stake in the case.

The foregoing examples collectively engender a larger, fundamental question: If funders are picking primarily winners – and more specifically winners that suit their business model – then what does real access to justice in international arbitration look like in an era of third-party funding? Would real access to justice need to involve third-party funders funding impecunious innocent respondents, or expensive long-shot claimants, or righteous injunctions with no monetary recovery, or unprofitable cases that espouse some worthy yet controversial position?

Much has been written about access to justice in international arbitration.[4] This Article contributes to the conversation by presenting one theoretical framework to assess

---

claim before determining whether to invest. But studying the form guide doesn't mean that the punter will pick the winning horse. The fact that the third-party funder has studied what is known about the case at a certain point (usually before anything is known of the respondent State's position) and is financially incentivized to bet on a winner does not mean that because the funder decides to invest, the case is bulletproof, or even that it is likely to end in a result favorable to the investor. It also does not mean that a fundamentally unmeritorious claim, which should never have been brought, will not receive third-party funding.") (parentheses in original).

3. There may be at least one notable exception. Narghis Torres, Co-Founder and CEO of LexFinance (<www.lex-finance.com>), publicly stated that his firm regularly finances respondent states in investment arbitration at an event titled "Third-Party Funding in Investor-State Dispute Settlement" hosted by Columbia Law School on 17 October 2017. This lends credence to the solution presented in Sect. IV of this Article, below.

4. See e.g., Ylli DAUTAJ and Bruno GUSTAFSSON, "Access to Justice: Rebalancing the Third-Party Funding Equilibrium in Investment Treaty Arbitration" (18 Nov. 2017), <http://arbitrationblog.kluwerarbitration.com/2017/11/18/access-justice-rebalancing-third-party-funding-equilibrium-investment-treaty-arbitration-2/> (last accessed 2 Feb. 2019); Jaroslav KUDRNA, "Arbitration and Right of Access to Justice: Tips for a Successful Marriage", Transnational Notes Blog (22 Feb. 2013) <https://blogs.law.nyu.edu/transnational/2013/02/ arbitration-and-right-of-access-to-justice-tips-for-a-successful-marriage/> (last accessed 2 Feb. 2019); Petra BUTLER

the level of access to justice that currently exists in international arbitration and determine pathways to increasing access to justice. This Article proposes a working definition of access to justice in international arbitration and then presents a simple thought experiment to assess which parties currently have access to justice in international arbitration and which parties may lack such access. This Article concludes by suggesting some next steps regarding how to increase access to justice in international arbitration.

II. ASSUMPTIONS MADE

First, what is access to justice? Access to justice could be defined in many ways depending on the context. For this Article, simple working definitions are appropriate. This Article defines "justice" as the assumption that the system of international arbitration and international arbitrators, viewed as a whole, reliably and regularly decides cases in a fair and enforceable manner that upholds due process of the law for all parties involved (leaving aside the idiosyncratic errors or biases of individual arbitrators). Of course, this is a seemingly rosy assumption that may be challenged by those critical of the international arbitration system. Nevertheless, for the purposes of this thought experiment, such an assumption is necessary – like a mathematical constant, if you will – to examine access from a financial perspective.

In addition, it is important to note that the definition of "justice" used in this Article does not address the merits of a particular claim or defense. In other words, this Article assumes that losers have just as much right as winners to bring their claims or marshal their defenses in international arbitration and, therefore, losers deserve as much *procedural* justice as winners do, even though the merits of their substantive positions may be shaky. Again, such an assumption could be challenged, but this Article adopts this assumption as necessary to the conclusions of this thought experiment, discussed further below.

This Article also assumes that "access" relates to the *financial* ability to proceed forward in arbitration. Thus, "access" in this context does not address non-financial barriers to arbitration, such as jurisdictional requirements, defective arbitration clauses, non-participating parties, substantive arbitrability, the availability of class or mass arbitration, or any similar non-financial barrier. In sum, this Article assumes that the phrase "access to justice" simply means having or acquiring the financial resources needed to bring your claim or muster your defense in international arbitration.

In applying this definition, there are an endless number of ways in which a party could have or acquire financial resources for pursing a claim in arbitration or defending against

---

and Campbell HERBERT, "Access to Justice vs Access to Justice for Small and Medium-Sized Enterprises: The Case for a Bilateral Arbitration Treaty", 26 New Zealand Universities Law Review (Dec. 2014) p. 186; Brooks W. DALY and Sarah MELIKIAN, "Access to Justice in Dispute Resolution" in Krista Nadakavukaren SCHEFER, ed., *Poverty and the International Economic Legal System: Duties to the World's Poor* (Cambridge University Press 2013) pp. 211-224; Francesco FRANCIONI, "Access to Justice, Denial of Justice and International Investment Law", 20 European Journal of International Law (1 Aug. 2009, issue 3) pp. 729-747 <https://doi.org/10.1093/ejil/chp057> (last accessed 2 Feb. 2019).

it. For example, many parties self-finance their claims or defenses. Parties may also acquire liability insurance or political risk insurance, which may include paying the costs of arbitration. Subsidiaries may be able to tap into the resources of their parent corporations. States may use their internal legal teams or tap into their treasuries to pay external law firms. A client may hire an attorney or law firm on a contingent or conditional fee basis, if allowed in the relevant jurisdiction. And then there's third-party funding. This Article adopts the ICCA-Queen Mary Task Force on Third-Party Funding definition of "third-party funding" in Chapter 3: Definitions, which reads as follows:

> "The term 'third-party funding' refers to an agreement by an entity that is not a party to the dispute to provide a party, an affiliate of that party or a law firm representing that party,
> (a) funds or other material support in order to finance part or all of the cost of the proceedings, either individually or as part of a specific range of cases, and
> (b) such support or financing is either provided in exchange for remuneration or reimbursement that is wholly or partially dependent on the outcome of the dispute, or provided through a grant or in return for a premium payment."[5]

Given the plethora of financing options, this Article must draw an arbitrary dividing line in the sand for the purpose of assessing access to justice. On one side of that line, the party definitely has access to justice and, on the other side, the party could potentially lack access to justice for the purpose of this thought experiment. It is important to note that this is not a line between the "haves" and the "have nots". Instead, this is a line between those who most certainly have access to justice and those whose access to justice is predicated on the outcome of the decision-making process of a financier not present at the time the dispute arises. Thus, for the purpose of this thought experiment, the line will be defined as whether the party's dispute financing is based on a *pre-existing* financial relationship with the financier *prior* to the incident that led to the claim in the arbitration. Of course, this line could be defined by other characteristics of a party or its case, but since this Article focuses on financial access to justice, the choice to draw the line according to the status of the source of a party's funding seems most appropriate.

To illustrate how this line functions, the simplest example is that a party with the financial resources to self-finance arbitration has a preexisting relationship with itself (the financier) before the claim arose; thus, that party has access to justice, according to this definition. Similarly, a subsidiary has a pre-existing relationship with a parent corporation prior to the claim in arbitration. If the parent corporation has the ability and willingness to provide financial support for a viable claim or defense, then the subsidiary has access to justice. Furthermore, if a party acquires liability insurance or political risk insurance at the outset of a contract or prior to making a foreign direct investment in a host state, and if such insurance covers the costs of arbitration, then the party has access to justice. On the other side of the line, an attorney or law firm will not enter into a

5. Chapter 3: Definitions, p. 50, The ICCA Reports No. 4: ICCA-Queen Mary University of London Task Force Report on Third-Party Funding in International Arbitration (International Council for Commercial Arbitration, 2018) (numbering and spacing in original), <www.arbitration-icca.org/publications/Third-Party-Funding-Report.html> (last accessed 2 Feb. 2019).

contingent or conditional fee arrangement with a client until after the incident that gives rise to the claim has taken place. Thus, if the party needs such contingent or conditional fee arrangement in order to pursue arbitration, then the party is in danger of not having access to justice if it is unable to obtain such an arrangement. Similarly, third-party funding – as traditionally envisioned – is tied to the existence of events that give rise to an arbitration claim.

It is important to note that, since the definition of "access to justice" articulated above involves engaging the machinery of the international arbitration process, this Article assumes that types of outside funding not tied to the existence of a dispute are more in the realm of corporate finance transactions and are not contemplated within this Article's definition of "access to justice". The assumption here is that if a party has the wherewithal to enter into a corporate finance transaction independent of any pending disputes, then it also likely has access to adequate resources to pursue a claim or defend itself in international arbitration; therefore, it has access to justice. Furthermore, any insurance agreement entered into *after* the incident that gives rise to the claim has taken place, which is often termed "after-the-event insurance", is categorized on the same side of the line as third-party funding and contingent or conditional fee arrangements.

This line in the sand is crucial, because the "access" in "access to justice" is an indicator of possibility, not certainty. In other words, having "access to justice" means that a party *could* financially pursue arbitration even if it chooses not to do so or is unable to do so for other non-financial reasons. For example, if a subsidiary could bring a viable claim with the help of the parent corporation, but *chooses* not to do so for business reasons, the subsidiary has access to justice, according to the definition in this Article. In addition, if the subsidiary could bring the claim with the help of the parent corporation, but the parent corporation believes that the claim is not viable enough to bring, then the subsidiary has access to justice, according to the definition in this Article. Furthermore, if a party is the respondent with sufficient financial resources to self-finance and nevertheless *refuses* to participate in the arbitration (thinking that the claim is bogus, for example), then the party has access to justice, according to the definition in this Article.

On the other hand, if a party is the *respondent* and does *not* have sufficient financial resources to self-finance while wanting to participate in the arbitration, then whether such a respondent has access to justice depends on the type of financier that could finance the party's defense. If the respondent can obtain a financier through a preexisting financial relationship, such as a parent corporation or a pre-existing insurance agreement, then the respondent has access to justice. If the respondent's financial relationship with the financier arises after the incident that led to the claim in the arbitration – such as a contingent or conditional fee arrangement with a law firm, after-the-event insurance or traditional third-party funding – then the respondent may have no access to justice if it is unable to create such a financial relationship.

This highlights a crucial point about access to justice, however it may be defined. Any proper assessment of "access to justice" must examine the situation of parties that have no choice in the matter: respondents. Respondents in all types of arbitration have no choice regarding whether the arbitration will bind them, regardless of whether they are financially able to participate in the arbitration or not. Thus, respondents *must* have access to justice – defined in this Article as having or acquiring the financial resources needed to muster their defenses in international arbitration – in order for the system to be considered "just" at all.[6]

There is also a cost component to access to justice, namely, whether the financier's willingness to pay the costs of arbitration is predicated on some relationship between the costs of arbitration and the magnitude of the claim. Some types of financiers – such as self-financiers, parent corporations, and liability insurance – will pay the costs of arbitration regardless of the amount of the claim or the type of defense. Other types of financiers – such as third-party funders or after-the-event insurers – might only agree to pay the costs of arbitration if the costs are some order of magnitude less than the amount of the claim, or if the party provides the financier with some other alternative form of remuneration. Attorneys on contingent or conditional fees are likely somewhere in the middle. While the amount of the attorney's fees may not be directly tied to the costs of the arbitration, the attorney may turn down a case that might be too expensive relative to the amount the attorney could expect to be paid if the party wins the case, especially since most jurisdictions have a legislative cap on attorney contingent or conditional fees.[7] In light of this, the cost of arbitration is a crucial component to consider when determining whether a party had adequate access to justice.

To further complicate the matter of costs, it is nearly impossible to calculate in advance precisely how much a case will cost. The only exception may be that certain types of financiers, such as third-party funders or law firms working on a contingent or conditional fee, may include in their contracts provisions capping the amount that they will spend on arbitration costs. In addition, there are different fee provisions under the various arbitral rules – whether calculated on an hourly or daily rate or based on the amount in dispute – and for *ad hoc* arbitration the basis for the fees is even more variable. Moreover, there are certain types of claims that may require more extensive resources – such as class arbitration – or that may require the services of an emergency arbitrator – such as an injunction. The costs of such types of proceedings may be highly variable and not at all connected to the economic value of the result. Furthermore, some types of claims have no damage award attached to them, such as injunctive or declarative relief, in which case the costs will always mathematically outweigh the dollars recoverable from the claim, even if the claim is otherwise worthy and winnable. Finally, there is the question of timing and settlement. If all other parameters are equal, a case that settles early usually results in cheaper costs than a case that goes all the way to an award, which

6. This same argument could potentially be applied in a domestic criminal prosecution context. In that context, the equivalent to a respondent state winner would be an innocent criminal defendant, for whom funding is non-existent, since all funding is currently limited to civil litigation in all the jurisdictions in which this Author found the existence or regulation of third-party funding (over sixty countries). See generally Lisa Bench NIEUWVELD and Victoria Shannon SAHANI, *Third-Party Funding in International Arbitration*, 2nd. ed. (Wolters Kluwer 2017). Presenting and analyzing this undoubtedly controversial argument in favour of allowing third-party funding in criminal defence cases is beyond the scope of this Article.
7. See generally Lisa Bench NIEUWVELD and Victoria Shannon SAHANI, *Third-Party Funding in International Arbitration*, 2nd. ed. (Wolters Kluwer 2017) (citing contingent or conditional fee caps in the Canada, China, New Zealand, South Africa, the United Kingdom and the United States). There are also likely many other countries that cap contingent or conditional fees, but which were not included in the aforementioned book due to the lack of information available from those countries regarding the availability of third-party funding.

in turn results in cheaper costs than a case that leads to enforcement or set-aside proceedings in a national court.

In sum, a case may be wildly expensive or may settle cheaply. One cannot predict in advance exactly which of these scenarios will happen in a particular case. Considering the high variability in cost structures and amounts, the thought experiment in this Article makes a simple assumption about costs. It assumes that the costs for a hypothetical party to an arbitration are reasonable and proportional for the type of case and type of claim or defense at issue, even though many cases may be extraordinarily expensive or surprisingly inexpensive. This assumption regarding costs is necessary for there to be any generalizable conclusions to be drawn from this thought experiment regarding access to justice.

There are a few less controversial assumptions in this thought experiment as well. This Article addresses only two types of international arbitration: commercial and investment arbitration. This Article does not address state-to-state arbitration, which may involve, for example, boundary or trade disputes. In addition, this Article addresses only single parties of three types: a corporation, a state, or an individual. A state-owned entity is categorized as a corporation for the purpose of this Article.[8] Multi-party actions – such as class, mass, or representative actions – are not contemplated. Furthermore, this Article categorizes the relief requested by a claimant as either damages or non-financial relief, such as an injunction, specific performance, or declarative relief. For respondents, the relief requested (that is, the respondents "claim") is characterized as "no liability" (namely, asking the tribunal to decide that the defendant is not liable for the injury the claimant alleges) in order to consider respondents and claimants together in this study. There may be other hybrid, unusual or less common types of relief that parties may request, but the aforementioned categories encompass the vast majority of types of claims or defenses brought in international arbitration.

Finally, since it is virtually impossible to predict with certainty the outcome of a case, this study addresses only two possibilities with respect to outcome – likely winner or likely loser – keeping in mind, however, that for some cases a party may be just as likely to win or lose. The reason that this study addresses only those two possibilities is that we know that all parties, including those who are self-financing, engage in some sort of analysis regarding the likelihood of winning the case when deciding whether or how to proceed. Most parties or their legal counsel have at least some expectation regarding whether the party is more likely to win or more likely to lose the case, and funders analyze this question and draw their conclusions often before the arbitration has even commenced. Moreover, some financiers enter the case at some point in the middle of the proceedings or finance enforcement proceedings at the end of the case, and those financiers will have a different viewpoint regarding the likelihood of winning than the financier who considers the case at the outset. Thus, the categories "likely winner" and "likely loser" are rough and inexact but help draw another necessary line in the sand,

---

8. For reasons beyond the scope of this Article, the Author takes the view that states and state-owned entities that are parties in a contractually-based international commercial arbitration are in a fundamentally different position than respondent states sued in investment treaty arbitration. For example, one key difference is that contractual rights are bilateral whereas rights under classic investment treaties are unilateral in favor of investors and against states.

similar to this Article's arbitrary dividing line in the sand for the purpose of assessing access to justice, as articulated above.

III. RESULTS OF THE THOUGHT EXPERIMENT

This Article now presents a thought experiment based on the aforementioned assumptions to assess what types of international arbitration parties are in danger of not having access to justice. This thought experiment begins by excluding parties that definitely have access to justice. From the foregoing assumptions, any party that has a preexisting financial relationship with the financier prior to the incident that led to the claim in the arbitration has access to justice. This means that any party that has the guaranteed ability to self-finance or to obtain funding from a parent corporation or preexisting insurance contract (liability insurance or before-the-event insurance) has access to justice. This is true regardless of whether the party is more likely to win or lose, regardless of the type of claim, and regardless of whether the party is a claimant or respondent. This is also true if the party chooses not to pursue the claim or defense, despite having the financial resources to do so. In contrast, a party in danger of lacking access to justice must enter into a new financial relationship after the incident that gives rise to the claim. This means that the thought experiment will focus on avenues for financial support for arbitration that are available only after the incident that gives rise to the claim has happened. These avenues include contingent or conditional fee agreements with attorneys, after-the-event insurance agreements, bank loans, and traditional third-party funding arrangements.

The second phase of the thought experiment narrows down the categories of international arbitration parties that need dispute financing by separating those likely to win from those likely to lose. Most avenues for dispute financing that are available after the incident that gives rise to the claim are tied to the likelihood of winning. Attorneys and law firms will generally only enter into a contingent or conditional fee agreement if they believe the case is a likely winner. Similarly, after-the-event insurers and third-party funders will generally only enter into an arrangement in which they expect to make money, which is usually tied to the party winning the case. There are some structures for third-party funding or after-the-event insurance (often, but not exclusively, on the defense side) in which the financier receives some remuneration even if the party loses the case. In most situations, however, financiers that enter into an agreement with a party after the dispute has arisen want to fund likely winners on the merits rather than likely losers, if such a characteristic can be gleaned at the outset. Thus, in contrast to the situation described in the prior paragraph in which the party is virtually guaranteed access to justice, a party with no preexisting financial relationship to the financier, and who is also likely to *lose* its claim or defense, has almost no access to justice. The word "almost" is used because there may be rare instances of financiers willing to back a case with a small chance of winning (sometimes called a "long shot"),[9] but doing so on a regular basis would likely not be lucrative for such financiers. Thus, parties likely to lose are likely to remain largely unfunded unless a preexisting financier

9. See e.g. K. BROWN DE VEJAR and C. BALDWIN, supra fn. 2, at p. 541.

is available. Therefore, such parties are likely to lack access to justice, according to the framework presented in this thought experiment.

This lack of access to justice for likely losers can be viewed in two different ways. On the one hand, one could argue that claimants who have a high likelihood of losing should not be able to bring their claims, perhaps (for example) because those claims might be frivolous. Similarly, one could argue that respondents who have a high likelihood of losing should not need to muster a zealous defense, perhaps because they truly did injure the claimant and the magnitude of that injury is equal to the relief that the claimant alleges. On the other hand, one could argue that both claimants and respondents may have a high likelihood of losing not because the claim or defense is invalid or frivolous, but rather due to a defect in the law applied to the case, or the party's lack of access to evidence to submit to the tribunal (for example, if the opposing party is in possession of the majority of the key evidence), or the party's (perhaps less expensive) legal counsel being inexperienced in international arbitration. In addition, even losers deserve the opportunity to zealously advocate for reducing the magnitude of their losses by arguing in favor of a set-off claim, a partial award, a lower cost award to the winner, or a lower interest rate on the damages (if applicable).

Nevertheless, since winning and losing on a spectrum is a matter of nuance (and perhaps even a philosophical query to some extent), this study focuses purely on winners or losers on the *merits only*. The result is that likely losers on the merits that need dispute financing typically do not obtain such financing and, therefore, lack access to justice. This is our first access to justice problem that this thought experiment has uncovered: *How can we provide access to justice for "unfunded losers"?*

If we remove the foregoing parties with preexisting access to funding and remove the unfunded losers, we are left with what our introduction calls "unfunded winners": claims or defenses that are likely to win on the merits if the party is able to obtain dispute financing. At this point it is useful to divide our "unfunded winners" according to the type of arbitration: commercial or investment arbitration. This is because types of parties and types of claims are treated differently depending on the type of arbitration. Beginning with commercial arbitration, the parties are all fungible, meaning that any party can be on any side and bring any claim. Jurisdictionally, since commercial arbitration arises from a contract, corporations, individuals and states can all serve as claimants or respondents. In addition, respondents in commercial arbitration can bring counterclaims or set-off claims, which gives them the ability to simultaneously serve as claimants while also serving as respondents. In light of this, the type of party is irrelevant to determining whether access to justice is available to unfunded winners in commercial arbitration.

Instead, one must examine the type of claim in order to assess access to justice for "unfunded winners" in international commercial arbitration. Damages claims are understandably attractive to dispute financiers, because there will be a pot of money to share if the party wins. Non-financial claims and "no liability" claims (defenses) are less attractive and may be completely unattractive because such claims do not automatically create a pot of money to share, even though such claims may be worthy on the merits. Dispute financiers that arrive on the scene after the dispute has arisen are typically looking for a cash profit. This is where the access to justice problem arises in commercial arbitration. The one exception is what one may call "not-for-profit" funders, which are funders that take an interest in the specific merits outcome of the case for non-financial reasons and do not expect to make a profit.[10] However, "not-for-profit" funders are not general market players in this space; they typically fund cases on a one-off, case-by-case basis and cannot be counted on to categorically fund all the cases regarding a certain industry, country, treaty or legal issue. Thus, "not-for-profit" funders cannot provide a solution that is generalizable to arbitration as a whole and, therefore, cannot solve the problem of access to justice in commercial arbitration. This brings us to our second access to justice problem that this thought experiment has uncovered: *How can we provide access to justice for "unfunded winners" with non-damages claims or defenses?*

Turning to investment arbitration, the picture becomes more complicated. "Unfunded winners" in investment arbitration must first be divided by party. Due to jurisdictional constraints, corporations or individuals are always claimants in investment arbitration and states are always respondents in investment arbitration.[11] Furthermore, jurisdictional constraints restrict the types of claims that can be brought. The treaty must specifically name the substantive rights that claimants may vindicate in investment arbitration. In vindicating those rights, the claimant may request damages or non-financial relief, such as restitution in kind[12] or specific performance, but only if such remedies are allowed by the treaty.

Traditional investment treaties do not provide for rights of the respondent state,[13] while some investment treaties negotiated in modern times do contain rights of respondent states and corresponding obligations of the individual or corporate investor.[14]

---

10. See Victoria Shannon SAHANI, "Revealing Not-for-Profit Third-Party Funders in Investment Arbitration", Oxford University Press Investment Claims Blog (1 Mar. 2017), <http://oxia.ouplaw.com/page/third-party-funders> (last accessed 2 Feb. 2019).

11. For arguments in favour of granting states jurisdiction to bring claims in investment arbitration, see, e.g., Victoria SHANNON, "The Structural Challenge of Investment Arbitration Viewed Through the Lens of Third-Party Funding", Oxford University Press Investment Claims Blog (9 Jun. 2015) <http://oxia.ouplaw.com/page/491/the-structural-challenge-of-investment-arbitration-viewed-through-the-lens-of-thirdparty-funding-> (last accessed 2 Feb. 2019); Gustavo LABORDE, "The Case for Host State Claims in Investment Arbitration", 1 Journal of International Dispute Settlement (1 February 2010, issue 1) pp. 97-122, <https://doi.org/10.1093/jnlids/idp008> (last accessed 2 Feb. 2019).

12. See, e.g., Michael E. SCHNEIDER, "Non-Monetary Relief in International Arbitration: Principles and Arbitration Practice" in *Performance as a Remedy*, ASA Special Series no. 30 (Juris 2011); Brooks E. ALLEN, "The Use of Non-Pecuniary Remedies in WTO Dispute Settlement: Lessons for Arbitral Practitioners" in *Performance as a Remedy*, ASA Special Series no. 30 (Juris 2011); Christoph SCHREUER, "Non-Pecuniary Remedies in ICSID Arbitration", 20 Arbitration International (2004, no. 4) pp. 325-332.

13. For a basic explanation of jurisdiction in investment treaty arbitration, See, e.g., Christoph SCHREUER, "Jurisdiction and Applicable Law in Investment Treaty Arbitration", 1 McGill Journal of Dispute Resolution (MJDR) (2014, issue 1) (republished in Transnational Dispute Management (2015, no. 6), available at <www.transnational-dispute-management.com> (last accessed 2 Feb. 2019)).

14. See, e.g., Tarcisio GAZZINI, "The 2016 Morocco–Nigeria BIT: An Important Contribution to the Reform of Investment Treaties" (26 Sep. 2017), <www.iisd.org/itn/2017/09/26/the-2016-morocco-nigeria-bit-an-important-contribution-to-the-reform-of-investment-treaties-tarcisio-gazzini/> (last accessed 2 Feb. 2019) (describing the innovations in this treaty, including putting obligations on investors to comply with the laws of the host state and providing a state the

Under traditional investment treaties, the respondent state has no rights under which to bring a counterclaim, so the only "claim" a respondent state could have is a claim of "no liability", which translates as its defense as defined above. Under more modern investment treaties, respondent states may have the jurisdictional ability to bring substantive counterclaims and the corresponding rights within the treaty that may be vindicated in investment arbitration.[15] Nevertheless, the right to bring a counterclaim is necessarily predicted on the claimant bringing the original claim first. Thus, it is exceedingly rare to see a host state bring an initial claim (rather than a counterclaim) against an investor under a treaty. Such a scenario would most certainly be possible under a contract, as discussed above. Therefore, in the context of pure treaty arbitration under traditional investment treaties, the host state appears to be perpetually stuck in the respondent role with almost no jurisdictional or substantive access to counterclaims. This means that the respondent always has a "no liability" claim but almost never will have any other type of claim under a traditional investment treaty.

In contrast, the individual or corporate investor has the ability to bring both damages claims and non-financial claims in investment treaty arbitration, and, if the respondent state were able to overcome a jurisdictional challenge to a counterclaim, then the investor would also have a "no liability" claim vis-à-vis that counterclaim. This means that the individual or corporate investor has the ability to subsidize the cost of bringing the non-financial claims through the damages claims, meaning that the marginal cost of bringing two (or three) claims instead of one is significantly reduced. In fact, most investors bring at least one damages claim even if they intend to raise non-financial claims as well. Thus, the potential recovery on the damages claim could be enough to cover the costs of the additional non-financial claims such that a dispute financier would agree to finance the representation. In contrast, a respondent state that is denied the ability to bring a damages claim or counterclaim through dispute financing is denied the ability to subsidize its "no liability" claim or other non-financial claim (such as a request for an injunction mandating that an investor stop polluting the environment in the host state). As mentioned above, not-for-profit dispute financiers may be willing to step into the breach for some respondents,[16] but they will not do so systematically, regularly or predictably and, therefore, do not present a viable solution to this problem.

---

opportunity to sue an investor in the courts of its home country for violations of the treaty obligations). While this treaty does not allow for a state to bring an investment arbitration claim against an investor, the treaty does provide a judicial route through which the state may be compensated for any wrongs the investor commits under the treaty. In addition, the treaty is silent regarding whether states may bring counterclaims against investors in investment treaty arbitration, which may open the door to jurisdiction over such claims. The effects of these provisions will be tested if a case is eventually commenced under the treaty.

15. For some examples of how tribunals have responded in cases in which host states have tried to bring counterclaims under traditional investment treaties, see Jean KALICKI, "Can States Assert Counterclaims Against Investors in BIT Proceedings?", Kluwer Arbitration Blog (16 Jan. 2012), <http://arbitrationblog.kluwerarbitration.com/2012/01/16/can-states-assert-counterclaims-against-investors-in-bit-proceedings/> (last accessed 2 Feb. 2018).

16. See Victoria Shannon SAHANI, Mick SMITH and Christiane DENIGER, "Third-Party Financing in Investment Arbitration" in Christina BEHARRY, ed., *Contemporary and Emerging Issues on the Law of Damages and Valuation in International Investment Arbitration* (Brill Nijhoff 2018) p. 49 ("In addition, not-for-profit funding may be a viable option for respondents in international arbitration –

Since both claimants and respondents in investment arbitration may have both damages claims and non-financial claims, the problem is not the type of claim, but rather the type of party. Unsurprisingly, respondents in investment arbitration generally are not attractive targets for investment by for-profit dispute financiers.[17] This brings us to our third and final access to justice problem that this thought experiment has uncovered: *How can we provide access to justice for respondents in investment arbitration?* The term "respondents" is appropriate instead of "respondent states", because, although exceedingly rare, a few treaties permit a host state to initiate a claim against an investor.[18]

IV. SUGGESTIONS FOR INCREASING ACCESS TO JUSTICE IN INTERNATIONAL ARBITRATION

The thought experiment above has raised the following question: *How can we provide access to justice for three types of parties in international arbitration: unfunded losers, unfunded winners with non-damages claims or defenses, and respondents in investment arbitration?* This Article concludes with a few ideas regarding how to address this question and thereby improve access to justice in international arbitration.

The first step is for the international arbitration community to decide whether the international concept of procedural due process requires that parties in these three

---

particularly respondent States in investment arbitration – since a financial return on investment would not normally be required."). For example, in *Philip Morris v. Uruguay*, Uruguay's defence was funded by a not-for-profit funder called the Campaign for Tobacco-Free Kids, and the Anti-Tobacco Litigation Fund (a Bloomberg Foundation and Gates Foundation collaboration) is funding respondent states facing similar challenges. See <www.bloomberg.org/press/releases/bloomberg-philanthropies-bill-melinda-gates-foundation-launch-anti-tobacco-trade-litigation-fund/> (last accessed 2 Feb. 2019). These are both not-for-profit funders, however, which invites the question, should only not-for-profit funders fund respondent states? This Article argues for answering this question in the negative, but cogent arguments could be made on the other side. For example, in the political campaign finance arena, arguments have been raised about the impropriety of corporate influence over elections and governmental functions through lobbying and financial contributions; one could argue that for-profit third-party funders funding states generally could yield similar negative effects. This Article avoids this question by choosing *respondent* states (not claimant states) as the paradigm. Respondent states, by definition, do not commence arbitrations and, therefore, theoretically there can be no corporate influence on the respondent state with respect to stirring up the arbitration itself. But some have argued that third-party funders may themselves fall within the definition of "investor" within a treaty and, thus, the same investor-host state problems that exist in the foreign direct investment system could thereby infect third-party funding, if funders begin to fund respondent states regularly. See, e.g., Duarté G. HENRIQUES, "Third-Party Funding: A Protected Investment?", Spain Arbitration Review (2017, no. 30).

17. There is potentially one dispute financier that would finance a respondent state's "no liability" claim (i.e. its defence), but one dispute financier is not enough to solve a systemic, structural problem. See description of LexFinance, supra fn. 3.

18. See supra fn. 14 (describing the 2016 Morocco-Nigeria BIT which allows host state claims against investors in national courts and, arguably, may allow host state counterclaims in an investment arbitration initiated by the investor under this treaty).

categories have adequate access to dispute financing. This is more of a philosophical question than an empirical one, and thus, this question is largely beyond the scope of this brief intervention. The short answer, from this Author's point of view, is that the right to adequate resources for loss mitigation – i.e., a party's right to argue for a tribunal to reduce the amount of the party's loss – is a right that the international arbitration community should recognize as part of the international concept of procedural due process. Arguing in favor of loss reduction may take the form of pursing a claim that is likely to lose, requesting an injunction or other non-monetary relief, arguing for paying less costs despite losing on the merits, or presenting a viable defense. This Article will assume that the international arbitration community would answer the question in the affirmative in order to proceed to the next step in the analysis, although compelling arguments could also be made on the opposing side.[19]

Assuming that these three categories of parties have a right to adequate financing for their claims or defenses, the next question is how to pay for this. This Article presents three categories of possible solutions. The first category of potential solutions involves donations of time or money. For example, perhaps third-party funders, after-the-event insurers, and law firms should engage in pro bono funding for a subset set of worthy claims or defenses that may be long-shot winners, which are seemingly worthy but likely to lose, or non-damages claims. One could include in this category worthy investment claims against judgment-proof sovereigns, meaning that the claimant investor would likely win the case but may be unlikely to be able to collect the award from the respondent. In the latter case, due to the push for transparency in investment arbitration, an unpaid award could perhaps have symbolic, political or public value that would make the award worthwhile for non-monetary reasons.

Another paradigm to consider is that the attorney Bar in some countries asks attorneys to donate a small percentage of their annual hours (e.g., fifty hours on average in the United States)[20] to pro bono efforts or for attorneys to donate money to the pro bono efforts of other attorneys, in lieu of performing the work directly. Similarly, perhaps law firms should take on some international arbitration cases pro bono, without any expectation of reimbursement, and third-party funders or after-the-event insurers should donate some small percentage of their portfolio funds toward pro bono efforts. Arbitrators could agree to hear some cases on a pro bono basis by not charging fees or expenses to the parties. In addition, a defense fund for needy respondents could be

19. For example, in *Essar v. Norscot* [2016] EWHC 2361 (Comm), the High Court upheld an ICC tribunal's ruling requiring the respondent to pay the claimant's cost of third-party funding because the court found that the respondent so damaged the claimant's financial position as to require the claimant to seek third-party funding in the first place. For a description of the *Essar* case, see, e.g., Maximilian SZYMANSKI, "Recovery of Third Party Funding Ordered by ICC Tribunal and Confirmed by the English High Court – An Under-Theorised Area of the Law", Kluwer Arbitration Blog (8 Oct. 2016) <http://arbitrationblog.kluwerarbitration.com/2016/10/08/recovery-of-third-party-funding-ordered-by-icc-tribunal-and-confirmed-by-the-english-high-court-an-under-theorised-area-of-the-law/> (last accessed 2 Feb. 2019).

20. See American Bar Association, Model Rules of Professional Conduct, Rule 6.1 ("Every lawyer has a professional responsibility to provide legal services to those unable to pay. A lawyer should aspire to render at least (50) hours of pro bono publico legal services per year.... In addition, a lawyer should voluntarily contribute financial support to organizations that provide legal services to persons of limited means.") (parentheses in original).

established, perhaps even from the funds donated pro bono by third-party funders, law firms, and after-the-event insurers.[21] Finally, crowdfunding by multiple individual donors – which already exists – may provide a potential solution in this context.[22]

The second category of potential solutions involves changes in the law or arbitration rules. For example, arbitral institutions could adjust their fee scales to give indigent parties a discount on the fees. Alternatively, arbitral institutions could adopt a rule that a party against whom an injunction is granted must pay the costs of the party awarded the injunction. This latter solution would allow law firms to take on injunction requests on a contingent or conditional basis on the theory that their fees will be repaid if the party is granted the injunction. This solution has the drawback, however, that it would only help parties likely to have their injunctions granted.

Another more controversial idea, which is also less likely to be implemented, is the renegotiation of investment treaties to allow for claims by host states against investors as well as counterclaims by respondents. This one is much harder to implement, since many countries no longer have the political will to ratify a renegotiated treaty, no matter how problematic the existing treaty may be. Nevertheless, countries whose investment treaties have expired, who are engaged in renegotiating their treaties for other reasons, or who are entering into new treaties could consider including provisions to allow for host state claims. Most notably, the recent European Court of Justice decision in *Slowakische Republik v. Achmea BV* may signal that all the investment treaties in Europe may soon need to be renegotiated, at least in part.[23] This is one provision that could be included in those renegotiated treaties or in any EU-wide investment treaty that may be negotiated in the future.

Finally, a third category of solutions involves financiers modifying their criteria when deciding which cases to fund. For example, a third-party funder might modify its algorithms and decision-making processes to include other ideals as factors to weigh in

21. For an example of a proposal for funding states in WTO dispute settlement, see, e.g., Mauritius NAGELMUELLER, "Guest Post: Dispute Finance for Sovereigns in WTO Disputes – Access To Justice for Developing Countries", International Economic Law and Policy Blog (12 Sep. 2017) <http://worldtradelaw.typepad.com/ielpblog/2017/09/dispute-finance-for-sovereigns-in-wto-disputes-access-to-justice-for-developing-countries.html> (last accessed 2 Feb. 2019) (proposing that for-profit dispute financiers should provide financing to developing states in WTO dispute settlement proceedings).
22. See, e.g., Manuel GOMEZ, "Crowdfunded Justice: On the Potential Benefits and Challenges of Crowdfunding as a Litigation Financing Tool", 49 U.S.F. L. Rev. (2015) p. 307; Ronen PERRY, "Crowdfunding Civil Justice", 59 B.C. L. Rev. (2018) p. 1357.
23. *Slowakische Republik v. Achmea BV*, Case C-284/16, Decision of the Court of Justice of the European Union, (6 Mar. 2018). For a description of the decision and its impact, See, e.g., Court of Justice of the European Union, Press Release: No. 26/18 – *The arbitration clause in the Agreement between the Netherlands and Slovakia on the protection of investments is not compatible with EU law* (6 Mar. 2018) <https://curia.europa.eu/jcms/upload/docs/application/pdf/2018-03/cp180026en.pdf> (last accessed 2 Feb. 2019); Reuters, "EU Court Rules Against Tribunals Settling Intra-EU Disputes" (6 Mar. 2018), <www.reuters.com/article/us-eu-court-arbitration/eu-court-rules-against-tribunals-settling-intra-eu-disputes-idUSKCN1GI1AY> (last accessed 2 Feb. 2019); Center for International Environmental Law, *Press Release: New European Court of Justice (ECJ) ruling could signal end of intra-EU investor-state dispute settlement* (6 Mar. 2018), <www.ciel.org/news/new-european-court-justice-ecj-ruling-signal-end-intra-eu-investor-state-dispute-settlement/> (last accessed 2 Feb. 2019).

determining whether to fund a case in order to increase access to justice in international arbitration. One of those ideals could be ensuring that respondent states have access to justice by having access to third-party funding. Notably, respondent states can fall into all five categories of unfunded winners mentioned in the introduction to this Article. Respondent states can be longshot winners, defendant winners, non-financial winners, and political winners all at the same time, depending on the facts and circumstances of the dispute. Respondent states – particularly ones that have viable counterclaims – can also be merit-based winners whose claims are too expensive to pursue relative to their claim value when offset by the cost to defend against the investor's original claim.

Furthermore, third-party funders have a much more dubious reputation in investment arbitration, when compared to commercial arbitration. Gallons of ink have been spent arguing against allowing third-party funding in investment arbitration for a variety of reasons.[24] If third-party funders financed some respondent states in investment arbitration, then perhaps the participation of third-party funders in investment treaty cases would be viewed as more balanced, perhaps even viewed positively. In addition, investment arbitration, as a whole, may be viewed as more legitimate if respondent states have more regular access to third-party funding. This Author would even go so far as to assert that, if third-party funders in international arbitration choose to fund only one category from the three categories of parties mentioned above in order to increase access to justice, then respondent states in investment arbitration are a prime category with which to begin.

To address a broader question, the solutions presented in this Article depart from the poverty paradigm that is often used to argue that dispute financiers should modify their choices regarding which cases to fund to promote access to justice.[25] For example, since so few respondent states are currently being funded, to this Author's knowledge, both poor and wealthy respondent states alike are equally denied third-party funding from most for-profit funders. Instead, this Article presents an argument that other worthy aspects of the case itself may be the true foundation of "access to justice" that funders should espouse and support financially, such as upholding the health and safety laws of a country,[26] defending against abusive investment practices, ensuring the stability of a country's legal system, stopping damaging environmental practices of investors, clarifying the meaning of ambiguous treaty language, and so on. This Article argues that

24. See supra fn. 1.

25. See, e.g., United Nations Office of the High Representative for the Least Developed Countries, Landlocked Developing Countries and Small Island Developing States (UNOHRLLS) and the International Development Law Organization (IDLO), *Investment Support Programme for the Least Developed Countries (ISP/LDCs): Programme Document*, p. 5 and fn. 11 (6 Sep. 2017), available at <https://res.cloudinary.com/lbresearch/image/upload/v1506335575/isp_ldcs_programme_document_6_september_258117_1133.pdf> (last accessed 2 Feb. 2019) (proposing a system for providing support to poor states for, among other endeavours, "[f]oreign investment-related dispute settlement between the Client and a foreign entity, including arbitration or any other alternative dispute resolution proceeding" and "if the applicable rules to the dispute allow, the ISP/LDCS may also seek to identify and field the Client's party-appointed arbitrator").

26. See supra fn. 16 for an example of a non-profit funder supporting a state's laws regarding packaging of tobacco products for public health and safety reasons.

those are worthy ideals worth pursuing and financing regardless of the wealth or poverty of the respondent nation or the potential for profit (or lack thereof).

V. CONCLUSION

The thought experiment presented in this Article intends to provoke discussion and deep thought about the legitimacy crisis in international arbitration and investment arbitration as viewed through the lens of financial access to justice. The assumptions made herein may seem rudimentary and the solutions presented may seem idealistic, but this is merely a starting point for a global discussion. This Author invites those readers who have far greater empirical skills to confer with those who have the data – the arbitral institutions and the financiers – to devise a way to measure empirically the availability of access to justice or lack of access to justice in international arbitration. If such research occurs, then targeted solutions could be developed that may be more viable to implement than those solutions presented herein.

The Economics of Access: Systemic Imbalances in ISDS

Kate Brown de Vejar[*] *and Chloe Baldwin*[**]

TABLE OF CONTENTS PAGE

I. INTRODUCTION

Investor-State dispute settlement ("ISDS") in the form of investment arbitration has been subject to significant criticism and increased scrutiny in recent years. Proposals for reform have been widely discussed within the international arbitration community. A number of States have altered their treaty practice in an attempt to give effect to some of these reforms in their future treaties. But there is also now a clear appetite for more sweeping, immediate, multilateral reform. A message is being delivered by States that "we created this system, and since our calls for reform have largely fallen on deaf ears, we *will* step in and make changes".

This message is manifest in two ongoing multilateral initiatives. The first is the current effort to update the International Centre for Settlement of Investment Disputes (ICSID) rules and regulations, which began in October 2016 with ICSID inviting member States to suggest topics that merit consideration. The second is the work of the United Nations Commission on International Trade Law (UNCITRAL) Working Group III on ISDS Reform.

ICSID's consultation process resulted in a list of sixteen topics for potential ICSID rule amendment.[1] Of these, topic nine in particular relates to the economics of access to investment arbitration, including (i) exploring a possible presumption in favor of

---

* Partner at DLA Piper LLP in New York and Mexico City.

** International Associate in the Washington DC office of Steptoe & Johnson LLP.

1. ICSID, "The ICSID Rules Amendment Process, Potential Areas for Amendment", available at <https://icsid.worldbank.org/en/Documents/about/List%20of%20Topics%20for%20Potential%20ICSID%20Rule%20Amendment-ENG.pdf> (last accessed 20 June 2018). The ICSID Secretariat is currently preparing background papers on each of these sixteen topics, which are expected to be available in or around August 2018. At the Annual Meeting of the American Society of International Law in April 2018, the Secretary General of ICSID provided some indication as to the areas which ICSID considered were ripe for reform. See "Kinnear sheds light on ICSID rules amendment", Global Arbitration Review (6 April 2018) available at <https://globalarbitrationreview.com/article/1167749/kinnear-sheds-light-on-icsid-rules-amendment> (last accessed 20 June 2018).

allocating costs to the prevailing party, (ii) considering a possible provision on security for costs.

Similar areas of concern were identified at the 27 November – 1 December 2017 meeting of UNCITRAL Working Group III on ISDS Reform.[2] Of the procedural issues discussed during the meeting, the issue of recovery of costs by States received the most attention. The meeting room was largely united that the practice of allocation of costs in proportion to success of claims, rather than each party bearing its own costs, was to be encouraged. There was a strong feeling that a State which successfully defends a claim should be able to recover the cost of its defense. In a similar vein, the need to review the issue of security for costs, and to ensure that there are assets from which a State would be able to recover its costs, was widely recognized. Third-party funding was another issue of general concern, both in terms of its impact on the number and type of claims brought, and regarding the need for increased transparency in this area. States continued to voice their concerns regarding the impact and lack of regulation of third-party funding in investment arbitration at the April 2018 meeting of UNCITRAL Working Group III.[3]

These concerns, which go to the economics of access to investment arbitration, are the focus of this paper. We first discuss the importance of ensuring that costs orders in investment arbitration are made regularly, and reflect the relative success of the parties' claims (taking into account the quantum claimed) and defenses. We then examine the need to revise the burden of proof and standard applied by investment arbitration tribunals when determining whether to grant an application for security for costs. Next, we look at some of the economic asymmetries and other distortions due to third-party funding of investment arbitrations. We end with a list of initiatives to address these issues.

II. ALLOCATION OF COSTS IN ISDS

At the 27 November – 1 December 2017 meeting of UNCITRAL Working Group III on ISDS Reform, the allocation of costs by investment arbitration tribunals was highlighted

2. The author, Kate Brown de Vejar, attended the session as an observer on behalf of the International Law Institute (see <www.ili.org> (last accessed 13 February 2018)). The official UNCITRAL report of Working Group III's deliberations on ISDS Reform at its 34th Session in Vienna, prepared by the Secretariat, is publicly available. See "Report of Working Group III (Investor-State Dispute Settlement Reform) on the work of its thirty-fourth session" (Vienna, 27 November – 1 December 2017), UN Doc. A/CN.9/930, available at <http://www.uncitral.org/pdf/english/workinggroups/wg_3/WGIII-34th-session/930_for_the_website.pdf> (last accessed 19 February 2018) (henceforth UNCITRAL WGIII ISDS Reform 34th Session Report). Sound recordings of the session are also publicly available at <http://www.uncitral.org/uncitral/audio/meetings.jsp> (last accessed 19 February 2018).
3. See "Report of Working Group III (Investor-State Dispute Settlement Reform) on the work of its thirty-fifth session" (New York, 23-27 April 2018), UN Doc. A/CN.9/935, available at <http://www.uncitral.org/pdf/english/commissionsessions/51st-session/a-cn9-935_-_clean_submitted_ADVANCE_COPY.PDF> (last accessed 15 June 2018) (henceforth UNCITRAL WGIII ISDS Reform 35th Session Report), paras. 89-92. Sound recordings of the session are also publicly available at <http://www.uncitral.org/uncitral/audio/meetings.jsp> (last accessed 15 June 2018).

as an area of real concern.[4] While there is no doubt that investment arbitration tribunals have the power and discretion to shift costs onto the losing party, or to apportion costs between the parties,[5] the concern raised was that this does not happen consistently, often leaving a respondent State to foot the bill of its own successful defense. As the report of the meeting records:

> "It was explained that arbitral tribunals in ISDS had historically followed the default rule under public international law and in inter-State cases that each party would bear its own costs. It was pointed out that the respondent State might find itself in the position of not being able to recover a substantial part or any of its costs in defending an unsuccessful, frivolous or bad faith claim by investors. In addition, it was stated that in the absence of allocation of costs, there was no incentive for the parties to limit their arguments and submissions."[6]

These concerns are justified by empirical evidence. Susan Franck's research on costs awards in investment treaty arbitrations, published in 2011 and surveying 102 treaty awards (publicly available before 1 June 2006), showed that the majority of investment treaty awards followed the practice of each side being responsible for its own party costs (the fees and expenses of legal counsel and any expert or factual witnesses) and for an equal share in the tribunal costs (the fees and expenses of the tribunal and the administering institution or appointing authority).[7] The study also revealed a concerning lack of consistency in tribunals' approaches to cost allocation, including a lack of any reliable relationship between cost shifting and the ultimate outcome of the case.[8] Awards "typically lacked citation to legal authority and provided minimal rationale, and the justifications for cost decisions exhibited broad variation".[9]

In their December 2016 article discussing the lack of reasoning for the cost award against claimants in the *Philip Morris v. Uruguay* case, Kenneth Reisenfeld and Joshua Robb mused:

> "It is possible that there was an unspoken rationale. The case was a controversial one, and some (including Uruguay's counsel) accused Philip Morris of using the arbitration process, and the expense it entailed, as a way to discourage relatively poor countries (not limited to Uruguay) from enacting anti-tobacco measures. The tribunal may have shifted costs to Philip Morris in part to send a message both to companies considering adopting such a strategy and to critics who pointed to

---

4. UNCITRAL WGIII ISDS Reform 34th Session Report, paras. 46-48.
5. In the context of UNCITRAL Working Group III's discussions, "Article 42 of the UNCITRAL Arbitration Rules (2010, as revised in 2013) was given as an example of a rule providing for allocation of costs among the parties." UNCITRAL WGIII ISDS Reform 34th Session Report, para. 47. See also Art. 61(2) of the ICSID Convention and ICSID Arbitration Rule 47(1)(j) (granting tribunals the power to decide how costs of the arbitration are allocated among the parties).
6. UNCITRAL WGIII ISDS Reform 34th Session Report, para. 46.
7. Susan D. FRANCK, "Rationalizing Costs in International Treaty Arbitration", 88 Wash. U. L.R. (2011, no. 4) p. 769 at pp. 777, 809.
8. *Ibid.*, pp. 777-778, 820-821, 826-827, 841.
9. *Ibid.*, p. 769.

> the case as an example of the abuses of investor-state dispute settlement. But whether justified or not, if that was the tribunal's justification, it would have been better to say so. Article 48 of the ICSID Convention, after all, requires that an award state the reasons on which it is based, and Article 52(1)(e) permits annulment when a tribunal fails to do so."[10]

The authors agree with these musings. In particular, in cases where costs are shifted because of the tribunal's concerns regarding the abusive behavior of a party, such as an investor's ulterior motive for bringing a claim, these reasons should be articulated so that they may act as an effective deterrent to such tactics going forward.

Since the Franck study was published, the situation has evolved to some extent. In the context of UNCITRAL Working Group III's discussion on costs in November-December 2017, Meg Kinnear, the Secretary General of ICSID, reported that in approximately half of recently issued ICSID awards, arbitral tribunals had ordered that the costs of the arbitration should either be borne by the unsuccessful party or be apportioned between the parties. Therefore, Ms. Kinnear noted, an emerging trend away from each party bearing its own costs could be identified.[11]

This emerging ICSID trend is in line with the results of a study conducted by Matthew Hodgson in 2013[12] and updated in 2017.[13] The 2013 study revealed that, in cases decided before 2006, investment arbitration tribunals adjusted costs in only 35% of cases, whereas in cases decided between 2006 and 2012, investment arbitration tribunals made some adjustment in the allocation of costs in 49% of cases.[14] The 2017 update to the study showed that, since the end of 2012, there has been a significant increase in the number of tribunals making adjusted costs orders, with 64% adjusting costs in some manner.[15]

---

10. See Kenneth REISENFELD and Joshua ROBBINS, "The Achilles' Heel of Investor-State Arbitration Awards", Law360 (6 December 2016) available at <https://www.bakerlaw.com/webfiles/Litigation/2016/Articles/12-07-2016-Law360-Robbins-Reisenfeld.pdf> (last accessed 22 February 2018).
11. UNCITRAL WGIII ISDS Reform 34th Session Report, para. 47.
12. The study involved a review of some 221 cases in which an award or decision was publicly available on 31 December 2012. After making other adjustments (including removing decisions reserving costs to a later stage of proceedings), the final data pool was 176 cases. For the results of the study, see Matthew HODGSON, "Counting the Costs of Investment Treaty Arbitration", Global Arb. Rev. (24 March 2014) available at <https://globalarbitrationreview.com/article/1033259/counting-the-costs-of-investment-treaty-arbitration> (last accessed 22 February 2018).
13. Matthew HODGSON, "Damages and Costs in Investment Treaty Arbitration Revisited", Global Arb. Rev. (14 December 2017) available at <https://globalarbitrationreview.com/article/1151755/damages-and-costs-in-investment-treaty-arbitration-revisited> (last accessed 23 February 2018). This update to the 2013 Hodgson study interpreted data from an additional 140 awards, which were publicly available as of 31 May 2017, including a number of awards that were handed down before the cut-off date of the first survey, 31 December 2012, but which only became public more recently). When combined with the 2013 study, the final data pool consisted of 324 awards and 52 decisions on annulment.
14. M. HODGSON, "Counting the Costs of Investment Treaty Arbitration", fn. 12 above.
15. M. HODGSON, "Damages and Costs in Investment Treaty Arbitration Revisited", fn. 13 above.

The 2013 Hodgson study noted a significant difference between UNCITRAL and ICSID tribunals, with UNCITRAL tribunals making some form of adjustment to costs in 69% of cases, while ICSID tribunals did so in just 36% of cases. This difference was attributed to the importance of the guidance provided in the applicable institutional rules.[16] The UNCITRAL Arbitration Rules state that the "costs of the arbitration shall in principle be borne by the unsuccessful party or parties",[17] whereas the ICSID Convention and Arbitration Rules provide no such guidance or default rule.[18] The 2017 Hodgson study update reveals, however, that since the beginning of 2013, 61% of ICSID tribunals issued an adjusted costs order, bringing them closer to the rate exhibited by UNCITRAL tribunals, which remained at 69%.[19]

The 2013 Hodgson study showed that, of those cases in which investment arbitration tribunals elected to apportion costs, they did so in respect of *both* tribunal costs and party costs 62% of the time.[20] This trend continued in cases decided after 2012.[21]

Both the 2013 Hodgson study and the 2017 update noted that the increasing trend of allocating both tribunal and party costs in line with the outcome of the case did not extend to annulment proceedings.[22] In both pre-2013 annulment decisions, and in decisions between 2013 and 2017, 85% of *ad hoc* committees ordered parties to bear their own party costs, and just 61% of *ad hoc* committees ordered the losing party to bear all of the committee costs.[23]

A particularly concerning trend noted in the 2013 Hodgson study was the disparity of treatment on costs between investors and States: successful claimants obtained an order for costs in 53% of cases, whereas only 38% of successful respondents also received a favorable costs award.[24] This result in pre-2013 awards certainly lends credibility to the complaints of States that they are, too often, left with a pyrrhic victory: no liability or a very low value payout, but a hefty legal bill. However, this disparity is greatly reduced in more recent awards. In awards from 2013 onwards, successful claimants obtained an

16. M. HODGSON, "Counting the Costs of Investment Treaty Arbitration", fn. 12 above.
17. 2010 UNCITRAL Rules, Art. 42(1). The 1976 UNCITRAL Rules contained a similar rule, but its scope is limited to tribunal costs. 1976 UNCITRAL Rules, Art. 40(1).
18. Art. 61(2) of the ICSID Convention leaves broad discretion to the tribunal to "assess the expenses incurred by the parties in connection with the proceedings" and "decide how and by whom those expenses, the fees and expenses of the members of the Tribunal and the charges for the use of the facilities of the Centre shall be paid", with no indication of the factors a tribunal may take into account in reaching its decision. Rule 47(1)(j) simply states that the award shall contain "any decision of the Tribunal regarding the cost of the proceeding".
19. M. HODGSON, "Damages and Costs in Investment Treaty Arbitration Revisited", fn. 13 above.
20. M. HODGSON, "Counting the Costs of Investment Treaty Arbitration", fn. 12 above. This is consistent with the Franck study, which also found that where tribunals shifted tribunal costs, they also tended to shift party costs. S. FRANCK, "Rationalizing Costs in Investment Treaty Arbitration", fn. 7 above, pp. 778, 833.
21. M. HODGSON, "Damages and Costs in Investment Treaty Arbitration Revisited", fn. 13 above.
22. *Ibid.*
23. M. HODGSON, "Counting the Costs of Investment Treaty Arbitration", fn. 12 above; M. HODGSON, "Damages and Costs in Investment Treaty Arbitration Revisited", fn. 13 above.
24. M. HODGSON, "Counting the Costs of Investment Treaty Arbitration", fn. 12 above.

adjusted costs award in 65% of cases, and successful respondents obtained an adjusted costs award in 63% of cases.[25]

While the very recent trend is toward greater consistency in cost awards in investment arbitrations, and less disparity of treatment between investors and States, the push by States for multilateral and institutional reform in this regard is understandable. Any disparity in the treatment of investors and States is unacceptable. First, allocation of costs in line with the outcome of the case should be the norm. The factors taken into account by investment arbitration tribunals when allocating costs should be discussed in awards, with a view to developing consistent approaches and standards, which can then be used to discourage investors from advancing frivolous claims, adopting a scorched earth approach to their claims, and exaggerating the quantum of their alleged damages. The latter point is important. Data shows that the cost of proceedings increases with the damages claimed by the claimant.[26] Moreover, the tactic of "anchoring" the tribunal's discussion of damages by initially advancing an unrealistically high number, in the hope of achieving a lower but still excessive award of compensation,[27] is misleading, abusive, and can lead to mistakes with disastrous consequences for States.[28] An effective way of discouraging this practice is to include the amount of damages claimed versus any amount ultimately awarded in the factors to be taken into account by investment arbitration tribunals when allocating costs. *Eastern Sugar v. Czech Republic* provides an example.[29] In that case, the tribunal ordered the investor, which had succeeded in establishing liability, to pay part of the respondent State's share of tribunal costs on the basis that the investor had originally claimed approximately € 109 million but was ultimately awarded only € 25 million, or roughly 25 percent of the claimed amount.[30] Another example is *Garanti Koza v. Turkmenistan*, where the claimant was awarded approximately five percent of the compensation it sought, prompting the following remark on costs from the tribunal: "The tribunal considers it appropriate to take the degree to which Garanti Koza prevailed into consideration, along with the fact that it prevailed, in ruling on the Parties' competing applications for costs."[31]

There is a good case for formalizing what appears to be the dominant trend, and making allocation of tribunal and party costs in line with the outcome of the case the default rule in investment arbitration. It is a practice well known in many national

25. M. HODGSON, "Damages and Costs in Investment Treaty Arbitration Revisited", fn. 13 above.
26. S. FRANCK, "Rationalizing Costs in Investment Treaty Arbitration", fn. 7 above, pp. 835-836, Chart 1. See also M. HODGSON, "Damages and Costs in Investment Treaty Arbitration Revisited", fn. 13 above.
27. For further discussion of this phenomenon in the context of third-party funding of ISDS case, see Sect. IV.*3* below.
28. George KAHALE III, "Rethinking ISDS", Transnat'l Disp. Mgmt (2018, no. 5) p. 1 at pp. 18-19.
29. *Eastern Sugar B.V. v. The Czech Republic* (SCC Case No. 088/2004), Partial Award (27 March 2007); and *Eastern Sugar B.V. v. The Czech Republic* (SCC Case No. 088/2004), Final Award (12 April 2007).
30. *Eastern Sugar B.V. v. The Czech Republic* (SCC Case No. 088/2004), Partial Award (27 March 2007) paras. 368 and 380; and *Eastern Sugar B.V. v. The Czech Republic* (SCC Case No. 088/2004), Final Award (12 April 2007) para. 6.
31. *Garanti Koza LLP v. Turkmenistan* (ICSID Case No. ARB/11/20), Award (19 December 2016) paras. 450-451.

jurisdictions,[32] and is now common practice in commercial arbitration cases.[33] And, as highlighted above, it is quickly becoming the dominant accepted approach in both UNCITRAL and ICSID investment arbitrations.[34]

As a matter of policy, a default rule that costs should be allocated in line with the outcome of the case creates incentives for desirable party behavior, such as admissions, settlement opportunities, and efficient management of procedural issues, and it discourages wasteful party behavior, including tactical delays, frivolous claims, and exaggerated damages.[35] The likely costs of a proceeding, and how these costs may be allocated between the parties by a tribunal, "are a part of the risk/reward assessment an investor makes before commencing an investment treaty case".[36] These factors are also relevant for the State as it considers its settlement options.[37] The existence of a default rule on the allocation of costs, and more thorough and detailed reasoning on costs in awards, will makes it easier for a party to an investment arbitration to understand its exposure and act accordingly.

Although, in recent years, both UNCITRAL and ICSID investment arbitration tribunals have shown a strong trend towards allocating costs in line with the outcome of the case, the current statistics also show there is a way to go before true consistency and predictability in costs awards is achieved. ICSID *ad hoc* committees should also adopt a stricter and more consistent practice of allocating costs to the losing party in annulment proceedings.[38] Three initiatives would help fast-track these initiatives. First, the authors would have liked to see an amendment to the ICSID Arbitration Rules establishing a default rule similar to Art. 42(1) of the 2010 UNCITRAL Rules, to the effect that the costs of the arbitration (or the annulment proceeding) shall in principle be borne by the unsuccessful party, but preserving the tribunal/*ad hoc* committee's discretion to apportion costs where reasonable in the circumstances of a given case, in line with Art. 61(2) of the ICSID Convention.[39] Based on the April 2018 public comments made by

32. M. HODGSON, "Counting the Costs of Investment Treaty Arbitration", fn. 12 above ("It is usual for a losing party to make at least some contribution to the costs of the winner in the national courts of many jurisdictions, including England & Wales, France, Germany, Hong Kong, Italy, the Netherlands, Poland, Russia, Singapore, Spain and Thailand.").
33. *Ibid.* ("According to a 2012 study by Queen Mary, University of London, this approach is common in commercial arbitration, being adopted in around one half of cases, with a further 30 per cent of cases seeing some apportionment of costs, leaving just 20 per cent of cases where costs were not adjusted.").
34. *William Nagel v. The Czech Republic* (SCC Case No. 049/2002), Final Award (9 September 2003) paras. 337-338; *Kılıç İnşaat İthalat İhracat Sanayi ve Ticaret Anonim Şirketi v. Turkmenistan* (ICSID Case No. ARB/10/1), Award (2 July 2013) paras. 9.2.5, 9.2.9; *İçkale İnşaat Limited Şirketi v. Turkmenistan* (ICSID Case No. ARB/10/24), Award (8 March 2016) para. 409; *Transglobal Green Energy, LLC and Transglobal Green Panama, S.A. v. Republic of Panama* (ICSID Case No. ARB/13/28), Award (2 June 2016), para. 130; *Windstream Energy LLC v. Government of Canada* (PCA Case No. 2013-22), Award (27 September 2016), para. 514.
35. S. FRANCK, "Rationalizing Costs in Investment Treaty Arbitration", fn. 7 above, pp. 795-797.
36. M. HODGSON, "Counting the Costs of Investment Treaty Arbitration", fn. 12 above.
37. *Ibid.*
38. M. HODGSON, "Damages and Costs in Investment Treaty Arbitration Revisited", fn. 13 above.
39. M. HODGSON, "Costs in Investment Treaty Arbitration: The Case for Reform", 11 Transnat'l Disp. Mgmt. (2014, no. 1) p. 1 at p. 9. Expressly preserving the tribunal/*ad hoc* committee's

Meg Kinnear, the Secretary General of ICSID, it appears that any forthcoming amendment to the ICSID Arbitration Rules on costs will stop short of establishing such a default rule. Rather, the only change currently envisioned is to provide ICSID arbitral tribunals and *ad hoc* committees with additional criteria to be taken into account when considering any allocation of costs, "including the outcome of the proceeding and conduct of the parties".[40] While in practice, ICSID tribunals seem to be adopting a loser-pays approach more frequently, even absent an express default rule, the presence of a default position would "be more likely to discourage speculative claims and dilatory tactics", and "encourage tribunals to provide more detailed reasoning when exercising their discretion to depart from the default approach".[41] Second, an option for States not content with the proposed ICSID rule change would be to include language on the allocation of costs in their treaty's ISDS provisions.[42] Third, parties to investment arbitrations and annulment proceedings need to demand that costs be treated in a fully reasoned manner in the award or decision, and investment arbitration tribunals and *ad hoc* committees need to respond to this demand, specifically identifying in the award or decision the party behavior which led to the allocation of costs in a particular manner.[43]

III. SECURITY FOR COSTS IN ISDS

Obtaining an order for the allocation of tribunal and party costs in line with the outcome of the case is only half the battle. Obtaining payment of the costs award is another matter altogether. It is also another area where there is significant imbalance between claimants in investment arbitrations and respondent States.

States' concerns in this regard were reflected in the discussions of UNCITRAL Working Group III on ISDS Reform in November-December 2017:

> "A further area of concern mentioned related to difficulties faced by successful respondent States in recovering costs from claimant investors. It was said that investors might use shell companies, or might be impecunious, which left States with no possibility of recovery. That was highlighted as another area of imbalance as States had a permanent and financial standing, which investors did not. It was said that that situation was aggravated by the fact that the possibility of obtaining

---

discretion to apportion costs would keep the default rule in line with the discretion to allocate costs embodied in Art. 61(2) of the ICSID Convention.

40. See "Kinnear sheds light on ICSID rules amendment", Global Arbitration Review (6 April 2018), available at <https://globalarbitrationreview.com/article/1167749/kinnear-sheds-light-on-icsid-rules-amendment> (last accessed 15 June 2018).
41. M. HODGSON, "Damages and Costs in Investment Treaty Arbitration Revisited", fn. 13 above.
42. A number of modern investment agreements have already adopted this approach. See the Comprehensive Economic and Trade Agreement (CETA) between Canada and the European Union and its Member States, provisionally entered into force 21 September 2017, Art. 8.39(5), and the EU-Singapore Free Trade Agreement, authentic text as of May 2015, Art. 9.26(1).
43. S. FRANCK, "Rationalizing Costs in Investment Treaty Arbitration", fn. 7 above, pp. 795-796.

security for costs was not provided for under investment treaties or in certain arbitration rules."[44]

This concern was also reflected in the results of a survey by Judith Gill and Matthew Hodgson published in September 2015.[45] That survey revealed "a common complaint from states that they are not on a level playing field since investors are often 'shell' companies with neither the intention nor the means to make good on an adverse costs decision".[46] This places the parties in an asymmetric position.[47] The following statistics from that survey are revealing:

– "In the investment treaty context at least, the suggestion that most awards are complied with voluntarily is not well founded, at least so far as costs awards are concerned. Only 52 per cent of costs awards in favor of claimants and 49 per cent in favor of respondents were paid in full."[48]

– "37 per cent of successful respondents were paid nothing at all, despite obtaining a costs award in their favour, whereas only 19 per cent of successful claimants suffered the same fate."[49]

– "Even taking account of settlements reached (almost all of which involved only partial payment), only 46 per cent of claimants paid (in full or part) on their own initiative, although 71 per cent of respondents did so."[50]

Anecdotal evidence also confirms the concerns of States that they are too often unable to recover the cost of successfully defending an investment arbitration:

– In *Kılıç v. Turkmenistan*, the tribunal awarded the respondent State over US$ 1 million in costs upon dismissal of the case for lack of jurisdiction, but the claimant refused to pay.[51] Despite its failure to pay the costs award, the claimant still managed to find funding for an annulment proceeding, which was also dismissed. The *ad hoc* annulment committee ordered *Kılıç* to post security in the amount of the costs award as a condition for stay of enforcement,[52] but no security was ever posted.

44. UNCITRAL WGIII ISDS Reform 34th Session Report, para. 49.
45. Judith GILL and Matthew HODGSON, "Costs Awards – Who Pays?", Global Arb. Rev. (15 September 2015), available at <https://globalarbitrationreview.com/article/1034757/costs-awards-%E2%80%93-who-pays> (last accessed 22 February 2018).
46. *Ibid.*
47. *Ibid.*
48. *Ibid.*
49. *Ibid.*
50. *Ibid.*
51. *Kılıç İnşaat İthalat İhracat Sanayi ve Ticaret Anonim Şirketi v. Turkmenistan* (ICSID Case No. ARB/10/1), Award (2 July 2013) para. 10.1.1(d).
52. *Kılıç İnşaat İthalat İhracat Sanayi ve Ticaret Anonim Şirketi v. Turkmenistan* (ICSID Case No. ARB/10/1), Decision on Applicant's Request for Continuation of Stay of Enforcement of the Award (5 June 2014) paras. 42, 47.

– In *Erhas et al. v. Turkmenistan*, a case discussed in Sect. IV(*1*) below in more detail, a group of unrelated claimants all financed by the same third-party funder and represented by its designated counsel attempted to bring a single arbitration proceeding to collectively adjudicate their unrelated claims. The tribunal dismissed the proceeding and issued a costs award, ordering the claimants to pay the respondent State more than US$ 1 million in legal fees and expenses.[53] However, the claimants and their funders have refused to pay any portion of the costs award.

The Gill and Hodgson survey reported the following incident:

– Counsel to another state complained that a subsidiary of one of the claimant companies was transferred (in potentially fraudulent circumstances) during the course of the proceeding and without disclosure to the tribunal. This ultimately prevented enforcement of the costs award since the claimants were left without substantial assets.[54]

The authors are also aware of an August 2016 UNCITRAL investment arbitration award dismissing all US$ 573 million in claims against the Islamic Republic of Pakistan, and ordering the claimants to pay to the respondent State £11 million in costs (out of an apparent total of £12 million spent by the state in defending the claims).[55] According to a 12 February 2018 report in connection with set-aside proceedings before the English courts, that costs award remains unpaid to this day.[56]

These outcomes are manifestly unsatisfactory, and calls for reform are well founded. As expressed by one respondent to the Gill and Hodgson survey, "increased availability of security for costs is the 'single change' [I] would propose to the investment arbitration regime precisely to discourage frivolous claims".[57] In investment arbitrations, interim orders which allow the respondent State to secure the amount representing its likely arbitration costs are seldom granted.[58] The main argument against making security for the respondent State's costs more frequently available is that it would create additional barriers to the bringing of (meritorious) claims by injured investors. However, in an age where third-party funding is readily available to claimants in investment arbitrations, the

53. "Turkmenistan Sees Off Group Claim", Global Arbitration Review (24 June 2015), available at <https://globalarbitrationreview.com/article/1034557/turkmenistan-sees-off-group-claim> (last accessed 22 February 2018).
54. J. GILL and M. HODGSON, "Costs Awards – Who Pays?", fn. 45 above.
55. Jarrod HEPBURN, "Fortier-Chaired UNCITRAL Tribunal Dismisses BIT Claim by Former Iraqi Government Minister Against Pakistan", Investment Arb. Rep. (4 September 2016), available at <https://www.iareporter.com/articles/fortier-chaired-uncitral-tribunal-dismisses-bit-claim-by-former-iraqi-government-minister-against-pakistan/> (last accessed 22 February 2018).
56. Jarrod HEPBURN, "English Court Orders Security for Costs Against Claimants in Set-Aside Proceedings Funded by Burford Capital, But Declines Security over Still-Unpaid Adverse Costs Order in Underlying Arbitration" Investment Arb. Rep. (12 February 2018), available at <https://www.iareporter.com/articles/english-court-orders-security-for-costs-against-claimants-in-set-aside-proceedings-funded-by-burford-capital-but-declines-security-over-still-unpaid-adverse-costs-order-in-underlying-arbitration/> (last accessed 15 February 2018).
57. J. GILL and M. HODGSON, "Costs Awards – Who Pays?", fn. 45 above.
58. Gary B. BORN, *International Commercial Arbitration*, 2nd edn. (Kluwer Law International 2014) p. 2496. Costs include legal costs, tribunal's fees and other administrative or miscellaneous costs.

weight of this argument is severely diminished. In fact, the prevalence of third-party funding in investment arbitration exacerbates the asymmetry of funding and cost recovery between claimants and States.

Claimants in investment arbitrations frequently turn to third-party funding because they are impecunious and unable to afford the cost of bringing the arbitration themselves. This is not uniformly the case, but it is certainly not unreasonable for a respondent State, faced with a funded claim, to have serious concerns regarding the claimant's ability to pay an adverse costs award. By definition, third-party funders are not parties to the arbitration and are not subject to the tribunal's jurisdiction. Accordingly, unless their funding agreement says otherwise, third-party funders are free to ignore any costs award rendered against the claimant they fund.[59] Hence the asymmetry: the impecunious claimant stands to benefit from a favorable award, but is judgment-proof insofar as an adverse costs award is concerned because it has few or no assets; the third-party funder stands to benefit from a favorable award, but is beyond the tribunal's jurisdiction to order payment of the other side's costs, and may be shielded from an adverse costs award against the claimant by the terms of the financing agreement. For the claimant and its funder, it's all upside, and no downside. By contrast, in this scenario, the respondent State must fund its own defense and has no possibility to recover the cost of its defense in the event of a favorable outcome and award of costs.

This asymmetry can have a direct effect on the manner in which a claimant presents its case, the incentive being to run every conceivable argument irrespective of merit and inflate the quantum claimed to impossible heights, because there are no cost consequences for such behavior.[60] These behaviors directly increase the cost of the respondent State's defense, exacerbating the problem.[61]

59. Aren GOLDSMITH and Lorenzo MELCHIONDA, "Third Party Funding in International Arbitration: Everything You Ever Wanted to Know (But Were Afraid to Ask) – Part 2", 2012 Int'l Bus. L.J. (2012, no. 2) p. 221 at p. 223 ("In theory, a respondent who is unable to satisfy an award of costs might attempt to act against the funder itself. However, under existing practices, which would generally qualify the funder as a non-party to the proceeding, it would likely be difficult, if not impossible, to obtain an arbitral award for costs against the source of TPF."); Edouard BERTRAND, "The Brave New World of Arbitration: Third-Party Funding", 29 ASA Bull. (2011, no. 3) p. 607 at p. 613 ("[A]n arbitral tribunal could never issue an award binding on the TPF funder in respect of the arbitration costs, because the TPF funder is not a party to the arbitration proceedings, and as such not a party to the arbitral proceedings."). See also *X v. Y and Z* (ICC Case), Procedural Order (3 August 2012), reproduced in Philippe PINSOLLE, "Third Party Funding and Security for Costs", 2 Cahiers de L'Arbitrage (2013) p. 399 at para. 40 ("The third party funding mechanism at hand makes it possible for the Funder to secure a comfortable share of the proceeds for itself in case the litigation is successful while (i) taking no risk whatsoever with regard to the costs that may have to be paid to the other party as a consequence of an unsuccessful litigation and (ii) retaining the possibility to walk out at any time by simply [']pulling the plug' on [the Claimant] should it appear ... that the case is going less well for the Claimant than had been anticipated.").

60. A. GOLDSMITH and L. MELCHIONDA, "Third Party Funding in International Arbitration: Everything You Ever Wanted to Know (But Were Afraid to Ask) – Part 2", fn. 59 above, p. 223 ("[C]laimants will be incentivised to generate and externalise excessive costs.").

61. See S. FRANCK, "Rationalizing Costs in Investment Treaty Arbitration", fn. 7 above, pp. 835-836 and Chart 1. See also Maxi SCHERER, Aren GOLDSMITH and Camille FLÉCHET, "Third Party

Another problem is that a third-party funder may decide to withdraw its funding at any time, leaving the claimant with no means to continue financing the case and the respondent State with no recourse to recover its costs. Most funding agreements contain provisions regarding discontinuance of the funding.[62] Such provisions "expose the opposing party to costs risks (i.e. the risk of being unable to collect costs from a defaulting entity no longer supported by [third-party funding]) in the event the funder should decide to withdraw funding because the claim appears to have weakened over time".[63] It is also well known that "some [funders] have no intention to finance the proceeding and do not even have money, they just hope to reach a settlement as quickly as possible and, if this does not occur, they abandon the client".[64] The result is that the respondent State is left high and dry.

These are not theoretical problems. The *Bozbey v. Turkmenistan* case is an example. There, the claimant postponed a hearing on jurisdiction and merits at the last minute after being unable to fund the litigation, despite having previously been supported by a third-party funder.[65] The case was suspended for over a year, presumably while the claimant tried to find alternative funding sources, and was eventually terminated by order of the tribunal, nearly three years after it had commenced.[66] The reader can guess whether the respondent State was ever able to recover the cost of its defense.

Valle Verde v. Venezuela provides another example.[67] That ICSID case was twice stayed in 2013-2014 for non-payment of the required advances.[68] In May 2015, the Secretary-

---

Funding of International Arbitration Proceedings – A View From Europe: Part 2: The Legal Debate", 2012(6) Int'l Bus. L.J. (2012) p. 649 at p. 651 ("[A] claimant with greater financial resources will have access to a larger number of experts and witnesses and their legal fees will be higher than those of a claimant with more limited resources. Accordingly, the costs of the respondent, who as a result will be likely to rely on more experts and witnesses, will also increase.").

62. The report of a roundtable attended by several third-party funders states that "[a]ll of the funders include clauses relating to the termination of the funding relationship in their contract". One of the funders also indicated that grounds for termination include "material changes in circumstances". Maxi SCHERER, Aren GOLDSMITH and Camille FLÉCHET, "Third Party Funding in International Arbitration in Europe: Part 1: Funders' Perspectives", Int'l Bus. L.J. (2012, no. 2) p. 207 at p. 218.
63. Aren GOLDSMITH and Lorenzo MELCHIONDA, "Third Party Funding in International Arbitration: Everything You Ever Wanted To Know (But Were Afraid To Ask)", 2012 Int'l Bus. L.J. (2012) p. 53 at p. 59.
64. Olivia DUFOUR, "*Prêts pour le Third Party Funding?*" *Lettre des Juristes d'Affaires* (September-October 2013, no. 1) p. 8 at p. 9 (quoting H.G. Gharavi; authors' translation).
65. "Turkmenistan Faces BIT Claim After Human Rights Ruling", Global Arb. Rev. (24 April 2013), available at <https://globalarbitrationreview.com/article/1032280/turkmenistan-faces-bit-claim-after-human-rights-ruling> (last accessed 22 February 2018).
66. Luke Eric PETERSON, "Central Asia Round-Up: Updates on Four UNCITRAL Investment Treaty Arbitrations in the 'Stans'", Investment Arb. Rep. (11 March 2014), available at <https://www.iareporter.com/articles/central-asia-round-up-updates-on-four-uncitral-investment-treaty-arbitrations-in-the-stans/> (last accessed 22 February 2018).
67. *Valle Verde Sociedad Financiera S.L. v. Bolivarian Republic of Venezuela* (ICSID Case No. ARB/12/18).
68. ICSID Case Details, *Valle Verde Sociedad Financiera S.L. v. Bolivarian Republic of Venezuela* (ICSID Case No. ARB/12/18), available at <https://icsid.worldbank.org/en/Pages/cases/casedetail.aspx?CaseNo=ARB/12/18> (last accessed 12 March 2018).

General of ICSID moved that the tribunal discontinue the proceeding for lack of payment.[69] That prompted the claimant to pay the required advances, but in June 2015, claimant's counsel withdrew.[70] In September 2015, the claimant again resurfaced, represented by new counsel, and filed another application requesting that Venezuela front some of the cost of bringing the case. The tribunal denied that request in January 2016, stating that "Valle Verde always knew about the possibility of having to cover Venezuela's share and therefore cannot claim a breach of its procedural rights once this possibility materialized".[71] In September 2017, the proceedings were again stayed for non-payment of the required advances, and the case remains stayed as of the date of the writing of this article.[72] This kind of stop-start behavior by a claimant is frustrating and costly for the respondent State, which is deprived of any legal certainly regarding the status of the case, and nonetheless has to keep its defense team in place to respond if and when the proceeding restarts, all with zero chance of recovering the cost of its defense if the proceeding is (finally) discontinued, or if the State prevails.

Again, increased availability of security for costs for respondent States is the obvious solution.[73]

It seems ridiculous that there is still any debate as to whether investment arbitration tribunals have the power to order security for costs. Even when there is no express reference to this power in the applicable arbitration rules,[74] the power to order security for costs falls clearly under the tribunal's general powers to grant interim relief to

---

69. *Ibid.*

70. Jack NEWSHAM, "ICSID Won't Make Venezuela Put Up Costs in Bank Row", Law360 (8 February 2016), available at <https://www.law360.com/articles/756357/icsid-won-t-make-venezuela-put-up-costs-in-bank-row> (last accessed 12 March 2018).

71. *Ibid.*

72. ICSID Case Details, *Valle Verde Sociedad Financiera S.L. v. Bolivarian Republic of Venezuela* (ICSID Case No. ARB/12/18), available at <https://icsid.worldbank.org/en/Pages/cases/casedetail.aspx?CaseNo=ARB/12/18> (last accessed 12 March 2018).

73. Jeffrey WAINCYMER, *Procedure and Evidence in International Arbitration* (Kluwer Law International 2012) p. 644 (stating that ordering security for costs is justified "where the claiming party is impecunious and is being funded by a related entity who will benefit if the claims succeed but be beyond exposure if they are lost".); Ph. PINSOLLE, "Third Party Funding and Security for Costs", fn. 59 above ("The fact that this [third-party funding] agreement may exclude the payment of arbitration costs in case of failure, as it appears to be most often the case, places the respondent against a claimant who, by definition, now has the means to move forward with his arbitration without really taking any risk regarding its outcome precisely because of his insolvency. It seems to us that this asymmetrical situation, when it is clearly established, justifies by itself granting security for costs. Indeed, absent such a guarantee, the claimant will be in a position, in case of failure, to hide behind his impecuniosity to refuse to pay costs, despite the fact that he was able to advance his claim thanks to the funds of the third party. The claimant would thus benefit from the best of both worlds, which does not seem like a desirable situation.").

74. Compare with London Court of International Arbitration, Arbitration Rules (2014), Art. 25, available at <http://www.lcia.org/dispute_resolution_services/lcia-arbitration-rules-2014.aspx#Article 25> (last accessed 15 February 2018); Singapore International Arbitration Centre, Arbitration Rules (2016), Rule 27, available at <http://www.siac.org.sg/our-rules/rules/siac-rules-2016#siac_rule27> (last accessed 15 February 2018).

protect a party's legitimate interest in ensuring that at least part of the cost of its defense will be recoverable.[75]

The ICSID tribunal in *RSM v. Saint Lucia* reasoned:

> "[S]ecurity for costs can be ordered based on Article 47 ICSID Convention and ICSID Arbitration Rule 39. The fact that ordering security for costs is not expressly provided for in those provisions does not exclude the Tribunal's jurisdiction to issue such measure."[76]

In the UNCITRAL context, Georgios Petrochilos explains that a tribunal's power to order security for costs is clearly encompassed in Art. 26(2)(c) of the 2010 UNCITRAL Rules, which refers to orders requiring a party to "preserv[e] assets out of which a subsequent award may be satisfied".[77] Investment arbitration tribunals constituted under the 1976 UNCITRAL Rules adopted a similar approach, also relying on Art. 26.[78]

Nonetheless, and for obvious reasons, claimants in ICSID proceedings continue to argue that the absence of an express provision on security for costs in the ICSID Convention and Arbitration Rules means that no power to make such orders exists. To put this (non)issue to rest, and as discussed by Meg Kinnear at the ICCA Congress in

75. Julian D.M. LEW, Loukas A. MISTELIS, and Stefan Michael KROLL, *Comparative International Commercial Arbitration* (Kluwer Law International 2003) pp. 600-601 ("The respondent against whom the proceedings were brought has an interest in ensuring that at least part of the fees incurred will be recoverable. To this end several arbitration rules contain provisions empowering the tribunal to grant security for costs.... However, even where no such express provisions exist, tribunals can grant such orders under their general power to grant interim relief."); Nicolas ULMER, "The Cost Conundrum", 26 Arb. Int'l (2010, no. 2) p. 221 at p. 230 ("[I]t is widely accepted that the ordering of security for costs is within the power of arbitrators to order interim measures"); *RSM Production Corporation et al. v. Government of Grenada* (ICSID Case No. ARB/10/6), Tribunal's Decision on Respondent's Application for Security for Costs (14 October 2010) para. 5.16; *Commerce Group Corp & San Sebastian Gold Mines, Inc v. Republic of El Salvador* (ICSID Case No. ARB/09/17), Decision on El Salvador's Application for Security for Costs (20 September 2012) para. 45 (finding that the ad hoc committee's power to safeguard the integrity of the proceeding included the power to order security for costs).

76. *RSM Production Corporation v. Saint Lucia* (ICSID Case No. ARB/12/10), Decision on Saint Lucia's Request for Security for Costs (13 August 2014) para. 54. See also *Lighthouse Corporation Ptd Ltd and Lighthouse Corporation Ltd, IBC v. Democratic Republic of Timor-Leste* (ICSID Case No. ARB/15/2), Procedural Order No. 2 (13 February 2016) para. 53 ("The Tribunal's power to grant security for costs as a provisional measure is undisputed. This power stems from Article 47 of the ICSID Convention and ICSID Arbitration Rule 39.").

77. Georgios PETROCHILOS, "Interim Measures Under the Revised UNCITRAL Arbitration Rules", 28 ASA Bull. (2010, no. 4) p. 878 at p. 885.

78. See *Guaracachi America, Inc. and Rurelec Plc v. The Plurinational State of Bolivia* (PCA Case No. 2011-17), Procedural Order No. 14 (11 March 2013) para. 6 ("[I]nvestment treaty tribunals clearly hold the power to grant provisional measures.... Article 26 of the [1976] UNCITRAL Rules expressly envisages this possibility."); *South American Silver Limited (Bermuda) v. The Plurinational State of Bolivia* (PCA Case No. 2013-15), Procedural Order No. 10 (11 January 2016) paras. 50, 52 ("The Tribunal considers that a request for security for costs should be encompassed in the category of interim or provisional measures, provided for in Art. 26 of the UNCITRAL Rules... . [S]everal decisions of arbitral tribunals in investment arbitrations, both under the ICSID Rules as well as the UNCITRAL Rules, confirm that arbitral tribunals are empowered to order security for costs.").

Sydney in April 2018, ICISD proposes to amend its Arbitration Rules to include a new provision on security for costs immediately after the current Rule 39 on provisional measures. This new provision will specifically confirm the (pre-existing) power of ICSID tribunals to issue orders for security for costs.

Closely related to this is the issue of the burden of proof and the standard to be applied by investment tribunals when considering an application for security for costs. Tribunals in ICSID proceedings have frequently required a State to show exceptional circumstances, such as an element of abuse of process, to justify the making of an order for security for costs.[79] One of the justifications for this high standard is that orders for security for costs create additional barriers to claims, and that it would be unfair for a respondent State to be able to prevent an impecunious claimant from bringing a claim in circumstances where the claimant's impecuniousness was caused by the respondent State in the first place. The purpose of this article is not to engage in a debate on the access-to-justice issue, but rather to point out that this concern falls away when the claim is funded by a third party.

For practical purposes, the funding for the security ordered will presumably be provided by the third-party funder, as a cost of the arbitration. Indeed, there are good reasons why this should be a requirement for international arbitrations funded by third-party funders where the claimant is unlikely to be in a position to satisfy an adverse costs award. As articulated by one ICC tribunal:

> "If a party has become manifestly insolvent and therefore is likely relying on funds from third parties in order to finance its own costs of the arbitration, the right to have access to arbitral justice can only be granted under the condition that those third parties are also ready and willing to secure the other party's reasonable costs to be incurred."[80]

79. Jean E. KALICKI, "Security for Costs in International Arbitration", 3 Transnat'l Disp. Mgmt. (2006, no. 5) p. 1 at p. 1. See, e.g., *Phoenix Action, Ltd. v. Czech Republic* (ICSID Case No. ARB/06/5), Decision on Provisional Measures (6 April 2007) para. 32; *Plama Consortium Limited v. Republic of Bulgaria* (ICSID Case No. ARB/03/24), Order (6 September 2005) para. 38; *Saipem S.p.A v. The People's Republic of Bangladesh* (ICSID Case No. ARB/05/7), Decision on Jurisdiction and Recommendation on Provisional Measures (21 March 2007) para. 175; *Occidental Petroleum Corporation and Occidental Exploration and Production Company v. The Republic of Ecuador* (ICSID Case No. ARB/06/11), Decision on Provisional Measures (17 August 2007) para. 59; *RSM Production Corporation et al. v. Government of Grenada* (ICSID Case No. ARB/10/6), Tribunal's Decision on Respondent's Application for Security for Costs (14 October 2010) para. 5.17; *Commerce Group Corp & San Sebastian Gold Mines Inc v. Republic of El Salvador* (ICSID Case No. ARB/09/17), Decision on El Salvador's Application for Security for Costs (20 September 2012) para. 44; *RSM Production Corporation v. Saint Lucia* (ICSID Case No. ARB/12/10), Decision on Saint Lucia's Request for Security for Costs (13 August 2014) para. 75; *Lighthouse Corporation Ptd Ltd and Lighthouse Corporation Ltd, IBC v. Democratic Republic of Timor-Leste* (ICSID Case No. ARB/15/2), Procedural Order No. 2 (13 February 2016) para. 59.
80. *X. S.A.R.L., Lebanon v. Y. AG, Germany* (ICC Case), Procedural Order No. 3 (4 July 2008) para. 21 in 28 ASA Bull. (2010, no. 1) p. 37.

Other tribunals and commentators share this view.[81] And if the third-party funder has done its homework and believes that the claim has a good chance of success, then there can be no real objection to fronting the security necessary for the claim to proceed. Selvyn Seidel of third-party funder, Fulbrook Management, has been quoted as saying, "[p]ersonally I like to assume an obligation to pay adverse costs – because, if I believe in the case, I don't think there are going to be adverse costs".[82]

The ICCA-Queen Mary Task Force Report on Third-Party Funding in International Arbitration (*ICCA-QM TPF Report*),[83] launched at the ICCA Congress in Sydney in April 2018, has recommended certain principles to be applied by arbitral tribunals in awarding security for costs, including that "applications for security for costs in international arbitration should be determined irrespective of any funding arrangement, and on the basis of, among other things, impecuniousness", and that "the burden should be on the moving party, and it is suggested that no party should have to defend a motion for

81. Ph. PINSOLLE, "Third Party Funding and Security for Costs", fn. 59 above, p. 399 at paras. 40, 43, reproducing *X. v. Y and Z* (ICC Case), Procedural Order (3 August 2012) (ordering security for costs after observing that the claimant's third-party funding arrangement "makes it possible for the Funder to secure a comfortable share of the proceeds for itself in case the litigation is successful while (i) taking no risk whatsoever with regard to the costs that may have to be paid to the other party as a consequence of an unsuccessful litigation and (ii) retaining the possibility to walk out at any time by simply [']pulling the plug' on [the Claimant] should it appear … that the case is going less well for the Claimant than had been anticipated."); *Swiss Entity v. Dutch Entity* (HKZ Case No. 415), Award (20 November 2001) in 20ASA Bull. (2002, no. 3) pp. 467-468, 471-472 (The respondent had applied for security for costs on the ground that the claimant was "not able to pay the costs of the proceedings and that it is therefore forced to obtain funds from external sources". The tribunal granted the request, stating that "it is most likely that if Respondent were to prevail in this arbitration, a future cost award in its favor could not be satisfied by Claimant".); Jarrod HEPBURN, "ICC Costs Award in Favor of Bulgaria Is Upheld, as Domestic Court Rejects Claimant's Allegation of Tribunal Bias Against Third-Party-Funded Claimant", Investment Arb. Rep. (19 October 2015) available at <https://www.iareporter.com/articles/icc-costs-award-in-favor-of-bulgaria-is-upheld-as-domestic-court-rejects-claimants-allegation-of-tribunal-bias-against-third-party-funded-claimant/> (last accessed 15 February 2018) ("Noting that [the claimant] Chematur's arbitral claim was funded by a third party, the tribunal had ordered Chematur to post a bank guarantee for $750,000."); M. SCHERER, A. GOLDSMITH and C. FLÉCHET, "Third Party Funding in International Arbitration in Europe: Part 1 – Funders' Perspectives", fn. 62 above, p. 215; Mick SMITH and Antonio WESOLOWSKI, "Mechanics of Third-Party Funding Agreements: A Funder's Perspective" in Lisa Bench NIEUWVELD and Victoria SHANNON, *Third-Party Funding in International Arbitration*, 2nd ed. (Kluwer Law International 2012) p. 19 at n. 16 ("It is also common for a third-party funder to be asked to provide additional capital either by way of provision for a future adverse cost orders, or for security for costs."); Jasminka KALAJDZIC, Peter CASHMAN, and Alana LONGMOORE, "Justice for Profit: A Comparative Analysis of Australian, Canadian and U.S. Third Party Litigation Funding", 61 Am. J. Comp. L. (2013, no. 1) p. 93 at p. 100 ("The [funding] agreement will often provide that the funder will … pay any amount required to be provided by way of security for costs.").

82. Alison ROSS, "The Dynamics of Third-Party Funding", Global Arb. Rev. (7 March 2012), available at <https://globalarbitrationreview.com/article/1031171/the-dynamics-of-third-party-funding-in-full> (last accessed 22 February 2018).

83. ICCA-Queen Mary Task Force on Third-Party Funding in International Arbitration, "ICCA-Queen Mary Task Force Report on Third-Party Funding in International Arbitration", The ICCA Rep. No. 4 (April 2008) (henceforth *ICCA-QM TPF Report*).

security unless and until the moving party makes a *prima facie* showing of impecuniousness. If no such showing is made, then the motion should be denied outright."[84] With respect, these recommendations do not respond to the growing asymmetries between investors and States in connection with third-party funded investment arbitrations. They are also unworkable in practice.

As a practical matter, the presence of a third-party funder may be the first, and perhaps the only indication that a claimant may be impecunious. While some claimants may have some publicly available financial information, this is extremely rare. For public companies, some financial information may be available at the group, or holding company level, but obtaining any information as to the assets or financial standing of the precise entity which is bringing the claim can be virtually impossible. The claimant may well be a special purpose vehicle which was set up for tax purposes, or to try to take advantage of certain treaty protections, but it may have little or no assets itself. For claimants who are private companies or individuals, finding any financial information at all, let alone accurate information, is even more difficult. The most likely scenario is that a respondent State becomes aware of the existence of a third-party funder, but is unable to find any publicly available information regarding the financial standing of the claimant. In these circumstances, putting the burden on the respondent State to make a prima facie showing of impecuniousness of the claimant, before the claimant needs to defend the motion, is illogical and unjust. It is the claimant which holds the relevant information.

The tool one would normally use when confronted with this type of information imbalance, in relation to jurisdictional or substantive issues in an investment arbitration, would be to request disclosures or document discovery. There is no good reason why a similar approach could not be used in relation to the issue of impecuniousness of the claimant. Once a respondent State becomes aware of circumstances suggesting that the claimant may be impecunious (including the fact that its claim is being funded by a third party, but also perhaps other circumstances, such as failure to pay an advance on costs, or an SEC disclosure) but not necessarily rising to the level of a prima facie showing, the respondent should disclose such circumstances to the tribunal and be permitted to request that the claimant provide information regarding its financial position and, in particular, for the claimant to make a showing that it has the financial wherewithal to cover an adverse costs order. Should the claimant fail to make such a showing, the tribunal must weigh the competing interests of access to justice versus the respondent's right to recover the costs of a successful defense. Where the claim is third-party funded, the scales tip markedly in favor of ordering security for costs.

ICSID Additional Facility case *Luis García Armas v. Venezuela*,[85] and UNCITRAL (PCA) case *Manuel García Armas and others v. Venezuela*,[86] provide an example of how this approach can work in practice. The same tribunal sits in both of these pending cases.[87]

84. *Ibid.* pp. 180-181.

85. *Luis García Armas v. Bolivarian Republic of Venezuela* (ICSID Case No. ARB(AF)/16/1).

86. *Manuel García Armas, Pedro García Armas, Sebastián García Armas, Domingo García Armas, Manuel García Piñero, Margaret García Piñero, Alicia García González, Domingo García Cámara and Carmen García Cámara v. Bolivarian Republic of Venezuela* (PCA Case No. 2016-08).

87. Tom JONES, "BIT Panel Orders Funded Claimants to Prove Solvency", Global Arb. Rev. (12 July 2017) available at <https://globalarbitrationreview.com/print_article/gar/article/1144330/bit-panel-orders-funded-claimants-to-prove-solvency?print=true> (last accessed 12 March 2018).

Following an application for US$ 5 million in security for costs by the respondent State based on "strong indications that the family had already or would become insolvent",[88] the claimants were first required to submit a redacted version of their funding agreement, with the full agreement being submitted in camera to the tribunal to review whether the redactions were appropriate. In the context of that in camera review, the tribunal found that respondent was indeed entitled to see the entirety of the document, as the funding agreement contained (otherwise redacted) language that showed that the funder would not cover any adverse costs order. The tribunal then proceeded, at the respondent's request, to order the claimants to show not only that they had sufficient assets, but also that they had sufficient revenue streams, to cover any adverse costs order.[89] The respondent State's application for security for costs is pending, but the tribunal's approach will ensure that it has access to all of the necessary information to determine whether an order for security for costs is appropriate and just in the circumstances of the case, and in June 2018, the tribunal ordered claimants to post a US$ 1.5 million bond as security, while declining to order respondent to pay any part of the advance on the tribunal's costs and fees.[90]

In this context, it is important to remark that a mere showing by the claimant that its third-party funder has agreed to pay any adverse costs award at the end of the proceeding is not sufficient to protect the respondent State's interests. First, the respondent State is not a party to that agreement and cannot enforce its terms. Second, the third-party funder is not subject to the jurisdiction of the arbitral tribunal which is, in any event, functus officio after the issuance of the final award and no longer in a position to coerce compliance through its jurisdiction over the claimant. Third, there is still the risk that the third-party funder will walk away from the funding agreement during the proceeding, rendering its promise to pay any adverse costs order of zero utility. Rather, if a third-party funder has agreed to pay any adverse costs award, then it should have no problem putting up a guarantee at the outset of the proceeding, or at the point when the issue of the claimant's impecuniousness otherwise arises.

A capable tribunal will manage the process of enquiring into the claimant's financial standing as well as its funding arrangements in an efficient manner to minimize delays. Any small delay will in any event be justified given the importance of protecting the interest of a respondent State in being able to enforce a favorable costs award. Moreover, what is at stake is much more than an unpaid costs award. Concrete measures must be taken to address the asymmetries in funding and cost recovery as between

88. *Ibid.*

89. *Ibid.* See also ICSID Case Details, *Luis García Armas v. Bolivarian Republic of Venezuela* (ICSID Case No. ARB(AF)/16/1), available at <https://icsid.worldbank.org/en/Pages/cases/casedetail.aspx?CaseNo=ARB(AF)/16/1> (last accessed 12 March 2018); PCA Case View, *Manuel García Armas, Pedro García Armas, Sebastián García Armas, Domingo García Armas, Manuel García Piñero, Margaret García Piñero, Alicia García González, Domingo García Cámara and Carmen García Cámara v. Bolivarian Republic of Venezuela* (PCA Case No. 2016-08), available at <https://www.pcacases.com/web/view/135> (last accessed 12 March 2018).

90. Tom JONES, "Funded BIT Claimants Ordered To Pay Security", Global Arb. Rev. (6 August 2018) available at <https://globalarbitrationreview.com/article/1172646/funded-bit-claimants-ordered-to-pay-security> (last accessed 19 December 2018).

investors and States in investment arbitration, which have been a key contributing factor to the diminished confidence of States in ISDS as a system.

During the public comment period on the Draft Report of the ICCA-Queen Mary Task Force on Third-Party Funding in International Arbitration,[91] one proposal to address this imbalance was "the adoption of a presumption that security for costs would be posted in every case, and a parallel presumption that the costs of security (i.e., the cost of funding, the cost of ATE insurance premiums, or the cost for a bank guarantee) would be shifted at the end of the case, along with other costs".[92] As the *ICCA-QM TPF Report* notes, "[u]nder this proposal, each party would be made financially whole at the conclusion of the case – if the state prevails it would be sure to recover on any costs award, and if the investor prevails it would recover not only its legal costs, but also costs associated with security".[93] Both parties would also arguably benefit by the reduction in, or elimination of, the time and costs associated with applying for, or resisting, an order for security for costs.[94] As noted in the *ICCA-QM TPF Report*, this proposal enjoyed (at least tentative) support from both funders and counsel who routinely represent States.[95]

In the search for a balanced approach, the rules on security for costs in jurisdictions with significant experience with third-party funding in domestic litigation are instructive. In the United Kingdom, for example, the Civil Procedure Rules allow courts to order security for costs to be provided by third parties who fund litigation on a commercial basis.[96] Addressing the issue of security for costs, the High Court has stated that the test was not whether the circumstances were "exceptional", but whether they were "just".[97] Traditionally, the English courts have limited the amount of a security for costs order against a third-party funder to the upper limit of the fund's contribution to funding the litigation.[98] However, a more recent decision makes it clear that the English courts have started taking a broader approach in exercising their discretion in relation to security for costs, scrutinizing the financial standing and resources of both claimants and their third-party funders, and awarding security for costs in excess of the funder's

91. ICCA-Queen Mary Task Force on Third-Party Funding in International Arbitration, "Draft Report for Public Discussion of the ICCA-Queen Mary Task Force on Third-Party Funding in International Arbitration" (1 September 2017) (henceforth *ICCA-QM Draft TPF Report*).
92. *ICCA-QM TPF Report*, pp. 224-225.
93. *Ibid.*
94. *Ibid.*, p. 225.
95. *Ibid.*
96. United Kingdom, Civil Procedure Rules 1998 (No. 3132 (L. 17) (as amended as of 1 October 2017)), Rule 25.14.
97. *The RBS Rights Issue Litigation* [2017] EWHC 1217 (Ch).
98. In *Arkin v. Borchard Lines, Ltd. No. 2*, the English Court of Appeal found the third-party funder liable for all costs up to the amount of its contribution to the litigation. *Arkin v. Borchard Lines, Ltd. No. 2* [2005] EWCA Civ. 655, paras. 37-45. See also Carolyn B. LAMM and Eckhard R. HELLBECK, "Third-Party Funding in Investor-State Arbitration: Introduction and Overview" in Bernardo M. CREMADES and Antonio DIMOLITSA, eds., *Dossier X: Third-Party Funding in International Arbitration* (ICC Institute of World Business Law 2013) p. 101 at pp. 111-112 (describing *Arkin v. Borchard Lines, Ltd. No. 2*, stating that "[t]he underlying rationale was that justice would be better served by allowing a right to recover from the professional funder whose intervention had permitted the continuation of a claim that had ultimately been found to lack merit".).

contribution where the interests of justice so require.[99] Likewise, in Australia, if the litigation is funded by a third-party funder, the court will generally order security for costs, considering that the third-party funder intends to benefit from any recovery.[100] Australian courts have general powers to make costs orders against parties and non-parties alike,[101] and courts can order costs against a third-party funder in circumstances where they have an interest in the subject of the litigation.[102] In 2016, for example, the Court of Appeal of the Supreme Court of Victoria went beyond the terms of the order for security for costs and upheld a non-party costs order against a third-party funder, where the amount ordered by way of security for costs was insufficient to cover the defendant's actual costs.[103] Like their English equivalents, the Australian courts scrutinize the funding agreement, and the capacity of both claimants and third-party funders to meet the costs,[104] and have focused on whether the "interests of justice" require orders for security of costs, and costs orders, rather than on whether or not "exceptional circumstances" exist.

The experience of these national jurisdictions with a history of dealing with funded litigation provides meaningful guidance as to the right balance to be struck when assessing security for costs applications in funded arbitrations. Requiring a respondent State to make a showing of "exceptional circumstances", such as abuse of process, is unreasonable and means that orders of security for costs have become the unicorns of investment arbitration. Everyone has heard of them, and apparently they are beautiful creatures, but no one has actually seen one. Investment arbitration tribunals should instead be striving to achieve just outcomes, having scrutinized the funding agreement, and the capacity of both claimants and their funders to meet any adverse costs order. Since they do not have jurisdiction to make adverse costs orders directly against third-party funders at the end of a case in the event that the claimant cannot pay, investment

---

99. *Sandra Bailey & Others v. GlaxoSmithKline UK Limited* [2017] EWHC 3195 (QB). In this case, the High Court ordered security for costs against the third-party funder in the amount of £1.75 million, when the third-party funder had provided only £1.2 million of funding toward the litigation in return for a share in the proceeds of any recovery. The case is notable in that it went beyond the cap established *Arkin v. Borchard Lines, Ltd. No. 2*, and opened the door to increased orders for security for costs and, consequently, increased liability for third-party funders.

100. *Idoport Pty Ltd v National Australia Bank Ltd* [2001] NSWSC 744.

101. See, e.g., Uniform Civil Procedure Rules 2005 (NSW), Rule 42.21(1A); Uniform Civil Procedure Rules 1999 (Qld), Rule 672. These statutes provide non-exhaustive lists of matters to which the Court may have regard in exercising its discretion whether to order security for costs.

102. *Knight v. FP Special Assets Ltd* [1992] HCA 28.

103. *Ryan Carter and Esplanade Holdings Pty Ltd v. Caason Investments Pty Ltd & Ors* [2016] VSCA 236.

104. For example, in *Domino's Pizza Enterprises Limited v. Precision Tracking Pty Ltd (No. 2)* [2017] FCA 211, the funded party opposed a security for costs order being made on the grounds that there was no risk that any costs order would not be satisfied owing to the combined effect of the litigation funding indemnity, an adverse costs insurance policy and proposed undertakings by Precision Tracking Pty Ltd to notify the parties of any relevant change of funding circumstances. However, the court upheld the application for security for costs, concluding that (1) Precision Tracking Pty Ltd did not itself have the capacity to meet an adverse costs order, (2) the funding agreement limited the indemnity to a counterclaim in the proceeding, and (3) the adverse costs insurance was taken out for the primary claim. Additionally, the funder had an absolute discretion to terminate its funding arrangements with Precision Tracking Pty Ltd at any time, including the adverse costs indemnity and the adverse costs insurance.

tribunals must make more frequent use of early orders for security for costs, which can then be advanced by the funder at a point in the proceeding when it is incentivized to do so. In short, third-party funders who stand to benefit from the outcome of a case by funding an impecunious claimant should also assume the risk of an adverse costs award.

IV. THIRD-PARTY FUNDING IN INVESTMENT ARBITRATION

At the April 2018 meeting of UNCITRAL Working Group III in New York, States continued to voice concerns regarding third-party funding in investment arbitration.[105] The report from that meeting records:

> "89. Regarding the practice of third-party funding, information was provided indicating that the practice was increasing in ISDS. Serious concerns were expressed in that regard. It was said that such practice raised ethical issues, and might have negative impact on the procedure. It was further pointed out that third-party funders might gain excessive control or influence over the arbitration process, which could lead to frivolous claims and discouragement of settlements. (….)
> 92. The following possible solutions were suggested for further consideration: (i) prohibiting third-party funding entirely in ISDS cases; (ii) regulating third-party funding, for example, by introducing mechanisms to ensure transparency in the arrangements (which could also assist in ensuring the impartiality of the arbitrators)."[106]

The *ICCA-QM TPF Report* also observes that "particularly in the international investment context, there were arguments to prohibit third-party funding because of its asserted consequences for the real and perceived legitimacy of investment arbitration".[107] The draft of that same report noted that the arguments surrounding third-party funding draw significantly on anecdotal evidence, and "are often premised on factual assumptions, for which empirical information regarding third-party funding specifically is not generally available".[108] Steinitz and Field observe that, despite the importance of the litigation funding industry and the robust academic debate surrounding the benefits and risks associated with it, there is a "complete absence of information about or discussion of litigation finance contracting".[109] That is, there is very little publicly known about the actual terms of litigation financing, despite the fact that it is precisely these terms which give rise to the benefits and risks that we all sit around discussing. In short, "[l]itigation finance is an opaque industry".[110]

105. UNCITRAL WGIII ISDS Reform 35th Session Report, paras. 89-92.
106. *Ibid.*
107. *ICCA-QM TPF Report*, p. 5.
108. *ICCA-QM Draft TPF Report*, p. 157.
109. Maya STEINITZ and Abigail C. FIELD, "A Model Litigation Funding Contract", 99 Iowa L. Rev. (2014, no. 2) p. 711 at p. 718.
110. *Ibid.* p. 719.

This article likewise relies on anecdotal evidence, drawing on real experiences which serve to highlight the distortive effects of third-party funding in investment arbitration, including its tendency to: (1) lead to speculative funding of cases lacking in merit; (2) incentivize the accumulation and coordination of claims by funders in the manner of a plaintiffs' attorney; (3) amplify the quantum claimed by investors; (4) alter the parties' normal settlement incentives; and (5) accord third-party funders disconcerting influence in the appointment of arbitrators, to the detriment of arbitrators' independent exercise of judgment.

1. *Speculative Funding of Cases Lacking in Merit*

The US Chamber of Commerce has characterized third-party litigation funding as a "clear and present danger to the impartial and efficient administration of civil justice in the United States".[111] In 2012, the Chamber made a proposal to regulate third-party litigation funding, in which it stated that litigation funding could be expected to increase the volume of abusive litigation, undermine the control of plaintiffs and lawyers over litigation, deter plaintiffs from settling and thus prolonging litigation, compromise the professional independence of attorneys, and more generally corrupt the attorney-client relationship.[112]

In response to the concern that third-party funding in ISDS will result in an increase in non-meritorious claims, the third-party funding industry has provided a number of responses and statistics, many of which were picked up in the *ICCA-QM TPF Report*. First, there is the claim that third-party funders are sufficiently detached, and skilled, to make an independent, realistic assessment of the merits and value of a case. In the abstract, this argument is not unreasonable. Certainly, third-party funders have no incentive to back a losing claim, and they generally have skilled teams of lawyers who assess the claim before determining whether to invest. But studying the form guide doesn't mean that the punter will pick the winning horse. The fact that the third-party funder has studied what is known about the case at a certain point (usually before anything is known of the respondent State's position) and is financially incentivized to bet on a winner does not mean that because the funder decides to invest, the case is bulletproof, or even that it is likely to end in a result favorable to the investor. It also does not mean that a fundamentally unmeritorious claim, which should never have been brought, will not receive third-party funding.

In this context, the authors of the *ICCA-QM TPF Report* apparently draw comfort from the following: "Leading funders report an average review-acceptance rate of 10-1, meaning that for every 10 cases they reviewed, they only agreed to fund one case."[113]

With respect, even if true, such a statistic is meaningless in qualitative terms. It tells us precisely nothing about the quality of that one-in-ten claim which receives funding;

111. John H. BEISNER and Gary A. RUBIN, U.S. Chamber Institute for Legal Reform, "Stopping the Sale on Lawsuits: A Proposal to Regulate Third-Party Investments in Litigation" (2012) available at <http://www.instituteforlegalreform.com/uploads/sites/1/TPLF_Solutions.pdf> (last accessed 15 February 2018) p. 1.

112. *Ibid*. pp. 1-2.

113. *ICCA-QM TPF Report*, p. 71.

only that, for any number of reasons, the third-party funder determined that it was better than nine other options.

The fact is that investing in a claim at the outset of a case, when so little is known about the asset, is highly speculative. Steinitz and Field draw a parallel between venture capital and litigation finance. They note that the two endeavors "have a similar risk profile: they invest in high-risk assets with the hope that, even if many of their investments fail, a handful will be wildly successful."[114] The same commentators observe that "[v]enture capitalists and litigation funders have similar (mid-length) investment timelines; they represent pools of investors' capital; and their profitability is measured across a portfolio of investments, not a single investment".[115] The comparison is apt, and the argument that there is no basis for any concern that third-party funders will ever back unmeritorious claims is terribly flawed. A funder may well back a claim which has a lower percentage chance of success (based on a very early assessment of the case), or which relies on a novel legal argument, or which has a high chance of failing on jurisdiction but good chances on the merits, provided the potential upside is sufficient, and provided the gamble fits into the risk profile of the funder's claim portfolio.

The authors' and their firm's own experience of third-party funding in investment arbitration underscores the point: third-party funders are willing to fund investment arbitrations which, from the outset, range from significantly to highly speculative when the potential upside is sufficient. This experience stems inter alia from a series of claims brought by Turkish investors against Turkmenistan under the Turkey-Turkmenistan bilateral investment treaty (BIT), all of which arose out of the construction industry.

The first of these cases was *Kılıç v. Turkmenistan*, which was registered before ICSID on 19 January 2010.[116] In its Decision on Art. VII.2 of the Turkey-Turkmenistan BIT dated 7 May 2012, the tribunal unanimously found that that provision requires an investor:

> "to submit its dispute to the courts of the Contracting Party with which a dispute has arisen, and must not have received a final award within one year from the date of submission of its case to the local courts, before it can institute arbitration proceedings in one of the fora in the manner permitted by Article VII.2".[117]

Then, in its 2 July 2013 award, the *Kılıç* tribunal ruled: (i) that the requirement to comply with Art. VII.2 of the BIT, and to have prior recourse to the Turkmen courts, constitutes a precondition to the existence of the Tribunal's jurisdiction, and (ii) that the claimant's failure to give effect to that requirement meant that the Tribunal did not have jurisdiction over the dispute. The claimant's claims were dismissed in their entirety for lack of jurisdiction, and the claimant was ordered to pay to the respondent State 50 percent of its reasonable legal costs and disbursements plus 75 percent of the costs

114. M. STEINITZ and A.C. FIELD, "A Model Litigation Funding Contract", fn. 109 above, p. 723.

115. *Ibid.*

116. *Kılıç İnşaat İthalat İhracat Sanayi ve Ticaret Anonim Şirketi v. Turkmenistan* (ICSID Case No. ARB/10/1), Decision on Article VII.2 of the Turkey-Turkmenistan Bilateral Investment Treaty (7 May 2012) para. 1.2.

117. *Ibid.*, para. 11.1(c).

incurred by the tribunal and ICSID following the Decision of 7 May 2012.[118] Arbitrator William W. Park issued a separate opinion in which he found that the claimant's failure to fulfill the requirement to submit the dispute to the local courts was a procedural flaw that went to the ripeness, or admissibility, of the claimant's claims, not to jurisdiction.[119] Under both approaches, the result was that, unless a Turkish claimant's claims against Turkmenistan had first been submitted to Turkmen courts and no final award had been received within one year from the date of submission, then the ICSID tribunal could not hear those claims under Art. VII.2 of the Turkey-Turkmenistan BIT.

On 20 December 2010, another case brought by a Turkish claimant against Turkmenistan under the Turkey-Turkmenistan BIT was registered before ICSID, *İçkale v. Turkmenistan*.[120] There, the respondent State's objections to jurisdiction on the basis of Art. VII.2 of the Turkey-Turkmenistan BIT were not bifurcated. In its award dated 8 March 2016, the *İçkale* tribunal decided by majority that the requirement to have prior recourse to the Turkmen courts in Art. VII.2 of the BIT was a procedural requirement that related to the admissibility of the claim rather than the tribunal's jurisdiction.[121] The majority also ruled that since a number of aspects of the dispute had been the subject of litigation before the Turkmen courts (e.g., for the application of delay penalties and termination of abandoned contracts), "it would be inappropriate ... to require that the Claimant subsequently commence further court proceedings under the relevant Contracts seeking relief thereunder and/or under the Treaty, given that the Contracts at issue had already been terminated by Turkmen courts".[122] Arbitrator Philippe Sands issued a Partially Dissenting Opinion on both points, finding (i) that the requirement for prior recourse to national courts went to the tribunal's jurisdiction, not merely to admissibility of the claims, and (ii) that in any event, the Turkmen court proceedings which had been brought did not fulfill the requirement for prior recourse to national courts: those proceedings had not been brought by the claimant, they involved certain breach of contract claims but did not concern any allegation of a violation of the BIT, and importantly, "six of the thirteen contracts appear never to have been raised before any national court in Turkmenistan, not for breach of contract or any other cause of action".[123]

---

118. *Kılıç İnşaat İthalat İhracat Sanayi ve Ticaret Anonim Şirketi v. Turkmenistan* (ICSID Case No. ARB/10/1), Award (2 July 2013) para. 10.1.1. See Luke Eric PETERSON, "Claimant's Failure to Pursue Local Remedies for 12 Months Derails $300 Million Claim Against Turkmenistan; Use of Local Courts Not Proven to Be Futile", Investment Arb. Rep. (5 July 2013) available at <https://www.iareporter.com/articles/claimants-failure-to-pursue-local-remedies-for-12-months-derails-300-million-claim-against-turkmenistan-use-of-local-courts-not-proven-to-be-futile> (last accessed 15 February 2018).
119. *Kılıç İnşaat İthalat İhracat Sanayi ve Ticaret Anonim Şirketi v. Turkmenistan* (ICSID Case No. ARB/10/1), Separate Opinion of Professor William W. Park (20 May 2013).
120. *İçkale İnşaat Limited Şirketi v. Turkmenistan* (ICSID Case No. ARB/10/24).
121. *İçkale İnşaat Limited Şirketi v. Turkmenistan* (ICSID Case No. ARB/10/24), Award (8 March 2016) para. 247.
122. *Ibid.*, paras. 262-263.
123. *Ibid.*, Partially Dissenting Opinion of Professor Philippe Sands QC (10 February 2016) paras. 14-15.

Despite their divergent views on Art. VII.2 of the Turkey-Turkmenistan BIT, all three members of the *İçkale* tribunal found that the claimant was not entitled to import the fair and equitable treatment, full protection and security, non-discrimination, and umbrella clause protections from other investment treaties concluded by Turkmenistan with third States on the basis of the most-favored-nation (MFN) clause in Art. II.2 of the BIT.[124] That meant that all of the claimant's claims, except for expropriation, were dismissed. The *İçkale* tribunal went on to find by majority that there had been no expropriation.[125] Thus, all of the claimant's claims were dismissed in their entirety for lack of merit, and the claimant was ordered to pay the respondent State more than US$ 1.7 million in costs.[126]

In parallel with the *İçkale* case, a third case was brought by a Turkish claimant and its main shareholder against Turkmenistan under the Turkey-Turkmenistan BIT. This case, *Muhammet Çap & Sehil v. Turkmenistan*, was registered at ICSID on 26 March 2012.[127] It emerged that a third-party funder was funding the claim. At the time funding was obtained for the *Sehil* claim:

– the *Kılıç* tribunal had not yet rendered its Decision on Art. VII.2 of the Turkey-Turkmenistan BIT which found that the local court requirement was a mandatory provision and ordered the claimant to pay costs;
– the *Kılıç* tribunal had not yet issued its Award dismissing the claimant's claims in their entirety for lack of jurisdiction and ordering the claimant to pay costs; and
– the *İçkale* tribunal had not yet issued its unanimous award finding that no substantive provisions could be imported into the Turkey-Turkmenistan BIT via the MFN clause, with the majority dismissing all of the claimant's claims and awarding costs to the respondent.

Nonetheless, these must have been issues which were examined by the funder's legal team prior to agreeing to fund the *Sehil* claim. The existence of the dissenting opinions of Professor Park in *Kılıç* and Professor Sands in *İçkale* of course show that different arbitrators were capable of having different views on, for example, the jurisdiction/admissibility issue. But that does not change the fact that, from its inception, the *Sehil* claim faced very significant legal hurdles, which were obvious from the plain language of the BIT in question, before anything was known about the respondent State's defenses on the merits or any proper exploration of the facts had been undertaken. And yet, the *Sehil* claim was apparently that one-in-ten case which received funding.

---

124. *İçkale İnşaat Limited Şirketi v. Turkmenistan* (ICSID Case No. ARB/10/24), Award (8 March 2016) para. 332.
125. *Ibid.*, paras. 350-355.
126. *Ibid.* para. 411(d)(e).
127. *Muhammet Çap & Sehil Inşaat Endustri ve Ticaret Ltd. Sti v. Turkmenistan* (ICSID Case No. ARB/12/6), Decision on Respondent's Objection to Jurisdiction Under Article VII(2) of the Turkey-Turkmenistan Bilateral Investment Treaty (13 February 2015) para. 11.

Erhas & others v. Turkmenistan, also brought under the Turkey-Turkmenistan BIT,[128] is another example. In this UNCITRAL case, twenty-two separate Turkish claimants sought to bring – in a single class action-type proceeding – eleven distinct claims against Turkmenistan, involving at least thirty-one different projects spanning a period of approximately twenty years and ranging across numerous industries, including a water bottling business, various factories, and a multitude of different construction projects. Indeed, the only common link between the claims was that a single third-party funder was funding them. As one commentator described it, FTI Consulting and Global Arbitration and Litigation Services essentially "convinced half a dozen Turkish companies ... to rely on its alleged financing to initiate arbitration against Turkmenistan".[129] Turkmenistan objected that it did not consent to such a joint arbitration claim, but ultimately agreed to appoint an arbitrator following agreement with the claimants that the tribunal would address Turkmenistan's preliminary objection at the outset of the case. In its 8 June 2015 award, the *Erhas* tribunal declined jurisdiction over the jointly submitted case, finding "'that consent to arbitration in a treaty based context does not imply the acceptance to the joint adjudication of entirely unrelated claims made by unrelated claimants in the context of different and unrelated investments'".[130] The claims in this case were, in the tribunal's words, "'entirely unrelated'".[131] The majority ordered the claimants to pay the costs of the proceedings and a reasonable portion of the respondent's legal fees and expenses.[132] Viewed under any lens, the *Erhas & others* claim was a highly speculative one. And yet, it received third-party funding.

The notion that third-party funders finance only meritorious claims, which too many in the international arbitration community seem to have swallowed, is patently naïve.[133] The *ICCA-QM TPF Report* comments on the existence, and rising prominence, of portfolio investment strategies by third-party funders, noting that a funder "may well provide funds for twenty or more cases at a time, each of them with different chances of success and different amounts at stake".[134] The Report acknowledges that this diversification of risk "may make initial assessment of risk less essential" and that, as a consequence, a funder's assessment of these cases may in practice be less rigorous than in individually selected cases.[135] On this issue, the Report concludes that, "[t]o the extent portfolio funding becomes more prevalent, it may require reconsideration of issues relating to

128. See generally Luke Eric PETERSON, "An UNCITRAL Tribunal Declines Jurisdiction over a Joint Treaty Claim Brought Against Turkmenistan by a Series of Unrelated Claimants", Investment Arb. Rep. (23 June 2015) available at <https://www.iareporter.com/articles/an-uncitral-tribunal-declines-jurisdiction-over-a-joint-treaty-claim-brought-against-turkmenistan-by-a-series-of-unrelated-claimants/> (last accessed 15 February 2018).

129. Hamid G. GHARAVI, "*Le Financement par un Tiers dans l'Arbitrage d'Investissement*", 2017 Belgian Rev. Arb. (2017, no. 1) p. 67 at para. 18 (authors' translation).

130. L.E. PETERSON, "An UNCITRAL Tribunal Declines Jurisdiction over a Joint Treaty Claim Brought Against Turkmenistan by a Series of Unrelated Claimants", fn. 128 above.

131. *Ibid.*

132. *Ibid.*

133. See Miriam K. HARWOOD, Simon N. BATIFORT and Christina TRAHANAS, "Third-Party Funding: Security for Costs and Other Key Issues" in Barton LEGUM, ed., *The Investment Treaty Arbitration Review*, 2nd edn. (Law Business Research 2017) p. 103 at pp. 108-109.

134. *ICCA-QM TPF Report*, p. 73.

135. *Ibid.* p.73.

how cases are assessed for funding".[136] It would seem, however, that the actual practices of funders are far more advanced along those lines than the *ICCA-QM TPF Report* contemplates. The following statement from Burford Capital's Annual Report from 2010 (eight years ago in a fast-moving industry) speaks for itself:

> "Not every investment will meet or exceed expectations. The model we use is very similar to that employed in venture capital, where poor results are expected from some investments and are balanced against high returns from other investments, in an effort to achieve desirable portfolio-wide returns.... [W]e regularly expect to have investments that disappoint, just as we regularly expect surprises to the upside as well.... If we shy away from risk for fear of loss, as some litigation investors do, we will not maximise the potential performance of this portfolio."[137]

As the co-founder of third-party funder Calunius Capital puts it, "[t]he perception that you need strong merits is wrong – there's a price for everything".[138]

During the preparation of this article and in the context of the authors' consultation with other law firms with significant experience representing States in investment arbitration, one lawyer commented:

> "Often, the funder is taking a flyer on a case that may have only a 40 percent chance of success, or worse. If you talk to funders (which I have), they will confide that they'll take a case on a coin flip chance (or worse). So the funding is not an access to justice issue, it's more like a patent troll issue. The funder is taking fairly worthless claims and then pumping them up into economic blackmail."

The fact is that the right price and terms of the funding agreement can make a weak case worth funding.[139] In addition, there are new products being developed by funders to further diversify their risk. Selvyn Seidel of Fulbrook Management explains:

---

136. *Ibid.*

137. Burford Capital 2010 Annual Report, available at <http://www.burfordcapital.com/investors/financial-reports-and-presentations/> (last accessed February 17, 2018) p. 5.

138. Pia EBERHARDT, et al., Corporate Europe Observatory and the Transnational Institute, "Profiting from Injustice: How Law Firms, Arbitrators and Financiers Are Fuelling on Investment Arbitration Boom" (November 2012) available at <https://corporateeurope.org/sites/default/files/publications/profiting-from-injustice.pdf> (last accessed 22 February 2018) p. 59 (quoting Mick Smith, Co-Founder of Calunius Capital).

139. *Ibid.* See also "Recent Developments in Investor–State Dispute Settlement (ISDS)", UNCTAD, IIA Issues Note No. 1, 2013, UN Doc. UNCTAD/WEB/DIAE/PCB/2013/3 (May 2013) n. 172 ("TPF companies, who build a 'portfolio' of claims, have an economic incentive to put money even into weak cases that have at least some chance of a high monetary award.") p. 25 ("[T]here are serious policy reasons against TPF of IIA claims – for example, it may increase the filing of questionable claims. From a respondent State's perspective, such frivolous claims, even if most of them fail, can take significant resources and may cause reputational damage."); John BEISNER, Jessica MILLER, and Gary RUBIN, U.S. Chamber Institute for Legal Reform, "Selling Lawsuits, Buying Trouble: Third-Party Litigation Funding in the United States" (October 2009)

> "There are other products we're considering.... Anything from derivatives, where we fund a single motion rather than the entire case, to a basket of five or six cases put together as a mini-portfolio to give some security through diversification. There is even the possibility – heaven forbid – that we could fund a case and then resell it to third parties, a bit like credit default swaps."[140]

This is no longer just a possibility. An arbitration practitioner with experience advising both established funds, and some investment banks which are now moving into the funding space, confirmed to the authors:

> "In the process of syndicating the debts attributable to funding, the level of scrutiny and due diligence by the hedge funds to which the funding is being syndicated is almost non-existent. They are acquiring such debt on trust, based on a combination of who the first reviewing law firm was for the funder and a ravenous desire to acquire risk."

The same lawyer compared this practice to the sub-prime market "where debt was wrapped and rated with little awareness of the underlying asset". His concern is the scenario where this debt becomes "a significant 'prop' for the arbitration market which might ultimately undermine its integrity".

In short, the fear that third-party funding will lead to more, and more speculative, claims is founded. The U.S. Chamber Institute for Legal Reform has recognized that third-party litigation funding can be "expected to increase the volume of abusive litigation" as funders "hedge any 'investment' against their entire portfolio of cases".[141] The risk which is supposed to moderate the bringing of frivolous claims is being diversified away to the point where there is no longer any sense of responsibility for the cost of bringing the claim, or the manner in which the case is run, or the costs incurred by the other party. The claimant, having started the claim, passes the risk to a funder, and "[i]f the money doesn't come, the claimant has nothing to lose, but the defendant (a government) has still been forced to pay top-tier firms for their services".[142]

---

available at <http://www.instituteforlegalreform.com/uploads/sites/1/thirdpartylitigationfinancing.pdf> (last accessed 22 February 2018) pp. 5-6 ("[A]lthough providing non-recourse loans to fund litigation is inherently risky, it does not follow that litigation-finance companies will only finance claims that are likely to succeed. These companies – like all sophisticated investors – will base their funding decisions on the present value of their expected return, of which the likelihood of a lawsuit's success is only one component. The other component is the potential amount of recovery.... Moreover, third-party funding companies are able to mitigate their downside risk in two ways: they can spread the risk of any particular case over their entire portfolio of cases, and they can spread the risk among their investors.").

140. A. ROSS, "The Dynamics of Third-Party Funding", fn. 82 above, p. 15.

141. John H. BEISNER and Gary A. RUBIN, U.S. Chamber Institute for Legal Reform, "Stopping the Sale on Lawsuits: a Proposal to Regulate Third Party Investments in Litigation" (October 2012) available at <http://www.instituteforlegalreform.com/uploads/sites/1/TPLF_Solutions.pdf> (last accessed 15 February 2018) p. 1.

142. P. EBERHARDT et al., Corporate Europe Observatory and the Transnational Institute, "Profiting From Injustice", fn. 138 above, available at <https://corporateeurope.org/sites/

2. *Accumulation of Claims in the Manner of a Plaintiffs' Attorney*

Even given all of the arguments above, one could still ask, what would make a third-party funder fund a case such as *Erhas & others v. Turkmenistan*?

The authors can imagine two possible answers. The first is relatively simple. In the tradition of plaintiffs' attorneys in the United States, collecting numerous claims means bargaining power and cost savings. A respondent State faced with the possible cost of defending eleven separate investor-State arbitrations brought by twenty-two different claimants relating to at least thirty-one different projects may indeed be inclined to settle. The effect of third-party funding on settlement incentives is discussed in more detail below. But there is no doubt that the more claims a single funder can collect against one respondent State, the more pressure it can bring to bear on that State, and the higher the likelihood of negotiating a quick settlement and a financially favorable outcome for the fund. This is yet another reason why the notion that third-party funders are financially incentivized to fund only meritorious claims rings hollow. Third-party funders are financially incentivized to reach early settlements where possible.[143] And what better way to increase the odds of early settlement than to accumulate as many claims as possible against the same respondent State?[144] The individual merits of each case are immediately of less importance: quantity, not quality.

The second reason is more complex, and even more concerning. Corporate Europe Observatory reports that "[i]n their quest for selling more services, some litigation funders are also exploring 'less passive business-models', providing for more influence

---

default/files/publications/profiting-from-injustice.pdf> p. 58 (quoting John Jones of risk insuring company Aon).

143. Maya STEINITZ, "Whose Claim Is This Anyway? Third-Party Litigation Funding", 8 Transnat'l Disp. Mgmt. (2011, no. 4) p. 1268 at p. 1313 (Noting that funders "have an incentive to settle early for a relatively low, but certain, recovery rather than incur the costs of going to trial and risking no or lesser recovery" and that this incentive is only exacerbated by the portfolio approach to investing.).

144. A number of States have already had, and continue to have, to weather this type of pressure. Luke Eric PETERSON, "Solar Investors File Arbitration Against Czech Republic; Intra-EU BITs and Energy Charter Treaty at Center of Dispute", Investment Arb. Rep. (15 May 2013) available at <http://www.iareporter.com/articles/solar-investors-file-arbitration-against-czech-republic-intra-eu-bits-and-energy-charter-treaty-at-center-of-dispute/> (last accessed 15 February 2018) (indicating that a bloc of at least ten investors brought claims against the Czech Republic under a number of treaties, including the Energy Charter Treaty and Czech bilateral investment treaties with the Netherlands, Germany, Cyprus, Luxembourg, and the United Kingdom); *Abaclat and Others v. The Argentine Republic* (ICSID Case No. ARB/07/5), Decision on Jurisdiction and Admissibility (4 August 2011) para. 1 (noting that, at the time of the initiation of the arbitration, the total number of claimants exceeded 180,000), para. 696 (finding that the consent of Argentina to jurisdiction "includes claims presented by multiple Claimants in a single proceeding"); "Spanish Arbitrator to Hear Abaclat Mass Claim", Global Arb. Rev. (23 January 2012), available at <https://globalarbitrationreview.com/article/1030917/spanish-arbitrator-to-hear-abaclat-mass-claim> (last accessed 21 February 2018) (reporting on *Abaclat v. Argentina*, noting that it was "the first mass claim in ICSID's history"); and *Bernardus Henricus Funnekotter and Others v. Republic of Zimbabwe* (ICSID Case No. ARB/05/6), Award (22 April 2009) para. 3 (indicating the claimants as being thirteen Dutch farmers bringing a consolidated claim).

on the management and strategies of arbitrations".[145] This includes managing and strategizing across multiple cases against the same respondent State. The authors have seen entire paragraphs from a claimant's memorial in one confidential investor-State proceeding appear word-for-word in a second investor-State case, brought by a different claimant, represented by a different law firm. This occurrence raised a few eyebrows, and inspired the questions: could the same third-party funder be behind both claims? Is that how the information was shared? Some letter-writing and an application for security for costs later and, indeed, the existence of a third-party funder was revealed. Putting aside any breach of confidentiality concerns, States need to understand that funders also coordinate multiple claims against a single respondent State to maximize the possibility of favorable outcomes across the claims, seeking out potential claimants with similar grievances (perhaps affected by the same State measure), and then deciding which claim in the series should proceed first as the most likely to generate a favorable "precedent" on which the other claimants, with perhaps lower initial probabilities of success, can then rely.

This cross-case coordination is unlikely to stop at cases against a single respondent State. If it is not already happening, Maya Steinitz predicts that financiers will likely "invest in rule change", selecting a claim to fund not because of its individual risk profile, but because it provides an opportunity to advance certain arguments or procedural changes which, if successful, will set a favorable precedent, leaving a lasting mark on the whole investment arbitration system and maximizing the future value of funders' portfolios.[146] One can indeed imagine this having been a consideration in the decision to fund the *Erhas* case. Imagine if the claimants had been successful in their petition to bring multiple, unrelated claims against a single respondent State in a single proceeding. For the fund, imagine the value of the accumulated claims (increased potential upside) and the cost savings (decreased investment) associated with bringing them all in one proceeding. In an *ad hoc* system with no precedent and no appeal structure, where arbitrators are free to render decisions on points of law in accordance with their own views,[147] and so, therefore, the choice of arbitrator can dictate the outcome of the case, no one can say that a finding on jurisdiction favorable to the *Erhas* claimants was an impossibility. For the fund, such a gamble on a very slim chance of success may indeed have been worthwhile.

A question in the minds of the authors is whether any of this can have been within the contemplation of the contracting States when they included ISDS provisions in their BITs. Could they have imagined that a very large portion of the benefit of the rights being accorded to the other State's investors would ultimately inure to a category of venture capitalists of undisclosed nationality? Did the contracting States contemplate and

145. P. EBERHARDT et al., Corporate Europe Observatory and the Transnational Institute, "Profiting From Injustice", fn. 138 above, <https://corporateeurope.org/sites/default/files/publications/profiting-from-injustice.pdf>, p. 59 (citing Luke Eric PETERSON, "Republic of Georgia Agrees to Pay 1/3rd of ICSID Award; Litigation Funders Eyes Recovery After Bumpy Ride", Investment Arb. Rep. (31 December 2011), available at <http://www.iareporter.com/articles/2011123 1_6> (last accessed 22 February 2018)).

146. M. STEINITZ, "Whose Claim Is This Anyway? Third-Party Litigation Funding", fn. 143 above, p.1312.

147. See generally G. KAHALE, "Rethinking ISDS", fn. 28 above, pp. 12-13.

consent to a system of ISDS where highly speculative claims would be brought against them, funded by third-party funders trying either to pressure a settlement or even to engineer legal outcomes which will favor their investment portfolios going forward?[148] It is not the purpose of this paper to discuss the jurisdictional implications for an investor's claim against a State when that claim is sold, or control over that claim is sold.[149] The broader issue is whether this phenomenon is changing the economics of access to investment arbitration in a way which is beyond what was originally contemplated by the States that designed it in the first place, and what can be done to manage these changes.

3. *Amplified Quantum Claimed by Investors*

The distortive effect of "anchoring" by claimants is not a new complaint.

It should come as no surprise that claimants in any legal system tend to begin their cases with exaggerated claims of compensation, whether it be a personal injury claim of millions of dollars for a coffee spill or a multibillion-dollar expropriation claim. The technique is known as "anchoring". The exaggerated claim is made in the hope that a less exaggerated but still indefensible amount will seem reasonable by comparison. In a mature legal system with professional judges, there are checks and balances to curb abuse, but in the world of ISDS, the risk of abuse is much higher. That is especially true in cases requiring complex valuations of businesses, often involving natural resources, which are typically at issue in investor-state arbitration.[150]

The practice of claiming a phenomenally high and unsupported quantum of damages in the hope of achieving an award of a lower, but still unsupported, amount is as old as dispute resolution itself, although certainly it has taken on a new significance in this age of mega-claims.[151] Anchoring is another area where the participation of third-party funders generates a perceptible negative impact.

Whatever a third-party funder's own internal estimates of reasonable recovery in a given investment arbitration might be, in the proceeding itself, a funder's only incentive is to inflate the damages claimed to the highest amount possible for the purpose of anchoring the damages discussion in the arbitration and achieving the best possible, if still unreasonably high, economic result. This is not a theoretical risk – it occurs. Moreover, there are currently no checks on, or consequences for, funders and claimants which engage in this practice. As discussed above, security for costs orders are rare, and if it turns out that the claim was exaggerated and the claimant is awarded significantly less, no one bats an eye.

---

148. The *ICCA-QM Draft TPF Report* does refer to concerns by critics that speculative portfolio claims may "expand the bases for liability for States beyond the originally intended meanings in investment and trade agreements", but these concerns are somewhat glossed over. *ICCA-QM Draft TPF Report*, pp. 159-161. The issue is not addressed in the final *ICCA-QM TPF Report*.

149. For further discussion on this point, see M.K. HARWOOD, S.N. BATIFORT and C. TRAHANAS, "Third-Party Funding: Security for Costs and Other Key Issues", fn. 133 above, pp. 114-116.

150. G. KAHALE, "Rethinking ISDS", fn. 28 above, p. 18 (internal citations omitted). See also Lucy REED, "The 2013 Hong Kong International Arbitration Centre Kaplan Lecture – Arbitral Decision-Making: Art, Science or Sport?", 30 J. Int'l Arb. (2013, no. 2) p. 85 at pp. 89-90.

151. G. KAHALE, "Rethinking ISDS", fn. 28 above, pp. 18-20.

In one recent investor-State case, evidence on the record revealed that, prior to the involvement of a third-party funder, the investor had valued its own losses as a result of the State's actions at approximately US$155 million. This amount was stated in the context of negotiations when legal action was already contemplated (suggesting that the investor had already received legal advice), and can reasonably be understood as representing the upper end of the investor's expected recovery. Moreover, there were no circumstances that would suggest that the investor was not sophisticated, or had not done sufficient work at that stage to come to a realistic estimation of its own losses.

Less than a year later, the investor entered into a third-party funding agreement and, in the months that followed, commenced an ICSID arbitration. In its request for arbitration, the investor claimed US$ 300 million, double the upper end of the investor's own expected recovery just eighteen months before. Nothing else had happened in the interim to increase the investor's alleged damage, just the signing of the third-party funding agreement. Now, if the terms of that funding agreement provided that the funder would receive 50 percent of any damages ultimately awarded, it makes perfect sense to try to increase the quantum claimed, by any means possible, so that 50 percent of the award will in fact fully compensate the investor for its alleged, real damage. After all, there is currently absolutely no reason not to do so. As discussed above, that needs to change.

4. *Alteration of the Parties' Normal Settlement Incentives*

The *ICCA-QM TPF Report* highlights a concern regarding the "extent to which the funder will take over control of the arbitration and the claimant's decision-making process (e.g., whether, when and at what level to settle the claim)".[152] Many funding agreements require the approval of the funder before the funded claimant can settle the dispute. Some funding agreements permit a claimant to settle without the funder's agreement, but only if the settlement offer is above a certain amount. The terms of a funding agreement may also reduce the claimant's percentage share of any recovery in the event of a settlement below a certain amount. These types of terms in a funding agreement can have a significant impact on the possibility for a State to settle a funded claim.

For example, even if it appeared reasonable to prevent or discourage settlement below a certain sum (or floor) when the third-party funder first evaluated a dispute, no matter how sophisticated the funder's review was, it occurred before anything was known of the respondent State's position, before significant development of the facts of the case, before document production, and before the hearing. As a case progresses and more is known, the prospects of a financial outcome above that floor can diminish. Imagine a respondent State's frustration upon learning from a claimant that, given how the case has proceeded, it would be happy to accept an offer of US$ x, but it cannot because of the terms of its third-party funding agreement.

The terms of a third-party funding agreement also often fail to take into account other incentives to settle. Where a claimant might otherwise settle a case, for example for non-economic reasons such as resuming business in the host country or obtaining injunctive relief, a third-party funder may be solely focused on financial gain.

152. *ICCA-QM TPF Report*, p. 28.

As Steinitz and Field observe:

> "A funder's objective is to maximize profits for the benefit of its investors. The funder also has a relationship with the plaintiff. These competing loyalties have a concrete consequence: in some scenarios, a funder may have objectives extrinsic to the claim, leading it to push for outcomes for its own benefit that disadvantage the plaintiff."[153]

Indeed, some have argued that third-party funding results in a "Bermuda Triangle" of divergent interests, often between the claimant, the counsel representing the claimant, and the third-party funders.[154]

Third-party funding not only affects a claimant's settlement incentives. Respondent States are less inclined even to enter into settlement negotiations when they know that a claim is funded by a third-party funder. No respondent State wants to get a reputation as a "settler". That will only incentivize more claims funded by funders against that State in the hope of a quick and painless settlement (a fast and lucrative return on the funder's investment). Rather, in this age of third-party funded investment arbitrations, a State has a strong incentive to generate a reputation as a "fighter", ensuring that obtaining any money from the State will be expensive, time-consuming, and difficult.

Respondent States also have a legitimate concern that the fruits of any settlement of what may be a meritorious claim should not go into the pocket of a fund which may then turn around and use that money to fund another suit against the same State (since the State is now known as a "settler"). Thus, settling even meritorious claims becomes more complicated when a third-party funder is involved.

Systematic disclosure of the existence and identity of a third-party funder in an investment arbitration is essential so that a respondent State can know who the real parties in interest are, with whom it is really negotiating, whether the funder is funding other claims against it, and whether it can impose conditions on any settlement of a claim which protect it from the ignominy of having its own money used to fund future claims against it.

5. *Funders' Influence in Arbitrators' Decision-Making*

The risk of potential conflicts of interest between a particular third-party funder and a given arbitrator is discussed at length elsewhere,[155] and there is an emerging consensus in favor of mandatory, systematic disclosure of the existence and identity of a third-party funder in any international arbitration claim as a potential solution.[156] This consensus is

153. M. STEINITZ and A.C. FIELD, "A Model Litigation Funding Contract", fn. 109 above p. 722.

154. C.B. LAMM and E.R. HELLBECK, "Third-Party Funding in Investor-State Arbitration Introduction and Overview", fn. 98 above, p. 107.

155. *ICCA-QM TPF Report*, pp. 81-115; M.K. HARWOOD, S.N. BATIFORT and C. TRAHANAS, "Third-Party Funding: Security for Costs and Other Key Issues", fn. 133 above, pp. 98-99.

156. See IBA Guidelines on Conflicts of Interest in International Arbitration, adopted on 23 October 2014, Guidelines 6(b) and 7(a) and Explanations to General Standards 6(b) and 7(a) (providing that a party shall disclose, "on its own initiative at the earliest opportunity", "any relationship, direct or indirect, … between the arbitrator and any person or entity with a direct economic

also reflected in the text of a number of recent treaties.[157] However, this solution does not address the risk of more general, systemic influence of third-party funders in arbitrators' decision-making.

One aspect of the third-party funders/arbitrators conflict discussion which has received less attention is the risk that, because arbitrators are aware of the role that third-party funders play in their appointment, or because they also have practices as counsel and have economic relationships with the funders that fund their clients' claims, they will be influenced to issue decisions favorable to the third-party funding industry, or influenced to not issue decisions viewed as unfavorable to the industry.

We discussed above the incentive for third-party funders to fund claims, not (or not solely) on the basis of the potential for economic return, but also in the hope of establishing procedural or substantive precedents tending to maximize the potential for future economic gain from the fund's investment portfolio. Is there a danger that arbitrators, conscious of the influence of third-party funders in the business of international arbitration, will be inclined to favor the interests of the third-party funding industry in their decisions?

In *Sehil v. Turkmenistan*, the tribunal ordered the claimants to disclose "whether their claims in this arbitration are being funded by a third-party/parties, and, if so, the names and details of the third-party funder(s) *and the terms of that funding*" (emphasis added).[158] The tribunal stated that it was "sympathetic to Respondent's concern that if it is successful in this arbitration and a costs order is made in its favour, Claimants will be

---

interest in ... the award", and recognizing that a third-party funder has a "direct economic interest" in the award); Catherine A. ROGERS, *Ethics in International Arbitration* (Oxford University Press 2014) para. 5.79 ("[F]or arbitrators to assess the potential for conflicts and make necessary disclosures, third-party funders' participation in particular international arbitration cases will necessarily have to be disclosed"); Burcu OSMANOGLU, "Third-Party Funding in International Commercial Arbitration and Arbitrator Conflict of Interest", 32 J. Int'l Arb. (2015, no. 3) p. 325 at pp. 339-340 ("[A]n obligation on the parties to disclose the presence of third-party funders in the arbitration proceedings is vital and would closely relate to the obligation of the arbitrators to disclose any relationship that they have with third-party funders that may imperil the arbitral tribunal's independence and impartiality."); Catherine KESSEDJIAN, "Good Governance of Third Party Funding", Columbia FDI Perspectives No. 130 (15 September 2014), pp. 1-2 ("Some of the best practices for arbitral tribunals confronted with third party financing could include the following: Financing by third parties must be disclosed for arbitration proceedings to be conducted appropriately."); Commision Financement de Procés par les Tiers, Club des Juristes, "*Financement du Procès par les Tiers*" (June 2014) p. 59 ("It is undeniable that the presence of a third-party funder in the arbitral proceeding may generate potential conflicts of interest. In this sense, the current situation that does not require anyone to disclose anything cannot persist.") (authors' translation); William STONE, "Third Party Funding in International Arbitration: A Case for Mandatory Disclosure?", 2015 Asian Disp. Rev. (2015, no. 2) p. 62 at p. 68 ("Absent disclosure of a funding relationship within the arbitration, the independence of an arbitrator cannot be assured.").

157. EU-Vietnam Free Trade Agreement, agreed text as of January 2016, Chapter 8: Trade in Services, Investment and E-Commerce, Chapter 2, Sect. 3, Art. 11.1; CETA, Art. 8.26; European Commission, Draft of Chapter II (Investment) of the Transatlantic Trade and Investment Partnership, released on 12 November 2015, Sect. 3, Art. 8.

158. *Muhammet Çap & Sehil Inşaat Endustri ve Ticaret Ltd. Sti. v. Turkmenistan* (ICSID Case No. ARB/12/6), Procedural Order No. 3 (12 June 2015) para. 8.

unable to meet these costs and the third-party funder will have disappeared as it is not a party to this arbitration".[159] When the claimants refused to disclose the funding agreement, the *Sehil* tribunal warned that it may draw adverse inferences.[160] In short, the *Sehil* tribunal determined that the terms of the funding agreement were relevant to the issue of security for costs and therefore ordered their disclosure. The terms of a funding agreement may also be of fundamental relevance to the issue of true ownership of a claim and jurisdiction.[161] Given that third-party funders have worked hard to maintain the confidentiality of the terms of their funding arrangements, one wonders how many arbitrators will be willing to order the disclosure of such agreements when necessary to properly consider a security for costs application or to ascertain whether a claimant remains the actual owner of the claim in dispute, and how many may, with one eye on their future income stream, decline to do so.

Arbitrator Gavan Griffith's opinion in *RSM v. Saint Lucia* was critical of the activities of third-party funders in investment arbitration, whom he characterized as "a new industry of mercantile adventurers".[162] He considered that third-party funding would normally provide the "exceptional circumstances" required to grant security for costs since otherwise the funder would enjoy the upside of the case but not assume the corresponding risk (a "gambler's Nirvana").[163] This led the claimant in that case to propose his disqualification,[164] and "drew a sharp response, especially from litigation financiers".[165]

The institution of safeguards to insulate arbitrators in investment arbitrations from the influence of individual third-party funders, and from the third-party funding industry in general, is long overdue. The only real solution to this, and indeed other conflicts of interest which are the direct and natural result of arbitrators also acting as counsel, is simply to ban the practice of "double-hatting". Lawyers who act as counsel should be prohibited from being appointed as arbitrators in investment arbitrations, or as *ad-hoc* committee members. Arbitrators and *ad hoc* committee members must also disclose as a matter of course any other relationship they may have with third-party funders, whether as a board member or an advisor, or in any other capacity. A consensus is growing, at least among States, that the practice of double-hatting should be prohibited in investment arbitration.

In March 2018, and in the context of their ongoing review and implementation of the Comprehensive and Progressive Agreement for Trans-Pacific Partnership (CPTPP),

159. *Ibid.* para. 12.
160. See Hamid G. GHARAVI, "*Le financement par un tiers dans l'arbitrage d'investissement*", fn. 129 above, p. 67 at para. 36.
161. M.K. HARWOOD, S.N. BATIFORT and C. TRAHANAS, "Third-Party Funding: Security for Costs and Other Key Issues", fn. 133 above, pp. 108-113.
162. *RSM Production Corporation v. Saint Lucia* (ICSID Case No. ARB/12/10), Decision on Saint Lucia's Request for Security for Costs, Assenting Opinion of Mr. Gavan Griffith QC (13 August 2014) para. 14.
163. *Ibid.*, paras. 13, 16.
164. *RSM Production Corporation v. Saint Lucia* (ICSID Case No. ARB/12/10), Decision on Claimant's Proposal for Disqualification of Dr. Gavan Griffith QC (23 October 2014) paras. 39-42.
165. J. GILL and M. HODGSON, "Costs Awards – Who Pays?", fn. 45 above.

New Zealand, Canada and Chile issued a Joint Declaration on Investor State Dispute Settlement. The Joint Declaration provides in relevant part:

> "Intend to promote transparent conduct rules on the ethical responsibilities of arbitrators in ISDS procedures, including conflict of interest rules that prevent arbitrators from acting, for the duration of their appointment, as counsel or party appointed expert or witness in other proceedings...."[166]

In May 2018, the Netherlands published a new draft model bilateral investment treaty, Art. 20.5 of which provides in relevant part:

> "Members of the Tribunal shall not act as legal counsel or shall not have acted as legal counsel for the last five years in investment disputes under this or any other international agreement."[167]

In April 2018, Meg Kinnear stated that ICSID would not – at this stage – be including a prohibition on the practice of double-hatting in its forthcoming rules amendment.[168] The authors view this as a lost opportunity for ICSID to lead the way in protecting investment arbitration as an institution from a practice that has severely damaged its reputation and credibility. States are encouraged to voice their views on this issue to ICSID, as well as in the context of their ongoing UNCITRAL WGIII discussions, and to adopt language in their treaties preventing the practice of double-hatting in ISDS.

V. SUGGESTED WAYS FORWARD

The above discussion highlights a number of areas where reform, regulation, and changes in States' treaty practice are required to correct systemic imbalances in investment arbitration. These imbalances include States bearing the economic burden of defending unmeritorious claims with little or no possibility of costs recovery, the funding of claims based on factors distinct from the underlying merits of the claim, the exponential inflation of the quantum claimed, the alteration of incentives to settle, and a concern that

166. New Zealand Ministry of Foreign Affairs and Trade, "Joint Declaration on Investor State Dispute Settlement", available at <https://www.mfat.govt.nz/assets/CPTPP/CPTPP-Joint-Declaration-ISDS-Final.pdf> (last visited 20 June 2018).

167. See "Radical Proposals in Draft Netherlands Model BIT", Global Arbitration Review (16 May 2018), available at <https://globalarbitrationreview.com/article/1169654/radical-proposals-in-draft-netherlands-model-bit> (last visited 20 June 2018). The text of the new Netherlands draft Model BIT is available in English at <https://globalarbitrationreview.com/digital_assets/820bcdd9-08b5-4bb5-a81e-d69e6c6735ce/Draft-Model-BIT-NL-2018.pdf> (last visited 20 June 2018). Notably, Art. 20.1 of the new Netherlands draft model BIT also provides that all arbitrators shall be appointed by the arbitral institution, thus eliminating the party-appointment system.

168. See "Kinnear Sheds Light on ICSID Rules Amendment", Global Arbitration Review (6 April 2018) available at <https://globalarbitrationreview.com/article/1167749/kinnear-sheds-light-on-icsid-rules-amendment> (last accessed 20 June 2018).

arbitrators may be influenced by economic incentives generated by the participation of third-party funders in the investment arbitration industry.

The following is a list of initiatives, current and future, aimed at addressing these imbalances for further consideration and debate:

– ICSID's current proposed rule amendment does not contemplate a default rule to the effect that the costs of the arbitration (both tribunal costs and party costs), or the annulment proceeding, shall in principle be borne by the unsuccessful party. The authors submit that such a default rule could be instituted in a manner consistent with Art. 61(2) of the ICSID Convention provided it is accompanied by language preserving the tribunal/*ad hoc* committee's discretion to apportion costs where reasonable in the circumstances of a given case.
– States should also include this type of default rule in their treaty's ISDS provisions.
– Parties to investment arbitrations and annulment proceedings should demand that costs be treated in a fully reasoned manner in the award or decision; investment arbitration tribunals and *ad hoc* committees need to meet this demand, specifically identifying in the award or decision the party behavior which led to the allocation of costs in a certain manner.
– The amount of quantum claimed by an investor, versus any amount ultimately awarded to it, should be a factor to be taken into account by investment tribunals when allocating costs, to discourage inflated damages claims.
– The current proposed amendments to the ICSID Arbitration Rules contemplate the addition of an article confirming the power of ICSID tribunals to issue orders for security for costs.
– The burden of proof applicable to, and standard for issuing, orders for security for costs in investment arbitrations need to change to reflect the reality of the availability of third-party funding in the market, the unavailability of accurate information regarding claimants' financial standing, and the asymmetries this creates.

• *Burden of proof*: Once a respondent State becomes aware of circumstances suggesting that the claimant may be impecunious (including the fact that its claim is being funded by a third party, but also perhaps other circumstances, such as failure to pay an advance on costs, or an SEC disclosure) but not necessarily rising to the level of a prima facie showing, the respondent should disclose such circumstance to the tribunal and be permitted to request that the claimant provide information regarding its financial position, and in particular make a showing that it has the financial wherewithal to cover an adverse costs order. Should the claimant fail to make such a showing, the tribunal must weigh the competing interests of access to justice versus the respondent's right to recover the costs of a successful defense. Where the claim is third-party funded, the scales tip markedly in favor of ordering security for costs.
• *Standard*: Investment tribunals should ensure that they have sufficient information regarding the relevant terms of a funding agreement, and the financial capacity of both the claimant and its funder, to be able to judge when the "interests of justice" (not "exceptional circumstances") require an order for security for costs to protect the respondent State from the risk of an unpaid cost award. Funders will factor such security

into the cost of funding the dispute, removing the access-to-justice concern from funded cases.

– Claimants in investment arbitrations should be required to disclose the existence of any third-party funding, and the identity of the funder, as a matter of course, at the earliest possible moment (including at the time of the notice of dispute or the request for arbitration, or as soon as a third-party funder becomes involved). This requirement should be incorporated into the ICSID Rules amendment procedure and the discussions of UNCITRAL Working Group III on ISDS Reform. States should include a similar requirement in their treaty's ISDS provisions.
– There should be mandatory, systematic, early disclosure of the existence and identity of third-party funders in all investment arbitrations, to ensure that:

• the respondent State in a given case knows who the real parties in interest are in the dispute, with whom it is really negotiating, whether the funder is funding other claims against it, and whether it can impose conditions on any settlement of a claim which protect it from the ignominy of having its own money used to fund future claims against it; and
• tactical behavior and coordination of multiple cases by third-party funders against different respondent States can be detected and monitored.

– There should be mandatory disclosure by arbitrators and *ad hoc* committee members of any relationship they may have with third-party funders (board member, advisor, or in any other capacity).
– In line with the growing consensus among States, lawyers who act as counsel or party-appointed experts in arbitrations, or who act as advisors or board members to third-party funders of arbitration proceedings, should be prohibited from being appointed as arbitrators in investment arbitrations, or as *ad hoc* committee members. This prohibition should form part of the current effort to amend the ICSID Arbitration Rules, as well as States' individual treaty practice, and the ongoing discussion regarding ISDS Reform taking place in UNCITRAL WGIII.

The Pandora's Box of Third-Party Funding: Some Practical Suggestions for Arbitrators in Light of Recent Developments

John Beechey, CBE[*]

TABLE OF CONTENTS PAGE

I. OVERVIEW OF RECENT DEVELOPMENTS IN THIRD-PARTY FUNDING

As more of the leading arbitral centres amend their legislation and lift restrictions upon the activities of third-party funders, international commercial and investor-State arbitration have become a rich and developing seam of business and revenues for the funders. There is no doubt that many of the entities, which are now active as funders are themselves well-funded, well-run and sophisticated operations. Their decision-making processes are based upon a careful and independent assessment of the potential for a level of recovery sufficient to justify the investment, but, and it is an important proviso, taking a view of each case in the context of their portfolios of investments as a whole.

For all that third-party funding has been described by Lord Neuberger, the recently retired President of the UK Supreme Court, as "the life-blood of the judicial system", the perception remains that this is an industry operating in the shadows, just as pressure is increasing at all levels, not least among lawmakers, for transparency in the arbitral process.[1] And it is true, too, that not every funder espouses the high standards of due

---

* Based in Hong Kong and London, active in commercial and investor-state arbitrations, serving as chairman, party-appointed arbitrator, or sole arbitrator in both "*ad hoc*" (including UNCITRAL) and institutional arbitrations under the rules of all major arbitral institutions. Former President of the International Court of Arbitration of the ICC (2009-2015); founding partner of the international arbitration practice of Clifford Chance LLP; ICCA Governing Board Member.

The author has been assisted in the preparation of this paper by Avv. Niccolo LANDI of Studio Legale Landi, Milan.

1. "It was observed that third-party funding had become a significant concern, in that it created a systemic imbalance and did not ensure a level playing field. It was added that issues of third-party funding related not just to costs, but also had an impact on other issues, such as conflicts of interest, collection and enforcement of costs awards." UNCITRAL Report of Working Group III (Investor-State Dispute Settlement Reform) on the work of its thirty-fourth session (Vienna, 27 November – 1 December 2017), para. 62; "... TPF can give rise to a host of important and complex ethical and procedural issues in international arbitration. These issues include the nature and degree of

diligence, management of the relationship with the funded party and its advisers and professionalism associated with the market leaders.[2] This is all grist to the mill in the increasingly politicized debate surrounding international arbitration generally and investment arbitration in particular.

Third-party funding is well established in the United States, the United Kingdom and Australia. It is gaining ground in Canada. In New Zealand, the maintenance and champerty rules remain on the statute book but the courts are said to be cautiously permissive of third-party funding arrangements. Ireland, however, remains a "no go" area. The old maintenance and champerty rules remain in place, as they did in Singapore and Hong Kong, too – until 2017.

These latter changes in two of the most prominent arbitration venues in Asia are of some significance, not least because they have been implemented at a time when the role of third-party funders is a matter of open debate and calls for regulation of the industry are strident in some political and business circles. It is not unreasonable to suppose that the legislators in these sophisticated jurisdictions would have fashioned their approach to third-party funding with an eye to the issues, which have attracted considerable attention internationally.

There are some noteworthy differences of approach between that adopted in Hong Kong and that in Singapore, which merit further comment, but it is striking that in both jurisdictions, the emphasis is on disclosure rather than regulation – at least for the time being.

1. *Singapore*

On 10 January 2017, the Singapore Parliament passed the Civil Law (Amendment) Act (Bill No. 38/2016) which entered into force on 1 March 2017 (the Act),[3] together with the Civil Law (Third-Party Funding) Regulations 2017 (the Regulations).[4]

The Act abolishes civil liability for the torts of maintenance and champerty[5] and allows third-party funding contracts, but it is not a blanket relaxation.[6] Third-party

influence of funders in the management of the dispute, issues of jurisdiction and admissibility (i.e. who owns the claim?), issues of transparency and disclosure of the funding arrangements, issues of attorney-client privilege, issues of conflicts of interest for tribunals, and issues of allocations of costs and security for costs": Stavros BREKOULAKIS, "The Impact of Third Party Funding on Allocation for Costs and Security for Costs Applications: The ICCA-Queen Mary Task Force Report", Kluwer Arbitration Blog, 18 February 2016, available at <http://arbitrationblog.kluwerarbitration.com/2016/02/18/the-impact-of-third-party-funding-on-allocation-for-costs-and-security-for-costs-applications-the-icca-queen-mary-task-force-report/> (last accessed 4 March 2018).

2. See the salutary case of *Excalibur Ventures LLC v. Texas Keystone Inc and Ors (Rev 2)* [2014] EWHC 3436.
3. The Act is available at <https://sso.agc.gov.sg/Bills-Supp/38-2016/Published/20161107?DocDate=20161107> (last accessed 4 March 2018).
4. The Regulations are available at <https://sso.agc.gov.sg/SL-Supp/S68-2017/Published/20170224?DocDate=20170224> (last accessed 4 March 2018).
5. Sect. 5A(1) of the Act: "It is declared that no person is, under the law of Singapore, liable in tort for any conduct on account of its being maintenance or champerty as known to the common law."

funding arrangements are permitted only in the context of international arbitration proceedings[7] and then subject to the proviso that they are made by eligible parties – that is to say: "a person who carries on the business of funding all or part of the costs of dispute resolution proceedings to which the person is not a party"[8] and who, in addition to carrying on that business in Singapore or elsewhere: "... has a paid-up share capital of not less than $5 million or the equivalent amount in foreign currency or not less than $5 million or the equivalent amount in foreign currency in managed assets".[9]

Other than within the ambit of international arbitration, however, third-party funding arrangements are still likely to fall foul of public policy considerations and to be deemed unenforceable on these grounds in Singapore.[10] The amendment does not "affect any rule of that law as to the cases in which a contract is to be treated as contrary to public policy or otherwise illegal".[11]

The Act forms part of a legislative "package" completed by the entry into force on 1 March 2017 of the amendments to the Legal Profession Act (Chapter 161) (the LPA)[12] and to the Legal Profession (Professional Conduct) Rules 2015 (the Singapore Professional Conduct Rules), which set out principles and standards of professional practice, etiquette and conduct to which lawyers are required to adhere.[13]

Sect. 107 of the LPA precludes solicitors from holding any interest of any party in any suit, action or other contentious proceeding and from acting on a contingency or success fee basis.[14] But the provision has been amended such that a solicitor may: (i) introduce or refer a third-party funder to the solicitor's client, provided he or she does so without receiving compensation; (ii) advise on or draft a third-party funding contract for the

---

6. Sect. 5B(10) of the Act gives the following definition of a "*third-party funding contract*": "... a contract or agreement by a party or potential party to dispute resolution proceedings with a Third-Party Funder for the funding of all or part of the costs of the proceedings in return for a share or other interest in the proceeds or potential proceeds of the proceedings to which the party or potential party may become entitled".
7. Sect. 3 of the Regulations 2017.
8. Sect. 5B(10) of the Act.
9. Sect. 4 of the Regulations 2017. Matthew Secomb and Adam Wallin point out that the definition of third-party funder and the criteria to be met in Singapore "seem to exclude respondent-side funding and non-commercial funders (such as pro bono funders, most individual persons, and businesses not principally engaged in funding)". Matthew SECOMB and Adam WALLIN, "Chapter 13, Singapore" in Leslie PERRIN, ed., *Third Party Litigation Funding Law Review* (Law Business Research 2017) p. 127.
10. See Matthew SECOMB and Adam WALLIN, fn. 9, p. 126: "Singapore law now permits third party funding in international arbitration (and related proceedings) if the funder meets certain qualifying criteria. Outside the international arbitration context, however, funding is generally prohibited on public policy grounds."
11. Sect. 5A(2) of the Act.
12. The LPA is available at <https://sso.agc.gov.sg/Act/LPA1966> (last accessed 4 March 2018).
13. The Legal Profession (Professional Conduct) (Amendment) Rules 2017 are available at <https://statutes.agc.gov.sg/SL-Supp/S69-2017/Published/20170224?DocDate=20170224> (last accessed 4 March 2018).
14. Sect. 107 of the LPA is available at <https://sso.agc.gov.sg/Act/LPA1966?ProvIds=P1VIII-#pr107-> (last accessed 4 March 2018).

solicitor's client or negotiate the contract on the client's behalf; and (iii) act on behalf of the client in any dispute arising out of the third-party funding agreement.

The amendments to the Singapore Professional Conduct Rules deal principally with two issues that apply to Singapore legal practitioners, namely: (i) a duty to disclose the existence of any third-party funding; and (ii) a financial interest prohibition.

As to the former, the new Sect. 49A of the Singapore Professional Conduct Rules requires legal practitioners to disclose to the court or the tribunal and to any other party involved in the proceedings: (i) the existence of any third-party funding contract related to the costs of those proceedings; and (ii) the identity and address of any funder. Disclosure must be made at the date the proceedings commence and, in any case, as soon as practicable after the third-party funding contract is entered into. In practice, this obligation may create some "inequalities" between Singapore legal practitioners and those qualified in other jurisdictions, where a similar disclosure obligation does not exist.[15]

So far as the prohibition against financial interest (and other interests) on the part of a Singaporean practitioner in a third-party funder is concerned, Sect. 49B of the Singapore Professional Conduct Rules proscribes any shareholding or other ownership interest in a third-party funder, whether direct or indirect: "(a) which the legal practitioner or law practice has introduced or referred to a client of the legal practitioner or law practice in relation to dispute resolution proceedings; or (b) which has a third-party funding contract with a client of the legal practitioner or law practice".

In addition:

– the Law Society of Singapore has issued a Guidance Note on Third-Party Funding (which entered into force on 25 April 2017). It sets out best practices for lawyers who refer, advise or act for clients which obtain third-party funding. The Note supplements the above-mentioned legislative amendments;[16]

– the Singapore International Arbitration Centre (SIAC) published the SIAC Investment Arbitration Rules (1 January 2017). They contain specific provisions directed towards

15. See Matthew SECOMB and Adam WALLIN, fn. 9, p. 132.

16. The Law Society of Singapore's Guidance Note on Third-Party Funding is available at <www.lawsociety.org.sg/For-Lawyers/Running-Your-Practice/Guidance-on-Professional-and-Practice-Issues> (last accessed 4 March 2018). Sect. 4 of the Note gives the following definition of third-party funding: "Third-party funding involves a commercial funder agreeing to pay some or all of the claimant's legal fees and expenses." On the lawyer's duty to disclose the existence of the third-party funder, the Note gives the following practical guidance: "You should consider informing your client at the start of your retainer that you have a professional duty to disclose whether your client is engaging third-party funding. It is good practice to check with your client at the start of the retainer on whether he/she intends to engage or is already engaged in third-party funding."

third-party funding.[17] SIAC has also produced its Practice Note PN-01/17 on Arbitrator Conduct in Cases Involving External Funding (on 31 March 2017);[18] and
– on 18 May 2017, the Singapore Institute of Arbitrators (SIArb) published the SIArb Guidelines for Third-Party Funders, which aim to promote best practices among third-party funders providing funding to parties in Singapore-seated international arbitrations.[19]

2. *Hong Kong*

Amendments to the Arbitration Ordinance (Cap. 609) followed from the approval on 14 June 2017 of the Arbitration and Mediation Legislation (Third-Party Funding) (Amendment) Ordinance Order No. 6 of 2017. The effect of these amendments is that the common law tort and offence of champerty and maintenance no longer applies to third-party funding of arbitration (including related court proceedings, emergency arbitrations and mediations) and mediation, both in respect of proceedings in Hong Kong and of work undertaken in Hong Kong relating to arbitrations and mediations outside Hong Kong.[20] On 23 June 2017, this legislation was (partially) enacted.[21] The Amendment Ordinance defines third-party funding as follows:

> "Third-party funding of arbitration is the provision of arbitration funding for an arbitration—
> (a) under a funding agreement;
> (b) to a funded party;
> (c) by a third-party funder; and

17. The SIAC Investment Arbitration Rules are available at <www.siac.org.sg/our-rules/rules/siac-ia-rules-2017> (last accessed 4 March 2018); see Arts. 24(l), 33.1 and 35.
18. The Practice Note PN-01/17 on Arbitrator Conduct in Cases Involving External Funding is available at <www.siac.org.sg/images/stories/articles/rules/Third%20Party%20Funding%20Practice%20Note%2031%20March%202017.pdf> (last accessed 4 March 2018).
19. See Sect. 1.1 of the SIArb Guidelines for Third-Party Funders, available at <https://www.siarb.org.sg/index.php/resources/third-party-funding> (last accessed 12 February 2019). Here, third-party funding is defined as follows: "Third party funding arises when a third party ... provides financial support to enable a party ... to pursue or defend an arbitration or related court or mediation proceedings. Such financial support is provided in exchange for an economic interest in any favourable award or outcome that may ensue."
20. See Melody CHAN, "Chapter 8, Hong Kong" in Leslie PERRIN, ed., *Third Party Litigation Funding Law Review* (Law Business Research 2017) p. 79: "Hong Kong had a long-standing general ban (with limited exceptions) on third party funding in litigation, arbitration and mediation."
21. See Caroline KENNY QC, "Third Party Funding of International Arbitrations", CIArb News, 1 November 2017, available at <https://www.ciarb.org/news/ciarb-news/news-detail/features/2017/11/01/third-party-funding-of-international-arbitrations> (last accessed 4 March 2018). Sect. 98K, Division 3 of the Amendment Ordinance states that: "The common law offences of maintenance (including the common law offence of champerty) and of being a common barrator do not apply in relation to third party funding of arbitration."; and Sect. 98L, Division 3 of the Amendment Ordinance states that: "The tort of maintenance (including the tort of champerty) does not apply in relation to third party funding of arbitration."

(d) in return for the third-party funder receiving a financial benefit only if the arbitration is successful within the meaning of the funding agreement."[22]

Whilst the funding agreement must be in writing and made after the effective date of the legislation, the funding may take the form of monetary or other financial assistance in respect of costs.

Notably, the obligation to disclose any such arrangements to every other party in the arbitration and to the tribunal to the extent of disclosing that such an arrangement exists; who the funder is; and the fact that a funding agreement has come to an end other than upon the conclusion of the proceedings is the subject of a specific carveout from the statutory confidentiality obligations concerning arbitral proceedings, which are a particular feature of Hong Kong law.[23]

In contrast to the narrow definition of a funder adopted in Singapore, the Hong Kong legislation extends to "any person who is a party to a funding agreement ... and who does not have an interest recognized by law in the arbitration other than under the funding agreement", including lawyers and law firms. But consistent with the longstanding prohibition in Hong Kong against the application by lawyers of conditional or contingency fees,[24] they are not permitted to fund an arbitration in which they are acting as counsel to one of the parties.[25]

There is not as yet a formal regulatory code governing the activities of third-party funders in Hong Kong, although there is a proposal that such a code should be issued and the Justice Secretary has the power to appoint an "advisory body" to draw it up and to monitor compliance. Sect. 98Q of the new enactment sets out a variety of practices and standards that might be thought appropriate, including capital adequacy requirements, confidentiality, conflicts of interest, disclosure, the extent to which the funder is in control of the proceedings and the bases upon which the funding agreement might be terminated. None of these proposals contemplates direct sanction in the event of non-compliance, but a failure to conform may be referred to a court or arbitral tribunal and be taken into account.[26]

3. United Kingdom

Regulation of third-party funders remains a topical issue in the United Kingdom. On 24 January 2017, responding to three written parliamentary questions asked by Lord Hodgson of Astley Abbots,[27] Lord Keen of Elie, for the UK government, stated that:

22. See Sect. 98G, Part 10A Arbitration Ordinance.
23. Idem, Sect. 98S.
24. Although such arrangements fall within the general definition of "third party funding".
25. Idem, Sect. 98NA.
26. Idem, Sect. 98S(b).
27. Written question – HL4213, available at <https://www.parliament.uk/business/publications/written-questions-answers-statements/written-question/Lords/2016-12-19/HL4213/> (last accessed 4 March 2018): "To ask Her Majesty's Government whether, in the light of the rapid expansion of third party litigation, they plan to introduce statutory regulation of funders"; written question – HL4214, available at <https://www.parliament.uk/business/publica

> "The Government does not believe that the case has been made out for moving away from voluntary regulation, as agreed by Parliament during the passage of the Legal Aid, Sentencing and Punishment of Offenders Act 2012. The market for third party litigation funding, remains at a relatively early stage in its development in this jurisdiction and we are not aware of specific concerns about the activities of litigation funders. The Government has not therefore undertaken a formal assessment of the effectiveness of the voluntary code of conduct or the membership of the Association of Litigation Funders. The last Government gave Parliament an assurance that it will keep third party litigation funding under review and this Government is ready to investigate matters further should the need arise."

In essence, the UK Government confirmed that it saw no immediate need to enact any legislation regulating third-party litigation funding in light of the fact that the present voluntary framework – i.e. the Code of Conduct for Litigation Funders[28] – had not created "specific concerns".

4. *Republic of Ireland*

On 23 May 2017, in its ruling in *Persona Digital Telephony Limited & Sigma Wireless Networks Limited v. The Minister for Public Enterprise, Ireland and the Attorney General*,[29] the Irish Supreme Court, with specific reference to the doctrines of champerty and maintenance, held that third-party funding is unlawful as a matter of Irish law in the context of litigation proceedings.[30] *Persona Digital* was the "first case to come before the Court which raises the issue of the potential use of a third-party professional funding agreement to support a party in legal proceedings".[31]

In her Judgment, Chief Justice Denham observed:

---

tions/written-questions-answers-statements/written-question/Lords/2016-12-19/HL4214/> (last accessed 4 March 2018): "To ask Her Majesty's Government whether it is the case that fewer than half the number of UK based firms, and no overseas based firms, have joined the Association of Litigation Funders; and what assessment they have made of the effectiveness of the voluntary code of conduct drafted by the Association"; written question – HL4216, available at <https://www.parliament.uk/business/publications/written-questions-answers-statements/written-question/Lords/2016-12-19/HL 4216/> (last accessed 4 March 2018): "To ask Her Majesty's Government whether they plan to introduce regulations to ensure that third party litigation funders are subject to the same statutory duties and obligations as apply to law firms operating in the same field."

28. The Code of Conduct for Litigation Funders is available at <http://associationoflitigationfunders.com/code-of-conduct/> (last accessed 4 March 2018).
29. *Persona Digital Telephony Limited & Sigma Wireless Networks Limited v. The Minister for Public Enterprise, Ireland and the Attorney General* [2017] IESC 27.
30. *Persona Digital Telephony Limited*, see fn. 29. At para. 54(ix), Chief Justice Denham stated: "I do consider that third party funding to support a plaintiff (where none of the exceptions apply) is unlawful by reason of the rules on champerty."
31. *Persona Digital Telephony Limited*, see fn. 29, para. 7.

> "The Court was asked not to be seduced into changing the law in the interests of what the Court may perceive to be just. It may be said that in light of modern issues, such as Ireland being an international trading State, issues arising on international arbitrations, and in the Commercial Court, it might well be appropriate to have a modern law on champerty and the third-party funding of litigation. However, this is a complex multifaceted issue, more suited to a full legislative analysis. This is re-enforced by the retention of the old statutes by the Act of 2007 [Statute Law Revision Act 2007], and by the work of the LRC [Law Reform Commission]."[32]

This judgment is in line with Irish law under which "maintenance and champerty are offences which evidence a public policy".[33] However, there are many legal practitioners and lawmakers in Ireland, who recognize that if the country wishes to play a significant role in the new, evolving third-party funding market, it will be necessary to develop a new law, which will allow third-party funding at least in international arbitration proceedings, following the recent examples of both Singapore and Hong Kong.

5. *France*

At about the same time as the legislative changes described above were being promulgated in Singapore, a Working Group of the Paris Bar published its Report.[34] Recourse to third-party funding is less common in the European civil law jurisdictions than in the leading common law jurisdictions, although it is growing in France, where the market is less mature than it is in Germany, but considerably more developed than it is in Italy, Spain and Switzerland, for example. It is noteworthy that, in line with the demand for disclosure of funding arrangements seen elsewhere in this string of recent developments, the Paris Bar Report emphasized the need for early and full disclosure of any third-party funding arrangements. That was a matter which it regarded as being of paramount importance.

6. *People's Republic of China*

On 1 October 2017, the Investment Arbitration Rules of the China International Economic and Trade Arbitration Commission (CIETAC Investment Rules) entered into force.[35] The CIETAC Investment Rules expressly allow recourse to third-party funding. As is the case in Singapore, the CIETAC Rules place considerable weight upon full and

32. *Persona Digital Telephony Limited*, see fn. 29, para. 54(vi).
33. *Persona Digital Telephony Limited*, see fn. 29, para. 26.
34. "*Le financement de l'arbitrage par les tiers* ("Third-party Funding")": 23 November 2016 (available at <http://bit.ly/2rQG3SY> (last accessed 9 April 2018) and Resolution 21 February 2017.
35. The CIETAC Investment Rules are available in Chinese at <www.yidaiyilu.gov.cn/wcm.files/upload/CMSydylgw/201709/201709260955044.pdf> (last accessed 4 March 2018). See also the Explanatory Note Regarding the CIETAC Investment Arbitration Rules (26 September 2017), available in Chinese at <www.yidaiyilu.gov.cn/zchj/zcfg/29165.htm> (last accessed 4 March 2018).

early disclosure of funding arrangements rather than regulation as the principal safeguard against abuse. Art. 27 requires a funded party to disclose, in writing and without delay, to any other party, the arbitral tribunal and the CIETAC Commission: (i) the existence and the nature of the funding arrangement; and (ii) the name and the address of the third-party funder. The arbitral tribunal has the power to compel disclosure of such information and, when ruling on costs of the arbitration, it may take into consideration the existence of a funding agreement and a party's compliance with its disclosure obligations.

7. *United Arab Emirates*

On 14 March 2017, the Dubai International Financial Centre (DIFC) Courts[36] adopted the Practice Direction No. 2 on Third-Party Funding in the DIFC Courts[37] (DIFC Direction). The DIFC Direction "sets out requirements to be observed by 'Funded Parties' in respect of their relationships, interactions and contracts with 'Funders' concerning legal 'Proceedings' in the DIFC Courts" where proceedings are commenced on or after the cited date.

Some of the most relevant features of the DIFC Direction are the following:

– disclosure that a funding agreement is in place. A funded party entering into a litigation funding agreement in respect of disputes filed in the DIFC Courts is required to provide every party to the relevant dispute with details of the identity of the funder, but it is not compelled to disclose a copy, or any part, of the litigation funding agreement "unless the Court orders otherwise";[38]
– the DIFC Courts may take account of the fact that a party is funded when making determinations on applications for security for costs, but the fact that a party is funded shall not by itself be determinative in making decisions on applications for security for costs;[39]
– the DIFC Courts have the "jurisdiction to make costs orders against third parties, including Funders, where the Court deems it appropriate, given the circumstances of the case".[40]

8. *Investment Treaties*

On 21 September 2017, the EU-Canada Free Trade Agreement (CETA) entered into force.[41] The CETA is remarkable for its acknowledgement that recourse to third-party

36. Available at <http://www.difccourts.ae/> (last accessed 4 March 2018).
37. Available at <http://www.difccourts.ae/2017/03/14/practice-direction-no-2-2017-third-party-funding-difc-courts/> (last accessed 4 March 2018).
38. Sub-sect. (4) of the DIFC Direction.
39. Sub-sect. (8) of the DIFC Direction.
40. Sub-sect. (9) of the DIFC Direction.
41. CETA is available at <http://ec.europa.eu/trade/policy/in-focus/ceta/index_en.htm> (last accessed 4 March 2018).

funding is not an anomaly in current investor-state arbitration and, in fact, it makes express provision for it. Art. 8.1 defines third-party funding as:

> "any funding provided by a natural or legal person who is not a disputing party but who enters into an agreement with a disputing party in order to finance part or all of the cost of the proceedings either through a donation or grant, or in return for remuneration dependent on the outcome of the dispute".

It will be appreciated that this definition includes not-for-profit funders ("through a donation or grant").

Provisions mirroring those in the CETA have been adopted in the Free Trade Agreement entered into between the EU and Vietnam.[42]

Once again, disclosure of third-party funding is a primary consideration. Art. 8.26 of CETA requires disclosure by the funded party of the name and the address of the funder:

> "at the time of the submission of a claim, or, if the financing agreement is concluded or the donation or grant is made after the submission of a claim, without delay as soon as the agreement is concluded or the donation or grant is made".

9. *ICCA-Queen Mary Task Force Report on Third-Party Funding in International Arbitration*

On 17 April 2018, the Task Force on Third-Party Funding in International Arbitration, established by the International Council for Commercial Arbitration (ICCA) along with Queen Mary College at the University of London,[43] published the ICCA-Queen Mary Task Force Report on Third-Party Funding in International Arbitration ("ICCA-QM Report").[44] The Report reflects upon the latest developments in the field.[45] It

42. An almost identical definition, which includes not-for-profit funders appears in Chapter 8, Chapter II, Sect. 3, Art. 2 of the Free Trade Agreement between the European Union and the Socialist Republic of Vietnam, available at <http://trade.ec.europa.eu/doclib/press/index.cfm?id=1437> (last accessed 4 March 2018): "'Third Party funding' means any funding provided by a natural or juridical person who is not a party to the dispute but who enters into an agreement with a disputing party in order to finance part or all of the cost of the proceedings in return for a remuneration dependent on the outcome of the dispute or in the form of a donation or grant." For a case in which a not-for-profit funder was involved, see *Philip Morris Brand Sàrl (Switzerland), Philip Morris Products S.A. (Switzerland) and Abal Hermanos S.A. (Uruguay) v. Oriental Republic of Uruguay* (ICSID Case No. ARB/10/7).
43. The ICCA-Queen Mary Task Force is co-chaired by William W. "Rusty" PARK, Stavros BREKOULAKIS and Catherine A. ROGERS and its work was coordinated by Lise BOSMAN and Lisa BINGHAM.
44. The ICCA-QM Report is available at <www.arbitration-icca.org/projects/Third_Party_Funding.html> (last accessed 1 May 2018).
45. Idem, p. 13: "The Task Force hopes that parties, counsel, and arbitrators may reference or invoke the Principles and analysis in the Report to address issues that arise in the course of an arbitration, in entering into a funding agreement, and in continued discussions and debates regarding third-party funding. The Report may also be useful for national courts in reviewing international arbitral

acknowledges that there were arguments in the international investment context to prohibit third-party funding because of its asserted consequences for the real and perceived legitimacy of investment arbitration.[46]

II. THIRD-PARTY FUNDING: THE POLEMIC

It is as well that the further development of a burgeoning third-party funding market should be the focus of review by lawmakers, professional bodies and regulators, and academics and institutions such as ICCA at this time. There is ample scope for change, but there is also a need to put this debate into a proper perspective.

These matters are under critical review well beyond the confines of the international arbitration community. Third-party funding seems to be one of those "red button" issues about which lawmakers, NGOs and other opinion formers have a lot to say, much of it, regrettably, based on little more than hearsay and reheated anecdote rather than fact. Moreover, the timing is unfortunate in that the third-party funding issue has been caught up in what has become a politicized debate about the standing of arbitration generally, perhaps most potently and, thus far, with the most significant consequences, in the context of both investor-state arbitration within the EU and of the putative negotiation of bilateral investment treaties to which the EU will be a party.[47]

There is room for legitimate concern that whatever agenda it is which drives the debate about ISDS in the European Parliament and the Commission, it takes precious little account of what is actually being done to address and to resolve the issues which have been identified – or to allow any credit for the changes that have been, and will be, made. The EU institutions have turned their backs on the investor-state arbitration model embodied in the International Centre for Settlement of Investment Disputes (ICSID) and they are seemingly determined to impose a "Multilateral Investment Court" in the constitution of the membership of which only the EU and the State with which it is contracting will have a say.[48]

Sentiment is as hostile across the Atlantic. Quite apart from Senator Elizabeth Warren's now notorious op-ed in the Washington Post, in which she saw fit to lambast

awards or in satellite litigation, and for regulatory bodies and arbitral institutions that seek to address issues relating to third-party funding in international arbitration."

46. Idem, p. 5.

47. See the EU Commission Decision (EU) 2015/1470, 30 March 2015, on State aid SA.38517 (2014/C) (ex 2014/NN) implemented by Romania – Arbitral award *Micula v. Romania* of 11 December 2013, available at <https://eur-lex.europa.eu/legal-content/EN/TXT/?uri=CELEX%3A32015D1470> (last accessed 9 April 2018) and the Judgment of the European Court of Justice in *Slovak Republic v Achmea BV* (Case 284/16, Judgment of 6 March 2018, available at <http://curia.europa.eu/juris/documents.jsf?num=C-284/16#>, last accessed 9 April 2018).

48. European Council Press Release 20 March 2018: "Multilateral investment court: Council gives mandate to the Commission to open negotiations", available at <www.consilium.europa.eu/en/press/press-releases/2018/03/20/multilateral-investment-court-council-gives-mandate-to-the-commission-to-open-negotiations/>, last accessed 9 April 2018.

investor-state tribunals as "rigged pseudo courts",[49] the US Chamber of Commerce has not restrained itself either, describing third-party litigation funding as a "clear and present danger to the impartial and efficient administration of civil justice in the United States".[50]

But it would be wrong to dismiss all of the criticism as mere "noise". There is a great deal in the old adage that not only must justice be done, it must be seen to be done.[51] Third-party funding is just one part of what is seen to be a much larger problem. The new disclosure requirements are a significant step in the right direction to address at least one area of concern. It remains to be seen whether voluntary codes of conduct will be sufficient – or even if they are, whether they will be seen to be sufficient. If they are seen to be toothless, as in at least one case, it is suggested they are,[52] pressure for a system of statutory regulation will inevitably build.

This is the battleground onto which the arbitrator, like or not, has strayed. While it might not be the lightning rod, there is no doubt that the conduct of arbitrators in cases involving third-party funders will be subject to rigorous scrutiny.

---

49. Senator Elizabeth WARREN: "The Trans Pacific Partnership Clause Everyone Should Oppose", Washington Post, 25 February 2015, available at <www.washingtonpost.com/opinions/kill-the-dispute-settlement-language-in-the-trans-pacific-partnership/2015/02/25/ec7705a2-bd1e-11e4-b274-e5209a3bc9a9_story.html?noredirect=on&utm_term=.96fb41b26e16> (last accessed 9 April 2018).
50. John H. BEISNER and Gary A. RUBIN, U.S. Chamber Institute for Legal Reform, *Stopping the Sale on Lawsuits: A Proposal to Regulate Third-Party Investments in Litigation* (2012) available at <www.instituteforlegalreform.com/uploads/sites/1/TPLF_Solutions.pdf> (last accessed 9 April 2018).
51. *R v. Sussex Justices, Ex parte McCarthy* [1924] 1 KB 256, [1923] All ER Rep 233.
52. The Code of Conduct for Litigation Funders has been strongly criticized by the U.S. Chamber Institute for Legal Reform:

    "... this self-regulation mechanism has no 'teeth' even for those that chose to join. The ALF [Association of Litigation Funders] is an independent body owned and directed by the member Funders. Adherence to the ALF Code is policed by the ALF. The maximum penalty the ALF has empowered itself to impose is a £500 fine, alongside possible exclusion from the association at the discretion of the organisation's board. However, even if a Funder were to violate every one of the principles of the ALF Code and eventually be excluded from the ALF, this would have no bearing at all on the Funder's ability to continue funding cases. In light of the above, it cannot be said that the ALF Code has led to any meaningful oversight of, or even monitoring of, the activities of an industry with assets under management of in excess of £1.5 billion"

    (U.S. Chamber Institute for Legal Reform, *Before the Flood – An Outline of Oversight Options for Third Party Litigation Funding in England & Wales* (April 2016) p. 3, <www.instituteforlegalreform.com/research/before-the-flood-an-outline-of-oversight-options-for-third-party-litigation-funding-in-england--wales> (last accessed 4 March 2018).

III. PRACTICAL ISSUES ARISING FOR ARBITRATORS FROM THE INVOLVEMENT OF A THIRD-PARTY FUNDER IN INTERNATIONAL ARBITRATION

1. *Impartiality and Independence of Arbitrators*

In principle, the existence of a funding agreement should have no bearing upon the progress and merits of the underlying arbitration[53] (although it may impact upon the tactics of the funded party). It could have (or could be perceived to have) a bearing upon the independence and the impartiality of an arbitrator, however,[54] and any relationship which links the arbitrator to the third-party funder is to be disclosed.[55] The classic

53. See *Oxus Gold v. The Republic of Uzbekistan*, UNCITRAL Case, Final Award, 17 December 2015, para. 127: "It is undisputed that Claimant is being assisted by a third-party funder in this arbitration proceeding. The Arbitral Tribunal has mentioned this fact in its Procedural Order Nos. 6 and 7. However, this fact has no impact on this arbitration proceeding."

54. Pursuant to General Standard 1 of the IBA Guidelines on Conflict of Interest in International Arbitration (2014), available at <https://www.ibanet.org/Publications/publications_IBA_guides_and_ free_materials.aspx> (last accessed 9 April 2018): "Every arbitrator shall be impartial and independent of the parties at the time of accepting an appointment to serve and shall remain so until the final award has been rendered or the proceedings have otherwise finally terminated." On the impartiality and independence obligation of the arbitrator, see, for example, Art. 5.3 of the London Court of International Arbitration (LCIA) Arbitration Rules 2014; Art. 11.1 of the International Chamber of Commerce (ICC) Rules of Arbitration (2017); and Art. 18.1 of the 2017 Arbitration Rules of the Arbitration Institute of the Stockholm Chamber of Commerce (SCC). Aren GOLDSMITH and Lorenzo MELCHIONDA, "Third Party Funding in International Arbitration: Everything You Ever Wanted to Know (But Were Afraid to Ask): Part 2", Int'l Bus. L.J. 53 (2012) p. 225, point out that:

"Arbitrators (or the law firms with which they are affiliated) may perform a number of professional services on behalf of funders, including representing funders for purposes of due diligence or as counsel retained at the request of the funder to conduct an unrelated claim.... Similarly, arbitrators may serve on advisory committees commonly established by funders or hold financial interests in funders (including common shares)."

James Egerton VERNON, "Taming the 'Mercantile Adventures': Third Party Funding and Investment Arbitration – A Report from the 14th Annual ITA-ASIL Conference", available at <http://arbitrationblog.kluwerarbitration.com/2017/04/21/taming-the-mercantile-adventurers-third-party-funding-and-investment-arbitration-a-report-from-the-14th-annual-ita-asil-conference/> (last accessed 4 March 2018), identifies the following potential conflicts between an arbitrator and a third-party funder: "... where the arbitrator is a member of the investment advisory panel of a funder; where he or she serves as a consultant to the funder; where the same arbitrator is regularly appointed in cases financed by a particular funder; or where the arbitrator has acted as counsel or an expert in other proceedings financed by the same funder".

55. Pursuant to Art. 3 of the Administrative Resolution 18/2016, *Recommendations regarding the existence of third-party funding in arbitrations administered by CAM-CCBC*, published by the Center for Arbitration and Mediation of the Chamber of Commerce Brazil-Canada (CAM-CCBC) on 20 July 2016 and available at <https://ccbc.org.br/Materia/2890/resolucao-administrativa-182016/en-US> (last accessed 4 March 2018): "The presence of a third-party funder can raise reasonable

example is the situation in which a lawyer acts as counsel in a funded case (maintaining regular contacts with, and being paid by, the funder) and is subsequently approached to serve as an arbitrator in another case in which the claimant receives its litigation funding from the same funder.

The ICC Note to Parties and Arbitral Tribunals on the Conduct of the Arbitration under the ICC Rules of Arbitration provides that: "Relationships between arbitrators, as well as relationships with any entity having a direct economic interest in the dispute or an obligation to indemnify a party for the award, should also be considered in the circumstances of each case."[56]

It is common practice that, before appointment or confirmation, a prospective arbitrator signs a truthful and complete statement of acceptance of appointment to confirm his or her impartiality, independence (and availability) and to disclose the existence of any conflict(s) of interest. Failure to make such disclosure creates an appearance of bias and may itself be a ground for disqualification. In fact, the rules of the principal arbitral institutions require a prospective arbitrator to disclose not only circumstances, which go to any actual conflict or relationship with a party or its advisors, but also any circumstances likely to give rise to doubts as to the arbitrator's independence and/or impartiality.[57]

The clear preponderance of opinion now is that the involvement of a funder with whom an arbitrator has a connection is a relevant circumstance to be disclosed by the arbitrator at the time of her/his appointment (or during the course of the arbitral proceedings).

That connection may be "direct" – as will be the case, if the arbitrator is a member of a law firm with which the third-party funder has a business relationship or if the arbitrator, in performing her/his ongoing duty reasonably to check for any potential conflict of interest,[58] discovers that a funder with which the arbitrator or the arbitrator's firm has an economic link is involved in the pending arbitration.

---

doubt as to the impartiality or independence of the arbitrators, due to possible past or current relationship between the arbitrator and the third-party funder."

56. Para. 24 of the ICC Note to Parties and Arbitral Tribunals on the Conduct of the Arbitration Under the ICC Rules of Arbitration, 30 October 2017, available at <https://cdn.iccwbo.org/content/uploads/sites/3/2017/03/icc-note-to-parties-and-arbitral-tribunals-on-the-conduct-of-arbitration.pdf> (last accessed 4 March 2018). See the new Sect. 49A of the Singapore Professional Conduct Rules, Sect. I.*1* above.

57. See, for instance: Art. 16.3 of the Vienna International Arbitral Centre (VIAC) Rules of Arbitration and Mediation (2018); Art. 31.1 of the CIETAC Arbitration Rules (2015); Art. 18 of the Arbitration Rule of the Chamber of Arbitration of Milan (2010). See also General Standard 3 of the IBA Guidelines on Conflicts of Interest in International Arbitration (2014), fn. 54.

58. General Standard 7(d) of the IBA Guidelines on Conflicts of Interest in International Arbitration (2014) fn. 54, provides that: "An arbitrator is under a duty to make reasonable enquires to identify any conflict of interest, as well as any facts or circumstances that may reasonably give rise to doubts as to his or her impartiality or independence. Failure to disclose a conflict is not excused by lack of knowledge, if the arbitrator does not perform such reasonable enquires." In the Explanation to General Standard 7, it is stated that: "In order to satisfy their duty of disclosure under the Guidelines, arbitrators are required to investigate any relevant information that is reasonably available to them." See also ICCA-QM Report, fn. 44, p. 112. See, too, *Compañía de*

It might also be "indirect"; the arbitrator may become aware of a potential conflict with a third-party funder in light of a disclosure by one of the parties.[59]

When an arbitrator has knowledge of the involvement of a third-party funder, then the arbitrator will be expected to evaluate whether that participation gives rise to a disclosure and if so, to make the requisite disclosure promptly to the parties (and to any administering arbitral institution).

But that begs a question. While the eminent Spanish arbitrator, Bernardo M. Cremades, suggests, that: "... the participation of third-party financiers in arbitration without the corresponding disclosure to the other party and arbitral tribunal could imply a breach of the procedural good faith with which the parties should conduct themselves",[60] is there, in fact, a binding obligation on a party (or the funder itself) to volunteer such a disclosure? The answer is that in some jurisdictions there is an obligation on the part of the funded party to disclose, and in some, there is not. And if there is no such disclosure, how can an arbitrator be responsible for a failure to make a disclosure, which could (and should) have been made, had he or she been in possession of the facts?

In the current environment, it may be that in the absence of any required disclosure (or voluntary disclosure) by a funded party, a prudent arbitrator, who believes that there are indications of the involvement of a funder (for example, a disinclination to contemplate what seem to be sensible opportunities to explore settlement options or a sudden and significant change in the strategy of a party) should raise the question. But that is not as easy to do in practice as it is to articulate the proposition in theory. First, the arbitrator may have misread the signals. Second, the funded party may be aggrieved that by being "bounced" into a disclosure other than at a time of its choosing, the arbitrator's actions have set it up for an application for security for costs. Either way, if

---

Aguas del Aconquija S.A. & Vivendi Universal v. Argentine Republic (ICSID Case No. ARB/97/3) Decision on Application for Annulment (10 August 2010) paras. 204-205, 222.

59. General Standard 7(a) of the IBA Guidelines on Conflicts of Interest in International Arbitration (2014), fn. 54, requires that:

"A party shall inform an arbitrator, the Arbitral Tribunal, the other parties and the arbitration institution or other appointing authority (if any) of any relationship, direct or indirect, between the arbitrator and the party (or another company of the same group of companies, or an individual having a controlling influence on the party in the arbitration), or between the arbitrator and any person or entity with a direct economic interest in, or a duty to indemnify a party for, the award to be rendered in the arbitration. The party shall do so on its own initiative at the earliest opportunity".

Art. 4 of the Recommendations regarding the existence of third-party funding in arbitrations administered by CAM-CCBC, fn. 55, states that: "In order to avoid potential conflicts of interest, CAM-CCBC recommends the parties to report the existence of third-party funding to CAM-CCBC at the earliest opportunity. The complete qualification of the funder should be included in this communication."

60. Bernardo M. CREMADES, "Third Party Funding in International Arbitration", available at <https://www.cremades.com/en/publications/78/third-party-funding-in-international-arbitration. aspx> (last accessed 4 March 2018).

the stakes are high (or the parties are playing "hardball"), any such enquiry, however well-intentioned, might be interpreted as a deliberate move by the arbitrator to prejudice the interests of the funded party contrary to the arbitrator's obligation to be even-handed as between the parties.

2. *Arbitral Tribunal Powers to Order Disclosure of Third-Party Funding*

a. *Commercial arbitration*

In its Report on Decisions on Costs in International Arbitration, the ICC Commission on Arbitration and ADR proposed that: "Where a tribunal has reason to believe that third-party funding exists, and such funding is likely to impact on the non-funded party's ability to recover costs if successful, the tribunal might consider ordering disclosure of such funding information as is necessary to ascertain that the process remains effective and fair for both parties."[61]

At the present time, no commercial arbitration rules provide for the mandatory disclosure of information pertaining to a third-party financing, nor do they vest in an arbitral tribunal the power to order that kind of disclosure.

It must be questionable whether that position is sustainable, not least given developments in the face of demands for change in investment arbitration, and whether the tentative proposal adumbrated in the ICC Commission Report to the effect that a tribunal "might consider" ordering disclosure is sufficient.

It is sometimes argued that many parties which initiate international arbitration proceedings do so on the back of borrowed funds rather than deploying their own resources. If third-party funding agreements had to be disclosed, so the argument runs, why should other financing agreements be any more inviolate from disclosure?

The answer is that there is a world of a difference between the use by a party to a dispute of funds borrowed from a bank or raised in the market and the source of which has no direct interest in the outcome of a particular court case or arbitration and that of a third-party funder, which has determined to support the action, having considered the specific merits of that case, and which invests specifically in that case with a view to a return. That involvement gives rise, not least, to questions as to the extent to which the funded party's strategy is to be determined by the funder; as to any "claim inflation" built in an attempt to secure a recovery in the event of a win sufficient to meet the funder's "cut" as well as the real loss suffered by the funded party; and as to the readiness of the funder to stand behind any adverse costs order in the event that expectations of success were not met.

It is acknowledged, after all, that funders do not support every case in the confident belief that it has a certain or very high prospect of success. As Kate Brown de Vejar and

61. ICC Commission Report, "Decisions on Costs in International Arbitration", 2015, para. 89, available at <https://cdn.iccwbo.org/content/uploads/sites/3/2015/12/Decisions-on-Costs-in-International-Arbitration.pdf> (last accessed 4 March 2018). Footnote 44 of this ICC Report gives the following definition of a third-party funder: "A third-party funder is an independent party that provides some or all of the funding for the costs of a party to the proceedings (usually the claimant), most commonly in return for an uplift or success fee if successful."

Chloe Baldwin point out in their paper for this Congress,[62] a decade ago, one leading funder described its business model as:

> "'similar to that employed in venture capital, where poor results are expected from some investments and are balanced against high returns from other investments in an effort to achieve desirable portfolio wide returns...'".

These are all matters, which go to the arbitrator's obligation to ensure an even-handed procedure as between the parties and in all cases – as it is put in Art. 22(4) of the ICC Rules of Arbitration – to:

> "act fairly and impartially and ensure that each party has a reasonable opportunity to present its case".

Quite apart from the obvious issues of conflict, these matters likewise militate in favour of requiring a funded party to make disclosure of the funder's participation at the earliest possible juncture and to leave beyond doubt the tribunal's ability to make enquiries about the terms of the funding arrangements to the extent that they might properly be said to have a bearing upon the conduct of the proceedings.

b. Investment arbitration

Pursuant to the 2017 SIAC Investment Arbitration Rules, an arbitral tribunal has the power to: "order the disclosure of the existence of a Party's third-party funding arrangement and/or the identity of the third-party funder and, where appropriate, details of the third-party funder's interest in the outcome of the proceedings, and/or whether or not the third-party funder has committed to undertake adverse costs liability".[63]

Similarly, the CIETAC Investment Rules give an arbitral tribunal the power to order disclosure of information relevant to the funding contract.[64] To date, there are no equivalent provisions in any other set of institutional rules on international investment arbitration, although the issue of third-party funding has been identified as a matter for consideration in the review of the ICSID Rules now underway.

It is hardly surprising that in the absence of a clear and consistent rules framework across the institutions, there should be little evidence of a consistent approach among arbitral tribunals as their power to confirm the existence of a third-party funding agreement and, if one is found to exist, to order disclosure of the terms of the agreement. These decisions have generally arisen in the context of an enquiry by the respondent State as to the likelihood that a funder would stand behind any adverse costs order that might be made against the funded party or in the context of an application for security for costs.

62. "The Economics of Access: Systemic Imbalances in ISDS", this volume, p. 520-557, citing the 2010 Annual Report of Burford Capital (fn. 137).
63. Art. 24(l) of the SIAC Investment Arbitration Rules, fn. 17.
64. CIETAC Investment Rules, fn. 35.

In the Permanent Court of Arbitration (PCA) case *South American Silver Limited (Bermuda) v. The Plurinational State of Bolivia*, the arbitral tribunal ordered the disclosure of the name of the third-party funder, but it rejected Bolivia's request for disclosure of the terms of the funding agreement.[65]

The arbitral tribunal observed that:

> "If the existence of these third parties alone, without considering other factors, becomes determinative on granting or rejecting a request for security for costs, respondents could request and obtain the security on a systematic basis, increasing the risk of blocking potentially legitimate claims."[66]

That decision might be thought problematic in that it rejected the proposition that the mere presence of a funder should be determinative of the grant or rejection of an application for security, yet the Tribunal did not permit access to the funding agreement which might well have shed light on the "other factors" to which it attached importance.[67]

In contrast, in *Muhammet Çap & Sehil Inşaat Endustri ve Ticaret Ltd. Sti. v. Turkmenistan*, the ICSID arbitral tribunal: "decided that Claimants should disclose whether their claims in this arbitration are being funded by a third-party/parties, and, if so, the names and details of the third-party funder(s) and the terms of that funding".[68]

In another ICSID case, *Eskosol S.p.A. in liquidazione v. Italian Republic*, the respondent – relying on the *Muhammet Çap* case – submitted a disclosure application. It contended that:

> "in order to protect its rights Italy needs to know whether the Claimant is funded by a third party and whether such third party would be financially sound as well as committed to execute a cost award adopted by the Tribunal against Eskosol".

Eskosol confirmed that it had required external funding to have access to justice and that, in light of the existence of an ATE insurance, the commercial soundness of the third-party funder was immaterial. The arbitral tribunal agreed. It denied Italy's disclosure application:

---

65. *South American Silver Limited (Bermuda) v. The Plurinational State of Bolivia* (PCA Case No. 2013-15), Procedural Order No. 10 (11 January 2016) paras. 79-80 and 84. See also, in this vein, *EuroGas Inc. and Belmont Resources v. Slovak Republic* (ICSID Case No. ARB/14/14).

66. *South American Silver Limited (Bermuda) v. The Plurinational State of Bolivia*, fn. 65, para. 77.

67. It is to be emphasized, however, that that tribunal accepted that it had the power to grant an order for security for costs pursuant to Art. 26 of the 1976 UNCITRAL Rules.

68. *Muhammet Çap & Sehil Inşaat Endustri ve Ticaret Ltd. Sti. v. Turkmenistan* (ICSID Case No. ARB/12/6), Procedural Order No. 3 (12 June 2015) paras. 8-9 and 13. See also *S&T Oil Equipment & Machinery Ltd v. Romania* (ICSID Case No. ARB/07/13), Order to Discontinue Proceedings (16 July 2010) and *S&T Oil Equipment & Machinery Ltd, et al v. Juridica Investment Limited, et al*, 456 Fed. Appx. 418, 2012 WL (5 January 2012) p. 2842, where a dispute arose on the termination of the funding agreement and it was litigated in the US Courts which ordered the disclosure of the funding agreement.

"It is now clear that the funder has made arrangements to support any cost award against Eskosol up to the amount of €1 million. It is neither necessary nor urgent at this point to investigate whether the funder would be in a position to arrange (or willing to arrange) insurance coverage or other security for a potentially higher amount of costs."[69]

ICSID arbitral tribunals to date have demonstrated a tendency to adopt a prudent and conservative approach to disclosure beyond the fact that funding is in place and the identity of the funder, as confirmed by the ICCA-QM Report:

"In most cases when disclosure has been ordered, the arbitral tribunal orders disclosure of the identity of the third-party funder, but only rarely disclosure of the terms of the funding arrangement and usually not for reasons related to arbitrator conflicts."[70]

It remains to be seen whether in the course of its rules revision, ICSID will amend the rules in such a way to accommodate a more expansive approach to disclosure of the nature of the funding arrangements in circumstances in which a tribunal determines that it would be appropriate to call for their production.[71]

3. *Third-Party Funding and Arbitral Institutions*

Since the arbitral institutions (for these purposes, that term includes the United Nations Commission on International Trade Law (UNCITRAL)) are the principal source of procedural rules applied in international arbitration, they have the potential substantially to influence the evolution of the role of third-party funding.[72]

Procedures and rules may be implemented to:

69. *Eskosol S.p.A. in liquidazione v. Italian Republic* (ICSID Case No. ARB/15/50), Procedural Order No. 3, Decision on Respondent's Request for Provisional Measures (12 April 2017) para. 40 et seq.
70. ICCA-QM Report, fn. 44, p. 106.
71. See, further, Sect. III.*3* hereof.
72. Jennifer A. TRUSZ, "Full Disclosure? Conflict of Interest Arising from Third-Party Funding in International Commercial Arbitration", 101 Geo L.J. (2013) 1649, available at <https://georgetownlawjournal.org/articles/111/full-disclosure-conflicts-of/pdf> (last accessed 4 March 2018) pp. 1673-1676, suggests that:

"The arbitral institutions should adopt rules to require disclosure of third-party funding in arbitration because the proliferation of funding in both domestic litigation and in international arbitration creates too great of a potential for conflicts of interest .... Upon notice by a party of a funding relationship, the arbitral institution shall conduct an automatic conflicts check. Because the arbitrators are required automatically to disclose information pertaining to third-party funding upon prospective appointment, the institution will have all information necessary to complete the check."

– oblige any party to disclose to the arbitral institution and to the other party or parties if it is funded and, if so, to reveal the identity of the funder(s);[73]
– empower an arbitral tribunal to require confirmation of the existence, or to order the disclosure, of a third-party funding agreement; and
– oblige an arbitrator to declare to the arbitral institution, to the parties and, if the case, to the other arbitrators the existence of a potential conflict of interest.[74]

The Hong Kong International Arbitration Center (HKIAC) is moving in this direction. In fact, this institution has established the HKIAC Rules Revision Committee to evaluate any possible amendments to the 2013 HKIAC's Administered Arbitration Rule to take account of the relaxation of the third-party funding rules in Hong Kong.[75]

So far as the disclosure of third-party funding agreements is concerned, the HKIAC Rules Revision Committee proposed the introduction of a new Art. 44 which provides as follows:

> "44.1 If a funding agreement is made, the funded party shall give written notice to all other parties, the arbitral tribunal and HKIAC of:
> (a) the fact that a funding agreement has been made; and
> (b) the name of the third-party funder.
> 44.2 The notice referred to in Article 44.1 must be given:
> (a) in respect of a funding agreement made on or before the arbitration commences in the Notice of Arbitration or Answer (as applicable); or
> (b) in respect of a funding agreement made after the arbitration commences, within 15 days after the funding agreement is made.
> 44.3 If a funding agreement ends (other than because of the end of the arbitration), the funded party shall give written notice to all other parties, the arbitral tribunal and HKIAC of:
> (a) the fact that the funding agreement has ended; and
> (b) the date the funding agreement ended.

---

73. At the start of the arbitration, this disclosure could be made a requirement for the validity and completeness of the request for arbitration. Jennifer A. TRUSZ, "Full Disclosure? Conflict of Interest Arising from Third-Party Funding in International Commercial Arbitration", fn. 72, p. 1675, considers that: "The arbitral rules should therefore be altered to require a party to disclose the fact that it is being financed by a third party. This duty should apply to both the claimant and the respondent in arbitration". See Sub-sect (4) of the DIFC Direction, fn. 37; and, Art. 27 of the CIETAC Investment Rules fn. 35.
74. To obtain this information, it will be sufficient to amend the form of the statement of acceptance, availability, impartiality and independence to be signed by the arbitrator by adding a reference to the third-party funder disclosed by the funded party in the request for arbitration. See Principle A.2, Chapter 4, of the ICCA-QM Report, fn. 44, p. 81: "Arbitrators and arbitral institutions have the authority to expressly request that the parties and their representatives disclose whether they are receiving support from a third-party funder and, if so, the identity of the funder."
75. The 2013 HKIAC's Administered Arbitration Rules are available at <https://www.hkiac.org/arbitration/rules-practice-notes/administered-arbitration-rules/hkiac-administered-2013-2#42> (last accessed 9 April 2018).

> 44.4 The notice referred to in Article 44.3 must be given within 15 days after the funding agreement ends."[76]

It is to be noted, too, that the HKIAC Rules Revision Committee is proposing to amend the confidentiality provision in the Rules such as to allow any party to publish, disclose or communicate any information pertaining to the relevant arbitration (including the award and any emergency decision) "to a person for the purposes of having, or seeking, third party funding of arbitration from the person".[77]

Another encouraging signal is the ICSID paper on the Rules Amendment Process, published on 15 May 2017 and aimed at updating the ICSID rules and regulations. The paper identifies sixteen topics which are to be examined in the next stage of the ICSID review. Third-party funding is one of them and the rationale for approaching this issue is described in these terms:

> "... views on third-party funding vary among jurisdictions, with some States expressly allowing such funding and others prohibiting it. The key issue identified for procedural reform is whether there should be disclosure of third-party funding for the purposes of conflict checking and/or for the purposes of security for costs."[78]

In light of ever-increasing pressure on the arbitral institutions to make good their stated commitment to greater transparency in their practices and procedures, it seems inevitable that express provision will need to be made to address some of the particular issues to which third-party funding gives rise. Those issues go beyond mere disclosure of the existence of a funding agreement and/or disclosure of its terms and obligations upon arbitrators of conflict disclosure that arise as a result. While it would be wrong (and impractical) to place the burden of policing the involvement of third-party funders in international arbitration entirely upon the shoulders of the institutions, they are well placed to monitor developments and to draw up proposals for future guidelines (or, should it be necessary, regulation) dealing with such matters as the extent of third-party funder intervention in the arbitral process. One such area is the vexed question of where the real control over a case lies when a funder is involved.

4. *Control of the Case*

Generally speaking, the third-party funder is not party to the arbitration, but it has a clear economic interest in the outcome of the dispute.[79] Quite apart from seeking to influence the tactics to be deployed once the case is underway, as to which, there is little

76. See the Proposed Amended HKIAC Administered Arbitration Rules, available at <https://www.hkiac.org/sites/default/files/ck_filebrowser/Proposed%20Amendments%20to%20th%20e%202013%20HKIAC%20Administered%20Arbitration%20Rules.pdf> (last accessed 4 March 2018).
77. Art. 45.3(e) the Proposed Amended HKIAC Administered Arbitration Rules, fn. 76.
78. The *ICSID Rules Amendment Process* is available at <https://icsid.worldbank.org/en/Documents/about/ICSID%20Rules%20Amendment%20 Process-ENG.pdf> (last accessed 4 March 2018).

to be done in terms of rules prescription, since the funding entity is not a party, the funder may seek to influence the constitution of the tribunal by dictating the nomination or appointment of a particular arbitrator. It is not axiomatic that such influence will be exercised improperly; a party which is inexperienced in proceedings of this kind may welcome such guidance and if exercised responsibly, it may actually benefit the conduct of the proceedings. But it does demonstrate the need for frank and prompt disclosure of the involvement of the funder and for full disclosure by both the funder and an arbitrator of any relevant connection between them.

5. *Costs Decisions in Light of the Existence of Third-Party Funding*

a. *Commercial arbitration; Recovery of third-party funding costs*

On 15 September 2016, the Commercial Court of England and Wales refused to set aside an award in which an arbitrator in an ICC arbitration seated in London awarded third-party funding costs to the successful party.[80] The Court further affirmed that the costs of litigation funding may be included in the expression "other costs of parties" provided under Sect. 59(1)(c) of the English Arbitration Act 1996.[81]

HHJ Waksman QC held that:

> "... litigation funding costs fall[s] within the arbitrator's general costs discretion. ... As a matter of justice, it would seem very odd and certainly unfortunate if the arbitrator was not entitled under s.59(1) (c) to include the costs of obtaining third party funding as part of 'other costs' *where they were so directly and immediately caused by the losing party*. ... In my judgment, therefore, I unhesitatingly conclude that the

79. Pursuant to General Standard 6(b) of the IBA Guidelines on Conflicts of Interest in International Arbitration (2014), fn. 54: "If one of the parties is a legal entity, any legal or physical person having a controlling influence on the legal entity, or a direct economic interest in, or a duty to indemnify a party for, the award to be rendered in the arbitration, may be considered to bear the identity of such party." Explanation to General Standard 6(b), clarifies that: "Third-party funders ... in relation to the dispute may have a direct economic interest in the award, and as such may be considered to be the equivalent of the party." Stavros BREKOULAKIS, "The Impact of Third Party Funding on Allocation for Costs and Security for Costs Applications: The ICCA-Queen Mary Task Force Report", fn. 1, points out that: "The TPF is not typically a party to the arbitration agreement, and has no involvement in the underlying dispute between the two parties in an arbitration. While funders may be involved in the proceedings, this cannot readily be interpreted as consent to arbitrate."

80. *Essar Oilfields Services Limited v. Norscot Rig Management PVT Limited*, [2016] EWHC 2361 (Comm). See the critical remarks on this decision of Duarte Gorjão HENRIQUES, "The *Essar v. Norscot* Case: A Final Argument for the 'Full-Disclosure-Wingers' of TPF in International Arbitration", available at <http://arbitrationblog.kluwerarbitration.com/2016/10/15/the-essar-v-norscot-case-a-final-argument-for-the-full-disclosure-wingers-of-tpf-in-international-arbitration/> (last accessed 4 March 2018).

81. Under the English Arbitration Act 1996, the costs of the arbitration which can be awarded consist of the fees and expenses of the arbitrators and any arbitral institution concerned, plus the legal or "other costs" of the parties. The Act is available at <https://www.legislation.gov.uk/ukpga/%201996/23/contents> (last accessed 4 March 2018).

> arbitrator's interpretation of 'other costs' was correct, in that it extended in principle to the costs of obtaining third party legal funding. Whether then to Award it is a matter of discretion."[82] (Emphasis added.)

While there is a perception that *Essar* is an important precedent for the recovery of third-party funding costs, it is to be borne in mind that there were exceptional circumstances in that case which were spelled out in the award by the arbitrator (a distinguished former English High Court Judge) and which led him to conclude that, in the proper exercise of his discretion, an award of third-party funding costs in that case was appropriate. It is not yet clear to what extent *Essar* will be a precedent to be applied as a matter of general principle in third-party funding cases; much may turn upon the facts of the case in question (as it did in *Essar*).

b. Security for costs in funded commercial arbitration cases

The ICC Commission on Arbitration and ADR considered that security for costs: "may be appropriate to protect the non-funded party and put both parties on an equal footing in respect of any recovery of costs".[83] However, Professor Stavros Brekoulakis has drawn attention to the following risk:

> "If the existence of [TPF] alone, without considering other factors, becomes determinative on granting or rejecting a request for security for costs, respondents could request and obtain the security on a systematic basis, increasing the risk of blocking potentially legitimate claims."[84]

In this respect, the Chartered Institute of Arbitrators (CIArb) provides the following guidance:

> "When security for costs is sought from a beneficiary of a claim, the arbitrators should consider whether the claiming party is a nominal claimant pursuing a claim for the benefit of another party, who does have funds, and who has a commercial interest in the outcome of the arbitration. Before determining whether to grant security for costs in such circumstances, arbitrators should also consider any additional factors including, inter alia, accepted business risk, who actually controls the proceedings, whether the person or entity who stands to benefit if

82. *Essar Oilfields Services Limited v. Norscot Rig Management PVT Limited,* fn. 80, paras. 68, 69 and 70.
83. Para. 90 of the 2015 ICC Commission Report, fn. 61. Under the arbitration rules of the major arbitral institutions, the arbitral tribunal has the power to order interim or conservatory measures, including security for costs: see, for example, Art. 28 of the ICC Rules of Arbitration (2017); Art. 25 of the LCIA Arbitration Rules 2014; Art. 24 of the International Centre for Dispute Resolution (ICDR) Arbitration Rules (2014).
84. Stavros BREKOULAKIS, "The Impact of Third-Party Funding on Allocation for Costs and Security for Costs Applications: The ICCA-Queen Mary Task Force Report", fn. 1.

the claimant wins will seek to escape liability and avoid paying any adverse costs, and any other relevant factors applicable to the dispute at hand."[85]

On 9 February 2018, the Commercial Court in London handed down a decision in *Progas Energy Ltd, Progas Holding Ltd and Sheffield Engineering Company Ltd v. The Islamic Republic of Pakistan*,[86] which considered two applications for security for costs arising out of an arbitration in which a third-party funder had been involved. The extent to which the Court considered that the involvement of the funder was relevant to its review (and the weight to be given to any commitment to meet an adverse costs order) is clear on the face of the judgment and instructive as to the approach to be adopted. Pakistan had obtained an award of its arbitration costs, plus interest. The first application was made under Sect. 70(6) of the English Arbitration Act 1996,[87] in respect of the claimants' challenge to the arbitral award under Sect. 68 of the English Arbitration Act 1996. The second was for a payment into court, under Sect. 70(7) of the English Arbitration Act 1996,[88] of the costs (together with interest on those costs) awarded to Pakistan in the challenged award. In the arbitration proceedings, the claimants had received funding from a subsidiary of Burford Capital Ltd.

With reference to the first application, the Court ordered the claimants to "provide security for costs in the sum of £ 400,000, either by paying that sum into Court or by providing an appropriate bank or other guarantee to the Defendant". In reaching this decision, the Court took into consideration two letters of the funder in which it stated that "it would ensure payment of any future adverse costs order made against the

85. CIArb Applications for Security for Costs, available at <http://www.ciarb.org/docs/default-source/ciarbdocuments/guidance-and-ethics/practice-guidelines-protocols-and-rules/international-arbitration-guidelines-2015/2015securityforcosts.pdf?sfvrsn=28> (last accessed 4 March 2018).

86. *Progas Energy Ltd, Progas Holding Ltd and Sheffield Engineering Company Ltd v. The Islamic Republic of Pakistan* [2018] EWHC 209 (Comm).

87. Sect. 70(6) of the English Arbitration Act 1996:

"The court may order the applicant or appellant to provide security for the costs of the application or appeal, and may direct that the application or appeal be dismissed if the order is not complied with. The power to order security for costs shall not be exercised on the ground that the applicant or appellant is—
(a) an individual ordinarily resident outside the United Kingdom, or
(b) a corporation or association incorporated or formed under the law of a country outside the United Kingdom, or whose central management and control is exercised outside the United Kingdom."

88. Sect. 70(7) of the English Arbitration Act 1996:

"The court may order that any money payable under the award shall be brought into court or otherwise secured pending the determination of the application or appeal, and may direct that the application or appeal be dismissed if the order is not complied with."

Claimants as part of these s. 68 proceedings up to the maximum amount of £ 482,029.19".

The Court took the view that these letters were nothing to the point:

> "... the letters from Burford do not constitute a contractual commitment to anybody (whether the Claimants or the Defendant) to meet any adverse costs order awarded in the Defendant's favour. It follows that the letters are not legally enforceable by the Defendant (or the Claimants for that matter) and I do not, therefore, see how ... the Defendant could obtain a 'simple order' from the Court requiring Burford to pay in accordance with the terms of the letters. Nor, I observe, do the Burford letters take the form of undertakings to the Court to meet the Defendant's costs. Even if they were, ... that would not entitle the Defendant to an order requiring Burford to pay its costs. The remedy for breach of an undertaking to the Court is committal, and that is not the same thing as obtaining payment of one's costs."[89]

On the second application, it is to be noted that it was:

> "the first occasion when an application under section 70(7) of the English Arbitration Act 1996 has been made where ... it is brought against a party funded by a professional third party funder who has not paid an adverse costs order by an arbitral tribunal, and is seeking (through the party which it is funding) to seek to re-run the arbitration which that party has lost, in circumstances where there was no ability on the part of the other party to seek an order against the funder in the underlying arbitration".[90]

The Court rejected Pakistan's second application, because it found no evidence of dissipation of assets by the claimants.[91] It made clear that, for the purposes of Sect. 70(7) of the English Arbitration Act 1996, the involvement of a third-party funder is irrelevant:

> "I consider that the authorities dealing with section 70(7) have identified an approach which should be regarded as applying whether the case involves commercial funding or not. ... I struggle to see why, as a matter of principle, there should be any special or different position where third party funders are involved ... 'the jurisdiction conferred on the court by section 70 should not be used a means of assisting a party to enforce an award which has been made in its

89. *Progas Energy Ltd, Progas Holding Ltd and Sheffield Engineering Company Ltd* v. *The Islamic Republic of Pakistan*, fn. 86, para. 35.
90. *Progas Energy Ltd, Progas Holding Ltd and Sheffield Engineering Company Ltd* v. *The Islamic Republic of Pakistan*, fn. 86, para. 69.
91. *Progas Energy Ltd, Progas Holding Ltd and Sheffield Engineering Company Ltd* v. *The Islamic Republic of Pakistan*, fn. 86, para. 65.

favour'. This seems to me to be a principle which is as appropriate in a case where there is litigation funding as in a case where there is not."[92]

c. *Investment arbitration*

The long prevailing convention in investor-state arbitration has been that, save in exceptional circumstances, the parties shall bear their own legal costs. Historically, it was also more likely than not that an application for security for costs brought by a respondent State would receive an unsympathetic hearing on the basis that if it was alleged that an investor was impecunious, the answer might lie in the actions of the State which had brought about that state of affairs and an order for security against an impecunious claimant might stifle the making of a meritorious claim by the investor.

There is an increasing propensity on the part of ICSID tribunals to move towards costs orders which reflect the outcome of the case, such that a State may find itself looking to an investor for recovery of what may be a substantial award of costs.

As the Minutes of the discussions of the UNCITRAL Working Group III on ISDS Reform record:

> "A further area of concern mentioned related to difficulties faced by successful respondent States in recovering costs from claimant investors. It was said that investors might use shell companies, or might be impecunious, which left States with no possibility of recovery. That was highlighted as another area of imbalance as States had a permanent and financial standing, which investors did not. It was said that that situation was aggravated by the fact that the possibility of obtaining security for costs was not provided for under investment treaties or under certain arbitration rules."[93]

The trend towards a shift in the costs burden is likely to increase the number of security for costs applications. The advent of third-party funding has also shifted the balance, but not necessarily to the advantage of a successful State party seeking recovery of costs from the funded party. There is no assurance for the State party that the presence of the funder in itself is a guarantee of payment of any award of costs against the funded party – or indeed that the case will run to a conclusion if the funder, for whatever reason, decides to cease funding.[94]

---

92. *Progas Energy Ltd, Progas Holding Ltd and Sheffield Engineering Company Ltd v. The Islamic Republic of Pakistan*, fn. 86, para. 78; see also para. 79:

> "In my view, to adopt an approach to section 70(7) which would, in effect, make up for the absence of such equivalents by permitting the Court to require that security in respect of costs awarded by arbitrators made against parties to arbitration proceedings should be provided by dint of the fact that those parties are in receipt of funding from commercial funders, would involve an illegitimate use of the power to be found in section 70(7)."

93. UNCITRAL WGIII ISDS Reform 34th Session Report, para. 49, available at <www.uncitral.org/uncitral/en/commission/working_groups/3Investor_State.html> (last accessed 9 April 2018).

94. *Farouk Bozbey v. Turkmenistan*, UNCITRAL Case, available at <https://www.italaw.com/cases/2465> (last accessed 8 April 2018).

What is an investment arbitration tribunal, faced with an application for security against a funded claimant, to do? First, while, as the UNCITRAL Working Group point out, it is right that there is not (yet) an express power to order security for costs in the ICSID Rules, there is little room for doubt that an ICSID tribunal may make such an order.[95] The same is true of investment tribunals operating under the UNCITRAL Rules.[96] In such a case, it might be argued that the focus of attention should be on the terms upon which funding is provided to the impecunious claimant rather than upon the parlous financial standing of the investor itself. Even if the funding agreement is disclosed and it appears to commit the funder to meet an adverse costs order, a tribunal might conclude that since the State party would not have any contractual standing under the funding agreement to enforce that commitment, the proper order would be to require security to be put up in any event to ensure that there were readily accessible funds, should, ultimately, an order for costs be made in favour of the respondent State party.

That said, the position remains that, to date, and with the exception of the *RSM Production Corporation v. Saint Lucia* case,[97] no ICSID tribunal has granted a request for security for costs.[98]

Investment arbitration tribunals have determined that the mere involvement of a third-party funder is not, in itself, a sufficient ground to justify an order for security for costs. As the Tribunal in *EuroGas v. Slovak Republic* pointed out, third-party funding is not now uncommon in investor-state arbitration and the mere fact that there is a combination of an impecunious claimant and third-party funding is not of itself grounds to order security for costs:

> "The Tribunal is of the view that financial difficulties and third-party funding – which has become a common practice – do not necessarily constitute per se

95. See *RSM Production Corporation v. St Lucia* (ICSID Case No. ARB/12/10), Decision on St. Lucia's Request for Security for Costs (13 August 2014) para. 54 and *Lighthouse Corporation Pty Ltd and Lighthouse Corporation Ltd., IBC v. Democratic Republic of Timor-Leste* (ICSID Case No. ARB/15/2), Procedural Order No. 2 (13 February 2016).
96. See *South American Silver* (fn. 65) and *Guaracachi America, Inc. and Rurelec Plc v. The Plurinational State of Bolivia* (PCA Case No. 2011-17), Procedural Order No. 14 (11 March 2013) para. 6.
97. *RSM Production Corporation v. Saint Lucia* (ICSID Case No. ARB/12/10), Decision on Saint Lucia's Request for Security for Costs (13 August 2014) (fn. 95).
98. See, for example, *Transglobal Green Energy, LLC and Transglobal Green Energy de Panama, S.A. v. Republic of Panama* (ICSID Case No. ARB/13/28), Decision on the Respondent's Request for Provisional Measures Relating to Security for Costs (21 January 2016); *Rafat Ali Rivzi v. Republic of Indonesia* (ICSID Case No. ARB/11/13), Award on Jurisdiction (16 July 2013) para. 23; *Commerce Group Corp. &San Sebastian Gold Mines, Inc. v. Republic of El Salvador* (ICSID Case No. ARB/09/17), Decision on El Salvador's Application for Security for Costs (20 September 2012) para. 45; *Burimi S.R.L. and Eagle Games SH.A. v. Republic of Albania* (ICSID Case No. ARB/11/18), Procedural Order No. 2 (3 May 2012) para. 41; *Rachel S. Grynberg, Stephen M. Grynberg, Miriam Z. Grynberg and RSM Production Corporation v. Grenada* (ICSID Case No. ARB/10/6), Decision on Respondent's Application for Security for Costs (14 October 2010) para. 5.20; *Saba Fakes v. Republic of Turkey* (ICSID Case No. ARB/07/20), Award (14 July 2010) para. 13.

> exceptional circumstances justifying that the Respondent be granted an order of security for costs."[99]

In the PCA case *Guaracachi America, Inc. and Rurelec PLC v. the Plurinational State of Bolivia*, the tribunal held that:

> "Respondent has not shown a sufficient causal link such that the Tribunal can infer from the mere existence of third-party funding that the Claimants will not be able to pay an eventual award of costs rendered against them regardless of whether the funder is liable for costs or not."[100]

In practice, it is fair to say that investor-State arbitral tribunals faced with an application for an order for security for costs tend to be very cautious. While the general approach to the making of costs orders may have changed, it remains the case that the exceptional circumstances test remains the criterion by which applications for security for costs are measured and only in the event of truly exceptional circumstances (similar to those in *RSM v. Saint Lucia*) will a tribunal order security for costs.

The ICCA-QM Report proposes as Principle No. D.1 of Chapter 6 on security for costs that: "An application for security for costs should, in the first instance, be determined on the basis of the applicable test, without regard to the existence of any funding arrangement."[101]

With reference to the need to disclose the funding agreement to the arbitral tribunal – if the funded party is found to be impecunious – the ICCA-QM Report proposes two options: (1) a limited disclosure of the "provisions that are strictly necessary to assess the extent to which the funder may cover (or not) an adverse costs order"; and (2) allowing "the funded party, its counsel or even the funder to provide the tribunal with a witness statement or affidavit stating its identity and whether under the third funding party agreements it can be held liable for adverse costs".[102]

There may be a "third way" which could reduce any potential objections based on confidentiality (option 1) and on the "quality" of any such affidavit (option 2): the appointment of an independent expert who – on the basis of a specific mandate agreed

99. *EuroGas v. Slovak Republic*, fn. 65, Procedural Order No. 3, 23 June 2015, para. 123.

100. *Guaracachi v. Bolivia* (PCA Case No. 2011-17), Procedural Order No. 14 (11 March 2013) paras. 6-7 (fn. 96).

101. ICCA-QM Report, fn. 44, p. 145. Jennifer A. TRUSZ, "Full Disclosure? Conflict of Interest Arising from Third-Party Funding in International Commercial Arbitration", fn. 72, p. 1677, suggests that:

> "The arbitral tribunal shall not be permitted to consider the existence of a third-party funding relationship itself in any decision regarding costs or security for costs. Third-party funders may be more willing to disclose their relationships with parties involved in litigation if rules are in place to ensure that tribunals will not use the relationships against them. Thus, institutions should expressly provide that the tribunal may not consider third-party funding in any decisions on costs or security for costs."

102. ICCA-QM Report, fn. 44, p. 181.

on between the parties – would be entitled to examine the funding agreement in its entirety and who would produce a report which would only be disclosed in full to the arbitral tribunal.

All that may be so, but why if, as appears to be the case, tribunals increasingly seek to award and apportion costs on the basis of the outcome of the arbitration rather than adopt the current conventional approach of letting the costs lie where they fall should a state that has successfully defended a case at great expense against a funded impecunious investor not be able to avail itself of a measure of the protection from exposure to costs that the impecunious investor itself sought to enjoy? And why should a funder, which backed the case in the expectation of a share of the winnings be allowed to walk away without any liability from any adverse costs award made against the party which it had funded?

In these changed circumstances, it may be appropriate for a tribunal not to focus simply on the impecuniosity of the investor and to ensure that it has a chance to bring an ostensibly meritorious claim to trial, but to consider whether the justice of the case calls for the costs of the State to be covered in the event that it were to prevail. If that is right, then *RSM v. St Lucia* may not be a lone outrider for very much longer.

IV. CONCLUSION

An arbitral tribunal faced with a party which it knows to be the recipient of third-party funding is in a position to consider issues of conflict disclosure and to embark upon the arbitration with that factor in mind. It will likely never be clear to a tribunal to what extent a funded party's approach to the arbitration is driven by the funder (any more than it might expect to be privy to a self-funded party's tactical considerations). If the party and its funder are "ad idem" from the outset that does not matter. But a tribunal with knowledge of a funder's involvement may be in a position to warn of consequences, not least in costs, if it perceives that tactics have been adopted by the funded party, the purpose of which is deliberately to derail, prolong or otherwise prejudice the efficient and effective prosecution of the arbitration and which would not otherwise be adopted by the funded party but for its ability to look to the funder for financial cover. That is a fine exercise in judgment, but it is one that may be undertaken on an informed basis.

A tribunal, which is kept in the dark about any such involvement labours under a very considerable disadvantage. Given the current (febrile) state of the debate about transparency in arbitration generally and the still present and palpable distrust about the role of third-party funding in particular, any measure which might assist to dispel the notion that some form of "black art" is in play, which operates, not least, to the detriment of State parties, should surely be adopted. Seen in this light, an obligation on the part of a funded party to make disclosure at the outset of the fact that it is funded and by whom ought to become the rule rather than the exception.

Arbitration Involving Public Bodies and Public Interests: Salient Issues

Arbitration Involving Public Bodies and Public Interests: Salient Issues

Part I: The Increasing Participation of Public Entities in International Arbitration

Arbitration Clauses and Disputes from the Central European Perspective: Blurring the Public-Private Divide

*Marie Talašová** *and Jaroslav Kudrna***

TABLE OF CONTENTS PAGE

I. INTRODUCTION

From the state's perspective, traditional separation between private commercial arbitration and public investment arbitration[1] is less relevant than one might think. Commercial and investment arbitrations both include private and public parties and often arise from similar economic transactions and state measures. Furthermore, important public interest implications and tax payer money are usually at stake in commercial as well as investment arbitrations.

Arbitrations involving Central European states offer excellent case studies of the ramifications that commercial and investment arbitrations can bring. After regaining their freedom after the fall of the communist regimes in 1989, Central European states were thrilled to move from a planned economy into a market-based economy. This gave rise to a multitude of state privatization processes. Former state-owned enterprises were sold to foreign buyers usually through a privatization agency or ministry. During negotiations, buyers from capital exporting countries often required the inclusion of arbitration clauses in privatization contracts. In the early 1990s, foreign buyers' home states negotiated bilateral investment treaties (BITs) – which also included arbitration clauses – with former communist countries to protect these new investments.

* Director at the International Arbitration and Investment Protection Unit at the Ministry of Finance of the Czech Republic.

** Legal Adviser at the International Arbitration and Investment Protection Unit at the Ministry of Finance of the Czech Republic.

The authors prepared this article in their personal capacity. The views expressed are those of the authors alone and do not necessarily represent the views of the Ministry of Finance or the Government of the Czech Republic. The authors would like to thank their colleague Katka Heroutová for her research assistance.

1. Stavros BREKOULAKIS, "The Protection of the Public Interest in Public Private Arbitrations", Kluwer Arbitration Blog (8 May 2017) at <http://arbitrationblog.kluwerarbitration.com/2017/05/08/the-protection-of-the-public-interest-in-publicprivate-arbitrations/> (last accessed 12 February 2018) ("In international arbitration, as in other fields of law, the divide between private and public – commercial arbitration and public international (including investment) arbitration – traditionally has been the generally, if uncritically, accepted belief.").

Central European states, eager to attract foreign investment, accepted arbitration clauses in both privatization contracts and BITs. As we will see, privatization gave rise to both commercial and investment arbitrations. Exploring arbitration clauses in privatization and investment contracts and related commercial and investment disputes is the main goal of the present article.

We will begin by discussing arbitration clauses in public-private contracts entered into by public entities with private foreign investors (II). The authors plunged into the Czech Republic's archives to dig out privatization contracts and look into dispute resolution mechanisms. The need for foreign investment, however, is not limited to the privatization process in the 1990s. It remains necessary for the development of natural resources, research and development, and other sectors. The authors thus also explore current practices used when signing memoranda of understanding and investment contracts with foreign investors in three Central European countries (Czech Republic, Slovakia and Poland).

Next, the authors will discuss public-private arbitration disputes (III). The focus will be on both commercial arbitrations arising out of public-private contracts and investment arbitrations. Legitimate state concerns for the public interest are present in both types of proceedings; therefore, referring to the public-private divide does not make much sense from a public interest perspective. The authors will also address how a state can deal with public interest concerns. Finally, this section will briefly explore the impact of public-private arbitrations on the public's opinion of arbitration in the three Central European countries.

II. ARBITRATION CLAUSES IN PUBLIC-PRIVATE CONTRACTS WITH FOREIGN INVESTORS

Foreign investors usually require including an arbitration clause in their contracts with public entities. This phenomenon was evident in older privatization contracts (*1*). The practice of including arbitration clauses also arises in current conclusions of memoranda of understanding and investment contracts with foreign investors (*2*). By comparing the practices from the 1990s with the current ones, the authors identify relevant changes in trends (*3*).

1. *Arbitration Clauses in Privatization Contracts*

Privatization was a significant undertaking for all former communist countries. In the Czech Republic, the process of privatization started at the beginning of 1990s and continued into the 2000s.

Privatization had several forms. The most prominent, called "big privatization",[2] involved the transfer of property managed by state enterprises. In the Czech Republic, it

2. Stanislav PLÍVA, "*Privatizace*" in Dušan HENDRYCH, et al., *Právnický slovník* (C.H. Beck 2009) [online version]. The term privatization in the Czech context also covered restitution and transfer of so called "operation units", i.e. property that was necessary for the function of state and regional bodies. *Ibid.*

was conducted by the newly created National Property Fund[3] and the Ministry of National Property Administration and Privatization (Privatization Ministry). The largest wave of big privatization, which will be our focus here, commenced in 1991 and ended with the dissolution of the Privatization Ministry in 1995.[4]

The process of privatization usually started with a project prepared by the state enterprise at stake. The Privatization Ministry (or sometimes the Government) then issued a privatization decision.[5] Assets were subsequently transferred to the National Property Fund, which negotiated purchase agreements with private buyers.

Privatization was conducted through public tender or direct sale.[6] The new buyers were foreign entities in over 150 privatization projects. In almost all projects, privatization was conducted through direct sale.

The authors were able to locate and review 126 privatization agreements concluded with foreign buyers. Most of them (102) contained an arbitration clause. The arbitration clauses greatly differed in their sophistication and content.

All arbitration clauses, except for two,[7] designated arbitration rules. The most popular arbitration rules were the UNCITRAL Arbitration Rules, which figured in 71 clauses, followed by the ICC Arbitration Rules (16 clauses), the Arbitration Rules of the Vienna International Arbitral Centre (VIAC) (5 clauses), the Rules of the Arbitration Court attached to the Czech Chamber of Commerce and the Agricultural Chamber of the Czech Republic[8] (4 clauses) and the International Arbitration Rules of Zurich Chamber of Commerce (2 clauses).

Six arbitration clauses only chose an arbitral institution. Meanwhile, all clauses that chose the UNCITRAL Arbitration Rules did not select an arbitral institution to administer the proceedings. Only one arbitration clause explicitly chose both rules and an administrating institution.[9]

Most of the arbitration clauses (84) selected the number of arbitrators and the place and the language of the arbitration. A majority of clauses (86) opted for three arbitrators. Most clauses designated Prague as the seat of arbitration (50), followed by Vienna (19), Zurich (8), Geneva (4), London (2), Paris (2), Munich (1), Amsterdam (1) and Brno (1). Thirteen clauses did not select the seat of arbitration. The most often

3. Act No. 171/1991, Coll., on the Competence of State Organs in the Matter of Transfer of Property to Other Person (entered into force on 24 May 1991).
4. This does not mean that there were no privatizations after 1995. For example, the privatization of banking sector mainly occurred between 1998 and 2002.
5. *Id.* Sect. 2(4).
6. Sometimes direct sales occurred through transformation from a state enterprise to a joint-stock company or transformation from a state joint-stock company to a private joint-stock company.
7. The first arbitration clause stated in the relevant part that "[the dispute] will be resolved in binding arbitral proceedings according to procedural rules" without specifying any arbitral institution or arbitration rules. The second clause stated that "[p]arties shall subject themselves to an arbitral award issued by three arbitrators" and then designated the way to appoint them.
8. The arbitration clauses referred to the Arbitration Court attached to the Czechoslovak Chamber of Commerce and Industry, which was the name of this arbitral institution before 1 January 1995.
9. The clause stated: "All disputes, controversies or claims between the Parties arising out of or connected with this Agreement, or the breach, termination or validity thereof ..., shall be finally settled by an arbitration ... administered by the International Chamber of Commerce ... in accordance with its Rules of Conciliation and Arbitration...."

selected foreign seat was Vienna. Historically, Vienna played a role as the seat of arbitrations between parties from Western and Eastern Europe, which might explain its popularity as the seat in the early 1990s. After Vienna comes Geneva and Zurich. This is not surprising because Switzerland is well known for its neutrality and as an arbitration-friendly jurisdiction.

Arbitrations were to be mostly held in English (79 clauses). In some marginal cases, the language of the proceedings was German (7 clauses) or both German and Czech (3). Czech alone was selected in just 2 clauses.

The most popular combination of elements, found in 42 arbitration clauses, was arbitration in English according to the UNCITRAL Arbitration Rules, with an arbitral tribunal consisting of three arbitrators and seated in Prague.

The majority of the privatization contracts (97) chose Czech (Czechoslovakian) law as the governing law.[10] Austrian law was selected in 4 contracts, German law in 3 and English law in 1. Most of these contracts were concluded in 1991 or 1992.

The majority of the arbitration clauses were brief and clear. However, one clause, for example, chose two sets of arbitration rules, stated that the tribunal was to be composed of two arbitrators and made the seat of the tribunal dependent on the seat of the claimant.[11]

In Slovakia, privatization contracts with an ICC arbitration clause were standard procedure. The particularity of the privatization agreements was that they usually included stabilization clauses protecting investors against future discrimination through taxation and regulation.

2. *Arbitration Clauses in Memoranda of Understanding and Investment Contracts*

The need for foreign direct investment is ongoing in Central European countries and was not limited to the privatization processes in the 1990s. It is therefore useful to explore current practices of memoranda of understanding (MoU) and investment contracts with foreign investors in the Czech Republic, Slovakia and Poland.

In the Czech Republic, there is a recent practice of signing MoU with foreign investors. The Czech Republic prefers to treat them as non-binding documents and includes specific language to that effect. If possible, the Czech Republic avoids the term MoU altogether and calls these documents "declarations" to highlight their non-binding nature. The State also likes to specify that the MoU or declarations cannot be enforced in judicial proceedings or investment arbitration under any bilateral or multilateral investment treaties. The State also includes language that the particular MoU does not limit the Government's right to regulate. The Czech Republic makes this effort to

10. In seven instances, the contracts stated that they were governed by the Czech commercial code and "other laws in force".

11. The clause read: "All legal disputes arising out of legal relationships governed by the contract or its annexes, and disputes regarding its validity, legal force, interpretation, cancellation or termination of this contract, will be decided solely by arbitrators appointed in accordance with the rules of arbitration of the Chamber of Commerce in Vienna and the Czechoslovakia's Commercial and Industrial Chamber in Prague. The tribunal shall be composed of two judges. The seat of the tribunal will be the seat of the claimant. The tribunal will rule pursuant to the laws of Czechoslovakia. The language of the arbitration will be German."

mitigate future disputes and avoid a public opinion backlash. The generally non-binding MoU can contain specifically listed binding provisions such as those related to confidentiality. In those cases, the Czech Republic agreed in the past to an ICC arbitration seated in Paris, which is a well-established arbitration venue acceptable to foreign investors. This is in contrast to the MoU investment contracts, which include specific obligations on behalf of the State and are thus approved by the Government. MoU or declarations are often signed at a lower level, for example by ministers or CzechInvest (an agency responsible for investment and business development).

In Slovakia, investment contracts with an ICC arbitration clause are standard procedure. They do not usually include stabilization clauses; rather, they only promise that an investor will be informed about future changes in legislation. Investment contracts are approved at the Government level.

In Poland, there is also a practice of concluding MoU with foreign investors. They are civil law contracts rather than administrative ones. The State aims at having Polish law as the governing law and having any disputes resolved by Polish courts. If an investor desires arbitration, there is a preference for the arbitration seat in Warsaw with a Polish arbitral institution (Lewiatan or National Chamber of Commerce (KIG)). Concerning international institutions, the usual choice is the ICC or an *ad hoc* arbitration under the UNCITRAL Arbitration Rules. The Stockholm Chamber of Commerce (SCC) Arbitration Rules are not accepted because of their emergency arbitration provisions.

3. *Overview of the State Practices*

An overview of state practices during the privatization processes in the 1990s and the current negotiations of public-private contracts with foreign investors reveals that commercial arbitration was a preferred choice for foreign investors during privatization processes in the 1990s and still today in the Czech Republic, Slovakia and Poland. The states in most cases agree to arbitrate future disputes.

A detailed review of archived Czech privatization contracts shows that there was a clear preference for *ad hoc* arbitrations under the UNCITRAL Arbitration Rules. This is in contrast with the current practice where parties seem to prefer an administered arbitration in commercial disputes. The use of the ICC Arbitration Rules is much more common than in the 1990s.

During the privatization, the Czech Republic was able to negotiate the seat of arbitration in Prague in slightly over half of the clauses (42 cases compared to 28 cases where the seat was abroad). The state has a legitimate interest to have the arbitration seated in its territory and thus subject it to its arbitration law and control of local courts to the extent permitted by the law. From the point of view of investors, the Czech 1994 Arbitration Act[12] was not based on the UNCITRAL Model Law and contains some

12. Act No. 216/1994 on Arbitral Proceedings and on Execution of Arbitral Awards (1994) at <https://is.muni.cz/el/1422/jaro2008/SOC026/um/216-1994_EN.pdf> (last accessed 16 February 2018). Arbitration clauses concluded before 1 January 1995 were governed by the Act No. 98/1963 Sb. on arbitration proceedings in international business and enforcement of arbitration awards (1963).

particularities (e.g., arbitrators cannot issue interim measures).[13] Foreign investors have a natural interest to have potential proceedings in a well-recognized arbitration seat to avoid any potential interventions by the courts of the host state, which is their counterparty (directly or indirectly through another public entity). From the reviewed contracts, the foreign investors were able to have the seat of arbitration abroad in less than a third of the cases.

Choosing the governing law of the host state in the vast majority of cases is not surprising as the transaction concerns a business activity in its territory. The choice of English as the language of the proceedings is also non-controversial.

III. CENTRAL EUROPEAN STATES' EXPERIENCE WITH PUBLIC-PRIVATE ARBITRATIONS

Central European states have rich experience with investment and commercial arbitration. The subject of this section will be the experience of the Czech Republic (*1*), Slovakia (*2*) and Poland (*3*) with public-private arbitrations as well as the public opinion of arbitration in these countries. Concerning the last point, investment arbitration has only recently received larger publicity in the EU countries because of its inclusion in the Transatlantic Trade and Investment Partnership (TTIP). Because of public pressure, the European Commission decided to reform investment arbitration provisions in the trade agreement with Canada (CETA) and other trade agreements, which have been recently negotiated. For the future, the European Commission has an aspiration to establish a multilateral permanent investment court.

1. Czech Republic

The Czech Republic's results in investment arbitrations are as follows: 16 wins,[14] 3 losses[15] and 3 settlements.[16] Four cases were discontinued by investors.[17] The Czech

13. Jaroslav KUDRNA, "Arbitration – Country Guides: Czech Republic", International Bar Association, Arbitration Committee (April 2015) at <https://www.ibanet.org/Article/NewDetail.aspx?ArticleUid=a646cf32-0ad8-4666-876b-c3d045028e64> (last accessed 12 February 2018).
14. *A11Y Ltd v. Czech Republic* (ICSID), Award (29 June 2018); *Antaris Solar, Michal Göde v. Czech Republic* (UNCITRAL), Final Award (2 May 2018); *Anglia Auto Accessories Limited v. Czech Republic II* (UNCITRAL), Final Award (10 March 2017); *I. P. Busta a J. P. Busta v. Czech Republic* (UNCITRAL), Final Award (10 March 2017); *WNC Factoring LTD v. Czech Republic* (UNCITRAL), Final Award (22 February 2017); *ECE v. Czech Republic* (UNCITRAL), Final Award (19 September 2013); *Jürgen Wirtgen, Stefan Wirtgen, JSW Solar (zwei) GmbH & Co.KG v. Czech Republic* (UNCITRAL), Final Award (27 June 2013); *InterTrade v. Czech Republic* (UNCITRAL), Final Award (28 May 2012); *Vöcklinghaus v. Czech Republic* (UNCITRAL), Final Award (19 September 2011); *Binder v. Czech Republic* (UNCITRAL), Final Award (15 July 2011); *Frontier Petroleum Services v. Czech Republic* (UNCITRAL), Final Award (12 November 2010); *European Media Ventures v. Czech Republic* (UNCITRAL), Final Award (8 July 2009); *Invesmart v. Czech Republic* (UNCITRAL), Final Award (26 June 2009); *Phoenix v. Czech Republic* (ICSID), Final Award (15 April 2009); *Nagel v. Czech Republic* (UNCITRAL), Final Award (9 September 2003); *Lauder v. Czech Republic* (UNCITRAL), Final Award (3 September 2001).

Republic currently has 11 pending cases,[18] of which 6 involve renewable energy sources. The older cases concerned media, banking, construction, etc. As a matter of policy, the Czech Republic publishes its past investment arbitration cases as there is important public interest involved.[19]

The first two investment treaty cases against the Czech Republic initiated by R. Lauder and CME in 1999 and 2000, respectively, are among the most controversial. There were two parallel investment arbitrations based on the same set of facts but with completely opposite results.

A Dutch company, CME, in cooperation with Czech company CET 21, operated the first Czech private TV station TV NOVA from 1993. In 1999, there was a split between the two partners, which ended with the Czech company CET 21, the holder of the license, terminating its cooperation with CME. The actions of the Media Council played a major role.

Both the ultimate beneficiary owner American billionaire R. Lauder and the company CME, which he controlled, initiated separate arbitration proceedings against the Czech Republic, which refused consolidation.

The tribunal in the *Lauder* case (R. Briner, L. Cutler, B. Klein) ruled that Mr. Lauder's harm was caused by private company CET 21.[20] Therefore, the tribunal rejected Lauder's claims for damages against the Czech Republic on 3 September 2001.[21]

On 13 September 2001, only ten days later, the majority in the *CME* case (W. Kühn, S. Schwebel) ruled that the Media Council, in its activities as market regulator, weakened the legal security and stability of CME's investment.[22] In addition, it ruled that in the course of the dispute between CME and CET 21 it clearly supported Czech

15. *CME v. Czech Republic* (UNCITRAL), Final Award (14 March 2003); *Eastern Sugar v. Czech Republic* (UNCITRAL), Final Award (12 April 2007); *Pren Nreka v. Czech Republic* (UNCITRAL), Final Award (22 July 2008).
16. *K+ Venture Partners v. Czech Republic* (UNCITRAL), Final Award (21 December 2006); *Mittal v. Czech Republic* (UNCITRAL), Final Award (6 May 2009); *Saluka v. Czech Republic* (UNCITRAL), Final Award (17 March 2006).
17. *Anglia and Busta v. Czech Republic* I (UNCITRAL); *Forminster v. Czech Republic* (UNCITRAL), Final Award (15 December 2014); *Nepolsky v. Czech Republic* (UNCITRAL), Final Award (5 February 2010); *Konsortium Oeconomicus v. Czech Republic* (UNCITRAL), Final Award (22 February 2012).
18. *Alcor Holdings v. Czech Republic* (UNCITRAL); *Voltaic Network v. Czech Republic* (UNCITRAL); *Photovoltaik Knopf Betriebs v. Czech Republic* (UNCITRAL); *I.C.W. Europe Investments v. Czech Republic* (UNCITRAL); *WA Investments – Europa Nova v. Czech Republic* (UNCITRAL); *Natland Investment Group N.V., Natland Group Limited, G.I.H.G. Limited, Radiance Energy Holding S.à.r.l. v. Czech Republic* (UNCITRAL); *WCV Capital Ventures Cyprus Limited, Channel Crossings Limited v. Czech Republic* (UNCITRAL); *A.M.F. Aircraftleasing Meier & Fischer GmbH & Co. KG v. Czech Republic* (UNCITRAL); *Pawlowski AG a Projekt Sever s.r.o. v. Czech Republic* (ICSID); *Diag Human and Josef Šťáva v. Czech Republic (ad hoc)*; *Fynerdale Holdings B.V. v. Czech Republic* (UNCITRAL).
19. See the Ministry of Finance of the Czech Republic's website at <https://www.mfcr.cz/cs/zahranicni-sektor/ochrana-financnich-zajmu/arbitraze/prehled-arbitraznich-sporu-vedenych-prot> (last accessed 31 January 2018).
20. *Ronald S. Lauder v. Czech Republic* (UNCITRAL), Final Award (3 September 2001), para. 235.
21. *Id.*, p. 74.
22. *CME Czech Republic B.V. v. Czech Republic* (UNCITRAL), Final Award (14 March 2003), paras. 592, 600-601.

company CET 21.[23] As a result, CME's investment was indirectly expropriated.[24] The majority awarded the claimant US$ 335 million.[25]

This controversial loss launched an avalanche of other investment claims. As a result, the Czech Republic ended 2016 with 34 cases, making it the number one most frequent respondent state in EU and third most frequent respondent state worldwide after Argentina and Venezuela, respectively.[26]

Based on this experience of parallel arbitrations with inconsistent results, the Czech Republic insists on prohibiting similar parallel proceedings brought by both the investor company and its shareholders in its revised BITs.[27]

The next case initiated against the Czech Republic in 2001 is connected to the privatization of the banking sector. One of the banks being privatized was Investiční a poštovní banka (IPB), one of the four largest banks in the Czech Republic. In 1998, after two years of negotiations, the Japanese bank Nomura concluded a share purchase agreement with the National Property Fund through which it acquired 36 percent of shares of the IPB. The same year, Nomura transferred the majority of the purchased shares to its Dutch subsidiary Saluka; the rest of the shares were transferred in February 2000. IPB had long had financial problems, which culminated on 16 June 2000, when IPB was put into forced administration by the Czech Central Bank. IPB's enterprise was then sold on 19 June 2000 for CZK 1 to another large Czech bank, Československá obchodní banka (CSOB), with substantial state guarantees for future non-performing loans.

The circumstances of the sale to CSOB led to an investment arbitration between Saluka and the Czech Republic initiated in 2001; Saluka sought CZK 40 billion in damages. In response, the Czech Republic initiated in 2002 an *ad hoc* commercial arbitration seated in Zurich against Nomura for breach of the privatization contract and sought damages amounting to CZK 263 billion.[28] In 2006, the Czech Republic lost the investment treaty case against Saluka.[29] However, before the tribunal issued a subsequent

23. *Id.*, para. 602.
24. *Id.*, para. 609.
25. *Id.*, para. 624.
26. UNCTAD, "World Investment Report 2017" (2017) p. 115, at <https://unctad.org/en/PublicationsLibrary/wir2017_en.pdf> (last accessed 31 January 2018).
27. Czech Republic Model BIT (2016), Art. 8(7) ("If an investment is held: /a/ by an investor of one Contracting Party in the territory of the other Contracting Party through a person of a third State or of the other Contracting Party; or /b/ by an investor, who is a legal person of one Contracting Party, in the territory of the other Contracting Party and such an investor is directly or indirectly owned or controlled by a person of a third State or of the other Contracting Party, the investor of a Contracting Party may not initiate or continue proceedings under this Article if the person of a third State or the person of the other Contracting Party submits or has submitted a claim with respect to the same measure or series of measures under any agreement between the other Contracting Party and the third State. The arbitral tribunal shall terminate the arbitral proceedings, if the dispute settlement procedure initiated by the person of a third State or a person of the other Contracting Party, is decided on the merits.").
28. Česká informační agentura, "Arbitráž: 263 mld.Kč - ČR může žalovat Nomuru a Saluku" (7 September 2004) at <www.kurzy.cz/zpravy/98084-arbitraz-263-mld-kc-cr-muze-zalovat-nomuru-a-saluku/> (last accessed 16 February 2018).
29. *Saluka Investments B.V. v. Czech Republic* (UNCITRAL), Partial Award (17 March 2006).

decision on damages, the State settled all the pending investment and commercial arbitrations with Nomura and Saluka for about US$ 175 million.[30]

Based on the state guarantees, CSOB then sued the Czech Republic in an ICC Arbitration seated in Vienna and in 2010 won CZK 1.6 billion in damages.[31] In 2016, CSOB won CZK 300 million against the Czech Central Bank, in an ICC arbitration seated in Prague, which was also connected with IPB's take over.[32]

From other cases, one can note that the company Diag Human, with which the Czech Republic has a long-running commercial arbitration dispute, has just started investment arbitration proceedings against the Czech Republic.[33]

Overall, investment arbitrations against the Czech Republic raise two major issues. First, the Czech Republic is often sued by its own nationals who invested in the Czech Republic through foreign companies set up for that purpose. For example, the Czech Republic is currently being sued by a former senator in the *AMF Aircraftleasing Meier & Fischer* case concerning bankruptcy proceedings[34] and by a current senator in the *WCV Capital Ventures Cyprus* case concerning gambling regulations.[35] Investment arbitration thus creates an uneven playing field where sophisticated domestic investors with necessary resources can act as foreign investors. Coming back to Professor Weil, it is reasonable to consider that states did not create foreign investment protection for their own nationals.[36] Despite that, tribunals keep interpreting BITs in a way that disregards states' fundamental rationale behind the creation of the BITs. The Czech Republic tries to remediate that in its new and revised BITs by requiring substantial business activity of the investor in its home state.[37]

30. Settlement Agreement between Nomura Holdings, Inc., Nomura International plc, Nomura Principal Investment plc, Saluka Investments B.V. and the Czech Republic (30 November 2006).
31. *CSOB v. Czech Republic* (ICC Ref. No. 15019/JHN/GZ), Award (20 December 2010).
32. Euro, "ČNB prohrála stamilionovou arbitráž s ČSOB" (25 January 2017) at <www.euro.cz/byznys/cnb-prohrala-stamilionovou-arbitraz-s-csob-1326129> (last accessed 15 February 2018).
33. *Diag Human and Josef Šťáva v. Czech Republic* (not yet specified). See Tom JONES, "Czech blood plasma saga leads to treaty claim", Global Arbitration Review (12 February 2018) at <https://globalarbitrationreview.com/article/1158723/czech-blood-plasma-saga-leads-to-treaty-claim> (last accessed 14 February 2018).
34. Novinky.cz, "*Kauza Fischerových boeingů se vrací. Podnikatel požaduje po Česku miliardy*" (6 December 2016) at <www.novinky.cz/ekonomika/422776-kauza-fischerovych-boeingu-se-vraci-podnikatel-pozaduje-po-cesku-miliardy.html> (last accessed 15 February 2018).
35. Lidové noviny, "*Konec tanečků. Senátor Valenta žaluje stát s právníky, kteří už Česko porazili*" (25 September 2015) at <https://byznys.lidovky.cz/konec-tanecku-senator-valenta-utoci-na-stat-s-pravniky-kteri-uz-cesko-porazili-194-/statni-pokladna.aspx?c=A150925_140049_statni-pokladna_sm> (last accessed 15 February 2018).
36. *Tokios Tokelés v. Ukraine* (ICSID Case No. ARB/02/18), Dissenting Opinion (Chairman Prosper Weil) (29 April 2004) para. 5 ("From this it appears that the ICSID arbitration mechanism is meant for international investment disputes, that is to say, for disputes between States and foreign investors. It is because of their international character, and with a view to stimulating private international investment, that these disputes may be settled, if the parties so desire, by an international judicial body. The ICSID mechanism is not meant for investment disputes between States and their own nationals.").
37. Czech Republic Model BIT (2016), Art. 1(3b) ("The term 'legal person' shall mean, with respect to either Contracting Party, any entity incorporated or constituted in accordance with, and

Second, despite rare losses, the Czech Republic has already paid almost US$ 100 million for legal services[38] and was only awarded costs in very few cases. In some of these cases, the claimants have yet to fulfill the order to pay the costs and the Czech Republic has thus been pursuing enforcement proceedings abroad for which it is incurring further legal costs. In some of those cases, the Czech Republic specifically asked for security for costs because it had serious reasons to believe that claimants would not pay its costs. However, given the extraordinarily high threshold for granting security for costs,[39] its requests have always been refused by the tribunals. More and more cases against the Czech Republic are third-party funded. The fact that third-party funders are not automatically obliged to cover adverse cost orders creates an imbalance in the system; the security for costs standard seems broken. The Czech Republic is trying to remediate this situation in its new and revised BITs by expressly giving tribunals the power to order security for costs and by lowering the threshold for granting them.[40]

Czech investors have initiated a few investment arbitrations in the past. Notably ČEZ, the biggest electricity producer in the Czech Republic, has initiated two investment arbitrations. The first arbitration against Albania[41] was settled in 2014.[42] The second arbitration was commenced against Bulgaria in 2016[43] and is still pending. Bulgaria is also currently facing a claim from another Czech power company, ENERGO-PRO.[44] Outside the energy sector, ČSOB defeated Slovakia in an earlier arbitration in 2004.[45]

Concerning public opinion on arbitration in the Czech Republic, investment arbitration received a negative image in 2003 when the Czech Republic lost its case against CME and had to pay a huge damages award. This negative public image has not changed since.

---

recognized as legal person by its laws, having the permanent seat and conducting substantial business activities within the territory of that Contracting Parties.").

38. See the Ministry of Finance of the Czech Republic's website at <http://www.mfcr.cz/cs/zahranicni-sektor/ochrana-financnich-zajmu/arbitraze/prehled-nakladu-za-pravni-sluzby> (last accessed 31 January 2018).

39. See, e.g., *RSM Production Corporation v. Saint Lucia* (ICSID Case No. ARB/12/10), Decision on Saint Lucia's Request for Security for Costs (13 August 2014).

40. Czech Republic Model BIT (2016), Art. 8(13) ("The arbitral tribunal may order security for costs at a proposal of the Contracting Party which is the party to the dispute. The arbitral tribunal shall especially consider ordering security for costs when there is a reason to believe: /a/ that the investor will be unable to pay, if ordered to do so, a reasonable part of attorney fees and other costs to the Contracting Party which is the party to the dispute; or /b/ that the investor has divested assets to avoid the consequences of the arbitral proceedings. Should the investor fail to pay the security for costs ordered by the arbitral tribunal, the arbitral tribunal shall terminate the arbitral proceedings.").

41. *ČEZ, a.s. v. Republic of Albania* (UNCITRAL).

42. ČEZ Group, "Agreement with Albania Confirmed: Parties Fulfilled All Conditions Precedent; ČEZ to Obtain Nearly CZK 3 bn" (16 October 2014), at <www.cez.cz/en/cez-group/media/press-releases/4877.html> (last accessed 26 January 2018).

43. *ČEZ, a.s. v. Republic of Bulgaria* (ICSID Case No. ARB/16/24).

44. *ENERGO-PRO a.s. v. Republic of Bulgaria* (ICSID Case No. ARB/15/19).

45. *Československa obchodní banka, a.s. v. Slovak Republic* (ICSID Case No. ARB/97/4), Award (29 December 2004).

2. *Slovakia*

Slovakia has won 6 investment arbitrations,[46] lost 2[47] and settled 2.[48] Another 2 cases were discontinued[49] and 2 cases are currently pending.[50] Investments concerned different sectors (insurance, banking) and industries (steel, mining industry, gas, etc.). Slovakia has the same approach as the Czech Republic in respect to transparency and publishes its arbitral awards.[51]

The key case for Slovakia was *CSOB v. Slovakia*. CSOB, a Czech commercial bank, started an ICSID arbitration against Slovakia for breach of the so-called Consolidation Agreement and sought US$ 1.4 billion in damages. The Czech Republic, Slovakia and CSOB concluded this agreement in 1993 to prepare CSOB's privatization. Under this agreement, Slovakia guaranteed payment for losses from non-performing loans.

The agreement included a reference to the Czech Republic-Slovakia BIT, which was actually never ratified. Nevertheless, the tribunal concluded that "by referring to the BIT, the parties intended to incorporate Art. 8 [concerning the dispute resolution mechanism] of the BIT by reference into the Consolidation Agreement, in order to provide for international arbitration as their chosen dispute-settlement method".[52]

After finding that it had jurisdiction, the tribunal decided that Slovakia breached the Consolidation Agreement by failing to cover the losses for the non-performing loans. It awarded CSOB SKK 24.8 billion (about US$ 782 million) as compensation and US$ 10 million in arbitration costs.[53]

The amount awarded in compensation would be equivalent to each of the 5.4 million Slovak citizens paying about US$ 145, in a context in which the average monthly salary in Slovakia was about US$ 500 in 2004.[54] It would be the same as if the United States was ordered to pay about US$ 290 billion in damages.

---

46. *Achmea v. Slovak Republic* II (UNCITRAL), Award (20 May 2014); *EURAM Bank v. Slovak Republic* (UNCITRAL), Award (20 August 2014); *Alps Finance v. Slovak Republic* (UNCITRAL), Award (5 March 2011); *Austrian Airlines v. Slovak Republic* (UNCITRAL), Award (9 October 2009); *HICEE v. Slovak Republic* (UNCITRAL), Award (17 October 2011); *Oostergetel v. Slovak Republic* (UNCITRAL), Award (23 April 2012). The information is based on UNCTAD, Slovakia – as respondent State, at <https://investmentpolicyhub.unctad.org/ISDS/CountryCases/191?partyRole=2> (last accessed 26 January 2018).
47. *Achmea v. Slovak Republic* I (UNCITRAL), Award (7 December 2012); *CSOB v. Slovak Republic* (UNCITRAL), Award (29 December 2004).
48. *Slovak Gas v. Slovak Republic* (UNCITRAL), Award (19 March 2013); *SPP v. Slovakia* (not known).
49. *Mensik v. Slovakia* (ICSID Case No. ARB/06/9); *U.S. Steel v. Slovakia* (UNCITRAL, PCA Case No. 2013-6).
50. *Muszynianka v. Slovak Republic* (UNCITRAL); *EuroGas v. Slovak Republic* (UNCITRAL).
51. See the Ministry of Finance of the Slovak Republic's website at <www.finance.gov.sk/Default.aspx?CatID=11173> (last accessed 15 February 2018).
52. *Ceskoslovenska Obchodni Banka, A.S. v. Slovak Republic* (ICSID Case No. ARB/97/4), Decision on Objections to Jurisdiction (24 May 1999), para. 55.
53. *Id.*, para. 374.
54. Ako-investovat.sk, "*Vývoj priemernej nominálnej mesačnej mzdy v SR*" at <http://ako-investovat.sk/grafy/makroekonomika/10/vyvoj-priemernej-nominalnej-mesacnej-mzdy-v-sr> (last accessed 31 January 2018).

Another interesting arbitration involving Slovakia is a case brought by Dutch insurer Achmea. The investor argued that the nationalization of the health system led to indirect expropriation of its health insurance business in Slovakia. The tribunal first found jurisdiction and then ordered Slovakia to pay € 22 million.[55]

Slovakia challenged the award before German courts, as the seat of the arbitration was in Frankfurt. The Federal Supreme Court sent the Court of Justice of the European Union (CJEU) three preliminary questions concerning the compatibility of the Slovakia-Netherlands BIT with EU law. In the opinion of Advocate General M. Wathelet, the Slovakia-Netherlands BIT is in compliance with the EU legal order.[56] Contrary to this opinion, the CJEU decided in March 2018 that the BIT was not compatible with the EU law.[57] The European Commission also separately started an infringement procedure against Slovakia for the non-compatibility of its intra-EU BITs with EU law and requested their termination.[58]

Slovak investors have initiated one case so far. A Slovak bank sued Greece over the changes to its government bonds. The tribunal, however, declined jurisdiction.[59]

In Slovakia, the public has had a neutral perception of arbitration in recent years. However, arbitration has recently attracted a lot of negative publicity when it became public that a lawyer was to be awarded a success fee of € 77 million after a victory of a state-owned company, which he represented in a commercial arbitration against Slovenské elektrárne, owned by Italian company Enel.[60] After the two-year representation, the success fee felt excessive to the public. The State was able to renegotiate the legal fees and decrease the total amount to € 17.6 million.[61] The legal fees have not yet been paid as there is a related ongoing criminal investigation.

3. *Poland*

Since its first investment arbitration in 1994, Poland has won 9 cases,[62] lost another 5[63] and settled 4.[64] One case was discontinued.[65] It currently has 4 pending investment

55. *Achmea B.V. v. Slovak Republic* (UNCITRAL, PCA Case No. 2008-13) (formerly *Eureko B.V. v. Slovak Republic*), Award (7 December 2012).
56. Advocate General's Opinion in Case C-284/16, *Slovak Republic v. Achmea BV* (19 Sept. 2017) at <eur-lex.europa.eu/legal-content/EN/TXT/HTML/?uri=CELEX:62016CC0284&from=EN> (last accessed 26 January 2018).
57. Court of Justice of the European Union, C-284/16, *Slovakia v. Achmea* BV (6 March 2018).
58. European Commission, "Commission asks Member States to terminate their intra-EU bilateral investment treaties" (18 Jun. 2015) at <europa.eu/rapid/press-release_IP-15-5198_en.htm> (last accessed 26 January 2018).
59. *Poštová banka, a.s. and ISTROKAPITAL SE v. Hellenic Republic* (ICSID Case No. ARB/13/8), Award (9 April 2015).
60. Nový Čas, "*Megaškandál v spore o Gabčíkovo: Advokát má od štátu dostať šokujúcu odmenu 77 miliónov eur!*" (28 September 2017) at <www.cas.sk/clanok/599803/megaskandal-v-spore-o-gabcikovo-advokat-ma-od-statu-dostat-sokujucu-odmenu-77-milionov-eur> (last accessed 31 January 2018).
61. Trend, "*Bžán si už vystavil faktúru na nechutnú odmenu, na analýzu o platnosti zmluvy nečakal*", (30 October 2017) at <www.etrend.sk/ekonomika/advokat-bzan-si-uz-vystavil-fakturu-na-12-5-miliona-eur.html> (last accessed 31 January 2018).
62. *Almås v. Poland* (UNCITRAL), Award (27 June 2016); *Seventhsun and others v. Poland* (UNCITRAL), Award (4 January 2016); *Enkev Beheer v. Poland* (UNCITRAL), Award (13 June

treaty cases in which investors claim about € 2 billion.[66] Activities of claimants span across various sectors (telecommunication, agriculture, banking, real-estate, energy and insurance) and industries (food, paper, metal, etc.).

Poland does not publish information about its investment arbitration proceedings or subsequent arbitral awards.[67] Attempts have been made under the Access to Information Act to change this practice. The Supreme Administrative Court of Poland decided in 2016 that "an arbitral award rendered against Poland is public information which should be disclosed to the public under the Access to Information Act".[68] The same court similarly decided that "a settlement reached before an investment arbitral tribunal is public information"[69] as well. These decisions of the Polish courts are sensible.

Poland is also in the process of revisiting its foreign investment policy. In early 2017, the Prime Minister appointed an inter-ministerial group for the legal and international aspects of the investment policy of Poland. One mentioned justification for that was that:

> "Polish investors do not benefit from the protection granted by BITs, but Poland is sued by foreign investors. According to the information from the State Treasury Solicitors' Office, despite the fact that 98% of cases against Poland are won (cases settled are considered to be won as well), Poland bears the costs of arbitral proceedings."[70]

2014); *Ryan and others v. Poland* (UNCITRAL), Award (24 November 2015); *Minnotte and Lewis v. Poland* (UNCITRAL), Award (16 May 2014); *Mercuria Energy v. Poland* (UNCITRAL), Award (December 2011); *TRACO v. Poland* (UNCITRAL), Award (5 September 2012); *Nordzucker v. Poland* (UNCITRAL), Award (23 November 2009); *Saar Papier v. Poland* (II) (UNCITRAL), Award (7 June 2001).

63. *Flemingo DutyFree v. Poland* (UNCITRAL), Award (12 August 2016); *Horthel and others v. Poland* (UNCITRAL), Award (2017); *Servier v. Poland* (UNCITRAL), Award (14 February 2012); *Cargill v. Poland* (UNCITRAL), Award (29 February 2008); *Saar Papier v. Poland* (I) (UNCITRAL), Award (16 October 1995).
64. *Vivendi v. Poland* (UNCITRAL), Settlement Agreement (April 2011); *Eureko v. Poland* (UNCITRAL), Award (19 August 2005); *Ameritech v. Poland* (UNCITRAL); *France Telecom v. Poland* (UNCITRAL).
65. *East Cement v. Poland* (UNCITRAL), Partial Award (26 August 2011).
66. *Lumina Copper v. Poland*; *Griffin Group v. Poland*; *PL Holdings v. Poland*; *Juvel and Bithell v. Poland*. See UNCTAD, Poland – as respondent State, at <https://investmentpolicyhub.unctad.org/ISDS/Country Cases/168?partyRole=2> (last visited 26 January 2018).
67. Marcin ORECKI, "Bye-Bye BITs? Poland Reviews Its Investment Policy", Kluwer Arbitration Blog (31 January 2017) at <http://arbitrationblog.kluwerarbitration.com/2017/01/31/bye-bye-bits-poland-reviews-investment-policy/> (last accessed 26 January 2018).
68. *Id.* citing Supreme Administrative Court of Poland, Judgment of 28 April 2016, Case No. I OSK 2456/14.
69. *Id.* citing Supreme Administrative Court of Poland, Judgment of 28 April 2016, Case No. I OSK 2706/14.
70. Marcin ORECKI, "Bye-Bye BITs? Poland Reviews Its Investment Policy", Kluwer Arbitration Blog (31 Jan. 2017) at <http://arbitrationblog.kluwerarbitration.com/2017/01/31/bye-bye-bits-poland-reviews-investment-policy/ > (last visited 26 January 2018).

This shows the common concern among Central European states that despite winning the cases they still bear substantial costs of legal proceedings as their legal costs are rarely granted.

In 2017, Poland unilaterally terminated its BIT with Portugal. It also requested to terminate the BIT with the Czech Republic. Poland will likely terminate all 23 intra-EU BIT.[71] It argues that they are against EU Law.

Polish investors initiated 7 investment arbitrations from which they lost 3,[72] discontinued 1[73] and 3 cases are pending.[74]

There is negative perception of arbitration in Poland. When terminating the Poland-Portugal BIT, the Polish Government justified its decision by stating that "it should be expected that [termination of the Poland-Portugal BIT] will be positively received due to the public criticism of intra-EU BITs and international investment arbitration in Poland".[75] Arbitration is considered an expensive and lengthy dispute resolution method.

IV. CONCLUSION

In conclusion, the Czech figures studied in regard to Central European states' experience with arbitration clauses show that foreign buyers had a strong negotiation position during the drafting period of the privatization contracts. The fact that the National Property Fund concluded over 150 privatization contracts that varied greatly in their content and complexity, yet pertained to fundamentally similar transactions, suggests that the differences can be attributed to the requests of the counterparties. Moreover, in the majority of cases (102 from 126 reviewed contracts), the Czech Republic gave up its own courts as the dispute resolution mechanism and opted for a less favorable method for the state. In 38 instances, the seat of arbitration was outside of the Czech Republic (in contrast, the seat was in Prague in 50 cases). In all but one of the cases, the Czech Republic agreed to hold proceedings in English.

This situation offers a parallel with the circumstances surrounding the conclusion of bilateral investment treaties in the first half of the 1990s. The Czech Republic also

71. Marcin ORECKI, "Let the Show Begin: Poland Has Commenced the Process of BITs' Termination", Kluwer Arbitration Blog (8 August 2017) at <http://arbitrationblog.kluwerarbitration.com/2017/08/08/let-show-begin-poland-commenced-process-bits-termination> (last accessed 26 January 2018).

72. *Cementownia "Nowa Huta" S.A. v. Republic of Turkey (I)* (ICSID Case No. ARB(AF)/06/2); *Europe Cement Investment and Trade S.A. v. Republic of Turkey* (ICSID Case No. ARB(AF)/07/2); *Robert Aleksandrowicz and Tomasz Częścik v. Cyprus* (SCC).

73. *Cementownia "Nowa Huta" S.A. and Polska Energetyka Holding S.A. v. Republic of Turkey (II)* (UNCITRAL).

74. *Zbigniew Piotr Grot, Grot Cimarron LLC, I.C.S. Laguardia SRL and Laguardia USA LLC v. Republic of Moldova* (ICSID Case No. ARB/16/8); *Yosef Maiman, Merhav (MNF), Merhav-Ampal Group, Merhav-Ampal Energy Holdings v. Arab Republic of Egypt* (PCA Case No. 2012/26); *Spółdzielnia Pracy Muszynianka v. Slovak Republic* (UNCITRAL).

75. Marcin ORECKI, "Let the Show Begin: Poland Has Commenced the Process of BITs' Termination", Kluwer Arbitration Blog (8 August 2017) at <http://arbitrationblog.kluwerarbitration.com/2017/08/08/let-show-begin-poland-commenced-process-bits-termination> (last accessed 26 January 2018).

agreed to conditions that were favorable to its capital exporting partners, including investment arbitration as the dispute resolution mechanism, which caused serious issues down the road. To illustrate, 20 out of the 23 investment arbitration cases concluded with an award or a settlement were based on BITs signed before the end of the year 1995.[76] Both the pressure and weaker position of the Czech Republic during the negotiation of privatization contracts and BITs brought negative consequences for states.

Given the great business opportunities offered by privatization,[77] there is a question of whether the Czech Republic could have enjoyed a stronger contractual position and avoided agreeing to commercial arbitration taking place abroad and investment arbitration.

Concerning disputes that arose out of the public-private contracts and BITs, we can find important public interest implications in both of them, particularly with regard to the lack of transparency. Both investment arbitration with Saluka and commercial arbitration with Nomura were kept outside of the public's sight, even though the claims were for more than CZK 300 billion. The settlement reached in 2006 was kept confidential until 2011. There is still a veil of secrecy around commercial arbitrations with CSOB. Although these are technically commercial arbitrations, given that they arise from state guarantees and the amounts at stake are substantial, the usual confidentiality cherished in business-to-business disputes should not be applied to the same extent in public-private disputes.

There is a trend to improve transparency in investment arbitration.[78] These efforts are currently pending at the EU level. The EU accession to the United Nations Convention on Transparency in Treaty-based Investor-State Arbitration (the Mauritius Convention on Transparency) requires unanimous support of the EU member states and this issue is awaiting decision of the EU Council. And given that this is an area of the shared competence, the EU member states cannot arguably adhere to the Mauritius Convention on their own without breaching the EU law. Nevertheless, nine member states have already at least signed the Mauritius Convention.[79]

However, there is no similar effort to improve transparency in public-private commercial arbitrations.

---

76. Six of the cases were based on the Czech Republic - Netherlands BIT (1991), 6 on the Czech Republic-Germany BIT (1990), 4 on the Czech Republic - United Kingdom BIT (1990), and 1 on the Belgium-Luxembourg Economic Union-Czech Republic BIT (1989), the Canada-Czech Republic BIT (1990), the Czech Republic-Switzerland BIT (1990) and the Czech Republic-United States of America BIT (1991).
77. Privatization offered an entry to a whole new market with no established competition. The access to this developing market could have been gained through a favorable purchase price.
78. See, e.g., UNCITRAL Rules on Transparency in Treaty-based Investor-State Arbitration (effective from 1 April 2014) ("Transparency Rules") (These rules do not apply to disputes arising out of treaties concluded prior to 1 April 2014, unless the contracting state parties to the treaty or disputing parties agree to their application); United Nations Convention on Transparency in Treaty-based Investor-State Arbitration (2014) (The Convention is an instrument by which contracting parties to investment treaties concluded before 1 April 2014 can consent to apply the UNCITRAL Transparency Rules).
79. These member states are Belgium, Finland, France, Germany, Italy, Luxembourg, Netherlands, Sweden and the United Kingdom. See <https://treaties.un.org/pages/ViewDetails.aspx?src=IND&mtdsg_no=XXII-3&chapter=22&lang=en> (last accessed 20 April 2018).

Because of the lack of transparency, commercial and investment arbitrations in some cases can hide the consequences of "bad" political decisions and deny the public the opportunity to hold politicians politically accountable for their past decisions.

In regards to transparency and the public interest perspective, the public-private divide in commercial and investment arbitrations between public and private parties does not make sense and is unjustified.

Challenges for Counsel in the Representation of States and State-Owned Entities in International Arbitration: A Practitioner's Perspective

*Paolo Di Rosa**

TABLE OF CONTENTS PAGE

I. INTRODUCTION

Counsel to sovereign States – in-house State counsel, international counsel, and external local counsel – confront myriad challenges during the course of an international arbitration, many of which are generally not faced in the representation of private sector parties. This paper addresses a few of those challenges, not just in the representation of States but also that of State- owned entities or instrumentalities (collectively, SOEs).

The experience of representing an SOE can vary significantly depending on the nature and corporate structure of the entity, and the degree of control or involvement of the State in the entity's operations and decision-making. In some instances, an SOE is run virtually like a private sector company; in those cases, representation of the SOE can be largely similar to that of a private corporation. In other instances, however, Government officials are heavily involved in the management of the SOE, which can render the experience for counsel akin to that of representing a State in an investment arbitration.

Although there is a sliding range between the two extremes posited above, we center our attention herein on the representation of (i) States in investment arbitrations, and (ii) SOEs in commercial arbitrations in instances in which State officials have a determinative degree of operational and managerial input with respect to the SOE. For convenience, where the considerations for both are similar, States and SOEs are referred jointly herein simply as "the State".

* Partner and International Arbitration Practice Group Chair, Arnold & Porter. The author has devoted most of his twenty-six-year legal career to the representation of sovereign States in public international law, international arbitration, and litigation matters. The author wishes to acknowledge the contribution to this paper of former Arnold & Porter associate (and former official of Ministry of Foreign Trade of the Republic of Colombia) José Antonio Rivas.

Sect. II below discusses the impact on counsel of the State's ability and willingness to assume control of the dispute early on, and to manage timing issues correctly; for those States that choose to hire specialized counsel for international arbitrations, the timing of the retention of such external counsel is a critical factor. Considering that investment disputes often concern concession contracts on natural resources, infrastructure and public utilities (which can involve a significant public interest dimension, and/or State measures that may have a public purpose), Sect. III below discusses the challenges that the State and its counsel may confront in a highly visible and political case, and the potential impact on the defense of media coverage and political dynamics. Sect. IV refers to challenges that often arise for counsel to the State with respect to evidentiary issues, including documentary evidence, fact witnesses, and experts. Sect. V discusses the factors that are relevant for a State in deciding on possible settlement of a dispute, and on whether or not to seek annulment or set-aside of an adverse arbitral award, and the potential impact of those factors on counsel's work. Finally, Sect. VI articulates some conclusions.

II. THE IMPORTANCE OF TIMING ISSUES IN THE REPRESENTATION OF STATES

For States that choose to engage specialized external counsel for international arbitrations, one of the principal mistakes can be to delay the retention of the specialized counsel until a point at which prejudice is caused to the State's legal position. Such delay can be deleterious, for example, when the specialized counsel is retained after the relevant arbitral proceeding has already begun, and especially once the arbitral tribunal has already been constituted, and the relevant procedural deadlines (e.g., for written submissions) are already running. In such circumstances, the challenges to external counsel are multiplied and magnified. Counsel no longer have the opportunity to advise the State on pre-arbitration strategy, including how best to position itself for an eventual arbitration in the event that the parties are unable to reach an amicable solution. Perhaps more importantly, in that scenario, counsel's ability to handle various tasks necessary for a successful defense become constrained – in some instances, critically so.

Simply put, time is the most valuable asset that the State has in an arbitration: time to understand the dispute and its underlying facts; to identify the relevant players within the Government; to assess relevant inter-agency dynamics; to obtain and deploy necessary resources; to organize the defense team; to obtain and assess relevant evidence; to develop a defense strategy; to identify and commit fact witnesses; to identify and engage expert witnesses; to handle political and media issues – in sum, time to properly manage the case and mount a solid defense.

1. *The State's Procedure for Selecting Specialized or External Counsel*

Joining a case after the relevant proceeding has already commenced presents significant challenges for the international specialized counsel in at least three critical respects. First, the arbitral tribunal may have been constituted in a way that is not ideal from the State's perspective, in terms of an adequate balance in the composition of the tribunal. Naturally, a tribunal with a less favorable composition can adversely affect the outcome of the arbitration. The situation is even worse if the State has outright forfeited its right to select a party-appointed arbitrator.

Failing to select a party-appointed arbitrator is one of the worst mistakes a State can make in an international arbitration, as the option to do so (where available) is one of the critical rights that a State enjoys. When the State is deciding on an arbitrator, it is not only selecting a person who would be more likely to side with the State (or at least sympathetic to the State's interests), but also – and perhaps more importantly – a person whose opinion would be likely to carry weight, respect and authority with other tribunal members. Specialized counsel typically conduct a due diligence exercise with respect to potential candidates for arbitrator, evaluating the candidates' respective experience, knowledge, and past records of decisions and awards, for the purpose of identifying to the extent possible each candidates' views on key aspects of the dispute at issue, as well as assessing potential conflicts of interest. The substantive research on the candidates can also involve a review of their publications and speeches, and intelligence-gathering pursuant to informal consultations with colleagues of the arbitration community.

Research about potential arbitrators and identification of the best choices for the State is a task for which specialized counsel is best positioned (due to past exposure to many of the candidates, whether in an arbitral, institutional or academic context), as a result of which engaging such counsel only after the arbitral tribunal has been constituted can ultimately – and unbeknownst to the State – play a critical role in the outcome of the arbitration. When the result of an arbitration ends up being adverse, it is impossible to ascertain what (if anything) might have yielded a different outcome; yet most knowledgeable and well-informed observers would agree that the composition of the tribunal can indeed be determinative.

Counsel's role can be important in the selection not only of the party-appointed arbitrator, but also of the tribunal chair. For example, it is often in the State's best interest to negotiate with the investor on the identity of the tribunal chair, and yet sometimes States are reluctant to engage with the opposing side on that issue. Instead, State officials often prefer to just allow the selection of the Chair to be made by the appointing arbitral authority or institution, for fear of subsequent criticism if the result of the arbitration is adverse to the State, and it is learned by critics that the opposing side had some influence on the identity of the Chair (or worse still, that the person had been proposed affirmatively by the opponent and accepted by the State's defense team).

The phenomenon of a protracted process for the selection of specialized counsel is understandable from the State's perspective, as in many instances there are significant budgetary, bureaucratic, and even political or ideological issues at play. Sometimes the relevant State officials face cumbersome procurement rules that they must observe before being able to hire international or specialized lawyers. However, considering the negative impact that a delayed selection of specialized counsel can have on the defense of the State, certain useful actions can be taken even in anticipation of a dispute.

Public bidding and procurement rules are designed to guarantee transparency and due process. The problem for selection of specialized counsel is that in various jurisdictions, if those rules are applied they may extend the duration of the selection process beyond what would be prudent to optimize the State's defense in the arbitration. For example, in ICSID cases, even before the request for arbitration ("RFA") is registered by ICSID, the State can assess the potential jurisdictional objections and merits of the case to determine whether it should explore an amicable solution. Having specialized counsel involved from an early stage in that process can be useful to explore an amicable resolution without causing prejudice to the State's legal position in an eventual arbitration. Counsel's involvement can also be useful for potentially important pre-arbitration tasks in cases that seem unlikely to settle. For example, before the ICSID Secretariat registers an RFA pursuant to Art. 36 of the ICSID Convention, the State may consider opposing registration of the RFA by the Centre if, on the basis of the information provided by the investor, the dispute is "manifestly outside the jurisdiction of the Centre".

A protracted public bidding process for the selection of specialized counsel can end up depriving the State of the advice of such counsel in the early stages of the dispute, which can be critical to the outcome thereof, not only in connection with the factors mentioned above (settlement negotiations, and a preliminary assessment of the case), but also with the assessment of potential candidates for party-appointed arbitrator and tribunal chair. Therefore, it is ideal for the State to implement some other mechanism (alternative to public bidding) for the selection of external counsel.

Some States use a closed bidding process in which they invite a number of pre-selected potential counsel with a proven track record in the defense of States, and apply clearly identified criteria that are based on factors such as the counsel candidates' past experience and success rate in investment arbitration, in disputes involving the relevant subject matter, and in the relevant geographic region, among other factors. Ultimately, the selection – even if not conducted pursuant to a public bidding – should still be competitive, transparent, and consistent with due process. In general, the basic procedure to select specialized counsel should be developed before a particular dispute crystallizes into an arbitration, thereby enabling the State and the agency leading the defense ("lead State agency") to apply an already established procedure once a notice of arbitration or RFA is presented.

With respect to the specific criteria to use for the bidding process, different States employ different mechanisms and formulae. So long as the process is reasonably expedited, the differences need not affect the State's interests adversely. That said, some criteria can be limiting or can generate unfavorable dynamics. For example, some States have a list of preferred providers that they first invite to bid, and then select the lowest-priced bid. Other States have other mechanisms to filter the bidders' technical qualifications, but then ultimately also select the lowest-price bid. This system does not always redound to the State's benefit (although naturally it helps with their short term budgetary situation). The reason that it can ultimately prove detrimental is because (a) at any given time, it is likely that at least one of the bidding firms – including respectable international firms – will have an incentive (for any of a number of possible reasons) to submit a "suicidal" bid; and (b) naturally a law firm will, on average, devote to the case a level of resources that is approximately commensurate with the allocated budget. The latter has to do with law firm economics, with which many State officials are not familiar.

To illustrate with an example, let us posit a case in which a State allocates a figure of US$ 1 million for legal fees for an international arbitration. That is of course a sizable sum of money in absolute terms. A State official might be tempted therefore to think: "We are giving this law firm a million US dollars, so surely they can organize themselves in a way that they can make that work for them financially." The problem with this reasoning is simply that most international firms focus at a managerial level not on the total amount that is contractually due or paid, but rather on the degree of correspondence between the amount paid (however high in absolute terms) and the value in dollars of the total hours worked, based on each time-keeper's hourly billing rate. Accordingly, if a given team devoted a specified number of hours to the case, and such hours correspond to US$ 1.5 million based on the relevant hourly rates and the number of hours worked, from a financial perspective the law firm's management may view that scenario by reference to the opportunity cost. In other words, it may perceive the case primarily as one that generated a "loss" of US$ 500,000 rather than US$ 1 million in income for the firm – the idea being that if that same team had devoted those extra hours to a different client, the firm might have received the additional US$ 500,000 for the time spent by the team. Some could argue about the range of profitability of the matter (which depends on different factors), but the bottom line is that from an internal perspective, law firm partners have a strong institutional incentive to allocate to a matter a level of personnel and hours that will fit the available budget (or at least that does not exceed that level by too much). That is just the reality of law firm economics, and anyone who argues otherwise is either naive or disingenuous, as no law firm partner who consistently asks his or her management for significant write-offs is likely to remain at that law firm for very long.

In any event, the adequacy of the resources that a State allocates to a given case can relate to the complexity of the case and to the level of resources that the opponent dedicates to its representation. If the opposing side in the arbitration is willing and able to devote significant resources to prosecute the case aggressively, such opponent will have an advantage over a State defense team that devotes fewer resources to the matter. No matter how skilled and experienced, a lawyer is ultimately just that: a lawyer, not a magician.

Many (or most) States conduct bidding contests to select external counsel for their defense or representation in international arbitrations. While that is helpful for purposes of transparency and the avoidance of irregularities in the hiring process, it can be harmful to the State's interests if the bidding requirements and mechanism are excessively cumbersome or time-consuming. For example, in some instances the bidding requirements are so extensive or onerous as to generate a disincentive for firms to even submit a bid in the first place. In other instances, States impose a bond requirement that can be viewed as prohibitively expensive, or not worth the risk of non-recoupment. It is best for the State to impose the least cumbersome and expensive bidding requirements possible, while still maintaining adequate transparency and competitiveness. Doing so can often be difficult in States where the regular government contracting rules and regulations apply to the selection of international counsel, as such norms often contain requirements that are not especially relevant to the context of hiring of counsel for international arbitrations, and can act as a deterrent for some firms from participating in the contest to begin with. For example, some States' procurement rules require the bidder to provide background information (e.g., bar good standing certificates, criminal background checks, academic diplomas), not just for the bidding firm's individual proposed team members (which can in itself be onerous), but for all partners of the bidding firm (which can be a non-starter for an international firm with hundreds of partners).

Other times the procurement rules require a multi-stage evaluation process that can be very time-consuming, lasting many months or even up to a year or more. This might not be problematic in government matters that are not especially time-sensitive, but can be downright devastating to the State's interests in an arbitral proceeding that lasts only two years (or even less, in the case of many commercial arbitrations). In some instances, for example, the proceeding is already in the briefing stage, which as explained above can pose significant practical, logistical, and ultimately substantive problems for the selected firm, because crafting and implementing a defense strategy can be very time-consuming. It is best therefore to maximize the amount of time available to the defense team to do its work.

To avoid these various difficulties, many States find a way to exempt the selection of external counsel in international arbitrations from the normal procurement rules, and instead grant at least some measure of discretion to the relevant government Ministry, agency or commission. Such discretion typically does not confer unbridled authority to handpick firms or lawyers (which in some instances and States could lend itself to irregularities), but rather to conduct a more streamlined process – imposing only those requirements that are relevant to the specific context; establishing a shorter overall timeline for completion of the selection process; and granting some latitude to select the bidder that seems best-suited for the case at hand.

A factor that is obviously relevant in any bidding contest conducted by a State to hire legal and advisory services is the cost of such services. While the price for legal representation must be considered (since public funds will be used for the purpose), allowing such factor to be the decisive factor in the choice of specialized counsel can be costly in the final outcome of the arbitration for at least two reasons. First, should price of representation drive the State's choice of specialized counsel, less experienced practitioners with a less effective track record might end up representing the State. Second, even if experienced practitioners are willing to submit a hyper-competitive economic proposal, the truth is that prices of specialized legal representation are often driven below what is financially healthy to provide adequate service. The implication for a given law firm of undertaking the representation of a State for suicidally low fees is either that such firm will have to have to subsidize the case (by devoting resources to it that will go unremunerated), or that the services provided will be more limited in nature than they would have been otherwise (for example, by means of the use of a lean team). In such circumstances, the breadth and depth of the State's defense could be impacted negatively.

Considering (1) the interests at stake, which often involve the public good and actions that may be justified by reference to a public purpose rationale, and (2) the funds spent by multinationals and other private sector companies to finance their own cases, the State should consider that its defense team comprising specialized international counsel should be competitive vis-à-vis opposing counsel. As international arbitration has evolved and international tribunals have moved closer to awarding costs and legal fees against the losing party, and especially when the State is at risk of losing hundreds of millions or even billions of dollars if the arbitration yields an adverse outcome, there are additional incentives for the State to allocate the necessary resources to enable the State's legal team to play on a level field with its adversaries.

2. *The Lead State Agency and Coordination of the State's Defense*

Engaging specialized counsel when the proceeding is already underway necessarily means that counsel for the State will face the daunting challenge of attempting to get up to speed on the case and to help put together an adequate defense in a limited period of time. As noted, time is usually the defense team's best friend in an international arbitration – especially in investment arbitrations. Several examples (aside from the one described above of a protracted bidding process) illustrate how a slow response time by the State can negatively affect its position in an arbitration. For example, there are often several different agencies or State institutions that are involved in the arbitration, and it usually takes some time for them to achieve an adequate degree of coordination. In some States it is even a legal requirement to establish a formal inter-agency body or commission, and doing so can be quite time-consuming if it is not a standing body. Also, the lead State agency will not necessarily be the agency that was involved in the facts underlying the dispute. Moreover, the agency responsible for funding the defense may be a third agency, which may also want to have a say in how the defense is conducted. All of this can end up being complex and time-consuming – and meanwhile the clock can be running in the arbitration.

As with the more efficient but still transparent and due process-based procedure suggested above for the selection of specialized counsel, establishing at an early stage the responsibilities of the different Government agencies that will be involved in an arbitration allows the State to handle in a more timely, efficient and effective manner the challenges presented by an arbitration. That in turn redounds to the benefit of the State's external counsel, whose task is enormously facilitated by not having to spend time on such matters at a juncture at which there are multiple competing demands on counsel's time.

Different States confer the lead agency role on different agencies: some on the trade or foreign trade ministry, some on the office of the general prosecutor, others on the ministry of foreign affairs, or the ministry of justice, and still others simply on the agency that has the main substantive connection to the dispute. This is a purely domestic and administrative decision, which should make sense from an organizational perspective taking into account the relevant legal and institutional considerations, as well as the human capital that would be most knowledgeable and experienced to represent the State or manage the case, and to provide support to international specialized counsel. Experience in international disputes is also generally a plus in the choice of the lead State agency.

However, adequate coordination transcends the mere establishment of an inter-agency body, or deciding which agency should be the lead State agency. It is also critical to establish administrative procedures to enable adequate cooperation by those agencies that are most knowledgeable about the facts underlying the dispute, such as for instance the tax authorities, the ministry of environment, the ministry of mining, or even a province or municipality. Pre-existing regulations that mandate full cooperation with the lead agency by the agency or agencies that allegedly breached the relevant contract or treaty could be instrumental during the course of the arbitration, in particular during the document production phase, and when counsel to the State are in the process of identifying and preparing witnesses. In addition to coordinating the management of the case with specialized international counsel, and coordinating the State's activities during the arbitration with those agencies involved in the facts and contested measures of the case, efficient procedures should also be in place to ensure prompt and sufficient funding of the costs of the arbitration. In various jurisdictions, the treasury or ministry of finance is in charge of providing the funds for the arbitration. In many of those States, if the funds are not budgeted in advance, the lead State agency may not have the wherewithal to hire specialized international counsel, local counsel, expert witnesses, translators, and other professionals, or to pay the administrative fees of the arbitral institution or the arbitrators for their work. Provisioning sufficient funds for the State's defense team for an international arbitration – either before a dispute arises, or as soon as the State learns that a request for arbitration is likely to be filed – can be critical to the success of external counsel in carrying out its mission.

III. POLITICAL AND MEDIA ISSUES

Particularly in investment arbitrations, which are generally more visible and can affect the public in a more significant – or at least more tangible – way, the handling of political and media issues by the State and its defense team can be especially important, and also can have a significant impact on the external counsel team. On a purely domestic and political level, Government officials may be keen on legitimizing certain decisions by invoking public purpose considerations, for example in connection with the termination of utility contracts with concessionaires on the basis of a deficient record in providing water, electricity, gas, or other services. Thus, when a public official or publicly elected figure speaks, while the domestic audience may welcome the words as a reflection of the official's intention to advance the public interest (e.g., by protecting the environment, providing water and energy, and promoting education, amongst many others), the consequences can be negative in the context of the arbitration. State officials are often tempted to launch very public attacks on certain foreign investors, based on political or populist considerations.

The problem with that is that in the realm of public international law and investment arbitration, the words of the State matter. This is why a sophisticated defense strategy must also include guidelines and principles concerning the handling by Government officials of political and media issues relating to the dispute. In general, prudence and restraint should guide State officials in their statements to the media about the case. In some instances, the media strategy of the investor is so vocal and aggressive, or the interests at issue are so visible or are made so visible by other interested parties (e.g., NGOs), that silence by the State is not an option. In those instances, the State, in consultation with specialized international counsel, should first determine the clear and simple message that State officials wish to convey to the public (e.g., that the State acted to protect the environment by issuing non-discriminatory measures that conformed with existing laws and regulations). Second, all statements by the State concerning the case should preferably be handled by a single spokesperson, instead of having several public officials opining publicly about the case. And third, any potential new statement by the State should first be discussed with the specialized international counsel, in order to assess the potential effect of such a statement on the arbitration. These guidelines are not especially complex, but, they require discipline and coordination between and amongst the lead State agency, other State actors involved in the case, and the specialized international counsel.

IV. PRACTICAL EVIDENCE-RELATED CHALLENGES FOR COUNSEL IN THE DEFENSE OF STATES IN INTERNATIONAL ARBITRATION

1. *Documentary Evidence*

It takes some time to collect the documents relevant to the State's defense in an arbitration, as such documents may be spread amongst different State entities or different offices within the same entity. Moreover, the adequacy of the evidence-gathering efforts by the State and its counsel will depend on the degree of file-keeping hygiene of the relevant State entity or entities, which can vary widely from State to State, from administration to administration, from agency to agency, and from individual to individual. Moreover, the relevant documentation often has been archived in a byzantine way, and can take some time to track down. In other instances, the relevant agency may have moved to a different location or merged into a different agency; that too can result in significant difficulties in obtaining documents. And of course, the older the vintage of the documents, the more difficult it is to track them down. All of this impacts on the State's ability to collect evidence for its defense, as well as to comply with its obligation as a disputing party in an arbitration to produce – in the context of the document production process – the relevant and material documents requested by the investor. That process takes time, in addition to political will and bureaucratic wherewithal.

The question is what can the State and counsel for the State do if – as occurs in many (if not most) countries – the information and document repository system is not ideal. To begin with, the consequence of not producing certain documents that the tribunal concludes exist or should exist could be that the tribunal draws adverse inferences against the State.

Such inferences, however, are neither automatic nor regularly reached by tribunals. Given the imperfect document-keeping systems that States often have, or the lack of any system at all, tribunals normally will want to ascertain the following:

(1) that the State engaged in good-faith efforts for the turnover of documents whose production the tribunal specifically ordered, or that the State agreed to produce;
(2) that any documents that are not produced by the State are in fact not in its possession; and
(3) the reason(s) why relevant documents were not produced.

Notably, if the opposing party complains to the tribunal that the State has failed to produce certain documents in its possession or is otherwise not cooperating during the document production phase, the information that the tribunal will need to assess how to respond to that complaint is in itself part of the narrative that the State should develop, for the purpose of demonstrating that despite diligent and reasonable efforts to find the relevant documents, it was unable to produce some of them.

For this purpose, from the time that the State is aware of the obligation to produce certain documents, the State should – under the specialized counsel's guidance – keep a historical log of all actions taken by State officials to identify and provide documents responsive to the investor's request for documents. In addition, if there are reasons – no matter how absurd they might sound at the beginning – that could explain why certain important documents were not kept, efforts to document and prove such situations should be made. For example, certain documents may not be in the possession of the State because the Ministry now in charge of the documents is new, or because certain documents were lost in a move or a fire, or because at the time there was no formal record-keeping policy for documents.

Whatever the reason may be, it would be important to provide supporting evidence that the circumstance in fact occurred and prevented the State from maintaining the relevant documents in its possession.

The first instance in which the party obligated to produce certain documents has to explain why certain documents are not being provided, is to the opposing party. If the opposing party perceives that the other side has undertaken diligent efforts to produce documents, the issue may not even get to the tribunal. If the opponent elevates a request for production of documents for decision by the tribunal, the suggested log and adequate documentation of the State's efforts to produce the relevant documents could provide sufficient confidence to the tribunal that the State was acting in good faith, and that adverse inferences against the State are not warranted.

2. *Fact Witnesses*

Often the State's principal witnesses will be officials who have already left the government and may be difficult to track down, and/or who may be reluctant to participate in the case, or too busy to do so. Potential witnesses who are former State officials may have no incentive to serve as a witness, and in some cases may even have a disincentive to do so (e.g., if the administration that is currently in place is from an opposite political party).

There are several factors that can hamper the procurement of key witnesses to testify in an arbitration. At the beginning, there may be preconceptions by incumbent Government officials about the likely unwillingness of former officials to testify, and even prejudices that they may hold about such officials, or about officials from different agencies, or about officials from a different political party. Any such preconceptions must be overcome if a potential fact witness is fundamental to the State's position in the case. On the other hand, presenting too many fact witnesses in an arbitral proceeding can be costly, inefficient, and potentially unnecessary. If the same facts can be established through documentary evidence, the testimony of a given fact witness might not be necessary.

For a witness whose participation is indeed considered necessary – either to testify affirmatively as to certain facts (especially ones that lack documentary support), or to contradict alleged evidence submitted by the opposing side, and that cannot otherwise be contradicted with documentary evidence – it is instrumental to coordinate with the lead State agency and the Government agencies that are knowledgeable about the facts of the case. Those State agencies and their officials generally are in a position to assess the reputation, credibility, strengths and weaknesses of potential witnesses, and therefore can constitute an important source of information for counsel to the State, both during witness selection and hearing preparation processes.

Commitment by State officials to the State's defense is of course an asset. However, it is incumbent upon specialized counsel to explain to the sovereign client why relying on a large number of witnesses may be unnecessary or even counterproductive; why a particular witness could present credibility risks before the tribunal; and ultimately why the selection of witnesses advised by specialized counsel makes sense in light of the narrative that the State is presenting to the tribunal.

3. *Expert Witnesses*

The hiring of expert witnesses to testify in the arbitral proceeding is often a critical component of the defense, but it can take States significant time to identify and hire relevant experts (especially since often for experts, too, local procurement rules require bidding contests).

The process for hiring expert witnesses (such as damages experts, or other subject-specific experts) should follow transparent but also efficient and dynamic rules. Depending on communication and/or linguistic skills, an expert may or may not possess the ability to easily communicate his or her views to the tribunal. A challenge that counsel to the State often face is that State officials may have their own views of who should act as an expert, and tend to prefer local experts. Yet, specialized counsel should be able to guide the State officials in assessing what experts are necessary to optimize the chances of success in the arbitration.

V. THE POLITICS OF SETTLEMENT, AND OF ANNULMENT OR SET-ASIDE

Although it often makes sense from a commercial or financial perspective for a State or SOE to settle a dispute, Government officials and managers of SOEs sometimes lack the wherewithal – political, bureaucratic, and sometimes even legal – to do so, even in circumstances in which they readily admit that settlement is warranted. This phenomenon is attributable to the fact that settling can be a thankless task for those who will be viewed as responsible for the decision, since whatever payment is made out to the opposing party will be subject to second-guessing (by members of the press, political opponents, civil society groups, etc.). In many instances it is simply too difficult for the State or SOE voluntarily to pay out a sizable sum to a litigation adversary when there is still some legal recourse or remedy available, and it is possible to continue battling in a legal proceeding (arbitral or judicial). In some circumstances, settling can envelop the relevant officials or SOE managers in a cloud of suspicion of corruption – even in instances where such individuals are acting entirely in good faith and in advancement of the State's best interests. This dynamic often generates a powerful disincentive for

Government or SOE officials to settle disputes, even where it would be highly advisable to do so. In some States, there can even be a requirement for the Government to exhaust legal remedies before settling, which removes any discretion and forces the State to continue litigating to the bitter end. The foregoing can place counsel in the uncomfortable position of litigating to conclusion a dispute that either will likely end in defeat or that makes absolutely no commercial sense to pursue further (for example, where the amount in dispute is proportionately so low in relation to the cost of litigating as to not make it worth the expense and effort, or when an adverse award has been received but the amount of damages granted to the opponent is low enough that seeking annulment makes no financial sense at all (although in such instances, the State might decide that it wishes to pursue annulment as a matter of principle). There is no simple or straightforward solution to the foregoing conundrums, but they do present dynamics of which external counsel need to be mindful, and which need to be handled with the requisite sensitivity to the pressures faced by the responsible officials or managers.

VI. CONCLUSIONS

The work of external counsel on behalf of States, and in some instances, on behalf of state-owned entities or instrumentalities, can present particular challenges that generally do not arise in the representation of private sector entities. Such challenges can relate to a multiplicity of factors, including bureaucratic and political considerations by the Government; budgetary limitations, and other factors. These elements can hinder the work of the defense team, complicate the State's legal position, and ultimately render more difficult the achievement of a positive outcome in the international arbitration. In this paper we have focused on some of the unique challenges of this nature, and explored some of their practical implications for external counsel and the State itself.

Protecting the Legitimacy of the Arbitral Process: Jurisdictional and Procedural Challenges in Public-Private Disputes

Reza Mohtashami QC[*]

TABLE OF CONTENTS

I. INTRODUCTION

There has been an inexorable trend towards ever-greater interaction between public and private sectors over the last century, and in particular over the last fifty years.[1] This is partly as a result of the privatization programmes implemented by developed economies during this period which have brought ever greater reliance on the private sector to perform public functions across a variety of economic sectors, ranging from operating airports to collecting municipal waste. In parallel, the process of globalization and the opening of emerging market economies to foreign investors have led to an increase in private foreign investment, which is no longer confined to the traditional North-South investment flows, but now includes capital from Asia and the Middle East being invested across the globe.[2]

These developments have led to a substantial increase in the number of public-private disputes, whether arising under contracts, many of which provide for international arbitration as the means to resolve disputes rather than reserving such matters for the national courts,[3] or claims brought by foreign investors under investment protection agreements alleging breaches by host states of their international law obligations. For

---

* Partner at Three Crowns LLP. The views expressed herein are solely those of the author. The author acknowledges the invaluable research assistance of Nicolas Zisis in preparing this paper.

1. Stavros BREKOULAKIS and Margaret DEVANEY, "Public-Private Arbitration and the Public Interest Under English Law", 80 M.L.R. (2017) p. 22.
2. Although much of this foreign investment is state-led and invested by state-owned enterprises and sovereign wealth funds from emerging market economies such as China, Qatar and Saudi Arabia: see Reza MOHTASHAMI and Farouk EL-HOSSENY, "State-Owned Enterprises as Claimants before ICSID: Is the Broches Test on the Ebb?", 3 BCDR Int. Arb. Rev. (2016) p. 371 at p. 374.
3. Guido TAWIL, "On the Internationalization of Administrative Contracts, Arbitration and the Calvo Doctrine" in *Arbitration Advocacy in Changing Times*, ICCA Congress Series no. 15 (Kluwer 2010) p. 325.

example, of the 810 cases filed with the International Court of Arbitration of the International Chamber of Commerce ("the ICC") in 2017, 15 percent involved states or state-entities;[4] whereas the number of investment treaty arbitrations has increased exponentially, with the number of cases filed in 2015 and 2016 standing at 77 (a record high) and 69, respectively.[5] The Permanent Court of Arbitration (PCA), moreover, has reported a new record in the number of public-private arbitrations that it administers involving a state or other public entity: 152 cases in 2017.[6]

The expansion of public-private arbitration, and the adoption of an essentially private dispute resolution mechanism to resolve disputes which may involve matters of public interest, has generated significant recent debate about the nature and conduct of such arbitrations and the possible need for procedural reform, especially in the investment-arbitration arena. Such discussion mainly has focused on concerns to safeguard the public interest and ensure the legitimacy of the process in light of the state's participation in the arbitration and the acknowledgement that the impact of the outcome of the arbitral process may not be confined to the litigating parties.[7] There has been much less focus, however, about protecting the integrity of the proceedings and ensuring a level playing field in circumstances where the involvement of a state party adds a dimension to the arbitration that is generally unknown in purely private disputes; or where the private party (or the arbitral tribunal itself) falls in some way within the scope of the state's coercive reach such that a multitude of tools can be brought to bear by way of national courts, law enforcement agencies, tax authorities and other municipal institutions; or even where instances of civil conflict or revolutionary movements call into question the standing of the government to represent the state in an arbitration, and thus potentially undermine the enforceability of an ensuing award . This is the focus of the present paper: to examine a number of jurisdictional and procedural challenges that apply uniquely in the context of public-private arbitrations, and which have the potential to undermine the legitimacy of the arbitral process.

II. STANDING TO REPRESENT A STATE IN INTERNATIONAL PROCEEDINGS IN TIMES OF CIVIL CONFLICT

It is a claimant's prerogative to designate the respondent to a lawsuit. In the context of an arbitration commenced under a contractual arbitration agreement, this should be a straightforward matter, even in circumstances where the responding party is a state or an

4. ICC press release dated 8 March 2018, available at <https://iccwbo.org/media-wall/news-speeches/icc-announces-2017-figures-confirming-global-reach-leading-position-complex-high-value-disputes/> (last accessed 30 May 2018).
5. According to UNCTAD, as of August 2017, the total number of reported treaty-based arbitrations stood at 817: <http://investmentpolicyhub.unctad.org/Upload/Documents/diaepcb2017d7_en.pdf> (last accessed 30 May 2018).
6. PCA press release dated 27 March 2018, available at <https://pca-cpa.org/en/news/permanent-court-of-arbitration-publishes-2017-annual-report/> (last accessed 30 May 2018).
7. Stephan SCHILL, "Crafting the International Economic Order: The Public Function of Investment Treaty Arbitration and Its Significance for the Role of the Arbitrator", 23 Leiden J. Int. Law (2010) p. 401 at p. 403.

emanation of the state.[8] Similarly, when commencing an arbitration pursuant to an investment protection treaty, it is a routine matter to notify the concerned ministries of the central government of the respondent state, in addition to the office of the head of state or government. Matters are less clear-cut when the state in question is in civil conflict, or amidst a revolutionary movement, or where there are competing political factions claiming legitimacy to represent the state. Leaving aside questions of the state's substantive liability under international law, and whether, for example, the state may be liable for the actions of a revolutionary movement,[9] there is an initial hurdle to overcome: establishing the standing of the government to represent the state as respondent in the arbitration. This is an issue that affects the legitimacy of the arbitral proceeding and may be critical to the eventual enforcement of an award against the state. No claimant wishes to complete an arbitration after several years of effort and cost, receive a favourable award, only then to be told that the award is unenforceable against the state because the respondent was not properly represented in the arbitration and did not have the opportunity to present a defence. This issue has regained urgency in light of the political turmoil and civil conflict that a number of Middle Eastern and North African states have undergone and continue to experience following the so-called "Arab Spring" revolutionary movements.

One way in which claimants can avoid these potential complications would be to wait for the political situation in the respondent state to stabilize and until a new government has established itself, and won international recognition, before initiating an arbitration. This is sound advice, but not always practicable in light of pressing commercial pressures or applicable limitation periods.[10] Alternatively, and if waiting until the political situation has settled is not an option, there may be a non-appearance by the respondent state. If the regime is still focused on the more pressing issues of restoring public order and establishing its authority, its representatives may not appear in the arbitration, and the tribunal may proceed on the basis of default.[11] There is however a third possibility, namely that a government representative appears in the arbitration but that the effectiveness of the government somehow comes under challenge during the

8. To be sure, complications may arise in the context of attempts to extend the arbitration agreement to non-signatories, or where there is a dispute as to whether a state or state-entity has acceded to an arbitration agreement: see, for example, the well-known *Pyramids* case (ICC Case No. 3493), ICCA *Yearbook Commercial Arbitration* IX (1984) (henceforth *Yearbook*) p. 111.

9. For a discussion of the international law rules on attribution in the context of states experiencing civil conflict, see Meriam AL-RASHID, Ulyana BARDYN and Levon GOLENDUKHIN, "Investment Claims Amid Civil Unrest: Questions of Attribution and Responsibility", 3 BCDR Int. Arb. Rev. (2016) p. 181; and Danielle MORRIS, "Revolutionary Movements and *De Facto* Governments: Implications of the 'Arab Spring' for International Investors", 28 Arb. Int. (2012) p. 721.

10. See, for example, the number of claims commenced against the Libyan Arab Republic since 2011 following the overthrow of the Gaddafi regime notwithstanding the continued civil conflict: <www.iareporter.com/articles/libya-round-up-state-reports-success-in-icc-arbitration-with-scandal-plagued-brazilian-contractor-french-investors-bit-claim-is-roiled-by-libyas-insistence-that-a-purported-settlement-was-not-ma/> (last accessed 30 May 2018).

11. See, for example, *Gamesa Eolica S.L. Unipersonal v. The Syrian Arab Republic* (PCA Case No. 2012-11), Award (5 February 2014), where the case was commenced after the start of the civil war in Syria and the proceedings continued without the substantive participation of the respondent.

proceedings.[12] Such challenge may come either in the form of an intervention in the arbitration from a competing political faction or regime claiming legitimacy to represent the state, or even may be raised by the claimant in seeking comfort as to the enforceability of an eventual award.

In such circumstances, an arbitral tribunal may be faced with the task of determining the legitimacy of the regime in question, as of the date of the arbitration, for the purposes of establishing the respondent's standing; and, then, also be required to determine the effectiveness of the regime, including an examination of the extent and nature of control of the state's territory by the regime, as part of determining whether the acts of the regime may be attributed to the state under international law. As discussed below, these two analyses involve different considerations.

1. Attribution of State Responsibility for the Acts of de facto Governments

The state is the only subject of international law to which responsibility can be attributed, and the attribution of conduct to the state is based on criteria determined by international law. State obligations, moreover, survive a change in government. It follows that internal political changes within a given state generally do not impact that state's international law obligations incurred prior to the change.[13]

In the regular course of events, a state is responsible for the acts of its de jure governments, which have been formally recognized by other states. Where the peaceful life of a nation is interrupted, however, the foregoing rule no longer provides a helpful guidepost, as revolutions or the rise of insurrectionary movements may result in the establishment of parallel governing structures that may become regarded as de facto governments. A general de facto government is one that controls the entire territory of the state (for example, following a successful revolution) and displaces the pre-existing government. Upon taking control of the state, such a de facto government takes over the levers of power and assumes responsibility as the actual government of the country. In so doing, the de facto government assumes the role of the prior de jure government and, thus, also assumes the responsibility of representing the state in international affairs; accordingly, its actions become binding on the state under international law.[14] In the case of a successful revolutionary movement, this means that the state is liable from the beginning of the revolution, on the theory that the revolution represented ab initio a changing national will crystallizing in the final successful result. Thus, the government created through a successful revolution becomes liable for all services rendered to the revolution; and the unlawful acts of successful revolutionists render the government equally liable.[15] The position under international law in relation to a general de facto government is now codified in Art. 10 of the International Law Commission's Draft

12. D. MORRIS, "Revolutionary Movements and *De Facto* Governments", fn. 9 above, p. 751.
13. James CRAWFORD, *The International Law Commission's Draft Articles on State Responsibility, Introduction, Text and Commentaries* (Cambridge 2002) p. 117, Art. 10, cmt. 5.
14. *Ibid.*, p. 115, Art. 9, cmt. 4 ("A general *de facto* government ... is itself an apparatus of the state, replacing that which existed previously. The conduct of the organs of such a government is covered by article 4 ...").
15. Edwin BORCHARD, "International Pecuniary Claims Against Mexico", 26 Yale L.J. (1917) p. 339 at p. 340.

Articles on State Responsibility (the ILC Articles).[16] By contrast an unsuccessful revolutionary movement remains merely an insurrection for which the state does not hold any responsibility.[17] As it is difficult, however, to predict whether a revolutionary movement will succeed, it is suggested that its international acts will be subject to a suspensive condition; unless and until the movement emerges as a government, its actions are not likely to bind the state.[18] Accordingly, an investor that chooses to do business with insurgents assumes the risks of its enterprise.

The position is less clear-cut in relation to a local de facto government, which exercises effective control over a part of the state's territory, but not the entire nation. The capacity of a local de facto government to create international obligations for the state is subject to a more complex analysis and depends upon the geographic, substantive and temporal limitations that constrain the effectiveness of such governments.[19] The position may be summarized as follows:

> "The temporary *de facto* government may legislate on all matters of local concern, and in so far as such legislation is not hostile to the subsequent *de jure* government which displaces it, its laws will be upheld. A military occupant as a general rule may not vary or suspend laws affecting property and private personal relations or those which regulate the moral interests of the community. If he does, his acts in so doing cease to have legal effect when the occupation ceases."[20]

International tribunals have held that the collection of taxes and customs duties within the territory and during the occupancy of a local de facto government relieves those taxpayers from a subsequent second payment upon the same goods to a succeeding de jure government.[21] In the *Guastini* case the Umpire held, for example, that annual licence fees

16. J. CRAWFORD, *Draft Articles on State Responsibility*, fn. 13 above, p. 116, Art. 10(1) ("The conduct of an insurrectional movement which becomes the new government of a State shall be considered an act of that State under international law.")
17. Although in relation to unsuccessful revolutionary movements, see the ILC Articles, Art. 9, which provides that the state is responsible for the conduct of a group of persons that in fact exercise "elements of governmental authority in the absence or default of the official authorities and in circumstances such as to call for the exercise of those elements of authority".
18. M. AL-RASHID, U. BARDYN and L. GOLENDUKHIN, "Investment Claims Amid Civil Unrest", fn. 9 above, p. 187.
19. D. MORRIS, "Revolutionary Movements and *De Facto* Governments", fn. 9 above, p. 729.
20. E. BORCHARD, "International Pecuniary Claims Against Mexico", fn. 15 above, p. 344.
21. Arbitral tribunals have distinguished between acts that are impersonal (i.e., that have the characteristics of ordinary governmental functions, for example, the payment of taxes and licence fees) and acts of a personal character, which provide support to a particular individual or group. An example of the latter was considered by the Umpire in the *Tinoco* Claims, which arose following the removal of the Tinoco regime which had governed Costa Rica. In that case, the Royal Bank of Canada asserted a claim against the government of Costa Rica to recover a loan to its predecessor, the Tinoco government. The Umpire considered the substance of the transaction and rejected the claim after having concluded that the Bank had known that the funds at issue were to be used for Tinoco's personal affairs (*Aguilar-Amory and Royal Bank of Canada claims* (*Great Britain v. Costa Rica*), 1 R.I.A.A. (1923) p. 369).

that were paid by an Italian merchant to the revolutionary movement that controlled the town of El Pilar in Venezuela before it was defeated bound the successor government.[22]

Although international tribunals have considered the grant of international recognition as part of their analysis in determining the status of a revolutionary movement, and whether such movement qualifies as a de facto government, international recognition has not been a determinative factor. Thus, for example, the Umpire in the *Tinoco* Claims held the non-recognition by Great Britain and its allies of a general interim government in Costa Rica as being neither determinative of the question of whether the administration constituted a de facto government nor as serving to estop a claim by Great Britain against the subsequent government of Costa Rica on behalf of its citizens.[23] Notwithstanding the absence of international recognition of the Tinoco government, the Umpire upheld the validity of a concession awarded to a British company by the deposed Tinoco regime, notwithstanding legislation by the new government invalidating contracts entered into by the previous regime.[24] In sum, an unrecognized local de facto government can bind the state under international law.

2. *A Government's Standing Before International Tribunals*

While the historical jurisprudence has focused on examining the binding nature of acts undertaken by de facto governments (whether general or local in their geographic scope) under international law, there has been less focus on the related – but distinct – issue of a government's standing to represent the state in relation to an international claim. This issue has been considered more recently before three different international courts and tribunals, where those panels have relied on the regime's international recognition – rather than examining the nature and extent of control of the regime over the nation's territory – as the means to resolve the question of whether a political faction claiming to be the legitimate government of a state is entitled to represent that state.

In the matter of *Cyprus v. Turkey*,[25] before the European Commission of Human Rights (the Commission), Cyprus, represented by the Greek Cypriot administration, had commenced a claim against Turkey arising out of the alleged violations by Turkey of the European Convention of Human Rights against Cypriot citizens during its occupation of part of the island of Cyprus. Turkey objected to the admissibility of Cyprus's claim and argued that the Greek Cypriot government was not entitled to represent the State of

---

22. *Guastini Case (Italian-Venezuelan Commission)*, 10 R.I.A.A. (1903) p. 561 at p. 580 ("Money paid, therefore to the *de facto* authorities in the shape of public dues must be considered lawfully paid, and receipts given by them regarded as sufficient to discharge the obligations to which they relate. Any other view would compel the taxpayer to determine at his own peril the validity of the acts of those exercising public functions in a regular manner.") See also the *Hopkins Case (U.S. v. Mexico)*, 4 R.I.A.A. (1926) p. 41, where the Umpire held that postal money orders issued by the Huerta administration in Mexico to the US claimant had to be recognized by Mexico's succeeding government.
23. *Tinoco Claims (Great Britain v. Costa Rica)*, 1 R.I.A.A. (1923) p. 371 at p. 383.
24. *Ibid.*, p. 381 ("Such non recognition for any reason, however, cannot outweigh the evidence disclosed by this record before me as to the *de facto* character of Tinoco's government, according to the standard set by international law.").
25. *Cyprus v. Turkey* (Application No. 8007/77 of 1978), Decision of 10 July 1978.

Cyprus. Turkey argued, moreover, that there were in fact two administrations – one Greek Cypriot and one Turkish Cypriot – and therefore neither administration could represent the state of Cyprus as a whole. The Commission dismissed Turkey's objection:

> "The Commission observes then that the applicant Government have been, and continue to be, recognised internationally as the Government of the Republic of Cyprus and that their representation and acts are accepted accordingly in a number of contexts of diplomatic and treaty relations and of the working of international organisations. In this respect the Commission refers to the practice mentioned in its previous decision and to more recent international practice both in the Council of Europe and in the United Nations."[26]

The criterion of international recognition also proved to be determinative for the International Centre for Settlement of investment Disputes (ICSID) tribunal in the case of *BUCG v. Yemen*,[27] a case that was commenced in 2014 by the Chinese claimant against the Republic of Yemen under an applicable investment protection treaty. The Yemeni state was represented in the case by international counsel and was participating in the proceedings notwithstanding the civil war in Yemen. During the proceedings, the Minister of Legal Affairs of the so-called Sana'a Government or Revolutionary Leadership in Yemen wrote to the tribunal to terminate the power of attorney of Yemen's international counsel pending instruction of new counsel. This intervention was denounced shortly thereafter by the Minister of Legal Affairs of the so-called Hadi Government, who denounced the authority of the Sana'a Government to represent Yemen and claimed that, as a matter of Yemeni law, she solely was authorized to oversee any international proceedings initiated by or against Yemen and to instruct international counsel. The tribunal was faced, therefore, with competing claims from two opposing regimes, each of whom claimed legitimacy in representing Yemen in the arbitration. After inviting both factions to make submissions in support of their respective standing to represent the state, the tribunal upheld the authority of the Hadi Government. In so doing, the tribunal focused exclusively on the international recognition of the Hadi Government as the legitimate government of Yemen, without any consideration of the effectiveness of that government, which, at the time, had lost control over much of Yemeni territory:[28]

> "The Tribunal notes that as recently as 23 September 2016 the UN General Assembly invited President Hadi to address it as the internationally recognized representative of the Republic of Yemen, which followed the 'affirmation' by the UN Security Council by Resolution No 2216 (dated 14 April 2015) of the 'legitimacy of the President of Yemen, Abdo Rabbo Mansour Hadi'. Although a

---

26. *Ibid.*, at para. 8.
27. *Beijing Urban Construction Group Co Ltd v. Republic of Yemen* (ICSID Case No. ARB/14/30).
28. In the absence of international recognition, the principal argument raised by the Sana'a Government concerned its control of Sana'a, Yemen's capital city, and the machinery of central government located therein, and the lack of effectiveness of the Hadi Government, which was described as a government in exile based in neighbouring Saudi Arabia.

> lot has happened on the ground in the last year, …, the legal status of the Hadi government appears to be unchanged. The Tribunal has carefully considered the opposing submissions of … and the material submitted to illustrate the state of hostilities existing in the Republic of Yemen, that the 'Revolutionary Leadership' controls the capital, Sana'a, in which the subject airport is located, and that the government of the 'resigned' President Hadi is no longer in control. Nevertheless the Tribunal has not been presented with any evidence that the international community recognizes a change of government."[29]

A second international arbitral tribunal reached a similar conclusion when confronted with the competing claims of the Hadi Government and the Sana'a Government to represent the interests of Yemen in the case of *Sabafon v. Yemen*, an arbitration commenced under Yemen's investment law pursuant to the Rules on International Commercial Arbitration of the United Nations Commission on International Trade Law (UNCITRAL).[30] In this case, the tribunal made it clear at the outset that it was not called upon to recognize or legitimize one government rather than the other, and defined its task as determining which government had standing to represent the state in the arbitration proceedings. In so doing, the tribunal was able largely to sidestep considerations of the practice of states and the international community when it comes to recognition of governments; although it did conclude that neither government exercised effective control over the entire territory of Yemen.

The tribunal instead addressed the issue of standing both from the perspective of domestic law and international law, and reached the same result under both scenarios. If Yemeni law were to apply, the tribunal held that the Hadi Government was the legitimate government of Yemen following a review of the Yemeni Constitution and administrative law provisions. Under its analysis of international law, the tribunal noted that "the Hadi Government has consistently been recognized by the international community and by third States as the de jure government of Yemen. At the same time, the Houthis have consistently been condemned for consolidating their de facto power over the capital Sana'a and surrounding provinces."[31] It concluded its analysis as follows:

> "[T]here can be no question that the Houthis exercise effective control over the entire territory of Yemen. Accordingly, the Tribunal finds that the facts on the ground do not support the application of the effective control doctrine, or, in other terms, the facts on the ground are not sufficient to disregard the recognition by the international community of the Hadi Government.
>
> The Tribunal therefore concludes that the Hadi Government is the legitimate government both as a matter of Yemeni law and international law. The Tribunal is

29. *Beijing Urban Construction Group Co Ltd v. Republic of Yemen* (ICSID Case No. ARB/14/30), Procedural Order No. 2 (8 November 2016) paras. 5 and 6.
30. *Yemen Company for Mobile Telephony-Sabafon v. The Government of the Republic of Yemen* (PCA Case No. 2010-03).
31. *Yemen Company for Mobile Telephony-Sabafon v. The Government of the Republic of Yemen* (PCA Case No. 2010-03), Procedural Order No. 11 (2 May 2018) para. 80.

> bound to take note of this state of affairs and to draw the necessary conclusions for the present case."[32]

The reference to international recognition as a means to determine the standing of a regime to represent the state in an international proceeding departs from the practice under international law in relation to determining the attribution to the state of acts committed by a governing regime. In the latter analysis, as discussed above, the international recognition (or lack thereof) of a de facto government or revolutionary movement has not been a determining factor.

The substantial reliance on the criterion of international recognition to determine challenges to the standing of a government to represent the state also departs from the practice of national courts when confronted with a similar scenario. For example, in England, the degree of international recognition of an alleged government is only one relevant factor in assessing whether it exists as the government of a state. The English courts instead undertake a multifaceted analysis and consider the following four factors in deciding whether a government exists as the government of a state:

> "(a) whether it is the constitutional government of the state; (b) the degree, nature and stability of administrative control, if any, that it of itself exercises over the territory of the state; (c) whether Her Majesty's Government has any dealings with it and if so what is the nature of those dealings; and (d) in marginal cases, the extent of international recognition that it has as the government of the state".[33]

This is a more complex analysis that considers not only the effectiveness of the government, but also its legality and constitutional status under the applicable municipal law. It is, arguably, a more stringent test than that applied by international courts and tribunals to determine the issue of standing and may arrive at a different result.

In commencing an international claim against a state that is experiencing civil unrest, a claimant should ensure – as best as it can – that the respondent state is represented by the internationally recognized government, even if the subject of the claims raised in the arbitration relate to the acts undertaken by a de facto government or insurrectionary movement with control over the whole or part of the state's territory.

III. FAILURE BY A STATE TO PARTICIPATE IN THE ARBITRATION

The problem of the defaulting respondent is common to all forms of arbitration, irrespective of whether the respondent is a state or not. On the one hand, a respondent in arbitration cannot be permitted to defeat its own consent to arbitration by refusing to participate. On the other hand, where the respondent has not taken active part, the arbitral tribunal (and the subsequent enforcing national court) must ensure that basic norms of due process have been observed. The arbitral tribunal's vigilance in this regard

32. *Ibid.*, paras. 88 and 89.
33. *Republic of Somalia v. Woodhouse Drake & Carey (Suisse) S.A. and Others*, [1993] 1 Q.B. 54, at p. 68. See also *Sierra Leone Telecommunications Co. Ltd. v. Barclays Bank plc.*, [1998] CLC 501.

will likely be heightened in the context of arbitrations against states (whether in the context of a commercial or investment arbitration). Where an award may potentially bind not just a single commercial entity but an entire nation, there may be additional concerns in deciding a case without a presentation of opposing factual accounts, or a full scale adversarial test of the claimant's legal arguments.[34] In light of these concerns, default by a respondent state can lead to significant disruption and delay, as arbitrators seek repeatedly to draw the defaulting respondent into the proceeding, request that claimants provide additional information as necessary to amplify the evidentiary record, or themselves undertake a factual investigation and engage in legal research.

This enhanced inquisitorial role is reflected in the procedural rules that govern ICSID arbitrations. Art. 45 of the ICSID Convention provides that "failure of a party to appear or to present his case shall not be deemed an admission of the other party's assertions". Art. 42 of the ICSID Arbitration Rules, moreover, sets out a specific procedure for circumstances of a defaulting respondent, such that the tribunal "shall examine the jurisdiction of the Centre and its own competence in the dispute" and, as regards the substance of the claims raised, "decide whether the submissions made are well-founded in fact and in law". Thus, although the ICSID system does not permit an absent respondent to prevent the case from being heard, it does not sanction the tribunal to accept the claimant's case at face value. The award in *LETCO v. Liberia*[35] describes the role of an ICSID tribunal faced with a defaulting state respondent:

> "Nevertheless the failure of the Government of Liberia to take part in the present arbitral proceedings does not entitle the claimant to an award in its favour as a matter of right. The onus is still upon the claimant to establish the claim which it has put forward in its Request for Arbitration and other documents.
> (....)
> In this way, the onus of testing the assertions made by the party appearing shifts onto the Tribunal itself. As it is put in the notes to Rule 42:
>
> 'After the Tribunal has, on the expiration of the period of grace, resumed consideration of the Request, the proceeding is no longer fully contentious in the sense that expression is used in national civil procedures; the initiative is shifted to the Tribunal as far as the substantiation of the submissions is concerned. The Tribunal must now *proprio motu* examine:
> ...
> (b) the substantive merit of the assertions made by both parties in order to satisfy itself whether their submissions are well founded in fact and law. To this end, it may call on the active party for observations, evidence or explanations.'
>
> It is this procedure which was followed by the Tribunal in the present arbitration. The Tribunal did not take for granted the assertions of law and fact

34. Noah RUBINS, "Particularities when Dealing with State Entities" in Günther HORVATH and Stephan WILSKE, eds., *Guerrilla Tactics in International Arbitration* (Kluwer 2013) p. 69.
35. *Liberian Eastern Timber Corporation v. Republic of Liberia* (ICSID Case No. ARB/83/2), Award (31 March 1986).

made by the claimant. On the contrary, it submitted them to careful examination: and its award is made on the basis of that examination."[36]

The procedure under ICSID may be contrasted with the position in commercial arbitration, where no provision similar to Art. 42 of the ICSID Arbitration Rules is found among the rules of the major international arbitral institutions. In ICC arbitration, for example, Art. 6(8) of the rules provides that 'if any of the parties refuses or fails to take part in the arbitration or any stage thereof, the arbitration shall proceed notwithstanding such refusal or failure'.[37] It has been argued that, in this sense, commercial arbitration adopts the burden of proof as recognized in many domestic legal systems.[38] Where one party has raised a fact, and provided sufficient evidence to prove that fact prima facie, the burden of proof shifts to the opposing side. If the fact remains uncontroverted by the opposing party, it is accepted by the decision-maker as established, without need for further independent corroboration. While this may be so in relation to a private commercial dispute, arbitral practice suggests that tribunals play an enhanced inquisitorial role when faced with a defaulting respondent state, irrespective of the applicable arbitration rules. For example, the arbitrators in the Libyan oil cases of the 1970s were disturbed by Libya's absence from the proceedings and undertook to fill in for the respondent state in critically reviewing the claimant's case. Judge Lagergren, the sole arbitrator in the *BP v. Libya*[39] *ad hoc* arbitration described his role in the following terms:

> "The facts deemed relevant and taken as established by the Tribunal have been gathered from evidence produced by the Claimant alone. With respect to certain facts the Tribunal has sought and received from the Claimant the submission of additional documentary evidence and explanations. The Tribunal deeply regrets the absence of further elucidation on the part of the Respondent.
>
> With respect to the analysis of the facts and their legal implications the Tribunal has had the benefit of argument presented by the Claimant alone. However, the Tribunal has felt both entitled and compelled to undertake an independent examination of the legal issues deemed relevant by it, and to engage in considerable legal research going beyond the confines of the materials relied upon by the Claimant. The conclusions in the Award therefore are based on a broader consideration of the issues than permitted by format of the Claimant's argument in support of its claims. Thus, the Tribunal to the greatest extent possible has endeavoured to eliminate any adverse effects for the Respondent of its decision not to appear as a party in the proceedings."[40]

---

36. *Ibid.*, paras. 44-47.
37. Although Art. 22.1(iii) of the LCIA Arbitration Rules does empower the arbitral tribunal to "conduct such enquiries as may appear to the Arbitral Tribunal to be necessary or expedient, including whether and to what extent the Arbitral Tribunal should itself take the initiative in identifying relevant issues and ascertaining relevant facts and the laws...".
38. N. RUBINS, "Guerrilla Tactics", fn. 34 above, p. 74.
39. *BP Exploration Co (Libya) Ltd v. Government of the Libyan Arab Republic,* Award (10 October 1973), 53 I.L.R. (1979) p. 297.
40. *Ibid.*, paras. 21 and 22.

In the more recent case of *Bogdanov v. Moldova*,[41] where the respondent state also failed to participate, the Stockholm Chamber of Commerce (SCC) tribunal made a similar observation about the broad scope of enquiry granted to the tribunal in relation to considering legal arguments that may not have been raised by the claimant:

> "[T]he Arbitral tribunal is not limited to the arguments made by the parties, as long as the Arbitral Tribunal limits its evaluation to the facts as presented by the parties, it remains free, within the borders of the applicable law (particularly as long as it remains within the frame of legal sources mentioned in the proceeding), to give the legal qualifications and determine the legal consequences that it deems appropriate, even if they are not pleaded by the parties."[42]

Indeed, it has been argued that the principle of *iura novit curia* (namely, that the tribunal knows the law and that it must apply the law ex officio) should be applied systematically in investment treaty arbitrations, precisely because of the participation of states and the public interest at stake.[43] In circumstances where the sovereign powers of the state are being scrutinized by an arbitral tribunal, it has been suggested that the tribunal should not take the risk of relying on under-researched and incomplete legal arguments presented by the parties.

If the public interest justification is accepted as a legitimate basis for unshackling the tribunal from relying solely on legal arguments raised by the parties in investment arbitration, then such practice should logically apply to all public-private arbitrations where the public interest is at stake and the award has broader implications than the mere parties to the dispute. This is especially so in the event of a defaulting respondent state, where arbitral tribunals appear reluctant to accept the claimant's case at face value without analysis of the substantive merit of the claimant's arguments in order to be satisfied of the claimant's case on the facts and the law.

---

41. *Iurii Bogdanov and Others v. Republic of Moldova* (SCC Case No. 93/2004), Award (22 September 2005).
42. *Ibid.*, para. 4.2.2.2. The cited passage sits uneasily, however, with the award's observations about the tribunal's independent analysis, at para. 3.2.2: "The Arbitral Tribunal did not engage in fact finding or legal investigations on behalf of the Respondent to compensate the latter's lack of assistance: it simply evaluated the facts and legal arguments as presented by the Claimant in order to satisfy itself of their soundness."
43. See, for example, S. SCHILL, "Crafting the International Economic Order", fn. 7 above, p. 422. ("Decision-makers exercising public functions, in particular when reviewing the legality of host state conduct, need to ensure, in view of the systemic impact of their decision, the correct and consistent application of the governing international law.... Consequently, arbitrators in investment treaty cases cannot rely solely on the presentation of the parties with respect to issues of the applicable international law, as is customary in commercial arbitration, and decide on that basis which arguments they consider more convincing. Instead, arbitrators in investment treaty cases, in applying and interpreting international investment treaties, should engage in independent legal research into the issues involved, comprising the recognized sources of international law, including customary law, treaty law, general principles, decisions by national and international courts and tribunals, and the writings of the most qualified publicists of international law.")

IV. REPUDIATION OF THE ARBITRATION AGREEMENT BY A STATE BASED ON ITS INTERNAL LAW

It is not normally improper for a respondent to contest the jurisdiction of an arbitral tribunal. Arbitration can only proceed with the consent of all parties, and it is not unusual for claimants to overreach in launching a case. In this context, jurisdictional objections are only natural. At the same time, such objections have become ubiquitous in arbitration against states. This is especially so in the context of investor-state arbitration where it is almost unheard of that a state would simply accept jurisdiction, such that states maintain, often as a matter of course, the same jurisdictional objections notwithstanding their repeated rejection in prior cases.[44] In the context of commercial arbitration, states seeking to evade arbitration to which they have agreed frequently raise provisions of their internal law that purport to prohibit the state from entering into an arbitration agreement with a private party, notwithstanding the fact that such jurisdictional pleas have been rejected consistently by arbitral tribunals. Indeed, a number of arbitral tribunals and commentators have acknowledged the existence of a substantive rule of "the common law of arbitration" to the effect that international arbitrators should reject a state's invoking its own law to contest the validity of its consent to an arbitration agreement.[45]

Arbitral tribunals have explained the origins of this substantive rule by invoking arguments of good faith or on the basis of international (or transnational) public policy or both. The tribunal in ICC Case No. 1939 first elaborated the rule as follows:

> "International public policy would be strongly opposed to the idea that a public entity, when dealing with foreign parties, could openly, knowingly, and willingly, enter into an arbitration agreement, on which its co-contractor would rely, only to claim subsequently, whether during the arbitral proceedings or on enforcement of the award, that its own undertaking was void."[46]

A number of awards have considered the invocation by the Iranian state or state entities of Art. 139 of the Iranian Constitution, which makes the submission to arbitration of disputes concerning state property conditional upon the approval of the Council of Ministers and notification to Parliament. Such jurisdictional pleas have been consistently rejected. In *Framatome v. Atomic Energy Organization of Iran*, the arbitral tribunal explained the basis for its decision as follows:

44. The motivation for doing so is presumably to increase the length and complexity of the proceedings.
45. Among the many commentaries on this issue, see Jan PAULSSON, "May a State Invoke Its Internal Law to Repudiate Consent to International Commercial Arbitration? Reflections on the *Benteler v. Belgium* Preliminary Award", 2 Arb. Int. (1986) p. 90; and Pierre LALIVE, "Transnational (or Truly International) Public Policy and International Arbitration", in *Comparative Arbitration Practice and Public Policy*, ICCA Congress Series no. 3 (1986) p. 258.
46. *Italian company v. African state-owned entity* (ICC Case No. 1939), Award, cited by Yves DERAINS, "*Le statut des usages du commerce international devant les jurisdictions arbitrales*", 1973 Rev. Arb. p. 122 at p. 145.

> "It is superfluous to add that there is a general principle, which today is universally recognized in relations between states as well as in international relations between private entities (whether the principle be considered a rule of international public policy, an international trade usage, or a principle recognized by public international law, international arbitration law or *lex mercatoria*), whereby the Iranian state would in any event – even if it had intended to do so, which is not the case – be prohibited from reneging on an arbitration agreement entered into by itself or, previously, by a public entity such as AEOI."[47]

Finally, while the tribunal in *Benteler v. Belgium* based its decision that the arbitration agreement in question was valid upon an interpretation of the 1961 European Convention on International Commercial Arbitration, it found support for its decision in the existence of a substantive rule of the "common law of arbitration" by reference to both international public policy and the doctrine of good faith:

> "A third formula, very widely used by international commercial arbitrators, consists in considering the prohibition on arbitration as being contrary to international public order....
>
> Without going that far, one can also conceive that the international arbitrator should dismiss the argument based on this prohibition when the circumstances of the case are such that the state would act *contra factum proprium* in raising it."[48]

It has been suggested that the application of this substantive rule should not be absolute in all circumstances, and that arbitral tribunals should be less ready to reject jurisdictional pleas invoking the state's domestic law without a closer examination of the specific circumstances at play.[49] It is argued, for example, that the principle of good faith would require the state to disclose to its private contracting party at the time of negotiating their contract that a domestic law prevented the state from submitting disputes to arbitration. If the state failed to do so, only a private party who was unaware that the state with which it was contracting was acting in bad faith would be entitled to invoke good faith to resist the jurisdictional challenge raised by the state. Conversely, if the private contractor knew that the state was acting in bad faith and, rather than confronting the state during the contract negotiation stage, accepted the risk of executing a contractual arbitration agreement, then the contractor has waived its right to rely on arguments of good faith.[50] Similarly, it is suggested that there should not be a blanket application of international public policy to dismiss such jurisdictional challenges by states in circumstances where the private contractor knew or should have known –

---

47. *Framatome S.A. v. Atomic Energy Organization of Iran* (ICC Case No. 3896), Award (30 April 1982), 111 J.D.I. (1984) p. 58. See also *Elf Acquitaine Iran v. NIOC*, Award (14 January 1982) *Yearbook* XI (1986) p. 97.
48. *Benteler v. Belgium*, Award (18 November 1993), 1989 Rev. Arb. p. 39.
49. Eduardo SILVA ROMERO, "Some Remarks on the Contribution of ICC Arbitrators to the Development of International Commercial Arbitration Involving States and State Entities" in Andrea CARLEVARIS, ed., *International Arbitration Under Review, Essays in Honour of John Beechey* (ICC 2015) p. 401.
50. *Ibid.*, p. 405.

through its contractual due diligence, which foreign investors now routinely conduct with the assistance of knowledgeable legal advisers – that the state was not permitted to submit disputes to arbitration.[51]

While it is suggested that basic justice militates against an unconditional protection of private contractors and application of a regime of unqualified liability in the event that the state seeks to elude the arbitration agreement, there is scant evidence that legislators and/or arbitrators are willing to undertake such a nuanced approach. Thus, not only have a number of national arbitration statutes adopted an unqualified approach to liability when arbitrators are confronted with a jurisdictional plea raised by the state invoking its internal law,[52] but the raising of such pleas and their endorsement by the domestic courts of the state have been held by arbitral tribunals to constitute a violation of the fair and equitable treatment obligation of states owed to foreign investors pursuant to investment protection treaties.[53]

V. A STATE'S INTERFERENCE WITH THE ARBITRATION PROCESS THROUGH THE EXERCISE OF ITS POLICE POWERS

The final part of this paper considers three instances where the state's exercise of its police powers have undermined, or at least threatened to undermine, whether deliberately or not, the integrity of the arbitration proceedings and prejudiced the private party's claim against the state. Faced with the state's coercive reach against the claimant, its witnesses and counsel (and even the arbitrators themselves), arbitrators have adopted a multitude of ways to maintain a level playing field in the arbitration and to safeguard the equality of arms between the public and private litigants, while recognizing a state's legitimate exercise of its police powers.

In *Libananco v. Turkey*,[54] an ICSID tribunal was confronted with an application, which the tribunal described as akin to a request for summary judgment, in the face of evidence that the Turkish public prosecutor had intercepted the email communications of the claimant and its arbitration counsel. It was alleged that Turkey had obtained access to nearly 2,000 privileged and/or confidential communications between the claimant's counsel and their clients, contacts and potential witnesses in Turkey. The claimant

51. *Ibid.*, p. 407.
52. Art. 177(2) of the Swiss Private International Law Act is a good example of such a statute: "A state, or an enterprise held by, or an organization controlled by a state, which is party to an arbitration agreement, cannot invoke its own law in order to contest its capacity to arbitrate or the arbitrability of a dispute covered by the arbitration agreement."
53. See, for example, *France Telecom Mobile International, S.A. and FTML S.A.L. v. the Lebanese Republic*, Award (31 January 2005) paras. 71-78. In this case, Lebanon had argued that an ICC arbitration agreement contained in the contract between the Lebanese government and FTML for the construction and operation of a mobile telephony network was null and void as a matter of Lebanese law, as was subsequently affirmed by the Lebanese Conseil d'Etat. The arbitral tribunal subsequently held that the state's revocation of the ICC arbitration agreement constituted a breach of Lebanon's obligation under the France-Lebanon bilateral investment treaty to accord French investors fair and equitable treatment.
54. *Libananco Holdings Co. v. Turkey* (ICSID Case No. ARB/06/8), Decision on Preliminary Issues (23 June 2008).

argued that the respondent's "conduct towards the claimant, counsel and its witnesses had made it impossible – indeed unsafe – to continue the prosecution of this case in its present form".[55] While the claimant had initially requested the tribunal to exclude the respondent from the rest of the proceedings, its position was later refined, with the claimant instead maintaining that the tribunal should determine the contested issues of jurisdiction and the merits of the claimant's claim on the basis of the evidence before it without receiving any further evidence from either party.[56]

Turkey acknowledged that the interception of the claimant's communications by the Turkish police had taken place as part of an investigation ordered by the public prosecutor, but the respondent argued that the investigation was not directed at the claimant's arbitration claim or its counsel, but rather was concerned with an alleged bank fraud. The respondent argued that it possessed "an undeniable entitlement to conduct investigation into crime, particularly serious crime, within its jurisdiction",[57], which could not be halted merely because an ICSID claim was pending. Moreover, while admitting that the claimant's counsel had been placed "on a comprehensive list of those [email addresses] thought to have been used for communication with a particular suspect", Turkey informed the tribunal that this did not reflect any desire to review attorney-client communications, much less any plan to pass those communications to Turkey's arbitration counsel. In reinforcement of this last point, Turkey's counsel gave personal assurances that they had neither been offered nor seen such materials. In sum, Turkey argued that "no actual prejudice" was caused to the claimant, and the matter should rest there.[58]

The tribunal made clear that it took this situation with utmost seriousness, finding that it struck at principles which lie at the heart of the ICSID arbitral process, including the principles of "basic procedural fairness, respect for confidentiality and legal privilege (and indeed immunities accorded to parties, their counsel, and witnesses under Articles 21 and 22 of the ICSID Convention); the right of parties both to seek advice and to advance their respective cases freely and without interference".[59] The tribunal described its duty to ensure a level playing field as follows:

> "Nor does the Tribunal doubt for a moment that, like any other international tribunal, it must be regarded as endowed with inherent powers required to preserve the integrity of its own process – even if the remedies open to it are necessarily different from those that might be available to a domestic court of law in an ICSID Member State. The Tribunal would express the principle as being that parties have an obligation to arbitrate fairly and in good faith and that an arbitral tribunal has the inherent jurisdiction to ensure that this obligation is complied with; this principle applies in all arbitration, including investment arbitration and to all parties, including States (even in the exercise of their sovereign powers)."[60]

55. *Ibid.*, para. 43.
56. *Ibid.*, para. 73.
57. *Ibid.*, para. 75.
58. *Ibid.*, para. 76.
59. *Ibid.*, para. 78.
60. *Ibid.*, para. 78.

The tribunal, nevertheless, declined to grant the relief sought by the claimant and accepted the state's assurances that no privileged information had been misused. It then set out a series of orders to ensure that this remained the case. In so doing, while the tribunal accepted that a "sovereign state does indeed have a right and duty to pursue the commission of serious crime, and that that right and duty cannot be affected by the existence of an ICSID arbitration against it", the tribunal rejected the state's comment that "the prosecutors' understanding, interest and patience for this offshore international arbitration ... are understandably limited".[61] Indeed, the tribunal warned Turkey that, going forward, its duty to investigate crime could not be exercised without regard to other rights and duties and a criminal investigation could not baulk an ICSID arbitration. In issuing orders in relation to the future conduct of the arbitration, the tribunal forewarned the respondent state that if it turned out that the respondent has used, in any way, privileged or confidential information obtained during the surveillance, "severe prejudice may apply" and the tribunal may consider other remedies "apart from the exclusion of improperly obtained evidence or information".[62]

Faced with challenging circumstances, the *Libananco* tribunal adopted a pragmatic approach in seeking to balance, on the one hand, the state's prerogative to exercise its police powers in a legitimate manner to combat crime notwithstanding the state's engagement in an international arbitration, with, on the other hand, the concern to ensure a level playing field is maintained between the litigants. In so doing, the tribunal affirmed its inherent powers to take the steps necessary to ensure the integrity of the proceedings – without spelling out what this may mean in practice – and set out a standard of conduct against which the parties would be assessed based on their duty to litigate fairly and in good faith. In this regard, and without expressly acknowledging it, the *Libananco* tribunal followed the reasoning previously adopted by the NAFTA tribunal in *Methanex v. US*,[63] where the claimant was alleged to have used private detectives to search through the garbage of a third party in an effort to find documents in support of its claim against the United States. The tribunal found that the company's evidence-gathering methods had involved trespassing and other illegal conduct and, thus, excluded the documents from the arbitration. In the process, the tribunal made the following observations about the standards of conducted expected of the parties:

> "The Disputing Parties each owed in this arbitration a general duty to the other and to the Tribunal to conduct themselves in good faith during these arbitration proceedings and to respect the equality of arms between them, the principles of 'equal treatment' and procedural fairness also required by Article 15(1) of the UNCITRAL Rules. As a general principle, therefore, just as it would be wrong for the USA to *ex hypothesi* misuse its intelligence assets to spy on [the claimant] (and its witnesses) and to introduce into evidence the resulting materials into this arbitration, so too would it be wrong for [the claimant] to introduce evidential materials obtained by [the claimant] unlawfully."[64]

61. *Ibid.*, para. 79
62. *Ibid.*, para. 80.
63. *Methanex Corporation v. United States*, Final Award on Jurisdiction and Merits (3 August 2005).
64. *Ibid.*, part II, para. 54.

Here again, the tribunal affirmed the parties' duty to respect the equality of arms and expressly curtailed the prospect of a state's resort to its police powers in a manner that perverted the principle of equal treatment and the obligation to litigate fairly and in good faith.

A more recent example of a state seeking to rely on documents procured through the exercise of its coercive powers arose in the contractual arbitration brought by Pearl Petroleum against the Kurdistan Regional Government of Iraq (the KRG).[65] In this case, the vehicle of one of the claimants' officers, also a witness in the arbitration, was intercepted at gunpoint while travelling to the airport in Erbil, the capital of the Kurdistan Region of Iraq. After having established his identity, the armed assailants confiscated the portable computer and mobile telephone of the claimants' witness and fled, without taking any other valuable items. The stolen computer contained an extensive record of confidential information relating to the dispute, including privileged communications with the claimants' arbitration counsel. Shortly thereafter, documents from the stolen computer began to be submitted in the arbitration by the respondent in support of its case, notwithstanding warnings from the claimants that using stolen documents would be a serious breach of professional duty by the KRG's counsel. In response, the respondent's counsel explained that the KRG was carrying out a criminal investigation of the claimants and their employees involving matters of national security and that "the KRG had obtained documents within the Kurdistan Region that are related to the Claimants' operations in the Kurdistan Region, pursuant to this investigation and in the exercise of the Kurdistan Region's security and policy powers". The respondent's counsel further explained that the KRG had provided counsel with documents in its possession and had confirmed that they were acquired lawfully. Further, that a third-party screening procedure was put in place to ensure that the KRG's counsel did not receive legally privileged documents or information.

The practical effect of this screening procedure was the drip-feed submission by the KRG in the arbitration of the claimants' internal documents in redacted form in support of the KRG's case. Leaving aside whether the documents had been obtained by the KRG through a lawful investigation or legal process (a matter which was contested), the conduct of the KRG and its counsel undermined the integrity of the arbitration and raised two questions of broader application. First, whether material obtained by the state in the context of a criminal investigation may be legitimately deployed in an international arbitration involving an unrelated commercial dispute; and, secondly, what are the obligations of the state's arbitration counsel to investigate the provenance of such material before they are deployed in the arbitration beyond accepting at face value the assurances of their client that they were lawfully obtained. While each case must be considered on its facts, the standards enunciated by the *Libananco* and *Methanex* tribunals as regards assessing the conduct of the parties against their duties of arbitrating fairly and in good faith establish a sound framework to consider the first question: a state may not misuse its police powers to obtain materials and to introduce the resulting materials in the arbitration. Exclusion of such material from the evidentiary record is necessary to preserve the equality of arms between the public and private parties. The position is less

65. *Pearl Petroleum Company Limited and others v. The Regional Government of the Kurdistan* (LCIA Case No. 132527).

clear-cut with respect to the second question, because of the relative paucity of sanctions that an international arbitral tribunal may bring to bear against counsel who have fallen short in their conduct. Notwithstanding recent efforts to empower arbitral tribunals to address matters of deficient conduct by counsel,[66] the knowing or uncritical use of ill-gotten materials in an arbitration may well lead to complaints being raised before the relevant professional bar associations, which are, arguably, more appropriate forums for assessing whether counsel's conduct falls short of the requisite ethical standards.[67]

Finally, while arbitral tribunals possess a variety of tools at their disposal to restrain the misuse of a state party's police powers at the expense of the opposing party in the arbitration, the tribunal's task becomes more complicated when the arbitrators themselves are the target of the state's coercive measures. The most brazen example of a state party's interference with the integrity of an arbitral tribunal arose in the *Himpurna* case.[68] In advance of a final hearing that was due to be held at The Hague (in defiance of injunctions issued by the Indonesian courts enjoining the arbitration subject to a penalty of US$ 1 million per day), the arbitrator appointed by the Indonesian state (Professor H. Priyatna Abdurrasyid) was intercepted upon his arrival at Schiphol airport in the Netherlands, prevented from participating at the arbitration hearing, and told that he would be accompanied back to Jakarta.[69] While Indonesia succeeded in ensuring that the evidentiary hearing would not proceed in the absence of Professor Priyatna, the arbitral tribunal nonetheless continued the case in truncated form and proceeded to complete its mandate and issue a final award.[70] The tribunal found support in international law for its decision to continue as a truncated tribunal:

> "Although the Republic of Indonesia's readiness to sabotage these proceedings gave rise to an extraordinary event, the Arbitral Tribunal has not found it necessary to innovate in order to ensure the fulfilment of its mandate under the Terms of Appointment. The weight of well-established international authority makes clear that an arbitral tribunal has not only the right, but the obligation, to proceed when, without legal excuse, one of its members fails to act, withdraws or – although not the case here – even purports to resign.
> (….)

---

66. See, for example, Art. 18.6 of the 2014 LCIA Arbitration Rules that empowers the tribunal to sanction the parties' legal representatives if their conduct falls short of the standards set forth in the General Guidelines for the Parties' Legal Representatives. Also, the remedies for misconduct available to arbitral tribunals under Arts. 26 and 27 of the IBA Guidelines on Party Representation in International Arbitration (2013), whenever the Guidelines have been adopted by the parties.
67. See, Bernard HANOTIAU, "Misdeeds, Wrongful Conduct and Illegality in Arbitral Proceedings" in *International Commercial Arbitration: Important Contemporary Questions,* ICCA Congress Series no. 11 (2002) p. 261 at p. 287.
68. *Himpurna California Energy Ltd. v. Republic of Indonesia*, Interim Award (26 September 1999), *Yearbook* XXV (2000) p. 109.
69. *Ibid.*, paras. 95 to 99, which include three eyewitness accounts of Professor Priyatna at Schiphol airport being escorted back to Jakarta by Indonesian agents.
70. *Himpurna California Energy Ltd. v. Republic of Indonesia*, Final Award (16 October 1999), *Yearbook* XXV (2000) p. 186.

> The Republic of Indonesia should not benefit from Professor Priyatna's absence. Finding that there is no valid excuse for it, the Arbitral Tribunal proceeds to fulfil its mandate and render this Final Award."[71]

Preventing an arbitrator from participating in the proceedings is certainly the most remarkable measure to which a state can resort – especially when it involves coerced repatriation. While such measures are certainly shocking and liable to be extremely disruptive, as the *Himpurna* case demonstrates, international arbitral tribunals have the necessary powers at their disposal to complete their mandate while maintaining the equality of arms between the parties and protecting the legitimacy of the arbitral process.

71. *Ibid.*, paras. 43 and 68. The tribunal relied upon the extensive writings of Judge Stephen Schwebel on the topic of truncated tribunals and drew upon past examples from international arbitral practice, including the practice of the Iran-U.S. Claims Tribunal, in support of its decision to continue in truncated form:

> "Withdrawal of an arbitrator from an international arbitral tribunal which is not authorised or approved by the tribunal is a wrong under customary international law and the general principles of law recognised and applied in the practice of international arbitration. It generally will constitute a violation of the treaty or contract constituting the tribunal, if not in terms then because the intention of the parties normally cannot be deemed to have authorised such withdrawal."

Public-Private Arbitrations: The Substantive Issues of Arbitrability, Mandatory Rules and Public Policy – The Latin American Experience

Gilberto Giusti[*]

TABLE OF CONTENTS PAGE

I. HISTORICAL BACKGROUND – LATIN AMERICAN NATIONALISM IN THE TWENTIETH CENTURY

The centrality of the state both in role and in concept was the prevailing component of politics in most Latin American countries until the mid-1980s. In the political arena, state paternalism and its consequent entrenched government bureaucracy have tremendously encumbered all aspects of private enterprise in Latin America over most part of the twentieth century. In the legal scenario, legislation was usually embedded with nationalism and protectionism.

As a result, the economic relationship between the state and the private sector practically boiled down to instruments in which the state played a supreme contract role with most of its rights labelled inalienable or not at the parties' free disposition (*direitos indisponíveis*) and therefore not subject to any dispute resolution method other than the respective national court system.

With respect to state investment disputes, investors were defenceless against the expropriation of their investments by the governments of host countries, as there were no effective channels or mechanisms available to recover what they had lost. In some cases, if an investor had political influence, it could exert pressure on the expropriating state to recover such investment, or at least some of it to mitigate losses. In other events, the investor resorted to its own state for diplomatic negotiations with the expropriating state and potential recovery of investments. Nonetheless, this solution could eventually lead to diplomatic conflicts, and the investor not always obtaining the protection expected from its state against the expropriating act of another state.

The alternative was to look to the Judiciary for investment protection. But this course of action faced even higher obstacles. When resorting to the courts of any state involved,

* Partner, Pinheiro Neto Advogados in São Paulo, Brazil.

the neutrality of jurisdiction would surely come to the fore, the more so if the courts sitting in the place of investment were chosen. In either case, the courts would be subject to political pressure, which would escalate in a direct relation to the values at issue.

On the other hand, if the courts of a (neutral) third state were chosen, an unbiased decision could indeed be obtained, but it would hardly be enforced by the defeated party of its own free will. In other words, this decision would figure as a moral victory only; its enforcement would once again be subject to the goodwill of the courts in the country of the defeated party, where the concepts of public interest and national sovereignty could be broadly interpreted by local courts.

As to resolution of commercial disputes arising out of a contractual relationship between public and private parties, uncertainty also prevailed. Irrespective of the nature of the contract at hand, the long-lasting concept of public interest would normally be invoked to set aside any dispute resolution method other than the jurisdiction of the courts of the domicile of the relevant public contracting party. In Brazil, for example, notwithstanding the enactment of the Arbitration Act in 1996, it took almost ten years for case law to consolidate the understanding that the state and its related entities can (in some cases they should, as seen below) indeed submit their contractual disputes with private individuals and corporations to arbitration.

These were all reminiscences of the Calvo Doctrine, a body of international rules that rejected international investment arbitration, as well as of the deeply rooted concept of national sovereignty and the supremacy of the state.

II. SIGNIFICANT CHANGES STARTING IN THE EARLY 1990S

As global capitalism developed, most Latin American countries realized that they would not properly benefit from the intensification of the international flow of capital without opening up their economies and modernizing their legal systems. Consequently, changes in the state, the society and the economy have occurred over the past three decades in the region in order to develop a set of new perspectives on Latin American politics and economics.

This important move to internationalism included the promotion of policies to encourage the entry and participation of foreign investment in the relevant host sates, the adoption of a set of rules to foster public-private contracts and related dispute resolution methods.

1. Investment-Related Disputes – The Washington Convention

In the late 1980s and early 1990s, many Latin American countries finally ratified the Convention on the Settlement of Investment Disputes between States and Nationals of Other States, also known as "the Washington Convention", as proposed by the World Bank in March 1965 and effective as from 14 October 1966:

State	Signature	Deposit of Ratification	Entry into Force
Argentina	21 May 1991	19 Oct 1994	18 Nov 1994
Chile	25 Jan 1991	24 Sep 1991	24 Oct 1991
Costa Rica	29 Sep 1981	27 Apr 1993	May 27, 1993
Dominican Republic	20 Mar 2000		
El Salvador	09 Jun 1982	06 May 1984	05 Apr 1984
Guatemala	09 Nov 1995	Jan 21, 2003	20 Feb 2003
Guyana	03 Jul 1969	11 Jul 1969	10 Aug 1969
Haiti	30 Jan 1985	27 Oct 2009	26 Nov 2009
Honduras	28 May 1986	14 Feb 1989	16 Mar 1989
Mexico	11 Jan 2018		
Nicaragua	04 Feb 1994	20 Mar 1995	19 Apr 1995
Panama	22 Nov 1995	Apr 08, 1996	08 May 1996
Paraguay	27 Jul 1981	07 Jan 1983	06 Feb 1983
Peru	04 Sep 1991	09 Aug 1993	08 Sep 1993

The adhesion of most Latin American countries to the Washington Convention and the respective World Bank's International Centre for Settlement of Investment Disputes (ICSID) three decades ago was enthusiastically celebrated in the international economic and legal communities. In practice, however, it ended up showing that such massive adhesion was a result of concerns by some Latin American states that hostility toward ICSID could hamper access to World Bank credit, rather than a genuine will to adopt and accept that dispute resolution system.

This may explain why Brazil did not follow this trend of adhesion to the ICSID and remains as the only major economy in Latin America that has never signed the Washington Convention.[1]

The Argentine Crisis of 2001 following the end of the peso's fixed exchange rate to the US dollar led to a large number of claims by international investors before the ICSID. Some controversial decisions by arbitration panels and the constant and sometimes virulent challenges to the course of the respective proceedings raised by Argentine authorities reignited for some time the protectionist wave in Latin America based on the traditional doctrine of national sovereignty and public interest.

The first Latin American country to denounce the Washington Convention was Bolivia in November 2007, followed by Ecuador in 2009 and Venezuela in 2013. Since then, there have been rumours that Argentina would also withdraw from the Convention, which has never materialized. Conversely, Mexico has very recently (January 2018) subscribed to the ICSID Convention and initiated the process for deposit of the respective instrument of ratification.

1. Mexico has subscribed to the ICSID Convention in January 2018 and initiated the process for deposit of the respective instrument of ratification.

Moreover, the apparent displeasure with ICSID in some Latin American countries has not significantly affected the number of investment disputes involving at least South American countries, as shown below:[2]

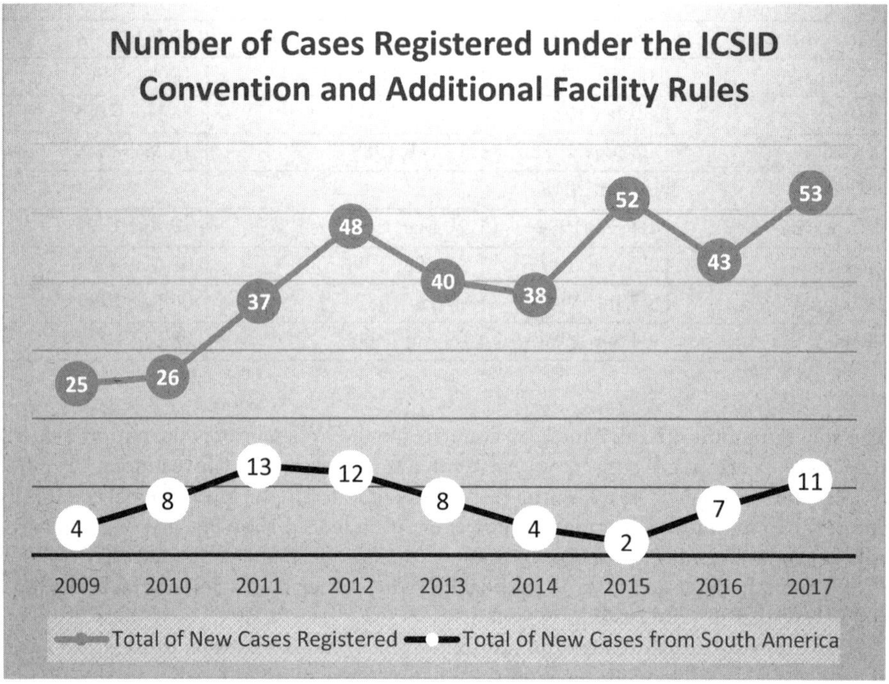

2. The classification of the geographic distribution since 2009 is available at: <https://icsid.worldbank.org/en/Pages/resources/ICSID-Caseload-Statistics.aspx>.

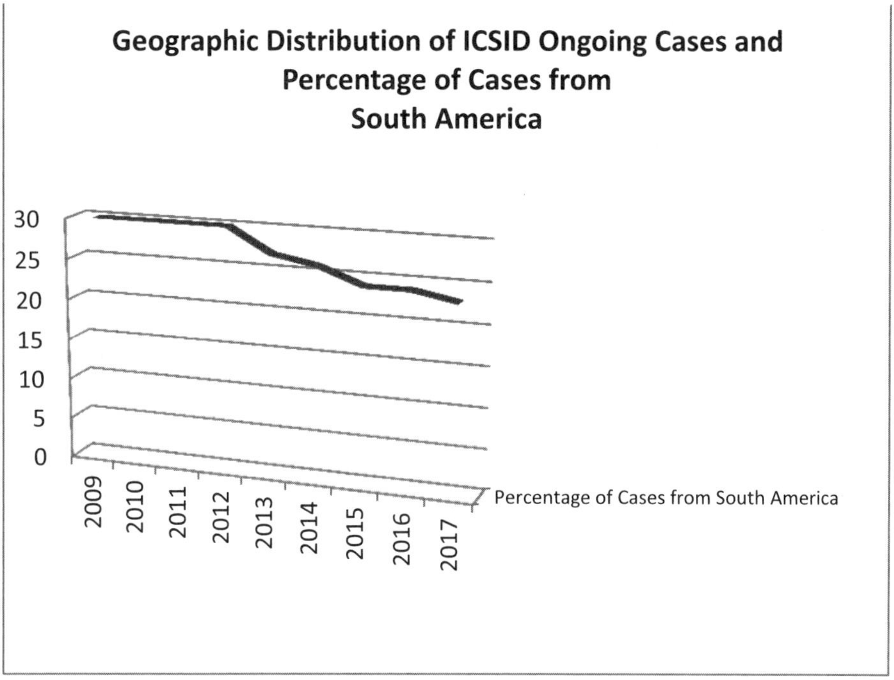

As can be seen, although the number of ICSID ongoing cases involving a South American country has decreased a little from 2009 to 2017 under a worldwide percentage perspective (second chart), the actual number of newly registered cases has indeed increased from four in 2009 to eleven in 2017 (first chart).

2. *Public-Private Arbitration*

While the discussion about adhesion to the Washington Convention was going on, and irrespective of its outcome, most Latin American countries realized that fostering public-private contractual instruments was also important (and actually indispensable in those countries that did not adhere to ICSID, such as Brazil) as a means of transforming the state in such a manner that it would be capable of adjusting to the new demands of the contemporary world. This proved particularly true in view of the privatization wave that spread over Latin America in the early 1990s.

Privatization occurred in different levels and even for different priorities in Latin America, depending on the relevant political and ideological streams prevailing at the time. Fiscal benefits have been a driving force, for instance, in Argentina when privatization was first launched. In Central America, the purpose of "social investment" has been emphasized to justify privatization. Mexico has valued privatization as part of the government's drive toward modernization and economic structural reform. In

Brazil, political expediency and the need to reduce the deficit played important roles in the government's privatization programme.

In common, all countries realized that the entrenched culture of statism – which was aggravated over the decades through large-scale nationalizations and the creation of parastatal enterprises impregnated with inefficient bureaucracies – was leading to the degeneration of the state apparatus itself. The consequences were (a) domestically, the rapid aggravation of the social and economic inequity between the rich and the poor; and (b) internationally, the risk of Latin America staying behind in the global distribution of wealth.

To correct[3] this course of events and related consequences, the regulation on public contracts as well as the concept of public-private partnership (PPP) were both reviewed and/or implemented in many Latin American countries since 1990 by means of modernization of local legislations.

At this point, it is important to emphasize that most Latin American countries are civil law jurisdictions in which a distinction may exist between public contracts such as concessions (where the private party provides a service directly to the public and takes end-user risk) and public-private partnerships (where the private party delivers a service to a public party against a fee).

For the purpose of this paper, whose main objective is to address current issues related to public-private arbitration, reference will be made – as applicable – to public contracts and/or to PPPs to define all types of instruments to which, as contract parties, on one side, government entities, autarchies, public foundations, state-owned companies and/or mixed-capital corporations stand, and, on the other side, individuals and/or corporations outside of the public sector stand.

The legal framework for public contracts and PPPs has steadily developed In Latin America over the past thirty years. Chile and Colombia have more than twenty-five years of experience and frameworks are extremely well developed. In Brazil, for example, the following legislation came into effect within this period: Public Procurement and Contract Law (1993), Concessions of Public Services Law (1995), Public-Private Partnerships Law (2004), among others. More recently, Argentina, Costa Rica and Nicaragua have also developed new legal frameworks for PPPs.

At the same time, many legal systems in Latin America have welcomed more efficient means of solving disputes, either by revising their judicial systems in order to make court proceedings more reliable and expeditious, or – and mainly – by introducing out-of-court proceedings such as arbitration.

In this sense, various countries have adopted arbitration laws based, in substantial part, on the Model Law on International Commercial Arbitration of the United Nations Commission on International Trade Law (the UNCITRAL Model Law), thus leading to legal convergence across the region. In addition, practically all Latin American countries have ratified the Convention on the Recognition and Enforcement of Foreign Arbitral Awards, also known as 1958 the New York Convention.

3. The author does not express any political and/or ideological opinion, but rather provides just an objective overview of historical facts.

The statistics of the International Chamber of Commerce (ICC) confirm that Latin America is currently one of the most active regions with respect to arbitrations. In 2016, the ICC Statistics show that:

– 339 parties from Latin America participated in ICC cases, out of 966 new ICC cases in 2016 (35.09%);
– as to the nationality of the Latin American parties, 123 were Brazilian (the fifth-most worldwide), 107 Mexican, 28 Peruvian, 13 Colombian, 13 Chilean, 12 Costa Rican and 11 Panamanian; and
– numerous Latin American arbitrators were confirmed by the ICC in 2016: 200 Brazilian, 32 Mexican and 17 Argentinian, among others.

Of the 966 new cases filed with the ICC in 2016, 106 (11.0%) had a state or a state entity as one or more of the parties.[4] For the purposes of comparison, in 2006, 590 cases were filed before the ICC[5], 62 of which (10.05%) involved a state or a parastatal entity:[6]

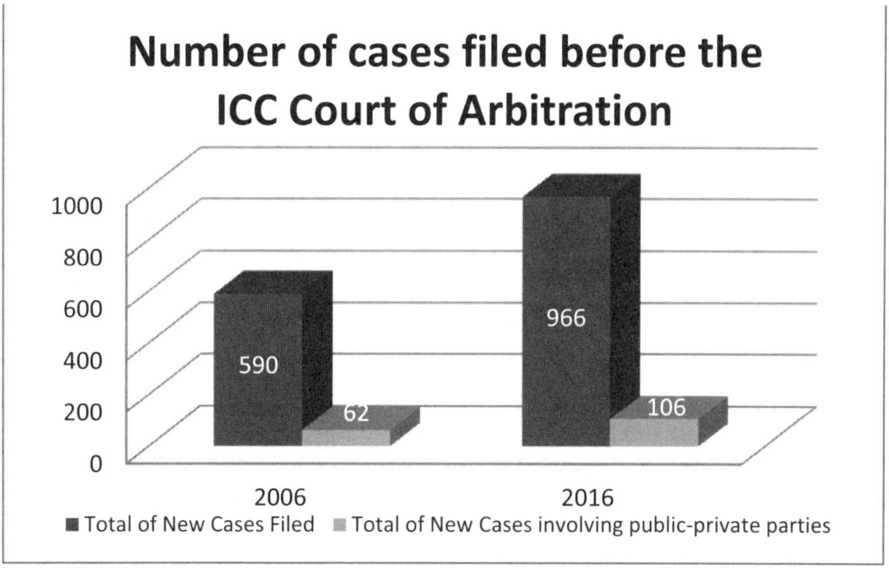

4. 2016 ICC Dispute Resolution Statistics. "Some 11% of cases filed in 2016 involved states or parties under state ownership (parastatals). The majority of the 123 state and parastatal parties in these filings came from countries with state-led economies, as reflected in the regional distribution shown below." Available at: <http://library.iccwbo.org/dr-bulletins.htm?AUTH=7677fd17-4350-&Timeframe=>.

5. The statistics considers not only ongoing arbitral proceedings, but all the Requests for Arbitrations submitted during a 1 year period.

6. 2006 ICC Dispute Resolution Statistics. Available at: <http://library.iccwbo.org/content/dr/STATISTICAL_REPORTS/SR_0023.htm?l1=Bulletins&l2=ICC+International+Court+of+Arbitration+Bulletin+Vol.18%2FNo.1+-+Eng&AUTH=7677fd17-4350-&Timeframe=#TOC_BKL1_1>.

As can be seen, although in terms of percentage of the total number of new cases there has been no significant increase between 2006 (10.05%) and 2016 (11.0%), the actual number of newly registered cases involving at least one state entity has increased from 62 to 106 (58.5%) in the same period. There is no indication as to how many of these 106 public-private arbitrations would involve a least one party from Latin America, but it is reasonable to infer that approximately the same 35.09% would apply, i.e., around 37 public-private arbitrations from Latin America.

III. THE SUBSTANTIVE ISSUES THAT PERSIST IN PUBLIC-PRIVATE ARBITRATIONS: ARBITRABILITY, MANDATORY RULES AND PUBLIC POLICY

Based on the foregoing, it is fair to say that Latin America has successfully moved from a rigid regime of statism and protectionism to a friendlier environment for international arbitration. This is a remarkable move if one considers that only thirty years ago there was no regulatory framework that accepted arbitration – even on a domestic level – as an effective and enforceable dispute resolution system.

When it comes to disputes involving public entities, however, special attention by the contracting parties should be given to the issues of arbitrability, mandatory rules and public policy.

1. *Arbitrability*

As mentioned above, resolution of disputes arising out of a contractual relationship between public and private parties in Latin America was invariably affected by uncertainty in view of the absolute supremacy of state's interests over private interests. Considering the reminiscences of the Calvo Doctrine referred to above, it is easy to understand that many scholars and judges in Latin America were reluctant – even under the newly enacted Arbitration Acts – to accept that the state and public entities could be subject to an out-of-court arbitration panel sometimes seating outside of the relevant country.

In the absence of a clear definition of or at least a consolidated case law on (i) those who were free to enter into an arbitration agreement and be bound by it (subjective arbitrability), and of (ii) the matters at the parties' disposition that could be decided by arbitration (objective arbitrability), uncertainty about public-private arbitration remained present in the legal system of some Latin American countries for quite a long time.

In Brazil, in the early 2000s, the *COPEL v. Araucaria* case put the credibility of arbitration to a test that caught the attention of the international legal community. UEG-Araucaria, the Brazilian subsidiary of a US company, initiated an ICC arbitration in Paris against COPEL, a Brazilian state-controlled power company in a dispute arising out of a turnkey contract for a power plant in Brazil. A series of first-instance and appellate-instance decisions ordered the stay of the arbitration proceedings under the argument that – irrespective of the fact that the parties had indeed agreed to refer their controversies to arbitration and that the dispute between the parties was of an economic nature – the dispute was not arbitrable because "it involved public interests".

The *COPEL* case was settled before a final decision was granted but the disruption it caused in the arbitral legal community only ceased in 2005 when the Brazilian Superior Court of Justice ruled on the *AES Uruguaiana v. CEEE* case. AES Uruguaiana was a private power company, CEEE was a mixed-economy company controlled by the state of Rio Grande do Sul, and the dispute related to a contract for the construction and operation of a 600MW gas-fired power plant. As in the *COPEL* case, the first-instance court ruled that the dispute could not be submitted to arbitration because it concerned a state-controlled entity whose assets were affected by "public finality" and therefore could not be disposed of. Furthermore, the appellate-instance court refused to recognize the negative effect of the arbitration agreement and invoked the principle of universal access to justice as set forth in the Brazilian Constitution[7] to conclude that the presence of an arbitration clause in the contract could not prevent a dispute from being heard by state courts.

In 2005, the Brazilian Superior Court of Justice overturned the *AES Uruguaiana v. CEEE* previous decisions and ruled that public entities (such as CEEE, a mixed-economy corporation controlled by the State of Rio Grande do Sul) are capable of entering into arbitration agreements and later on should be subject to the competent arbitration proceedings as long as the dispute relates to secondary public interests (i.e., those concerning financial and economic aspects only). It was expressly decided that:

> "Contract is valid when signed by the mixed capital companies exploiting economic activity such as production or commercialization of goods or services (Federal Constitution, Article 173, Sect. 1) and stipulating arbitration as the means to solve any disputes arising from the adjustment."[8]

The issue of arbitrability of rights and obligations arising from public contracts is so sensitive in civil law jurisdictions that were influenced by the Napoleonic Code that the Brazilian legislator deemed it appropriate to make the law clearer on this. In 2015, some of the dispositions of the Brazilian Arbitration Law (enacted in 1996) were amended and paras. 1 and 2 were added to Art. 1 of the Law:

> "Article 1. Those who are capable of entering into contracts may make use of arbitration to resolve conflicts regarding freely transferable property rights.
> *Paragraph 1*. Direct and indirect public administration may use arbitration to resolve conflicts regarding transferable public property rights.
> *Paragraph 2*. The competent authority or direct public administration entity that enters into arbitration agreements is the same entity that enters into agreements or transactions"

7. Brazilian Federal Constitution, Art. 5, Sect. XXXV – "The law shall not exclude any injury or threat to a right from the consideration of the Judicial Power."
8. Brazilian Superior Court of Justice, Second Chamber, Special Appeal No. 612.439/RS, Reporting Justice João Otávio de Noronha, ruled on 25 October.

Besides the main arbitration acts adopted by most Latin American countries, the principle of the arbitrability of disputes involving state entities is reaffirmed in the specific legislation on PPPs and other public contracts.[9]

2. *Mandatory Rules*

One of the most crucial questions in international arbitration is whether relevant mandatory rules that are foreign to the parties' designated applicable law of the contract can or should be applied by the arbitral tribunal. Generally, mandatory rules protect the social and economic interests of a society.

As a rule, arbitrators should respect to the greatest possible extent the general principle of party autonomy as to the law chosen by the parties to govern the relevant contractual obligations, as well as the arbitration procedural rules. Application of mandatory rules foreign to the freely elected set of rules should be accepted by the arbitrators mainly with a view to guaranteeing future enforcement of the award, especially in the jurisdiction that contemplates said rules. The most commonly cited mandatory rules are competition law, securities regulation, public service regulations and currency control.

This approach is valid for disputes arising out of contracts to which all parties are private, as well as for those involving public and private parties. As far as public-private arbitration is concerned, however, arbitrators should take special caution in applying mandatory rules that derive from a legal system outside of the chosen law of the contract.

If the mandatory rules applied by the arbitrators derive from the legal system of the state party, the result of the arbitration may be considered oppressive to the private party. In case the mandatory rules derive from the legal system of the private party, the state party may question the result of the arbitration because it violated the more strict will that is proper to public entities. When deciding whether to apply relevant mandatory rules in this scenario, arbitrators should therefore be particularly mindful of the award's enforceability.

Mandatory rules of relevant national legal systems that may be applied by the arbitrators are of a substantive nature, i.e., a substantive law that will guide the tribunal's decision on the merits. The laws that regulate and support the procedural aspects of the arbitration (lex arbitri) are usually the laws of the seat of arbitration, which is freely chosen by the parties.

Some of the recent Latin American legislations on public-private contracts, however, have prescribed the place where any arbitral tribunal should seat, as well as the language in which the arbitration should be conducted, which in principle collides with the free will principle.

This is the case, for example, of Art. 11, item III, of the Brazilian PPP Law of 2004, which provides that any arbitration relating to a PPP contract (both domestic and international) must be conducted in Brazil and in the Portuguese language. This extravagant legal provision has not been scrutinized by any local or foreign court or

9. In Brazil, Article 23-A of Law No. 8.987 of 1995 (Concessions Law), Article 11, III, of Law No. 11.079 of 2004 (the PPP Law).

arbitration panel yet, and therefore it remains uncertain whether it will be regarded as a mandatory rule to which the parties and the arbitrators should be bound.

In any event, this legal provision makes recourse to arbitration in disputes related to PPPs unattractive and once again reveals that nationalism and protectionism have not been completely extirpated from the Latin American legal scenario yet.

3. *Public Policy*

The broad concept of public policy, together with the concept of national sovereignty, has supported the nationalistic and protectionist position taken by Latin American countries until the last quarter of the twentieth century, as seen above. Since then, both concepts have been adapted to reflect the opening-up of most jurisdictions in the region to international methods of resolution of disputes.

The public policy exception to recognition and enforcement of foreign arbitral awards[10] is currently interpreted more narrowly by most Latin American states, if compared with the region's legal scenario thirty years ago, when a mere inconsistency with local substantive laws could easily bar enforcement of a foreign award.

It should be emphasized, however, that enforcement of a foreign arbitral award in Latin America may be subject to a previous recognition process at the competent court of the country where enforcement is sought. Although this recognition process in most cases is limited to the analysis of formal requirements, it may cause a significant delay in the enforcement itself, thus frustrating the party interested in an expeditious solution.

In Brazil, the recognition process prior to actual enforcement is required by the Federal Constitution. The process of recognition of a foreign award is carried out before the Superior Court of Justice and aims at transforming said award into an enforceable decision within the Brazilian territory, i.e., equivalent to any judgment rendered in Brazil.

The defendant cannot raise merits-based defences or any other defences related to the scope of the foreign award. Through the process for recognition of the foreign award, the Superior Court of Justice will solely analyze the compliance of formal requirements under Brazilian law, as well as whether the foreign award is in accordance with national sovereignty, public policy and the dignity of the human person.

Despite the lack of currently available reliable statistics, it is well known in the region (through articles, reports, conferences) that in most Latin American countries courts have been constantly refusing opposition to enforcement on grounds of public policy. In the vast majority of the cases, recognition is granted and subsequent enforcement is allowed provided that it is evidenced that the local defendant has been duly served process and given full opportunity to present its case before the arbitrators, thus conforming with public policy.

---

10. The New York Convention, Article V(2)(*b*).

IV. CONCLUSION

The environment for public-private partnerships and other contractual instruments between state/parastatal entities and the private sector in Latin America is expected to continue developing as countries still need major improvements in infrastructure to sustain economic growth and social progress in the years to come.

Several countries in the region have developed new legal frameworks with a view to facilitating the entering of public-private contracts with special attention to arbitration as the most efficient method of solving disputes arising therefrom. Considering that this is still a brand new reality in the region, where until recently the state centralized practically all economic activity and all disputes were resolved before local courts only, it is an exciting and challenging experience for legal professionals to follow closely what is going on in this part of the world.

Bibliography

Lawrence S. GRAHAM
The State and Policy Outcomes in Latin America (Praeger 1990)

Luiz Carlos Bresser PEREIRA and Peter SPINK
Reforming the State: Managerial Public Administration in Latin America (Lynne Rienner Publishers 1999)

Mariana Hernández CRESPO
"Securing Investment: Innovative Business Strategies for Conflict Management in Latin America" in Arnold INGEN-HOUSZ, ed., *ADR in Business: Practice and Issues Across Countries and Cultures*, Vol. 2 (Kluwer 2011)

F. M. MANIRUZZAMAN
"International Arbitration and Mandatory Public Law Rules in the Context of State Contracts: An Overview", 7 Journal of International Arbitration (1990, no. 3) pp. 53-64

United Nations Department of Economic and Social Affairs Division for Public Economics and Public Administration
"Privatization in Latin America in the Early 1990s" (NY, 1999) <https://publicadministration.un.org/publications/content/PDFs/E-Library%20Archives/1999%20Privatization%20in%20Latin%20America%20in%20the%20Early%201990s.pdf>

Arbitration Involving Public Bodies and Public Interests: Salient Issues

Part II: Confidentiality, Transparency and Public Participation: Too Far or Not Far Enough?

The Contribution of Non-State Actors to the Development of Transparency Regimes in Investment Treaty Arbitration

Chester Brown[*]

TABLE OF CONTENTS

I. INTRODUCTION

The purpose of this chapter is to consider the contribution of non-State actors to the development of the transparency regimes in investment treaty arbitration. It is convenient to begin by recalling the proceedings of the first meeting of the United Nations Commission on International Trade Law (UNCITRAL) Working Group III from 27 November – 1 December 2017, at which Working Group III decided in a rather pointed way that its work on the reform of investor-State dispute settlement would be "government-led with high-level input from all governments".[1] This mantra was understood as a form of rebuff by States to the involvement by non-State actors (including private practitioners) in UNCITRAL's work on previous topics in Working Group II, such as the revision of the UNCITRAL Arbitration Rules, the drafting of the UNCITRAL Rules on Transparency in Treaty-based Investor-State Arbitration (the Transparency Rules),[2] and the negotiation of the United Nations Convention on Transparency in Treaty-based Investor-State Arbitration (the Mauritius Convention).[3] In this regard, the mantra that the work of Working Group III will be "government-led" may be interpreted as an effort by States to ensure that they would be in control of UNCITRAL's work, and this (along with other issues) made for a rather provocative opening to Working Group III's session.[4] It may be overdramatizing the goings-on at the

* Professor of International Law and International Arbitration, University of Sydney Law School; Barrister, 7 Wentworth Selborne Chambers, Sydney; and Overseas Associate, Essex Court Chambers, London.

1. Report of Working Group III (Investor-State Dispute Settlement Reform) on the Work of Its Thirty-Fourth Session Vienna, 27 November – 1 December 2017, UN Doc. No. A/CN.9/930, para. 6.
2. UNCITRAL Rules on Transparency in Treaty-based Investor-State Arbitration (effective as of 1 April 2014), available at <www.uncitral.org> (Transparency Rules).
3. United Nations Convention on Transparency in Treaty-based Investor-State Arbitration, opened for signature 17 March 2015, UNTS Registration No. 54749 (entered into force 18 October 2017) available at <www.uncitral.org> (Mauritius Convention).
4. See, e.g., Luke PETERSON, "UNCITRAL Meetings on ISDS Reform Get Off to a Bumpy Start, as Delegations Can't Come to a Consensus on Who Should Chair Sensitive Process – Entailing a Rare

UNCITRAL to say that this represented a "line in the sand" moment in investment treaty arbitration, where States said "no more". But the issues now being discussed in Working Group III are arguably of greater significance to States than some of the previous topics in Working Group II (such as the revision of the UNCITRAL Model Law, which occupied UNCITRAL's Working Group II between 1999-2006;[5] the revision of the UNCITRAL Arbitration Rules, which was considered by Working Group II between 2006-2010;[6] and the Enforcement of Settlement Agreements, which was on Working Group II's agenda from 2015-2018).[7]

But this episode highlighted the questions: who is it, and who should it be, that contributes to the work of UNCITRAL, and the reform agendas of other bodies which operate in the field of investment treaty arbitration, and set rules and standards which become mandatory or represent best practice? Should it be States, or should it be non-State actors, or should it be both, as it has been in the past? And how does this reflect on the past work of UNCITRAL's Working Groups, in particular Working Group II; are States right to be concerned (if indeed they are concerned) about how that work has progressed and been developed? In particular, what influence have non-State actors had in UNCITRAL's work, particularly on the development of rules on transparency in investment treaty arbitration?

This all has to be prefaced with the obvious point that there are various types of non-State actors which have contributed to the work of UNCITRAL's Working Groups II and III. There are inter-governmental organizations which are involved in revisions to and the reform of investor-State dispute settlement procedures, such as the International Centre for Settlement of Investment Disputes (ICSID) and the Permanent Court of Arbitration (PCA).[8] There are also professional non-governmental organizations (NGOs), such as the International Bar Association (IBA) and the International Chamber of Commerce (ICC).[9] And there are also NGOs which form part of what is loosely

---

Vote", IA Reporter (9 December 2017) at <www.iareporter.com> (last accessed 18 October 2018).

5. See, e.g., Report of the Working Group on Arbitration and Conciliation on the Work of Its Forty-Fourth Session, (New York, 23-27 January 2006), paras. 1-2 (UN Doc. No. A/CN.9/592 (27 February 2006)).
6. See, e.g., Report of Working Group II (Arbitration and Conciliation) on the Work of Its Fifty-Second Session (New York, 1-5 February 2010), paras. 1-3 (UN Doc. No. A/CN.9/688 (19 February 2010)).
7. See, e.g., Report of Working Group II (Dispute Settlement) on the Work of Its Sixty-Eighth Session (New York, 5-9 February 2018), paras. 1-4 (UN Doc. No. A/CN.9/934 (19 February 2018)).
8. See, e.g., Report of Working Group III (Investor-State Dispute Settlement Reform) on the Work of Its Thirty-Fifth Session (New York, 23-27 April 2018), paras. 7(a)-(b) (UN Doc. No. A/CN.9/935 (14 May 2018)), noting that the PCA and ICSID attended the Working Group's session.
9. See, e.g., Report of Working Group III (Investor-State Dispute Settlement Reform) on the Work of Its Thirty-Fifth Session (New York, 23-27 April 2018), para. 7(c) (UN Doc. No. A/CN.9/935 (14 May 2018)).

known as "civil society", such as the International Institute for Sustainable Development (IISD), and the Centre for International Environmental Law (CIEL).[10]

Against this background, this chapter examines the contribution made by these various non-State actors, particularly the NGOs, to developments in the field of confidentiality and transparency in international arbitration. This is an area where there have been many developments in the past ten or fifteen years, which culminated with the adoption of the Transparency Rules, and the Mauritius Convention. And it is an area where States have not necessarily led the way and consistently spoken with one voice. What is evident is that NGOs and civil society have made a significant contribution, which can be described as having come in three areas of activity. First, non-State actors have contributed to the development of the rules on transparency through their petitions to tribunals to be granted amicus curiae status. Secondly, non-State actors have contributed to transparency as advocates for change to the procedural rules that apply in investment arbitration proceedings. And thirdly, they have contributed to transparency through their publishing activities.

II. CONTRIBUTION OF NON-STATE ACTORS

1. *Petitions for Amicus Curiae Status*

Beginning with the first of these contributions, non-State actors have made an important contribution to the development of the rules on confidentiality and transparency as petitioners for amicus curiae status. They have done so in cases brought under the UNCITRAL Rules, and in cases under the Convention on the Settlement of Investment Disputes between States and Nationals of Other States (the ICSID Convention), at a time when neither set of arbitral rules contained any relevant provisions on transparency. And the petitions of non-State actors arguably led arbitral tribunals to interpret their procedural powers broadly enough to allow them into proceedings in appropriate circumstances.

There are various cases which are well known, but it is convenient to begin with *Methanex Corporation v. United States*,[11] which concerned a Californian government measure which prohibited the use of MTBE, a gasoline additive, for which one of the main ingredients was methanol, one of Methanex's products. In this case, there were applications for amicus curiae status by the IISD and the Earth Justice Legal Defense Fund, on behalf of Communities for a Better Environment, the Bluewater Network, and CIEL.[12]

10. See, e.g., Report of Working Group III (Investor-State Dispute Settlement Reform) on the Work of Its Thirty-Fifth Session (New York, 23-27 April 2018), para. 7(c) (UN Doc. No. A/CN.9/935 (14 May 2018)).
11. *Methanex Corporation v. United States* (Decision of the Tribunal on Petitions from Third Persons to Intervene as "*Amicus Curiae*" of 15 January 2001).
12. *Methanex Corporation v. United States* (Petition of IISD to the Arbitral Tribunal of 25 August 2000), *Methanex Corporation v. United States* (IISD's Final Submissions to the Arbitral Tribunal of 16 October 2000); *Methanex Corporation v. United States* (Amended Petition of Communities for a

As is well known, the *Methanex* tribunal decided that it had the power under the UNCITRAL Rules to accept amicus curiae submissions. This tribunal, which was (then) composed of VV Veeder QC (chair), William Rowley QC, and Warren Christopher, began by noting that its mandate was to decide a substantive dispute between the claimant and respondent, and that it had no jurisdiction over any third parties.[13] But it considered that its receipt of written submissions from a person other than the Disputing Parties was not equivalent to adding that person as a party to the arbitration.[14] It considered that allowing a third person to make an amicus submission could fall within its procedural powers over the conduct of the arbitration, within the general scope of Art. 15(1) of the UNCITRAL Arbitration Rules (1976).[15] It also observed that this had been accepted by the Iran-US Claims Tribunal, and the authoritative guide to the exercise of the Iran-US Claim Tribunal's discretion under Art. 15(1), as well as at least one award "demonstrate[d] that the receipt of written submissions from a non-party third person [did] not necessarily offend the philosophy of international arbitration involving States and non-State parties".[16] The tribunal also referred to the practice of World Trade Organization (WTO) panels, which had accepted amicus briefs.[17] The *Methanex* tribunal noted the claimant's position that the acceptance of amicus curiae briefs would add to the burden on the parties in having to respond to them, but the tribunal considered that it would be able to devise procedures to manage that risk, and it did not consider that there was any immediate risk of unfair or unequal treatment for either of the disputing parties.[18] The tribunal then considered relevant provisions of the North American Free Trade Agreement (NAFTA) and the UNCITRAL Rules of Arbitration, and noted that there was "no provision in Chapter 11 [of NAFTA] that expressly prohibit[ed] the acceptance of *amicus* submissions, but likewise nothing that expressly encourage[d] them".[19] As for the UNCITRAL Rules, the tribunal observed that Art. 25(4) required that the hearings be held in camera; this was not relevant to the tribunal's power to accept amicus curiae submissions, but it was relevant to the petitioners' request "to attend hearings and to receive copies of all submissions and materials adduced before the Tribunal".[20] The tribunal accepted that this was consistent with the duty of privacy in international arbitration, but did not agree that this also conferred a duty of confidentiality (noting, inter alia, the judgment of the High Court of Australia in *Esso v. Plowman*).[21] The tribunal ultimately concluded that:

Better Environment, the Bluewater Network of Earth Island Institute, and CIEL, to Appear Jointly as *Amicus Curiae* of 13 October 2000).

13. *Methanex Corporation v. United States* (Decision of the Tribunal on Petitions from Third Persons to Intervene as "*Amicus Curiae*" of 15 January 2001) para. 29.
14. *Ibid.*, para. 30.
15. *Ibid.*, para. 31.
16. *Ibid.*, para. 32, referring inter alia to *Iran v. United States* (Case A/15), Award No. 63, reprinted in 2 Iran-United States Claims Tribunal Reports 40, 42.
17. *Ibid.*, para. 33, referring to *United States – Imposition of Countervailing Duties on Certain Hot-Rolled Lead and Bismuth Carbon Steel Products Originated in the United Kingdom*, WT/DS138/ABR (7 June 2000) para. 39.
18. *Ibid.*, paras. 35-37.
19. *Ibid.*, paras. 38-39.
20. *Ibid.*, para. 41.
21. *Ibid.*, paras. 43-45, referring to *Esso v. Plowman* (1995) 183 CLR 10.

> "by Article 15(1) of the UNCITRAL Arbitration Rules it has the power to accept *amicus* submissions (in writing) from each of the Petitioners, to be copied simultaneously to the legal representatives of the Disputing Parties, Canada and Mexico. In coming to this conclusion, the Tribunal has not relied on the fact that *amicus* submissions feature in the domestic procedures of the courts in two, but not three, NAFTA Parties. The Tribunal also concludes that it has no power to accept the Petitioners' requests to receive materials generated within the arbitration or to attend oral hearings of the arbitration. Such materials may however be derived from the public domain or disclosed into the public domain within the terms of the Consent Order regarding Disclosure and Confidentiality, or otherwise lawfully; but that is a quite separate matter outwith the scope of this decision."[22]

The *Methanex* tribunal did not immediately decide whether it should exercise its discretion to accept such amicus submissions; it left that for a later decision.[23] It is significant that it supported its approach by reference to the public interest that was at stake in this NAFTA arbitration, in a passage that has been frequently quoted:

> "There is an undoubtedly public interest in this arbitration. The substantive issues extend far beyond those raised by the usual transnational arbitration between commercial parties. This is not merely because one of the Disputing Parties is a State: there are of course disputes involving States which are of no greater general public importance than a dispute between private persons. The public interest in this arbitration arises from its subject-matter, as powerfully suggested in the Petitions. There is also a broader argument, as suggested by the Respondent and Canada: the Chapter 11 arbitral process could benefit from being perceived as more open or transparent; or conversely be harmed if seen as unduly secretive. In this regard, the Tribunal's willingness to receive *amicus* submissions might support the process in general and this arbitration in particular; whereas a blanket refusal could do positive harm."[24]

More than two years later, in January 2003, the IISD and Earth Justice Defense Fund filed further petitions to be admitted as amicus curiae in the proceedings.[25] And on 7 October 2003, the NAFTA Free Trade Commission regularized the procedure for making applications for amicus status; the relevant considerations in granting amicus curiae status were the extent to which "the non-disputing party submission would assist the tribunal in the determination of a factual or legal issue related to the arbitration by bringing a perspective, particular knowledge or insight that is different from that of the

22. *Ibid.*, para. 47.
23. *Ibid.*, para. 48.
24. *Ibid.*, para. 49; see, e.g., *Biwater Gauff (Tanzania) Ltd v. Tanzania* (ICSID Case No. ARB/05/22), Procedural Order No. 5 of 2 February 2007, para. 51; see also *Philip Morris Brands SARL v. Uruguay* (ICSID Case No. ARB/10/7), Procedural Order No. 3 of 17 February 2015, para. 26.
25. Joint Motions to the Tribunal Regarding the Petitions for *Amicus Curiae* Standing of the IISD, Communities for a Better Environment, Bluewater Network, and the Centre for International Environmental Law (31 January 2003).

disputing parties"; the extent to which "the non-disputing party submission would address matters within the scope of the dispute"; whether "the non-disputing party [had] a significant interest in the arbitration"; and whether there was "a public interest in the arbitration".[26] Having considered the NAFTA Free Trade Commission's statement on non-disputing party participation, the disputing parties in *Methanex* reached agreement on the applicable procedure for admission of amicus curiae briefs, which was communicated to the tribunal.[27]

The Free Trade Commission's list of matters to be taken into account in exercising discretion as to whether to accept amicus curiae submissions is interesting, because it is largely consistent with the conditions that were suggested as relevant by the IISD in its Final Submission in Support of its Application for *Amicus Curiae* Status in the *Methanex* case of 16 October 2000. In that final submission (which was authored by Professor Don McRae and Howard Mann), the IISD argued that the test should consist of asking (i) whether the petitioner could demonstrate that it had an interest in the issue;[28] (ii) whether the petitioner's submissions would be useful to the tribunal (considering whether the petitioner's submissions would add anything to those of the parties);[29] and (iii) whether there was a broader public interest in the dispute.[30]

The two amicus curiae submissions were ultimately considered by the *Methanex* tribunal.[31] It is unclear as to how influential they were on the outcome, given that both submissions were essentially supportive of the United States' position, and the United States successfully defended the Californian measure.[32]

The *Methanex* tribunal was not the first international court or tribunal to find that it had the power to accept amicus submissions, even though the power was not made express; as noted above, the *Methanex* tribunal referred to previous practice of WTO panels and the Iran-US Claims Tribunal. But it was a significant decision, as it arguably laid the path for subsequent developments.

The next case was *United Parcel Services, Inc v. Canada*,[33] in which the arbitration proceeded largely in parallel with *Methanex*. This was a claim in which the American package delivery company United Parcel Services, Inc (UPS) argued that Canada's provision of public funds to Canada Post and the subsidization of its package delivery and courier business breached obligations under Chapter 11 of NAFTA. In this case, various applications for amicus status were made, including by the Canadian Council of Postal Workers, the Council of Canadians (both of which were sympathetic to Canada's position), and the Chamber of Commerce of the United States which was supportive of UPS's claim). The first two of these entities petitioned the tribunal for the right to be

26. Statement of the Free Trade Commission on Non-Disputing Party Participation (7 October 2003).
27. Letter to the Tribunal dated 31 October 2003 Recording the Parties' Agreement on *Amicus Curiae* Participation.
28. IISD, "Petitioner's Final Submissions Regarding the Petition of the IISD to the Arbitral Tribunal for *Amicus Curiae* Status" (16 October 2000) para. 33.
29. *Ibid.*, para. 33.
30. *Ibid.*, para. 38.
31. *Methanex v. United States* (Award of 3 August 2005), Part II, Chapter C, paras. 26-29.
32. *Ibid.*, Part VI.
33. *UPS v. Canada* (Decision of the Tribunal on Petitions for Intervention and Participation as *Amicus Curiae* of 17 October 2001).

made parties to the proceedings, and in the alternative they sought standing to intervene in the proceedings, with full rights of audience.[34] They argued that they both had an interest in the broader public policy implications of this dispute, as they "not only implicate the full array of Canada Post services, but many other public service sectors as well".[35] The *UPS* tribunal, which was chaired by Sir Kenneth Keith, who sat with Dean Ronald Cass and Yves Fortier CC QC, accepted that it had the power within Art. 15(1) of the UNCITRAL Rules to accept amicus curiae briefs, and held that it was "part of its power to conduct the arbitration in such manner as it considers appropriate",[36] although it added that "the receiving of such submissions from a third person is not equivalent to making that person a party to the arbitration".[37] In deciding that the parties had permission to file amicus briefs,[38] the *UPS* tribunal accepted the relevant criteria identified by the petitioners, most particularly the Canadian Council of Postal Workers, which had referred to the important public character of the issues in dispute, to the petitioners' own real interests in the case, and the ability of the petitioners to "provide assistance beyond that provided by the parties".[39] So in this case, the non-State actor played an important role in shaping the test accepted by the *UPS* tribunal as relevant.

The next case is *Aguas del Tunari v. Bolivia*, which is the first of the cases involving an amicus petition that was brought under the ICSID Convention. The tribunal consisted of Professor David Caron, Henri Alvarez QC, and José Luis Alberro-Semerena. In this case, a petition was submitted by CIEL and the Earth Justice Legal Defense Fund on behalf of eight NGOs.[40] These interveners sought an extensive range of orders, including (i) standing to participate as parties in the arbitration, including "all rights of participation accorded to other parties in the claim",[41] and in the alternative, (ii) the right to participate as amicus curiae and make submissions on the procedure of the arbitration, the issues of jurisdiction and merits; (iii) public disclosure of documents; (iv) open hearings; (v) a site visit by the tribunal to Cochabamba, with public hearings; (vi) a right to respond to any comments of the parties to the petition; and (vii) a right to amend the petition as further details became known to the petitioners.[42] But this case had a different outcome from *Methanex* and *UPS*; the ICSID tribunal wrote to the petitioners, denying

34. Petition of the Canadian Union of Postal Workers and the Council of Canadians (8 November 2000).
35. *UPS v. Canada* (Decision of the Tribunal on Petitions for Intervention and Participation as *Amicus Curiae* of 17 October 2001), para. 3(ii).
36. *Ibid.*, para. 61.
37. *Ibid.*, paras. 60-63.
38. *Ibid.*, paras. 60-63.
39. *Ibid.*, para. 70.
40. These included the "Coalition for the Defence of Water and Life", "Friends of the Earth Netherlands", and various concerned individuals (including a priest – Father Luis Sanchez) and a congressman (Congressman Jorge Alvarado): see Petition of the La Coordinadora para la Defensa del Agua y Vida, Oscar Olivera, La Federación Departamental Cochabambina de Organizaciones Regantes, Omar Fernandez, SEMAPA Sur, Father Luis Sánchez, Congressman Jorge Alvarado, and of Friends of the Earth-Netherlands to the ICSID tribunal in *Aguas del Tunari v. Bolivia* (29 August 2002).
41 *Ibid.*, para. 3.
42 *Ibid.*, para. 3.

their requests.[43] The tribunal found that the requests were beyond the power or authority of the tribunal to grant, and held that the BIT and the ICSID Convention "place[d] the control of the issues raised with the parties, not with the Tribunal".[44] So in the context of NGOs seeking to intervene in investment cases, this was a firm rebuff.

The next case was *Suez, Sociedad General de Aguas de Barcelona SA, and Vivendi Universal SA v. Argentine Republic*.[45] In this case, various NGOs (including, again, CIEL) tried again, and applied for access to the hearings, for permission to make submissions as amicus curiae, and to allow them timely access to all the documents of the case.[46] This claim was subject to the pre-2006 ICSID Rules, which did not make provision for non-disputing party submissions, as has been seen in the *Aguas del Tunari* case. The petitioners referred to and relied on the decisions of the UNCITRAL tribunals in *Methanex* and *UPS*, and this tribunal (chaired by Professor Jeswald Salacuse, and including also Professor Gabrielle Kaufmann-Kohler, and Professor Pedro Nikken) decided the issue differently from the ICSID tribunal in *Aguas del Tunari*. In its Order of 19 May 2005, the tribunal denied the petitioners access to the hearing,[47] but it held that Art. 44 of the ICSID Convention gave it the power to accept amicus curiae submissions.[48] It went on to consider the relevant conditions for exercise of the power, which were "(a) the appropriateness of the subject-matter of the case", i.e., whether it was of broader public interest; "(b) the suitability of a given non-party to act as *amicus* in that case", which would require considerations of expertise, experience and independence, and whether the submission would assist the tribunal; and "(c) the procedure by which the *amicus* submission would be made and considered", which must safeguard due process and equal treatment of the parties.[49] These same factors were also applied by the identically composed tribunal in the other (later) *Suez* case, *Suez, Sociedad General de Aguas de Barcelona SA, and InterAgios Servicios SA v. Argentine Republic*.[50]

In applying the first of these factors, the *Suez* tribunal found that

> "19. ... [T]he present case potentially involves matters of public interest. This case will consider the legality under international law, not domestic private law, of various actions and measures taken by governments. The international responsibility of a state, the Argentine Republic, is also at stake, as opposed to the liability of a corporation arising out of private law. While these factors are certainly matters of public interest, they are present in virtually all cases of

43. Letter from the *Aguas del Tunari v. Bolivia* tribunal to Earth Justice (29 January 2003).

44. *Aguas del Tunari v. Bolivia* (ICSID Case No. ARB/ 02/3), Decision on Jurisdiction of 21 October 2005) para. 17.

45. *Suez, Sociedad General de Aguas de Barcelona SA, and Vivendi Universal SA v. Argentine Republic* (ICSID Case No. ARB/03/19), Order in Response to a Petition for Transparency and Participation as *Amicus Curiae* of 19 May 2005.

46. *Ibid.*, para. 1.

47. *Ibid.*, paras. 6-7.

48. *Ibid.*, para. 16.

49. *Ibid.*, para. 17.

50. *Suez, Sociedad General de Aguas de Barcelona SA, and InterAguas Servicios SA v. Argentine Republic* (ICSID Case No. ARB/03/17), Order in Response to a Petition for Participation as *Amicus Curiae* of 17 March 2006, para. 17.

> investment treaty arbitration under ICSID jurisdiction. The factor that gives this case particular public interest is that the investment dispute centers around the water distribution and sewage systems of a large metropolitan area, the city of Buenos Aires and surrounding municipalities. Those systems provide basic public services to millions of people and as a result may raise a variety of complex public and international law questions, including human rights considerations. Any decision rendered in this case, whether in favor of the Claimants or the Respondent, has the potential to affect the operation of those systems and thereby the public they serve.
> 20. These factors lead the Tribunal to conclude that this case does involve matters of public interest of such a nature that have traditionally led courts and other tribunals to receive *amicus* submissions from suitable nonparties. This case is not simply a contract dispute between private parties where nonparties attempting to intervene as friends of the court might be seen as officious intermeddlers."[51]

The *Suez* tribunal also recognized the broader benefits to the system of investment arbitration of greater transparency:

> "The acceptance of *amicus* submissions would have the additional desirable consequence of increasing the transparency of investor-state arbitration. Public acceptance of the legitimacy of international arbitral processes, particularly when they involve states and matters of public interest, is strengthened by increased openness and increased knowledge as to how these processes function. ... Through the participation of appropriate representatives of civil society in appropriate cases, the public will gain increased understanding of ICSID processes."[52]

As for the second factor (the suitability of specific non-parties to act as amicus curiae), the *Suez* tribunal considered that the following information about the petitioner was relevant: (a) the identity and background of the petitioner, (b) the nature of the petitioner's interest in the case, (c) whether the petitioner had received any form of support from one of the parties, or from any person connected with the parties in the case.[53] And as for the third factor (the appropriate procedure governing the submission of amicus briefs), the *Suez* tribunal deferred its decision on the appropriate procedure, noting that it would address this issue if it "decided to grant leave to a particular non-disputing party".[54]

The *Suez* tribunal had the chance to consider its own procedure when, on 1 December 2006, the various petitioners filed an application for amicus curiae standing. In its Decision of 21 February 2007, the *Suez* tribunal noted that, in the intervening period

51. *Suez, Sociedad General de Aguas de Barcelona SA, and Vivendi Universal SA v. Argentine Republic* (ICSID Case No. ARB/03/19), Order in Response to a Petition for Transparency and Participation as *Amicus Curiae* of 19 May 2005, paras. 19-20.

52. *Ibid.*, para. 22.

53. *Ibid.*, para. 25.

54. *Ibid.*, para. 29.

since its Order of 19 May 2005, ICSID had amended its rules and introduced an express provision in ICSID Rule 37(2) dealing with amicus submissions, with effect from 10 April 2006; however, the revised ICSID Rules were not applicable to the case.[55] The new Rule 37(2) permitted the tribunal to "allow a person or entity that is not a party to the dispute ... to file a written submission with the Tribunal regarding a matter within the scope of the dispute". In determining whether to allow such a submission, the Tribunal would "consider, among other things", the extent to which:

> "(a) the non-disputing party submission would assist the Tribunal in the determination of a factual or legal issue related to the proceeding by bringing a perspective, particular knowledge or insight that is different from that of the disputing parties;
> (b) the non-disputing party submission would address a matter within the scope of the dispute;
> (c) the non-disputing party has a significant interest in the proceeding."[56]

Rule 37(2) also requires that the tribunal "ensure that the non-disputing party submission does not disrupt the proceeding or unduly burden or unfairly prejudice either party, and that both parties are given an opportunity to present their observations on the non-disputing party submission."[57]

Although Rule 37(2) was not formally applicable to the *Suez* case, the *Suez* tribunal considered that the relevant considerations contained in Rule 37(2) were consistent with the factors that it had identified in its earlier order, and granted the five petitioners permission to file a joint amicus brief.[58]

The next case to consider is *Biwater Gauff (Tanzania) Ltd v. Tanzania*.[59] This tribunal, which was composed of Bernard Hanotiau, Gary Born, and Toby Landau QC, considered a claim by a British investor which had a contract to provide water and sewerage services in Tanzania, and which alleged that its investment had been expropriated. A petition to intervene as amicus curiae was submitted by the IISD and CIEL, as well as by three Tanzania-based NGOs.[60] Although this arbitration was commenced in 2005, the petitioners' application was considered under the revised ICSID Rules, which (as noted above) were amended in April 2006 to expressly cater for

55. *Suez Sociedad General de Aguas de Barcelona SA, and Vivendi Universal SA v. Argentine Republic* (ICSID Case No. ARB/03/19), Order in Response to a Petition by Five Non-Governmental Organizations for Permission to Make an *Amicus Curiae* Submission of 21 February 2007, paras. 14-15.
56. ICSID Rules of Arbitration (2006), Rule 37(2), reproduced in *Suez Sociedad General de Aguas de Barcelona SA, and Vivendi Universal SA v. Argentine Republic* (ICSID Case No. ARB/03/19), Order in Response to a Petition by Five Non-Governmental Organizations for Permission to Make an *Amicus Curiae* Submission of 21 February 2007, para. 14.
57. ICSID Rules of Arbitration (2006), Rule 37(2).
58. However, it did not allow them access to documents or to attend the hearing: *Suez Sociedad General de Aguas de Barcelona SA, and Vivendi Universal SA v. Argentine Republic* (ICSID Case No. ARB/03/19), Order in Response to a Petition by Five Non-Governmental Organizations for Permission to Make an *Amicus Curiae* Submission of 21 February 2007, para. 27.
59. *Biwater Gauff (Tanzania) Ltd v. Tanzania* (ICSID Case No. ARB/05/22), Award of 24 July 2008.
60. Petition for *Amicus Curiae* Status of 27 November 2006.

amicus curiae submissions. The tribunal granted the petitioners an opportunity to file a written submission under ICSID Arbitration Rule 37(2).[61] The amici duly submitted amicus curiae briefs, which addressed "broad policy issues concerning sustainable development, environment, human rights and governmental policy".[62] And the amici appear to have been influential; the *Biwater* tribunal noted that: "[T]he Arbitral Tribunal has found the *Amici's* observations useful. Their submissions have informed the analysis of claims set out below, and where relevant, specific points arising from the *Amici's* submissions are returned to in that context."[63]

One such issue concerned the content of the fair and equitable treatment (FET) standard, on which the tribunal observed that, in deciding to apply the general standard which was articulated by the *Waste Management (No. 2)* tribunal, it had taken account of the amici's submission, particularly on the relevance of taking into account the responsibility of foreign investors in terms of "prior due diligence and subsequent conduct", and on the limits of legitimate expectations, where an investor takes on risks in entering a particular investment environment.[64] And so to the extent that the *Biwater* tribunal adopted a balanced approach to the FET standard, which takes into account all of the facts and circumstances of the case, including as relevant the investor's conduct, the amici in *Biwater* have arguably contributed to the development of this substantive standard of protection.

In *Electrabel v. Hungary*, another arbitration in which the tribunal was chaired by VV Veeder QC, issues of European law arose. In its Procedural Order No. 5 (18 August 2009), the tribunal ordered that the European Commission would be granted permission under ICSID Arbitration Rule 37(2) to file a written submission as a non-disputing party. As the tribunal explained:

> "[T]he Tribunal notes that while the European Commission is an expert commentator on European Community law and could accordingly assist the Tribunal by addressing several legal issues, the scope of its legal opinion should in principle be directed to addressing the following issues: (a) European Community Law and its connection with the Energy Charter Treaty; (b) Community Law and the State Aid investigation concerning the Power Purchase Agreements signed by Hungary; and (c) the Effect of Community Decisions on the European Union's Members States, particularly Hungary."[65]

In its award, the tribunal placed on record "its thanks and appreciation to the European Commission for its Submission, as regard both applicable law and jurisdiction. It is a lengthy, scholarly and important document for these arbitration proceedings; and only

61. *Biwater Gauff (Tanzania) Ltd v. Tanzania* (ICSID Case No. ARB/05/22), Award of 24 July 2008, para. 62.
62. *Ibid.*, para. 366.
63. *Ibid.*, para. 392.
64. *Ibid.*, para. 601.
65. *Electrabel SA v. Hungary* (ICSID Case No. ARB/07/19), Procedural Order No. 5 of 18 August 2009, para. 24.

part of it is cited in this Decision."[66] And the tribunal lamented that the European Commission had not played a more active role in the arbitration proceedings:

> "[I]t is unfortunate that the European Commission could not play a more active role as a non-disputing party in this arbitration, given that (as was rightly emphasised in the European Commission's Submission), the European Union is a Contracting Party to the ECT in which it played from the outset a leading role; and, moreover, that the European Commission's perspective on this case is not the same as the Respondent's and still less that of the Claimant. In short, the European Commission has much more than 'a significant interest' in these arbitration proceedings. Unlike the two Parties, the Commission has made a jurisdictional objection based on EU law as the law applicable to the Parties' arbitration agreement."[67]

Although there are multiple other cases which could be mentioned, one case in which an amicus curiae submission arguably had an impact is *Philip Morris Brands SARL v. Uruguay*.[68] In this case, the World Health Organization (WHO) and the Secretariat of the Framework Convention on Tobacco Control (FCTC) sought and were granted permission to submit an amicus brief under ICISD Arbitration Rule 37(2), and the Pan American Health Organization (PAHO) was also granted permission to file an amicus brief.[69] Another application for amicus curiae status was received from the "Avaaz Foundation", but this application was rejected by the tribunal, on the basis that it would not bring any new perspective to bear on the dispute.[70] The "Inter-American Association of Intellectual Property" also filed a request, but this too was rejected, on the basis of the close relationship between that organization and the claimants.[71]

In this case, the amicus curiae briefs were clearly taken seriously by the tribunal and were extensively relied on. If you review the footnotes of the *Philip Morris* award, you will find that the WHO amicus brief and the PAHO amicus brief are referred to at least twenty-one times in the footnotes of the section containing the tribunal's findings. It is obviously not possible to tell if the amicus briefs had any material effect on the decision; clearly Uruguay was represented by excellent counsel and had submitted its own expert evidence, so perhaps the relevant information would have found its way before the tribunal even without the amicus briefs. But it is still quite remarkable that the tribunal saw fit to appear to place such weight on the amicus briefs in making its factual determinations.

66. *Ibid.*, para. 4.91.
67. *Ibid.*, para. 4.92.
68. *Philip Morris Brands SARL v. Uruguay* (ICSID Case No. ARB/10/7), Award of 8 July 2016.
69. *Ibid.*, paras. 35-48.
70. *Ibid.*, paras. 49-52.
71. *Ibid.*, paras. 53-55.

2. *Changes to Arbitral Rules*

The second contribution that has been made by non-State actors is that they have advocated for and changes to the Rules of Arbitration – both the ICSID Arbitration Rules and the UNCITRAL Rules.

The revision of the ICSID Rules in 2006 saw the introduction of the two transparency measures, and this followed the few ICSID cases where petitions for amicus curiae status had been made to ICSID tribunals – *Aguas del Tunari* and the two *Suez* tribunals, with inconsistent results. As Aurelia Antonietti has explained:

> "[t]raditionally, hearings are conducted behind closed doors and are held by the tribunal in presence of the parties, their agents, counsel, advocates, witness and experts. Former ICSID Arbitration Rule 32(2) specified that the tribunal would decide, with the consent of the parties, which other persons may attend the hearings."[72]

Rule 32(2) was ultimately amended such that, "unless either party objects", the tribunal, after consultation with the Secretary-General, may allow non-parties "to attend or observe all or part of the hearings, subject to appropriate logistical arrangements".[73] The change brought about by this provision is not all that dramatic, since it remains open to either party to object, and the hearing remains closed.

By far the greater development was the inclusion of Rule 37(2). As Antonietti explained:

> "[T]he Discussion Paper suggested in 2004 that ICSID tribunals may accept and consider written submissions from a non-disputing party after consulting both parties to the proceeding as far as possible. It appears that certain governments had a strong preference that the consent of both parties be made a condition for a tribunal allowing such submissions. However, the adopted amendment of Arbitration Rule 37 leaves the decision to the tribunal, and only provides for consultation with the parties. One could think that if a party refuses to make itself available for such consultations, the tribunal could go ahead with its decision."[74]

And of course ICSID is currently considering further amendments to its Rules.[75] In the public consultation process, non-State actors have made various submissions, in which a number of proposals relating to confidentiality and transparency have been made.[76]

---

72. Aurelia ANTONIETTI, "2006 Amendments to the ICSID Rules and Regulations and the Additional Facility Rules", 21 ICSID Review – Foreign Investment Law Journal (2006) p. 427.
73. ICSID Rules (2006), Rule 32(2).
74. A. ANTONIETTI, above fn. 72.
75. E.g., "Proposals for Amendment of the ICSID Rules – Synopsis" (2 August 2018), available at <www.worldbank.org/icsid> (last accessed 18 October 2018); see also "States Discuss Proposed Rule Amendments" (28 September 2018), available at <www.worldbank.org/icsid> (last accessed 18 October 2018).
76. "Proposals for Amendment of the ICSID Rules – Synopsis" (2 August 2018) paras. 43-49, available at <www.worldbank.org/icsid> (last accessed 18 October 2018); see also Columbia Centre on

Turning to the UNCITRAL Rules, it is well known that during UNCITRAL Working Group II's work on the revision of the UNCITRAL Rules of Arbitration, a proposal was made to the Working Group that transparency provisions should be included. As Working Group II reported:

> "65. In order to take account of the public interest aspects of investor-State arbitrations, a proposal was made to amend a limited number of provisions of the UNCITRAL Arbitration Rules. In that connection, the delegation that referred to the Milan Club of Arbitrators also referred to two non-governmental organizations (the Center for International Environmental Law (CIEL) and the International Institute for Sustainable Development (IISD)) and the Working Group had no objection to hearing their proposal. The Working Group did not discuss the contents of that proposal and decided to reproduce the substance of the statement by the two non-governmental organizations in annex III to this report."[77]

In its submission to Working Group II, IISD and CIEL sought "a very limited number of additions to the UNCITRAL Arbitration Rules in order to take account of the important public interest aspects of investor-State arbitrations".[78] They claimed that their amendments would "leav[e] untouched the Rules' application to other types of arbitrations and avoiding undue delay, disruption or cost".[79] There were only four provisions which were proposed to be inserted or amended. These concerned the publication of the notice of arbitration and information concerning the constitution of the tribunal;[80] the publication of all documents in an investor-State claim (subject to redaction of confidential information);[81] the participation of amicus curiae by filing written submissions;[82] holding open hearings in investor-State cases,[83] and the publication of awards.[84]

However, the Working Group decided not to take up this suggestion of considering the inclusion of transparency measures in the UNCITRAL Rules of 2010. It decided that:

> "to embark at this stage on the preparation of Rules governing transparency and possibly other issues since the complex negotiation would delay the current work

---

Sustainable Investment, "Illustrative Suggestions for Amendments to the ICSID Arbitration Rules" (31 March 2017) available at <www.worldbank.org/icsid> (last accessed 18 October 2018).

77. UNCITRAL Working Group II, Report of the Working Group on Its 48th Session (4-8 February 2008, New York), UN Doc. No. A/CN.9/646 (29 February 2008) para. 65.
78. *Ibid.*, Annex III.
79. *Ibid.*, Annex III.
80. *Ibid.*, Annex III, proposed amendment to Art. 3(5).
81. *Ibid.*, Annex III, proposed amendment to Art. 15(3).
82. *Ibid.*, Annex III, proposed amendment to Art. 15(4).
83. *Ibid.*, Annex III, proposed amendment to Art. 25(4): "(4) *Except in an arbitration brought by an investor against a State under the terms of a treaty,* hearings shall be held in camera unless the parties agree otherwise … ."(Emphasis added.)
84. *Ibid.*, Annex III, proposed amendment to Art. 32(5): "*Except in an arbitration brought by an investor against a State under the terms of a treaty,* the award may be made public only with the consent of both parties." (Emphasis added.)

of revising the Rules. There was an expectation that the revised Rules would be available to users of commercial arbitration as soon as feasible."[85]

As is of course well known, Working Group II took up the issue of transparency and its work – with the active contribution of non-State actors – this led to the adoption of the UNCITRAL Transparency Rules and the Mauritius Convention, the details of which have been well traversed elsewhere.[86] This is not to say that States did not play their role in the development of the transparency provisions. For instance, the Government of Canada submitted a paper in support of transparency measures in the UNCITRAL Rules, which was influential.[87] But non-State actors played an important role in putting this onto the agenda in the first place, and for tenaciously ensuring that it led to a successful outcome.

3. *Publishers of Information Concerning Investment Treaty Arbitration*

The third and final way that non-State actors have played an important role in developing the rules on transparency is through carrying out investigative reports and publishing information on investment treaty arbitration. Today we all think of Global Arbitration Review (GAR), which is a very useful publication, but before there was GAR there was the Investment Treaty News (ITN) service, which was published by Luke Peterson at the IISD, and then Luke Peterson started "Investment Arbitration Reporter". These newsletters reveal information about cases which is not just useful for a policy agenda, but also for lawyers as a tool to find relevant decisions and awards, so that they can develop arguments based on materials which are otherwise hard to find. It might therefore be said that they have indirectly led to the development of the jurisprudence in this field.

III. CONCLUDING REMARKS

In closing, I return to where I began, which is the activities of UNCITRAL's Working Group III and its project of examining whether reform is necessary to the ISDS system. In spite of the mantra that Working Group III's work is to be "government-led", it is hoped that the States in Working Group III will recognize that a rather large contribution has been made by non-State actors to the development of transparency rules in investment arbitration, and that a similar contribution can be expected from

85. *Ibid.*, para. 68.
86. See especially Esme SHIRLOW, "The Dawn of a New Era? The UNCITRAL Rules and UN Convention on Transparency in Treaty-based Investor-State Arbitration", 31 ICSID Review – Foreign Investment Law Journal (2016) p. 622; Jansen CALAMITA, "The Changing Landscape of Transparency in Investor-State Arbitration: The UNCITRAL Transparency Rules and Mauritius Convention", *Austrian Yearbook on International Arbitration* (2016) p. 271; and Esme SHIRLOW, "Three Manifestations of Transparency in International Investment Law: A Story of Sources, Stakeholders, and Structures", 8 Goettingen Journal of International Law (2017) p. 73, pp. 85-89.
87. Revision of the UNCITRAL Rules, Observations of the Government of Canada, UN Doc A/CN.9/662 (12 June 2008).

many stakeholders in the question of ISDS Reform. Indeed, the delegations of many States include private practitioners; they are often the members of the delegation with most expertise, so it is likely that the ISDS Reform project will benefit from the input of a broad range of participants. It is trite to say it, but the reform of the ISDS system is not only important for States; it is important for all stakeholders, and non-State actors have an important role to play in this project.

The Investor-State Dispute System Trinity and Early State Practice in Investor-State Arbitration

Patrick W. Pearsall[*]

TABLE OF CONTENTS PAGE

I. INTRODUCTION

Third-party participation in investor-State arbitration is now nearly universally possible. Institutions, states, arbitrators, and most practitioners have accepted the concept of third-party participation with exceptional speed. The number of third-party submissions has grown steadily since 2001 and the renewed public attention to the investor-State dispute system (ISDS) will almost certainly result in even more submissions in the years to come.[1] As the breadth of these submissions increases, so too has the sophistication of the practice.

Many have written on this topic.[2] Much of the discussion centers on how best to calibrate third-party participation within a system that is meant to depoliticize and

* Partner, Chair of Public International Law, Jenner & Block LLP, Washington D.C.

1. Sophie LAMB, et. al., "Recent Development in the Law and Practice of Amicus Briefs in Investor-State Arbitration", 5 Indian J. Arb. L. (2017, issue 2) p. 87, fn. 72 (noting that "[t]he ratio of tribunal decisions on amicus applications to cases registered with ICSID was approximately 1:6 in 2015 and 1:7 in 2016 (January to September). These ratios stood at 1:31 in 2001 and 1:23 in 2006 (ICSID tribunals did not make any decisions on amicus applications between 2002 and 2005).").
2. There have been well over 120 articles on third-party participation in investor-State arbitration published between 2001 and 2018. Some of the more recent and comprehensive works include: A. SARAVANAN and Dr. S.R. SUBRAMANIAN, "The Participation of Amicus Curiae in Investment Treaty Arbitration", 5 Journal of Civil & Legal Sciences (2016, no. 4); J. Christopher THOMAS, "Amicus Curiae in ICSID Arbitration" in Meg KINNEAR et. al., eds., *Building International Investment Law: The First 50 Years of ICSID* (Kluwer Law International 2015) pp. 685-698; Laurence BOISSON De CHAZOURNE and Rukia BARUTI DAMES, "Transparency in Investor-State Arbitration: An Incremental Approach", 2 BCDR Int'l Arb. Rev. (2015, no. 1) pp. 59-76; Mariel DIMSEY, "Article 4. Submission by a Third Person" in Dimitrij EULER, et. al., eds., *Transparency in International Investment Arbitration* (Cambridge University Press 2015) pp. 128-195; Chiara RAGNI, "The Role of Amicus Curiae in Investment Disputes" in Tullio TREVES et. al., eds., *Foreign Investment, International Law and Common Concerns* (Routledge 2014); Paul COATES, "The UNCITRAL Rules on Transparency in Treaty-based Investor-State Arbitration: Continuing the Evolution of Investment Treaty Arbitration", 17 Int'l Arb. L. Rev. (2014, no. 6); Lucas

provide efficient adjudication.[3] Within these debates, and indeed within the evolution of third-party participation in general, states have a unique role to play.[4] The role of the state as it relates to third-party participation is sometimes divergent and sometimes inconsistent – but it is always important. Indeed, from the perspective of other systemic actors, the role of the state is always primary. And the role of the state is no more crucial than at the early design stages of a procedural innovation.

States are the "ISDS Trinity" sitting at the center of the investor-State dispute system: they are the lawgivers (through their treaty- and rule-making function); they are the protectors of investment (through their establishment of transnational obligations and a depoliticized system for efficient adjudication of disputes); and they are the respondents (through their offers to arbitrate in international investment treaties and subsequent participation in the arbitral process).

States' stewardship of the system, especially on matters of transparency, is not without its difficulties. Some observers suggest that states have been slow or unsophisticated in responding to criticisms of "secrecy", resulting in a "democracy deficit" and an almost perpetual crisis of legitimacy.[5] Just how third-party participation

---

BASTIN, "Amici Curiae in Investor-State Arbitration: Eight Recent Trends", 30 Arb. Int'l (2014, no. 1) pp. 125-144; Maciej ZACHARIASIEWICZ, "Amicus Curiae in International Investment Arbitration: Can it Enhance the Transparency of Investment Dispute Resolution?", 29 J. Int'l Arb. (2012, no. 2), pp. 205-224; Katia Fach GÓMEZ, "Rethinking the Role of Amicus Curiae in International Investment Arbitration: How to Draw the Line Favorably for the Public Interest", 35 Fordham Int'l L. J. (2012, no. 2) pp. 510-564; Eugenia LEVINE, "Amicus Curiae in International Investment Arbitration: The Implications of an Increase in Third-Party Participation", 29 Berkley J. Int'l L. (2011); Noah RUBINS, "Investment Arbitration – "Transparency" in Investment Arbitration: A Call to Cost-Benefit Analysis" in Christian KLAUSEGGER, et. al., eds., *Austrian Yearbook on International Arbitration 2010* (Manzsche Verlags- und Univeristätsbuchhandlung 2010) pp. 293-305; Stanimir A. ALEXANDROV and Marinn CARLSON, "The Opportunity to Be Heard: Accommodating Amicus Curiae Participation in Investment Treaty Arbitration" in Miguel Angel FERNÁNDEZ-BALLESTER and David ARIAS, eds., *Liber Amicorum Bernando Cremades* (La Ley 2010) pp. 49-64; Nigel BLACKABY and Caroline RICHARD, "Amicus Curiae: A Panacea for Legitimacy in Investment Arbitration?" in Michael WAIBEL, et. al., eds., *The Backlash Against Investment Arbitration* (Kluwer Law International 2010), pp. 253-274; Karl-Heinz BÖCKSTIEGEL, "Transparency and Third-Party Participation in Investment Arbitration" in Rainer HOFMANN and Christian J. TAMS, eds., *The International Convention on the Settlement of ICSID Disputes (ICSID): Taking Stock after 40 years* (Nomos 2007) pp. 209-212.

3. See e.g., Noah RUBINS, "Investment Arbitration – Opening the Investment Arbitration Process: At What Cost, for What Benefit?" in Christian KLAUSEGGER, et. al., eds., *Austrian Arbitration Yearbook 2009* (Manzsche Verlags- und Univeristätsbuchhandlung 2009) pp. 483-492; Charles BROWER and Stephan SCHILL, "Is Arbitration a Threat or a Boon to the Legitimacy of International Investment Law?", 9 Chi. J. Int'l L. (2009, no. 2) p. 471.
4. The role of the "state" in investment arbitration has long been the subject of many excellent works of scholarship. Without necessarily aligning myself with the views expressed therein one way or another, perhaps one of the best discussions of the many roles of the state in investment treaty practice is Anthea ROBERTS, "Power and Persuasion in Investment Treaty Interpretation: The Dual Role of States", 104 Am. J. Int'l L. (2010, no. 2) pp. 179-225.
5. Anthony DEPALMA, "NAFTA's Powerful Little Secret; Obscure Tribunals Settle Disputes, but Go Too Far, Critics Say", New York Times, A1 (11 March 2001) ("Their meetings are secret. Their members are generally unknown. The decisions they reach need not be fully disclosed. Yet the way a small group of international tribunals handles disputes between investors and foreign

fits into these challenges, and whether third-party participation is properly understood as a component of "transparency" at all, is itself up for debate.[6]

The focus of this short paper, however, is not to engage with this debate. Nor will the paper dwell on the development of the practice generally or discuss how one might properly account for third-party participation without negatively impacting the integrity of the proceedings.[7] To be sure, we should continue to have these discussions and I am confident they will continue long beyond this ICCA Congress.

Instead, my modest aim is to: (1) consider how the tripartite role of the state helps us understand its behavior within the investor-State dispute system, (2) examine how the first cases to deal with third-party participation provide an example of how the system can evolve, and (3) present a few brief observations on how states react to innovation within this framework. In short, to better anticipate how the system will evolve one should recognize the different interests that a state must balance when making a decision at a moment of innovation (or reform). How to understand these moments of innovation is very much at the center of this Congress, including on issues related to third-party participation and its future within investor-State arbitration.

II. THE "ISDS TRINITY": THE TRIPARTITE ROLE OF THE STATE IN THE INVESTOR-STATE DISPUTE SYSTEM

States are unique in the investor-State dispute system. As a class of participants, states occupy three distinct yet interconnected roles within the framework. What I call the ISDS Trinity can be understood as shorthand for the state's systemic role as (1) lawgiver, (2) protector, and (3) respondent. Each role has different attendant interests and thus each state necessarily calibrates the emphasis it puts on these three roles in its own

---

governments has led to national laws being revoked, justice systems questioned and environmental regulations challenged. And it is all in the name of protecting the rights of foreign investors under the North American Free Trade Agreement."). This now famous passage put the transparency debate front and center, literally, within the United States. See also Barnali CHOUDHURY, "Recapturing Public Power: Is Investment Arbitration's Engagement of the Public Interest Contributing to the Democratic Deficit?" 41 Vand. J. Transnat'l L. (2008) p. 775 (quoted from same in N. BLACKABY and C. RICHARD, "Amicus Curiae: A Panacea for Legitimacy in Investment Arbitration?", fn. 71, "[o]ne method of reducing the democratic deficit is to enhance public debate and participation in the investment arbitration process such that the public feel as though they have a meaningful say in the arbitral tribunal outcomes".); OECD, *Transparency and Third Party Participation in Investor State Dispute Resolution* (2005) para. 1, noting that "confidential in camera proceedings has come under increased scrutiny and criticisms".

6. See N. BLACKABY and C. RICHARD, "Amicus Curiae: A Panacea for Legitimacy in Investment Arbitration?", fn. 2 above (citing at fn. 7, Thomas N. HALE and Anne-Marie SLAUGHTER, "Transparency: Possibility and Limitations", 30 Fletcher Forum of World Affairs (2006) pp. 153, 163 as describing "the term transparency as an 'egregiously overused and poorly understood buzzword'".); M. ZACHARIASIEWICZ, "Amicus Curiae in International Arbitration: Can It Enhance the Transparency of Investment Dispute Resolution?", fn. 2 above.
7. State action in the formative years of third-party participation circumscribed this inquiry within the text of various arbitration rules and international treaties themselves. Contrast this, for example, with the more reticent action by states concerning security for costs or so-called "double hatting" by arbitrators.

parochial way based on its perceived needs. By definition states are different from one another.[8] Thus, while every state must take account of its role within the ISDS Trinity, no state is likely to fulfill its role identically to any other. In perfect balance, a visual depiction of the ISDS Trinity might look like this:

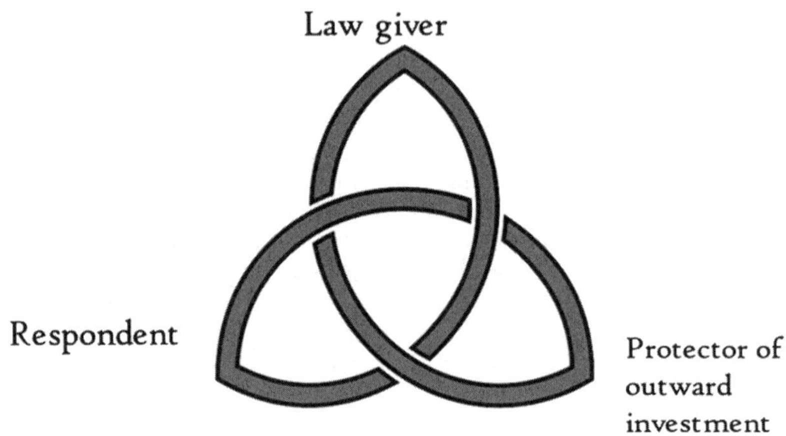

For any given state the ISDS Trinity is not static and almost never in balance. Indeed, a state's posture within the ISDS Trinity shifts internally depending on the dominant role it is playing. For example, a state may privilege certain interests when it is sitting as a lawgiver (e.g., at the negotiating table of a bilateral investment treaty (BIT) or at a United Nations Commission on International Trade Law (UNCITRAL) Working Group it may prioritize international norms) and other interests when it is a respondent in an active investor-State arbitration (e.g., sovereignty). These shifts in emphasis do not necessarily mean that the state is acting solely in its own self-interest or without care to its other roles within the system (i.e., the other points of the Trinity). The state must understand the interests underpinning each of the roles it plays within the ISDS Trinity at every systemic decision-point. When lawgiver, it must also be mindful of its role as respondent and protector. When respondent, it must be mindful of its role as lawgiver and protector, etc. Viewed in relation to the ISDS Trinity, one can observe state action on the "evolution" of investor-State arbitration in a new light.

One could apply the Trinity framework to any number of moments when a state must make a decision within the investor-State dispute system. For illustrative purposes, and in part because it is the topic of our panel, I focus on the innovation of third-party participation within the system.

8. Ian BROWNLIE, *Principles of Public International Law*, 5th ed. (Oxford University Press 1998) pp. 83-85.

Role in Trinity	Application of Interest
The state as lawgiver	As lawgiver the state has a broad interest in transparency, legitimacy, the rule of law, and the consistency and correctness of trans-substantive principles of treaty interpretation. States have obligations primarily to other states when acting as lawgiver.
The state as respondent	As respondent the state has a broad interest in protecting its regulatory power and general public welfare measures. This interest manifests with a specific concern of acceptance of process by local constituencies. States have obligations primarily to investors, other states, and their domestic population when acting as respondent.
The state as protector	As the protector of its nationals who also invest abroad, the state has a broad interest in the depoliticization of disputes and in the efficiency of a neutral dispute resolution system. States have obligations primarily to domestic constituencies when acting as protector.

III. THE PUNCTUATED EVOLUTION OF THIRD-PARTY PARTICIPATION: *METHANEX*, *UPS*, *AGUAS DEL TUNARI*, AND *VIVENDI*

Professor Chester Brown, in his article entitled "The Contribution of Non-State Actors to the Development of Transparency Regimes in Investment Treaty Arbitration", contained in this volume, does an excellent job placing third-party participation's origins in context.[9] I won't endeavor to walk the same ground here, but some basic framing of the evolution of third-party participation is important for my purposes as well. Evolution, the theme of this ICCA Congress, provides an evocative vocabulary for this undertaking. Indeed while the evolution of third-party participation in investor-State arbitration is reasonably well documented, recounting a few key moments of punctuation is helpful.[10] Third-party participation did not evolve gradually – it burst

9. Chester BROWN, this volume, pp. 653-668.
10. S. J.GOULD, *Punctuated Equilibrium* (Belknap Press 2007).

upon the scene and found a home within the system almost immediately. Looking selectively at some of these formative moments and how states responded at the time nicely demonstrates two additional ideas of the paper: (1) states were reactive – not proactive or innovative – as third-party participation evolved; and (2) once the concept of third-party participation evolved to a point of viability, states were exceptionally quick to tear down the systemic barriers to its growth in nearly every forum. In many ways, as the primary actors within the system, states' quick reaction to these innovations became more important than the innovation itself.

The debt to commercial arbitration for many of the procedures found in investor-State arbitration is well known.[11] Also well known are the differences between commercial arbitration and investor-State arbitration on fundamental concepts of privity, confidentiality, and party autonomy.[12] At first, the design of the investment arbitration system left almost no room for third parties to participate in the process. Just under two decades ago the participation of third parties in investor-State arbitrations was non-existent. But as the world becomes smaller and information becomes more available to the historically disenfranchised, "newness" has a way of entering an otherwise homogenous discourse.[13] In what context such moments occur, and when, often informs how the system's dominant actors react.

1. *Methanex Corporation v. United States*

Newness arrived within investor-State arbitration early in this century in the form of a request for participation by a third party who was not involved in the underlying dispute. On 25 August 2000, at the height of the global cosmopolitan effort to bring human rights norms within the international legal paradigm,[14] for the first time, a third party requested permission to participate in an investor-State arbitration as an "amicus curiae".[15] Under the sage direction of Professor Donald McRea and Howard Mann, a

11. Karl-Heinz BÖCKSTIEGEL, "Commercial and Investment Arbitration: How Different Are They Today?: The Lalive Lecture 2012", 28 Arb. Int'l (2012, no. 4) pp. 577-590.
12. Jan PAULSSON, "Arbitration Without Privity", 10 ICSID Rev. – Foreign Investment L. J. (1995, no. 2) pp. 232-257.
13. Homi K. BHABHA, "How Newness Enters the World: Postmodern space, postcolonial times and the trials of cultural translation" in Homi K. BHABHA, *The Location of Culture* (Routledge 1994).
14. F. FUKUYAMA, *The End of History and the Last Man* (Perennial, New York 2002); cf. Costas DOUZINAS, *The End of Human Rights: Critical Legal Thought at the Turn of the Century* (Hart Publishing 2000).
15. The term "amius curiae" was used by the petitioners in the *Methanex* Chapter 11 dispute and has been used by many scholars, practitioners, applicants, and tribunals since. Use of this term is unsurprising because it is the term used for similar submissions in common law jurisdictions. The NAFTA Parties themselves at first adopted the term "amicus curiae" when providing their views in the *Methanex* arbitration. Thereafter in their FTC Statement, discussed below, the NAFTA Parties referred to these submissions as "non-disputing party submissions", with a lower-case letter "p" perhaps in an attempt to bring this new practice more clearly within the terminology of the NAFTA itself in NAFTA Art. 1128. That choice by the NAFTA Parties has become confusing to some in relation to the terminology of NAFTA Art. 1128, which concerns "non-disputing Party," with a capital "p" and refers to submissions on matters of treaty interpretation by the other NAFTA Parties. NAFTA Parties, however, need not seek special leave from the tribunal to submit

Canadian NGO called the "The International Institute for Sustainable Development" (IISD) asked the *Methanex Corporation v. United State of America* NAFTA Chapter 11 tribunal (V.V. Veeder, Warren Christopher, and J. William Rowley) for "permission to submit an *Amicus Curiae* brief to the Tribunal on critical legal issues of public concern in the arbitration[.]"[16]

The application was concise, spare, and persuasive. In explaining why they should be permitted to file, the petitioners anticipated much of the substantive criteria that would later govern such motions, noting that "[t]he legal issues raised in this case are of immense public importance", that the ruling "will have a critical practical impact on environmental and other public welfare law-making at the federal, state and provincial levels throughout the NAFTA region", and that the subject under consideration "are matters of public interest distinct from the commercial issues that arbitration processes normally handle".[17]

The true innovation of the request, however, was the legal basis on which it argued for the tribunal's authority to permit third-party participation. Arguing that the UNCITRAL Arbitration Rules allow "broad discretion and flexibility in the conduct of the arbitral proceedings" and relying on Art. 15(1), the petitioner asserted that nothing "prohibits the Tribunal from granting the *amicus* status requested here".[18] Everyone, including the petitioner, recognized that this request was something completely new.[19]

---

their views. The status of a non-NAFTA Party that seeks to provide a submission is therefore different and the nuance of a lower-case letter has occasionally been overlooked. Arbitral rules have also used various formulations as the practice developed. Indeed the United States has at times returned to calling these submissions "amicus curiae" submissions in its public statements relating to its more recent ISDS provisions. To make matters even more complicated, recent multilateral treaties and efforts to harmonize the practice have used the term "third-party" submissions. In this regard, the use of that term by the UNCITRAL Rules on Transparency is particularly noteworthy. It may yet take a few years to coalesce around terminology. The ICSID Rules amendment process, currently under way during the writing of this paper, is proceeding in the shadow of the UNCITRAL Rules on Transparency, which uses the term "third-party". What terminology the ICSID Rules use will have a significant impact on whether we begin to coalesce around the term "third-party" or continue to have multiple terms across various institutions and treaties. All things being equal, in accord with the UNCITRAL Rules on Transparency, I find the term "third-party" to be more precise than "amicus curiae" and less confusing than "non-disputing party" and have opted to use that term throughout.

16. *Methanex Corporation v. United States of America*, NAFTA Ch. 11/UNCITRAL Arbitration, Petition to the Arbitral Tribunal by the International Institute for Sustainable Development ("IISD") (25 August 2000) para. 1.1. Methanex Corp., a major producer of methanol, brought this suit in response to California's ban on MTBE, a chemical compound used to treat unleaded gasoline. Methanol is a key component of MTBE. Methanex claimed that the California ban violated multiple provisions of the NAFTA and was tantamount to an expropriation of its investment.
17. *Methanex Corporation v. United States of America*, NAFTA Ch. 11/UNCITRAL Arbitration, Petition to the Arbitral Tribunal by the International Institute for Sustainable Development (25 August 2000) paras. 3.1-3.3.
18. *Methanex Corporation v. United States of America*, NAFTA Ch. 11/UNCITRAL Arbitration, Petition to the Arbitral Tribunal by the International Institute for Sustainable Development (25 August 2000) paras. 4.1-4.3.
19. The petitioner acknowledged that it is "not aware of any previous cases under the UNCITRAL process where third parties have petitioned the Tribunal to submit an *amicus* brief" and that "this issue is a matter of first impression for this Tribunal". *Methanex Corporation v. United States of*

Within just a few days, on 31 August 2000, the Claimant filed in opposition to the petition of the IISD, citing the importance of confidentiality to the proceedings and noting that Art. 15(1) of the UNCITRAL Arbitration Rules is addressed toward procedural matters and not matters such as third-party participation which it argued are more substantive rather than procedural.[20] Just a few days later, on 6 September 2000, a second petition was received by the tribunal by yet another third party seeking leave to file in the arbitration, this time by a coalition of United States–based NGOs (Communities for a Better Environment, the Blue Water Network of Earth Island Institute, and the Center For International Law).[21] The coalition sought leave to present arguments about how best to balance property rights and the government's authority to implement environmental regulations – a kind of precursor to the "right to regulate" concerns that dominate the debate today.

On the same day, 6 September 2000, the *Methanex* tribunal held a procedural conference and set a briefing schedule for third-party participation. The tribunal decided to permit applications up to a deadline of 13 October 2000, later extended to 16 October 2000, and specifically allowed for the NAFTA Parties to submit views on these questions soon thereafter.

IISD responded to the Claimant's objection a few weeks later and elaborated on its argument in support of its petition, including by highlighting the "troubling" failure of the recently issued *Metalclad* Award[22] to make "any reference to the environmental and sustainable development goals" recognized in the NAFTA – a perspective it promised to provide if accepted as participants.[23]

The stage was now set for the NAFTA Parties to make their views known. It was the first time in any investor-State arbitration where a state was to address the issue of third-party participation. It was clearly a pivotal moment. All three NAFTA Parties submitted views: the United States (in this case in its express role as a Disputing Party) on 27 October 2000,[24] and both Mexico and Canada (as non-disputing Parties pursuant to a

---

America, NAFTA Ch. 11/UNCITRAL Arbitration, Petition to the Arbitral Tribunal by the International Institute for Sustainable Development (25 August 2000) para. 4.3.

20. *Methanex Corporation v. United States of America*, NAFTA Ch. 11/UNCITRAL Arbitration, Submissions of Claimant Respecting Petition of the International Institute for Sustainable Development (31 August 2000).
21. *Methanex Corporation v. United States of America*, NAFTA Ch. 11/UNCITRAL Arbitration, Petition to the Arbitral Tribunal by Communities for a Better Environment, The Blue Water Network of Earth Island Institute, and the Center For International Law (5 September 2000); see also *id.* (13 October 2000).
22. *Metalclad Corporation v. The United Mexican States* (ICSID Case No. ARB(AF)/97/1), Award (30 August 2000).
23. *Methanex Corporation v. United States of America*, NAFTA Ch. 11/UNCITRAL Arbitration, Petitioner's Final Submissions Regarding the Petition of the International Institute for Sustainable Development to the Arbitral Tribunal for Amicus Curiae States (16 October 2000) paras. 10-18.
24. *Methanex Corporation v. United States of America*, NAFTA Ch. 11/UNCITRAL Arbitration, Statement of Respondent United States of America Regarding Petition for Amicus Curiae Status (27 October 2000).

request by the tribunal and the express authority granted by NAFTA Art. 1128) on 10 November 2000.[25]

When it comes to the NAFTA Parties and interpretation of NAFTA Chapter 11, commonality in views is typically the norm. Nothing prohibits a NAFTA Party, including the Disputing Party, from speaking with another NAFTA Party on questions of treaty interpretation. Often this is done in advance of a NAFTA Art. 1128 submission (also called a non-disputing Party submission) and helps ensure that whenever possible the NAFTA Parties are speaking with one voice – a common view provides guidance to investors and tribunals alike. In the autumn of 2000, however, the three states each had a unique and divergent view on the question of third-party participation.

That the NAFTA Parties did not have a consensus view is, upon reflection, not necessarily surprising. States are different and have different views. Difference is a core principle of the Westphalian notion of sovereignty. From another perspective, perhaps it should have been expected that the NAFTA Parties would adopt different positions – they were, after all, representing somewhat divergent interests in the arbitration. Mexico and Canada, as non-disputing Parties, were firmly in their role as "lawgivers" – by considering the petition's implications for future arbitrations' legitimacy, for example – and as "protectors of outward investment" – by considering how the introduction of third-party submissions would impact their efforts to attract foreign investment, or in Canada's case impact their investors' rights under the treaty. The United States, on the other hand, was obliged to not only take those viewpoints into account, but also to take a position first and foremost as "respondent" – that is, the party whose immediate and concrete interests were the subject of the dispute. In that capacity, the United States had to keep an eye toward preserving both its own regulatory authority vis-à-vis investors and its responsibility for the public welfare of its constituents (i.e., its own citizens).

The United States supported "Petitioners' requests to make written *amicus* submissions", arguing that under "the rules governing this arbitration, the Tribunal may properly consider petitions for leave to make *amicus* submissions and allow such submissions in instances it deems appropriate". The United States submitted that Methanex's position amounted to treating the UNCITRAL Arbitration Rules and the NAFTA as analogous to "an arbitration between private parties brought under the arbitration clause of a commercial agreement".[26] That position, it argued, was without merit.[27] In particular, reasoned the United States, the tribunal's exercise of discretion was especially appropriate "where, as here, the arbitration is against a sovereign State and also implicates substantial public interests".[28] The case, it explained, was "a dispute brought by a private party against a State that (1) challenges sovereign acts under

25. *Methanex Corporation v. United States of America*, NAFTA Ch. 11/UNCITRAL Arbitration, Mexico's Submission in Response to Application for Amicus Standing (10 November 2000); and Submission of the Government of Canada (10 November 2000).

26. *Methanex Corporation v. United States of America*, NAFTA Ch. 11/UNCITRAL Arbitration, Statement of Respondent United States of America Regarding Petition for Amicus Curiae Status (27 October 2000) pp. 1-3.

27. *Id.*, pp. 2-3.

28. *Id.*, p. 2.

international law pursuant to a trilateral trade agreement, and (2) implicates substantial public interests such as public health and the environment".[29]

Throughout its response, however, the United States clearly also kept its roles as "lawgiver" and "protector of investment" front-of-mind. In making its conclusions, the United States argued that an investor-State arbitration has a "fundamentally different nature than a typical international commercial dispute" and that the tribunal's decision on the merits "may have a significant effect beyond the two parties to the dispute".[30] Finally, the United States found no difficulty in the application of the UNCITRAL Arbitration Rules and the NAFTA as permitting the tribunal to exercise its discretion[31] and believed that such discretion in favor of acceptance of third-party submissions was particularly apt "upon a showing by a non-disputing party of knowledge or expertise, and upon a determination by the Tribunal that the submission would be both relevant and helpful to the Tribunal – yet would not prejudice the rights of the parties or interfere with the efficient advancement of the proceedings" and that failure to do so may "reinforce the growing perception that Chapter Eleven dispute resolution is an exclusionary and secretive process".[32]

Mexico, which occupied a different role in the arbitration as a non-disputing Party, did not agree with the United States. In its submission, Mexico drew a clear line within the NAFTA itself. It noted that the definition of "disputing Parties" provided by application of Art. 1139 as "the disputing investor and the disputing Party", that apart from non-disputing Parties under Art. 1128, "no other person has a legal interest in the dispute, and therefore, Chapter Eleven does not provide for the intervention of other persons".[33] Moreover, because NAFTA Parties must limit themselves to submissions on matters of treaty interpretation only, Mexico pointed out that third parties would thus "have greater rights than the NAFTA Parties themselves" and would "render Article 1128 meaningless, contrary to the principle of effectiveness in international treaty interpretation, because the NAFTA Parties would then be able to make submissions on questions on interpretation of the Agreement under Article 1128, and file *amicus* briefs for other purposes".[34]

Furthermore, Mexico raised a concern customary to any "lawgiver" – namely, the need to protect the integrity of both its own legal system and its obligations under a multinational agreement. Mexico pointed out that third-party participation is not

29. *Id.*, pp. 2-3.

30. *Id.*, pp. 4-5.

31. The United States recognized the tension between third-party participation and non-disputing Party submissions as provided for in NAFTA Chapter 11 and sought to clarify lest there be any confusion. Toward that end the United States noted that "Article 1128 does limit the Tribunal's discretion in one sense: it grants non-disputing State Parties a *right* to make submissions to tribunals on questions of interpretation of the NAFTA. It therefore removes any discretion the Tribunal might otherwise have had to decline to accept such a submission. Article 1128's grant of a *right* to non-disputing State Parties to make certain submissions, however, does not speak to whether the Tribunal may exercise its discretion to accept, *as a matter of permission*, submissions by other non-parties as a general matter." See *Id.*, p. 11. (Emphasis in original.)

32. *Id.*, pp. 14-15.

33. *Methanex Corporation v. United States of America*, NAFTA Ch. 11/UNCITRAL Arbitration, Mexico's Submission in Response to Application for Amicus Standing (10 November 2000) paras. 1-2.

34. *Id.*, para. 7.

provided for in civil law jurisdictions and that the tribunal must be sensitive to the fact that the investor-State dispute system provided for in the NAFTA draws "a careful balance between the procedures of common law countries and those of civil law countries (such as Mexico)" and that the "fact that a specific procedure or legal concept may exist in a Party's domestic law cannot serve as grounds to transport it into the international plane".[35] No doubt mindful of the *Methanex* tribunal's common law background, Mexico cautioned:

> "Even though in this arbitration both the disputing Party and the Party of the disputing investor are common law countries, Mexico is concerned that concepts or procedures that are alien to its legal tradition and which were not agreed to as part of the NAFTA may be imported into NAFTA dispute settlement proceedings, and set a precedent for future cases in which Mexico is involved as the disputing Party."[36]

Canada adopted a more cautious approach and sought to encourage consensus among the NAFTA Parties. In its relatively short submission, Canada agreed with the United States that although "only NAFTA Parties have the right to make submissions on questions of interpretation of the NAFTA" and that a third party has no such right, but that it too was "mindful" of "the public interest in these matters" and therefore "sympathetic to the interests of the Petitioners". Because nothing in the NAFTA or the UNCITRAL Arbitration Rules expressly prohibited third-party participation, Canada was inclined to suggest that "in this case, the Tribunal should accept the written submissions of the Petitioners".[37] Canada, however, expressly disclaimed the precedential value of its statement and stated that it "is without prejudice to the position Canada may take in other NAFTA Chapter Eleven cases".[38]

Nevertheless, Canada recognized the "importance of ensuring uniformity and predictability in the rules and procedures governing the settlement of investment-state disputes" and that there "are numerous complex legal and technical issues raised by the question of whether and how a NAFTA Chapter Eleven tribunal should receive submissions from persons other than the disputing Parties or the non-disputing NAFTA Parties" and therefore implored the "NAFTA partners to work together on the issue of *amicus curiae* participation as a matter of urgency in order to provide guidance to Chapter Eleven tribunals".[39] In this respect, Canada can be seen as representing the "protector of investment" viewpoint by calling for a predictable, uniform interpretation of the NAFTA dispute resolution process – an important concern for investors – as well as the viewpoint of "lawgiver" concerned about consistency and legitimacy of the system.

The tribunal's decision on this request in *Methanex Corporation v. United States of America* was not only "new", it was groundbreaking. Relying on Art. 15(1) of the

35. *Id.*, para. 13.
36. *Id.*, para. 14.
37. *Methanex Corporation v. United States of America*, NAFTA Ch. 11/UNCITRAL Arbitration, Submission of the Government of Canada (10 November 2000) para. 3.
38. *Id.*
39. *Id.*, para. 4.

UNCITRAL Arbitration Rules, the tribunal reasoned that it had broad and discretionary powers on questions of procedure and that it therefore "has the power to accept *amicus* submissions (in writing) from each of the Petitioners, to be copied simultaneously to the legal representatives of the Disputing Parties, Canada and Mexico".[40]

The thoughtful and thorough decision of the unanimous tribunal directly replied to the submissions by the NAFTA Parties. With respect to the role of third parties vis-à-vis non-disputing Parties (i.e., the other NAFTA Parties both of whom had a right to participate pursuant to NAFTA Art. 1128) and the concerns raised in each NAFTA Party's submissions, the tribunal was categorical that in its view: "receipt of written submissions from a person other than the Disputing Parties is not equivalent to adding that person as a party to the arbitration" and therefore the "rights of the Disputing Parties in the arbitration and the limited rights of a Non-Disputing Party under Article 1128 of NAFTA are not thereby acquired by such a third person". Focusing on the limited nature of third-party participation, and in direct response to concerns raised by the NAFTA Parties, the tribunal made it clear that the NAFTA Parties' "rights, both procedural and substantive, remain juridically exactly the same before and after receipt of such submissions; and the third person acquires no rights at all".[41]

As for the difficulties in responding to third-party submissions, the tribunal noted that "[i]t would always be the Tribunal's task, assisted by the Disputing Parties, to adopt procedures whereby any burden in meeting written submissions from a Petitioner was mitigated or extinguished".[42] As a nod in that direction, and consistent with what the tribunal understood as its authority under the UNCITRAL Arbitration Rules and the NAFTA, it limited the scope of third-party participation to just written submissions, noting that "it has no power to accept the Petitioners' requests to receive materials generated within the arbitration or to attend oral hearings of the arbitration".[43]

Finally, the tribunal addressed several points that were more systemic in nature. First, it directly addressed Mexico's express concern that a decision to allow third-party submissions would be privileging one legal tradition (namely, common law) over another. "In coming to this conclusion," the tribunal stressed, "[it] has not relied on the fact that *amicus* submissions feature in the domestic procedures of the courts in two, but not three, NAFTA Parties."[44]

Second, it associated itself with the views of the United States and Canada that "the Chapter 11 arbitral process could benefit from being perceived as more open or transparent; or conversely harmed if seen as unduly secretive". The tribunal thereby aligned itself as a lawgiver and asserted that its "willingness to receive *amicus* submissions might support the process in general and this arbitration in particular; whereas a blanket refusal could do positive harm".[45]

---

40. *Methanex Corporation v. United States of America*, NAFTA Ch. 11/UNCITRAL Arbitration, Decision of the Tribunal on Petitions from Third Persons to Intervene as "Amici Curiae" (15 January 2001) para. 47.
41. *Id.*, para. 30.
42. *Id.*, para. 37.
43. *Id.*, para. 47.
44. *Id.*
45. *Id.*, para. 49.

Third, and finally, the tribunal expressly limited (or at least purported to limit) the power of its decision and stated that it "can set no legal precedent, in general or at all" and "has no power to determine for other arbitration tribunals how to interpret Article 15(1)" and "in a later arbitration, there may be other circumstances leading that tribunal to exercise its discretion differently".[46] Implicitly echoing Canada's call for consistency and placing its totality of the circumstances-based approach directly to the NAFTA Parties, the tribunal concluded with: "For each arbitration, the decision must be made by its tribunal in the particular circumstances of that arbitration only."[47]

2. *United Parcel Service of America, Inc. v. Government of Canada*

Another NAFTA tribunal was confronting the same questions on an overlapping time frame. On 8 November 2000 – more than two months before the *Methanex* tribunal issued its decision – another coalition submitted an application to the Chapter 11 tribunal in *United Parcel Service of America Inc. v. Government of Canada* NAFTA (Dean Ronald A. Cass, L. Yves Fortier, and Kenneth Keith). The application was brought on behalf of the Canadian Union of Postal Workers (which represented approximately 46,000 operational employees of the Canadian Postal Service) and the Council of Canadians (a non-partisan Canadian NGO) requesting, inter alia, standing as Parties in the proceedings, or, in the alternative, "the right to intervene in such proceedings in accordance with the principles of fundamental justice".[48]

In their application, the petitioners acknowledged "the relative novelty of [their] application" and noted that "[w]hile the issue of third party intervention in arbitral proceedings is not without precedent, it has very rarely arisen in the modern era of international commercial arbitration".[49] In explaining why they should either be admitted standing as Parties to the proceedings, or the right to intervene in the proceedings, the petitioners argued: (i) they had direct interests in the outcome of the case; (ii) "this claim has broader public policy implications that are also of vital concern to the Petitioners"; and (iii) the UNCITRAL process reserved "exclusively to those with standing as Parties, certain matters that are of vital concern to the Petitioners. These issues include the extent to which Canadian courts will maintain judicial oversight of these proceedings, and the lack of transparency that traditionally characterizes such arbitral processes."[50] The petitioners further argued that the authority to grant third-party standing was provided for by a number of international conventions, customs, and jurisprudence including, for example, Art. 15(1) of the UNCITRAL Arbitration Rules.[51]

---

46. *Id.*, para. 51.
47. *Id.*
48. *United Parcel Service of America Inc. v. Government of Canada*, NAFTA Ch. 11/UNCITRAL Arbitration, Submissions of the Canadian Union of Postal Workers and the Council of Canadians (8 November 2000) paras. 1-15. United Parcel Service of America Inc., a delivery company, brought this claim against the Government of Canada in connection with alleged unfair advantages accorded by Canada to Canada Post in its direct competition with UPS Canada.
49. *Id.*, para. 23.
50. *Id.*, paras. 24-60.
51. *Id.*, paras. 61-89.

Without directly addressing the threshold question of its authority to consider third-party applications, on 17 April 2001, the tribunal ordered the petitioners to file briefs in respect of their petition by 14 May 2001, with the Parties replying on 28 May 2001.[52] Consequently, on 10 May 2001, the Canadian Union of Postal Workers and the Council of Canadians filed a second petition repeating their requests of 8 November 2000.[53]

All three NAFTA Parties submitted comments on the application: Canada (in its role as a Disputing Party) on 28 May 2001;[54] and both Mexico and the United States (as non-disputing Parties) on 11 June 2001.[55]

In its submission, Canada stated that it "supports greater openness in NAFTA Chapter Eleven proceedings and appreciates the contribution that transparency brings to building public confidence in the investor-state dispute settlement process".[56] In this submission, however, it went further than it had in *Methanex*, setting forth a legal argument in affirmative support of acceptance, rather than expressing a mere inclination. Canada argued that, whilst the tribunal had no explicit jurisdiction to add the petitioners as Parties to the proceedings, it did have discretion, pursuant to Art. 15(1) of the UNCITRAL Arbitration Rules, to receive written briefs from third parties. Canada further argued that, in deciding whether to accept requests for intervention, the tribunal should consider whether:

> "(a) There is a public interest in the arbitration;
> (b) The Petitioners have sufficient interest in the outcome of the arbitration;
> (c) The Petitioner's submissions will assist in the determination of a factual or legal issue related to the arbitration by bringing a perspective or particular knowledge that is different from that of the disputing parties; and
> (d) The Petitioners' submissions can be received without causing prejudice to the disputing parties."[57]

Mexico agreed with Canada's argument that the tribunal had no jurisdiction under the NAFTA and the UNCITRAL Arbitration Rules to add the petitioners as additional disputing Parties to the proceedings.[58] But, consistent with its arguments in *Methanex*,

---

52. *United Parcel Service of America Inc. v. Government of Canada*, NAFTA Ch. 11/UNCITRAL Arbitration, Procedural Decision No. 2 (17 April 2001).
53. *United Parcel Service of America Inc. v. Government of Canada*, NAFTA Ch. 11/UNCITRAL Arbitration, Petition to the Arbitral Tribunal Canadian Union of Postal Workers and of the Council of Canadians (10 May 2001).
54. *United Parcel Service of America Inc. v. Government of Canada*, NAFTA Ch. 11/UNCITRAL Arbitration, Canada's Submission on Canadian Union of Postal Workers and the Council of Canadians Petition for Intervention (28 May 2001).
55. *United Parcel Service of America Inc. v. Government of Canada*, NAFTA Ch. 11/UNCITRAL Arbitration, First Mexican 1128 Submission (11 June 2001); and First US 1128 Submission (11 June 2001).
56. *United Parcel Service of America Inc. v. Government of Canada*, NAFTA Ch. 11/UNCITRAL Arbitration, Canada's Submission on Canadian Union of Postal Workers and the Council of Canadians Petition for Intervention (28 May 2001) para. 6.
57. *Id.*, paras. 9-58.
58. *United Parcel Service of America Inc. v. Government of Canada,* NAFTA Ch. 11/UNCITRAL Arbitration, First Mexican 1128 Submission (11 June 2001) para. 6.

Mexico disagreed with Canada's view on the tribunal's ability to allow third-parties to file written submissions. Mexico argued that "the absence of express language in [the NAFTA] means that the Tribunal cannot take it upon itself to authorize actions that the sovereign States party to the Treaty did not authorize".[59]

Conversely, the United States agreed with Canada's views that tribunals are not authorized under the NAFTA to grant third parties standing in arbitral proceedings, but that "in proceedings governed by the UNCITRAL Arbitration Rules, tribunals are authorized to accept written submissions of such third parties as *amici curiae*".[60] This view was again consistent with the United States' arguments in *Methanex*.

On 17 October 2001, the tribunal issued its decision on the petition. The tribunal held that it had the authority to permit third-party participation pursuant to Art. 15(1) of the UNCITRAL Arbitration Rules, stating "[t]he Tribunal declares that it has power to accept written *amicus* briefs from the Petitioners".[61] The tribunal, however, deferred consideration of receiving briefs until the merits stage of the arbitration following consultation with the Parties.

On 20 October 2005, the tribunal received another application from the Canadian Union of Postal Workers and the Council of Canadians for "standing to participate in these proceedings".[62]

In explaining why they should be permitted to file a submission, the petitioners relied on some of the same substantive criteria that were relied upon by the petitioners in the *Methanex* case. In particular, the petitioners argued:

> "[t]here is also a considerable public interest in the subject matter of the arbitration that arises from the potential of this claim to impugn the validity of an important Canadian cultural program, and to expand the scope of investor-state litigation in a manner that will encourage future claims assailing Canadian policy and law as it relates to other public services, such as those relating to health care and libraries."[63]

The petitioners further argued that (i) their "submissions would assist the Tribunal in the determination of factual and legal issues related to this arbitration and bring a perspective, particular knowledge and insight that is different from that of the disputing parties"; (ii) they "ha[d] a significant and direct interest in this arbitration"; and (iii) their "views on several of the issues that arise in these proceedings are likely to be quite distinct from those of Canada and Canada Post".[64]

---

59. *Id.*, para. 7.
60. *United Parcel Service of America Inc. v. Government of Canada*, NAFTA Ch. 11/UNCITRAL Arbitration, First US 1128 Submission (11 June 2001) para. 3.
61. *United Parcel Service of America Inc. v. Government of Canada*, NAFTA Ch. 11/UNCITRAL Arbitration, Decision of the Tribunal on Petitions for Intervention and Participation as Amici Curiae (17 October 2001) paras. 59-68 and 73.
62. *United Parcel Service of America Inc. v. Government of Canada*, NAFTA Ch. 11/UNCITRAL Arbitration, Application for Amicus Status by the Canadian Union of Postal Workers and the Council of Canadians (20 October 2005).
63. *Id.*, para. 22.
64. *Id.*, paras. 20-21 and 23.

On the same day, the tribunal received an application from the US Chamber of Commerce, a business federation representing "the interests of United States investors abroad".[65] The US Chamber of Commerce argued that the criteria tribunals should consider in exercising their discretion to allow third-party participation were derived from decisions in *Methanex*, *Aguas Argentinas S.A. et al v. The Argentine Republic*, and from the *UPS* tribunal's 17 October 2001 decision discussed above. It argued that those decisions established the following criteria: (i) will the submissions assist the tribunal in providing perspective, knowledge, expertise, insight or material not provided by the parties? (ii) will the submission address matters within the scope of the dispute? (iii) does the applicant have a significant interest in the arbitration? and (iv) is there a public interest in the subject matter of the arbitration? The petitioners further argued that such considerations are to be balanced against the possibility of unduly burdening or unfairly prejudicing the parties or the process.[66]

On 10 November 2005, Canada filed a response to the US Chamber of Commerce's application in which it did not object to the filing of a submission.

Although no formal decision was issued with respect to the third-party applications, the tribunal's eventual Award indicates in its report on the procedural history that it accorded the US Chamber of Commerce amicus status. The Award further suggests that the submission of the Canadian Union of Postal Workers and the Council of Canadians was also accepted.[67]

3. *The FTC Statement*

In the midst of this rapidly changing environment, the NAFTA Parties took up Canada's call from its submission in *Methanex* to seek consensus on third-party participation. Throughout the next several months the NAFTA Parties, now acting primarily in their roles as "lawgivers", worked to develop a common approach for third-party participation. The speed with which the NAFTA Parties acted is remarkable. Only two years after the tribunals' decisions on third-party participation in *Methanex* and *UPS,* the three NAFTA Parties had come to a compromise consensus position and, sitting as the authoritative Free Trade Commission (FTC),[68] issued an official statement favoring the availability of third-party participation.[69] Without question, the *Methanex* tribunal's decision that it had discretion to permit third-party submissions and would exercise that discretion in favor of acceptance was instrumental in the ultimate decision by the

---

65. *United Parcel Service of America Inc. v. Government of Canada*, NAFTA Ch. 11/UNCITRAL Arbitration, Application for Amicus Status by the US Chamber of Commerce (20 October 2005) para. 3.
66. *Id.*, paras. 7-8.
67. *United Parcel Service of America Inc. v. Government of Canada*, NAFTA Ch. 11/UNCITRAL Arbitration, Award on the Merits (24 May 2007) para. 3.
68. NAFTA Art. 2001(2); Gabrielle KAUFMANN-KOHLER, "Interpretive Powers of the Free Trade Commission and the Rule of Law" in Emmanuel GAILLARD, ed., *Fifteen Years of NAFTA Chapter 11 Arbitrations* (Juris 2011).
69. Statement of the Free Trade Commission on non-disputing party participation (7 October 2003).

NAFTA Parties to issue the FTC Statement.[70] The FTC Statement adopted much of the *Methanex* tribunal's approach and read: "No provision of the North American Free Trade Agreement ("NAFTA") limits a Tribunal's discretion to accept written submissions from a person or entity that is a not a disputing party…."[71] It further set out the considerations a tribunal should take into account when determining whether to grant leave to file a third-party submission, which included the extent to which:

> "(a) the [third-]party submission would assist the Tribunal in the determination of a factual or legal issue related to the arbitration by bringing a perspective, particular knowledge or insight that is different from that of the disputing parties;
> (b) the [third-]party submission would address matters within the scope of the dispute;
> (c) the [third-] party has a significant interest in the arbitration; and
> (d) there is a public interest in the subject-matter of the arbitration."[72]

The FTC Statement offered further guidance to NAFTA Chapter 11 tribunals that in exercising its discretion to allow third-party participation, the tribunal must ensure that "(a) any [third] party submission avoids disrupting the proceedings; and (b) neither disputing party is unduly burdened or unfairly prejudiced by such submissions".[73] At the 2003 annual meeting of the FTC, at which the FTC Statement was issued, US Trade Representative Robert B. Zoellick commented: "We are pleased that we have been able to take further steps to enhance the public participation and understanding of the dispute settlement process."[74]

4. *Aguas del Tunari S.A. v. Bolivia*

Meanwhile, third-party participation was first considered by an ICSID tribunal in *Aguas del Tunari S.A. v. Bolivia* (David D. Caron, José Luis Alberro-Semerena, Henri C. Alvarez). On 29 August 2002, various NGOs and individuals submitted a petition to intervene in the arbitration as Parties, or, in the alternative, to participate as "amicus curiae".[75] Like the third parties in *Methanex*, the petitioners asserted that the tribunal's decision was "likely to affect issues of broad public concern", including water rights and the environment, and that petitioners were uniquely situated to "represent the concerns of a broad sector of the public in Bolivia and throughout the world".[76] But the petitioners also invoked systemic arguments directed at investor-State arbitrations writ large,

70. It was not until 2004, however, following the issuance of the NAFTA Free Trade Commission's Statement on non-disputing party participation in 2003 that the *Methanex* tribunal admitted the briefs.
71. Statement of the Free Trade Commission on non-disputing party participation (7 October 2003) para. 1.
72. *Id.*, para. 6.
73. *Id.*, para. 7.
74. Richard MILLS and Ricardo REYES, "NAFTA Commission Announces New Transparency Measures" (7 October 2003), available at <https://ustr.gov/archive/Document_Library/Press Releases/2003/October/NAFTA_Commission_Announces_New_Transparency_Measures.html> (last accessed 23 February 2018).

claiming that "fundamental fairness and the legitimacy of the Tribunal's award requires that the Tribunal allow Petitioners to intervene in these proceedings".[77] The petition included a detailed list of specific requests, including the right to make submissions regarding procedures, jurisdiction, arbitrability, and the merits; permission to attend hearings and make oral presentations; and secure immediate access to the Parties' submissions. The petition made additional requests in support of its appeal to transparency and legitimacy, including public disclosure of the Parties' submissions, reports, and hearing transcripts; making all hearings open to the public; and holding a public hearing in Cochabamba, the city at the heart of the dispute, to develop the facts of the case.[78]

The petition's legal argument echoed the third-party petition in *UPS*, albeit in a different legal framework – it claimed that the decision as to the petitioners' participation was a procedural issue rather than a substantive one. Noting that the ICSID Convention was silent on the question of their participation, the petitioners directed the tribunal to Art. 44, which "explicitly allows [it] to decide on any question of procedure not covered by those instruments or by a rule agreed by the parties".[79] They further argued that the tribunal's discretion could override any objection of the Parties in appropriate circumstances, such as when the "character of claims ... raises broad issues of public concern".[80] And, citing an "authoritative text" requiring that arbitrations avoid acting in a manner contrary to public policy in the state where the arbitration is held, the petitioners argued that their participation was acceptable because Bolivian public policy gives third parties the opportunity to participate in disputes.[81]

The tribunal was no doubt aware of the *Methanex* and *UPS* rulings on third-party participation, not least because petitioners had addressed both cases at length.[82] Nonetheless, the tribunal proclaimed itself constrained in its authority under the ICSID Convention and the Netherlands-Bolivia BIT. It did not engage in a comparison between its own perceived authority and that vested to a NAFTA Chapter 11 tribunal operating

75. *Aguas del Tunari, S.A. v. Republic Of Bolivia* (ICSID Case No. Arb/02/3), Petition (29 August 2002). The dispute concerned claims related to a concession contract to provide water and sewage services to the City of Cochabamba. The following collectively brought a petition to intervene: (1) La Coordinadora Para La Defensa Del Agua Y Vida (self-described as "a coalition of community organizations, labor groups, human rights organizations, farmers associations, students and other broad-based networks of civil society in the region of Cochabamba, Bolivia"); (2) La Federación Departamental Cochabambina De Organizaciones Regantes (self-described as representing "thousands of small-scale producer families"); (3) SEMAPA Sur (self-described as a "grassroots organization dedicated to bringing water to the neighborhoods in the southern part of Cochabamba"); (4) Friends Of The Earth-Netherlands (self-described as a "Dutch environmental association with 30,000 members, working at the local, national and international level for ecologically sustainable development"); and (5) four associated individuals: Oscar Olivera, Omar Fernandez, Father Luis Sánchez, and Congressman Jorge Alvarado. *Id.*, paras. 5-17.

76. *Id.*, para. 2.

77. *Id.;* see also paras. 23, 29-34.

78. *Id.*, para. 3.

79. *Id.*, para. 37.

80. *Id.*, para. 40.

81. *Id.*, paras. 38, 41.

82. *Id.*, paras. 33, 40, 43-44, 51-52, 59-62.

under the UNICTRAL Arbitration Rules.[83] Although it appears that neither Party filed formal submissions responding to the petition, the tribunal noted that it had requested and received the Parties' views, and the petition was discussed at the arbitration's First Session on 9 December 2002.[84]

In a letter dated 29 January 2003, the tribunal unanimously concluded that the third parties' request was beyond the power or authority of the tribunal. In its reasoning, the tribunal commented that "[t]he interplay of the two treaties involved [*i.e.*, the ICSID Convention and the 1992 Netherlands-Bolivia BIT] and the consensual nature of arbitration places the control of the issues ... with the parties, not the Tribunal".[85] It found that without the Parties' consent, it could not grant to third parties permission to intervene in the proceedings, and could not provide access to hearings or transcripts for either third parties or the public.[86] It also commented that there was no present need to call witnesses or seek third-party submissions.[87] The tribunal hastened to express its respect for the petitioners, however, emphasizing that the "briefness of our reply should not be taken as an indication that your request was viewed in other than a serious manner" and noting that it appreciated the petitioners' concern with the matter's resolution.[88]

5. *Suez, Sociedad General de Aguas de Barcelona S.A., and Vivendi Universal S.A. v. Argentina*

A few years after the *Aguas* decision, an ICSID tribunal came to the opposite conclusion. On 28 January 2005, the tribunal in *Suez, Sociedad General de Aguas de Barcelona S.A., and Vivendi Universal S.A. v. Argentina* (Gabrielle Kaufmann-Kohler, Pedro Nikken and Jeswald W. Salacuse), received an application from four Argentine-based NGOs and one international NGO, inter alia, for permission to "present legal arguments as *amicus curiae*".[89]

The Claimants and Argentina both filed observations on the application. The Claimants asked the tribunal to refuse the request, whilst Argentina "expressed its approval".[90] The Parties' observations are not publicly available, so we cannot evaluate how Argentina balanced its tripartite roles as "lawgiver", "protector of outward investment", and "respondent" in addressing the petition.

---

83. *Aguas del Tunari S.A. v. Bolivia* (ICSID Case No. ARB/02/3), Letter from the President of the Tribunal (29 January 2003) para. 3.
84. *Id.*, para. 2.
85. *Id.*, para. 3.
86. *Id.*, para. 3.
87. *Id.*, para. 5.
88. *Id.*, para. 6.
89. *Suez, Sociedad General de Aguas de Barcelona S.A., and Vivendi Universal S.A. v. Argentina* (ICSID Case No. ARB/03/19), Order in Response to a Petition for Transparency and Participation as Amicus Curiae (19 May 2005) para. 1. Four investors (two French, one Spanish and one English) brought this claim in connection with concessions entered into by the Claimants and the Argentine government for water distribution and waste water treatment services in Buenos Aires and the surrounding municipalities, and actions taken by the Argentine Republic in relation to those concessions.
90. *Id.*, para. 8.

On 19 May 2005, the tribunal issued its decision on the application, commenting that

> "[n]either the ICSID Convention nor the Arbitration Rules specifically authorize or specifically prohibit the submission by nonparties of *amicus curiae* briefs or other documents. Moreover, to the knowledge of the Tribunal, no previous tribunal functioning under ICSID Rules has granted a nonparty to a dispute the status of *amicus curiae* and accepted *amicus curiae* submissions."[91]

The tribunal then proceeded to discuss each element of its decision in turn.

First, it considered whether it had the power to accept and consider submissions by third parties. Relying on the "grant of residual power to the Tribunal to decide procedural questions..." in Art. 44 of the ICSID Convention, the tribunal found that it did have power to admit submissions from "suitable nonparties in appropriate cases".[92] The tribunal commented that "[t]he admission of an *amicus curiae* submission would fall within this definition of procedural question since it can be viewed as a step in assisting the Tribunal to achieve its fundamental task of arriving at a correct decision in this case".[93]

Borrowing from the key turning point in the evolution of third-party participation in the NAFTA context, the tribunal referenced the decision in *Methanex*, noting that it "supports the conclusion of the present Tribunal with respect to its power to admit *amicus* submissions in this case. The *Methanex* tribunal, interpreting Art. 15(1) of the UNCITRAL Arbitration Rules, which is substantially similar to Art. 44 of the ICSID Convention, concluded that the UNCITRAL Rules gave it power to accept *amicus* briefs."[94]

The tribunal then went on to consider the conditions for the admission of third-party submissions. Basing its conclusions on "a review of *amicus* practices in other jurisdictions and fora", the tribunal found that the power to accept third-party submissions should depend on three basic criteria: "(a) the appropriateness of the subject matter of the case; (b) the suitability of a given nonparty to act as *amicus curiae* in that case, and (c) the procedure by which the *amicus* submission is made and considered".[95] In relation to the tribunal's second criterion, it further commented that it would only accept submissions from "persons who establish to the Tribunal's satisfaction that they have the expertise, experience, and independence to be of assistance in this case".[96] The tribunal commented that the application of these criteria "will enable it to balance the interests of concerned nondisputant parties to be heard and at the same time protect the substantive and procedural rights of the disputants to a fair, orderly, and expeditious arbitral process".[97]

In applying the three criteria set out above, the tribunal commented that:

---

91. *Id.*, para 9.
92. *Id.*, paras. 10-16.
93. *Id.*, para. 11.
94. *Id.*, para. 14.
95. *Id.*, para 17.
96. *Id.*, para 24.
97. *Id.*, para 17.

> "[t]he acceptance of *amicus* submissions would have the additional desirable consequence of increasing the transparency of investor-state arbitration. Public acceptance of the legitimacy of international arbitral processes, particularly when they involve states and matters of public interest, is strengthened by increased openness and increased knowledge as to how these processes function. It is this imperative that has led to increased transparency in the arbitral processes of the World Trade Organization and the North America Free Trade Agreement. Through the participation of appropriate representatives of civil society in appropriate cases, the public will gain increased understanding of ICSID processes."[98]

The tribunal concluded, however, that in order to make a decision as to whether the petitioners should be allowed to file a written submission, further information was needed in relation to, inter alia, their identity and backgrounds and interest in the case.[99] Subsequently, on 1 December 2006, the petitioners filed a further petition.[100] Again, both the Claimants and Argentina filed observations on the petition; again, those observations are not publicly available.

The tribunal's ultimate Order, however, provides a high-level overview of the Parties' responses in its recitation of the case's procedural history. The Claimants had asked the tribunal to reject the petition for a number of reasons, including that: (i) the petitioners offered no new factual elements to the arbitration and would only make inappropriate legal arguments; (ii) none of the issues the petitioners proposed to raise concerned the public interest in the dispute or fell within the subject matter of the dispute; and (iii) the petition had been filed too late and was likely to cause disruption to the proceedings. On the contrary, Argentina had submitted that it had no objection to the petition. The Order provides no additional detail with respect to Argentina's submission.[101] Based on the further information provided, on 12 February 2007, the tribunal granted the petitioners permission to file a joint submission of no more than thirty pages.[102] The submission was filed on 4 April 2007, subsequent to which it was transmitted to the Parties for their observations.[103] It is not clear from the publicly available documents whether the Parties did in fact file any observations on the submission.[104]

98. *Id.*, para 22.
99. *Id.*, paras. 25-27 and 33b.
100. *Suez, Sociedad General de Aguas de Barcelona S.A., and Vivendi Universal S.A. v. Argentina* (ICSID Case No. ARB/03/19), Order in Response to a Petition by Five Non-governmental Organizations for Permission to Make an Amicus Curiae Submission (12 February 2007) para. 7.
101. *Id.*, paras. 8-10.
102. *Id.*, para. 27.
103. *Suez, Sociedad General de Aguas de Barcelona S.A., and Vivendi Universal S.A. v. Argentina* (ICSID Case No. ARB/03/19), Decision on Liability (30 July 2010) paras. 18 and 256.
104. Another case against Argentina being decided in parallel was *Suez, Sociedad General de Aguas de Barcelona S.A., and InterAgua Servicios Integrales del Agua S.A. v. Argentina* (ICSID Case No. ARB/03/17). The tribunal in this case also received a petition from third parties to participate in the proceedings. The tribunal similarly concluded that the third parties had provided insufficient information to enable it to determine whether or not they were

IV. CONCLUSION

So why did third-party submissions, and by that I mean written amicus submissions, became so evolutionarily preferred? My point of interest in recounting the above is to take a quick look at state action at the moment of innovation. The advent of third-party submissions did *not* evolve gradually – it burst upon the scene and found a home within the system almost immediately. The example that I and several of my co-panelists discuss in our papers is rightly the moment when the innovation of third-party submissions first occurred. The NAFTA Parties quickly assessed the viability of the concept – I argue within the framework of the Trinity as lawgiver, respondent, and protector – and accepted the possibility of third-party submissions with unprecedented speed. The debates at the time make clear that they found comfort that the divergent and sometimes conflicting interests of the Trinity were in sufficient balance and that the concept of third-party submissions vindicated several of the key interests of each role. Once brought in, the NAFTA Parties and thereafter tribunals and institutions quickly tore down the obstacles to third-party submissions.

We are now in a time of rising populism and resurgent nationalism. The question of ISDS reform echoes within a larger conversation regarding global trade and investment. Many governments are beginning to question whether foreign investment – and the accompanying investor-State dispute system – is a transnational and cosmopolitan good. These dynamics are likely to further complicate the debate currently underway at the UNCITRAL Working Group III meetings and elsewhere in international investment agreement negotiations.

Realignment of preferred trading partners will test the universality of transparency as being in the public's interest and increased regional segmentation will test the cultural bias of these norms. What quickly evolves is not always durable. Finally, the various efforts underway to redesign aspects of the ISDS adjudicatory process may result in significant changes to what is understood as transparency. It is an open question, for example, whether states are more comfortable with secrecy within a "standing court" procedure versus in an *ad hoc* tribunal process. What is *clear* to me at least is that all of these challenges will be assessed by states that participate in the investor-State dispute system. Whether knowingly or not, the states that participate in the investor-State dispute system will test the various innovations to transparency in the years to come against the crucible of their roles within the Trinity.

---

suitable to act as amicus curiae and, therefore, requested that further information be filed. See *Suez, Sociedad General de Aguas de Barcelona S.A., and InterAgua Servicios Integrales del Agua S.A. v. Argentina* (ICSID Case No. ARB/03/17), Order in Response to a Petition for Participation as Amicus Curiae, 17 March 2006, paras. 24-26 and 29-34. The third parties did not, however, file the further information requested by the tribunal.

Transparency in International Investor-State Arbitration: Commendable in Theory, Complicated in Practice

Stanimir A. Alexandrov and Patrick Childress***

TABLE OF CONTENTS PAGE

Over the past decade or so, a consensus has emerged among advocates, arbitrators, governments, academics, and civil society, that increasing transparency in international investor-State arbitration is a laudable goal. Yet, despite this broad agreement, fully transparent arbitral proceedings remain the exception rather than the rule. This commentary explores this disconnect, focusing on why transparency is commendable in theory, but challenging to implement in practice.

Before proceeding further, a brief discussion of what it means for an arbitration to be "transparent" is in order. For the purposes of this commentary, a "transparent" arbitration is one in which all written briefing is public, oral hearings are live streamed on the internet, and third-party participation via amicus curiae submissions is available. The benefits of this level of transparency are discussed in Sect. I, the practical challenges that transparency creates are discussed in Sect. II, and Sect. III contains brief concluding remarks.

I. TRANSPARENCY IN THEORY: AN ANSWER TO CRITICS OF INVESTOR-STATE ARBITRATION?

One of the central benefits of increasing transparency in investor-State arbitration is that open proceedings blunt many of the core criticisms of the investment arbitration system. Investor-State arbitration has come under fire from many sides in the past several years, including from non-governmental organizations (NGOs), politicians, and even certain governments. The criticisms vary in substance and volume, but, as a general matter, they fall into three main categories: (i) arbitration is unnecessarily secretive; (ii) arbitration is skewed in favor of corporations; and (iii) arbitration shuns public involvement, even though public funds and important issues of public policy are at stake. Enhanced transparency can address all three concerns.

* Founding partner of Stanimir A. Alexandrov PLLC; ICCA Governing Board Member.
** Associate at Sidley Austin LLP.

1. *Secrecy*

With respect to secrecy, critics disparage investor-State tribunals for operating behind closed doors, shielded from public scrutiny and accountability. A recent book criticizing investor-State arbitration coined the pejorative term "shadow courts" to describe investment treaty tribunals.[1] This criticism is not without foundation. However, it is a simple critique to address. Publishing written pleadings, opening hearings to the public, and permitting amicus submissions are obvious, direct, and effective ways to allay concerns regarding secrecy. Making these three practices widespread would strip critics of the "secrecy" talking point, without altering the substance of the investor-State dispute settlement system. This is a clear benefit of increased transparency.

2. *Corporate Skew*

Over the past few years, detractors of arbitration have raised a second criticism, the so-called "corporate skew" in arbitration, more frequently. In fact, it is often the central argument upon which opponents of investor-State arbitration rely. The following statement from the prominent US-based NGO Public Citizen sums up the position well:

> "At the heart of today's 'trade' agreements like NAFTA are provisions that grant multinational corporations shocking new rights and powers that make it easier to outsource jobs and attack the environmental and heath laws on which we all rely.
>
> Individual foreign corporations are empowered to sue governments before a panel of three corporate lawyers to demand unlimited compensation from taxpayers if they think a law or government action violates their new rights.
>
> (....)
>
> Not only do corporations get a special system of 'justice' outside our courts, but it's totally rigged in their favor. One day a corporate lawyer can sit on an ISDS tribunal deciding cases and the next day they can attack our laws on behalf of a corporation."[2]

Inflammatory statements of this nature make good headlines and attract attention, but the data does not back them up. In 2017, the United Nations Conference on Trade and Development (UNCTAD) released statistics regarding the outcomes of all of the investor-State arbitrations concluded between 1987 and 2016.[3] UNCTAD found that only 27% of those cases ended with an award favoring a foreign investor, while tribunals found in favor of the State 36% of the time.[4] In a further 2% of cases, the tribunal found

1. Haley Sweetland EDWARDS, *Shadow Courts: The Tribunals that Rule Global Trade* (Columbia Global Reports 2016).
2. Public Citizen, "Investor-State Dispute Settlement (ISDS): Extraordinary Corporate Power in 'Trade' Deals", at: <www.citizen.org/our-work/globalization-and-trade/investor-state-system> (last accessed 8 March 2018).
3. UNCTAD "World Investment Report 2017, Investment and the Digital Economy", at p. 117.
4. UNCTAD "World Investment Report 2017, Investment and the Digital Economy", at p. 117.

a treaty breach but awarded no damages, in 10% of cases there was a discontinuance, and the remaining 25% of cases settled.[5]

These statistics, which demonstrate that States are more successful in investment disputes than investors, would seem to undercut the "corporate skew" argument entirely. Critics point out that States never actually "win" anything in investor-State cases – the best they can hope for is to "not lose".[6] That is a fair point, but it does not change the fact that the UNCTAD statistics show that States prevail (or at least do not lose) more than investors do. Indeed, one would expect the UNCTAD statistics to tell a very different story if a systemic and pervasive corporate bias in the system existed. But despite all this, critics of investor-State arbitration remain unconvinced.

If statistics will not sway arbitration's detractors, perhaps transparency will. Pulling back the curtain and allowing the public – including opponents of investor-State arbitration – to observe all phases of these proceedings, would likely allay concerns regarding a pro-corporate bias. Critics of the system characterize international arbitrators as corporate shills, but if they actually observed a hearing, they likely would come away with a starkly different view. Indeed, arbitrators receive appointments based on their reputations as substantive experts and fair-minded adjudicators. Observing tribunals in action would reassure critics that investor-State arbitration proceedings are professional, serious, and even-handed affairs. One would expect – or at least hope – that this exposure (in combination with clear statistical data) would be sufficient to convince critics that their concerns regarding a pro-corporate bias are unfounded.

3. *Lack of Public Involvement*

A third criticism of investor-State arbitration is that these proceedings exclude important public voices (NGOs, civic groups, local populations, etc.) even though investment arbitrations often have serious consequences for the public in the respondent State. Enhanced transparency – principally in the form of increased amicus curiae submissions – can go a long way to addressing this concern. Amicus submissions allow the public to weigh in on issues of public concern that are relevant to the tribunal. For instance, if an arbitration involves the revocation of an oil production license due to groundwater contamination, the tribunal hearing the case might benefit from amicus submissions from local civic groups, environmental NGOs, etc.

Arbitral tribunals have recognized that the use of amicus submissions is a positive development. For instance, the *Methanex v. United States* tribunal recognized noted that:

> "there is an undoubtedly public interest in this arbitration. The substantive issues extend far beyond those raised by the usual transnational arbitration between commercial parties. This is not merely because one of the Disputing Parties is a State: there are of course disputes involving States which are of no greater general public interest than a dispute between private persons. The public interest in this

5. UNCTAD "World Investment Report 2017, Investment and the Digital Economy", at p. 117.
6. Howard MANN, "ISDS: Who Wins More, Investors or States?" at: <www.iisd.org/itn/wp-content/uploads/2015/06/itn-breaking-news-june-2015-isds-who-wins-more-investors-or-state.pdf> (last accessed 9 March 2018).

> arbitration arises from its subject-matter, as powerfully suggested in the Petitions. There is also a broader argument, as suggested by the Respondents and Canada: the ... arbitral process could benefit from being perceived as more open or transparent; or conversely be harmed if seen as unduly secretive. In this regard, the Tribunal's willingness to receive *amicus* submissions might support the process in general and this arbitration in particular, whereas a blanket refusal could do positive harm."[7]

In short, the *Methanex* tribunal held that amicus submissions were appropriate given the public interests at issue in that specific case, and desirable generally because transparency increases the legitimacy of the investment arbitration system.

In the more recent *Bear Creek v. Peru* arbitration, the tribunal accepted an amicus submission from the Association of Human Rights and the Environment – Puno (DHUMA). DHUMA is an NGO based in southern Peru, which focuses on the protection of indigenous rights and the environment.[8] The *Bear Creek* case related to a mining concession in southern Peru, which generated intense, widespread protests from nearby indigenous communities that feared that the mine would cause environmental damage. DHUMA was an ideal vehicle to voice the concerns of the local indigenous populations.

The *Bear Creek* tribunal accepted DHUMA's amicus submission, noting that: "DHUMA's local knowledge of the facts may add a new perspective that differs from that of the Parties,"[9] and that "DHUMA has information and experience specific to the background and development of the Santa Ana Project which may contribute a new perspective."[10]

In addition to making a detailed written submission, DHUMA representatives also attended the hearing (wearing traditional indigenous dress), which enhanced the sense of inclusiveness and legitimacy of the proceedings. The *Bear Creek* tribunal cited DHUMA's brief in its final award, at one point quoting three entire paragraphs of the amicus submission.[11] In a separate opinion, one of the arbitrators noted that:

> "DHUMA assisted the Tribunal by bringing a perspective, particular knowledge or insight that is different from that of the disputing parties. Its participation in

7. *Methanex Corporation v. United States of America*, Decision of the Tribunal on Petitions from Third Persons to Intervene as *Amici Curiae* (15 January 2001) at para. 49.
8. *Bear Creek Mining Corporation v. Republic of Peru* (ICSID Case No. ARB/14/21), *Amicus Curiae* Brief submitted by the Association of Human Rights and the Environment – Puno, 9 May 2016.
9. *Bear Creek Mining Corporation v. Republic of Peru* (ICSID Case No. ARB/14/21), Procedural Order No. 6 (21 July 2016) para. 40.
10. *Bear Creek Mining Corporation v. Republic of Peru* (ICSID Case No. ARB/14/21), Procedural Order No. 6 (21 July 2016) para. 44.
11. *Bear Creek Mining Corporation v. Republic of Peru* (ICSID Case No. ARB/14/21), Award (30 November 2017) para. 218.

> these proceedings was helpful and polite at all times, and added to perceptions of the legitimacy of ICSID proceedings of this kind."[12]

In sum, DHUMA's involvement increased transparency, assisted the tribunal, and added an important perspective that would have been absent otherwise.

Amicus submissions from individuals or entities based in the respondent State deserve particular consideration from tribunals. Taxpayer money from citizens of the respondent State – sometimes many millions or billions of dollars – is at stake in these arbitrations. Given that their money is on the line, those taxpayers deserve to be involved in the process if and when it makes sense to do so. This is not to suggest that tribunals should accept all amicus submissions from citizens of respondent States, but these applications do deserve particular attention.

For the reasons set out above, increased transparency is a goal that all stakeholders – States, claimants, counsel, arbitrators, civil society, etc. – should champion. However, as discussed in the section below, enhancing transparency can generate practical challenges that tribunals must handle with care.

II. TRANSPARENCY IN PRACTICE: PUBLIC PARTICIPATION PRESENTS COMPLEX CHALLENGES

Given the clear benefits of transparency, the lack of transparency in international arbitration proceedings is striking. An analysis of the adoption of the Mauritius Convention on Transparency brings this issue into clear focus. The Mauritius Convention obliges contracting parties to consent to broad transparency measures in future investor-State arbitrations, including publishing written submissions, holding public hearings, and permitting amicus submissions.[13] Thus far, just 22 of the world's 193 countries (about 11 percent) have signed the Mauritius Convention, and of those, a mere three (Canada, Switzerland, and Mauritius) have ratified the treaty.[14] The scarce adoption of the Mauritius Convention leaves one to ponder the question: if transparency is so sensible in theory, why are States reluctant to agree to it in practice? At least three factors are at play: (i) the hesitancy of States to publicize disputes where State conduct is under attack; (ii) confidentiality concerns; and (iii) increased costs connected to third-party involvement.

12. *Bear Creek Mining Corporation v. Republic of Peru* (ICSID Case No. ARB/14/21), Partial Dissenting Opinion of Professor Philippe Sands, QC (30 November 2017) para. 36 (internal quotations omitted).
13. See United Nations Convention on Transparency in Treaty-based Investor-State Arbitration (New York, 2014).
14. UNCTAD, "Status: United Nations Convention on Transparency in Treaty-based Investor-State Arbitration (New York, 2014)," <www.uncitral.org/uncitral/en/uncitral_texts/ arbitration/ 2014Transparency_Convention_status.html> (accessed on 8 March 2018).

1. *Reputational Concerns*

A central reason that States may not be eager to include transparency provisions in their investment treaties is a reluctance to publicize arbitrations that focus on States' alleged mistreatment of foreign investors. States sign investment treaties hoping to improve their reputations as stable destinations for foreign investment. A highly public investment arbitration in which the State is accused of serious malfeasance (illegal expropriation, unfair and inequitable treatment, etc.) can erase that reputational boost entirely. The issue of reputational risk has become particularly salient in the past few years, as States have increased their use of corruption allegations in defending against investment claims. Fighting jurisdiction by arguing corruption can be an effective litigation strategy, but corruption reflects poorly on the investor *and* the State. After all, for every corrupt investor paying for access, there must also be a corrupt government official accepting the bribe.

For these reasons, if a State's goal is to maximize foreign investment, one could argue that the best strategy would be to sign investment treaties liberally, but demand that those treaties limit transparency as much as possible. If a State can keep its treaties public, but its treaty disputes private, it can reap the reputational benefits of signing investment treaties while limiting the downside risks of fighting embarrassing treaty claims in public.

Yet, this cannot be the right strategy. If States subject themselves to broad transparency requirements, their desire to avoid bad press and protect their reputations may make them more open to negotiation and settlement. In this way, transparency could encourage States to avoid arbitration altogether, which generally is a positive outcome for all parties involved. Further, transparency would greatly contribute to increased accountability by States and enhance the opportunities for public discussion of a State's conduct and policies. Thus, in the long run, transparency will impose on States – at various levels – more discipline in regulating investors' conduct in a fair and reasonable manner.

2. *Confidentiality*

Increased transparency also raises the specter of confidentiality concerns. Arbitral parties worry that as proceedings become more transparent, the risk of sensitive information in written submissions and oral testimony becoming public increases. This concern is justified, but tribunals have the tools necessary to manage confidentiality issues effectively in the context of both written submissions and oral testimony.

With respect to written submissions, in most cases, a simple confidentiality order with specific guidance on redactions is sufficient. Confidentiality orders have become commonplace in investor-State practice, and parties and counsel generally are comfortable with these agreements and the protections they afford. The process of redacting confidential information can be time-consuming and costly for the parties (especially if parties object to the opposing party's redactions), but this seems a small price to pay given the overall benefits of transparency.

Another challenge for arbitrators is protecting confidential information during oral testimony being streamed online in real time. Tribunals should, of course, order that the cameras be turned off whenever confidential information is discussed, but this sounds easier in theory than it is in practice. It can be difficult to predict when precisely confidential material will come up during testimony, and turning the cameras on and off repeatedly can waste time and interrupt the flow of a witness examination. To minimize these downsides, tribunals should ask counsel to notify the tribunal before beginning a series of questions regarding a topic likely to involve confidential information. Tribunals can then turn off the cameras for that entire line of questioning, rather than switching them on and off repeatedly. For instance, if counsel notifies the tribunal that it plans to ask a quantum expert about a company's sensitive financial information, the tribunal can order the cameras be turned off for that series of questions. Sensitive information involving States' secrets can be dealt with in a similar fashion.

In sum, although increased transparency does indeed raise confidentiality concerns, these issues typically are manageable, particularly if experienced counsel and skilled arbitrators are handling the case.

3. *Amicus Submissions: Costs and Procedural Issues*

A third concern regarding increased transparency is that involving more parties – in particular through amicus submissions – will increase costs and cause procedural delays. These are serious issues, which tribunals must confront and address proactively. In quite a few cases, tribunals receive applications to intervene from several, if not many, NGOs and other organizations. These applications prompt an array of submissions from the parties, including:

– Written comments on each application to participate as amicus curiae;
– Potentially responsive comments by each applicant to participate as amicus curiae, and further comments by the parties;
– Extensive submissions by each party on the substance of each amicus brief, potentially responsive comments by the amici, and further comments by the parties;
– Written arguments related to whether the arbitral record should include certain documents attached or related to the amicus brief(s); and
– Various other correspondence and in-person discussions at the hearing regarding the extent of the amici's participation and the content of every amicus brief.

Those submissions increase costs for the parties, who pay higher fees to counsel and to the tribunal for the time spent preparing and considering amicus-related arguments and issues. In addition, the time devoted to discussing amicus applications and amicus briefs can extend the proceeding and can even be disruptive, if, for example, a hearing must be rescheduled.

Therefore, tribunals must be careful to manage amicus submissions in order to limit costs. Tribunal can do so in at least three ways.

First, tribunals should be selective. At first glance, allowing multiple amici and considering as many perspectives as possible might seem like an attractive option. Tribunals should resist this impulse given the significant burden amicus submissions impose on the parties. Tribunals should only accept amicus submissions from third parties with a unique and valuable perspective to add.

Second, tribunals should consider imposing page limits on the parties' submissions regarding amicus submissions.

Third, tribunals should exercise caution when considering whether to allow representatives of the amici to participate in the hearing.

Each of these practices will reduce costs, minimize the disruptions, and help the parties and the tribunal maintain focus on the parties' main briefing. In short, once again, proper management by the tribunal can limit the downsides of increasing transparency through amicus participation.

III. CONCLUDING THOUGHTS

Stakeholders are nearly unanimous in their belief that investor-State arbitration should be a more open and transparent process. Increasing transparency enhances the legitimacy of the system, and blunts many of the core criticisms of investor-State arbitration. However, additional transparency in the arbitral process presents practical challenges, including increased costs and confidentiality concerns. Tribunals can and should take steps to limit these downsides. If managed properly, the benefits of transparency appear to outweigh the potential problems.

Investor-State arbitrations typically involve important issues of public policy and many millions – if not billions – of public, taxpayer dollars. Given the strong public interests at play, making investor-State arbitration proceedings as open and transparent as possible is a worthy goal.

What Has Been the "Spillover" Effect of the Transparency Debate On Commercial Arbitrations?

Constantine Partasides QC[*]

TABLE OF CONTENTS

I. INTRODUCTION

Transparency is a modern "buzzword" that is sweeping like a growing tidal wave through investor-state dispute resolution.[1] Public issues should be addressed, so the argument goes, in a public process. "If the institution of arbitration has no "hidden agendas", then open your doors", has been the challenge, and our world of arbitration has started to respond positively.

But surely commercial arbitration is different? Surely, disputes arising under contracts deserve to be resolved with the confidentiality that has always been implicit in the process? Or is contractual arbitration now, too, at risk from "spillover" from the wave of transparency sweeping through its more public form? This paper addresses that last question by asking two further questions: Is the more private world of contract arbitration safe from the prying eyes of the world? More fundamentally, should it be?

II. THE TIDAL WAVE OF TRANSPARENCY SWEEPING OVER INVESTOR-STATE ARBITRATION?

The wave of transparency sweeping through investor-state arbitration is impossible to deny. A crescendo of criticism from civil society, or at least the many interest groups who claim to speak for it, has proven irresistible, and has led to the following widely (and rightly) heralded rule changes over the last decade.

---

* Founding partner of Three Crowns LLP; ICCA Governing Board Member. The author acknowledges and thanks Richard Trinick, an associate in the firm's London office, for his contribution to this paper.

1. The author is aware that his use of this metaphor is not original in the context of commentary on confidentiality. See the description of the Australian High Court's 1995 decision in *Esso v. Plowman* as crashing "like a giant wave – a veritable Australian tsunami – on the shores of jurisdictions around the world" in Yves FORTIER, "The Occasionally Unwarranted Assumption of Confidentiality", 15 Arb Int'l (1999) p. 131 at p. 134.

In 2006, the Arbitration Rules of the International Centre for Settlement of Investment Disputes (ICSID) were changed to allow for open hearings, submissions by third parties and publication of "excerpts of the legal reasoning of the Tribunal".[2] In 2010, the Arbitration Rules of the United Nations Commission on International Trade Law (UNCITRAL) were changed to allow for the publication of awards with the consent of the parties.[3] In 2014, the UNCITRAL Rules on Transparency in Treaty-based Investor-State Arbitration were promulgated (the UNCITRAL Transparency Rules) in relation to treaties concluded after 1 April 2014, providing for automatic publication of all submissions, orders, hearing transcripts and awards. In October of 2017, and momentously, the Mauritius Convention on Transparency in Treaty-based Investor-State Arbitration entered into force, applying the UNCITRAL Transparency Rules to all treaty-based arbitrations where both the host state and investor's home state are parties thereto. And in addition to all of these significant changes, various individual arbitral institutions have amended their rules in ways that will allow greater transparency when their rules are used specifically for investor-state arbitration.[4]

In a legal field better known for incremental reform, this truly constitutes a veritable regulatory tsunami. So is this wave likely to spill over into contractual arbitration?

III. SPILLOVER INTO THE WORLD OF CONTRACTUAL ARBITRATION?

One simple answer is no. Contract arbitration is quite different from its more public treaty form, and each of the major transparency initiatives referred to above has often been accompanied by a clear recognition of that difference.

Thus, the UNCITRAL Report of the Working Group on Arbitration and Conciliation on the work of its forty-eighth session (4-8 February 2008) made a clear demarcation between investor-state and so-called "purely private arbitration" as follows: "General agreement was expressed by the Working Group regarding the desirability of dealing with transparency in investor-State arbitration, *which differed from purely private arbitration, where confidentiality was an essential feature.*"[5] (Emphasis added.)

In the same vein, the UNCITRAL 2016 "Notes on Organizing Arbitral Proceedings" explicitly recognize that: "*the specific characteristics of investor-State arbitration* arising under an investment treaty have prompted the development of transparency regimes for *such* arbitrations."[6] (Emphasis added.)

---

2. ICSID Rules 32(2), 37(2) and 48(4) respectively.
3. UNCITRAL Rules 2010, Art. 34(5).
4. See, for example, the SIAC 2017 Investment Arbitration Rules, which deem consent to publication of certain information about a case, including redacted excerpts of the reasoning of the Tribunal (Rule 38.2). See also the Stockholm Chamber of Commerce (SCC) 2017 rules, which provide for submissions by third parties, but only in treaty-based investor-state arbitration (Appendix III).
5. UNCITRAL Report of the Working Group on Arbitration and Conciliation on the work of its forty-eighth session (4-8 February 2008) para. 57.
6. UNCITRAL "Notes on Organizing Arbitral Proceedings" (2016) para. 55.

Similarly, the recent transparency amendments made by the Stockholm Chamber of Commerce (SCC) and the Singapore International Arbitration Centre (SIAC) are stated only to apply to treaty-based investor-state arbitration.[7]

And Australia has very deliberately adopted different standards of transparency for investor-state and commercial arbitration. It has sought to include transparency provisions for investor-state arbitration in all of its recent trade deals (including with China, Chile, Korea and the ASEAN and TPP agreements). But in parallel, Australia made legislative amendments in October 2015 that replaced its confidentiality "opt-in" system with an "opt-out" system (i.e. confidential unless you agree otherwise) for contractual arbitrations.[8]

But will the well-recognized distinction between treaty-based and contract-based arbitration fully insulate the latter from this surge in transparency? As our process attracts widespread public attention as never before, will such distinctions always be respected? And should they be?

IV. EXAMINING THE DISTINCTION BETWEEN TREATY-BASED AND CONTRACT-BASED ARBITRATION?

There are reasons not to be confident that the distinction will always hold firm. The public versus private distinction between treaty and contract arbitration can be overstated. Commercial arbitrations can often involve state entities and, as such, can have just as much of an impact on a state's public policy and finances as investor state arbitration. By way of example, the ICC reports that around 10 percent of its caseload involves a state entity, and we can be sure that only a fraction of these are treaty-based investor-state cases.[9]

In this way and others, there can be significant public interest in a contractual arbitration in the same way as a treaty arbitration. So it surely follows that calls for greater arbitral transparency will not always stop at the door of contractual arbitration. Let us consider a handful of prominent examples.

Probably the most notorious recent example is *L'affaire Tapie*. Bernard Tapie was a high profile French businessman, football club owner and television celebrity who had owned Adidas AG. On becoming a government minister in 1992, he entered into a deal with Crédit Lyonnais, to repay his debts to the bank by transferring his equity in Adidas AG. The same ownership interest in Adidas AG was subsequently sold on by Crédit Lyonnais at a much higher price. When Crédit Lyonnais then fell into bankruptcy, and its liabilities were assumed by the Consortium de Realisation on behalf of the French Government, Mr. Tapie chose to make a claim against the Government for the alleged undervaluation of his shareholding. Following various proceedings before the French courts, which Mr. Tapie largely lost, the French Government agreed to refer the

7. See fn. 4 above.
8. See the amendments made to the International Arbitration Act 1974 (Cth) by the Civil Law and Justice (Omnibus Amendments) Act 2015 (Cth).
9. See the ICC's 2016 Statistical Report (<https://iccwbo.org/media-wall/news-speeches/full-2016-icc-dispute-resolution-statistics-published-court-bulletin/>).

ongoing dispute to arbitration. That later decision to refer the dispute to arbitration was taken by the government of Nicolas Sarkozy, to whom Mr Tapie had made political donations.[10]

In those confidential arbitral proceedings, and despite the earlier judicial decisions that had gone against him, Mr Tapie was awarded € 403 million. The award was not challenged within the period prescribed by French law, but certain confidential information was leaked to the press indicating that the arbitration may have been tainted by fraud, in particular a "fraudulent collaboration" between Mr Tapie, his counsel and one of the arbitrators. President Sarkozy's government was then accused of referring the dispute involving a political donor to confidential arbitration so as to increase Mr Tapie's chances of winning, and a criminal investigation was subsequently launched, ultimately resulting in a number of convictions and the award being annulled.

"*L'affaire Tapie*" demonstrates how keen the public interest can be in a so-called private (i.e. non-treaty based) arbitration. Moreover, the confidential nature of the arbitration, coupled with later fortuitous revelations of criminal activity, have left many in France scandalized that a legal determination of this nature could be rendered against a state-controlled entity behind closed doors.

Similar public interest can exist in commercial arbitrations that do not feature the same political dimension. In the recent case of *Microsoft Mobile v. Sony Europe*,[11] Microsoft brought a tortious claim in England for alleged anti-competitive "cartel conduct" by Sony and others in relation to the sale of lithium ion batteries, an essential component in smartphones.

Microsoft's allegations of "cartel conduct" were far-reaching, and encompassed alleged price-fixing, market allocation and bid-rigging in the EU, Brazil, China, India, Japan and elsewhere.

On Sony's application for a stay in favour of arbitration pursuant to Sect. 9 of the Arbitration Act 1996, the English High Court held that Microsoft's claim against Sony should be heard by an arbitral tribunal, rather than by the English courts, pursuant to an arbitration agreement contained within the product purchase agreement that those parties had entered into.

As a consequence, many third parties who undoubtedly have a direct interest in that commercial arbitration – including other members of the alleged "cartel" against whom Microsoft may have an action, and other entities who may have been unlawfully overcharged when purchasing batteries from Sony – will have access to little or no information about it. More broadly, the public at large may ultimately be kept in the dark as to whether or not they were victims of anti-competitive practices that generally inflated smart-phone prices for consumers.

So there are commercial arbitrations in which the same "public interest" argument can be made in favour of transparency as for treaty arbitration. The word "commercial" alone is, therefore, unlikely to insulate contractual arbitration entirely from the wave of transparency, and perhaps rightly so. This in turn raises the following question: how can

10. See "Tapie: the end of the affair", published on globalarbitrationreview.com on 30 June 2016. See also "Tapie: the end of the end of the affair?", published on globalarbitrationreview.com on 20 May 2017.
11. *Microsoft Mobile Oy (Ltd) v. Sony Europe Limited and Ors* [2017] EWHC 374 (Ch).

we protect confidentiality where it is appropriate and valuable in commercial arbitration, while balancing it with competing demands to make the process less opaque? And one of those competing demands arises from the generally growing public interest in the system of arbitration as a whole. For arbitration is no longer what it was when many of us began our careers; a rarefied procedural exoticism for a relatively small number of users that chose the jurisdictional exception, rather than the norm. Arbitration has now become the mainstream; in the words of Jonathan Mance LJ (as he then was) that now date back more than a decade: "Arbitration is an important feature of international, commercial and financial life, and there is legitimate interest in its operation and practice."[12]

What does this new reality mean for the place of privacy and confidentiality in the modern process of arbitration more generally?

Perhaps a first answer to this question is that systemic concerns must surely be subordinated to the choices made by the parties to an individual arbitration. For arbitration is surely *their* process, and party autonomy is surely the *single* principle in commercial arbitration that prevails over all others. Such an argument appears to this author to be unassailable. But further reflection perhaps yields a further answer, which is not inconsistent with this first answer, and it is this: the *further* step of "systemic secrecy", regardless of party intention, is now perhaps more difficult to justify in the modern world.

And so I turn to the implied duty of confidentiality that still prevails in some jurisdictions.

In truth, the number of jurisdictions that recognize such an implied duty is diminishing. Sweden has not recognized an implied duty since the turn of the new millennium. The year was 2000, the case was *Bulbank*, and the court was the Swedish Supreme Court,[13] which rejected the existence of an implied duty of confidentiality on the basis that, unlike privacy, there was no international consensus regarding the place of confidentiality in arbitration. And it is difficult to contradict that conclusion when one surveys the law of many different jurisdictions.

A similar position has long existed in the United States, where the US Federal Arbitration Act is silent on confidentiality, and US courts have been reluctant to recognize any implied duty to fill the legislative gap.[14] In *United States v. Panhandle E. Corp.*, the federal government sought to have Panhandle, a US company, produce documents from an ICC arbitration between Panhandle's subsidiary and Sonatrach, the Algerian state oil company. Refusing to infer any implied duty of confidentiality, the Delaware District Court refused a protective order to prevent such disclosure.[15]

12. Mance LJ in *Department of Economics, Policy and Development of the City of Moscow v. Bankers Trust* [2005] QB 207 at para. 39.
13. *Bulgarian Foreign Trade Ltd v. AI Trade Finance Inc.*, Case No. T 1881-99 (Swedish Sup. Ct. 27 October 2000).
14. See, for example, *United States v. Panhandle E. Corp.* (118 F.R.D. 346 (D. Del. 1988); *Contship Containerlines, Ltd. v. PPG Industries, Inc.*, 2003 WL 1948807 (S.D.N.Y. 2003). The New York Civil Practice Law and Rules (CPLR) are also silent as to confidentiality.
15. *United States v. Panhandle E. Corp.* (118 F.R.D. 346 (D. Del. 1988) at 349-350; *American Cent. E. Tex. Gas Co. v. Union Pac. Res. Group*, 2000 WL 33176064, at *1 (E.D. Tex. 27 July 2000); see also

Continental Europe is not so very different. In Switzerland, arbitrators are bound by an implicit duty of confidentiality with respect to the proceedings, but this does not apply to the parties themselves or to third parties involved in the arbitration. It is, therefore, for the parties to provide for confidentiality in their agreement with third parties or to agree on the general confidentiality of the arbitration, either expressly or by reference to arbitration rules containing confidentiality obligations. In Germany, Austria and Bulgaria, commentators and courts are divided as to whether a duty of confidentiality may be implied into an arbitration agreement.

France, long considered a home of international arbitration, provides barely more comfort for those looking for implied confidentiality. Following the implementation of Decree No. 2011-48 of 13 January 2011, there is no express obligation of confidentiality in international arbitration (although there is in domestic arbitration). And for their part, the French courts have been inconsistent as to the existence of a presumption of confidentiality in international arbitration.[16]

That leaves England, and those jurisdictions that still take their lead from its common law. For the duty of confidentiality in England still does rely on implication, in the absence of any legislative provision in the English Arbitration Act of 1996.

The silence of the 1996 Act on the issue of confidentiality is not an indication of the lack of importance its drafters attached to the subject. To the contrary, at the time the 1996 Act was enacted, confidentiality was considered a major competitive advantage of arbitration. The Departmental Advisory Committee recorded that "there is ... no doubt whatever that users of commercial arbitration in England place much importance" on privacy and confidentiality "as essential features" of arbitration.[17] However, it was the difficulty of reaching a statutory formulation, in the light of "the myriad exceptions" and qualifications that would have to follow, that led the drafters to conclude that the courts should be left to grapple with the issue "on a pragmatic case-by-case basis".[18]

The first thoroughgoing judicial attempt to do so occurred in 1997 in *Ali Shipping Corporation v. Shipyard Trogir*.[19] In that case, the defendant shipyard concluded six shipbuilding contracts with six separate companies in common ownership. The claimant, *Ali Shipping*, was one of the six purchasers, and it successfully obtained an award against the yard. In separate arbitrations with the other purchasers the shipyard attempted to deploy materials obtained in the *Ali Shipping* arbitration, including the award, written submissions and transcripts. The Court of Appeal granted Ali Shipping an injunction

---

Caringal v. Karteria Shipping, Ltd., 2001 WL 874705, at 1 (E.D. La. 24 Jan. 2001) (ordering production of documents from a London arbitration).

16. See Paris Court of Appeal, 18 Feb 1986, 1986 Rev Arb 583; Paris Court of Appeal, 22 Jan. 2004, 2004 Rev Arb 647.
17. The Departmental Advisory Committee on Arbitration (DAC) Report on Arbitration Bill 1996, p. 12. The Report also approved the observation of Sir Patrick Neill QC (see, 12 Arbitration International (1996) p. 287) that it would be difficult to conceive of any greater threat to the success of English arbitration than the removal of the general principles of confidentiality and privacy.
18. DAC Report, p. 10.
19. *Ali Shipping Corporation v. Shipyard Trogir* [1997] EWCA Civ 3054; [1999] 1 WLR 314. For an overview of English law on confidentiality in international arbitration see T. APLIN, L. BENTLY et al, *Gurry on Breach of Confidence*, 2nd edn, (OUP 2012) Chapter 9L, Chapter 2.

restraining the shipyard from using the documents for this purpose, finding that the arbitration agreement contained an implied duty of confidentiality. The Court of Appeal determined that the term upon which confidentiality rested was implied as a matter of law, not as a matter of fact, and accordingly arose in the same way in every arbitration regardless of the presumed intentions of the parties.[20]

This analytical approach was subsequently criticized by the Privy Council in *Associated Electric & Gas Insurance Services Ltd v. European Reinsurance Company of Zurich (Bermuda).*[21] For its part, the Privy Council found that it "runs the risk of failing to distinguish between different kinds of confidentiality which attach to different kinds of documents or to documents which have been obtained in different ways and elides privacy and confidentiality".[22] In the words of the Privy Council, "[g]eneralisations and the formulation of detailed implied terms are not appropriate".[23]

When the Court of Appeal was next called upon to consider such questions, in the 2008 case of *Emmott v. Michael Wilson Partnership*,[24] it took note of the Privy Council's critique.[25] In *Emmott*, the Court of Appeal granted permission to disclose pleadings generated in a London-seated arbitration to parties in overseas court proceedings, in order to prevent the overseas courts from being misled. In the London arbitration, the defendants had originally alleged fraud against the claimant, and the points of claim had been disclosed to the overseas court. However, the allegations of fraud were abandoned in the arbitration, and the claimant successfully applied for permission to disclose the amended points of claim and skeleton argument generated in the arbitration in the overseas court proceedings. In the light of the prior disclosures, the Court of Appeal held that such further disclosure was necessary in the interests of justice.[26]

Delivering the leading judgment, Lawrence Collins LJ (as he then was) described the implied agreement as "really a rule of substantive law masquerading as an implied term".[27] Nevertheless, the Court ultimately confirmed the existing position in the following terms:[28]

> "Documents in arbitration may, as I have said, be inherently confidential, as where they contain trade secrets. But it is clear that what has emerged from the recent authorities in England is that there is, separate from confidentiality in that sense,

---

20. *Id.*, at 326. This approach has been followed in some other common law jurisdictions, including Singapore (see *Myanma Yaung Chi Oo Co Ltd v. Win Win Nu* [2003] SGHC 124; *AAY v. AAZ* [2011] 1 S.L.R. 1093); New Zealand (see Arbitration Act 1996, Sect. 14B); and Hong Kong, where the common law duty of confidentiality has been incorporated as an express duty in to the Hong Kong Arbitration Ordinance (see Cap 609 Sect. 18).
21. *Associated Electric & Gas Insurance Services Ltd v. European Reinsurance Company of Zurich (Bermuda)* [2003] UKPC 11.
22. *Id.*, para. 20.
23. *Id.*
24. *Emmott v. Michael Wilson Partnership* [2008] EWCA Civ 184.
25. *Id.*, at 1381-1382.
26. The court also indicated that the issue of confidentiality, arising as between parties to the arbitration, should have been determined by the arbitrator, and that had the defendant applied for a stay this would probably have been granted. See *id.*, at 1380.
27. *Id.*, at 1380.
28. *Id.*, at 1379-1380.

> an implied obligation (arising out of the nature of arbitration itself) on both parties not to disclose or use for any other purpose any documents prepared for and used in the arbitration, or disclosed or produced in the course of the arbitration, or transcripts or notes of the evidence in the arbitration or the award, and not to disclose in any other way what evidence has been given by any witness in the arbitration, save with the consent of the other party, or pursuant to an order or leave of the court.... The obligation is not limited to documents which contain material which is confidential, such as trade secrets. The *obligation arises, not as a matter of business efficacy, but is implied as a matter of law*." (Emphasis added.)

In so holding, the court recognized that the duty of confidentiality could not be implied in the normal way, i.e. as a term that must have been intended by the parties because it is necessary for their agreement (in this case, their arbitration agreement) to work. Instead, as Lawrence Collins plainly recognized, it was imposed as a matter of law, regardless of party intention or consent. In this age of ever-greater transparency, the question that will increasingly be asked is whether such a presumption – for which perhaps read *policy* – is truly apposite in the world in which we live today.

To address that question, let me recount the story of a small dinner I was invited to some months ago. It was a dinner hosted by one of the many investigations firms that now regularly advertise their services to law firms in international arbitration. Although I do not say yes to many of those invitations, on this occasion I did decide to accept, because the guest speaker was a former chief of England's Secret Intelligence Service, MI6, known as "C" in the real "spy world", or "M" for all those who are fans of Dame Judi Dench in the James Bond films. And "C's" subject that evening was: "Survival in the Age of Populism".

It was a fascinating talk, filled with interesting insights on a variety of pressing geopolitical issues, which regrettably I cannot share, because we agreed at the very beginning of the dinner that we would all be subject to the "Chatham House Rule". But there is one thing "C" said that I can share, because it involved no controversial view on non-public information, and it is this: "The states, institutions, companies and individuals who will prosper in this new age of populism are those that recognise what it demands." Now that statement might sound too obvious to be worth repeating. But is it? How many of us are actually in determined denial about the transformations that recent political events have brought upon our society? How many of us are proving slow to turn our minds to how we might have to adjust to the implications of this new age?

So I do not think that the insight that "C" offered is so obvious. And I do think that it is worth pondering in the context of the procedural institution of international arbitration. Because there is one way in which this new age may impinge on our process. For we appear to be moving: from an age in which transparency is valued as an end in itself, (which, as we have seen, is imposing its own pressures on the confidentiality of the arbitral process); to an age in which the absence of transparency or information is likely to be replaced by an avalanche of misinformation, or "fake news", to fill the void that the lack of transparency leaves.

Considering that recent evolution in the context of the arbitral process leads to various thoughts, such as: let us keep our process away from the prying eyes of those inclined to senseless soundbites; the less publicity our process attracts, the better it will be able to perform its justice function. But there is one question that keeps bubbling to the surface from amongst these purists' thoughts, and it is this:

> *In an age in which an absence of information is often replaced by an abundance of misinformation, is it acceptable – or even wise – for a process that now accounts for such a significant proportion of commercial dispute resolution around the world to be automatically confidential?*

My answer to that question is that, over time, it will become less and less acceptable, and less and less wise. This is not because some parties – possibly many parties – will not continue to elect to make their processes confidential. Many will, and of course they should always be able to. But the *implied* duty of confidentiality – again – goes much further than this; it draws the curtain of confidentiality down over every arbitration, as a matter of course, whether the parties have selected it or not. Such an implied duty is not based on party consent, and its disappearance will not erode in any way parties' ability to choose to make their arbitration confidential.

So I anticipate the implied duty of confidentiality will come under increasing pressure where it still exists. And as that pressure on the implied duty mounts, so more jurisdictions will perhaps move to deal with confidentiality expressly in their arbitration statutes, either by providing an "opt-out" system (automatic confidentiality unless the parties agree otherwise), or an "opt-in" (no confidentiality unless the parties choose to make it so).

We see examples of both approaches in different jurisdictions. By way of example, in its 2004 statute, Norway adopted an "opt-in" system, providing that "[t]he arbitral proceedings and the arbitral award shall not be subject to a duty of confidentiality, unless otherwise agreed by the parties in respect of each arbitration".[29] Australia included a similar provision in its 2010 amendments to the International Arbitration Act 1974. Following these amendments, Sect. 22(3) of the Act provided that the Act's confidentiality provisions would only apply "to arbitral proceedings commenced in reliance on an arbitration agreement if the parties to the agreement agree (whether in the agreement or otherwise in writing) that they will apply". However, in December 2015, as mentioned above, as part of certain "omnibus amendments" to civil justice legislation, Australia reversed the "confidentiality opt-in" in the 2010 Amendment, so that the confidentiality provisions will now apply unless the parties to the arbitration agreement opt out, i.e. agree that they should not.

Both approaches are already out there. So let me end by gazing into a crystal ball, and asking which of these two legislative approaches will likely predominate in the years to come?

The arguments in favour of confidentiality in arbitration, which might be thought to auger in favour of an "opt-out" system, are well known. Some – perhaps many – of our clients prize it. For them arbitration is, above all, a means of resolving their particular commercial disputes that rarely will be helped by unnecessary publicity. And such individual commercial objectives must be prioritized; that is precisely why the potential for confidentiality is such a virtue of our process.

---

29. Act of 14 May 2004 No. 25 relating to Arbitration (The Arbitration Act), Chapter 1, Sect. 5.

But let us also recognize the costs of confidentiality, because they may be less obvious, but they are no less real, for those same users of our process.

– "Cost No. 1": The resulting paucity of information about what takes place in arbitrations undoubtedly makes our process less predictable for all participants. Various initiatives from within the arbitral community have sought somewhat to address this growing user complaint, from greater transparency shown by some institutions on how arbitrator challenges are decided,[30] to private initiatives such as Professor Catherine Rodgers's Arbitrator Intelligence project.[31] But for now such initiatives are perhaps more significant for evidencing the growing demand for more information, than for fully satisfying that demand.

– "Cost No. 2": That paucity of information also allows misinformation to flourish, as I've noted, which in turn undermines the legitimacy of a process that those same users depend upon. Already we are experiencing the backlash against investment arbitration that finds its loudest voice in complaints about a lack of transparency. And it would be naïve to presume that such complaints are not also polluting the reputation of international arbitration more generally. Manifestly, they already are, that is why the New York Times spoke in recent years of "arbitration everywhere *stacking* the deck of justice" in relation to consumer arbitration.[32] (Emphasis added.)That is why the Economist has even more recently bemoaned "the *craze* for mandatory arbitration" in relation to employment arbitration.[33] (Emphasis added.) These are not compliments, and here is a rather easy prediction to make: accusations denigrating "shadowy, secretive, private courts" will not get any easier to rebut or explain over time.

– And mixed in with all of this is "Cost No. 3": the absence of the behavioural advantages that will come with the scrutiny that public information will allow on the performance of the participants in our process (arbitrators and counsel alike).

For these reasons, this author's view is that, as the premium of transparency increases ever more in our modern world (together with the costs of non-transparency), so we might expect – and perhaps should look for – the default setting in commercial arbitration to shift increasingly to an "opt-in" system too.

Such an evolution to a default setting of greater transparency should be no concern at all for those parties still interested in agreeing a duty of confidentiality expressly for their arbitration. Indeed, the most powerful criticism that can be made of this prediction is that it won't actually change very much at all, because most users will expressly choose to make their process confidential.

But if that is so, then why oppose a change that will not change the practice at all for those who don't want it to change, but will nevertheless help to reinforce the modern legitimacy of our process. Because our process will no longer have to explain why it is

30. See the LCIA's widely welcomed practice to publish sanitized versions of its reasoned challenge decisions.

31. See <www.arbitratorintelligence.org/>.

32. See <www.nytimes.com/2015/11/01/business/dealbook/arbitration-everywhere-stacking-the-deck-of-justice.html>.

33. See <www.economist.com/news/leaders/21735590-millions-american-employees-have-no-recourse-courts-problem-craze>.

indiscriminately secret, as a matter of the system, whether the parties have expressed an intention to have a confidential process or not.

So let me end by inviting us to turn our eyes beyond the present to the future. And let me do so by asking another question: *Can we imagine international arbitration's automatic, indiscriminate, confidentiality remaining acceptable in our modern world in ten years', twenty years' or thirty years' time?*

If the answer to that last question just might be no, here's a further question: why wait to make a change grudgingly in twenty or thirty years that may by then be considered to be long overdue? Why not make the change before the criticisms from beyond our field begin to mount?

General de Gaulle famously said that it was essential to be able to tell the difference between a passing breeze and the winds of history — *"entre les courants d'air et le vent de l'Histoire"*. Although the clamour for transparency may have seemed a seasonal gust in the early years of the new millennium, it has not gone away, and seems destined to assume historical importance.

Building Better Arbitration Proceedings: Practical Suggestions

Building Better Arbitration Proceedings: Practical Suggestions

Part I: Revisiting the Conventional Wisdom in the Organization of Arbitral Proceedings

Prayers for Relief – The Focus for Organization

Klaus Reichert SC[*]

TABLE OF CONTENTS

I. INTRODUCTORY QUESTION

What is the object or purpose of organizing arbitral proceedings? Unless the answer to this question is clearly understood, and such understanding is shared between all counsel and the tribunal, from the outset of a case, there is a real risk that the organization does not actually achieve the fair, efficient and expeditious conduct of the arbitration.

This paper proposes a short answer to that question. The object or purpose of arbitral proceedings is the disposition by the tribunal of the parties' respective prayers for relief. The tribunal does not resolve any and every difference of opinion, or disputed fact, or indeed slight, as its sole task (derived from the agreement to arbitrate) is to grant or withhold the prayers for relief. Every step in the organization of the case should be directed towards that task.[1] This paper will now develop support for the answer proposed to the introductory question with the following points in mind: (II) how are disputes settled by arbitration; (III) what is the fundamentally important characteristic of an award; and (IV) how comparisons with national litigation are apt to mislead.

II. HOW ARE DISPUTES SETTLED BY ARBITRATION?

One starts with the basis and uncontroversial premise that an arbitration only exists because of an agreement to resolve disputes by that procedure. Taking a typical example of an arbitration agreement, namely the International Chamber of Commerce (ICC) standard clause:

> "All disputes arising out of or in connection with the present contract shall be finally settled under the Rules of Arbitration of the International Chamber of

* Barrister at Brick Court Chambers, London; ICCA Governing Board Member.

1. The topic discussed in this paper arises from a number of lectures given, first in November 2017, as the Scholar-in-Residence at the Center for Transnational Litigation, Arbitration, and Commercial Law at New York University School of Law, and then in February 2018 at the International Arbitration Institute of the University of Miami.

> Commerce by one or more arbitrators appointed in accordance with the said Rules."

While much focus in the past has been on the introductory words to such clauses (*all disputes arising out of or in connection with...*) debating on the scope of an agreement to arbitrate with linguistic contortions on whether a dispute arises *under* or *out of*, those debates are largely now over. Perhaps what may have been overlooked is what exactly is meant by the words *shall be finally settled*. Those words are often skipped over as one might readily assume that they speak for themselves. For present purposes they will be looked at in a little more detail.

There is another basic premise which can readily be stated without much fear of contradiction, namely, a dispute is settled by a remedy or relief being granted (or refused) by the tribunal. While the innumerable legal systems and governing laws around the world have a vast array of differing rules and approaches to contract interpretation (for example), one commonly finds that each has remedies to resolve disputes. Legal systems generally do not resolve disputes by having a general enquiry into what happened between parties and thereafter coming up with a just solution. Rather, parties assert that the material facts, by reference to applicable legal principles, give rise to certain remedies.

III. WHAT IS FUNDAMENTALLY IMPORTANT ABOUT AN AWARD?

The answer is: the disposition of the claims made as set out at the end of the award. That is what the parties are told to do, or not to do.

The importance of remedies for the purposes of arbitral proceedings is sitting in plain (legal) sight. Three examples are now considered: (*1*) a reasoned award can be dispensed with by agreement of the parties; (*2*) infra petita as a recourse against an award; and (*3*) certain institutional rules and practice.

1. Reasons – Fundamental, or Dispensable

Consider the United Nations Commission on International Trade Law Model Law on International Commercial Arbitration (the UNCITRAL Model Law) which provides as follows:

> "*Article 31. Form and contents of award*
>
> ....
>
> (2) The award shall state the reasons upon which it is based, unless the parties have agreed that no reasons are to be given...."

In a similar vein, one sees in Sect. 52(4) of the English Arbitration Act 1996:

> "The award shall contain the reasons for the award unless it is an agreed award or the parties have agreed to dispense with reasons."

Thus, parties are free to agree that reasons can be dispensed with – the articulation by a tribunal of reasons, or grounds, is clearly not considered to be so crucial as to be rendered sacrosanct. Of course it is most unusual for reasons to be dispensed with, but that is not the point; the UNCITRAL Model Law and the English Arbitration Act both permit parties to dispense with reasons. An award rendered under such circumstances is no less an award than one with reasons because, critically, the operative part decides on the prayers for relief advanced by each side. That operative part, deciding on the prayers for relief, brings the dispute to an end.

2. *Infra (or Ultra) Petita*

Consider Art. 1485 of the French Code of Civil Procedure (CCP) which provides as follows (in relevant part, translated):

> "... once an award is made, the arbitral tribunal shall no longer be vested with the power to rule on the claims adjudicated in that award. However, on application of a party, the arbitral tribunal may interpret the award, rectify clerical errors and omissions, or make an additional award where it failed to rule on a claim. The arbitral tribunal shall rule after having heard the parties or having given them the opportunity to be heard."

Thus, Art. 1485 CCP provides that an arbitral tribunal can complete its award when it failed to rule on a head of claim ("*le tribunal arbitral peut interpréter la sentence ... ou la compléter lorsqu'il a omis de statuer sur un chef de demande*"). It follows that not all omissions give rise to a claim for infra petita. The omission must be related to a claim ("*chef de demande*"), as opposed to a ground for relief put forward in support of a claim ("*moyen*"). A claim is to be understood as a formal request, made by a party to the tribunal, to give a ruling on a specific point. The claim(s) submitted by the parties form(s) the subject matter of a dispute. Grounds, on the other hand, are the reasons forming the basis of a claim.

In Switzerland, the Private International Law Act provides as follows:

> "*Article 190*
>
> ....
>
> 2. The award may only be annulled:
>
> ...
>
> (c) if the arbitral tribunal's decision went beyond the claims submitted to it, or failed to decide one of the items of the claim[.]"

Similarly with the UNCITRAL Model Law:

> "*Article 33*
>
> ....
>
> (3) Unless otherwise agreed by the parties, a party, with notice to the other party, may request, within thirty days of receipt of the award, the arbitral tribunal to

make an additional award as to claims presented in the arbitral proceedings but omitted from the award...."

In short summary: the *chef de demande* is the critical matter for disposition, not the *moyen*.

3. Certain Institutional Rules and Practice

First, consider the current ICC Rules (in relevant part):

> "*Article 23: Terms of Reference*
> (1) As soon as it has received the file from the Secretariat, the arbitral tribunal shall draw up, on the basis of documents or in the presence of the parties and in the light of their most recent submissions, a document defining its Terms of Reference. This document shall include the following particulars:
> ...
> (c) a summary of the parties' respective claims and of the relief sought by each party, together with the amounts of any quantified claims and, to the extent possible, an estimate of the monetary value of any other claims;
> ....
> (4) After the Terms of Reference have been signed or approved by the Court, no party shall make new claims which fall outside the limits of the Terms of Reference unless it has been authorized to do so by the arbitral tribunal, which shall consider the nature of such new claims, the stage of the arbitration and other relevant circumstances."

Secondly, the current ICC Award Checklist provides as follows (in relevant part) for tribunals to consider when preparing an award:

> "7. *Dispositive Section, Place of Arbitration, Date, Signature –*
> A. Award contains a dispositive section mentioning all orders (including the decision on jurisdiction, if applicable) and nothing more.
> B. Award deals with all of the issues and parties' claims (which should be stated clearly and precisely somewhere in the award and compared to the Terms of Reference), including the parties' most recent requests for relief, and decides nothing more than those issues and claims (state clearly if certain claims are reserved for one or more future awards)."

While the word "claims" and the phrase "requests for relief" appear to be two different things, one might venture to suggest that these are simply interchangeable labels for the same thing, namely, *chef de demande* and not *moyen*. One might consider the French version of Art. 23(1)(c) and 23(4) respectively of the ICC Rules to illustrate this point:

> "*un exposé sommaire des prétentions* [the claims] *des parties et des décisions sollicitées* [prayers for relief] *par chacune d'elles ainsi que le montant de toute demande quantifiée et, dans la mesure du possible, une estimation de la valeur pécuniaire de toute autre demand*"

and

> *"Après la signature de l'acte de mission, ou son approbation par la Cour, les parties ne peuvent former de* ***nouvelles demandes*** [the exact language, *prétentions*, used in Art. 23(1)(c) is not replicated, but rather the word *demandes* is used] *hors des limites de l'acte de mission, sauf autorisation du tribunal arbitral qui tient compte de la nature de ces* ***nouvelles demandes****, de l'état d'avancement de la procédure et de toutes autres circonstances pertinentes.*" (Emphasis added.)

Indeed, in French legal thought[2] a claim is defined as:

> "What is required from the judge or the arbitrator by one of the parties: the result it wishes to obtain."

4. Conclusion

It is tentatively suggested that the three foregoing points, namely the dispensable nature of reasons, infra petita, and arbitral rules-cum-practice, demonstrate that the disposition of the prayers for relief is the most significant part of any award. The oft-noted practice, namely that the very first thing counsel does when receiving an award is go to the last page, bears this out. While one might thereafter dwell on the reasoning, ultimately that which is to be paid (or not), and enforced if necessary, is to be found on that key last page. In less subtle terms, if one has to enforce and then execute an award as against the assets of a respondent, the bailiff will not be looking at the reasons, but at the last page for the amount of money ordered. Perhaps this is the starkest example of what arbitration is ultimately all about, the satisfaction of an award; hence the importance of the prayers for relief.

IV. IS THIS NOT THE SAME AS A NATIONAL COURT?

One might observe that all of this is fairly similar to the manner in which a national court goes about its task in deciding the remedy to give to a party, and therefore one often encounters parties approaching the formulation of claims or prayers for relief, and indeed their "pleadings" or "submissions" or "statements" or "memorials" in a manner which roughly corresponds to the domestic litigation rules in the jurisdiction where their lawyers qualified. This national court influence also can carry through into the conception of parties as to how arbitral proceedings evolve, when evidence is adduced, how it is adduced, and when one makes arguments as to the consequences of such evidence. Specifically, there are legal cultures where the trial (i.e., the evidential hearing) is more important than any other aspect of the case, and that is the occasion when the evidence comes out. Thereafter the court can fashion the legal remedy.

2. P. GIRAUD, "*La confomité de l'arbitre à sa mission*", sous la direction de Charles Jarrosson, para. 158)."

This is apt to mislead in the context of arbitration. A national court (subject of course to its rules, laws, and inherent powers) has the full original or general jurisdiction accorded to a state court. It can fashion remedies having heard evidence. It has a panoply of powers (e.g., in a constitutional context) which engage a public function. An arbitral tribunal has no such wide-ranging constitutionally-backed powers, and its existence and function have a much more limited lifespan with jurisdiction only insofar as is necessary to undertake its task. Once the award is rendered, and any time period for corrections (and the like) is past, the tribunal is functus officio.

An illustration of the general jurisdiction of a national court comes from the English Civil Procedure Rules, Part 16(2)(5) (Part 16 sets the requirements of a statement of case in municipal litigation): "The court may grant any remedy to which the claimant is entitled even if that remedy is not specified in the claim form."

One might readily ask where such a provision can be found in any set of arbitration rules, or in any arbitration law. Which leads one to an observation made during the presentation of these remarks during the ICCA Congress in Sydney, namely, what does *further or other relief* actually mean in the context of international arbitration? One, of course, sees it in virtually every request, answer, memorial, or submission, but what does it mean? Does it mean anything? Or is it an unwarranted cross-over from municipal litigation?

The *Carnelli* case[3] is historically, and legally, engaging. The arbitration was based on the Treaty of Peace between the United States and Italy involving a claim by a US national for war damage done to her property in Salerno in 1943. The United States requested the Commission to:

> "(a) Decide that the claimant is entitled to receive from the Italian Republic, a sum sufficient at the time of payment to make good the loss suffered, which sum is estimated to be on September 28, 1943, 185,300 lire, subject to the necessary adjustment for variation in value between 1943 and the final date of payment.
> (b) Order that the costs of and incidental to this claim be borne by the Italian Republic.
> (c) Give such further or other relief as may be just and equitable."

The Commissioners (Scanlan and Sorrentino) dealt with the third request in the following terms (the quotation is long but a rewarding read) at pp. 94-96:

> "*In the Brief submitted at the conclusion of the case*, and the Commission desires to emphasize the manner in which the request was raised for the first time in this case, *the Agent of the United States requests a determination by the Commission that the giving of 'such further or other relief as may be just and equitable' calls for the payment to the claimant by the Italian Government 'of an appropriate amount of interest'*.
> (....)
> The request for interest contained in the Brief presented by the Agent of the United States must fail because the Commission does not believe that the question

3. Decision No. 5 of 4 March 1952 of the Italian-United States Conciliation Commission, Vol. XIV, pp. 86-96, *Recueil des Sentences Arbitrales*.

of interest on the claim is before it in the instant case; this is a preliminary question to any consideration of the more general question of the responsibility of the Italian Government for the payment of interest on the claim.

Article 7 (a) of the Rules of Procedure of this Commission adopted and promulgated in Rome on June 29, 1950, by the Representatives of the two Governments provides that proceedings before the Commission shall be initiated by the formal filing of a Petition signed by the Agent of the claiming Government, and *that the Petition must contain*:

...
(iii) a clear and concise statement of the facts in the case; each material allegation should be set forth in a separate paragraph in so far as possible;
(iv) a clear and concise statement of the principles of law upon which the dispute is based;
(v) a complete statement setting forth the purpose of the Petition and the relief requested.

The fifth requisite of Article 7 of the Rules of Procedure is clear and unequivocal. There must be contained in the Petition 'a complete statement setting forth the purpose of the Petition and the relief requested'.

The Petition presented by the Agent of the United States of America on behalf of the claimant herein was deposited with the joint Secretariat on August 28, 1950, about two months after the promulgation of the Rules of Procedure. The relief requested in the Petition has been set out in full in the Statement of the Case, *supra*. There is no direct or indirect reference to interest in the Petition. The request for 'such further or other relief as may be just and equitable' contained in the Petition is not a statement which sets forth that one of the purposes of the Petition is the obtaining of interest on the claim or that one of the measures of relief requested is the granting of interest as part of the award.

Inasmuch as the desire for clearly informing the Italian Government of the nature of the case and the relief requested by the Government of the United States was one of the reasons, if not the principal reason, for the requirement laid down in Article 7 (*a*) of the Rules of Procedure, including the specific requirement that the Petition shall contain a complete statement setting forth the purposes of the Petition and the relief requested, *the request for 'such further or other relief as may be just and equitable' contained in the Petition submitted in the instant case by no means achieves the purpose of informing the Italian Government of a request for interest*.

That the Italian Government did not infer from the request for 'such further or other relief as may be just and equitable' that the Government of the United States was making a request for interest appears clearly from the Answer and the supplemental Answer submitted by the Agent of the Italian Government. When the Agent of the United States for the first time raised the question of interest in the Brief by specifically requesting that interest be allowed on the claim, the Reply Brief of the Italian Government denies vigorously the responsibility of the Italian Government for interests. *If the Petition had included a clear request for interest, it is probable that the same vigorous denial would have been asserted by the Agent of the Italian*

> *Government in his Answer or supplemental Answer to the Petition, and the issue would have been clearly developed by the Agents of the two Governments prior to concluding the formal submission of proof.* In any event, the Agent of the Italian Government denied the responsibility of his Government for the payment of interest as promptly as he could after the Agent of the United States had informed him in the Brief that interest was being requested.
>
> The Agent of the United States at no time requested this Commission to permit the amending of the Petition in this dispute in order to include an express request for interest. It was not until July 16, 1951, that the Commission issued an Order, as requested by the Agent of the United States, that formal submission of proof had been concluded by the Agents of the two Governments. In that Order a period of time was granted to the Agent of the United States to file a Brief in support of his Petition.
>
> Article 11 of the Rules of Procedure of the Commission, entitled 'Briefs and Oral Arguments', makes it clear that Briefs and oral arguments were not intended to include either amendments or additions to the Petitions, Answers, or any other pleadings. The request for interest contained in the Brief in this case is an addition to the request contained in the Petition and cannot be deemed to have been submitted in accordance with the Rules of Procedure of the Commission. It is, therefore, not a request which can be considered by the Commission.
>
> Although Article 18 of the Rules of Procedure reserves to the Commission the right to deviate from these Rules in individual cases, the Commission is satisfied that the Rules of Procedure are in conformity with justice and equity as required by the express provision of Article 83, paragraph 3, of the Treaty of Peace. Therefore, no reason is perceived in the instant case for any deviation under Article 18 of the Rules from the requirements established in Article 7 (a) of the Rules of Procedure, particularly since there is a lack of any evidence in the record that a request for interest on the claim has ever been raised between the two Governments either as a general question under Article 78 or in this specific case at any time prior to the presentation of the Brief in this case by the Agent of the United States of America." (Emphasis added.)

In relatively short order, the conclusion can be drawn that a tribunal does not have general authority to fashion the reliefs to which it feels a claimant is entitled based on the evidence. Secondly, the expression "further or other relief" is meaningless in the arbitration context, and does not rescue a party which should have included a prayer for relief in respect of a claim it might well have made from the outset had the case been thoroughly investigated. Indeed, one might wonder, based on the foregoing, whether the equally oft-used phrase, "the right to amend or supplement these claims is reserved", has the meaning and effect to allow late-blooming prayers for relief such as that advanced by the United States in the *Carnelli* case.

Recollecting that the tribunal's task is, essentially, to resolve the dispute in a binding manner by the grant, or withholding of the prayers for relief sought by the parties. It does not have the authority to give a party something it did not ask for, or decide something which is not legally "alive" merely because it might have been argued at length. Take the example of a claim for a debt amount against which four different defences are raised. If one of the defences succeeds (e.g., the tribunal prioritizes one of the lines of defence for disposition first by way of a partial final award), then the tribunal no longer has jurisdiction over the claim as it has been finally determined. The claimant might well wish to have the other three defences (e.g., if something important for a long-term relationship has arisen) decided, but strictly speaking, the tribunal has no authority to do so as the claim which was before it for decision is now legally "dead" or moot.

In England, for the purposes of Sect. 68(2)(d) of the Arbitration Act 1996[4] Merkin and Flannery note:

> "... an 'issue' for the purposes of section 68(2)(d) is one that is of decisive effect on the outcome, and not an incidental or peripheral matter, whose resolution is largely immaterial to the overall result or that falls away in the light of other holdings".[5]

Thus, there is no duty under English law on the part of a tribunal to render an award on defences (for example) which have become moot.

V. CONCLUSION

If one bears in mind that one of the cornerstones of arbitral proceedings is due process, and there is now an expectation that parties are not taken by surprise in any way whatsoever, combining that expectation with the importance of the prayers for relief as set out above, the conclusion one reaches is as follows. The organization of arbitral proceedings must, from the very beginning, focus on what is essential for the disposition of the prayers for relief advanced by the parties. It is essential for the efficient organization of the case that parties must articulate as fully as is possible their prayers for relief at the outset, and no later than the first memorial. Later additions (or "refinements" – a comforting word which belies what is actually meant often in practice by wholesale changes) only give rise to additional expense and investigations. Time must be taken at the outset so that parties advance the prayers for relief they consider they need to make, but also those which they consider that they can support.

On reflection of the wider topic developed during the ICCA Sydney Congress, the conventional wisdom which attaches now to the organization of arbitral proceedings is that all such organization is directed towards articulating everything in writing in

---

4. "*Sect. 68.*
(1) A party to arbitral proceedings may (upon notice to the other parties and to the tribunal) apply to the court challenging an award in the proceedings on the ground of serious irregularity affecting the tribunal, the proceedings or the award. ....
(2) Serious irregularity means an irregularity of one or more of the following kinds which the court considers has caused or will cause substantial injustice to the applicant—....
(d) failure by the tribunal to deal with all the issues that were put to it...."

5. R. MERKIN and L. FLANNERY, *Arbitration Act 1996*, 5 ed. (Informa Law from Routledge 2014) p. 313.

advance of any hearing. It is simply inconceivable that anyone now can be taken by surprise at a hearing. If one considers all of the various guidelines, rules, and so on, the overriding message is that the pre-hearing work, all written, is directed towards making sure that the full case and all evidence is plainly laid out before one gets to a hearing. One does not detect any appetite internationally for that to change so that trial by ambush would become the norm. Thus, if that is a working assumption, namely that the organization of arbitral proceedings should continue to have as its object the clear notification of everything before a hearing, then it becomes all too obvious that the risk of overblown and unmoored proceedings is heightened. If one has the key task of the tribunal in mind from the outset, namely, the granting or withholding of the relief sought, then such risks can be abated insofar as is practically possible. Parties must know this from the outset, and be aware that they must bring forward their prayers for relief in full at the earliest opportunity.

What Is Conventional Wisdom in the Organization of Arbitral Proceedings?

Nayla Comair-Obeid[*]

TABLE OF CONTENTS PAGE

I. INTRODUCTION

1. *What Is "Conventional Wisdom"?*

The expression "conventional wisdom" results from an association of "convention" and "wisdom". Thus, while certain wisdoms can be unconventional, and conventions, far from being always wise, "conventional wisdom" refers to those principles which are both conventional and wise. In other words, they ally the rooting power of traditions with the insight that comes with wisdom.

John Kenneth Galbraith has defined "conventional wisdom" in the following way:

> "What is conventional wisdom? It will be convenient to have a name for the ideas which are esteemed at any time for their acceptability, and it should be a term that emphasizes this predictability. I shall refer to these ideas henceforth as the conventional wisdom."

Three elements in this definition deserve particular attention. In the words of John Kenneth Galbraith, conventional wisdom refers to ideas which are "esteemed ... for their acceptability", i.e. generally recognized as sound and as a vehicle of wisdom. The second element of this definition has a time component. A conventional wisdom is not one which is temporarily in vogue but rather one that has endured the test of time. Finally, because the principles which can be categorized as "conventional wisdom" are generally accepted and have remained steadfast across time, they are a source of reliability and predictability.

---

* Founding Partner of Obeid Law Firm and Professor of international commercial arbitration at the Lebanese University; Past President of the Chartered Institute of Arbitrators (CIArb) 2017 and CIArb Companion; author of *Law of Business Contracts in the Middle East* and numerous other publications in Arabic, French and English covering a range of legal fields.The author has an extensive career in litigation and international arbitration. Her areas of expertise cover international business law, Islamic Finance, and Middle Eastern legislations.

2. *Relevance of the Topic*

Analyzing the meaning of conventional wisdom and identifying the principles which constitute it require going back to the foundations of international arbitration, which is of particular relevance at a moment when the role of arbitrators and counsel in international arbitration is being called into question. Among the criticisms that international arbitration faces are the increased time and costs of its proceedings and the quality of arbitrators' decisions,[1] with criticisms against investor-State arbitration being particularly acute.[2] In such a context, conventional wisdom bears an element of acceptability as mentioned above and as such, if properly observed, should have an ability to unite, to inspire trust of the end users and to strengthen a system which has been a source of discontent.

However, does the fact that the principles identified as conventional wisdom are *recognized as "wise"* mean that they represent the *"right"* principles to apply in any circumstances? This is probably not the case, mainly for two reasons:

(1) First, the way arbitrators work has evolved over the years, not only due to the technological innovations, but also as a result of an increased arbitration caseload over the years. I therefore do believe that wisdom requires a constant adaptation of arbitral procedures to the changing environment in which arbitrators operate.
(2) Second, the specificities of each case sometimes require a deviation from admitted practice.

This paper will attempt to analyze the role of conventional wisdom in the promotion of efficient arbitration proceedings. In doing so, the paper will identify a number of ideas and principles which are generally accepted and ensure the good functioning of the arbitration process (Sect. II). Next, the paper will question the element of acceptability and predictability included in John Kenneth Galbraith's definition by analyzing how conventional wisdom is influenced by perceptions (Sect. III). Finally, it will explore some innovative techniques in international arbitration, focusing on the way they can contribute to consolidating conventional wisdom and improving the practice of international arbitration (Sect. IV).

---

1. See, e.g., William W. PARK, "Arbitration and Fine Dining: Two Faces of Efficiency" in P. SHAUGHNESSY and S. TUNG, eds., *The Powers and Duties of an Arbitrator: Liber Amicorum Pierre A. Karrer* (Kluwer 2017) at p. 251; Steven SEIDENBERG, "International Arbitration Loses Its Grip", 96 A.B.A. Journal (2010) at p. 50; Peter YUEN and John CHOONG, "Is Arbitration Value for Money? Assessing Some Common Complaints about the Costs of International Arbitration", 3 Asian Dispute Review (2008) at pp. 90-95; Leon E. TRAKMAN and Hugh MONTGOMERY, "The 'Judicialization' of International Commercial Arbitration: Pitfall or Virtue?", 30 Leiden Journal of International Law (2017) at p. 405; Jennifer KIRBY, "Efficiency in International Arbitration: Whose Duty Is It?", 32 Journal of International Arbitration (2015, no. 6) at pp. 689-696.
2. Alison ROSS, "'Game of Tribunals' — Winter Is Coming, Warns Born", Global Arbitration Review (2016) available at <http://globalarbitrationreview.com/article/1067197/-game-of-tribunals-%E2%80%93-winter-is-coming-warns-born> last accessed on 22 May 2018.

II. CONVENTIONAL WISDOM AS A SET OF GENERALLY ACCEPTED PRINCIPLES

A number of principles in international arbitration are generally recognized principles which have been constantly applied throughout the times. The below is not intended to be an exhaustive list of such principles but rather a description of some accepted wisdoms in international arbitration and of where they can be found.

1. *Some Commonly Accepted Wisdoms in International Arbitration*

a. *Constitution of an arbitral tribunal: A preference for three arbitrators?*

At the stage of the constitution of the arbitral tribunal, one idea which has been described as a conventional wisdom relates to the preferability of having a three-member tribunal, whenever the economics of a case can bear it.[3]

The first reason advanced in favour of this conventional wisdom is that having three arbitrators improves the quality of the arbitral process and the award, since three arbitrators allows for "true deliberation – the sharing of ideas, perspectives reasoning and drafting",[4] and a more thorough consideration of the issues from different points of view.[5]

The second argument in support of appointing three arbitrators rather than only one is that having the ability to nominate a co-arbitrator generally increases party confidence in the arbitral process, since the parties "believe that there is at least one member of the arbitral tribunal who will listen attentively and sympathetically to its case, understand its position, and ensure that the party gets a fair hearing and that its views are considered during the deliberations".[6]

When arbitrators have the same ethical and professional values, as well as good knowledge of the applicable law or, at least, an open and flexible approach to the application of a foreign law, three-member tribunals' deliberations can be very fruitful, particularly in complex procedures where the complementary approaches of three well-versed individuals are most often beneficial to the decision-making process.

---

3. Jennifer KIRBY, "With Arbitrators, Less Can Be More: Why the Conventional Wisdom on the Benefits of Having Three Arbitrators May Be Overrated", 26 Journal of International Arbitration (Kluwer Law International 2009, no. 3) p. 337 at p. 338.
4. Stephen JAGUSCH, "Starting Out as an Arbitrator: How to Get Appointments and What to Do When You Receive Them", 71 Arb. (2005) p. 329 at p. 335.
5. Julian D. M. LEW, Loukas A. MISTELIS and Stefan M. KROLL, *Comparative International Commercial Arbitration* (Kluwer Law International 2003) at pp. 227-228; Jan PAULSSON, "Ethics, Elitism, Eligibility", 14 Journal of International Arbitration (1997) at p. 13; Wendy MILES, "Practical Issues for Appointment of Arbitrators", 20 International Arbitration (2003) p. 219 at p. 226.
6. See Jennifer KIRBY, fn. 3 above, at p. 342. In a survey conducted by Queen Mary University London in 2012 on "Current and Preferred Practices in the Arbitral Process", a significant majority of interviewees further state that they prefer selection of the two co-arbitrators in a three-member tribunal by each party unilaterally, for the following reasons: (i) it gives the parties control over the constitution of the tribunal and inspires confidence in the arbitral process, which consequently raises the legitimacy of the final award; (ii) parties are better placed to know what skills and knowledge are required for resolving the dispute; and (iii) many interviewees expressed some distrust in arbitral institutions selecting arbitrators.

However, criticism against three-arbitrator tribunals has developed, underlining the potential risks for excesses coming principally from party-appointed arbitrators such as: co-arbitrators having ex parte communication with "his/her" party; resigning at a time designed to disrupt the proceedings; making himself unavailable for deliberations; encouraging the filing of challenges; secretly feeding information about deliberations to "his/her" party; failing to deal with an award that needs only his signature before it can be notified to the parties; secretly sending "his/her" party the draft of a forthcoming award; taking months to draft a promised dissenting opinion; filing a dissenting opinion designed to undermine the enforceability of the award.[7]

The risk of excesses with three-member tribunals is indeed not negligible but could probably be attenuated if a proper system of sanctions was in place in cases of abuse. The Chartered Institute of Arbitrators (the CIArb or the Institute), for example, has adopted its own Code of Conduct for arbitrators who are also members of the Institute. Pursuant to Art. 15.2 of the Code of Conduct, the misconduct of an arbitrator may involve "a significant breach of professional or ethical conduct which shall include the Code of Professional and Ethical Conduct or other similar document published from time to time by the Institute".[8] Such mechanisms are still in their infancy though, and could be further developed to ensure stricter observance of arbitrators' ethical duties.

b. Conventional wisdom at the preliminary stages of the arbitral proceedings

The experiences I have encountered in the course of my career as an international arbitrator have taught me that the initial stages of the arbitral proceedings are essential for the conduct of the rest of the proceedings, as they constitute the key moment to set the tone for the arbitration and to build the basis for efficient proceedings.

The procedural planning of an arbitration requires that the arbitral tribunal ascertain at a very early stage of the arbitration the source of the dispute, the delimitation of factual and legal issues, as well as how the parties contemplate the arbitral proceedings and timetable.[9] Appendixes to the International Chamber of Commerce Arbitration Rules (the ICC Rules) of 2012 and 2017 include a number of specific "Case Management Techniques" which the arbitral tribunal is encouraged to consider in conjunction with the "Case Management Conference" or "Preliminary Meeting".[10]

The Preliminary Meeting is indeed key since it allows for a dialogue between the arbitrator(s), and both counsel for the claimant and for the respondent. The presence of the parties themselves at this stage is highly recommended, since it represents the best occasion for the arbitrator(s) to explain to them how the arbitration proceedings work, particularly when they are unfamiliar with such proceedings.

Further, the Preliminary Meeting allows the arbitrator(s) to ensure that the parties are aware of other mechanisms available for the resolution of their dispute, and is in my experience, the best occasion to encourage settlement. As such 11 percent of my cases

---

7. Jennifer KIRBY, fn. 3 above, at p. 344.
8. The Chartered Institute of Arbitrators Code of Professional and Ethical Conduct for Members (2009).
9. Gary B. BORN, "Chapter 15: Procedures in International Arbitration" in *International Commercial Arbitration,* 2nd edn. (Kluwer Law International 2014).
10. Appendix IV to the ICC Rules of 2012 and 2017.

have been settled following the Preliminary Meeting, after the parties had acquired a full understanding of the arbitral procedure, including the time and costs involved.

c. Conventional wisdom in the conduct of the arbitration

The international arbitral process seeks to achieve a number of objectives which can be described as conventional wisdoms. As put forward by Gary Born, some of the most important characteristics of the arbitral procedure are procedural fairness, efficiency, expertise and tailoring procedures to specific disputes and parties.[11]

With international arbitration disputes involving parties coming from different jurisdictions, one of the fundamental objectives of international arbitration is indeed that disputes will not be resolved in accordance with the procedures of any of the parties' home jurisdictions, but rather with a neutral procedure during which both parties will be treated fairly and equally.

It is also conventional wisdom that international arbitration proceedings should be efficient and as expeditious as possible, with most arbitral institutions imposing extendable limitations for the rendering of the arbitral award, the new trend being to impose sanctions on arbitrators who are delayed in rendering their award.

Finally, the use of arbitral procedures that are flexible and tailored to the parties' specific dispute and wishes is another well-known, essential feature of international arbitration. The parties' ability to tailor the arbitration procedure to their own requirements, by choosing where the arbitration is to be held, which language should be used, whether the arbitrators require any qualification and expertise, is indeed an important advantage over court proceedings for international business actors and investors.

2. Conventional Wisdom in the Organization of Arbitral Proceedings and the Role of Arbitral Institutions

Efforts have been made by international organizations and arbitral institutions to codify and regularize the organization of arbitral proceedings.

Produced by the United Nations Commission on International Trade Law (UNCITRAL), the UNCITRAL Notes on Organizing Arbitral Proceedings (the UNCITRAL Notes) gather a number of non-binding principles developed over the years of practice of international arbitration around the world, and as such are a useful guide of principles applicable to the management of arbitration cases. The UNCITRAL Notes are meant as a reference tool to be used during the initial stages of an arbitration, aimed at producing a well-organized, efficient arbitral proceeding by identifying issues for the tribunal and the parties to address.[12]

As stated in the Introduction to the UNCITRAL Notes:

> "Laws governing the arbitral procedure and arbitration rules that parties may agree upon typically allow the arbitral tribunal broad discretion and flexibility in the conduct of arbitral proceedings. This is useful in that it enables the arbitral

11. Gary BORN, fn. 9 above, p. 2120.
12. *Ibid.* at 2235-2236.

> tribunal to take decisions on the organization of proceedings that take into account the circumstances of the case, the expectations of the parties and of the members of the arbitral tribunal, and the need for a just and cost-efficient resolution of the dispute."[13]

The UNCITRAL Notes provide for guidelines in relation to the adoption of procedural rules; language, translation and costs; seat of the arbitration and location of the hearings; administrative matters and appointment of a secretary; deposits for costs and arbitrators' fees; timetable for written submissions, evidence, witness testimony and hearing; hearing procedures; possible settlement issues; and issue definition.

Other institutions have produced useful guidance on the management of arbitration proceedings. In addition to Appendix IV to the ICC Rules of 2012 and 2017 containing "Case Management Techniques",[14] the ICC Task Force on Controlling Time and Costs in International Arbitration, for instance, provides for useful recommendations regarding case management. The CIArb also has published a Guideline on "Managing Arbitrations and Procedural Orders" which can be a useful source of conventional wisdom in the management of arbitration cases.[15]

III. CONVENTIONAL WISDOM AND PERCEPTIONS

Although the principles which constitute conventional wisdom aspire to a certain universality and are theoretically "esteemed at any time for their acceptability", the practice of international arbitration shows that although there might be general consensus as to the formulation of certain principles, the perception of the way such principles should apply is likely to be influenced by the background of the party representatives or arbitrators involved in a specific arbitration proceeding.

1. *Perceptions Influenced by Legal Background*

The legal tradition of an arbitrator or counsel often does influence the perception of the best ways to conduct arbitral proceedings and to apply the substantive law.

As Pierre Tercier explained in a lecture at the American University Washington College of Law, justice is not dispensed in the same way everywhere around the globe, meaning that the preferred way of applying the law in one legal system can be inconceivable in another legal system. This implies that arbitrators, facing the inherent diverse backgrounds of parties and of their representatives in international arbitration, should be ready to understand and apply rules with which they are not necessarily

13. UNCITRAL Notes on Organizing Arbitral Proceedings (New York, 2012) Introduction, para. 4.
14. See fn. 10 above.
15. CIArb Guideline on "Managing Arbitrations and Procedural Orders" (2015). Other institutions have published guidelines for the organization of arbitral proceedings. See, e.g., the Singapore International Arbitration Centre (SIAC) Practice Note for Administered Cases (1 September 2013); the SIAC Practice Note for UNCITRAL Cases (2 January 2014); the London Court of International Arbitration (LCIA) Notes for Arbitrators (26 October 2017); the International Bar Association (IBA) Rules on the Taking of Evidence in International Arbitration (2010).

familiar. This also implies that counsel should be ready to adapt to a different way of approaching the legal proceedings from the other party's side.[16]

By way of example, while applying the principle of equality of arms is a conventional wisdom recognized in both civil and common legal traditions, the application of this principle by counsel in document production differs significantly between both traditions. Thus, the common law adversarial approach requires the disclosure of both supportive and adverse documents to a disputing party's case and ensures that "cards face up on the table" to secure equality of arms.[17] By contrast, in the civil law inquisitorial approach, document production is initiated by the disputing party and limited to the discharge of each party's burden of proof. Therefore, each party has to make out its own case in reliance on the evidence in its own possession, and document requests are only admissible in the most exceptional circumstances.[18]

2. *Perceptions Influenced by Cultural Background or Personal and Specific Industry Experience*

At the 2002 ICCA Congress, Shari Diamond, professor of law, whose research and interests include the psychology of the decision-making process, described three main psychological influences on an arbitrator's decision-making:

> "decision-makers are influenced by their cultural backgrounds, their prior experiences and their personal associations in formulating their understanding of and judging the behaviour they must consider in reaching their decisions."[19]

While the legal tradition is essential in an arbitrator's or lawyer's perception of fairness, due to a developed habit of applying rules in a certain way, the cultural or professional background of arbitrators can also influence the decision-making process and their perception of the best application of conventional wisdoms, e.g., their perception of a fair procedure.

Justice Holmes explained how the legal culture in which an arbitrator is schooled can have a significant impact not only on the procedures the arbitrator adopts but also on how he or she interprets the legal principles applicable:

> "The life of the law has not been logic: it has been experience. The felt necessities of the time, the prevalent moral and political theories, intuitions of public policy, avowed or unconscious, even the prejudices which judges share with their fellow-

16. "Washington DC: Tercier on Harmonisation", Global Arbitration Review (11 December 2015) available at <https://globalarbitrationreview.com/article/1035003/washington-dc-tercier-on-harmonisation> last accessed on 22 May 2018.
17. Gordon BLANKE, "Document Production in International Arbitration: From Civil and Common Law Dichotomy to Operational Synergies", 83 Arbitration (2017, no. 4) p. 423 at p. 424.
18. *Ibid.*
19. Shari DIAMOND, "Psychological Aspects of Dispute Resolution: Issue for International Arbitration" in *International Commercial Arbitration: Important Contemporary Questions*, ICCA Congress Series no. 11 (Kluwer Law International 2003) p. 336.

> men, have had a good deal more to do than the syllogism in determining the rules by which men should be governed."[20]

A number of studies have been conducted on the influence of arbitrators' industry backgrounds on arbitration outcomes, including with a focus on the securities industry[21] or the construction industry,[22] some of them concluding that a specific industry experience indeed has an impact on the decisions arbitrators take.[23]

In light of the foregoing, ideas have been developed on how to minimize the impact of cultural differences or of personal experience, in order to ensure a more harmonized approach to the application of conventional wisdom. As explained by Edna Sussman:

> "While arbitrators are often selected because of their backgrounds and experience, arbitrators should take care to assess the case that is actually presented before them, and to consciously endeavor to overcome any affinity they might have for any of the parties as a result of their background. Counsel should take care in the selection of arbitrators to appoint arbitrators accustomed to assessing witnesses from different cultural backgrounds and who have a reputation for independence and impartiality in their decision-making."[24]

A number of suggestions have been formulated to improve arbitral procedures and to ensure the best application of and respect for the principle of due process. Having a thorough review of the evidentiary record and a strong focus on the factual evidence submitted by both parties, for instance, can help to avoid being influenced by internal bias.[25]

IV. CONVENTIONAL WISDOM AND INNOVATION

Innovative tools and platforms in international arbitration represent another way to improve the arbitral process and to ensure respect for conventional wisdom.

20. Oliver WENDELL HOLMES Jr., *The Common Law* (Dover Publishing 1991).
21. Stephen J. CHOI, Jill E. FISCH and A.C. PRITCHARD, "The Influence of Arbitrator Background and Representation on Arbitration Outcomes", Penn Law: Legal Scholarship Repository (2014).
22. George OSSMAN III, Mehmet Emre BAYRAKTAR and Qingbin CU, "Consistency and Reliability of Construction Arbitration Decisions: Empirical Study", 26 Journal of Management in Engineering (2010, no. 2).
23. See Stephen J. CHOI, Jill E. FISCH and A.C. PRITCHARD, fn. 21 above; see also Edna SUSSMAN, "Chapter 3: Biases and Heuristics in Arbitrator Decision-Making: Reflections on How to Counteract or Play to Them" in Tony COLE, ed., *The Roles of Psychology in International Arbitration*, (Kluwer Law International 2017) p. 40 at pp. 45-74.
24. Edna SUSSMAN, fn. 23 above, at p. 65.
25. Edna Sussman advances that reviewing the evidentiary record before preparing the award, and reviewing evidence in favor of what has preliminarily been assessed to be the losing side can be a remedy to the expression of bias. *Ibid.* at pp. 67-68.

1. *Innovative Tools and Better Application of Conventional Principles in International Arbitration*

As described above, it is commonly accepted that arbitration proceedings should be quick, efficient and predictable to ensure access to justice. This is also essential to make sure that they maintain the advantages attributed to alternative means of dispute resolution over national court proceedings which often suffer the consequences of an overloaded schedule.[26] The development of innovative tools is even more necessary in an ever-evolving society with an increasing need for speed and swift resolution of disputes.

Once a swift and cost-efficient method of resolving international disputes, international arbitration is now often stalled by long and costly procedures.[27]

Yet, long and costly procedures can be avoided if the arbitration is organized and managed effectively. A number of ideas have been developed over time to improve the efficiency of the arbitral process.

2. *Examples of Innovations*

Below are examples of procedural innovations which can improve both time and cost efficiency of the arbitral process.

a. *Procedural innovations*

In a survey conducted by Queen Mary University London on "Improvements and Innovations in International Arbitration",[28] the procedural innovation perceived as most effective at controlling time and cost in international arbitration was the requirement for tribunals to commit to a schedule for deliberations and delivery of final awards.[29] Such internal commitment of the arbitral tribunal is essential and can be achieved only if the proceedings are efficiently organized, an efficiency which can be maximized when arbitrators are fully knowledgeable of the details of the case when they attend the evidentiary hearing.

b. *Innovative tools*

Three qualitative analytical models have been identified by Iain Sheridan as models that may contribute to the processes and outcomes in international arbitration, namely mind map diagrams; simplified evidence charts and cause and effect diagrams.[30] These are only

---

26. See e.g. Frank Sander's 1976 speech at the Pound Conference on "The Causes of Popular Dissatisfaction with the Administration of Justice", widely seen within the legal academy as the birth of the Alternative Dispute Resolution (ADR) movement in the United States and then worldwide. During this speech, Franck Sander explained that ADR should help avoid case overload in courts, which slows down the judicial process.
27. See fn. 1 above.
28. Queen Mary University London Survey, "Improvements and Innovations in International Arbitration" (2015).
29. *Ibid.* at p. 24.
30. Iain SHERIDAN, "Qualitative Analytical Models for Arbitration", 33 Journal of International Arbitration (2016, no. 2) pp. 171-184.

examples of innovative software, among a myriad of tools which are being developed and used to simplify and organize complex fact matrices and ideas.

i. Mind map diagrams

Mind map diagrams summarize a case in a non-linear way, replicating how the human brain often analyzes knowledge and problems. The essential elements of any mind map are (1) a main topic represented with a central image; (2) important themes radiating from the central image as branches; (3) branches comprised of a key image or key word printed on an associated line to form a connected nodal structure, and (4) the incorporation of color to clarify or emphasize connections.[31]

This tool allows for complex, voluminous facts to be summarized with links to other types of documents, such as party requests and responses, as well as expert spreadsheets.[32]

ii. Simplified evidence charts

Simplified evidence charts can set out with succinct clarity either side's arguments alongside supporting evidence and accepted generalizations. Well-drafted simplified evidence charts help counsel in preparing for and delivering their oral arguments and also aid arbitrators' decision-making.[33]

iii. Fishbone diagrams

Fishbone diagrams or cause and effect diagrams can help in brainstorming and in the identification of possible causes of a problem and in sorting ideas into useful categories. They are a visual way to look at cause and effect and as such can help clarify causation matters in the most sophisticated cases.[34]

c. *Online platforms*

Recourse to Online Dispute Resolution (ODR) through diverse online platforms can be key to saving time and costs, particularly in situations where the parties are not based in the same countries, and where the amount in dispute and nature of the dispute allows for such procedure.[35]

By way of example, the European Commission has sponsored an innovative online platform for ODR, "The ODR Platform" that can be used for any contractual dispute arising from online purchases of goods or services where the trader and consumer are both based in the European Union or Norway, Iceland, and Liechtenstein. The platform

31. Page VITULLI and Rebecca M. GILES, "Mind Mapping: Making Connections with Images and Colors", 6 Delta State University Journal (2016, no. 2).
32. Iain SHERIDAN, "Dispute Resolution: Three Tools to Improve International Arbitration", IFLR1000 (12 October 2015).
33. *Ibid.*
34. *Ibid.*
35. Julio Cesar BETANCOURT and Elina ZLATANSKA, "Online Dispute Resolution (ODR): What Is It and Is It the Way Forward?", 79 International Journal of Arbitration, Mediation and Dispute Management (2013, no. 3). See also Derrick YEOH, "Is Online Dispute Resolution the Future of Alternative Dispute Resolution?", Kluwer Arbitration Blog (29 March 2018).

is designed as a mechanism that is aimed to provide the speed and high quality required by the current world business sector.[36]

The World Intellectual Property Organization (WIPO) Arbitration and Mediation Center is also developing an online, internet-based system for administering disputes. Digital communication tools will allow the parties to file requests by completing electronic forms and to submit documents and exchange correspondence online through secure channels. The parties, the neutrals and the Center will thus communicate electronically (in addition to using any available audio and video facilities), reducing the need for other potentially time-consuming and expensive means of communication and in-person meetings and hearings.[37]

V. CONCLUSION

The 2018 edition of the ICCA Congress has invited us to look to the future of international arbitration and to think about how to build better arbitration proceedings, notably by analyzing conventional wisdom in the organization of arbitral proceedings.

Essential in many different professions, the concept of "wisdom" has been extensively analyzed by Greek philosophers in the fifth century B.C. and is central in the five virtues described as follows by Aristotle in *The Nicomachean Ethics*:

(1) Science (*episteme*) allows to draw conclusions in a logical, demonstrable fashion, from given facts and principles;
(2) Intelligence (*nous*) is the intuition of self-evident truths and can be referred to as "common sense";
(3) Theoretical wisdom (*sophia*) is a combination of science and intelligence;
(4) Prudence or practical wisdom (*phronesis*) involves not only the ability to decide how to achieve a certain end, but also the ability to reflect upon and determine good ends;
(5) Art (*technē*) is the ability to use one's skills to produce and create.[38]

As practitioners of international arbitration, and particularly as arbitrators, it is useful to keep in mind the five virtues described by Aristotle more than two millennia ago. Arbitrators indeed have to approach the decision-making process in a scientific fashion, while using common sense, wisdom, prudence, and a sense of creation to reach just and fair solutions.

According to Aristotle, we learn moral virtue primarily through habit and practice rather than through reasoning or instruction. It is up to us, as members of the arbitration community, to uphold these essential virtues by practicing them as habits, if we wish to ensure the perennity of international arbitration in the years to come.

---

36. See the website of the European Commission, "Online Dispute Resolution", at <https://ec.europa.eu/consumers/odr/main/?event=main.trader.register> last accessed on 22 May 2018.
37. WIPO Arbitration and Mediation Center, at <www.wipo.int/amc/en/> last accessed on 22 May 2018.
38. ARISTOTLE, *Nicomachean Ethics*, Book VI.

Revisiting Conventional Wisdom in the Organization of Arbitral Proceedings: Perspectives from Chinese Users and Institutions

Fuyong Chen *

TABLE OF CONTENTS PAGE

I. WHY IS REVISITING CONVENTIONAL WISDOM FROM THE PERSPECTIVE OF USERS NEEDED?

It has always been a very difficult task to clearly define what the "conventional wisdom" is when it comes to how arbitral proceedings are organized. But most practitioners in this field of dispute resolution often have a general sense of how to run an arbitration case. For example, in international arbitrations, most practitioners likely agree to refer to the United Nations Commission on International Trade Law (UNCITRAL) Notes on Organizing Arbitral Proceedings. However, is the conventional wisdom we are able to derive from current norms satisfactory in achieving the aims of the arbitral process?

Before touching upon this question, we should first consider: What is the aim of the arbitral process? Some may propose that we are seeking to achieve an enforceable award and therefore we should look at the limitations as set out in the 1958 New York Convention. Obviously, this is a perspective mainly from the arbitral tribunal. The disputing parties, or arbitration users, are more likely concerned about the quality of the award, which at a minimum means the substance of the award should be fair with the issues in dispute duly heard and considered by the arbitral tribunal. In addition, the users usually would like to obtain the award in an efficient and cost-effective way. Considering these aims we find the conventional wisdom may not always be satisfactory in achieving all aims. The common complaints from the users are inefficiency and high cost of arbitration.

As we know, the contractual foundation of the arbitral process calls for the acceptance of arbitration by every party to the contract. To shape arbitration as an attractive user-orientated dispute resolution mechanism, we should revisit the conventional wisdom in

---

* Deputy Secretary-General, the Beijing Arbitration Commission/Beijing International Arbitration Center; Vice-President, Asia Pacific Regional Arbitration Group (APRAG). The author wishes to thank Weixia GU, Wei SUN, Ke HU, Arthur MA, Kaishen HUANG, Xi ZHANG and Chenxi LIN for their constructive comments on earlier versions of this article.

the organization of arbitral proceedings from the perspective of arbitration users rather than merely from the perspective of arbitration practitioners. Traditionally, the main attraction for users to insert arbitration clauses in their transnational contracts is the international enforceability supported by the New York Convention. In the near future, this key advantage of arbitration may be substantively diluted due to the possible international enforceability of settlement agreements resulting from mediation and court judgments. Working Group II UNCITRAL, for example, has finalized and submitted, for approval at the UNCITRAL Conference 2018, an instrument to deal with the enforcement of international commercial settlement agreements resulting from mediation. In addition, the Hague Conference on Private International Law (HCCH), in 2016, proposed a draft text on the Recognition and Enforcement of Foreign Judgments. It may not take long to see the final draft. Against this background, the users' concern should be placed in a higher position than before. Otherwise, if the international enforceability of both settlement agreements and court judgments becomes a reality in the future, the original users of arbitration may turn more to mediation or litigation.

Adopting a user-focused perspective on commercial arbitration also allows for more diverse voices in the field of international arbitration. As a result of China's continuous economic growth over the last three decades, more and more Chinese participate in international arbitration. Moreover, with the implementation of the Belt and Road Initiative, international cases involving Chinese parties are likely to increase significantly in the future. Chinese users' expectations and attitudes toward arbitration, especially their perception and understanding of the ways in which arbitral proceedings are organized, will likely have considerable impact on the future landscape of international arbitration.

II. WHAT MEASURES ARE EMPLOYED BY CHINESE ARBITRATION INSTITUTIONS TO RELIEVE THE CONCERNS OF USERS ON TIME AND COST?

For this discussion, the "conventional wisdom" is considered to be an equivalent of the "widely accepted norms" of international arbitration. However, to what extent can a norm be regarded as "widely accepted"? We might need to consider the problem of representation here. As a matter of fact, many so-called "widely" accepted norms were primarily developed by practitioners mainly from a small group of countries with a strong presence in the field of international arbitration. For the rest, including China, some of these norms are not home-grown but rather foreign and therefore far from "widely accepted".

It is natural for a user to compare the norms of international arbitration with practices at home. With their increasing involvement in international arbitration, Chinese users also have a desire to revisit the "widely accepted norms", particularly when they find that the problems of time and cost caused by these norms may not be problems at all in China's practice. Traditionally, Chinese users prefer institutional arbitration over *ad hoc* arbitration. When it comes to the organization of arbitral proceedings, most professionals think of the roles of counsel and arbitrators. However, in the context of institutional arbitration, the arbitration institution could be more sensitive to the needs of the users with different background and play a very important role to improve efficiency and to control the costs of the arbitration.

In the next part, I will take the practice of the Beijing Arbitration Commission/ Beijing International Arbitration Center (BAC) as an example to illustrate what kinds of measures an institution may employ to relieve the concerns of the users on efficiency and cost.

1. *Measures to Increase Efficiency*

As the following figures show, the BAC has maintained a high caseload over the past 5 years. If we look at the cases concluded in each year, the time from the establishment of the arbitral tribunal to the conclusion of the case ranges from 61 to 75 days on average for the expedited procedure and from 126 to 150 days for the common procedure.

Year	**2013**	**2014**	**2015**	**2016**	**2017**
Total caseload	1,627	2,041	2,944	3,012	3,550
Average number of days/ case for expedited procedure	70	61	75	64	64
Average number of days/case for common procedure	150	140	148	126	133

How does the BAC achieve this high level of efficiency? Measures employed by the BAC to increase efficiency include the following:

(a) Limitation on arbitrators' caseloads: According to the BAC's Code of Ethics for Arbitrators, an arbitrator is not allowed to accept a new appointment when there are ten or more pending cases under his or her name. This requirement encourages arbitrators to conclude their cases as efficiently as possible so they can accept more new appointments.

(b) Availability requirement: If an arbitrator may not be available for a first hearing within sixty days after the constitution of the tribunal, he or she is not allowed to accept the appointment.

(c) Prompt delivery of the award: The presiding arbitrator is expected to provide the draft award within thirty days from the last hearing or the last submission of the parties, and the co-arbitrators are expected to provide comments within five days of receiving the draft. An arbitrator with undue delays in more than three cases in the arbitrator's history

of arbitrating with the BAC will not be offered new appointments from the arbitration institution for one year. Those with seriously undue delays will be removed from the list of BAC arbitrators.
(d) Mobile access and notification: All cases are run using a state-of-the-art case-management system which can automatically record every step of the proceedings. Arbitrators are provided with mobile access to the system and can easily check the procedural history and current status of each of their cases. When one arbitrator uploads the draft award or any comments on the draft, the system will immediately send a reminder text message to the other members of the tribunal.
(e) Electronic signing: When the award is finalized, arbitrators can sign it by using the electronic signing system, which works even via mobile phone.

2. *Measures to Reduce Costs*

The BAC is devoted to providing dispute resolution services of an international caliber at local fee standards. It seems to be an impossible mission. However, the BAC basically accomplishes it by helping the disputing parties control costs.

(a) Distance filing: When filing a case, neither claimants nor their counsel, especially those residing outside Beijing, are required to come to the BAC in person. The BAC provides a free case-filing consultation service: a telephone call, fax or email will be enough to obtain answers to their questions. The submission of documents can be done by post or courier or through the online case filing system.
(b) Strict ad valorem charges: Unless otherwise agreed by the parties, the BAC charges an arbitration fee calculated on the basis of the sum in dispute. This makes the arbitration fee predictable. The fee charged by the BAC, which includes both its administrative fee and the fee of the arbitrators, is lower than that of most international arbitration institutions.
(c) Arbitrator intelligence: The BAC publishes comprehensive background for each arbitrator listed on its website. Besides the usual information, the BAC provides information on the number of past cases (i.e. how many times he or she has acted as co-arbitrator, sole arbitrator or presiding arbitrator before the BAC and how many cases are still pending). With the help of this transparent information on the listed arbitrators, the disputing parties can make an informed decision – at nearly zero research cost – regarding the appointment of the arbitrator in a specific case.
(d) Fee allocation: The BAC Arbitration Rules provide that when applying the Rules, the arbitral tribunal, the parties and their representatives shall act in accordance with the principles of good faith, collaboration and appropriate resolution of the dispute. Where there exist any breaches of the Rules that cause delay in the arbitral proceedings, the allocation of arbitration costs to the party at fault shall not be limited by the principle of costs following the event.
(e) Facilities and recording services: The BAC offers hearing rooms and recording services in Beijing at no additional charge.
(f) Use of Arb-Med: With the consent of the parties, arbitral tribunals tend to proactively organize mediation after hearings; in practice, around 20 percent of the cases at the BAC are concluded by mediation and hence substantially reduce the time and costs.

(g) Appraisals: The BAC maintains a list of highly-competent appraisal institutions for construction disputes. For specialized matters related to project settlement or quality, an arbitral tribunal may submit matters for appraisal to an appraisal institution agreed upon by the parties or to the appraisal institution appointed by the arbitral tribunal if it deems such appraisal to be necessary. Compared with allowing each party to bring their own expert evidence, the introduction of a common appraiser usually reduces the cost.
(h) Publishing select awards: The BAC has published select awards on certain areas of law, such as company law, contributing to the development of law on frontier issues and providing higher predictability for the parties.

III. WHERE MAY THE CHINESE CONVENTIONAL WISDOM AND THE WESTERN CONVENTIONAL WISDOM MEET?

The "widely accepted" norms generally are regarded as reflecting best practices in the field. However, if the time and cost to follow these norms cannot be justified by the complexity of the case, the norms will seem to be mainly in the interest of arbitrators and practitioners rather than the users of arbitration. Market forces will then push the practitioners to adjust the norms. As such, many proposals have been raised in recent years to address concerns on time and cost from arbitration users.

In China, arbitration is something transplanted from other countries. Bringing the arbitration rules in line with international practice has long been a mainstream topic in the field. However, if we look at all the proposals so far to improve the "widely accepted" norms in international arbitration, we may find that some of the international norms that China is trying to learn may be in the process of evolving towards the domestic norms that China currently follows. Highlighting some differences between arbitration practices in China and those elsewhere might be of help for us to understand where the Chinese conventional wisdom and the Western conventional wisdom in the organization of arbitral proceedings may meet in the future.

1. *A Basic Mode Beyond the Differences Between Civil and Common Law*

The continuous efforts in encouraging the internationalization of Chinese arbitration has made it possible for foreign lawyers to argue arbitration cases in Beijing similarly to how they do before tribunals in the other leading arbitration centers, such as Hong Kong, Singapore, London and Paris. According to Global Arbitration Review's Guide to Regional Arbitration 2018, the BAC's Rules are the most flexible of those offered in China in terms of party autonomy, where they approach the international norm. You are very likely able to arbitrate a dispute pretty much in any way you want, even "when it comes to the vexed topic of which laws should apply".[1]

It is not, however, safe to assume that all relevant procedural matters are the same or that they are simply a complete transplantation of international norms. Although China is

1. *The Global Arbitration Review, Guide to Regional Arbitration 2018*, available at <https://globalarbitrationreview.com/benchmarking/guide-to-regional-arbitration-volume-6-2018/1150107/welcome-to-gar's-guide-to-regional-arbitration> (last accessed 12 March 2018).

seen as a civil law jurisdiction, this does not mean that Chinese arbitration proceedings will necessarily always apply the core civil law principles, such as the inquisitorial approach and a focus on documents, which are often referred to as some of the key features of Chinese litigation practice. Rather, the BAC Arbitration Rules clearly state that, in respect of any matters not expressly provided for in the Rules, the BAC may administer and the arbitral tribunal may conduct the arbitration in such manner as they consider appropriate to ensure the efficient and fair resolution of the dispute between the parties.

This does not mean that common law procedures will automatically be adopted by the tribunal either. For users who prefer common law procedures, it is advisable to put in a special agreement on the specific procedures that will make sure that common law procedures or international arbitration practices are adopted in the Chinese arbitration.

2. *Style of Pleading*

There is a tendency for the tribunal in international arbitration to require the parties to limit their submissions to a certain number of pages (as appropriate) and focus their pleadings on the key issues. The style and approach to pleading in China is generally shorter and more concise than equivalents in international arbitration outside China. A party is expected to serve supporting witness statements along with its pleading and the documentary evidence that supports its case. Unless as a matter of procedure already agreed upon by the parties or decided upon by the arbitral tribunal, there is no specific provision or limitation on the rounds of pleadings. However, the usual expectation in practice is not only to set out the basics but actually also to include the content of a full statement of the case/statement of defense in the request for arbitration/defense and the answer.

3. *Document Production*

There are many complaints concerning the abuse of document production in international arbitration. In China, if parties want specific document production, it is advisable for them to agree to the use of the International Bar Association (IBA) Rules on the Taking of Evidence in International Arbitration in advance in their arbitration agreement. If parties do not specify a set of rules, the rules of evidence that arbitrators in Chinese arbitrations will apply include the evidence rules from the Arbitration Law of the PRC and institutional arbitration rules. Under these rules, there is no express power for a tribunal to make orders for the specific production of documents. However, if a party submits an issue in a case and can show that the relevant evidence is only in the possession of the other party, the other party is expected to disclose the evidence. If it refuses to disclose the evidence without any justifiable reason, and the evidence would have had an adverse impact on the case of the party possessing the evidence, adverse inferences may be drawn from the refusal to disclose.

4. *Hearing*

There are more and more tribunals in international arbitration who try to limit the evidentiary hearing and rely more on documents. Normally, hearings in China last for only a half day or one day, which is substantially shorter than the hearings before major international arbitration institutions. This is largely a result of the fact that Chinese parties in arbitrations seldom introduce witnesses in the proceedings if they believe that the documentary evidence they have submitted will be sufficient to prove their claims. However, more complex disputes can have oral hearings lasting several days or have several hearings in non-consecutive days.

When there are several hearings over non-consecutive days, the first hearing actually plays a role similar to that of the mid-arbitration "Case Review Conference", an idea developed by Neil Kaplan and later developed by Constantine Partasides and Scott Vesel that advocates splitting an arbitration in two halves, with an in-person case review conference mid-way through in which there is a "meaningful discussion" about the merits of the case, allowing the arbitrators to streamline certain aspects and better define the document disclosure and evidentiary process.

Unless otherwise agreed by the parties, the arbitral tribunal may adopt an inquisitorial or adversarial approach in hearing the case, having regard to the circumstances of the case. In practice, a tribunal will commonly adopt a combination of the inquisitorial and the adversarial approach, which means the hearing will include the tribunal's investigation, on its own initiative, concerning some issues aside from the parts driven by the parties.

Before closing the hearing but after consulting the disputing parties, the tribunal usually will give directions for post-hearing procedures. Typically, the parties are expected to submit additional evidence (if any) within the time specified by the tribunal. Then, the parties are allowed to submit written comments on the new evidence within a certain number of days from receipt of said evidence. Further, both parties may be directed to submit post-hearing briefs within a specified time. It is important for the tribunal to limit the post-hearing submissions to dealing with those matters that arose in the hearing itself, in order to prevent opening up new issues or evidence. The post-hearing briefs should also contain the parties' respective submissions on costs.

5. *The Role of Case-Handling Secretary*

Traditionally, Chinese arbitral institutions will assign to each individual case a case-handling secretary who plays much more important roles than those of the case manager in international arbitration. Usually the secretary will directly handle most logistical and even procedural matters in arbitration, for instance, the service of documents and the issuing of procedural notices, and allows arbitrators to focus on substantive issues. Some experts in China advocate limiting the role of the case-handling secretary and encourage the tribunal to assume more work. However, the growing practice, in international arbitration, of introducing a secretary to the tribunal in recent years seems to justify the Chinese practice of allowing a case-handling secretary to take on broader duties than those of a case manager.

In conclusion, compared with the lawyer-driven and lengthy western conventional practice, the Chinese conventional wisdom is to allow the arbitral tribunal and the arbitration institution to play more active roles so that the arbitration proceeding can be run in an efficient and cost-effective way and be tailored as appropriate for each dispute. Although currently it is not clear yet where the Chinese conventional wisdom and the Western conventional wisdom will meet, but they definitely will meet somewhere in the future.

When Does the Use of an Arbitral Secretary Detract from the "*Intuitu Personae*" Principle?

Funke Adekoya, SAN[*]

TABLE OF CONTENTS PAGE

I. INTRODUCTION

It is accepted by all that since the appointment of an arbitrator is personal to the person appointed – "*intuitu personae*"; the arbitrator is expected to be personally responsible for the conduct of the arbitration and the issuance of the award. The arbitrator having been selected based on his or her particular expertise or skills, the person is contractually required to conduct the proceedings without being in any way subject to any external input. Any delegation of duties will be viewed as a dereliction or abdication of his or her functions.

A typical arbitration requires that the arbitrator perform the following functions:

(i) receive the parties' case materials and documents;
(ii) receive and deal with correspondence from the parties;
(iii) organize and schedule meetings;
(iv) manage appointments;
(v) review and respond to routine or substantive applications;
(vi) take evidence at the hearing and review each side's case filings;
(vii) conduct necessary legal research;
(viii) draft and issue the award.

Each function above may involve a significant investment of time.

Over time, it has become increasingly common for the arbitral tribunal to seek external support for some of these tasks by appointing an arbitral secretary. It is not clear when arbitral secretaries were first used in *ad hoc* arbitral proceedings. However, there is a decision of the Italian courts,[1] stating that using arbitral secretaries for legal analysis was a delegation of the arbitral tribunal's adjudicative functions.

---

* Senior Advocate of Nigeria; Head of Dispute Resolution and Litigation, AELEX; ICCA Governing Board Member.

1. Reported in XVI ICCA *Yearbook Commercial Arbitration* (Kluwer Law International 1991) p. 156.

The conventional wisdom regarding the role of the arbitrator in organizing arbitral proceedings would seem to be that the use of an arbitral secretary in providing purely administrative support does not violate the "*intuitu personae*" principle. Legal analysis provided by an arbitral secretary may however impinge upon the personal role of the arbitrator.

II. NOTES, GUIDELINES AND REGULATIONS ON THE ROLE OF THE ARBITRAL SECRETARY

In the last twenty years, various arbitral institutions have issued notes and guidelines which seek to "regulate" the functions of the arbitral secretary. A review of the various documents indicates an expansion of the role, from the conduct of purely administrative tasks into areas that may indicate a shift in the extent of the application of the "*intuitu personae*" principle

When parties appoint an arbitrator in institutional arbitration proceedings, depending on the arbitral institution, it is possible that the institution will undertake some of the administrative tasks involved in managing the arbitration. The parties, by selecting institutional arbitration, have impliedly agreed that some part of what would otherwise have been the arbitrator's responsibilities will be handled by a third party.

In International Chamber of Commerce (ICC) administered arbitrations, the first two of the administrative duties outlined above, which the arbitrator in *ad hoc* proceedings would have to deal with, are handled by the ICC Secretariat.[2]

In International Centre for Settlement of Investment Disputes (ICSID) arbitrations, the ICSID Administrative and Financial Regulations provide that a secretary shall be appointed to each ICSID tribunal. The Regulations state that the secretary of the tribunal shall "keep summary minutes of hearings" and "perform other functions with respect to the proceeding at the request of the ... Tribunal ... or at the direction of the [ICSID] Secretary-General".[3]

In practice, the ICSID secretariat provides the arbitrators with a case team consisting of an ICSID legal counsel, paralegal, legal assistant and hearing organizer. The legal counsel acts as secretary to the arbitral tribunal. The ICSID Arbitration Rules clearly state that secretaries cannot attend tribunal deliberations unless the tribunal consents: "Only members of the Tribunal shall take part in its deliberations. No other person shall be admitted unless the Tribunal decides otherwise."[4]

This is similar to the administrative support the Permanent Court of Arbitration (PCA) can provide in arbitrations administered by it, with a staff member being appointed as registrar or administrative secretary for a case. The staff member will carry out administrative tasks at the direction of the arbitral tribunal. [5]

2. Art. 5(2):- "The Secretariat may grant the respondent an extension of the time for submitting the Answer...."; Art. 5(3): "The Answer shall be submitted to the Secretariat in the number of copies specified by Article 3(1)."; Art. 5(4): "The Secretariat shall communicate the Answer and the documents annexed thereto to all other parties."
3. Regulation 25 of the Administrative and Financial Regulations.
4. Rule 15(2) of the ICSID Arbitration Rules.
5. <https://pca-cpa.org/en/services/arbitration-services/case-administration/>.

The implication is that for some, if not most institutional arbitrations, the arbitrators receive administrative support, leaving them free to deal with the substantive dispute between the parties.

The extent to which an arbitral secretary (other than the arbitral institution itself) participates in the arbitration proceedings depends on the institution, tribunal and parties who have made the appointment. In some institutional arbitrations, the institutional rules set out the roles of the arbitral secretaries. Although the ICC Secretariat performs some of the functions of an arbitral secretary, its Rules do not provide for such an appointment. By way of guidance, in 2017, the Secretariat of the ICC International Court of Arbitration issued a Note to Parties and Arbitral Tribunals on the Conduct of the Arbitration Under the ICC Rules of Arbitration (the ICC Note).[6]

Sect. XVII of the ICC Note states the policy and practice of the ICC Court with respect to the appointment, duties and remuneration of arbitral tribunal administrative secretaries or other assistants in ICC administered tribunals. The ICC Note applies to the appointment of an Administrative Secretary after 1 August 2012, the date of its previous two-page "Note on the Appointment, Duties and Remuneration of Administrative Secretaries".

Sect. XVII provides that should a tribunal in an ICC administered arbitration wish to appoint a secretary, it must first submit the proposed secretary's curriculum vitae and a declaration of independence and impartiality to the parties. The declaration contains "an undertaking on the part of the Administrative Secretary to act in accordance with the present Note and an undertaking on the part of the Arbitral Tribunal to ensure that this obligation on the part of the Administrative Secretary shall be met".[7]

Para. 150 of the ICC Note lists the "organisational and administrative tasks" that an Administrative Secretary may perform as:

– transmitting documents and communications on behalf of the arbitral tribunal;
– organizing and maintaining the arbitral tribunal's file and locating documents;
– organizing hearings and meetings;
– attending hearings, meetings and deliberations; taking notes or minutes or keeping time;
– conducting legal or similar research; and
– proof-reading and checking citations, dates and cross-references in procedural orders and awards, as well as correcting typographical, grammatical or calculation errors.

6. The Note to Parties and Arbitral Tribunals on the Conduct of the Arbitration Under the ICC Rules of Arbitration was revised in January 2019. The numbering and quotations referred to in this Article reflect the 2017 version (henceforth the ICC Note). The ICC Note as revised in January 2019 is available at <https://cdn.iccwbo.org/content/uploads/sites/3/2017/ 03/icc-note-to-parties-and-arbitral-tribunals-on-the-conduct-of-arbitration.pdf>.

7. Para. 147.

After listing these functions, para. 151 of the ICC Note then states that:

> "Under no circumstances may the arbitral tribunal delegate decision-making functions to an Administrative Secretary. Nor should the arbitral tribunal rely on the Administrative Secretary to perform any essential duties of an arbitrator."

The ICC reinforces its support for the "*intuitu personae*" principle as para. 153 of its Note which says that

> "A request by an Arbitral Tribunal to an Administrative Secretary to prepare written notes or memoranda shall in no circumstances release the Arbitral Tribunal from its duty personally to review the file and/or to draft any decision of the Arbitral Tribunal."

Clearly, the position of the ICC is that "conducting legal or similar research" is not one of the "essential duties" for which an arbitrator is appointed, and as such the delegation of those duties to a third party does not detract from the "*intuitu personae*" principle.

Perhaps reinforcing the position that the arbitral secretary acts under the supervision of the arbitral tribunal, the ICC Note states that an ICC tribunal cannot pass the fees of the arbitral secretary on to the parties: the arbitrators must pay the secretary's fees from their own fees.[8] However, the parties will pay all "justified reasonable expenses for hearings and meetings",[9] which may include expenses incurred by the arbitral secretary in arranging hearings and meetings.

Other arbitral bodies have also walked a fine line between preserving the personal nature of the arbitrator's appointment and expanding the scope of duties that an arbitral secretary can perform. Some institutions attempt a list (though expressed to be non-exhaustive) of what tasks an arbitral secretary can undertake.

Similar to the ICC, the Arbitration Rules of the London Court of International Arbitration (LCIA) do not contain specific provisions on the role of the tribunal secretary. The LCIA, however, in October 2017 updated its Notes to Arbitrators (the LCIA Notes), to include guidance on the role of an arbitral secretary. Sect. 8 of the LCIA Notes opens with para. 68 which prescribes that "... an Arbitral Tribunal may obtain assistance from a tribunal secretary in relation to an arbitration. However, in no circumstances may an Arbitral Tribunal delegate its fundamental decision-making function."

The LCIA goes further than the ICC however in demarcating the role of the arbitral secretary from the appointment of the arbitrator being a personal one, which does not permit delegation. While the ICC takes the view that an arbitral secretary conducting research does not derogate from the personal responsibilities of the arbitrator, the LCIA goes even further. For the LCIA, should the arbitrators so propose it as part of the secretary's tasks, an arbitral secretary's participation in "substantive tasks, such as summarising submissions, reviewing authorities, and preparing first drafts of awards, or

8. Para. 157.
9. Para. 155.

sections of awards, and procedural orders",[10] is not part of the arbitral tribunal's "fundamental decision-making function" as long as such tasks are "carried out in accordance with the Arbitral Tribunal's specific instructions".

Introducing the 2017 changes to the Notes for Arbitrators on its website, the LCIA states that:

> "One of the most contentious issues regarding tribunal secretaries regards the tasks a tribunal secretary should be entitled to carry out. Previously, the LCIA has dealt with this by providing a list of activities that the tribunal secretary should limit themselves to. In light of the broad spectrum of opinions on this matter, the Notes for Arbitrators still provide a list of tribunal secretary tasks, but the list is now a list of tasks that tribunals "may wish to propose". The list is a starting point for the discussion between tribunals and parties – parties must expressly consent to the tasks proposed, ensuring that all arbitrators and parties are comfortable with the tribunal secretary's role at the outset."

In its "Note on the Use of a Secretary",[11] the Arbitration Institute of the Finland Chamber of Commerce (FAI) also lists what an arbitral secretary can do. In addition to performing routine administrative tasks, such as transmitting documents and communications on behalf of the arbitral tribunal, organizing meetings and hearings, taking notes or minutes of meetings, and recording witness testimonies at a hearing, the FAI Note states that an arbitral secretary may undertake the following tasks:

> "(i) proofreading and checking the accuracy of cross-references, citations, dates and other figures in draft procedural orders and awards as well as correcting any clerical, typographical or computational errors found in the drafts;
> (ii) collecting case law or published commentaries on legal issues defined by the arbitral tribunal, preparing summaries from case law and publications as well as producing memoranda summarising the parties' respective submissions and the evidence supporting those submissions, provided that the arbitral tribunal refrains from relying solely on a secretary's work to the exclusion of its own review of the file and legal authorities."[12]

Maintaining the concept of the "*intuitu persona*" principle, it emphasizes that

> "The mandate of an arbitrator is personal. By accepting appointment, an arbitrator undertakes not to delegate the mandate to any other person, including any tribunal-appointed secretary. An arbitrator may under no circumstances rely on a secretary to perform any essential duties of an arbitrator."

10. Para. 71.
11. <https://arbitration.fi/wp-content/uploads/sites/22/2016/07/note-on-the-use-of-a-secretary.pdf>. Accessed on 13 January 2018
12. Art. 3.4 of the FAI Note.

It prescribes that the arbitral tribunal must however ensure that by performing these tasks, the arbitral secretary does not assume any part of "the decision-making function of the tribunal, or otherwise influence the tribunal's decisions in any manner".[13]

The FAI Note also provides that the tribunal is responsible for the secretary's fee out of its own fees.[14]

The table below shows how the two major arbitral institutions – the ICC and the LCIA – regulate the arbitral secretary's role.

	ICC	LCIA
Appointment	An appointment may be made at any time during proceedings; Tribunal must seek consent of parties; Parties can object to appointment, which shall be binding on the tribunal	In making an appointment, the Tribunal must seek consent of parties; A Party can object to appointment, which shall be binding on the tribunal
Role	Spells out the roles of the arbitral secretary	Makes this subject to consent of the parties; however, the tribunal may set out the extent, if any, to which the tribunal secretary carries out substantive tasks, such as summarizing submissions, reviewing authorities, and preparing first drafts of awards, or sections of awards, and procedural orders.
Remuneration	Apart from reasonable personal disbursements; remuneration of the arbitral secretary is to be paid by the tribunal without cost to parties	Remuneration subject to agreement of parties
Qualification	Does not make any provision	Does not make any provision
Standards	Same independence and impartiality requirements as those which apply to arbitrators under the Rules.	

13. *Ibid*.
14. Art. 4.2

Where the arbitrator is appointed in *ad hoc* proceedings, he or she does not have the administrative guidance or support provided by an arbitral institution; it is the tribunal that decides the remit of the roles of arbitral secretaries, either solely or after consultation with the parties.

To fill that gap, the United Nations Commission on International Trade Law (UNICITRAL) has promulgated guidance notes for *ad hoc* arbitrations. In 2016 UNCITRAL published its 2nd Edition of its "Notes on Organizing Arbitral Proceedings".[15] UNCITRAL's Notes are not procedural rules; their purpose is to guide arbitrators in *ad hoc* proceedings through the various issues that may arise in organizing arbitral proceedings.

UNCITRAL's Notes reiterate that as a general rule, arbitral secretaries provide organizational support, although some arbitral tribunals may want the arbitral secretary to provide more substantive support such as conducting legal research, preparing the recitals or the procedural history portion of the award, or even preparing draft procedural decisions.

In spite of this UNCITRAL, supports the generally agreed position "that secretaries are not involved and do not participate in the decision-making of the arbitral tribunal…".[16]

III. THE CASE LAW

So where are we today? As of 2014, in *Sonatrach v. Statoil*, Algeria's Sonatrach challenged an ICC award in favour of Norwegian state oil company Statoil on the basis that the ICC tribunal had improperly delegated authority to the secretary and impermissibly allowed the secretary to participate in its deliberations. The evidence was that the arbitral secretary had produced three notes on legal issues which the arbitral tribunal had refused to release to the Claimant upon receiving the secretary's fee note, on the ground that a release would breach the confidentiality of the tribunal's deliberations. However, the High Court of Justice of England and Wales ultimately dismissed Sonatrach's application, noting that " it is standard practice in ICC arbitrations for administrative secretaries to be used and for them to produce notes to assist the tribunal" and going on to find that the tribunal's reference was that the documents prepared by the arbitral secretary constituted a part of the arbitral tribunal's deliberations, and not the secretary's personal participation.[17] It would seem that the English High Court position is in line with the ICC Note, such that the delegation of research duties to an arbitral secretary is not a delegation of the personal functions which an arbitrator is expected to undertake. Perhaps the position being taken is that the personal skills of the arbitral tribunal are the ability to analyze the legal research conducted by others, and not the ability to personally undertake the research function itself.

---

15. <http://www.uncitral.org/pdf/english/texts/arbitration/arb-notes/arb-notes-2016-e.pdf>. Accessed on 14 January 2018.
16. Para. 36 of the Notes.
17. *Sonatrach v. Statoil* [2014] EWHC 875 (Comm) (2 April 2014), paras. 46-50.

In *Veteran Petroleum Limited (Cyprus) v. the Russian Federation* (the Yukos set-aside case),[18] Russia sought to set aside the arbitral award because (in addition to other grounds), the time sheets obtained from the arbitral tribunal showed that the arbitral secretary spent more time on the arbitration than the arbitrators. Russia's argument on this issue was that the extensive time spent on the arbitral proceedings by the arbitral secretary indicated a breach of the "*intuitu personae*" principle "goes to the essence of the arbitral function", which is that the arbitral tribunal had delegated to the arbitral secretary primary responsibility "to review the evidence and arguments and to decide the case personally, without delegation".[19]

While the award was eventually set aside on other grounds, the award and entire proceedings were at risk of being set aside because of how the arbitral secretary was used.

The "*intuitu personae*" principle was also the basis of the argument put forward in a 2015 Swiss case[20] where an award was challenged before the Swiss Supreme Court because the sole arbitrator who was not a lawyer had appointed both a legal consultant and an administrative secretary to assist him with the procedural issues.

The unsuccessful respondent's position was that the arbitral tribunal was improperly constituted because while the arbitration agreement provided for a sole arbitrator, the sole arbitrator did not decide the case personally but in conjunction with the legal consultant and the arbitral secretary.

And in 2017, in *P v. Q and ors*,[21] the Claimant applied pursuant to Sect. 24(1)(d)(i) of the English Arbitration Act 1996 to remove the Second and Third Defendants as arbitrators for failing to properly conduct the arbitration proceedings. The overall complaint was that the arbitral tribunal had improperly delegated its functions to the arbitral secretary. In support of its case, the Claimant relied on an email which the tribunal chairman had mistakenly sent to a paralegal at the Claimant's lawyer's offices, and which was intended for the arbitral secretary. The Chairman's email attached the Claimant's lawyer's application for an extension of time and the covering email and asked, "Your reaction to this latest from [Claimant]?" The Claimant alleged as Ground 2 of its complaint that the Chairman had breached his mandate as an arbitrator and his duty not to delegate by seeking the views of a person who was neither a party to the arbitration nor a member of the tribunal on substantial procedural issues (i.e. the Secretary).

The court however held that whilst the acts of the arbitral tribunal may be construed as a failure to follow arbitral best practice, they did not amount to failing to properly conduct proceedings within the meaning of Sect. 24(1)(d) of the Act. The judge said that

> "Soliciting or receiving any views of any kind from a tribunal secretary on the substance of decisions does not of itself demonstrate a failure to discharge the

18. PCA Case No. AA 228, Final Award, 18 July 2014.
19. Brief of Russian Federation dated 28 Jan. 2015, para. 468 on p. 179.
20. Referred to in 9 Bundesgericht [BGer] [Federal Supreme Court] 21 May 2015, 4A_709/2014 (Switz.).
21. <https://www.judiciary.gov.uk/wp-content/uploads/2017/03/p-v-q-and-ors-2017-ewhc-194-comm-20170209.pdf>. Accessed on 14 February 2018.

> arbitrator's personal duty to perform the decision-making function and responsibility himself. That is especially so where, as in this case, the relevant arbitrator is an experienced judge who is used to reaching independent decisions which are not inappropriately influenced by suggestions made by junior legal assistants."[22]

The trial court was very likely swayed in reaching its decision by its review of the guidelines on the use of arbitral secretaries issued by various arbitral institutions and organizations including extensive reference to the *Young ICCA Guide on Arbitral Secretaries*, noting that "It was compiled by authors with collective experience of acting as tribunal secretary in over 90 arbitrations. They took account of a survey in 2012 sent to a cross section of international arbitration practitioners, users and providers, and a second more focussed survey of about 100 practitioners in 2013."[23]

The judge also referred to the below quoted portions of a 2006 report by joint committees of the New York City Bar Association[24] which stated that:

> "'The role of the arbitrator is characterised by its *intuitu personae* nature. The appointment of a secretary may be reconciled with this fundamental principle so long as the arbitral tribunal exercises both close supervision of and has ultimate authority over the decision-making process.' (p.586).
>
> and
>
> 'There is concern that a secretary permitted substantial involvement may exercise undue influence over the arbitral tribunal and, as a result, affect the disposition. This concern is best addressed by disclosure, transparency and informed consent of the parties.' (p. 591)."[25]

In all the cases reviewed, it was not the use of arbitral secretaries per se that was being challenged, but the scope of their role. While there is consensus on using arbitral secretaries for administrative and clerical roles, it is not the same for tasks that involve legal analysis, case reviews and writing parts of the award. Some legal writers believe that these tasks are integral to the decision-making function of the arbitral tribunal and as such should not be delegated.

In the *P v. Q and ors* case, the court reconciled the personal nature of the arbitrator's appointment with the expanding role currently being played by arbitral secretaries by saying that:

> "Care must be taken to ensure that the decision-making is indeed that of the tribunal members alone. The safest way to ensure that that is the case is for the secretary not to be tasked with anything which involves expressing a view on the

22. Para. 69 of the judgment.
23. Para. 56 of the judgment.
24. 17 The American Review of International Arbitration (2006, no. 4).
25. Para. 64 of the judgment.

> substantive merits of an application or issue. If he is so tasked, there may arise a real danger of inappropriate influence over the decision-making process by the tribunal, which affects the latter's ability to reach an entirely independent minded judgment.... Best practice is therefore to avoid involving a tribunal secretary in anything which could be characterised as expressing a view on the substance of that which the tribunal is called upon to decide."[26]

IV. THE COMMENTARY

Most commentators agree that the use of arbitral secretaries enhances time and cost efficiency in arbitral proceedings. They take care of the administrative and clerical aspects of proceedings, thereby leaving the tribunal to deal with the substantive issues. According to the *Young ICCA Guide on Arbitral Secretaries*, this is particularly so in complex cases likely to involve voluminous submissions as well as considerable documentary evidence. It is their use in conducting legal and other research, drafting preliminaries and other parts of the award that raise concern.

There are no uniform standards, or consensus on who decides the roles of arbitral secretaries. In fact, it is due to the absence of uniform standards that the *Young ICCA Guide on Arbitral Secretaries*[27] attempts to codify existing best practices and provide guidance in areas of controversy.

To what extent does the use of an arbitral secretary impact the *intuitu personae* principle governing the appointment of an arbitrator? Disquiet has been expressed where arbitral secretaries may be required to provide assistance such as:

- researching questions of law;
- researching discrete questions relating to factual evidence and witness testimony
- drafting the award or parts of the award.

The research functions are a significant input into the decision-making function of the arbitrator. Also, there may be instances where the legal opinion or conclusions of an arbitral secretary may not fully articulate the issues or salient points of a research, and an arbitrator relying on those conclusions may be in jeopardy of reaching erroneous conclusions. As a result, any party appointing an arbitrator may rightly be concerned about the impact using a secretary may have on the quality of the arbitral process.

In spite of these concerns, the use of arbitral secretaries has become a permanent fixture of the arbitral process. In 2012 and 2013 the Young ICCA Task Force conducted surveys into the use of arbitral secretaries.[28] Results showed that the arbitral community is moving towards an increased role for the secretary, with 68.8% of respondents in the 2012 Young ICCA Survey (increasing to 85.7% of respondents in the following year's

26. Para. 68 of the judgment.
27. <www.arbitration-icca.org/media/3/14235574857310/aa_arbitral_sec_guide_composite_10_feb_2015.pdf>. Accessed on 17 February 2018.
28. Annex B and Annex C to the Young ICCA Guide.

survey) supporting the use of arbitral secretaries to conduct legal research and check referenced legal authorities for the arbitral tribunal.

In the 2012 Survey, 60.2% of respondents indicated their approval (subject to subsequent review and approval by the arbitral tribunal) of the drafting by the arbitral secretary of procedural orders or similar documents such as terms of reference; with the figure rising to 71.4% of respondents in the 2013 Survey.

The 2015 edition of the Queen Mary International Arbitration Survey[29] asked respondents which tasks they felt a tribunal secretary should perform. Ninety-three percent felt the arbitral secretary could undertake organizational tasks, 81% supported communications with the parties, while 75% felt it was permissible for tribunal secretaries to prepare drafts of procedural orders and non-substantive parts of awards.

In spite of the overwhelming support for the use of arbitral secretaries, a vast majority of the respondents do not consider it appropriate for tribunal secretaries to conduct substantive or merits-related tasks.

The fact that many Notes and Guidelines propose that the fees for the arbitral secretary be paid by the arbitrators[30] supports the position that the functions being performed by the arbitral secretary are those of the arbitrators. That would mean that the *intuitu personae* principle has been impacted by the appointment of arbitral secretaries. Another view is that the concept of *intuitu personae* still remains in place, but its scope has been eroded by the appointment of arbitral secretaries. Those Rules and Guidelines which propose that an arbitral secretary should be able to conduct case and other legal research for the arbitral panel, and draft procedural orders and the recitals in the award (subject to the guidance and review of the arbitral tribunal) also state categorically that arbitral secretaries should not participate in the "decision-making" functions of the arbitral tribunal. It would seem that the *intuitu personae* principle is being redefined such that the personal functions of the arbitrator are limited to the decision-making process.

V. CONCLUSION

Perhaps, it is time to revisit conventional expectations of parties about the scope of an arbitrator's functions vis-à-vis the *intuitu persona* principle. If wisdom is the correct application of knowledge, then the results of the various surveys indicate that arbitral secretaries working in a more than purely administrative role are the new conventional wisdom.

If this reflects the true position, then the arbitration community needs to agree on universally acceptable standards of regulation for arbitral secretaries, such that the increased role of arbitral secretaries does not turn the arbitral secretary into the "fourth arbitrator", thus impugning the *intuitu personae* principle. This is in line with the results of the 2015 edition of the Queen Mary International Arbitration Survey, in which 68% of the respondents felt that the use of tribunal secretaries should be regulated in some way.

---

29. <www.arbitration.qmul.ac.uk/docs/164761.pdf>. Accessed on 22 February 2018.
30. The ICC Note, the Finnish Chamber, SCC and Swiss Chambers Rules.

Such universally acceptable regulatory standards, perhaps coordinated through ICCA or/and UNCITRAL may help bridge regulatory gaps. Any such international effort must involve all the major arbitral institutions in order to ensure universal acceptance of the final document. The present regime that comprises piecemeal guidance notes from some institutions creates uncertainty and must be addressed. The *Young ICCA Guide on Arbitral Secretaries* may be a good place to start.

Building Better Arbitration Proceedings: Practical Suggestions

Part II: Efficiency and the Lessons to Be Learned from Other Dispute Resolution Frameworks

Building Better Arbitration Proceedings

The Honourable P.A. Bergin SC *

TABLE OF CONTENTS

It is a pleasure to have been invited to participate in the proceedings today. My task is to discuss the procedural attractiveness of arbitration and litigation respectively and in doing so to challenge some recent negative stereotyping of the litigious process. It is also to discuss one particular significant lesson (and some others) that may be learned from the procedures adopted in the Commercial List[1] of the Equity Division of the Supreme Court of New South Wales (the NSW Commercial Court). Finally, it is intended to make some short observations about the need to take up opportunities for the development of more innovative commercial dispute resolution mechanisms.

I. LITIGATION AND ARBITRATION

In previous years it has been observed that the boost in the popularity of arbitration has been due in part to the perceived negative aspects of the litigious process. The complaints about the litigious process have been described as "manifold" in the areas of "cost, time, discovery" and "sluggish courts".[2] In contrast it has been said that arbitration offers less costly and simpler processes with the very attractive attribute of confidentiality.[3] However, in recent times it has been observed that there is now "wide, deep and loud" dissatisfaction with the arbitral process including complaints that "costs are too high, proceedings are too slow, arbitrator selection is too opaque, tribunals are too homogenous, conflicts of interest and issue conflict are scandalous".[4]

---

* Judge of the Supreme Court of NSW from 1999 to 2017; serving as Commercial List Judge (2003 to 2009) and the Chief Judge in Equity (2009 to 2017); International Judge of the Singapore International Commercial Court since 2015.

1. Administered since 2009 by Hammerschlag J.
2. Daniel HOCHSTRASSER and Nadja JAISLI, "Commercial Litigation in State Courts – Why Arbitration Is Not Always the Better Choice in Swiss Domestic Disputes", Global Arbitration Review (October 2015).
3. Chief Justice Sundaresh MENON, "International Commercial Courts: Towards a Transnational System of Dispute Resolution", Opening Lecture for the Dubai International Financial Centre (DIFC) Courts Lecture Series 2015. para. 7.
4. Professor Lucy REED, "International Dispute Resolution Courts: Retreat or Advance?", John E.C. Brierley Memorial Lecture (11 September 2017).

Commentators have entered both the litigious and arbitral arenas with predictions that would alarm even the most hardened practitioners. The predictions are in part reliant upon the proposition that the commercial community is turning its face away from the courts in favour of arbitration. A recurring theme has been that the increase in arbitrations is to the detriment of the vitality and proper development of commercial law.

Take for instance the prediction ten years ago by Peter L Murray, the Robert Braucher Visiting Professor at Harvard Law School, that "public justice" in the United States of America was in danger of erosion by the "privatization of justice".[5] Professor Murray referred to "the extraordinary growth of private dispute resolution modalities and the development of an entrepreneurial industry of private dispute resolution service providers".[6]

Professor Murray identified four key characteristics of the civil justice system that are comprehended by the concept of the "due process of the law" as: (1) the transparency of its processes; (2) the insulation of the public decision makers from influence by the parties; (3) the expectation that decisions are based on publicly known legal norms; and (4) the oversight and control by the appellate structure.[7] These are not the characteristics of the arbitral system which is a process pursuant to the private contractual choice of commercial parties.

Although Professor Murray accepted that a large number of litigants still used the courts and that there was a great deal of "pre-trial activity", he suggested that what was disappearing was the ultimate submission of civil disputes to public decision makers and the resolution of disputes by court judgments with the consequential impact on the development and vitality of the law with the potential loss of judicial precedent.[8]

Seven years later (in 2015), the (now former) Attorney-General of Singapore, the Honourable V K Rajah SC went a little further in an article entitled "*W(h)ither adversarial commercial dispute resolution?*"[9] (the Article) propounding the very provocative conclusions and predictions that: (1) "commercial parties appear to have retreated from the courts;"[10] (2) there has been a "freezing of the common law caused by the marked decline in court litigation";[11] (3) "something has to be done to arrest the alarming decline in litigation before the courts";[12] and (4) the "disdain for adversarial forums will have a seismic impact on the landscape of transnational dispute resolution".[13]

The significant statistics upon which these conclusions and predictions were based were represented graphically in the Article as follows:[14]

5. Peter L. MURRAY, "Privatization of Civil Justice", 91 Judicature (May-June 2008, no. 6) at p. 272; and the fuller version of which is published in 15 Willamette Journal of International Law and Dispute Resolution (2007, no. 2, Winter).
6. *Ibid.*, at p. 272.
7. *Ibid.*, at p. 272.
8. *Ibid.*, at pp. 273-274.
9. 33 Arbitration International (2017, no. 1) p. 17.
10. *Ibid.*, at p. 20.
11. *Ibid.*, at p. 24.
12. *Ibid.*, at p. 26.
13. *Ibid.*, at p. 34
14. *Ibid.*, at p. 19.

W(h)ither adversarial commercial dispute resolution? • **19**

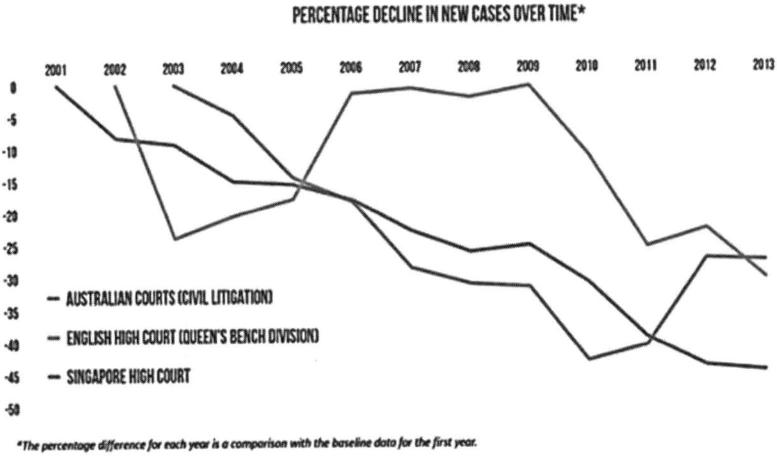

Figure 1.

The "Australian Courts" are represented by the line starting at 2001 suggesting that they are in a far more parlous state than the English High Court and the High Court of Singapore.

The Article records that "in the five mainland states of Australia, for example, the amount of civil litigation per capita from 2000-01 to 2012-13 declined by a sharp 46 per cent"; and that in Singapore there was a general decline in the "number of civil originating processes filed in the Supreme Court over the period 2003 to 2013".[15] This is referred to as a "trend" with the observation that there was a notable exception in the Commercial Court of England and Wales which had seen an increase in its caseload over the past decade. However, it was also reported that when one includes the "other branches of the English High Court's Queens Bench Division" there was a similar trend of a 30 percent decline in the number of "civil proceedings commenced in London" during the period.[16]

The statistics from which this graph was created for the High Court in England and the High Court of Singapore were drawn respectively from the official statistics on the UK Government website and the Supreme Court of Singapore Annual Reports for the relevant years.[17]

15. *Ibid.*, at pp. 18-19.
16. *Ibid.*, at p. 19.
17. *Ibid.*, fns. 5 and 6.

However, the source of the statistics for the Australian courts is identified as an online article at the http address adelaidehillslawyersonline.com.au. The Courts of Tasmania, the Northern Territory and the Australian Capital Territory were excluded from the statistics because it was concluded that "most of Australia's resident population can be found in the five mainland states".[18] The Article is about "*commercial*" dispute resolution. However, the only statistics in the Article that are purely "commercial" are those referred to in the Commercial Court of England and Wales that are not separately extracted. Accordingly, it appears that the figures for all "civil" litigation – not purely commercial litigation – are used as the basis for these provocative conclusions and predictions.

The figures in the online Adelaide Hills Lawyers paper (relied upon in the Article) are drawn from figures provided to the Australian Productivity Commission which exclude specialist courts, the various State tribunals and the High Court of Australia. There is an inconsistent selection of court-types or case mixes. For instance, there are the single courts of England and Singapore; whereas the figures for Australia are for general (as opposed to purely commercial) litigation in courts at various levels including the Local Courts, County and District Courts and Supreme Courts for five out of the six States and neither of the Territories.[19] There is also an inconsistent baseline used for each of the countries with the additional problem of the Australian figures having been based on a per capita basis, rather than being linked to the litigious commercial community and the number of filings.[20]

The official figures published by the busiest commercial court in Australia, the NSW Commercial Court, extracted in the table below demonstrate a very different outcome to that reported in the Article.[21]

18. *Ibid.*, fn. 4 and Bernard O'BRIEN *The Rise and Fall of Commercial Litigation in Australia* (2014).
19. This excludes all the Courts of that State and those Territories and approximately 4.8 percent of the Australian population from the per capita analysis.
20. 2003 for Singapore; 2002 for the UK; and 2000-2001 for Australia.
21. Statistical appendices of the Supreme Court of New South Wales Annual Reviews 2004 to 2015 and provisional statistical data for 2016 (published on the website of Supreme Court of NSW).

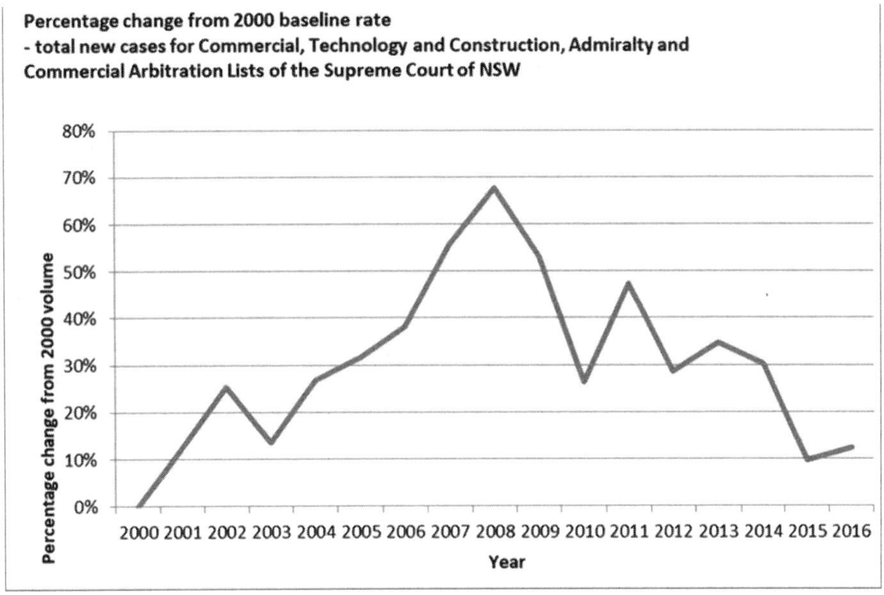

While it can be seen that the there is some volatility in the numbers over the relevant years, these figures do not support the contention that there has been a 46 percent decline in commercial litigation in the relevant period.

The reality is that there is a great deal of confidence in the NSW Commercial Court and the litigious process. Cases are well managed and resolved very expeditiously. If there is a case that requires even speedier resolution than usual, the Court accommodates it. Where questions arise in commercial arbitrations (international or otherwise) the Court also deals with it in an expeditious fashion. Far from retreating from the Court, the commercial community seems to choose the mechanism of litigation and arbitration as appropriate for each case.

VK Rajah SC also referred to the torrent of criticism in recent years levelled at the cost and delay in arbitrations and what was labelled as the "judicialization" of the international commercial arbitration process with the suggestion that the arbitral process now "mimics litigation in many respects".[22] If that is so, then it is a shame that it has mimicked the outmoded processes that have now been shed in the NSW Commercial Court. Mimicking the processes of the NSW Commercial Court could only enhance the cost-efficiency of any arbitral process.

In New South Wales, there is no evidence that commercial parties are retreating from the courts or holding them in disdain; nor, thankfully, is there any evidence of the freezing of the common law.

22. 33 Arbitration International (2017, no. 1) at pp. 24-25.

Further warnings about the stultification of the common law by reason of the increase in arbitrations were issued in 2017 by the former Lord Chief Justice of England and Wales, the Right Hon The Lord Thomas of Cwmgiedd.[23] In a rather unpopular move with arbitrators, Lord Thomas advocated legislative amendment to make appeals in respect of arbitrations more readily available so that the Commercial Court would have a better diet from which to develop and keep the commercial law dynamic.[24] Lord Thomas also referred to the proposal for the publication of anonymized awards to avoid the prospect of the commercial law going "underground".[25]

More recently steps have been taken to publish anonymized challenges to arbitration;[26] and the Mauritius Convention on Transparency has been ratified in October 2017 in respect of investor-state arbitration proceedings.[27] It has been reported that the move towards greater transparency in treaty-based investor arbitration has been accompanied by "a decline in emphasis on confidentiality among parties".[28]

Although these concerns have been expressed about the vitality of the commercial law being challenged by the popularity of the arbitration process, the only published figures of purely commercial cases in the two leading Commercial Courts[29] suggest that the operation of the commercial law in the courts is vibrant, flexible and trusted by the commercial community.

II. LESSONS FROM THE COURT PROCESS

V K Rajah SC's Article also included the claim that "court proceedings are notorious for being onerous, slow and expensive" and that the "flag bearer" for this criticism is the "formal discovery process". Although there was reference in the Article to new technological tools that have been endorsed by courts to facilitate more effective discovery,[30] there was no mention of the most innovative and cost-efficient development

23. The Jill Poole Memorial Lecture, "Keeping Commercial Law Up to Date", Aston University (8 March 2017); The National Judges College, Beijing Commercial Dispute Resolution; Courts and Arbitration (6 April 2017).
24. The Jill Poole Memorial Lecture, "Keeping Commercial Law up to Date Aston University" (8 March 2017) paras. 41-43; The National Judges College, Beijing Commercial Dispute Resolution; Courts and Arbitration (6 April 2017) paras. 29-30.
25. A suggestion made by Sir Bernard Rix in the Jones Day Professorship in Commercial Law Lecture, SMU, Singapore (12 March 2015) referred to by Lord Thomas in the Jill Poole Memorial Lecture, "Keeping Commercial Law Up to Date", Aston University (8 March 2017).
26. LCIA Challenge Decisions Database issued 12 February 2017.
27. Ratified by Mauritius, Canada and Switzerland. It was also signed by a number of other countries, including Australia in July 2016, but is yet to be ratified by those nations.
28. Douglas THOMSON, "The Mauritius Convention; A New Era of Transparency", GAR Review (January 2018).
29. Commercial List of the Equity Division of the Supreme Court and the Commercial Court in London.
30. Including endorsement of Technology Assisted Review (TAR) or Predictive Coding and *Rio Tinto PLC v. Vale* SA No. 14 Civ 3042 (SDNY, 2 March 2015).

in this area introduced in March 2012 in the Supreme Court of NSW in Practice Note SC Eq 11 *Disclosure in the Equity Division* (the Disclosure Practice Note).[31]

The issue of the crippling costs of discovery in commercial litigation in New South Wales courts came to a head in 2007 when senior practitioners at law firms in Sydney informed the Chief Justice of the Supreme Court[32] that the "usual flag fall" for discovery in commercial cases was $2 million.[33] In this context the Chief Justice suggested that "business lawyers" may be "bypassed" unless the legal services they delivered were seen to be more cost-effective.

Debate continued for some years as to how these costs could be controlled. Options including discovery by categories of documents (rather than general discovery), electronic discovery and the capping of costs were considered and tried.

The process for the disclosure of documents by categories allowed the parties to draft descriptions of classes of documents they regarded as relevant to the issues in dispute and serve them on their opponents requiring disclosure within a specified timeframe. The introduction of this process spawned a growth industry in interlocutory applications in which the parties parsed and teased the categories drafted by their opponents contending that they should not be required to search for or produce the documents in the categories the subject of the challenge. This delayed the preparation of the evidence and increased the costs of the litigation.

The introduction of the process of electronic discovery followed its adoption in the United States of America. However rather than simply producing those documents that were already stored electronically, the parties set about creating electronic databases of their hard copy documents and then produced them electronically. This was an added cost at the time which, once identified, was clarified in the Rules of Court. This did not cure the problem of the very expensive flag fall for commercial litigation.

Whilst ever the step of discovery/disclosure was taken before the step of the filing of evidence, it was not feasible to control the costs of discovery and thus the costs of commercial litigation.

At the beginning of 2012 an informal pilot scheme was introduced into the NSW Commercial Court in which the parties were required to serve their evidence prior to any discovery being permitted. The reception from the profession was initially lukewarm but improved over the ensuing weeks. In late March 2012 the Chief Justice[34] issued the Disclosure Practice Note applicable to all cases in the Equity Division of the Court. It provides relevantly:

> "*Disclosure*
>
> 4. The Court will not make an order for disclosure of documents (disclosure) until the parties to the proceedings have served their evidence, unless there are exceptional circumstances necessitating disclosure.

31. The Hon Justice P A BERGIN, "The New Regime of Practice in the Equity Division of the Supreme Court of New South Wales", 11 The Judicial Review (2014) p. 399.
32. At that time, the Honourable JJ Spigelman AC.
33. The Honourable JJ SPIGELMAN AC, "Access to Justice and Access to Lawyers", 35th Australian Legal Convention, Sydney (24 March 2007).
34. The Honourable TF BATHURST AC.

> 5. There will be no order for disclosure in any proceedings in the Equity Division unless it is necessary for the resolution of the real issues in dispute in the proceedings."

If at some stage there is to be an application for disclosure, the applicant has the onus of establishing necessity. The Practice Note also provides that the Court may impose a limit on the amount of recoverable costs in respect of disclosure.

This has resulted in a marked difference in the commercial litigation landscape in New South Wales. It has resulted in the enhancement of the Court's capacity to control the process of document disclosure, the speedier resolution of commercial cases and the reduction of costs of commercial litigation.

Many arbitrators adopt the Memorials approach which has the Statement of Case and Defence filed with witness statements and exhibits and first expert reports. It is after this first round of evidence that the parties then embark upon the process of "disclosure" or request for documents. This differs from the system under the Disclosure Practice Note which requires all the evidence, both in chief and in reply, to be filed before an application for disclosure will be entertained (unless it falls into the exceptional circumstance category).

In the arbitration field there are recent reports of "growing frustration" with the way the Redfern Schedule is used for complex and document-heavy cases.[35] The purpose of the Redfern Schedule is to record the request for documents and the reasons for the requests, the responses thereto and, where necessary, the tribunal's determination. It is reported to have become a "cumbersome" process, with a disconnect between document requests and the real issues in dispute.[36] Although some recommendations for reform, including the use of horizontal rather than vertical cells and the filing of short submissions with the Schedule have been made, it seems that the process is governing the debate rather than the debate focusing on the need for an overhaul of the system. Once an order is made that allows the creation and development of a Redfern Schedule with competing and numerous requests and responses, the capacity to control the process and the costs of the process is greatly diminished or even lost.

May I suggest that if Procedural Order No. 1 requires the parties to prepare their evidence without discovery in line with the Disclosure Practice Note, the system will not be cumbersome but will be far more cost efficient. It will move to a necessity-based determination by the tribunal rather than the protracted inter partes processes documented in a Redfern Schedule.

Another area from which lessons may be learned from the litigious process that leads to the time-efficient and cost-effective determination of the real issues in dispute is close case management with requirements for compliance with agreed or court-imposed timetables. The majority of timetables are agreed by the parties in the knowledge that they will be given a hearing date to suit the case preparation. On occasions the Court will fix the trial date at an early stage of the process and then fix the timetable to accommodate that date. The capacity of the parties to bring the case back before the NSW Commercial Court List Judge at short notice also focuses the parties on achieving

35. "Compendium of Arbitration Practice", IBA Arb40 Subcommittee (October 2017) p. 6, para. 1.2.
36. *Ibid.*, p. 15, Chapter 4.1.

compliance with the case preparation regime. There is a culture within the legal profession that if there is to be slippage in the timetable, the parties agree on an adjustment to the timetable and notify the Court immediately; or they relist the matter for argument about those adjustments, particularly where a trial date may be in jeopardy.

It must be recognized that this system is made possible because there is a judge available at all times (including out of hours for urgent applications) to manage the cases; and to impose sanctions for non-compliance, costs or otherwise, where appropriate. It may not be so easy to convene the arbitral tribunal to deal with these case management issues on an urgent basis. Anecdotal evidence suggests that although the arbitral tribunal may favour expeditious management, the parties (in private rather than institutional arbitrations) for commercial or other reasons, may favour a more leisurely timetable. This is quite a different setting to that of a court where public funds and resources have to be considered in achieving cost efficient outcomes. It will all depend upon the particular case. However, the inculcation of a culture of close case management will ensure that the real issues are identified early and that the steps taken in the process focus the tribunal and the parties on the determination of those real issues.

III. OTHER MATTERS

Whilst I have respectfully disagreed with the Hon VK Rajah SC's statistical analysis and thus the conclusions reached therefrom, the former Attorney-General's suggestions in relation to the future growth of the hybrid processes of mediation-arbitration (med-arb) and/or arbitration-mediation-arbitration (arb-med-arb), supported by the figures from the Singapore International Arbitration Centre (SIAC) and the Singapore International Mediation Centre (SIMC), are compelling.[37]

There are so many innovative ideas that are being promoted throughout the world for the more effective and efficient additional mechanisms for dispute resolution.

Take for example, the establishment of the Singapore International Commercial Court (SICC). That Court is one of a kind.[38] It is part of the Supreme Court of Singapore, constituted by the Judges of the Supreme Court and fifteen International Judges drawn from both common law and civil jurisdictions.[39] The SICC was established in January 2015 amidst some concern from the Singaporean and international arbitral community that it might have an adverse impact on its work. This concern has now abated. The work of the SICC is international commercial litigation. The work of the Singaporean and international arbitral community is arbitration.

The idea for an international commercial court or tribunal in Australia was first promoted in 2013, albeit as a "radical possibility" and a "lofty goal", by the Honourable

37. 33 Arbitration International (2017, no. 1) at p. 32.
38. Compared to the Global Market Court in Abu Dhabi; the Dubai International Financial Centre Courts; and the recently established Astana International Finance Centre Court in Kazakhstan.
39. The International Judges are presently drawn from Australia; Canada; France; Hong Kong SAR; Japan; the United Kingdom; and the United States of America.

T.F. Bathurst AC, the Chief Justice of the Supreme Court of NSW.[40] The Chief Justice expressed the view that "such a system would have considerable advantages" and in an observation now relevant to the SICC, the Chief Justice said:[41]

> "An international commercial court, for use consensually by commercial parties, and dealing with a limited range of matters involving international commercial disputes, would not impinge on the judicial sovereignty of any state and could well increase confidence in parties participating in international trade and investment. It would also, in my view, play an important role in the development of the law applicable to international commercial contracts and cross-border disputes and to the promotion of convergence in commercial legal systems in our region."

Three years later, in April 2016, the then Chief Justice of the Supreme Court of Victoria, the Honourable Marilyn Warren AC[42] suggested that "the opportunities offered by an Australian international court are almost boundless".[43] Boundless they may be, but these opportunities are not being exploited.

Perhaps the task of bringing all the States and Territories together to create an Australian International Commercial Court is not one that is attractive to the respective governments. If that is so, you may think that this is certainly a missed opportunity.

40. The Honourable T.F. BATHURST AC, *The Importance of Developing Convergent Commercial Law Systems in Core Values of an Effective Judiciary* (2015 Academy Publishing). A record of the Biennial Conference of Chief Justices of Asia and the Pacific held in Singapore in 2013.
41. *Ibid.*, at p. 192.
42. Jointly with the Hon Justice Clyde Croft.
43. The Hon Marilyn WARREN AC and The Hon Justice Clyde CROFT, "An International Commercial Court for Australia – Looking Beyond the New York Convention: Remarks at the Commercial CPD Seminar Series, Melbourne", available online at <http://assets.justice.vic.gov.au/supreme/resources/2a7ead53-9ae9-4e26-9bad-56ef25d7d34c/aninternationalcommercialcourtforaustralialookingbeyondthenewyorkconvention.pdf>.

The Future of Arbitration – Identifying Processes That Could Usefully Be Adopted in International Commercial Arbitration

Flip Petillion[*]

TABLE OF CONTENTS

In this article, we identify processes that were developed in dispute resolution rules and practices of different alternative dispute resolution (ADR) institutions, as they could usefully be adopted in international commercial arbitration. We first list the role and mission of each institution we will refer to and briefly summarize the ADR proceedings that we have experienced. We then list relevant processes of these proceedings in the order in which they may be useful in the chronological flow of (international) commercial arbitration proceedings.

I. RELEVANT INSTITUTIONS AND PROCEEDINGS

1. *American Arbitration Association (AAA) International Centre for Dispute Resolution (ICDR))*

a. *Independent Review Processes (IRP)*

We have used the services of the International Centre for Dispute Resolution (ICDR), a division of the American Arbitration Association (AAA), as international dispute resolution provider for Independent Review Processes (IRPs), which were introduced as an ICANN accountability mechanism in 2002.[1] ICANN is the acronym for 'Internet Corporation for Assigned Names and Numbers'. It is a not-for-profit public-benefit

* Founder and partner of PETILLION, an independent law firm based in Brussels with a focus on dispute resolution. The author is regularly invited to serve as an arbitrator in complex international commercial arbitration proceedings administered by leading arbitration institutions.

1. ICANN, *Bylaws as adopted effective 15 December 2002 (the New Bylaws)*, 15 December 2002, <www.icann.org/resources/unthemed-pages/bylaws-2002-12-15-en>.

corporation formed in September 1998.[2] ICANN's primary mission is to coordinate, at the highest level, the Internet's systems of unique identifiers globally,[3] and in particular to ensure the stable and secure operation of the Internet's unique identifier systems, the Domain Name System or DNS.[4]

ICANN sought to increase competition at the registry level (i.e., increase the number of extensions such as .com or .gov), and posted a call for new top-level domain (TLD) applications in 2000, 2004 and 2011.The IRP became operational after April 2004, when ICANN elected ICDR as IRP provider.[5] As a result, applicants as of the 2004 TLD round had the opportunity to challenge the decisions of the ICANN Board before an independent ICDR Panel. All IRP Declarations rendered by the ICDR Panels, having acted in IRPs pursuant to the Procedure set out by ICANN and the ICDR Rules for Expertise, are published on ICANN's websites. Since the IRP inception, eighteen cases have been initiated and one case is still pending.[6]

b. Expert determination

We also know the ICDR as a provider of an Expert Determination procedure pursuant to ICANN's 2011 new generic top-level domain (gTLD) program, which gave various categories of third parties the opportunity to challenge the application for a particular gTLD via ADR mechanisms. Such challenges (called "objections") could be initiated with independent Dispute Resolution Service Providers (DRSP) according to a pre-established set of rules.[7]

Under these rules, objections could be based on the following grounds:

– *String Confusion*:[8] The applied-for gTLD string is confusingly similar to an existing TLD or to another applied-for gTLD string in the same round of applications. Objectors could be existing TLD operators or gTLD applicants in the current round.
– *Legal Rights*: The applied-for gTLD string infringes the existing legal rights of the objector. Objectors could be rights holders; in practice all were trademark holders.
– *Community*: There is substantial opposition to the gTLD application from a significant portion of the community to which the gTLD string may be explicitly or implicitly targeted. Objectors could be an established institution associated with a clearly delineated community.

---

2. See California Secretary of State, Business information for entity number 2121683, available on <http://kepler.sos.ca.gov/>.
3. ICANN, Articles of Incorporation, Art. 3; ICANN, Bylaws, Art. I(1).
4. ICANN, Bylaws, Art. I(1).
5. ICANN, *Resolution 04.33 adopted at Special ICANN Board Meeting*, 19 April 2004, <www.icann.org/resources/board-material/resolutions-2004-04-19-en>.
6. For a critical assessment of IRP decisions, see Flip PETILLION and Jan JANSSEN, *Competing for the Internet: ICANN Gate – An Analysis and Plea for Judicial Review Through Arbitration* (2017 Wolters Kluwer) 478 p.
7. ICANN, *New gTLD Applicant Guidebook 4 June 2012*, <https://newgtlds.icann.org/en/applicants/agb/guidebook-full-04jun12-en.pdf>, Attachment to Module 3: New gTLD Dispute Resolution Procedure.
8. "String" refers to the sequence of letters that the gTLD is composed of.

– *Limited Public Interest*: The applied-for gTLD string is contrary to generally accepted legal norms of morality and public order that are recognized under principles of international law such as racially abusive strings.[9]

The ground for objection dictates which DRSP was to manage the dispute process: String Confusion Objections (SCOs) were managed by the ICDR.

Parties were not prevented from taking a matter to court. However, decisions obtained through the ADR mechanisms established within the framework of the new gTLD program were likely to be quicker and easier to execute. All Expert Determinations rendered by the ICDR Expert Panels, having acted in new gTLD related disputes pursuant to the New gTLD Dispute Resolution Procedure set out by ICANN and the ICDR Supplementary Procedures for String Confusion Objections, are published on ICANN's websites. ICDR has administered sixty-seven cases. In March 2015, at the request of ICANN, the ICDR developed specific review procedures to evaluate and finally review selected expert determinations that were perceived inconsistent or unreasonable.[10]

2. *International Chamber of Commerce (ICC)*

a. *Commercial arbitration*

In international commercial arbitrations, we have been working with the International Chamber of Commerce's (ICC) International Court of Arbitration, which is the world's leading arbitral institution.

b. *Expert determination*

The ICC is also known as another provider of an Expert Determination procedure from ICANN's 2011 new gTLD program (see I.*1* above). ICC's International Centre for ADR managed the Limited Public Interest Objections and the Community Objections. All Expert Determinations rendered by the ICC Expert Panels, having acted in new gTLD-related disputes pursuant to the New gTLD Dispute Resolution Procedure set out by ICANN and the ICC Rules for Expertise, are published on ICANN's and ICC's website. The ICC has administrated 127 cases.

3. *World Intellectual Property Organization (WIPO)*

a. *ADR*

The Arbitration and Mediation Center of the World Intellectual Property Organization (WIPO) is a neutral, international and non-profit dispute resolution provider that offers ADR options. WIPO mediation, arbitration, expedited arbitration, and expert

9. For more information on ICANN's objection procedures, see Flip PETILLION and Jan JANSSEN, "A Critical Assessment of Litigation in the New Domain Name Landscape", Computerrecht (2013, no. 5) pp. 259-263; Flip PETILLION and Jan JANSSEN, *Competing for the Internet: ICANN Gate – An Analysis and Plea for Judicial Review Through Arbitration* (Wolters Kluwer 2017) pp. 59-60, 126-128.

10. ICDR, Procedures for Final Review of Perceived Inconsistent or Unreasonable String Confusion Objection Expert Determinations, 15 March 2015, available at <icdr.org>.

determination enable private parties to settle their domestic or cross-border intellectual property and technology disputes out of court. The WIPO Center is also the global leader in the provision of domain name dispute resolution services under the WIPO-designed Uniform Domain Name Dispute Resolution Policy (UDRP).

b. Uniform Domain Name Dispute Resolution Policy (UDRP)

The Arbitration and Mediation Center of WIPO is the major DRSP in the Uniform Domain Name Dispute Resolution Policy (UDRP), which has been adopted by ICANN (see I.*1*.*a* above) and is incorporated by reference into the Registration Agreement between a registrant of a domain name and a registrar. The UDRP dictates the terms and conditions in relation to a dispute between the registrant and any party (complainant) over the registration and use of an Internet domain name. The complainant must prove that:

(i) the domain name is identical or confusingly similar to a trademark or service mark in which the complainant has rights; and
(ii) the registrant has no rights or legitimate interests in respect of the domain name; and
(iii) the domain name has been registered and is being used in bad faith.

The UDRP decisions are published on WIPO's website. WIPO has administered near to 40,000 cases since 1999.

c. Expert determination

WIPO was yet another provider of an Expert Determination procedure from ICANN's 2011 new gTLD program (see I.*1*.*b* above). In that program, WIPO managed the Legal Rights Objections (LROs). Through the LRO, trademark owners and intergovernmental organizations (IGO) could file a formal objection to a third party's application for a new TLD. An independent panel of one or three neutral experts determined whether an applicant's potential use of the disputed applied-for new TLD would cause impermissible infringement of the objector's existing trademark, or IGO name or acronym. The resulting expert determinations may be viewed at the WIPO Center's LRO webpages. WIPO has administrated sixty-nine cases.

4. FORUM

FORUM is another important DRSP in the UDRP adopted by ICANN (see I.*1*. above).

FORUM also handles Uniform Rapid Suspension (URS) procedures. The URS System complements the UDRP by offering a cheaper and faster path to relief for rights holders experiencing the most clear-cut cases of infringement by domain name registrants. Under the URS procedure, rights holders may only claim the suspension of a domain name, whereas under the UDRP, other remedies are available, such as the transfer or the cancellation of the domain name.

The UDRP and URS decisions are published on FORUM's website. FORUM has administrated almost 24,500 UDRP cases since 2000 and over 800 URS cases since 2013.

5. *Czech Arbitration Court (CAC)*

The Czech Arbitration Court (CAC) is the sole provider of ADR.EU, which is, along with WIPO, one of the two ADR providers for .eu domain name disputes. ADR.EU also provides a UDRP service for several generic top-level-domains.

The UDRP decisions are published on CAC's website. CAC has administrated over 800 cases since 2009.

6. *Nominet*

Nominet is the biggest registry in the United Kingdom, responsible for the .uk, .cymru, and .wales TLDs. Nominet provides a Dispute Resolution Service (DRS) as a fast and efficient way to resolve .uk domain name disputes. The DRS Policy and the UDRP are different systems. In some places they share very similar wording, but there are significant differences and the citation of UDRP decisions in a dispute under the DRS Policy is rarely considered helpful.

The DRS decisions are published on Nominet's website. Nominet has administrated about 8,000 cases since 2001.

7. *Belgian Centre for Arbitration and Mediation (CEPANI)*

a. *Commercial arbitration*

CEPANI is the Belgian centre for arbitration and mediation. We have both used the centre in our arbitrations as well as been invited by the centre to act as arbitrator in commercial arbitrations.

b. *ADR*

The centre is locally also well known as the provider of ADR to solve domain name disputes in the .be domain.

The ADR decisions are published on the websites of CEPANI and DNS Belgium, the registry managing the .be domain.

8. *Stichting Internet Domeinregistratie Nederland (SIDN)*

The Stichting Internet Domeinregistratie Nederland (SIDN) is the Dutch registry managing the .nl domain. Similarly to Nominet in the UK and CEPANI in Belgium, SIDN provides its own ADR for domain name disputes within the .nl domain. Its approach is more similar to ICANN's UDRP compared to Nominet's or CEPANI's DRS, as SIDN exclusively relies on WIPO for the provision of this service.

The ADR decisions are published on the websites of WIPO. WIPO has administrated over 400 .nl cases since 2008.

9. *International Trademark Association (INTA)*

The International Trademark Association (INTA) is a global association of brand owners and professionals dedicated to supporting trademarks and related intellectual property rights to foster consumer trust, economic growth, and innovation. It is not an ADR institution. However, it has set up a Panel of Trademark Mediators and it collaborates with the WIPO Center in the promotion of the use of ADR amongst potential users. It does this by harnessing the international experience of the WIPO Center and the special expertise of INTA's Panel of Trademark Mediators. This collaboration provides value to INTA members by making available an administered mediation option at special rates. INTA expects that this collaboration between two recognized organizations in this area will stimulate the use of mediation by parties and thus reduce the negative impact of disputes in the productive use of trademark rights.

II. PRE-ARBITRATION PROCEEDINGS

Several specific industry associations and organizations encourage the use of different forms of dispute resolution or provide rules that facilitate settlement opportunities, even before any expert or panelist[11] is appointed. In this way, disputes are more rapidly resolved without the need for lengthy or costly procedures. A few of these are listed below.

1. *Pledge*

a. *World Intellectual Property Organization (WIPO) Mediation Pledge for Intellectual Property and Technology Disputes*

Being aware that parties to commercial disputes related to intellectual property (IP) assets are increasingly concerned about the time and cost caused by such disputes, WIPO has recently started to promote a pledge.

Without binding the parties, the WIPO Mediation Pledge for IP and Technology Disputes promotes mediation as an alternative to court litigation in order to reduce the impact of disputes in innovation and creative processes. By subscribing to the WIPO Mediation Pledge, users of the Patent Cooperation Treaty (PCT), Madrid, and Hague systems, as well as all other IP stakeholders can contribute to time- and cost-efficient resolution of IP and technology disputes.

Companies, universities and R&D Centers, and law firms may sign the WIPO Mediation Pledge. The form is available on WIPO's website.[12] While not formal signatories, other IP stakeholders may expressly support the WIPO Mediation Pledge.

b. *International Trademark Association (INTA) Law Firm Pledge*

The International Trademark Association (INTA) has also published a pledge form which is meant to be signed by law firms. By executing the pledge, law firms recognize that for many trademark disputes more effective methods of resolution exist apart from traditional litigation or trademark office proceedings, and that these methods can

---

11. We have opted to use the word "panelist" over "panellist" as it is the format used by ICANN and WIPO. We use "panellist" or "panel member" as general term and where appropriate we use "mediator", "expert" and "arbitrator".
12. <https://www.wipo.int/amc/en/mediation/pledge.html>.

significantly reduce the costs and burdens of proceedings and result in business solutions not available in court or trademark office tribunals.

Law firms subscribe to the following statements of policy on behalf of their firm: first, appropriate lawyers in the firm are knowledgeable about ADR and familiar in particular with the INTA Panel of Trademark Mediators as well as with the applicable guidelines and rules; second, where appropriate, the responsible attorney will discuss with the client the availability of ADR procedures so that the client can make an informed choice concerning the resolution of the dispute.

c. Appraisal

Signing the WIPO Mediation Pledge or the INTA Law Firm Pledge shows willingness to consider mediation in intellectual property disputes. Broad adherence to the Pledge promotes two shared goals; first, increased consideration of the inclusion of mediation clauses in contracts, and second, increased consideration of using mediation in the absence of such clauses (e.g., for non-contractual disputes).

The pledges create positive conditions for intellectual property dispute resolution, but the pledges are not binding commitments and do not create legally enforceable rights or obligations. Also, mediation may not be suitable for every dispute and, in any event, does not limit a party's other dispute resolution options, including court litigation.

2. Recommended Cooperation

a. The Internet Corporation for Assigned Names and Numbers (ICANN) Cooperative Engagement Process

On 11 April 2013, the Internet Corporation for Assigned Names and Numbers (ICANN) introduced the Cooperative Engagement Process (CEP).[13]

The CEP is a voluntary process that can be initiated before filing a Request for IRP. The IRP is an arbitration process in which a panel is asked to determine whether ICANN acted within the scope of its mission and whether it complied with its Articles of Incorporation and Bylaws.[14] The CEP aims to resolve the contested issue and to determine if any issues remain for the IRP, or whether the matter should be brought to the ICANN Board's attention. Although the CEP is voluntary, parties are urged to enter into a period of cooperative engagement. A party's decision not to participate in good faith in the cooperative engagement, can have important cost implications in future proceedings: in such cases, and provided ICANN prevails in the IRP, the IRP Panel is obliged to award ICANN all reasonable fees and costs incurred by ICANN during the proceedings, including legal fees.[15]

The CEP proceeds as follows: Within fifteen days of the posting of the minutes of an ICANN Board meeting, a party may file a request for CEP. The requesting party should identify the Board action(s) at issue, as well as the provisions of the ICANN Bylaws or

13. The CEP is established by Art. IV, Sect. 3, paras. 14, 16 and 17 of the ICANN Bylaws. The actual operation of the CEP was posted in a note on ICANN's website, and is considered to be incorporated into ICANN's Bylaws.
14. ICANN Bylaws, as amended on 22 July 2017, Art. 4(3).
15. ICANN Bylaws, as amended on 22 July 2017, Art. 4(3)(e).

Articles of Incorporation that have allegedly been violated. The requesting party is also expected to designate a single point of contact for the resolution of the issue. ICANN expects the CEP to be between ICANN and the requesting party, without reference to outside counsel.[16] However, nothing prevents a requesting party from designating outside counsel as the single point of contact if it believes that this will help to advance the process.

Within three business days following the initiation of a CEP, ICANN will designate a single executive to serve as the point of contact for the resolution of the issue and provide notice of the designation to the requesting party. ICANN expects the requesting party and ICANN's representative to confer (either by telephone or in person) within two business days of ICANN providing notice of its designated representatives, in order to attempt to resolve the issue, and to determine if any issues remain for the IRP or whether the matter should be brought to the ICANN Board's attention. If, during the first conference, the representatives are not able to resolve the issue or agree on a narrowing of issues, or a reference to the ICANN Board, they will be expected to meet in person at a location mutually agreed upon within seven calendar days of the initial conference. At this second conference, the parties will attempt to reach a definitive agreement on the resolution of the issue or on the narrowing of issues remaining for the IRP, or whether the matter should be brought to the ICANN Board's attention. The time schedule and process may be modified if both ICANN and the requesting party agree in writing. In practice, the time schedule is often extended in view of the complexity of issues that can be raised within a CEP.[17]

The CEP request suspends the deadline to file an IRP for a maximum of fourteen days, unless parties agree on a longer suspension.[18] In practice, ICANN has consistently agreed to longer suspensions in cases when the CEP has taken longer than initially expected. ICANN is currently in the process of redefining the IRP Rules of Procedure and recent drafts set no specific deadline to file an IRP.[19]

Within a CEP, all matters discussed during the cooperative engagement phase are to remain confidential and are not to be subject to discovery or used as evidence for any purpose within the IRP, and this without prejudice to either party.

b. Appraisal

Participation in multiple CEPs has shown us that the CEP can be a useful mechanism for instigating open and frank discussions with ICANN's General Counsel and his team. Although a CEP may not result in a negotiated agreement in circumstances where

16. ICANN, *Cooperative Engagement Process – Requests for Independent Review*, 11 April 2013, <https://www.icann.org/en/system/files/files/cep-11apr13-en.pdf>.
17. ICANN, *Cooperative Engagement Process – Requests for Independent Review*, 11 April 2013, <https://www.icann.org/en/system/files/files/cep-11apr13-en.pdf>.
18. ICANN, *Cooperative Engagement Process – Requests for Independent Review*, 11 April 2013, <https://www.icann.org/en/system/files/files/cep-11apr13-en.pdf>.
19. ICANN Bylaws, as amended on 22 July 2017, Art. 4(3)(n)(iv)(A); for a recent status, see ICANN, *Draft Report of IRP-IOT Following Public Comments on the Updated Supplementary Procedures for the ICANN Independent Review Process*, 20 February 2018, <https://community.icann.org/display/WEIA/WP-IOT+-+IRP+Implementation+Oversight+Team?preview=/59643726/79436450/IRP.IOT.ReportonPubComments.Rules(V2).pdf>.

interests and positions are diametrically opposed between parties, it remains an excellent process that can create goodwill between the parties and ensure the efficient handling of further proceedings. The CEP also offers a unique opportunity for ICANN to obtain advanced knowledge of the arguments that a party may be planning to raise as part of an IRP. However, for a party that believes in its arguments, this is a small price to pay for the increased efficiency a CEP can bring to the dispute resolution.

3. *Mandatory Mediation*

a. *Nominet*

Nominet provides for a mandatory mediation period if the respondent, a holder of the domain name in the .uk domain, responds to a filed complaint. Nominet's trained mediators handle the mediation proceedings, which may last no longer than ten days. If no acceptable solution is found, Nominet notifies the parties that a panelist will be appointed subject to payment of a fee by the complainant.

To be enforceable, any settlement reached by the parties must be in writing or similar electronic form.

Nominet ensures confidentiality. The panelist appointed in the DRS is informed whether or not a mediation occurred, but he or she is not informed of the mediation discussions or the reason why mediation was not successful and the parties failed to resolve the dispute.

b. *Stichting Internet Domeinregistratie Nederland (SIDN)*

SIDN provides for a dispute resolution service before referring the case to WIPO for further administration. Similar to Nominet's DRS, an automatic and free-of-charge mediation period is initiated if the respondent files a response to the complaint. This mediation period lasts for a maximum of thirty days but may be extended twice with the consent of both parties, for periods of up to thirty days.

If the mediation is not successful, the complainant must pay the administration fee and the panelist's fee to WIPO before the case is further handled.

c. *Facilitating a settlement*

On 31 July 2015, ICANN updated its UDRP Rules, hereby impacting complaint filing modalities and party settlement practices.

To facilitate settlements, parties may ask for the suspension of the proceedings to allow them to discuss settlement options. When the ADR provider understands from the file that the respondent may be willing to settle, the provider will generally invite the claimant to ask for the suspension. If and when the parties reach a settlement, they complete a Standard Settlement Form and return a signed copy to the ADR provider.

The Standard Settlement Form is not intended to be a copy of the settlement agreement. It merely summarizes the essential terms of the parties' agreement. The ADR provider does not disclose the completed Standard Settlement Form to any third party. But the form can help third parties implement the agreement without the need for an order by a panel.

The complainant must subsequently confirm to the ADR provider that the settlement agreement has been honoured before the proceedings can be terminated.

d. Appraisal

Although mediation is not always offered as an option, the provision of a short period enabling parties to consider mediation can be useful to resolve a dispute. The mandatory mediation period may lead to a better understanding of the parties' respective interests and position and clarify the parties' respective chances of success if they intend to continue the proceedings. This will undoubtedly be the case in matters where the subject matter of the dispute is well defined, which is very often the case in disputes involving trademarks and domain names.

A form such as the Standard Settlement Form is a simple process allowing the ADR provider to close proceedings while keeping the full settlement agreement confidential.

III. APPOINTMENT PROCEDURES

1. *The Benefits of Specialist Knowledge*

The attractiveness of ADR can be explained in part by the fact that proceedings are handled faster and more efficiently by panelists who are specialized in the appropriate area. For example, parties may succeed in that goal if they nominate and get appointed panelists with sufficient specialist knowledge. It is one of the first things for parties and appointing institutions to examine which person would be most suitable given the economic sector or industry setting in which the dispute takes place and taken into account the applicable law.

Arbitral institutions have become increasingly involved in the appointment of arbitrators. These institutions have built up unique knowledge about arbitrator competencies, areas of expertise and working methods. Even if it is true that some institutions tend to make repeat appointments of the same individuals, new talent does seem to be given a fair chance. And in our view, repeat appointments need not be a problem: better to appoint an arbitrator more than once than to appoint a less qualified or less experienced individual merely for the sake of diversity.[20]

2. *The Pros and Cons of a Standing Panel*

A way to structure appointment proceedings is the creation of standing panels. If organized efficiently, these standing panels may expedite the appointment process and even augment the parties' trust in single-member tribunals. In this section we discuss the advantages and pitfalls of standing panels. In the next section, we will discuss the use of single-member panels.

A standing panel can take different forms. At one side of the spectrum, one may find a simple list or roster of panelists (mediators, experts, arbitrators) selected by an institution and available for party consideration. The list may be exhaustive or not. At the other end of the spectrum, the standing panel is composed of the panelists selected by an institution to preside over all disputes that may arise over a certain development or

20. For a detailed analysis on this subject, see Flip PETILLION "Choosing the Arbitrator" in Fabienne BRISON, et al., eds., *Liber Amicorum M. Flamée* (Die Keure 2016) p. 381.

period; and, alternatively, the panel may be composed of panelists from which benches may be made by the institution.[21]

a. Policy arguments for and against standing panels

i. Costs are foreseeable

When an institution selects a fixed panel of panelists, it may get a better view on the costs. Either it can agree a fixed fee with the panelists when serving on the standing panel, regardless of the number of expected disputes, or it can agree on the parameters that will determine the fee in case disputes arise. As a result, no surprises can arise from a party's nomination of an arbitrator who charges fees that are beyond the standard rate for similar disputes. Alternatively, in situations where parties are allowed to nominate panelists who are not listed, they may be appointed by the institution, but subject to the institution's fees or parameters to determine the fees.

The downside may be that the panelists on the standing panel may require a fee for keeping themselves available and free from conflicts to serve on the panel. In some, usually smaller, standing panels, the panelists receive an annual stipend. That is for instance the case with the Public Interest Commitment Dispute Resolution Procedure (PICDRP) and IRP standing panels that ICANN has installed or plans to install (cf. infra). If few or no disputes take place, the costs of maintaining a standing panel may largely outweigh the normal costs for dispute resolution. Absent any disputes, there would be no party to share the cost with. In cases where an administrative authority were to insist on installing standing panels to handle disputes related to its decisions (like ICANN, cf. infra), it is a cost that the authority would need to bear on its own.

ii. Nomination of knowledgeable experts

When composing a standing panel, the institution selecting the arbitrators can apply detailed criteria, organize a tender process, or even require prospective panelists to pass specific tests. As their appointment does not take place in the context of an existing dispute, timing is not of the essence and care can be taken in the selection process. Once appointed, the institution can organize mandatory trainings for the arbitrators to ensure that they keep on top of developments in the applicable regulatory framework.

The fact that the appointment of a standing panel happens outside the context of an existing dispute also has negative effects. As it is impossible to predict the precise subject-matter of future disputes, the standing panel may lack expected expertise.

iii. Time saving

With a standing panel in place, the parties need not agree on an appointment procedure and they can move directly to other procedural aspects and the merits of the case.

Without a standing panel, the appointment of an adequate panel can be a source of delay. E.g., prospective arbitrators may be challenged, co-arbitrators may experience difficulties in finding a mutually acceptable president, and parties may prefer to grant the

21. Charles PU Jr, "'Wheel of Fortune' or 'Singled Out?': How Rosters 'Matchmake' Mediators", 3 Dispute Resolution Magazine (1997) pp. 10, 11.

co-arbitrators a delay over having an arbitral institution or competent court select the presiding arbitrator.

iv. Predictability

A standing panel which is active for multiple years is likely to rule on similar cases over the years. As a result, standing panels have the potential to develop coherent jurisprudence, thereby building a more predictable environment.

What about independence and impartiality?

Proponents of standing panels will argue that party-appointed arbitrators are unable to remain neutral because they are directly appointed by the disputing parties.[22] We tend to disagree.[23]

It is true that parties will try to appoint an arbitrator with a maximum predisposition to their case, but that should not affect a party-appointed arbitrator's neutrality. Members of the arbitral tribunal are aware that party-appointed arbitrators may be selected for their inclination to ascribe to the legal theories advanced by the party who appointed them. But the balance is restored by the fact that adversaries are generally each allowed to nominate an arbitrator. Of course, it may happen that a party appointed an arbitrator who does not act as a neutral. The lack of neutrality will be quickly noticed by the other arbitrators on the panel. The arbitrator who gives the impression of partisanship not only damages his or her own reputation, the partisan arbitrator will generally have a hard time convincing the other arbitrators on the tribunal of a biased opinion. Unless the party who appointed that arbitrator clearly has the stronger case, the chairman can more easily ignore the opinion and abandon the goal of reaching a unanimous decision.

For the parties, it is comforting to know that, by carefully selecting a prospective arbitrator, they have an arbitrator on the panel who is likely to be receptive to the points they will raise. It will reassure them that their position will be heard, even if not followed.

Depending on how a standing panel is organized, the balance might shift in the complete opposite direction. For example, an administrative authority that provides for ADR proceedings for disputes related to the authority's own decisions could not only choose the institution that will administer the cases, but also impose a standing panel and even select the members of the panel itself. In its selection it can ensure that only panelists who are likely to follow its position are appointed. The situation where the administrative authority is to become a party to disputes decided by (members of) the standing panel, is obviously problematic. Parties in dispute with the authority will be subjected to arbitration proceedings administered by a panel that may be more

---

22. See e.g., Hans SMIT, "The Pernicious Institution of the Party-Appointed Arbitrator", 33 Columbia FDI Perspectives (2010) pp. 1, 2, <http://ccsi.columbia.edu/files/2014/01/FDI_33.pdf>; Jan PAULSSON, "Moral Hazard in International Dispute Resolution", 25 ICSID Review – Foreign Investment Jaw Journal (2010) pp. 339, 348.

23. We are not alone in our views; See, e.g., Charles N. BROWER, Charles B. ROSENBERG, "The Death of the Two-Headed Nightingale: Why the Paulsson–Van den Berg Presumption that Party-Appointed Arbitrators are Untrustworthy Is Wrongheaded", 29 Arbitration International (1 March 2013, issue 1) pp. 7-44.

predisposed to the position of the authorities. The balance that exists on a more conventional arbitration panel is completely gone.

v. What about party autonomy?

The parties' involvement in the appointment procedure contributes to the smooth and transparent running of proceedings. If the parties are able to contribute to the composition of the panel, they have greater confidence in the competence, independence and impartiality of the panelists than when a panel is appointed with no or very little involvement by the parties.

However, having to agree on an appointment procedure may make the proceedings less antagonistic. But without this step in the process, parties may more quickly tackle the core issues of the dispute and enter into the aspects that oppose them.

We are experiencing an evolution in the customs of arbitration. In an international context, ADR practitioners increasingly meet new faces and some may not always be accustomed to the collegial atmosphere that typically exists in the arbitration world. Aggressive litigation techniques, which may be commonplace in certain jurisdictions or sectors, sometimes get introduced in arbitration, making proceedings more adversarial. However, this observation should not hinder those parties that are able to treat their opponent courteously from agreeing on efficient appointment procedures, best suited for their case.

vi. What about case-specific expertise?

If the ADR agreement only allows for the appointment of panelists who appear on the standing panel, the standing panel must be sufficiently diverse to ensure adequate appointments. The narrower a standing panel is, the less likely the members of the standing panel have the necessary case-specific expertise. A major advantage of *ad hoc* appointments, in contrast to a standing panel, is that the parties have more freedom in finding the panelists that are best suited for the case.

b. Practical examples of standing panels

i. Standing panels for domain name disputes under the UDRP

Relatively soon after its formation, ICANN adopted the UDRP and Rules for UDRP in August 1999 and had the implementation documents approved in October 1999. The first UDRP case was brought in December 1999, and for nearly two decades the UDRP has been a tremendous success, providing an efficient tool for the online protection of trademarks.

Without naming it as such, the Rules for UDRP require that the approved dispute resolution service providers install a standing panel. Panelists must be appointed by the provider and each provider must maintain and publish a publicly available list of panellists and their qualifications.[24] This requirement has not changed over time.[25]

---

24. ICANN, *Rules for Uniform Domain Name Dispute Resolution Policy,* as approved by the ICANN Board of Directors on 28 September 2013, <www.icann.org/resources/pages/udrp-rules-2015-03-11-en>, para/ 6(a). For prior versions of these rules, see ICANN, *Rules for Uniform Domain Name Dispute Resolution Policy,* as approved by the ICANN Board of Directors on 30 October 2009,

The first approved UDRP provider, WIPO, takes pride in the fact that its panellists "come from different regions of the world and are well reputed for their impartiality, sound judgement and experience as decision-makers, as well as their substantive experience in the areas of IP law, electronic commerce and the Internet".[26] Panelists are not paid for appearing on the standing panel. They are paid a fixed fee for the cases they handle. The roster of panelists is sufficiently broad to make sure that WIPO can appoint a panelist who is free from conflicts of interest. Before each appointment, the UDRP provider will check with each prospective panelist whether there are any facts or circumstances, past or present, or that could arise in the foreseeable future, that might call into question that person's independence in the eyes of one or both of the parties in the administrative proceeding.

Taking into consideration the envisioned procedural schedule in a case, UDRP providers also check whether the prospective panelist is able to commit the time required to discharge his or her duties responsibly and within the required deadlines.[27]

As the roster is sufficiently broad and the disputes sufficiently narrow, the standing panel works well for UDRP. FORUM[28] and CAC[29] have adopted a similar approach and this specific dispute resolution model was successfully copied for domain name disputes relating to country code top-level domains (ccTLDs) such as .be[30] and .eu.[31]

ii. Expert determination standing panels

WIPO also installed a standing panel to handle Legal Rights Objections (LRO) against new gTLD applications. WIPO's roster comprised 107 panelists from 30 countries, with corresponding linguistic and regional diversity as well as significant expertise in trademark, e-commerce and Internet law. WIPO could build on the expertise it had acquired by maintaining a UDRP standing panel, and it used its pool of UDRP panelists to populate the LRO standing panel. Between them, these panelists had decided

<www.icann.org/resources/pages/rules-be-2012-02-25-en>; ICANN, *Rules for Uniform Domain Name Dispute Resolution Policy*, as approved by ICANN on 24 October 1999, <https://archive.icann.org/en/dndr/udrp/uniform-rules-24oct99-en.htm>.

25. ICANN, *Rules for Uniform Domain Name Dispute Resolution Policy,* as approved by the ICANN Board of Directors on 28 September 2013, <www.icann.org/resources/pages/udrp-rules-2015-03-11-en>, para. 6(a). For prior versions of these rules, see ICANN, *Rules for Uniform Domain Name Dispute Resolution Policy,* as approved by the ICANN Board of Directors on 30 October 2009, <www.icann.org/resources/pages/rules-be-2012-02-25-en>; ICANN, *Rules for Uniform Domain Name Dispute Resolution Policy*, as approved by ICANN on 24 October 1999, <https://archive.icann.org/en/dndr/udrp/uniform-rules-24oct99-en.htm>.
26. WIPO, *WIPO Domain Name Panelists*, <www.wipo.int/amc/en/domains/panel.html>.
27. See e.g., WIPO, *WIPO Domain Name Panelists*, <www.wipo.int/amc/en/domains/panel.html>.
28. The FORUM's Supplemental Rules to ICANN's Uniform Domain Name Dispute Resolution Policy, para. 9; FORUM Arbitration and Mediator Qualifications, available at <www.adrforum.com/Neutrals>.
29. CAC's UDRP Supplemental Rules of the Czech Arbitration Court, para. 6.
30. Rules for Domain Name Dispute Resolution of CEPANI, Art. 7.
31. ADR.eu -.eu Alternative Dispute Resolution Rules (the ADR Rules), para. 4(a).

approximately 11,500 out of a total of 20,000 WIPO panel decisions that had been rendered until then under the WIPO-initiated UDRP.[32]

All LROs needed to be filed within a designated filing window. Once the filing window had ended, all compliant objections were published at the same time, and the applicants concerned were notified of the objection. If no response and response fee was filed before the predetermined deadline, the LRO was automatically accepted.[33] Hence, expert panelists were only appointed after an administratively-compliant response was received.

The LRO standing panel was sufficiently large to handle the LRO case load. Expert determinations were rendered in sixty-three proceedings. The vast majority – fifty-four out of the sixty-three proceedings – were handled by single-member expert panels. In total, WIPO appointed 49 out of the 107 panelists to handle these cases.[34]

As WIPO knew the names of all counsel in LRO proceedings, it was able to avoid the appointment of panelists who acted as counsel to any of the parties in LRO proceedings. In our view, that was not strictly necessary. Nothing would prevent counsel from representing parties in one case and acting as expert panelist in an unrelated case between different parties, as is often the case in UDRP proceedings. In many jurisdictions, practicing counsel are asked from time to time to sit as deputy judges. Many respected arbitrators combine their work as arbitrator with their work as counsel. It is our personal conviction that the combination of both occupations makes one a better arbitrator and counsel.

Nevertheless, we agree that, in the context of LRO proceedings, it was probably prudent not to appoint panelists who also served as counsel in a different LRO. Although it must be possible for a panelist to dissociate his or her expert opinion from his or her role as counsel, the appointment of a LRO panelist who also serves as counsel in LRO proceedings would almost certainly have given rise to criticism. WIPO's roster was populated with enough competent experts to ensure that adequate panelists were appointed in every case without having to call upon experts who also served as counsel in similar cases. The easiest way to deal with criticism was by avoiding it. And to ensure that parties accepted the expert determinations, it was wise to make sure they were spared from unnecessary critique.

The mandate of LRO panels was sufficiently precise and narrow. LRO expert determinations did not give rise to much controversy. We know of one expert determination which was challenged in court and one which was challenged in an IRP. Both challenges were quickly dismissed.[35]

---

32. WIPO, *WIPO Arbitration and Mediation Center End Report on Legal Rights Objection Procedure 2013*, December 2013, available at <www.wipo.int/export/sites/www/amc/en/docs/lroreport.pdf>, p. 9.
33. New gTLD Dispute Resolution Procedure, Art. 11(g).
34. WIPO, *WIPO Arbitration and Mediation Center End Report on Legal Rights Objection Procedure 2013*, December 2013, available at <www.wipo.int/export/sites/www/amc/en/docs/lroreport.pdf>, p. 9.
35. US District, Court Central District of California, *Del Monte International GmbH v. Del Monte Corporation*, Order of Dismissal, CV 13-5912, 5 February 2014; ICDR Case No. 01-14-0000-9604, *Merck KGaA v. ICANN*, Final Declaration of the Independent Review Process Panel, 11 December 2015; For a critical assessment of the IRP involving Merck KGaA, see Flip PETILLION

To summarize, WIPO's standing panel worked well for LROs. WIPO had the advantage of being able to rely on a large pool of experts who regularly handle comparable cases.

Other types of expert determinations in the context of new gTLD applications – administered by either the ICC or ICDR – were much more controversial. But the controversy did not focus much on the appointment of panelists; it can be attributed to the fact that the panelists had to work within a completely new framework using untested standards.[36]

In any event, the experience in the context of new gTLD applications shows that, with careful preparation, standing panels can prove useful to handle a relatively large number of similar disputes in a short timeframe.

iii. Independent Review Process (IRP) standing panel

Ever since its Bylaws modification on 11 April 2013, ICANN has envisioned the installation of a standing panel for handling IRPs, ICANN's external accountability mechanism to review ICANN's actions and inactions for compliance with its Articles of Incorporation and Bylaws.[37] However, to date, an IRP standing panel has never been in place.

ICANN reconfirmed its willingness to install such a standing panel and to work out more detailed rules. But ICANN is still figuring out the process for selecting candidates almost five years after it decided to work with a standing panel. In January 2018, ICANN's legal staff informed the ICANN community as follows:

> "[W]e've identified that not only do we need to jumpstart the community conversation to identify the next steps but it's also really important for us to gain an understanding of the full timeline of what the selection process is prior to sending out the call for expressions of interest for people to serve as panelists. We need to know and we need to be able to explain to them if it's going to be a six-month process or a one year process for example. We also need to understand and be able to explain to the applicant the level of community involvement and the community access to information such as their identities just for the fact of applying, et cetera."[38]

For ICANN, the installation of a standing panel clearly is a slow process, and we do not exclude that suitable candidates may have lost interest in serving on the IRP standing panel by the inertness of the selection process. It is also unclear whether the IRP standing panel will be regularly called upon to serve in IRPs. Until now, IRPs have always been initiated in connection with ICANN's allocation of licenses to operate gTLDs. These

---

and Jan JANSSEN, *Competing for the Internet: ICANN Gate – An Analysis and Plea for Judicial Review Through Arbitration* (Wolters Kluwer 2017) pp. 243-254.

36. Flip PETILLION and Jan JANSSEN, *Competing for the Internet: ICANN Gate – An Analysis and Plea for Judicial Review Through Arbitration* (Wolters Kluwer 2017) p. 126.
37. ICANN, Bylaws as amended 11 April 2013, Art. IV(3).
38. ICANN, *Transcription Independent Review Process Webinar*, 17 January 2018, <www.icann.org/en/system/files/files/transcript-establishment-irp-standing-panel-process-webinar-17jan18-en.pdf>, p. 3.

licenses have been allocated in different application rounds. If past experience helps to predict the future, one might expect that, once installed, the IRP standing panel is not likely to be a hive of activity until ICANN allocates new licenses for gTLDs. At this stage, it is unclear when ICANN will organize a next round of gTLD applications or open a permanent window for gTLD applications. Until then, there seems to be a high likelihood that few cases will be brought to IRP. Maintaining a standing panel could place an unwanted financial burden upon ICANN.

In 2016, when the ICANN community reviewed ICANN's accountability, it favoured the institution of a standing panel for IRPs,[39] although ICANN had no actual experience with the appointment of a standing panel or with dispute resolution by such panel. The choice is surprising. It is not clear how the community would benefit from the institution of a standing panel as opposed to relying on more liberal appointment methods, which have worked well until now.

A possible explanation for the ICANN community's choice may be that the community considered that the appointment of arbitrators created unnecessary delays and that proceedings took too long. However, in our experience, delays in the appointment of IRP panelists were mostly attributable to ICANN. ICANN, as the party involved in all IRPs, could perhaps be expected to have a list of pre-selected individuals for nomination as co-panelists. A prior list of interested panelists could certainly contribute to the efficiency in establishing IRP panels in a timely fashion. But this goal can be achieved without the institution of a standing panel.

We understand the benefits to ICANN of a standing panel, as it would be easier to guide a small group of panelists who are supposed to serve for five years. ICANN's new Bylaws provide that the members of the standing panel will receive training provided by ICANN on the workings and management of the Internet's unique identifiers.[40] However, there is a risk that panelists could be prejudiced by ICANN's interpretation of its obligations as a result of this training. It is difficult to see how a standing panel, trained by one party to the IRP proceedings, would improve ICANN's accountability, especially since the system of *ad hoc* appointments has been shown to work and gives parties the opportunity to appoint a balanced panel.

The absence of a standing panel has not been an impediment to the appointment of appropriately qualified IRP panelists. In our view, there is no pressing need to limit the pool of individuals who can serve as IRP panelists. Significant legal expertise is one of the most important qualifications required of an IRP panelist – particularly in international law, corporate governance, and regulatory and administrative processes – as is experience in dispute resolution and arbitration. A strong understanding of the DNS is obviously a prerequisite, but experience shows that open-minded panelists can quickly make up for an initially limited knowledge of the DNS. It is much more important to have independent and impartial panelists with an open mind than to have a DNS subject-

39. CCWG-Accountability, *Supplemental Final Proposal on Work Stream 1 Recommendations*, 23 February 2016, <www.icann.org/en/system/files/files/ccwg-accountability-supp-proposal-work-stream-1-recs-23feb16-en.pdf>, p. 35.
40. ICANN, Bylaws as amended on 1 October 2016, Art. 4(3)(j)(i).

matter expert who may be involved with various ICANN stakeholder groups or advisory committees.[41]

In our view, the disadvantages largely outweigh the advantages of a standing panel for IRPs.

iv. Public Interest Commitment Dispute Resolution Procedure (PICDRP) standing panel

In December 2013, ICANN adopted a Public Interest Commitment Dispute Resolution Procedure or PICDRP. The PICDRP is designed to offer some form of redress to the internet community towards a gTLD registry who breaches specific contractual commitments that must serve the public interest. The PICDRP intends that the parties self-resolve the issue. If amicable settlement discussions fail, ICANN may analyze the situation or refer the issue to a standing panel for independent evaluation.[42]

The PICDRP standing panel operates at ICANN's expense.[43] Each panel member is compensated in the form of an annual stipend and a per matter fee for each service on a panel.[44] The terms of standing panel members are supposed to be staggered for the purpose of continuity and consistency. Initially, ICANN's plan was to have two of the standing panel members serve for two years and a third member serve for one year. Subsequent terms of new members and the renewal of terms would then be two years. With agreement from ICANN, standing panel members would be allowed to renew for a maximum of two terms.[45] However, the implementation of the staggered terms is yet unclear. In 2014, three members were appointed on the standing panel. In 2015, four members were added to the roster. All initially appointed members are still on the standing panel today.[46]

So far, the members of the PICDRP standing panel did not have many opportunities to ensure consistency in their evaluations, as only one complaint has been referred to the panel.[47] In its evaluation report, the PICDRP panel took a narrow view on its mandate.[48]

It remains to be seen whether new complaints will follow. The mandate of the PICDRP panel might indeed be too specific for the panel to be called upon on a regular basis. Unlike the UDRP, it is debatable whether the PICDRP responds to a real and pressing need. The UDRP was introduced to deal with the issue of cybersquatting and

41. Flip PETILLION and Jan JANSSEN, *Competing for the Internet: ICANN Gate – An Analysis and Plea for Judicial Review Through Arbitration* (Wolters Kluwer 2017) pp. 374-375.
42. ICANN, *Public Interest Commitment Dispute Resolution Procedure*, 19 December 2013.
43. ICANN, *Public Interest Commitment Dispute Resolution Procedure*, 19 December 2013, Sect. 4(1).
44. ICANN, *Call for Expressions of Interest: PICDRP Standing Panel*, 2 December 2014.
45. ICANN, *Announcement on Call for Expressions of Interest for PICDR Standing Panel Members*, 19 December 2014, <https://newgtlds.icann.org/en/announcements-and-media/announcement-4-19dec13-en>.
46. For the current composition of the PICDRP standing panel, see <www.icann.org/resources/pages/picdrp-2014-01-09-en>.
47. ICANN PICDRP, *Adobe Systems Incorporated et al. v. Top Level Spectrum, Inc., d/b/a Fegistry LLC et al.*, PIC Report VNE-236-30027, 14 March 2017, available at <www.icann.org/uploads/compliance_notice/attachment/911/serad-to-westerdal-16mar17.pdf>.
48. ICANN PICDRP, *Adobe Systems Incorporated et al. v. Top Level Spectrum, Inc., d/b/a Fegistry LLC et al.*, PIC Report VNE-236-30027, 14 March 2017, available at <www.icann.org/uploads/compliance_notice/attachment/911/serad-to-westerdal-16mar17.pdf>.

misappropriation of trademarks on the Internet, which posed a real threat to the protection of trademarks. The PICDRP was introduced before practical problems had arisen.

The future will tell whether it will be worth maintaining a standing panel to handle these complaints. If the current trend of scarce complaints under the PICDRP continues, it might be worth abandoning the idea of a PICDRP standing panel or revisiting the panel's role.

c. Lessons learned

Standing panels that receive repeat appointments can bring relevant expertise to a dispute, allowing them to quickly grasp and efficiently solve the issue with specialized knowledge. Experience shows that they work well when (i) their mandate is sufficiently precise and narrow, and (ii) there is either a constant flux of new cases or when a relatively large number of cases must be handled in a short timeframe. In our view, both requirements must be fulfilled to make a standing panel a success.

Standing panels may be less appropriate when the contours of the dispute or of the panel's mandate are less clear or less predictable. If a policy instrument can be applied to a wide variety of disputes, the disputing parties may be better served with party autonomy in the selection of arbitrators.

Finally, a standing panel should not be installed merely for the purpose of having such a standing panel. If relatively few disputes are expected or if the number of expected disputes is uncertain, the better option may be to have a list of pre-selected individuals who might be interested in serving on a panel should the need arise.

3. Small Is Beautiful: The Use of Single-Member Panels

a. Policy arguments for and against single-member panels

i. Cost and time-efficient

The use of single-member panels can mean a significant reduction in costs and quicker turnaround times. A panelist appointed as sole arbitrator does not need to concert with co-panelists nor adapt himself to their agenda. Procedural orders can be issued without a need to consult among panelists. Less time will be spent during deliberations, as there is no need for seeking consensus or a majority among arbitrators.

ii. Increased availability

An often heard complaint is that some arbitrators take on too many cases, serve on too many panels and experience difficulties in issuing their decisions. Part of the problem is that arbitrators are often requested to serve on three-member panels, whereas the case could be handled more efficiently, and as proficiently, by a single-member panel. If panels are less populated, arbitrators will obtain increased availability to serve on different panels and to issue timely awards.

iii. No compromise decisions

Most arbitration laws and institutional rules will provide that arbitral awards must be decided by a majority.[49] Nevertheless, the vast majority of arbitral tribunals will try to reach consensus before having to revert to a majority decision, often followed by a dissenting opinion.

The need for compromise may not only delay decisions, it is also a source for criticism. The consensus-driven dynamics in the decision-making of panels composed of more than one arbitrator may indeed be one of the reasons for the importunate perception that arbitral tribunals tend to "split the baby" when making decisions.[50] Many studies have been made on the topic, and recent research confirms that there continues to be no real evidence of arbitral tribunals "splitting the baby".[51] Nevertheless, the myth continues to exist. The fact that many awards in commercial arbitration remain confidential makes this a difficult research topic. Nurturing this myth is the fact that many parties who are not awarded the entirety of their claim have the impression that the decision is the result of a compromise between arbitrators, whereas there may be judicious reasons to accept only part of a claim.

This perception, which is often voiced loudly together with the misconception that party-appointed arbitrators are partisan, sparks the distrust that exists with those who are less familiar with the arbitration community and the ADR community more generally. By favouring the appointment of single-member panels, greater trust can be

49. See e.g., UNCITRAL Model Law (2006), Art. 29; UNCITRAL Arbitration Rules (2013), Art. 33; ICC Rules of Arbitration (2017), Art. 32; LCIA Arbitration Rules (2014), Art. 26(5); Arbitration Rules of the Arbitration Institute of the Stockholm Chamber of Commerce (2017), Art. 41; SIAC Rules 2016, Art. 32(7).

50. See Ana Carolina WEBER, Carmine A. PASCUZZO S., Guilherme de SIQUEIRA PASTORE, Ricardo DALMASO MARQUES, "Challenging the 'Splitting the Baby' Myth in International Arbitration", 31 Journal of International Arbitration (Kluwer Law International 2014, issue 6) pp. 719-734.

51. John FISHER, Sarah JOHNSON and Matthew FRITZSCHE, *PwC International Arbitration damages research*, 2017 update, <www.pwc.co.uk/forensic-services/assets/pwc-international-arbitration-damages-research-2017.pdf>, p. 3; Soia MENTSCHIKOFF, "Commercial Arbitration", LXI Colum.L.Rev. (May 1961) p. 846; J. Kirkland GRANT, *Securities Arbitration for Brokers, Attorneys and Investors* (Greenwood Publishing Group 1994); Carl F. INGWALSON, Jr., "Dispelling Arbitration Myths", Utah State Bar 2011 Summer Convention, San Diego, California; James R. DEYE and Lesly L.BRITTON, "Arbitration by the American Arbitration Association", 70 N.D. L. Rev. (1994) pp. 287-288; Stephanie E. KEER, Richard W. NAIMARK, "Arbitrators Do Not 'Split the Baby' – Empirical Evidence from International Business Arbitration", 18 J. Int'l Arb. (2001, issue 5) p. 573; Christopher R. Drahozal, "Arbitration by the Numbers: The State of Empirical Research on International Commercial Arbitration", 22 Arb. Int'l (2006, no. 2) p. 304; "Splitting the Baby: A New AAA Study" (9 Mar. 2007); Christopher DRAHOZAL, "Busting Arbitration Myths", 56 U. Kan. L. Rev. (April 2008, no. 3) pp. 673-674; Douglas SHONTZ, Fred KIPPERMAN, Vanessa SOMA, *Business-to-Business Arbitration in the United States – Perceptions of Corporate Counsel, Report of RAND Institute for Civil Justice* (2011), available at <www.rand.org/pubs/technical_reports/TR781.html>, pp. 12-13; AAA/ICDR Awards Do Not Split the Baby – Countering Counsel Perception in Commercial B2B Arbitration Cases (2016), available at <https://ss-usa.s3.amazonaws.com/c/2345/media/578e637693d2c/2016_Split_the_Baby_WhitePaper.pdf>.

built in arbitral decision-making, especially if statistics show similar outcomes between the decisions of single-member panels and those populated by three or more arbitrators.

iv. No dissenting opinions

A related, but not less controversial, issue is the practice of dissenting opinions in international arbitration. Proponents of this practice will argue that dissenting opinions play an important role in the development of the law. They might also argue that a well-reasoned and earnest dissent can help build confidence in the process by showing the losing party that the case was thoroughly assessed and evaluated.[52] In our view, such confidence should exist also without a dissent. It is not the task of a dissenting arbitrator to build confidence in the process; that is the task of the entire panel.

Critics of dissenting opinions are skeptical about their contribution to the development of the law.[53] They observe a relaxed attitude towards dissenting opinions[54] and raise questions about the fact that virtually all dissenting opinions written by a co-arbitrator are in favour of the party that nominated them.[55] Some critics see this as an illustration that "too many co-arbitrators still have difficulties in being fully impartial".[56] Of course, a carefully selected party-appointed arbitrator is likely to be more predisposed to the legal theories advanced by the party that nominated him or her. That does not mean that a party-appointed arbitrator who drafts a dissenting opinion in favour of the party that appointed him or her is not fully impartial. After all, the dissent will normally be its own judge. A partisan or poorly reasoned dissenting opinion will harm its author. It will not hinder the arbitral process.

A rampant increase in dissenting opinions that are partisan or that appear inspired mainly by an arbitrator's desire to appease the party that appointed him or her, would undermine the credibility of the practice of dissenting opinions and of arbitration in general. In our view, the arbitration community should be extremely cautious about dissenting opinions, as unbridled dissents are an attack to the legitimacy of the arbitral process.

---

52. R. MOSK and T. GINSBURG, "Dissenting Opinions in International Arbitration" in M. TUPAMÄKI, ed., *Liber Amicorum Bengt Broms* (1999).
53. See Albert Jan VAN DEN BERG, "Dissenting Opinions by Party-Appointed Arbitrators in Investment Arbitration" in M. ARSANJANI, et al., eds., *Looking to the Future: Essays on International Law in Honor of W. Michael Reisman* (Brill 2010).
54. See Alan REFERN, "Dissenting Opinions in International Commercial Arbitration: The Good, the Bad and the Ugly", 20 Arb. Int'l. (2004, issue 3) pp. 223, 242.
55. See Albert Jan VAN DEN BERG, "Dissenting Opinions by Party-Appointed Arbitrators in Investment Arbitration" in M. ARSANJANI, et al., eds., *Looking to the Future: Essays on International Law in Honor of W. Michael Reisman*; Yves DERAINS, "The Deliberations of the Arbitral Tribunal – "*Retour au délibéré arbitral*" in Markus WIRTH ed., *The Resolution of the Dispute – From the Hearing to the Award: ASA Special Series No. 29* (2007) p. 17; Albert Jan VAN DEN BERG, "Charles Brower's Problem with 100 per cent—Dissenting Opinions by Party-Appointed Arbitrators in Investment Arbitration", 31 Arbitration International (1 September 2015) pp. 381-391.
56. Yves DERAINS, "The Deliberations of the Arbitral Tribunal – *'Retour au délibéré arbitral'*" in Markus WIRTH, ed., *The Resolution of the Dispute – From the Hearing to the Award: ASA Special Series No. 29* (2007) p. 17

A moratorium on the use of dissenting opinions by party-appointment arbitrators, as advocated by Professor van den Berg (albeit in the context of investment arbitration),[57] may be too drastic a measure to curtail the lenience towards dissents. But the arbitration community should embrace initiatives to limit the number of dissenting opinions.

Having more cases decided by single-member panels will automatically result in fewer dissenting opinions and avoid abuse of this practice. If there are fewer cases in which a dissenting opinion is expressed, the dissenting voice is likely to be louder and more likely to serve its role in the development of the law.

v. Default option for default cases?

It occurs that arbitration agreements require the appointment of three arbitrators, irrespective of the amount in dispute. Even when the respondent did not react to the request for arbitration, the claimant may need to proceed with the appointment of a three-member panel (via court proceedings or with the assistance of an arbitral institution). The installation of a three-member panel in default cases will almost always be an unnecessary financial burden and create unwanted delays.

Parties can easily avoid this situation by agreeing on a more streamlined appointment procedure in case of default. However, practice shows that parties rarely provide for alternative rules in case of default. Arbitral institutions can fill this gap by providing e.g., that, in case of default, a single arbitrator will be appointed unless the parties have explicitly agreed that three or more arbitrators must also be appointed in case of default.

b. Practical examples

i. International Chamber of Commerce (ICC) expedited procedures

The ICC has taken a step towards having more cases decided by single-member panels with the adoption of its Expedited Procedure Rules in 2017. According to these new rules, the ICC Court of Arbitration may appoint a sole arbitrator in expedited arbitration proceedings, notwithstanding any contrary provision of the arbitration agreement.[58] Practice will show whether party autonomy will be limited effectively by the ICC Court of Arbitration if parties expressed their agreement to have their dispute decided by a three-member panel. In any event, the new rules clearly demonstrate the ICC's intention of having more disputes decided by sole arbitrators.

The ICC seeks to have the expedited procedure apply to most cases that do not exceed US$ 2,000,000. For agreements concluded after 1 March 2017, parties must explicitly opt out of the Expedited Procedure Rules if they do not want these rules to apply to their disputes below this threshold. For agreements concluded before that date, or for disputes above the US$ 2,000,000 threshold, parties may opt in to the Expedited

57. Albert Jan VAN DEN BERG, "Dissenting Opinions by Party-Appointed Arbitrators in Investment Arbitration" in M. ARSANJANI, et al., eds., *Looking to the Future: Essays on International Law in Honor of W. Michael Reisman*; Albert Jan VAN DEN BERG, "Charles Brower's Problem with 100 per cent—Dissenting Opinions by Party-Appointed Arbitrators in Investment Arbitration, 31 Arbitration International (1 September 2015) pp. 381-391

58. ICC Arbitration Rules (2017), Appendix VI, Art. 2(1).

Procedure Rules. Nevertheless, the ICC Court of Arbitration may determine that it is inappropriate in the circumstances of the case to apply the Expedited Procedure Rules.

ii. Uniform Domain Name Dispute Resolution Policy (UDRP) panels

Single-member panels are preferred in UDRP cases. The vast majority of domain name disputes under the UDRP are decided by sole panelists. Nevertheless, either party may elect to have the dispute decided by a three-member panel.[59] If claimants elect a three-member panel, they must pay the fees for such panel in their entirety. If the respondent elects a three-member panel, the applicable fees are shared equally between parties.[60] Practice shows that parties rarely elect three-member panels. The additional costs may be one reason. More importantly, a predictable body of case law has developed over the years and single-member panels give a sufficient amount of legal certainty. The success of the UDRP is even more remarkable as panel decisions are not binding and parties may initiate "regular" court proceedings within a certain time frame.

c. Outlook

The arbitration community has sought ways to appease critics and to build confidence in appointment procedures. Examples include the joint identification of the presiding arbitrator before making unilateral appointments, or the screened selection of party-appointed arbitrators, meaning that the party-appointed arbitrators are contacted by the arbitral institution and do not get to know which party nominated them.[61] It remains to be seen whether these fairly recent and imaginative approaches will create greater trust in ADR, since they also risk adding more complexity to the appointment procedure.

Having more cases decided by sole panelists may be a more efficient way to soothe arbitration foes. The appointment of single-member panels is easily understood both within and outside the arbitration community. The efficiencies resulting from smaller arbitration panels are likely to get noticed outside the inner circle of arbitration practitioners.

IV. THE EX OFFICIO EXAMINATION OF EVIDENCE

1. Policy Arguments For and Against Ex Officio Examination

The quest to uncover the truth is one of the most important aspects in administering justice. Whenever a judge, panelist or arbitrator is asked to decide on a legal issue, he or she will want to have the facts straight. Even when allegations are not contradicted, e.g., in default proceedings, panels may want to see – and the applicable standard of proof

59. ICANN, *Rules for Uniform Domain Name Dispute Resolution Policy,* as approved by the ICANN Board of Directors on 28 September 2013, <www.icann.org/resources/pages/udrp-rules-2015-03-11-en>, para. 6.
60. ICANN, *Rules for Uniform Domain Name Dispute Resolution Policy,* as approved by the ICANN Board of Directors on 28 September 2013, <www.icann.org/resources/pages/udrp-rules-2015-03-11-en>, para. 6.
61. For a practical example of the screened selection method, see 2014 CPR Rules for Administered Arbitration of International Disputes, Rule 5.4.

may require – convincing evidence. After all, it is the parties' job and the role of counsel to convince a panel and to create what we call "substantiated credibility".[62]

When the file is lacking evidentiary support for easily verifiable information, it may be tempting for the panel members to perform its own research ex officio to assess the case merits or to rely on facts they consider well known. The situation may be delicate when the panel was selected precisely because of its expertise or experiential background in a particular sector and its familiarity with the customs and practices in a particular field. The parties may expect the panel to bring its experience to the deliberations. Without a proper understanding of all relevant facts – that is including the ones that were not presented – the legal truth risks being misconstrued. Panelists should be wary of importing their own subjective appreciation of factual matters into the decision-making. A decision that is influenced by the panel's own experiences rather than being based solely on the facts presented to it, may give the impression that the panel was prejudiced.

A simple way to overcome the controversy could be to ignore one's own experiences and to determine that a party failed to carry its burden of proof. But that approach might not satisfy the parties and could intensify the dispute or make it more complex from a procedural point of view. This "solution" might also not satisfy panelists, who are committed to serving the parties in their attempt to resolve the dispute.

Seasoned arbitrators will often find ways to make the parties fill evidentiary gaps, while observing due process rights and without creating any appearance of bias.

It is unlikely for arbitrators to ignore what came to their attention. If, through preliminary research or otherwise, they have stumbled upon facts that may be relevant to the case, they cannot simply disregard them. In this case, a procedural order notifying the parties and inviting them to comment on evidence that was not presented by the parties will often solve the issue with respect to the parties' due process rights and the principle of equality of arms, which requires a contradictory debate. Requiring parties to comment may be perceived as overly formalistic and frustrate the procedural economy, e.g., when allegations are undisputed and the evidence to support the allegations is readily accessible to the public, and not capable of being reasonably disputed.

2. *Practical Examples*

a. *Domain name disputes under UDRP*

In domain name litigation under the UDRP, it has been accepted that a panel may undertake limited factual research into matters of public record if it considers such information useful to assess the case merits and reach a decision.[63] It would indeed make the proceedings unduly complex if a UDRP panelist were to invite the parties to

62. We have lectured about this concept at the Fourth Annual Juris Conference on Damages in International Arbitration in Vienna in 2015 and were invited to elaborate on it at the Annual Arbitration Conference of the ICC United Kingdom in London in 2016.

63. WIPO, *WIPO Overview of WIPO Panel Views on Selected UDRP Questions, Third Edition (WIPO Jurisprudential Overview 3.0)* (2017) <www.wipo.int/amc/en/domains/search/overview3.0/>, Sect. 4.8.

comment each time he or she wants to verify the truthfulness of an allegation by consulting, e.g., a dictionary or a trademark registration database.

An unwanted consequence of panelists making enquiries of their own is that some parties seem to have become sloppy in presenting their case as they count on the professionalism of the panelist to fill obvious gaps in the case file. The panelist loses time by retrieving information that should have been presented by the parties. On the other hand, the panelist would lose much more time if he or she were to issue a procedural order to allow the parties to complete their file.

b. Nominet

Some ADR centres try to avoid this situation by making clear that it is the parties' responsibility to include within their submissions *all* evidence upon which they wish to rely.[64] Nominet's DRS policy for .uk domain name disputes sets forth that, in the ordinary course, its experts will not perform any research into a dispute or check the parties' assertions. However, an expert may, at his or her entire discretion, check any material which is generally available in the public domain.[65]

3. Appraisal

Parties are better served by a panel that is eager to understand all aspects of a case and the details of a trade than by an insufficiently informed panel. One may expect that a panel's curiosity and critical thinking will generally lead to better and fairer decisions. To avoid a panel's own research and study – both in and outside the context of a dispute – clouding the panel's judgment, transparency is key. If a panel's reasoning is likely to be impacted by its own knowledge or research, it is imperative that the parties be informed accordingly and, in some instances, even be invited to debate. While a panel may expect parties to submit all evidence relevant to properly assess the case, limited and transparent ex officio examination by the panel may be essential to fully establish the legal truth.

V. EFFICIENCIES IN REASON-GIVING

1. Reasons Not to Give Reasons?

The reasons for giving reasons in judgments, administrative decisions and arbitral awards are manifold. To give but one example, reason-giving is thought to improve the quality of the decision. It concentrates the mind, thereby avoiding arbitrary decision-making. Or, as the late Lord Justice Bingham put it:

> "I cannot, I hope, be the only person who has sat down to write a judgment, having formed the view that A must win, only to find in the course of composition

64. See e.g., NOMINET, Dispute Resolution Service – Experts' Overview, Foreword to Version 3 by Nick Gardner, Chair of the Panel of Experts, December 2016.
65. NOMINET, Dispute Resolution Service Policy, applicable as of 1 October 2016, Sect. 18(1).

> that there are no sustainable grounds for that conclusion and that on any rational analysis B must succeed."[66]

Lord Bingham is definitely not the only person who was courageous enough to reconsider his initial position and to let his mind take precedence over his intuition. However, a number of psychologists suggest that the reasoning process will often come down to *post hoc* constructions that are made to justify one's intuitions.[67] At best, such *post hoc* rationalizations are legally sound and correspond to the reasoning that would have applied without being led by intuition. But, if the decision-maker's intuition was incorrect and not reconsidered, parties can only hope that the outcome can be overturned. In this respect, reason-giving can prove immensely useful for contestation purposes. A court or tribunal's written reasoning may allow for a meaningful judicial review. Historically, the possibility for such review and possible annulment was exactly the reason not to give reasons. Courts in Ancient Rome and in premodern, continental Europe deemed it valuable not to give reasons to avoid an appearance of uncertainty and to avoid criticism.[68]

Naturally, we do not advocate a return to the judicial practices and conflict-resolution mechanisms of the pre-modern era. A corresponding lack of reasoning is a catalyst for abuse and arbitrary decision-making. On the other hand, in specific situations, and in the context of alternative dispute resolution in particular, one may question the desirability of reason-giving and of extensive possibilities for judicial review. Considerations of efficiency may prevail over the need for a detailed rationale. And, if applied with care, they may further due process, rather than being an impediment to fairness.

2. *Deference as a Reason Not to Give Reasons – The Example of Expert Determinations*

The speed and the possibility of calling upon subject-matter experts are often invoked as benefits of alternative dispute resolution mechanisms. The deference which parties grant to an expert may be a sufficient reason for them not to challenge his or her opinion. For this reason, it is common to provide in contracts that expert determination is binding, sometimes completed with the possibility to challenge it in court or before an arbitral tribunal, if done before a certain deadline.[69] If the parties want to resolve their dispute fast and if they can fall back on capable experts, it may be counterproductive to require extensive reasoning.

66. Rt Hon. Lord Justice BINGHAM, "The Differences Between a Judgment and a Reasoned Award", 16 The Arbitrator (May 1997, no. 1).
67. See Mathilde COHEN, "When Judges Have Reasons Not to Give Reasons: A Comparative Law Approach", 72 Wash. & Lee L. Rev. (2015, Issue 2), <http://scholarlycommons.law.wlu.edu/wlulr/vol72/iss2/3>, p. 483, at p. 518 and references there.
68. See Mathilde COHEN, "When Judges Have Reasons Not to Give Reasons: A Comparative Law Approach", 72 Wash. & Lee L. Rev. (2015, Issue 2) p. 483, <http://scholarlycommons.law.wlu.edu/wlulr/vol72/iss2/3, 486-487> and references there.
69. Queen Mary University of London, School of International Arbitration, Pinsent MASONS, *Pre-empting and Resolving Technology, Media and Telecoms Disputes – International Dispute Resolution Survey*, <www.arbitration.qmul.ac.uk/docs/189659.pdf>.

Because the parties may still take recourse to more judicial forms of dispute resolution, the absence of reasoning in the expert determination does not risk impeding their rights. If the expert's opinion did not resolve the dispute, the parties may take the matter further to court or arbitration. Should the expert's opinion be relevant to subsequent proceedings, nothing would prevent the parties jointly asking the expert to explain his or her opinion after it was issued if needed.

The rules on expert determinations of leading institutions provide that the experts must give reasons for their findings, unless otherwise agreed by all of the parties.[70] The choice for reason-giving as default option seems justified by the expectations of most parties. In many cases, the authority of the expert alone will not give sufficient comfort to the parties. Many organizations have become accustomed to more or less detailed reasoning in expert opinions and they will often expect a statement of reasons, even in low-profile cases.

On average, the balance may have shifted too much in the direction of reason-giving, meaning that too much time and effort is sometimes spent on details. The course of action is usually chosen by the party initiating the proceedings. And, once proceedings have started, it is often difficult for a party to convince its opponent that the dispute would be better served in a different setting.

To avoid situations where the proceedings are too cumbersome for the purpose, it is preferable that parties consider upfront what situations may give rise to a dispute and how a particular type of dispute must be handled. This exercise will help prevent parties falling back on full-fledged arbitration or litigation for relatively simple disputes. The need for reasons may be best assessed on a case by case basis; the parameters for making such decision are best agreed upfront. When assessing the parameters, one should be mindful, however, about how the lack of reason-giving may be an impediment to the enforceability of the third-party decision.

3. *Standardization in Reason-Giving*

Specialized institutions have thought of different ways to facilitate reason-giving. We generally distinguish two models: (i) summary decisions and (ii) case preparation by staff.

a. *Summary decisions*

Obvious cases can be decided more quickly and at a lesser cost. Some ADR institutions offer summary decisions in "obvious" cases where the respondent defaulted, but the practical organization of summary decisions differs.

Some institutions accept that a summary decision contains no reasons at all. Under Nominet's DRS Policy, a mere statement that the claimant has shown his allegations to reasonable satisfaction may suffice.[71] Some panelists complete this statement with optional comments, listing the main reasons for their decision in bullet form.

---

70. See ICC Rules for the Administration of Expert Proceedings (1 February 2015), Art. 8(1); WIPO Expert Determination Rules (Effective from 1 January 2016), Art. 17(c)(iii).

71. Under Nominet's Dispute Resolution Service Policy for abusive registrations of domain names in the.uk domain, plaintiffs have the option to apply for a summary decision if the respondent did not

CAC also offers "summary" decisions in default cases. However, it still requires that these decisions contain reasons.[72] The panelist fee will be lower for a summary decision, unless the panel determines that a normal fee is appropriate in view of the complexity of the proceeding. In practice, there is hardly any difference between the summary decisions of this institution and the decisions in complex cases or in cases where a defence was presented. The bulk of the default cases are indeed clear-cut cases, for which the outcome is quickly decided. However, requiring the decision to contain reasons similar to the rationale in standard cases (i.e., cases where the respondent did not default) means that a disproportionate amount of time is put into writing down the reasons for the decision. The practical result is that the panelist will be paid less, even though the amount of work put into a reasoned administrative decision in default cases is similar to the work put into a decision where a response was submitted.

If the primary aim of summary decisions is to shorten the throughput time and to facilitate the work of the panel, a more sensible option is to allow for decisions with no or limited reasons. If the decision does not limit the parties' right to seek recourse in court, the absence of reasoning only has a limited impact on the parties.[73] However, a determination to allow no or only limited reasons cannot be made by the UDRP dispute resolution providers, such as WIPO, CAC and FORUM, as it would require a change in the Rules for UDRP for which ICANN is responsible.

Institutions will wish to maintain accurate decision-making. In our view, the single most important action will be to appoint dutiful panelists, who remain on top of case law developments. The institutions can assist in having panelists maintain and improve their expertise by organizing regular training sessions, appointing deciders in both obvious cases and more complex cases that require elaborate reasoning, etc. Other means of improving the accuracy of decision-making are the indexing of decisions, the development of checklists, the scrutiny of decisions and the publication of case law overviews (cf. infra).

b. Case preparation by staff

Institutions can be of tremendous value in ensuring the efficient administration of cases, e.g., by reviewing compliance with formal requirements, by helping parties remedy deficiencies and by facilitating communication and notifications via online portals and

---

submit a response. The request will be granted if the appointed expert considers that (i) the complainant has shown that he or she has rights in respect of a name which is identical or similar to the domain name and the domain name is an abusive registration, and (ii) no other factors apply which would make a summary decision unconscionable in all the circumstances (Nominet's DRS Policy, Sect. 12).

72. The Czech Arbitration Court offers dispute resolution at a reduced fee for UDRP cases in which the respondent defaulted, unless the panel determines that an additional fee is appropriate in view of the complexity of the proceeding (CAC's UDRP Supplemental Rules of the Czech Arbitration Court applicable for proceedings where the complaint is submitted on or after 31 July 2015, Annex A). However, the rules for UDRP require that the decisions provide the reasons on which they are based (Rules for Uniform Domain Name Dispute Resolution Policy, as approved by the ICANN Board of Directors on 28 September 2013, Sect. 15(d)).

73. Without reasoning, it might be more difficult for the prevailing party to maintain that the decision must be upheld. If the plaintiff was given the choice to opt for a summary decision, the difficulties that may result from the absence of reasons can be attributed to the plaintiff's choice.

otherwise. Online case management systems, if administered well, can facilitate the examination of exhibits and submissions. Text recognition software can make documents searchable, thereby helping panelists analyze the case material.

Some institutions have gone a step further in their assistance to panelists. They have staff prepare a memorandum for the panelist with references to case law that is deemed relevant to the case and that provides arguments for both parties. Although these memoranda may expedite the writing process and create more standardized decisions, the practice also opens the door for criticism.

i. Research and drafting assistance in judicial processes

Judicial assistants and law clerks have legal research and drafting functions in different legal systems. Their involvement has often been instrumental in reducing judicial backlog. In various jurisdictions, judicial assistants prepare bench memoranda to streamline proceedings and to facilitate deliberations. In some jurisdictions, they take part in the deliberations and make a first draft of judgements upon instruction of the judge.[74]

In complex arbitrations, arbitrators sometimes ask arbitral secretaries to perform targeted factual or legal research and to collect their findings in a bench memorandum. If agreed with the parties, and if the secretary is acting upon clear instructions of the arbitrator, that practice is acceptable. However, it is much more controversial whether secretaries may assist arbitrators in making draft awards. Recently, the alleged involvement of arbitral secretaries in the drafting of substantive portions of arbitral awards gave rise to controversy.[75] Distinguished authors advocated against allowing a secretary to draft awards.[76]

How must one situate the preparation of bench memoranda by the ADR institution's staff within this debate? ADR institutions may simply offer the bench memorandum, even if unsolicited by the panelist. The panelist may be unable to interact with or give instructions to the author of the bench memorandum. If a panelist were then to base the decision largely on a bench memorandum prepared by the ADR institution's staff, the effects of such memorandum would be similar to the contentious issue of having arbitral secretaries draft substantive portions of arbitral awards.

74. For a critical review of different judicial assistant models, see Nina HOLVAST, "The Power of the Judicial Assistant/Law Clerk: Looking Behind the Scenes at Courts in the United States, England and Wales, and the Netherlands", 7 International Journal for Court Administration (21 April 2016, no. 2).

75. The controversy started after the Russian Federation filed a writ of summons before the district court in The Hague on 10 November 2014 in the matter that is known as the *Yukos* case. See Writ of Summons of 10 January 2014 of the Russian Federation, available in English at <www.italaw.com/sites/default/files/case-documents/italaw4158_0.pdf>, paras. 486-515.

76. See e.g., Constantine PARTASIDES, "The Fourth Arbitrator? The Role of Secretaries to Tribunals in International Arbitration", 18 Arbitration International (2002, issue 2) <http://arbitration.oxfordjournals.org/content/18/2/147>, p. 1; Gary BORN, *International Commercial Arbitration* (Kluwer 2014) p. 2000.

ii. Defining the roles of judicial assistants, arbitral secretaries and the ADR institution's staff

Judicial assistants and law clerks have not gone through the same selection process and they are not always subject to the same ethical, deontological and disciplinary rules as judges. Yet, their opinions may influence the judge's decision-making. That is not problematic per se. Having judicial assistants perform targeted research and act as a sounding board may actually improve the judge's reasoning. One may expect judges to apply the highest ethical standards and professionalism. They should be able to identify whether research is done properly or whether the proposed legal reasoning is sound. It is essential that the judge remains in control and that the resulting judicial opinion is his or her own. That may be even more important in common law systems, where the judicial opinion may set a precedent and where judges have the ability to make law.

The roles of judicial assistants and law clerks are often formed by practice and may vary not only between jurisdictions, but also depending on the working methods of the judges they serve. Their adjudicative tasks and ethical rules are seldom codified.[77] Nevertheless, their presence in the judicial corps is visible and their adjudicative tasks can be derived from public job descriptions. Legislators can intervene relatively easily if they observe abuse or consider that the role of judicial assistants must be modified.

The precise role of arbitral secretaries risks being less transparent. Arbitral secretaries are often presented to the parties as fulfilling purely administrative tasks. The fees charged by the arbitral secretary in the *Yukos* case suggests that the secretary did more than looking after the smooth administration of the case.[78] That should not be a problem if openly communicated to and agreed with the parties.[79] Parties should be able to challenge a proposed secretary and to object if a secretary outsteps his or her original mandate. Unless the absence of a secretary would frustrate the proceedings, parties should be able to object to the use of secretaries altogether, preferably before the arbitral tribunal is constituted. Otherwise, the parties might feel uncomfortable about objecting to the use of arbitral secretaries when proposed by the tribunal.

The scope of institutional involvement in the conduct of arbitrations and ADR proceedings differs from one institution to another. Similarly, the mandate of staff members within those institutions may vary substantially between institutions. An institution's primary mandate will be to ensure the smooth administration of the proceedings. Many ADR institutions will perform administrative completeness checks and provide assistance in the appointment of panelists. An increasing number of ADR institutions develops detailed training programs for panelists and prospective panelists. However, when, in the context of a dispute, institutions do not limit their involvement to administering the dispute from an organizational point of view and when they participate in the substantive part of the proceedings, transparency is key to increase, or

77. In Belgium, law clerks operate under the authority and the instructions of judges, whom they assist in preparing their legal task (Art. 162(2) Belgian Judicial Code). They must take an oath and are subject to ethical and disciplinary rules (see e.g., Arts. 289, 299*bis*, 412 Belgian Judicial Code).

78. Writ of Summons of 10 January 2014 of the Russian Federation, available in English at <www.italaw.com/sites/default/files/case-documents/italaw4158_0.pdf>, paras. 491-499.

79. To ensure that the use of secretaries is a truly free choice for the parties, it is best that the willingness of an arbitral tribunal to appoint one or more secretaries is disclosed and agreed upon during the arbitrator selection stage.

preserve, the centre's legitimacy. When parties are informed that an institution provides panels with bench memoranda, performs scrutiny of the decisions, or is otherwise involved in substantive parts of the proceedings, they may deliberately choose those institutions. However, that should be communicated openly to the parties. It is also desirable that institutions and panelists follow clear guidelines for creating *casu quo* considering bench memoranda.

iii. Possible impact beyond the context of the dispute?

For many years, arbitration has been commonly understood as lacking a doctrine of precedent.[80] That would mean that arbitrators have a lesser ability to make law than judges have. Arbitral secretaries would then have fewer motives for pushing their policy views than judicial staff. But the belief that arbitration is not precedent-setting must be nuanced, as was cogently argued by Professor Kaufmann-Kohler.[81] In commercial arbitration, there may indeed be no meaningful precedential value; in specific sectors, there is a strong reliance on previous awards. At a lecture in 2006, Professor Kaufmann-Kohler identified strong reliance on precedents in sports arbitration and a progressive emergence of rules in investment arbitration.[82]

Also in domain name dispute resolution under the UDRP, there is a consistent application of the rules and a strong body of case law that is largely followed.[83] With respect to ICANN's accountability mechanisms, there is an expressed desire from ICANN to create consistent jurisprudence and legal precedent.[84] Many IRP panels considered that IRP decisions did not set binding precedent. Nevertheless, some IRP panels have blindly adopted the reasoning made by previous panels.[85] It is still too early to tell how the rule of precedent will develop under ICANN's accountability mechanisms, as relatively few cases have been decided so far, the accountability

80. See, e.g., Richard M. ALDERMAN, "Consumer Arbitration: The Destruction of the Common Law", 2 Journal of American Arbitration (2003, no. 1); U of Houston Law Center No. 2006-A-18. Available at SSRN: <https://ssrn.com/abstract=923462)>; Carrie MENKEL-MEADOW, "Whose Dispute Is It Anyway? A Philosophicla and Democratic Defense of Settlement (In Some Cases)", 83 Geo. L.J.(1995) p. 2663; William M. LANDES and Richard A. POSNER, "Adjudication as a Private Good", University of Chicago Law School, Working Paper No. 263 (July 1978).

81. Gabrielle KAUFMANN- KOHLER, "Arbitral Precedent: Dream, Necessity or Excuse", 23 Arbitration International, LCIA (2007, no. 3) pp. 357-378.

82. Gabrielle KAUFMANN- KOHLER, "Arbitral Precedent: Dream, Necessity or Excuse", 23 Arbitration International, LCIA (2007, no. 3) pp. 357-378.

83. See WIPO Jurisprudential Overview 3.0, Sect. 4.1; See also *F. Hoffmann-La Roche AG v. Relish Enterprises*, 17 December 2007, WIPO Case No. D2007-1629; *Mile, Inc. v. Michael Burg*, 7 February 2011, WIPO Case No. D2010-2011.

84. ICANN Bylaws, as amended on 22 July 2017, Art. 4(3)(a)(vi); The desire for IRP Declarations to have precedential value was first stated in the ICANN Bylaws, as amended on 11 April 2013, Art. IV(3)(21).

85. Flip PETILLION and Jan JANSSEN, *Competing for the Internet: ICANN Gate – An Analysis and Plea for Judicial Review Through Arbitration* (Wolters Kluwer 2017) pp. 287, 309-310; 333-334.

framework seems in a constant flux, and many unaltered rules have not been addressed in sufficient detail so far.[86]

The succinct overview above illustrates that arbitrators and panelists in ADR proceedings in general have the ability to make law in an increasing number of fields, yielding their effects globally. Therefore, the impact of an arbitral secretary pushing his or her agenda could be similar, if not greater, than the impact of a judicial staff member assisting panelists in their adjudicative duties.

iv. Best practices for dealing with bench memoranda

The author of the bench memorandum must be equally as impartial and independent as the arbitrator. If a bench memorandum is provided by an institution without the arbitrator's involvement, the institution should have processes in place to guarantee the author's independence and impartiality. Ideally, the arbitrator and the parties involved are made aware of the background, qualifications and affiliations of the bench memorandum's author.[87]

An appropriate way to consider bench memoranda prepared by staff or arbitral secretaries would be for the arbitrators to perform a complete analysis of the case prior to reading the bench memorandum. The bench memorandum could then either strengthen the arbitrator's opinion or make the arbitrator reflect on, and potentially reconsider, his or her initial assessment. The arbitrator should approach the bench memorandum in a manner similar to his or her consultation of topical expert opinions or legal treatises.

In complex cases with voluminous submissions and evidence, a bench memorandum can help structure the evidential record and facilitate the identification of key documents. However, it is imperative that such a bench memorandum is made under clear and precise instructions of the arbitrators involved. This type of bench memorandum should not be prepared before the arbitrators have gone through the file and been able to identify the issues that require factual research that can be handled more efficiently and cost-effectively by arbitral secretaries.[88] One ought not to forget that the appointment of arbitrators is *intuitu personae*. In no event may an arbitral tribunal delegate its decision-making authority to a third party. An arbitrator cannot rely on a bench memorandum without analyzing the underlying evidence and making his or her own impartial and independent assessment of the case.

---

86. Flip PETILLION and Jan JANSSEN, *Competing for the Internet: ICANN Gate – An Analysis and Plea for Judicial Review Through Arbitration* (Wolters Kluwer 2017) pp. 346-348, 358-360.

87. See International Council for Commercial Arbitration (ICCA), *Young ICCA Guide on Arbitral Secretaries*, The ICCA Reports No. 1, available at <www.arbitration-icca.org>, Commentary to Art. 2(2):

> "It is imperative that the parties are provided with sufficient information to make an informed decision as to the appropriateness of a particular candidate. Requiring the arbitral tribunal to submit the candidate's *curriculum vitae* for review before his or her appointment should address any concerns the parties may otherwise have regarding potential conflicts."

88. See International Council for Commercial Arbitration (ICCA), *Young ICCA Guide on Arbitral Secretaries*, The ICCA Reports No. 1, available at <www.arbitration-icca.org>, Arts. 3(f) and 4(1).

VI. SCRUTINY OF AWARDS

1. *International Chamber of Commerce (ICC)*

a. *Scrutiny of arbitral awards*

Scrutiny of arbitral awards is a distinctive feature of ICC arbitration. No arbitral award is issued without the approval of the ICC Court of Arbitration (the Court).

The Court's scrutiny is a mandatory process from which the parties cannot derogate. Despite the principle of party autonomy in international arbitration, the ICC may refuse to administer proceedings if the parties' requests are at odds with this fundamental and distinctive feature of ICC arbitration. In rare circumstances, the parties may de facto circumvent the scrutiny process by agreeing that an award must not contain reasoning. However, the Court will only occasionally approve unreasoned awards and will assess on a case-by-case basis whether the requirement to give reasons can be dispensed with.[89]

The Court's scrutiny of awards is recognized as reducing the risk of arbitral awards being set aside.[90] To the extent practicable, the Court considers the requirements of mandatory law at the place of arbitration.[91] The scrutiny process involves the assessment of formal, editorial, substantial and legal points.[92] The Court may require changes as to form, but will only recommend changes as to substance. The Court's suggestions do not affect the arbitral tribunal's liberty of decision.[93] In this respect, the Court will not scrutinize the award to see whether the decisions are correct or not.[94] Substantive comments are aimed at ensuring that all legal claims are dealt with or at identifying weaknesses in the reasoning or inconsistencies.[95]

b. *Scrutiny of expert determinations*

The scrutiny process is also applied when the ICC International Centre for ADR (the Centre) administers expert proceedings. As is true for the Court, the Centre may require change as to form, but will only recommend changes as to substance.[96]

Whereas the scrutiny of arbitral awards is a mandatory process, parties to expert proceedings may jointly request that the expert report is issued without the Centre's

89. Gustav Flecke GIAMMARCO, "The ICC Scrutiny Process and Enhanced Enforceability of Arbitral Awards", 24 Journal of Arbitration Studies (1 September 2014, no. 3) p. 57.
90. Jason FRY, Simon GREENBERG, Francesca MAZZA, *The Secretariat's Guide to ICC Arbitration*, ICC Publication No. 729E (2012) p. 328, para. 3-1182; Gustav Flecke GIAMMARCO, "The ICC Scrutiny Process and Enhanced Enforceability of Arbitral Awards", 24 Journal of Arbitration Studies (1 September 2014, no. 3) pp. 47-77.
91. ICC Rules of Arbitration, Appendix II, Art. 6.
92. Gustav Flecke GIAMMARCO, "The ICC Scrutiny Process and Enhanced Enforceability of Arbitral Awards", 24 Journal of Arbitration Studies (1 September 2014, no. 3) p. 62.
93. ICC Rules of Arbitration, Art. 34.
94. Michaël W. BÜHLER, Thomas H. WEBSTER, *Handbook of ICC Arbitration* (Sweet & Maxwell 2014) p. 504.
95. Jason FRY, Simon GREENBERG, Francesca MAZZA, *The Secretariat's Guide to ICC Arbitration*, ICC Publication No. 729E (2012) p. 335; Gustav Flecke GIAMMARCO, "The ICC Scrutiny Process and Enhanced Enforceability of Arbitral Awards", 24 Journal of Arbitration Studies (1 September 2014, no. 3) pp. 68-69.
96. ICC International Centre for ADR, Expert Rules, Art. 9.

scrutiny. The Centre will consider whether the issuance of an unscrutinized report is appropriate under the circumstances of the case.[97]

2. Nominet

Nominet does not check the decisions issued under its dispute resolution policy. It provides for an independent six-member Expert Review Group (ERG) that is concerned with quality control of the decisions.[98] Each fully reasoned draft decision is reviewed by a member of the ERG before it is published. The ERG member reviews the draft decision and provides feedback to the expert. However, the experts will remain responsible for the decision and will not be required to make any changes to the draft decision that they do not wish to make.

The aim of the ERG's review is to make sure that decisions are consistent with the applicable policy and previous decisions, which strengthens legal predictability.[99]

3. Appraisal

The scrutiny of awards and administrative decisions undoubtedly contributes to the quality of the decision-making. In the first place, the review by experienced members of the arbitration community or an independent group of experts benefits the parties, as the resulting decisions are likely to be more authoritative for having passed the scrutiny, and therefore easier to enforce. But the experience of those who scrutinize the decisions also benefits the arbitrators and experts who drafted the decision. The fresh pair of eyes and the reviewer's outsider perspective will help the panelist understand whether his or her reasoning is sufficiently clear and unambiguous. Comments and suggestions by the reviewers will also help the panelist to make better decisions in the future, taking into account previous observations. In that way, one may expect there to be fewer recurring issues and that the scrutiny is further fine-tuned.

The ICC's scrutiny of expert reports and the review performed at the request of Nominet shows that scrutiny processes need not necessarily be limited to more complex arbitrations. They may also be useful in more narrow or targeted forms of dispute resolution.

However, the purpose of the review seems different under the ICC rules compared to Nominet's DRS Policy. Scrutiny under the latter rules aims at ensuring a consistent application of a fixed set of applicable rules. In contrast, the ICC does not assess consistency between different arbitral awards or expert reports. The cases administered by the ICC are more diverse and are mostly confidential in nature. The purpose of the proceedings is different and calls for a different kind of scrutiny. Arbitral awards are scrutinized mainly to avoid the risk of their being set aside. The ICC scrutinizes expert reports to ensure that the expert's message is conveyed clearly. The authors of these reports may be experts in their field, but less accustomed to the drafting of reasoned

97. ICC International Centre for ADR, Expert Rules, Art. 9(2).
98. Art. 1, Nominet DRS Policy
99. See "Expert Review Group" on Nominet's website, <www.nominet.uk/wp-content/uploads/2015/08/Expert-Review-Group.pdf>.

opinions in the context of resolving a dispute. Nevertheless, it is not to be excluded that specific sectors will call for ADR mechanisms that are tailored to their needs and ask for consistency checks within defined categories of decisions in order to obtain more predictable ADR outcomes.

VII. ADVANTAGES AND DISADVANTAGES OF APPEAL MECHANISMS IN ADR

The possibility of an appeal mechanism in commercial arbitration has always felt unnatural to us. If the purpose of the appeal is simply to redo the proceedings and give the parties another shot, than there is little merit in organizing an appeal. Why would the first panel of arbitrators be less well positioned to render an award than the appeals panel? One would expect that the parties, who (in most cases) have agreed upon the procedure for appointing a panel, submitted the case to the best possible panel for deciding their case. If the aim is to obtain, in an expedited fashion, an enforceable award which finally resolves the dispute, parties are not served by allowing the award to be appealed.

The situation would be different if the power of the parties in the arbitrators' selection process was curtailed. In many jurisdictions, limiting the power of one of the parties to the benefit of another party will be considered unlawful for being contrary to the parties' right to equal treatment.[100] But a party's autonomy in the appointment procedure may also be limited without shifting the balance between parties. Disputes may be referred to standing panels or appointments may be made by third parties and institutions. In these circumstances, appeal mechanisms could be beneficial. This is even more the case if awards are capable of setting legal precedent and influence future decisions. In such situations, the litigants and potential future litigants may be served by an appeal mechanism, where precedent-shaping awards can be reviewed by an *en banc* standing panel or by specialist arbitrators.

Appeal mechanisms exist, inter alia, in sports arbitration with the Court of Arbitration for Sport[101] and in administrative proceedings related to country-specific domain names.[102] In country-specific domain name litigation, these appeal mechanisms have certainly contributed to a more coherent body of law. Only a small fraction of the decisions is appealed, but the appeal mechanism allows that the most controversial cases are given extra scrutiny, usually by the most established authorities in the field.

100. See, e.g., France: Art. 1510, Code of Civil Procedure; French *Cour de Cassation*, 7 January 1992, Rev. Arb., 1992, p. 470; Belgian Arbitration Law: Art. 1699 Belgian Judicial Code; Switzerland: Art. 11 International Arbitration Convention; UNCITRAL Model Law on International Commercial Arbitration (1985), with amendments as adopted in 2006, Art. 18; see also Ricardo UGARTE and Thomas BEVILACQUA, "Ensuring Party Equality in the Process of Designating Arbitrators in Multiparty Arbitration: An Update on the Governing Provisions", 27 Journal of International Arbitration (2010, Issue 1) pp. 9-49.

101. Code of Sports-related Arbitration, in force as from 1 January 2017, Sect. S20.

102. See, e.g., Nominet's DRS Policy, Sect. 20; Cepani, Rules for Domain Name Dispute Resolution, 1 January 2018, Art. 18.

Appeal mechanisms are less common in commercial arbitrations, but they are offered by some institutions.[103] As long as there is no precedent rule in commercial arbitration and when the party autonomy in selecting the panel is not curtailed, we see no added value in organizing appeal procedures. Depending on the seat that is chosen, there may be a possibility to submit questions of law to judicial review by the courts.[104] Organizing appeals within the arbitral proceedings would only add another layer to the dispute, increasing both time and expense of the proceedings.

In conclusion, when parties can autonomously decide upon the selection of an arbitral tribunal, we see no value in appeal mechanisms. If, on the other hand, standing panels are organized in specific sectors and there is a move towards *stare decisis* in a subset of commercial arbitration, there are legitimate reasons for organizing appeals to have controversial cases reviewed by a panel of experts. Otherwise, the possibility of setting aside awards and of raising defences in enforcement proceedings should offer sufficient protection against defective awards.

VIII. PUBLICATION OF DECISIONS AND CASE LAW OVERVIEWS

The benefit of publishing case decisions is obvious. Third parties discover trends in case law. It helps them to assess the chances of success in their own case. Arguments discussed in decisions may help when drafting a new claim or a response. The publication enhances both legitimate expectations and legal certainty.

Case law analysis and overviews add to the utility of the publication. Many jurisdictions have a long tradition of these. Readers attach importance to them when they are prepared by a recognized learned and distinct author. Some institutions have gone a step further and prepared their own case law overviews and enhanced the accessibility of decisions by linking them to a searchable interface. Below is an overview.

1. *International Chamber of Commerce (ICC)*

The ICC makes available a digital library for payment of a fee. The library contains key awards, procedural decisions, doctrine and articles. The library is a useful tool for the practitioner to acquire more insight in specific ADR mechanisms and to understand how recurring issues have been dealt with in previous cases.

2. *World Intellectual Property Organization's (WIPO) Jurisprudential Overview*

Apart from the expert determinations released in the framework of the ICANN third round of new gTLD applications, WIPO publishes all UDRP panel decisions on its website, together with a regularly updated list of all pending UDRP cases. The Center also makes available a Legal Index covering all WIPO UDRP panel decisions. The index is keyword-searchable on topics covered in WIPO panel decisions. WIPO also provides

103. See JAMS Optional Arbitration Appeal Procedure, June 2003, <www.jamsadr.com/files/Uploads/Documents/JAMS-Rules/JAMS_Optional_Appeal_Procedures-2003.pdf>.
104. See, e.g., Arbitration Act 1996 of England, Sect. 69.

a search tool that allows for a search of cases by domain name, by name of the complainant and by name of the respondent. Full text search is also available.

WIPO prepared a jurisprudential overview of the UDRP panel decisions. It published the third version in 2017. The original and second editions of WIPO's Overview continue to be accessible on WIPO's website for reference. As of early 2018, WIPO has processed 40,000 UDRP-based cases decided by nearly 500 experts covering some 65 nationalities and 21 languages and involving parties from over 175 countries.

Under the UDRP, decision-making authority rests exclusively with the appointed external panels, based on the facts and circumstances of each case. While the UDRP does not operate on a strict doctrine of binding precedent, it is important for the overall credibility of the UDRP system that filing parties can reasonably anticipate the result of their case. WIPO panels strive for consistency with prior decisions, often noting the existence of similar facts and circumstances or identifying distinguishing factors. In so doing, WIPO panels seek to ensure that the UDRP operates in a fair and predictable manner for all stakeholders while also retaining sufficient flexibility to address evolving Internet and domain name practices.

With this collective aim, WIPO's Overview summarizes consensus panel views on a range of common and important substantive and procedural issues. Following a review of thousands of WIPO panel decisions, the third edition includes express references to almost 1,000 representative decisions from over 265 WIPO panelists. The number of issues covered in WIPO's Overview has significantly increased over the course of more than fifteen years to reflect a range of incremental DNS and UDRP case evolutions.

While the overall purpose of the WIPO Jurisprudential Overview is to improve the predictability of decisions, differences of opinion may still exist on some specific issues and in certain outlier cases, all the more so where panelists and parties come from a multitude of jurisdictions. Furthermore, neither the WIPO Jurisprudential Overview nor prior UDRP decisions are strictly binding on panelists, who are expected to consider the particular facts and circumstances of each individual proceeding in a manner they consider fair. At the same time, panel findings tend to fall within the views summarized in this WIPO Jurisprudential Overview. Finally, the WIPO Jurisprudential Overview cannot serve as a substitution for each party's obligation to argue and establish their particular case under the UDRP, and it remains the responsibility of each party to make its own independent assessment of prior decisions relevant to its case.

The consensus views laid out in this WIPO Jurisprudential Overview have been welcomed by UDRP panellists, inter alia, at WIPO's panelists meetings convened in Geneva through 2016. The contents reflect the meetings' constructive dialogue, as well as substantial contribution and informal review from a number of the most experienced WIPO panelists.

3. *Nominet*

Nominet has so far prepared three Dispute Resolution Service – Experts' Overviews. The last version was released in December 2016. The purpose of these overviews has remained the same: to assist all participants or would-be participants in disputes under the DRS Policy by explaining commonly raised issues and how experts, the members of

Nominet's panel of independent adjudicators, have dealt with those issues in past decisions. It also draws attention to areas where experts' views differ.

Nominet strongly recommends participants in a dispute under the DRS Policy to review the sections of the Overview relevant to their case, as well as the extensive range of other explanatory material that Nominet publishes on its website.

Previous versions of the Overview have been frequently cited in expert decisions. Nominet has received positive feedback from parties and practitioners, who value it as a useful resource.

The third version includes additional material following the decisions and the expert meetings which have occurred since the first and second version.

While there is no system of precedent under the DRS Policy, for the DRS Policy to be effective there must be a measure of consistency in the decisions. The panel of experts does its best in that regard, although there are a few areas where differing views prevail.

If anyone involved in a dispute under the DRS Policy proposes to rely upon the rationale of any previous DRS decision, the more recent decisions (particularly at appeal level) are more likely to represent current thinking.

4. *Czech Arbitration Court (CAC)*

CAC Requires panelists to categorize their decision in accordance with pre-defined criteria. CAC publishes a regularly updated list of all pending UDRP cases. It also publishes all UDRP panel decisions. The categorization of decisions facilitates searching for relevant decisions.

5. *FORUM*

Panelists are invited to categorize their decision on a voluntary basis and FORUM publishes a searchable database of cases. Unlike the WIPO database which is searchable on the basis of keywords, FORUM users must enter appropriate information in specific fields to obtain results.

6. *Outlook*

As a growing number of ADR decisions and arbitral awards get published, an increasing number of decisions refer to past determinations. Panelists are guided by the solutions advanced by their peers and one can observe panelists promoting adjudicatory consistency in specific sub-domains. When parties start adapting their behaviour as a result of past decisions, this may result in legitimate expectations as well as *opinio juris*, the belief that one's actions are carried out as a legal obligation. Case overviews may be the testimony of the formation of a coherent set of norms and customary practices. In specific sub-domains, the paradigm of ADR as a form of private and *ad hoc* dispute resolution seems to have shifted towards a more public and normative form of resolving disputes.

How will the world of international commercial arbitration respond to these developments? Will a modern-day version of the lex mercatoria emerge beyond the domain of cyberspace, where self-regulation gets an increasingly prominent place? Do today's global customers of ADR favour tailored dispute resolution mechanisms and a substantive international framework of commercial, antitrust, maritime, construction, and contract law?

IX. CONCLUSION: THE FUTURE OF ARBITRATION

In this article, we have identified a number of trends and processes in the dispute resolution rules and practices of the ICDR, ICC, WIPO and other alternative dispute resolution institutions. Some of these processes and developments can prove useful in international commercial arbitration generally. We think of the use of rosters of arbitrators with specific expertise and that favour single-member panels, of increased transparency, and of case law overviews.

We mainly see a specialization in dispute resolution approaches: specific procedures are developed to address specific issues, creating efficiencies that may have gone astray in modern-day arbitrations. At the same time, we notice encroaching judicialization of modern-day arbitration. It is often perceived as a threat.[105] In our view, this evolution is mainly due to parties and counsel, who are unfamiliar with the pragmatism that has been characterizing arbitration, importing aggressive litigation techniques and guerrilla tactics into the arbitration proceedings. The judicialization of arbitration is a logical consequence and may even be a necessary defence to ensure arbitration's survival. It remains important to discern public policy concerns that could threaten the legitimacy of arbitral proceedings. If one is forced to choose between more efficient proceedings and an enforceable award, the choice is quickly made.

International commerce requires increased efficiencies. For international commerce to succeed in its quest for more efficient dispute resolution, two prerequisites should be met in our view.

First, international commercial arbitration should embrace other forms of dispute resolution by getting a deep understanding of new methods of dispute resolution and by allowing these methods to narrow down the dispute before it is brought to arbitration.

Private initiatives for more efficient dispute resolution tailored to sector-specific needs have resulted in the administration of justice becoming more fragmented and specialized. Exemplifying this evolution are specialists in their field who jointly develop new standards in multi-disciplinary teams and who become increasingly involved in enforcing those standards through self-regulation. This is especially apparent in fields of new technologies and cyberspace.

In response to this trend, more international business lawyers and in-house counsel should familiarize themselves with these self-regulatory initiatives and introduce these into dispute resolution formats. When negotiating deals, more attention should go to the rise of possible disputes and the means of tackling the dispute early on in the conflict. Specific problems may call for different solutions. Do parties really need to submit their dispute to arbitration or can they resolve their dispute by submitting a targeted question

105. See Queen Mary University of London, School of International Arbitration, PwC, *2013 International Arbitration Survey – Corporate Choices in International Arbitration, Industry Perspectives*, <www.arbitration.qmul.ac.uk/docs/123282.pdf>, pp. 5, 21-22.

to an agreed-upon expert? If the source of the dispute can be identified early on in the process and narrowed down to its core, a more tailored approach is feasible. Financial, accounting, legal, commercial, administrative, technical or other issues can be evaluated in function of sector-specific practices by calling upon appropriately qualified experts or targeted dispute resolution policies before escalating issues to a more litigious setting. The disputes that cannot be resolved accordingly may funnel through to arbitration. By reserving arbitration for complex and multi-layered disputes, arbitration is capable of building bridges between these different practices.

The second prerequisite stems from the expectation that arbitrations, under their present format, are unlikely to become less judicial. The Model Law on International Commercial Arbitration of the United Nations Commission on International Trade Law (UNCITRAL) has been broadly adopted and an increasing number of jurisdictions require arbitral awards to be reasoned. To realize efficiencies in reason-giving, there should be increased transparency about recurring issues. Arbitration as a form of *ad hoc* dispute resolution may become the exception. Arbitration customers should consider whether they want to acknowledge the more judicial nature of arbitration and distil an international normative framework out of this evolution. In the long run, that might make commercial arbitration proceedings more predictable, and as a consequence, less judicially complex. And who knows, one day we might drop the "A" in "ADR" here.[106]

106. <www.arbitration-icca.org>.

The Moving Face of Technology

Part I:
Technology as Facilitation

Technology as Facilitation: Transcript of the Session*

TABLE OF CONTENTS — PAGE

I. INTRODUCTION: EXCERPT FROM TRANSCRIPT OF ICCA YEARBOOK (XCIII) 2068

As is customary, we devote this portion of the Yearbook to reflect on ICCA Congresses past. 2068 marks the fiftieth anniversary of the 2018 ICCA Congress in Sydney (at the time part of the nation-state of Australia, back when ICCA Congresses were held in a single location rather than virtually or holographically). The topic of the Congress, fittingly enough for this retrospective, was *Evolution and Adaptation: The Future of International Arbitration*.

A review of the program shows that there were many interesting sessions touching on what at the time was perceived as arbitration's looming crisis of legitimacy and how to address it, as international dispute resolution passed from what today we mark as its golden age into the more uncertain period of the 2020s and 2030s.

One session, however, that struck us particularly apt for review from our vantage point fifty years later was titled *Technology as Facilitation*. In that session, the panelists explored technology emerging at that time that they believed might affect and improve the conduct of arbitral proceedings.

The extant video of the conference shows Hugh Carlson,[1] Gabrielle Nater-Bass,[2] Rashda Rana SC,[3] and moderator Paul Cohen[4] demonstrating what today seem like extraordinarily rudimentary versions of augmented reality, instant translation, and machine learning systems. As with so much footage from the time, viewers will note that the panelists look considerably older than they do today. Such was the era before regenerative therapy.

The panelists of course knew that their prognostications for the benefits of technology in arbitration would not be entirely accurate. Taking as their *caveat* Niels Bohr's famous

---

* The General Editors would like to thank Justin R. Rassi, Associate in the International Dispute Resolution Group and Public International Law Group, Debevoise & Plimpton, LLC, for his assistance in preparing the Transcript. Thanks also to Steve Fleming of Opus 2 for his participation and considerable technical assistance.

1. Director of Practice and Senior Associate, Three Crowns LLP; adjunct professor, Georgetown Law School; co-director, International Arbitration Workshop, Harvard Law School
2. Partner, Homburger, Zurich; Co-head, ICCA-ASIL Task Force on Damages.
3. Commercial and construction infrastructure lawyer; Past-President and Member of the Advisory Board of ArbitralWomen; Past-President. Australian Branch of the Chartered Institute of Arbitrators.
4. Barrister and US-trained lawyer practicing at 4-5 Gray's Inn Square Chambers and in San Francisco; Editor-in-Chief, Journal of Technology in International Arbitration; Co-chair, International Task Force of the Silicon Valley Arbitration and Mediation Center.

quip "Predictions are hard to make – especially about the future," the panelists attempted to extrapolate what arbitration might look like five or ten years hence, based on the technology developing at that time. They could not then have known about or predicted the scope of innovations such as the Comprehensive Brain-Computer Interface, the Instanet [Internet that instantly and precisely answers any specific question you have], or the transformational power of quantum computing.

Given the technology then on the horizon, the panelists focused on how augmented reality, instant translation, and machine learning might affect the arbitrations of the day. Those of us old enough to remember augmented reality will recall that it was an early attempt to superimpose computer-generated images onto the real world, through lenses such as glasses, goggles, or (in the case of the ICCA Congress), old-fashioned smartphones.

The panelists explained that augmented reality technology could be helpful in resolving aspects of construction disputes (recall that, prior to the widespread use of AI architecture and 3D printing for most infrastructure, construction disputes were relatively commonplace.) For example, augmented reality could effectively show images of what a particular construction design looked like, how it might have gone wrong, and where there were any structural flaws. These would be especially useful in lieu of site visits where the site was inconvenient, unsafe, or largely destroyed.

To illustrate the uses of augmented reality in this context, the panelists devised a mock arbitration proceeding around the destruction of the Death Star, the fictional weapon in the twentieth century science fiction classic *Star Wars*. Rashda Rana cross-examined Darth Vader (Steve Fleming of Opus 2), appearing via video conference. The audience had been instructed at the beginning of the session on how to download an augmented reality app on their smartphones. At various points during the cross-examination, the audience was invited to train their smartphones onto the main screen, where they could see images of the Death Star in motion.

Even by the standards of the day, this was a relatively primitive demonstration. Headsets such as the Microsoft HoloLens delivered a more intense and sophisticated augmented reality experience; but at a cost of US$ 3,000 each (pre e-currency), this was not an effective option for an audience of several hundred people.

The panel then turned to a demonstration of instant translation technology. Here too some viewers of the video today might be forgiven for sniggering at the state of the art. "Instant translation" was neither instant nor entirely accurate.

Once again using the ubiquitous smartphones of the era, the panelists used the Microsoft Translation app, one of several then on the market. The translation functions of the time needed the user to select the language in which they were speaking and the language into which they wished their speech to be translated. Written translation accompanied the spoken words.

The results were mixed. The translation app appeared to have trouble with Gabrielle Nater-Bass's Swiss-accented German, although it translated her French and Italian adequately. Members from the polyglot audience were invited to speak in various languages. The app tended to do better with European languages than with others – perhaps because of their greater structural similarity to English.

It did not seem as though instant translation software would make human translators redundant any time soon – and indeed the neural implants that facilitated the so-called

Babel Fish function (named after the quasi-telepathic creatures from the twentieth century science fiction *Hitchhiker's Guide to the Galaxy*) would not become commonplace until the late 2030s. Nonetheless, the panelists noted that the speed with which the translation apps were improving was exponential. By the mid-2020s, they predicted, the accuracy rates of these programs would approach human levels.

The panel explained that the translation apps were a form of what at the time was called machine learning – the process now very familiar to us whereby an algorithm would absorb immense amounts of data and use it to develop the ability to mimic or perform particular functions that until then had been the exclusive province of human minds. Thus, the audience heard computer-generated music styled after Bach, based on inputs from all of the composer's works.

Turning to the potential applications of machine learning for the arbitrations of the day, the panel devised yet another mock arbitration. This one centered on the travails of the fictional Mr. Spock, an alien from the television show and later movie series *Star Trek* (often confused today with the above-mentioned, equally science-fictional *Star Wars*.) Steve Fleming of Opus 2 once again played the witness, via video conference. His firm had downloaded all the scripts from *Star Trek* episodes and movies into a machine learning database. Hugh Carlson cross-examined the witness. His questions were scripted, but the responses from the database based on those questions were unknown. Thus, Hugh would ask the database (addressed as "Computer," consistent with *Star Trek* lore) to find instances anywhere in the scripts in which Spock had made a particular kind of statement. The database would comb through the scripts, find what it believed to be language matching Hugh's query, and then show video from the series corresponding to the script excerpt.

According to the panelists, the database worked well, although it did show a couple of excerpts different from the ones that the panelists had expected. This demonstrated the surprising flexibility of machine learning, even in its early stages fifty years ago.

After a very entertaining mock examination of Mr. Spock, it was time to leave the galaxy far away and come back to planet earth. As augmented reality technology was still not widely available back in the day, the panelists then discussed "equality of arms" – or concerns regarding due process – sharing with the audience certain "tips" if they were to make use of such technology in their arbitration proceedings.

The session concluded with a round of questions from the audience, touching on all the topics that the panel had broached. The video of the session is available in the ICCA archives; a Real-Feel™ holographic augmentation can be found on the Instanet at Insta.ICCA2018.TechasFacilitation/RealFeel.

For those of you who are old-fashioned, a transcript of the session's proceedings can be found below.

II. TRANSCRIPT OF THE ICCA SYDNEY 2018 CONGRESS SESSION "TECHNOLOGY AS FACILITATION"

Cohen: Hello everyone, please take your seats. Welcome. This is going to be a rather different, very different panel to the other ones, for better or worse. We are talking this afternoon about technology in arbitration and there are a series of panels this afternoon.

This one is technology as facilitation, which is to say, some of the ways in which technology can make our lives better or easier in arbitration. We will see if that's the case or not as we go through.

The operating principle here is something that a science fiction writer named William Gibson once wrote which was: the future is already here, it's just not evenly distributed. What he meant by that is that there are various technologies which are in use somewhere in the world today, but are too unwieldy, not fit for purpose or too expensive to be used more ubiquitously. So we are going to test that proposition and take a bunch of technologies that are in use today so we will see how and whether they might work in the arbitration context.

None of this would be possible without our friends at Opus Two. I have to give them great thanks. Opus Two, if you don't know, is a software and services business at the cutting edge of legal tech. How many of you have used LiveNote in a hearing? Pretty much all of you. LiveNote was invented by Graham Smith Bernal, who is the creator of Opus Two, as well. So the flagship Opus Two device, Opus Two Magnum, has all sorts of wonderful bells and whistles, is cloud-enabled and you can basically have real-time transcription services used in hearings; LiveNote, of course; and all sorts of other things. It can be entirely paperless, which I know is not a development that's universally welcome but probably ought to be.

It's all very twenty-first century and the Chief Technology Officer of Opus Two, Steve Fleming, will be up on the screen to your right later on in the program. And also there are some representatives in Booth 8. Taryn Auchecorne and Katie Beth Jones, who are in the back, will be able to show you some of these demos afterwards.

I should also thank Daniel Mason of Mason Videos. It depends on if the AR works whether I thank him or kill him. Full disclosure, he is my brother-in-law.

The state of the art in this stuff – augmented reality – that Daniel helped with, is the Microsoft HoloLens and it's a wonderful device. You just stick it on, there's a headset, and you can see all these fantastic things happening. But it costs US$ 3,000 a pop. We asked them if they would be willing to lend us any. They were not willing to lend us one, let alone several dozen. So good news for those who like to play around with their phones as some you are no doubt doing now, we need your phones. We are going to use the phones to do some of this technology.

Before I do that, let me introduce your panel to you. I'm not going to bother going into long introductions, we are much better looking in real life, as you can tell. They are probably well known to you in any event.

We are going to show you three different types of technologies: (i) augmented reality [AR], (ii) instant translation and (iii) real-time analysis. I apologize: some of you will have to move around to get a better view during parts of this presentation. We didn't design the set-up here with two different projection screens. The folks here have been terrific helping us and in accommodating us. Thanks for all the help, which has been essential.

Let's talk about augmented reality. Those of you who have not yet done this probably have not downloaded this app. If you take the time now to start downloading it, that would be helpful if you're interested in seeing this demo. Go to the app store if you have an iPhone, or if you have an Android phone, which is pretty much anything which is not an iPhone, go to Google Play. If you have a Blackberry .... 2005 called. It wants it back.

You download HP reveal and you should get different kinds of apps, it will depend whether it's an app store or Google play, but it should be fairly easy to download.

So, what is augmented reality? You've probably heard of virtual reality where you stick stuff over your head and you're in a different world like in that movie *Ready Player One*. Augmented reality is slightly different. You superimpose images on top of the world as you see it, as will be familiar to anyone who has played Pokemon Go, where you see fake Pokemon in the real world, or to anyone who has played with Snapchat and can add filters.

We'll start with the virtual reality demonstration in a moment. For those of you who have not got there yet, scroll through introductory steps and go to "log in", not "sign up", and put in the user name "Icca" and password "Icca". Hopefully you will see the seven little white dots scrolling around. That will be sign that you are in the app ready to go.

Can I have a show of hands of who is there already? Now let me tell you before we go any further, and again I apologize for the set-up, it's probably better if you're further back because you won't get a good look of the screen. Hopefully you'll get the best view of the screen a few rows back. And you'll be able to see the AR.

What's AR good for? Well it's useful for construction arbitration. You have a bunch of schematics and diagrams and sites and site visits and things like that where it would be very helpful or certainly easier to be able to visualize and see what's going on in an augmented reality set-up. You would put on glasses like this and all of a sudden here's the bridge, here's the building or what have you.

We have designed for you an augmented reality hypothetical. It involves a construction dispute and it is called *Galactic Empire v. Deathstar Manufacturers Inc.* A long time ago, in a galaxy far, far away, the claimant, the Empire, is an autocratic regime engaged in interstellar conquest and domination. The respondent, Deathstar Manufacturers [DSM], is a maker of giant weapons of mass destruction. The Empire hired DSM to build a weapon and the weapon was destroyed by a group of rebels.

The Empire asserts that DSM's design of the Deathstar was either deliberately or negligently flawed, thus permitting its destruction. The respondent denies any such design flaws. So let's imagine now we've had the star witness for the Empire, the claimant, show up in direct examination and they are about to show up in cross-examination.

And I need to introduce the other "half" of technology we are doing here. We've talked about the three. The "half" is video conferencing. You've seen video conferencing and it's nothing new to you because this is one of the technologies that has become sufficiently cheap and ubiquitous that you can use at no cost. If the witness is not actually in another galaxy, he is rumored to be in New York. Counsel, if you're ready we will ask the witness to come to the video. The witness will be on the right.

> **STAR WARS MUSIC**
>
> *Counsel (Rana)*: Thank you Mr. Arbitrator. Thank you, witness. What was your role on the Deathstar, Mr. Vader?
> *Witness (Fleming)*: Lord Vader.
> *Counsel:* Sorry, Lord Vader.

Witness: I was sent by the Emperor himself to supervise the destruction of the rebels.
Counsel: And I take it that things didn't quite go to plan.
Witness: One of the rebels is strong in the Force.
Counsel: Can we stick to the facts Mr. Vader. What was the cause of the Deathstar's destruction, in your opinion?
Witness: I have given you my answer.
Counsel: Perhaps I can rephrase the question. What was the physical, rather than the metaphysical, cause of the Deathstar's destruction?
Witness: The rebels dropped a torpedo into the thermal exhaust port causing a chain reaction.
Counsel: It's the Empire's position that this thermal exhaust port was improperly exposed permitting the kind of destructive effect that occurred with the rebel attack. So, in your opinion, all the rebels had to do was swan up to the Deathstar, drop a bomb into the thermal exhaust port, and Bob's yer uncle.
Witness: This is exactly what they did.
Counsel: Well, it was a little bit more complicated than that, wasn't it? The rebels had to breach all the Deathstar's defenses, fly through innumerable crenellations and laser towers and then launch a device into a space only 2 meters wide while flying approximately 10,000 kilometers per hour.
Witness: If you use the Force, it is not so difficult.
Counsel: So you keep saying, Lord Vader. But really this was a one-in-a-million shot. No reasonable building company could have foreseen that this kind of catastrophic event would occur.
Witness: They could and they did. The Deathstar was fatally flawed, deliberately so.
Counsel: Well, we'll let the Tribunal be the judge of that. Obviously we can't take them on a site visit because the Deathstar was completely destroyed. Although I understand that the Empire has commissioned a new one?
Witness: That is correct.
Counsel: So, my client's work could not have been all that shoddy, could it? In any event, I want to take you through a simulation of the events leading up to the Deathstar's destruction so we can show the Tribunal what we think occurred. Can I ask our technical support team to pull up a model of the Deathstar, please?

Cohen: Okay, now folks, on these slides if you have the app and you're pointing your phones with any luck the Deathstar should appear. The little dots should coalesce into one dot and, presto, you have a Deathstar.

Counsel: Mr. Vader, is this a realistic depiction of the Deathstar?
Witness: It is.
Counsel: Can we look at the thermal exhaust port, please.

Cohen: Okay, there should be another image now, hopefully of the thermal exhaust port. Anyone? No one. Okay

Counsel: The Tribunal is moving forward. Lord Vader, how big was the Deathstar?
Witness: I'm not exactly sure, but well over 100 kilometers across, the size of a moon.
Counsel: And again, the thermal exhaust port was 2 meters wide?
Witness: Correct.
Counsel: All right. Now, let's look at the Deathstar's defenses. Technical assistance, could you please zoom out again.

Cohen: I have no idea what this actually shows. If it shows something we will be happy.

Counsel: Lord Vader, can you guide us through the Deathstar's defenses, please.
Witness: In the outer perimeter, there are a number of laser cannons. Similar weapons can be found inside the canyons. And of course, the Deathstar has a large number of single person spacecraft known as TIE fighters that can be scrambled in defense.
Counsel: And where was the thermal exhaust port in relation to all those defenses?
Witness: Beyond that, at the end of a long ravine in the outer hull.
Counsel: So let me see, if we can see what it must have taken to destroy the Deathstar. Simulation please.

Cohen: Okay, next slide. Anything? Getting some yesses.

Counsel: So first you need a small one-person spacecraft, is that right?
Witness: Several of them could attack at once.
Counsel: Okay, several could attack. In any event, one of those spacecraft needs to dodge the incoming fire from the laser cannons, needs to avoid all the TIE fighters, dip into the ravine, then dodge all the crenellations in the ravine, which is not much wider than the spacecraft itself, then avoid the laser cannons inside the ravine, avoid the TIE fighters in hot pursuit, and fire a bomb into a smaller space than the arm span of a wookie.
Witness: It's actually a proton torpedo, not a bomb.
Counsel: Is that similar to a photon torpedo in Star Trek?
Witness: I have no idea what you're talking about.
Counsel: Never mind. The point, Lord Vader, that I'm making is that this is all a highly improbably series of events, is it not? When lightning strikes a tree we don't blame it for having negligently grown in the wrong place.
Witness: The emperor can make lightning strike where he wishes.
Counsel: Good for him. Now, will you agree with me, Lord Vader, that if a manufacturer were setting out to make a shoddy device prone to self-destruction or sabotage, he would probably use a somewhat simpler design flaw? Specifically, one liable to be less lethal to any would-be saboteur.
Witness: I withdraw my case on behalf of the Empire.
Counsel: I beg your pardon.
Witness: I have heard your words and see your wiles. You are clearly also from the Dark Side. Join me, and we will conquer the galaxy. You may never again have

fear of the IBA Guidelines or will need to seek third-party funding, and all your arbitrators will be partial.
Counsel: Sounds good to me.

Cohen: Alright, thank you very much, Lord Vader. You are excused. [Applause] Ok, we'll leave that slide up for a minute but I think we're done for the moment with the AR, so thank you. You can all sit down if you want to.

So Gabrielle, do you have some thoughts about the possibilities and pitfalls of AR in international arbitration?

Nater-Bass: Yeah. After that very entertaining cross-examination of Lord Vader, it's unfortunately time to leave the galaxy and come back to planet earth. While you just saw how augmented reality can really enhance arbitration proceedings, I would like you now to focus with me on two aspects that are absolutely key for the arbitration practice. And that is due process and effectiveness.

How can we ensure that augmented reality technologies as you just saw them do not compromise due process and effectiveness? In this regard, I would like to share with you an experience I just had a couple of weeks ago in an arbitration in which I was an arbitrator. It was a complex construction case, not as complex as we have just seen, but the case actually concerned defects and alleged design defects in a granulation process facility. Just the Friday before a Monday the hearing was supposed to start, claimant announced that it wanted to use augmented reality, by way of a special software where they would actually take the tribunal – and they planned to use that for the opening pleadings but also for a cross- and direct examination – through the facility and would show them the effects and design problems they have identified.

While one can easily see that that in fact would have been really interesting, it maybe would have facilitated also the tribunal to understand the technology. The tribunal was all of a sudden, of course, confronted and not unexpectedly with questions of due process as respondent heavily disputed the use of such augmented reality, not having had a chance to look at the software, to test it, to see whether it actually reflects reality where one can see in this facility.

There are some key takeaways I would like to share with you today. As I said, there is no doubt that augmented reality can increase effectiveness and it can also probably save time and costs, such as travel costs. But in order to make sure that due process and fair treatment is not jeopardized, you always have to ask yourself whether the contemplated use of said technology does not in any way jeopardize the party's right to be heard, the party's right to equal treatment and the party's right to present his or her own case. As you all are aware, if there is a "yes" to any of these questions, your award is at risk, not only of being challenged but probably of not being recognized and enforced.

That's why there are some do's and don'ts or practical tips if you use augmented reality that I would like to share with you. First of all, address the potential use of the technology as early as possible in the proceedings and reach an agreement thereon. While ideally, you would start discussing augmented reality use at the outset of an arbitration, it is not very realistic. Most likely, you will start thinking of such technology when you start approaching the evidentiary hearing phase. So the latest stage may be the organizational conference. And there, you should not only discuss and reach agreement what type of technology to use, but also how you plan to use it. In the example I was just explaining to you, we ended up at the end using it because there was no time to just allow it for the opening and presentation, but only after the opposing party and its expert had time over the weekend to use and test the technology, but not for cross-examination. So you should prevent any surprises.

And this actually brings me to the next practical tip: ensure that the other party and its tactical experts, as well as the tribunal, had the possibility to get, access, tests, and get familiar with the technology, as well.

And, please, that's my next tip, use appropriate, accessible and – for both parties – affordable technology. Make sure that the technology is sophisticated enough so that it is credible enough, but at the same time, it should be easy. It should be possible to test and get familiar with this technology within a fairly short period of time so that the tribunal, as well as opposing party and expert can use it. If the technology requires a license, make sure that that license also allows you to let the tribunal and opposing party use the software.

With that, I come to tip number four and I think that in preparing these sessions we understood how important that tip is. Test all technology you intend to use before D-day, as you will remember there is Murphy's principle and it's true for that, as well. If it can go wrong, it will go wrong at that adverse moment.

And my last tip, please make sure that whatever you try or intend to use is in compliance with the applicable law and the procedural rules, the arbitration rules and the seat of the arbitration. These may have certain restrictions which, for example, force a hearing to take place in person. Thank you very much and now I think the show can go on.

Cohen: The show goes on. Thank you very much, Gabrielle. I was remiss, in all my excitement about AR, in not telling you about how this video conferencing works and how easy it is. This happens to be a video conference system called Zoom which I use all the time and it's basically free. I have the upgraded version for $15 US dollars a month and all I need to do is on my iPad or phone or computer I start the Zoom video and I invite a participant. The participant receives an email and she clicks on the link in the email and she is in the video conference, presto. So that's what we're using right now with Darth Vader who happened to have been in New York and I believe the other witnesses are also in New York.

Let's move on. Let's talk about instant translation. I personally am constantly in awe of this community, where there are so many people who are able to handle unbelievably complex disputes in a language that is not necessarily their first language.

But what could happen if everyone could speak in their native language and make themselves heard and understood? The technology, believe it or not, is almost there. It's not quite there, as you'll see. But it's made amazing strides over the past couple of years and we're going to demo it in a moment, again with our polyglot panel's help, specifically, Gabrielle. She fulfills the polyglot quota.

But before we do that, we just wanted to run the real-time transcription service on this, through another video that we affectionately like to call, Science Fiction Icons and Their Friends Talk Past Each Other. So, it's a very short and, frankly, not terribly coherent tale about the search for truth, dry cleaning, breach of contract and arbitration.

Here we go. So the video will be on your, at your left. The transcription will be on your right.

[Short video with clips from science-fiction films and TV shows follows]
[Laughter]

Cohen: All right; hopefully you can see both the video and the transcription. Now, can I ask Opus Two's CTO Steve Fleming to join? I know he's on the other line. We have the translation set up, is that right, Steve?

Fleming: That's right, Paul. All ready.

Cohen: Okay, so, I guess we'll get going. Gabrielle, if you'd like to get started. Let's see what happens. Fingers crossed.

Nater-Bass: I will now interrogate this system in different languages using my iPhone app that I have downloaded and I hope you bear with me with a small demonstration. I get started. Hello! Hello! [German speaking]
[English translation]
Nater-Bass: The app we just see costs nothing.
[German speaking]
[English Translation]
Nater-Bass: What is the cost of the license?
[German Translation]

Fleming: Thanks, Gabrielle. So, as you switch languages, I think I'll also sort of just address the question. I think it's worth stating we were using Microsoft Translate which is a consumer application really. The technology itself is not really mature enough for prime-time usage. But it definitely serves as a useful illustration of how far this technology has advanced. Voice recognition is, as you know, advancing at a very quick pace – near 95 percent accuracy with Siri, Alexa, Google, etc. At present Opus Two, you know we only really seek to provide the services of skilled simultaneous or consecutive interpreters, I should say, for arbitration hearings worldwide.

Nater-Bass: Good. I will continue.
Let's test French now. [French speaking]
[Translation] How much is it to use the license?

Fleming: Well, that's a tricky question to answer. I think you know in theory, if this service were available, there would be some degree of cost attached to it, for all this technology, as Paul will explain when we look at the analytics piece. There's a significant investment really needed in developing, training and perfecting it, particularly when it comes to legal models of equal parlance, etc. I think the long-term benefit for this type of translation technology would be that it would effectively circumvent the need for human professionals at a hearing. But I must stress this is very much theoretical and you know we would still use highly skilled humans for the foreseeable future.

Nater-Bass: Thank you very much. Let's go on and test Italian once. [Italian speaking] [Translation] Do you have customers in the legal field? In the case of affirmative reply also just in the field of international arbitration law?

Fleming: Yes, again I think the question there is tied to whether this type of technology is ultimately useful in arbitration. And you know, clearly it is not at this time, but we are very much sort of moving towards a world where a tourist, if you can imagine these days, the next generation of tourists amongst us will have no concept of what it is to be lost or not to be able to communicate in a foreign country by use of smart phones and apps like these. The complexities around legal and speech recognition, etc. within that sphere are very difficult and involve a lot of machine learning which we'll come to talk about shortly.

Nater-Bass: Thank you very much for this informative answer. Let's continue. You can see you can switch really quite fast from one language to the next one. [French speaking] Assume that the software is being used by a court, more technical devices are needed to put it all in place.

Fleming: Yes, in theory one can imagine this actually working with a very small device whether that be a smart phone or something similar or certainly interfacing through the softwear that you're using within the hearing. You know, ultimately it's the type of thing that we would integrate into our platform to run an electronic arbitration. As I said, the technology isn't there yet but Opus recently fitted out a high-tech court room project in Abu Dhabi, and it's actually built with this kind of technology in mind, behind the scenes at least for sort of some degree of speech recognition, etc.

Nater-Bass: Thanks also for this. I have one other interesting question before I open this to the audience for questions.
Nater-Bass: [German speaking]
[Translation] Is it possible to program specific terms? If so, how is this done?

Fleming: Yes, I think for this app, deep learning is a really key part of artificial intelligence. As I said, Paul's going to look at this in layman's terms. But in an ideal world actually these models will continue to train themselves. If you look at the world of what's becoming known as ambient computing, which is household devices like an Amazon Alexa, etc, those are going to be a major driver behind effecting speech technology and recognizing human speech. I think it's predicted about 75 percent of households in the US are expected to have one of these devices by 2020. So, all of that will go towards perfecting the models, etc., etc. You know, what's key for a technology business in the legal space is to utilize where possible your data set and expertise to help train models in speech and in particular, types of disputes, instruction, etc. and give it sort of language packs, if you will. So, all of this stuff is terribly interesting and exciting, love to get into it in greater detail but there's probably not enough time for all of that right now.

Cohen: All right, thank you very much. We have time for one volunteer who speaks a language that is not German, Italian or French. Australian does not count. Anyone? I see somebody there. What's your language?

Audience Member: Arabic.

Cohen: Arabic? Let's just see. Hold on. Okay, we're just going to hit the Arabic function if it's there and then you can try out a question and we'll see how it works, and only you will know whether it's accurate.

Nater-Bass: Ready?

Cohen: Okay. Do you want to come up here, sir? Can we have this? Thank you. Congratulations. Get a prize. Okay. You need the phone, though. Speak in the microphone here and when you're ready, sit down and then let's see. Ready?

Audience Member: Should I ask a question?

Cohen: Yeah, yeah any question. Say anything you like. Say whatever. Ready?

Audience Member: [Arabic speaking]

Nater-Bass: You have to hold it while you say the language.

Audience Member: Ok. [Arabic speaking]

Nater-Bass: Hold the microphone and then slowly speak in.

Audience Member: [Arabic speaking]

Cohen: Well, it doesn't like you, I'm sorry. Oh, well. Thank you for doing that anyway. All right, Rashda is going to try one. Which language are you trying, Rashda? Let us know.

Rana: I will just say something in Urdu. It's a language I can speak, yes.

Cohen: Let's see if they have Urdu. They should. Just waiting for it, Steve.

Fleming: No problem.

Cohen: Technical difficulties.

Nater-Bass: Sorry, it's giving up the ghost.

Cohen: Okay, now it's working.

Nater-Bass: I just have to restart it if you give me one second.

Cohen: Okay. We will do that demo, but let's move on until the demo is ready. That was instant translation. Before we get back to it let's talk about the third demo, which is real time analytics. What the heck is real-time analytics? Well, without putting too fine a point on it, it's a form of artificial intelligence. And AI appears to be sort of the flavor of the month in so many sectors, but as a legal community we don't know an enormous amount about it, which is hardly surprising. We're not computer scientists, we're lawyers. Is it working? Still not working. Okay, so at the risk of straying very far afield from my fields of strength, which are mostly Premier League soccer and Star Trek episodes, I am going to try to give you a little primer on what AI is.

So first of all, AI – first slide of what AI is, Steve. It's a form of computer programming obviously. Not all computer programs are AI. A lot of them are, these days. If you go to an ATM or something like that, the cash machine, the programs that are involved in spitting out the cash and figuring out your bank account are probably not AI programs. The really excellent demo web app that was shown at the Damages Breakfast yesterday, I suspect – from what little I've seen of it – is not an AI program. Nonetheless, it is a very effective program.

But AI is increasingly becoming sort of, if not dominant, at least very prominent in all forms of computer programming. I have gone to the next slide but I should probably explain again where AI came from. The name is about sixty-some years old and it really dates to an article that Alan Turing, the mathematician and code breaker wrote in the early 1950s, sort of half tongue in cheek, saying that the computer will have reached the level of human intelligence when you can have a remote conversation with a human on one hand and a computer on the other hand and not be able to functionally tell the difference between them. Now, AI went through a number of different iterations. In the 1980s, it was very popular to do something called "expert systems" whereby you interrogated experts at what they were good at so you would take very prominent arbitrators and say: how did you decide the case? How does this work? What did you do? Take us through this. And then you would try to translate all of that into a logic-based computer program. If you're interested, it was usually Lisp or Prolog. Well, that didn't work. Well, it didn't work very well.

So the modern form for about the past fifteen or so years of AI that's really come to dominate AI is something called "machine learning". Okay, so you've probably heard this term quite a lot. I'll go to the next slide. Machine learning is a form, again vastly oversimplifying it, but it's a form of programming whereby you give a computer inputs and the computer program learns from those inputs and improves as it does it. So if you can see the slides, there are a number of examples of different kinds of machine learning algorithms. There's ones that you have for Netflix for example, you know, if you like this movie you'll love that movie; to examine whether people are good credit risks or bad credit risks. Not the most popular, possibly not the most effective of all of them. The spam filter on your email is a machine-learning programming, probably a Bayesian algorithm that says, is this spam, is this not spam? Sometimes it gets it right. Sometimes you get an email about Viagra and it can't be helped.

And the form of machine learning that is coming in turn to dominate machine learning is something called a "neural network." A neural network is an attempt to mimic the way the brain works. So we have a bunch of neurons and synapses and they fire and we get inputs from those and we build them up into incredibly complex layers that allow us to see, hear, talk, arbitrate, do whatever it is that we're doing. They do a bunch of things. Facial recognition systems are usually neural network apps, game-playing artificial intelligence like the stuff that you can play Go or win Jeopardy with, self-driving cars. Computer-generated art and music – the sound doesn't appear to be working on the slide, which is a shame. Let's see if it works. In any event, what would have been playing, if you could hear it, was a rather nice little computer-generated – okay, a rather tinny but otherwise maybe nice computer-generated – tune which was done simply by giving the computer program all of Bach and saying, here's all of Bach, now do something that sounds like it, okay?

How does that work? Without getting too technical about it, there are lots and lots of inputs that you get into the computer and some of them get it right and some of them get it wrong and the computer favors the inputs that get it right through something called back-propagation. So something says: this is a human being in front of the car, please stop. The input that gets that right gets weighted better than the input that drives thru the human being in the simulation – it obviously wouldn't happen in real life.

As you do that, you build up, as your brain does, a series of dos and don'ts and this works and this doesn't and hence with more data it becomes more sophisticated. So how does that actually work? Well it is like the old joke, how do you get to Carnegie Hall? I guess we can adapt it now. How do you get to the Sydney Opera House, when you ask someone in the street, how do you get to the Sydney Opera House? The answer: practice, practice, practice, as the joke goes.

So data, big data, is how you're meant to practice. We just speed the vast amounts of data and they get better and better, hopefully, at identifying stuff and doing what they do: the same way that we do, when you think about it. We are born, we have no data, we are pretty useless and then we grow up and slowly we absorb things and learn how to walk and so on and so forth. So that is the theory. We are not going to talk about robots and robot masters taking over and all that stuff, but we will in the next panel – a much different panel.[5] We are just going to focus on the positive uses or potentially positive uses of data.

So now go to the next slide. We have yet another demonstration for you with a remote witness and this one is: *Spock v. United Federation of Planets*. It is going to employ the real-time analytics that we are talking about and I will explain how it works.

Why would we care about this kind of technology, real-time analytics, the practical application? Well I don't know about you, but there are a number of times in a case where I have thought: I know the witness said something, somewhere, sometime about something; I can't remember the exact words but it had to do with some theme or other. And you have no idea where it is. Similarly with a document: there is something in the zillions of documents; you know you saw it but you can't quite put your finger on it. You can't do a specific word search because you can't remember the exact word, you just get a sense of what it was about.

Well, this is the kind of thing that real-time analytics will really excel at and we will see, we will test it out. We have designed this cross-examination of a witness to elicit

5. See "Technology as Disruption", this volume, pp. 837-868.

specific kinds of evidence, but the exciting bit is we are not exactly sure whether it will elicit the specific evidence that we think it will elicit. Hopefully it will elicit either that evidence or something similar to it so we will find out again.

Here's the hypothetical, in case you are wondering. The claimant, Mr. Spock, is a former officer in Starfleet. He alleges that the respondent passed him over for promotion because of his unusual appearance. The respondent – this is important – respondent counterclaims that the claimant is a confirmed mutineer who once tried to hijack a Starship.

Now the data that we are using here, obviously because this is not a real case, is we have downloaded every *Star Trek* episode – and this is my field of expertise, I am happy to say. We downloaded every single *Star Trek* episode, a few of the movies. We are going to use that to comb through some of the questions, to comb through the evidence and see what happens. Let's see how it works.

Can I ask the witness now to come for cross-examination if he is there? On the screen on your left, your right, sorry. Hello, witness. Are you ready for the witness?

> *Counsel (Carlson)*: Good afternoon, Mr. Spock. Mr. Spock, can you hear me?
> *Witness (Fleming)*: I can hear you.
> *Counsel*: Perfect. Mr. Spock, you claim that the federation denied you a promotion to captain on the basis of your non-human appearance. Is that right?
> *Witness*: Affirmative.
> *Counsel*: You are of course aware, Mr. Spock, that the Federation is an interplanetary, multicultural organization in which one's color, shape and size ceased to be relevant centuries ago.
> *Witness*: Indeed; my being passed over was a triumph of human emotion over the precepts of federation law.
> *Counsel*: But isn't it a fact, Mr. Spock, that you were once court-martialed for having mutinied and hijacked the *Enterprise*?
> *Witness*: That information is classified and inadmissible
> *Counsel*: Well, Mr. Spock, that information is essential to the Federation's defense in this case. The Tribunal has ruled that it can come in.
> *Witness*: Most illogical.
> *Counsel*: Mr. Spock, were you not arrested for conspiring to take over the Starship *Enterprise* from the Captain?
> *Witness*: I decline to answer under Starfleet Regulation 5.4.
> *Counsel*: Be that as it may, Mr. Spock. We have the logs of the *Enterprise* for the entirety of the five-year mission. I now propose to have the Tribunal review those logs. Computer, please pull the transcripts from the *Enterprise* logs.

Cohen: This is all, if you haven't figured it out, on the screen on your right.

> *Counsel*: Computer, please identify language corresponding to the prior question?
> [Excerpt from *Star Trek* episode]
> *Counsel*: Mr. Spock, do you deny that these logs reflect that you submitted yourself to court martial on a charge of mutiny?

Witness: I see no purpose in responding to questions premised on the possibility that a computer is flawed.
Counsel: Indeed, Mr. Spock. So let us take this further. Mr. Spock, on this mission did you order a communication blackout?
Witness: Same answer.
Counsel: Then this communication blackout was ordered under false Starfleet mission instructions to take command of the *Enterprise* from Captain Kirk, wasn't it?
Witness: I fail to see the purpose of this line of questioning.
Counsel: It's something we call cross-examination, Mr. Spock. Allow me to try again. Did you order a communication blackout under the guise of false Starfleet mission instructions to take command of the *Enterprise* from Captain Kirk for what you claim were medical reasons and did you then instruct the crew to trust your orders?
Witness: I believe the relevant response is objection: compound question.
[Laughter]
Counsel: Enough of this. Computer: identify relevant logs corresponding to my previous question.
[Excerpt from *Star Trek* episode]
Counsel: So in fact, Mr. Spock, you had no authorization from Captain Kirk to take the *Enterprise* toward Talos IV?
Witness: There were extenuating circumstances.
Counsel: Be that as it may, Mr. Spock. The record clearly reflects that you admitted your guilt. Well, Mr. Spock?
Witness: I do not believe you have asked a question, sir.
Counsel: You submitted yourself for court martial because you knew you had taken the ship to Talos IV without the Captain's authorization and you lied about it, didn't you?
Witness: Vulcans are incapable of lying.
Counsel: Is that so?
Witness: Indeed, you will find evidence of the fact in the ship's logs.
Counsel: Well there were a lot of episodes – I mean missions. Where exactly in the logs do you contend that there is evidence that Vulcans don't lie?
Witness: I refer to the so-called *Enterprise* Incident, in which the ship crossed the Neutral Zone into Romulan space on a spy mission.
Counsel: You were a spy?
Witness: Affirmative.
Counsel: All right. Computer: identify log entries corresponding to when Spock, and the Enterprise, raided Romulan space for a Federation spy mission.
[Excerpt from *Star Trek* episode]
Counsel: Hmm, Mr. Spock, you clearly lied when you told the *Enterprise* crew that you were taking command with Captain Kirk's authorization. How do you explain that?
Witness: Frustrating. The only logical explanation is that the writers were quite inconsistent in their conception of Vulcan attributes.
Counsel: Do you have anything else to say, Mr. Spock?

> *Witness*: Yes. May I have a mask like your previous witness's? It will serve to cover my ears.
> [Laughter]

Cohen: Thank you very much, Captain Carlson. Thank you, Mr. Spock.

As you saw, we weren't quite sure what would necessarily come up with those. We actually had different clips in here than the ones we thought would come, but there were related ones that came up. So the technology does work, and it works in sort of interesting ways.

Rashda, tell us in general terms about what you think of these kinds of AI programs for facilitating arbitration.

Rana: I am actually interested in what all of you have to say about some of the technology that we've shown you, but I want to just deal with two particular points about technology and the dispute resolution community. We are not atypical in the sense that I see a great deal of resistance to the use of technology.

I don't know if Justice Lindgren is in this room. Is he? Justice Lindgren was a federal court judge, Federal Court of Australia judge, and I actually did the very first entirely electronic court case with him. How long ago do you think that might be? It was entirely electronic, meant to have no paper at all.

Cohen: Last month.

Rana: Just guess. How long ago do you think it might have been?

Carlson: Last year.

Rana: Last year, any other guesses?

Audience Member: Ten years?

Rana: 1997.

Cohen: Wow.

Rana: Entirely electronic. We all had computer screens, we had a technical person bringing up all the documents as we set them. They were all bar-coded so we had to read a bar code and the document came up. When we handed in submissions, it was a case that went for, I don't know, ten months or something. We gave him forty-seven folders of paper for our submissions because nobody could get the hang of the electronic stuff and I must say since 1997 – so what's that, twenty-one years ago – the uptake on technology has been really slow. And I am afraid it is actually us, it is the lawyers; it is not the technology because the pace of advancement of technology has been extremely fast and even between now, what we've shown you and if we were to repeat this next year you will see that it has advanced quite a great deal.

So I just wonder what the resistance is, and I know that some of the résistance seems to be the potential for self-interest, in fact the potential possibility that we are going to lose our jobs as either lawyers – or perhaps the even bigger fear arbitrators – and whether AI in particular can actually replace what people are talking, the soft areas of decision-making, the ethical areas of decision making and whatever is the human ingredient that goes into decision-making.

I don't see it as a problem. I hope I am not robotic in my own mentality but I don't see it as a problem. So, I would be quite interested to see where the resistance actually is and if, quite a lot of you probably follow OGEMID and you may have seen the recent discussion on AI but it is actually a very disturbing kind of resistance to taking up where we have got to. I will give three examples:

(1) One is the Care Vault, which I always use because there are robots that are nurses and they are absolutely brilliant. They make fabulous decisions, correct decisions much more quickly and actually nurturing in a way that a nurse might be.
(2) The other one is self-driving cars. I mean they are a no-brainer and we will all have one soon. It will be a similar resistance to when email and iPhones came up. It will all be forgotten in a couple of years.
(3) The other one is, I am just trying to tackle the resistance in terms of the soft stuff. Caring, emotional stuff that seems to come in when people talk about AI, and that is the use of pets, AI pets, to help people who are housebound, whether they are old or disabled or sick, as replacement of real pets and they seem to serve the same purpose. So when old, sick, disabled people or housebound people have been tested, the responses that they have shown in terms of progress and health are the same as if they had a real dog. Perhaps we are beginning to turn in terms of our minds to what is a useful way of using AI. I spoke at lunchtime with some people about the international citizen of Saudi Arabia, the robot Sophia. She is a bit creepy, but she is probably a form of what we should expect as your next tribunal.

Cohen: You are looking to quash the resistance. Hugh, your thoughts?

Carlson: I thought that I might to attempt to bridge the gap between the topic of this panel, which is titled Technology as Facilitation, and the topic of the next panel, which is Technology as Disruption. And I thought I might do so by identifying that these two topics are very much a question of timing: the further we move away from the status quo, I think – and perhaps we disagree here a little bit – the greater the likelihood the technologies may disrupt rather than facilitate. What would be of interest to us is what will happen as we move away from facilitation and towards disruption; that is, if we think perhaps simply of facilitation as a sunny day and disruption as a blackened night sky, what do we make of that twilight? So if I may be permitted for a moment to gaze into the early dusk glow to offer a few observations, they would be these:

First, international arbitration will prove resilient to direct disruption by AI. What do I mean by disruption? In the context of law, I offer the following crude definition: widespread replacement of junior associates by Artificial Intelligence For those of you in the audience with an Amazon Echo think: "Alexa, prepare for me three to four paragraphs explaining why discounted cash flow is an inappropriate valuation methodology in this case and send me highlighted PDFs of the authorities upon which you rely." If and when AI should be able to accomplish reliably tasks like these, disruption will have arrived.

So why will international arbitration be resilient to disruption as I just have clearly defined? A couple of words on complexity and data: with regard to complexity: in international arbitration, little of what junior associates do, as many people in this room know, is the form of gruntwork that can easily be automated. There are of course exceptions to this – document production and reviews, perhaps – but by and large the type of work that they are doing is generally distinguishable than that of their compatriots in different practice groups.

With regard to data, I think this benefits from Paul's helpful summary. As a general principle, Artificial Intelligence is only as intelligent as its data is copious and useful. Because international arbitration has a far smaller data set than exists in many other practices, in part due to a lack of transparency, what AI is capable of doing in international arbitration is quite limited, at least for the time being. Unless the move to transparency more meaningfully informs our processes, AI will lag in international arbitration as compared against other practices, including litigation.

The second observation I have for you is that, just because international arbitration is likely to prove comparatively resilient to disruption doesn't mean that we are out of the woods. This is because litigation is going to become more competitive, potentially more competitive, due to large, rapidly-growing data sets as well the benefit of much more AI investment in litigation than in arbitration. Litigation in many jurisdictions will become increasingly automated, it will become correspondingly less expensive, and it will become quicker. In addition, the predictability of outcomes will continue to increase.

These advantages, and they will continue to grow, I submit to you are going to make it more palatable to clients weighing litigation against arbitration.

The third and final observation is to encourage the people in this room to keep an eye on AI outside of the legal space. Significant advancements in Artificial Intelligence across various industries will cause lasting change in the international arbitration market place, to our clients well before AI directly disrupts our own niche industry. We can't reliably predict how it is going to happen but we can say with near certainty that this transformation will be widespread and profound.

I have heard the expression that AI is the new electricity. Seemingly overnight new industries will emerge and others will fade away. To paraphrase Robert Depito, the co-founder of the US Financial Services firm Blackrock, Apple was not in the music industry, Google was not in the mobile phone industry and Amazon was not in the groceries industry – until they were. So too will technology companies soon enter and disrupt other industries, likely including at least several of those we consider to be staples in the international arbitration market place. As a community we will want to follow closely these developments and adapt rapidly as the market's place procedural needs change and to the title of this conference evolves. Thanks.

Cohen: Thank you very much Rashda. Thank you, Hugh.

To my immense shock and delight, we actually have a few minutes left over. So we are going to let you out early. Kidding. We are going to take questions.

Can I ask Steve to come to the Zoom? Let's have a look at you. It will be more fun that way. Thanks, Steve. So, questions for any of the panel or comments. Let's leave out "AI is going to take us all over and be our robot masters." Save that for the next panel that is coming right after the break.

Audience Member: Thank you, I have a question. My name is Alice from the VIAC [Vienna International Arbitral Centre]. I have a question with respect to the translation issue and with respect to confidentiality. I am just wondering what about the live translation, where is it done and who is translating and is that secure. You know we are talking about confidential proceedings and then you know who could possibly access and I think some of the concerns that I would have when using the service.

Cohen: Before I let Steve answer that, let me just observe that we are talking about cybersecurity as well,[6] right after we talk about AI. So it is a very timely question. Thank you. Steve.

Fleming: That is a great question, actually. So obviously I have seen in court hearings and various other disputes, even some arbitrations, the use of tools like Skype for video conferencing and I think that by and large that is going out encrypted over the internet. However, for a tool such as translation which is obviously working through the data and producing in effect a transcript of what is holding the recording of the audio. You would not want to be utilizing any kind of cloud service, because of the security and sensitivity around that data, for any of the technologies that we have been developing in that space. But we have localized versions of the software running. So in essence, it would be running purely on our systems and it wouldn't be subject to any sort of any public cloud service. The data could be kept in accordance with the policies agreed at the start of the case.

Audience Member: Fantastic.

Audience Member: Vismay Shroff, I am an attorney from Bombay, India. I had a question about language translation options. We saw German, French and Italian translated to English. What options do you have for English to be translated into other languages? I suppose this may be of interest to everybody here as well.

Fleming: Should I take that one?

Cohen: Yes, go ahead Steve.

Fleming: Very quickly, yes that particular application that we used actually works – works from any language to any language that it supports. So if you are on the receiving end, as Gabrielle was using on her phone in French or in whatever language she was logged in at the time, if I were to speak back to her in English it would actually play back that in the native language selected. So it does do it both ways and again it is a great

6. See "Technology as Disruption", this volume, pp. 837-868.

application if you are a tourist. There are a number of these devices that you can actually get now, some of which are completely offline, which you speak into and it will send things back and vice-versa. That technology does exist.

Cohen: Thank you for your question.
[Translation into Hindi]

Audience Member: Damn it, it is showing it on there, it is now saying it.

Audience Member: A question for Steve, please: one of the messages that you are going to hear in the next panel is that it is going to be primordial for the tribunal to be able to understand how algorithms or any form of technology works on the side, obviously, of counsel but also very importantly the arbitrators. My question to you: how prepared are you, as the technical side of this, to put it to naughty lawyers who are very backwards in technical terms in order to be able to understand how your technology comes to the decisions that they do? How they work, opening the black box for us essentially. How prepared are you, how ready are you to put this information to us?

Fleming: Right, that is a good question. I think, if I heard the question correctly, from the technologies we looked at today the third technology which was the text analytic piece, something we are actually launching in BETA form quite shortly. We will be launching it in the summer. We are just in the middle right now of testing it and productizing it and our philosophy really is the technology business in the legal space. It has never been to blind anyone with science. LiveNote is a technology that has significant benefits with a very minimal learning curve.

So, that's a great example of sitting in front of the piece of technology and immediately getting the benefit without having to do anything. What we are looking at when it comes to AI, I think (we almost prefer the term IA, which is Intelligence Automation or sort of automated intelligence), what we are looking to serve users are useful and relevant extracts that are semantically similar to the piece of text that a witness has given in their evidence. The mock-up you saw today is really a working prototype. We are actually working with a lot of our user groups and users and really anybody who wants to come and have a look at it. We will have it available to folks to play with. We wouldn't introduce a technology that effectively doesn't work or could not be relied upon. What we are really interested in doing is making it as accurate as possible, as useful as possible sort of provides an easy benefit.

Cohen: Time for two more questions: the gentlemen here and then one other.

Audience Member: Michael Patrick Joyce. As an arbitrator how do I tell the difference between augmented reality and distorted reality? In other words, it is a question of control. How do I know that I am not being hoodwinked? How do I know that I am not being blinded by science?

Cohen: That is a good question. One of the slides I insisted on deleting was one my brother-in-law stuck in with me turning into Sean Connery, it is his version of me in a distorted-augmented sense.

Fleming: Maybe I can answer your question also by referring back to what I have just explained. I think in order to ensure due process, and also for the tribunal, you have to check there is no other way to make this augmented reality technology in advance. Actually, they have to be shown and explained to the tribunal. They have to be shown and explained to those technical experts, and used only if everybody is in agreement. This is not just reflecting something which is not reality; it can be used. In other words, you have to test it, get familiar with it. You have to get comfortable with it and that needs time and preparation. I think that is key.

Cohen: Time for one more question. If there is anyone. Fine if there isn't. Is that Kathleen?

Audience Member: I am not sure that this question is better for this panel or next. So if it is better for the next, Sophie will say it and take it. I was interested in what Hugh has to say about how AI is likely to affect court litigation versus arbitration, availability of data etc. I wonder what your position is with respect to how AI made an impact on existing inequality of arms between parties and how the availability of technology will either increase or decrease what we see already as being the disparate capabilities of parties with more resources, and it seems to be that AI has the possibility of actually narrowing that gap if it is available to all or greatly increasing it if it is not. From my perspective you can see a world in which this technology was available relatively widely or one in which it is not available at all, which will boil down to cost and data. I don't know what your thoughts are about that.

Carlson: I think it is a very good question and it is one that is really being grappled with it at the moment. I am involved in a project with Harvard Law School, its International Development Society, in which access to justice through Artificial Intelligence is the subject. I think that could be extrapolated and applied in the international arbitration context.

My inclination is that it will do more to narrow the gap as opposed to widen it for the reason you have described. I think the technology will not prove prohibitively expensive in due course. It may take some time to arrive to that, but once we do I think parties will have available to them tools that will permit them to generate comprehensive briefs at a fraction of the cost that is currently available with, for example, international counsel. Now that is not to suggest that counsel won't play a role in that process, but it will be a comparatively reduced role permitting parties that perhaps presently don't have access to the system to indeed gain that and have a voice that they may not know.

Rana: I would just like to add that I think Hugh is right and I think, Kathleen, you anticipated it in terms of the narrowing of the inequality of inequity of arms. An online dispute resolution system has just gone live in England and one of the bases behind it was in fact to allow litigants in person to actually go through the process in quite a mechanical way which is a little bit harder when you have to fill in forms and come to court and speak to an opponent, perhaps a lawyer opponent as well as a judge, so the idea is that fairly simple mechanical claims can now be deal with online. And I am not just talking about filing on line, it is actually the whole dispute that gets dealt with and decided online by the computer. Certainly we are beginning to see that in other jurisdictions as well, small cases but I just want to reiterate what I said: the pace of advancement is enormous, so you can start with little cases but we will very quickly be looking at big cases where quite a lot of the dispute will be dealt with online – so not just with a robot but just online, and again algorithms are developing very quickly to enable that sort of thing to happen.

In the nineteenth century when the phone was developed, it was actually regarded with a great deal of suspicion. It was devil's work. Now we have moved on from that, and I think Hugh mentioned where we are at is like the new electricity and it as well was regarded with great suspicion. The notion that you could switch a switch and you had light and you were actually interfering with nature – not just devil's work but interfering with nature. This is the resistance I would like you all to get over. Your life will be much better for it.

Cohen: On that note, it remains to me just to give enormous thanks to Steve. It is 1:00 in the morning for him. So, thank you for staying up and being Darth Vader and being Mr. Spock. Thank you for everything. Thank you to the AV people, John over there, and of course to our fabulous panel. Thank you for coming.
[Applause]

Part II:
Technology as Disruption

Cybersecurity and Cyber Insurance

Alana Maurushat[*]

TABLE OF CONTENTS PAGE

I. INTRODUCTION

Cybersecurity focuses on protecting computers, networks, programs and data from unintended or unauthorized access, change or destruction.[1] More broadly speaking, cybersecurity involves protecting systems and processes from malice, error, or mischance. This, in turn, requires cross-disciplinary expertise. Cybersecurity is about so much more than computers and systems engineering. It involves cryptography, computer security, economics, risk management, applied psychology, software engineering and the law. While this paper contains insights applicable to organizations located anywhere in the world, it focuses on Australia and the United States.

More than 94 percent of Australian businesses have access to the internet, this is increasing year on year, thus making cybersecurity more important than ever.[2] A major concern amongst businesses at the moment is the challenge that cyber risks present.[3] Some companies are reporting that there are over twenty serious cyberattacks every day.[4] There are many recent high-profile incidents where businesses' information systems have been compromised, leading to sensitive data being accessed. Cybersecurity is important, as no organization – no matter how skilled – is immune from the risks and associated costs of dealing with cyberthreats.

Although this article will not extensively cover all the current risks, it will aim to cover some risks in the current threat landscape, the costs associated with data breaches, and the use of cyber insurance as a method of mitigating cyber incidents. The paper relies on previous published research by the author and co-authored with Ciaran

---

* Professor of Cybersecurity and Behaviour at Western Sydney University; Member of the Board of Directors and Special Cyber Advisor for the cybercrime investigations firm IFW Global.

1. University of Maryland University College, *Cyber Security Primer* <www.umuc.edu/cybersecurity/about/cybersecurity-basics.cfm>.
2. Australian Bureau of Statistics, *Business Use of Information Technology, 2013*-14 (16 July 2015) <www.abs.gov.au/ausstats/abs@.nsf/mf/8129.0>.
3. Price Waterhouse Coopers, *CSFI/PwC Insurance Banana Skins Australia 2015*.
4. *Ibid*.

Finnane,[5] as well as the recent and only empirical study of cyber insurance policies done by Sasha Romanovsky, Lillian Ablon, Andreas Kuehn, and Therese Jones from RAND.org.[6]

II. SECURITY THREAT AND RISK LANDSCAPE

Organizations face a number of cyberthreats and risks when an organization's security is breached. Table 1 below lists some of these threats which may include:

Table 1. Cybersecurity Threats

Term	Definition
Denial of service attacks[7]	An attack that prevents or impairs the authorized use of information system resources or services
Unauthorized access to data and networks for corporate espionage, activism, fraud, and extortion/blackmail[8]	Any access that violates the stated security policy
Discovery of vulnerability[9]	A characteristic or specific weakness that renders an organization or asset (such as information or an information system) open to exploitation by a given threat or susceptible to a given hazard
Interference with data and networks (Intrusion)[10]	An unauthorized act of bypassing the security mechanisms of a network or information system
Data breaches[11]	The unauthorized movement or disclosure of sensitive

5. Ciaran FINNANE and Alana MAURUSHAT, "Managing Cybersecurity Risks through Cyber Insurance", Precedent (2016, issue 32).
6. Sasha ROMANOSKY, Lillian ABLON, Andreas KUEHN, and Therese JONES, "Content Analysis of Cyber Insurance Policies: How Do Carriers Price Cyber Risk", 2017 Workshop on the Economics of Information Security.
7. Department of Homeland Security, A Glossary of Common Cybersecurity Terminology, National Initiative for Cybersecurity Careers and Studies <https://niccs.us-cert.gov/glossary>.
8. *Ibid.*
9. *Ibid.*
10. *Ibid.*

Term	Definition
	information to a party, usually outside the organization, that is not authorized to have or see the information
Ransomware[12]	Malicious software (malware) that locks your keyboard or computer to prevent you from accessing your data until you pay a ransom (usually through cryptocurrencies such as Bitcoin)
Credential Harvesting Malware / Spyware[13]	Software that is designed to gather data from a computer or other device and forward it to a third party without the consent or knowledge of the user. This often includes collecting confidential data such as passwords, PINs, credit card numbers, monitoring keyword strokes, tracking browser habits and harvesting email addresses
Social Engineering[14]	The art of gaining access to buildings, systems or data by exploiting human psychology, rather than by breaking in or using technical hacking techniques

An organization hit with a cybersecurity incident may react in a number of ways. Mitigation of damages is the key priority for most organzations when under threat. The most important component in mitigation against damage is protecting assets not already compromised such as data that has not yet been stolen.[15] This could require the stopping of the denial of service attack as soon as possible through various means – technical measures, paying a bribe, isolating data, making immediate data backups, or launching a counter denial of service attack. Damage control may also mean ensuring that there is no media attention to the matter. Mitigating against damage is one facet in the aftermath of a cyber incident.

Of these threats data breach is one of the most prevalent. High profile data breaches locally and abroad highlight the high costs and damage caused by breaches of personal information covered under the Australian Privacy Act. The Office of Australian Information Commission (OAIC) recommends that all entities have a data breach

11. *Ibid.*
12. Kim ZETTER, "What Is Ransomware? A Guide to the Global Cyberattack's Scary Method", Wired (14 May 2017) <https://www.acsc.gov.au/publications/ACSC_Threat_ Report_ 2017.pdf>.
13. Kaspersky Lab, "What is Spyware?" <www.kaspersky.com.au/resource-center/threats/ spyware>.
14. George HULME and Joan GOODCHILD, "What is Social Engineering? How Criminals Take Advantage of Human Behavior", CSO (3 August 2017) <www.csoonline.com/article/2124681/ social-engineering/what-is-social-engineering.html>.
15. Alana MAURUSHAT, "Hack Counter-Attack: Its Uses and the Need for Legislation", 6 E-Finance & Payments: Law & Policy Issue 12 (December 2012).

response plan. OAIC recommend a four-step plan: (1) contain the breach and do a preliminary assessment; (2) evaluate the risk associated with the breach; (3) notification; and (4) prevent future breaches. Having a data breach plan is one method of mitigating against damages and costs. Having a data breach response plan may also reduce cyber insurance premiums. There are similar data breach notification laws throughout many parts of the world including the United States, Europe and China.[16]

While implementing a data breach response plan can assist in mitigating these costs, businesses are increasingly turning to cyber insurance as a means of deflecting associated costs of cyber incidents.[17]

III. THE COST OF DATA BREACHES

Research suggests that the cost to an organization for a data breach can be significant.[18] When attackers are successful in breaching systems, it can have significant financial and non-financial consequences for the affected business. The average financial cost for a business of a data breach in 2014 was US$ 2.8 million, with roughly 30 percent of these costs associated with legal, forensic, and investigation.[19] In 2017, the average total cost of a data breach is now US$ 3.62 million. The IBM Security/Ponemon study revealed that US$ 141 was the average cost per lost or stolen record.[20] There is a further 27.7 percent likelihood of a recurring data breach within the next two years. A large part of the total cost though is the loss of business and reputational loss.[21] The successful attacks take an average of twenty-three days to resolve; with it increasing to fifty days if it was an attack from within the business.[22] Aside from the financial and nonfinancial losses, the most alarming statistic is that over 60 percent of businesses that experience a cyberattack, such as those listed above, go out of business within six months.[23]

IV. RISK REDUCTION

There is a need to manage and reduce these risks to business. Although there are many ways to reduce the risk, the threats will always be present and ever evolving. As a way to

16. Alana MAURUSHAT, "Data Breach Notification Law Across the World from California to Australia", Privacy Law and Business International (2009). This research was updated from 2016-2017.
17. Price Waterhouse Coopers, *CSFI/PwC Insurance Banana Skins Australia 2015*.
18. Ponemon Institute, *2015 Cost of Data Breach Study: Australia*, p. 1 shows that the average organizational cost for a data breach has reached US$ 2.82 million or US$ 144 per lost or stolen record of personal information, see <www-03.ibm.com/security/data-breach/>.
19. *Ibid.*
20. Ponemon Institute, 2017 Cost of Data Breach Study: Global Overview (IBM Security, June 2017).
21. Department of Communications and the Arts, Australian Government, *Stay Smart Online 'Small Business Guide'* Stay Smart Online <https://www.communications.gov.au/sites/g/files/net301/f/SSO%20Small%20Business%20Guide.pdf>.
22. *Ibid.*
23. *Ibid.*

offset some of the damage of cyberattacks, some may consider taking out a cyber insurance policy. Cyber risk is currently ranked the top risk in Australia by businesses for the 2015 Banana Skins Insurance Survey, moving up from thirteenth place in 2013.[24] Whilst regulation remains the main concern globally, cyber risk currently rates fourth in 2015, moving from twenty-second place in 2013.[25] This survey of over 806 respondents shows how much of a concern cyber risk has become for businesses in Australia and also worldwide, it shows how much of a growing issue this has become and the need to manage and reduce these risks. Cyber insurance is one way to manage and offset this risk.

Although businesses are increasingly seeing the need for cyber insurance, the reality of acquiring insurance policies that cover cyberthreats, is not as pressing. A 2016 AusCert and BDO survey of Australian and New Zealand businesses as covered by Computer World[26] revealed that only 13.8 percent of respondents had cyber coverage under their various insurance policies, 7.4 percent thought that they might be covered through other polices, with another 9.4 percent stating that they have separate cyber insurance policies.[27] Close to 70 percent were not covered for cyber related incidences in their policies. Furthermore only 48 percent had a cyber response plan with 41 percent also having a cyber incident response team.

V. WHAT IS CYBER INSURANCE?

Cyber insurance generally is taken out to protect businesses from risks associated with online activities;[28] the insurance can cover things such as lost business due to a system breach, or compensation for stolen data.[29] Traditional insurance policies cover tangible assets such as computers and related hardware. Cyber insurance aims to cover items associated with a breach, such as network interruption, reputation loss, notification and monitoring costs.[30] Like any insurance policy, there are numerous inclusions and exclusions depending on what level of cover is chosen.

The cyber insurance market is currently worth US$ 1.5 billion with the United States accounting for approximately US$ 1 billion, European countries US$ 150 million, with the rest of the market shared between other countries.[31] The uptake of cyber insurance in the United States has been far more rapid than in other countries around the world. Forty-seven states in the United States currently require businesses to notify customers

---

24. Price Waterhouse Coopers, *CSFI/PwC Insurance Banana Skins Australia 2015*.
25. *Ibid.*
26. Stuart CORNER, "What Cyber Insurers Look For" Computerworld (20 Nov. 2017) <https://www.computerworld.com.au/article/630214/what-cyber-insurers-look/>.
27. AusCert BDO, 2016 Cyber Security Survey <https://www.bdo.com.au/en-au/2016-cybersecurity-survey-results>.
28. Centre for Internet Security, *Cyber Insurance Research Paper*, p. 7 <www.canberra.edu.au/cis/storage/CIS%20Cyber%20Insurance_FINAL.pdf>.
29. *Ibid.*
30. *Ibid.*, p. 8.
31. Keith KIRKPATRICK, "Cyber Policies on the Rise", 58 *Communications of the ACM* (2015) p. 21.

and government of a data breach, and this may be one reason why cyber insurance in the United States is more prevalent.[32]

Businesses need to consider numerous things when assessing whether cyber insurance is suitable for them and the level of cover required. Some things that need to be considered are the reputation loss, monitoring and notification costs, and network interruption associated with the breach.[33] It is also necessary to evaluate the type of data being held by the business and the consequence of losing such data.[34]

Insurable losses include both first-party losses and third-party losses. As Bailey explains: "First-party losses concern claims made by an insured for financial harm suffered directly by the insured organization as a result of an insured occurrence whereas third-party losses concern claims made against an insured, by a third party, for losses related to an insured occurrence."[35]

Table 2 below highlights different types of insured losses.

Table 2. Insurance Losses

Insured First Party Losses	Insured Third Party Losses
Property damage of tangible assets (servers, computers)	Damage to third party property both tangible and intangible
Property damage of intangible assets (data, software)	Denial of access or use
Theft of proprietary information or data	Insufficient measures to protect third party from consequences of malware
Business interruption	Unauthorized use of third party data
Damage to company assets from malware	Unauthorized use of confidential information
Incident management costs	Failure to prevent unauthorized access, use or interference of data or networks

32. *Ibid.*
33. Centre for Internet Security, *Cyber Insurance Research Paper*, p. 8 <www.canberra.edu.au/cis/storage/CIS%20Cyber%20Insurance_FINAL.pdf>.
34. *Ibid.*
35. Liam BAILEY, "Mitigating Moral Hazard in Cyber-Risk Insurance", 3 Journal of Law & Cyber Warfare (2014, issue 1).

Insured First Party Losses	Insured Third Party Losses
Replacement of damaged or destroyed goods such as software, hardware	Defense expenses for legal costs incurred
Fraudulent transfer of funds or data	

In the United States cyber insurance has gained serious momentum after a decade of underwriting thousands of polices. In Australia, there is comparatively little reliable data for the local market.[36] The lack of local data is a problem in many jurisdictions.

There is little research in cyber insurance, and what is there is mostly theoretical. A recent study (the first of its kind) by Romanovsky et al., however, produced a comprehensive analysis of losses covered by cyber insurance policies, exclusions, underwriting approaches to risk and factors used to determine premiums.[37] Researchers examined 180 cyber insurance policies in the States of New York, Pennsylvania and California. The researchers noted that the term “cyber insurance” did not indicate stand-alone policies. Instead, cyber insurance was captured in policies such as “Commercial Property”, “Internet Liability”, “Burglary and Theft”, and so on.

The insurance questions did not cover the substance of a particular cybsercurity protocol, or corporate structure. The policies merely asked if there was, for example, the role of Chief Information Security Officer or Privacy Officer. Or was there a management or IT security management. The protocols and roles themselves were not questioned.

International Organization for Standardization (ISO) standards and National Institute of Standards and Technology (NIST) cybersecurity frameworks were only mentioned once but the authors note that these frameworks are beginning to be integrated with the policies of major insurance companies. Some companies merely looked at competitors rates in order to set their own. Researchers note that there were few cases where the insurance companies had the requisite experience and confidence to develop their own pricing model. They cannot, for instance, use claim counts for data due to the paucity of related claims.

1. A Case Study – Ashley Madison

There are many high profile cases in which a business’s data has been breached, with many millions of customers affected. A recent example is the Ashley Madison incident where millions of customer records were breached and then placed in a publicly

36. Interview with Leon Fouche, partner and national leader of Cybersecurity at insurance advisory firm BDO in Sam WORTHINGTON, “Is Cyber Security Insurance Really Worth it?” Security Brief Australia (6 August 2016).
37. Sasha ROMANOSKY, Lillian ABLON, Andreas KUEHN, and Therese JONES, “Content Analysis of Cyber Insurance Policies: How Do Carriers Write Policies and Price Cyber Risk?”, WEIS Conference 2017. Available at <https://weis2017.econinfosec.org/wp-content/uploads/sites/3/2017/06/WEIS_2017_paper_28.pdf>.

available database for anyone to search. The Ashley Madison incident was global news for quite a while, with two affected customers reportedly taking their own lives when their identities were disclosed.[38] The Ashley Madison incident is still unfolding and represents a large breach, the next example is of a small professional firm. The firm discovered that a virus had infected its small network of twenty-two computers, including two virtual servers and associated hardware. The firm had antivirus software installed on all computers and definitions were up to date. When the virus was first discovered the firm notified its information technology providers and insurers who attempted to remove the virus without success. The only way to rectify the virus was to wipe all the computers and restore data from a back-up. The firm lost three days of business due to the down time. As the firm having a cyber insurance policy, the insurance company deployed their response team who minimized reputational damage and harm to the business. Although this is a relatively small incident, it shows the effect that a cyberattack can have on a company, and the importance of procedures to minimize and reduce the effects of the attack. The insurers paid out a total US$ 35,265 to cover the incident.[39] Without the cyber insurance policy, restoration of the affected systems might have taken many more days.

2. *A Case Study – Sony*[40]

On 8 December 2014, Sony informed its employees, that personally identifiable information about employees and their dependents may have been obtained by unauthorized individuals as a result of a "brazen cyber-attack", including names, address, social security numbers and financial information.[41] On 7 December 2014, C-SPAN reported that the hackers stole 47,000 unique Social Security numbers from the Sony Pictures Entertainment (SPE) computer network.[42] Although personal data may have been stolen, early news reports focused mainly on celebrity gossip and embarrassing details about Hollywood and film industry business affairs gleaned by the media from electronic files, including private email messages, released by the computer criminals. The leak revealed multiple details of behind-the-scenes politics on Columbia Pictures' current Spider-Man film series, including emails between head of Sony pictures Amy Pascal and others to various heads of Marvel Studios.[43] In addition to the emails, a copy of the script for the upcoming James Bond film *Spectre*, which was due to be released in

38. Chris BARANIUK, "Ashley Madison: 'Suicides' over Website Hack", BBC News (24 August 2015) <www.bbc.com/news/technology-34044506>.
39. Centre for Internet Security, *Cyber Insurance Research Paper*, p. 10 <www.canberra.edu.au/cis/storage/CIS%20Cyber%20Insurance_FINAL.pdf>.
40. Paper on file with author (Draft). Adib HAQUE and Alana MAURUSHAT, "Why Attribution is Hard – the Sony Hack Analysed".
41. State of California Department of Justice Office of the Attorney General, Sony Pictures Entertainment Notice Letter (8 Dec. 2014).
42. C-Span, "Hacking and Cybersecurity Threats" (7 Dec. 2014).
43. Julie MAKINEN, "North Korea Decries U.S. Allegations on Sony Hack; U.S. Turns to China", Los Angeles Times (20 Dec. 2014).

2015, was obtained.[44] As a result of this breach, later in December, former Sony Pictures Entertainment employees filed four lawsuits against the company for not protecting their data that was released in the hack, which included Social Security numbers and medical information.[45] In January 2015, details were revealed of the Motion Picture Association of America's lobbying of the United States International Trade Commission to mandate US internet service providers (ISPs) either at the internet transit level or consumer-level internet service.

While some experts estimate that the Sony hack cost the company US$ 100 million, Sony CEO Michael Lynton is reported as stating, "I would say the cost is far less than anything anybody is imagining and certainly shouldn't be anything that is disruptive to our budget," and was "well within the bounds of insurance".[46]

VI. AUSTRALIAN CYBER INSURANCE MARKET

Some people have argued that the cyber insurance market is immature, with insufficient data to perform effective actuarial analysis of the risk. Others have refuted this claim citing that at least in the United States, the cyber insurance market is now over a decade old with advanced threat analytics, cyberattack incidents, thousands of data breaches publicized and analyzed, the introduction of new security and privacy laws and the correlating lawsuits for data breaches and security incidents.[47]

There are two hurdles in Australia preventing companies from venturing into cyber insurance. The first is that Australian insurance companies may genuinely not have enough data about Australian cyber incidents. The second is that there is no legal duty in Australia to report data breaches, and the publication of detailed cyber incidents and threat analysis is newer to the Australian landscape – we have traditionally had fewer statistics. In many other jurisdictions data breach notification is compulsory and comes with heavy fines for failure to notify the appropriate authority and customers of the breach.[48]

---

44. Phil HELSEL, "North Korea Insults Obama, Blames U.S. for Internet Outgages", NBC News (26 Dec. 2014).
45. Ralph ELLIS, "Lawsuits Say Sony Pictures Should Have Expected Security Breach", CNN (20 Dec. 2014).
46. Mary MILLIKEN, "For Sony Picture CEO, Cyberattack Won't Set Studio Back", Reuters (8 Jan. 2015) <www.reuters.com/article/2015/01/09/us-northkorea-cyberattack-sony-idUSKBN0KI02420150109#2iLM0p9aTU3BBxUE.97>.
47. Sasha ROMANOSKY, "Comments to the Department of Commerce on Incentives to Adopt Improved Cybersecurity" (April 2013) <www.ntia.doc.gov/files/ntia/romanosky_comments.pdf>.
48. Alana MAURUSHAT, "Data Breach Notification Law Across the World from California to Australia", Privacy Law and Business International (2009). Updated Report 2015 forthcoming.

VII. CONCLUSION

Even the best designed systems are vulnerable to attacks, and businesses need to assess and take steps to minimize the risk.[49] Minimizing the risk of an attack is not just about spending money on information technology security, it is also about implementing appropriate procedures and making the culture of a business security-aware.[50] The type of attacks will continue to evolve, and the number of businesses affected will rise. The Australian Government is considering introducing mandatory data breach notifications for businesses, and this may increase the uptake of cyber insurance.[51]

49. *Ibid*.
50. *Ibid*.
51. Attorney General for Australia, "The Australian Government has responded to the inquiry of the Parliamentary Joint Committee on Intelligence and Security (PJCIS) into the Telecommunications (Interception and Access) Amendment (Data Retention) Bill 2014" (Media Release, Recommendation p. 38) <www.attorneygeneral.gov.au/Mediareleases/Pages/2015/FirstQuarter/Government-Response-To-Committee-Report-On-The-Telecommunications-Interception-And-Access-Amendment-Data-Retention-Bill.aspx>.

Cyber Intrusion as the Guerrilla Tactic: An Appraisal of Historical Challenges in an Age of Technology and Big Data

Edna Sussman[*]

TABLE OF CONTENTS PAGE

"*There is a new mantra in cybersecurity today: 'It's when not if.'*"[1]

I. INTRODUCTION

Cyber intrusion and hacking are in the news almost daily with damaging invasions of law firms, corporations, governmental agencies, and political entities. "Security breaches are becoming so prevalent that there is a new mantra in cybersecurity today: 'It's when not if,' a law firm or other entity will suffer a breach."[2] Those who monitor information technology (IT) systems report dozens of attempted attacks on a daily basis. Arbitration participants have not been immune.[3]

---

* Full-time independent arbitrator and Distinguished ADR Practitioner in Residence at Fordham University School of Law; former litigation partner at White & Case LLP and has served as an arbitrator in over 200 complex commercial arbitrations, both international and domestic, under many institutional rules and *ad hoc*; member of the panel of many of the leading dispute resolution institutions around the world and fellow of the Chartered Institute of Arbitrators; sits on the Board of the American Arbitration Association; chair of the AAA-ICDR Foundation; Chair of the New York International Arbitration Center; past President of the College of Commercial Arbitrators; graduate of Barnard College and Columbia Law School; has lectured and published widely on arbitration, mediation, energy and environmental issues.

1. David REIS, *ABA Tech Report 2017*, ABA, <https://www.americanbar.org/groups/law_practice/publications/techreport/2017/security.html> (last visited 23 May 2018).
2. *Id.*
3. See, e.g., Allison ROSS, "Cybersecurity and Confidentiality Shocks for the PCA", Glob. Arb. Rev. (23 Jul. 2015) <https://globalarbitrationreview.com/article/1034637/cybersecurity-and-confidentiality-shocks-for-the-pca> (reporting on an attempted hack of the PCA website during the hearing of the maritime border dispute between the Philippines and China); Zachary ZAGGER, "Hackers Target Anti-Doping, Appeals Bodies Amid Olympics", Law360.com (12 Aug. 2016, 5:00 PM) <https://www.law360.com/articles/827962/hackers-target-anti-doping-appeals-bodies-

At the ICCA Congress in 2018, a consultation draft of the Cybersecurity Protocol for International Arbitration was circulated for comment.[4] The Protocol is

> "intended to encourage participants in international arbitration to become more aware of cybersecurity risks in arbitration and to provide guidance that will facilitate collaboration in individual matters about the cybersecurity measures that should reasonably be taken, in light of those risks and the individualized circumstances of the case to protect information exchange and the arbitral process".[5]

It is hoped that adherence to the Protocols coupled with adherence to practical guidance on how to protect against cyber intrusion[6] will diminish the number of incidents in international arbitration.

While guerrilla tactics such as fabricated or illegally obtained evidence are not new, cyber intrusion requires a review of pertinent issues that might arise where fabricated or illegally obtained evidence is made possible by virtue of cyber intrusion. This paper seeks to flag for further analysis: (a) the issues that may arise and that may require consideration by arbitrators in instances in which evidence is introduced at the hearing which is, or is claimed to be, hacked or fabricated through cyber manipulation; (b) unconscious influences that can impact decisions where such evidence is an issue; and (c) the arbitrator's duties when confronted with such evidence. The discussion will provide an overview of the admissibility of illegally obtained documents, authentication of documents, sanctions, the psychological impact on decision-making of inadmissible evidence, the influence of one's native legal culture on decision-making and the arbitrator's duty to report.

amid-olympics> (A group of hackers attempted to infiltrate the website of the Court of Arbitration for Sport during the Rio Olympic Games.).

4. *Cybersecurity in International Arbitration ICCA-NYC Bar-CPR Working Group*, Arbitration-ICCA.org, <www.arbitration-icca.org/projects/Cybersecurity-in-International-Arbitration.html> (last visited 23 May 2018).
5. *Draft Cybersecurity Protocol for International Arbitration – Consultation Draft*, ICCA-NYC Bar-CPR, <http://www.arbitration-icca.org/media/10/43322709923070/draft_cybersecurity_protocol_final_10_april.pdf> at p. 5 (last visited 23 May 2018).
6. Following are some of the currently available sources that address cybersecurity measures, but technology is constantly evolving and hackers are increasingly sophisticated and developing new cyber weapons. Thus, keeping up to date on the latest guidance is essential. See, e.g., Stephanie COHEN and Mark MORRIL, "A Call to Cyber Arms: The International Arbitrator's Duty to Avoid Digital Intrusion", 40 Fordham Int'l. L. J., 981, 1012–1018 (2017); Jill D. RHODES and Robert S. LITT, *The ABA Cybersecurity Handbook: A Resource for Attorneys, Law Firms, and Business Professionals*, 2d ed. (ABA 2018); Maud PIERS and Christian ASCHAUER eds., *Arbitration in the Digital Age: The Brave New World of Arbitration* (Cambridge 2018); ARIAS, *U.S, Practical Guide for Information Security in Arbitration* (ARIAS 2017) <https://www.arias-us.org/wp-content/uploads/2017/08/ARIAS-US-Practical-Guide-for-Information-Security-in-Arbitration_6.6.17.pdf>; Philip Doyle GRAY, *The Pillars of Digital Security: How to Ethically Use Technology in Legal Practice* (2017).

II. ADMISSIBILITY

Arbitrators have broad discretion in dealing with evidence. They may admit or reject evidence and have full discretion in evaluating and weighing the evidence in determining what weight, if any, the evidence should be given. Art. 19(2) of the United Nations Commission on International Trade Law (UNCITRAL) Model Law on International Commercial Arbitration provides that "[t]he power conferred upon the arbitral tribunal includes the power to determine the admissibility, relevance, materiality and weight of any evidence". National laws governing the arbitration provide similar powers to the arbitrators.[7]

The International Bar Association (IBA) rules and various institutional rules grant broad discretion to the arbitral tribunal in the taking of evidence. Art. 9(1) of the 2010 IBA Rules on the Taking of Evidence in International Arbitration provides that "[t]he arbitral tribunal shall determine the admissibility, relevance, materiality and weight of evidence". Art. 20(6) of the 2014 International Centre for Dispute Resolution (ICDR) International Arbitration Rules provides that "[t]he tribunal shall determine the admissibility, relevance, materiality and weight of the evidence". Rule 34(a) of the 2013 American Arbitration Association (AAA) Commercial Arbitration Rules provides that "[C]onformity to legal rules of evidence shall not be necessary." Rule 22.1(vi) of the 2014 London Court of International Arbitration (LCIA) Arbitration Rules provides that the tribunal "shall have the power ... to decide whether or not to apply any strict rules of evidence (or any other rules) as to the admissibility, relevance or weight of any material tendered by a party on any issue of fact...".

The courts recognize the discretion afforded to arbitrators, and consistent with the deference courts generally give arbitral decisions, courts have confirmed that arbitral tribunals are not bound by domestic rules of evidence.[8] "In practice, international arbitral tribunals typically do not apply strict rules of evidence, particularly rules of evidence applicable in domestic litigations."[9]

Given this wide discretion and the binding nature of arbitral awards, tribunals generally admit evidence to avoid risking vacatur for failure to provide a full and fair opportunity to present the case, and then consider its credibility, weight and value.[10] However, on a proper showing, evidence may be excluded by the arbitral tribunal. Where it is demonstrated that evidence has been obtained illegally the arbitral tribunal is faced with a difficult choice. With the prevalence of cyber intrusions in today's world, it

---

7. See Gary BORN, International Commercial Arbitration, 2d ed. (Kluwer 2014) Sect. 15.09(A) (citing the U.S. Revised Uniform Arbitration Act; the English Arbitration Act; the French Code of Civil Procedure; German ZPO; Austrian ZPO; Hong Kong Arbitration Ordinance; Japanese Arbitration Law; Korean Arbitration Act; and Costa Rica Arbitration law).
8. See, e.g., Bell Aerospace Co. Div. of Textron, Inc. v. Int'l Union, United Auto., etc., 500 F.2d 921, 923 (2d Cir. 1974) ("In handling evidence an arbitrator need not follow all the niceties observed by the federal courts.").
9. G. Born, supra fn. 7, at 2310.
10. Edna SUSSMAN, "The Arbitrator Survey – Practices, Preferences and Changes on the Horizon", 26 Am. Rev. Int'l Arb. (2015) pp. 517, 521 (survey results demonstrated that only 11 percent of arbitrators excluded evidence that would not be admissible under national evidentiary standards more than 75 percent of the time).

is inevitable that tribunals will be increasingly required to address the question of whether or not they should admit illegally obtained evidence. Reporting on a dispute before a federal court in New York, an aptly named article in The Wall Street Journal was titled "Hackers for Hire are Easy to Find".[11] As described, hundreds of personal emails of a Kuwaiti billionaire were posted online and available to all. It was reported that the cost for the hackers was US$ 400, demonstrating the low cost and ease with which computer hacking can be accomplished.

However, no clear line of authority has developed to guide tribunals as to how they should treat illegally obtained evidence. Tribunals have arrived at different conclusions on the question.[12]

The *Corfu Channel* case, heard before the International Court of Justice between 1947 and 1949 was an early instance in which the tribunal dealt with illegally obtained evidence.[13] The United Kingdom in violation of Albania's sovereignty conducted a mine sweeping operation in Albanian waters to find evidence in support of its case that Albania had failed to give warning to the United Kingdom about mines in the channel as was required by international law, which caused several British warships to be struck by submerged mines. While the court found that the United Kingdom's actions were unlawful, the court did not exclude the evidence and did not apply any material sanctions against the United Kingdom.

Taking a different position in the prominent arbitration decision in *Methanex v. United States* (*Methanex*), long before WikiLeaks, the tribunal declined to admit the wrongfully obtained evidence.[14] Methanex attempted to rely on documents obtained by going through wastepaper and rubbish in support of its position. The tribunal stressed the general duty of good faith and the fundamental principles of justice and fairness:

"[I]t would be wrong to allow Methanex to introduce this documentation into these proceedings in violation of its general duty of good faith and, moreover, that Methanex's conduct, committed during these arbitration proceedings, offended basic principles of justice and fairness required of all parties in every international arbitration."[15]

The *Methanex* tribunal, however, also considered the question of materiality of the evidence and concluded that it was only of "marginal evidential significance".[16]

In the well-known *Yukos* award which granted $ 50 billion in damages, the tribunal relied extensively on confidential diplomatic cables from the United States Department

11. Cassell BRYAN-LOW, "Hackers for Hire Are Easy to Find", The Wall Street Journal (23 Jan. 2012) <https://www.wsj.com/articles/SB10001424052970203471004577145140543496380>.
12. See generally, Cherie BLAIR and Ema Vidak GOJKOVIĆ, "WikiLeaks and Beyond: Discerning an International Standard for the Admissibility of Illegally Obtained Evidence", 22 ICSID Rev. – For. Inv. L. J. 1 (2018, issue 1); J. H. BOYKIN and M. HAVALIC, "Fruits of the Poisonous Tree: The Admissibility of Unlawfully Obtained Evidence in International Arbitration", 5 Transnat'l Disp. Mgmt. J. (2015); Jessica O. IRETON, "The Admissibility of Evidence in ICSID Arbitration: Considering the Validity of WikiLeaks Cables as Evidence", 30 ICSID Rev. – For. Inv. L. J. (2015, issue 1) p. 231.
13. *Corfu Channel (Merits) (U.K. v. Alb.)*, 1949 I.C.J. Rep. 4 (9 Apr.).
14. NAFTA Chapter Eleven Arbitral Tribunal: *Methanex Corporation v. United States of America*, Final Award on Jurisdiction and Merits (3 August 2005) Text of Decision, 44 I.L.M. 1345 (2005).
15. *Id.*, at para. 59.
16. *Id.*, at para. 56.

of State that had been illegally obtained and published on WikiLeaks.[17] The tribunal specifically referenced the views expressed by officials in the US Embassy's cables published by WikiLeaks in support of its decision stating that the cables revealed the "candid" and "unguarded" views of PwC's senior management, an important issue in the case.[18] The tribunal provided no analysis of whether evidence illegally obtained should be admitted.

In *Libananco v. Turkey* (*Libananco*),[19] while the arbitration was in progress, Turkish authorities were intercepting electronic communications, including between Libananco and its legal counsel, and obtained 2,000 legally privileged and confidential emails. Turkey maintained that the surveillance activities had nothing to do with the arbitration and the files intercepted were not shared with the department that was handling the arbitration. The tribunal referenced as having been affected: basic procedural fairness, respect for confidentiality and legal privilege, the right of parties to advance their respective cases freely and without interference, and respect for the tribunal itself. The tribunal expressed the principle that "[p]arties have an obligation to arbitrate fairly and in good faith and that an arbitral tribunal has the inherent jurisdiction to ensure that this obligation is complied with".[20] The tribunal directed that any document which had been intercepted which related to the arbitration be destroyed and held that any privileged documents or information which may be introduced in the future, as well as any evidence derived from possession of such documents or information, would be excluded from evidence.

In *Caratube v. Kazakhstan*,[21] Caratube attempted to introduce eleven documents that had been made publicly available on the Internet as a consequence of a hacking of the Kazakhstan government's IT system. Hackers had uploaded about 60,000 documents onto a website known as "Kazakhleaks". The tribunal allowed the admission of all non-privileged leaked documents but excluded from the record all illegally leaked privileged documents finding that the tribunal must afford privileged documents the utmost protection.[22]

The application for reconsideration of an interim decision in *Conoco Phillips v. Venezuela* provides an example of the potential for flashpoints between the search for

---

17. *Hulley Enters. Ltd. (Cyprus) v. Russian Fed'n*, (PCA Case No. AA 226), Final Award (18 Jul. 2014) paras. 1185-1186 (hereinafter *Hulley*). The District Court of The Hague quashed the final award from *Hulley* on other grounds on 20 April 2016. See *Rechtbank* Den Haag, Pronunciations, De Rechtspraak (20 Apr. 2016) <http://deeplink.rechtspraak.nl/uitspraak?id=ECLI:NL:RBDHA:2016:4230> [https://perma.cc/4RHA-YHZ5]. As of this writing the appeal is pending.
18. *Hulley*, supra fn. 17, at para. 1189.
19. *Libananco Holdings Co. Ltd. v. Republic of Turkey* (ICSID Case No. ARB/06/8), Decision on Preliminary Issues (23 Jun. 2008) (hereinafter *Libananco*).
20. *Id.*, at para. 78.
21. *Caratube Int'l Oil Co. LLP & Devincci Salah Hourani v. Republic of Kazakhstan* (ICSID Case No. ARB/13/13), Award of the Tribunal, (27 Sep. 2017) paras. 150-166 (hereinafter *Caratube*) (summary of the decision on the claimants' request for the production of "leaked documents"). See also, Alison ROSS, "Tribunal Rules on Admissibility of Hacked Kazakh Emails", Glob. Arb. Rev. (22 Sep. 2015) <https://globalarbitrationreview.com/article/1034787/tribunal-rules-on-admissibility-of-hacked-kazakh-emails> (discussing the parties' positions and the decision).
22. *Caratube*, supra fn. 21, at para. 166.

truth and other values.[23] Venezuela, in an application for reconsideration of an interim decision, relied on US Embassy cables made available on WikiLeaks which showed that Venezuela had attempted to negotiate in good faith with the claimant, Conoco Phillips, including about compensation for the expropriation and which directly contradicted previous factual findings of the tribunal. The challenge was rejected based on the tribunal's analysis of the right to reconsider a prior decision under the ICSID rules, concluding that its prior decision had res judicata effect and could not be reconsidered. In a strong dissent Professor George Abi-Saab, concluding that the revelations of the WikiLeaks cables, which he found to be reliable, radically contradicted the factual analysis of the prior decision, stated:

> "In the circumstances, I don't think that any self-respecting Tribunal that takes seriously its overriding legal and moral task of seeking the truth and dispensing justice according to the law on that basis, can pass over such evidence, close its blinkers and proceed to build on its now severely contestable findings, ignoring the existence and the relevance of such glaring evidence.
>
> It would be shutting itself off by an epistemic closure into a subjective make-believe world of its creation; a virtual reality in order to fend off probable objective reality; a legal comedy of errors on the theatre of the absurd, not to say travesty of justice, that makes mockery not only of ICSID arbitration, but of the very idea of adjudication."[24]

That the discretion afforded to arbitrators calls upon them to balance the search for truth and other values is not new. It is just being presented in a new context in our digital world. As William Park said, "Nothing new resides in balancing truth-seeking against values that further public goals rather than adjudicatory precision."[25] As William Park elaborated:

> "Arbitrators are supposed to arrive at some understanding of what actually happened and what legal norms determine the parties' claims and defenses. In finding facts and applying law, arbitrators should aim at getting as near as reasonably possible to a correct view of the events giving rise to the controversy, and to consider legal norms applied in other disputes that raise similar questions.
>
> This does not mean that arbitrators do not balance truth-seeking against other goals. Indeed, they do so all the time, notably in connection with document production (which competes with economy and speed), and attorney-client privilege (which inhibits attempts to get at what corporate officers really knew).

---

23. *ConocoPhillips Petrozuata, ConocoPhillips Hamaca B.V. and ConocoPhillips Gulf of Paria B.V v. Bolivarian Republic of Venezuela* (ICSID Case No. ARB/07/30), Decision on Respondent's Request for Reconsideration (10 Mar. 2014).
24. *ConocoPhillips Petrozuata, ConocoPhillips Hamaca B.V. and ConocoPhillips Gulf of Paria B.V v. Bolivarian Republic of Venezuela* (ICSID Case No. ARB/07/30), Decision on Respondent's Request for Reconsideration – Dissenting Opinion of Georges Abi-Saab (10 Mar. 2014) para. 66.
25. William W. PARK, "Truth Seeking in International Arbitration" in Markus WIRTH, et al., eds., *The Search for "Truth" in Arbitration: Is Finding the Truth What Dispute Resolution Is About?* (Juris 2011) pp. 1, 10.

However, such balancing of interests does not require abandonment of truth taking as an aspiration."[26]

In short, there are no bright lines that govern the admissibility of illegally obtained evidence, as is the case with many of the instances in which the tribunal is called upon to balance competing values. The decisions appear to emphasize who committed the wrongful act, whether the documents are privileged, and whether the information revealed was material to the decision on the merits.

Cherie Blair and Ema Gojković, in their comprehensive article analyzing the existing jurisprudence, conclude that a trend may be discerned based on existing case law. They posit that the "legal and policy elements which have been taken into account when deciding admissibility of illegally obtained evidence include:[27]

(1) Has the evidence been obtained unlawfully by a party who seeks to benefit from it?
(2) Does the public interest favour rejecting the evidence as inadmissible?
(3) Do the interests of justice favour the admission of evidence?"

As decisions continue to explicate the question of admissibility of evidence that is the fruit of a cyber intrusion, other issues and concerns present themselves that bear analysis.

III. AUTHENTICATION

While this discussion focuses on emails, similar issues can arise with text messages,[28] Facebook entries and postings on other social media outlets,[29] and evidence from the "internet of things".[30] Litigation positions taken by parties with the ascendance of cyber

---

26. William W. PARK, "Arbitrator Integrity: The Transient and the Permanent", 46 San Diego L. Rev. (2009) pp. 629, 695.
27. C. BLAIR and E.V. GOJKOVIĆ, supra fn. 12, at p. 25. See also, J.H. BOYKEN and M. HAVALIC, supra fn. 12 (distilling the decisions to provide a roadmap for analysis of admissibility).
28. See Rena ANDOH and James SALEM, "Text Messages as Evidence: The Current State of Affairs in New York State Courts", N.Y.L. J. (9 Feb. 2018, 3:00 PM) <https://www.law.com/newyorklawjournal/sites/newyorklawjournal/2018/02/09/text-messages-as-evidence-the-current-state-of-affairs-in-new-york-state-courts/?slreturn=20180428133423>; Sara E. COSTELLO, "Establishing That Text Messages Are Admissible", A.B.A. (1 Apr. 2013) <http://apps.americanbar.org/litigation/litigationnews/top_stories/040113-text-message-admissible.html>; P.W. GRIMM, et al., infra fn. 37, at p. 19.
29. See Siri CARLSON, "When Is a Tweet Not an Admissible Tweet? Closing the Authentication Gap in the Federal Rules of Evidence", 164 U. Pa. L. Rev. (2016) p. 1033; John G. BROWNING, "Introducing Social Media Evidence", 74 The Advoc. (Texas) (2016) p. 112; Honorable Paul W. GRIMM, et al., "Authentication of Social Media Evidence", 36 Am. J. Trial Advoc. (2013) p. 433.
30. Ronald J. HEDGES and Kevin F. RYAN, *The Internet of Things: What Is It, What Can Happen with It, and What Can Be Done When Something Happens*, N.Y.S. Bar Assn., <http://www.nysba.org/Journal/2018/Apr/What_Is_It,_What_Can_Happen_With_It,_and_What_Can_Be_Done_When_Something_Happens/> (last visited 23 May 2018).

intrusion are presented in a variety of ways. A party may contend that the documents were "stolen" by hacking into his or her IT system; thus, illegally obtained.[31] That contention raises questions of admissibility discussed above. A party may contend that it no longer has the documents available for production because it was hacked.[32] That contention raises questions of proof as with any assertion that documents no longer exist, although a forensic examination may be required for the production of such proof in the context of digital evidence. Or illegally hacked emails might be posted publicly on WikiLeaks or some other platform on the web that is publicly available.[33] Again, that raises a question of admissibility discussed above. The party may contend that the emails were fabricated by a hacker and that they did not write them. That contention raises questions of authenticity discussed in this section.

Authentication is not an issue frequently encountered in international arbitration. However, it is likely that with the prevalence of cyber intrusions and the ease with which it seems to be possible to intrude, arbitrators will likely be required to review an increasing number of objections to admissibility based on lack of authenticity.

In the famous case of *Ceglia v. Zuckerberg*,[34] plaintiff, Paul Ceglia, alleged that while he was at Harvard, Facebook's CEO, Mark Zuckerberg, entered into a "work-for-hire" contract pursuant to which the plaintiff helped fund the development of Facebook in exchange for a one-half interest in Facebook. The authenticity of the purported contract and of several related emails was challenged. Given the magnitude of what was at stake, a variety of forensic examination tools were employed, including a review of the metadata, backdating anomalies, formatting anomalies, and a linguistic analysis. Each of these forensic tests is discussed by the court at length in its decision. Based on its conclusion that the purported contract and the emails were not authentic but recently created fabrications, the court relying on its inherent authority concluded that the case could not go to the jury and dismissed.[35]

In the United States, Rule 902 of the Federal Rules of Civil Procedure was recently amended to provide for self-authentication of digital evidence. A record generated by an electronic process, or system that produces an accurate result and data copied from an electronic device, storage medium, or file if authenticated by a process of digital identification, as shown by a certification of a qualified person is self-authenticating, without the need for a testifying witness.[36] However, as the comments to the new rule

31. See discussion on *Caratube v. Kazakhstan* above.
32. See, e.g., *Ousterhout v. Zukowski*, No. 11 CV 9136, 2016 WL 3675564 (N.D. Ill. 5 Apr. 2016); *DeCastro v. Kavadia*, 309 F.R.D. 167 (S.D.N.Y. 2015).
33. See, e.g., *Republic of Kazakhstan v. Ketebaev*, No. 17-CV-00246-LHK, 2017 WL 6539897 (N.D. Cal. 21 Dec. 2017) (describing a hacking of emails of Kazakh government employees, which were posted on a website and posted on personal Facebook pages and newspaper websites, and included attorney-client communications between Kazakh officials and their attorneys; the case was dismissed for lack of personal jurisdiction).
34. *Ceglia v. Zuckerberg*, No. 10-CV-00569-A, 2014 WL 1224574 (W.D.N.Y. 25 Mar. 2014), aff'd, 600 F. App'x 34 (2d Cir. 2015).
35. *Id.*
36. CARL A. AVENI, "New Federal Evidence Rules Changes Reflect Modern World", A.B.A. Litigation News (23 Apr. 2018) <https://www.americanbar.org/groups/litigation/publications/litigation-news/featured-articles/2018/new-federal-evidence-rule-changes-reflect-modern-world.html>.

note, authenticity does not preclude other grounds for objection and parties remain free to object on other grounds including that the digital evidence was not placed there by them. Thus, while self-authentication does relieve one aspect of proof, it does not, and is not intended to, resolve claims that the computer was hacked and false evidence was introduced.

For arbitrators faced with determining authenticity, a review of factors which had been considered under earlier versions of the U.S. Federal Rules of Evidence to test authenticity may be instructive in determining authenticity. In addition to evidence as to digital hash values and testimony from a forensic witness as to when the email issued and from which device based on the metadata and other features, Hon. Paul W. Grimm, Daniel J. Capra, and Gregory P. Joseph, Esq. identify a variety of circumstantial factors that may be considered and could be useful to arbitrators confronted with this issue.[37]

They conclude that

> "[w]hile it is true that an email may be sent by anyone who, with a password, gained access to another's email account, similar questions could be raised with traditional documents.... The mere fact that hacking, etc., is possible is not enough to exclude an email or any other form of digital evidence.... If the mere possibility of electronic alteration were enough to exclude the evidence, then no digital evidence could ever be authenticated."[38]

IV. SANCTIONS

The question of what sanctions a tribunal has authority to impose, and when and how sanctions should be imposed has been the subject of extensive discussion in recent years in the wake of the issuance of the 2013 International Bar Association Guidelines on Party Representation in International Arbitration (IBA Guidelines).[39] Various proposals have been made as to who should be responsible for sanctioning counsel.[40] Guerrilla tactics, including cyber intrusion, bring that issue to the fore.

---

37. Hon. Paul W. GRIMM, et al., "Authenticating Digital Evidence", 69 Baylor L. Rev. (2017) pp. 1, 9. See also, Hon. Paul W. GRIMM, "Authenticating Digital Evidence, 31 GP Solo – Litigation (2014, no. 5) p. 46, <https://www.americanbar.org/content/dam/aba/publications/gp_solo_magazine/september_october_2014/gpsm_v031n05_14sep_oct.authcheckdam.pdf>; Robert MORGESTER, "Introducing Digital Evidence in California State Courts (N. Am. & Caribbean Conf., 2016), <www.iap-association.org/getattachment/Conferences/Regional-Conferences/North-America-and-Caribbean/4th-North-American-and-Caribbean-Conference/Conference-Documentation/4NACC_Jamaica_WS1B_Morgester_CA-Digital-Evidence.pdf.aspx> (last visited 23 May 2018).
38. Hon. P.W. GRIMM, et al., supra fn. 37.
39. International Bar Association, IBA Guidelines on Party Representation in International Arbitration (2013) (hereinafter IBA Guidelines).
40. See, e.g., Elliott GEISINGER, "'Soft Law' and Hard Questions: ASA's Initiative in the Debate on Counsel Ethics in International Arbitration" in Daniele FAVALLI, ed., *The Sense and Non-sense of Guidelines, Rules and Other Para-regulatory Texts in International Arbitration* (Juris 2015) p. 17 (proposing a global arbitration ethics council); Tom JONES and Alison ROSS, "Mourre Calls for Institutions to Join Forces", Glob. Arb. Rev. (9 Mar. 2018) <https://globalarbitrationreview.

Tribunals are appropriately concerned about guerrilla tactics, and consideration of remedies beyond the exclusion of evidence may be appropriate in cases of cyber intrusion. As the tribunal stated in *Libananco*:[41]

> "The Tribunal attributes great importance to privilege and confidentiality, and if instructions have been given with the benefit of improperly obtained privileged or confidential information, severe prejudice may result. If that event arises the Tribunal may consider other remedies available apart from the exclusion of improperly obtained evidence or information."

The IBA Guidelines empower the tribunal to address "misconduct" by a party representative after giving the parties notice and a reasonable opportunity to be heard. Misconduct is broadly defined by the IBA Guidelines to include "breach of the present guidelines, or any other conduct that the arbitral tribunal determines to be contrary to the duties of a party representative".[42] The nature of the "misconduct" intended to be covered has not been established but, certainly, cyber intrusion would fall into that category. The guidelines give the tribunal power to respond and specifically identify admonishing the party representative, drawing inferences, apportioning costs, and taking other "appropriate measures in order to preserve the fairness and integrity of the proceeding". In determining the remedy, the tribunal is to consider the nature and gravity of the misconduct, the good faith of the party representative, the extent to which the party representative knows about or participated in the misconduct, the potential impact of a ruling on the rights of the parties, the need to preserve the integrity and fairness of the arbitral proceedings, and the enforceability of the award.[43] These considerations clearly outline the matters to be considered in deciding whether or not to impose a sanction on a party for cyber intrusions, if it is concluded that the tribunal has

---

com/article/1166513/mourre-calls-for-institutions-to-join-forces> (noting that ASA's proposal did not attract international consensus because important institutions took the view that counsel misconduct is for the arbitrators to deal with, along with the support of the institutions); Carlos A. CARMONA, "Considerations on the IBA Guidelines on Party Representation in International Arbitration: A Brazilian Point of View", 1 Les Cahiers de l'Arbitrage (2014) pp. 29, 44; Felix DASSER, "A Critical Analysis of the IBA Guidelines on Party Representation" in D. FAVALLI, ed., *The Sense and Non-sense of Guidelines, Rules and Other Para-Regulatory Texts in International Arbitration* (Juris 2015) pp. 33, 47; Jarred PINKSTON, "The Case for Arbitral Institutions to Play a Role in Mitigating Unethical Conduct by Party Counsel in International Arbitration", 32 Conn. J. Int'l L. (2017) pp. 177, 201; Vincent S. DATTILO, "Ethics in International Arbitration: A Critical Examination of the LCIA General Guidelines for the Parties' Legal Representatives", 44 Ga. J. Int'l & Comp. L. (2016) pp. 637, 645 (By incorporating ethical standards in arbitral rules, the arbitrators themselves would become the enforcers of these rules, therefore, empowered to sanction attorneys for applicable misconduct). See also, William W. PARK, "A Fair Fight: Professional Guidelines in International Arbitration", 30 Arb. Int'l (2014, issue 3) p. 409.

41. *Libananco*, supra, fn. 19, at para. 80.
42. IBA Guidelines, supra fn. 39, at p. 3.
43. IBA Guidelines, supra fn. 39, at p. 16 (Guidelines 26 and 27 on remedies for misconduct). See also, Edna SUSSMAN, "Can Counsel Ethics Beat Guerrilla Tactics?: Background and Impact of the New IBA Guidelines on Party Representation in International Arbitration", N.Y. Disp. Resol. Law (Fall 2013) at p. 47.

authority to do so. Others have added disqualification of counsel, and even in particularly egregious cases, a dismissal of the entire case with prejudice as possible sanctions.[44]

On must start with the question of whether there is authority to impose the sanction. Authority for sanctions might be found in institutional rules, party adoption of the IBA Guidelines, party agreement, and perhaps even the tribunal's inherent power.[45] Much has been written about the inherent powers of arbitrators but the scope of the tribunal's inherent power is an unresolved question and a continuing subject of debate.[46]

Drawing negative inferences, often cited and on occasion applied, raises less serious questions about the authority of the tribunal. But depending on the circumstances and the relationship of the inference to the wrongful conduct even that may raise questions of punitive measures in violation of due process and risk vacatur.[47]

The question of whether the tribunal has the power to impose cost sanctions on the parties – and even more questionably, on the counsel – has not been firmly settled.[48] Pierre Mayer opined that "punishing a counsel, or a party through a decision on costs is an abuse of the power to sanction. This is because an arbitrator is not allowed to impose a penalty without a basis in law: '[W]ithout a power specifically conferred either by the law or by the parties ... an arbitrator is not allowed to impose a penalty.'"[49] Others have taken a different view.[50] Yet, others have suggested that the power to impose cost

44. See generally, Abba KOLO, "Witness Intimidation, Tampering, and Other Related Abuses of Process in Investment Arbitration: Possible Remedies Available to the Arbitral Tribunal", 26 Arb. Int'l (2010, issue 1) p. 43.

45. J. PINKSTON, supra fn. 40; Philip D. O'NEILL, "The Power of Arbitrators to Award Monetary Sanctions for Discovery Abuse", Disp. Resol. J. (Nov. 2005 – Jan. 2006) at p. 60 (discussing the different approaches courts have taken to potential sources of authority for this power); Sarah WHITTINGTON, "*Timor-Leste v. Australia:* 'Guerrilla Tactics' and Schoolyard Bullies in State Arbitration", 6 Y.B. on Arb. & Mediation (2014) pp. 429, 437 ("Recent studies of 'guerrilla tactics' in arbitration present divergent views on how to effectively sanction or prevent these actions."); Pedro J. MARTINEZ-FRAGA, "Good Faith, Bad Faith, but Not Losing Faith: A Commentary on the 2010 IBA Rules on the Taking of Evidence in International Arbitration", 43 Geo. J. Int'l L. (2012) pp. 387, 421 (discussing inherent authority of arbitrators to impose sanctions).

46. See Margaret L. MOSES, "Inherent Powers of Arbitrators to Deal with Ethical Issues" in Arthur ROVINE, ed., *Contemporary Issues in International Arbitration and Mediation, The Fordham Papers* (Brill/Nijhoff 2014) p. 93; Andrea BJORKLUND and Jonathan BROSSEAU, "Sources of Inherent Powers in International Adjudication", 6 Eur. Int'l Arb. J. (2018, no. 2) p. 1.; 76 Int'l L. Ass'n Rep. Conf. (2014) pp. 823-851 (International Law Association's report on the inherent and implied powers of arbitrators in international commercial arbitration); Martins PAPARINSKIS, "Inherent Powers of ICSID Tribunals: Broad and Rightly So" in Ian A. LAIRD and Todd J. WEILER, eds., *Investment Treaty Arbitration and International Law*, Volume 5 (Juris 2011) p. 9;

47. W. PARK, supra fn. 40, at p. 422; Menalco J. SOLIS, "Adverse Inferences in Investor-State Arbitration", 34 Arb. Int'l (2018, issue 1) p. 79.

48. G. BORN, supra, fn. 7, at Sect. 15.10.

49. "Mayer on Arbitrators' Powers and Limits", Glob. Arb. Rev. (25 Oct. 2017) <https://globalarbitrationreview.com/article/1149346/mayer-on-arbitrators-powers-and-limits>.

50. Richard KREINDLER and Mariel DIMSEY, "Sanctioning of Party Conduct Through Costs: A Reconsideration of Scope, Timing and Content of Costs Awards" in Patricia SHAUGHNESSY and Sherlin TUNG, eds., *The Powers and Duties of an Arbitrator, Liber Amicorum Pierre A. Karrer*, 2d ed. (Kluwer 2017) p. 201.

sanctions should be more vigorously pursued,[51] as arbitration users have urged.[52] Some courts have confirmed the tribunal's authority to impose costs as a sanction.[53]

Whether or not the tribunal has the authority to disqualify counsel in international arbitration has also not been definitively decided. The historical view has been that arbitral tribunals do not have the power to disqualify or sanction counsel.[54] However, that may be evolving. In a leading case, *Hrvatska Elektroprivreda, d.d. v. Republic of Slovenia*, the tribunal disqualified the counsel brought into the representation shortly before the hearing, which presented a conflict with one of the arbitrators, based on the inherent power of the tribunal to take measures to "preserve the integrity of the proceedings".[55] In a subsequent case, the tribunal in *The Rompetrol Group N.V. v. Romania* declined to disqualify the counsel and, while not deciding the limits of the tribunal's powers, stated that "such powers as may exist would be one to be exercised only rarely, and in compelling circumstances".[56] Given the right of the parties in arbitration to select a representative of their choosing, any power to disqualify counsel will certainly be very sparingly exercised.[57] Some courts have found disqualification to be beyond the powers of an arbitrator.[58] Courts, however, in appropriate circumstances, have disqualified counsel who have engaged in cyber guerrilla tactics.[59]

The dismissal of the entire case with prejudice as a sanction for guerrilla tactics would be an extreme measure and not likely to be the remedy chosen by a tribunal. Gunther Horvath, Stephan Wilske, and Jeffrey Leng report that no tribunal has done so.[60] Courts

---

51. Gunther J. HORVATH et al., "Dealing with Guerrilla Tactics at Different Stages of an Arbitration" in Gunther HORVATH, et al., eds., *Guerrilla Tactics in International Arbitration* (Kluwer 2013) pp. 33, 48-50.
52. Queen Mary Univ. of London Sch. of Int'l Arb., *International Arbitration Survey: Current and Preferred Practices in the Arbitral Process* (2012) p. 41 (reporting that according to the survey, an overwhelming majority of respondents believe tribunals should take into account improper conduct by a party or its counsel when allocating costs).
53. BORN, supra fn. 7, at pp. 2316-2317.
54. Catherine ROGERS, *Ethics in International Arbitration* (Oxford 2014) pp. 135.
55. *Hrvatska Elektroprivreda, d.d. v. Republic of Slovenia* (ICSID Case No. ARB/05/24), Tribunal's Ruling Regarding the Participation of David Mildon QC in Further Stages of the Proceeding (6 May 2008).
56. *The Rompetrol Group N.V. v. Romania* (ICSID Case No. ARB/06/3), Decision of the Tribunal on the Participation of a Counsel (14 Jan. 2010).
57. Alan Scott RAU, "Arbitrators Without Powers? Disqualifying Counsel in Arbitral Proceedings", 30 Arb. Int'l, (2014, issue 3) pp. 457, 511 ("Precisely because of their regulatory spareness, transnational rules will have the virtue of directing the attention of arbitral tribunals to the core of what alone is critical – that is, to what is minimally necessary to ensure the fairness of proceedings.").
58. *Nw. Nat. Ins. Co. v. Insco, Ltd.*, 866 F. Supp. 2d 214, 217 (S.D.N.Y. 2011).
59. See, e.g., *Bona Fide Conglomerate, Inc. v. Sourceamerica*, No. 314CV00751GPCDHB, 2016 WL 4361808, at *6 (S.D. Cal. 16 Aug. 2016) (where privileged documents were leaked to WikiLeaks, the court disqualified the counsel overriding the magistrate's recommendation of the lesser remedy of evidence exclusion, while noting that "an order of disqualification of counsel is a drastic measure, which courts should hesitate to impose except in circumstances of absolute necessity").
60. G. HORVATH, et al., supra fn. 51, at pp. 51-52; Gunther J. HORVATH, et al., "Lessons to be Learned for International Arbitration" in Gunther Horvath, et al., eds., *Guerrilla Tactics in International Arbitration* (Kluwer 2013) pp. 278-279.

have not always been so restrained and have dismissed complaints lodged by parties who have engaged in illegal conduct in the collection of evidence by cyber intrusion.[61]

V. THE IMPACT ON DECISION-MAKING OF INADMISSIBLE EVIDENCE

National laws provide exclusionary evidentiary rules where the prejudicial effect of the evidence outweighs its probative value, where the nature of the evidence has limited reliability and therefore limited probative value, or where policy considerations dictate exclusion as is the case in disincentivizing illegal behavior. While these exclusionary evidentiary rules authorize and, in some cases, require the fact-finder to exclude the evidence, the fact is that the fact-finder has already seen the evidence.

Study after study has established that fact-finders cannot ignore inadmissible information and are influenced in their decision-making by that information, even if it has been excluded. As Doron Teichman and Eyal Zamir sum up the literature:

> "[n]umerous studies have documented the effects of inadmissible evidence in ... legal domains, such as hearsay evidence, pretrial media reports, and illegally obtained evidence. These studies show that inadmissible evidence affects judicial decision-making in civil as well as criminal settings, irrespective of whether that evidence favors the prosecution or the defense. A recent meta-analysis concluded that 'inadmissible evidence produced a significant impact.'"[62]

Illustrative study outcomes include one study which demonstrated that there was a spread in finding liability as between judges who saw inadmissible privileged information damaging to the plaintiff (29 percent found for plaintiff) as compared to judges who did not see that information (55 percent found for the plaintiff). There was a spread of 25 percent in the damages awarded between judges who saw evidence of an unrelated criminal conviction which was suppressed as unduly prejudicial and those who were not informed of the prior criminal conviction.[63] Recognition of unconscious influence is undoubtedly the rationale for not permitting parties to introduce evidence of settlement discussions.

---

61. See, e.g., *Leor Expl. & Prod., LLC v. Aguiar*, No. 09-60136-CIV, 2010 WL 3782195 (S.D. Fla. 28 Sept. 2010), on reconsideration in part, No. 09-60136-CIV, 2011 WL 4345294 (S.D. Fla. 15 Sept. 2011) (dismissing the case in which the party had engaged in computer hacking relying on the court's inherent power to impose sanctions for bad-faith conduct and finding that no lesser sanction would suffice under the circumstances); *Salmeron v. Enter. Recovery Sys., Inc.*, 579 F.3d 787 (7th Cir. 2009) (dismissing the case as a sanction for the willful leak of documents which were ultimately posted on WikiLeaks).
62. Doron TEICHMAN, et al., "Judicial Decision-Making: A Behavioral Perspective" in Eyal ZAMIR, et al., eds., *Oxford Handbook of Behavioral Economics and the Law* (Oxford 2014) pp. 1, 9. See also, Andrew J. WISTRICH, et al., "Can Judges Ignore Inadmissible Information? The Difficulty of Deliberately Disregarding", 153 U. Pa. L. Rev. (2005) pp. 1251, 1279-1281.
63. Edna SUSSMAN, "Arbitrator Decision-Making: Unconscious Psychological Influences and What You Can Do About Them", 24 Am. Rev. Int'l Arb. (2013) pp. 487.

As the courts have found it can be "difficult to 'unring the bell'".[64] Arbitrators should be sensitive to this unconscious influence and carefully assess the evidence upon which they rely to ensure that it supports their conclusions without reference to excluded evidence. Advocates should be sensitive to the fact that highlighting evidence to urge its exclusion may cause it to make an even deeper impression on the fact-finder.

VI. THE IMPACT ON DECISION-MAKING OF NATIVE LEGAL CULTURE

At a recent conference, a well-known arbitrator suggested that looking to the law of one's own jurisdiction is very useful in considering whether the governing law makes sense. Those in attendance were surprised by that comment, but it was perhaps just a conscious recognition of the fact that at an unconscious level one's own legal culture, whether native or the one in which an individual has predominantly practiced, may influence one's analysis and decision.

Supporting this conclusion Joshua Karton found in his study of the evolution of contract law in arbitration, that tribunals considered extrinsic evidence where they were charged with applying the law of a common law jurisdiction even though the law of that jurisdiction would have precluded such evidence.[65] We can surmise that this outcome resulted from the influence of the arbitrators' native legal culture. As Giuditta Cordero-Moss aptly put it "the legal background of the arbitrator is recognized as playing an important role, a sort of imprinting, which will influence the approach taken...."[66] Thus, while the award may be written with reference to the applicable law, the conclusion may be driven by an arbitrator's legal culture. As Justice Scalia pointed out, quoting Chancellor James Kent who said, "I almost always found [legal] principles suited to my views of the case."[67] National laws may vary as to the admissibility of unlawfully obtained evidence and influence decisions on the admissibility of evidence obtained through cyber intrusion.[68]

A comprehensive decision reviewing prior relevant authorities was issued by the Singapore Court of Appeals in 2016, which directly addressed the question of the balance between the competing policy imperatives of truth and privilege in the context of WikiLeaks exposure.[69] A former employee sought to introduce into evidence communications of his former employer with its counsel, which had been hacked by unknown parties and uploaded onto WikiLeaks. The court concluded that even though the WikiLeaks material submitted as evidence was publicly available, because it constituted a minute fraction of the approximately 500 GB of data that had been pilfered just from the former employee's system, it was highly probable that few, if any, knew of

64. *N.L.R.B. v. Jackson Hosp. Corp.*, 257 F.R.D. 302, 307 (D.D.C. 2009).

65. Joshua D. H. KARTON, *The Culture of International Arbitration and the Evolution of Contract Law* (Oxford 2013) pp. 195-232.

66. Giuditta CORDERO-MOSS, "Non-national Sources in International Commercial Arbitration and the Hidden Influence by National Traditions", 63 Scandinavian Stud. of L. (2017) p. 22.

67. Antonin SCALIA, et al., *Making Your Case: The Art of Persuading Judges* (2008) p. 27.

68. See Jane COLSTON, "The Fruit from a Poisoned Tree – Use of Unlawfully Obtained Evidence", IBA Int'l Litig. Newsl. (Sep. 2017) at p. 20.

69. *Wee Shuo Woon v. HT S.R.L.*, [2017] S.G.C.A. 23 (Sing.).

its existence, and therefore the contents were not public knowledge and retained their confidential status. The court considered the fact that the employee had not been the perpetrator of the cyberattack but concluded that there was little doubt that the employee knew that the emails were privileged. The court held that the confidential character of the information in the emails had not been lost by its posting on WikiLeaks because to hold otherwise would be to "sanction and to encourage unauthorized access and pilferage of confidential information". The court further examined whether or not the documents supported the conclusions the employee sought to draw from them and concluded that they did not. The court concluded that "the balance between the competing imperatives of truth and privilege is ... struck in favor of the latter".[70]

Historically, case law from the United Kingdom supported accepting evidence which had been obtained in violation of law or ethics.[71] In 1980, the High Court of Justice, Chancery Division, opined that in civil cases "the judge cannot refuse it [evidence] on the ground that it may have been unlawfully obtained in the beginning".[72] That statement of principle may be in the process of evolving,[73] and considerations of competing values are being reviewed in light of subsequent enactments. In a decision issued in 2003, the English Court of Appeal considered violations of the Human Rights Act committed by an insurer which filmed a video of the claimant in her home without her knowledge, having obtained access to the claimant's home by deception. The court weighed the circumstances against the relevance of the evidence and concluded "this is not a case where the conduct of the defendant's insurers is so outrageous that the defence should be struck out .... It would be artificial and undesirable for the actual evidence, which is relevant and admissible, not to be placed before the judge who has the task of trying the case."[74]

In an even more recent case in 2010, documents had secretly been accessed and copied for the wife from the husband's server in his office and passed on to the wife's solicitor. The English Court of Appeal narrowed the *Hildebrand* rule which was previously thought to permit access to information about the other spouse whether or not it was confidential to assist in proceedings concerning financial provision. The court held that where rights pursuant to Art. 8 of the Human Rights Act and expectations of privacy are breached turnover of the documents to the husband's counsel was required, and the wife was restrained from using any information contained in the documents. The court also noted that the wife was at liberty to commence ancillary proceedings to obtain information to which she is entitled with respect to the husband's finances. The court noted that the conduct in question might also have constituted criminal offenses under the Computer Misuse Act 1990 and the Data Protection Act 1998. In rendering its

70. *Id.*, at 29.
71. Nigel COOPER, *The Fruit of the Poisoned Tree – The Admissibility of Evidence in Civil Cases* (unpublished manuscript) (on file with author) <www.bgja.org.uk/wp-content/uploads/2014/02/NigelCooper.pdf> (last visited 24 May 2018) (discussing the English case laws on the admissibility of evidence obtained in violation of law or ethics).
72. *Helliwell v. Piggott-Sims*, [1980] F.S.R. 356 (Eng.).
73. N. COOPER, supra, fn. 71, at p. 1.
74. *Jones v. University of Warwick* [2003] EWCA (Civ) 151 (Eng.).

decision, the court stated that it had given due regard to the competing right to a fair trial, right to preserve confidence and right to rely on evidence.[75]

In the United States, to safeguard the Fourth Amendment rights, the exclusionary rule does not permit the admission of evidence seized during an unlawful search as proof against the defendant at a criminal trial. The courts have developed the "fruit of the poisonous tree" doctrine which extends the exclusionary rule to require suppression of other evidence that is derived from and is tainted by the illegal search or seizure. The doctrine is not applicable in civil cases.[76] How courts handle evidence derived through illegal or unethical means in civil cases is not uniform and is generally fact specific. Courts have said that "[g]enerally in civil cases, the manner in which evidence is obtained is irrelevant to the issue of admissibility."[77] On the other hand, the courts have noted that "courts routinely preclude [the] use of evidence obtained in violation of the ethical rules in order to appropriately remedy that violation".[78]

Addressing an application to strike references to documents that had been released by others on WikiLeaks from the complaint, a US District Court declined to do so. The court found that since the

> "documents have been available in the public domain for more than five years, and this Court does not have the power or ability to limit its access. ... '[I]t is unlikely that the court can now effectively enforce an injunction against the internet in its various manifestations, and it would constitute a dubious manifestation of public policy were it to attempt to do so.' ... [The] complaint does not put this material 'in the public eye' any more than the internet has already done so."[79]

In France, views on the issue have been split between the "Civil" and the "Criminal" divisions of the French Supreme Court (*Cour de Cassation*). In civil matters, the legality of evidence has been considered through the prism of a more general notion of "fairness" (*loyauté*) in the administration of evidence, established by the decision of *Cour de Cassation* in 2011. In that case, a company produced in support of its application audio tapes containing recorded telephone conversations with representatives of two of its competitors. The Paris Court of Appeals held that while the recordings were obtained in an unfair manner, they could not be completely excluded from the debate by the mere application of an "abstract principle" of fairness, without showing that production of such evidence had a specific impact on the right to a fair trial of the parties in question. The

75. *Tchenguiz v. Imerman*, [2010] EWCA (Civ) 908 (Eng.).

76. *Lingo v. City of Salem*, 832 F.3d 953, 958 (9th Cir. 2016); *White v. City of Birmingham, Ala.*, 96 F. Supp. 3d 1260, 1271 (N.D. Ala. 2015), as amended (27 May 2015) (noting that the Supreme Court has "repeatedly declined to extend the exclusionary rule to proceedings other than criminal trials" and permitted the evidence, noting its immense probative value); *United States v. Janis*, 428 U.S. 433, 460 (1976).

77. *Carr v. Ferrell-Duncan OBGYN Clinic*, 538 S.W.3d 360, 363 (Mo. Ct. App. 2018); *accord, Radder v. CSX Transp., Inc.*, 68 A.D.3d 1743, 1744-1745 (2009).

78. *Scranton Prod., Inc. v. Bobrick Washroom Equip., Inc.*, 190 F. Supp. 3d 419, 434 (M.D. Pa. 2016), reconsideration denied, No. 3:14-CV-00853, 2016 WL 7173786 (M.D. Pa. 8 Dec. 2016).

79. *Bible v. United Student Aid Funds, Inc.*, No. 1:13-CV-00575-TWP, 2014 WL 1048807, at *4 (S.D. Ind. 14 Mar. 2014), rev'd and remanded on other gds., 799 F.3d 633 (7th Cir. 2015).

Cour de Cassation disagreed and held that the recordings, made unbeknownst to their subjects, were not admissible as evidence.[80] In its decision, the Court relied on Art. 9 of the French Civil Procedure Code, Sect. 1 of Art. 6 of the European Convention on Human Rights, and the "principle of fairness in the administration of evidence".

Yet, the prohibition is not absolute. For example, the *Cour de Cassation* admitted findings, derived from the surveillance by a bailiff of a person, when such surveillance was made in public, holding that "any harm caused to the privacy of Mr. Z., in public spaces or places open to public, without any incitement to go there [...] were not disproportionate".[81] In a more recent decision, the court has further clarified that "the right to prove one's case can only justify the production of evidence which causes harm to privacy, where such production is indispensable to the exercise of that right, and where the harm was proportionate to the aim pursued".[82]

The Criminal Division of the *Cour de Cassation*, on the other hand, is less concerned with the principle of *loyauté*. It relies in particular on Art. 427, para. 1 of the Criminal Procedure Code, which states that "[e]xcept where the law provides otherwise, offenses may be established by any means of evidence and the judge shall rule based on his personal conviction", to admit evidence obtained in an illegal or unfair way.[83] In general, the Criminal Division admits a victim's use of unfairly obtained evidence, if it is a condition for her access to justice, as well as where admission of such evidence is a condition to establish the innocence of the person. It also rules on a regular basis that there is no legal provision allowing criminal judges to exclude evidence submitted by an individual to the investigative authorities on the sole basis that such evidence would have been obtained illegally or unfairly, and that it is only up to the judges, pursuant to Art. 427 of the Criminal Procedure Code, to assess the probative value of such evidence, having submitted it to an adversarial debate. This includes, notably, cases where the illegally obtained evidence includes the content of a person's communications with her lawyers.[84]

In light of the unconscious influence of one's native legal culture, there may be situations where counsel would wish to consider emphasizing differences, if there are any, between the applicable law and the native legal culture of the arbitrators.

---

80. Ass. plén., 7 January 2011, Bull. 2011, Ass. plén., No. 1. See also, Com., 13 October 2009, n°08-19.525 (barring transcript of a telephone conversation overheard unbeknownst to the interlocutor).
81. Civ. 1ère, 31 October 2012, Bull. 2012, I, No. 226.
82. Civ. 1ère, 25 February 2016, n°15-12.403.
83. Notably, and contrary to the stance of the civil division of *Cour de Cassation*, the criminal division has recognized as admissible recordings of private telephone conversations. See Crim., 31 January 2007, Bull. crim. 2007, No. 27, p. 100.
84. Crim., 11 June 2002, Bull. crim. 2002, No. 131; Crim., 31 January 2007, Bull. crim., No. 27, p. 100; Crim., 27 January 2010, Bull. crim. 2010, No. 16; Crim., 7 March 2012, Bull. crim. 2012, No. 64; Crim., 31 January 2012, Bull. crim. 2012, No. 27.

VII. DUTY TO REPORT

Cyber intrusion is a crime in jurisdictions around the world.[85] Violations of privacy laws are also implicated. What, if any, is the arbitrator's duty to report a cybercrime? And to whom? Local authorities? Counsel's bar association? The administering institution? While arbitrators must first consider whether they are under any legal or ethical obligation that requires them to take action,[86] the resolution of the question presents the tension between reporting wrongdoing and the confidentiality of the arbitration proceeding.[87]

Elliott Geisinger and Pierre Ducret distinguish between doctored documents and witnesses lying on the stand, which they consider sufficiently dealt with by the tribunal's disregard of such evidence on the one hand and what they referred to as a "Balrog"[88] on the other hand. A Balrog is a violation of fundamental national or supranational rules close to transnational public policy. They cite as examples, money laundering, corrupt practices, gross violation of competition law, fraudulent conveyances, financing of terrorism, violation of embargoes, traffic of cultural property, and gross violations of

---

85. See, e.g., Directive 2013/40/EU, of the European Parliament and of the Council of 12 August 2013 on Attacks Against Information Systems and Replacing Council Framework Decision 2005/222/JHA; Tony KRONE, "Hacking Offences", Austl. Inst. Crim., <https://aic.gov.au/publications/htcb/htcb005> (24 last visited May 2018) (describing how computer hacking crimes are defined in Australia); Nat'l Conf. on St. Legis, *Computer Crime Statutes*. (12 May 2016) <http://www.ncsl.org/research/telecommunications-and-information-technology/computer-hacking-and-unauthorized-access-laws.aspx> (All fifty US states have computer crime laws; most address unauthorized access or computer trespass. Some state laws also directly address other specific types of computer crime, such as spyware, phishing, denial of service attacks, and ransomware); Computer Fraud and Abuse Act, 18 U.S.C. Sect. 1001 (1986); Computer Misuse and Cybersecurity Act, No. 19, c. 50A, 1993 (Sing.); The Information Technology Act, No. 21, Acts of Parliament, 2000 (Ind.).
86. C. ROGERS, supra fn. 54, at p. 97; Alexis MOURRE, "Arbitration and Criminal Law: Reflections on the Duties of the Arbitrator", 22 Arb. Int'l (2006, issue 1) p. 95.
87. Steven C. BENNETT, "Who Is Responsible for Ethical Behavior by Counsel in Arbitration", Disp. Resol. J. (May-Jul. 2008) at pp. 38, 44 (Attorneys have an obligation under the rules of professional conduct to report unethical conduct of other members of the bar. If this obligation applies to attorneys when they serve as arbitrators, the arbitrators would have conflicting ethical obligations – to maintain confidentiality and to report unethical conduct by counsel in arbitral proceedings.). Cf. Carrie MENKEL-MEADOW, "Ethics Issues in Arbitration and Related Dispute Resolution Processes: What's Happening and What's Not", 56 U. Miami L. Rev. (2002) pp. 949, 955 (suggesting that the answer may depend on whether the arbitration process is purely private or sponsored by a court). Also see, Robert BLACKETT, "The Very Naughty List: What Happens If Arbitrators Suspect Criminal Activity by the Parties", The Arbiter: Int'l Disp. Newswire (Winter 2014) p. 6 (discussing what should arbitrators in an English-seated arbitration do – legally and/or ethically – when they suspect one or both parties have committed, is committing, or intends to commit a criminal offence); Kristen M. BLANKLEY, "Lying, Stealing, and Cheating: The Role of Arbitrators as Ethics Enforcers", 52 U. Louisville L. Rev. (2014) pp. 443, 462-491 (discussing why arbitrators should be acting as ethics enforcers); S. COHEN and M. MORRIL, supra fn. 6; JEFFREY WAINCYMER, *Procedure and Evidence in International Arbitration* (2012) p. 105 (discussing the powers, rights and duties of arbitrators).
88. The Balrog reference draws upon Tolkien's *Lord of the Rings* tale of miner dwarves who dug too deeply and unleashed "a terrible daemon from ancient times", the Balrog.

environmental regulations.[89] If a party hacks into another parties' computer system, or worse yet, posts it publicly or provides it to others to post publicly, one might well conclude that the matter involves no ordinary doctored document, but rather rises to the level of a Balrog.

However, Geisinger and Ducret conclude that finding a reporting duty is in complete contradiction with the confidential nature of international commercial arbitration and suggest that most legal systems would not impose any such duty even with respect to Balrogs.[90] They allow for possible exceptions for extremely serious violations of fundamental legal principles such as human trafficking where the confidentiality of the arbitration becomes a "minor consideration".

Two anecdotes confirm the historic general acceptance of Geisinger and Ducret's conclusion. It became clear to the tribunal in the course of one hearing some years ago, when the testimony of one witness was interrupted and both counsel requested an adjournment, that the testimony revealed a Balrog which had not previously been identified. The tribunal approached the arbitral institution and requested a formal legal opinion as to their duties. A British QC was retained to deliver an opinion virtually overnight. He opined that the tribunal did not have a duty to report the Balrog. The tribunal relied on that advice. In another case, it became apparent from the testimony that a bridge was in imminent danger of collapse because the steel that had been used in its construction was not of sufficient thickness. The tribunal advised counsel that if they did not report it to the authorities promptly the tribunal would take it upon itself to do so.

Perhaps the historic bright line between reporting a Balrog and preserving confidentiality as drawn where there is a danger to life and limb is applicable to cyber intrusion. But with the advent of criminal statutes around the globe dealing with corruption and money laundering, some of which impose reporting requirements that vary across jurisdictions, coupled with the emergence of these issues in arbitration, the duty to report criminal activity has gained attention with no clear answer as to the scope of the arbitrator's duties to report.[91] Data breach notification laws and regulations have been enacted in many jurisdictions[92] making the issue of the duty to report potentially relevant to cybercrimes as well.

---

89. Elliott GEISINGER and Pierre DUCRET, "The Uncomfortable Truth: Once Discovered What to Do with It" in Markus WIRTH, et al., eds., *The Search for "Truth" in Arbitration: Is Finding the Truth What Dispute Resolution Is About?* (Juris 2011) pp. 113, 114.

90. *Id.*, at pp. 128-130; See also, A. MOURRE, supra fn. 86.

91. See, e.g., Inan ULUC, *Corruption in International Arbitration* (Wildy, Simmonds and Hill 2018) pp. 192-200; A. MOURRE, supra fn. 86. Sara NADEAU-SEGUIN, "Commercial Arbitration and Corrupt Practices: Should Arbitrators Be Bound by a Duty to Report Corrupt Practices?, 10 Transnat'l Disp. Mgmt. J. (2013, issue 3); A. Timothy MARTIN, "International Arbitration and Corruption: An Evolving Standard", 1 Transnat'l Disp. Mgmt. J (2006, issue 2); A. MOURRE, supra, fn. 86.

92. See, e.g., U.S.: Conf. on St. Legis. *Security Breach Notification Laws* (all fifty states have statutory breach notification laws); Regulation (EU) 2016/679 of the European Parliament and the Council of 27 April 2016 on the Protection of Natural Persons with Regard to the Processing of Personal Data and on the Free Movement of Such Data, and Repealing Directive 95/46/EC (General Data Protection Regulation), 2016 O.J. L 119/1, Art. 33.

The countervailing considerations of arbitrator confidentiality and the privacy of the proceedings, the obligation to make every effort to ensure that the award is enforceable, and the emerging view that arbitrators have a responsibility to uphold the international rule of law and must be concerned with international public policy will thus likely be a subject of concern not only in the context of corruption and money laundering but perhaps in the area of cyber intrusion as well.

While dealing with the obligations of lawyers with respect to the criminal act of money laundering, the bar associations which collaborated on the effort noted in their report the "essential ethical obligations of the legal profession not to support or facilitate criminal activity". The report further noted the fact that specific laws and regulations in many countries "have been extended to lawyers and require, in a formal sense, lawyers to take specific actions" including "in some jurisdictions an obligation to inform the authorities". Based on the development of these recent legal requirements the report strikes a final cautionary note.

> "The obligation by lawyers to report is highly controversial and is seen by many to endanger the independence of the legal profession and to be incompatible with a lawyer client relationship. However, in some countries lawyers can themselves be prosecuted for failure to carry out appropriate due diligence and report suspicious transactions to the authorities. It is important that lawyers in such countries are fully aware of these obligations and the actions they need to take."[93]

Arbitrators who are attorneys may or may not be bound by the duties of attorneys, and which law would apply is far from clear, but if confronted with a cyber intrusion an arbitrator might be wise to heed this admonition with respect to cyber intrusion as well and consider what obligations, if any, he or she has to report.

VIII. CONCLUSION

The ease with which it appears cyber intrusion can be accomplished and the almost daily reports of hacks suggests that arbitrators are likely to be presented with issues related to breaches of cyber security. The issues are not new. They are merely presented in a new guise. It is hoped that this article will assist arbitration practitioners in understanding the issues as presented in this context and provide guidance as to how to approach them.

93. *A Lawyer's Guide to Detecting and Preventing Money Laundering*, a collaborative publication of the International Bar Association, the American Bar Association and the Council of Bars and Law Societies of Europe (2014) at p. 2 <https://www.anti-moneylaundering.org/About AML.aspx> (last visited 3 November 2018).

Hot Topics and New Voices

Hot Topics and New Voices

Part I:
Hot Topics

Report of the Rapporteur for the "Hot Topics" Panel

Marina Kofman[*]

TABLE OF CONTENTS PAGE

I. INTRODUCTION

The Hot Topics Panel was a round-table discussion of some "hot topics" in arbitration at the time of the 2018 ICCA Sydney Congress. The panel featured Mark Kantor, Independent Arbitrator, as Moderator, with Judith Levine, Permanent Court of Arbitration; Joongi Kim, Yonsei Law School and Natalie Reid, Debevoise and Plimpton, making up the panel. The topics discussed were improperly obtained evidence, the Belt and Road Initiative (BRI), parallel proceedings and arbitration for claims of discrimination and sexual misconduct. This is an edited summary of the panel discussion.

II. IMPROPERLY OBTAINED EVIDENCE

Levine: Last night while returning from your respective cocktail receptions, you may have smelled smoke lingering in the Sydney air. As a local, I can tell you that the smoke was not on account of the sizzling hot topics we will be delivering to you this afternoon, but, as you may have read in our local press, some bushfires resulting from extraordinarily hot April weather. In addition to our changing climate, other front-page stories in the local press leading up to the ICCA week have included dubious sporting practices, reprimand of a dubious lawyer, a spotlight on the extent of Chinese development of ports in our Pacific neighbors, and allegations of cyber-attacks across the West. Some of the same headline themes will pop up during our discussion this afternoon.

I will be kicking off with the topic of improperly obtained evidence. If a piece of evidence has been obtained as a result of dumpster-diving, email hacking, unauthorized wiretapping or large-scale national security breach, can it ever be relied upon in an international arbitration? I will answer, yes it can. But that answer may depend on who did the dirty work, how material is the evidence, and who got hurt by the unlawful act. Due to time constraints I will not be dealing with fraudulent creation of evidence, such

* Associate at Norton Rose Fulbright.

as the allegedly fabricated documents in the *Lighthouse/East Timor*[1] and *Sanum*[2] cases, but rather, I will focus on where evidence is questionable not on account of its authenticity, but rather the manner in which it was obtained.

A preliminary consideration will be whether the party seeking to rely on the evidence, was itself involved in unlawfully obtaining it. Some examples where this was the case were *Methanex v. United States*,[3] in which claimants sought to admit documents obtained by acts of trespass, searching trash cans and dumpsters to retrieve private correspondence.[4] In *Libananco v. Turkey*,[5] Turkey sought to rely on thousands of privileged and confidential emails obtained through court-ordered surveillance in an unrelated investigation.[6] What were the consequences? Generally speaking, in these circumstances the evidence will not be admitted. Both tribunals ruled that evidence was inadmissible, with the *Methanex* tribunal basing its conclusions on principles of unclean hands and bad faith. The *Methanex* tribunal said that the conduct committed during the arbitration offended basic principles of justice and fairness. However, they did leave the door slightly ajar if the evidence would have been material, by examining whether and ultimately concluding that it only would have been of marginal evidential significance in support of Methanex's case.

What about when the evidence was originally obtained in an unlawful manner, but the party relying on it simply found it (in the public domain, for example)? Is that party an innocent but fortunate bystander, or a tainted conspirator? Examples where the original means of obtaining evidence may be questionable, but the party seeking to rely on it was not involved, include a number of Court of Arbitration for Sport (CAS) match-fixing cases, for example, a FIFA fee-fixing case where a Sunday Times investigation revealed unauthorized wiretapping of players admitting to match-fixing. FIFA then found the players were involved in the match-fixing based on that evidence.[7] Likewise, in *Metalist v. UEFA*, a team was sanctioned on the basis of match-fixing admissions obtained through illegal phone tapping.[8]

---

1. *Lighthouse Corporation Pty Ltd and Lighthouse Corporation Ltd, IBC v. Timor-Leste* (ICSID Case No. ARB/15/2), Award (22 December 2017) para. 226; see also "Debevoise censured over 'fraud' in casino dispute", Global Arbitration Review (2 February 2018) at <https://globalarbitrationreview.com/article/1153317/debevoise-censured-over-%E2%80%9Cfraud%E2%80%9D-in-casino-dispute> (last accessed 12 November 2018).
2. *Laos v. Lao Holdings NV and Sanum Investments Ltd* (SIAC Case No. 143 of 2014) Award (29 June 2017) para. 210.
3. *Methanex v. United States of America* (UNCITRAL Rules).
4 *Methanex v. United States of America*, Final Award (Jurisdiction and Merits), (3 August 2005) pt. 2, ch. I, para 55.
5. *Libananco Holdings Co. Limited v. Republic of Turkey* (ICSID Case No. ARB/06/8).
6. *Libananco Holdings Co. Limited v. Republic of Turkey* (ICSID Case No. ARB/06/8), Award (2 September 2011) para. 22.
7. *Fusimalohi v. FIFA* (CAS Case No. 2011/A/2425), Award (8 March 2012) para. 10.
8. *Football Club Metalist. v. UEFA & PAOK FC* (CAS Case No. 2013/A/3297), Award (29 November 2013) para. 8.10; Natalia KISLIAKOVA, "Using Illegally Obtained Evidence in the Court of Arbitration for Sport", CIS Arbitration Forum (16 February 2018) at <http://www.cisarbitration.com/2018/02/16/using-illegally-obtained-evidence-in-the-court-of-arbitration-for-sport/> (last accessed 15 October 2018).

You may be familiar with various cases involving WikiLeaks cables, which in 2010 were released on a massive scale into the public domain. These were US State Department diplomatic cables, and the release was contrary to US espionage laws and international norms on diplomatic immunity. This provided something of a treasure trove for parties in international arbitration and litigation. For example, in the *Chagos Marine Protected Area Arbitration (Mauritius v. United Kingdom)*,[9] brought by Mauritius against the UK, Mauritius sought to rely on a diplomatic cable which recorded a British official telling US diplomats that it would become "difficult if not impossible" for former inhabitants to pursue their claim of resettlement on the islands if the entire Chagos Archipelago were a marine reserve. This was used as evidence to question the true intention behind the UK's declaration of a marine protected area. The UK acknowledged that the document was unfortunate but cited UK court decisions questioning its accuracy. It did not claim archival immunity.[10]

In the *Yukos* cases, diplomatic cables recording meetings between former auditors of Yukos, PwC, and staff at the US Embassy in Moscow were similarly relied on by the claimants to show Russian authorities pressured PwC to withdraw their audits as part of a broader campaign to destroy Yukos and take its assets. Russia did not object to the admissibility of the cables and did not disagree that they reflected the "candid" and "unguarded" views of the auditors held at the time.[11]

In *ConocoPhillips v. Venezuela*, Venezuela relied on WikiLeaks cables to ask the tribunal to revisit a decision on liability alleging the cables showed the claimants made false representations to the tribunal.[12] In the case of *Caratube v. Kazakhstan*,[13] the claimants sought to admit evidence from a site similar to WikiLeaks following a hacking attack against the Kazakh Government's computer network. There Kazakhstan did object on the basis of privilege.[14]

What are the consequences? The action taken by tribunals has been varied. In practice, one factor is whether or not the other side has actually objected. So, if there is no objection, the tribunal might admit the evidence either as probative or corroborative

9. Chagos Marine Protected Area Arbitration (Mauritius v. United Kingdom) (PCA Case No 2011-03).
10. *Chagos Marine Protected Area Arbitration (Mauritius v. United Kingdom)* (PCA Case No. 2011-03), Award (18 March 2015) para. 494.
11. *Hulley Enterprises Ltd v. Russian Federation* (PCA Case No. AA 226), Award (18 July 2014) para. 1189; *Yukos Universal Ltd v. Russian Federation* (PCA Case No. AA 227), Award (18 July 2014) para. 1189; *Veteran Petroleum Ltd v. Russian Federation* (PCA Case No. AA 228), Award (18 July 2014) para. 1189; see also James H. BOYKIN and Malik HAVALIC, "Fruits of the Poisonous Tree: The Admissibility of Unlawfully Obtained Evidence in International Arbitration", 5 Transnational Dispute Management (August 2015).
12. *ConocoPhillips Petrozuata B.V., ConocoPhillips Hamaca B.V. and ConocoPhillips Gulf of Paria B.V. v. Bolivarian Republic of Venezuela* (ICSID Case No. ARB/07/30), Interim Decision (7 January 2017) para. 135.
13. *Caratube International Oil Company LLP and Devincci Salah Hourani v. Republic of Kazakhstan* (ICSID Case No. ARB/13/13).
14. *Caratube International Oil Company LLP and Devincci Salah Hourani v. Republic of Kazakhstan* (ICSID Case No. ARB/13/13), Award (27 September 2017) paras. 150-156.

of other evidence, which is how the *Yukos* tribunal dealt with it.[15] A tribunal might choose to consider evidence as not reliable or material, which is how the *Chagos* tribunal dealt with it, citing UK court decisions that the report was not accurate, but making a passing comment that it did not consider it appropriate to place weight on a record of such provenance.[16] Or, a tribunal may choose to ignore it altogether, as the majority in *ConocoPhillips v. Venezuela* did. By contrast, the dissenting arbitrator in that case found those cables to be highly probative and accused his colleagues of "closing their blinkers" instead of "seeking the truth and dispensing justice".[17]

If there is an objection by the other side, what have tribunals done? Cherie Blair, in a speech last year, argued for "grabbing the bull by the horns".[18] An example of this is a series of Swiss Federal Supreme Court decisions reviewing a CAS decision. Those courts and tribunals went through a balancing act of looking at the interest of establishing the truth on the one side, against the interest in preserving the legally protected rights that have been infringed by the taking of evidence. That Swiss approach led to upholding the CAS decision based on wiretaps, by which they ultimately deferred to the public interest and sports interest involved in the fight against match-fixing.[19]

Some tribunals have acknowledged that even if a document was initially obtained unlawfully, the disclosure could not be damaging because of its extensive prior and public disclosure, which is how some of the UK[20] and US courts[21] have dealt with WikiLeaks cables.

---

15. *Hulley Enterprises Ltd v. Russian Federation* (PCA Case No. AA 226), Award (18 July 2014) para. 1223; *Yukos Universal Ltd v. Russian Federation* (PCA Case No. AA 227) Award (18 July 2014) para. 1223; *Veteran Petroleum Ltd v. Russian Federation* (PCA Case No. AA 228), Award (18 July 2014) para. 1223.
16. *Chagos Marine Protected Area Arbitration (Mauritius v. United Kingdom)* (PCA Case No. 2011-03), Award (18 March 2015) para. 542.
17. *ConocoPhillips Petrozuata B.V., ConocoPhillips Hamaca B.V. and ConocoPhillips Gulf of Paria B.V. v. Bolivarian Republic of Venezuela* (ICSID Case No. ARB/07/30), Dissenting Opinion of Georges Abi-Saab (10 March 2014) para. 66.
18. Alison ROSS, "Blair's Two-Step Test for Illegally Obtained Evidence", Global Arbitration Review (27 April 2017) at <https://globalarbitrationreview.com/article/1140718/blair's-two-step-test-for-illegally-obtained-evidence> (last accessed 16 October 2018).
19. Decision of the Swiss Federal Supreme Court 4A_448/2013 of 27 March 2014, para. 3.2.2; Decision of the Swiss Federal Supreme Court 4A_362/2013 of 27 March 2014, para. 3.2.2; see also Luca BEFFA, "Does an award based on illegally obtained evidence violate public policy? Not necessarily according to the Swiss Federal Supreme Court", Global Arbitration News (24 April 2015) at <https://globalarbitrationnews.com/does-an-award-based-on-illegally-obtained-evidence-violate-public-policy-not-necessarily-according-to-the-swiss-federal-supreme-court-20150424/> (last accessed 16 October 2018) discussing two "almost identical" decisions by the Swiss Federal Supreme Court.
20. In *R (Bancoult) v. Secretary of State for Foreign and Commonwealth Affairs* (No 3) [2014] EWCA Civ 708, para. 58, the Court found "if a relevant document has found its way into the hands of a third party, even in consequence of a breach of inviolability, it is prima facie admissible.", subsequently affirmed [2018] UKSC 3 (Lord Mance, J), paras. 10-21.
21. *Bible v. United Student Aid Funds, Inc.*, No. 1:13-CV-00575-TWP-TAB, 2014 WL 1048807, at *4 (S.D. Ind. 14 Mar. 2014), where the Court noted WikiLeaks documents had been in public domain for more than five years, and plaintiff "does not put this material 'in the public eye' any more than the internet has already done so.", subsequently reversed on other grounds, 799 F.3d 633 (7th Cir. 2015).

In *Caratube v. Kazakhstan*, the tribunal appreciated the need to protect against cybercrime and acknowledged the potential unfairness of allowing confidential evidence obtained through hacking, but also referred to the need for the tribunal to have access to potentially relevant information already in the public domain, and allegedly relevant and material to the dispute. Only non-privileged leaked documents were to be admitted.[22] Finally, another possibility is for a tribunal to appoint an independent confidentiality advisor to review the documents and make privilege determinations. This happened in a Permanent Court of Arbitration (PCA)-administered NAFTA case – *St Marys v. Canada*, which settled very quickly after the advisor issued his report.[23] The process avoids the problem of a tribunal having to put the "genie back into the bottle" so to speak or having to un-see the already seen "fruit of the poisonous tree".

I do not think this is a topic which is going to go away, with more and more data vulnerable to security breaches, as is being discussed now by the technology panel.[24] I do have questions for my panellists arising from these issues, so from Natalie, I would like to know, what role, if any, do you see the IBA [International Bar Association] Guidelines or other soft law instruments having to play?

Reid: Thank you Judith. I think when we talk about soft law we start from the question of what is the role that soft law generally plays. We think of perhaps three roles. They can aspire to and sometimes succeed in reflecting a widely held consensus; they can reflect best practices, or they can attempt to progressively develop the law. We all know that depending on where particular soft law or guidelines fall, they may have more or less acceptance in the given field. When we come to the particular question of illegally obtained evidence, the two sets of rules or guidelines that come to mind are the IBA documents: the IBA Guidelines on Party Representation, regarding the conduct of party representatives (counsel), and the IBA Rules on the Taking of Evidence.

Let us start with the Guidelines on Party Representation. I find it interesting that when discussing evidence, they speak about false evidence and they speak about whether or not the witnesses' or expert's evidence is his or her own. But they are silent on illegally obtained evidence. I think the one conclusion we can draw from this is that the focus of the Guidelines and other soft law instruments when it comes to arbitration proceedings is more on accuracy of the evidence as it is presented to the tribunal, leaving questions about how information is obtained for other debates in other fora at other times.

---

22. *Caratube International Oil Company LLP and Devincci Salah Hourani v. Republic of Kazakhstan* (ICSID Case No. ARB/13/13) Award (27 September 2017) paras. 150-156; Nikki O'SULLIVAN, "Lagging Behind: Is There a Clear Set of Rules for the Treatment of Illegally Obtained Evidence in International Arbitrations?", Practical Law Arbitration Blog (31 August 2017) at <http://arbitrationblog.practicallaw.com/lagging-behind-is-there-a-clear-set-of-rules-for-the-treatment-of-illegally-obtained-evidence-in-international-arbitrations/> (last accessed 16 October 2018).
23. *St Marys VCNA LLC v. Canada*, Confidentiality Order (24 October 2012) and Consent Award (12 April 2013).
24. See the contribution of Edna SUSSMAN for the Technology as Disruption panel: "Cyber Intrusion as Guerilla Tactic: An Appraisal of Historical Challenges in the Age of Technology and Big Data", this volume, pp. 849-868.

To move on to the IBA Rules on the Taking of Evidence, again the question is, what if anything do they have to say about it? Again, there is surprisingly little, at least on their face. Art. 9.2(b) contemplates exclusion of evidence on the basis of "legal impediment or privilege under the legal or ethical rules determined by the Arbitral Tribunal to be applicable", leaving open the basis for an argument that illegally obtained evidence would breach ethical rules. When we look to the very next provision however, Art. 9.3, building out and expanding on what Art. 9.2(b) is supposed to mean, again we see a focus on attorney-client privilege and suitable confidentiality. This underscores two points of reference, number one, what were the parties' expectations, and number two, the need to maintain fairness and equality in proceedings.

It is perhaps not surprising that what we see is a certain willingness in tribunals to accept illegally obtained evidence, except where it is proved that it affects the integrity of the proceeding itself, such as where one of the parties is alleged to be involved in the illegal activity to obtain the evidence for use in the case. Or, where it has an adverse effect on the equality of arms. The instances where tribunals have been inclined to bar evidence allegedly illegally obtained is where it implicates privilege, which is sacrosanct, for example in *Caratube*[25] and *Libananco*.[26]

Levine: Yesterday, Chief Justice Menon said that ethics is a big issue.[27] To the extent ethical issues are posed by these cases, what are the tools available to address them?

Kim: Thank you Judith, I think there are two ways to think about this. One way is "what" can be done and the other is "who can do it". With reference to the "what" part, as we know from the Queen Mary surveys, there is very little a tribunal can do. What they can do depends upon how egregious the misconduct in the way the evidence was obtained, and of course, the involvement – whether it is the parties or counsel. We know that the tribunal can take appropriate measures and they can safeguard integrity of proceedings. What is left is of course the obvious tool in the tribunal's possession, which is costs – but is that enough? Is that what is going to be able to control how we deal with this problem? How far should a tribunal go? What else could they do?

Then the next question of course would be "who". Is it the tribunal or is it the opposing counsel? Is it the seat of where the dispute is occurring or is it perhaps the bar association of counsel, or the bar association where opposing counsel is from? It is very complex. Another issue we should consider is, if you are the tribunal and you have this evidence that is suspect – it is easier if it is very clear. But what if it is "sufficient" and it just "does not look right"? One of my favourite analogies is Michael Hwang's analogy. He has framed it as to whether the tribunal should be a watchdog or a bloodhound. Yes you should be a watchdog and guarantee these things, but should you be a bloodhound when the evidence is suspect? That is where he draws the line, so we should think about that.

25. *Caratube International Oil Company LLP and Devincci Salah Hourani v. Republic of Kazakhstan* (ICSID Case No. ARB/13/13).
26. *Libananco Holdings Co. Limited v. Republic of Turkey* (ICSID Case No.ARB/06/8).
27. Sundaresh MENON, "The Influence of Public Actors on Lawmaking in International Arbitration: Domestic Legislatures, Domestic Courts and International Organizations", this volume, pp. 112-150.

Kantor: The topic of illegally obtaining evidence always raises the issue of conduct of counsel and conduct of the arbitrators. Judith, do you see a role either formal or informal for the arbitral institution in the context of illegally obtained evidence?

Levine: I am not sure that it always raises the issue of ethics and conduct of the arbitrators unless they have somehow been complicit in the collection of that evidence. As for institutions, it may depend on the institution's involvement if we are talking about items that are exhibited to pleadings within the context of the case with dozens of pleadings. For an institution like the ICC that handles thousands of cases, as a practical matter that may simply not be possible. Some of the arguments and issues that can be raised with respect to even the arbitrators who do have authority and inherent power over the conduct of proceedings, even have power over the reporting or disciplining of counsel, then I think it would be even a further stretch to say that the institutions do that. They may not be aware of what is going on. To the extent we see dubious practices amongst arbitrators or counsel anecdotally or first-hand in the course of our work, institutions might be able to take that into account informally, considering for example, not putting their names on a list of potential arbitrators for appointment in a particular case, but I do not expect that there is any duty to get into the nitty gritty of particular items of evidence from the institution's point of view. That is more a matter for the parties and the arbitrators.

Kantor: Institutions are important not only in connection with the question you have just answered but also obviously in the Belt and Road Initiative. Joongi, you are the next person up and that is your talk.

III. BELT AND ROAD INITIATIVE

Kim: I was thinking about how to frame this. If you look at our panel, on my right Judith is from Australia and to my far left is Mark who is from the United States and of course both are very large countries. In contrast, Natalie and I are from very small countries. We are easily intimidated. What we do in Korea to encourage ourselves, to inspire ourselves – we have a very simple saying, we say that the small pepper is hot. I think my topic is the hottest of course! The Belt and Road Initiative, I think, is a cauldron – it is smoldering and I think it is going to generate a tremendous number of transactions, projects and ultimately disputes. There is no question about this. If there is one thing I would like you take away when you leave – it is the meaning of Belt and Road itself. But if you look at the deeper meaning, if you understand Chinese text, it is very simple but it is counter-intuitive. "Belt" refers to the land and the "Road" – literally "road" means "route". So actually it refers to the maritime route. So it is two things – it is maritime and land. The land Road is the Silk Road economic belt. Maritime of course is the maritime Silk Road. This is a massive undertaking.

There is a recent Economist article that has compared the Belt and Road Initiative – that it is anywhere between seven to ten times the scale of the Marshall Plan.[28] This is extraordinary. I think this is a game changer. It covers all of Central Asia, Africa, Europe, the Middle East – over seventy-one countries and jurisdictions are involved. The Asian Infrastructure Investment Bank [AIIB], with one hundred billion dollars in capital, will potentially provide synergy. The BRI is supposed to lead to in excess of over one trillion dollars in projects. Eventually economists tell us this could lead to over 20 trillion dollars in GDP. This is extraordinary, and if you dig a little deeper – the numbers which are interesting to us, is of the seventy-one jurisdictions, fifty-five have BITs [bilateral investment treaties], usually with China and there are a number that have multilateral investment treaties as well. Of course the big challenge, and this comes inbound and outbound, will be that a lot of the jurisdictions involved among the seventy-one are challenging jurisdictions, where those that are accustomed to liberal democracy and rule of law will not necessarily find it. For example, inadequacies can exist in terms of the competence and independence of judiciaries, which presents serious challenges.

Among recent developments in January, we note Chinese experts here will know very well, but in January 2018 the Supreme People's Court announced they will have three special courts – one will be in Xi'an which is supposed to cover more land-orientated disputes, and one in Shenzen, which will deal with more maritime disputes and Beijing is supposed to act as the headquarters. So the first issue of course is these are courts and they are not arbitration tribunals.

The second thing to note is that CIETAC [China International Economic and Trade Arbitration Commission] has recently adopted its own investment rules, and it has also set up a Silk Road Arbitration Centre in Xi'an. As well as that, the Wuhan Arbitration Commission has announced a One Belt One Road Arbitration Centre for international Public-Private Partnership projects. The last interesting thing that is developing and simmering is the Department of Justice in Hong Kong has an interesting initiative – it is called the EBRAM (E-Belt and Road Arbitration and Mediation Centre), a planned online platform to attract BRI disputes. My first question will go to Judith on my right and the question is, how, where and under what circumstances will these disputes be resolved?

Levine: It is hard not to notice the level of excitement generated by the potential of disputes around the Belt and Road. Many institutions have responded enthusiastically. For example, the ICC [International Chamber of Commerce] announced last month a commission to address BRI dispute resolution potential.[29] The HKIAC [Hong Kong International Arbitration Centre] has been particularly active in promoting its suitability for the "Belt and Road" disputes and their brochure on this is available at the Congress

28. The Economist, "Will China's Belt and Road Initiative Outdo the Marshall Plan?" (8 March 2018) <https://www.economist.com/finance-and-economics/2018/03/08/will-chinas-belt-and-road-initiative-outdo-the-marshall-plan> (last accessed 16 October 2018).
29. "The International Court of Arbitration of the International Chamber of Commerce (ICC Court) has announced the establishment of a commission to address dispute resolution potential in relation to China's Belt and Road Initiative." ICC (5 March 2018) at <https://iccwbo.org/media-wall/news-speeches/icc-court-launches-belt-road-initiative-commission/> (last accessed 9 November 2018).

booth.[30] In 2017, there were BRI-related events in Malaysia dedicated to investment disputes along the Belt and Road. I actually see some parallels between the excitement about potential arbitrations of Belt and Road disputes and potential arbitrations in the context of climate change disputes that will come as a result of the new green economy created by the Paris Agreement.[31] Both Paris and the BRI are massively ambitious projects that will entail billions if not trillions of dollars in investment and infrastructure, and they both promise a web of new projects and legal relationships that will bring with them the potential for disputes.

In both contexts, because of the cross-border nature of these relationships there will be a desire for neutrality, enforceability and flexibility. International arbitration is seen as an attractive dispute resolution option. But I do not think in either context that there is a one-size-fits-all approach to arbitration, given the wide range of possible disputes. It will depend on the constellation of stakeholders, specializations, public or private nature, governing law, and any required technical expertise. Joongi, you mentioned the Asian Infrastructure Investment Bank, which was formed in 2015 and has eighty-four member states, and which looks ready to commit billions in finance related to Belt and Road initiatives. I took a look at their General Conditions for Sovereign-backed Loans[32] and these contain an arbitration clause for disputes among the bank and the loan parties, typically a state or project-implementing entity. The clause provides that the governing law shall be international law, disputes shall be submitted to arbitration under the UNCITRAL Rules, the appointing authority shall be the Secretary-General of the Permanent Court of Arbitration and the place of arbitration shall be The Hague.[33]

Other interesting elements in these General Conditions include incorporation of social and environmental policy,[34] and reference to an operational policy recently adopted on international relations, which includes funding projects in areas where the

---

30. "HKIAC announces Belt and Road Programme", HKIAC (26 April 2018) at <http://www.hkiac.org/news/hkiac-announces-belt-and-road-programme> (last accessed 9 November 2018).
31. Judith LEVINE, "Adopting and Adapting Arbitration for Climate Change-Related Disputes" in Wendy MILES, ed., *Dispute Resolution and Climate Change: The Paris Agreement and Beyond* (International Chamber of Commerce 2017) p. 24.
32. "General Conditions for Sovereign-backed Loans", Asian Infrastructure Investment Bank (1 May 2016) at <https://www.aiib.org/en/policies-strategies/_download/general-conditions/policy_general_conditions_sovereign_backed_loans.pdf> (last accessed 16 October 2018).
33. "General Conditions for Sovereign-backed Loans", Asian Infrastructure Investment Bank (1 May 2016) Sect. 7.04, at <https://www.aiib.org/en/policies-strategies/_download/general-conditions/policy_general_conditions_sovereign_backed_loans.pdf> (last accessed 16 October 2018).
34. "General Conditions for Sovereign-backed Loans", Asian Infrastructure Investment Bank (1 May 2016) Sect. 4.01(b), at <https://www.aiib.org/en/policies-strategies/_download/general-conditions/policy_general_conditions_sovereign_backed_loans.pdf> (last accessed 16 October 2018); Environmental and Social Framework", Asian Infrastructure Investment Bank (February 2016) at <https://www.aiib.org/en/policies-strategies/_download/environment-framework/20160226043633542.pdf> (last accessed 16 October 2018); "Directive on Environmental and Social Policy", Asian Infrastructure Investment Bank (4 December 2017) at <https://www.aiib.org/en/policies-strategies/_download/environment-framework/environ menttal-and-social-directive.pdf.> (last accessed 16 October 2018).

international boundaries are disputed.[35] I think in cases where there are inter-state elements, which may arguably arise for disputes between state-owned enterprises [SOEs] and host countries under investment arrangements, some institutions will be particularly experienced for that type of dispute, but, for say a construction dispute with sub-contractors, other types of institutions may be more appropriate.

Either way, I think it is important to find neutral institutions who can appoint arbitrators with relevant experience, relevant legal knowledge and skills, capacity to hold proceedings in the region if that makes practical sense, and also – given China's stated preference for mediation as a first step – experience with alternative forms of dispute resolution. As with climate change disputes, there may also be the need for technical expertise, procedural flexibility and account to be taken of the interest of affected communities,[36] for example, those displaced by the Laos railway project. I will leave my remarks there.

Kim: Thank you Judith. So Natalie, given your expertise, the burning question would be – how do you think the Belt and Road region will be affected in terms of ISDS, do you think there will be anything brought by Chinese investors or claims brought against China, or other investors? It is a massive project.

Reid: It is a massive question! I think that what we will see – certainly as a feature, if we take a step back and remind ourselves of the features that you highlighted, this is a series of infrastructure projects that is unprecedented in human history. The purpose of it really is to deepen connections, whatever one may think of the motivations behind this project – but certainly to deepen the connections between China and markets across the Belt and Road: Asia, Middle East and Europe. More than 70 countries are involved as you said, a host of bilateral investment treaties and multilateral instruments, by the latest count, China is party to over 100 bilateral investment treaties that are in force and has investment agreements in force with all but 10 of the countries that would be involved in One Belt One Road. The question becomes less "whether or not" Chinese investors may have claims, speaking not just as an investment arbitration practitioner, but as the daughter of a civil and structural engineer – infrastructure and construction will generate disputes. But the question rather is whether there will be an accessible forum for the substantive claims that may be generated. For those of us who have been involved with disputes governed at least in part by Chinese BITs, we know that there are different types of BITs, and different types of Chinese BITs and they are not all created equal and certainly there are varying degrees of access to that international forum.

Even if investments by Chinese investors, including of course the state-owned enterprises, would be covered under the definition of investor and definition of investment, I do think there would be a greater need – and with the increased

35. "Operational Policy on International Relations", Asian Infrastructure Investment Bank (21 March 2017) at <https://www.aiib.org/en/policies-strategies/_download/operational-policy-on-international-relations/operational-policy-on-international-relations.pdf.> (last accessed 16 October 2018).

36. Judith LEVINE, "Adopting and Adapting Arbitration for Climate Change-Related Disputes", in Wendy MILES, ed., *Dispute Resolution and Climate Change: The Paris Agreement and Beyond* (International Chamber of Commerce 2017) p. 24.

sophistication of these players – a greater demand for a comprehensive and uniform approach that provides greater access to the international forum. In the absence of which, you know the risk that you are in the truly unenviable position of having a claim, and perhaps a valid claim that is worth a very large sum, but no impartial forum in which you can bring that claim.

I noted that you have mentioned not just the flocking to One Belt One Road of international arbitration centres, but the prospective creation of courts. That may provide some release out, but again there may be some question as to whether that would be a fully adequate alternative solution because there would be the question of whether those courts would have jurisdiction over sovereigns against whom Chinese investors may wish to bring a claim.

Kim: Another issue is, as we know, the Chinese government traditionally has pushed for multi-tiered clauses, so negotiation, mediation, arbitration, but then there is recently some conflicting evidence that a lot of the Chinese SOEs actually are not interested in mediation and would rather go straight to arbitration. What do you think of the future of these multi-tiered clauses?

Reid: The multi-tiered clause is not unfamiliar to those of us in practice. We see it frequently where there are parties who expect to have long-standing professional relationships – the idea is that this kind of clause, if well designed and well implemented, will maximize the opportunities to resolve the dispute before they threaten that long-standing relationship. I think the perceived wisdom or conventional wisdom, harking back to an earlier panel, is that Chinese parties were supposed or believed to have an aversion to the direct conflict of arbitration. To the extent that, whether it is by past practice or current preference that you will still be seeing multi-tiered clauses, I would not be surprised. Again, in any kind of negotiation it is the party that has the leverage in that negotiation that tends to help decide what the dispute resolution clause looks like. The question again I think is, it is infrastructure, and that I think brings with it a set of different considerations – the potential delay that could be generated by protracted dispute resolution would be in great tension with the way in which construction disputes are ideally resolved. A delay can make or break a project, it can certainly bankrupt a contractor or a supplier, so what you would expect is to see a multi-step process that reflects all of the best practices and innovations of construction arbitration. Seeing that in mega-projects, or what used to be called "mega-projects" before One Belt One Road – you have the Channel Tunnel, the Hong Kong International Airport – it is an opportunity to deploy those lessons learnt as well as a source of lots of work for those of us in the room.

Kantor: Joongi, I was struck by the fact that Judith's response to your question drew our attention to an arbitration clause that has very familiar features to it. Also the first question you put, that triggered an investor-state set of issues, which again are very familiar issues to people who attend ICCA Congresses. Another issue that is very familiar is the tension between confidentiality and transparency that we have seen particularly in investor-state world, but also in state-sponsored initiatives more generally – pressure towards transparency. Is that same tension playing out in Belt and Road, or is it instead something that is left to the individual projects and individual dispute resolution forums? Are we seeing any trend there?

Kim: I think the one thing just off the top of my head, is the new courts that they are planning to set up. These are courts, so they will be transparent, they will not be confidential. Depending on how actively these courts will be used I think that sends a very good signal in terms of transparency.

Kantor: You do make an assumption there about transparency. I remind you, that if you went to Western Europe you would find much greater practical barriers, to access to court filings and other court documents than you might find if you were, for example, Canadian. So the extent to which we see transparency in national court systems varies as a practical matter from country to country and indeed from court to court.

Kim: I have been told that they have been looking at things like the Singapore International Commercial Court and I am sure for some things, the DIFC [Dubai International Financial Centre]. So that is something to think about – whether they are going to go in that direction and to what extent. I do not think they are going to go as far as Canada.

Kantor: Be it all as it may – the multiplicity of forums that you have mentioned almost guarantees parallel proceedings. Does it not, Natalie?

IV. PARALLEL PROCEEDINGS

Reid: What is it in particular that I am going to be focusing on, given how many of us have dealt with parallel proceedings before – what actually makes this a hot topic? What I will not be talking about is many of the broad kinds of parallel proceedings we are familiar with: multiple contract-based or treaty arbitrations arising from the same facts or simultaneous treaty or contract arbitrations, or many other examples where there are simultaneous international and domestic proceedings. The reason I will not be talking about most of those is because that basic phenomenon is not new, and we are familiar with the means that have been developed and deployed to manage potential conflicts between fora, whether it is Art. II of the New York Convention and anti-suit injunctions, to the practical solution of appointing the same tribunal in newer cases.

Perhaps what we are interested in here, and part of my own personal interest, is that recent years have seen increased incidence or at least increased public knowledge of a kind of parallel proceedings that raises a whole host of procedural questions and questions of principle. International arbitration of a commercial or investment matter, on one hand, and simultaneous domestic criminal proceedings involving the same entities, the same transactions or the same individuals on the other. The trend that we are seeing – or at least the phenomenon that I find interesting is that the tribunals seem increasingly willing to issue provisional measures in those circumstances. A caveat, in terms of setting this topic up, I focus on investor-state cases for a couple of reasons – one is that they are public, and therefore we know about the cases and second, because the state is respondent in almost all cases, or at least a party, the potential tensions that are inherent in these kinds of parallel proceedings are brought into sharp relief.

I think they offer solutions available to tribunals in a way that would be difficult to replicate in purely private commercial disputes. We can trace the evolution of this issue – from the *Tokios Tokelés v. Ukraine*[37] case in 2003, which I think many of you know was the first tribunal to hold that it had the authority to grant provisional measures to enjoin a host state in continuing with criminal prosecution, even though it declined to grant the provisional measures in that case; through to *Caratube*[38] which Judith had already talked about, in which that tribunal announced what perhaps is still seen as the clearest articulation of the standard that is often applied, in concluding that a particularly high threshold must be overcome before a tribunal, an ICSID [International Centre for Settlement of Investment Disputes]Tribunal, it said, can indeed recommend provisional measures regarding criminal investigations conducted by the state. Perhaps unsurprisingly under that particularly high threshold it concluded that it was not satisfied in that case. Again, we follow the trend through to *Quiborax v. Bolivia*,[39] where that tribunal, in contrast, did order Bolivia to suspend the criminal proceedings because it concluded that the criminal prosecutions at issue in that case were a defence strategy that had appeared to target the claimants in the arbitration precisely because they had initiated the arbitration, and ordered provisional measures in order to protect the procedural integrity of the arbitration.

So what is new and hot? In the last four years alone, and this is perhaps skipping over 2010-2014, we have seen publicly disclosed decisions in more than half a dozen cases in which provisional measures have been sought regarding domestic criminal proceedings. Not all of them have come out the same way, and I think that looking at the outcomes in the way in which tribunals have weighed the particular factors provides food for further discussion and some guidance on the ways in which the case law in this area is developing. The cases in which provisional measures have been granted are cases which are familiar to many, *Laos v. Lao Holdings*,[40] *Hydro v. Albania*,[41] *Nova Group v. Romania*[42] and *Pugachev v Russia*.[43] Cases in which they were denied – *Churchill Mining v. Indonesia*,[44] where the tribunal concluded that the party against which the criminal proceedings were apparently directed was not a party to the arbitration and it would have no effect on the proceeding; *Teinver v. Argentina*,[45] where the criminal prosecutions or investigations were happening too late to have any effect on the arbitral proceeding and *Italba v. Uruguay*,[46]

37. *Tokios Tokelés v. Ukraine* (ICSID Case No. ARB/02/18).
38. *Caratube International Oil Company LLP and Devincci Salah Hourani v. Republic of Kazakhstan* (ICSID Case No. ARB/13/13).
39. *Quiborax S.A., Non Metallic Minerals S.A. and Allan Fosk Kaplún v. Plurinational State of Bolivia* (ICSID Case No. ARB/06/2).
40. *Lao Holdings N.V. v. Lao People's Democratic Republic* (ICSID Case No. ARB(AF)/12/6).
41. *Hydro S.r.l. and others v. Republic of Albania* (ICSID Case No. ARB/15/28).
42. *Nova Group Investments, B.V. v. Romania* (ICSID Case No. ARB/16/19).
43. *Sergei Viktorovich Pugachev v. The Russian Federation* (UNCITRAL).
44. *Churchill Mining PLC and Planet Mining Pty Ltd v. Republic of Indonesia* (ICSID Case No. ARB/12/14).
45. *Teinver S.A., Transportes de Cercanías S.A. and Autobuses Urbanos del Sur S.A. v. The Argentine Republic* (ICSID Case No. ARB/09/1).
46. *Italba Corporation v. Oriental Republic of Uruguay* (ICSID Case No. ARB/16/9).

where there was no effect on the proceedings because the witnesses were released and the party seeking the provisional measures had not established that the witnesses would be impaired.

Coming to what might be the most recent decision in this area – a February 2018 SCC order,[47] where the emergency arbitrator partially granted and partially denied the request. In a split decision, the emergency arbitrator denied the portion of the request which involved the principal of the claimant, who was imprisoned, and sought an order directing his release from prison. No absence of aggressive lawyering there. The emergency arbitrator denied that portion, saying that it was essentially the final release sought, and concluded that the individual in question could pursue the claim while incarcerated but ordered Mongolia to permit reasonable access to local and international counsel in order to ensure that the individual could in fact pursue the claims.

What are the conclusions we can draw from this? What has been driving tribunals' decisions? The considerations we have seen highlighted in this line of cases is the tribunal will weigh, on one hand, the sovereign right – and some of them will even say it is a duty – to pursue criminal proceedings in the sphere of their jurisdiction. Recognition that the mere fact that you have initiated an arbitral proceeding, even an ICSID proceeding, does not confer immunity on you from domestic criminal action. But on the other hand, recognizing that there are important, perhaps fundamental concerns, about due process, about access to the international forum and the integrity of the proceedings. Again, we see tribunals being more and more willing to issue provisional measures, certainly around the ability of a party to participate in proceedings or to obtain the evidence in order to present the case, that has been impaired or threatened, especially where it would directly impact the evidence that is relevant to the case and that the tribunal views as necessary towards deliberations.

I will pause there and kick it to Judith first. I have talked about instances in which tribunals have been willing or not willing to halt ongoing criminal investigations or prosecutions. There are some interesting questions of practice and procedure about what to do when those criminal proceedings are not halted. How do you in fact continue to manage an arbitration and protect the integrity of that arbitration when you have these ongoing criminal proceedings? Let us start with testimony of witnesses.

Levine: I will speak about some of the more practical elements of managing testimony of witnesses and will reflect on a recently concluded confidential case which was a claim brought by a state against an investor pursuant to a shareholder agreement. It concerned an alleged bribe of a high-ranking official and had parallel ICSID investor-state proceedings, parallel criminal prosecutions in the home state of the investor against the person alleged to have made the bribe, and parallel criminal prosecutions in the host state against the official alleged to have received the bribe. All of these people were of interest to the tribunal. Some practical solutions were required for one witness who was physically able to come to The Hague, but had concerns for their safety and being arrested because there were still live Interpol arrest warrants.

47. *Mohammed Munshi v. Mongolia* (SCC CASE No. 2018/007), Award on Emergency Measures (5 February 2018).

The PCA would make safe passage arrangements under its Headquarters Agreement with the Netherlands for key witnesses to attend, in that case, for a key witness to attend a merits hearing.[48] These arrangements include a supplement to our Headquarters Agreement, which provides the protocol for liaising with the Dutch Ministry of Foreign Affairs, who communicates with officials at the airport and allows entry without arrest to the witness entering. They mirror similar privileges and immunities and arrangements of other courts and tribunals in The Hague. We use them to facilitate entry of witnesses in the *Yukos* arbitrations and several others since. We have also replicated them in our host country agreement with other member states and negotiated them on an *ad hoc* basis for a site visit to a country where participants in a site visit were concerned about being arrested.[49]

In the case I mentioned, the tribunal also had to go to Switzerland to examine witnesses, and the one witness that the tribunal was keen to hear from was the high-ranking official who was alleged to have received the bribe. During the course of proceedings, he was released from prison and moved to England, and the tribunal on its own initiative decided to question him and they travelled to London to conduct that examination. One final interesting procedural aspect of that case was that there were some objections to admissibility of evidence that was obtained in the courts in a separate national investigation – which harks back a bit to my earlier presentation on questionable methods of obtaining evidence – one of the parties called experts to testify on the forensic and procedural shortcomings in the investigation. Ultimately, the tribunal did not treat the evidence as relevant so did not have to tackle that judgment call head on. Those are some issues that have come up with parallel criminal proceedings. There are of course many examples of how we coordinate other types of parallel proceedings.[50]

---

48. Agreement Concerning the Headquarters of the Permanent Court of Arbitration between the Permanent Court of Arbitration and The Kingdom of the Netherlands (30 March 1999).

49. *Chevron Corporation and Texaco Petroleum Company v. The Republic of Ecuador* (PCA Case No. 2009-23), Second Partial Award (30 August 2018).

50. An example of harmonious coordination of parallel proceedings is a case that initially started as three cases against the same State at the SCC (brought under the Energy Charter Treaty (ECT)), at the ICSID (brought under a BIT) and at the PCA (brought under the UNCITRAL Rules and a different BIT). The tribunal had already been constituted in the PCA-administered case. The parties drafted a formal consolidation agreement that provided that the three cases would be heard by the UNCITRAL tribunal. The SCC and ICSID cases were deemed to have commenced under the UNCITRAL Rules and formally terminated at other fora. In another case, there were parallel proceedings commenced at the ICSID and at the PCA. Co-arbitrators were the same in both proceedings, but presiding arbitrators were different. The parties adopted parallel timetables and had the two tribunals sit together in hearing both cases. Bangladesh Accord Arbitrations represent an example of coordinated contract-based arbitrations. There, two separate complaints were brought by the same two global workers unions, but against two separate fashion brands. All of the parties involved were signatories to the Accord on Fire and Building Safety in Bangladesh signed on 15 May 2013 referring to the UNCITRAL Rules. The parties agreed that while remaining formally distinct, the cases would be heard by the same tribunal. In investor-state arbitration, some cases can be technically separate but coordinated as a single proceeding. Proceedings brought by Stabil LLC and Ukrnafta as claimants against the Russian Federation is one of such examples ("Arbitration Between PJSC Ukrnafta as Claimant and The Russian Federation — Arbitration Between Stabil LLC and Ten Others as Claimants and The Russian Federation", Permanent Court

Reid: A question to Joongi about what happens when the parallel proceedings are no longer parallel. So, the domestic criminal case has yielded a conviction of the individual and let us say it is the individual claimant or the individual is the principal of the entity that is the claimant. What happens in the international arbitration? There are questions of the effect that that conviction would have on the tribunal.

Kim: The questions are how much weight can you give it and does it rise to the level of res judicata. I think generally the way it is viewed is, in a criminal case, if you think about it in terms of the standard of proof, it is much higher. So, do you grant more weight to these criminal cases than to civil and administrative cases? I think the general view is it would not reach the level of res judicata. Particularly for an investor-state case, that domestic jurisdiction does not affect a res judicata on an international tribunal.

We do have very interesting cases, one going on right now, that – to the extent we are able to disclose – is *Mol v. Croatia*.[51] It is a very interesting case where there was conviction at the first level, it got upheld all the way to the supreme court and then the separate constitutional court, and the Croatian constitutional court has remanded it back for retrial. Specifically, in the decision apparently they say, "this decision is not subject to *res judicata* for an international tribunal", because there are apparently two parallel cases going. I have never seen that before. From the tribunal's perspective, they do not necessarily have a verdict. But let us say they deny the weight of the evidence on which the criminal decision has been made, then that award can proceed on. But in a New York Convention scenario – could that lead to a public policy challenge on the award, which is another interesting question to think about.

Kantor: Natalie, as I have mentioned to all three of you before, I face a little bit of conflict here because I am sitting as an arbitrator in a matter where questions of corruption have arisen, and national court proceedings have consequences for the arbitration in which I am an arbitrator. So let me change the focus just a little bit and thereby avoid that. Some disputes are extremely large – they involve large quantities of money and large interests from the parties. The two examples of that are the softwood lumber dispute that has been going on for decades between interests in the United States and interests in Canada. The second is the extraordinary case of the Lago Agrio *Chevron v. Ecuador* dispute[52] – $ 9 billion in damages. One of the interesting things to me about both of those disputes is the multiplicity of forums in which the parties seek to have some or all of the issues adjudicated or delayed or obfuscated or clarified. Is there something about large disputes that triggers parallel proceedings, and if so, are there lessons we can draw from them?

Reid: It is a great question. Large disputes at least in my experience and observation and particularly when they are very large – the stakes are so large – if you have motivated

of Arbitration (2 May 2016) at <https://pcacases.com/web/sendAttach/1701> (last accessed 12 November 2018)).

51. *Republic of Croatia v. MOL Hungarian Oil and Gas Company Plc* (PCA Case No. 2014-15).

52. *Chevron Corporation and Texaco Petroleum Corporation v. The Republic of Ecuador* (UNCITRAL, PCA Case No. 2009-23).

parties and competent, creative counsel on both sides it will turn into the proverbial, three-dimensional chess game. But it will be played out as a three-dimensional chess game in almost every possible forum. Whether it is an attempt to obtain strategic advantage or to create leverage, whether it is an effort to obtain or generate evidence for use in one of the other proceedings, for example the Lago Agrio and *Chevron* cases have produced a wealth of case law in the US for how you can actually use a 1782 proceeding to get the kind of evidence that nobody ever believed you could use, for use in an international arbitration. The lessons learnt I think, may be that when you have those kinds of cases which are more likely to occur, perhaps in natural resources cases, whether it is oil and gas or mining, again because of the stakes, is they push the boundaries of what is viewed as possible. How many proceedings can we juggle at once, how can we devise a kind of strategy to continue to pursue and hopefully accomplish our client's goals, so that we can make it a little bit more feasible so it now becomes conceivable within the realm of the possible, when before, people might not have imagined it because it was just too big.

Kantor: One of the consequences of these kinds of disputes is that we lose finality, which we often think of as a positive in the world of international arbitration. Am I right about that, that the bigger the dispute the less likely to see finality or am I being too gloomy? But let us move on to my topic and then open it up to the floor for comments.

V. ARBITRATION FOR CLAIMS OF DISCRIMINATION AND SEXUAL MISCONDUCT

Kantor: It is not unusual in arbitration conferences to hear discussions today of diversity and the need for more diversity in the world of arbitration, whether it is gender, race, colour, or national origin. That is not what I am raising here. What I am raising is the use of arbitration as a tool to hide discriminatory misconduct, including sexual harassment. Let me offer you three illustrations from the United States. The first, you may have noticed claims being brought in by anchors and former anchors and reporters against Fox News, women alleging sexual harassment – and their employment contracts provided for mandatory arbitration and for that arbitration to be confidential. Some of those women have gone into US national courts in an effort to avoid those arbitration clauses, and seeking public accounting of those allegations. The second example, very recently – there is an American law firm based out on the West Coast – it had in its employment contracts for summer law clerks an arbitration clause. Because it was well advised and because it was primarily based in California, it was sensitive to Californian jurisprudence so in that arbitration clause, it listed every single statute that may be implicated in employment-related claims, most obviously, civil rights statutes and statutes that could give rise to anti-discrimination claims or gender or sexual harassment claims.

A law lecturer at Harvard Law School came across this clause courtesy of a student who gave it to him and he proceeded to tweet out the clause together with his outrage that this was intended to prevent public discussion of claims of sexual misconduct or civil rights violations. That triggered quite a controversy in the law school world – among faculty and law students alike. In my own institution, where I am an adjunct at Georgetown, that led one faculty member who was familiar with arbitration from consumer protection issues to discuss the topic on an email listserve for permanent faculty and the law school visitors committee proposing that any law firm that had such an arbitration clause be prohibited from interviewing students at Georgetown Law School. That triggered a fair amount of supportive conduct as well as some opposition. In the meantime, the law firm that had been the object of this issue withdrew the arbitration clause generally. They did not, as they could have, withdraw the portion of the arbitration clause that might breach sexual misconduct or civil rights misconduct, instead they simply withdrew the entire arbitration clause because what mattered to them was recruiting at major law schools.

That is by the way what some major business organizations have done in the United States. Rather than face the public reputation consequences – simply avoid the entire issue by moving away from arbitration and back into national courts. Now that did not resolve the issue for law schools. Instead, the issue at least in Georgetown is now quite live and the deans responsible for those subject areas have now raised them with other peer law schools and with the National Association for Law Placement, which is an organization that acts as a clearing body for law placement by law schools for their law students. So this will continue to be an issue as to whether or not arbitration clauses in employment contracts with law students seeking law clerk jobs or possibly even with associates seeking permanent employment with law firms will be a ground for law faculties to seek to deny those law firms interviewing rights at the law schools.

The third example has nothing whatsoever to do with employment law, and that is important because the United States and Canada are somewhat unusual in the world in permitting mandatory pre-dispute arbitration agreements for employment contracts. The third dispute involves Stephanie Clifford and Donald Trump. Stephanie is perhaps better known as Stormy Daniels. They had what appears to be a consensual arrangement – not an employment arrangement – I might add. But, at some point the idea arose that there ought to be a payment of money in return for confidentiality and that contract contained an arbitration clause. The arbitration clause provided for confidentiality, and now Ms. Clifford would like to be free from her arbitration clause and free from the confidentiality, and that has ended up in the US District Court in California to determine whether or not the appropriate forum is confidential arbitration or the public courts.

The issue which pervades all three of these types of disputes – let me quote you Stormy Daniels's lawyer in announcing they will oppose a motion to compel arbitration – what he said was "We will vigorously oppose the just filed motion from 'DJT' and 'MC' to have this case decided in a private arbitration, in a private conference room, hidden from the American public. This is a democracy and this matter should be decided in an open court of law owned by the people."

The two themes at issue there are transparency and public accountability. In arbitration, including commercial arbitration, historically we have asserted that confidentiality and privacy are positive attributes of commercial arbitration. We kind of like the idea of private arbitrators. The counter-pressure began in the world of consumer arbitration in America, but applies in employment arbitration and now goes beyond to address confidentiality agreements which are ubiquitous in the world of international commerce. Those same themes are apparent – transparency and public accountability. They are counter-pressure to attributes of international commercial arbitration that we have often seen as positives. So the issue for us here, when we look at issues that have public interest associated with them, for example, discriminatory conduct, including sexual harassment, is whether arbitration is antithetical to those ideals. Judith let me ask you for your thoughts on this.

Levine: This does not relate to sex or employment or harassment or Donald Trump, I am afraid, but it does raise questions about an employment context in the sense of women's rights and trying to achieve a balance between confidentiality and transparency. I am referring to two recent arbitrations conducted at the PCA[53] under the Bangladesh Accord on Building and Fire Safety in Bangladesh,[54] which affects the ready-made garment industry in Bangladesh. Perhaps some of you are wearing clothes that were made in Bangladesh and might be aware of the legally binding agreement that came out as a result of the Rana Plaza tragedy in 2013 and that led to two arbitrations being brought by trade unions representing millions of workers against two of the fashion companies that signed up to the Accord. The case involves workers' rights and certainly high reputational stakes. Last year, a tribunal at the PCA chaired by ICCA's President Donald Donovan was handling two parallel claims by global unions against two fashion companies. The second procedural order,[55] which you can find on the PCA website, tackled the confidentiality and transparency balance, which was also the subject of Constantine Partasides's presentation on the transparency topic earlier.[56]

The parties had agreed to apply the UNCITRAL Rules, which do not provide much guidance beyond private hearings and the non-publication of the award without party consent. The unions argued for full transparency given the millions of stakeholders involved and the hundreds of companies who had signed up and the involvement of states and intergovernmental organizations. The respondents however preferred full confidentiality given that they were contesting liability and considered themselves in compliance with the Accord and did not want the reputational damage that resulted just from naming them in the context of such a claim.

Both sides argued that the governing law was on their side irrespective of whether it was Bangladeshi or Dutch law. Both sides found in both of those laws, either arguments in favour of an implied duty of confidentiality, or in favour of transparency. Ultimately, the tribunal struck a balance between those transparency concerns on the one hand and the public interest elements to the case. But on the other hand, the tribunal had to look at the terms of the Accord itself and found that the drafters of the Accord provided the transparency about supply factories but preserved confidentiality of linking that to the names of the companies. They acknowledged that to have named the companies would inevitably have caused reputational damage before any findings on liability, and not served the purposes of the Accord.[57] As a result of this decision, you can read about the cases, you can read about the Accord and how it has been interpreted. The unions have

53. <https://pca-cpa.org/en/cases/152/> (last accessed 17 October 2018).
54. Signed on 15 May 2013. See <http://bangladeshaccord.org/> (last accessed 17 October 2018).
55. Bangladesh Accord Arbitrations, Procedural Order No. 2 (4 September 2017).
56. Constantine PARTASIDES, "What Has Been the 'Spillover' Effect of the Transparency Debate on Commercial Arbitrations?", this volume, pp. 699-710.
57. Bangladesh Accord Arbitrations, Procedural Order No. 2 (4 September 2017).

announced that the cases have settled and praised the process as a turning point for arbitration of Business and Human Rights disputes.[58] It seems that the fashion industry also endorses the process because a new version of the Accord, which comes into effect in a couple of weeks, has already been signed by over 140 fashion companies. Its arbitration clause is new and improved[59] – the previous one was somewhat pathological – but it does maintain the balance with respect to confidentiality and transparency that was already in the Accord that has been interpreted by those tribunals. It also contains some whistle-blower protections for workers to raise concerns about health and safety in a confidential way through a hotline. I thought I would throw out that example because it is interesting. It may be discussed tomorrow in the New Frontiers panel[60] and it carries on the theme of the transparency panel earlier today.

Kantor: I would very much like to ask difficult and searching questions of Joongi and Natalie but I'm conscious of time and it really is important to allow the audience to ask questions and make comments on it so perhaps we could raise up the lights in the room and bring out the roaming microphones.

VI. AUDIENCE QUESTIONS

Audience member: You can add to your list investment treaty arbitration because these issues which you are discussing – and my question to you – are they not directly related to the fact that in all issues leaving the core subject of international trade – one thing is international trade and all classical arbitration developing pressure from the public, like from journalists, who have been pressing for public viewing the moment that you have issues of public importance which go beyond the core normal trade stuff. That is my question to you.

Kantor: My answer was more sensitive to that issue but we were also aware that there were a number of excellent panels at the conference dealing directly with investor-state arbitration. We tried to choose topics that would not duplicate or overlap with some of those other panels and that is why you have not heard as much from us about investor-state as perhaps you might have anticipated given the background of the four people sitting up here in the room.

---

58. "The 2013 Bangladesh Accord, and its more recent 2018 iteration show that businesses are willing to work with national governments, IGOs, NGOs, and groups representing affected individual workers to agree on arbitration as a neutral, enforceable and flexible means to address grievances relevant to business and human rights." (Judith LEVINE and Kashpee WAHID, "Business and Human Rights: A 'New Frontier' for International Arbitration?", 5 The ACICA Review (2017, no. 2) pp. 35, 39).
59. 2018 Accord on Fire and Building Safety in Bangladesh (May 2018) Art. 3, at <http://bangladeshaccord.org/wp-content/uploads/2018-Accord-full-text.pdf> (last accessed 9 November 2018).
60. Campbell MCLACHLAN, "Scope for Enlarged Participation in International Arbitration", this volume, pp. 1061-1076.

Audience member: I have two comments on the Belt and Road Initiative. The first is the Belt and Road Initiative is really a moving target, it is not really fixed. Today there are sixty-five countries. Tomorrow if the US wants to join or Japan, there will be sixty-seven, so it is a moving target. For certain, I think that the arbitration institutions should not be over-excited about this One Belt One Road Initiative because a lot of the investments are really policy bank investments in those countries – China Development Bank, China Export-Import Bank – they are not going to be ready to sue the government for that kind of project. The secondary remark I want to add is about AIIB versus the One Belt One Road Initiative. Asia Infrastructure Investment Bank is an international financial institution and is not a Chinese financial institution. I am working for AIIB and so far there is no single project invested in by AIIB in those Belt and Road Initiative countries. That is why the governing body of AIIB, they are criticized somehow by the Chinese government who say, "you are not really pushing for our One Belt One Road Initiative." I think the people should distinguish between AIIB on the one hand and One Belt One Road on the other hand.

Audience member: Thank you very much for this interesting debate. I would just add to the debate about your question to Judith regarding the direct involvement of an institution regarding legal evidence. I think there can be direct involvement. I am not talking about a real case but, for example, if there is a challenge against an arbitrator and this challenge is supported by legal evidence, then the institution would have to decide on balance whether to accept the challenge or reject it based on the main other factors. I would like to hear the point of view of Ms. Levine, on whether she agrees with me or not. I would like to make a second comment regarding the Belt and Road Initiative. The Cairo Regional Centre For International Commercial Arbitration, the Beijing Arbitration Commission and KLRCA [Kuala Lumpur Regional Centre for Arbitration][61] – have entered into a Belt and Road Cooperation Agreement last year and there have been several events in Beijing and Cairo about this.

Levine: When deciding a challenge, an institution is acting in a decision-making function so it is different from providing administrative support to the decision makers, which was the subject of Mark's earlier question. Secondly, I would add that we have been called on to provide assistance in identifying forensic experts to decide forgery of signature and also experts on computer forensics so the PCA can support tribunals in getting an independent expert to come in and help decide on the authenticity of documents.

Audience member: This is primarily to Judith, although others may be inclined to jump in. The question is in regard to everybody's favourite case *Chevron* and Lago Agrio and the 28 USC 1782 issues, which Natalie identified. For those of you who do not know about this, there is a wacky little US law that allows interested parties who may not even be the litigants to obtain US style discovery of materials and information in the US "in aid of a proceeding in front of a foreign or international tribunal", and there has been a lot of dispute as to whether arbitration tribunals, either investment or commercial, constitute

61. Now called the Asian International Arbitration Centre (AIAC).

a foreign or international tribunal under the meaning of this particular statute. I have written on numerous occasions that neither investment nor commercial proceedings do, unfortunately with respect to investment proceedings the weight of courts has gone against me so I am still battling it out. It is still open on the commercial front and my question to Judith is, certainly as Natalie suggested this might be an improper use of 28 USC 1782 from the perspective of the parties although the courts have taken different views. Could the arbitrators or could the parties enter into some contract or agreement or could the arbitrators enter an order prohibiting this type of information from being allowed into the proceedings and how would that be construed? Most importantly, would we be able to stop any interested party from even getting this information because once it is out, it is out and can be used for a variety of different purposes?

Levine: I do not have a view on the *Chevron v. Ecuador*[62] case and I have had no involvement with that case. In the *Yukos* case, there was an interesting use of Sect. 1782 in the context of the criminal prosecution of Mikhail Khodorkovsky in Russia. The Criminal Court, and I think it was his lawyers in the criminal proceedings, sought a deposition of the PwC auditors that I mentioned in connection with WikiLeaks, and a Californian court granted that deposition. How it relates to the arbitration is the transcript of that deposition was then proffered by the Russian Federation as evidence in the context of the international arbitration.[63]

62. *Chevron Corporation and Texaco Petroleum Corporation v. The Republic of Ecuador* (UNCITRAL, PCA Case No. 2009-23).

63. *Hulley Enterprises Ltd v. Russian Federation* (PCA Case No. AA 226), Award (18 July 2014) paras. 1222-1223; *Yukos Universal Ltd v. Russian Federation* (PCA Case No. AA 227), Award (18 July 2014) paras. 1222-1223; *Veteran Petroleum Ltd v. Russian Federation* (PCA Case No. AA 228), Award (18 July 2014) paras. 1222-1223; see also Judith LEVINE, "Can Arbitrators Choose Who to Call as Witnesses? (And What Can Be Done If They Don't Show Up?)" in *Legitimacy: Myths, Realities, Challenges*, ICCA Congress Series no. 18 (2014) p. 315.

Hot Topics and New Voices

Part II:
New Voices

Arbitration of Disputes Arising in Conflict and Post-Conflict Zones: Managing the Risks

Samantha Lord Hill *

TABLE OF CONTENTS

I. INTRODUCTION

Since 2000 alone there have been over twenty armed conflicts in the Middle East region resulting in hundreds of thousands of casualties and the destruction of towns and cities, the most widely reported being the Iraq Wars (2003-2011 and 2014-present), the Yemeni Crises and Civil War (2004-present), the Egyptian Crisis (2011-2014) and the Syrian Civil War (2011-present).

These types of armed conflicts have had a significant impact on both the global and domestic economies. In December 2016, the Institute for Economics and Peace (IEP) released a report titled "The Economic Value of Peace – Measuring the Global Economic Impact of Violence and Conflict", in which it stated that the total economic impact of violence on the global economy in 2015 was estimated to be US$ 13.6 trillion, or 13.3 percent of world GDP.[1] On a domestic scale, taking Syria as an example, the economic impact of the conflict was estimated at 54.1 per cent of GDP in 2015.[2]

While much attention on the world stage is paid to armed conflicts and their effects, as countries have become less inclined to use military force to achieve their foreign objectives they have increasingly turned to the use of sanctions as a lower risk and arguably more cost-effective alternative. The purpose of sanctions has been described as "to try to alter strategic decisions of state and non-state actors that threaten [a state's] interests or violate international norms of behaviour"[3] such as democracy, human rights

* Senior Associate, Dispute Resolution, Freshfields Bruckhaus Deringer, Dubai (UAE) and Singapore, LLB (Hons), LLM, ACIArb, Any views set out in this article are the views of the author only and do not represent the views of Freshfields Bruckhaus Deringer. The author would like to thank Erin Miller Rankin and Sami Tannous (Partners, Freshfields Bruckhaus Deringer) and Monty Taylor (Associate, Arnold & Porter) for their support in the preparation of this paper.

1. Institute for Economics and Peace, "The Economic Value of Peace 2016: Measuring the Global Economic Impact of Violence and Conflict" (15 December 2016) p. 4 (available at <https://reliefweb.int/report/world/economic-value-peace-2016-measuring-global-economic-impact-violence-and-conflict>).
2. *Ibid.*, p. 3.
3. J. MASTER, "What Are Economic Sanctions?", Foreign Affairs (7 August 2017) (available at <https://www.cfr.org/backgrounder/what-are-economic-sanctions>).

or the rule of law. One of the most recent examples in the Middle East region is the sanctions imposed on the State of Qatar in June 2017 by regional governments including Saudi Arabia, United Arab Emirates, Bahrain, Egypt, Jordan, Chad, Djibouti, Comoros, Maldives, Mauritania, Senegal and Yemen (Hadi government), on the basis of Qatar's alleged support of terrorism.[4] Such sanctions have ranged from the blocking of airspace to Qatari aircraft and the suspension of all flights and sea contacts to Qatar[5] to the freezing of accounts, deposits and investments held by certain Qatari entities and nationals in the countries which have imposed sanctions against Qatar.[6]

Notwithstanding the challenges of doing business in conflict zones (whether armed or otherwise), the need for foreign investment and assistance to support humanitarian and security goals during the conflict period, and to facilitate the restoration of any affected areas during and post-conflict, represents an attractive and lucrative opportunity for foreign investors and businesses. Taking three recent examples:

– As at February 2018, the World Bank had secured approximately US$ 4.7 billion to be invested in rebuilding and restoring Iraq's electricity generation and distribution networks, water and sewage treatment plants, oil and gas facilities, telecommunication systems, hospitals, schools, housing, and transportation networks.[7]
– Efforts to rebuild Syria have already begun with the International Monetary Fund estimating that approximately US$ 100 to 200 billion will be needed for physical reconstruction alone.[8]
– The Minister of Industry, Mine and Trade in Iran has said that, since the lifting of economic sanctions against Iran in January 2016 as a result the nuclear deal signed in the Joint Comprehensive Plan of Action in 2015, US$ 9.7 billion in investment has already

4. See for example, "UAE supports statements of Kingdom of Bahrain and Kingdom of Saudi Arabia on Qatar", Emirates News Agency (5 June 2017) (available at <http://wam.ae/en/details/1395302617576>).
5. See for example UAE Cabinet Resolution No. 18 of 2017 which implements the UAE's measures against Qatar; see also "Emirates suspends flights to and from Qatar", Emirates News Agency (5 June 2017) (available at <http://wam.ae/en/details/1395302617600>); "Etihad suspends flights to and from Qatar", Emirates News Agency (5 June 2017) (available at <http://wam.ae/en/details/1395302617604>); "Saudi Arabian Airlines announces suspension of all flights to and from Qatar", Emirates News Agency (5 June 2017) (available at <http://wam.ae/en/details/1395302617640>); "Gulf Air suspends flights to and from Qatar", Emirates News Agency, (5 June 2017) (available at <http://wam.ae/en/details/139530 2617645>); K. PAUL, S. AZHAR and J. MERRIMAN, "Saudi Arabia Revokes Qatar Airways' Licences", Reuters (6 June 2017) (available at <http://uk.reuters.com/article/uk-gulf-qatar-license-idUKKBN18X0XS>).
6. Dubai Financial Services Authority letter dated 12 June 2017; See "UAE Central Bank Issues Instructions for Freezing Accounts, Deposits, Investments of Designated Terrorists, Terror Organisations", Emirates News Agency (9 June 2017) (available at <http://wam.ae/en/details/1395302618302>).
7. "World Bank's Commitment to Iraq Reaches US$ 4.7 Billion", World Bank, (14 February 2018) <www.worldbank.org/en/news/press-release/2018/02/13/world-banks-commitment-to-iraq-reaches-us47-billion>.
8. International Monetary Fund, "Syria's Conflict Economy", IMF Working Paper WP/16/123, (International Monetary Fund, 2016) p. 21.

been registered in Iran,[9] and China's state-owned CITIC Group has recently agreed to grant a US$ 10 billion line of credit, which is likely to fund infrastructure projects throughout Iran as part of China's Belt and Road Initiative.[10]

Against the myriad of risks facing entities that wish to do business in these conflict and post-conflict zones, the incorporation of an arbitration agreement into the relevant contract is just one of the measures that businesses usually take to try to mitigate their potential exposure. This, coupled with the challenges faced in the performance of contractual obligations in conflict and post-conflict zones, unsurprisingly leads to a rise in both domestic and international arbitration: if one looks at the Middle East, the London Court of International Arbitration (LCIA) statistics show that Middle Eastern parties made up 3 percent of its caseload in 2006,[11] with an increase to 6.4 percent in 2016.[12]

While the agreement to arbitrate in a stable, foreign jurisdiction, with a well-established arbitration regime (such as London, Paris or, for Middle Eastern disputes in particular, the Dubai International Financial Centre (DIFC) or the Abu Dhabi Global Market (ADGM)) and the designation of the arbitration rules of a leading and internationally-recognized arbitral institution (such as the International Chamber of Commerce (ICC), LCIA or DIFC-LCIA) will go a long way towards providing a robust dispute resolution mechanism, there are risks that may arise (and have in fact arisen) in the arbitration of disputes concerning conflict and post-conflict zones. Such risks give rise to interesting questions of arbitral practice which will be considered further in this paper.

II. RISKS ARISING IN ARBITRATION INVOLVING CONFLICT AND/OR POST-CONFLICT ZONES

1. *Institutional Arbitration in a Conflict or Post-Conflict Zone*

When choosing arbitration as the agreed dispute resolution mechanism, parties have the choice of agreeing to either *ad hoc* arbitration, for example under the UNCITRAL Arbitration Rules 2010, or institutional arbitration where an arbitral institution such as the ICC, LCIA, or DIFC-LCIA is designated to administer the arbitration in accordance with its own procedural arbitration rules. The procedural certainty and efficiency that comes with institutional arbitration appears to make it the preferred option with, for

9. "Iran Attracts $10bn in Foreign Investment Post-JCPOA", Iran Business News (21 February 2018) <www.iran-bn.com/2018/02/21/iran-attracts-10bn-in-foreign-investment-post-jcpoa/>.
10. "Iran, China Sign $10 Billion Finance Deal", Finance Tribune, (14 September 2017) <https://financialtribune.com/articles/economy-business-and-markets/72363/iran-china-sign-10-billion-finance-deal>.
11. LCIA, "Director's Report 2006", p. 4.
12. LCIA, "Facts and Figures – 2016: A Robust Caseload", p. 6.

example, the ICC recording a total of 966 new cases filed in 2016 alone, involving 3,099 parties from 137 countries.[13]

Where parties choose institutional arbitration, the risk of the institution ceasing to operate as a result of conflict can arise where the designated institution is physically located within the conflict zone. By way of example, the Beirut Chamber of Commerce and Industry had a Conciliation and Arbitration Commission in 1974 but its activities were suspended during the Lebanese Civil War, which occurred from 1975 to 1990.[14] It was only later in 1995 that the Lebanese Arbitration Center was founded and arbitration activities resumed.[15] Similarly, the author understands that the Yemeni Centre for Conciliation and Arbitration is not presently functioning as a result of the Yemeni Civil War. While the lack of a functioning arbitral institution creates clear administrative difficulties, the more fundamental risk is that it might render the arbitration agreement between the parties inoperable and/or incapable of being performed.

Where the designated arbitral institution remains in operation, practical difficulties may arise in the administration of the arbitration. As a result of the sanctions presently imposed upon the State of Qatar, for example, the postal services between Qatar, on the one hand, and the various states that have cut diplomatic ties with Qatar on the other hand have been suspended.[16] Art. 3.1 of the Arbitration Rules of the Qatar International Center for Conciliation and Arbitration (QICCA) provides that all notices, data, memoranda, documents and other correspondence shall be delivered either by hand or by registered mail.[17] It is only after the formation of the arbitral tribunal that the parties may agree to use electronic means of communication pursuant to Art. 3.2.[18] Therefore, a party residing in a state that has imposed postal restrictions against Qatar is likely to face difficulties in filing its notice of arbitration[19] or its response[20] (as applicable) under the QICCA Arbitration Rules. Where a party is unable to file its notice of arbitration, the arbitration clearly cannot commence;[21] where a party is unable to file its response, there is a risk of the arbitration proceeding without the participation of the respondent.[22]

In addition, where sanctions operate to restrict the transfer of funds into a state, difficulties can arise in paying the arbitration registration fee to the arbitral institution, with the result that, if the fee is not paid in time, the institution will not register the case.[23] Similarly, where the parties fail to make the deposit on costs to the institution

13. "ICC Reveals Record Number of New Arbitration Cases Filed in 2016", ICC News Bulletin (18 January 2017); ICC, "2016 ICC Dispute Resolution Statistics" (2017).
14. N. NAJJAR, *Arbitration and International Trade in the Arab Countries* (Brill/Nijhoff, Leiden, Boston 2018) p. 213.
15. For more information on the Lebanese Arbitration and Mediation Center, see <www.ccib.org.lb>.
16. "UAE and Saudi Arabia cut ties with Qatar – live updates", The National (5 June 2017) (available at <https://www.thenational.ae/world/uae-and-saudi-arabia-cut-ties-with-qatar-live-updates-1.24574>).
17. QICCA Rules, Art. 3.1.
18. QICCA Rules, Art. 3.2.
19. QICCA Rules, Art. 4.1.
20. QICCA Rules, Art. 5.1.
21. QICCA Rules, Art. 4.2.
22. QICCA Rules, Art. 5.4.
23. See for example QICCA Rules, Art. 44.2.

within the relevant time frame, the institution may suspend or terminate the proceedings (or request the arbitral tribunal to do so).[24]

The above types of risks can be alleviated by designating a well-established arbitral institution physically located outside the conflict or post-conflict zone, which is accustomed to dealing with procedurally complex disputes such as the LCIA or the ICC. For example, the LCIA Arbitration Rules 2014 allow for the filing of the request for arbitration and the answer in hard copy or by electronic means and so the risk of a party being unable to file its request for arbitration or its answer is more limited, even if that party is located in a conflict zone.[25] Similarly, while the ICC Arbitration Rules 2017 require that the request for arbitration be delivered in hard copy to one of the ICC offices (even if the request is filed by email),[26] a claimant has a choice as to which office it may deliver the request to thereby allowing greater scope for compliance with the Rules. Moreover, the LCIA Arbitration Rules 2014 allow for the arbitration to proceed notwithstanding that the request for arbitration is incomplete or the answer is missing, late or incomplete.[27]

With respect to the filing fee and deposit on costs, both the LCIA Arbitration Rules 2014 and the ICC Arbitration Rules 2017 allow for a party to make a substitute deposit on costs to the institution where the other party fails to make such payment in order to allow the arbitration to proceed.[28] The party effecting the substitute payment may then request the arbitral tribunal to make an order or award in order to recover the amount paid as a debt immediately due together with any interest.[29]

Interestingly, the question of the effect of sanctions on arbitration procedure was addressed expressly by the ICC, LCIA and the Arbitration Institute of the Stockholm Chamber of Commerce (SCC) in the context of the sanctions imposed by the European Union on Russia in connection with the Crimea and Eastern Ukraine crisis in March 2014. In June 2015, the ICC, LCIA and SCC confirmed in a joint statement that those sanctions do not explicitly target arbitration proceedings, but that the asset-freezing restrictions might require additional administrative steps on the side of the affected party.[30] In addition, the joint statement clarified that "the sanctions do not impose a general prohibition for Russian parties to seek arbitration before European arbitral institutions, and Russian parties are not treated differently from other parties".[31]

Accordingly, when entering into a contract connected with a conflict or post-conflict zone, designation of a leading arbitral institution situated outside the conflict zone and accustomed to dealing with procedurally complex disputes ought to be one of the first steps taken in order to manage the risks that may arise in any future arbitration.

24. See for example QICCA Rules, Art. 48.2.
25. LCIA Arbitration Rules 2014, Arts. 1.2 and 2.2.
26. ICC Arbitration Rules 2017, Art. 4.1.
27. LCIA Arbitration Rules 2014, Art. 5.1.
28. LCIA Arbitration Rules 2014, Art. 24.4; ICC Arbitration Rules 2017, Art. 37(5).
29. LCIA Arbitration Rules 2014, Art. 24.3 to 24.5.
30. ICC, "LCIA and SCC Joint Statement" (17 June 2015) p. 6 (available at <http://sccinstitute.com/media/80988/legal-insight-icc_lcia_scc-on-sanctions_17-june-2015.pdf>).
31. *Ibid.*

2. *Appointment of the Tribunal*

In any arbitration there is a risk that a party may be unable or unwilling to appoint an arbitrator in accordance with the procedure agreed between the parties; that risk is increased where a party is located in a conflict or post-conflict zone and may have difficulties communicating with potential arbitrator candidates. Most, if not all, modern arbitral institutions contain default provisions for the appointment of the arbitral tribunal by the institution or a designated appointing authority in the event that either party is, or both parties are, unable to participate in the appointment process.

Under the LCIA Arbitration Rules 2014, the LCIA Court alone is empowered to appoint the arbitral tribunal and it may do so by having regard to any nomination of an arbitrator made by a party.[32] However, the LCIA Court may proceed to appoint the arbitral tribunal notwithstanding any absent or late nomination by a party.[33] Similar provisions can be found in the ICC Arbitration Rules 2017, which provide the ICC Court with the power to appoint the arbitral tribunal in the event of any default by a party or parties.[34] For their part, the UNCITRAL Rules 2010 designate the Secretary-General of the Permanent Court of Arbitration at The Hague as the appointing authority in the absence of a designation by the parties.[35]

Therefore, even where a party is located in a conflict or post-conflict zone and cannot, for any reason, take the procedural steps necessary for the appointment of an arbitrator, provided that the parties have chosen a well-established set of arbitration rules containing a reliable default appointment mechanism, any risk posed to the appointment process ought to be mitigated.

3. *Jurisdictional Objections: Who Is the Real Respondent Now?*

Where claims are brought against a state or state-owned entity, jurisdictional or procedural objections may be raised where the legitimacy of the government of the state against which the claim has been brought is in question.

The author is aware of one recent case against a Middle East state in which the tribunal was advised by an "acting" minister that the power of attorney of the law firm appointment to represent the state had been revoked and that a new ministry had taken over the defence of the state. The "acting" minister represented a revolutionary group which claimed that it superseded the government of the state. The tribunal found that the onus was on the "acting" minister to demonstrate that the government had been superseded and that the law firm appointed by the government was no longer authorized to act.

Following submissions from all concerned parties, the tribunal found that although the revolutionary group had taken control of parts of the state, including the capital city, there was no evidence on the record in the arbitration to demonstrate that the international community recognized a change in government. In particular, in dismissing

32. LCIA Arbitration Rules 2014, Art. 5.7.
33. LCIA Arbitration Rules 2014, Art. 7.2.
34. ICC Arbitration Rules 2017, Art. 12.
35. UNCITRAL Arbitration Rules 2010, Art. 6(1).

the contentions of the "acting" minister, the tribunal relied upon evidence from the UN General Assembly, the UN Security Council and the Council of the Arab League which referenced and reaffirmed the legitimacy of the government to act on behalf of the state.

Accordingly, where there is a risk of objections, whether jurisdictional or procedural, being raised in respect of the legitimacy of the respondent or its representatives, additional care must be taken by the claimant to identify the proper respondent in the request for arbitration and a suitable procedure ought to be proposed for dealing with such objections efficiently and cost-effectively in order that they do not frustrate the arbitration of the underlying dispute.

4. *Jurisdictional Objections: Arbitrability of the Dispute*

Where the substance of a dispute involves matters arising as a result of, or in connection with, conflict, or where a party to a dispute is subject to certain sanctions, questions can arise as to whether the dispute is capable of settlement by arbitration or whether it concerns matters that are reserved exclusively for national courts.

As two authors have commented: "practice indeed shows that arbitral tribunals and domestic courts have accepted that the existence of a sanctions regime does not render a dispute inarbitrable, but rather that the public policy character of a sanctions regime should be taken into account by the tribunal in rendering its decision."[36]
This statement is in line with the decision in *Fincantieri Cantieri Navali Italiani SpA and OTO Melara SpA v. Ministry of Defence of Iraq,*[37] in which an ICC tribunal seated in Switzerland held that the application of the UN sanctions regime against Iraq in the 1990s was a matter of mandatory law applicable to the merits of the dispute as distinct from a matter applicable to the arbitrability of the dispute. The Italian parties sought to have the decision set aside before the Swiss Federal Tribunal but it supported the tribunal's decision and confirmed that the matter was arbitrable pursuant to Swiss law.[38] However, the Italian parties had also referred the matter to the Italian courts and the Court of Appeal of Genoa reached a different conclusion, holding that, as a matter of Italian law, the dispute was inarbitrable.[39] This approach was later criticized by the Paris Court of Appeal, which refused to enforce the Genoa Court's decision in France.[40]

A further example can be seen in the case of *La Campagnie Nationale Air France v. Libyan Arab Airlines*, in which an UNCITRAL arbitral tribunal seated in Montreal, Canada, the Montreal Superior Court and the Quebec Court of Appeal each rejected an argument

36. E. DE BRABANDERE and D. HOLLOWAY, "Sanctions and International Arbitration" in L. VAN DEN HERIK, ed., *Research Handbook on UN Sanctions and International Law* (Edward Elgar Publishing 2017) p. 307.
37. ICC Award 6719 (Interim Award) Journal du droit international (1994) 1071 discussed in E. DE BRABANDERE and D. HOLLOWAY, "Sanctions and International Arbitration" in L. VAN DEN HERIK, ed., *Research Handbook on UN Sanctions and International Law* (Edward Elgar Publishing 2017) p. 307.
38. *Fincantieri Cantieri Navali Italiani SpA and OTO Melara SpA v. M et Tribunal Arbitral* (23 June 1992) ATF 118 II 353 Swiss Federal Tribunal 355.
39. *Fincantieri Cantieri Navali Italiani SpA v. Iraq* (1994) Riv. Dell'arb Court of Appeal Genoa 510.
40. *Legal Department of the Ministry of Justice of the Republic of Iraq v. Fincantieri Cantieri Navali Italiani* (15 June 2006) Rev Arb (2007) Paris Court of Appeal 87.

that the dispute was inarbitrable because of sanctions imposed on Libya by the UN Security Council.[41] Rather, the question as to the effect of the sanctions regime was seen as one concerning the admissibility of the claim to be decided by the tribunal rather than one of arbitrability of the dispute.[42]

While a party cannot prevent the opposing party from raising an objection to jurisdiction based on the arbitrability of the dispute, a party can seek to manage the disruption to the arbitration process by proposing a suitable procedure for dealing with such objections efficiently and cost-effectively.

5. *Party Non-Participation*

Where a party is physically located in a conflict or post-conflict zone, there is a risk that that party may be unable, or may choose not, to participate in the arbitration. As indicated earlier in this paper, most modern arbitration rules include default provisions to address the situation in which a respondent fails to provide an answer or response to a request for arbitration, enabling the arbitration to continue in any event. However, the more complex question arises in circumstances where a party becomes unable or unwilling to participate in the arbitration because of events that have arisen after the arbitration commenced.

Arbitral tribunals are usually given broad discretion to conduct arbitral proceedings in the manner they deem appropriate provided that they comply with the applicable arbitral rules (in particular those relating to impartiality, independence and a reasonable opportunity to be heard) and any agreement of the parties.[43] However, in circumstances where a party is no longer able or willing to participate in the arbitration, great care has to be taken in order to limit the risk of a challenge to the award.

It is widely accepted that where a party fails to participate in the arbitration, the tribunal has an inherent power to continue the proceedings so that the arbitration is not frustrated by a party's non-participation.[44] The Chartered Institute of Arbitrators (CIArb) Guideline on Party Non-Participation provides that, before proceeding with the arbitration, the arbitrators should satisfy themselves, to the extent they are able to do so, that the claimant has a prima facie case, that all parties were properly notified of the proceedings, and that the non-participating party has no acceptable excuse for its non-participation.[45] Where a party's non-participation is caused by "unforeseeable circumstances that are beyond the control of the party concerned" and the party informs the tribunal accordingly, this excuse is likely to be acceptable such that the arbitrators may extend any applicable time limits in order to allow the party to re-engage in the proceedings.[46]

41. E. DE BRABANDERE and D. HOLLOWAY, "Sanctions and International Arbitration" in L. VAN DEN HERIK, ed., *Research Handbook on UN Sanctions and International Law* (Edward Elgar Publishing 2017) pp. 308-309.
42. *Ibid.*, p. 310.
43. See generally ICC Arbitration Rules 2017, Art. 22.
44. CIArb Guideline on Party Non-Participation, para. 4.
45. CIArb Guideline on Party Non-Participation, Art. 1.1.
46. CIArb Guideline on Party Non-Participation, para. 1(c).

Where a party does not provide an acceptable excuse and the tribunal proceeds with the arbitration, the tribunal should ensure that the non-participating party is given a fair opportunity to take part in the arbitration in order to present its case and to comment on the arguments and evidence submitted by the opposing party.[47] Therefore, the tribunal should ensure that all parties are copied in all correspondence, and that the non-participating party is provided with copies of all notices, procedural orders, directions and submissions.[48] Where a party fails to attend a scheduled hearing, the arbitrators may decide to continue with the hearing in its absence or call a temporary adjournment while enquiries are made regarding the non-attendance.[49]

Accordingly, where a party is unable or unwilling to participate in an arbitration as a result of events that have occurred in a conflict or post-conflict zone, an experienced arbitral tribunal ought to be able to navigate its way through the obstacles presented to allow the arbitration properly to progress, while at the same time ensuring that both parties are given a fair and reasonable opportunity to present their case and limiting the risk of a challenge to any awards rendered.

6. *Access to Documentary Evidence*

One of the key risks affecting many, if not all, disputes in conflict or post-conflict zones is the security of evidence. Documents or other evidence may be seized or destroyed, whether purposely or by mistake. This risk is especially acute in disputes with an element of political sensitivity, or in areas of heightened violence, where bombing or other forms of physical destruction are ongoing. Access to project areas may be limited or non-existent, or simply unsafe.

A lack of access to documentary evidence carries with it two main risks: (1) that a party will be unable to comply with its disclosure obligations in the arbitration, as a result of which adverse inferences may be drawn against that party; and (2) that a party will not have the documentary evidence required to support and prove its case.

Tribunals have excused a party from the duty to disclose evidence where it is shown that the evidence was lost due to the occurrence of civil strife, war, riots and revolution or other forms of disaster.[50] However, such explanations have not been accepted without substantiation.[51] If a party's claim that documents have been destroyed is prima facie inconsistent with known facts, or reasonable business practice of parties in similar circumstances, the party claiming that it is unable to produce the required documents must be able to provide a satisfactory explanation to the tribunal.[52]

In *William J Levitt v. The Islamic Republic of Iran,*[53] the tribunal determined that reasonable record keeping practices would dictate that copies of original documents would be stored in a location away from the area affected by civil strife:

---

47. CIArb Guideline on Party Non-Participation, para. 1(c).
48. CIArb Guideline on Party Non-Participation, para. 4(a).
49. CIArb Guideline on Party Non-Participation, Art. 4.
50. N. O'MALLEY, *Rules of Evidence in International Arbitration: An Annotated Guide* (2012) p. 300.
51. *Ibid.*
52. *Ibid.*
53. *William J Levitt v. The Islamic Republic of Iran*, Case no. 210, Concurring and Dissenting Opinion of Richard C. Allison, 3 September 1991 regarding Chamber Three Award No. 520-210-3.

> "It must be recognized that the record in this Case is further obscured by Claimant's alleged inability himself to supply documents supporting his version of the facts. The failure to maintain virtually any records outside Iran is rather inexplicable in a corporation with experienced and sophisticated management. Also, the failure to produce as a witness a key former employee who had been in charge of the irrigation project in Iran left an important gap in Claimant's proof."[54]

If, on the other hand, a party is concerned that the opposing party may have documentary evidence that is at risk of destruction, it can seek a preservation order in order to compel the owner or custodian of the documents to maintain them and protect them against loss or damage. A preservation order can be sought as a preliminary measure either from the local court in whose jurisdiction the documents are located (if such court is functioning), the court at the seat of arbitration, or from the arbitral tribunal.

Where a party fails to produce a document and/or fails to comply with a preservation order, without reasonable explanation, a tribunal may draw adverse inferences against that party as a result of its failure, the inference being that the document is likely to be damaging the party's case in the arbitration.[55]

The guidelines regarding adverse inferences in international arbitration were set out in the 1992 version of the International Bar Aassociation Rules on the Taking of Evidence in International Commercial Arbitration and modified in the 2010 version (IBA Rules). Art. 9(5) of the 2010 IBA Rules provides:

> "If a Party *fails without satisfactory explanation to produce any Document requested in a Request to Produce* to which it has not objected in due time or *fails to produce any Document ordered to be produced by the Arbitral Tribunal, the Arbitral Tribunal may infer that such document would be adverse to the interests of the party*."[56] (Emphasis added.)

However, the power to draw adverse inferences ought to be used in exceptional cases only. This principle was expressed in a 2010 award[57] in which the sole arbitrator said:

> "It is a well-established principle in international commercial arbitration that arbitrators may draw adverse inferences against a party that refuses, *without reasonable excuse*, to disclose documents and information under its control, essential to prove or disprove claims asserted against it. *The use of such power by an*

54. *Ibid.*
55. N. O'MALLEY, *Rules of Evidence in International Arbitration: An Annotated Guide* (2012) pp. 300-301; S. GREENBERG, F. LAUTENSCHLAGER, "Adverse Inferences in International Arbitral Practice", 22 ICC International Court Bulletin (2011, no. 2).
56. IBA Rules, Art. 9(5).
57. S. GREENBERG, F. LAUTENSCHLAGER, "Adverse Inferences in International Arbitral Practice", 22 ICC International Court Bulletin (2011, no. 2); see also J. SHARPE, "Drawing Adverse Inferences from the Non-production of Evidence", 22 Arbitration International (2006, no. 4) pp. 549-572.

> *arbitrator is an exceptional one, and should only be used when the arbitrator is satisfied that certain requirements are met.*"[58] (Emphasis added.)

In *George Edwards v. Government of the Islamic Republic of Iran*,[59] the principle of adverse inferences was considered in circumstances where the claimant had fled Iran amidst the Islamic Revolution, and, in the process, had abandoned business records that he said were essential to his contract claims. The claimant alleged that the Iranian Government had gained access to the documents that the claimant had left behind and so the claimant requested that adverse inferences be drawn against the Government for its failure to produce such documents. The tribunal refused the claimant's application. It acknowledged the evidentiary hurdles confronting claimants displaced by the Islamic Revolution, but held that "where there is no evidence that the Respondent came into actual possession of the document in question, the Tribunal cannot shift the burden of proof"[60] to Iran or draw adverse inferences from Iran's non-production.

A similar issue arose in *H. A. Spalding Inc. v. Ministry of Roads and Transport*,[61] in which both parties alleged that all of the records that were kept in Teheran were in the custody and control of the Iranian Government. The tribunal held that "even though Claimant's Teheran records are no longer available to Claimant it does follow that they are available to Respondents and that inferences may be drawn against them". [62]

In order to mitigate the risk that a party is unable to access documentary evidence to support its case and/or comply with an order for document production because of the disappearance or destruction of documents in a conflict zone or post-conflict zone, parties operating in such zones should implement document management procedures to ensure that copies are kept outside the affected areas and, preferably, outside the jurisdiction. Where electronic documents are concerned, back-up versions of the documents should be stored overseas. The risk of a party being unable to provide a justifiable reason for the inability to produce documents might also be reduced where such party has kept a record of the steps it has taken to keep its documents safe and secure.

7. *Absent Witnesses*

Difficulties may also arise in arbitrations concerning conflict or post-conflict zones in respect of the availability of fact witness evidence. This is particularly so where there are travel restrictions in place between the country of residence or nationality of a fact witness and the country in which the arbitration will take place. By way of example, as a

---

58. S. GREENBERG, F. LAUTENSCHLAGER, "Adverse Inferences in International Arbitral Practice", 22 ICC International Court Bulletin (2011, no. 2). See also *Marvin Feldman v. Mexico* (ICSID Case No. ARB(AF)/99/1) (16 December 2002).
59. *George Edwards v. Government of the Islamic Republic of Iran*, Award No 451-251-2 (5 December 1989).
60. *George Edwards v. Government of the Islamic Republic of Iran,* Award No 451-251-2 (5 December 1989), para. 11.
61. *H. A. Spalding Inc. v. Ministry of Roads and Transport*, Award No 212-437-3 (24 February 1986).
62. *H. A. Spalding Inc. v. Ministry of Roads and Transport*, Award No 212-437-3 (24 February 1986) para. 31.

result of the sanctions imposed on Qatar in June 2017, citizens of the United Arab Emirates (UAE), Saudi Arabia and Bahrain were banned from entering Qatar and Qatari citizens residing in those countries were forced to leave and other Qatar citizens were banned from entering.[63]

Where a fact witness has provided a witness statement in an arbitration and is required by the opposing party to appear at the hearing for cross examination, the consequences of a witness's failure to appear at the hearing may be significant. Art. 4.7 of the IBA Rules provides that:

> "a witness whose appearance has been requested pursuant to Article 8.1 fails without a valid reason to appear for testimony at an Evidentiary Hearing, the Arbitral Tribunal *shall disregard any Witness Statement related to that Evidentiary Hearing by that witness* unless, in exceptional circumstances, the Arbitral Tribunal decides otherwise".[64] (Emphasis added.)

Accordingly, the default position under the IBA Rules is that a witness who fails to appear at a hearing shall have his or her evidence disregarded.[65] Exceptional circumstances may exist where the witness's failure to appear is due to circumstances beyond his or her control; however, it is for the party presenting the witness to demonstrate that such exceptional circumstances exist.[66] In making such a determination, the tribunal is likely to consider the extent to which the witness, and the party presenting the witness, might have been able to make alternative arrangements for the witness to provide his or her testimony, for example by video conference under Art. 8.1 of the IBA Rules.

Where the evidence of a fact witness is taken by video conference, care has to be taken to ensure that equality and fairness is maintained for both parties, including by ensuring that the technology used is of sufficient quality to approximate live testimony and that exhibits can be shared with the witness and the hearing room simultaneously.[67] In addition, it is important to ensure that the evidence is taken in accordance with the laws applicable at the location of the witness on giving evidence in foreign proceedings.[68] In many instances, the taking of such evidence will be governed by international treaties

63. "UAE supports statements of Kingdom of Bahrain and Kingdom of Saudi Arabia on Qatar", Emirates News Agency (5 June 2017) (available at <http://wam.ae/en/details/1395302617576>).
64. IBA Rules, Art. 4.7.
65. N. O'MALLEY, *Rules of Evidence in International Arbitration: An Annotated Guide* (Informa Law 2012) para 4.50.
66. N. O'MALLEY, *Rules of Evidence in International Arbitration: An Annotated Guide* (Informa Law 2012) para. 4.53.
67. 1999 IBA Working Party and 2010 IBA Rules of Evidence Review Subcommittee, "Commentary on the Revised Text of the 2010 IBA Rules on the Taking of Evidence in International Arbitration", pp. 17-18.
68. M. DANIS, "Strategic Options with Foreign Witnesses in International Arbitration" (Association of Corporate Counsel, 23 May 2012).

such as the Hague Convention on the Taking of Evidence Abroad in Civil or Commercial Matters or the Vienna Convention on Consular Relations.[69]

Lastly, where a party fails without satisfactory explanation to make available a fact witness for cross-examination (whether in person or by video conference), the arbitral tribunal may infer that such evidence would be adverse to the interests of that party. This principle is enshrined in Art. 9.6 of the IBA Rules.[70]

Accordingly, when arbitrating disputes involving individuals who are located in conflict or post-conflict zones, it is necessary to plan ahead and ensure that steps are taken in advance so that procedures are put in place to ensure fact witnesses are available and able to attend the hearing to provide their oral testimony. Such procedures may include agreeing to hold the hearing in a place to which the fact witnesses can travel and/or arranging the formalities and logistics of video conferencing well in advance.

8. Dealing with Local Courts

While most modern arbitration rules provide the arbitral tribunal with broad powers to order interim measures,[71] sometimes it is necessary to seek assistance from local courts at the seat of the arbitration, the place of residence or business of a party to the arbitration or the place(s) where a party's assets are located. A party may require assistance from a local court in respect of matters such as the preservation and/or production of documentary evidence, subpoenaing witnesses, the preservation of assets, including by placing a prohibition on their sale or other dissipation out of the relevant jurisdiction, and/or by way of injunction refraining a party from commencing or pursuing proceedings in another jurisdiction while the arbitration is ongoing.

In times of conflict, it is often the case that the courts physically located in a conflict zone cease to operate properly with judges, administrative staff and lawyers having fled the area during the conflict. Moreover, where new factions take control of conflict areas issues arise as to which courts, if any, form part of the official judicial system. Taking Syria as an example, the International Legal Assistance Consortium (ILAC) Rule of Law Report: Syria 2017 noted that "[t]he sheer number of different armed opposition groups, each of which have formed their own separate administrative and judicial institutions, means that there is no single system of justice in areas outside of government control".[72]

In order to limit the risk, therefore, of the effect of a lack of a functioning court system in a conflict or post-conflict zone, a party's first step ought to be to choose a seat of arbitration outside the conflict zone, preferably in a well-established, arbitration-friendly, robust jurisdiction such as England or France so as to ensure that the courts having supervisory jurisdiction over the arbitration are not subject to or affected by the circumstances in the relevant conflict or post-conflict zone.

---

69. M. DANIS, "Strategic Options with Foreign Witnesses in International Arbitration" (Association of Corporate Counsel, 23 May 2012).
70. IBA Rules, Art. 9.6.
71. See for example, ICC Arbitration Rules 2017, Art. 28; LCIA Arbitration Rules 1998, Art. 25; LCIA Arbitration Rules 2014, Art. 25.
72. International Legal Assistance Consortium, "Rule of Law Report: Syria 2017" (available at <www.ilacnet.org/wp-content/uploads/2017/04/Syria2017.pdf>).

Where the arbitration is seated outside the affected zone, and the parties have chosen a modern set of procedural arbitration rules that empower the tribunal to order interim measures, the parties to the arbitration ought to have a good level of protection through the supervisory courts at the seat and the tribunal itself in respect of any interim relief they may wish to seek. That does not, however, extinguish the risk that a recalcitrant party may choose not to comply with orders made by the courts at the seat of arbitration or the tribunal or that it may seek its own orders from the local courts in the conflict or post-conflict zone in an attempt to frustrate the arbitration process or any award rendered therein. In these latter situations, the question becomes one of strategy, requiring an assessment of which court(s) outside the conflict or post-conflict zone might be most appropriate to approach in order to obtain assistance.

9. *Enforcing the Award*

In many instances, parties which have endured an arbitration will voluntarily honour the resulting award rendering the process for recognition and enforcement of the award unnecessary; in one study, 86 percent of corporate counsel interviewed indicated that in more than 76 percent of their arbitration proceedings, the unsuccessful party voluntarily complied with the award.[73] However, where a party fails to comply with an award, for example by not making payment of amounts awarded to the successful party, it will be necessary for the successful party to take steps to have the award recognized and enforced in order that it can then have the award executed against the assets of the unsuccessful party.

To the extent that the unsuccessful party has assets located outside a conflict or post-conflict zone, the procedural risks associated with dealing with local courts situated inside the conflict zone can be overcome by targeting the conflict-free assets in the first instance. However, even where such an approach is taken, there remains a risk that the unsuccessful party may seek to resist recognition and enforcement of the award on one or more of the grounds set out in Art. V of the 1958 New York Convention on the Recognition and Enforcement of Foreign Arbitral Awards (New York Convention). The most likely Art. V candidates to be relied upon when seeking to resist recognition and enforcement of an award concerning a dispute connected with a conflict or post-conflict zone are considered below.

a. *"Not given proper notice" or "otherwise unable to present his case"*

Art. V(1)(*b*) of the New York Convention provides that a court may refuse recognition and enforcement where "the party against whom the award is invoked was not given proper notice of the appointment of the arbitrator or of the arbitration proceedings or was otherwise unable to present his case".[74]

It is well established that Art. V(1)(*b*) of the New York Convention is to be interpreted narrowly, with the result being that it has seldom been invoked

73. Queen Mary University of London, "International Arbitration: Corporate Attitudes and Practices 2008" (available at <www.arbitration.qmul.ac.uk>).

74. New York Convention, Art. V(1)(*b*).

successfully.[75] In fact, a 2010 survey of 136 reported court decisions over the past 35 years concerning an alleged violation of Art. V(1)(*b*) shows that the article was successfully invoked in only 10 percent of cases.[76] The survey found that only where the parties had effectively been denied an opportunity to be heard would a challenge based on Art. V(1)(*b*) of the New York Convention be successful.[77] In this vein, Born has asserted that the phrase "unable to present his case" has extended the procedural fairness ground only to "cases in which extraordinary circumstances, akin to *force majeure,* prevented a party from presenting its case".[78] In addition, in general, enforcing courts will reject an argument made under Art. V(1)(*b*) of the New York Convention where the defendant has been given the opportunity to participate in the arbitration.[79] A party alleging that it has not been able to present its case must show that its failure to participate in the proceedings did not result from its own conduct.[80]

Notwithstanding the above, one can easily see how an unsuccessful party who has been unable to participate in the appointment of an arbitrator or has been unable to properly present his case, for example because of a lack of documentary evidence as a result of conflict activities or the inability of a witness to appear at the hearing, may seek to resist recognition and enforcement on this ground. It is for this reason that it is particularly important that tribunals appointed to deal with disputes connected with conflict or post-conflict zones take care in their approach to the conduct of proceedings and ensure that the parties are each given a reasonable opportunity to be heard and that the matters affected by virtue of events within the conflict or post-conflict zone are properly considered.

b. Procedural irregularity

Similar arguments as those under Art. V(1)(*b*) may be raised under Art. V(1)(*d*) of the New York Convention which provides that a court may refuse recognition and enforcement where "the composition of the arbitral authority or the arbitral procedure was not in accordance with the agreement of the parties, or, failing such agreement, was not in accordance with the law of the country where the arbitration took place".[81]

---

75. H. VERBIST, "Challenges on Grounds of Due Process Pursuant to Article V(1)(b) of the New York Convention" in E. GAILLARD and D. DI PIETRO, eds., *Enforcement of Arbitration Agreements and International Arbitral Awards: The New York Convention in Practice* (Cameron May 2008) p. 692.
76. *Ibid.*
77. A. JANA, A. ARMER, J. KLEIN KRANENBERG, "Article V(1)(b)" in H. KRONKE, et al., eds., *Recognition and Enforcement of Foreign Arbitral Awards: A Global Commentary on the New York Convention* (Kluwer Law International 2010) p. 231.
78. G. BORN, *International Commercial Arbitration* (Kluwer Law International, 2001) p. 832.
79. A. JANA, A. ARMER, J. KLEIN KRANENBERG, "Article V(1)(b)" in H. KRONKE, et al., eds., *Recognition and Enforcement of Foreign Arbitral Awards: A Global Commentary on the New York Convention* (Kluwer Law International 2010) p. 253; *Geotech Lizenz AG v. Evergreen Systems Inc.*, 697 F.Supp. 1248, 1253 (E.D.N.Y. 1988); *Biotronik Mess- und Therapiegeräte GmbH & Co. v. Medford Medical Instrument Co.*, United States District Court, 12 May 1976 reported in ICCA *Yearbook Commercial Arbitration* II (1977) (henceforth *Yearbook*) p. 250, p. 250.
80. A. JANA, A. ARMER, J KLEIN KRANENBERG, "Article V(1)(b)" in H. KRONKE, et al., eds., *Recognition and Enforcement of Foreign Arbitral Awards: A Global Commentary on the New York Convention* (Kluwer Law International 2010) p. 253.
81. New York Convention, Art. V(1)(*d*).

In line with the pro-arbitration, pro-enforcement bias of the New York Convention, the courts in many (if not all) Contracting States require there to be a substantial defect in the composition of the arbitral tribunal or the arbitral procedure in order for Art. V(1)(*d*) of the New York Convention to be successfully engaged.[82] As Born states: "[i]t is clear that a serious violation of the procedural law of the arbitral seat is necessary in order to justify non-recognition of an award under Article V(1)(*d*). It is insufficient to deny recognition of an award that a minor or incidental violation of the procedural law occurred."[83]

The preferred approach appears to be to consider whether the defect in the composition of the arbitral tribunal or in the arbitration procedure had a material impact on the outcome of the arbitration,[84] i.e. would the outcome of the arbitration be different, had the procedural irregularity not have occurred? However, and again, while Art. V(1)(*d*) has only been invoked successfully in a small number of cases,[85] there is a clear risk that an unsuccessful party who has been unable properly to participate and present his case because of events occurring in a conflict or post-conflict zone may seek to rely on this article to resist recognition and enforcement. This serves as yet another reason why arbitrators dealing with cases involving conflict or post-conflict zones must take extra care in their approach to the conduct of proceedings.

c. *Matter not capable of settlement by arbitration*

Art. V(2)(*a*) of the New York Convention expressly allows the enforcing court of a Contracting State to refuse to enforce a foreign arbitral award where "[t]he subject matter of the difference is not capable of settlement by arbitration under the law of that country.[86]

Under this article, an enforcing court can make enquiries into the arbitrability of a dispute ex officio, even if neither party to the dispute has raised an objection to enforcement based on arbitrability.[87] While the concept of arbitrability is posited in the New York Convention,[88] the Convention does not set a criterion for what constitutes an arbitrable matter and what does not. This is because Art. V(2)(*a*) of the New York

82. G. BORN, *International Commercial Arbitration*, 2nd ed. (Kluwer Law International 2014) p. 3581.
83. *Ibid.*
84. *Ibid.*, p. 3582; 41, *X SA v. Y*, Swiss Federal Tribunal, 28 July 2010 reported in *Yearbook* XXXVI (2011) p. 337 [17]; Case No. 411, Oberlandesgericht Karlsruhe, 14 September 2007 reported in *Yearbook* XXXIII (2008) p. 541 at p. 546; Case No. 82, Oberlandesgericht Bayern, 23 September 2004 reported in *Yearbook* XXX (2005) p. 568; *Pacific China Holdings Ltd v. Grand Pacific Holdings Ltd* [2011] HKCFI 424, 102-103 (Hong Kong Court of First instance); *Pacific China Holdings Ltd v. Grand Pacific Holdings Ltd* [2012] HKCU 971 (Hong Kong Court of Appeal).
85. A. J. VAN DEN BERG, "New York Convention of 1958: Refusals of Enforcement 2007", 18 ICC International Court of Arbitration Bulletin (2007, no. 2) p. 26; D. DUSHYANT, "A Review of Most Common Grounds for Refusing Enforcement Including 'Public Policy'", Paper of the Speech held at the 11th International Arbitration Day and United Nations New York Convention Day "The New York Convention: 50 Years" in New York, 1 February 2008.
86. New York Convention Art. V(2)(*a*).
87. New York Convention Art. V(2)(*a*); D. DI PIETRO, "General Remarks on Arbitrability Under the New York Convention" in L. A. MISTELIS and S. L. BREKOULAKIS, eds., *Arbitrability: International and Comparative Perspectives* (Kluwer Law International 2009) p. 96.
88. New York Convention Arts. II(1), V(2)(*a*).

Convention provides that the difference must be capable of settlement by arbitration according to the 'law of that country'.[89] It seems undisputed that the enforcing court is bound by its own *lex fori* and, as such, must determine whether an award has violated any rules of its own country in relation to arbitrability.[90] The general principle adopted by most states is that matters that involve such sensitive public policy issues should be resolved by state courts and not by arbitration.[91]

Where the dispute in question arises out of events which have occurred as a result of conflict, or brings into question the effect of measures imposed by state governments or international bodies during crises periods, one can envisage arguments by the unsuccessful party as to why the dispute involves sensitive issues of public policy rendering the dispute inarbitrable. However, on balance, and while each case is of course fact-sensitive, it appears that the strong public policy in favour of resolving disputes by arbitration is likely to prevail, in particular where ultimately the dispute is one of a contractual or economic nature between commercial entities.[92] Indeed, steps can be taken to manage the risk associated with a negative finding on arbitrability at the enforcement stage by seeking recognition and enforcement in an arbitration-friendly jurisdiction where possible.

d. Public policy

Lastly, Art. V(2)(*b*) of the New York Convention permits the enforcing court to refuse recognition and enforcement of the award ex officio where it finds that recognition and enforcement would be contrary to the public policy of the country in which enforcement is sought.[93] In the 1824 case of *Richardson v. Melisch*,[94] the court famously stated that "public policy is a very unruly horse and once you stride it, you never know where it will carry you".[95] This quote elegantly captures the unpredictable nature of public policy arguments and it is for this reason that public policy is often viewed as the catch-all ground on which a party may try to resist recognition and enforcement of an arbitral award.[96] For this reason, this ground is one of the most often invoked.

89. New York Convention Art. V(2)(*a*).
90. G. BORN, *International Commercial Arbitration*, 2nd ed. (Kluwer Law International 2014) p. 3694; D. DI PIETRO, "General Remarks on Arbitrability Under the New York Convention" in L. A. MISTELIS and S. L. BREKOULAKIS, eds., *Arbitrability: International and Comparative Perspectives* (Kluwer Law International 2009) pp. 85, 109; P. BERNARDINI, "The Problem of Arbitrability in General" in E. GAILLARD and D. DI PIETRO, eds., *Enforcement of Arbitration Agreements and International Arbitral Awards: The New York Convention in Practice* (Cameron May 2008) p. 503, p. 516.
91. G. BORN, *International Commercial Arbitration* , 2nd ed. (Kluwer Law International 2014) p. 994.
92. T. CUMMINS, R. MEADE and L. YOUNGMAN, "Economic Sanctions: Implications for International Arbitration", Global Arbitration Review (19 April 2017) (available at <https://globalarbitrationreview.com/insight/the-middle-eastern-and-african-arbitration-review-2017/1139759/economic-sanctions-implications-for-international-arbitration>).
93. New York Convention, Art. V(2)(*b*).
94. *Richardson v. Melisch* (1824) 2 Bing 229.
95. *Ibid.* 252.
96. G. BORN, *International Commercial Arbitration*, 2nd ed. (Kluwer Law International 2014) pp. 3650-3651.

In recent times, the public policy ground of the New York Convention has sparked debate in particular in respect of cases where the enforcement and subsequent execution of an award might be contrary to a sanctions regime.

The United States District Court for the Southern District of New York considered Art. V(2)(*b*) of the New York Convention in *MGM Productions Group, Inc v. Aeroflot Russian Airlines*.[97] In that case, MGM Productions Group Inc (MGM) was the assignee of an arbitral award obtained by Russo International Ventures, Inc (Russo), a New York corporation, against Aeroflot Russian Airlines (Aeroflot). The award was rendered by a Stockholm Chamber of Commerce arbitral tribunal seated in Sweden and ordered Aeroflot to pay to Russo approx. US$ 13.1 million plus interests and costs. MGM sought recognition and enforcement of the award in the United States but its application was opposed by Aeroflot, which contended that confirmation of the award would be contrary to public policy of the United States because the agreement the subject of the dispute concerned transactions relating to Iran which were prohibited by the US sanctions against Iran.[98] The question of whether the agreement violated US sanctions had already been considered by the arbitral tribunal, which had found that the agreement did not violate such sanctions.[99] The Court agreed with the arbitral tribunal and found that even if the agreement had violated US sanctions, Aeroflot had not convinced the Court that the public policy defence under the New York Convention supported its case.[100] Accordingly, the Court recognized and enforced the award.

In addition, the United States Court of Appeals for the Ninth Circuit considered Art. V(2)(*b*) of the New York Convention in *Ministry of Defense of Iran v. Cubic Defense Systems,*[101] in which the Court found that economic sanctions and foreign policy disputes are not sufficient to override the strong public policy in favour of the recognition of international arbitration awards. The case concerned recognition and enforcement of an ICC award rendered in Switzerland in May 1997 in which the tribunal had ordered Cubic Defense to pay US$ 2.8 million plus interests and costs to the Ministry of War of the government of Iran (predecessor to the Ministry of Defense and Support for the Armed Forces of the Islamic Republic of Iran) (the Ministry). The dispute had arisen out of contracts for the sale and service of an air combat manoeuvring range for use by Iran's military but the Iranian Revolution had resulted in non-performance of the contracts by Cubic Defense.

In June 1998, the Ministry filed a petition before the courts in the United States seeking recognition and enforcement of the ICC award, which petition was granted. Cubic Defense then appealed, arguing, under Art. V(2)(*b*) of the New York Convention, that confirmation of the ICC award was contrary to a fundamental public policy of the United States against trade and financial transactions with the Islamic Republic of Iran.[102] In particular, Cubic Defense pointed to the sanctions the United States has imposed on Iran, including the Iranian Assets Control Regulations, the Iranian Transactions

97. 573 F.Supp.2d 772 (S.D.N.Y. 2003).
98. *MGM Productions Group, Inc v. Aeroflot Russian Airlines*, 573 F.Supp.2d 772 (S.D.N.Y. 2003) p. 774.
99. *MGM Productions Group, Inc v. Aeroflot Russian Airlines*, 573 F.Supp.2d 772 (S.D.N.Y. 2003) p. 776.
100. *MGM Productions Group, Inc v. Aeroflot Russian Airlines*, 573 F.Supp.2d 772 (S.D.N.Y. 2003) p. 776.
101. *Ministry of Defense of Iran v. Cubic Defense*, 665 F.3d 1091 (9th Circ. 2011).
102. *Ministry of Defense of Iran v. Cubic Defense*, 665 F.3d 1091 (9th Circ. 2011) p. 21001.

Regulations and the Weapons of Mass Destruction Proliferators Sanctions Regulations.[103] Cubic Defense further contended that the existence of a policy prohibiting payment of the award was sufficient to demonstrate the existence of a fundamental public policy against confirmation of the award and that, even though the sanctions did not specifically prohibit confirmation of the award, they constituted evidence of a comprehensive US policy against trade, investment and economic support for Iran such that confirmation of the ICC's award was repugnant to the public policy of the United States.[104]

On hearing Cubic Defense's submissions, Judge Fisher commented as follows:

> "We are not persuaded by Cubic's argument, which gives too little weight to this country's strong public policy in support of the recognition of foreign arbitration awards, and too much weight to the regulatory restrictions governing payment of the ICC's award. ... we conclude that the Ministry, and the United States as amicus curiae, have the better argument."[105]

Further, the Court stated:

> "Our analysis begins with the strong public policy favoring confirmation of foreign arbitration awards. 'The goal of the Convention, and the principal purpose underlying American adoption and implementation of it, was to encourage the recognition and enforcement of commercial arbitration agreements in international contracts and to unify the standards by which agreements to arbitrate are observed and arbitral awards are enforced in the signatory countries.'[106] ... To prevail, therefore, Cubic must demonstrate a countervailing public policy sufficient to overcome this strong policy favoring confirmation of the ICC's award. Cubic has not met that 'substantial' burden."[107]

The Court confirmed that the ICC's award was not contrary to the public policy of the United States under Art. V(2)(*b*) of the New York Convention and that Cubic Defense had not identified a public policy sufficient to overcome the strong federal policy in favour of recognizing foreign arbitral awards.[108] In doing so, the Court drew a distinction between "confirming" the award under the New York Convention (i.e. recognition and enforcement) and ordering payment of the award (i.e. execution), stating that "we should not refuse to confirm an arbitration award because payment is prohibited when payment may in fact be authorized by the government's issuance of a specific license".[109]

Similarly, in January 2014, the Swiss Federal Supreme Court[110] recognized and enforced an award rendered by a three-member tribunal seated in Teheran, in which the tribunal ordered an Israeli-controlled Swiss company to pay US$ 97 million in damages

103. *Ministry of Defense of Iran v. Cubic Defense*, 665 F.3d 1091 (9th Circ. 2011) p. 21001.
104. *Ministry of Defense of Iran v. Cubic Defense*, 665 F.3d 1091 (9th Circ. 2011) p. 21002.
105. *Ministry of Defense of Iran v. Cubic Defense*, 665 F.3d 1091 (9th Circ. 2011) p. 21003.
106. Quoting *Scherk v. Alberto-Culver Co.*, 417 U.S. 506, 520 n.15 (1974).
107. *Ministry of Defense of Iran v. Cubic Defense*, 665 F.3d 1091 (9th Circ. 2011) p. 21003.
108. *Ministry of Defense of Iran v. Cubic Defense*, 665 F.3d 1091 (9th Circ. 2011) p. 21006.
109. *Ministry of Defense of Iran v. Cubic Defense*, 665 F.3d 1091 (9th Circ. 2011) pp. 21005-21006.
110. Swiss Federal Supreme Court, Case 4A_250/2013, 21 January 2014.

plus interest to an Iranian company. The tribunal had rendered its award in 2001 but when it remained unpaid in 2011, the Iranian company commenced enforcement proceedings in Switzerland. The Court of First Instance in Geneva granted enforcement of the award which was affirmed by the Court of Justice. However, the Israeli-controlled Swiss company appealed to the Federal Supreme Court arguing that enforcement should be refused under Art. V(2)(*b*) of the New York Convention on the basis that the payment of the award would violate international economic sanctions against Iran, which in turn would be contrary to the public policy of Switzerland. The Swiss Federal Supreme Court rejected the arguments and found that the Swiss company had failed to make out its case. It went on to say that the Swiss company had not developed or substantiated its arguments on the relationship between Swiss and international law or properly explained why the payment of the award would violate the sanctions regime or be incompatible with public policy.

In line with the pro-enforcement bias underpinning the New York Convention, it is likely to be difficult for an unsuccessful party to an arbitration to resist enforcement on the public policy ground simply by virtue of the connection between the dispute and a particular conflict. However, clearly a party's chances of successfully enforcing an award are increased when enforcement is sought in a jurisdiction renowned for being arbitration-friendly and which has minimal connection to or involvement with the conflict.

III. CONCLUDING REMARKS

The lucrative business opportunities presented by the need for foreign investment across industries in conflict and post-conflict zones, coupled with the status of arbitration as the preferred method of dispute resolution for the international business community, has given rise and will continue to give rise to an increase in the number of arbitrations involving conflict and post-conflict zones.

Such arbitrations will inevitably raise complex questions of arbitral procedure and concomitant risks, many of which can be managed provided that parties are alive to such risks and take steps to mitigate them at the outset of a project or transaction. This requires parties to give careful consideration to their arbitration agreement when entering into the initial contract in order to minimize the risk of the chosen arbitration mechanism being affected by events occurring in the conflict or post-conflict zone. It also requires parties to put measures in place during the life cycle of the project, even before a dispute arises, to ensure that it is in a position, in the event that a dispute does arise, to properly support its case and comply with its obligations to the tribunal, for example in respect of document disclosure. Lastly, it requires that both the parties and the arbitrators are aware of the procedural issues that might arise by virtue of the connection of the dispute to a conflict or post-conflict zone and that these issues are dealt with in such a way as to limit the risk, in so far as possible and practicable, of a challenge to a subsequent arbitral award.

Date of Breach, Contributory Fault, and Mitigation of Damages in Investment Arbitration

Jawad Ahmad[*]

TABLE OF CONTENTS PAGE

I. INTRODUCTION

Depending on the date when a breach is established, a tribunal may view the investor's conduct as either contributory fault or a failure to mitigate. Importantly, this distinction in treatment results in dramatic variations in the amount by which an award is discounted. This paper argues that the date of breach may determine how the investor's conduct is categorized – as either contributory fault or a failure to mitigate. Before discussing these principles, it is worth briefly mentioning what is understood by full reparation under international law.

Under international law, the purpose of full reparation is to restore the position of the injured party by wiping out all of the consequences of the illegal act. This principle stems from the *Chorzów Factory Case*.[1] Notably, "the amount of compensation must not be more than the loss actually incurred by the injured party",[2] so as to avoid overcompensation.

---

* Associate, Mayer Brown International LLP in London; former private law clerk for Judge Charles N. Brower, 20 Essex Street Chambers, London, physically based in Washington, D.C., where he acted as a tribunal assistant in both investor-State and commercial arbitrations; previously, Judge Brower's Legal Adviser at the Iran-United States Claims Tribunal in The Hague where he worked on State-to-State arbitrations; Associate Editor, Kluwer Arbitration Blog; Editor, Arbitration International.

1. *Factory at Chorzów (Germany v. Poland) (Merits)* (1928 P.C.I.J. (ser. A) No. 17), Judgment (13 September 1928) at 47.

   "[R]eparation must, as far as possible, wipe out all the consequences of the illegal act and reestablish the situation which would, in all probability, have existed if that act had not been committed. Restitution in kind, or, if this is not possible, payment of a sum corresponding to the value which a restitution in kind would bear; the award, if need be, of damages for loss sustained which would not be covered by restitution in kind or payment in place of it – such are the principles which should serve to determine the amount of compensation due for an act contrary to international law."

2. Stephan WITTICH, "Compensation", Max Planck Encyclopedia of Public International Law, Oxford Public International Law (May 2008) at <http://opil.ouplaw.com/view/10.1093/law:

This is achieved by principles limiting compensation. How they are applied will depend on a number of factors, "including the facts of the individual case, the conduct of the parties, the underlying treaty, and possibly other equitable considerations".[3]

Both contributory fault and mitigation "share an essential feature: 'being defenses pleaded by the debtor [...] they are not affirmative claims'".[4] Both principles focus on investor conduct and behavior so as to reduce the award sum substantially. The date of breach of the primary obligation separates the operation of these principles. Contributory fault analysis takes place prior to the breach, while mitigation analysis occurs after.

The parties should have this distinction at the forefront of their minds when framing their respective cases. Recalling the theme of the 2018 ICCA Congress being "evolution and adaptation", all arbitration stakeholders should reflect on how these principles can be re-approached effectively.

II. CONTRIBUTORY FAULT AND MITIGATION OF DAMAGES

Contributory fault requires the tribunal to take into account any contribution to the loss by the injured party. Art. 39 of the International Law Commission Draft Articles on Responsibility of States for Internationally Wrongful Acts (ARSIWA) encapsulates the principle under public international law.[5] This principle also finds its source in domestic legal systems under similar terms, such as "contributory negligence", "comparative fault", "*faute de la victime*" and "contribution to the injury".[6] Significantly, contributory fault assessment centers on "the occurrence of damage in the first place"[7] and, thus, *before* the breach, in the form of the internationally wrongful act. This is distinct from the

epil/9780199231690/law-9780199231690-e1025?rskey=GOucGQ&result=2&pid=EPIL> (last accessed 2 January 2018) para. 16.

3. Borzu SABAHI, Kabir DUGGAL and Nicholas BIRCH, "Principles Limiting the Amount of Compensation" in Christina L. BEHARRY, ed., *Contemporary and Emerging Issues on the Law of Damages and Valuation in International Investment Arbitration* (Brill/Nijhoff 2018) p. 325 at p. 346.
4. Horia CIURTIN, "A Hermeneutical Perspective upon the 'Mitigation of Damages' Principle: The Metamorphosis of a Concept in International Law", 12 Transnational Dispute Management (2015, no. 6) p. 1 at p. 17.
5. Draft Articles on Responsibility of States for Internationally Wrongful Acts, Art. 39, <https://www.law.umich.edu/facultyhome/drwcasebook/Documents/Documents/International%20Law%20Commission%202001%20Draft%20Articles%20on%20State%20Responsibility.pdf>. "In the determination of reparation, account shall be taken of the contribution to the injury by wilful or negligent action or omission of the injured State or any person or entity in relation to whom reparation is sought."
6. Commentary 5 to Art. 39 of the ARSIWA. "Draft Articles on Responsibility of States for Internationally Wrongful Acts, with commentaries" International Law Commission, 53rd Sess., UN Doc. A/56/10 (New York, 23 April – 1 June and 2 July – 10 August 2001), <http://legal.un.org/ilc/texts/instruments/english/commentaries/9_6_2001.pdf>; See also B. SABAHI, K. DUGGAL and N. BIRCH, "Principles Limiting the Amount of Compensation", fn. 3 above, p. 326.
7. Irmgard MARBOE, *Calculation of Compensation and Damages in International Investment Law*, 2nd ed. (Oxford 2017) para. 3.241.

mitigation of damages, which, as discussed further below, centers on the injured party's steps to reduce its loss *after* the breach.[8]

Only willful or negligent actions or omissions may amount to contributory fault, which should result in more than a *de minimis* contribution to the injury.[9] Commentators also opined that the action or omission should constitute "reproachable behavior".[10]

There are presently two types of contributory fault cases.

First, where the contributory fault of the investor, while it increased the loss that the investor sustained, was unrelated to the wrongful act of the State. *MTD v. Chile*[11] and *Iurii Bogdanov et al. v. Moldova*[12] both involved situations where the investor had a "reckless manner and/or ha[d] exercised bad or poor business judgment".[13]

---

8. H. CIURTIN, "A Hermeneutical Perspective Upon the 'Mitigation of Damages' Principle: The Metamorphosis of a Concept in International Law", p. 6; see also Irmgard MARBOE, *Calculation of Compensation and Damages in International Investment Law*, fn. 7 above, para. 3.241.
9. Commentary 1 to Art. 39 of the ARSIWA. "Draft Articles on Responsibility of States for Internationally Wrongful Acts, with commentaries" International Law Commission, 53rd Sess., UN Doc. A/56/10 (New York, 23 April – 1 June and 2 July – 10 August 2001), <http://legal.un.org/ilc/texts/instruments/english/commentaries/9_6_2001.pdf>.
10. I. MARBOE, *Calculation of Compensation and Damages in International Investment Law*, fn. 7 above, para. 3.243 (footnote omitted).
11. *MTD Equity Sdn. Bhd. and MTD Chile S.A. v. Republic of Chile* (ICSID Case No. ARB/01/7), Award (25 May 2004) paras. 242-243. In *MTD v. Chile*, the tribunal found the respondent to be in breach of the fair and equitable treatment standard in the Chile-Malaysia BIT, as the respondent had induced the claimants to enter into the project, but later did not grant necessary permissions. The tribunal, however, found that the claimants had contributed to their losses by "fail[ing] to protect themselves from business risks inherent in their investment in Chile". According to the tribunal, "a wise investor" would not have paid the full amount up front for the land but would have staged future payment to project progress.

    It is debatable whether *MTD v. Chile* falls under the category of contributory fault. One commentator has suggested that the claimants' conduct was related arguably to the respondent's conduct. Cf. Mark KANTOR, "Chapter 38: The Impact of Contributory Investor Conduct: Only with Difficulty Commensurable" in Meg N. KINNEAR, Geraldine R. FISCHER, Jara MINGUEZ ALMEIDA, Luisa Fernanda TORRES, Mairée Uran BIDEGAIN, eds., *Building International Investment Law: The First 50 Years of ICSID* (Kluwer Law International 2015) p. 533 at p. 548. "The situation in *MTD v. Chile*, as explained above, encompassed investor conduct unrelated to Chile's unlawful conduct (the business risk of dealing with a potentially unreliable partner in the project), but also investor conduct that was arguably related to Chile's conduct (relying on a land valuation that presumed the development permits later denied by Chile would be forthcoming)."
12. *Iurii Bogdanov, Agurdino-Invest Ltd. and Agurdino-Chimia JSC v. Republic of Moldova* (SCC), Arbitral Award (22 September 2005) pp. 3, 15-17. The first claimant, a Russian citizen, had established Agurdino-Invest Ltd., a wholly owned investment company in the Republic of Moldova, the second claimant. The second claimant had entered into a privatization contract with the respondent pursuant to which it would sell its assets to the respondent in Agurdino–Chimia JSC, the third claimant. In exchange for the sale, the second claimant would acquire shares held by the respondent in state-owned entities that were not specified. Despite numerous requests to the respondent, the respondent did not deliver shares on the ground that the third claimant's share requests were not eligible for acquisition. The issue turned on whether the respondent's criteria for eligible shares deprived the claimants of any compensation as required by the privatization contract. The respondent rejected the third claimant's request for shares. While the tribunal found that the respondent had breached its treaty obligation to accord fair and equitable treatment (FET), the claimants were found to have contributed to their loss by failing to specify in the

Second, where the contributory fault of the investor provoked the wrongful act of the respondent. In these cases, the tribunal determines whether there is a sufficient causal link between the investor's conduct and the respondent's wrongful act as per Arts. 31(1) and 39 of the ARSIWA.[14] There are more cases falling within this latter category than the former category. *Occidental v. Ecuador*,[15] *Yukos v. Russia*,[16] and *Copper Mesa v. Ecuador*[17]

---

privatization contract the criteria on which the shares would be chosen and because the second claimant had "enter[ed] into the Privatization Contract on such vague terms, the Claimant[s] must have been aware of the risk that the compensation in Compensation Shares at their face value might not be fully satisfactory". The tribunal found that while the respondent had breached the FET standard, the claimants had contributed to their loss by failing to ensure more specificity in their contract with the respondent on the conditions of their compensation. The tribunal did not specify the percentage or amount that represented the claimants' contribution to their loss.

13. B. SABAHI, K. DUGGAL and N. BIRCH, "Principles Limiting the Amount of Compensation", fn. 3 above, p. 326.

14. See also Commentary 13 to Art. 31 of the ARSIWA. "Draft Articles on Responsibility of States for Internationally Wrongful Acts, with commentaries" International Law Commission, 53rd Sess., UN Doc. A/56/10 (New York, 23 April – 1 June and 2 July – 10 August 2001), <http://legal.un.org/ilc/texts/instruments/english/commentaries/9_6_2001.pdf>. "It is true that cases can occur where an identifiable element of injury can properly be allocated to one of several concurrently operating causes alone. But unless some part of the injury can be shown to be severable in causal terms from that attributed to the responsible State, the latter is held responsible for all the consequences, not being too remote, of its wrongful conduct...."

15. *Occidental Petroleum Corporation and Occidental Exploration and Production Company v. The Republic of Ecuador* (ICSID Case No. ARB/06/11). Award (5 October 2012) para. 680. In *Occidental v. Ecuador*, the tribunal found the respondent to have both expropriated and breached the relevant treaty's FET standard by issuing the *caducidad* decree that terminated the contract with the respondent with immediate effect. The tribunal, however, noted that the claimants provoked the respondent by failing to obtain ministerial authorization in executing a transfer of partial ownership to a third party, which led to the *caducidad* decree. The tribunal was unanimous that the claimants contributed to their loss but split on the claimants' percentage of contribution.

16. *Hulley Enterprises Limited (Cyprus) v. The Russian Federation* (PCA Case No. AA 226), Final Award (18 July 2014) paras. 1585, 1614 and 1621 (*Hulley* Final Award). In *Yukos*, the tribunal found that the respondent had unlawfully expropriated the claimants' investment and used tax violations as a pretext to justify its acts. The tribunal, however, found that the claimants had provoked the respondent by abusing the tax regime in Russia, specifically the low-tax regions and the Double Taxation Treaty between Cyprus and Russia, which enabled the respondent to rely on that conduct as justification to expropriate the claimants' investment.

    Note that *Hulley* Final Award; *Yukos Universal Limited (Isle of Man) v. The Russian Federation* (PCA Case No. AA 227), Final Award (18 July 2014); and *Veteran Petroleum Limited (Cyprus) v. The Russian Federation* (PCA Case No. AA 228), Final Award (18 July 2014) (collectively the "*Yukos*" awards) are nearly identical. For simplicity, this article will only cite to the *Hulley* Final Award and not to the other two.

17. *Copper Mesa Mining Corporation v. Republic of Ecuador* (PCA Case No. 2012-2), Award (15 March 2016), paras. 1.111, 4.265, 5.65, 6.66-6.67, 6.85, 6.98-6.99, 6.100-6.102, 6.123, and 6.129-6.130. The tribunal found the respondent to have expropriated two of the claimant's concessions, Junín and Chaucha, and, with respect to the Junín concessions, also breached fair and equitable treatment and full protection and security protections under the Canada-Ecuador BIT for failing to support the claimant against anti-miner protesters. The tribunal found that there was no expropriation of the third concession, Telimbela. With respect to the Junín concession, the respondent issued termination resolutions that were deemed to have been arbitrary and issued without due process, which amounted to unlawful expropriation. The respondent contended that

involved situations where the investor was found to have undertaken an act that provoked the respondent to commit an internationally wrongful act. The dissenting arbitrators in *Burlington Resources v. Ecuador*[18] and *Bear Creek v. Peru*[19] also found that the respective investors' acts had provoked the State in question.

---

it issued the termination resolutions on the ground of legitimate public policy as the claimant had failed to acquire the approval of local communities during the time it held the concession. The tribunal, however, considered the claimant's conduct as contributing to its loss. The Junín concessions spawned years of anti-miner and pro-miner protests, both groups having engaged in a series of violent acts. The tribunal found that the claimant's local company had by itself and through contractors and sub-contracts employed armed men in uniform using tear gas canisters and firing weapons at local villagers more than two years prior to the termination notice for the Junín concessions. Thus, the claimant "had substantially reduced its chances of turning the Junín concessions into a commercial success". Notably, the tribunal found that the claimant's senior personnel in Ecuador had violated Ecuadorian criminal law and that claimant's senior management in Canada, while not privy to the planning and execution of the violent acts, was negligent.

18. *Burlington Resources Inc. v. Republic of Ecuador* (ICSID Case No. ARB/08/5), Decision on Reconsideration and Award (7 February 2017) paras. 572-581 and n. 1113. A majority of the tribunal rejected the respondent's argument that the claimant contributed to its loss. First, the claimant's non-payment of taxes under the contested tax measure was not the triggering event for the expropriation. A majority of the tribunal found that, even if the claimant had paid the taxes, the respondent would have expropriated the claimant's investment in any event (the dissenting arbitrator, however, believed that claimant's refusal to pay its taxes played a role in the chain of events leading to the expropriation). Second, the claimant's threat to suspend operations did not aid the respondent's case on contributory fault. Both parties violated the procedural order recommending that the parties refrain from aggravating the dispute. Thus, the reference to the claimant's threat was not helpful to the respondent. Third, the claimant's refusal to sign an agreement with the respondent concerning its property rights also did not contribute to its loss. The claimant could not be forced to negotiate an agreement against its will.

19. *Bear Creek Mining Corporation v. Republic of Peru* (ICSID Case No. ARB/14/21), Award (30 November 2017) paras. 149, 202, 406, 411-412. The claimant was granted a supreme decree permitting its mining project in Santa Ana to go forward, but soon afterwards social unrest and protests ensued prompting the respondent to revoke the decree over three years later. Leading up to the revocation decree, the claimant engaged in a series of community outreach workshops with both communities falling within the project's direct and indirect area of influence. One issue was whether further outreach contributed to the social unrest that justified the revocation decree. A majority of the tribunal found that the respondent had not proven a causal link between the claimant's outreach activities concerning its project and the revocation decree. The majority found that the respondent's authorities were aware of the activities and they "were conducted with their approval, support, and endorsement, and that no objections were raised by the authorities in this context". *Bear Creek Mining Corporation v. Republic of Peru* (ICSID Case No. ARB/14/21), Partial Dissenting Opinion of Professor Philippe Sands QC (30 November 2017) paras. 4, 19, and 39. The dissenting arbitrator, however, opined that the claimant was responsible for the social unrest "that left the Peruvian government in the predicament it faced, and the need to do something reasonable and lawful to protect public well-being". The dissenting arbitrator found the claimant's contribution to be both significant and material. The dissenting arbitrator noted that the claimant's project failed because it did not manage to ensure harmony between the project and those it affected in the community. The dissenting arbitrator noted that discontent arising from a significant number of communities falling within the claimant's project influence were not addressed by the claimant in its outreach activities and, further, there was disparate treatment of communities. Essentially, according to the dissenting arbitrator, the protests were caused by the

Contributory fault requires a comparison of the parties' respective contributions to the loss sustained by the injured party. The analysis is complex "and the [t]ribunal ha[s] a corresponding margin of estimation".[20] These "estimations" by tribunals have generated high discount figures. In *MTD* the tribunal reduced the compensation amount by 50 percent (approximately US$ 5.871 million),[21] in *Occidental* by 25 percent (approximately US$ 589.8 million),[22] in *Yukos* by 25 percent (approximately US$ 16.6 billion),[23] and in *Copper Mesa* by 30 percent (approximately US$ 4.793 million).[24]

There is ample writing that "adjustment is performed as a blanket percentage discount over the value of damages that have been calculated"[25] with insufficient reasoning.[26] Coupled with the fact that *Occidental* and *Yukos* represent two of the largest awards in investment arbitration history[27] and "[t]here is nothing as likely to fuel a backlash as damages awards that are seen as excessive and are not founded on satisfactory reasoning".[28]

The conduct assessed under contributory fault analysis in the second category of cases was also found to have violated domestic law. In *Occidental*, the claimants were found to

---

claimant because it did not "take real or sufficient steps to address those concerns and grievances, and to engage the trust of all potentially affected communities".

20. *MTD Equity Sdn. Bhd. and MTD Chile S.A. v. Republic of Chile* (ICSID Case No. ARB/01/7), Decision on Annulment (21 March 2007) para. 101.
21. *MTD Equity Sdn. Bhd. and MTD Chile S.A. v. Republic of Chile* (ICSID Case No. ARB/01/7), Award (25 May 2014) paras. 242-243.
22. *Occidental Petroleum Corporation and Occidental Exploration and Production Company v. The Republic of Ecuador* (ICSID Case No. ARB/06/11), Award (5 October 2012) para. 687.
23. *Hulley* Final Award, para. 1634.
24. *Copper Mesa Mining Corporation v. Republic of Ecuador* (PCA Case No. 2012-2), Award (15 March 2016) paras. 6.133 and 7.30-7.32.
25. Carla CHAVICH and Pablo LÓPEZ ZADICOFF, "Economics in Investor-State Arbitration Beyond Quantum" in Marion JANSEN, Joost PAUWELYN and Theresa CARPENTER, eds., *The Use of Economics in International Trade and Investment Disputes* (Cambridge 2017) p. 335 at p. 347 (footnotes omitted).
26. See Wolfgang ALSCHNER, "Aligning Loss and Liability – Toward an Integrated Assessment of Damages in Investment Arbitration" in Marion JANSEN, Joost PAUWELYN and Theresa CARPENTER, eds., The Use of Economics in International Trade and Investment Disputes (Cambridge 2017) p. 283 at p. 317. "Given its significant impact on damages, contributory fault is one of the areas where more law and more economics would be desirable to move from a discretion-based case-by-case analysis to a more predictable methodology clarifying how we measure fault legally and how we quantify it monetarily." (Footnotes omitted); B. SABAHI, K. DUGGAL and N. BIRCH, "Principles Limiting the Amount of Compensation", fn. 3 above, p. 328. "The percentage (or the amount) by which tribunals should reduce damages for contributory fault, however, has not received careful attention and is not based on any particular formula." (Footnotes omitted); Wojciech SADOWSKI, "Yukos and Contributory Fault", 12 Transnational Dispute Management (2015, no. 5) p. 27. "[A] simple split expressed as a percentage more approximates to a business deal or a decision taken *ex aequo et bono* rather than the outcome of a legal determination made in accordance with transparent and predictable criteria." (Emphasis in italics in original) (footnotes omitted).
27. M. KANTOR, "Chapter 38: The Impact of Contributory Investor Conduct: Only with Difficulty Commensurable", fn. 11 above, p. 552.
28. Thomas WÄLDE and Borzu SABAHI, "Compensation, Damages and Valuation in International Investment Law", 3 Transnational Dispute Management (2006, no. 5) p. 2.

have carried out an "unlawful act" by failing to acquire the necessary ministerial authorization.[29] In *Yukos*, the claimants were found to have violated Russian tax law[30] and their conduct formed part of a larger alleged pattern of the claimants' illegal and bad faith conduct.[31] In *Copper Mesa*, the claimant's "senior personnel in Quito were guilty of directing violent acts committed on its behalf, in violation of Ecuadorian criminal law".[32] In *Bear Creek*, the dissenting arbitrator maintained that the claimant had failed to obtain a "social license"[33] that required community consent and support for the project, which had its source in both international and domestic law.[34] In *Burlington*, the conduct in question was the investor's non-payment of taxes, which the dissenting arbitrator maintained "played a major role in the chain of events leading to the expropriation".[35]

Allegations of domestic law violations may serve as grounds either to dismiss a case for want of jurisdiction or to attack the merits or admissibility of the claim.[36] Contributory fault, however, serves as a "rider" argument when the investor conduct in question does not rise to the level that could compel the dismissal of the case on jurisdictional, merits, or admissibility grounds.

---

29. *Occidental Petroleum Corporation and Occidental Exploration and Production Company v. The Republic of Ecuador* (ICSID Case No. ARB/06/11), Award (5 October 2012) paras. 672 and 680.
30. *Hulley* Final Award, paras. 1614 and 1621.
31. *Ibid.*, para. 1607.
32. *Copper Mesa Mining Corporation v. Republic of Ecuador* (PCA Case No. 2012-2), Award (15 March 2016) para. 6.100.
33. *Bear Creek Mining Corporation v. Republic of Peru* (ICSID Case No. ARB/14/21), Partial Dissenting Opinion of Professor Philippe Sands QC (30 November 2017) para. 3.
34. *Bear Creek Mining Corporation v. Republic of Peru* (ICSID Case No. ARB/14/21), Award (30 November 2017) para. 406.

    "Even though the concept of '*social license*' is not clearly defined in international law, all relevant international instruments are clear that consultations with indigenous communities are to be made with the purpose of obtaining consent from all the relevant communities. In its application for a public necessity declaration, Claimant listed 5 communities as falling within the Project's area of direct influence and 21 communities within the Project's indirect area of influence. Claimant continuously emphasized – including at the Hearing – that it went far beyond the minimum requirements of Article 4 of Ministerial Resolution No. 304527 by, amongst others, conducting over 130 community outreach workshops. Still, the question remains whether Claimant took the appropriate and necessary steps to engage all of the relevant and likely to be affected local communities, and whether its approach contributed significantly to the nature and extent of the opposition that followed."

    (Emphasis in italics in original) (footnotes omitted).
35. *Burlington Resources Inc. v. Republic of Ecuador* (ICSID Case No. ARB/08/5), Decision on Reconsideration and Award (7 February 2017) paras. 577-580 and n. 1113.
36. *For example, Bear Creek Mining Corporation v. Republic of Peru* (ICSID Case No. ARB/14/21), Award (30 November 2017) para. 328. In *Bear Creek*, the lack of "social license" was used as a basis to dismiss claims on admissibility; *Hulley* Final Award, para. 1374. In *Yukos*, the tribunal dismissed the respondent's argument based upon the "unclean hands" doctrine, but noted that it would assess the allegations through the lens of contributory fault; *Copper Mesa Mining Corporation v. Republic of Ecuador* (PCA Case No. 2012-2), Award (15 March 2016) para. 5.65. In *Copper Mesa*, the tribunal also rejected the respondent's reliance upon the "unclean hands" doctrine and, instead, treated the issue under "analogous doctrines of causation and contributory fault".

Mitigation of damages requires the injured party to take reasonable steps to reduce the loss it has incurred after the breach of the obligation. Commentary 11 to Art. 31 of the ARSIWA recognizes the principle, highlighting that the expression "duty to mitigate" does not entail a legal obligation rising to the level of international responsibility. Rather, a failure to take reasonable steps to reduce the loss "may preclude recovery to that extent".[37] Investment tribunals have recognized it frequently as a general principle of law.[38]

Mitigation is a duty to be performed, but a failure to conduct mitigation efforts "may not be to the detriment of the claimant".[39] The respondent carries the burden of proving that the claimant did not mitigate its losses.[40] If the respondent succeeds in discharging its burden, then the tribunal will attribute the losses to the claimant's failure to mitigate those losses.[41] The ultimate objective is to determine "if it was unreasonable for the claimant to go for that particular mitigation opportunity, but not whether that opportunity was the next best alternative available".[42] The Respondent, thus, seeks:

> "to build a new hypothetical situation in which the claimant takes a reasonable mitigation opportunity that it did not take in the actual world. The recoverable damages would be the difference between the claimant's hypothetical situation but for the breach, and the claimant's hypothetical situation if it had mitigated."[43]

The respondent's objective to build a hypothetical extends to situations where (a) the injured party has failed to mitigate at all; and (b) where the injured party has mitigated, but the steps taken were not, in the respondent's view, reasonable.

---

37. Commentary 11 to Art. 31 of the ARSIWA. "Draft Articles on Responsibility of States for Internationally Wrongful Acts, with commentaries" International Law Commission, 53rd Sess., UN Doc. A/56/10 (New York, 23 April – 1 June and 2 July – 10 August 2001), <http://legal.un.org/ilc/texts/instruments/english/commentaries/9_6_2001.pdf>; See also *Gabčíkovo-Nagymaros Project (Hungary v. Slovakia)*, 1997 I.C.J. 7, Judgment (25 September 1997) paras. 80-81.
38. *Middle East Cement Shipping and Handling Co. S.A. v. Arab Republic of Egypt* (ICSID Case No. ARB/99/6), Award (12 April 2002) para. 167. "The duty to mitigate damages is not expressly mentioned in the BIT. However, this duty can be considered to be part of the General Principles of Law which, in turn, are part of the rules of international law which are applicable in this dispute."; *AIG Capital Partners, Inc. &CJSC Tema Real Estate Co. v. Republic of Kazakhstan* (ICSID Case No. ARB/01/6), Award (7 October 2003) para. 10.6.4(1). "Mitigation of damages, as a principle, is applicable in a wide range of situations. It has been adopted in common law and in civil law countries, as well as in International Conventions and other international instruments."; *CME Czech Republic B.V. v. Czech Republic* (UNCITRAL Arbitration), Final Award (14 March 2003) para. 482. "One of the established general principles in arbitral case law is the duty of the party to mitigate its losses."
39. Herfried WÖSS, Adriana SAN ROMÁN RIVERA, Pablo T. SPILLER, and Santiago DELLEPIANE, *Damages in International Arbitration Under Complex Long-Term Contracts* (Oxford 2014) para. 5.106 (footnotes omitted).
40. *Ibid.*
41. *Ibid.*, para. 5.107.
42. *Ibid.*, para. 5.108.
43. *Ibid.* (footnotes omitted).

Determining "reasonable steps" is a factual inquiry, "although common ones would include renegotiation of contracts, redeployment of resources, or even the abandonment of a losing investment".[44] Investment tribunals have rarely found investors to have failed to mitigate damages. In *EDF v. Argentina* "the tribunal decided that the company's [i.e., EDFI, the investor] lack of diligence in negotiating the sale of a massive lot of shares to a third party constitutes a failure to mitigate."[45] EDFI had sold its shares in the investment vehicle, EDEMSA, to another shareholder, IADESA, and kept its claims in the arbitration. Significantly, the investor had disregarded the possibility of successfully obtaining a renegotiated tariff with the local government in its agreement with EDEMSA, thus leaving any possible benefit derived from the renegotiation process to the buyer.[46] The tribunal appeared to be conscious that both EDFI and IADESA were shareholders of EDEMSA and knew "that a tariff change was being discussed with the [local government]".[47]

There is a consistent pattern of investment tribunals deferring to the injured parties' efforts to mitigate their loss. As a result, there are more investment treaty cases where the tribunal has rejected the respondent's arguments that the investor failed to mitigate. Some examples of this trend are discussed below.

In *Saar Papier v. Poland,* the claimant claimed compensation for the damage suffered to its investment due to an import ban on secondary raw material for the production of toilet and tissue paper. The tribunal ruled that the claimant did not fail in its duty to mitigate because it did everything it could to challenge the import ban by challenging the customs office's decision rejecting importation the second time. Additionally, the tribunal found that there were no reasonable substitutes for the claimant's secondary raw material and, thus, it had not failed to mitigate by exploring alternatives.[48]

In *Middle East Cement v. Egypt*, the tribunal rejected the respondent's argument that the claimant failed to mitigate by not continuing to supply cement as the decree banned only a certain type of cement.[49] Moreover, the tribunal was not persuaded by the respondent that the alternative types of cement and their exportation from Egypt to other countries had been proven feasible. Additionally, exporting the non-banned cement was not an economically feasible alternative.[50] As to the argument that the claimant could have resumed its business activities after the lifting of the ban three years after it was introduced, the tribunal determined that "[a]n investor who has been subjected to a revocation of the essential license for its investment activity, three years earlier, has good

44. B. SABAHI, K. DUGGAL and N. BIRCH, "Principles Limiting the Amount of Compensation", fn. 3 above, p. 332.
45. H. CIURTIN, "A Hermeneutical Perspective Upon the 'Mitigation of Damages' Principle: The Metamorphosis of a Concept in International Law", p. 17 (footnotes omitted).
46. *EDF International S.A., SAUR International S.A. and León Participaciones Argentinas S.A. v. Argentine Republic* (ICSID Case No. ARB/03/23), Award (11 June 2012) paras. 1301-1309.
47. *Ibid.*, paras. 1298 and 1307.
48. *Saar Papier Vertriebs GmbH v. Republic of Poland* (UNCITRAL), Final Award (16 October 1995) paras. 98-102.
49. *Middle East Cement Shipping and Handling Co. S.A. v. Arab Republic of Egypt*, (ICSID Case No. ARB/99/6), Award (12 April 2002) para. 168.
50. *Ibid.*, paras. 168-169.

reason to decide that, after that experience, it shall not continue with the investment activity, after the activity is again permitted".[51]

In *AIG v. Kazakhstan*, the claimants made a certain equity investment in Kazakhstan. An ordinance issued by the authorities stopped all works related to the investment project. The tribunal found that the respondent had expropriated the claimants' investment. The respondent, however, argued that the claimants failed to mitigate by not accepting its offer for an alternative site. The tribunal rejected that argument as "it would be wrong in principle to impose on the injured party (the creditor or foreign investor) a 'duty' to examine (and if reasonable, to accept) an alternative solution"[52] where there has been a taking of property.

In *HEP v. Slovenia*, the respondent argued that by declining its offers to sell electricity, as well as by not seeking to import electricity from outside Slovenia, the claimant failed to mitigate its damages. The tribunal found that the State's offers materially differed in economic aspects from what the claimant was supposed to have obtained if the respondent had not breached the treaty. Thus, the tribunal decided that the claimant acted reasonably in rejecting those offers. Moreover, the tribunal considered whether the claimant's use of expensive sources of electricity was reasonable in reaction to the respondent's failure to resume delivery of energy by the prescribed date. The tribunal ultimately ruled that the claimant acted reasonably and chose not to "second-guess" the claimant's decision.[53]

In *Dunkeld v. Belize*, the tribunal considered whether the claimant failed to mitigate its damages by not using "'a fair and independent mechanism'"[54] through the Government-offered compensation process following the respondent's compulsory acquisition of the claimant's investment.[55] The tribunal noted that pursuing local remedies "is not strictly linked to the mitigation of losses, such that any duty to mitigate should require the exhaustion of local remedies".[56] But local remedies may provide a remedy that appears "more rapid or certain than that of an international claim, such that a party would be derelict in failing to attempt the local process".[57] The tribunal concluded that the investors had pursued "local compensation without a successful result, and the

51. *Ibid.*, para. 169.

52. *AIG Capital Partners, Inc. and CJSC Tema Real Estate Company v. Republic of Kazakhstan* (ICSID Case No. ARB/01/6) Award (7 October 2003) para.10.4.6.(5)(a).

53. *Hrvatska Elektroprivreda d.d. v. Republic of Slovenia* (ICSID Case No. ARB/05/24), Award (17 December 2015) paras. 214-216.

54. *Dunkeld International Investment Limited v. The Government of Belize* (PCA Case No. 2010-13), Award (28 June 2016) para. 195.

55. *Ibid.*, paras. 4 and 197.

56. *Ibid.*, para. 197.

57. *Ibid.* See also *William Ralph Clayton, William Richard Clayton, Douglas Clayton, Daniel Clayton and Bilcon of Delaware Inc. v. Government of Canada* (PCA Case No. 2009-04), Government of Canada – Counter-Memorial on Damages (9 June 2017) paras. 86-98; Government of Canada – Rejoinder on Damages (6 November 2017) paras. 92-113. Canada argued, citing inter alia *Dunkeld*, that the claimants should have sought judicial review of the joint review panel's decision, which a majority of the tribunal found to be in breach of the minimum standard of treatment, as it would have fully restored their lost opportunity.

Respondent ha[d] not identified any other steps that the Claimant could reasonably have taken to mitigate its losses."[58]

In *National Grid v. Argentina*, the respondent introduced emergency measures in reaction to the 2002 economic crisis that required renegotiation of public utility contracts. By the time the claimant filed its statement of claim, the renegotiations had achieved nothing. Soon afterward, the claimant sold its shares in the investment vehicle to a third party for US$ 14 million without prejudice to its rights in arbitration and in mitigation of its loss. The respondent maintained that the claimant's decision to sell its shares was negligent and an intentional attempt "to inflict a serious economic burden on the Respondent".[59] The tribunal concluded that the claimant had sold its stake for the best price it could obtain and that it would not "second-guess" the claimant's business judgment to sell in lieu of accepting the pre-conditions for renegotiation with the respondent.[60]

The above awards confirm the observations shared in scholarship that "investment tribunals are rather cautious in accepting a violation of the duty to mitigate damages".[61] Tribunals may be reluctant to see past the wrong committed by the respondent. Once an internationally wrongful act is deemed to have occurred, there would be little logic in scrutinizing efforts undertaken (or not taken) by the injured party in reaction to the breach.[62] Moreover, the wrongful act by the respondent may have completely prevented the injured party from carrying out any mitigation efforts.[63] The respondent must show

58. *Dunkeld International Investment Limited v. The Government of Belize* (PCA Case No. 2010-13), Award (28 June 2016) para. 199.

59. *National Grid P.L.C. v. Argentina Republic* (UNCITRAL), Award (3 November 2008) para. 273.

60. *Ibid.* The tribunal also noted that the respondent's threats to the buyer of shares affected the price ultimately paid by the third party: "Furthermore, the Respondent made it known at the time of the sale that it would hold buyers of shares, such as Dolphin, responsible for any compensation awarded to claimants such as National Grid. There seems to be little doubt that announcements of this sort would have weighed on the price paid by Dolphin, or any other buyer, pressures which would not seem to have been present in other comparable transactions."

61. I. MARBOE, *Calculation of Compensation and Damages in International Investment Law*, fn. 7 above, para. 3.265.

62. Georg Schwarzenberger was skeptical to require the injured party to act when the breaching party had committed a wrongful act. I. MARBOE, *Calculation of Compensation and Damages in International Investment Law*, fn. 7 above, Chapter 3, at n. 549, citing Georg SCHWARZENBERGER, *International Law as Applied by International Tribunals* (Stevens and Sons Ltd., London 1957) p. 663.

63. *S.D. Myers, Inc. v. Government of Canada* (UNCITRAL), Second Partial Award (21 October 2002) at paras. 98, 164-167. Canada had introduced a temporary boarder closure of polychlorinated biphenyl (PCB) from Canada to United States which significantly curtailed the claimant's business in exporting PCB from Canada to United States for remediation during the period of the ban. This temporary closure was in breach of Arts. 1102 and 1105 (national treatment, full protection and security, and the international minimum standard of treatment). The tribunal's objective was to award the claimant damages for the "'window of opportunity'" to export PCB it would have had but for the respondent's breach. In this regard, the tribunal rejected the argument that the resumption of claimant's activities after the ban was lifted eighteen months after it was first introduced was an issue of mitigation. "If CANADA's measure were to have destroyed SDMI's opportunity to develop its business of remediating the Canadian PCB inventory (and this is a position that is advanced by SDMI) it could not *mitigate* that damage by doing what it allegedly had lost the opportunity to do. Logically, the two do not fit." (Italics in original.)

something far more imprudent on the investor's part. Respondents thus face an uphill battle in demonstrating that the claimant failed to mitigate.

In comparison to percentages applied in contributory fault cases discussed above, quantifying the effect of mitigation of damage tends to produce "hard numbers" that represent the financial gain acquired (or that could have been acquired) by the injured party. For example, in *EDF v. Argentina*, the tribunal reduced the award sum by approximately US$ 14.1 million,[64] in *National Grid v. Argentina* by US$ 14 million,[65] and in *Bridas v. Turkmenistan*, a non-investment case, the tribunal reduced the award by US$ 50 million representing the claimant's failure to mitigate as it had continued to incur operating costs despite not being able to obtain revenues.[66] Thus, computing the mitigation amount tends to be more precise, quantifiable, and involves less of a judgment call.

III. DISTINGUISHING CONTRIBUTORY FAULT AND MITIGATION: THE RELEVANCE OF THE DATE OF BREACH

Both contributory fault and mitigation focus on "the fact that due to the conduct of the injured party the damage is more substantial".[67] Drawing "a distinction between them is at times hard to make"[68] because an act or an omission could be either contributory fault or a failure to mitigate. A bright line can be drawn if the focus of the inquiry centers on the date of breach.

The distinction becomes apparent when focusing on what obligation has been breached. In *LaGrand*, the International Court of Justice (ICJ) found the United States to have breached Art. 36(1) of the Vienna Convention on Consular Relations by not informing two German nationals of their rights under the Convention following their arrest, which thereby deprived Germany of the opportunity to provide assistance to its nationals under the Convention.[69] The ICJ case is identified in Commentary 3 to Art. 39 of the ARSIWA as an example of contributory fault.

---

64. *EDF International S.A., SAUR International S.A. and León Participaciones Argentinas S.A. v. Argentine Republic* (ICSID Case No. ARB/03/23), Award (11 June 2012) para. 1317.
65. *National Grid P.L.C. v. Argentina Republic*, UNCITRAL, Award (3 November 2008) para. 290. One could add *Hrvatska Elektroprivreda d.d. v. Republic of Slovenia* to this list as well. The final phase of the arbitration exclusively concerned the cost of replacing the electricity HEP (the claimant) should have received from Slovenia but for the breach. HEP's conduct in replacing electricity in reaction to the breach was mitigation of damages, which the tribunal computed to be € 77,205,000. *Hrvatska Elektroprivreda d.d. v. Republic of Slovenia* (ICSID Case No. ARB/05/24), Award (17 December 2015) para. 470(b).
66. *BRIDAS SAPIC and ors v Turkmenistan* (International Chamber of Commerce Case No 9058/FMS/KGA), Third Partial Award and Dissent (6 September 2000) paras. 46-53. Reported in Investment Claims (Oxford 2015).
67. S. WITTICH, "Compensation", fn. 2 above, para. 40.
68. *Ibid.*; See also James CRAWFORD, *State Responsibility – The General Part* (Cambridge 2013) p. 501. "The principle of contribution to injury and that of mitigation of damages are closely related and a clear distinction between them is at times hard to make."
69. *LaGrand (Germany v. US)* (2001 I.C.J. Rep.), Judgment (27 June 2001) at 515.

> "(3) In the *LaGrand* case, ICJ recognized that the conduct of the claimant State could be relevant in determining the form and amount of reparation. There, Germany had delayed in asserting that there had been a breach and in instituting proceedings. The Court noted that 'Germany may be criticized for the manner in which these proceedings were filed and for their timing', and stated that it would have taken this factor, among others, into account 'had Germany's submission included a claim for indemnification'."[70]

Thus, the ICJ regarded Germany as having contributed to its injury due to the United States' breach of the provisional measures order because Germany delayed commencing proceedings.[71] The provisional measures order in question was granted on 3 March 1999 and ordered the United States to take all measures to ensure Walter LaGrand, one of the German nationals, was not executed pending the final disposition of the case.[72] The ICJ did not consider, however, "Germany's delay in the context of the United States' breaches of Article 36 of the Vienna Convention on Consular Relations as contributing to the damage flowing from those injuries (a failure to mitigate damage)".[73]

Investment treaty tribunals, and counsel, have used language that blurs the two principles of contributory fault and mitigation. In *CME v. Czech Republic*, the respondent raised both mitigation and contributory fault arguments,[74] which the tribunal appears to have conflated.[75] In *EDF v. Argentina*, the tribunal seems to have blended the concept of contributory fault with mitigation of damages.[76] In *Yukos*, the tribunal concluded that the date of expropriation was on 19 December 2004, the date of Yuganskneftegaz's auction,[77] yet the tribunal considered the investor's conduct *after* the date of

70. Commentary 3 to Art. 39 of the ARSIWA. "Draft Articles on Responsibility of States for Internationally Wrongful Acts, with commentaries" International Law Commission, 53rd Sess., UN Doc. A/56/10 (New York, 23 April – 1 June and 2 July – 10 August 2001), <http://legal.un.org/ilc/texts/instruments/english/commentaries/9_6_2001.pdf>. (Italics in original) (footnotes omitted).
71. J. CRAWFORD, *State Responsibility – The General Part*, fn. 68 above, p. 501.
72. *LaGrand* (*Germany v. US*) (2001 I.C.J. Rep.), Order (3 March 1999) at 16.
73. J. CRAWFORD, *State Responsibility – The General Part*, fn. 68 above, p. 501.
74. *CME Czech Republic B.V. v. Czech Republic* (UNCITRAL), Final Award (14 March 2003) paras. 300-304.
75. *Ibid.*, paras. 481-483. The *CME v. Czech Republic* tribunal did not find that the claimant contributed to its own loss by firing the general director of its majority shareholder and withholding daily broadcasting logs from a third company. The tribunal titled the section as "Respondent's Request for Re-litigation of the Partial Award on the basis of 'Mitigation' or 'Contributory Fault'" which was misleading as any alleged contributory fault would have been assessed prior to the breach and any conduct after the breach would have been assessed as mitigation. The tribunal also appears to have viewed the respondent's arguments as an attempt to re-litigate the Partial Award on liability.
76. *EDF International S.A., SAUR International S.A. and León Participaciones Argentinas S.A. v. Argentine Republic* (ICSID Case No. ARB/03/23), Award (11 June 2012) para. 1301. "It would be patently unfair to allow Claimants to recover damages for loss that could have been avoided by taking reasonable steps. In other words, the injured party must be held responsible for its own contribution to the loss."
77. *Hulley* Final Award, para. 1762.

expropriation in its contributory fault analysis: Yukos's non-payment of a loan and how that contributed to its bankruptcy,[78] which occurred in March 2006.[79]

Identifying and being clear on the date of breach keeps these principles distinct. The date of breach serves as the dividing line between contributory fault and mitigation of damages. In other words, contributory fault analysis ends where mitigation begins. Determining the date of breach is, however, far from clear in many cases as it will depend on the content of the obligation that is breached and the factual circumstances of the case. The tribunals in *Yukos*[80] and *Renta 4*[81] arrived at different dates of expropriation despite both disputes stemming from the same factual context, highlighting that there are many different ways to characterize the same set of facts.[82]

An outright expropriation would be an instantaneous breach[83] whereby the date of taking would be the date of the breach. However, determining the date of breach may be more challenging if the expropriation is "creeping", in that it involves a series of measures taken by the accused State.[84] A similar difficulty may extend to determining the

78. *Ibid.*, para. 1630.

79. *Ibid.*, paras. 1074-1075. See also W. SADOWSKI, "Yukos and Contributory Fault", fn. 26 above, p. 18.

80. *Hulley* Final Award, para. 1762. The *Yukos* tribunal ruled that the date of expropriation was 19 December 2004, the date of the Yuganskneftegaz's auction.

81. *Renta 4 S.V.S.A, Ahorro Corporación Emergentes F.I., Ahorro Corporación Eurofondo F.I., Rovime Inversiones SICAV S.A., Quasar de Valors SICAV S.A., Orgor de Valores SICAV S.A., GBI 9000 SICAV S.A. v. The Russian Federation* (SCC No. 24/2007), Award (20 July 2012) para. 189. The *Renta 4* tribunal accepted 23 November 2007 as the date of expropriation which was when Yukos "was removed from the Unified Register of Companies in the wake of the end of the bankruptcy proceedings as pronounced by the Moscow Arbitrazh Court". See also Manuel A. ABDALA and Alan ROZENBERG, "Assessing Investor Damages Involving Publicly Traded Companies – with Examples from the Yukos Cases" in Marion JANSEN, Joost PAUWELYN and Theresa CARPENTER, eds., *The Use of Economics in International Trade and Investment Disputes* (Cambridge 2017) p. 349 at p. 359, in which the authors argue that 14 April 2004 could have been the date of expropriation.

82. *RosInvestCo UK Ltd. v. The Russian Federation* (SCC No. 079/2005), Final Award (12 September 2010) para. 674. The third case, *Rosinvest*, does not indicate the precise date of expropriation, but instead identifies the valuation date to be 24 January 2007, which was the date when the Participation Agreements were terminated with Elliot International, a Cayman Island company, that controlled and owned the investments (Yukos shares) at issue.

83. Art. 14(1) of the ARSIWA. "Draft Articles on Responsibility of States for Internationally Wrongful Acts, with commentaries", International Law Commission, 53rd Sess., UN Doc. A/56/10 (New York, 23 April – 1 June and 2 July – 10 August 2001) <http://legal.un.org/ilc/texts/instruments/english/commentaries/9_6_2001.pdf>.

84. J. CRAWFORD, *State Responsibility – The General Part*, fn. 68 above, pp. 257-258.

> "A further area which is the cause of disagreement is that of expropriation of property. It may be considered that the taking of the property itself is an instantaneous act, with the situation of deprivation that follows reflective only of its consequences, as opposed to the act itself.... An outright, acknowledged expropriation (e.g., by decree or judicial decision) may well occur and be completed on a given day, whereas a 'creeping' expropriation consisting of a series of acts together amounting to virtual deprivation is in a different category – even though the source of obligation may be the same."

relevant date at which the investor has not received fair and equitable treatment or full protection and security, vis-à-vis a series of persistent measures.[85]

Depending upon the type of expropriation, a party may be able to frame the dispute by putting forward a specific date as the alleged date of expropriation. In direct expropriations, the expropriating State "determines in the first instance the moment of expropriation".[86] If the investor disputes that determination, then it is reviewed by the designated jurisdiction to decide the issue. In "creeping" expropriation cases, however, the investor's initial allegation "'determines' in the first instance the moment of expropriation".[87] The initial allegation would also be subject to final determination by the designated jurisdiction.

In two cases, the respondent elected not to advance dates of breach as part of its liability strategy, leaving to the investors considerable freedom to frame the dispute in this regard.[88] Insofar as contributory fault and mitigation are concerned, the parties may be incentivized to propose a date or range of dates of breach helpful to their particular positions. The below hypothetical demonstrates this point.

1. *Hypothetical*

Suppose a foreign investor (Investor A) operates a coal mine in Country B. On 1 November 2017, Country B introduces a series of measures, including tax assessments,

---

See also W. Michael REISMAN and Robert D. SLOANE, "Indirect Expropriation and its Valuation in the BIT Generation", 74 The British Yearbook of International Law (2004) p. 115 at p. 143. "In the circumstances of a creeping or consequential expropriation, however, where the state takes property rights indirectly and unlawfully, it becomes difficult if not impossible to discern when, precisely, the foreign investor 'irretrievably lost' the value of its investment." (footnotes omitted).

85. *Azurix Corp. v. The Argentine Republic* (ICSID Case No. ARB/01/12), Award (14 July 2006) paras. 313 and 417.

86. W. Michael REISMAN and Robert D. SLOANE, "Indirect Expropriation and Its Valuation in the BIT Generation", fn. 84 above, p. 115 at p. 143.

87. *Ibid.*, p. 144.

88. *Renta 4 S.V.S.A, Ahorro Corporación Emergentes F.I., Ahorro Corporación Eurofondo F.I., Rovime Inversiones SICAV S.A., Quasar de Valors SICAV S.A., Orgor de Valores SICAV S.A., GBI 9000 SICAV S.A. v. The Russian Federation* (SCC No. 24/2007), Award (20 July 2012) para. 190.

"The Respondent questions the date of 23 November 2007, asking 'how Claimants can argue that the alleged expropriation occurred in November 2007, which was several years after most of the alleged expropriatory events of which they now complain, and over a year after they gave notice of their expropriation claim.' (SoRej para. 443.) The Respondent further asserts that as it denies that 'any expropriation occurred at all, it is certainly not incumbent on the Respondent to put forward alternative dates on which such a non event may have occurred.' (SoD para. 477, n. 822.) If the Respondent could propose more appropriate dates, it might prudently have advanced such contentions in the alternative, rather than simply denying that its measures had the effect of an expropriation. Having rejected that denial, the Tribunal accepts the Claimants' logic in putting forward the date as 23 November 2007."

Hulley Final Award, para. 1738. "While Respondent does not propose any specific alternative date when Claimants lost control of their investments, Professor Dow suggested at the Hearing that such a date would, in any event, have to be before the end of 2004." (Footnotes omitted).

affecting all coal mine operators. On 1 December 2017, Investor A starts selling assets at its factory to minimize its financial exposure in Country B. On 1 January 2018, Country B directly expropriates investor A's investment such that the entirety of Investor A's business is now State-owned.

a. Scenario 1

Tribunal concludes that the date of expropriation is 1 November 2017, the date of Country B's first measure, which crystalizes as the date of breach. All of Investor A's conduct after 1 November 2017 could be evaluated through the lens of mitigation. Hence, Investor A's move to sell its assets on 1 December 2017 could be argued to constitute steps taken by Investor A to reduce its loss. Country B could either argue that proceeds of the asset sale should be discounted from the damages awarded to Investor A or that Investor A failed to mitigate because it could have sold the assets for a higher price. In the latter event, the burden will be on Country B to put forward a hypothetical asset sale.

b. Scenario 2

Tribunal concludes that the date of expropriation is 1 January 2018, which is the date of the final measure undertaken by Country B and, hence, the date of breach. All of Investor A's conduct prior to 1 January 2018 could be evaluated through the lens of contributory fault. Thus, Investor A's move to sell assets at its factory on 1 December 2017 may be viewed as provoking the wrongful conduct of Country B's expropriation one month later, i.e., 1 January 2018. (In this connection, one commentator even suggested that Yukos's steps to remove assets from the grips of the Russian authorities in the course of the tax enforcement proceedings could be seen as contributory fault.)[89]

89. W. SADOWSKI, "Yukos and Contributory Fault", fn. 26 above, pp. 25-26.

> "The third important area of the company's potential contribution is concerned with the alleged steps taken by Yukos in the course of the tax enforcement proceedings in order to remove assets from the reach of the Russian authorities. This was noted, in particular, by the *Quasar* tribunal who called it a '*perfectly understandable reaction would be to save what could be saved of what is, after all, presumptively the property of any corporate entity's owners*'. In this respect, two observations seem to be pertinent. First, it is possible that the conduct of the Yukos owners moving the assets away in response to the conduct of the state, contributed to the ultimate demise of the company and the pace thereof. Given that the company's assets were being liquidated not only through tax enforcement proceedings, but also through the acts of the company itself, its equity value was decreasing at an even faster rate. Yet in the light of the *Hulley* tribunal's determination that Russia intended to expropriate Yukos, a passive approach of the shareholders and managers of the company would not have saved it. Hence, although the conduct of Yukos was not without the influence on the actual insolvency of the company, a causal link between the conduct and the injury cannot be established. However, as shall be shown in the next section, that conduct should not be without consequences regarding the level of damages."

(Emphasis in italics in original) (footnotes omitted); see also *Hulley* Final Award, para. 1810. "The Tribunal notes that even after the tax assessments at issue in the present arbitration were issued, Claimants and their owners were able to divert money earned by Yukos out of Yukos, and into the two Stichtings, and therefore away from the tax authorities. The Tribunal cannot exclude the possibility that, but for the expropriation, the very same mechanism would have been resorted to

Country B may argue that Investor A was attempting to reduce its asset base so that Country B could not enforce, for example, its tax assessments issued on 1 November 2017. Selling assets while a tax assessment is pending would amount to contributory fault because it is equivalent to an asset-stripping scenario. This exposes the investor to injunctions and civil and criminal fines, all of which harm the investment before the State takes it over and could potentially provoke the subsequent expropriation. Country B may even argue that what Investor A was doing was illegal under the law of Country B. Investor A may argue, however, that Country B had its mind set on destroying Investor A's investment and that Country B used illegality as a pretext to expropriate.[90]

2. *Analysis*

The above hypothetical illustrates how the date of breach affects the availability of contributory fault and failure to mitigate as defenses to the respondent state. As discussed above, depending upon how the conduct is assessed, through the lens of contributory fault or mitigation, there may be vast economic consequences in the final award sum. Finding that the investor contributed to its loss tends to result in discounting the final award sum by a percentage figure of the entire award, but discounting on the ground of mitigation tends to generate more precise numbers. All things being equal in the above hypothetical, the respondent has an interest in insisting on a date of expropriation as late as possible so that it can cast all of the investor's conduct as going to contributory fault. Conversely, the investor would want to insist on an earlier date of expropriation to portray its subsequent conduct as mitigation of damages, reducing the discount on the final award sum. Of course, this hypothetical cannot account for all of the various reasons a party may have for putting forward a particular date of breach.

---

by Claimants under different circumstances to divert some of the money earned by Yukos." (footnotes omitted). The diversion of funds was analyzed in the fair market value of Yukos; *Renta 4 S.V.S.A, Ahorro Corporación Emergentes F.I., Ahorro Corporación Eurofondo F.I., Rovime Inversiones SICAV S.A., Quasar de Valors SICAV S.A., Orgor de Valores SICAV S.A., GBI 9000 SICAV S.A. v. The Russian Federation* (SCC No. 24/2007), Award (20 July 2012) para. 123.

"The response to this argument can be very succinct. If Yukos' owners and management concluded that the Russian Government had set its face against them and was pursuing an objective of confiscation, they would hardly have been encouraged to keep profits sitting nicely where they could be taken by state power. If the storm clouds were so ominous, there was no reason to invest in assets within the jurisdiction (because they would be susceptible to dispossession by force) and the perfectly understandable reaction would be to save what could be saved of what is, after all, presumptively the property of any corporate entity's owners."

90. See, for example, *Renta 4 S.V.S.A, Ahorro Corporación Emergentes F.I., Ahorro Corporación Eurofondo F.I., Rovime Inversiones SICAV S.A., Quasar de Valors SICAV S.A., Orgor de Valores SICAV S.A., GBI 9000 SICAV S.A. v. The Russian Federation* (SCC No. 24/2007), Award (20 July 2012) paras. 122-124. The tribunal appeared to have accepted that Yukos's reaction to divert funds from Russia's grip was not "outlandish or exaggerated".

IV. CONCLUSION

Why does ISDS exist? To ascertain who, as between a foreign investor or a host State, ought to bear the economic burden concerning an international investment dispute. In short, it is all about the damages:

> "[I]nvestment arbitration is about money. Investors initiate investment claims to recover monetary losses and respondent states defend against these claims to prevent paying money out of the taxpayers' pockets."[91]

Revolt against ISDS is the flavor of the decade with States and interest groups campaigning to replace or otherwise alter the existing ISDS model with a permanent court. Ample academic writing and debate have enriched the arbitration community, investigating both the possibility and (non)-practicability of such a court. Critics of the system should, however, not lose focus of the "bottom line" and should consider strategies that could serve to reduce the compensation amount payable by States.

Despite the obvious importance to compensation, lawyers and academics regard quantum of damages "as the 'poor cousin' of more important legal battles about jurisdiction over claims and their merits, and hence [questions of damages and compensation] have received less systematic attention".[92] Such predisposition may be understandable. If respondent counsel, for example, can secure the dismissal of a case on jurisdiction or the merits, then a quantum strategy may find itself relegated to a subsidiary concern. Rarely, however, will counsel for the respondent possess such foresight on the strength of its case at the inception of the dispute. Whether the case is bifurcated or not may also have a bearing on developing an effective quantum strategy. One commentator has noted that the non-bifurcation of the *Yukos* hearings between merits and quantum may have had a significant impact on the contributory fault analysis in that case.[93]

We live in a world of the US$ 50 billion ISDS award.[94] To date, the *Yukos* Awards hold the record as the highest award in investment arbitration. Even excluding the *Yukos* Awards, the last five years have shown an increase in the amount awarded to successful claimants. According to a recent survey, in cases since 2013 the average amount awarded to successful claimants is US$ 171 million, which is an increase of over 124 percent when compared to the US$ 76.3 million average in an earlier version of the same survey based on publicly available awards as of 31 December 2012.[95] The overall average

91. W. ALSCHNER, "Aligning Loss and Liability – Toward an Integrated Assessment of Damages in Investment Arbitration", fn. 26 at p. 283 (footnotes omitted).
92. Charles N. BROWER and Michael OTTOLENGHI, "Damages in Investor-State Arbitration", 4 Transnational Dispute Management (2007, no. 6) p. 2.
93. M. KANTOR, "Chapter 38: The Impact of Contributory Investor Conduct: Only with Difficulty Commensurable", fn. 11 above, pp. 551-552.
94. *Yukos* Awards.
95. "Investment Treaty Arbitration: cost, duration and size of claims all show steady increase", Allen & Overy LLP (14 December 2017) at <www.allenovery.com/publications/en-gb/Pages/Investment-Treaty-Arbitration-cost-duration-and-size-of-claims-all-show-steady-increase.aspx>; See also Matthew HODGSON and Alastair CAMPBELL, "Damages and costs in

"amount across all cases to date (a data pool of 132 excluding *Yukos*) is now US$ 110.9 million."[96] To emphasize the point differently, "the median amount awarded to successful claimants ... in cases from 2013 onwards, was US$ 40 million (compared to US$ 10.7 million prior to 2013)."[97] This is "a 274% rise of the median, which might be considered a better reflection of a 'typical' case".[98] Thus, the financial stakes in investment arbitration are more than a final cadence and warrant a serious reflection on a quantum strategy at an early stage. Quantum is the implicit beat of ISDS and both contributory fault and mitigation have powerful implications for its rhythm.

investment treaty arbitration", Global Arbitration Review (14 December 2017) at <http://globalarbitrationreview.com/print_article/gar/article/1151755/damages-and-costs-in-investment-treaty-arbitration-revisited?print=true>.

96. M. HODGSON and A. CAMPBELL, "Damages and costs in investment treaty arbitration", fn. 95 above. As mentioned, this figure excludes the approximately US$ 50 billion award in the *Yukos* Awards. Including the *Yukos* Awards, the overall average comes to US$ 486.1 million.

97. *Ibid.*

98. *Ibid.*

Sovereign Wealth Funds: The New Kids on the Block

Solomon Ebere[*]

TABLE OF CONTENTS PAGE

I. INTRODUCTION

Sovereign Wealth Funds (SWFs), which manage the foreign assets of States, have recently emerged as a significant class of global investors. Although they have been making headlines in the mainstream press following several high-profile investments in major Western banks amid the 2008 financial crisis, as well as their involvement in corruption-related scandals spanning from Eastern Europe to South-East Asia, limited attention has been devoted to SWFs in international arbitration. Yet, they have become active players at both ends of the spectrum, i.e. as claimant and as respondent, and it looks like this is just the beginning. This presentation attempts to shed some light on the critical issues relating to international arbitrations in which this unique type of investor is involved.

SWFs are not your typical foreign investors. According to the International Working Group of Sovereign Wealth Funds (IWG), comprising twenty-six States maintaining SWFs, which put in place best practices known as the "Santiago Principles", SWFs are

> "special purpose investment funds or arrangements that are owned by the general government. Created by the general government for macroeconomic purposes, SWFs hold, manage, or administer assets to achieve financial objectives, and employ a set of investment strategies that include investing in foreign financial assets."[1]

---

* Senior Associate at Omnia Strategy LLP, London; international arbitration lawyer with more than six years of experience; admitted to the New York and Paris Bars; participated in proceedings conducted under the ICC, ICDR, Swiss, UNCITRAL and ICSID Arbitration Rules, as well as in court proceedings before the US and the UK courts; J.D., Georgetown Law; Global Law Scholar, Georgetown Law; founder and former chair of the Georgetown International Arbitration Society; post-graduate degree in comparative law and a J.D. equivalent, both from the University of Paris I (La Sorbonne).

1. IWG, *Sovereign Wealth Funds – Generally Accepted Principles and Practices – "Santiago Principles"* (October 2008) at <http://www.ifswf.org/sites/default/files/santiagoprinciples_0_0.pdf>.

This definition highlights two key aspects of SWFs: they are State-owned entities whose purpose is to invest in foreign assets. One would be remiss not to mention another key aspect that sets SWFs in a class of their own: they are of a very significant financial size, as they manage trillions of dollars.

Their investments have raised some concerns, particularly in host States. Whilst traditionally the bulk of SWFs' investments was in the financial sector, they have diversified their portfolios, investing in other sectors, such as natural resources, defence and infrastructure. Host States have suspected that States behind these SWFs, some of whom are at odds with the international community, may be inclined to invest in these strategic sectors to foster their geopolitical interests, rather than for purely commercial goals. For instance, the potential acquisition of several ports in the United States in 2006 by Dubai Ports World, owned by the Government of Dubai, gave rise to national security concerns in the US Congress.[2] As a result of these suspicions, many countries have established pre-screening procedures applicable to SWF investments (e.g., Canada, China, France, Germany, Japan, Korea, Russia and the United States).

SWFs have also come under considerable scrutiny due to their implication in scandals over fraud and corruption of high-level government officials of host States. This is the case of the Malaysian SWF, 1Malaysia Development Berhad (1MDB). According to the US Department of Justice, between 2009 and 2015, more than US$ 4.5 billion in funds belonging to 1MDB were misappropriated by high-level officials of 1MDB, including Malaysia's former prime minister who set up 1MDB in 2009, as well as officials and executives of International Petroleum Investment Company (IPIC), an Abu Dhabi SWF that had injected US$ 3.5 billion in 1MDB.[3]

Another noteworthy aspect of SWFs is their increasingly important role in the economic development of emerging jurisdictions. Asia, along with Africa and Latin America, have been key destinations for sovereign funds in recent years – an important dimension of ever-expanding "south-south" trade and investment, given that some of the most prominent and active SWFs are themselves funded and controlled by emerging economies.

This unique blend of politics, banking, national security concerns and emerging jurisdictions makes SWFs natural candidates for many more international arbitrations to come, whether commercial or treaty-based.

This presentation endeavours to capture some of the salient issues these disputes could involve. First, we will look in more detail at what makes SWFs such "unique" actors. Second, we will analyze the disputes SWFs have been involved in to date, as respondents or as claimants against their contractual counterparts and/or host State of investment. Third, we will describe the jurisdictional hurdles SWFs could face in an investment treaty arbitration context, as well as the protections they could rely upon to redress the wrong they have suffered.

---

2. See "Dubai Seeks to Calm the Storm Over Ports", The Economist (10 March 2006) at <http://www.economist.com/node/5620236>.
3. See "Justice Department Complaint Seeking 1MDB Assets", New York Times (16 June 2017) at <https://www.nytimes.com/interactive/2017/06/16/world/asia/1mdb-malaysia-complaint.html>.

II. SWFS: A GROWING BUT CONTROVERSIAL FORCE

1. *SWFs Are Strange Creatures*

> "Sovereign wealth funds are special purpose investment funds or arrangements, owned by the general government. Created by the general government for macroeconomic purposes, SWFs hold, manage, or administer assets to achieve financial objectives, and employ a set of investment strategies that include investing in foreign financial assets. The SWFs are commonly established out of balance of payments surpluses, official foreign currency operations, the proceeds of privatizations, fiscal surpluses, and/or receipts resulting from commodity exports."[4]

SWFs are thus creatures of governments, whose purpose is to invest in foreign financial assets. However, these features do not make them unique. Throughout the history of international arbitration are disputes in which the claimants have been State-owned entities, including ones investing in foreign financial assets.[5]

So what differentiates SWFs from other State-owned entities? First and maybe foremost, is the sheer financial size and potential growth of these funds. They manage trillions of assets – US$ 7.4 trillion as of September 2017 according to the Sovereign Wealth Fund Institute – and could grow to a staggering amount in the years to come given that they have more than doubled in the last decade.[6] The current size of the fifteen largest SWFs is summarized in the table below:

4. International Monetary Fund and International Forum of Sovereign Wealth Funds, "Santiago Principles", (October 2008) at <http://www.iwg-swf.org/pubs/eng/santiagoprinciples.pdf>.
5. See, e.g., *Cskoslovenka Obschodni Banka, A.S. v. Slovak Republic* (ICSID Case No. ARB/97/4), Decision on Jurisdiction (24 May 1999) (dispute in which the claimant was a commercial bank in which its home State, the Czech Republic, had an interest); *CDG Group plc v. Republic of Seychelles* (ICSID Case No. ARB/02/14), Award (17 December 2003) (CDC Group, a development finance institution owned by the United Kingdom, brought a claim in 2002 against the Seychelles); *Telenor Mobile Communication AS v. Hungary* (ICSID Case No. ARB/04/15), Award (13 September 2006) (in 2004, Telenor Mobile, a telecommunications company majority owned by Norway, commenced arbitration against Hungary); *Hrvataska Elektroprivreda d.d. v. Republic of Slovenia* (ICSID Case No. ARB/05/24), Award (17 December 2015); *Flughafen Zürich A.G. and Gestión e Ingenería IDC S.A. v. Bolivarian Republic of Venezuela* (ICSID Case No. ARB/10/19), Award (18 November 2014).
6. Sovereign Wealth Fund Institute, "Sovereign Wealth Fund Market Size by Quarter 1998 to 2017" (updated February 2018), at <https://www.swfinstitute.org/sovereign-wealth-fund-rankings/>; CNBC, "The World's Biggest Sovereign Wealth Funds in 2017" (17 July 2015) at <https://www.cnbc.com/2015/07/17/the-worlds-biggest-sovereign-wealth-funds.html#slide=1>.

Rank	Sovereign Wealth Fund	Home Jurisdiction	Assets (US$ billion)
1	Government Pension Fund Global	Norway	737.2
2	SAMA Foreign Holdings	Saudi Arabia	675.9
3	Abu Dhabi Investment Authority	UAE	627.0
4	China Investment Corporation	China	575.2
5	SAFE Investment Company	China	567.9
6	Kuwait Investment Authority	Kuwait	386.0
7	Hong Kong Monetary Authority Investment Portfolio	Hong Kong (China)	326.7
8	Government of Singapore Investment Corporation	Singapore	285.0
9	National Welfare Fund	Russian Federation	239.3
10	Temasek Holdings	Singapore	173.3
11	National Social Security Fund	China	160.6
12	Qatar Investment Authority	Qatar	115.0
13	Australian Government Future Fund	Australia	88.7
14	Revenue Regulation Fund	Algeria	77.2
15	Investment Corporation of Dubai	UAE	70.0

Second, both governments and the press alike have viewed them suspiciously. While during the financial crisis in 2007-2008, western governments and western banks welcomed with open arms much-needed capital from SWFs to bail them out, the suspicion that the States behind these SWFs made these investments for national strategic purposes remained. As Germany's chancellor, Angela Merkel, told the financial newspaper *Handelsblatt*, "The question is whether the participation of a state fund is motivated by the willingness to exercise political influence."[7] Whether these national security concerns are legitimate or not, they have led a number of western governments to add pre-screening procedures to SWF investments.[8] The press did not spare SWFs

7. Le Figaro, "Europe Looks at Sovereign Wealth Funds" (20 July 2007) at <http://www.lefigaro.fr/economie/2007/07/20/04001-20070720ARTFIG90040-l_europe_se_penche_sur_les_fonds_souverains.php>; see also Laurence DUBIN, "*Les Fonds souverains: Propos Introductifs*", pp. 10-11, in *Les Fonds Souverains entre Affirmation et Dilution de l'Etat Face à la Mondialisation* (2014).
8. See infra Sect. IV.*1*, "Jurisdiction Ratione Materiae: Whether Pre-admission Screening of Proposed Investments by SWFs Breaches Treaty Obligation".

either. Maybe partly for the sake of publicity and newspaper sales, a lot of sensationalist ink was spilled writing about them, and not all the coverage was accurate.[9]

Third, the fact that some of these SWFs are at the centre of recent corruption scandals involving high-profile officials and business people has added to their controversial appearance and the perceived lack of transparency of their operations. Some scholars have argued that these funds could be legitimately disguised as supporting domestic development when in reality they were used to deepen the pockets of the political leaders.[10] One such example is the high profile corruption scandal involving the alleged channelling of several hundreds of millions of funds from 1MDB to the former Malaysian Prime Minister Najib Razak's personal accounts.

2. *SWFs in Five Continents*

The number of SWFs is rapidly growing. In simplistic terms, three generations of SWFs can be identified. The first generation was born in the 1970s in the Gulf countries, in Norway and in Canada, resulting from the necessity to invest the proceeds of the sale of commodities, in particular oil. The second generation, which was born more recently, involved major geopolitical actors, such as China and Russia. The third generation, contemporaneous, was born in emerging markets which disposed structural surpluses of commodities, such as Libya.[11] Finally, it has emerged that African States are catching up and have established their own SWFs in the past few years.[12]

9. See, e.g., Adriano B. LUCATELLI, "A Swiss Sovereign Wealth Fund: Not Such a Smart Idea", Market Mogul (11 August 2015) ("sovereign wealth funds are open to abuse, as they inspire political covetousness. Politicians may be tempted to earmark profits on foreign investments for politically motivated means, or to use the sovereign wealth fund as a means of exercising greater influence over their central bank, which by definition should be independent.") at <https://themarketmogul.com/swiss-sovereign-wealth-fund-not-smart-idea/>; see also Samantha PEARSON, "Sovereign Wealth Funds: Foreign Cash Has Its Drawbacks", Financial Times (26 April 2011) ("there is a sense of unease about SWFs' lack of transparency and their exploitation of local resources") at <https://www.ft.com/content/e5e4f274-6ef5-11e0-a13b-00144feabdc0>; see also Peter GALUSZKA, "Sovereign Wealth Funds: Benefit or Threat?", Moneywatch (5 May 2008) ("Just when CEOs thought they had a handle on secretive and powerful hedge funds, they must consider a quieter but even bigger monster – Sovereign Wealth Funds.") at <https://www.cbsnews.com/ news/sovereign-wealth-funds-benefit-or-threat/>.
10. See, e.g., Daniel W. DREZNER, "White Whale or Red Herring?: Assessing Sovereign Wealth Funds", Stockholm: Glasshouse Forum 2008 (in which the author argues that SWFs can serve as slush fund vehicles for corruption).
11. Laurence DUBIN, "*Les Fonds souverains: Propos Introductifs*" in *Les Fonds Souverains entre Affirmation et Dilution de l'Etat Face à la Mondialisation* (2014) p. 9 ("*Les Fonds souverains: Propos Introductifs*": "*on peut distinguer trois générations de fonds. La première date des années 70 et est apparue dans les Etats du Golfe, en Norvège et au Canada en raison de la nécessité d'investir les recettes de l'exportation des matières premières. La deuxième génération, plus récente, est marquée par la création de fonds souverains par des acteurs géopolitiques majeurs, comme la Chine et la Russie. La troisième génération, contemporaine, provident des pays émergents disposant d'excédents structurels de matières premières.*").
12. The Economist, "Sovereign-Wealth Funds Catch on in Africa" (16 March 2017) available at <https://www.economist.com/news/finance-and-economics/21718893-countries-disagree-about-how-use-them-sovereign-wealth-funds-catch>; see also Financial Times, "Sovereign Funds

While the largest SWF is European, specifically Norway, two regions dominate the landscape in terms of total number of entities and total assets: Asia Pacific and the Middle East.[13] SWFs traditionally invested in high-profile assets in western banks. Yet, many of them are now turning to emerging markets, as they believe that economic growth in the decade to come will be dominated by the emerging world, including in Asia, sub-Saharan Africa and Latin America.[14] Sub-Saharan Africa is expected to show the largest growth in terms of percentage although total assets are expected to remain comparatively modest.[15]

III. SWF LITIGATION AND ARBITRATION

The emerging role of SWFs in world affairs has recently led to a flurry of high-stake litigations and arbitrations.

During the financial crisis back in 2007 and 2008, several SWFs stepped in and invested much-needed capital in a number of capital-starved corporations, including in and/or through leading western banks such as Citigroup, Goldman Sachs or Société Générale. However, the market continued to plummet and the SWFs suffered heavy losses. Soon thereafter, these SWFs commenced legal actions against the aforementioned banks, both before national courts and before arbitral tribunals. Arbitrations and litigations in this category that are public knowledge as of the date of writing include the following:

– The Abu Dhabi Investment Authority, one of the world's largest SWFs, initiated two arbitrations against Citigroup over a 2007 deal in which the SWF had agreed to pay US$ 7.5 billion to acquire a 4.9 percent stake in Citigroup. In the first arbitration initiated in 2009, the SWF sought US$ 4 billion in damages before an American Arbitration Association/International Centre for Dispute Resolution (AAA/ICDR) tribunal on the ground that Citigroup had fraudulently induced it into buying the stake. The SWF claimed that Citigroup had issued preferred shares to other investors and

Expand in Africa" (15 December 2013) available at <https://www.ft.com/content/515caa8e-5750-11e3-9624-00144feabdc0>.

13. See Elizabeth WHITSITT and Todd WEILER, "Sovereign Wealth Funds and Bilateral Investment Treaties' New Models: Issues, New Trends and State Practice" in Fabio BASSAN, *Research Handbook on Sovereign Wealth Funds and International Investment Law* (Edward Elgar 2015) p. 278. For a more up-to-date ranking, see Sovereign Wealth Fund Institute, "Sovereign Wealth Fund Rankings" (updated February 2018), at <https://www.swfinstitute.org/sovereign-wealth-fund-rankings/>.
14. Mahmoud KASSEM, "Adia Targets Emerging Markets as Long-Term Gains Slow", The National (4 July 2017) at <https://www.thenational.ae/business/adia-targets-emerging-markets-as-long-term-gains-slow-1.91754>. Sheikh Hamed bin Zayed Al NAHYAN, Adia's managing director, said in the fund's annual review, published on 4 July 2017, "We expect that over two-thirds of the growth in global GDP over the coming ten years will come from those emerging economies; with roughly half coming from China and India alone."
15. PwC, "Sovereign Investors 2020: A Growing Force", p. 10, at <https://www.pwc.com/ee/et/publications/pub/sovereign-investors-2020.pdf>.

thereby diluted the value of the shares the SWF had purchased. In 2011, the tribunal dismissed that claim.[16]

In 2013, the SWF filed a second claim worth US$ 2 billion also with the AAA/ICDR but before a different tribunal, alleging that Citigroup had breached their investment agreement and an implied covenant of good faith and fair dealing by failing to use "commercially reasonable efforts" to ensure the SWF received the best possible return on its investment. The second tribunal also dismissed this claim. It held that the "narrow language" of the contract meant that Citigroup was only required to make commercially reasonable efforts to consummate the transactions contemplated in the agreement. It did not require Citigroup to operate its business so as to maximize the SWFs' return. Moreover, Citigroup could not have breached the implied covenant on the facts alleged as there was no evidence that it had acted purposefully to deprive it of the fruits of the contract. Finally, the tribunal rejected any allegations that Citigroup's acts and omissions had been commercially unreasonable.[17]

– The Libyan Investment Authority (LIA), Libya's SWF created towards the end of Qaddafi's regime, brought a US$ 1.2 billion claim against US leading investment bank, Goldman Sachs, before the English High Court over a series of trades. The LIA claimed that it was too unsophisticated to understand what it was buying and that Goldman Sachs exercised undue influence over it. It also argued that the trades entered into were unconscionable bargains. On either basis, the LIA contended that it was entitled to rescind the trades and to the return of its premium. In October 2016, the High Court dismissed the LIA's claim.[18]

– In 2014, the LIA brought another claim before the English High Court against another leading investment bank, Société Générale, for US$ 2.1 billion regarding trades executed between 2007 and 2009. This time, the LIA claimed that Société Générale had obtained the contract through corruption, involving the payment of US$ 58.5 million to a Panama-registered company called Leinada, controlled at the time by Libyan businessman Walid Giahmi. On 3 May 2017, on the eve of the start of the hearing, the parties settled for an alleged amount of € 963 million.[19]

Another type of dispute involving SWFs pertains to high-level corruption scandals. Arbitrations in this category that are public knowledge as of the date of writing include the following:

16. See Global Arbitration Review, "US Court Allows Abu Dhabi Fund's Claim to Proceed" (27 November 2013) at <http://globalarbitrationreview.com/article/ 1032829/us-court-allows-abu-dhabi-funds-claim-to-proceed>.
17. See Global Arbitration Review, "Abu Dhabi Fund Won't Challenge Citigroup Award" (22 March 2017) at <http://globalarbitrationreview.com/article/1138494/abu-dhabi-fund-won%E2%80%99t-challenge-citigroup-award>.
18. *The Libyan Investment Authority v. Goldman Sachs International*, [2016] EWHC 2530 (Ch) at <www.20essexst.com/sites/default/files/judgments/Libyan%20Investment%20Authority%20v%20Goldman%20Sachs.pdf>.
19. See the Financial Times, "SocGen Agrees € 963m Settlement with Libyan Investment Authority" (4 May 2017) at <https://www.ft.com/content/7dc88450-3094-11e7-9555-23ef563ecf9a>.

– On 22 October 2015, the State General Reserve Fund of the Sultanate of Oman, Oman's SWF, initiated arbitration proceedings against the Republic of Bulgaria before the International Centre for Settlement of Investment Disputes (ICSID).[20] The claim relates to the Omani SWF's shareholding in the Bulgarian bank, Corporate Commercial Bank (Corpbank) that collapsed in 2014. As widely reported in the foreign and financial press, Corpbank was Bulgaria's fourth largest lender until it saw a run on deposits in 2014. Since then, the bank's license has been revoked and bankruptcy proceedings initiated, amidst allegations from Bulgarian authorities and parliamentarians that the bank's management hid gaping losses by engaging in a pyramid scheme. It has also been reported that the bank's largest shareholder, controversial businessman Tsvetan Vassilev, faces charges of alleged embezzlement, which he contests.[21]
– In June 2016, the IPIC, one of Abu Dhabi's SWFs, and its subsidiary Aabar Investments launched a US$ 6.5 billion London Court of International Arbitration (LCIA) claim against 1MDB, the scandal-plagued Malaysian SWF. The dispute is rooted in a 2012 deal wherein IPIC agreed to guarantee two sets of bonds worth US$ 3.5 billion that 1MDB issued to finance the purchase of power plants. After 1MDB struggled to honour its debts, the parties signed a bailout agreement in May 2015, in which IPIC agreed to provide 1MDB with an immediate US$ 1 billion cash loan and temporarily assume its obligations to pay interest on the bonds. IPIC was to assume liability for all payments under the bonds and forgive other debts upon receiving a transfer of assets of equivalent value from 1MDB. However, in April 2016, IPIC declared that it was terminating the agreement, contending that 1MDB had repeatedly defaulted on interest payments under the bonds, which IPIC had continued to honour as guarantor. This dispute has arisen in the wake of a much bigger scandal over alleged misappropriation of funds from 1MDB, which is US$ 11 billion in debt. Anti-corruption investigations have been launched in Singapore, Switzerland, the United Arab Emirates (UAE) and the United States amid allegations that the funds landed in the hands of former Malaysian Prime Minister Najib Razak's friends and associates, as well as officials and executives from IPIC. The US Department of Justice is still trying to recover US$ 1 billion that they say was ultimately spent on luxury homes in Manhattan and Los Angeles, Picasso and Monet paintings, and financing for Hollywood blockbuster *The Wolf of Wall Street*. In April 2017, IPIC and 1MDB agreed to settle the dispute for US$ 1.2 billion.[22]
– In a London-based arbitration, the LIA secured a US$ 380 million award against Zambia for nationalizing Zamtel, a Zambian telecom company in 2011. The LIA owned

20. See ICSID website at <https://icsid.worldbank.org/en/Pages/cases/casedetail.aspx?CaseNo=ARB/15/43>.

21. See Luke E. PETERSON, "Oman's Sovereign Wealth Fund Is the Latest Claimant to Try to Hold a Sovereign State – this Time Bulgaria – Liable for Losses Tied to a Bank Failure", IA Reporter (23 October 2015) at <https://proxy.ppl.nl:2094/articles/omans-sovereign-wealth-fund-is-the-latest-claimant-to-try-to-hold-a-sovereign-state-this-time-bulgaria-liable-for-losses-tied-to-a-bank-failure/>.

22. See Sebastian PERRY, "Malaysia State Fund Faces Claim over Debt Bailout", Global Arbitration Review (14 June 2016) at <https://globalarbitrationreview.com/article/1036405/malaysian-state-fund-faces-claim-over-debt-bailout>; see also Tom JONES, "Malaysia's 1MDB Settles LCIA Claim", Global Arbitration Review (24 April 2017) at <https://globalarbitrationreview.com/article/1139957/malaysia%E2%80%99s-1mdb-settles-lcia-claim>.

a 75 percent share of Zamtel through its subsidiary LAP Green, while the Zambian government owned 25 percent.

– It was also reported that the LIA brought similar claims against other African countries, including Rwanda and Chad. The LIA claims that these countries took advantage of "Libya's political turmoil to nationalise assets belonging to the country's US$ 66 billion sovereign funds" following the eight-month-long conflict that brought a brutal end to Muammar Gaddafi's forty-year rule.[23]

IV. JURISDICTIONAL ISSUES IN INVESTMENT ARBITRATIONS

In order for an SWF to benefit from the protection of an international investment agreement (IIA), its claim must vest a tribunal with jurisdiction ratione temporis, ratione personae and ratione materiae.

There are four jurisdictional issues of particular relevance to SWFs. The first and second concern issues of jurisdiction ratione materiae: whether pre-admission screening of proposed investments of SWFs breaches treaty obligations and whether the purchase of foreign assets qualifies as an *investment* under bilateral investment treaties and under ICSID. The third and fourth concern issues of jurisdiction ratione personae: whether SWFs qualify as foreign investors under bilateral investment treaties and under the Convention on the Settlement of Disputes between States and Nationals of Other States (the ICSID Convention), since the ICSID Convention does not permit arbitration between states. Each of these questions raises interesting legal issues. We will look at them in seriatim.

1. *Jurisdiction Ratione Materiae: Whether Pre-admission Screening of Proposed Investments by SWFs Breaches Treaty Obligations.*[24]

Considering the political sensitivity involved, many countries have established pre-screening procedures applicable to SWF investments. This is typically done pursuant to a domestic statute that empowers national government agencies to review potential investments by foreign persons to determine the effect of these investments on, inter alia, national security.[25] Similar procedures have been developed in Australia, Canada, China, France, Germany, Japan, Korea and Russia.[26]

---

23. See I-ARB, "Zambia Pays First Installation of 380 Million USD Award" (undated) at <https://www.iarbafrica.com/en/news-list/17-news/544-zambia-pays-first-installation-of-380-million-usd-award?utm_source=ActiveCampaign&utm_medium=email&utm_content=I-Arb+Weekly&utm_campaign=I-Arb+Weekly-2018-5>.
24. See Grant HANESSIAN and Kabir DUGGAL, "The Role of Sovereign Welfare Funds and National Oil Companies in Investment Arbitrations", Global Arbitration Review (9 June 2016); see also Anna JOUBIN-BRET, "Admission and Establishment in the Context of Investment Protection" in A. REINISH, ed., *Standards of Investment Protection* (OUP 2008) pp. 9 et seq.
25. See, e.g., the Committee on Foreign Investment in the United States (CFIUS).
26. See Mathias AUDIT, "*Le Règlement des Litiges Relatifs à l'Activité des Fonds Souverains*", pp. 107-110 (Les Fonds Souverains entre Affirmation et Dilution de l'Etat Face à la Mondialisation 2014).

Whether such procedures may violate obligations under an investment treaty depends on the language of the BIT. There appear to be three prevalent approaches to pre-admission review of investments in BITs:

– If the BIT is silent on the issue, no protection is afforded to the investor.
– The so-called "admission model": host States are obligated to create favourable conditions; however, the actual admission of an investment is conditional upon host State laws and policy. Only if there is a breach of these requirements, would there be a breach of the applicable BIT.[27]
– The so-called "pre-establishment model":[28] national treatment is guaranteed to investors at the pre-investment stage. If the claimant can establish it was in "like circumstances" and not given equal treatment to domestic investors, there could be a potential breach of the BIT. However, finding an investor that is "in like circumstances" might not be a simple task: "The test requires comparison. The identification of a national 'comparator' is important. Such a comparator would be difficult to find, as it is unlikely that any national investor would have the deep pockets of the SWF, its association with a foreign state, or possess motivation by national as well as commercial interest."[29]

2. *Jurisdiction Ratione Materiae: Whether the Purchase of Foreign Assets Qualifies as an "Investment" Within the Meaning of the Applicable BIT and ICSID Convention*

SWFs must also satisfy the criteria for determining the existence of an "investment" under the ICSID Convention. A common formulation for this was developed by the tribunal in the *Salini v. Morocco* case, which lists four characteristics of investment: contribution, duration of performance, risk, and promotion of the economic development of the host State. Of the four criteria, there are concerns that an SWF may have trouble with the "promotion of the economic development" standard as (1) an SWF investment may not make a sufficiently meaningful long-term contribution to the economy of the host State, and (2) by definition, an SWF would be more concerned with the protection of a sovereign's wealth rather than participating in the economic development of the host State.

A similar question may also arise under some BITs, in particular the latest ones, such as the Morocco-Nigeria BIT, wherein *"investment"* is defined inter alia as "contribut[ing] sustainable development", which is itself defined as "the reduction of poverty, increase of

---

27. See, e.g., the India-Kazakhstan BIT, Art. 3(1) ("Each Contracting Party shall encourage and create favourable conditions for investors of the other Contracting Party to make investments in its territory, and admit such investments in accordance with its laws and policy.").
28. See, e.g., the 2012 U.S. Model BIT, Art. 3(1) ("Each Party shall accord to investors of the other Party treatment no less favorable than that it accords, in like circumstances, to its own investors with respect to the establishment, acquisition, expansion, management, conduct, operation, and sale or other disposition of investments in its territory.").
29. M. SORNARAJAH, "Sovereign Wealth Funds and the Existing Structure of the Regulation of Investments", 1 Asian Journal of International Law (2011, issue 2) pp. 281-282.

productive capacity, economic growth, the transfer of technology, and the furtherance of human rights and human development".[30]

3. *Jurisdiction Ratione Personae: Whether SWFs Qualify as Foreign Investors Under BITs*

SWFs differ from traditional private corporations as they are State-owned and, generally, State-controlled. The question that arises is whether they qualify as "*investors*" under the applicable BIT. Again, the answer will depend on the language of the applicable BIT. There appear to be three common approaches:

– The BIT defines the term "*enterprise*" as including state-owned entities: in this situation, SWFs would qualify as "*investors*" under the BIT.[31]
– The BIT defines the term "*investor*" as including state corporations registered under the laws of X: in this situation, an SWF would qualify as an "*investor*" under the BIT if it is set up as a state corporation.[32]
– The BIT is silent on the issue: a tribunal is likely therefore to adopt a plain meaning analysis to see if SWFs would qualify as "*investors*" under the BIT.[33]

While a review of BITs reveals that the definition of "*investors*" or related term differs widely depending on the BIT, unsurprisingly, Middle Eastern States that are home to the largest SWFs (e.g., Kuwait, Qatar, Saudi Arabia and the UAE) usually negotiate BITs containing a broad definition of "*investors*". By contrast, other significant SWF jurisdictions, such as China, Norway, Russia or Singapore, or barely include State-owned entities in the definition of "*investors*".[34]

30. See The Preamble and Art. 1(3) of the Morocco-Nigeria BIT, dated 3 December 2016.
31. See, e.g., NAFTA, Arts. 1139 and 201(1) ("enterprise means any entity constituted or organized under applicable law, whether or not for profit, and *whether privately-owned or governmentally-owned*, including any corporation, trust, partnership, sole proprietorship, joint venture or other association").
32. See, e.g., the Ghana-China BIT, Art. 1(b) ("The term 'investor' means.... In respect of Ghana ... (ii) *state corporations* and agencies and companies under the laws of Ghana which invest or trade abroad."); see also Czech Republic-Kuwait BIT, Art. 1(2)(b); see also US-Rwanda BIT, Art. 1.
33. See, e.g., South Korea – Kazakhstan BIT, Art. 1(2)(b); see also the Japan-Pakistan BIT, Art. 1.
34. Elizabeth WHITSITT and Todd WEILER, "Sovereign Wealth Funds and Bilateral Investment Treaties' New Models: Issues, New Trends and State Practice" in Fabio BASSAN, *Research Handbook on Sovereign Wealth Funds and International Investment Law* (Edward Elgar 2015) pp. 291-296. ("It is not surprising that the States members of the United Arab Emirates (UAE), Saudi Arabia, Kuwait and Qatar, which are home to five of the 15 largest SWFs (ADIA, SAMA Foreign Holdings, KIA, Qatar Investment Authority and Investment Corporation of Dubai), are most consistent in their practice and almost always negotiate BITs containing the broadest definition of investor for their SWFs (....) Similar to China, BITs entered into by significant SWF jurisdictions other than the Middle East States suggest that including government-owned or –controlled entities in the definition of investor is more the exception than the rule and often contain ambiguous terminology.").

4. *Jurisdiction Ratione Personae: Whether SWFs Qualify as Foreign Investors Under the ICSID Convention?*

The question here is whether SWFs, given that they are State-owned, satisfy the objective requirement under Art. 25(2) of the ICSID Convention, which defines "*National of another Contracting State*" as follows:

> "any juridical person which had the nationality of a Contracting State other than the State party to the dispute on the date on which the parties consented to submit such dispute to conciliation or arbitration and any juridical person which had the nationality of the Contracting State party to the dispute on that date and which, because of foreign control, the parties have agreed should be treated as a national of another Contracting State for the purposes of this Convention".

Aaron Broches, who was the general counsel to the World Bank and a founding father of ICSID, answered the question in the affirmative and set forth the following test:

> "There are many companies whose shares are owned by the government, but who are practically indistinguishable from the completely privately owned enterprise both in their legal characteristics and in their activities. It would seem, therefore, that for purposes of the Convention *a mixed economy company or government-owned corporation should not be disqualified as a 'national of another Contracting State' unless it is acting as an agent for the government or is discharging an essentially governmental function*. I believe it is fair to say that there was a consensus on this point among those participating in the preparation of the Convention." (Emphasis added.)[35]

ICSID case law confirms that the so-called Broches test is the appropriate test to determine whether a State entity's activities fall outside the scope of the ICSID Convention. For instance, in *CSOB v. The Slovak Republic*, the tribunal concluded that even though CSOB was owned by the Czech Republic, its activities were primarily commercial as opposed to governmental in nature.[36] Similarly, in *CDC v. The Slovak Republic*, the tribunal concluded that CDC, an entity wholly owned by the UK government, conducted activities that were commercial in nature, not governmental.[37]

V. SUBSTANTIVE PROTECTIONS AVAILABLE TO SWFS IN INVESTMENT ARBITRATIONS

Assuming a tribunal determines that it possesses jurisdiction to hear a claim brought by an SWF, the next questions to arise concern the substantive protections available to SWFs under IIAs. The case law on that point has been limited to date for at least two

---

35. Aron BROCHES, "The Convention on the Settlement of Investment Disputes between States and Nationals of Other States", 136 Recueil des Cours (1972) pp. 354-355.
36. See *CSOB v. The Slovak Republic* (ICSID Case No. ARB/97/4), Decision on Jurisdiction (24 May 1999) para. 20.
37. See *CDC v. The Seychelles* (ICSID Case No. ARB/02/14), Award (17 December 2003) para. 17.

reasons. First, SWFs have only recently engaged in investment treaty arbitrations. Second, the only publicly available investor state arbitration, *State General Reserve Fund of the Sultanate of Oman v. Republic of Bulgaria*, is still in the early stage of the proceedings. Notwithstanding, once jurisdiction has been established, SWFs should be entitled to all the protections afforded to investors under the applicable IIAs, including the core ones such as protections against discrimination; expropriation; and fair and equitable treatment and full protection and security.

1. Prohibitions Against Discrimination: National Treatment and Most-Favoured-Nation Clauses

The principle of non-discrimination is one of the basic protections for foreign investors and investments in host nations.[38] IIAs most commonly provide guarantees against discrimination in two ways. First, national treatment (NT) ensures that foreign investors will be treated no less favourably than similarly situated domestic investors, unless such differential treatment can be justifiably related to a non-discriminatory public policy rationale. Second, most-favoured-nation (MFN) treatment ensures that foreign investors will not be treated less favourably than investors from any third country. Claims brought by SWFs arising out of alleged violations of (1) the national treatment and (2) MFN standard seem likely given that SWF investments are sometimes prohibited at the entry level or pre-establishment stage due to their State-ownership and/or control.[39]

a. National Treatment Standard

The standard framework for applying the NT standard in a particular case requires an arbitral tribunal to consider three questions. First, whether the foreign investor and the domestic investor are in comparable circumstances.[40] Second, whether the treatment accorded to the foreign investor is less favourable, in result, than the treatment accorded to domestic investors – arbitral tribunals do not necessarily require an intent to discriminate but are satisfied with the factual existence of less favourable treatment.[41] Third, whether different treatment can be justified on the basis of its relation to valid grounds of public policy.[42]

As described above, the host State has the sovereign right to establish pre-screening procedures applicable to SWF investments. An SWF will be protected against

38. See Todd WEILER, "Prohibitions Against Discrimination in NAFTA Chapter 11" in Todd WEILER, ed., *NAFTA Investment Law and Arbitration: Past Issues, Current Practice, Future Prospects* (Transnat'l Publishers 2004) p. 27.
39. See infra Sect. IV.*1* on pre-admission screening.
40. Some tribunals require foreign and domestic investors to be in the same line of business (see, e,g., *Feldman v. Mexico* (ICSID Case No. ARB (AF)/99/1), Final Award (16 December 2002) while other tribunals have determined that such comparisons need not be made only within the same industry sector (see, e.g., *Occidental Exploration v. Ecuador* (LCIA No. UN 3467), Final Award (1 July 2004).
41. See, e.g., *Thunderbird v. Mexico* (UNCITRAL), Award (16 December 2002) para. 183.
42. Elizabeth WHITSITT and Todd WEILER, "Sovereign Wealth Funds and Bilateral Investment Treaties' New Models: Issues, New Trends and State Practice" in Fabio BASSAN, *Research Handbook on Sovereign Wealth Funds and International Investment Law* (Edward Elgar 2015) p. 282.

discriminatory measures only under the so-called "admission model" and "pre-establishment model".[43] Even then, a number of hurdles remain for the SWF to prove that the host State has violated the NT standard, such as finding a "comparator". Given the unique nature of SWFs, it may be difficult to find a national investor that shares similar characteristics.

b. Most-Favoured-Nation Standard

MFN clauses, like NT clauses, are extremely common in IIAs. In contrast with NT clauses, which focus on discrimination in favour of local investors, the focus of an MFN clause is on discriminatory treatment as between foreign investors. As with the NT standard, finding a "comparator" may be an issue.

2. Expropriation, Fair and Equitable Treatment and Full Protection and Security

Other core protections, including against uncompensated expropriations[44] or violations of the fair and equitable treatment (FET) standard[45] and full protection and security[46] may also be invoked. For instance, SWFs could be subject to treatment that violates the FET standard, including their legitimate expectations, as well as the full protection and security standard.

---

43. See infra Sect. IV.*1* "Jurisdiction Ratione Materiae: Whether Pre-admission Screening of Proposed Investments by SWFs Breaches Treaty Obligations."
44. Elizabeth WHITSITT and Todd WEILER, "Sovereign Wealth Funds and Bilateral Investment Treaties' New Models: Issues, New Trends and State Practice" in Fabio BASSAN, *Research Handbook on Sovereign Wealth Funds and International Investment Law* (Edward Elgar 2015) pp. 285-286 ("While the language of such clauses varies somewhat, all generally protect investors from both direct and indirect expropriations. In determining whether a host State's measure(s) amounts to indirect expropriation, tribunals have often considered factors such as: (i) the impact of the measure (which encompasses a relative appraisal of: alleged destruction of economic value, deprivation of control and permanence of measure), and (ii) the legitimate expectations of the investor, in establishing and maintaining the investment, considered in proportion with/to (iii) the nature, objectives and character of the measure and the means of its introduction and application.").
45. Elizabeth WHITSITT and Todd WEILER, "Sovereign Wealth Funds and Bilateral Investment Treaties' New Models: Issues, New Trends and State Practice" in Fabio BASSAN, *Research Handbook on Sovereign Wealth Funds and International Investment Law* (Edward Elgar 2015) pp. 283-284 ("The exact contours of the FET standard are ... not easily defined.... Notwithstanding its seemingly enigmatic character, it appears beyond doubt that the FET standard is informed by principles such as due process, transparency, good faith, and stability, mediated by a principle of proportionality."); see also Katia YANNACA-SMALL, "Fair and Equitable Treatment Standard: Recent Developments" in A. REINISCH, ed., *Standards of Investment Protection* (OUP 2008) pp. 111-130; see also Christopher F. DUGAN, Don WALLACE, Jr., Noah RUBINS, Borzu SABAHI, *Investor-State Arbitration*, "Chapter XVII 'Fair and Equitable Treatment' and 'Full Protection and Security'" (OUP 2008) pp. 491 et seq.
46. Elizabeth WHITSITT and Todd WEILER, "Sovereign Wealth Funds and Bilateral Investment Treaties' New Models: Issues, New Trends and State Practice" in Fabio BASSAN, *Research Handbook on Sovereign Wealth Funds and International Investment Law* (Edward Elgar 2015) pp. 286-287 ("Tribunals largely agree that the full protection and security standard imposes an obligation of vigilance and due diligence on a host State, to prevent wrongful injuries to foreign investors and to punish the perpetrator responsible for such injuries.").

If a host State's measures have a severe, lasting impact on an investment, the measure might also potentially breach the applicable expropriation clause.

VI. RESERVATIONS AND EXCEPTIONS OR "EXIT PROVISIONS"

One of the mechanisms most commonly employed by States in managing concerns about regulatory sovereignty has been to include reservations and/or exceptions in their IIAs. Reservations and exceptions serve as a key means of safeguarding the exercise of the police power and, as such, should also be considered in addressing concerns arising from the alleged targeting of strategic sectors by SWFs (such as the supposed threat that they might obtain access to sensitive technologies, critical infrastructure or enjoy controlling interests in enterprises that exploit a host State's natural resources). For example, more contemporary BIT practice in some countries permits a host State to derogate from its investment treaty obligations in relation to the financial sector if such measures are taken for "prudential reasons". In addition, certain IIA provisions appear intended to permit States to take reservations in respect of substantive IIA disciplines for both existing and future non-conforming measures. Finally, some IIAs appear to permit a host State to essentially derogate from its treaty obligations, should the subject matter of its regulatory measures relate to its national or essential security interests.[47]

1. *Prudential Measures and Transfer of Funds Exception*

Prudential measures typically ensure the host State's ability to maintain the integrity of its financial institutions and safeguard the stability of its financial system, by allowing the host State to provide less favourable treatment to foreign investors in respect of the establishment and operation of investments in the financial sector. Similarly, a transfer of funds exception permits the host State to limit fund transfers by financial institutions to their affiliates for the same purpose, i.e., maintaining the integrity of the host State's financial system.[48]

These types of provisions are, however, rare and can mostly be found in the Canadian BITs and the 2012 US Model BIT.[49] By contrast, the BITs entered into by the States hosting the largest SWFs do not contain such provisions.[50] Furthermore, Canada or the

47. Elizabeth WHITSITT and Todd WEILER, "Sovereign Wealth Funds and Bilateral Investment Treaties' New Models: Issues, New Trends and State Practice" in Fabio BASSAN, *Research Handbook on Sovereign Wealth Funds and International Investment Law* (Edward Elgar 2015) p. 302.

48. Elizabeth WHITSITT and Todd WEILER, "Sovereign Wealth Funds and Bilateral Investment Treaties' New Models: Issues, New Trends and State Practice" in Fabio BASSAN, *Research Handbook on Sovereign Wealth Funds and International Investment Law* (Edward Elgar 2015) pp. 303.

49. See, e.g., Art. 20 of the 2012 U.S. Model Bilateral investment Treaty, at <https://ustr.gov/sites/default/files/BIT%20text%20for%20ACIEP%20Meeting.pdf>; see also Art. 10(2) of Canada's 2004 Model Foreign Investment Protection Agreement (FIPA), at <https://www.italaw.com/ documents/Canadian2004-FIPA-model-en.pdf>.

50. Elizabeth WHITSITT and Todd WEILER, "Sovereign Wealth Funds and Bilateral Investment Treaties' New Models: Issues, New Trends and State Practice" in Fabio BASSAN, *Research Handbook on Sovereign Wealth Funds and International Investment Law* (Edward Elgar 2015) pp. 304-305.

United States has very rarely relied on these types of provisions in prior investor-State disputes.[51] Yet, it would be interesting whether these provisions become more popular following the resurgence of nativist and populist sentiments following the 2007-2008 financial crisis.

2. *Reservations for Existing and Future Non-conforming Measures*[52]

Some IIAs also contain general reservations for non-conforming existing and future measures. Their purpose is to exempt a wide range of existing and future measures from the core substantive protections typically afforded to investors. Similarly to prudential measures and transfer of funds exceptions, these reservations are in practice rare – they can only be found in Chinese and Canadian BITs.[53] Sometimes, these reservations operate to exempt all such measures from the NT obligation only. In other instances, these reservations are more expansive and exempt measures from the MFN and FET obligations as well as from the prohibitions against arbitrary and discriminatory treatment.

3. *Public Policy / National Security Concerns Exception*

Finally, SWFs must be prepared to answer the host State's objection that the former's investment contravenes the latter's public policy or national security concerns, justifying the host State's violation of its IIA obligations. As explained by a commentator, this "exception" may take different forms:

> "An essential security interest exception purports to allow a host State to derogate from its BIT obligations, including investor treatment standards (e.g., NT, MFN treatment and minimum treatment standards), performance requirement and expropriation obligations, if the impugned measure is necessary to protect the essential security interests of the host State.... Concerns have largely focused on the alleged self-judging nature of the exception ....
>
> It may be helpful, in this regard, to view such provisions as existing on a spectrum. At one end would be the broadest essential security interest exception clause – as illustrated by the 2012 US Model BIT, which appears to have been designed to be unabashedly 'self-judging', with few restrictions. Somewhere in the middle is the 2004 Canada Model FIPA, which appears to have been intended

51. Elizabeth WHITSITT and Todd WEILER, "Sovereign Wealth Funds and Bilateral Investment Treaties' New Models: Issues, New Trends and State Practice" in Fabio BASSAN, *Research Handbook on Sovereign Wealth Funds and International Investment Law* (Edward Elgar 2015) p. 306.
52. Elizabeth WHITSITT and Todd WEILER, "Sovereign Wealth Funds and Bilateral Investment Treaties' New Models: Issues, New Trends and State Practice" in Fabio BASSAN, *Research Handbook on Sovereign Wealth Funds and International Investment Law* (Edward Elgar 2015) pp. 306 et seq.
53. Elizabeth WHITSITT and Todd WEILER, "Sovereign Wealth Funds and Bilateral Investment Treaties' New Models: Issues, New Trends and State Practice" in Fabio BASSAN, *Research Handbook on Sovereign Wealth Funds and International Investment Law* (Edward Elgar 2015) pp. 306 et seq.

to be 'self-judging' from the perspective of the host State, but which nevertheless expressly restricts its use to times of war and related circumstances. And at the other end of the spectrum are IIAs that do not even contain an essential security interest exception, but which would leave open the possibility that some form of *de facto* reservation might exist as a matter of customary international law."[54]

54. Elizabeth WHITSITT and Todd WEILER, "Sovereign Wealth Funds and Bilateral Investment Treaties' New Models: Issues, New Trends and State Practice" in Fabio BASSAN, *Research Handbook on Sovereign Wealth Funds and International Investment Law* (Edward Elgar 2015) pp. 310 et seq.

The Excessive Scope for "the Individual" in Decision-Making in Investment Arbitration: Views from Younger Practitioners

Lucas Bastin[*]

TABLE OF CONTENTS PAGE

I. ORIGINS AND PURPOSE

The origins of this contribution lie in a London classroom. At a lecture by a senior practitioner in investment arbitration, the topic of "the backlash" in investment arbitration arose. The senior practitioner took the time to explain what this shorthand reference meant. He touched on familiar points. The unexpected scope of the substantive protections in investment treaties. *Tecmed* para. 154. The *CME/Lauder* difficulty. The lack of transparency. The perceived early high rate of success of claims. The lack of consistency in decisions. The sense that policy and politics, as truer expressions of sovereignty, receive insufficient voice.

The explanation was clear and powerful. But at the end of it, one of the students asked simply: how were such "mistakes" made? It seemed obvious to this student that, in particular, a system that produced inconsistent decisions and thereby unpredictable legal outcomes would lose attractiveness to repeat users of that system. That a "backlash" followed was something that was so likely that the mistakes ought not to have been made.

It is easy to criticize with hindsight. Understanding the consequences of an approach to an issue at the time it is taken is far harder than doing so a decade or more later. One can explain in reply to enquiries such as this, from those who are emerging into the investment arbitration field only now and were not directing the development of the system prior to the "backlash", that the system was young, previous guidance was minimal, and nothing was written into investment treaties to protect against the causes of the backlash developing. While *Tecmed* para. 154 might not be written today, it was a reasonable approach to a new and difficult question fifteen years ago.

But such an answer to the question would not be a complete one. Infancy of the system is not necessarily an explanation, or certainly a complete explanation, for why people versed in the field universally believe a backlash occurred. As such, the initial

* Barrister, Essex Court Chambers, London. Thanks are due to Monty Taylor, and participants in and attendees at the New Voices Panel at the ICCA Sydney 2018Congress for comments.

purpose of this contribution was to discern what problems had in fact arisen in investment arbitration to tarnish its reputation and lead States to reconsider its scope. And because this consideration was being undertaken in the context of a presentation on the as-advertised "provocative" New Voices Panel at the ICCA Sydney 2018 Congress, it followed that the views consulted and represented should be those of the younger generation of investment arbitration practitioners.

With this objective in mind, this contribution was originally predicated on obtaining the views of a significant number of "younger" (that is, under the age of forty, in line with the composition of the ICCA New Voices Panel) investment arbitration practitioners as to which parts of the system had been a success, and which parts a failure. This contribution was to act as an intergenerational report card: a fresh perspective on the state of the system that the "older" generation might find interesting (if a touch impudent), and one that would give a voice to a younger generation and articulate the way in which that generation might start to contribute to the improvement of a system of international rights protection that was unprecedented in international law.

However, as discussions with those younger investment arbitration practitioners took place,[1] the purpose of this contribution evolved. It became clear that one issue with the investment arbitration system attracted a greater level of attention and energy than others. It was true that concerns existed among the younger practitioners about the persistent lack of a *jurisprudence constante* on core legal issues and the resulting "battle of authorities", the lack of any structured entry into the profession, the lack of diversity, the lack of an international investment court, the treatment of amici curiae, the level of engagement with civil society's views of the profession, and the monetization of investment treaty arbitration. These were imperfect aspects of the system that the younger practitioners believed required attention.

But the issue that recurred and prompted deepest concerns was the scope the system allowed to the personal preferences, approaches and even biases of individual decision-makers, and the way such personal matters could generate procedural and substantive consequences – a facet of the investment arbitration system that came in the discussions to be referred to as the role of "the individual" in that system. Concern was expressed by the younger practitioners that the influence of "the individual" could be so great that it could redirect the course of an arbitration and the procedural balance between the parties, prompt a departure from settled legal principle, or lead someone to engage in conduct that, though not regulated expressly as inappropriate and thus not forbidden, placed the integrity of the process in doubt. Systemically, the scope of operation allowed to "the individual" was too broad, extending beyond mere discretion that facilitated appropriate decision-making.

This space for arbitrator individuality, which one might have regarded as a key strength of the system, emerged as a source of frustration among the younger practitioners. A measure of faith in the decision-making in the system had been lost. There was a sense that the persuasiveness of substantive submissions had ceded too much

1. With some two dozen younger investment arbitration practitioners. The methodology employed in preparing this contribution based on those interviews is set out in fn. 4 below.

ground to the intractability of personal preference, to the unknowable extent of the influence granted to "the individual".

It may be that the emergence of this theme was, in truth, a reflection of the growing maturity of the younger practitioners – it was not that this balance was new or had tipped in a different direction, but it was simply that these younger practitioners now saw the real position, as it is and was. But even if that were so, the question still remained much the same as the one which the student in the classroom asked: how was it that those with the capacity to influence the profession had left these matters unregulated? If the scope for "the individual" was so large in investment arbitration decision-making, why were greater efforts not expended to limit such variables to an appropriate level of discretion that facilitated proper decision-making?

Hence the ultimate scope of this contribution. Rather than a report card from the young to the old on the shortcomings in the system generally, the content of which would perhaps surprise no one and merely parrot concerns about the system that experienced practitioners and academics had articulated many times before, the issue that falls to be considered is the extent to which the space for "the individual" in the decision-making ranks of the investment arbitration system is excessive, damages the system, and ought to be limited.

In essaying this issue, this piece has two broad steps. The first is to identify the character of the alleged shortcoming, to assess in what ways the excessive space for "the individual" in the decision-making of the investment arbitration system manifests itself. The second stage is to discuss what remedies might be implemented to limit any such excess of such space.

II. THE EXCESSIVE SPACE FOR "THE INDIVIDUAL" IN THE DECISION-MAKING OF THE INVESTMENT ARBITRATION SYSTEM

1. *Introduction – Difficulty or Value of Proof by Anecdote*

Proof by anecdote is among the most unreliable proof that exists. It needs to be treated with caution. But collective experience is equally not something that should be ignored, because from it broader truths may be inductively identified. This is not a novel concept, even if it is out of vogue. As Aristotle put it:

> "From perception then, as we hold, memory results, and from repeated recollections of the same phenomenon comes experience, for memories which are numerically many form but a single experience. Next, from experience, or from the entire universal which is retained in the soul ... comes the elementary principle of art and science; if the concern be with production, of art, if with reality, of science."[2]

The ethnographic method relies on the truth underlying Aristotle's observation. The rise of ethnographic research as a discipline reflects the acceptance that, ultimately, one must

2. ARISTOTLE, *Posterior Analytics* (trans., Bouchier, Oxford 1901) at 127-128.

have for consistent anecdotal evidence. If one experiences a phenomenon enough, a measure of truth associates to that phenomenon. The instinct then is to analyze and regulate that truth, rather than allowing it to remain "anecdotal" or "relativized" – that is, rather than allowing it merely to be, as Nietzsche describes it, "a mobile army of metaphors, metonyms, anthropomorphisms, in short a sum of human relations which have been subjected to poetic and rhetorical intensification, translation and decoration".[3]

While the present contribution does not pretend to be a rigorous ethnographic study that tries to characterize any perception that arises from discussions with younger practitioners as a principle of science or something more elevated than an anecdotal or relativized truth, it is expected that the strength of its observations will derive from the recognition by readers of the validity of the examples discussed as to how excessive space for "the individual" in the decision-making of the investment arbitration system is proving problematic.

To that end, five such shortcomings were key among those identified by the younger practitioners interviewed.[4]

2. *The Shortcomings*

The first shortcoming related to the space for "the individual" in respect of decisions by arbitrators concerning the procedure used in a given arbitration. This shortcoming was the one that appeared most frequently at the forefront of the comments by the young practitioners interviewed, even if it was one of the less trenchant. That perhaps is inevitable, as shortcomings in the procedural balance of an arbitration are the most ostensible, and thus most obvious and memorable. One nonetheless needs to be clear to what this shortcoming refers once one puts aside complaints about a procedural issue merely being decided adversely to a party in a way that imposed a large or inconvenient burden on it. Rather, the shortcoming is one whereby personal preference on the part of the arbitrator plays an active part in the determination of procedural questions.

On this topic, younger practitioners expressed concern about how, seemingly in the absence of express regulation of the precise matter before the arbitrators, those arbitrators were able to take steps such as resigning from arbitrations shortly after a substantive hearing but before any Award for reasons of personal convenience, leaving a hearing during sitting hours to attend to personal matters while procedural decisions were being taken for the conduct of the hearing and post-hearing, and in one instance liaising ex parte with an appointing party during the pendency of an arbitration about the content of the arbitration.

The shortcoming in these matters was not the fact that certain individuals made decisions that one might think were inadvisable in the circumstances – human error

3. Friedrich NIETZSCHE, "On Truth and Lying in a Non-Moral Sense" in *The Norton Anthology of Theory & Criticism* (Norton 2001) at p. 878.

4. The following account is a summary of the shortcomings thus identified and the consequences they produce. The account is not intended in the present contribution to be tendentious, but rather an attempt to summarize the collective observations made by those interviewed. The younger practitioners who participated in the discussions are not identified to preserve the anonymous basis on which the comments were given. Records of discussions are kept on file with the author. Unless otherwise stated or obvious, quotations below are from the younger practitioners themselves.

cannot be eliminated entirely. Rather, the shortcoming identified was that these decisions placed the procedural balance of the arbitration at risk, seemingly on the basis that personal considerations were prioritized above the procedural integrity of the arbitration. It seemed an elementary failure of regulation of decision-making conduct for "the individual" to influence procedural outcomes in an arbitration in such ways.

The second shortcoming was derived less from case-by-case experience. It related to the space for "the individual" to dictate substantively how a case would be presented and decided. The concern here was a familiar one – through an individual's public positioning of his or her views on substantive issues in investment arbitration, it became possible to predict with a degree of accuracy how he or she would decide a particular legal issue or even a case as a whole. This ramified consequences which the younger practitioners identified as giving excessive scope to individual preferences to exert disproportionate influence in investment arbitration.

In a context where the individual in question was not (yet) sitting as arbitrator, the younger practitioners pointed out that it meant would-be arbitrators could in effect "advertise" their views and "pitch" for arbitral appointments by a party with which his or her publicly expressed views aligned. It could even incentivize would-be arbitrators to adopt exaggerated forms of certain views in order to attract attention and appointments by such a party. It exposed the profession to criticism that ideology rather than, or at least in addition to, legal merits was a key characteristic for eligibility for such appointments. It risked entry to arbitrator ranks based on "form rather than substance". And it made the diligence appointing parties completed on arbitrators extensive, even "invasive".

As to the context where the individual was already an arbitrator in the field, this shortcoming was also noted by the younger practitioners as resulting in the concentration of appointments among a relatively small number of arbitrators who had "proven themselves". The volume of appointments some individuals received, often by claimants or respondents only, both resulted from and encouraged a "doubling down" on views on certain legal issues, where the specific facts of the dispute then had to meet a higher practical burden to "turn" that arbitrator in favour of a conclusion he or she would otherwise not be expected to adopt. This facilitated the rise of the "professional arbitrator" – someone who could obtain enough appointments in the field of investment arbitration, notwithstanding the relative paucity of new cases each year, to sustain a full-time practice. It meant that the "tie-breaker" of the presiding arbitrator, and the capacity of that person to act decisively in that role, became of outsized importance to the substantive outcome of the dispute – almost a return to the time where the third member of a tribunal was an umpire rather than an arbitrator. And, perhaps of greatest systemic concern, it meant that a small number of arbitrators were able to secure a large number of appointments, and through that privileged position to generate and propagate new legal principles or lines of authorities that received endorsement in the (multiple) cases on which they sat and eventually thereby gained a currency or prominence disproportionate to the number of arbitrators who had endorsed such a principle.[5]

5. For an articulation of the danger that lies in such a situation, see the dissent of Arbitrator Stern in *Impregilo S.p.A. v. Argentine Republic* (ICSID Case No. ARB/07/17), Award (21 June 2011) para. 5.

The shortcoming in this regard was the way in which these highly personalized features of the path to becoming, and then gaining eminence as, an arbitrator could have substantive results. The concern was not that people had views and had expressed them publicly, but rather that these views became "commoditized" in "the market" of investment arbitration appointments. To even be "on the supermarket shelf", as put by one younger practitioner with a turn of phrase, "you had to be branded, because no one buys 'no name' in this field". In subtle ways (or not), the capacity for three individuals to form a tribunal with neutral and impartial views on the submissions made to them was eroded by the space "the individual" was afforded in investment arbitration to signal, articulate and decide matters of substance.

The third shortcoming is related to the capacity for "the individual" to issue a minority decision in an investment arbitration context. The ability of an arbitrator to decide a case as he or she thinks correct is of course not objectionable. Hence the proper place for dissenting opinions in investment arbitration, and the lack of any formal doctrine of *stare decisis*.

However, in the absence of any requirement of consensus or binding precedents, the space for "the individual" to issue decisions without reference to the work of other tribunals that have considered or are considering the same issues is very broad. It was no surprise that the decision-making that resulted in the *CME/Lauder* controversy, or the "battle of authorities" that ensues when deciding a legal issue that has generated multiple lines of authority, was noted by the younger practitioners as at times unhelpful. It was also described to be not an exclusive product of the variability of the legal norms in issue, but as a product at least in part of the individuals who happen to be appointed as arbitrators in one case to the next.

Complaints about this feature of the system, while retaining some validity, do feel well worn. Beyond such points, though, a further aspect of the shortcoming was cited by a number of the younger practitioners interviewed. In recent years, one can point to decisions that departed markedly from what was perhaps, by this point, considered a settled principle of international investment law. Naming the cases and arbitrators would be caddish, even self-defeating, but they are well known. And the point arising from the interviews is not that some decisions are wrong and deserving of censure. Rather it is that they have been rendered with what appears to be either insufficient regard to previous consistent authorities, or with an excessive reliance on the absence of a formal doctrine of *stare decisis* in investment arbitration.

This feature is something one would expect investment arbitration to have overcome by now, as a result of its "adolescence".[6] It is of course doctrinally correct that international fora such as investment arbitration tribunals do not have a formal doctrine of *stare decisis*.[7] But a recent trend in discussions of the value of previous authorities is

6. As phrased in: Jean KALICKI, "A Talk by Jean Kalicki '89", Harvard Law School, 30 October 2015, available at <https://www.youtube.com/watch?v=nTE0Z4e6qrQ>.

7. See, as a small selection of examples: *AES Corporation v. Argentine Republic* (ICSID Case No. ARB/02/17), Decision on Jurisdiction (26 April 2005) para. 23 (which view was specifically endorsed in *AES Summit Generation Limited and AES-Tisza Erömü Kft. v. Republic of Hungary* (ICSID Case No. ARB/07/22), Decision of the *ad hoc* Committee on the Application for Annulment (29 June 2012) para. 99); *Wintershall Aktiengesellschaft v. Argentine Republic* (ICSID Case No. ARB/04/14), Award (8 December 2008) paras. 187 and 194; *Bureau Veritas, Inspection, Valuation,*

beginning to reflect something more than their having "persuasive" value only.[8] Decisions in the area have begun to accept that the earlier decisions exert a stronger normative force on tribunals. There is an emerging notion in more recent cases that, even in the absence of a formal doctrine of *stare decisis*, arbitrators have a "duty" to take account of previous decisions in an effort to facilitate the formation of consistent legal principles and interpretations, with the purpose of enhancing the predictability of international investment law and of the scope of protection it afforded to investment.[9] As Judge Kannan Ramesh of the High Court of Singapore, who might be thought to have come to the issue with fresh eyes with the assistance of eminent counsel, concluded:

> "There is no system of precedent in international law. Past decisions have no precedential value even where the same treaty or State is involved. That said, a *de facto* doctrine of precedent for investment treaty arbitration definitely exists and investment tribunals approach their task by carefully considering the work of other tribunals. The consensus appears to be that this is both conducive to the development of a *jurisprudence constante* in international investment law, and helpful to individual tribunals in examining how similar issues have been resolved or as illustrating the application of established principles."[10]

Assessment and Control, BIVAC B.V. v. Republic of Paraguay (ICSID Case No. ARB/07/9), Decision on Jurisdiction (29 May 2009) para. 58; Víctor Pey Casado and President Allende Foundation v. Republic of Chile (ICSID Case No. ARB/98/2), Award (8 May 2008) para. 119; Caratube International Oil Company LLP v. Republic of Kazakhstan (ICSID Case No. ARB/08/12), Award (5 June 2012) para. 234.

8. This expression of the (limited) value of precedents, albeit sometimes half-heartedly and over competing commentary on the point by a dissenting arbitrator, is reflected in, e.g.: *Impregilo S.p.A. v. Argentine Republic* (ICSID Case No. ARB/07/17), Award (21 June 2011) para. 108 (but note the dissent of Arbitrator Stern on this issue, para. 5); *Burlington Resources Inc. v. Republic of Ecuador* (ICSID Case No. ARB/08/5), Decision on Reconsideration and Award (7 February 2017) para. 46 (but note the dissent of Arbitrator Stern on this issue, para. 46); *Daimler Financial Services AG v. Argentine Republic* (ICSID Case No. ARB/05/1), Award (22 August 2012) para. 52; *Quasar de Valors SICAV S.A. and others (formerly Renta 4 S.V.S.A and others) v. Russian Federation* (SCC Case No. 24/2007), Award on Preliminary Objections (20 March 2009) para. 16; *Murphy Exploration and Production Company International v. Republic of Ecuador* (PCA Case No. 2012-16; formerly AA 434), Partial Final Award (6 May 2016); *Republic of Ecuador v. United States of America* (PCA Case No. 2012-5), Award (29 September 2012) para. 188.
9. *Khan Resources Inc., Khan Resources B.V. and CAUC Holding Company Ltd. v. Government of Mongolia* (UNCITRAL), Decision on Jurisdiction (25 July 2012) para. 417; *KT Asia Investment Group B.V. v. Republic of Kazakhstan* (ICSID Case No. ARB/09/8), Award (17 October 2013) para. 53; *Churchill Mining Plc/Planet Mining Plc v. Republic of Indonesia* (ICSID Case No. ARB/12/14 and 12/40), Decision on Jurisdiction (24 February 2014) para. 85; *Renée Rose Levy and Gremcitel S.A. v. Republic of Peru* (ICSID Case No. ARB/11/17), Award (9 January 2015) para. 76. This line of cases recalls the earlier expressed view of Professor Wälde that a tribunal should not depart from established practice (in the NAFTA and ICSID context, such as the case before him) without in-depth reasoning and after hearing the Parties in writing and orally on the precise issue, and even then it may still not be proper for a tribunal to do so: *International Thunderbird Gaming Corporation v. United Mexican States* (UNCITRAL), Separate Opinion (1 December 2005) paras. 130-131.
10. *Swissbourgh Diamond Mines (Pty) Limited and others v. Kingdom of Lesotho* (PCA Case No. 2013-29), Set Aside Judgment of the High Court of Singapore (14 August 2017) para. 103 (citations omitted).

The choice for arbitrators, therefore, ought not to be whether they agree or disagree with what has been said before. It ought rather to be whether they see such an analytical error in previous decisions so as to mean those decisions ought not to be followed. Reasons for departure from settled principle ought to be given that go beyond a personal dislike for that principle, or the mere ability to articulate an arguable line of reasoning alternative to the one adopted by many arbitrators previously (and which, indeed, may have been expressly rejected by those previous, numerous arbitrators).

Instances where this reassertion of minority views results in an outlier decision departing from a settled line of principle thus appear to be more an expression of "the individual" in investment arbitration rather than an example of the system correcting a mistake that many arbitrators have made previously. Indeed, it may even have reached the point whereby insisting that an arbitrator is entitled to decide a case without reference to previous decisions – which position has been maintained even by very prominent arbitrators who have been involved in many previous cases – openly elevates the influence of "the individual" above the influence of the system.

The fourth shortcoming is related to the capacity for "the individual" to engage in conduct which, though not proscribed by any rule or guideline, is nonetheless questionable. While this conduct is often hard to index against precise procedural or substantive consequences in an investment arbitration, the concern was expressed that the conduct gives rise to doubts about the investment arbitration system that are needless.

The younger practitioners interviewed cited several examples of this. Most connected one way or another to the appropriateness of an individual accepting an arbitral appointment. The old debate about "double-hatting" – or what Professor Sands, almost a decade ago in the same city that the 2018 ICCA Congress is taking place, called the "revolving door" of the same person acting both as counsel and arbitrator[11] – remained an issue. So too did the maintenance of personal or professional relationships while the two relevant individuals were counsel and arbitrator in the same case. Excessively narrow interpretations of what constituted a conflict of interest, in the absence of regulation of the precise situation in the International Bar Association (IBA) Guidelines or elsewhere, were also a concern. This was especially so in a context where challenges to arbitrators were becoming more commonplace, and the high degree of interconnection in a small profession was reaching a level whereby arbitrators may be challenged for connections not only with counsel, but also with agents,[12] parties,[13]

11. Luke Eric PETERSON, "Arbitrator Decries 'Revolving Door' Roles of Lawyers in Investment Treaty Arbitration", IA Reporter (25 February 2010) available at <https://www.iareporter.com/articles/arbitrator-decries-revolving-door-roles-of-lawyers-in-investment-treaty-arbitration/>.
12. See *Arbitration Between the Republic of Croatia and the Republic of Slovenia* (PCA Case 2012-04), Partial Award (30 June 2016) para. 130.
13. See Luke Eric PETERSON, "After ICSID Tribunal Is Constituted, US Investor Big Sky Energy Corporation Seeks to Disqualify Arbitrator Nominated by Kazakhstan", IA Reporter (30 January 2018) available at <https://www.iareporter.com/articles/after-icsid-tribunal-is-constituted-us-investor-big-sky-energy-corporation-seeks-to-disqualify-arbitrator-nominated-by-kazakhstan/>.

entities related to parties,[14] experts or witnesses,[15] or even a law firm not involved in the case at hand but involved in other cases against a disputing party.[16] An impression among some younger practitioners was that this developing web of situations that might prompt an arbitrator challenge was not being met with additional care about accepting appointments, but rather with what one practitioner called a "bring it on!" attitude.

The fifth and final shortcoming about the excessive space given to "the individual" in decision-making in investment arbitration that arose out of discussions with younger practitioners was one entirely unrelated to the foregoing shortcomings. It related to the lack of guidelines that existed for the discharge of the duties of an appointing authority.

A meaningful number of arbitrators, especially presiding arbitrators, in investment arbitrations are appointed by an appointing authority. In the ICSID context, the Secretary General in 2016 calculated that ICSID was responsible for appointing 15 percent of "all" ICISD tribunal members.[17] That is one in seven of the total arbitrators in ICSID arbitrations. One assumes that the majority of these appointments concern the presiding arbitrator, such that the percentage of presidents appointed by ICSID is in fact much higher. In addition, a number of younger practitioners had experience of cases where the Secretary-General of the Permanent Court of Arbitration (or his designee) or the President of the International Court of Justice was involved in the appointment of an arbitrator in a non-ICSID arbitration.

The function of the appointing authority in the investment arbitration context is thus an important one. But no guidelines exist as to how an appointing authority identifies the person who will be appointed. ICSID has in this lacuna developed a ballot procedure, which it describes on its website, but no other appointing authority has done likewise. Yet, even in the ICSID context, as with other appointing authorities, there is little guidance given to appointing authorities as to who an appropriate appointee (or, in a ballot process, candidate) might be. The latitude for an appointing authority thus to appoint any arbitrator at all outside the ICSID context, and any arbitrator from the Panel of Arbitrators within the ICSID context, is very wide. This latitude means that appointing authorities are free to consider not only who might be a good appointee as

---

14. See *Suez, Sociedad General de Aguas de Barcelona S.A. & Vivendi Universal S.A. v. Argentina* (ICSID Case No. ARB/03/19), Decision on Second Challenge to Gabrielle Kaufmann-Kohler (12 May 2008) paras. 36-40.
15. See Luke Eric PETERSON, "Co-arbitrators Declare Themselves to Be 'Equally Divided' on Challenge to Third Tribunal Member, thus Putting ICSID in the Driver's Seat", IA Reporter (21 October 2017) available at <https://www.iareporter.com/articles/co-arbitrators-declare-themselves-to-be-equally-divided-on-challenge-to-third-tribunal-member-thus-putting-icsid-in-the-drivers-seat/>.
16. See, e.g.: Luke Eric PETERSON, "Venezuela Hires Private Investigator to Examine Ties of Yves Fortier's Secretary to his Former Law Firm, but Again Fails to Make Out Its Case for Disqualification", IA Reporter (9 May 2017) available at <https://www.iareporter.com/articles/venezuela-hires-private-investigator-to-examine-ties-of-yves-fortiers-secretary-to-his-former-law-firm-but-again-fails-to-make-out-its-case-for-disqualification/>.
17. Claire LIPMAN, "An Interview with Meg Kinnear, Secretary General of ICSID: Part 2/4: ICSID Arbitration Procedure", Practical Law Arbitration Blog (3 February 2016) available at <http://arbitrationblog.practicallaw.com/an-interview-with-meg-kinnear-secretary-general-of-icsid-part-24-icsid-arbitration-procedure/>.

presiding arbitrator in a given case, but also whether desirable objectives such as increased diversity among the arbitrator ranks can be concurrently advanced.[18]

It also means, however, that considerable power is vested in a few people, who operate without regulation as to whom an appropriate appointee might be in a given case. This is a large space in which "the individual" in investment arbitration generates substantive consequences. The size of this space prompted two core comments by the younger practitioners. The first is that those few appointing authorities become natural magnets for those seeking appointments. That may be the way of the world, and there have been precious few alternatives proposed,[19] but such magnetic power exacerbates the difficulty that was identified by the younger practitioners. The second consequence is that it leaves the investment arbitration system generally, and the prominent appointing authorities specifically, open to criticism.[20] Irrespective of whether one believes the major appointing authorities in investment arbitration exercise their powers appropriately or otherwise, it is the vesting of those powers and the consequent vulnerability to such criticism that the younger practitioners noted was an example of the excessive space given to "the individual" in decision-making in investment arbitration.

3. *The Macroscopic Problem*

The foregoing shortcomings are ones which, in the impression of the younger practitioners interviewed, cumulatively result in the investment arbitration system affording excessive scope for "the individual" in the decision-making that defines and mobilizes that system. However, a natural response to this is that, at some point, the system needs to vest decision-making power in someone. It is inherent in the nature of a system that has competing arguments determined by human beings that "the individual" is going to play a part in that determination. The lens is too microscopic if one criticizes a system as a whole by reference to specific shortcomings.

While that reply is fair, the above shortcomings are not without a macroscopic unity: virtually all of the shortcomings arise in one way or another out of a lack of regulation. The extent of discretion given to decision-makers left enough room for "the individual" to exert an influence on the decision-making which had no regulatory check.

---

18. A lack of diversity remains a problem in investment arbitration, as in international arbitration generally: see as a leading contribution on the issue Lucy GREENWOOD and Mark BAKER, "Getting a Better Balance on International Arbitration Tribunals" 28 Arbitration International (2012) p. 653.
19. See the proposal for, inter alia, "constituting a collegial body for the appointment of *ad hoc* committee members [for ICSID annulment committees] sending its recommendations to the president of the Administrative Council", Hamid GHARAVI, "ICSID Annulment Committees: The Elephant in the Room", Global Arbitration Review (24 November 2014) available at <www.derainsgharavi.com/2014/11/icsid-annulment-committees-the-elephant-in-the-room/>.
20. See Hamid GHARAVI, "ICSID Annulment Committees: The Elephant in the Room", Global Arbitration Review (24 November 2014) available at <www.derainsgharavi.com/2014/11/icsid-annulment-committees-the-elephant-in-the-room/>. It is in such a context that the OECD is now investigating systemically the way in which appointing authorities act in investment arbitrations, and how that system of designation and appointment can be improved: see <www.oecd.org/investment/Consultation-ISDS-appointing-authorities-arbitration.htm>.

It is of course true that the number of actors in international arbitration is large, and it is arguable that the number is higher in investment arbitration where sovereign decisions, a public purse and civil society are engaged uniquely. That diversity of actors in investment arbitration makes it difficult to regulate all, or even most, situations in which an inappropriate expression of "the individual" might arise. But lack of regulation – especially when it is to such an extent that the cumulative effect of the shortcomings arising from the expression of "the individual" damages the system as a whole – can be addressed. After all, as Professor Gaillard recalls, "one cannot forget that arbitration is intended for the parties and not for all the other actors that gravitate around it."[21]

Professor Gaillard's reminder on this point explains why the macroscopic problem arising from the shortcomings discussed above is so important. Through allowing unregulated expressions of "the individual" to damage the system as a whole, it is the "symbolic capital" of the actors in the system that suffers the most.[22] Moreover, in a system where arbitrators "demonstrate some of the markers of professionalization and have consciously invoked the nomenclature of professionalism",[23] loss of symbolic capital by decision-makers by reference to their conduct giving rise to the above shortcomings also produces a loss of symbolic capital by the system of investment arbitration as a collective.

This observation results from the fact that the decision-makers are more than functionaries. They oversee the "rituals" of the system.[24] They also act as "value leaders", who formulate and execute an "ambition ... to provide guidance as to the way international arbitration should develop and arbitral social actors should behave ... [and] are recognized, at varying degrees of legitimacy, as having the social ability to provide such guidance".[25] When "the individual" is given too much scope in the decision-making within the investment arbitration system such that the above shortcomings occur, it is not just personal reputations that suffer. It is, rather, the symbolic capital of the system as a whole and the value leadership within that system that is impaired.

What is more, the specificities of the structure of the investment arbitration system highlight how viral the damage done by an undue influence of "the individual" in decision-making can be. Of particular relevance is the ability of one person to play multiple functions within the system – at once counsel, arbitrator, academic commentator, media commentator, professional organization leader, among others. In performing a concurrent variety of functions, however, it is open to that person, even expected, to maintain a consistent "role" – that term referring to the "activity consisting

21. Emmanuel GAILLARD, "Sociology of International Arbitration", 31 Arbitration International (2015) p. 1 at p. 4.
22. Emmanuel GAILLARD, "Sociology of International Arbitration", 31 Arbitration International (2015) p. 1 at p. 2.
23. Catherine ROGERS, "The Vocation of International Arbitrators", 20 American University International Law Review (2005) p. 957 at pp. 976-977.
24. For a fuller exploration of the sociological import of such "rituals" and how they manifest in the international arbitration world, see Emmanuel GAILLARD, "Sociology of International Arbitration", 31 Arbitration International (2015) p. 1 at pp. 10-13.
25. Emmanuel GAILLARD, "Sociology of International Arbitration", 31 Arbitration International (2015) p. 1 at p. 7.

in defending certain values or beliefs", which in investment arbitration is sometimes reduced to the unhelpful dichotomy whereby "a given player may perceive his or her role as defending States or defending the interests of foreign investors".[26] This is not a mere theoretical observation. It has very practical consequences relating to how the investment arbitration system understands conflict of interests that can exclude a person from fulfilling a particular function in that system. As Professor Gaillard elaborates on this point:

> "The current trend in assessing conflicts of interests in international arbitration is to focus on functions. It is sometimes argued that a social agent routinely performing the function of counsel has a structural conflict of interest which should preclude him or her from acting as co-arbitrator, president or member of an *ad hoc* committee in ICSID arbitration. An analysis focusing on roles as defined above, rather than on functions, or at least in conjunction with the concept of function, might be a more fruitful exercise, as it is the role, not the function, which polarizes the field."[27]

At a subcutaneous level of analysis, therefore, the problem arising from the shortcomings noted above about the excessive scope given to "the individual" in the decision-making in investment arbitration is that insufficient regulation leaves room for the "role" a particular decision-maker adopts to influence those decisions. Questions of "double-hatting", conflicts of interest, who appoints and is appointed, departures from settled legal principles, the path to eminence as an arbitrator, ex parte communications – all these are cast in a different light if their common cause is the assimilation by decision-makers of "the individual" with an adopted "role". Such a conclusion, if correct, would mean decision-making is at risk of being defined by a decision-maker viewing his or her mandate as being the defence of personalized values or beliefs. That is not, one would hope to posit without controversy, how most would characterize the objective and impartial duty of determining disputes by reference to a transparent and predictable system of legal rules.

Macroscopically, therefore, the lack of regulation and the way in which "the individual" can operate in that absence when engaging in decision-making within the investment arbitration system is both the unifying shortcoming to which almost all the concerns of the younger practitioners related, and also the cause of the excessive influence over such decision-making that is exerted by "the individual" and any corresponding "role" a decision-maker may have adopted.

4. *The Need for Regulation*

It ought to go without saying that none of the younger practitioners involved in the discussions, and certainly not the younger practitioner presently collating those remarks

26. Emmanuel GAILLARD, "Sociology of International Arbitration", 31 Arbitration International (2015) p. 1 at p. 14.
27. Emmanuel GAILLARD, "Sociology of International Arbitration", 31 Arbitration International (2015) p. 1 at p. 15.

and commenting on them, adopts a "holier than thou" position. Younger practitioners are not decision-makers. They have never had to transition from a predominantly counsel role to a predominantly arbitrator role. They are not value leaders, not guardians of rituals, and possess little symbolic capital. They know little of the difficulties that come with being decision-makers in the investment arbitration system, and little of how much space "the individual" in that system truly has when sitting in a room with other decision-makers trying to reach consensus.

But, equally, younger practitioners are part of the investment arbitration system. They are part of the same collective of which the decision-makers are also a part. And it is from that base commonality that many of the younger practitioners' comments raised the need for additional regulation, tailored to limiting the excessive scope afforded to "the individual" in decision-making within investment arbitration.

It seems apparent from the nature and extent of the shortcomings discussed above that a significant uptick in the regulation of decision-makers' conduct in the investment arbitration system is required. Arbitration practitioners have shown themselves perfectly capable of doing this. The 2010 IBA Rules on the Taking of Evidence in International Commercial Arbitration, the 2014 IBA Guidelines on Conflicts of Interest in International Arbitration and the 2013 IBA Guidelines on Representation in International Arbitration are all good examples from the last handful of years as to how regulation can keep pace with events. The 1987 IBA Rules of Ethics for International Arbitrators are perhaps due an overhaul, but it runs alongside the emergence of an increasing number of ethical codes for arbitrators being issued by arbitral institutions or professional bodies,[28] and the work of scholars such as Professor Rogers.[29]

None of these codes, however, are tailored to the investment arbitration system, or to limiting the space afforded to "the individual" in the decision-making within that system. That is why the various shortcomings discussed above are mostly unregulated. But given the existence of those shortcomings and the macroscopic problem they suggest, the case for a supplement to the IBA Rules/Guidelines focused on investment arbitration is convincing. A supplement of this kind could answer the specific manifestations of "the individual" that are problematic.

Thus, for instance, principles of precedent in investment arbitration could be expressly stated, such as by reference to an express duty for arbitrators to take account of previous decisions in an effort to facilitate the formation of consistent legal principles and interpretations. A limit on the total number of appointments in investment arbitrations a person can accept may be worth considering, if only to ensure that a person's "role" does not gain undue influence over his or her decision-making or over a significant portion of the decision-making in the investment system as a whole. Express regulations on what constitutes acceptable "double-hatting" and what does not – perhaps by reference to whether a party or its counsel would gain an insight into an arbitrator's

28. See, e.g., the codes issued by the American Arbitration Association, the Milan Chamber of National and International Arbitration, the Singapore International Arbitration Centre, and the Cairo Regional Centre for International Commercial Arbitration.

29. See, e.g.: Catherine ROGERS, "The Vocation of International Arbitrators", 20 American University Journal of International Law and Policy (2005) p. 959; Catherine ROGERS, "Regulating International Arbitrators: A Functional Approach to Developing Standards of Conduct", 41 Stanford International Law Review (2005) p. 53.

approach to an issue that is not shared by the opposing party or its counsel – might warrant attention. So too would express regulation of the matters to be taken into account by appointing authorities when appointing arbitrators. A revisiting of the "lists" in the IBA Guidelines on Conflicts of Interest in light of peculiarities of investment arbitration, and in particular the reality that fewer actors participate in that system more often when compared to (say) commercial arbitration, may also be merited.

Some of these nascent proposals may seem like significant departures from the *status quo*. A cap on total number of appointments, for example, may even impinge on party autonomy. But, at a minimum, the unique nature of the investment arbitration system and of the various shortcomings discussed above means serious consideration ought to be given to significant alterations to the regulation of the space afforded to "the individual" in the decision-making in investment arbitration.

III. CONCLUSION

"How sharper than a serpent's tooth it is to have a thankless child."

None of the younger practitioners consulted during the preparation of this contribution were insensitive to the fact that the decision-makers in the investment arbitration system to date had to find answers to difficult questions in a new field with sparse guidance and regulation. None, equally, were insensitive to the fact that the terms of the applicable investment treaty, contract or legislation often are cast in broad language that inevitably admits of a variety of approaches and viewpoints. A genuine appreciation pervaded of the distance that international investment law, and the regulatory framework within which decision-makers operated, had come in what is still a relatively short period of time. We younger practitioners are no thankless Gonerils.

But nor are we Lear blind. The identification of the shortcomings discussed in this contribution is the product of reflection and a measure of insight. In many cases, the younger practitioners spoke in terms of real devotion to their field of practice and those who have led that field to date. It is that devotion that spurs a desire to rectify shortcomings by way of more detailed regulations focused on the problems in this field. The proposals noted briefly above are not offered as a panacea. They are offered certainly with the awareness that difficult discussions would need to follow to achieve more detailed regulation of the specific shortcomings in the field of investment arbitration. However, it is hoped that, in the context of a forum such as the ICCA Sydney 2018 Congress, the voice of a younger generation might be heard by the decision-makers, and such discussions, both difficult and rewarding, might follow.

Plenary Session

New Frontiers in International Arbitration

Plenary Session
New Frontiers in International Arbitration

Part I:
Potential of Arbitration Involving New Types of Claims

Arbitration of Internal Trust Disputes: The Next Frontier for International Commercial Arbitration?

S.I. Strong[*]

TABLE OF CONTENTS PAGE

I. INTRODUCTION

Although "external" trust disputes[1] have long been subject to arbitration at both the national and international levels, recent years have seen increasing interest in "internal" trust arbitration, meaning proceedings that address matters involving trustees and/or beneficiaries. While arbitral specialists do not find the concept of internal trust arbitration particularly problematic, many trust lawyers view the procedure with trepidation if not outright horror.[2] To some extent, differences in how trust arbitration is perceived can be explained by a mutual lack of understanding about the intricacies of the secondary body of law: on the one hand, trust lawyers often fail to appreciate the sophistication of contemporary arbitration law while on the other hand, arbitral specialists overlook the special challenges associated with trusts.

Unfortunately, experts in the two fields of law seldom communicate, which leads to a variety of problems in practice. For example, experts in trust law often propose model clauses and procedural rules that do not comply with best practices in arbitration law, while experts in arbitration frequently promote or adopt procedures that are not sufficiently tailored to the special needs of trust disputants. If trust

---

* Ph.D. (law), University of Cambridge; D.Phil., University of Oxford; J.D., Duke University; M.P.W., University of Southern California; B.A., University of California, Davis. The author, who is admitted to practice as an attorney in New York, Illinois, and Missouri and as a solicitor in England and Wales and in Ireland, is the Manley O. Hudson Professor of Law at the University of Missouri, Senior Fellow at the Center for the Study of Dispute Resolution, and Adjunct Professor at Georgetown University Law Center. Prof. Dr. Strong sits as an arbitrator on a variety of international commercial and trust-related matters.

1. "External" trust arbitration involves disputes between trusts and third parties, such as financial advisors or other entities bound to the trust by contract.

2. American College of Trust and Estate Counsel, Arbitration Task Force Report (Sept. 2006), available at <www.mnbar.org/sections/probate-trust/ACTEC%20Arbitration%20Task%20 Force%20Report-2006.pdf> (discussing the "blinding prejudice" against trust arbitration in some segments of the trust law community) pp. 4-7.

arbitration is to flourish, individuals and institutions in both fields – trust law and arbitration law – must work together to develop a mechanism that complies with the unique requirements of both bodies of law.

Trust arbitration is an extremely complicated subject, and it is impossible to provide a comprehensive analysis of all of the relevant issues in the space provided here.[3] However, it is useful to introduce some of the key concepts and authorities so that experts in international commercial arbitration can appreciate the importance of trusts in the global marketplace and can begin to recognize the special challenges involving arbitration of these types of disputes. This discussion will therefore proceed as follows.

First, Sect. II provides some basic background on trusts and their importance to the international commerce. Next, Sect. III outlines some of the problems that can arise in this area of law, particularly from a trust law perspective. Sect. IV discusses recent legislative, judicial and institutional developments in this area of law, including examples from Europe, Australasia and the Americas. Finally, Sect. V concludes the discussion.

II. TRUSTS IN THE INTERNATIONAL COMMERCIAL CONTEXT

The trust is traditionally considered a creature of the common law, since the device was originally developed in medieval England as a means of conveying and protecting property through the division of legal and beneficial ownership.[4] However, many civil law jurisdictions have seen the benefit of this particular mechanism and have adopted similar devices known as *Stiftungen* (foundations) or associations. While the precise requirements for creating a trust will vary across jurisdictional lines, the Hague Convention on the Law Applicable to Trusts and on Their Recognition states that:

> "the term 'trust' refers to the legal relationships created ... by a person, the settlor, when assets have been placed under the control of a trustee for the benefit of a beneficiary or for a specified purpose".

A trust has the following characteristics –

(a) the assets constitute a separate fund and are not a part of the trustee's own estate;

3. Additional reading is available. See generally S.I. STRONG, ed., *Arbitration of Trust Disputes: Issues in National and International Law* (Oxford University Press 2016); Grant JONES and Peter PEXTON, *ADR and Trusts: An International Guide to Arbitration and Mediation of Trust Disputes* (Spiramus Press 2015); S.I. STRONG, "Mandatory Arbitration of Internal Trust Disputes: Improving Arbitrability and Enforceability Through Proper Procedural Choices", 28 Arbitration International (2012) p. 591 (hereinafter STRONG, *Arbitrability*); S.I. STRONG, "Arbitration of Trust Law Disputes: Two Bodies of Law Collide", 45 Vanderbilt Journal of Transnational Law (2012) p. 1157 (hereinafter STRONG, *Two Bodies*).
4. Strong, *Two Bodies,* supra fn. 3, at p. 1169.

(b) title to the trust assets stands in the name of the trustee or in the name of another person on behalf of the trustee;
(c) the trustee has the power and the duty, in respect of which he is accountable, to manage, employ or dispose of the assets in accordance with the terms of the trust and the special duties imposed upon him by law.[5]

Traditionally, trusts have been characterized almost exclusively as an estate planning tool for wealthy individuals and families. However, trusts are routinely used in high-value commercial matters and operate in many jurisdictions as the functional equivalent of corporations.[6] Some of the more common types of "commercial" or "business" trusts include pension trusts, investment or unit trusts (which include mutual funds, real estate investment trusts (REITs), oil and gas royalty trusts, and asset securitization trusts) and trusts relating to the issuance of bonds.[7] International elements frequently exist with respect to both commercial and intergenerational trusts, with beneficiaries living in jurisdictions that are different from the place of the trust or the place where other beneficiaries reside.[8]

III. PROBLEMS WITH TRUST ARBITRATION

While internal trust disputes can be made subject to post-dispute arbitration agreements (*compromis*) with relative ease, the real question is whether and to what extent arbitration can be mandated on a pre-dispute basis by including an arbitration provision in the trust itself. Unfortunately, these types of provisions have experienced some difficulties because of the traditional conceptualization of trusts as donative rather than contractual in nature.[9] Although the notion of trusts as donative instruments has been criticized by a variety of commentators, particularly with

---

5. See Convention on the Law Applicable to Trusts and on Their Recognition, Art. 2, 1 July 1985, 23 I.L.M. 1389 (1984).
6. S.I. STRONG, "Congress and Commercial Trusts: Dealing With Diversity Jurisdiction Post-*Americold*", 69 Florida Law Review (2017) p. 1021 (hereinafter STRONG, *Commercial Trusts*).
7. See John H. LANGBEIN, "The Secret Life of the Trust: The Trust as an Instrument of Commerce", 107 Yale Law Journal (1997) p. 165 at pp. 168-176; STRONG, *Arbitrability,* supra fn. 3, at pp. 599-604. A number of these types of trusts have been subject to arbitration in various countries. See *Hastings v. Wilson*, 516 F.3d 1055, 1059 (8th Cir. 2008); *Bortrager v. Central States, Southeast and Southwest Areas Pension Fund*, 425 F.3d 1087, 1092 n. 1 (8th Cir. 2005); *Contract Serv. Emp'ee Trust v. Davis*, 55 F.3d 533, 535 (10th Cir. 1995); *Reeves v. Tarvizian*, 351 F.2d 889, 890-892 (1st Cir. 1965); *Stender v. Cardwell*, Civ. No. 07-cv-02503-REB-MJW, 2009 WL 3416904, at *2 (D. Colo. 20 Oct. 2009); See also *The Law Debenture Trust Corp. plc v. Elektrim Fin. B.V.* [2005] EWHC 1412, paras. 38-47 (Ch.) (Engl.).
8. STRONG, *Arbitrability,* supra fn. 3, at pp. 599-604; STRONG, *Commercial Trusts,* supra fn. 6.
9. See David HAYTON, et al., *Underhill and Hayton Law Relating to Trusts and Trustees* para. 11.83 (18th edn., LexisNexis 2010) (stating that "[a] trust is not a contract but a unilateral transfer of assets to a person prepared to accept the office of trustee with the benefits and burdens attached to such office"); STRONG, *Two Bodies,* supra fn. 3, at p. 1174.

respect to commercial trusts, which clearly reflect a bargained-for exchange,[10] trusts are routinely viewed as something other than contracts.

Early commentary identified five criteria that must be satisfied if an arbitration provision in a trust is to be considered enforceable. While these elements are not embodied in a particular statute, they nevertheless resonate with judges, legislators and commentators. Thus, it is often said that an arbitration provision in a trust will only be considered valid if:

(1) the court's jurisdiction is not being ousted in an unacceptable fashion;
(2) the clause purporting to be an arbitration clause is an agreement that is both (a) operable, effective and capable of being performed and (b) covers the dispute at issue;
(3) the clause is binding on the party seeking to avoid arbitration;
(4) all interested parties, including unascertained, unborn and legally incompetent beneficiaries, are properly represented in the proceeding; and
(5) the subject matter of the dispute is arbitrable.[11]

A detailed analysis of each of these issues is beyond the scope of the current discussion, although there are a number of works that can be consulted.[12] Instead, the focus here will be on illustrating in broad outline how two of the above-mentioned concerns – in this case, points (3) and (4) – can raise issues that do not exist in other forms of international commercial arbitration.

1. *Can an Arbitration Provision in a Trust Bind All Parties to the Arbitration?*

The first item to consider involves the question of whether an arbitration clause found in a trust can bind the party seeking to avoid arbitration. The problem usually relates to beneficiaries, who typically do not sign the trust instrument or accept any burdens thereunder.[13] However, it is possible, even in jurisdictions that view trusts as donative in nature, for the deed of trust to be drafted in such a way that benefiting from the trust would be deemed an agreement to submit trust disputes to arbitration. By accepting the gifts or invoking any rights under the trust deed, the beneficiaries would be deemed to agree to settle any dispute in accordance with the arbitration agreement contained in the trust deed.[14]

This technique is known in England as "deemed acquiescence" and indicates that beneficiaries who receive some sort of benefit under the trust are bound by the terms

10. LANGBEIN, supra fn. 7, at pp. 166-167; See also STRONG, *Commercial Trusts,* supra fn. 6; STRONG, *Two Bodies,* supra fn. 3, at p. 1172.
11. See Lawrence COHEN and Marcus STAFF, "The Arbitration of Trust Disputes", 7 Journal of International Trust and Corporate Planning (1999) p. 203 at p. 209.
12. See *id.*; STRONG, *Arbitrability,* supra fn. 3, at p. 591; STRONG, *Two Bodies,* supra fn. 3, at p. 1157.
13. It is possible to bind trustees to arbitration through a side contract.
14. Tina WÜSTEMANN, "Arbitration of Trust Disputes" in Christoph MÜLLER, ed., *New Developments in International Commercial Arbitration* (Schulthess Verlag 2007) p. 33 at p. 45.

of the instrument, including any mandatory arbitration clause contained therein.[15] Under this doctrine, "any beneficiary (even an unborn or unascertained one) who derives his entire interest in the trust from the settlor, and whose rights and obligations under the trust are hence determined by the trust deed, is deemed to acquiesce to the arbitration provision."[16]

The United States has adopted a similar approach under a theory known as "conditional transfer".[17] Under this doctrine, provisions found in the trust are binding on beneficiaries to the extent that the beneficiary's "rights" in the corpus of the trust are seen as "wholly derivative" of the settlor's "right to pass her property to the persons of her choosing".[18] Because the beneficiary has "rights" in the trust only because the settlor granted those rights, the settlor may condition receipt of any benefits on compliance with arbitration provisions contained in the trust.[19] Courts in civil law countries (most notably Switzerland) have used similar techniques to bind beneficiaries to arbitration provisions found in trust instruments.[20]

Deemed acquiescence and conditional transfer would appear to raise few concerns within the arbitral community because they resemble certain theories used in arbitration law to extend an arbitration agreement to non-signatories.[21] For example, deemed acquiescence and conditional transfer could easily be analogized to implied consent, estoppel or third-party beneficiaries in the arbitral context.

Although there appears to be something of a split of authority in the United States regarding the application of arbitral principles on non-signatories to trust disputes,[22] international practice would seem to support such an approach. Indeed, the United

---

15. This approach relies in part on language found in the Arbitration Act 1996 stating that an arbitration agreement binds any person claiming "under or through" a party to the agreement. Arbitration Act 1996, Sect. 58(2); See also *id.* Sect. 82(2); Lawrence COHEN and Joanna POOLE, "Trust Arbitration – Is It Desirable and Does it Work?", 18 Trusts & Trustees (2012) pp. p. 324 at p. 328; Michael HWANG, "Arbitration of Trust Disputes" in LEGAL MEDIA GROUP, ed., *Guide to the World's Leading Experts in Commercial Arbitration* (2009) p. 83 at p. 84.
16. Paul BUCKLE, "Trust Disputes and ADR", 14 Trusts & Trustees (2008) p. 649 at pp. 655-656.
17. See *American Cancer Soc., St. Louis Division v. Hammerstein*, 631 S.W. 2d 858, 864 (Mo. App. 1981); *Tennant v. Satterfield*, 216 S.E.2d 229, 232 (W. Va. 1975).
18. E. Gary SPITKO, "Gone but Not Conforming: Protecting the Abhorrent Testator from Majoritarian Cultural Norms Through Minority-Culture Arbitration", 49 Case Western Reserve Law Review (1999) p. 275 at p. 300.
19. See *id.*
20. See WÜSTEMANN, supra fn. 14, at pp. 45-46.
21. See *Thomson-CSF, SA v. Am. Arbitration Ass'n*, 64 F.3d 773, 776 (2d Cir. 1995) (discussing "agency (actual and apparent), alter ego, implied consent, 'group of companies,' estoppel, third-party beneficiary, guarantor, subrogation, legal succession and ratification of assumption"); STRONG, *Two Bodies*, supra fn. 3, at p. 1212.
22. Compare *Zisman v. Lesner*, No. 6:08-cv-1448-Orl-31DAB, 2008 WL 4459029, at *3-4 (M.D. Fla. 29 Sept. 2008) (allowing used principles of equitable estoppel to overcome the technical absence of a "writing" in a trust-related dispute), and *Decker v. Bookstaver*, No. 4:09-CV-1361, 2010 WL 2132284, at *1-2 (E.D. Mo. 26 May 2010) (allowing arbitration of internal trust dispute based on incorporation by reference of an arbitration provision found in a side agreement), with *McArthur v. McArthur*, 168 Cal. Rptr. 3d 785 (Cal. Ct. App. 2014) (refusing to adopt a theory of direct benefit estoppel).

Nations Commission on International Trade Law (UNCITRAL) issued a formal recommendation in 2006 stating that form requirements relating to the definition of an "agreement in writing" under the United Nations Convention on the Recognition and Enforcement of Foreign Arbitral Awards (New York Convention) should be relaxed and given an expansive interpretation.[23] While the recommendation does not specifically indicate what can now be considered an "agreement in writing" under the New York Convention,[24] a 2005 report from an UNCITRAL working group suggests that the concepts of deemed acquiescence and conditional transfer (which incorporate principles of estoppel) could fall within the expansive approach to an "agreement in writing" advocated by UNCITRAL, which would allow international trust arbitration to benefit from the pro-enforcement bias of the New York Convention.[25]

Parties and courts seeking additional guidance on how to interpret an "agreement in writing" can also look to the 2006 version of the Model Arbitration Law for assistance.[26] Option I and Option II of the revised version of Art. 7 of the Model Arbitration Law both eliminate the need for the parties to have signed the arbitration agreement in question.[27] Option II goes even further, stating that an "'[a]rbitration agreement' is an agreement by the parties to submit to arbitration all or certain disputes which have arisen or which may arise between them in respect of a defined legal relationship, whether contractual or not".[28] Because Option II does not mention the need for the arbitration provision to appear in a contract, jurisdictions adopting this provision would likely have few, if any, problems enforcing a mandatory arbitration provision found in a trust. However, Option I and Option II would both be very useful in overcoming concerns about whether an arbitration provision in a trust instrument can bind all relevant parties.

---

23. See Convention on the Recognition and Enforcement of Foreign Arbitral Awards, Art. II, 10 June 1958, 21 U.S.T. 2518, 330 U.N.T.S. 3 (hereinafter New York Convention); UNCITRAL, Recommendation Regarding the Interpretation of Article II, Paragraph 2, and Article VII, Paragraph 1, of the Convention on the Recognition and Enforcement of Foreign Arbitral Awards, U.N. Doc. A/6/17 (7 July 2006) (hereinafter UNCITRAL Recommendation) (recommending that Art. II(2) of the New York Convention "be applied recognizing that the circumstances described therein are not exhaustive"); STRONG, *Two Bodies,* supra fn. 3, at pp. 1214-1216.

24. New York Convention, supra fn. 23, Art. II(2); See also UNCITRAL Recommendation, supra fn. 23.

25. See Note by the Secretariat, UNCITRAL, Working Group II (Arbitration), Settlement of Commercial Disputes: Preparation of Uniform Provisions on Written Form for Arbitration Agreements, U.N. Doc. A/CN.9/WG.II/WP.139 (14 Dec. 2005) paras. 16-21 (hereinafter UNCITRAL Note); STRONG, *Two Bodies,* supra fn. 3, at pp. 1216-1218.

26. See UNCITRAL Model Law on International Commercial Arbitration, Art. 7, UNCITRAL, 18th Sess., Annex 1, U.N. Doc. A/40/17 (21 June 1985), revised by Revised Articles of the UNCITRAL Model Law on International Commercial Arbitration, UNCITRAL, 39th Sess., Annex, U.N. Doc. A/61/17 (7 July 2006) (hereinafter Model Arbitration Law).

27. See *id.*; UNCITRAL Note, supra fn. 25, paras. 11-12; Gerard MEIJER and Josefina GUZMAN, "The International Recognition of an Arbitration Clause in the Articles of Association of a Company" in C.J.M. KLAASSEN et al., eds., *Onderneming en ADR*, (Wolters Kluwer 2011) pp. 117 at pp. 143-145.

28. See Model Arbitration Law, supra fn. 26, Art. 7, Option II.

2. *Identifying Proper Parties to a Trust Arbitration*

Even if trusts are considered capable of binding parties through an arbitration provision in the trust deed, questions exist about the propriety of using arbitration when some parties in interest may be unascertained, unborn or legally incompetent (such as through legal minority) at the time the dispute arises.[29] Concerns about the legal status of beneficiaries are most often seen in the context of inter-generational trusts. These types of devices can endure over several lifetimes, which means that a trust dispute might arise before one or more beneficiaries are born[30] or ascertained.[31] Commercial trusts are unlikely to generate the same level of concern about unborn or unascertained beneficiaries, since beneficial interests in commercial trusts are typically reflected in certificates or shares that are conveyed in a manner similar to that seen in the corporate context.[32] However, it is possible that some shares in a commercial trust could be held by minors or other legally incapacitated persons.

Specialists in international commercial arbitration may find these kinds of concerns somewhat challenging, since arbitration seldom involves the rights of persons who are not actually present in the dispute. However, courts have traditionally characterized trust disputes to operate *in rem,* with decisions binding "all persons having adequate notice, whether or not they actually participate in the proceeding".[33] As a result, courts and arbitral tribunals must give special attention to questions involving who should have notice of a trust proceeding, how notice must be given to those persons and what sort of procedures must be used to protect the rights of all interested parties, regardless of whether they are present or not.[34]

The first task – identifying who should be given notice of a trust dispute – requires a careful reading of the trust document as well as a detailed knowledge of the context in which the trust operates. For example, some beneficiaries may not be identified in the trust by name. Although this practice may seem strange to commercial specialists, it has long been condoned by trust law. Trusts can endure for a very long period of time, which means that the terms of the trust must be sufficiently flexible so as to anticipate a variety of different circumstances, including those relating to the possibility that some beneficiaries might not yet be born or ascertained or might not have legal capacity.

---

29. See COHEN and STAFF, supra fn. 11, at p. 209.
30. An example might be a trust for the benefit of "my grandchildren", not all of whom may be born at the time the trust is created or at the time the dispute arises.
31. An example might be a trust created for the benefit "those of my grandchildren who graduate from college". Not only might the number of grandchildren change, but the limiting condition (graduation from college) could be fulfilled at any time up until the death of a potential beneficiary.
32. See STRONG, *Commercial Trusts,* supra fn. 6.
33. Blaine Covington JANIN, "Comment, *The Validity of Arbitration Provisions in Trust Instruments*", 55 California Law Review (1967) p. 521 at p. 529.
34. See STRONG, *Arbitrability,* supra fn. 3, at pp. 637-649; S.I. STRONG, "Empowering Settlors: How Proper Language Can Increase the Enforceability of a Mandatory Arbitration Provision in a Trust", 47 Real Property, Trust and Estate Law Journal (2012) p. 273 at pp. 309-325 (hereinafter STRONG, *Language*).

These types of issues have been resolved in litigation by allowing judges to appoint a person to represent the interests of any unnamed, unascertained or legally incompetent beneficiaries.[35] In England, the person named to protect the beneficiaries' claims, called a "special representative," cannot have any independent interest in the dispute itself.[36] Other jurisdictions, such as the United States, either appoint an independent representative similar to a special representative or allow an existing beneficiary who shares the absent beneficiary's interests to protect the absent beneficiary's claims in a practice known as "virtual representation".[37] Minors and other legally incompetent persons may have legal representatives, typically referred to as guardians, already in place.[38]

The question then becomes whether these sorts of representative mechanisms can be used in arbitration. The answer may depend on whether the trust instrument specifically describes the representative mechanism that is to be used. For example,

> "[t]here appears to be no reason why the court would not grant a stay [of litigation] to the trustee on the sole ground that the beneficiary is not properly represented in the arbitration. If the arbitration provision is properly drawn to provide for adequate representation, then the child [or other beneficiary] should be bound to take the benefit of it."[39]

In drafting such a provision, the settlor should be sure to "provide how incapacitated, unascertained and unborn beneficiaries can come (or be brought) forward to make their claims.... The arbitral tribunal could determine who should be served with notice of the arbitration, in the same way as, in court proceedings, a judge can."[40] Furthermore, "[t]o avoid problems the trust deed should provide for payment of ... [special or virtual representatives] out of the trust fund".[41] Notably, this technique appears to be equally appropriate in the context of both commercial and inter-generational (family) trusts.

Trustees who are not given explicit powers to appoint special or virtual representatives could attempt to do so based on their general discretionary powers to resolve trust disputes. This approach would likely be bolstered by statutory provisions allowing trustees to pursue non-judicial means of dispute resolution.[42] While some within the trust law community have questioned whether an arbitral

35. See BUCKLE, supra fn. 16, at pp. 649-650.
36. See Gail E. MAUTNER and Heidi L.G. ORR, "A Brave New World: Nonjudicial Dispute Resolution Procedures Under the Uniform Trust Code and Washington's and Idaho's Trust and Estate Dispute Resolution Acts", 35 American College of Trust and Estate Counsel (ACTEC) Journal (2009) p. 159 at pp. 161, 163-164.
37. See William M. MCGOVERN, et al., *Wills, Trusts and Estates: Including Taxation and Future Interests*, 4th edn. (West 2010) pp. 613-614.
38. See *id.* at pp. 660-663.
39. COHEN and STAFF, supra fn. 11, at pp. 222-223.
40. *Id.* at p. 223.
41. David HAYTON, "Future Trends in International Trust Planning", 13 Journal of International Trust and Corporate Planning, (2006) p. 55 at p. 72.
42. See STRONG, *Two Bodies,* supra fn. 3, at pp. 1188-1191 (discussing the Uniform Trust Code and related legislation).

tribunal can be relied upon to appoint a competent representative, then-Professor (now Judge) David Hayton has said that "[o]ne can leave it to the good sense of the arbitrator to provide for due process and a fair hearing by appointing appropriate skilled independent persons to represent minors and unborn and unascertained beneficiaries".[43]

IV. THE RISE OF TRUST ARBITRATION AROUND THE WORLD

Although trust arbitration faces some very real jurisprudential challenges, the outlook for this particular procedure has never been more positive. Not only have numerous common law and civil law jurisdictions adopted legislation specifically providing for arbitration of internal trust disputes, but a number of courts and arbitral institutions have also supported advances in this field.

1. *Legislative Developments*

Numerous jurisdictions from around the world have begun to adopt legislation allowing arbitration of internal trust disputes. Although the shape and form of these provisions can vary widely, they all demonstrate that the traditional animus toward trust arbitration is waning.

The United States has enacted perhaps the most diverse array of pro-trust arbitration legislation. At the time of writing, five US states (Arizona, Florida, Missouri, New Hampshire and South Dakota) have adopted statutes explicitly recognizing the validity of an arbitration provision found in a trust.[44] Support for trust arbitration can also be found in the Uniform Trust Code (UTC), a model enactment that has been adopted in whole or in part by thirty-one US states and the District of Columbia, and in the laws of two other states (Washington and Idaho), although these provisions do not specify whether the settlor or the trustee is the holder of the authority to choose arbitration as a means of resolving disputes.[45]

Other countries have also embraced legislation on trust arbitration. For example, Guernsey and the Bahamas have both adopted extremely wide-ranging legislation, with other common law jurisdictions, most notably New Zealand, poised to follow suit.[46] Several civil law jurisdictions, most notably Liechtenstein, Malta, Panama and

---

43. HAYTON, supra fn. 41, at p. 72.
44. See Ariz. Rev. Stat. Ann. Sect. 14-10205; Fla. Stat. Ann. Sect. 731.401(2); Mo. Rev. Stat. Sect. 456.2-205.1; N.H. Rev. Stat. Sect. 564-B:1-111A ; S.D. Codified Laws Sect. 55-1-54.
45. See Idaho Code Ann. Sects. 15-8-101, 15-8-103; Wash. Rev. Code Sects. 11.96A.010, 11.96A.030; National Conference of Commissioners on Uniform State Laws (NCCUSL), Uniform Trust Code (2000), Sect. 111, last revised or amended in 2005, <www.law.upenn.edu/bll/archives/ulc/uta/2005final.htm>; STRONG, *Two Bodies,* supra fn. 3, at pp. 1189-1190.
46. See Arbitration Amendment Bill 2017 (N.Z.) (proposing a new Sect. 10A in the Arbitration Act 1996 (N.Z.) that would "deem" arbitration clauses in trusts to be arbitration agreements under the 1996 Act and would give arbitrators the ability to appoint representatives empowered to act for minor, unborn or unascertained beneficiaries); David BROWNBILL, "Arbitration of Trust Disputes Under the Bahamas Trustee Act 1998", in *Arbitration of Trust*

Paraguay, allow arbitration of internal disputes involving trusts or trust-like devices.[47] Although Switzerland does not recognize trusts as a matter of national law, Swiss courts appear capable of enforcing awards arising out of arbitration of foreign trusts pursuant to the Swiss statute on private international law.[48]

Relatively little authority exists regarding the enforcement of arbitral awards generated by internal trust arbitration other than *Weizmann Institute of Science v. Neschis*, a US decision that considered whether and to what extent an arbitral award rendered in Liechtenstein should be given preclusive effect in a US court proceeding.[49] The court provided for enforcement of the award, even though Liechtenstein had not yet acceded to the New York Convention. No known case exists under the New York Convention, although various commentators have argued that trust arbitration falls within the terms of the New York Convention.[50]

2. *Judicial Developments*

Skeptics in this area of law routinely claim that trust arbitration can only develop as a statutory device. However, a number of courts have upheld arbitration of an internal trust dispute despite the absence of any specific legislation on the subject.

The most well-known of these decisions is *Rachal v. Reitz* from the Supreme Court of Texas.[51] In *Rachal*, the Texas Supreme Court overcame concerns about the contractual nature of trusts by embracing the direct benefits theory of estoppel (essentially, the doctrine of conditional transfer) and applying all terms of the trust, including the arbitration provision, against the beneficiary because the beneficiary had

---

Disputes, supra fn. 3, p. 313 at p. 313; Paul BUCKLE, "Trust Arbitration in Guernsey" in *Arbitration of Trust Disputes*, supra fn. 3, p. 289 at p. 289; S.I. STRONG, "The Future of Trust Arbitration: Quo Vadis?" in *Arbitration of Trust Disputes*, supra fn. 3, p. 531 at p. 533 (hereinafter STRONG, *Quo Vadis*).

47. See Maltese Arbitration Act, ch. 387, Sect. 15A; Dante FIGUEROA, "Civil Law Trusts in Latin America: Is the Lack of Trusts an Impediment for Expanding Business Opportunities in Latin America?", 24 Arizona Journal of International and Comparative Law (2007) p. 701 at pp. 704-707; Edgardo MUÑOZ and Sofía LLAMAS, "Arbitration of Mexican Trust Disputes: A Couple Made For Each Other?", 23 University of Miami International & Comparative Law Review (2015) p. 1 at pp. 81-83; Georg VON SEGESSER and Katherine BELL, "Arbitration of Trust Disputes", 35 ASA Bulletin (2017) p. 1 at p. 35; Rafael IBARRA GARZA, "(Un)enforceability of Trust Arbitration Clauses in Civil and Common Law", 22 Trusts & Trustees (2016) p. 759.
48. See Tina WÜSTEMANN and Roman HUBER, "Trust Arbitration in Switzerland" in *Arbitration of Trust Disputes*, supra fn. 3, at pp. 383, 386, 406-407.
49. See 421 F.Supp.2d 654, 674-83 (S.D.N.Y. 2005).
50. See Sarah GANZ, "Enforcement of Foreign Arbitral Awards Arising from an Internal Trust Arbitration: Issues Under the New York Convention" in *Arbitration of Trust Disputes*, supra fn. 3, at p. 494; Margaret L. MOSES, "International Enforcement of an Arbitration Provision in a Trust: Questions Involving the New York Convention" in *Arbitration of Trust Disputes*, supra fn. 3, at pp. 467, 493; STRONG, *Two Bodies*, supra fn. 3, at pp. 1213-1219.
51. See *Rachal v. Reitz*, 403 S.W.3d 840 (Tex. 2013); See also Mary F. RADFORD, "Trust Arbitration in the United States Courts" in *Arbitration of Trust Disputes*, supra fn. 3, p. 175 at p. 175-202; STRONG, *Two Bodies*, supra fn. 3, at pp. 1207, 1245 (discussing case law in other states, including New York, Michigan and California).

clearly indicated acceptance of the terms and validity of the trust by accepting the benefits of the trust and suing to recover damages for violation of the terms of the trust.[52] The court approved of this type of "equitable defensive" theory because it "promote[d] fairness by holding a party to its position in the performance of an agreement or in bringing litigation".[53]

The Texas approach can be contrasted with that that taken in California. In 2014, the California Court of Appeal held in *McArthur v. McArthur* that an arbitration provision in a trust was unenforceable against an objecting beneficiary.[54] However, in so doing, the court did not reject the direct benefit estoppel theory seen in *Rachal* but instead noted that the beneficiary did not seek to claim benefits or enforce her rights under the trust; to the contrary, she sought to set the trust aside in its entirety. As a result, the arbitration provision could not be held against the beneficiary, and her claim had to be heard in litigation.

Another California case – *Roehl v. Ritchie* – saw the California Court of Appeal upholding an award arising out of trust arbitration after one of the parties claimed that the arbitrator had exceeded the scope of his powers in issuing a series of awards relating to an accounting issue.[55] Notably, the court at no point suggested the arbitration provision might be unenforceable, even though the relevant language was found in the trust itself.

This is not to say that all US decisions have been positive. Indeed, a number of early cases involving trust arbitration were relatively negative, although many of these decisions can no longer be considered good law. The most well-known of these decisions comes from Arizona. In *Schoneberger v. Oelze,* the Arizona Court of Appeals denied enforcement of an arbitration provision in a trust on the grounds that a trust is not a contract.[56] Although this case is still sometimes referred to in comparative analyses, it has since been superseded by statute, as recognized by the Arizona Court of Appeals in *Jones v. Fink*.[57]

Another case that is frequently cited as curtailing the arbitration of trust disputes is *In re Jacobovitz' Will*, a New York state court decision from 1968 that held that wills (and, by extension, trusts) were non-arbitrable as a matter of public policy.[58] However, *In re Jacobovitz' Will* was called into question by *In re Blumenkrantz,*[59] which allowed arbitration of internal trust matters.

Michigan underwent a similar shift at about the same time. For years, *Meredith's Estate,* a 1936 decision from the Supreme Court of Michigan, was frequently cited as

52. See 403 S.W.3d 840 (Tex. 2013).
53. *Id.* at 848.
54. See 168 Cal. Rptr. 3d 785 (Cal. Ct. App. 2014).
55. See 54 Cal. Rptr. 3d 185 (Cal. Ct. App. 2007).
56. See *Schoneberger v. Oelze*, 96 P. 3d 1078 (Ariz. Ct. App. 2004), superseded by statute, Ariz. Rev. Stat. Ann. Sect. 14-10205.
57. See *Jones v. Fink*, No. CA-SA 10-0262, 2011 WL 601598 (Ariz. Ct. App., 22 Feb. 2011) (discussing Ariz. Rev. Stat. Ann. Sect. 14-10205).
58. See *In re Jacobovitz' Will*, 295 N.Y.S. 2d 527, 529 (Sur. Ct. Nassau Co. 1968), superseded by implication by *In re Blumenkrantz*, 824 N.Y.S. 2d 884, 887 (Sur. Ct. Nassau County 2006).
59. See *Blumenkrantz*, 824, N.Y.S. 2d at 887.

prohibiting trust arbitration because trust disputes are in rem proceedings.[60] However, *Meredith's Estate* was superseded by implication by *In re Nestorovski Estate,*[61] which concluded that an arbitration proceeding did not improperly oust the court of jurisdiction over probate concerns.

3. *Institutional Developments*

The final set of developments to consider involves institutional rules. While there is no requirement that parties to an internal trust dispute must use a specialized rule set (indeed, there are examples of trust arbitrations proceeding under the general rules of the American Arbitration Association (AAA), the International Chamber of Commerce (ICC) and the International Centre for Dispute Resolution (ICDR)),[62] the numerous challenges associated with trust arbitration[63] suggest that a dedicated rule set might be useful even if it is not required. Indeed, certain types of commercial trust disputes have been arbitrated for decades[64] largely, though not exclusively, as a result of a set of specialized rules developed by the AAA in conjunction with the International Foundation of Employee Benefit Plans (IFEBP).[65]

While the AAA/IFEBP rules do not address the precise types of internal disputes under discussion in this paper, they doubtless inspired the AAA to create a more general set of rules – the AAA Wills and Trusts Arbitration Rules – applicable to a

60. See *Meredith's Estate*, 266 N.W. 351, 354, 356 (Mich. 1936), superseded by implication by *In re Nestorovski Estate*, 769 N.W. 2d 720, 732 (Mich. Ct. App. 2009).
61. See *Nestorovski Estate,* 768, N.W. 2d at 732.
62. See *Municipality of San Juan v. Corporacion para el Fomento Economico de la Ciudad Capital*, 597 F.Supp.2d 247, 248-249 (D. Puerto Rico 2008) (upholding terms of a pre dispute, mandatory arbitration provision in the trust deed calling for arbitration under the ICDR Arbitration Rules); *Burlington Resources Oil & Gas Co. LP v. San Juan Basin Royalty Trust*, 249 S.W.3d 34, 36, 38 (Tex. App. 2007) (involving a post-dispute arbitration agreement concerning accountings and audits of the trust and invoking the AAA Commercial Arbitration Rules); *New South Federal Savings Bank v. Anding*, 414 F.Supp.2d 636, 646-647 (S.D. Miss. 2005) (upholding mandatory arbitration agreement in trust deed rider invoking the AAA Commercial Arbitration Rules); *Newbridge Acquisition I, L.L.C. v. Grupo Corvi, S.A. de D.V.*, No. 02 Civ. 9839(JSR), 2003 WL 42007, at *1 (S.D.N.Y. 6 Jan. 2003) (involving an arbitration provision in a trust agreement invoking the ICC Arbitration Rules).
63. See COHEN and STAFF, supra fn. 11, at p. 209.
64. See *Hastings v. Wilson*, 516 F.3d 1055, 1059 (8th Cir. 2008); *Bortrager v. Central States, Southeast and Southwest Areas Pension Fund*, 425 F.3d 1087,1092 n.1 (8th Cir. 2005); *Contract Serv. Emp'ee Trust v. Davis*, 55 F.3d 533, 535 (10th Cir. 1995); *Reeves v. Tarvizian*, 351 F.2d 889, 890-92 (1st Cir. 1965).
65. See AAA/IFEBP Multiemployer Pension Plan Arbitration Rules for Withdrawal Liability, effective 1 Sept. 1986, <www.foreclosuremediationfl.adr.org/sp.asp?id=22108>; AAA/IFEBP Impartial Umpire Rules for Arbitration of Impasses Between Trustees of Joint Employee Benefit Trust Funds, effective 1 Jan. 1988, available at <www.foreclosuremediation fl.adr.org/sp.asp?id=22111>; *Teamsters-Employers Local 945 Pension Fund v. Waste Management of New Jersey, Inc.*, No. 11-902 (FSH), 2011 WL 2173854, at *2 (D.N.J. 2 June 2011); *I.L.G.W.U. Nat'l Retirement Fund v. Meredith Gray, Inc.*, 94 Fed. Appx. 850, 852 (2d Cir. 2003).

wider range of trust disputes.[66] At this point, the AAA is the only arbitral institution to have created a rule set dedicated entirely to trust disputes.

That is not to say that other arbitral institutions have ignored internal trust arbitration entirely. In 2008, the ICC issued a report indicating that the ICC considered its standard arbitration rules to be sufficient in any matter involving an internal trust dispute and suggesting that parties use a special model arbitration clause that was to be placed in the trust in question to ensure that all parties would be bound by the clause.[67] In 2018, the ICC adopted several revisions to its model clause for trust arbitration, although the basic approach remained the same.[68]

Both the ICC and AAA approach trust arbitration from an arbitration perspective, which has its benefits. However, both regimes have been criticized for failing to appreciate fully the special concerns associated with arbitration of trust disputes, a problem that perhaps could have been avoided had trust lawyers been more closely involved in the process of developing the various rules and clauses.[69] As a result, it is not surprising that trust lawyers have taken matters into their own hands.

The most ambitious initiative from the trust law community has come from the American College of Trust and Estate Counsel (ACTEC). In a 2006 report, ACTEC proposed a number of initiatives, including model legislation concerning trust arbitration and model clauses for use in trusts.[70] While these provisions have the support of the trust law community, they reflect significant shortcomings from an arbitral perspective.[71]

Interestingly, the most promising procedural approach to trust arbitration comes from the world of corporate law. Trust arbitration is conceptually similar to shareholder arbitration, particularly with respect to the need to bind potentially large numbers of parties through a document that does not meet the technical requirements of a contract.[72] Therefore, it has been suggested that the German Arbitration Institute (DIS) Supplementary Rules for Corporate Law Disputes could provide a very helpful basis for a new set of rules for internal trust law arbitration.[73]

---

66. See AAA Wills and Trusts Arbitration Rules, effective 1 June 2012, available at <http://www.adr.org>.
67. See ICC Arbitration Clause for Trust Disputes, 19 ICC International Court of Arbitration Bulletin (2008) p. 9.
68. See ICC Arbitration Clause for Trust Disputes, 29 ICC International Court of Arbitration Bulletin (2018, no. 3) pp. 92 and 94; see also <https://iccwbo.org/publication/icc-arbitration-clause-trust-disputes-explanatory-note/>.
69. See E Gary SPITKO, "A Critique of the American Arbitration Association's Efforts to Facilitate Arbitration of Internal Trust Disputes" in *Arbitration of Trust Disputes*, supra fn. 3, at pp. 59, 73; STRONG, *Arbitrability,* supra fn. 3, at pp. 629-637; STRONG, *Language,* supra fn. 34, at pp. 309-325.
70. See Robert W. GOLDMAN in *Arbitration of Trust Disputes*, supra fn. 3, at pp. 74, 86-98 (reproducing the various ACTEC proposals).
71. See S.I. STRONG, "Institutional Approaches to Trust Arbitration: Comparing the AAA, ACTEC, DIS, and ICC Mechanisms" in *Arbitration of Trust Disputes*, supra fn. 3, at pp. 99, 103-140 (hereinafter STRONG, *AAA, ACTEC, DIS and ICC*).
72. See STRONG, *Two Bodies,* supra fn. 3, at p. 1167 n. 39.
73. See DIS Supplementary Rules for Corporate Law Disputes, effective 15 Sept. 2009, available at <www.dis-arb.de/download/DIS_SRCoLD_%202009_Download.pdf>; STRONG, *AAA,*

V. CONCLUSION

Although it is impossible to provide a comprehensive analysis of the special challenges associated with trust arbitration in a work of this nature, hopefully this discussion has provided a working introduction to the subject. Trust arbitration is very much at the cusp of a major breakthrough, and it is important that arbitral specialists understand the unique nature of this particular procedure. Indeed, proponents of trust arbitration will need to address a number of critical questions if the process is to reach its full potential.[74] Hopefully, the points raised in this chapter will prove helpful to those future discussions.

ACTEC, DIS and ICC, supra fn. 71, at pp. 103-140; STRONG, *Arbitrability,* supra fn. 3, at pp. 637-649.

74. STRONG, *Quo Vadis,* supra fn. 46, at pp. 544-547.

International Arbitration of Corporate Disputes: A Workable Balance Between Two Dimensions of Party Autonomy

Massimo V. Benedettelli[*]

TABLE OF CONTENTS PAGE

I. CORPORATE DISPUTES AS A NOVEL FRONTIER OF INTERNATIONAL ARBITRATION

Corporate disputes may become a novel frontier of international arbitration once their peculiarities are identified and properly dealt with (I). It is a fact that an array of distinct kinds of disputes may arise from the formation, operations and winding-up of a company (II). It is also a fact that in this specific sector of international business many legitimate reasons may lead the parties to prefer private adjudication to State court litigation, there being in principle no obstacles to the settlement via arbitration of corporate disputes (III). Arbitrating corporate disputes, however, poses several problems regarding all facets of an arbitration, be it the jurisdiction of the arbitral tribunal, the organization of the proceedings, the determination of the applicable law, or the effects, review and enforcement of the award (IV). Solving these problems is not an easy task. Only a few arbitration laws address them with provisions *ad hoc*, and when the dispute at bar is international different laws may potentially apply, so that the coordination of the relevant legal systems for identifying the applicable law becomes a necessary and preliminary step (V). This article submits that arbitral tribunals should approach corporate disputes by considering that in this area of business two equally important dimensions of party autonomy cross and overlap, namely the parties' power to have recourse to arbitration for settling their disputes and the parties' power to incorporate a company by choosing among the different models of corporate organization laid down by State law for the carrying out of entrepreneurial activities. Thus, the issue becomes how party autonomy in arbitration and party autonomy in corporate matters can be balanced

* Partner, ArbLit, Milan; Professor of International Law, University "Aldo Moro", Bari.

so that the will of the parties, as reflected in the arbitration agreement and in the corporate contract, is best protected (VI). This article further submits that this balancing would be best achieved if arbitral tribunals would handle the regulatory problems raised by the arbitration of corporate disputes through a two-pronged method: firstly, by trying to combine to the largest possible extent the law of the seat of the arbitration and the law under which the company has been incorporated; secondly, by giving precedence to the latter when a "true" conflict-of-laws materializes (VII).[1] Such a method would have the benefit of enhancing party autonomy, predictability and legal certainty. It would also create the conditions for a "virtuous" forum shopping whereby entrepreneurs would be able to select the *lex societatis* and the *lex arbitri* that best fit their needs, without jeopardizing the legitimate interests States have in the regulation of corporations (VIII).

II. DO "CORPORATE DISPUTES" REALLY EXIST?

Disputes may arise with respect to the various acts that are required for the formation of a company. For instance, founders may fail to fulfil obligations as to the subscription and payment of the company's capital, members of the company's administrative bodies may be held liable for debts incurred on behalf of the company before the company is incorporated, the very existence of the company may be challenged by any interested party with the purpose of lifting the corporate veil when the process of incorporation has not been properly complied with.

Disputes may also result from the operations of the company. Resolutions taken by the company's administrative bodies (including resolutions of the shareholders' meeting approving the company's financial statements) may be challenged as to their existence, validity or effectiveness. Individuals holding positions in bodies charged with the company's administration or control (board of directors, management board, supervisory board, board of statutory auditors) may be sued for damages when they fail to comply with fiduciary and other duties which under applicable law or contractual arrangements regulate the performance of their activities. Disputes may also arise when said individuals are removed from office and their employment or service contract is terminated, as well as when a shareholder is excluded from the company or forced transfers of shares are carried out.

Shareholders of the company may enter into agreements regulating the exercise of their voting rights (within the shareholders' meeting or other corporate bodies) and patrimonial rights (as to the collection of dividends or the distribution of assets in case of liquidation of the company). They may also regulate the disposal of shares or other instruments issued by the company (whether through sales, usufructs, collaterals or other types of acts) by granting to each other pre-emption, "first offer/refusal", "tag-

1. These propositions were first advanced in a presentation given during the XV Congress of the Comitê Brasileiro de Arbitragem held in Florianopolis on 25-27 September 2016 (*Trabalhos do XV Congreso Internacional de Arbitragem do Comitê Brasileiro de Arbitragem, Consentimento na Arbitragem Internacional* (CBAr 2017) p. 52 et seq.), and further developed in M.V. BENEDETTELLI, "*Sull'arbitrato societario 'internazionale'*", XXVII Rivista dell'arbitrato (2017) p. 299, and *Id.*, "*Patti parasociali ed arbitrato estero: sul possibile equilibrio tra autonomia societaria e autonomia compromissoria*", LXII Rivista delle società (2017) p. 631.

along" or "drag-along" rights, or by setting-up "lock-up" periods during which such disposals are prohibited. Shareholders may also undertake commitments of other kinds with respect to transactions (capital increases, capital decreases, mergers, de-mergers, transformations of the corporate form, defences from hostile take-overs) which affect the structure of the company's capital or its control and governance. The validity, interpretation and performance of all such agreements and commitments may be controversial, leading to disputes (e.g., in the context of a merger with respect to the determination of the share exchange ratio or the protections granted to minority shareholders, bondholders and creditors).

Additional types of disputes may arise in two situations which change the "status" of the company. The company may decide to enter into a capital market by listing shares, bonds or other financial instruments or by carrying out transactions (including take-over offers) over instruments of other listed companies. By so doing the company becomes subject to the rules which regulate the relevant market, the breach of which may lead to controversies with the market authorities and other market participants. The "status" of the company changes also when the company becomes insolvent. This triggers additional obligations on the company's administrative and control bodies the respect of which can be vindicated by any interested party. Moreover, to maximize the insolvency assets and achieve the equal treatment of the creditors the bankruptcy administrator may terminate or avoid contracts, payments or other acts of the company, which may also generate disputes.

Finally, disputes may result from the winding-up of the company, for instance with respect to decisions taken by the competent corporate body on the liquidation of the company's assets and the distributions of the proceeds between the creditors and the shareholders.

All these disputes share the common feature of being directly or indirectly connected with the formation, operations and winding-up of companies. In other important respects, though, they differ from each other.

First, they differ as to their cause of action, which could be grounded, alternately or cumulatively, in: the law under which the company is incorporated (the *lex societatis*); the disputed contract (deed of incorporation, shareholders' agreement, investment agreement, merger/de-merger deed) or act of private autonomy (take-over offer) and the relevant applicable law (the *lex contractus*); the law governing issues of liability in tort (the *lex loci delicti*); the law governing the company's insolvency (the *lex fori concursus*) or the capital market where the company is active (the *lex mercatus*).

Second, the relief requested may also be of quite distinct kinds. Claimants in corporate disputes may alternatively seek: condemnations to pay amounts of money as damages or as overdue debts vis-à-vis the company; declarations as to the inexistence, invalidity or ineffectiveness of the company, of corporate acts, of acts of disposal of shares or other instruments issued by the company; the fixing of terms of corporate transactions (e.g., the merger/de-merger share exchange ratio); the removal of directors or other company officers. Moreover, the claimants may request, or the applicable law may provide, that the relevant decisions have *erga omnes* effects, i.e. that they bind not only the parties in dispute but also third parties belonging to a qualified class (shareholders, creditors, corporate bodies).

Third, the dispute may arise between different subjects such as founders/shareholders, the company, individuals holding positions in the company's administrative and control bodies, the company's creditors, financial market authorities, administrators of the company's bankruptcy.

Given all such differences one could question whether it makes any sense at all to speak of "corporate disputes": legal categories should not just be a tribute to scholarly ingenuity or intellectual narcissism, they should also be of real use to the practice of the law. However, the experience of some jurisdictions shows that the submission to arbitration of disputes connected with the formation, operations and winding-up of companies poses some peculiar problems and triggers the need of *ad hoc* regulations. Whether or not this happens will depend on the case at bar and on the applicable law. When this happens, corporate disputes must be singled out from the broader category of commercial disputes so that parties, counsel and arbitrators are provided with adequate tools for properly handling their settlement through arbitration.

III. REASONS FOR ARBITRATING CORPORATE DISPUTES

The reasons which normally lead the actors of international business to prefer arbitration to court litigation may find further grounds when the dispute at bar relates to the formation, operations or winding-up of a company.

The search for an independent adjudicator with the aim of avoiding the parochialism which may sometimes affect State courts can be justified by the specific desire of ousting the jurisdiction of the courts of the company's State of incorporation, i.e. those courts which could often be the "natural" forum for corporate disputes. This may be the case, for instance, when the dispute arises from a shareholders' agreement which some or all shareholders have executed with the purpose of derogating from the company law rules governing the company's affairs. In this case the parties may be concerned that the courts of the State of incorporation may not fully enforce or properly interpret such agreement and rather give a priori precedence to the forum's *lex societatis*. This concern may be higher when the company is a special purpose vehicle which has been incorporated in a foreign jurisdiction by investors who originate from another country, or from countries sharing the same legal tradition, particularly when the law of incorporation of the vehicle is one with which the investors have little familiarity, or which materially departs from the company laws of the investors' State of origin, and the shareholders' agreement serves the objective of bringing the "rules of the corporate game" back to what the investors are more accustomed to. In this scenario the choice of arbitration may be also driven by the parties' desire to have an adjudicator with the required level of expertise, an expertise that foreign courts may not necessarily have when facing those sophisticated mechanisms of corporate governance which are often reflected in shareholders' agreements.

The higher level of "finality" that awards may have if compared to court judgments, and the higher "speed" that arbitration may offer vis-à-vis court proceedings, may be crucial when selecting the method for settling corporate disputes. This is certainly the case when the dispute relates to matters that need to be decided quickly if one wants to avoid disruptions to the company's business, as is for instance the case when the dispute deals with the existence, validity or effectiveness of resolutions of corporate bodies, or with the existence, validity or effectiveness of transactions on shares carried out in breach of limits set out in the company's articles of association, and consequently with the entitlement of the relevant shareholders to cast their vote in the shareholders' meeting.

The confidentiality which may govern arbitral proceedings, as opposed to the publicity which normally accompanies court proceedings, may also be a prominent feature. It is quite often the case, in fact, that undertakings relating to corporate governance or shareholding structures are documented through shareholders' agreements or investment contracts, rather than being incorporated into the company's articles of association, because for various, and not necessarily illegitimate, reasons the contracting parties prefer such instruments not to become known by the public-at-large. More in general, investors may consider it harmful for the company's business if the market becomes aware that disputes have arisen between the company's shareholders, or between the company and the members of its administrative and control bodies, or about a shareholders' meeting resolution.

The worldwide recognition of arbitration agreements and circulation of foreign awards which is guaranteed by the 1958 New York Convention may also justify a preference for arbitration. Lacking equivalent multilateral instruments, the recognition and enforcement of choice-of-court agreements and foreign court judgments is regulated by the private international laws in force in the relevant States. Such laws not only differ in significant respects, sometimes they also provide for the exclusive jurisdiction of the forum courts with respect to corporate disputes involving domestic companies. When, as also happens, the recognition and enforcement of a foreign judgment is made conditional upon the requirement that the foreign court has acknowledged jurisdiction on a ground known by the law of the forum,[2] this will mean that foreign judgments rendered by courts of a State other than the State of incorporation of the relevant company, including judgments rendered by courts selected by the parties pursuant to choice-of-court agreements, may be denied recognition. More in general, the predictability and legal certainty which result from a contractual choice of the dispute resolution method will be enhanced if the parties enter into an arbitration agreement, rather than a choice-of-court agreement, given the wide territorial reach of the New York Convention.

Whatever benefits the parties may draw from submitting their corporate disputes to arbitration, this would be a non-issue if one were to consider such disputes a priori non-arbitrable.[3] Two arguments could be raised in this respect, both of which, however, do not withstand scrutiny.

2. This is what happens under French law with the requirement of the *compétence indirecte* of the foreign court: see B. AUDIT, "*Le droit international privé en quête d'universalitè: cours general (2001)*" in *Collected Courses of The Hague Academy of International Law*, Volume 305 (Brill-Nijhoff 2003) at p. 640 et seq.
3. On this issue see, also for further references, B. HANOTIAU, "*L'arbitrabilité*" in *Collected Courses of The Hague Academy of International Law*, Volume 296 (Brill-Nijhoff 2003) at p. 164 et seq.; G. B. BORN, *International Commercial Arbitration,* 2nd edn. (Kluwer Law International 2014) I, at p. 1029 et seq.

Corporate disputes could be held not arbitrable on the ground that they often trigger the application of mandatory rules set out by the applicable *lex societatis, lex mercatus* or *lex fori concursus*. This position reflects the old-fashioned "public law taboo"[4] according to which only magistrates of the State to which a given mandatory rule belongs can be entrusted with the delicate task of interpreting/applying it and can properly implement the underlying public policies. In most jurisdictions this taboo has been overcome, and since long. If no one any more doubts that disputes involving issues of antitrust law can be arbitrated,[5] there are no reasons why the same should not be true for disputes involving issues of company law, financial markets law, insolvency law.

A different, and more articulated, argument could be brought forward by reference to those provisions which in some countries, as mentioned, reserve to the forum's courts jurisdiction over corporate disputes involving domestic companies. This is what happens, for instance, in all Member States of the European Union pursuant to Art. 24, no. 2, of the so-called Brussels I-*bis* Regulation,[6] establishing the exclusive jurisdiction of the courts of the Member State in which the company has its seat over "proceedings which have as their object the validity of the constitution, the nullity or the dissolution of companies ... or the validity of the decisions of their organs". It could be maintained that if a State does not trust foreign magistrates with respect to the interpretation and application of its company law, it should trust private adjudicators such as arbitrators even less, particularly when, as is often the case in international arbitration, they may not be trained in the law which is going to be applied to the merits of the dispute. This line of reasoning is flawed, as the law in force in some Member States of the European Union confirms. Indeed, the *travaux préparatoires* of the 1968 Brussels Convention, where such provision was first contemplated, and of subsequent treaties whereby new Member States have adhered to such instrument, demonstrate that its true rationale was that of ensuring the "*forum/jus*" identity, i.e. the coincidence between the adjudicating court and the applicable law, in consideration of the special expertise which is required when issues of *lex societatis* are at bar.[7] Evidently, a proper construction of company law issues was deemed important, also for the spillover effects that wrong decisions may have on other disputes by creating precedents, and litigation on such issues before foreign courts was

4. H. MUIR WATT, "Private International Law Beyond the Schism", 2 Transnational Legal Theory (2011) p. 347 at p. 362.

5. See, also for comparative law references, P.M. PATOCCHI, P. MARZOLINI, "*La deroga convenzionale della giurisdizione in favore dell'arbitrato*" in M.V. BENEDETTELLI, C. CONSOLO, L. RADICATI di BROZOLO, eds., *Commentario breve al diritto dell'arbitrato nazionale ed internazionale*, 2nd edn. (Wolters Kluwer CEDAM 2017) p. 754 et seq.

6. Council Regulation (EC) 44/2001 of 22 December 2000 on jurisdiction and the recognition and enforcement of judgments in civil and commercial matters in the European Union, in E.C.O.J., L 012, 2001, 1, as recasted through Regulation (EU) 1215/2012 of the European Parliament and of the Council of 12 December 2012, E.U.O.J., L 351, 2012, 1.

7. Many commentators agree that this is the *ratio* of Art. 24, no. 2, of the Brussels I-*bis* Regulation (and of the equivalent provision contained in the 1968 Brussels Convention): see, inter alia, G.A.L. DROZ, *Compétence judiciaire et effets des jugements dans le Marché Commun (Etude de la Convention de Bruxelles du 27 septembre 1968)* (Librairie Dalloz 1972) p. 103; J. KROPHOLLER, *Europäisches Zivilprozeßrecht. Kommentar zum EuGVÜ und Lugano Übereinkommen*, 6th edn. (Verlag Recht und Wirtschaft 1998) p. 213 et seq.; M. VIRGÒS SORIANO, F. GARCIMARTÌN ALFÈREZ, *Derecho procesal civil internacional – Litigaciòn internacional* (Civitas 2000) p. 188.

considered in this respect risky. It was feared that foreign judges either could have ended up applying a different company law on the basis of their own conflict-of-law rules, or could have wrongly applied/interpreted the foreign law of incorporation, being influenced in its construction by the domestic company law with which they presumably were more familiar. These considerations cannot be extended *pari passu* to arbitrators, though.[8] Arbitrators, in particular when sitting in international tribunals, are not, and should not behave as if they were, organs of any State, including the State where their arbitration is seated. As such, they are not bound by the private international law of any given State. They are also accustomed to applying laws of jurisdictions other than the one in which they have qualified without being influenced by the peculiarities of their legal culture of origin. No wonder, then, that in some EU Member States the provision of Art. 24, no. 2, of the Brussels I-*bis* Regulation providing for the exclusive jurisdiction on certain corporate disputes lives well together with other provisions that expressly admit their arbitrability.[9]

Moreover, general prohibitions to settle corporate disputes by arbitration would run counter to the *favor arbitratus* which inspires the New York Convention,[10] justifying a restrictive interpretation of those treaty provisions which allow the contracting States not to enforce arbitration agreements or awards when their subject-matter is not arbitrable.[11]

IV. PROBLEMS RAISED BY THE ARBITRATION OF CORPORATE DISPUTES

Statutes and case-law of some jurisdictions evidence that the arbitration of corporate disputes poses special problems, leading to deviations from the regime which governs, in general, the arbitration of commercial disputes. Spain[12] and Italy[13] have *ad hoc* arbitration laws. In Russia certain corporate disputes are arbitrable only by domestic arbitration.[14]

8. See P. SCHLOSSER, "Report on the Association of the Kingdom of Denmark, Ireland and the United Kingdom of Great Britain and Northern Ireland to the Convention on jurisdiction and the enforcement of judgments in civil and commercial matters and to the Protocol on its interpretation by the Court of Justice", in E.C.O.J., C 59, 1971, at Sect. 63(a).
9. This is the case of Italy and Spain: see fn. 12 and fn. 13 below.
10. See, inter alia, N. BLACKABY, C. PARTASIDES, A. REDFERN, M. HUNTER, *Redfern and Hunter on International Commercial Arbitration*, 5th edn. (Oxford Univ. Press 2009) Sects. 11.37, 11.61, 11.107.
11. New York Convention, Arts. II(2)(3) and V(2)(*a*).
12. Arts. 11-*bis* and 11-*ter* of Law 23 December 2003 no. 60, as amended by Law 20 May 2011 no. 11, (Spanish Law no. 2003/60), on which see CLUB ESPAÑOL DE ARBITRAJE, *Informe sobre el arbitraje societario en España* (2013), available at <www.clubarbitraje.com/sites/default/files/cea_Arbitraje_Societario_1.pdf> (last accessed 24 May 2018); I. ARROYO, "*El arbitraje en el derecho societario español*", XXVII Rivista dell'arbitrato (2017) p. 283.
13. Arts. 34-36 of Legislative Decree 17 January 2003, no. 5 ("Italian Legislative Decree no. 2003/5").
14. This results from the reform of Russian arbitration law enacted with Laws 29 December 2015, no. 382-FZ and no. 409-FZ, in particular from new Art. 225(1)(3) of the *Arbitrazh* Procedure Code: see Freshfields Bruckhaus Deringer, "Russian M&A Deals in the Context of the Arbitration Reform: Practical Guidance", available at <http://knowledge.freshfields.

The Supreme Courts of Germany[15] and Austria[16] have set out conditions that need to be satisfied when the arbitration deals with resolutions of a company's shareholders' meeting or other matters which also require the relief to be enforceable vis-à-vis the company. In Brazil companies can be admitted to listing in a certain regulated market only if their by-laws provide for arbitration[17] and commentators have long discussed whether arbitration clauses inserted in the by-laws by a majority resolution can bind

---

com/en/Global/r/3641/russian_arbitration_reform___first_results_and_outstanding> (last accessed 24 May 2018). See also High Court, *Maximov v OJSC Novolipetsky Metallurgichesky Kombinat* [2017] EWHC 1911 (Comm), refusing enforcement in England of an award which had been annulled in Russia on the ground, inter alia, of non-arbitrability of corporate disputes.

15. Bundesgerichtshof, 6 April 2009, no. II ZR 255/08, (reversing 29 March 1996, no. II ZR 124/95) and 6 April 2017, no. I ZB 23/16, holding that disputes concerning resolutions of shareholders' meeting of German companies incorporated in the form of a limited liability company or of a limited partnership, as well as disputes between partners of a German partnership, can be submitted to arbitration only if the following conditions are satisfied: (i) the consent of all shareholders to arbitrate results from the fact that an arbitration agreement is set out in the company's by-laws or in a shareholders' agreement (executed also by the company); (ii) all shareholders and other stakeholders such as members of the corporate bodies (a) are informed about the existence of the dispute and the development of the proceedings, (b) are entitled to participate in the appointment of the members of the arbitral tribunal unless all members are appointed by an independent institution, and (c) are entitled to join the arbitral proceedings; (iii) the consolidation of arbitral proceedings having the same subject-matter is possible. On this case-law see N. SCHMID-AHRENDTS, A. COVI, "Arbitrability of Corporate Disputes: A German Perspective", 4 International Commercial Arbitration Review (2014) p. 116. In order to allow arbitral proceedings to comply with these requirements the German Arbitration Institute (DIS) has enacted special rules for corporate law disputes ("DIS Supplementary Rules", in force from 15 September 2009; a slightly amended version of such rules is also attached as Annex 5 to the DIS Arbitration Rules in force from 1 March 2018). For a commentary of the DIS Supplementary Rules see C. BORRIS, "Collective Arbitration: The European Experience – Germany and the DIS Supplementary Rules for Corporate Law Disputes (DIS-SRCoLD)" in B. HANOTIAU, E.A. SCHWARTZ, eds., *Class and Group Actions in Arbitration* (ICC Institute of World Business Law 2016) p. 80 et seq.
16. Oberster Gerichtshof, 22 October 2010, no. 7 Ob 103/10p, holding that when the relief requested is intended to produce effects over the company or the disputed relationship is characterized by *litisconsortium* corporate disputes can be arbitrated only upon the condition that (i) all shareholders have agreed to refer the matter to arbitration, and (ii) all shareholders and the company are entitled to intervene in the arbitral proceedings. See C. LIEBSCHER, "Arbitration and Company Law in Austria", 12 European Company Law (2015) p. 128.
17. See Art. 39 of the Rules governing the *Novo Mercado*, a market of financial instruments managed by *Bovespa*, the Sao Paulo stock exchange (available at <www.bmfbovespa.com.br/en_us/listing/equities/listing-segments/novo-mercado/>, last accessed 24 May 2018). The submission to arbitration of corporate disputes is admitted, in principle, by Brazilian company law: see Arts. 109.3 and 136.A of Law 15 December 1976, no. 6404, as amended. See D. DE ANDRADE LEVY, "*Aspectos Polêmicos da Arbitragem no Mercado de Capitais*", VII Revista Brasileira de Arbitragem (2010, no. 27) p. 7. For a decision of a US federal district court declining jurisdiction and referring the parties to arbitration over a class action filed by shareholders of a Brazilian company listed both in the Bovespa and (through ADRs) in the New York Stock Exchange see *In re Petrobras Securities Litigation*, 2015 WL 4557364 (S.D.N.Y. 2015).

dissenting or new shareholders.[18] In other countries it is debated whether corporate disputes are at all arbitrable and, if so, if special rules are needed.[19]

Looking at the experience of these jurisdictions may help to detect which specific problems the arbitration of corporate disputes raises, even when the applicable laws are silent and gaps need to be filled.

First, corporate disputes may pose problems with respect to the jurisdiction of the arbitral tribunal, in terms of subject-matter arbitrability, admissibility and extension of the arbitration agreement to non-signatory parties.

As noted, it would be wrong to consider *all* disputes relating to the formation, operations and winding-up of a company not arbitrable, in principle and a priori. This does not exclude, however, that the applicable law may provide that some corporate

18. For opposing views see M. CARVALHOSA, *Comentàrios à la lei de sociedades anònimas*, 4th edn. (Sariava 2008) p. 308 and D. De ANDRADE LEVY, "*Aspectos Polêmicos da Arbitragem*", fn. 17 above, at p. 26 et seq.
19. On the debate in the United States as to whether "derivative actions" by shareholders against company's directors for breach of their "fiduciary duties" can be submitted to arbitration see for conflicting views P. HERZFELD, "Prudent Anticipation? The Arbitration of Public Company Shareholders Disputes", 24 Arbitration International (2008) p. 312 and A. LIPTON, "Manufactured Consent: The Problem of Arbitration Clauses in Corporate Charters and Bylaws", 104 Georgetown Law Journal (2016) p. 583. On the arbitrability of corporate disputes in Belgium, England, France, the Netherlands, Sweden, Central/Eastern Europe jurisdictions, Singapore and India see, respectively: D. VAN GERVEN, M. BERLINGIN, "Arbitration and Company Law in Belgium", 12 European Company Law (2015) p. 132 and O. CAPRASSE, *Les sociétés et l'arbitrage* (Brylant 2002); J. CARTER, S. PAYTON, "Arbitration and Company Law in England and Wales", 12 European Company Law (2015) p. 138 and Court of Appeal, *Fulham Football Club (1987) Ltd. v. Richards*, [2012] 1 All ER (Com) 1148 (holding that corporate disputes are arbitrable as long as, also in light of the relief requested, they do not engage the rights of creditors or impinge on any statutory safeguards imposed for the benefit of third parties); T.A. BRABANT, M. DEPLATS, S. SALEM, "Arbitration and Company Law in France", 12 European Company Law (2015) p. 144, D. COHEN, *Arbitrage et Société* (L.G.D.J. 1993) and Cour d'Appel de Paris, 20 January 2015, *Coralsa Corporation Alimentaria S.A. c. Société Ingelco* n. 12/16039; H. DE MOL VAN OTTERLOO, "Arbitration and Company Law in the Netherlands", 12 European Company Law (2015) p. 160 and Hoge Raad der Nederlanden, 10 November 2006, *Groenselect*, R05/063HR; K. LÖF, A. STEEN, "Arbitration and Company Law in Sweden", 12 European Company Law (2015) p. 166 and Svea Court of Appeal, *Folgerö v. Isaksson, Lummi and Strandbacke*, Case Ö 2116-03; E. VERESS, ed., *Arbitrability of Company Law Disputes in Central and Eastern Europe* (Forum Iuris 2018); Singapore Court of Appeal, 26 October 2015, *Tomolugen Holdings v. Silica Investors*, [2015] SGCA 57 and 9 January 2017, *L Capital Jones Ltd. v. Maniach Pte Ltd*, [2017] SGCAS 03, holding that an oppression claim by a minority shareholder is arbitrable; Bombay High Court, 20 August 2014, *Rakesh Kumar Malhotra v. Rajinder Kumar Malhotra*, reported in <http://arbitrationblog.kluwerarbitration.com/2016/06/16/a-false-start-uncertainty-in-the-determination-of-arbitrability-in-india/> (last accessed 24 May 2018) with a comment by A. KURLEKAR, holding that claims by a shareholder against the companies' directors for oppression and mismanagement are not arbitrable. See also Arts. 147-149 of the Uniform Act on Commercial Companies and the Economic Interest Group, adopted on 30 January 2014 by the Organization for the Harmonization of Business Law in Africa, allowing the submission to arbitration of "any dispute among members or among one or more member(s) and the company".

disputes may not be settled via arbitration[20] or, more likely, that they may be settled via arbitration but only if certain conditions are complied with.[21]

The rationale for such special treatment may be twofold. Corporate disputes often impinge on the interests of wider categories of stakeholders (shareholders, creditors, the company, members of the corporate bodies, investors, the company's employees) other than the parties to the dispute at bar. This is certainly the case when the claimant challenges the existence, validity or effectiveness of a resolution of a corporate body by reference to the applicable company law or the existence, validity or effectiveness of a transfer of shares by reference to limitations set out in the company's by-laws, particularly if the relief requested is a declaratory or constitutive decision, rather than damages. It may also be the case when a claim is raised against the company's directors

20. See DIS Supplementary Rules, Preamble, stating that according to the prevailing view arbitration agreements cannot be validly inserted in the by-laws of a German stock corporation (*Aktiengesellschaft*) whose shares are listed on a stock exchange, being unclear whether the same prohibition applies also to "small" stock corporations having a limited number of shareholders and not being listed in a capital market. See CLUB ESPAÑOL DE ARBITRAJE, *Informe*, fn. 12 above, Sects. 20, 22 clarifying that the regulation of corporate disputes set out in Spanish Law no. 2003/60 applies only to corporations (including corporations whose shares are listed on a regulated market), i.e. companies incorporated under Spanish law in the form of *sociedades anònimas*, *limitadas* and *comanditarias por acciones* (*contra* I. ARROYO, "*El arbitraje en el derecho societario español*", fn. 12 above, at pp. 287, 297, arguing that also corporate disputes relating to partnerships, such as a *sociedad colectiva* and a *sociedad en comandita*, can be submitted to arbitration, and recalling that a pending proposal for the reform of Spanish company law expressly excludes the arbitrability of corporate disputes involving listed companies). See Art. 225(1)(2) of the Russian Arbitrazh Procedure Code, referred to at fn. 14 above, providing that disputes concerning Russian "strategic" companies (within the meaning of Federal Law no. 57-IZ of 29 April 2008) are not arbitrable. See Arts. 34.1, 34.4 and 34.5 of Italian Legislative Decree no. 2003/5, according to which the by-laws of companies incorporated under Italian law can contain arbitration agreements devolving to arbitration disputes between shareholders, or between shareholders and the company, or between members of the company's administration and control bodies and the company or the company's shareholders, provided that (i) the company's shares are not listed in a capital market or are otherwise owned in a relevant measure by retail investors, (ii) the subject-matter of the dispute is a disposable right relating to the corporate relationship (as is not the case for disputes on resolutions of the shareholders' meeting which approve the company's financial statements: see, inter alia, Corte di Cassazione, 20 August 2015, no. 17283) and (iii) the dispute is not one where the intervention of the public prosecutor is mandatorily required.

21. See DIS Supplementary Rules, Sect. 2, fn. 1, stating that failure to comply with the provisions on the joinder of shareholders to the proceedings affect the arbitrability of the dispute as a matter of German law. See CLUB ESPAÑOL DE ARBITRAJE, *Informe*, fn. 12 above, Sects. 39-45, clarifying that the provisions of Art. 11-*bis*.3 of Spanish Law no. 2003/60, which regulate the constitution of the arbitral tribunal and the organization of the proceedings when the dispute relates to a shareholders' meeting resolution, are mandatory, so that the parties would not be entitled to submit such disputes to arbitration pursuant to different rules (unless the parties agree on such alternative rules after the dispute has arisen). See M.V. BENEDETTELLI, "*Sull'arbitrato societario 'internazionale'*", fn. 1 above, at p. 320, holding that the mandatory rules set out by Arts. 34.2, 35 and 36 of Italian Legislative Decree no. 2003/5 (regulating the constitution of the arbitral tribunal, the organization of the proceedings, the law applicable to the merits, the remedies against the award) should be construed as conditions to the arbitrability of corporate disputes involving Italian companies.

for breach of their "fiduciary" or other duties by the company or by shareholders exercising a "derivative action".

Moreover, the settlement of a corporate dispute may require the interpretation of rules of the applicable company law for solving issues which the relevant State of incorporation may wish to be correctly adjudicated. This may justify a stricter control of the awards to avoid that errors in law can "spread" around, due to the force of precedent that may attach to any adjudicatory decision even when rendered by arbitral tribunals.

Such "conditional arbitrability" of corporate disputes may take different forms. It may require that the seat of the arbitration be placed in the State of incorporation of the relevant company under the assumption that the State of incorporation would then be in a better position to ensure that the proceedings are conducted consistently with the interests that it deems worthy of protection.[22] This solution, however, results in an almost absolute prohibition to submit corporate disputes to international arbitration, which may not satisfy the needs of international business, and may be also at odds with the State's undertakings under the New York Convention, if a pro-arbitration construction of Art. II is maintained. An alternative, and more arbitration-friendly, solution may be that of allowing corporate disputes to be arbitrated in a State other than the State of incorporation, but to require that the proceedings are carried out in compliance with special rules, so that the peculiarities of corporate disputes are duly taken into account.[23]

Corporate disputes may also justify *ad hoc* admissibility requirements. In particular, when the dispute potentially affects subjects other than the parties, it may be provided that the arbitral tribunal should not proceed unless evidence is given that the request for arbitration has been made known to the public at large or has otherwise been communicated to such other subjects (e.g., by serving them, or the company, with a copy of the request[24] or by recording its existence with the competent companies' register[25] or by giving public notice of the request through the means used for mass-claims litigations). This to ensure that all such subjects may protect their interests with any instrument (e.g., joinder as an additional party or as an intervenor, *tierce-opposition*) which the applicable law grants them for such purpose.

Arbitration agreements for the settlement of corporate disputes may be deemed to bind also non-signatory parties. This may be the case when the arbitration agreement is

22. E.g., this is what happens under Russian law, with the result that certain corporate disputes involving Russian companies cannot be settled through international arbitration: see fn. 14 above.
23. E.g., this is what happens under Italian law: while the already mentioned provisions of Arts. 34.2, 35 and 36 of Italian Legislative Decree no. 2003/5 regulating the arbitration of corporate disputes involving Italian companies are mandatory, nowhere does Italian law forbid such arbitrations to be seated abroad (see M.V. BENEDETTELLI, "*Sull'arbitrato societario 'internazionale'*", fn. 1, at p. 316).
24. See DIS Supplementary Rules, Sects. 2.1. and 2.2, providing that when the dispute requires a single decision binding all shareholders and the company, the claimant who wishes to extend the effects of the award to such parties without naming them as respondents must identify them in the statement of claim giving their address so that they can be served by the arbitral institution, and Sect. 5.1, providing that if such parties elect not to join the proceedings the arbitral tribunal must keep them informed of any development by delivering them a copy of written pleadings, procedural orders and decisions.
25. E.g., this is required by Art. 35.1 of Italian Legislative Decree no. 2003/5.

contained in the by-laws of the company so that it may be considered one of the rules which govern the company's organization with *erga omnes* effects, and its acceptance may be deemed implied when someone acquires shares of the company or accepts to serve as a company's officer.[26] It may also be the case when the arbitration agreement is embodied in a compromissory clause and the contract (shareholders' agreement, investment agreement) has been executed also by the company with the intention of becoming a party to it.[27]

Second, special procedural rules may be required for the arbitration of corporate disputes. This may be the case with regard to the modalities for the constitution of the arbitral tribunal.[28] Even when the dispute is only between two parties, or multiple parties who represent two groups of opposed interests, the fact that the award may produce effects on subjects other than those which are eventually litigating may justify restrictions on the parties' freedom to form the arbitral tribunal through the "classic" mechanism whereby each party appoints one arbitrator and may rather require that all members of the arbitral tribunal be selected by an independent institution.

The need to protect subjects other than the claimant(s) and the respondent(s) whose interests may be affected by the award may also justify their joinder in the pending arbitral proceedings as additional parties or as intervenors[29] and rules aimed to ensure

---

26. See CLUB ESPAÑOL DE ARBITRAJE, *Informe*, fn. 12 above, Sects. 21-22, 69-70, confirming that arbitration agreements set out in the by-laws of the company bind all the shareholders, including those that have acquired shares after the arbitration agreement was inserted in the by-laws and those who have voted against the relevant resolution, and I. ARROYO, *El arbitraje en el derecho societario español*, fn. 12 above, at p. 289, holding that such agreements bind also the company's directors. See Italian Legislative Decree no. 2003/5, Art. 34.3 and Art. 35.5, providing, respectively, that the arbitration clause set out in the company's by-laws binds the company and all the shareholders and that the award binds also the company.
27. A company may execute a shareholders' agreement between two or more of its shareholders for different reasons: for the sole purpose of acknowledging the existence of the shareholders' agreement, so that any future cooperation by the company's directors to breaches committed by one shareholder will not be deemed innocent, entitling the non-defaulting shareholder to claim for damages; in order to make any right that the shareholders have assumed to the company's benefit irrevocable; for becoming a party to the shareholders' agreement (as long as this is possible under the applicable company law) so that it directly assumes rights and obligations towards the shareholders. These different scenarios trigger different effects as to whether an arbitration agreement contained in the shareholders' agreement binds, or can be "extended" to, the company: see M.V. BENEDETTELLI, *Patti parasociali ed arbitrato estero*, fn. 1 above, at p. 631.
28. See Spanish Law no. 2003/60, Art. 11-*bis*.3, providing that when the dispute concerns the challenge of a resolution of the shareholders' meeting all members of the arbitral tribunal must be appointed by an arbitral institution, which must also be in charge of the administration of the proceedings, and CLUB ESPAÑOL DE ARBITRAJE, *Informe*, fn. 12 above, Sect. 38, recommending that this provision be used for all types of corporate disputes. See Italian Legislative Decree no. 2003/5, Art. 34.2, providing that an arbitration clause set out in the by-laws of a company is null and void if it fails to provide that all members of the arbitral tribunal must be appointed by a subject who has no ties with the company. In an unpublished award (referred to in M.V. BENEDETTELLI, "*Sull'arbitrato societario 'internazionale'*", fn. 1 above, at p. 315) an arbitral tribunal seated in Switzerland has found such provision not to be inconsistent with the ICC Rules.
29. See DIS Supplementary Rules, Sects. 3.1 and 4, clarifying that other shareholders and the company which have not been originally named as respondents may join the proceedings, at their choice, on claimant's or on respondent's side, either as a party or as a compulsory intervener,

that their right to take part in the proceedings is effective, particularly when they are numerous and cannot individually afford the costs of a litigation.[30] The likelihood that the same or connected issues are the subject of concurrent arbitral proceedings (as may happen when a corporate resolution is challenged) may require rules on consolidation.[31]

Similar reasons may lead to the enactment of rules mandating that, by departing from the confidentiality that often accompanies arbitration, awards rendered on corporate disputes be published[32] or made otherwise known to interested third parties through the same means that can be used for informing them about the existence of a request for arbitration, so that such third parties can have recourse to any instrument which the applicable law grants them for challenging the validity of the award or for resisting its enforcement. Such rules may also be justified by the interest that the State of incorporation may have in ensuring transparency for decisions on company law issues so that a consistent body of precedents can be created and made known to market operators.[33]

Moreover, the subject-matter of the dispute may justify that the arbitral tribunal be empowered to grant interim measures of a special kind, e.g., the suspension of resolutions of the shareholders' meeting,[34] the appointment of *ad hoc* administrators, the issuance of injunctions addressed to shareholders or directors.

Third, as to the rules applicable to the merits the arbitral tribunal may be required to adjudicate any company law issue arising in the arbitration, including when it arises as an

---

within the meaning of Sect. 69 of the German Code of Civil Procedure when they are going to be bound by the award. See CLUB ESPAÑOL DE ARBITRAJE, *Informe*, fn. 12 above, Sect. 86, stating that in the field of corporate disputes it is "*imprescindible regular la intervenciòn de un tercero*" either as co-claimant or as co-respondent. See Italian Legislative Decree no. 2003/5, Art. 35.2, providing that third parties can join the proceedings as interveners either on a voluntary basis, or, if they are shareholders, upon request of a party or by order of the arbitral tribunal pursuant to, respectively, Arts. 105, 106 and 107 of the Italian Code of Civil Procedure.

30. The failure to give to third parties the opportunity to join the arbitral proceedings when under applicable law the award is able to affect their interests could be deemed a ground for refusing recognition of the award under an extensive interpretation of Art. V(1)(*b*) of the New York Convention.

31. See DIS Supplementary Rules, Sect. 9, requiring consolidation before the arbitral tribunal first seized of multiple proceedings when the subject-matter of the dispute requires a single decision. See CLUB ESPAÑOL DE ARBITRAJE, *Informe*, fn. 12 above, Sect. 86, pointing out that when institutions administer the arbitration of corporate disputes it is "*imprescindible ampliar el campo de la acumulacion*" of proceedings dealing with the same dispute.

32. See Italian Legislative Decree no. 2003/5, Art. 35.5-*bis*, providing that when the subject-matter of the dispute is the validity of resolutions of the shareholders' meeting the tribunal's orders which suspend the effectiveness of the challenged resolution and awards deciding on the merits must be filed by the company's directors with the companies' register. See also Spanish Law no. 2003/60, Art. 11-*ter*, mandating that awards which annul resolutions of the shareholders' meeting must be recorded in the *Registro Mercantil*.

33. See CLUB ESPAÑOL DE ARBITRAJE, *Informe*, fn. 12 above, Sects. 52-56.

34. See Italian Legislative Decree no. 2003/5, Art. 35.5. This provision is remarkable since it embodies an exception to the general rule of Art. 818 of the Italian Code of Civil Procedure whereby arbitral tribunals are not empowered to grant interim relief. Also under Spanish law arbitral tribunals are entitled to order the suspension of resolutions of shareholders' meeting, through an award if the decision has to be registered in the *Registro Mercantil*: see CLUB ESPAÑOL DE ARBITRAJE, *Informe*, fn. 12 above, Sects. 95-96.

incidental question only, on the basis of the *lex societatis* of the State of incorporation, or, to say it otherwise, the arbitral tribunal may be prohibited from adjudicating such issues ex aequo et bono, or by reference to laws of other States.[35]

Fourth, special rules may apply to the award. Such rules may relate to its effects, since there may be circumstances in which the award binds not only the claimant(s) and the respondent(s), or other parties to the arbitration agreement who have elected not to participate in the arbitration, but also third parties (other shareholders, members of the company's administrative bodies), particularly if under applicable law they were informed of the request for arbitration and entitled to join the proceedings.[36]

A special regime may be contemplated also with regard to the means for challenging the award. The importance that the State of incorporation may give to a proper interpretation and application of its company law may justify that the parties are granted the non-waivable right to request the setting-aside of the award,[37] also for errors in law.[38] Furthermore, the impact that the award may have on subjects other than those which were parties to the dispute may justify granting them the power to react to the award by making use of special instruments (e.g., *tierce opposition*) which some legal systems devise for the purpose of protecting third parties from the indirect/"reflex" effects that an award may have on them.[39]

---

35. See CLUB ESPAÑOL DE ARBITRAJE, *Informe*, fn. 12 above, Sects. 57-58, stating that while Art. 11-*bis* of Spanish Law no. 2003/60 does not exclude the possibility for the arbitral tribunal to decide ex aequo et bono the parties would be well advised to provide for the application by the arbitral tribunal of (Spanish) law since companies are "*creaciones de la ley y sus controversias tienen una naturaleza eminentemente juridica*". See Italian Legislative Decree no. 2003/5, Art. 36.1, providing that even if the arbitration clause authorizes the tribunal to decide ex aequo et bono the award must always decide on the basis of the applicable law when the subject-matter of the dispute is the validity of a resolution of a shareholders' meeting or when in order to reach its decision the tribunal needs to adjudicate (on an incidental basis) upon issues which are not arbitrable.
36. See DIS Supplementary Rules, preamble, and Sect. 11, providing that the effects of the award extend also to those shareholders which have been served with a copy of the statement of claim pursuant to Sect. 2.2, irrespective of whether they have made use of the right to join the proceedings. See CLUB ESPAÑOL DE ARBITRAJE, *Informe*, fn. 12 above, Sect. 81, clarifying that the award binds all shareholders, irrespective of whether they have taken part in the proceedings.
37. See Italian Legislative Decree no. 2003/5, Art. 35.3, providing that the remedies set out by Art. 829 of the Italian Code of Civil Procedure for setting the award aside are not waivable by the parties.
38. See Italian Legislative Decree no. 2003/5, Art. 36.1, providing that irrespective of any waiver contained in the arbitration clause, the award must always be challengeable for errors in law when the subject-matter of the dispute was the validity of a resolution of a shareholders' meeting or when in order to reach its decision the tribunal has adjudicated (on an incidental basis) upon issues which are not arbitrable. See also CLUB ESPAÑOL DE ARBITRAJE, *Informe*, fn. 12 above, Sect. 76, and I. ARROYO, "*El arbitraje en el derecho societario español*", fn. 12 above, at p. 291, noting that corporate disputes may trigger the application of mandatory rules or public policy principles of the company's law of incorporation which the arbitral tribunal will be obliged to enforce and the respect of which will be checked by Spanish courts in the context of annulment proceedings.
39. See Italian Legislative Decree no. 2003/5, Art. 35.3, providing that the award is always subject to the extraordinary means of challenge of *opposizione di terzo* and of *revocazione* pursuant, respectively, to Art. 395, nn. 1), 2) 3) and 6) and Art. 404 of the Italian Code of Civil Procedure.

V. COORDINATING THE DIFFERENT LAWS POTENTIALLY APPLICABLE TO THE ARBITRATION OF CORPORATE DISPUTES

In the context of international business transactions, corporate disputes may trigger the application of different laws, with the consequent need of coordinating the relevant legal systems.

This is certainly true concerning the law applicable to the merits. The settlement of these disputes may likely give rise to issues of company law, to be decided in principal or incidentally, with the consequence that the arbitral tribunal will have to deal with the preliminary question of identifying the *lex societatis* which governs the relevant company. As is well known, States determine the scope of application of company law on the basis of the alternative theories of the "registered seat" and of the "real seat", with the risk that if a company has been formed in one jurisdiction but is de facto administered from another jurisdiction two different laws could claim to be the applicable law of incorporation.[40] Even when there is no doubt about the identity of the State of incorporation, company law rules of other States with which the company has important connections (a branch, a permanent establishment or other relevant links) could apply. Rules affecting the operations of the company may be laid down also by the State whose laws govern a financial market in which the company is active, and by the State where proceedings for the insolvency of the company have been opened.[41] Corporate disputes may also originate from contracts (shareholders' agreements, investment agreements) or other acts of party autonomy (take-over offers), the governing law of which may belong to a State different than the company's State of incorporation. Finally, corporate disputes may also result from tortious claims, leading to the application of a still different law based on the customary connecting factor of the place where the harmful event has occurred.

Different laws may also apply with specific regard to the regulation of the arbitration of corporate disputes. The State of incorporation may treat the settlement by arbitration of disputes relating to the formation, operations and winding-up of a company as a matter which impacts on the functioning of the company and therefore needs to be regulated through its company law. In the practice of international arbitration it may easily happen, though, that the State of incorporation of the company to which the corporate dispute at bar refers does not coincide with other States involved in the arbitration, namely the State where the parties want the arbitration to be seated, the State whose law governs the arbitration agreement, the State whose law the parties have chosen to regulate the procedural aspects of the arbitration, the State whose courts act as *juge d'appui* (in connection with the constitution of the arbitral tribunal, the instruction of the case, the granting of interim measures), the State where recognition and enforcement of the award is sought. The laws of all such States may provide rules addressing one or more of the problems which, as pointed out above, corporate disputes typically pose. The relevant regulations may differ, or even be contradictory with each

40. See M.V. BENEDETTELLI, "Five Lay Commandments for the European Private International Law of Companies", XVII Yearbook of Private International Law (2015/2016) p. 209, at p. 217 et seq.
41. *Ibid.*, at p. 224 et seq.

other, as would happen, for instance: if the *lex societatis* would provide for the non-arbitrability of a dispute that under the *lex arbitri* can be settled via arbitration or if the *lex societatis* would contemplate grounds for vacating the award that the *lex arbitri* ignores; or if the *lex societatis*, in contrast to the *lex arbitri* or to the *lex contractus* governing the arbitration agreement, would allow the "extension" of the arbitration agreement to the company or to other non-signatory stakeholders, and would require that such subjects are allowed to participate in the arbitral proceedings by procedural means which the *lex arbitri* does not contemplate; or if the law of the State where the award is enforced would not allow its recognition vis-à-vis third-party subjects that have not taken part in the arbitral proceedings, notwithstanding that the *lex societatis* or the *lex arbitri* admits that the award can produce such effects.

Thus, more than other kinds of commercial disputes, corporate disputes can generate conflict-of-laws situations, triggering the need to coordinate the relevant legal systems. Such coordination will be carried out in each State in accordance with its own private international rules, subject to limits stemming from international treaties. An important role in this respect will obviously be played by the New York Convention, with respect to matters for which it provides harmonized rules. The New York Convention can be indirectly relevant also for matters which it leaves unregulated (e.g., arbitrability) since also in this case the contracting States will have to exercise their legislative discretion having regard to the *favor arbitratus* which inspires the Convention, and their arbitration laws will have to be construed accordingly.

By contrast to State courts, arbitral tribunals, which have "no forum", will not be necessarily bound by a sole source of private international law and will rather resort to one of the different methods that the practice of international arbitration has developed to address conflict-of-laws issues. Whatever method they choose, arbitral tribunals will normally be guided by certain paramount values. They shall respect the will of the parties, since it is the parties' agreement that grounds their jurisdiction. They shall ensure predictability and legal certainty through the application of laws that the parties could have reasonably expected to become relevant in the settlement of their corporate disputes. They shall make any effort to secure the enforceability of their awards both in the State of the seat of the arbitration as well as in those other States where the parties have an actual interest in having them enforced. When determining the applicable law, arbitral tribunals may also wish to avoid lending themselves to fraudulent schemes that the parties may have set up, should they realize that the arbitration is instrumental to escaping from the reach of State overriding mandatory rules.

It is this author's opinion that all these values could be better protected if arbitral tribunals would handle conflict-of-laws issues which arise in the arbitration of corporate disputes by a *voie directe* reference both to the law of the State of incorporation of the relevant company and to the law of the State of the relevant arbitral seat. This cumulative application of two laws should take place by trying to combine their regulations to the largest extent possible, and, when this proves to be unworkable since the conflict of laws is "true", by giving precedence to the law of the State of incorporation.

The main reason which justifies this solution is that in this area two equally important dimensions of party autonomy overlap and may contradict each other: arbitration autonomy, i.e. the power to derogate to the jurisdiction of State courts by referring the dispute to private adjudicators, and corporate autonomy, i.e. the power to carry out entrepreneurial activities by making use of an organizational model devised by the company law of a given State. Were arbitral tribunals to solve the problems raised by the arbitration of corporate disputes by reference to the *lex arbitri* only, this would imply disrespect of another law, the *lex societatis*, that the same parties to the dispute have also chosen for regulating their relationships (as founders, shareholders, members of corporate bodies).

Indeed, arbitration autonomy and corporate autonomy stand, in principle, on an equal footing. When the *lex societatis* dictates rules which directly or indirectly deal with the settlement of corporate disputes, their consideration by the arbitral tribunal would be consistent with the parties' will, and certainly would not take the parties by surprise. This would be a necessity, if the arbitral tribunal has to render an enforceable award, when the type of relief sought[42] shows that the jurisdiction of the State of incorporation is the only one (or the main one) where the parties have an actual interest in having the award recognized and enforced. Considering the *lex societatis* may be proper also when no such interest exists, or there is even evidence that the parties wish to avoid any "contact" between their dispute and the State of incorporation (this could happen, e.g., when the claim arises out of a shareholders' agreement which the parties have stipulated with the intention of derogating from provisions of the *lex societatis* and the enforcement of which has been secured through collaterals over assets located outside the State of incorporation). Even in this scenario, in fact, the arbitral tribunals will have to look to the *lex societatis* in order to determine whether the interest pursued by the parties is legitimate or, rather, evidences a *fraude à la loi*, recourse to arbitration being just instrumental to the avoidance of overriding mandatory rules of the State of incorporation.

The suggested approach for managing conflict-of-laws issues in the context of the arbitration of corporate disputes imposes on the arbitral tribunal the task of finding the proper balance between potentially different regulations set out by the *lex arbitri* and by the *lex societatis*. This becomes easier if one correctly understands what arbitration autonomy and corporate autonomy really are. Such understanding may also justify the precedence that should be given to the *lex societatis* over the *lex arbitri* when conflicts between the two laws cannot be solved by means of interpretation.

VI. ARBITRATION AUTONOMY *VERSUS* CORPORATE AUTONOMY: REDUCING AND SOLVING CONFLICTS

Party autonomy is not just self-regulation of private interests. Party autonomy is self-regulation of private interests through norms. Thus, it requires a legal system, "external" to the parties, to which the parties can refer when the norms which they have agreed upon need to be enforced. In the practice of international business the parties mostly rely on State institutions to perform such function.

42. E.g., a declaratory judgment on the invalidity of a shareholders' meeting resolution or of a transfer of shares in breach of restrictions set out in the by-laws.

When protecting party autonomy through their institutions, however, States set out limits and conditions to the parties' power to self-regulate their interests so as to ensure that the exercise of such power does not jeopardize the public good. This obviously happens when the parties decide to set up a company, since the incorporation of a company takes place by reference to models of entrepreneurial organization devised by State law and with the cooperation of State bodies. It also happens when the parties decide to oust the jurisdiction of State courts by settling their disputes through private adjudication, since it is to State courts that the parties mostly and ultimately look when they need to enforce their arbitration agreements or awards that are pronounced on their basis.

Party autonomy is the blood which makes companies alive. If it is true that companies are "creatures of the law",[43] i.e. legal fictions through which States set out alternative organizational models for the carrying out of entrepreneurial activities, it is also true that their actual existence ultimately depends on the founders' and shareholders' will to make use of such legal instrument, as such will is expressed by the execution or adherence to the deed of incorporation, which is a contract. Other contracts surround the operations of the company and may impact on the company's capital structure and corporate governance, such as shareholders' agreements, investment agreements, contracts documenting transactions carried out on financial markets. Contracts may also be stipulated to regulate a company's winding-up.

In the field of company law, freedom of contract finds quite important limits and conditions, though. In fact, company law lays down special rules which deviate from the contract and tort law regime that would normally apply to the regulation of private relationships, in particular in areas such as the liability for one's own debts and agency.[44] Because of such special rules companies are a powerful instrument made available to those who own/control or manage the company for dealing with various categories of more or less "weak" counterparties (creditors, minority shareholders, employees, financial market participants, other stakeholders affected by the company's activity). Therefore, it does not come as a surprise that when granting the "privilege of incorporation" States lay down mandatory rules which become an essential component of their company law and provide mechanisms to ensure that such mandatory rules are duly complied with by their addressees, be they the company's founders, the shareholders or the directors.

States put limits and conditions also on party autonomy in arbitration. Arbitration is not just a mechanism for the settlement of disputes, arbitration is the settlement of disputes through adjudication. Indeed, arbitral tribunals are not asked to render whatever type of decision may settle the dispute, they are asked to decide on the basis of legal syllogisms, i.e. by applying rules to facts, at the end of adversarial proceedings and through measures that can have res judicata effects and be the ground for forced execution. No wonder, then, that when cooperating with the enforcement of arbitration agreements and awards States may wish to check that the ousting of the jurisdiction of courts and the conferral of adjudicatory powers to private bodies does not run counter to

43. See E.C.J., 27 September 1988, 81/87, *The Queen* ex parte *Daily Mail and General Trust Plc*, [1988] ECR I-5505, para. 19.

44. See M.V. BENEDETTELLI, "Five Lay Commandments", fn. 40 above, at p. 216.

any public interest. States do so by declaring certain matters non-arbitrable, by requiring that the arbitral proceedings comply with principles of fair trial and due process equal or similar to those applicable to court proceedings, by controlling that the awards are not at odds with their public policy or other rules the respect of which is intrinsic to the proper exercise of an adjudicatory function.

By inserting arbitration agreements in a company's deed of incorporation or by-laws, in a shareholders' agreement, in an investment agreement, or in any other contract related to the formation, operations or winding-up of the company, the parties interconnect the laws that govern the relevant company and the relevant arbitration. As mentioned, in the context of international business transactions such laws may belong to different legal systems and may provide for different or even contradictory rules on issues such as arbitrability, extension of the arbitration agreement to non-signatories, the conduct of the arbitral proceedings, effects of the award, means to challenge the award or to resist its enforcement. By contrast to other situations where conflicts of laws materialize, this is a peculiar one to the extent that the conflict is generated by two acts of party autonomy, the arbitration agreement and the corporate contract, both of which have been freely executed by the parties and represent the parties' will. This justifies an approach which, as mentioned, tries to combine the *lex arbitri* and the *lex societatis*, before determining which one trumps the other in case such "cumulative application" proves to be impossible.

Indeed, a proper and "smart" construction of the provisions of the *lex arbitri* and of the *lex societatis* regulating the arbitration of corporate disputes may show that their clash is only apparent. Different instruments can serve this purpose.

First, it has to be checked whether such provisions "want" to be applied in the circumstances. Even when broadly formulated, those set out by the *lex societatis* may apply only when the dispute is not limited to issues arising from the interpersonal relationship of the claimant(s) and the respondent(s) but affects the organization of the company and the interests of other subjects, whether directly or indirectly. For instance, the *lex societatis* may wish to regulate disputes on whether a shareholders' resolution is valid, or a shareholder has the right to attend and cast his/her vote in a shareholders' meeting, given that their outcome will have effects *erga omnes*, while it may be less concerned about the way damage claims for breaches of undertakings contained in a shareholders' or investment agreement are settled. Similarly, provisions of the *lex arbitri* may not intend to be applied to situations where the only link between the relevant jurisdiction and the dispute comes from the fact that such jurisdiction has been chosen to be the seat of the arbitration. For instance, provisions that would exclude the subject-matter arbitrability of corporate disputes or the parties' waiver to remedies against the award could be deemed not to apply, respectively, when the company is incorporated under a foreign law and when there is no other connection between the dispute and the State of the *lex arbitri* but for the seat.

Second, it must be checked whether the rules of the *lex arbitri* and of the *lex societatis* potentially in conflict are dispositive or mandatory, mandatory rules of the *lex societatis* having to prevail over dispositive rules of the *lex arbitri*, and vice versa. For such purpose both the arbitration agreement and the corporate contract will have to be interpreted on the basis of the hermeneutic principle *ut magis valeat*, i.e. by preferring among alternative constructions the one that allows both acts of party autonomy to be valid and effective under their governing law. In most contemporary jurisdictions both arbitration law and company law are to a large extent disposable, i.e. they can be derogated by the parties, or by their agents (arbitral institutions and arbitral tribunals, founders/shareholders and company's directors, respectively), in order to make them consistent with the parties' actual needs. Such derogations normally have to be expressly set out in the relevant contracts. It may well be, though, that when inserting an arbitration clause in a deed of incorporation or other corporate contract and when providing for an arbitral seat in a State different than the State of incorporation the parties may have not fully appreciated the complex conflict-of-laws problems to which such choices could lead. It is then legitimate to presume, failing any indication to the contrary, that the parties would have exercised all the powers granted to them by the applicable *lex arbitri* and *lex societatis* as far as necessary to ensure their coexistence and the effectiveness of both the arbitration agreement and the corporate contract.[45]

Third, the conflict between *lex arbitri* and *lex societatis* may be "false" when one set of rules still allows the achievement of the ultimate objectives pursued by the other set of (different) rules. Statutes are often drafted by taking a merely domestic perspective, i.e. without considering the possibility that the matter that is the object of regulation could end up being connected with other legal systems and therefore trigger a conflict-of-laws issue. Then, it does not necessarily go against the intentions of the legislator to hold that with respect to cross-border matters the strict application of rules of a given statute, even when mandatory, may leave room for the application of a foreign law, as long as such law performs the same function, though through different means. This technique for dealing with situations of (apparent) conflict-of-laws may found further justification when one is faced with different, but functionally equivalent, provisions of the *lex arbitri* and of the *lex societatis* and the relevant States have to honour their obligations under the New York Convention. The New York Convention, in fact, carries with it the duty to interpret the contracting parties' domestic law as far as possible in light of the treaty, of the *favor arbitratus* by which it is inspired, and of the contracting States' obligation to recognize, in principle, foreign arbitrations.

A few examples may clarify how the suggested approach could work.[46]

The *lex societatis* may mandatorily require that all the members of the arbitral tribunal be appointed by an independent institution, even when the dispute does not involve a plurality of parties, while the *lex arbitri* (or the arbitration rules to which the parties may have referred) may contemplate the "classic" default mechanism according to which each party appoints its own arbitrator and the arbitrators so appointed designate the president of the tribunal. If the arbitration clause set out in the corporate contract is silent on this issue, it will have to be interpreted in the sense that the (implied) will of the parties was

45. When the respondent does not challenge the arbitral tribunal's jurisdiction, i.e. when both parties want their dispute to be settled through an arbitration seated in a State other than the State of incorporation, such presumptions could be given stronger legitimacy if the parties were to expressly confirm, in the terms of reference or in an equivalent instrument, that this is indeed what they really wanted when the arbitration agreement was executed. In such a case the arbitral proceedings would start on more solid grounds, and the enforceability of the award also in the State of incorporation of the relevant company could be better secured.

46. See, *amplius*, M.V. BENEDETTELLI, "*Sull'arbitrato societario 'internazionale'*", fn. 1 above, at p. 321 et seq.

both to dispose of such default rule in order to comply with the *lex societatis* and to grant the power to appoint the members of the tribunal to the institution which under the law of the seat of the arbitration (or under the selected arbitration rules) performs such function.[47]

The *lex societatis* may attribute powers of *juge d'appui* to the court of the place where the company has its registered or its administrative seat, in connection with various matters such as the constitution of the arbitral tribunal, the monitoring of the independence and impartiality of the arbitrators, the gathering of evidence, the issuance of interim measures. Lacking any express indication to the contrary, provisions of this kind will have to be construed as mere rules on territorial venue, laid down on the implicit assumption that the arbitration is domestic, rather than as rules on international jurisdiction aimed to preclude the exercise of the relevant powers by foreign courts or arbitral tribunals and institutions.

The *lex societatis* may restrict the parties' freedom to choose the law or the rules applicable to the merits or to request the arbitral tribunal to adjudicate ex aequo et bono, by prescribing that corporate disputes must necessarily be decided by applying the law under which the company has been incorporated, whether in general or only when the dispute relates to specific issues of corporate law (e.g., validity of resolutions of corporate bodies). By contrast, the *lex arbitri* (or the arbitration rules) may provide that the arbitral tribunal must always comply with the mandate received from the parties and apply the law that they have chosen or adjudicate on equitable grounds if this is what the parties have agreed. It may also grant to the arbitral tribunal wide powers to select the law or the rules that it deems more proper in the circumstances when there is no parties' agreement on the point. When the arbitration clause in the corporate contract does not contain any agreement on the applicable law or rules, it will have to be construed as if it incorporates by reference the above-mentioned conflict-of-laws rule set out by the *lex societatis*. If it rather contains the agreement to apply a foreign law (i.e., the law of a State other than the State of incorporation) or mandates the arbitral tribunal to adjudicate ex aequo et bono, it will have to be construed as if such agreement was meant to cover only those disputes, if any, which under the *lex societatis* can be so decided (e.g., because the *lex societatis* characterizes them as contractual).

The *lex societatis* may protect third parties whose interests may be directly or indirectly affected by the dispute (other shareholders, the company, members of the corporate bodies, creditors) first by requiring that they be informed of any pending arbitration and of any award rendered at its outset. Whatever is the prescribed means of publicity (recording the request for arbitration and the award on the companies' register, individual service of process, notice by instruments used for mass claims) such publicity may run counter to provisions of the *lex arbitri* (or of the arbitration rules) aimed to secure the confidentiality of the arbitral proceedings. This conflict of regulations could be overcome, though, by construing the arbitration agreement as if it contained an implied waiver of the applicable provisions on confidentiality, which normally are disposable by the parties.

---

47. This solution has been followed in the unpublished Swiss ICC award referred to at fn. 28 above.

The *lex societatis* may secure the protection of third parties who are affected by the arbitration of corporate disputes also by granting them the right to join the proceedings or to seek the consolidation of concurrent proceedings, to apply for the setting aside of the award or to resist its enforcement. By so doing, the *lex societatis* may lay down *ad hoc* procedural rules or may refer to the regime which applies to commercial arbitration in general. It could be the case that the *lex arbitri* allows the joinder in pending arbitral proceedings or their consolidation, or that it contemplates instruments to challenge the award and its effect, though through procedures which do not coincide with those set out by the *lex societatis*. This difference in regulation should not be an obstacle to the application of the *lex arbitri* for the reasons given above: in this case the conflict-of-laws is "false", since provisions of the *lex societatis* which have been laid down on the assumption that the arbitration was domestic should leave room in cross-border situations for provisions of the applicable foreign law which, though different, are equivalent as to function and effects.

Moreover, some apparent clashes of regulation between *lex societatis* and *lex arbitri* may be overcome by an interpretation *in favor validitatis* of the arbitration agreement. In particular, if the *lex arbitri* permits the joinder only if there is the consent of all the parties of the pending arbitration and/or of the arbitral tribunal, such consent could be deemed given by the claimant(s) and respondent(s) when they have become parties to the arbitration agreement, and by the arbitrators when they have accepted their mandate to adjudicate the dispute, being aware that the company was governed by the relevant *lex societatis* and that the arbitration was governed by the relevant *lex arbitri*.

Finally, the *lex societatis* may prescribe that awards that have settled the corporate dispute by adjudicating on company law issues should always be challengeable on the ground of errors in the application of the law and that such remedy should not be waivable in advance by the parties. Should the *lex arbitri*, as it sometimes happens, provide for such remedy only if the parties have expressly consented to it in the arbitration agreement, such consent will have to be considered implicitly given pursuant to the already referred criterion which requires that all efforts be made to make the arbitration agreement valid also under the *lex societatis*. If, as will be the case for most jurisdictions, the vacation of an award for errors in law is simply not contemplated, then a possible solution to the conflict of laws could be found by checking if the *lex arbitri* allows the parties to waive their right to have the award set aside by the courts of the State of the seat. If this condition is satisfied, the *lex arbitri* could be construed in the sense that it allows not only such full waiver, but also the different and partial waiver that would occur if the parties agree that the jurisdiction on claims for setting the award aside should be conferred on the courts of a State other than the State of the seat. Then, an interpretation *in favor validitatis* of the arbitration clause set out in the corporate contract could be that the parties have accepted to grant jurisdiction on set-aside claims for errors in law to the courts of the State of incorporation of the relevant company.

Arbitral tribunals may resort to all these interpretative instruments in order to overcome apparent clashes between the *lex societatis* and the *lex arbitri* and to implement to the largest possible extent the parties' will, as reflected in the arbitration agreement and in the corporate contract. There may be situations, though, where the conflict-of-laws is "true" since the two laws which are potentially applicable provide for opposite regulations of the same issue. This may be the case, in particular, when the *lex societatis* contains a straightforward prohibition to settle by arbitration a certain class of corporate disputes which under the *lex arbitri* would be arbitrable or when the *lex societatis* makes such arbitrability conditional to procedural requirements which are incompatible with the *lex arbitri*.

In such situations the conflict of laws will have to be solved, in principle, in favour of the *lex societatis*, which will trump the *lex arbitri*. The reason is that the mandatory provisions of the *lex societatis* which give rise to the conflict will likely aim to protect the interests of those third parties which may be directly or indirectly affected by the corporate dispute, or the general interest of the State of incorporation to ensure that its company law is correctly interpreted and applied so as to ensure a level-playing field among all market participants. Obviously, such interests do not belong to the parties in dispute and cannot be disposed of through the mere execution of an arbitration agreement and by choosing to have the arbitration seated in a jurisdiction whose arbitration law is at odds with the law of incorporation. Indeed, arbitration agreements cannot bind subjects which are not privy to them, even less when the dispute arises or is connected to a legal instrument, i.e. the company, that the litigating parties themselves have freely accepted to use, thus accepting also to be bound by any rule of the law of incorporation which may prove to be incompatible with rules governing the arbitration under the *lex arbitri*.

VII. INTERNATIONAL ARBITRATION OF CORPORATE DISPUTES AS A TOOL FOR A "VIRTUOUS" FORUM AND LAW SHOPPING

In the era of globalization entrepreneurs often conduct regulatory arbitrages by selecting among different laws potentially applicable to their operations the one they believe best fits their needs. They do so when they choose the law under which their company is going to be incorporated by looking at the alternative types of company models which States "offer" in the "market of corporate charters". They may also choose the stock exchange where their shares are going to be listed or their financial transactions are carried out by considering the regulations which govern the relevant financial market. They may even try to have insolvency proceedings opened in the State whose insolvency courts and laws are preferred, particularly when their purpose is the restructuring rather than the liquidation of the debtor.[48]

Regulatory arbitrages may also underlie the selection of the method for the settlement of commercial disputes. When entering into choice-of-court agreements or choosing to file an application in one of the alternative fora that may have jurisdiction on the relevant claim, as well as when selecting the seat of the arbitration or the State in which to seek assistance for enforcing the arbitration agreement and the award, entrepreneurs consider (educated entrepreneurs should consider) also the "qualities" of the different judicial systems and procedural laws, and the impact that such systems and laws may prospectively have on the outcome of their dispute.[49]

---

48. See M.V. BENEDETTELLI, "Five Lay Commandments", fn. 40 above, at p. 246 et seq.
49. F. FERRARI, ed., *Forum Shopping in the International Commercial Arbitration Context* (Sellier European Law Publishers 2013).

It is debated whether regulatory arbitrages are a positive or negative phenomenon. In a free market perspective there is no reason why the law applicable to business should not be considered as a "commodity" that the entrepreneurs freely select, as they freely select other factors of the productive process, it being then up to the market to "price" such choice and ultimately assess whether or not the entrepreneurial calculus has been correct. It has been argued, however, that such a freedom would inevitably result in a "race to the bottom" as to the quality of the regulation of business, since entrepreneurs would inevitably prefer rules which are less restrictive. As a result, "regulatory lift-offs" would be allowed, jeopardizing the States' sovereign power to govern their economies and structure their markets consistent with what is required by the public good.[50]

This position suffers from a double misconception. It is obvious that entrepreneurs pursue their "egoistic" interests, but this does not mean that they will always and necessarily aim to escape the reach of State regulations or try to be governed by the lowest regulatory standards, also because consumers, lenders, authorities and other stakeholders may give value to the "regulatory profile" of their corporate counterparties. On the other hand, even when entrepreneurs do pursue "regulatory lift-offs", sooner or later there will be the need for a "jurisdictional touch-down" (e.g., when arbitration agreements or awards are not spontaneously complied with), so that the State where the relevant transaction or dispute finally "lands" will be able to check whether party autonomy has been properly exercised and to secure the implementation of its mandatory rules.[51]

Indeed, shopping for the best forum and for the best laws can be a "virtuous" exercise as long as the fundamental right of the parties to self-regulate their interests finds the correct balance with the fundamental right of the States to pursue the wealth of their national communities.

The submission of corporate disputes to international arbitration shows that this balancing exercise is possible.

There is no reason why entrepreneurs should be precluded from getting the benefits that normally attach to international arbitration when a dispute arises with respect to the formation, operations and winding-up of a company. This, however, should not put at risk the safeguards which the State of incorporation provides to the benefit of third parties with whom the company, its owners/controlling entities and its managers interact, or for the purpose of creating a level playing field in the market as to the interpretation and application of its company law. The real problem, then, is how to address potential conflicts that may arise between the *lex arbitri* and the *lex societatis* in the regulation of the settlement by arbitration of corporate disputes.

Arbitral tribunals may contribute to reducing such conflicts to the minimum and solving them on a rational and predictable basis if the method proposed in this article is followed. It requires them to reconcile apparently conflicting provisions of the *lex arbitri* and of the *lex societatis* as far as possible through the interpretation devices suggested above, and to grant priority to the *lex societatis* over the *lex arbitri* when the conflict is

50. See W. BRATTON, J. MCCAHERY, S. PICCIOTTO, C. SCOTT, eds., *International Regulatory Competition and Coordination* (Oxford Univ. Press 1996).

51. See R. WAI, "Transnational Liftoff and Juridical Touchdown: The Regulatory Function of Private International Law in an Era of Globalization", 40 Columbia J. Transn'l L. (2002) p. 209.

"true". Were this approach to be adopted, the problems that the settlement of corporate disputes by arbitration poses could find a solution. Arbitrating corporate disputes could then become a new frontier of international arbitration.

New Arbitration Frontiers: Climate Change

Annette Magnusson[*]

TABLE OF CONTENTS PAGE

> *"... this is the first time in history that we have to act on a threat collectively made to ourselves, to act on it at scale, to act before the full consequences are felt, and to act on behalf of a generation that has not yet been born – and to do it before all the planetary boundaries have been breached."*[1]

At the Mauritius ICCA Congress in 2016, UN Secretary General Ban Ki-Moon concluded his keynote address with the following words: "I ask all of you to use the great power of arbitration to help the world overcome conflict and hatred and build a future of dignity for all on a healthy planet."

Are we living up to the expectations reflected in the speech by the UN Secretary General? Are we using the full potential of international arbitration to address the challenge of climate change? If not, how can we increase our efforts to use international arbitration in the best possible way?

The purpose of this paper is to explore how international arbitration could contribute to a better world in the Anthropocene Age.[2] I hope it will inspire to act and to a part in the battle against climate change.

---

* Secretary General of the Arbitration Institute of the Stockholm Chamber of Commerce (SCC).The author wishes to acknowledge the invaluable assistance of Sukma Dwi Andrina in preparing this text, and is grateful for additional input from Anja Ipp and Alexey Vyalkov.

1. Thomas FRIEDMAN, *Thank You for Being Late: An Optimist's Guide to Thriving in the Age of Accelerations* (Farrar, Straus and Giroux 2016) p. 183.
2. "Humans are now the most significant driver of global change, propelling the planet into a new geological epoch, the Anthropocene." "The Stockholm Memorandum: Tipping the Scales Towards Sustainability", presented at the 3rd Nobel Laureate Symposium on Global Sustainability, 18 May 2011, available at <www.nobel-cause.de/stockholm-2011/download/Memorandum_EN.pdf>; Additional reading Andrew J. HOFFMAN, P. Deveraux JENNINGS, and Lianne M. LEFSRUD, "Climate Change in the Era of Anthropocene – An Institutional Analysis" (June 2015) available at <https://deepblue.lib.umich.edu/bitstream/handle/2027.42/111880/1280_Hoffman.pdf?sequence=1&isAllowed=y> (last accessed 20 June 2018).

I. THE STARTING POINT

Today we see a triumvirate of digitalization, globalization and climate change affecting societies all over the planet at an ever-increasing pace.[3] We see the consequences of these forces at work on many levels and in many arenas, be it global, regional or national.

International arbitration is already a fact of life in many arenas of global change. But could more be done to align the potential of international arbitration specifically with climate change targets? International arbitration adds force behind the words of international agreements. And it enjoys a uniquely strong international support. These are valuable features in the pursuit of efficient climate-change response tools.

1. How Climate Change Affects Society

To state that global warming is happening is no longer controversial. Nor is it controversial to state that human activities are a dominant cause.[4]

A warmer planet involves potentially dramatic consequences. In 2015 the Intergovernmental Panel on Climate Change (IPCC) reported that the warming of the climate system is unequivocal,[5] and that the global surface temperature is projected to rise over the twenty-first century under all emission scenarios assessed so far to date.[6]

The effects of climate change are not only about the weather. Socially destabilizing events directly or indirectly associated with climate change risks are already causing tremendous challenges. This is expected to increase.[7] In February 2018, the World Threat Assessment report from the US Intelligence Community concluded that climate change is likely to give rise to "economic and societal discontent – and possibly upheaval".[8] Water scarcity risks heightening tensions between countries, turning control of water supplies into a weapon of war. Extreme weather events compound with other

3. T. FRIEDMAN, *Thank You for Being Late: An Optimist's Guide to Thriving in the Age of Accelerations*, fn. 1 above, p. 156.
4. A report published in 2015 examined 69,406 peer-reviewed articles on global warming. Only 0.005 per cent of the authors rejected anthropogenic global warming, see James Lawrence POWELL, "Climate Scientists Virtually Unanimous: Anthropogenic Global Warming Is True", 35 Bulletin of Science, Technology and Society (2015, issue 5-6) available at <http://journals.sagepub.com/doi/10.1177/0270467616634958> (last accessed 20 June 2018).
5. IPCC, *Climate Change 2014: Synthesis Report. Contribution of Working Groups I, II and III to the Fifth Assessment Report of the Intergovernmental Panel on Climate Change* [Core Writing Team, R.K. PACHAURI and L.A. MEYER, eds. (IPCC, Geneva 2015) pp. 2-4 available at <http://ar5-syr.ipcc.ch/topic_summary.php> (last accessed 2 July 2018).
6. *Ibid.*, pp. 10-13.
7. T. FRIEDMAN, *Thank You for Being Late: An Optimist's Guide to Thriving in the Age of Accelerations*, fn. 1 above, p. 156; Nicholas STERN, *The Economics of Climate Change. The Stern Review* (Cambridge University Press 2007) pp. 119-123.
8. Daniel R. COATS, "Statement for the Record: Worldwide Threat Assessment of the US Intelligence Community", p. 16, available at <www.dni.gov/files/documents/Newsroom/Testimonies/2018-ATA---Unclassified-SSCI.pdf> (last accessed 11 June 2018).

drivers to cause humanitarian disasters, population migrations, water and food shortages and social disruption.[9]

Climate change impacts witnessed in recent years also include forced human migration and displacement as a consequence of rising sea levels and other weather events.[10] A recent report from the Intergovernmental Science-Policy Platform on Biodiversity and Ecosystem services (IPBES) concludes that 50-700 million people risk being forced to migrate in the next thirty years due to land degradation and climate change.[11] The 2014 International Bar Association (IBA) report *Achieving Justice and Human Rights in an Era of Climate Disruption* concludes that "both at the state and international level, climate change will create new pressures and challenges that will affect every region of the world".[12]

The need to cover the costs of climate change mitigation and adaptation is another societal consequence. Costs associated with the impact of climate change are in the order of trillions of US dollars, or several per cent of GDP.[13] Just in the period May 2013 – April 2014, it is estimated that governments spent US$ 92 billion as a consequence of floods, droughts and other disasters.[14]

2. *International Arbitration and Climate Change – An Odd Couple?*

International efforts to address climate change are conducted in an arena governed by political negotiations which at times resembles a battle of numbers for emissions targets and temperature caps. The battle includes potentially sensitive discussions about who is to blame, and who should pay. In this context, does international arbitration as an operational legal tool have any role to play?

At first sight, the answer appears to be – no. For example, a quick check of the index in the recently published treatise *International Climate Change Law*[15] reveals that arbitration is not part of the picture. Indeed, it is not even mentioned once. The result is similar in other texts on climate change and the law. Compliance with agreements in the climate change regime tends to rely on a measure of assurance to states that if they act, others

9. *Ibid.*, p. 16.
10. IBA Presidential Task Force on Climate Change Justice and Human Rights, *Achieving Climate Change Justice and Human Rights in an Era of Climate Disruption* (International Bar Association 2014) p. 42.
11. IPBES Secretariat, "Media Release (March 2018): Worsening Worldwide Land Degradation Now 'Critical', Undermining Well-Being of 3.2 Billion People", available at <www.ipbes.net/news/media-release-worsening-worldwide-land-degradation-now-%E2%80%98critical%E2%80%99-undermining-well-being-32> (last accessed 20 June 2018).
12. IBA Presidential Task Force on Climate Change Justice and Human Rights, *Achieving Climate Change Justice and Human Rights in an Era of Climate Disruption*, fn. 10 above, p. 43.
13. N. STERN, *The Economics of Climate Change. The Stern Review*, fn. 7 above, p. 264 and p. 471; Overview by Robert BLACKETT, "Ten Inconvenient Truths About Climate Change Tort Claims", The Arbiter (Spring 2018).
14. "Up in Smoke?" The Economist (26 November 2016) p. 53.
15. Daniel BODANSKY, Jutta BRUNEE, Lavanya RAJAMANI, *International Climate Change Law* (Oxford University Press 2017) p. 363.

will reciprocate.[16] It is this reliance that fosters implementation, not specific provisions on enforcement, including arbitration.

From a global governance perspective, this is not surprising. International law contains few examples of strong tools to secure both participation and compliance in efforts to resolve collective action issues.[17] A description which fits well with the climate change crisis: it is a long-term global issue requiring initiatives in concert. Efforts to tackle it have consistently relied on consensus rather than confrontation.[18] Peer pressure or public pressure are the practical mechanisms used to enforce agreed norms on climate change, not formal dispute resolution. Different tools for transparency are also the most commonly used mechanism for influencing state behaviour in the international environmental regime as a whole, including efforts to mitigate climate change.[19] Although some other treaties that target environmental issues do include language on state-to-state arbitration, these provisions, with the exception of the United Nations Convention on the Law of the Sea (UNCLOS), have rarely – if ever – been applied. [20]

In summary: details of enforcement have been left out of international instruments to achieve sufficient state participation towards global climate change goals. In the period leading up to the Paris Agreement in 2015, the then Executive Secretary of the UNFCC noted that any system agreed should be "collaborative rather than punitive". [21]

International arbitration, in contrast, ensures compliance with binding legal obligations, be they in a public or private context.

Against this background, it is tempting to conclude that arbitration is unlikely to be used to enforce international climate change law any time soon. Without an agreement to arbitrate, no arbitration is possible. And a scenario where states buy into an arbitration agreement under the climate change law regime is not very likely.

But the battle for climate change mitigation and adaptation is being played out in more than one arena, and this paper will try to demonstrate how international arbitration could still play an important role.

As we have seen, climate change is already having substantial effects on society. A large share of global disruption and conflict could be argued to include elements of climate change. In parallel, recognition that climate change is jeopardizing fundamental human rights is gaining momentum.[22]

Where climate change contributes to geopolitical conflicts, international arbitration can potentially make important contributions, as indeed it has done in the past.

---

16. *Ibid.*, p.3.
17. *Ibid.*
18. *Ibid.*, p. 26, p. 50.
19. *Ibid.*, p. 2, p. 242; also p. 16; Paris Agreement (opened for signature 22 April 2016, entered into force 4 November 2016), Art. 13 available at <https://unfccc.int/process-and-meetings/the-paris-agreement/the-paris-agreement> (last accessed 4 July 2018).
20. Examples of environmental disputes within the UNCLOS system include *The Mox Plant case* (*Ireland v. the United Kingdom*) and *The Chagos Archipelago case* (*Mauritius v. the United Kingdom*).
21. Alister DOYLE, "Enforcing a Global Climate Deal: Speak Loudly, Carry No Stick", Reuters Global Energy News (12 October 2015) available at <www.reuters.com/article/us-climatechange-summit-sanctions-insigh-idUSKCN0S506320151012> (last accessed 20 June 2018).
22. IBA Presidential Task Force on Climate Change Justice and Human Rights, *Achieving Climate Change Justice and Human Rights in an Era of Climate Disruption*, fn. 10 above, p. 41.

Arbitration can untie challenging geopolitical knots through use of the rule of law and diplomacy, as opposed to use of force. In the book *Arbitrating for Peace*,[23] published by the Stockholm Chamber of Commerce (SCC) on the occasion of the SCC Centennial in 2017, authors describe how arbitration has contributed to avoiding continued conflicts over the transfer of natural gas, the seal trade, civil war, and construction of a diplomatic mission – just to mention a few examples. There is no reason to believe that arbitration cannot continue to contribute in this way to human co-existence in the future as well.

3. *Climate Change and Human Rights*

The interconnection between climate change and human rights has been confirmed by international courts[24] and in international governmental bodies.[25] In 2014, the IBA published the comprehensive report *Achieving Justice and Human Rights in an Era of Climate Disruption*,[26] assessing the need to reform legal frameworks at national, regional and international level to protect human rights threatened by climate change. One of the report's key recommendations is the creation of a new international dispute resolution structure for climate change issues, and it encourages arbitral institutions "to take appropriate steps to develop rules and/or expertise specific to the resolution of environmental disputes".[27]

While recognizing the importance of the interconnection between climate change and human rights, it will not be specifically addressed in this paper.

4. *Along the New Frontier of Climate Change and Arbitration*

Existing and well-established legal instruments, the commercial activities necessary to reach climate change targets, and the viability of states' international obligations on climate change are some of the building blocks along the new frontier of international arbitration and climate change.

The public international law chapter in Sect. II describes international commitments for climate change mitigation and adaptation as laid down in the United Nations Framework Convention on Climate Change (UNFCCC) and the Paris Agreement, two of the main instruments of what has been referred to as the "relatively small body of international law" dealing with climate change.[28] As will be seen, they are not very

23. Ulf FRANKE, Annette MAGNUSSON, Joel DAHLQUIST, eds., *Arbitrating for Peace, How Arbitration Made a Difference* (Wolters Kluwer 2016).
24. Inter-American Court of Human Rights, Advisory Opinion OC 23/17, 15 November 2017, available at <https://aida-americas.org/sites/default/files/resources_files/resumen_seriea_23_eng%20%281%29.pdf> (last accessed 21 June 2018).
25. Report of the Office of the United Nations High Commissioner for Human Rights on the relationship between climate change and human rights, dated 15 January 2009, available at <https://documents-dds-ny.un.org/doc/UNDOC/GEN/G09/103/44/PDF/G0910344.pdf?OpenElement> (last accessed 21 June 2018).
26. IBA Presidential Task Force on Climate Change Justice and Human Rights, *Achieving Climate Change Justice and Human Rights in an Era of Climate Disruption*, fn. 10 above.
27. *Ibid.*, p. 14.
28. *Ibid.*, p. 44.

strong in language of enforcement, but a paper on climate change and dispute resolution would be incomplete without them. In addition, this Section will discuss new contexts or models for bilateral investment treaties (BITs).

Sect. III will address the commercial side. Foreign investments of relevance for climate change mitigation and adaptation will be decisive, and here international arbitration can contribute to vehicles for change.

And finally, there is the potential for cross-fertilization between established legal norms and procedures, and climate change mitigation and adaptation objectives. This area needs to be further explored to unleash the full force of the law to combat climate change, and is discussed further in Sect. IV.

II. PUBLIC INTERNATIONAL LAW

In the widely-discussed *The Economics of Climate Change*, economist Nicholas Stern points out that effective action on climate change "will require international frameworks that allow countries to establish mutual responsibilities across the full range of dimensions of action".[29]

The Stern report was published in 2007. Since then, awareness of the consequences of climate change has increased, the Paris Agreement negotiated and entered into force, and renewable energy is on the rise – just to mention a few examples of positive signs in the years since the report was first published.

But global ambitions to mitigate climate change still lack efficient enforcement mechanisms. Could international arbitration fill this gap?

1. *Dispute Resolution in International Climate Change Law Instruments*

There is a sentiment that international environmental law tends to under-achieve because enforcement is so difficult – there is simply no obvious court or jurisdiction to hear cases in the event of an alleged breach of an international environmental treaty.[30] Although a number of environmental treaties give states the option to accept the jurisdiction of the International Court of Justice (ICJ) or even arbitration, states' willingness to do so is low. The vague language of the obligations of international environmental law instruments also adds to the difficulty of enforcement.

All of this would explain why, historically, courts and tribunals in general appear to have played a modest role in the development of international environmental law.[31] And where international dispute settlement procedures do exist, they are considered weak

29. N. STERN, *The Economics of Climate Change. The Stern Review*, fn. 7 above, p. 643. The Stern Report has been widely debated but also criticized. See, among others, Robert O. MENDELSOHN, "A Critique of the Stern Report", available at <www.environment.research.yale.edu> (last accessed 19 June 2018). In Dieter HELM, *The Carbon Crunch* (Yale University Press 2012) p. 18, it was pointed out that the Stern Report has not been peer reviewed (however, it also noted that this does not necessarily translate into "a criticism of the content of the report itself").
30. Polly BOTSFORD, "Environmental Law Gets Radical", IBA Global Insight (October 2012).
31. D. BODANSKY, J. BRUNEE, L. RAJAMANI, *International Climate Change Law*, fn. 15 above, p. 283.

due to lack of compulsory jurisdiction or enforcement,[32] and so in practice fall short in reducing emissions.[33]

The same description also fits the UNFCCC and the Paris Agreement. The language in these texts is weak or incomplete as far as enforcement goes. However, this does not mean that these instruments do not matter. They do. The Paris Agreement in particular has been hailed as a great victory for the international community, a victory that communicates an important message about joint priorities.

But even if rightfully described as a breakthrough and a success, the Paris Agreement in isolation will not resolve the climate change crisis.[34] Although a strong manifestation of intent, it contains no strong tools to incentivize actual action on the ground.

The principal elements of the Paris Agreement are laid out below. But first, a brief introduction is needed to the framework convention under the auspices of which the Paris Agreement was negotiated.

a. United Nations Framework Convention on Climate Change (UNFCCC)

The United Nations Framework Convention on Climate Change (UNFCCC) was adopted on 9 May 1992 after negotiations initiated in 1990. It remains at the centre of the UN climate change regime, together with additional texts which have materialized as a result of the yearly Conference of the Parties (COP).[35] COP decisions can play – and have played – a significant role in carving out the details of the international climate regime.[36] The most widely-known COP results outside the immediate sphere of climate change expertise are probably the Kyoto Protocol (COP3) and the Paris Agreement (COP21).

The UNFCCC establishes a basis for future action. Although it contains few substantive obligations, its broad scope is presented through the Preamble and specific articles on Objective (Art. 2), and Principles (Art. 3). The Convention lays out commitments (Arts. 4-6), including mitigation, adaptation, financial support and technology transfer, an institutional framework (Arts. 7-11), and finally implementation and compliance mechanisms (Arts. 7.2 and 12-14). Following the traditional model of multilateral environmental agreements, implementation is primarily governed by transparency, in the UNFCCC regime, through a system of reporting on a country's performance under the Convention. However, the consequence of absence of reports – or "communication of information related to implementation" as the text of Art. 12 reads – is not addressed.

Art. 13 foresees a multilateral consultative process to resolve questions regarding implementation, and calls on the COP to carve out the details of the process at its first

32. *Ibid.*, p. 289.

33. *Ibid.*

34. *Ibid.*, p. 209. The United Nations Environment Program also noted that the Nationally Determined Contribution under the Paris Agreement only covers around one-third of emissions reductions needed by 2030. See UN Environment, *The Emission Gap Report 2017: A UN Environment Synthesis Report* (United Nations Environment Program, November 2017), pp. xiv and 1.

35. D. BODANSKY, J. BRUNEE, L. RAJAMANI, *International Climate Change Law*, fn. 15 above, p. 118.

36. *Ibid.*, pp.19-20.

session. Again, this issue has so far been left unaddressed by the COP, and no multilateral process has yet been established.[37]

Art. 14 of the UNFCCC contains provisions on dispute resolution. These primarily seek to have any "dispute between any two or more parties concerning the interpretation or application of the Convention" decided "through negotiation or any other peaceful means of their own choice". [38] Parties can also declare in advance that they accept the jurisdiction of the ICJ over disputes arising under the Convention.[39] So far, only 1 of the 197 parties[40] has declared that it accepts the jurisdiction of the ICJ.[41]

Art. 14 also enables parties to declare that they accept arbitration "in accordance with procedures to be adopted by the Conference of the Parties" in "an annex on arbitration".[42] Similarly, "additional procedures relating to conciliation" are foreseen to be added to the Convention by the COP in an annex.[43]

Procedures for arbitration or conciliation have not yet been addressed by a COP. The potential of arbitration to promote and support the work of the parties to the Paris Agreement was recently discussed at COP23 (2017). Together with the IBA, several arbitral institutions seized the opportunity in Bonn to raise awareness of the potential of dispute resolution in the field of climate change.[44] This initiative at the crossroads of international arbitration and climate change is expected to continue at future COPs.

The current state of affairs thus means that implementation and enforcement mechanisms under the UNFCCC are either absent or weak.[45] Joint decisions by states under the regime are for the most part not legally binding under international law, and it is left to each state to decide on implementation measures.[46] This may well lead to governments choosing later rather than sooner when faced with the dilemma of short-term political priorities prompting immediate decisions, decisions which may not necessarily be aligned with long-term and non-binding international obligations.

Voiced concern for the effectiveness of the climate change regime has long pointed towards the fact that there is "no truly effective mechanism to take states to task for

37. *Ibid.*, pp. 153-54.
38. United Nations Framework Convention on Climate Change (opened for signature 4 June 1992, entered into force 21 March 1994), 1771 UNTS 107, Art. 14.1.
39. *Ibid.*, Art. 14.2(a).
40. UNFCCC, "Status of Ratification of the Convention", available at <http://unfccc.int/essential_background/convention/status_of_ratification/items/2631.php> (as of 22 February 2018).
41. UNFCCC, "Declarations of Status of Ratification of the Convention", available at <http://unfccc.int/essential_background/convention/items/5410.php> (last accessed 21 June 2018).
42. United Nations Framework Convention on Climate Change, fn. 38 above, Art. 14.2(b).
43. *Ibid.*, Art. 14.7.
44. International Chamber of Commerce, "What Role for Dispute Resolution in Supporting the Paris Climate Agreement?", available at <https://iccwbo.org/media-wall/news-speeches/role-dispute-resolution-supporting-paris-climate-agreement/> (last accessed 22 June 2018).
45. D. HELM, *The Carbon Crunch*, fn. 29 above, p. 156; D. BODANSKY, J. BRUNEE, L. RAJAMANI, *International Climate Change Law*, fn. 15 above, p. 16.
46. Jorge E. VIÑUALES, *Foreign Investment and the Environment in International Law* (Cambridge University Press 2012) p. 274.

failure to comply"[47] and that the international community "is largely reliant on individual states to commit to honour the object and the purpose of an agreement and monitor compliance".[48]

But reliance on the goodwill of governments to ensure that targets are achieved is seen as inadequate.[49] One commentary summarizes the frustration in the following way: "Despite the fact that the Framework Convention is a binding treaty, that goal seems to be long gone, and it's a bit unclear whom you would sue if, say, your island nation is disappearing under the rising seas."[50]

b. Paris Agreement

The Paris Agreement was concluded in Paris on 12 December 2015 as a result of COP21, and formally as an agreement under the UNFCCC.[51] It has been welcomed and celebrated in numerous global arenas and in climate change contexts.

The Agreement entered into force on 4 November 2016, i.e. thirty days after the date on which at least fifty-five parties to the Agreement, accounting for at least an estimated 55 per cent of total global greenhouse gas emissions, deposited their instruments of ratification, approval or accession with the Depository.[52] As of 11 June 2018, the Paris Agreement has 197 Signatories and 178 Parties.[53]

The Paris Agreement seeks to progress climate change work through the use of nationally determined contributions (NDCs). The idea of NDCs is that each party reports its intended climate action for the purpose of reducing greenhouse gas (GHG) emissions. And in the work leading up to the Paris negotiations, parties were invited at COP19 in 2013 to prepare and submit intended nationally determined contributions (INDCs).[54]

The NDC provision in the mitigation section of the Paris Agreement (Art. 4) is characterized as "the most significant legal obligation" in the Agreement.[55] It could be said to represent a middle ground, i.e. it seeks to achieve concrete targets while simultaneously privileging sovereign autonomy. NDCs are to be prepared, communicated and maintained by signatory parties.[56] In addition, each party is to

47. Neil HODGE, "Acts or Emissions", IBA Global Insight (February 2012), citing Hans Corell, former Under-Secretary-General for Legal Affairs and the Legal Counsel of the United Nations and Co-Chair of the IBA's World Organizations Committee.

48. *Ibid.*

49. *Ibid.*

50. Gernot WAGNER and Martin WEITZMAN, *Climate Shock. The Economic Consequences of a Hotter Planet* (Princeton University Press 2015) p. 43.

51. D. BODANSKY, J. BRUNEE, L. RAJAMANI, *International Climate Change Law*, fn. 15 above, p. 212.

52. Paris Agreement – Status of Ratification, available at <https://unfccc.int/process/the-paris-agreement/status-of-ratification>, 22 June 2018.

53. *Ibid.*

54. D. BODANSKY, J. BRUNEE, L. RAJAMANI, *International Climate Change Law*, fn. 15 above, p. 214.

55. *Ibid.*, p. 231.

56. Paris Agreement, fn. 19 above.

provide the information necessary to track its progress in implementing and achieving those targets.[57]

Inclusion of the NDC rules has been described as "the outer edge of what was politically achievable ..." during the Paris negotiations.[58] The fact that NDCs represent procedural obligations, in contrast to obligations of result[59] might have been one element of the rules which in the end facilitated their inclusion in the Paris Agreement.

Complementing the language on mitigation, Art. 4 of the Paris Agreement also addresses Adaptation (Art. 7), Loss & Damage (Art. 8) and Finance (Art. 9). Provisions for implementation, or enforcement, are found in Arts. 13, 14 and 15.

As in other agreements in the multilateral environmental law (MEA) regime as a whole, the Paris Agreement primarily relies on transparency for the purpose of oversight and implementation. The Agreement does not include binding obligations of result relating to NDCs, and the transparency framework is the "main mechanism to hold states accountable for doing what they say they will do".[60]

The Paris Agreement also includes provisions that foresee a mechanism to facilitate implementation of and compliance with the agreement (Art. 15). But as yet there is no language on the details: this is left for further elaboration by the COP. It remains to be seen whether any language on dispute resolution can be agreed upon in upcoming negotiations.

In summarizing enforcement under the UNFCCC and the Paris Agreement, a picture thus emerges of an international system by which action for climate change mitigation and adaptation is safeguarded by a system relying on co-operation, or peer pressure, rather than formal rules. This leads to vulnerability and hampers efficiency.[61]

The current system for addressing climate change at the international level could also be described as a system where "stringency, participation, and compliance are interlinked" and where weakness along any of these three dimensions will undermine the regime's effectiveness, regardless of how strong the other two dimensions are.[62] So far, it appears that states have been reluctant to hand over any authority to arbitral tribunals for the purpose of safeguarding stringency and participation.

But could there be other areas of international law where arbitral tribunals might make a difference?

---

57. *Ibid.*, Art. 13.7 (b).
58. D. BODANSKY, J. BRUNEE, L. RAJAMANI, *International Climate Change Law*, fn. 15 above, p. 215.
59. *Ibid.*, pp. 231-232.
60. *Ibid.*, p. 242.
61. N. STERN, *The Economics of Climate Change. The Stern Review*, fn. 7 above, p. 509. Practical examples illustrating the weakness of the system include the United States' withdrawal from the Paris Agreement, see Valerie VOLVOVICI, "US Submits Formal Notice of Withdrawal from Paris Climate Pact", available at <www.reuters.com/article/us-un-climate-usa-paris/u-s-submits-formal-notice-of-withdrawal-from-paris-climate-pact-idUSKBN1AK2FM> (last accessed 25 June 2018); Canada's abandonment of the Kyoto Protocol, see "Canada to Withdraw from Kyoto Protocol, available at <www.bbc.com/news/world-us-canada-16151310> (last accessed 25 June 2018); Japan's refusal to extend the Kyoto Protocol, see Ministry of Foreign Affairs of Japan, "Japan's position regarding the Kyoto Protocol", available at <www.mofa.go.jp/policy/environment/warm/cop/ kp_pos_1012.html> (last accessed 25 June 2018).
62. D. BODANSKY, J. BRUNEE, L. RAJAMANI, *International Climate Change Law*, fn. 15 above, p. 6.

2. *Investment Arbitration and Climate Change*

In the absence of strong tools for enforcement in international environmental law as a whole, including climate change law, models and mechanisms created elsewhere in international law could be worth examining.[63]

In this context, international investment law and investment arbitration are a potential arena for climate change–related disputes. Perhaps this is how international arbitration will indeed be used in the future to add force to the words of climate change obligations as agreed in the UNFCCC or the Paris Agreement.

Since 1959, states have entered into over 3,000 bilateral treaties for the purpose of protecting foreign investments. A majority of these treaties provide for arbitration between investors and the state in a situation of potential breach of the investment protection provisions of the treaty. By the end of 2017, a global total of 855 investor-state cases were known to have been heard.[64]

The inclusion of international arbitration in bilateral investment agreements represents what some would call a revolutionary development in international law. It confirms a development by which not only states are the subject of international law. Judge Stephen Schwebel, former President of the ICJ, summarizes the development in a speech from 2014 as follows: "That entitlement to international arbitration is one of the most progressive developments in the procedure of international law in the last fifty years, indeed in the whole history of international law."[65]

Keeping the inherently evolutionary character of international law in mind, could investment treaty arbitration be "a force for good" used to motivate a change of state behaviour in compliance with international agreements, including climate change policies? Some have argued affirmatively – yes.[66]

Where the treaty basis for the tribunal's jurisdiction is expressed in broad terms, for example "all disputes relating to an investment", this could support a broad approach to the sources of obligations that form the basis of investors' claims, including environmental or climate change obligations.[67] It has been held that "there is no obstacle preventing a tribunal from interpreting the fair and equitable standard .... in a manner that is sensitive to the legitimate regulatory objectives of the host state as defined by international environmental law".[68]

---

63. Zachary DOUGLAS, "The Enforcement of Environmental Norms in Investment Treaty Arbitration" in Pierre-Marie DUPUY and Jorge E. VIÑUALES, eds., *Harnessing Foreign Investment to Promote Environmental Protection* (Cambridge University Press 2013) p. 417.
64. United Nations Conference on Trade and Development, "Investor-State Dispute Settlement: Review of Developments in 2016", IIA Issues Note (May 2018, issue 1) available at <http://investmentpolicyhub.unctad.org/Publications/Details/172> (last accessed 2 July 2018).
65. Judge Stephen M. SCHWEBEL, "Keynote Address: In Defence of Bilateral Investment Treaties" in *Legitimacy: Myths, Realities, Challenges*, ICCA Congress Series no. 18 (Kluwer 2015) p. 5.
66. Anatole BOUTE, "Combating Climate Change Through Investment Arbitration", 35 Fordham International Law Journal (The Berkeley Electronic Press 2012, issue 3) p. 613.
67. Zachary DOUGLAS, "The Enforcement of Environmental Norms in Investment Treaty Arbitration" in Pierre-Marie DUPUY and Jorge E. VIÑUALES, eds., *Harnessing Foreign Investment to Promote Environmental Protection*, fn. 63 above, p. 424.
68. *Ibid.*, p. 418.

Another common standard in BITs is that of full protection and security. This standard typically targets the state's obligation to protect the investor's property from actual damage, including by the actions of others in situations where the state has an obligation to exercise due diligence.[69] At a minimum, the standard is seen as protecting the physical integrity of the investor's property.[70]

Could state behaviour harming the environment constitute a violation of the full protection and security standard found in investment protection treaties? Perhaps, as illustrated by an award from 2016 under the Canada-Barbados Bilateral Investment Treaty.

In *Peter A. Allard v. The Government of Barbados*, the Canadian investor argued that the government was in breach of its treaty obligations due to failure to enforce both domestic and international environmental laws, including international environmental treaties, and therefore harmed his investment.[71] The claim was dismissed, but the arbitral tribunal noted in the award rendered on 27 June 2016 that "consideration of a host State's international obligations may well be relevant" in the application of the standard of full protection of security. The reasoning of the arbitral tribunal has been described as a legal standard which "may pave the way for future cases that environmentalists could help investors against governments", including a potential argument that a government's actions and inactions on climate change violate the obligation of full protection and security.[72]

A similar line of reasoning had been raised earlier, in late 2015, when haze originating from forest fires in Indonesia caused severe air pollution problems in several neighbouring countries in South-East Asia.[73] The haze gave rise to a debate on whether pollution caused by the forest fires constituted a violation of international law, and whether it could give rise to treaty claims.[74] The argument was raised that the standard

69. Campbell MCLACHLAN, Laurence SHORE, Matthew WEINIGER, *International Investment Arbitration: Substantive Principles,* 2nd edn. (Oxford University Press, Oxford 2010) p. 247 and p. 262; *Asian Agricultural Products Ltd (AAPL) v. The Republic of Sri Lanka* (ICSID Case No ARB/87/3), Final Award (27 June 1990) paras. 50, 53; *Peter A. Allard v The Government of Barbados* (PCA Case No. 2012-06), Award (27 June 2016) paras. 243-244.

70. *Saluka Investments BV v. The Czech Republic* (UNCITRAL), Partial Award (17 March 2006) para. 483.

71. *Peter A. Allard v. the Government of Barbados* (PCA Case 2012-06), Award (27 June 2012), for more information about the case see <https://pcacases.com/web/view/112> and <http://graemehall.com/legal/papers/BIT-Complaint.pdf>.

72. SIMON LESTER, Cato Institute, "What If ISDS Lawsuits Were Used to Fight Climate Change?", at Huffington Post Blog, 3 October 2016 <www.huffingtonpost.com/simon-lester/what-if-isds-lawsuits-wer_b_12311892.html?guccounter=1>.

73. Nash JENKINS, "The Current Haze over Southeast Asia Could Be Among the Worst Ever", available at <http://time.com/4060786/haze-singapore-indonesia-malaysia-pollution/> (last accessed 25 June 2018).

74. Mark MANGAN and Henry DEFRIEZ, "Does the Haze over Southeast Asia Violate International Law?", Eco-Business (8 October 2015) available at <www.eco-business.com/opinion/does-the-haze-over-southeast-asia-violate-international-law/> (last accessed 25 June 2018).

of full protection and security includes an obligation by the state to prevent damage caused by "egregious pollution".[75]

Could the standard of full protection and security be said to include a state obligation to take all necessary steps to prevent damage to investments caused by GHG emissions? At the time of writing, this remains an open question.

a. Investments in renewable energy

Investments closely aligned with climate change mitigation are investments in renewable energy, where growth has been very strong in recent years. Examples include wind and solar parks, which are now being built at an unprecedented rate.[76]

In 2016, global renewable power generation rose by 9 per cent, and solar power alone demonstrated a growth of more than 30 per cent. Renewable energy represents more than half of new power capacity added worldwide in 2016.[77]

The US Energy Information Administration predicts that renewable energy will be the fastest growing energy source between 2015 and 2040.[78] And the International Energy Agency forecasts that the gas and renewables share of global energy supply could reach 54 per cent in 2040 – if governments adopt stronger climate policies.[79]

In short, investment in renewable energy has demonstrated strong growth – growth which is expected to continue. This is essential for the Paris Agreement targets.[80] The Financial Times editorial in September 2016 notes: "If the world is to reduce the risk of catastrophic global warming to acceptable levels, there will have to be a huge reallocation of capital away from fossil fuels and towards low-emissions energy sources."[81]

But the sharp increase in investment in renewable energy has not been without its challenges. In many jurisdictions, investments in renewable energy have been supported by feed-in tariffs, investment support, tax exemptions or other incentive schemes.[82] As

75. "Does the Smoke Haze Over South East Asia Violate International Law?", Dechert LLP Legal Update (September 2015) p. 3.
76. PILITA CLARK, "The Big Green Bang", Financial Times (19 May 2017) available at <www.ft.com/content/44ed7e90-3960-11e7-ac89-b01cc67cfeec> (last accessed 2 July 2018). See also US Energy Information Administration, *International Energy Outlook 2017* (September 2017) p. 81, available at <www.eia.gov/outlooks/ieo/pdf/0484(2017).pdf> (last accessed 25 June 2018).
77. "The Big Green Bang", Financial Times (19 May 2017) fn. 76 above.
78. See also US Energy Information Administration, *International Energy Outlook 2017*, fn. 76 above.
79. Anjli RAVAL and David SHEPPARD, "Oil Industry's Swagger Takes Knock from Gas Boom", Financial Times (19 February 2018) available at <www.ft.com/content/b8ac0cf6-1269-11e8-8cb6-b9ccc4c4dbbb>.
80. International Energy Agency, *World Energy Outlook 2016* (OECD/IEA 2016) and International Energy Agency, *World Energy Outlook 2017* (OECD/IEA 2017).
81. "Investment Threats in a Changing Climate", editorial, Financial Times, 12 September 2016.
82. For additional details see for example European Commission, *Commission Staff Working Document: Guidance for the Design of Renewables Support Schemes*, SWD (2013) 439 final (5 November 2013) available at <https://ec.europa.eu/energy/sites/ener/files/documents/com_2013_public_intervention_swd04_en.pdf> (last accessed 26 June 2018).

economies have shifted, a number of these programmes have later been revised.[83] And where policy has changed there are numerous examples of investors seeking compensation from governments, arguing that changing legal regimes have constituted a violation of their rights under various investment protection treaties, most notably the Energy Charter Treaty (ECT).[84]

The public domain currently includes close to sixty claims under investment treaties pending against states relating to investments in renewable energy.[85] Of all known investor-state cases in the environmental or sustainability sphere,[86] most arise out of investments in renewable energy.[87] A majority of these cases are based on investments in solar energy.[88]

The first award in one of these so-called solar energy cases was rendered on 21 January 2016, as the result of ECT arbitration under the SCC Rules. The award has thereafter become publicly available.[89]

The policy targeted in the arbitration included a special legal regime introduced by Spain for the purpose of favouring and promoting energy production from renewable sources. Following a change in this regime, the Dutch company Charanne B.V. and the Luxembourg entity Construction Investments S.à.r.l. commenced arbitration against Spain, arguing that the government's action violated the investment protection afforded to investors under the ECT. One of the grounds advanced by the investors was that the changes constituted a violation of the investors' legitimate expectations.

The arbitral tribunal stated that the existence of legitimate expectations on the part of the investor is a relevant factor in analyzing whether a violation under the treaty has occurred, and that the standard meant that an investor should be entitled to a legitimate expectation that a state will not act "unreasonably, disproportionately or contrary to the public interest".[90] The *Charanne* Tribunal concluded that Spain had not acted in violation of these obligations, and the claim was dismissed in its entirety.[91]

---

83. For an overview see Norah GALLAGHER, "ECT and Renewable Energy Disputes" in Maxi SCHERER, ed., *International Arbitration in the Energy Sector* (Oxford University Press 2017) p. 257.
84. *Ibid.*, p. 258.
85. See, among others, "List of All Investment Dispute Cases" available at <www.energycharter.org>, <www.italaw.com>, Mena Chambers, "ECT Dispute Settlement List", available at <www.menachambers.com/expertise/energy-charter-treaty/dispute-settlement/>; SCC internally-produced statistics on investment disputes related to renewable energy, updated as of 29 December 2017.
86. This would include cases dealing with green investments, for example renewable energy, and cases where environmental policy has played a role.
87. Based on research on investor-state arbitration in the public domain by the Arbitration Institute of the Stockholm Chamber of Commerce, as of 31 August 2017 thirty-two awards have been rendered in investor-state arbitration cases that dealt with questions of measures to protect the environment and public health. See the cases on <www.italaw.com>.
88. Annette MAGNUSSON, "Climate Disputes and Sustainable Development in the Energy Sector: Bridging the Enforceability Gap" in Maxi SCHERER, ed., *International Arbitration in the Energy Sector* (Oxford University Press 2017) p. 384.
89. *Charanne and Construction Investments v. Spain* (SCC Case No. V062/2012), Award (21 January 2016) available at <www.italaw.com/cases/2082> (hereinafter *Charanne v. Spain*).
90. *Ibid.*, para. 514.
91. *Ibid.*, The quotes above are taken from the unofficial translation available at <www.italaw.com/sites/default/files/case-documents/italaw7162.pdf>.

Following the award in 2016, additional awards have been rendered in what has come to be described as renewable energy treaty arbitrations, with different factual backgrounds and outcomes.[92] A common denominator, however, appears to be elaboration by the different tribunals on the standard of legitimate expectations in terms of change of policy.

In *Charanne*, the arbitral tribunal noted that the standard of legitimate expectations includes the notion that an investor should be able to expect that the state will act in the "public interest".[93] Could an overarching ambition to reduce CO_2 emissions in turn be deemed part of that public interest?

None of the awards in the solar energy arbitrations published to date contain any factual conclusions or arguments regarding CO_2 emissions. GHG emissions appears not to have been argued, nor have any international obligations relating to climate change mitigation.

In *Eiser v. Spain*,[94] emissions targets form part of the factual background of the policy subjected to the tribunal's review. A direct reference to the UNFCCC is made in the award when the EU policy for reduction of GHG through development of renewable energy is said to build "from multilateral agreements including the 1992 Framework Convention on Climate Change".[95]

In the Tribunal's Reasons in *Novenergia v. Spain*, the tribunal notes that the policy being targeted in the case was "clearly enacted with the objective of ensuring that the Kingdom of Spain achieved its emissions and RE targets".[96] Apart from this, no general reference either to GHG emissions or international obligations relating to climate change is found in the award.

In summary, it appears that the potential legal territory where an arbitral tribunal could find itself charged with the task of balancing international investment law – for example as contained in the definition of public interest as an element of the notion of legitimate expectations – and climate change law, including GHG-curbing ambitions or NDC commitments under the Paris Agreement, remains unchartered.[97]

---

92. For an overview see *Legitimate Expectations in Renewable Energy Treaty Arbitrations: The Lessons So Far* <http://arbitrationblog.kluwerarbitration.com/2018/03/22/legitimate-expectationsrenewable-energy-treaty-arbitrations-lessons-far/>.
93. *Charanne v. Spain*, fn. 89 above, paras. 510 and 513-514.
94. *Eiser Infrastructure Limited and Energía Solar Luxembourg S.à r.l. v. Kingdom of Spain* (ICSID Case No. ARB/13/36), Final Award (4 May 2017) available at <www.italaw.com/search/site/Eiser?f%5B0%5D=sm_field_case_document_type%3Aaward> (hereinafter *Eiser v. Spain*).
95. *Ibid.*, para. 101.
96. *Novenergia II – Energy & Environment (SCA) (Grand Duchy of Luxembourg), SICAR v. The Kingdom of Spain* (SCC Case No. 2015/063), Final Arbitral Award (15 February 2018), para. 665.
97. On the potential normative conflict between international environmental law and international investment law, see Francisco FRANCIONI, "The Private Sector and the Challenge of Implementation", p. 26 and Magnus Jeko LANGER, "Key Instruments of Private Environmental Finance: Funds, Project Finance and Market Mechanism" in Pierre-Marie DUPUY and Jorge E. VIÑUALES, eds., *Harnessing Foreign Investment to Promote Environmental Protection* (Cambridge University Press 2013) p. 134.

b. Are BIT carve-outs the key?

One model commonly advocated and used to address environmental issues in modern BITs is so-called carve-outs where states seek to reserve policy space for measures motivated by environmental considerations.[98] In these BITs, the investment protection afforded to investors under the treaty is excluded where measures attributed to the state are motivated by environmental protection objectives (usually with the caveat that such measures are not applied in a manner which would constitute arbitrary or unjustified discrimination).[99] The intent is to preserve policy space for contracting states for such measures.

The model by which environmental issues are addressed through carve-outs has developed as a result of concern that the absence of such carve-outs in a BIT would in practice prevent states from taking necessary action, also referred to as regulatory chill.[100] The fear has been that states would refrain from taking measures to protect the environment, including climate change mitigation and adaptation measures, where such measures might potentially be seen as a breach of their international investment protection obligations.

But the use of carve-outs as a tool to achieve global environmental goals has its limitations.

First, a review of publicly available awards in investor-state arbitrations demonstrates that very few cases in fact involve environmental issues. In a survey conducted by the SCC, fewer than forty environment-related awards were identified in the public domain between 1995 and August 2017.[101] This can be compared with the total number of 548 awards up to 31 December 2017, as reported by the United Nations Conference on Trade and Development (UNCTAD).[102] Most of the known 548 awards have been based on BITs dating back to the 1980s and 1990s,[103] that is, when carve-outs were not part of a standard BIT. This would lead to the conclusion that even in the absence of carve-outs, environmental issues are rare in the available public docket of investor-state arbitration.

98. Manjiao CHI, Integrating Sustainable Development in International Investment Law: Normative Incompatibility, System Integration, and Governance Implication (Routledge 2018) p. 116.

99. Kathryn GORDON and Joakim POHL, "Environmental Concerns in International Investment Agreements: A Survey" in OECD Working Papers on International Investment 2011/01 (OECD Publishing 2011), available at <www.oecd.org/daf/inv/investment-policy/WP-2011_1.pdf>, pp. 14-15 (last accessed 25 June 2018).

100. Eckhard JANEBA, "Regulatory Chill and the Effect of Investor State Dispute Settlement" in CESIfo Working Papers No. 1688 (November 2016) p.1, available at <www.cesifo-group.de/DocDL/cesifo1_wp6188.pdf> (last accessed 2 July 2018).

101. The SCC has conducted internal research on ISDS Awards within the Environmental Sphere, see the cases on <www.italaw.com>. See also Pierre-Marie DUPUY, "International Environmental Law: Looking at the Past to Shape the Future" in Pierre-Marie DUPUY and Jorge E. VIÑUALES, eds., *Harnessing Foreign Investment to Promote Environmental Protection* (Cambridge University Press 2013) p. 18.

102. UNCTAD, "Investor-State Dispute Settlement: Review of Development in 2016", IIA Issues Note: International Investment Agreements (UNCTAD May 2017), available at <http://investmentpolicyhub.unctad.org/Publications/Details/172> (last accessed 27 June 2018).

103. *Ibid.*, p. 3.

The current regime of international investment law thus appears not to be an arena in which international arbitration and environmental concerns typically cross paths.

Second, creating a regulatory space for governments in BITs specifically for action addressing environmental protection, including climate change, achieves very little if this space is de facto kept empty, that is, if states do not take concrete action for climate change mitigation and adaptation.

Typically, the language of carve-outs in international investment agreements contains nothing that incentivizes the state to take action. In the policy space effectively created by carve-outs, traditional hurdles for climate change policy are therefore likely to play out.

The most common hurdle is probably the shift in political priorities. Policy objectives considered necessary when signing a multilateral environmental agreement may not necessarily enjoy the same status some years later, when other pressing issues enter the political agenda.[104] For many governments, failure to meet climate change objectives involves fewer immediate consequences than failure to address a current problem. An economic crisis could easily shift priorities. This has been described as "the iron law of climate policy"; that is, where climate policy is designed in a manner which puts it on a confrontational course with policy focused on economic growth, climate policy will lose every time.[105] And even when the costs of implementing a long-term agreement for climate change are low and seen to offer clear advantages, the risk is always the short-term negative impact on certain groups.[106] When this gives rise to conflict, it is a conflict that policymakers can seldom afford to ignore. And yet another hurdle for climate change policy is raised.

In summary, the potential new frontier of arbitration and climate change under the umbrella of public international law is still in its infancy. And although arguably signs of change are on the future horizon, including in international investment law, given the dynamics of international climate change law, perhaps expectations should not be set too high.

So, let us turn to the traditional role played by international commercial arbitration in international trade and economic development. At the intersection between international business and climate change resides another new frontier for arbitration and climate change.

---

104. Examples include Henry VOY, "Poland on Course for Battle on New EU Climate Change Target", Financial Times (1 October 2014) available at <www.ft.com/content/4ec9373c-495e-11e4-8d68-00144feab7de> (last accessed 2 July 2018); "Electricity Industry Absorbs the Shock of Reforms", Financial Times (24 June 2014); "UK Climate Effort Hit by Carbon Capture Reverse", Financial Times (25 September 2015). The 2016 US election represents a recent and dramatic shift of policy in this regard, see, for example, Michael D. SHEAR, "Trump Will Withdraw U.S. from Paris Climate Agreement", The New York Times (1 June 2017); Demetri SEVASTOPULO, Barney JOPSON and Pilita CLARK, "Trump Takes US Out of Paris Climate Deal" in Financial Times (2 June 2017).

105. Roger PIELKE, JR., *The Climate Fix* (Basic Books 2010) p. 46.

106. Urs LUTERBACHER, "The Political Environment of Environmental Law" in Pierre-Marie DUPUY and Jorge E. VIÑUALES, eds., *Harnessing Foreign Investment to Promote Environmental Protection* (Cambridge University Press 2013) p. 65.

III. INTERNATIONAL COMMERCIAL ARBITRATION

Climate change mitigation and adaptation require not only "unprecedented levels of international cooperation"[107] but also enormous capital investment.

In a report from 2013, UNCTAD points out that foreign direct investment plays a key role in building low-carbon economies.[108] Many other organizations have made similar statements,[109] and in the work leading up to the Paris Agreement it was clear that for the first time in UNFCCC history, the private sector was fully on board.[110]

Today climate change mitigation and adaptation are not only a matter for governments, international organizations and international law. The private sector is equally important, if not even more important. The role of the private sector in global environmental governance, including climate change mitigation issues, has moved "from marginal to central".[111] Priorities established and initiatives taken by private actors, be they large corporations or individuals, are essential. Already in the Stern report it was pointed out that dangerous climate change cannot be avoided only through high-level international agreements, but that it will take behavioural change by individuals and communities.[112] Private companies are part of the equation.

This course of action is already under way. Large corporations are increasingly turning to renewable energy to power their operations. Companies in general are investing in clean technology and energy-efficiency measures. Not only does this make good business sense, but it also demonstrates leadership in a broader corporate sustainability and climate commitment.[113] In an interconnected world where strong values are increasingly connected with profitability,[114] this matters. As one commentator

107. Daniel M. FIRGER, "The Potential of International Climate Change Law to Mobilise Low-Carbon Foreign Direct Investment" in Pierre-Marie DUPUY and Jorge E. VIÑUALES, eds., *Harnessing Foreign Investment to Promote Environmental Protection* (Oxford University Press 2013) p. 177.

108. United Nations Conference on Trade and Development, *Promoting Low-Carbon Investment,* UNCTAD Advisory Series A, No. 7 (United Nations Publication 2013).

109. OECD, *Investing in Climate, Investing in Growth* (OECD Publishing 2017) p. 264.

110. Kevin MOSS, "Business Helped Make the Paris Agreement Possible" (17 December 2015), available at <www.wri.org> (last accessed 27 June 2018); "The World Bank, Private Sector – An Integral Part of Climate Action Post-Paris" (30 December 2015) available at <www.worldbank.org> (last accessed 27 June 2018).

111. P. DUPUY, "International Environmental Law: Looking at the Past to Shape the Future" in Pierre-Marie DUPUY and Jorge E. VIÑUALES, eds., *Harnessing Foreign Investment to Promote Environmental Protection*, fn. 101 above, p. 9

112. N. STERN, *The Economics of Climate Change. The Stern Review*, fn. 7 above, p. 448.

113. David GARDINER & Associates, LLC, *Power Forward: Why the World's Largest Companies Are Investing in Renewable Energy* (Calvert Investment, CERES, WWF 2013) p. 4, available at <www.ceres.org> (last accessed 26 June 2018).

114. See LRN, *The HOW Report. A Global, Empirical Analysis of How Governance, Culture and Leadership Impact Performance* (LRN 2016), available at <http://lrn.com/governance-culture-leadership/> (last accessed 26 June 2018): "Those [companies] that align behaviors to sustainable, human values and conduct business with integrity outperform and deliver disproportionate long-term value."

says: "Being 'green' is no longer presented as a matter of responsibility, but as one of profitability and competitiveness in the economy of the future."[115]

The impact when global corporations establish global renewable energy commitments across their entire operation can be quite substantial.[116] The mere size of corporations, in combination with their ambitions, may even affect the renewable energy market as a whole. When global corporations make the shift towards renewable power supply, it may give renewable energy producers and policymakers certainty, and encourage business models and policy strategies for an increase in renewable energy demand.[117]

Private capital and individuals thus play a decisive role, as does the market economy and its instruments. International commercial arbitration is one of those instruments.

If predictions are right, we should see a large increase in the number of commercial contracts relating to climate change mitigation and adaptation in the coming years. And the momentum seems to be building. In September 2017, the Financial Times carried a report of an "ethical investment boom", seeking to capture the opportunity represented by clean technologies, including renewable energy.[118] Funds that uphold environmental, social and governance standards are also reported to outperform funds that do not. In short, investors are finding that "if they are good to the planet and to people, they also end up, on average, benefiting themselves".[119]

The investment needed for climate change is diverse and global. Increasing demands for energy due to higher living standards globally and a growing world population need to be met. Renewable energy plants must replace carbon-heavy ones; energy-efficient transportation will be needed to carry an increasingly mobile world population; sustainable agriculture and reforestation must substitute unsustainable land use and deforestation; and climate-resilient infrastructures must be built where global warming and rising sea levels are already putting communities at risk. Investment is also needed to support innovation of new technologies and to bring existing technologies to scale.[120]

Deploying new technologies and other steps necessary for societal transitions prompted by climate change will require considerable funds worldwide, and many stakeholders have ventured figures.[121] In May 2017 the Organisation for Economic

115. P. DUPUY, "International Environmental Law: Looking at the Past to Shape the Future" in Pierre-Marie DUPUY and Jorge E. VIÑUALES, eds., *Harnessing Foreign Investment to Promote Environmental Protection*, fn. 101 above, p. 13.

116. David Gardiner & Associates, LLC, *Power Forward: Why the World's Largest Companies Are Investing in Renewable Energy*, fn. 113 above, p. 6.

117. *Ibid.*, p. 24.

118. James KYNGE, "The Ethical Investment Boom" in Financial Times (4 September 2017) <www.ft.com/content/9254dfd2-8e4e-11e7-a352-e46f43c5825d>.

119. *Ibid.*

120. N. STERN, *The Economics of Climate Change. The Stern Review*, fn. 7 above, p. 393.

121. See, e.g., UNFCCC, *Report on the Analysis of Existing and Potential Investment and Financial Flows Relevant to the Development of an Effective and Appropriate International Response to Climate Change* (UNFCCC 2007), available at <http://unfccc.int/cooperation_and_support/financial_mechanism/items/4053.php>; International Energy Agency, *Energy Technology Perspectives 2012. Pathways to a Clean Energy System,* (OECD/IEA 2012) available at <www.iea.org/publications/freepublications/publication/ETP 2012_free.pdf> ; Ethan ZINDLER and Ken LOCKLIN, *Mapping the Gap: the Road from Paris* (Bloomberg Energy Finance 2016) available at <www.ceres.org/press/press-releases/report-on-12.1-trillion-investment-in-renewable-power-

Cooperation and Development (OECD) published a study which estimates that US$ 6.3 trillion of investment in infrastructure will be required annually between 2016 and 2030.[122] This includes investment in energy demand; telecoms; power and electricity transmission and distribution; water and sanitation; primary energy supply chains; and transport.[123]

Against this background, legal frameworks – including the model offered by international arbitration – will certainly play a decisive role. In this setting, arbitration must continue to do what it has always done: enforce contracts.

Should arbitration procedure be adapted where the substantive issues relate to climate change? This question is addressed next.

IV. THE NEW FRONTIERS

International arbitration could potentially make a difference for climate change through procedural innovations, along with development of entirely new instruments for green growth supported by international arbitration. This section explores some of these ideas.

1. *Procedure*

Procedure is one natural starting point when exploring international arbitration in a climate change context. Could procedural mechanisms be put in place to ensure that climate change elements are not marginalized in the course of resolving disputes through arbitration?[124]

a. *Confidentiality*

A potential hurdle for arbitration playing a role in climate change awareness could be its inherent characteristic of confidentiality. Although investor-state arbitration represents a new trend in this respect – through adoption of the United Nations Commission on International Trade Law (UNCITRAL) Rules on Transparency in Treaty-based Investor-State Arbitration[125] – parties to international commercial arbitration tend not to be interested in having their dispute, or details of it, being made public. Perhaps there is reason to revisit this principle where cases involve climate change–related matters.

As we have seen, transparency has traditionally been the main incentive to achieve compliance in international environmental law. In recent years, the general publicity offered by climate change litigation has also contributed to public involvement in the

---

needed-to-limit-climate-change>; Green Growth Action Alliance, *The Green Investment Report. The Ways and Means to Unlock Private Finance for Green Growth* (World Economic Forum 2013) available at <www3.weforum.org/docs/WEF_GreenInvestment_Report_ 2013.pdf> (all last accessed 26 June 2018).

122. OECD, *Investing in Climate, Investing in Growth*, fn. 109 above, Executive Summary.

123. *Ibid.*, p. 28.

124. M. CHI, *Integrating Sustainable Development in International Investment Law: Normative Incompatibility, System Integration, and Governance Implication*, fn. 98 above, p. 138.

125. UNCITRAL Rules on Transparency in Treaty-based Investor-State Arbitration, available at <www.uncitral.org/uncitral/en/uncitral_texts/arbitration/2014Transparency.html>.

threat of climate change.[126] When climate change becomes a story about a person, or a community, rather than a scientific report focusing on GHG concentrations and large-scale weather phenomena, awareness tends to become more tangible, more focused, and potentially more effective.[127] Traditional international arbitration lacks this element.

Should we consider deviating from the confidentiality norm in cases involving issues with a bearing on climate change mitigation and adaptation? There is a clear parallel to the debate which preceded the UNCITRAL Rules on Transparency, and later the United Nations Convention on Transparency in Treaty-based Investor-State Arbitration (the Mauritius Convention), where arguments of public interest spearheaded development. A similar argument could be made in a climate change context.

Of course, not all cases with a climate change element will include public interest. But absent public interest, there could still be valuable – and even inspiring – details to be shared on how the private sector is in fact building a low-carbon society.

A tool for transparency already in place where a case raises matters of public interest is the instrument of amicus curiae.[128]

Provisions on submissions from third parties or non-disputing parties to the treaty have been included in the UNCITRAL Transparency Rules, but are also found in other arbitration rules.[129] Parties to the North American Free Trade Agreement (NAFTA) have for example issued a specific Statement on non-disputing party participation, where public interest is one of the elements listed for consideration by the tribunal when deciding to grant leave to file an amicus brief.

b. Applicable law

Applicable law and its sources provide another potential area for innovation. Could interpretation of provisions on applicable law be expanded for the purpose of addressing all issues of relevance for a particular dispute? And might this include laws or rules of law regulating matters of relevance for climate change?

126. D. BODANSKY, J. BRUNEE, L. RAJAMANI, *International Climate Change Law*, fn. 15 above, p. 287; Giulio CORSI, "New York City v. Big Oil: A New Opportunity to Address Climate Change in the Trump Era?" (Climate Institute, 25 February 2018) available at <http://climate.org/new-york-city-v-big-oil-a-new-opportunity-to-address-climate-change-in-the-trump-era/> (last accessed 27 June 2018).

127. Examples include Attracta MOONEY and Ed CROOKS, "2018 New York Sues Big Oil Companies over Climate Change" in the Financial Times (10 January 2018) <www.ft.com/content/4de8e4fc-f62b-11e7-88f7-5465a6ce1a00>; Agence France Presse, "Peruvian Farmers Sue German Energy Giant for Contributing to Climate Change", The Guardian (14 November 2017) available at <www.theguardian.com/world/2017/nov/14/peruvian-farmer-sues-german-energy-giant-rwe-climate-change>; James CONCA, "Children Win Another Climate Change Legal Case in Mass Supreme Court", Forbes (19 May 2016) available at <www.forbes.com/sites/jamesconca/2016/05/19/children-win-another-climate-change-legal-case-in-mass-supreme-court/#7566498c5822> (all last accessed 26 June 2018).

128. M. CHI, *Integrating Sustainable Development in International Investment Law: Normative Incompatibility, System Integration, and Governance Implication*, fn. 98 above, p. 127.

129. See ICSID Rules of Procedure for Arbitration Proceedings, Rule 37(2) and SCC Arbitration Rules Appendix III, Arts. 3 and 4.

A parallel example is offered by the debate on arbitration and human rights, with particular focus on investment arbitration. Where a dispute has consequences beyond the immediate parties to the dispute, tribunals arguably need to consider the wider interest and possibly apply competing norms when calibrating standards for an investment protection treaty, including human rights.[130] Could there be cases where one such competing norm is international climate change law?

A common obstacle to achieving coherent application of parallel or competing norms is that each area of international law tends to operate in isolation. Just as in the human rights context, the silo of international investment law is rarely confronted with the law as contained in the silo of climate change law, while climate change commitments rarely play out in disputes involving states under international investment law.

But climate change litigation in recent years has offered some interesting examples where attempts have been made to tear down the walls between the silos. In these cases, reliefs sought have been formulated with the aim of forcing governments to act, or to refrain from taking certain action. A common denominator is what could be characterized as cross-fertilization, or cross-referencing, of legal norms.

International law obligations have been brought into court proceedings, and arguments put forward that national statutory law should be interpreted through the lens of international obligations as laid down in the UNFCCC (*Urgenda*) or the Paris Agreement (*Arctic Oil*).

In *The People v. Arctic Oil* in the Oslo district court, the NGOs Greenpeace Nordic Association and Natur og Ungdom challenged the Norwegian government's decision to grant licences for drilling in the Arctic, a decision taken a little less than one month after Norway signed the Paris Agreement. The state's undertakings in its capacity as a signatory to an international instrument of climate change mitigation and adaptation were, in the opinion of the plaintiffs, highly relevant for assessing the state's action. In its claim to have the decision by the Norwegian government declared unconstitutional, the plaintiffs argued that international law as represented by the Paris Agreement and international human rights should be applied when interpreting the state's obligation under the constitution.[131] In addition, the plaintiffs argued that the impact assessment preceding the grant of a licence was inadequate in relation to "Norway's national GHG emission reduction targets and *international obligations*" (emphasis added).[132] After dismissal by the Oslo district court in January 2018, the case is currently pending appeal.[133]

In *Urgenda vs. The Netherlands*, the Urgenda Foundation and a group of Dutch citizens brought a legal action against the Dutch state, arguing that by not adequately regulating and curbing Dutch GHG emissions, the state had committed the tort of negligence against its citizens. Urgenda held that international obligations, such as those of a signatory to the UNFCCC, should be relevant in defining the standard of the duty of care

130. LSE Laboratory for Advanced Research on the Global Economy, *Toby Landau QC on arbitration and human rights* (28 March 2014) <www.youtube.com/watch?v=bJaoADpICjs>.

131. *People v. Arctic Oil Climate Lawsuit*, Notice of Proceedings (18 October 2016), p. 43, available at <www.savethearctic.org/en/peoplevsarcticoil/background-documents/> (last accessed 4 July 2018)

132. *Ibid.*, p. 37.

133. *Ibid.*

attributable to the Dutch government vis-à-vis its citizens, even if the resolutions at issue have no legally binding force between governments.

In its decision, the District Court of The Hague reasoned that "the Parties agree that due to current climate change and the threat of further change with irreversible and serious consequences for man and the environment, the State should take precautionary measures for its citizens".[134] The Court further observed that "the State is obliged to take measures in its own territory to prevent dangerous climate change (mitigation measures)",[135] and noted that "it is an established fact that the State has the power to control the collective Dutch emissions level (and that it indeed controls it)".[136] In conclusion, the Court held that current Dutch climate policies were inadequate and unlawful, labelled them as hazardous negligence and ordered the Dutch government to limit the joint volume of Dutch annual GHG emissions.[137] According to the same Court, the duty of care as contained in the Dutch Civil Code translates into a legal obligation by the Dutch state to abide by targets as defined in international instruments to which it is a signatory, including the UNFCCC.

The Dutch and Norwegian examples illustrate how public policy as laid down in statutory law, or a duty of care attributable to the government, have been used as arguments to prompt a government or a public authority to live up to promises made at national and international level, including action to reduce carbon emissions.

Could the same model have been applied had the case been heard before an arbitral tribunal? This represents yet another open question for arbitration and climate change, but might be an interesting area to explore going forward.

2. *New International Models*

A certain amount of cross-fertilization is already emerging in a formalized way through cross-references between treaties. In addition, new instruments connecting the dots between climate change, investment needs and economic development are on the horizon. Policies other than those based directly on international instruments of climate change law can play a role in the global response to climate change.[138] This could include policy for low-carbon investment, energy efficiency improvements or natural conservation programmes.[139]

134. *Urgenda Foundation v. the State of the Netherlands (Ministry of Infrastructure and the Environment)* (Case Number C/09/456689), Judgment (2015), The Hague District Court, HA ZA 131396, para. 4.64, available at <www.elaw.org/system/files/urgenda_0.pdf> (hereinafter *Urgenda*).

135. *Ibid.*, para. 4.65

136. *Ibid.*, para. 4.66.

137. The Dutch government appealed the case on 23 September 2015. The appeal is currently pending and was heard at The Hague Court of Appeal on 28 May 2018. The verdict is expected to be rendered on 9 October 2018. More information available here <www.urgenda.nl/en/themas/climate-case/>.

138. D.M. FIRGER., "The Potential of International Climate Change Law to Mobilise Low-Carbon Foreign Direct Investment" in Pierre-Marie DUPUY and Jorge. E. VIÑUALES, eds., *Harnessing Foreign Investment to Promote Environmental Protection*, fn. 107 above, p. 178.

139. *Ibid.*, p. 203.

a. Bridging agreements

Perhaps greater emphasis could be put on the connection between different international legal instruments going forward, for the purpose of achieving enforcement of climate change commitments.

The award in *Allard v. Barbados* mentioned earlier is interesting from the point of view of enforcement of international environmental law in general, as it reasons on the connection between bilateral investment treaties and other international obligations of the state. The investor had argued that the state was in breach of its obligations under international environmental law and that had caused damage to his investment, which in effect constituted a breach of the investment protection provisions of the BIT.[140] On this point, the arbitral tribunal stated: "The fact that Barbados is party to the *Convention on Biological Diversity* and the *Ramsar Convention* does not change the standard under the BIT, although consideration of a host State's international obligations may well be relevant in the application of the standard to particular circumstances."[141]

Although not leading to the conclusion that there had been a violation of the BIT involved, the arbitral tribunal appears to open the door to bringing in obligations as defined by international environmental law when calibrating BIT standards. Could this be a bridge to international climate change law in treaty-based investment arbitration?

Another example of bridging agreements is the Peru-US Trade Promotion Agreement of 2009, which includes specific language to that effect. In essence, the Peru-US TPA requires the parties to use their best endeavours to fulfil their obligations under a number of multilateral environmental agreements listed in the TPA.[142] In addition, the TPA contains a chapter on dispute resolution, including international arbitration.[143] This in turn enables enforcement through international arbitration for agreements that do not contain provisions or other enforcement mechanisms.

The Peru-US TPA has been characterized as the first trade agreement to directly incorporate environmental agreements in a dispute settlement-enforced system.[144] This could be one way forward for arbitration and climate change.

In addition to the Peru-US agreement, other recent BITs and FTAs include language addressing sustainability in general.[145] A recent OECD study reveals that more than 75 per cent of recently concluded IIAs include language referring to sustainable development targets, and the trend is increasing; almost all treaties concluded between 2012 and 2013 contained language to that effect.[146]

---

140. *Peter Allard v. Barbados*, fn. 71 above, paras. 178, 230.

141. *Ibid.*, para. 244.

142. The United States-Peru Trade Promotion Agreement (12 April 2016), Chapter Eighteen, available at <https://ustr.gov/trade-agreements/free-trade-agreements/peru-tpa/final-tex>.

143. *Ibid.*, Chapter Twenty One.

144. IBA Presidential Task Force on Climate Change Justice and Human Rights, *Achieving Climate Change Justice and Human Rights in an Era of Climate Disruption*, fn. 10 above, p. 171.

145. *Ibid.*, p. 169.

146. Kathryn GORDON, Joachim POHL and Marie BOUCHARD, "Investment Treaty Law, Sustainable Development and Responsible Business Conduct: A Fact Finding Survey", *OECD Working Papers on International Investment* (OECD Publishing 2014).

The general aims of sustainable development as defined in the Sustainable Development Goals (SDGs)[147] of 2015 can also be directly aligned with climate change targets. SDG 13 specifically targets Climate Action, and the energy goals of the SDGs are also closely aligned with climate change mitigation targets covered by the Paris Agreement.[148] Reference to sustainable development in instruments upon which arbitration is based could thus in effect contribute to inclusion of climate change perspectives.

Another possible model to build a link with international climate change obligations and other state commitments is to use COP decisions under the UNFCCC as interpretive guidance for international commitments.[149] Although technically not binding under international law, a COP decision could be understood as an expression of the understanding of states regarding their joint commitments, and thus potentially bridge a gap needed to establish that a certain measure of relevance for climate change is governed by international law. As far as is known, no arbitral tribunal has yet been presented with such an interpretive exercise.

b. New instruments

The private sector will play an important role in climate change mitigation and adaptation efforts, but it remains the task of government to provide a stable policy framework.[150] However, a recurring theme following the Paris negotiations has been that although the money for green investments exists, investors are hesitant to deploy their funds in the absence of stable and transparent legal frameworks, including neutral and reliable enforcement mechanisms. Today, no international legal instrument specifically incentivizes and protects cross-border investment aimed at climate change mitigation and adaptation.

New models for international agreements are needed – agreements that address the specific needs of states as a consequence of climate change mitigation and adaptation efforts, but at the same time provide investors with the necessary long-term stability.

Against this background, in 2017 the Arbitration Institute of the Stockholm Chamber of Commerce, with partners including the IBA and the crowd sourcing platform HeroX,[151] initiated the Stockholm Treaty Lab contest.[152] The Stockholm Treaty Lab is

147. United Nations General Assembly Resolution, *Transforming Our World: The 2030 Agenda for Sustainable Development*, A/RES/70/ (25 September 2015) available at <www.un.org/ga/search/view_doc.asp?symbol=A/RES/70/1&Lang=E>.
148. Paris Agreement, fn. 19 above.
149. Jorge. E. VIÑUALES, "The Environmental Regulation of Foreign Investment Schemes Under International Law" in Pierre-Marie DUPUY and Jorge E. VIÑUALES, eds., *Harnessing Foreign Investment to Promote Environmental Protection* (Oxford University Press 2013) p. 275.
150. N. STERN, *The Economics of Climate Change. The Stern Review*, fn. 7 above, p. 409; also see among others, OECD, *Tackling Climate Change and Growing the Economy: Key Messages and Recommendations from Recent OECD Work*, available at <www.oecd.org>; UNCTAD, "Investment Policy Framework for Sustainable Development" (2015) available at <www.unctad.org/diae> (last accessed 4 July 2018).
151. See <www.herox.com/stockholmtreatylab>.
152. A. MAGNUSSON, *Innovation Prize to Increase Green Investments* <www.hagainitiativet.se/en/blogg/Annette-Magnusson-Innovation-Prize-to-Increase-Green-Investments>; see also <http://stockholmtreatylab.org/>.

using crowd-sourcing to find an effective legal instrument for climate change mitigation and adaptation. In this innovation contest the grand prize will be awarded to the contestant team that drafts a model treaty with the greatest potential to increase investment in climate change adaptation and mitigation.

The contest meets a need voiced that policymakers should "seek out new ways to use international law as a catalyst, not a hurdle, for private investments in low-carbon growth".[153] The objective is to create a new model for an international treaty that, if implemented, can be expected to create transparent, stable and enforceable investment policy regimes to incentivize the investment needed to meet Paris Agreement targets.

One of the assessment criteria in the competition is enforceability, which is spelled out as follows: "The Model Treaty is binding and enforceable. It contains an effective dispute resolution mechanism, through which both investors and states can bring claims related to the Treaty."[154]

At the time of writing, the competition is under way and the jury is reviewing the submissions. The competition has attracted attention from innovators in more than twenty-five jurisdictions, organized in teams representing a wide variety of expertise.[155] There appears to be a global and multidisciplinary consensus that a gap needs to be filled to get the necessary investment for climate change mitigation and adaptation off the ground.

153. D.M. FIRGER, "The Potential of International Climate Change Law to Mobilise Low-Carbon Foreign Direct Investment" in P. DUPUY and J. E. VIÑUALES, eds., *Harnessing Foreign Investment to Promote Environmental Protection*, fn. 107 above, p. 204.

154. See <www.herox.com/stockholmtreatylab/guidelines>.

155. See <www.sccinstitute.com/about-the-scc/news/2017/stockholm-treaty-lab-what-s-next/>.

What Can Arbitration and Human Rights as Mechanisms of Dispute Resolution Learn from Each Other in Order to Meet the Challenges of Climate Change?

Ana Stanič * *and Petra Butler* **

TABLE OF CONTENTS PAGE

According to the International Bar Association (IBA) Presidential Task Force on Climate Change Justice and Human Rights, "[g]lobal climate change is a defining challenge of our time".[1] It "poses an effective obstacle to the continued progress of human rights" further exacerbating the "existing inequities that afflict a world already riven with vast inequality, poverty and conflict".[2]

Courts are becoming the "new front line of climate change action".[3] In particular, there is a rise in tortious and other claims being brought by affected populations against

* English lawyer specializing in arbitration, EU and international law; founder of E&A Law; visiting lecturer at the Centre for Energy, Petroleum and Mineral Law and Policy in Dundee, the Technische Universität in Berlin, and the UIBE in Beijing; represents states and energy companies in commercial and investment treaty arbitrations, has appeared before the Court of Justice of the EU and filed a number of cases before the Court.

This is a longer version of a paper presented by the author at the ICCA 2018 Conference in Australia during the panel on Potential of Arbitration Involving New Types of Claims. The paper was prepared after extensive discussions with Petra Butler. Sect. VI of this paper was written by Petra Butler and represents her views on what arbitration can learn from human rights.

** Professor, Victoria University of Wellington; co-director, Centre for Small States; and Visiting Professor, Queen Mary University of London. The author of Sect. VI of this paper would like to thank Christoph Katerndahl for his valuable research assistance.

1. International Bar Association, "Achieving Justice and Human Rights in an Era of Climate Disruption, International Bar Association Climate Change Justice and Human Rights Task Force Report" (November 2012) available at <https://www.ibanet.org/PresidentialTaskForceCCJHR2014.aspx> (last accessed 12 June 2018).
2. *Ibid.*
3. Damian CARRINGTON, "Can climate litigation save the world?", available at <https://www.theguardian.com/environment/2018/mar/20/can-climate-litigation-save-the-world> (last accessed on 12 June 2018).

corporations in national courts including in respect of climate change.[4] At the same time, claims are increasingly being brought against states in national courts and international human rights courts, including for contributing to climate change.[5] For example, claims are being brought against states for breaches of Art. 8 of the European Convention on Human Rights (ECHR) including for failing to take steps to stop serious pollution from a waste treatment plant operated by a private company[6] and for granting a permit to operate a goldmine using the cyanidation process.[7] Specifically in *Guerra and Others v. Italy* the European Court of Human Rights (the Court) found "that severe environmental pollution may affect individuals' well-being and prevent them from enjoying their homes in such a way as to affect their private and family life adversely", holding Italy in breach of its obligation under Art. 8 by failing to provide the affected individuals information on the serious pollution risk from a factory near them.[8]

At the same time private corporations are increasingly bringing claims against states for breaches of human rights, whether as part of investment treaty claims or as stand-alone claims in national courts and international human rights courts.

There is no doubt that the number of climate change, environmental and human rights cases being brought against states as well as private corporations will rise in the future. Given the nature and the complexity of these cases, the way in which national

---

4. Numerous cases are ongoing in national courts around the world. By way of example on 3 March 2015 four victims of the fire in a factory in Pakistan filed claims against the German retailer Kik in the court in Dortmund in Germany. Kik was the main buyer of goods produced in the factory. On 30 August 2016, the Dortmund court accepted jurisdiction and granted legal aid to the claimants to cover their costs. In February 2019 the same court dismissed the case on the basis that the claims were statute barred. At the time of the publication of this article, the claimants were planning to appeal the decision. For more information on the case see <https://www.ecchr.eu/en/case/kik-paying-the-price-for-clothing-production-in-south-asia/> (last accessed on 18 April 2019). *Saul v. RWE – Case of Huaraz* is the first case brought before courts in Europe against an energy company for its alleged contribution to climate change. Information on the case and the pleadings by the parties in the case are available at <https://germanwatch.org/en/huaraz> (last accessed on 12 June 2018). *Okpabi and others v. Royal Dutch Shell Plc and Shell Petroleum Development Company of Nigeria Ltd* [2018] EWCA Civ 191 is an example of an unsuccessful attempt to sue two companies in the Shell group (domiciled in the United Kingdom and Nigeria respectively) in the UK Courts for alleged pollution in the Niger Delta in Nigeria. More information is available at <www.bailii.org/ew/cases/EWHC/TCC/2017/89.html> (last accessed on 12 June 2018).
5. One of many such cases around the world is the case brought by the Urgenda Foundation together with 900 Dutch citizens against the Dutch government for failing to set ambitious enough targets for cutting greenhouse emissions by 2020. On 4 June 2015, the District Court of The Hague ordered the Dutch government to cut the country's greenhouse gas emissions by at least 25 percent by the end of 2020. On 9 October 2018, The Hague Court of Appeal upheld the decision of the lower court, finding that the Netherlands had breached its duty of care by failing to pursue more ambitious targets. More information on the case is available at <www.urgenda.nl/en/themas/climate-case/> (last accessed on 18 April 2019).
6. *Lopez Ostra v. Spain* (Application no. 16798/90), (9 December 1994) available at <http://hudoc.echr.coe.int/eng?i=001-57905> (last accessed on 12 June 2018).
7. *Taşkın and Others v. Turkey* (116/1996/735/932), (30 March 2005) para. 104, available at <http://hudoc.echr.coe.int/eng?i=001-67401> (last accessed on 12 June 2018).
8. *Guerra and Others v. Italy* (Application no. 46117/99), (19 February 1988) para. 60, available at <http://hudoc.echr.coe.int/eng?i=001-58135> (last accessed on 12 June 2018).

courts, international human rights courts and arbitral tribunals resolve these disputes will thus need to change to ensure that there is no enforcement gap.

Through the prism of the *Yukos* cases this article examines the differences in approach adopted by the Court and the investment treaty arbitral tribunal (the Tribunal) set up under the Energy Charter Treaty[9] (ECT) to resolving, in essence, the same dispute, and thereby highlights what investment treaty arbitration and human rights litigation can learn from each other in order to meet the challenges of climate change and thereby ensure there is no enforcement gap.

By way of background Sect. I sets out the key facts giving rise to the dispute in the *Yukos* cases heard before the Court and the Tribunal. Sect. II examines the approach and reasoning adopted by the Tribunal established to resolve the dispute between the three controlling shareholders of Yukos and the Russian Federation (Russia) under the ECT. Sect. III in turn examines the approach and reasoning adopted by the Court in proceedings brought by Yukos against Russia for breaches of the ECHR. The key reasons for the difference in the approaches of the two bodies are presented in Sect. IV. Sect. V discusses the ways in which the enforcement of human rights can be bolstered by using the reasoning and powers adopted by arbitral tribunals in investment treaty arbitrations. As finally, Sect. VI sets out what investment treaty arbitration can learn from human rights law from the point of view of a human rights lawyer.

I. KEY FACTS GIVING RISE TO THE *YUKOS* CASES

OAO Yukos Oil Company (Yukos) was a Russian company engaged in the exploration, production, refining, marketing and distribution of crude oil, natural gas and petroleum products. In 2003 it had around 100,000 employees and a market capitalization of over US$ 33 billion which ranked it among the ten largest oil and gas companies in the world by market capitalization.[10]

The fact that Yukos had reallocated its trading operations to low-tax jurisdictions in order to maximize profits was at the heart of the dispute between Yukos and Russia. Although initially the Russian Tax Ministry had not objected to Yukos' "tax optimization structure", in December 2003 it ordered a tax re-audit for the year 2000. On 29 December 2003 the Tax Ministry demanded that Yukos pay approximately US$ 3.5 billion for tax owed for 2000.

Shortly thereafter, given the size of the tax liability and the alleged fear that Yukos would dissipate its assets the Russian Government proceeded to freeze shares Yukos held in its subsidiaries as well as its other assets.

In November 2004 the Tax Ministry had re-assessed Yukos' tax liabilities for the years 2000 to 2003 at US$ 14.36 billion.

9. The text of the Energy Charter Treaty is available at <https://energycharter.org/fileadmin/DocumentsMedia/Legal/ECTC-en.pdf> (last accessed on 12 June 2018).
10. *Yukos Universal Limited (Isle of Man) v. The Russian Federation* (PCA Case No. AA 227), Final Award (18 July 2014) para. 73, available at <https://www.italaw.com/sites/default/files/case-documents/italaw3279.pdf> (last accessed on 12 June 2018) (Award).

Given the size of the tax liabilities, Russia sold Yukos' core asset, Yuganskneftegaz (YNG), in December 2004. YNG was sold to Baikal Finance Group, a company incorporated only a few days before, and participating as the only bidder in, the auction for US$ 9.37 billion although Dresdner Bank had previously valued it at between US$ 15.7 billion and US$ 18.3 billion and JP Morgan at between US$ 16 billion and US$ 22 billion. A few days later Baikal Finance Group sold YNG to the Russian state-owned company, Rosneft. Thereafter, Yukos' remaining assets were nearly all acquired by Gazprom and Rosneft in subsequent bankruptcy auctions raising a total of US$ 31.5 billion. In November 2007, Yukos was liquidated and struck off the register of legal entities.

During the period from 2003 to 2006 criminal investigations were initiated by Russia against Yukos' management. The Tribunal had found that by 2006 "no fewer than 35 top managers and employees of Yukos had been interrogated, arrested or sentenced".[11] In particular, Mr. Khodorkovsky, the director and main shareholder of Yukos, was arrested at gunpoint in October 2003 and taken to Moscow where he was charged with economic crimes including fraud, tax evasion and embezzlement. He was in prison for over ten years until his much-publicized release in December 2013.

Russia denied that Yukos and its officers were targeted in a discriminatory way, contending that taxation measures had also been applied to other tax offenders and that the searches and seizures were taken as part of legitimate taxation measures and conducted in accordance with usual practice and the appropriate procedural protections available under Russian law.

II. THE DECISION OF THE TRIBUNAL

The three controlling shareholders of Yukos commenced investment treaty arbitrations against Russia under the ECT in 2005. Claiming damages of US$ 114 billion, Yukos' shareholders alleged that Russia had (i) failed to treat their investments in Yukos in a fair and equitable manner and on a non-discriminatory basis in breach of Art. 10(1) of the ECT;[12] and (ii) expropriated their investments in breach of Art. 13(1) of the ECT.[13] The three arbitrations were consolidated into a single arbitration by the parties agreeing to appoint the same arbitrators to resolve them. The award on the merits was rendered on

11. *Id.*, para. 83.
12. Pursuant to Art. 10(1) Russia had undertaken to "encourage and create stable, equitable, favourable and transparent conditions for Investors ... to make Investments.... Such conditions shall include a commitment to accord at all times to Investments ... fair and equitable treatment. Such Investments shall also enjoy the most constant protection and security and no Contracting Party shall in any way impair by unreasonable or discriminatory measures their management, maintenance, use, enjoyment or disposal...."
13. Under Art. 13 of the ECT Russia had undertaken that investments of investors would "not be nationalized, expropriated or subjected to a measure or measures having effect equivalent to nationalization or expropriation (hereinafter referred to as 'Expropriation') except where such Expropriation is: (a) for a purpose which is in the public interest; (b) not discriminatory; (c) carried out under due process of law; and (d) accompanied by the payment of prompt, adequate and effective compensation".

18 July 2014,[14] over nine years after the original proceedings were commenced. The Tribunal's reasoning in respect of these claims as well as regarding damages is examined below.

1. *Breach of Art. 13 of the ECT*

When considering the claim of expropriation, the Tribunal acknowledged that the ECT expressly circumscribes the jurisdiction of the ECT in respect of tax in recognition of states' sovereign rights in international law concerning taxation and their reluctance to subject taxation measures to review by international arbitral tribunals. In particular, the Tribunal noted that it had to determine whether actions taken by the Russian tax authorities fell within the scope of the jurisdictional carve-out set out in Art. 21(1) concerning taxation and/or were "brought back within the Tribunal's jurisdiction by the claw-back of Article 21(5) of the ECT".[15] Thus, albeit not applying the doctrine of the margin of appreciation of the Court, the Tribunal acknowledged that the threshold for the reviewability of a state's actions in respect of tax under the ECT is high. In this regard the Tribunal noted that the investors had "no issue with the right of the Russian Federation to enact tax provisions or with the content of Russian tax law", but with "the manner in which Russian tax law was grossly distorted, misapplied and abused to effect the destruction of Yukos".[16]

The Tribunal held that the carve-out of Art. 21(1) "appl[ied] only to *bona fide* taxation actions, i.e., actions that are motivated by the purpose of raising general revenue for the State".[17] Having examined the facts, and in complete contrast to the conclusions reached by the Court (discussed in Sect. III below), the Tribunal concluded that "the tax assessments levied against Yukos by the Russian Federation, which the Tribunal has found were designed mainly to impose massive liabilities based on VAT and related fines, and were essentially aimed at paralyzing Yukos rather than collecting taxes, are not exempt from scrutiny under the ECT".[18] Furthermore, it found that the "subsequent steps in the enforcement of the tax assessments [were] not captured by the carve-out", because "they too were exigently pursued by means that indicate that Yukos was not just being chased to pay taxes, but was being driven into bankruptcy".[19] It therefore concluded that it had both direct and indirect jurisdiction over claims under Art. 13 of the ECT as the carve out of Art. 21(1) did not apply in the case and that, in any event, the claw-back of Art. 21(5) could be invoked.

In reaching the opposite conclusion to the Court regarding expropriation, the Tribunal noted that it was not bound by the findings of the Court as *ordre public* as per Art. 31(3)(c) of the Vienna Convention of the Law of the Treaties.[20] It then went on to find that the auction of YNG and the bankruptcy of Yukos amounted to an effective

14. Award, fn. 10, para. 63.
15. *Id.*, para. 1406.
16. *Id.*, para. 1381.
17. *Id.*, para. 1407.
18. *Id.*, para. 1444.
19. *Id.*, para. 1445.
20. The text of the Convention is available at <https://treaties.un.org/doc/publication/unts/volume%201155/volume-1155-i-18232-english.pdf> (last accessed on 12 June 2018).

expropriation of Yukos and thus a breach of Art. 13. It is clear from the tone of the award that the Tribunal was convinced that Russia's actions were politically and economically motivated, rather than aimed at legitimate tax enforcement.

2. *Breach of Art. 10 of the ECT*

One of the key reasons for the Tribunal's finding that Russia breached Art. 10 was the refusal of the Russian Tax Ministry and, subsequently, of its courts to reattribute to Yukos its trading companies' VAT refunds. The Tribunal noted that Russia had sought to convince it to adopt a broad interpretation to Russia's anti-tax abuse policy in order to reassign VAT obligations from the subsidiaries located in low-tax regions to Yukos, whilst at the same time seeking to rely on Yukos' error in filing VAT returns annually rather than monthly as a basis to prevent Yukos from claiming such refunds for itself.

In contrast with the Court, the Tribunal held that "it was arbitrary and contradictory for the authorities to re-attribute the trading companies' oil, revenues, profits, tax liabilities and activities to Yukos but to refuse to re-attribute to Yukos those companies' entitlement to VAT refunds".[21]

Interestingly, the Tribunal went out of its way to explain why its conclusions differed from those of the Court. Referring to the ECHR principle of proportionality, it noted that such principle requires a state "not to go further than is necessary to attain the objectives of ensuring the correct levying and collection of the tax and the prevention of tax evasion".[22] The Tribunal noted that the Court seemed to "have entirely missed the point being made, namely that if the tax authorities were going to attribute to Yukos the transactions carried out in the names of its trading companies, they should also have attributed to Yukos the submission of normal VAT documentation by the trading companies".[23] It criticized the Court for adopting an entirely formalistic approach when finding "that relevant rules made the procedure for VAT refunds sufficiently clear and accessible for the applicant company to [be] able to comply with it"[24] and that Yukos "failed to submit any proof that it had made a properly substantiated filing in accordance with the established procedure".[25]

In particular, the Tribunal strongly disagreed with the Court's conclusion that Yukos had not received "any adverse treatment in this respect",[26] finding that Yukos had received "some thirteen billion dollars-worth of adverse treatment by reason of the imposition on it of VAT liabilities earlier excluded by the undisputed export of the oil in question".[27]

As evidence corroborating its finding that Russia "would have done whatever was necessary to ensure that the VAT liability was imposed on Yukos" the Tribunal made reference to the second trial and conviction of Mikhail Khodorkovsky noting that after having been convicted of various tax-related crimes and sentenced for a term of nine

21. Award, fn. 10, para. 656.
22. *Id.*, para. 677.
23. *Id.*, para. 698.
24. *Id.*, para. 699.
25. *Ibid.*
26. *Ibid.*
27. *Id.*, para. 700.

years of imprisonment in May 2005 he was sentenced to an additional thirteen years and six months in prison essentially on the basis of the same circumstances surrounding Yukos that led to his original conviction for tax evasion.[28]

Turning next to the fines imposed by Russia for failing to pay liabilities, the Tribunal found these to be disproportionate and in breach of Russia's obligation under Art. 10. In this regard the Tribunal noted that the Court held that the retroactive application of Resolution 9–P violated the fundamental principle of legality and breached Art. 1 of Protocol No. 1 of the ECHR. The Tribunal concluded that the fines levied in relation to the 2000 tax year were therefore barred by the statute of limitations.[29]

The following facts persuaded the Tribunal to find that Russia had further breached its obligations under Art. 10. First, and unlike the Court, the Tribunal found that Yukos had made good faith attempts to settle its tax claim. Second, it noted that soon after Yukos was acquired by Rosneft, a significant portion of the tax assessments levied against YNG were set aside or vastly reduced by Russian courts. Third, and again unlike the Court, the Tribunal concluded that the price paid by Baikal at the auction for YNG was far below the fair value of those shares. Fourth, and contrary to the Court, the Tribunal was persuaded that the western banks "were actively 'encouraged' to enter into the confidential sale agreement in order to accomplish their objective of being paid".[30] The Tribunal held that although Yukos was to shoulder some of the blame for not paying the western banks and thereby increasing its exposure to the risk that it could be petitioned into bankruptcy, it appeared undeniable "that initiating bankruptcy was not the goal of the Western banks, but rather the objective of Rosneft, in the interests of its owner, the Russian Federation".[31] Finally, the Tribunal relied on the events surrounding the formal withdrawal by PricewaterhouseCoopers of all of its prior audit reports for Yukos as evidence "that Yukos was the object of a series of politically-motivated attacks by the Russian authorities that eventually led to its destruction".[32]

In view of the above, the Tribunal concluded that Russia had breached the shareholders' right to fair and equitable treatment "by failing to meet basic requirements of procedural propriety and due process, engaging in conduct that was unreasonable, arbitrary, disproportionate and abusive, and failing to ensure a stable and transparent legal and business framework".[33] Furthermore, it held that the removal of judges refusing to rule in Russia's favour and the lack of independence and impartiality of judges hearing Yukos' cases constituted a denial of justice in breach of the fair and equitable treatment standard of Art. 10(1). Finally, it held that Russian authorities had discriminated against the shareholders' investments by (i) singling out Yukos and treating it in a markedly different manner from other similar oil companies in Russia, (ii) treating YNG differently before and after its acquisition by Rosneft, and (iii) ensuring a differential treatment in the bankruptcy proceedings between creditors related to Yukos, on the one hand, and state-related creditors, on the other hand.

28. *Ibid.*
29. The Court reached the same decision.
30. Award, fn. 10, para. 1148.
31. *Ibid.*
32. *Id.*, para. 1253.
33. *Id.*, para. 108.

3. *Damages*[34]

In assessing damages suffered by the shareholders as a result of Russia's breaches of the ECT the Tribunal observed that there was an agreement between the parties that "in the event of an expropriation through a series of actions, the date of the expropriation is the date on which the incriminated actions first lead to a deprivation of the investor's property that crossed the threshold and became tantamount to an expropriation".[35]

The Tribunal then found that "a substantial and irreversible deprivation of Claimants' assets occurred on 19 December 2004, the date of the YNG auction"[36] since YNG was its main production asset.

Turning to the methodology for assessing damages the Tribunal noted that as the case before it was one of unlawful expropriation (the requirements set out in paras. (a) to (d) of Art. 13(1) not having been complied with by Russia) the shareholders were "entitled to select either the date of expropriation or the date of the award as the date of valuation".[37] In this regard the Tribunal made reference to Art. 36 of the International Law Commission's (ILC) Draft Articles on State Responsibility and noted that in case of an illegal expropriation investors "must enjoy the benefits of unanticipated events that increase the value of an expropriated asset up to the date of the decision, because they have a right to compensation in lieu of their right to restitution of the expropriated asset as of that date".[38]

In determining Yukos' value as of 21 November 2007 the Tribunal opted for the comparable companies method and then used the RTS Oil and Gas Index to calculate Yukos' value as at the date of the award, being 30 July 2014.

Loss of dividends which would have been paid to the shareholder but for the expropriation was considered by the Tribunal as the second element of the damages suffered by them as a result of expropriation of their investment. In the case of the value of Yukos, the Tribunal determined the value of the lost dividends on the date of the expropriation and the date of the award. The Tribunal concluded that "Yukos' dividends in 2004 would have been USD 2.5 billion, and the sum of Yukos' dividends over the period from 2004 through the first half of 2014 would have been USD 45 billion".[39]

It accordingly concluded that the damages suffered by shareholders (including interest) due to Russia's breach of Art. 13 of the ECT, based on a valuation date of 30 June 2014, amounted to US$ 66.694 billion.[40]

34. For a good analysis of the Tribunal's reasoning concerning damages see Irmgard MARBOE, *Yukos Universal Limited (Isle of Man) v. The Russian Federation* (Case Comment), 30 ICSID Review – Foreign Investment Law Journal (2015, no. 2) p. 326.
35. Award, fn 10, para. 1761.
36. *Id.*, para. 1762.
37. *Id.*, para. 1763.
38. The text of the International Law Commission's Draft Articles on the Responsibility of States for Internationally Wrongful Acts is available at <https://casebook.icrc.org/case-study/international-law-commission-articles-state-responsibility> (last accessed on 12 June 2018).
39. Award, fn. 10, para. 1812.
40. *Id.*, para. 1825.

Since the Tribunal had determined that the shareholders had contributed 25 percent to the prejudice they suffered at the hands of Russia, the total amount of damages awarded was reduced by 25 percent to US$ 50,020,867,798.

III. THE DECISION OF THE COURT

Yukos lodged a case against Russia for breaches of inter alia its rights under Arts. 6 and 18 of the ECHR and Art. 1 of Protocol No. 1 to the Convention on 23 April 2004. A one-day hearing was held on 4 March 2010.[41] The Court rendered its decision on the merits on 20 September 2011, just under three years before the Tribunal rendered its decision in respect of the ECT.

1. *Exclusion of Jurisdiction*

Before turning to the merits of the case, the Court had to determine whether it had jurisdiction to hear the case as arbitral proceedings discussed in Sect. II were underway. In particular, the Court had to determine whether its jurisdiction was excluded pursuant to Art. 35(2) of the ECHR.

Art. 35(2) provides that the Court cannot consider a matter which is "substantially the same" as one already being submitted to another procedure of international investigation or settlement.[42] Accordingly, the Court had to determine whether the case brought under the ECT was substantially the same as the matter put before it.

In reaching its decision on this point the Court adopted the triple identity test approach regularly adopted by arbitral tribunals in investment treaty cases in respect of "fork in the road" provisions.[43] Applying this test the Court found that although the proceedings before it and the Tribunal refer "to the same events"[44] the parties before them are different and that therefore the two matters were not "substantially the same".[45]

41. *OAO Neftyanaya Kompaniya Yukos* v. *Russia,* (Application No. 14902/04), (8 March 2012) available at <https://hudoc.echr.coe.int/eng#{%22itemid%22:[%22001-106308%22]}> (last accessed on 12 June 2018) (Decision).
42. The text of the ECHR is available at <https://www.echr.coe.int/Documents/Convention_ENG.pdf> (last accessed on 12 June 2018).
43. *Vivendi v. Argentina* (ICSID Case No. ARB/97/3), Award (21 November 2000) para. 53-5, available at <https://www.italaw.com/sites/default/files/case-documents/ita0206.pdf> (last accessed on 12 June 2018), *Azurix v. Argentina* (ICSID Case No. ARB/01/12), Decision on Jurisdiction (8 December 2003) paras. 37-41, 86-92, available at <https://www.italaw.com/sites/default/files/case-documents/ita0060.pdf> (last accessed on 12 June 2018). For further cases see fn. 166 in Rudolf DOLZER and Christopher SCHREUER, *Principles of International Investment Law,* 5th edn. (OUP 2012) p. 267.
44. Decision, fn. 41, para. 524.
45. *Ibid.*, para. 526.

2. *Breach of Art. 6*

Turning to the first substantive claim made by Yukos against Russia the Court examined the facts in the case through the prism of the obligations imposed on Russia under Art. 6 of the ECHR.[46] The Court found that Yukos had not been given enough time during the trial court or the appeal phase to study "the entirety of these documents and, more generally, to prepare for the hearings on the merits of the case on reasonable terms".[47] It also held that the "appeal court failed to acknowledge, let alone to remedy the shortcomings committed by the first-instance court as regards the applicant company's restricted access to the case file".[48] It therefore found Russia in breach of its obligation to accord Yukos a fair trial pursuant to Art. 6(1), taken in conjunction with Art. 6(3)(b).

3. *Breach of Art. 1 of Protocol No. 1*

Turning next to Russia's obligations under Art. 1 of Protocol No. 1, taken alone and in conjunction with Arts. 1, 7, 13, 14 and 18 of the ECHR, the Court noted that Yukos alleged that the "imposition and enforcement of the 2000-2003 Tax Assessments"[49] as well as the auction of YNG "were unlawful, arbitrary and disproportionate".[50]

Pursuant to Art. 1 of Protocol No. 1

> "[e]very natural or legal person is entitled to the peaceful enjoyment of his possessions. No one shall be deprived of his possessions except in the public interest and subject to the conditions provided for by law and by the general principles of international law. The preceding provisions shall not, however, in any way impair the right of a State to enforce such laws as it deems necessary to control the use of property in accordance with the general interest or to secure the payment of taxes or other contributions or penalties."[51]

Accordingly, the Court had to determine whether the actions taken by Russia as related to the tax re-assessment, the auctioning of YNG and the bankruptcy of Yukos amounted to interferences with its property rights and met the requirement of lawfulness, pursued a legitimate aim, were proportionate to the aim pursued and were not discriminatory within the meaning of Art. 14 of the Convention, taken in conjunction with Art. 1 of Protocol No. 1.

Contrary to the Tribunal, the Court started its analysis by finding that Yukos' decision to structure its operations in low-tax jurisdictions was a sham. The Court described its

46. Art. 6(1) provides that "[i]n the determination of his civil rights and obligations or of any criminal charge against him, everyone is entitled to a fair and public hearing within a reasonable time by an independent and impartial tribunal established by law". Art. 6(3) guarantees that "[e]veryone charged with a criminal offence has the following minimum rights: ... (b) to have adequate time and facilities for the preparation of his defence;...". ECHR, fn. 43.
47. Decision, fn. 41, para. 540.
48. *Id.*, para. 545.
49. *Id.*, para. 552.
50. *Ibid.*
51. *Id.*, para. 553.

role in quite a different manner to how the Tribunal saw its own. It noted that "[a]s regards the compliance with the domestic law, the Court has limited power ... since it is a matter which primarily lies within the competence of the domestic courts ... and that [a]s regards the quality of the law, the Court's task (was) to verify whether the applicable provisions of domestic law were sufficiently accessible, precise and foreseeable...".[52] Importantly, it noted that in respect of tax it had to afford Russia "an exceptionally wide margin of appreciation"[53] in the exercise of its fiscal functions under the lawfulness test given that the third sentence in Art. 1 of Protocol No. 1 expressly reserved the right of "[c]ontracting States to pass 'such laws as they may deem necessary to secure the payment of taxes'".[54]

Turning to the facts in question the Court held that "notwithstanding the [s]tate's margin of appreciation in this sphere", the Court found "that there has been a violation of Article 1 of Protocol No. 1 on account of the change in interpretation of the rules on the statutory time-bar resulting from the Constitutional Court's decision of 14 July 2005 and the effect of this decision on the outcome of the Tax Assessment 2000 proceedings".[55] It then went further to note that Yukos' "conviction under Article 122 of the Tax Code in the 2000 Tax Assessment proceedings laid the basis for finding the applicant company liable for a repeated offence with a 100% increase in the amount of the penalties due in the 2001 Tax Assessment proceedings", and thus found "that the 2001 Tax Assessment in the part ordering [Yukos] to pay the double fines was not in accordance with the law, as required by Article 1 of Protocol No. 1".[56]

Turning to the tax authorities' refusal to allow Yukos to claim a refund for the VAT reattributed to it, the Court simply found that Yukos "failed to submit any proof that it had made a properly substantiated filing in accordance with the established procedure".[57] As noted in the preceding Section, the Tribunal had found that the refusal of the tax authorities to allow Yukos to claim the refund resulted in a VAT obligation of US$ 13 billion. Therefore, the Court's conclusion that Yukos "did not receive any adverse treatment in this respect"[58] is perplexing.

Turning next to examine the actions of the Russian authorities to enforce the debt resulting from the tax assessments for the years 2000-2003, the Court noted that these involved the seizure of Yukos' assets, the imposition of a 7 percent enforcement fee on the overall amount of the debt and the forced sale of YNG. The Court, in stark contrast to the Tribunal, saw these actions as having the "common and ultimate goal ... to force the company to meet its tax liabilities".[59] It noted that it had "no reason to doubt that throughout the proceedings the actions of various authorities had a lawful basis and that the legal provisions in question were sufficiently precise and clear to meet the Convention standards concerning the quality of law".[60]

52. *Id.*, para. 559.
53. *Id.*, para. 566.
54. *Ibid.*
55. *Ibid.*
56. *Ibid.*
57. *Id.*, para. 602.
58. *Ibid.*
59. *Id.*, para. 646.
60. *Id.*, para. 647.

Although the Court found that the choice of auctioning YNG "as the first item"[61] to be auctioned in satisfaction of Yukos' liability was capable of dealing a fatal blow to its ability to survive the tax claims and to continue its existence, it nevertheless found that "in principle" the choice of auctioning YNG was not "entirely unreasonable".[62] The Court therefore found that the auctioning of YNG was disproportionate to the objectives of enforcing tax obligations but not arbitrary.

Turning to the 7 percent enforcement fee the Court found that "in the circumstances of the case the resulting sum was completely out of proportion to the amount of the enforcement expenses which could have possibly been expected to be borne or had actually been borne by the bailiffs".[63] It, therefore, held that "domestic authorities failed to strike a fair balance between the legitimate aims sought and the measures employed".[64] Without any detailed reasoning the Court held that an enforcement fee of 4 percent rather than 7 percent would have been proportionate.

4. *Breach of Art. 18 of the ECHR*

Turning next to Art. 18, the Court refused to find that the overall effect of the actions taken by Russia was "to destroy the company and to take control of its assets".[65] Accordingly, and unlike the Tribunal, the Court held that Yukos had not been able "to furnish the Court with an incontrovertible and direct proof in support of his or her allegations"[66] that the restrictions applied in respect of its rights under Art. 1 of Protocol No. 1 were in fact being applied for a purpose other than the one for which it was prescribed.[67]

The Court noted that it was Yukos which had to substantiate its allegations that the actions taken against it were politically motivated. It found that although it was "true that the case attracted massive public attention and that comments of different sorts were made by various bodies and individuals in this connection ... [t]he fact remained ... that those statements were made within their respective context and that as such they are of little evidentiary value for the purposes of Article 18".[68] The Court thus concluded that "there has been no violation of Article 18 of the Convention, taken in conjunction with Article 1 of Protocol No. 1, on account of the alleged disguised expropriation of the company's property and the alleged intentional destruction of the company itself".[69]

---

61. *Id.*, para. 633.
62. *Id.*, para. 654.
63. *Id.*, para. 655.
64. *Id.*, para. 657.
65. *Id.*, para. 623.
66. *Id.*, para. 663.
67. Art. 18 of the ECHR provides that "[t]he restrictions permitted under [the] Convention to the said rights and freedoms shall not be applied for any purpose other than those for which they have been prescribed". Fn. 42, p. 14.
68. Award, fn. 10, *id.*, para. 665.
69. *Id.*, para. 666.

5. *Assessment of Damages*

The Court turned to the question of the assessment of damages in its decision dated 15 December 2014.[70] Invoking the powers granted to it under Art. 41 of the ECHR the Court noted that it could not "speculate as to what the outcome of court proceedings might have been had the violation of the Convention not occurred"[71] and that there was "insufficient proof of a causal link between the violation found and the pecuniary damage allegedly sustained by the applicant company".[72] It therefore found that in respect of the breaches of Art. 6 there was "no ground for an award [of damages]".[73]

Turning to the assessment of damages in respect of the breaches of Art. 1 of Protocol No. 1 the Court found that the amount Yukos should be compensated on account of the retroactive imposition of the penalties, the payment of the enforcement fee and the conduct of enforcement proceedings was € 1,866,104,634. Although it had found that the auctioning of YNG was a disproportionate act, it did not award any damages in respect thereof.

IV. KEY REASONS FOR THE DIFFERENCES IN THE TWO DECISIONS

As Sects. II and III reveal the Tribunal and the Court reached starkly different decisions, with the Tribunal awarding damages in excess of US$ 50 billion and the Court awarding damages of € 1.86 billion. Given that the same facts are the basis for both decisions, the question is: What is the reason for this?

At first glance it may seem that the key reason for this difference is the different legal basis for reviewing Russia's actions vis-à-vis Yukos as between the Tribunal and the Court. However, it is clear from a careful review of the decisions that the key reason for the difference is their different findings of facts in the cases.

Whereas the Tribunal looked at the totality of the actions directed at Yukos, the Court did the opposite, dissecting the actions in turn. In fact, some of the most striking actions taken by the Russian authorities against Yukos, such as the commencement of the bankruptcy proceedings and its ultimate winding up, were only reviewed by the Court in a cursory manner.

Moreover, it is evident that the Tribunal perceived Russia's actions in a completely different light than the Court. By way of example, whereas the Tribunal found the fact that within forty-eight hours of issuing their payment demands for the year 2000 the tax authorities required Yukos to pay in full US$ 3.48 billion in alleged tax arrears, interest and fines and prohibited Yukos from selling or encumbering the company's shareholdings in its Russian subsidiaries as arbitrary and unfair, the Court found "no indication of arbitrariness or unfairness ... in this connection".[74]

---

70. *OAO Neftyanaya Kompaniya Yukos v. Russia,* (Application No. 14902/04) (15 December 2014) available at <http://hudoc.echr.coe.int/eng?i=001-145730> (last accessed on 12 June 2018) (Damages Decision).
71. *Id.*, para. 18.
72. *Id.*, para. 19.
73. *Ibid.*
74. Decision, fn. 41, para. 535.

Moreover, whereas the Tribunal considered the imprisonment of Mr. Khodorkovsky and other members of the management of Yukos as facts corroborating its findings, the Court dismissed their relevance, insisting that the burden of proof was on Yukos to establish the political motivation behind the actions taken by the Russian authorities.

The approach taken by the Court is surprising and disappointing. Given the nature of allegations concerning breaches of human rights, one would have expected the Court to adopt a broad approach to the review of the relevant facts rather than a narrow one. Adopting a highly technical and formalistic approach to reviewing the facts in cases of breaches of human rights runs the risk of failing to identify the heart of the breach. Governments are increasingly sophisticated in the manner in which they breach human rights of their citizens and deal with their political opponents. Consequently, the Court and other international institutional mechanisms for holding states to account must rise to that challenge.

As noted in Sect. II, the Tribunal accused the Court of being overly formalistic in its reasoning. From reading the Court's decision one does not get at all a sense of the gravity of the actions taken nor even the sheer amount of the tax liabilities, which exceeded US$ 31 billion, imposed on Yukos. Even the tone of the decisions is completely different, with the Court taking a more deferential view.

One possible way of explaining the different understanding of the facts could be the difference in the nature of the proceedings themselves. Whereas the hearing lasted only one day in the Court, the hearing on the merits in the arbitration took a month and was preceded by a hearing on jurisdiction of ten days. Moreover, the hearing before the Tribunal was preceded by several rounds of exchanges of written submissions and expert evidence and extensive document production. The Court did not have the benefit of detailed legal submissions nor the ability to cross-examine experts or witnesses.

The second key reason for the difference between the decisions is likely to stem from the presumption of bona fides on the part of a State to which the Court referred in its judgment. In fact the entire judgment is replete with statements of deference to Russia. No such presumption or deference exists under international investment law or general public international law.

The effect the operation of this presumption has on the outcome of a case can be seen from the different way in which the Court and the Tribunal approached the determination of the existence and significance of various so-called "anti-abuse" doctrines under Russian law. Unlike the Court, the Tribunal held that "at the time of the tax assessments against Yukos, the 'business purpose' doctrine ... had not yet been explicitly adopted into Russian law".[75] This important difference between the findings of the Tribunal and the Court is particularly stark since the Tribunal acknowledged that it had chosen not to accept in full the evidence put forward by Russia's expert concerning the anti-abuse doctrine even though the shareholders had not put forward any testimony challenging his evidence and chose not to cross-examine him on the existence of the doctrine. The readiness of the Tribunal to find against Russia has been criticized by human rights lawyers used to the Court taking a much more deferential view of a state's actions.

75. *Id.*, para. 663.

The third reason for the difference between the two decisions stems from their different approaches to the assessment of damages and causation further discussed in Sect. V below.

V. WHAT CAN HUMAN RIGHTS LEARN FROM ARBITRATION TO MEET THE CHALLENGES OF CLIMATE CHANGE LITIGATION?

Now that the key reasons for the difference between the two decisions have been identified, this Section discusses the four key ways in which the system of protecting human rights ought to be enhanced to meet the challenges of climate change litigation by adopting the rules of procedure used in commercial and investment treaty arbitration and by granting powers regularly exercised by arbitral tribunals to the Court and other international human rights institutions.

First, the procedural rules of the Court ought to change to allow for several rounds of pleadings, exchanges of expert reports, and the cross-examination of experts and witnesses. As noted in Sect. IV, whereas the hearing on the merits before the arbitral tribunal lasted fourteen days the hearing on the merits of the *Yukos* claim in the Court was only one day.[76] This is simply inadequate to deal with the complexity of climate change and environmental cases going forward.

Moreover, the idea that such a complex case as *Yukos*, where there was a considerable difference between the parties' pleadings on Russian law, could be determined by the Court without probing the experts or witnesses is at odds with how such matters are resolved in arbitration and, for that matter, in national courts. As discussed at the beginning of this article, in the future many more claims for breach of proprietary rights are likely to be brought before the Court and other human rights institutions whether relating to climate change or otherwise. These claims will be factually and legally much more complex than the types of claims heard to date by these institutions and will likely be largely based on expert evidence. The rules of procedure concerning pleadings and hearings, as well as the format of the application form, will need to be changed to allow the Court to fulfil its function as the protector of human rights.

Second, the presumption of the bona fide nature of state actions applied by the Court when analyzing actions of States must be abolished. The Court underlined the importance of this presumption in the Khodorkovsky case when it noted that the "whole structure of the Convention rests on the general assumption that public authorities in the member States act in good faith".[77] The Court does not provide any authorities for the existence of this assumption in international or national laws. It is often claimed that such a presumption is the corollary of a state's obligation under customary international law to act in good faith.[78] But how can a state's international law obligation to act in

76. In fact typically cases before the ECHR are decided on documents only.

77. *Khodorkovskiy v. Russia* (Application no. 5829/04), Judgement (28 November 2011), available at <http://hudoc.echr.coe.int/eng?i=001-104983> (last accessed on 12 June 2018).

78. William BURKE-WHITE and Andreas VON STADEN, "The Need for Public Law Standards of Review in Investor-State Arbitrations" in Stephan W. SCHILL, ed., *International Investment Law and Comparative Public Law* (OUP 2010) p. 705.

good faith be turned into a presumption that it does in fact act in good faith? This simply cannot be correct.

Moreover, how can such a "general assumption" be defended in the twenty-first century especially within a body of law concerned with ensuring the defence of human rights and by a court whose purpose is to act as the objective enforcer of human rights? The operation of this presumption together with the requirement of exhaustion of local remedies and the doctrine of the margin of appreciation unjustifiably limit the ability to hold states to account in respect of human rights, and in a way that the reviewability of acts *iure gestionis* is not limited in national courts.

Third, the Court must start using its power to grant interim measures under Art. 39 of the ECHR more robustly. The power to grant injunctions is a powerful tool at the disposition of tribunals in international commercial and investment treaty arbitrations. The readiness of tribunals and national courts to use this power is key to an efficient and effective legal system as it provides a mechanism to address the situation where irreparable damage would otherwise be caused to a claimant. The ability to obtain freezing of assets orders and other interim measures significantly reduces the likelihood of breaches and, as such, the mere threat of the power being used acts as an important deterrent.

Although the test for granting an injunction adopted by international arbitral tribunals is substantially the same as that under Art. 39 of the ECHR, the Court has interpreted its power extremely narrowly. The Court has to date held that torture, house eviction and extradition are the only instances of "an imminent risk of irreparable harm".[79]

Such a narrow interpretation of the Court's power under Art. 39 further and seriously undermines the effectiveness of the international human rights legal system, especially when combined with the requirement of exhaustion of local remedies. The fact that multinational companies are able to obtain interim measures in respect of proprietary claims whereas individuals are not able to get them in respect of breaches of human rights is difficult to justify in modern democracies. This difference in standards of protection is putting the credibility of the entire system of enforcement of human rights at stake.

Fourth, there is a wide consensus amongst human rights lawyers that awards of damages granted by the Court are "relatively low compared to damages awarded by domestic courts of some Council of Europe states".[80] Compared to awards in arbitration they are very low. The difference in the amount of damages awarded by the Court in the *Yukos* case when compared to that of the Tribunal is revealing. The key reason for this difference is the "prevailing view that the primary remedy in Strasbourg is the finding of a violation of the Convention itself".[81] The support for this narrow interpretation of the Court's powers cannot be found in the actual wording of the ECHR.[82] There is nothing

79. ECHR, Interim measures (1 February 2018), available at <https://www.echr.coe.int/Documents/FS_Interim_measures_ENG.pdf> (last accessed on 12 June 2018).
80. Philip LEACH, *Taking a Case to the European Court of Human Rights*, 3rd edn. (OUP 2011) p. 600.
81. *Ibid.*
82. Art. 41 of the ECHR provides that "[i]f the Court finds that there has been a violation of the Convention or the Protocols thereto, and if the internal law of the High Contracting Party concerned allows only partial reparation to be made, the Court shall, if necessary, afford just satisfaction to the injured party". Fn. 48.

in the wording of Art. 41 to support the argument that the finding of breach should double up as a remedy.

As Judge Bonello said in *Aquilina v. Malta* it is "wholly inadequate and unacceptable that a court of justice should 'satisfy' the victim of a breach of fundamental rights with a mere handout of legal idiom".[83]

The Court has a lot to learn from investment treaty tribunals as well as from commercial arbitral tribunals and national courts with regard to the assessment of damages and causality. In cases of breaches of political rights under Art. 6 the Court regularly refuses to grant damages on the grounds that there is no clear link between the damages claimed and the alleged violation.[84] Many ECHR judges have expressed their dismay at the continued reluctance of the Court to even ensure that redress for fundamental rights at the international level is at least the same as that granted in national courts. For example, Judge Casadevall and Judge Kovler noted in *Kingsley v. UK*[85] that the Court could have made an award of damages by reference to loss of opportunities or damage to reputation.

How stark the gap is in the approach taken by the Court and arbitral tribunals is revealed by looking at the *Yukos* case. Whereas the Court refused to award damages in respect of the breach of an Art. 6 right, the Tribunal had no difficulty in respect of the same facts granting damages for the breach of fair and equitable treatment applying the "but for" test.

That the principle which the Court should apply when assessing pecuniary damages is the same as that taken by an investment treaty or commercial arbitral tribunal is clear from the ECHR's Practice Directions on Just Satisfaction of Claims. It provides that "the applicant should be place[d] as far as possible in the position in which he or she would have been had the violation found not taken place, in other words *restitutio in integrum*".[86]

The same basis for the assessment was adopted by the Tribunal. However, unlike the Court the Tribunal noted that since restitution can only take place at the time of the award, the value of an asset at the time of the award was decisive. It therefore held that shareholders (i) should enjoy the benefits of unanticipated events that increase the value of the expropriated assets up to the date of the decision, and (ii) should not bear risks of unanticipated events which diminish the value of the assets. By granting the shareholders the right to choose between the date of expropriation and date of the award as the date of assessment of damages, the shareholders were able to receive over US$ 44 billion more in damages.

83. *Aquilina v. Malta* (Application no. 25642/94), (29 April 1999) p. 20, available at <http://hudoc.echr.coe.int/eng?i=001-58239> (last accessed on 12 June 2018).

84. ECHR, *Practice Direction: Just Satisfaction Claims* (September 2016) at paras. 7 and 8, available at <https://www.echr.coe.int/Documents/PD_satisfaction_claims_ENG.pdf> (last accessed 12 June 2018).

85. *Kingsley v. United Kingdom* (Application no. 35605/97), (28 May 2002) available at <http://hudoc.echr.coe.int/eng?i=001-60487> (last accessed on 12 June 2018).

86. ECHR, fn. 84, para. 10. For a discussion on how the approach taken by the Court in assessing damages in case of expropriation differs from that adopted in public international law see Héléne RUIZ FABRI, "The Approach Taken by the European Court of Human Rights to the Assessment of Compensation for 'Regulatory Expropriations' of the Property of Foreign Investors", 11 N.Y.U. Envtl L.J. (2002-2003) p. 148.

VI. WHAT CAN INTERNATIONAL ARBITRATION LEARN FROM HUMAN RIGHTS – A HUMAN RIGHTS LAWYER'S POINT OF VIEW[87]

The task of the state to protect and to foster its citizens' rights inevitably results in conflict: between the rights of the individual – natural or legal – on the one hand, and the right of the community represented by the state on the other.[88] Decision-makers tasked with resolving investment disputes have to take account of that conflict and must develop a framework that aids the reconciliation of the actors' competing rights and duties. The Court has been a pioneer in the creation of a framework balancing the right of the individual and the right of the state as a place-holder for the community of citizens it represents.

An analysis of the Court's judgment in *Yukos* and the *Yukos* Tribunal's final award reveals substantive similarities in the reasoning of the two bodies. Both the Court and the Tribunal put an emphasis on the Russian authorities' "excessive harshness"[89] and their "unyielding" inflexibility as to the pace of the proceedings.[90] Both considered the rights-infringements on the part of Russia to be so severe that they granted the Claimant a record amount of compensation. In that respect, the *Yukos* case confirms that a human rights analysis does not significantly differ in its outcome from the analyses of tribunals under an investment treaty.

Similarities notwithstanding, the decisions are far from identical. The Tribunal refused to examine the procedural improprieties of the case under "fair and equitable treatment" standard, whereas the Court conducted an in-depth analysis of a violation of the Claimant's right to a "fair trial". And the two bodies advanced diametrically opposed views on the Claimant's "political motivation" charge. Since investment tribunals and human rights courts do not operate in "parallel universes" it should be the aim of either regime to learn from the other and to adopt, albeit modified, proven paradigms to avoid divergence regarding fundamental legal principles. The following briefly outlines four principles arising out of the Court's judgment which in the author's view should be adopted by investment arbitral tribunals to aid the reconciliation of the actors' competing rights and duties.

87. This Section was written by Petra Butler and represents her views on what arbitration can learn from human rights.

88. *Soering v The United Kingdom*, Application No. 14038/88 (7 July 1989) p. 89; Rolv RYSSDAL, "Opinion: The Coming Age of the European Convention on Human Rights", 1 EHRLR (1996) p. 18, p. 26. This is a very simplistic statement – being the core/starting point-issues arise in all shades of grey. For the purpose of the argument advanced in this addendum the core statement is sufficient.

89. Award, fn. 10.

90. Decision, fn. 41, para. 1583.

1. *Balancing of Conflicting Rights' Positions*

Human rights methodology provides for a balancing of conflicting rights' positions.[91]

The *Yukos* case illustrates the importance of this balancing. While the Tribunal did not accept that Russia's measures had pursued the legitimate aim of collecting taxes,[92] the Court considered that the Russian authorities' actions "pursued a legitimate aim of securing the payment of taxes", and that the 2000-2003 assessments were proportionate measure in pursuit of that aim.[93] The Court went further – adopting the domestic authorities' assessment that the Claimant's trading companies were "sham entities"[94] and accepting the "fact"[95] that the Claimant had been found guilty of running a tax evasion scheme.

All this testifies to the Court's opinion that Russia had not acted arbitrarily. However, the Court's determination that measures pursued the legitimate aim of collecting taxes was not determinative. Instead, the Court proceeded through a wider proportionality analysis, in which it considered whether the measures were suitable, necessary and proportional in view of the legitimate aim. Ultimately, the court determined that the measures were not.

It is this proportionality analysis to which tribunals should pay particular note. The analysis formed the focal point of the Court's reasoning whether Russia's actions were justified.[96] According to well-established Court jurisprudence, the proportionality analysis has four limbs: (1) the measure in question is prescribed by law; (2) the measure has a legitimate aim; (3) the measure is necessary to achieve that aim;[97] and (4) there is a reasonable relationship of proportionality between the measure and the aim sought to be realized.[98] A fair balance must be struck between the demands of the general interest of the community and the requirements of the protection of the individual's fundamental rights.[99]

A full account of the Court's analysis is beyond the scope of this addendum,[100] but the important point to note for the instant purpose is that the Court acknowledged Russia's

91. Petra BUTLER, "Red Riding Hood – Is Investor-State Arbitration the Big Bad Wolf?", 5 Penn. St. J.L. & Int'l Aff. (2017) p. 328, p. 362.
92. Holding that the respondent was "not engaged in a true, good faith tax collection exercise" (*Yukos* Award, fn. 2, p. 985), and was "not driven by motives of tax collection", p. 1037.
93. Decision, fn. 41, para. 606.
94. *Id.*, para. 592.
95. *Id.*, para. 649.
96. See Christoph GRABENWARTER and Katharina PABEL, *Europäische Menschenrechtskonvention: Ein Studienbuch*, 6th ed. (C. H. Beck, München 2016) Sect. 18 paras. 14 et seq.
97. Monica CARSS-FRISK, "A Guide to the Implementation of Article 1 of Protocol No. 1 to the European Convention on Human Rights", Human Rights Handbook No. 4 (Council of Europe, Strasbourg 2003) p. 109 et seq.
98. *James v. the United Kingdom*, A98 (1986) p. 50; and *Lithgow v. the United Kingdom*, A102 (1986) p. 120
99. *Sporrong and Lönnroth v. Sweden*, A52 (1982) p. 69 and 73; *Tre Traktörer Aktiebolag v. Sweden*, A159 (1989) p. 59; *Hentrich v. France*, A296-A (1994) p. 45-49; *Holy Monasteries v. Greece*, A301-A (1994) p. 70.
100. Decision, fn. 41, paras. 606 et seq.

legitimate aim to pursue the collection of taxes[101] (relying on Art. 1(2) of Protocol No. 1 to the ECHR)[102] and the wide margin of appreciation Russia enjoyed in the tax sphere in order to implement its policies. However, when ascertaining whether Russia struck a fair balance between the legitimate interest in enforcing the tax debt in question and the protection of the Claimant's rights set forth in Art. 1 of Protocol No. 1[103] it found that Russian authorities did not employ the least infringing measures to pursue their aim.[104] The Court stressed that the crux of the case did not lie in the attachment of the Claimant's assets and cash per se, but rather in: (1) the speed with which the authorities demanded the company make payment, (2) the decision that that Claimant's main production unit would be the first asset to be compulsorily auctioned, and (3) the speed with which the auction had been carried out.[105] Thus, Russia had violated the Claimant's right to property under Art. 1 of Protocol No. 1 by instituting the enforcement proceedings against the Claimant.[106]

2. *Reliance on Well-Established Legal Standards*

Investment treaty arbitration proceedings generally evolve around standards that are "re-phrased" human rights standards, such as "fair and equitable treatment", denial of justice, or expropriation. In the Award the parties argued about the standard for expropriation laid out in Art. 13(1) ECT, and the level of protection guaranteed by the "fair and equitable" treatment standard in Art. 10(1) ECT (minimum standard or higher level of protection?).

The Court's jurisprudence, as well as the jurisprudence of other human rights tribunals, provides arbitral tribunals with an important extra resource to interpret those standards. As Harris et al. note, the ECHR is the "most advanced instrument of this kind. It has generated the most sophisticated and detailed jurisprudence in international human rights law."[107]

Having regard to Court jurisprudence would have added to the robustness of the Tribunal's reasoning.[108]

---

101. *Id.*, para. 606.
102. David HARRIS et al., *Law of the European Convention on Human Rights*, 2nd ed. (OUP 2009) p. 668. Compare also Clare OVEY and Robin WHITE, *The European Convention on Human Rights*, 4th ed. (OUP 2006) p. 370, p. 373; Nußberger observes that only rarely will an interference with the right to property be unlawful due to an illegitimate aim, as states enjoy a very wide margin of appreciation in this respect: Angelika NUßBERGER, "*Enteignung und Entschädigung nach der EMRK*" in Otto DEPENHEUER and Foroud SHIRVANI, ed., *Die Enteignung: Historische, vergleichende, dogmatische und politische Perspektiven auf ein Rechtsinstitut* (Springer, Berlin 2018) p. 89 p. 102.
103. Decision, fn. 41, paras. 646, 648.
104. *Id.*, para. 653.
105. Decision, fn. 41, para. 650.
106. *Id.*, para. 658.
107. David HARRIS et al., fn. 102, p. 30.
108. E.g., the Court has continuously stressed that under Art. 6 ECHR it is only concerned with the question whether the proceedings as a whole have been fair: see *Gäfgen v. Germany*, Judgment, ECtHR App. No. 22978/05, paras. 162-188 (1 June 2010); Decision, fn. 41, para. 534; see also

3. *Implementation of Judicial Self-Restraint*

Tribunals should include a human rights analysis in their decision-making process. In the author's view, the inclusion of such a process will lead to judicial self-restraint.

The "margin of appreciation" doctrine plays a crucial role in this respect. The baseline of the doctrine was first explained by the Court in *Handyside v. the United Kingdom*, which noted that state authorities are in a better position than an international judge to take a view on the content of moral requirements and on the "'necessity' of a 'restriction' or 'penalty' intended to meet them".[109] This discretion is encapsulated in the "fourth instance" doctrine, which states that the Court does not constitute a further court of appeal from the decisions of national courts applying domestic law.[110]

The implementation of the margin of appreciation meant that the Court was not called upon to scrutinize the legality of the Russian tax authorities' measures under domestic law. It was "sufficient" for the Court to satisfy itself that the findings of the domestic courts had neither been arbitrary nor manifestly unreasonable.[111]

In the author's view arbitral tribunals should develop a margin of appreciation doctrine within investment arbitration. A state must have some scope to decide on how to fulfil its function. Margin of appreciation is part of the proportionality analysis, and speaks to whether the measure has a legitimate aim and whether or not the state has to choose the least infringing measure available to the state if the result of doing so is that other legitimate goals can also be achieved. The margin of appreciation has to be assessed in light of the investment treaty (or in the *Yukos* case, the ECT). By entering into an investment treaty a state circumscribes its policy choices, with the result that it may only be able to limit the rights of an investor in the most severe circumstances.[112]

4. *Standard of Proof*

The Tribunal and the Court differ in the standard of proof they each apply. The Court defines the standard of proof for the party who bears the burden of persuasion with regard to a certain factual question or mixed factual and legal questions. The jurisprudence of the Court reveals that the state's standard of proof can fall into three categories: strict, intermediate, and lenient scrutiny.[113] The nature of the violation and

---

Petra BUTLER, "Human Rights" in Andrea BJORKLUND et al., *Cambridge Compendium of International Commercial and Investment Arbitration* (CUP, forthcoming).

109. See *Handyside v. the United Kingdom*, Judgment, ECtHR App No 5493/72, para. 48 (7 December 1976).
110. See David HARRIS, et al., fn. 102, p. 14.
111. Decision, fn. 41, para. 594.
112. See Art. 9 of the Hong Kong – ASEAN Free Trade Agreement (FTA) (12 Nov 2017) which sets out explicitly when the state can adopt measures necessary to maintain public morals or the protection of privacy of individuals.
113. Depending on the width of the margin of appreciation. Mónika AMBRUS, "The European Court of Human Rights and Standards of Proof" in Lukasz GRUSZCZYNSKI and Wouter WERNER, eds., *Deference in International Courts and Tribunals: Standard of Review and Margin of Appreciation* (OUP, 2014) p. 235. The Canadian Supreme Court also has noted that the right in question and the facts of a case are determinative on the level of standard of proof required (*R v. Oakes* [1986] 1 RCS 103, 137, 138 (SCC)).

the importance of the right are the most important factors in determining which standard the Court applies.[114] For example, the Court requires a high standard of proof in cases concerning the right to life and the freedom from torture.[115]

Tribunals should look to adopt a more nuanced approach to standard of proof – one which is linked to the margin of appreciation. By adopting a more bespoke approach, tribunals will be better equipped to strike fair balance between safeguarding the individual's rights on the one hand, and the rights of the community on the other.

5. *Conclusion*

Arbitral tribunals are tasked with balancing the rights of the investor with those of the state's community. Using a human rights framework in an arbitral tribunal's decision-making will not necessarily lead to a different outcome. However, it will lead to a more robust methodological approach and reliance on well-established legal principles. The inclusion of a human rights analysis into its decision-making process will increase an investment arbitration tribunal's legitimacy and public acceptance. In terms of Darwinian theory, "evolution by means of adaptation" might be one in a range of the silver bullets for mastering the current challenges of investment arbitration.

VII. CONCLUSION

Human rights protection and the protection of foreign investment have the same objective: to protect non-state entities from state power.[116] In order to meet the challenges posed by climate change both arbitration and human rights must learn from each other. In particular, rather than lowering the bar of investor protection we must raise the bar for the protection of human rights by ensuring that the Court exercises its powers to grant interim measures and award damages, and by changing the way it takes evidence.

114. See, e.g., *Guiliani and Gaggio v. Italy* (App. no. 23458/02), ECtHR 2011; *Nachova and others v. Bulgaria* (app. nos. 43577/98, 43579/98), ECtHR (Chamber) 2004.

115. *Guiliani and Gaggio v. Italy*, above; The Court's jurisprudence regarding Arts. 2 and 3 reveals that strict scrutiny is akin to "beyond reasonable doubt".

116. Erik DE BRABANDERE, "Complementarity or Conflict? Contrasting the *Yukos*-case before the European Court of Human Rights and the Investment Tribunals", 30 ICSID Review – Foreign Investment Law Journal (2015, no. 2) p. 345.

Plenary Session
New Frontiers in International Arbitration

Part II:
Potential of Arbitration Involving New Stakeholders

Scope for Enlarged Participation in International Arbitration

Campbell McLachlan QC[*]

TABLE OF CONTENTS

I. INTRODUCTION

Two great innovative arbitrations that bookend the last decade–*Abyei*[1] and the first cases under the *Bangladesh Accord*[2] – provide the inspiration for this closing panel. At first blush these cases, however individually remarkable, look unlikely companions. *Abyei* concerned the delimitation of a territorial boundary between a national liberation movement and a sovereign state whilst the *Bangladesh Accord* case involved a claim between trade unions and international buyers from the Bangladesh garment industry on building safety. Neither of them appears to provide an obvious precedent for a more general expansion of participation in international arbitration when set against the backdrop of the great engine of commercial arbitration that is the prime focus of this Council.

---

* Professor of Law, Victoria University of Wellington; *Associé Institut de Droit International*; Associate Member, Bankside Chambers (Auckland & Singapore), Essex Court Chambers (London); Senior Research Fellow 2019 KFG Berlin-Potsdam Research Group "International Rule of Law: Rise or Decline?".

1. *Sudan v. The Sudan People's Liberation Movement/Army (the Abyei Arbitration)* (Final Award, 22 July 2009) XXX RIAA 145 (*Abyei*), as to which see: V. LOWE and A. TZANAKOPOULOS "Introduction: The Abyei Arbitration" in L. BOSMAN and H. CLARK, eds., *The Abyei Arbitration*, Permanent Court of Arbitration Award Series, Volume 9 (2012) p. 1; W. MILES, "The *Abyei* Arbitration: A Model for Peaceful Resolution of Disputes Involving Non-state Actors" in U. FRANKE, A. MAGNUSSON and J. DAHLQUIST, *Arbitrating for Peace: How Arbitration Made a Difference* (Kluwer, Alphen aan den Rijn 2016), p. 223; cf. G. BORN and A. RAVIV "The Abyei Arbitration and the Rule of Law", 58 Harv ILJ (2017) p. 177.
2. *IndustriALL Global Union v. Respondent* (PCA Case Nos. 2016-36 and 2016-37), case details available at: <https://pca-cpa.org/en/cases/152/> (*Bangladesh Accord Arbitrations*); Accord on Fire and Building Safety in Bangladesh (13 May 2013) available at: <http://www.industriall-union.org/sites/default/files/uploads/documents/2013-05-13_-_accord_on_fire_and_building_safety_in_bangladesh_0.pdf> (last accessed 21 January 2019) (Bangladesh Accord). The 2013 Accord had a five-year duration (Preamble, para 2). It has now been replaced by the 2018 Accord, which will expire on 31 May 2021, at which time "the work will be handed over to a national regulatory body, supported by the International Labor Organization" (Preamble, para. 2).

Yet these two cases, when considered together, are significant both for what they demonstrate about the gaps in the contemporary system of international dispute resolution that arbitration is uniquely able to fill and the essential conditions and qualities needed if arbitration is in fact going to be able to meet the needs of enlarged participation on a more general basis. The cases are significant in at least three key respects: (a) the pre-conditions needed for the insertion of binding third-party determination according to law into a complex international dispute; (b) the capacity of the arbitral process to accommodate group claims that would otherwise not have an available and effective international forum; and (c) the core attributes of the arbitral process that justify its privileged place in international dispute resolution.

Arbitration does not hold such a position simply by virtue of party autonomy. As the International Law Commission put it:

> "It is not the fact alone that the *compromis* may provide that the award is binding on the parties which makes it so binding. The view of States that international law makes an arbitration award binding, the circumstance that the tribunal faithfully has adhered to the fundamental principles of law governing its proceedings, these are the ultimate sources of the binding authority of an international arbitral award."[3]

The argument presented here is that arbitration does have the capacity to determine complex disputes on the international plane that could not otherwise be effectively determined in any court, national or international. Its capacity to do so is always dependent on the willingness of the parties to subject themselves to third-party binding adjudication of a particular dispute. It is no accident that both of the cases examined here arose from major crises in which other means of dispute resolution had been tried but found insufficient and a special framework had to be created to provide for arbitration. If these precedents are to have any more general benefit, that will require a determination on the part of States and private stakeholders to build a framework that enables more general resort to arbitration and addresses the limitations that arbitration ordinarily has in facilitating group claims.

The paper will develop this argument under five heads:

(1) The particular context that lead to the arbitration agreement in each case;
(2) The gap in participation in international dispute resolution that each agreement was designed to fill;
(3) The significance of the cases in terms of the core elements of the arbitral process;
(4) The implications of two arbitral processes as possible precedent; and,
(5) The elements that would have to be addressed if the potential of international arbitration in this regard were to be fully realized.

3. International Law Commission, "Commentary on the Draft Convention on Arbitral Procedure adopted by the International Law Commission at its Fifth Session, prepared by the Secretariat of the United Nations" (A/CN.4/92, 1955) p. 105.

This last point is not merely technical. The larger point that invites consideration in the light of both of these cases is that the process of international arbitration serves not only the needs of international commerce, but also serves a wider purpose in the pacific settlement of international disputes.[4] These two purposes are neither distinct nor antithetical. They are mutually interdependent goals. Not only is peace and security an essential condition for economic development; but also "the fullest collaboration between all nations in the economic field with the object of securing, for all, improved labour standards, economic advancement, and social security" (to borrow the language of the Atlantic Charter)[5] is a key means of promoting peace and security.

II. CONTEXT

Though they are both arbitrations conducted under the auspices of the Permanent Court of Arbitration (PCA) in The Hague, each of *Abyei* and the *Bangladesh Accord* arbitrations took place under special arbitration agreements concluded between the Parties following major crises. They are anything but usual cases.

1. Abyei

In the case of *Abyei*, as the Award relates, the context was two long-running civil wars in Sudan: "The Abyei Area is said to be at the geographical centre of this civil war, which is the longest running conflict in Africa and has caused some two million deaths, significant economic destruction and untold suffering, particularly for the people of Southern Sudan."[6] Negotiations for Peace had led to a series of agreements entered into between the Government of Sudan and the Sudan People's Liberation Movement/Army (SPLM/A) representing Southern Sudan, including an agreement to establish an Abyei Boundaries Commission (ABC) to define and demarcate the Abyei Area.[7] These agreements were in turn reconfirmed in the Comprehensive Peace Agreement concluded on 9 July 2005.[8] The ABC carried out its work and delivered its Experts' Report on 14 July 2005. But disagreements arose between the Parties as to whether the ABC Experts exceeded their mandate.[9] In order to resolve these disagreements, the

4. Art. 33(1) Charter of the United Nations (signed 26 June 1945, entered into force 24 October 1945) 59 Stat. 1031, 145 UKTS 805 provides: "The parties to any dispute, the continuance of which is likely to endanger the maintenance of international peace and security, shall, first of all, seek a solution by negotiation, enquiry, mediation, conciliation, *arbitration*, judicial settlement, resort to regional agencies or arrangements, or other peaceful means of their own choice." (emphasis added).
5. Fifth Principle, Declaration of Principles known as the Atlantic Charter issued by the Prime Minister of the United Kingdom and the President of the United States of America (signed 14 August 1941) 204 LNTS 384.
6. *Abyei*, [109].
7. *Ibid.*, [113]-[117]; Abyei Protocol (26 May 2004) and Abyei Appendix (17 December 2004).
8. *Ibid.*, [118].
9. *Ibid.*, [133].

Parties agreed to submit their dispute to arbitration.[10] They agreed to apply the PCA Optional Rules for Arbitrating Disputes between Two Parties of which only one is a State.[11] They provided that the Award "shall be final and binding"[12] and that "the Presidency of the Republic of Sudan shall ensure [its] immediate execution".[13] The Tribunal issued its Award on 22 July 2009.

2. *Bangladesh Accord*

The context for the conclusion of the Bangladesh Accord, including its arbitration agreement, also concerned a major humanitarian crisis, but in a very different context. The Accord was concluded on 13 May 2013 in the immediate aftermath of the April 2013 Rana Plaza building collapse in the Bangladesh garment industry that led to the death of more than 1,100 people and injured more than 2,000. Its signatories now include over 200 global brands, retailers and importers in 20 countries in Europe, North America, Asia and Australia and 10 trade unions.[14] The Accord commits the Parties to "a safe and sustainable Bangladeshi Ready-Made Garment ('RMG') industry in which no worker needs to fear fires, building collapses, or other accidents that could be prevented with reasonable health and safety measures".[15] It "covers all suppliers producing products for the signatory companies", which the signatories "shall require ... to accept inspections and implement remediation measures in their factories".[16] If a supplier fails to implement remediation measures required by the Accord Safety Inspector, the signatory is required to implement a process that, if the default is not remedied, leads to termination of the business relationship.[17]

The Accord is governed by a Steering Committee, with equal representation of trade union and company representatives and a (non-voting) chair appointed by the International Labour Organization.[18] Disputes between the Parties relating to the implementation of the Accord must first be submitted to the Steering Committee for decision by majority vote. "Upon request of either party, the decision of the SC may be appealed to a final and binding arbitration process," the resulting award to be enforceable in the courts of the domicile of the relevant signatory and subject to the 1958 New York Convention where it is applicable.[19]

In the two arbitrations to have arisen to date under the Accord, the Steering Committee was deadlocked. It reached the decision that it was unable to agree on the merits of a complaint brought by two trade unions, noting that the trade unions have the

10. *Ibid.*, [134]-[135]; Abyei Arbitration Agreement (7 July 2008), reproduced in L. BOSMAN and H. CLARK at p. 453.
11. Art. 1(1) Abyei Arbitration Agreement.
12. Art. 9(2).
13. Art. 9(5).
14. *Bangladesh Accord Arbitrations*, Procedural Order No. 2 (4 September 2017) ("PO No 2"), [4].
15. Bangladesh Accord, preamble para 1.
16. *Ibid.*, "Scope."
17. *Ibid.*, "Supplier Incentives" [21].
18. *Ibid.*, [4].
19. *Ibid.*, [5]; Convention on the Recognition and Enforcement of Foreign Arbitral Awards (signed 10 June 1958, entered into force 7 June 1959) 330 UNTS 38 (New York Convention).

right to proceed to arbitration.[20] The tribunals were constituted; confirmed their jurisdiction to determine the claims; and rejected the Respondents' admissibility objection.[21] The claims were settled in December 2017 and January 2018 respectively and terminated by agreement in July 2018.[22]

In 2018, the parties to the original Accord adopted a revised "Transition Accord on Fire and Building Safety in Bangladesh".[23] This revised Accord continues the fire and building safety programme until 2021. Clause 3 deals with dispute resolution. It continues to refer in the first instance to the Steering Committee, which is now mandated to adopt a dispute resolution process, including the opportunity for mediation. Nevertheless, arbitration remains the backstop form of dispute resolution. The revised dispute resolution clause specifies arbitration under the last revision of the UNCITRAL Arbitration Rules, seated in The Hague, administered by the Permanent Court of Arbitration. The applicable law of the revised Accord is the law of the Netherlands.[24]

III. JURISDICTION RATIONE PERSONAE

In each case, the arbitration agreement concluded between the Parties filled a critical gap in the reach of binding third-party adjudication of disputes and demonstrated the capacity of the arbitral process to address that gap.

1. *Abyei*

Since World War II, the majority of armed conflicts have been internal rather than international disputes. Where an intra-State peace agreement can be negotiated, the secure demarcation of territorial disputes is often a key element. Yet many such peace agreements fail, in part for want of an available means of third-party dispute settlement.[25]

The nature of such agreements means that they fall outside the jurisdiction of established courts. The national courts of the home State are unlikely to be acceptable to both parties. On the international plane, the Statute of the International Court of Justice

20. *Bangladesh Accord Arbitrations* PO No. 2, [53].
21. *Ibid.*, [104].
22. Termination Orders dated 17 July 2018 available at: <https://pca-cpa.org/en/cases/152> (last accessed 21 January 2019).
23. Available at: <https://admin.bangladeshaccord.org/wp-content/uploads/2018/08/2018-Accord.pdf> (last accessed 21 January 2019).
24. *Ibid.*, [24]. On 19 May 2019, the Accord, which had been subject to legal challenge in the Bangladesh courts, reached a settlement under which its functions will be transferred to a national Bangladesh safety entity, all other elements of the Accord remaining in place: <https://bangladeshaccord.org/updates/2019/05/19/accord-reaches-resolution-on-continua tion-of-its-work-in-bangladesh> (last accessed 28 May 2019).
25. M. BOLTJES, *Implementing Negotiated Agreements: The Real Challenge to Intra-State Peace* (Cambridge UP 2007); N. CASPERSEN, *Peace Agreements* (Wiley 2016).

provides that "Only States may be parties in cases before the Court."[26] National liberation movements enjoy a measure of legal personality at international law.[27] But they are not competent to bring a case before the Court.

In the case of Sudan, the SPLM/A had been recognized as the appropriate representative of the people of Southern Sudan. In that capacity it had negotiated and entered into the Comprehensive Peace Agreement and the specific accords and agreements relating to the Abyei Area. The delineation of the Abyei Area nevertheless had particular implications for the potential creation of a new State. The Abyei Protocol provided for a referendum of the "residents of the Abyei Area" simultaneously with a referendum of the people of Southern Sudan. The latter would determine whether to confirm the unity of Sudan or to vote for secession. The Abyei Referendum would decide whether the residents of Abyei wished to remain a special administrative region in the north or to become part of a southern province. As the Tribunal put it, the consequences of the choice to be made by the residents of the Abyei Area were that "they may find themselves north or south of an international boundary if South Sudan secedes".[28]

If, then, the submission of the *Abyei* dispute to arbitration was a prelude to the possible emergence of a new State in the future, the decision to do so challenged conventional conceptions of arbitration. As at the date of the arbitration agreement, the dispute was not, in the terms of the 1907 Hague Peace Convention, an "[i]nternational arbitration [which] has for its object the settlement of differences between States".[29]

Yet this was not ultimately an impediment. The PCA "is competent to place its offices and staff at the disposal of the Contracting Powers for the use of any special Board of Arbitration"[30] and its Council may settle "rules of procedure".[31] The PCA has since 1934 accepted the administration of cases between a non-State party and a State[32] and has developed specific rules for such cases, which rules were applied in *Abyei*.[33] Moreover the

26. Art. 34(1) Statute of the International Court of Justice (signed 26 June 1945, entered into force 24 October 1945) 59 Stat 1055; UKTS 67 (1946); R. KOLB, *The International Court of Justice* (Hart, Oxford 2013) p. 263.
27. R. JENNINGS and A. WATTS, eds., *Oppenheim's International Law*, 9th ed., (Longmans 1992) vol. 1, pp. 161-165.
28. *Abyei*, [594]. In the event, from 9 to 15 January 2011, an internationally monitored referendum was held in South Sudan in which 98.83 percent of the voters voted in favour of independence: Southern Sudan Independent Referendum Commission "Final Results Report, 7 February 2011", p. 94. On 9 July 2011, South Sudan seceded from the Republic of Sudan and became a sovereign, independent State, the Republic of South Sudan. South Sudan was admitted to membership of the United Nations on 14 July 2011. No official Abyei Referendum could be held and the status of the Area remains contested and subject to UN supervision: UNSC Res 2386 (2017).
29. Art. 37, Convention for the Pacific Settlement of International Disputes (adopted 18 October 1907, entered into force 26 January 1910) (1907) 205 CTS 233.
30. *Ibid.* Art. 47.
31. *Ibid.* Art. 49.
32. *Radio Corporation of America v. China* (Award, 13 April 1935) III RIAA 1621, 8 ILR 26; J.D. AMADO, J.S. KERN and M.D. RODRIGUEZ, *Arbitrating the Conduct of International Investors* (Cambridge UP 2018) p. 11.
33. PCA, Optional Rules for Arbitrating Disputes Between Two Parties of Which Only One Is a State 1993.

use of international arbitration for the determination of territorial disputes at the sub-national level is not unprecedented, tribunals finding that they are entitled to refer, in addition to any specific agreements between the parties and applicable constitutional provisions within the State, general principles of international law.[34]

2. *Bangladesh Accord*

The arbitration agreement in the *Bangladesh Accord* is no less remarkable for the way in which it extended the ordinary reach of international arbitration. As recently as 2015 a general survey of the use of arbitration in international labour disputes pointed out that the creation of a standing tribunal to resolve international labour disputes "remains an ideal".[35]

The Bangladesh Accord deals with one set of international labour issues only (fire and building safety) and then only in respect of one industry in one country. Yet within this framework it breaks new ground. It binds together in a direct contractual relationship that includes an arbitration agreement two parties that otherwise would not have been so bound: the international brands that buy the garments manufactured in Bangladesh and the unions representing the factory workers.[36]

A significant development on the workers' side of the dispute has been the establishment of global trade unions, with the capacity to act on behalf of a group of national unions in order to negotiate and conclude global framework agreements with multinational corporations.[37]

These distinctive features are well summarized by the Tribunal:

> "In the Tribunal's view, this case cannot be characterized either as a classic 'public law' arbitration (involving a State as a party) or as a traditional commercial arbitration (involving private parties and interests), or even as a typical labor dispute. A number of features distinguish the Accord from such categorizations, including (a) the creation of the Accord in the wake of the Rana Plaza tragedy; (b) the number of signatories to the Accord (over 200 as the date the arbitrations were commenced); (c) the number of supplier factories affected by the Accord (over 1600); (d) the number of workers in the Ready-Made Garment industry

34. *Kanton Wallis v. Kanton Tessin* (Swiss Federal Court, 2 July 1980) BGE 106 Ib 154; *Dubai-Sharjah Border Arbitration* (19 October 1981) 91 ILR 543, cited in *Abyei* [430]-[431]; and see also: *Brčko Inter-Entity Boundary (Bosnia v. Republika Srpska)* (Interim Award, 14 February 1997) 36 ILM 396, (Final Award, 5 March 1999) 38 ILM 534, on which see: R.J. HARRY, "The Brčko Arbitation" in U. FRANKE (2016) Ch. 11; Ch. SCHREUER 11 Leiden JIL (1998) p. 71, 12 Leiden JIL (1999) p. 575. For a recent example of the use of arbitration to determine a title dispute between Maori tribal groups in New Zealand see: *Ngāti Whakaue v. Ngāti Wahiao* [2016] NZHC 1486, [2017] NZCA 429, [2017] 3 NZLR 770, citing *Abyei* at [66]-[68].

35. K. CLAUSSEN, "The Use of Arbitration to Decide International Labour Issues" in A. BLACKETT and A. TREBILCOCK, *Research Handbook on Transnational Labour Law* (Edward Elgar 2015) Ch. 28, p. 395.

36. For a critique see: C. SCHEPER, "Labour Networks Under Supply Chain Capitalism: The Politics of the Bangladesh Accord", 48 Development and Change (2017) p. 1069.

37. <http://admin.industriall-union.org/issues/confronting-global-capital/global-framework-agreements> (last accessed 16 February 2017).

protected by Accord (over 2 million); (e) the involvement of international organizations in the negotiation and governance of the Accord (including the ILO); (f) the involvement of States and State entities in the negotiation and oversight of the Accord (including the government of Bangladesh); (g) the involvement of Bangladeshi and international non-governmental organizations as witnesses to the Accord and in an advisory capacity; and (h) the public nature of the Accord itself and many associated documents, as well as detailed information about factory remediation under the Accord."[38]

For present purposes, the Accord is distinctive because it furnishes standing consent on the part of 200 international brand companies to submit to international arbitration a claim by a union representing workers in supplier factories that the companies have failed to abide by their Accord undertakings. It is not a "multi-stakeholder initiative". The supplier factories are not directly party to it; nor are the workers themselves. Rather the Accord places the responsibility directly on the purchasing company to ensure that its suppliers comply with the remediation requirements under the Accord. It subjects the purchasing company to arbitration in the event of an alleged default and empowers the unions to bring arbitral proceedings in the event that a dispute over building safety cannot be resolved within the Steering Committee. For this purpose, the Accord relies upon the enforcement mechanism of the New York Convention. It adopts and incorporates the provisions of the UNCITRAL Model Law on International Commercial Arbitration as applicable to the process of the arbitration.[39]

IV. THE ARBITRAL PROCESS

The two cases have important implications for the operation of the arbitral process. In the first place, in both cases the parties chose arbitration as part of a larger dispute resolution process.

In *Abyei*, the first step had been an expert determination by the Abyei Boundaries Commission (ABC). Their procedure was explicitly technical and not legal. The experts were to be knowledgeable in history and geography; they were required to listen to the representatives of the people and to consult the archives in order to arrive at a decision that "shall be based on scientific analysis and research".[40] By contrast, the arbitral tribunal was asked to decide "[w]hether or not the ABC experts had ... exceeded their mandate" and to do so according to the applicable law.[41]

In *Bangladesh Accord* the parties were required first to present their dispute to the Steering Committee (consisting of an equal number of company and union representatives) for decision. The Accord then permitted either party to appeal the

38. *Bangladesh Accord Arbitrations* PO No. 2, [93].
39. Bangladesh Accord, [5]. The reference to the UNCITRAL Model Law may have been intended to be to the UNCITRAL Arbitration Rules. The tribunals in the *Bangladesh Accord Arbitrations* applied the latter to their proceedings: PO No. 1, [14.1].
40. Abyei Appendix, Sect. 4, cited at *Abyei* [116].
41. Arts. 2 and 3 Abyei Arbitration Agreement, reproduced in L. BOSMAN and H. CLARK at pp. 456-457.

decision of the Committee to a final and binding arbitration process.[42] The provision for arbitration performs a useful ultimate adjudicatory role in the rare case where the Steering Committee either cannot reach a decision or its decision is not accepted. Nevertheless its significance must be seen in the context of the inspection and remediation process, which is being carried out on a very large scale and which, in view of the ultimate remedy of business termination in the event of non-compliance, has led to a high level of compliance without the need for an adjudicatory process.[43]

In both cases the reference to arbitration sought to support the alternative forms of dispute resolution by ensuring that, in the event that either party was dissatisfied with their outcome, they could resort to a formal determination according to law. But the parties' arbitration agreement in each case led to a quite different scope of review.

In *Abyei*, the Tribunal, construing the terms of the agreement in light of the jurisprudence of the International Court of Justice, determined that it "must limit itself to assessing whether the ABC Experts' findings can be understood as a not unreasonable discharge of their mandate, that is, as an exercise that does not amount to a manifest breach of the competence assigned to them".[44] Although this element of its reasoning did not go uncontested,[45] it has proved to have a much wider application in guiding international tribunals charged with the review of the decisions of other bodies.[46]

The Tribunal also found as a general principle that a failure on the part of the Commission to state reasons for a decision may lead to an excess of mandate.[47] The Parties were entitled to expect that "an award should contain sufficient ratiocination to allow the reader to understand how the tribunal reached its binding conclusions (regardless of whether the ratiocination might persuade a disengaged third party that the award is substantively correct)".[48] Awards might be set aside if the conclusions were not supported by any reasons at all, where the reasoning is incoherent or obviously incoherent or frivolous. This part of its decision has also been subject to criticism.[49] No doubt the adequacy of reasoning required will depend upon the nature of the particular arbitration and the issues. But the *Abyei* standard has proved to be influential in subsequent cases concerning the review of arbitral awards.[50]

---

42. Bangladesh Accord, [5].
43. Bangladesh Accord "Quarterly Aggregate Report" (October 2018) available at: <https://admin.bangladeshaccord.org/wp-content/uploads/2018/12/Accord_Quarterly_Aggregate_Report_October_2018.pdf> (last accessed 21 January 2019).
44. *Abyei*, [510].
45. Dissent of Judge *Al-Khasawneh*, [181]-[182], [192]; G. BORN and A. RAVIV "The Abyei Arbitration and the Rule of Law", 58 Harv ILJ (2017) p. 177.
46. As in the case of an application for the annulment of an arbitral award on the ground that "the Tribunal has manifestly exceeded its powers" under Art. 52(1)(b) ICSID Convention: *Fraport AG v. Philippines* (ICSID Case No ARB/03/25), Decision on Annulment (2010) [44]; LOWE and TZANOPOULOS, [65]-[66].
47. *Abyei*, [518]-[535].
48. *Ibid.*, [531].
49. G. BORN and A. RAVIV, pp. 193-200.
50. *Ngāti Whakaue v. Ngāti Wahiao* [2017] NZCA 429, [2017] 3 NZLR 770, [66]-[68]. For discussion of the reasoning requirement in domestic commercial cases see: *Westport Ins Corp v. Gordian Runoff Ltd* [2011] HCA 37, 244 CLR 239, 281 ALR 593; D. WILLIAMS and A KAWHARU, *Williams & Kawharu on Arbitration*, 2nd ed. (LexisNexis, Wellington 2017) [14.10.1].

By contrast, the terms of the Bangladesh Accord does not limit the reference to arbitration to the question of excess of mandate. Rather it provides that the decision of the Steering Committee may be "appealed to a final and binding arbitration process". The Tribunal found that on its own the term "appeal" does not denote whether the tribunal's task was to be a de novo review or something more limited. However "considering the non-legal, industry-based character of the first level of decision-making, there is every reason to believe that the Accord signatories considered that the 'arbitration' to which that initial decision could be 'appealed' would involve the full fact-finding and law-deciding authority of standard arbitral processes".[51]

V. IMPLICATIONS FOR ENLARGED PARTICIPATION GENERALLY

Both *Abyei* and the *Bangladesh Accord Arbitrations* are each the product of their respective particular set of circumstances. They are important in themselves for their contribution of a legal framework to the resolution of complex problems, even if they have not resolved all aspects of the wider matrix of those problems. As Lowe and Tzanopolous conclude: "decisions of tribunals cannot be expected to settle disputes unless the parties intend to cooperate fully in the implementation of the decision ... but they can make a major contribution in clarifying the position by identifying strong legal rights and dismissing untenable claims".[52]

They are also important as precedents for the ability of the arbitral process to bring together before an independent international tribunal parties that otherwise would not be so subject.

The question that this leaves is the extent to which this experience is capable of being generalized and how this might be achieved. It is tempting to say that, arbitration agreements being the expression of the will of the parties, this is simply a matter of party autonomy: that parties, whether political, private, commercial or industrial should simply be left to determine for themselves whether they wish to choose arbitration as their preferred means for the resolution of their disputes. Yet this would be to ignore the fact that, as in the *Bangladesh Accord Arbitrations*, the parties may not otherwise be in a contractual relationship that would ordinarily provide a basis for an arbitration agreement; or that, as in *Abyei*, the dispute may be seen as internal within a State so as not ordinarily to admit of international adjudication.

Moreover it would be to underrate the significance of the wider international institutional support that facilitated the resort to arbitration: in the case of *Abyei* the Parties were assisted to reach agreement through the involvement of the wider international community, notably the Inter-Governmental Authority on Development (IGAD) and the African Union.

Submission to international arbitration for the resolution of intra-state disputes has continued in South Sudan. A "Revitalised Agreement on the Resolution of the Conflict in

51. *Bangladesh Accord Arbitrations* PO No. 2, [63].
52. V. LOWE and A. TZANOPOULOS, [64]. On the continuing difficulties in resolving the *Abyei* dispute and securing compliance with the Award see: UNSC Res 2386 (2017); G. BORN and A. RAVIV, pp. 222-224.

the Republic of South Sudan" was concluded under the auspices of IGAD on 12 September 2018.[53] The Parties include both the Transitional Government of South Sudan and various opposition and other political parties. One element of the Agreement is the establishment of a Technical Boundary Committee "to define and demarcate the tribal areas of South Sudan as they stood on 1 January 1956 and the tribal areas in dispute in the country".[54] In the event that any tribe claims that the report of this Committee is violated, that tribe is entitled to resort to arbitration against the Government of South Sudan before the Permanent Court of Arbitration in The Hague.[55]

In the case of the *Bangladesh Accord* the International Labour Organization has had a strong role in facilitating the Accord and its implementation through the Steering Committee. In both cases, the process of arbitration was facilitated by the availability of the Permanent Court of Arbitration, which served as Registry and provided substantial administrative support. In both cases, the arbitrations were conducted under internationally developed procedural rules: the PCA's "Optional Rules for Arbitrating Disputes between Two Parties of which only one is a State" in the case of *Abyei* and the UNCITRAL Arbitration Rules 2010 in the case of the *Bangladesh Accord*.

The *Bangladesh Accord* has three further features that may have more general implications. In the first place, it brings together a large number of corporate and union parties in a standing agreement that, inter alia, provides for arbitration in the event of a dispute that cannot be resolved by other means. It does so within an umbrella contractual framework that lies outside the dense network of contract relations between particular buyers and their suppliers, though the *Accord* makes plain that a failure to abide by remediation required under its terms may produce real effects at the supply contract level. The result is that the resolution of disputes is not left to *ad hoc* agreements concluded after a dispute has arisen nor is such agreement left to the decision of individual buyers.

Second, all of the parties to the Accord participate in a standing framework that is designed to address the problems of building safety in the Bangladesh garment industry. They have a collective voice in decision-making through the Steering Committee (and related bodies). Arbitration performs only part of that wider process, existing to support it where the parties cannot otherwise agree on the solution in a particular case.

Third, the Parties specifically agree that any Award will be internationally enforceable under the New York Convention in the courts of the domicile of the signatory against whom enforcement is sought. This represents a major advance in international enforcement that only arbitration can provide. The courts of the host State would only exceptionally be able to exercise jurisdiction to enforce building safety standards as a matter of public law against international buyers. Such companies would likely not be subject to the personal jurisdiction of host state courts. In the normal case, the responsibility for building safety would fall on the local occupier. In any event, any

53. Intergovernmental Authority on Development, "Revitalised Agreement on the Resolution of the Conflict in the Republic of South Sudan" (signed 12 September 2018) available at: <https://igad.int/programs/115-south-sudan-office/1950-signed-revitalized-agreement-on-the-resolution-of-the-conflict-in-south-sudan> (last accessed 1 February 2019).

54. *Ibid.*, Art. 1.15.18.1.

55. *Ibid.*, Art. 1.15.18.7

judgment of the host state courts imposing such a liability for breach of public law standards as the suit of the state would only exceptionally be enforceable abroad.[56] By agreeing to arbitration and applying the enforcement mechanism of the New York Convention, the Parties to the Bangladesh Accord ensured that the responsibility for implementation assumed by the international brands is reinforced, where ultimately necessary, by enforceability at home.

The New York Convention itself takes liberal view of the kinds of disputes that may be validly submitted to arbitration and in turn the subject of an enforceable award. It applies to disputes "in respect of a defined legal relationship, whether contractual or not, concerning a subject matter capable of settlement by arbitration".[57] It extends "not only to awards made by arbitrators appointed for each case but also those made by permanent arbitral bodies to which the parties have submitted".[58]

This example offers potential in many other contexts, in which international arbitration can offer a neutral forum for the resolution of disputes that may otherwise founder for want of a forum. An example is the field of environmental disputes. Arbitration is widely, though not universally, agreed to as the preferred means of dispute resolution between states in multilateral environmental treaties.[59] But such agreements are unlikely to apply directly to disputes involving private parties that are alleged to cause environmental harm.

International arbitration is capable of resolving such disputes. The Permanent Court of Arbitration has developed a specific set of Optional Rules for Arbitration of Disputes relating to the Environment and/or Natural Resources (PCA Environmental Arbitration Rules), which have been used in several disputes.[60] The prospect for using arbitration to decide such claims has also arisen with increasing frequency in the context of counterclaims in investment arbitration. Of course a State may not wish to pursue such claims in arbitration. It may prefer, for good public reasons, to enforce the obligations of all private parties (whether domestic or foreign) under its own environmental regulations before host state courts.

---

56. See further C.A. MCLACHLAN *Foreign Relations Law* (Cambridge UP 2014) Ch. 11, esp. [11.73]-[11.84].
57. Art. II, New York Convention. Note however that, pursuant to Art. I(3) a State may, when it becomes party to the Convention "declare that it will apply the Convention only to differences arising out of legal relationships, whether contractual or not, which are considered as commercial under the national law of the State". At the time of writing, 47 of the 157 States Parties have made such a declaration: <http://www.uncitral.org/uncitral/en/uncitral_texts/arbitration/NYConvention_status.html> (last accessed 16 February 2018). On the construction of this declaration see: UNCITRAL, "Guide on the Convention on the Recognition and Enforcement of Foreign Arbitral Awards" (New York 1958) (2016 ed.) UN Sales No E.16.V.7, [83]-[91].
58. Art. I(2).
59. T. STEPHENS, *International Courts and Environmental Protection* (Cambridge UP 2009) pp. 28-36. Art. 14(2)(b) United Nations Framework Convention on Climate Change (signed 9 May 1992, entered into force 21 March 1994) 1771 UNTS 107 provides for the adoption by the Conference of Parties of an Annex on Arbitration, which has not yet been adopted.
60. J. LEVINE "Information About the Activities of the Permanent Court of Arbitration in Environmental Disputes in the Context of Energy Projects" (PCA 2014); J. LEVINE, "Adopting and Adapting Arbitration for Climate Change-related Disputes" in W. MILES, ed., *Dispute Resolution and Climate Change: The Paris Agreement and Beyond* (ICC 2017) Ch. 3.

Where the State does wish to avail itself of arbitration as an alternative means of resolving such a dispute (securing in the process the advantage of international enforceability of any award against the foreign investor), it will be necessary for the tribunal to find that it has a basis for jurisdiction over such a counterclaim; that it is admissible, being sufficiently closely related to the investor's claims; and that the investor owes a duty under the applicable law.[61] The majority of counterclaims asserted in investment arbitration to date have failed on the view taken by the tribunal on the proper interpretation of the investment treaty as instrument of consent pursuant to one or more of these grounds.[62]

A study recently prepared with the support of the Permanent Court of Arbitration and published in January 2018 explores the limitations of the current structure of investment treaties in facilitating such claims, whether by way of counterclaim or original action and proposes a number of alternative models should States wish to amend their treaty arrangements to facilitate such claims.[63] The framers of the Convention on the Settlement of Investment Disputes between States and Nationals of Other States (the ICSID Convention) expressly envisaged both possibilities. Art. 25 makes provision on a fully bilateral basis for "any legal dispute arising directly out of an investment between a Contracting State ... and a national of another Contracting State".[64] Art. 46 requires a tribunal, save in the case of contrary agreement, to "determine any incidental or additional claims or counterclaims arising directly out of the subject-matter of the dispute provided that they are within the scope of the consent of the parties and are otherwise within the jurisdiction of the Centre".[65]

Despite the limitations that have been encountered in practice, the recent examples of the Decisions on Counterclaims in the *Burlington* and *Perenco v. Ecuador* cases[66] show that, where there is jurisdiction (in those cases by consent), an international arbitral tribunal is fully competent to determine very complex claims for environmental remediation. In so doing, it may, pursuant to Art. 42(1) (second sentence) of the ICSID Convention, apply the tort law of the host state to determine the applicable legal standards.[67]

---

61. *Urbaser SA v. Argentina* (ICSID Case No ARB/07/26), Award (8 December 2016) Pt XII.
62. For discussion see: M. TORAL and T. SCHULTZ, "The State, a Perpetual Respondent in Investment Arbitration?" in M. WAIBEL et al., eds., *The Backlash Against Investment Arbitration* (Kluwer 2010) p. 577; BUBROWSKI, "Balancing IIA Arbitration Through the Use of Counterclaims" in A. DE MESTRAL and C. LÉVESQUE, eds. *Improving International Investment Agreements* (Routledge 2013) p. 212; D. ATANANSOVA, A.M. BENOIT and J. OSTRANSKY, "Legal Framework for Counterclaims in Investment Treaty Arbitration", 31 J Int"l Arb (2014) p. 357.
63. J.D. AMADO, J.S. KERN and M.D. RODRIGUEZ, *Arbitrating the Conduct of International Investors* (Cambridge UP 2018).
64. Art. 25, Convention on the Settlement of Investment Disputes between States and Nationals of Other States (signed 18 March 1965, entered into force 14 October 1966) 575 UNTS 159 (ICSID Convention).
65. *Ibid.*, Art. 46.
66. *Burlington Resources Inc v. Ecuador* (ICSID Case No ARB/08/5), Decision on Counterclaims (7 February 2017); *Perenco Ecuador Ltd v. Ecuador* (ICSID Case No ARB/08/6), Interim Decision on the Environmental Counterclaim (11 August 2015).
67. *Burlington* [71]-[74]; *Perenco* [319] et seq.

Important though they are, these decisions do not however resolve the difficult questions of jurisdiction, admissibility and applicable law that otherwise arise for tribunals to whom application is made to accept such claims in the absence of *ad hoc* agreement between the parties. Nor do they challenge the bilateral paradigm of an investment dispute. To be sure, in such cases the State stands as *parens patriae*, claiming damages in order to secure remediation for the benefit of the people. But the decisions do not have direct implications for the admission of new parties to arbitral proceedings. By contrast, the Bangladesh Accord demonstrates the potential value of bringing together a number of parties under the umbrella of the same standing agreement. It is to the significance of this aspect of that case as a precedent that attention must finally turn.

VI. CONDITIONS FOR ENLARGED PARTICIPATION

The question whether arbitration is capable of providing for the aggregation of claims where the parties have an identity of interest arising out of the same dispute is critical to its ability to deal fairly with a larger range of complex transnational issues that either present common issues or involve multiple claimants or defendants.[68]

Courts, whether national or international, typically have procedural rules at their disposal that can facilitate the aggregation or consolidation of claims or provide for the identification of test cases. Such procedures promote efficiency, but they also implement important elements of the principle of legality: by promoting equal access to justice and ensuring consistency of approach between like cases. The standing of arbitration as a dispute resolution mechanism will ultimately be imperilled if arbitration clauses are upheld, particularly in contracts of adhesion, but the consolidation of claims refused.[69] There is a real risk that this can lead to a denial of justice if it has the effect of rendering otherwise valid claims uneconomic to pursue on an individualised basis.[70] More

68. See generally S.I. STRONG, *Class, Mass and Collective Arbitration in National and International Law* (Oxford UP 2013) and, in the context of investment arbitration: C. MCLACHLAN, L. SHORE and M. WEINIGER, *International Investment Arbitration: Substantive Principles*, 2nd ed. (Oxford UP 2017) Ch. 4, esp. [4.200]–[4.214], discussing *Abaclat and Others v. Argentina* (ICSID Case No ARB/07/5), Decision on Jurisdiction and Admissibility. IIC (2011) 504; *Ambiente Ufficio SpA. and Ors v. Argentina* (ICSID Case No ARB/08/09), Decision on Jurisdiction and Admissibility IIC 576 (2013); *Alemanni and Ors v. Argentina* (ICSID Case No ARB/07/8), Decision on Jurisdiction and Admissibility) IIC 666 (2014). For proposed models to deal with such claims see J. AMADO, "Mass Proceedings and Settlement Agreements", Ch. 4 in *Arbitrating the Conduct of International Investors*.
69. See, for example, the US Supreme Court jurisprudence upholding (by narrow majority) limits on the aggregation of claims in consumer cases under the Federal Arbitration Act: *Stolt-Nielsen SA v. Animal Feeds International Corp* 130 S. Ct. 1758 (2010); *AT&T Mobility LLC v. Conception* 131 S. Ct. 1740 (2011); *DIRECTV Inc v. Imburgia*, 136 S. Ct. 463 (2017) cf. Sect. 11 Arbitration Act 1996 (NZ) (arbitration agreements in consumer contracts unenforceable in the absence of separate written agreement after the dispute has arisen).
70. G. BORN, "The US Supreme Court and Class Action Arbitration: A Tragedy of Errors", <www.kluwerarbitrationblog.com> (1 July 2011) (last accessed 8 February 2018); "Arbitration Everywhere: Stacking the Deck of Justice", New York Times (31 October 2015, 1 November 2015).

generally, a limitation on the ability of arbitral tribunals to consolidate or marshal cases arising out of the same dispute heightens the risk of inconsistent decisions.[71]

The need to expand consolidation in order to ensure access and consistency is an illustration of a larger point made at the outset of this paper. International arbitration has considerable potential to resolve disputes involving parties that may otherwise not be amenable to effective dispute resolution. Its ability to do so depends in the first instance on the willingness of the parties, in the exercise of party autonomy, to commit to arbitration. But the ultimate source of legitimacy and binding effect of an international award is not simply a product of that agreement. It is also, as the International Law Commission observed "the circumstance that the tribunal faithfully has adhered to the fundamental principles of law governing its proceedings".[72]

71. As in *Lauder v. Czech Republic* (Award) 9 ICSID Rep 62, IIC 205 (UNCITRAL, 2001); *CME Czech Republic BV v. Czech Republic* (Partial Award) 9 ICSID Rep 121, IIC 61 (UNCITRAL, 2001); (Final Award) 9 ICSID Rep 264, IIC 62 (UNCITRAL, 2003), described as "the ultimate fiasco in investment arbitration": A. REINISCH "The Proliferation of International Dispute Settlement Mechanisms" in I. BUFFARD, et al., *International Law Between Universalism and Fragmentation: Festschrift in Honour of Gerhard Hafner* (2008) pp. 107, 116. The problem also arises where a number of claims arise out of the same state measure and give rise to a common legal issue.

72. Above fn. 3.

Closing Keynote Address

Closing Keynote Address

The Hon T.F. Bathurst *

TABLE OF CONTENTS | PAGE

I. INTRODUCTION

I would like to begin by acknowledging the traditional owners of the land on which we meet, the Gadigal people of the Eora nation, and pay my respects to their elders past, present and emerging.

It is a pleasure to have the opportunity to speak at the closing of this 24th ICCA Congress in Sydney. I have had the immense privilege of attending many of the sessions over the past three days – and of course enjoyed the social functions that attend these gatherings. It is also my great pleasure that the Congress this year has been held in my hometown of Sydney, and I hope that alongside all the learning and networking, you have had an opportunity to get outside and enjoy the weather, the beaches and the views.

Of course, of more importance than social functions and excursions, was the rigorous academic program that we have been exposed to. A significant amount of work has gone into each of the speakers' presentations and I thank them for devoting their time and expertise to the big issues that are facing international arbitration. Too often these events descend into an orgy of self-congratulations with little constructive being said. To the contrary, in this Congress we have been privileged to hear from over fifty speakers, all renowned experts on international arbitration, expressing what could only be described as a cosmopolitan view of the issues which will confront international arbitration in the coming years and the best means to deal with them. Now in the face of the quality of the presentations I will not try to compete with them but rather focus this morning on some of the key themes emerging from the past few days.

These themes are ultimately what you all, the players in this field, have determined are "The Future of International Arbitration". They seem to me to be, firstly, the internal challenge of legitimacy and associated with that issues of institutional design, costs, delays and transparency and secondly, the external challenges and opportunities that the coming years will bring in terms of technology. It is these two topics to which I will now turn.

* Chief Justice of New South Wales.

II. LEGITIMACY

Thomas Schultz on Monday helped frame this issue of legitimacy in practical terms – why do we care about legitimacy in international arbitration? He made the point that a regime that is not legitimate to the actors who can change it is likely to be unstable – that is, it is likely to change – and those who operate in that regime need to anticipate such changes.[1] One way we can think about legitimacy, therefore, is from the perspective of each actor who has change-making power. It is entirely sensible when one considers that any effort to define values that mean arbitration is "legitimate" needs to balance the myriad interests of its many players.

I think in the context of international arbitration and treating it as a process as distinct from a series of cases governed by particular rules of proceedings, legitimacy involves the concept of a process which is acceptable to the parties directly or indirectly affected by it. Legitimacy of commercial arbitration in that sense is vital. Quite apart from investor-state disputes it is the most common way of resolving international commercial disputes, its importance being enshrined in the 1958 New York Convention and the UNCITRAL Model Law on International Commercial Arbitration. It is thus a contributor to the rule of law and international commerce and order. This Congress can only be congratulated for paying such close attention to this issue. Confidence in the process or institution, whichever you prefer to call it, is critical in those circumstances.

One of the problems facing this community is a prevailing public perception that arbitration is not a legitimate means of resolving disputes that affect them. Of course the "legitimacy-elephant" in the room is Investor State Dispute Settlement. This issue, as we heard on Monday from Chief Justice Allsop,[2] caused significant public concern in this country around ratification of the TPP – or the new TPP-11– because of the Australian experience with the Philip Morris plain packaging tobacco dispute.

Unfortunately we are operating in an era where mistrust in public institutions is rife. It seems this sentiment is only amplified in relation to international institutions. The expropriation obligation has collided with notions of the public interest and states' rights.[3] When considering expropriation disputes, tribunals take into account whether measures taken are "proportional to the public interest presumably protected".[4] I think it is trite to say that questions of proportionality inevitably involve value judgments. The legitimacy of tribunals making these judgments, when they operate outside accountable domestic governments is in sharp focus. This is particularly so in countries such as Australia and perhaps other common law countries where the concept of proportionality as a legal tool is not perhaps as well understood and accepted as in civil law jurisdictions.

1. Thomas SCHULTZ, "Legitimacy Pragmatism in International Arbitration: A Framework for Analysis", this volume, pp. 25-59.
2. Chief Justice James ALLSOP AO, "Keynote Address", this volume, pp. 3-22.
3. As discussed by Melida HODGSON and Patricia Cruz Trabanino, "The Evolution of the Expropriation Obligation in Investment Arbitration and Its Adaptation in Treaties to Reflect State Rights", this volume, pp. 226-256.
4. *LG&E Energy Corp., LG&E Capital Corp., and LG&E International, Inc. v. Argentine Republic* (ICSID Case No. ARB/02/1), Decision on Liability (3 October 2006) [195] citing *Técnicas Medioambientales Tecmed S.A. v. The United Mexican States*, ICSID Case No. ARB (AF)/00/02 Award para. 154 (29 May 2003) [122].

We are already seeing pushback from this uncomfortable intersection – one example being the Court of Justice of the European Union (CJEU) ruling last month in *Slovak Republic v. Achmea*[5] – that the investor-state dispute arbitration clause in the Netherlands-Slovakia bilateral investment treaty is not compatible with EU law. In the CJEU's view, this arbitration clause removes disputes involving the interpretation of EU law from judicial review as provided for by the EU legal framework.[6]

A second issue is the provision in the "TPP-11" last month, for a senior level Commission with authority to issue interpretations of the agreement that are binding on tribunals considering it.[7] That Commission comprises government representatives of each party at the level of Ministers or senior officials.[8] Thus at least to a limited extent any arbitral tribunal's power to interpret the treaty potentially is limited.[9] Of course that has all been thrown up in the air just last week, but of course I am making no comment about that....

In this context of increasing involvement of public bodies in international arbitration, Chief Justice Menon posed the following question to consider: "Under what conditions is the exercise of power [over persons] ... which is mediated through the laws of international arbitration, rightful? And to what extent is it appropriate for certain actors to have a role in shaping the rules by which such power is acquired and exercised?"[10]

So at the same time we are questioning the legitimacy of private arbitration resolving disputes of a public nature, there is also a real question to be asked about the legitimacy of the involvement of public bodies in arbitration, as against the arbitration precepts of party autonomy and minimal curial intervention.

This involvement is problematic, firstly, because of state sovereignty and the effect of changing national attitudes towards arbitration, when domestic policies can "profoundly affect the global complexion of arbitration".[11] The second concern is accountability, where public actors make decisions as to arbitration with no accountability to the affected private parties. Thirdly, is legislative and judicial overreach to the extent that party autonomy and other interests of arbitration users are trampled in pursuit of public policy concerns. Fourthly is the inconsistency that results when different jurisdictions produce conflicting rules and norms as they seek, for example, to fill the gaps in the lex arbitri. This is affected by the fifth concern, being that of legal precision.[12]

The challenge for the future, in line with what Professor Schill contended at the Congress in 2016,[13] is to develop a "constitutional legal mindset in thinking about the

5. *Slowakische Republik v. Achmea BV* (Case C-284/16).
6. *Ibid.* [56].
7. Comprehensive and Progressive Agreement for Trans-Pacific Partnership, Art. 9.25(3) <http://dfat.gov.au/trade/agreements/not-yet-in-force/tpp-11/official-documents/Pages/official-documents.aspx>,
8. *Ibid.* chapter 27.
9. Discussed by Professor Lucy REED, "Lawmaking by Arbitrators", this volume, pp. 52-85.
10. Chief Justice Sundaresh MENON, "The Influence of Public Actors on Lawmaking in International Arbitration: Domestic Legislatures, Domestic Courts and International Organizations", this volume, pp. 112-150.
11. *Ibid.*
12. *Ibid.*
13. Stephan W. SCHILL, "Developing a Framework for the Legitimacy of International Arbitration" (ICCA Congress Series No 18, *Legitimacy: Myths, Realities, Challenges*).

functioning and legitimacy of international arbitration".[14] As Chief Justice Menon has suggested, what this requires is a concerted effort from all stakeholders to develop a set of core principles to articulate and guide the proper relationship between public actors and international arbitration.[15]

This is part of a broader need for arbitration to develop a certain level of "self-regulation" in order to maintain its autonomy.[16] Alexis Mourre made the point, and I believe it was well made, that the "development of procedural soft law is a fundamental condition for the establishment of trust in arbitration".[17]

But these sets of rules – such as guidelines on conflicts, best practices guides and the like – in turn require legitimacy. This requires that the process of rule-making is representative, transparent and consultative. An arbitral body engaged in a rule-making exercise should draft under the auspices of a representative task force, submit the draft for consultation with persons likely to participate in the process and engage in periodic review.[18] The harmonization of arbitration rules depends on consensus in this community, which is possible if you perceive yourselves as part of a global group sharing the same vision of arbitration as an "autonomous global system of justice".[19] Congresses such as these go a long way to helping establish this common mindset.

1. *Institutional Design*

It may be that some of legitimacy challenges stem from a perception of investor-state regimes being a "bad deal". Won Kidane suggested on Monday that this may be because of the impression that the expropriation obligation confers all the benefits on investors, with no commensurate benefit on the individuals those investors affect.[20] Concern over this imbalance has led to the imposition of some substantive obligations on investors under some contemporary treaties, such as through counterclaim provisions, but by and large it remains a one-way street. From an access point of view we were challenged as to whether it is necessary to rethink this aspect of structural design to temper the pivot away from its use.

The other big legitimacy discussion that has been had is over the issue of party appointment. Alfonzo Gomez-Acebo expressed the view on Monday afternoon that there is a problem with party appointments if it is thought the appointing party has a role to play in ensuring "their" party's position is understood by the tribunal.[21] This is because such a notion is hard to reconcile with precepts of impartiality and independence. There

---

14. *Ibid.* p. 826.
15. S. MENON, above fn. 10.
16. Alexis MOURRE, "Arbitral Institutions and Professional Organizations as Lawmakers", this volume, pp. 86-111 at p. 87.
17. *Ibid.*
18. *Ibid.*
19. *Ibid.*
20. Won KIDANE, "Sustainable Development Obligations and Access to Treaty Remedies in Contemporary Investment Treaties and Models", this volume, pp. 292-314.
21. Alfonso GOMEZ-ACEBO, "A Special Role of Party-Appointed Arbitrators?", this volume, pp. 318-416.

may be a role for soft-law producers, like the Chartered Institute of Arbitrators, to eliminate any such ambiguity.

There is however the converse side, that party appointment of arbitrators offers disputing parties confidence in the process. This is an important part of considering legitimacy from the perspective of party self-interest.[22] An important factor to remember, and one that is easily forgotten, is the reputation element for arbitrators – it is difficult to build up yet easily destroyed – and this can work against any incentive to taint a decision in favour of a party to secure future appointments.[23]

For commercial parties, the ability to select an arbitrator engenders a sense of control and proximity to the proceedings. It always has been an integral part of party autonomy in arbitration. Taking it away may diminish corporate users' preference for arbitration in the first instance.[24] The other issue is whether corporate users have faith in institutions to make appointments for them. In this context I think the point was well-made by Chief Justice Allsop on Monday, that it would be unwise to transmogrify concerns about ISDS into concerns about international commercial arbitration, as each needs to be understood from its own perspective.[25] The degrees of concern attending each field are different, and the solutions may need to be different too.

2. *Costs and Delays*

Perhaps it is trite to say it at this point, but a point of continued concern throughout this Congress has been the need to address costs, delays and transparency. Surveys from 2015 confirm this – respondents perceived the worst characteristic of international arbitration to be "cost".[26] Corporate decision-makers historically selected international arbitration as their contractual dispute mechanism because it was a faster, more effective way of deciding disputes. Its continued popularity is dependent on maintaining this competitive advantage.

It has been instructive at this Congress to hear perspectives from a variety of jurisdictions, offering ideas that I personally had never considered. It can serve as a timely reminder that what we might consider "arbitration orthodoxy" may represent only a fraction of what is possible. The organization of arbitration proceedings was, by and large, developed by practitioners from a narrow group of countries, who historically dominated its practice.

For example, the contribution of the Deputy General of the Beijing Arbitration Commission, Dr Fuyong Chen, offered insight into the manner in which that Commission relieves the concerns of users on efficiency and cost – by imposing a

22. Natalie Y. MORRIS-SHARMA, "The T(h)reat of Party Autonomy in ISDS Arbitrator Selection: Any Options for Preservation?", this volume, pp. 432-447.
23. *Ibid.*
24. Ruth STACKPOOL-MOORE, "Institutional Appointment of Arbitrators", this volume, pp. 417-431.
25. J. ALLSOP, above fn 2.
26. Queen Mary University of London, *2015 International Arbitration Survey: Improvements and Innovations in International Arbitration*, 7.

limitation on caseloads, requiring prompt delivery of awards and using technology to enable mobile access, notification, electronic signing and distance filing.[27]

Patricia Bergin, the former Chief Judge in Equity of the NSW Supreme Court, also raised the possibility that the arbitral process can learn from initiatives implemented in domestic courts, which face many common challenges. As she said, the current issues with the Redfern Schedule bear some analogy to the challenges faced with the formal discovery process in the NSW Supreme Court. In an attempt to control the burgeoning cost of the process a Practice Note was issued, requiring service of evidence prior to discovery except in exceptional circumstances, and limiting discovery to the issues in dispute as revealed by that evidence.[28]

I agree with the comments of Patricia at this Congress that this procedure has resulted in "the enhancement of the Court's capacity to control the process of document disclosure, the speedier resolution of commercial cases and the reduction of costs".[29] I appreciate that the Practice Note is not unique and that steps similar to that required by it have been adopted in many arbitrations. However it does demonstrate that proactive steps either by use of the rules, or by case management in individual proceedings, can significantly limit both costs and delay. I also appreciate concerns about due process but I do not think that due process requires more than giving parties a fair opportunity to present their respective cases. It does not include permitting the parties to chase every conceivable rabbit down every conceivable burrow, or giving them unlimited time to undertake that fruitless task.

3. *Transparency*

Finally, there is transparency. I think there is probably consensus that increasing transparency in investor-state disputes is a laudable goal, in response to the sledges in recent years that it is, apparently, secretive, skewed in favour of corporations, and excludes the public whose funds and interests are at stake.[30]

So far each of the major transparency initiatives in recent years has been accompanied by a clear recognition of the difference between ISDS and contract arbitration – where confidentiality is assumed to be an essential feature.

However, it may be that certain disputes are of such a "public" nature that the distinction is not tenable. One example we heard was the *Microsoft Mobile v. Sony Europe*[31] case, involving a tortious claim brought by Microsoft in England for alleged anti-competitive cartel conduct. The claim was ordered to be heard by an arbitral panel

27. Fuyong CHEN, "Building Better Arbitration Proceedings: Practical Suggestions", this volume, pp. 736-743.

28. Supreme Court of NSW, Practice Note SC Eq 11, *Disclosure in the Equity Division* <http://www.lawlink.nsw.gov.au/practice_notes/nswsc_pc.nsf/pages/574>.

29. Patricia A. BERGIN, "Building Better Arbitration Proceedings", this volume, pp. 759-768 at p. 766.

30. Stanimir A. ALEXANDROV and Patrick CHILDRESS, "Transparency in International Investor-State Arbitration: Commendable in Theory, Complicated in Practice", this volume, pp. 691-698.

31. [2017] EWHC 374 (Cth), as discussed by Constantine PARTASIDES QC, "What Has Been the "Spillover" Effect of the Transparency Debate on Commercial Arbitrations?", this volume, pp. 699-710.

rather than the English courts pursuant to an agreement between the parties. The issue resulting is that third parties who may also have been the victim of unlawful conduct will have access to little or no information about it, and the public is kept in the dark about conduct that could have had an impact on consumer prices. One interesting issue which could have arisen out of the *Microsoft Mobile* case is whether production of material tendered in the arbitration and the arbitrator's award, could be compelled in either regulatory proceedings or proceedings in which the plaintiff was not bound by an arbitration agreement. The privacy protection might not be as absolute as originally perceived.

Part of the issue stems from what I think most of us here would be quite happy about – the exponential growth in the use of international arbitration. But it also means that arbitration can now longer claim some exotic status – it is no longer litigation for the "hip" – it is purely mainstream.[32] I hope this doesn't disappoint you too much. What we were challenged to rethink this week is whether this new reality means the idea that party autonomy prevails over all else will still hold true in ten, twenty or thirty years' time – and what this means for the place of privacy and confidentiality.

A pessimistic scenario is that the absence of transparency will start to mean misinformation – alternative facts, "post-truth" opinions and "fake news" abound. Constantine Partasides QC posed the following question, and I will simply quote it: "In an age in which an absence of information is often replaced by an abundance of misinformation, is it acceptable – or even wise – for a process that now accounts for such a significant proportion of commercial dispute resolution around the world to be automatically confidential?".[33]

What is interesting to note is that transparency was also a complaint we heard this year from corporate users. Laura Abrahamson posited that from a corporate user's perspective, there is significant demand for the publication of awards, whether in full, redacted or summary form – and also for greater data around arbitrators to guide selection decisions.[34] It might be premature to presume that the interests of the public and the interests of corporations in this area will always conflict.

However, at the risk of offending some of my fellow judges, lack of transparency or for that matter the reference of a body of international disputes to arbitration, has not in my view, inhibited the development of the common law at least in this country. Commercial arbitration has been around for decades, if not centuries, and the common law seems to have muddled along. In that context it must be remembered that a huge majority of cases in the courts don't involve any point of principle, but rather the application of established principle to the facts. It is the curse of an appellate judge these days to be bombarded by first instance decisions raising no point of principle and merely having the effect of raising the judge's blood pressure as he or she has to wade through them. I regret that the same could probably be said of a great number of awards

However, I should say, that in the case of arbitrations that do raise a point of principle, courts would benefit from access to the reasoning of the arbitrators. If that

32. C. PARTASIDES, above fn. 31, at p. 703.

33. *Ibid.*

34. Laura ABRAHAMSON, "Costs, Delay and Transparency – A Comment on Continued Legitimacy Concerns from the User's Perspective", this volume, pp. 354-360.

could be achieved it would be desirable. However, I would not subscribe to the view that it is a serious policy matter, at least in this country, at the present time.

III. TECHNOLOGY

Now we can't be at a Congress with the word "future" in the name without some mention of how robots are going to be doing all our jobs soon. I would be lying if I said it doesn't keep me up some nights. When one googles "what makes a good judge", the first attribute that comes up is "legal ability". Anyone who has seen the YouTube video "paralegal vs robot" should have no doubt that robots are far better at law than humans. And while some lawyers no doubt seem like robots in terms of their lack of apparent need for sleep or sustenance – I'm not sure how they will compete with the real deal. It seems every day there is a new headline to the effect of "Are we ready for robot judges?".... "AI to replace lawyers". It is enough to make the best of us nervous. I imagine the sessions yesterday exploring how much more effective artificial intelligence will be than humans as arbitrators has had much the same effect on you.[35] Although, I suspect these things worry the younger "digital natives" among us far less than the "digital immigrants" such as myself.

The future of technology both in arbitration and litigation is at once both an opportunity and a challenge. It offers solutions to the challenges such as unconscious bias and managing voluminous documents. This Congress has shown us first-hand how the use of different technologies will revolutionize arbitration – such as the use of augmented reality in a proceeding.[36] I was grateful for an explanation of what this means at the time, so I will pass on the favour – it refers to the superimposition of images on the world as you see it – like Pokémon Go, for those who have also been confronted with robotic-like children chasing imaginary creatures in their suburbs.

In line with the academic rigour that has attended this entire Congress, it was not all fun and games and cross-examination of Darth Vader. There were also the difficult questions of how we can ensure tech is used in a way that does not impinge on due process, and how we can ensure there is equality of access to these programs. The other point made, that I would repeat, is that technology is not only relevant to the process of arbitration, but also the content of future disputes. It will change your clients' worlds well before it changes yours. If for nothing than pure economic benefit, it is incumbent on us to understand and embrace it.

35. Carsten VAN DE SANDE, "Technology as Disruption" (Panel Discussion at the 24th ICCA Congress, Sydney, 17 April 2018).
36. Paul H COHEN, Hugh CARLSON, Rashda RANA SC and Gabrielle NATER-BASS, "Technology as Facilitation", this volume, pp. 813-836.

IV. NEW VOICES

Finally, I would like to make mention of the young practitioners who spoke yesterday afternoon – on topics as varied as arbitration in conflict zones,[37] sovereign wealth funds in investor-state dispute settlement,[38] the principles limiting compensation in arbitration[39] and their views on the state of the system.[40] These young practitioners come to the table, it is evident, with a genuine devotion to the practice of arbitration, and a desire to see it flourish. I think in a congress dedicated to thinking about the future of international arbitration, these young voices are the ones that deserve particular attention, and I commend them for their contributions.

The past few days have offered an unparalleled opportunity to engage in thoughtful introspection about the future of this industry. I hope you have each found it as useful as I have. I thank the organizing committee for the opportunity to speak, and I look forward to meeting again at the next ICCA Congress.

37. Samantha Lord HILL, "Arbitration of Disputes Arising in Conflict and Post-Conflict Zones: Managing the Risks", this volume, pp. 897-916.
38. Solomon EBERE, "Sovereign Wealth Funds: The New Kids on the Block", this volume, pp. 936-952.
39. Jawad AHMAD, "Date of Breach, Contributory Fault, and Mitigation of Damages in Investment Arbitration", this volume, pp. 917-935.
40. Lucas BASTIN, "The Excessive Scope for 'the Individual' in Decision-Making in Investment Arbitration: Views from Younger Practitioners", this volume, pp. 953-966.

ICCA-ASIL
Task Force on Damages
Breakfast

Damages in International Arbitration: ICCA-ASIL Web Application

Catherine Amirfar[*] *and Gabrielle Nater-Bass*[**]
Co-Chairs of the ICCA-ASIL Task Force on Damages

TABLE OF CONTENTS

I. INTRODUCTION

On 16 April 2018, the ICCA-ASIL Task Force on Damages (the "Task Force") held a one-hour seminar titled "Damages in International Arbitration: ICCA-ASIL Web Application." The seminar introduced a prototype of the new web-based application ("web app") that is the culminating project of the joint ICCA and ASIL Task Force on Damages. The panel discussed the genesis and purpose of the project: to create a free resource for international arbitration practitioners across the globe, and to serve as a foundational guide to the core concepts in damages, as well as the tricky or even undecided issues relating to damages. Utilizing the prototype version of the web app, the panel demonstrated how the web app can assist practitioners to strengthen their understanding of damages concepts, identify thorny issues to address, and locate sources for further research.

The Task Force developed this web app with an eye towards providing the starting point on the topic of damages for a broad swathe of practitioners, ranging from experts who seek a refresher or an update on a particular point, to leading practitioners seeking to use the web app as a research resource, to those who are new to the field of damages in international arbitration seeking a primer on the topic. The Task Force believes that this web app has the potential to change the way practitioners approach damages in international arbitrations – to engage every damages phase with a rigorous review of the issues and questions at play and to promote a comprehensive understanding of how each issue fits together.

---

* Partner in the International Dispute Resolution Group at Debevoise & Plimpton LLP in New York since 2008, serves as the Co-Chair of the firm's Public International Law Group; spent two years as the Counselor on International Law to the Legal Advisor at the US Department of State.

** Partner at Homburger in Zurich since 2006; President of the Arbitration Court of the Swiss Chambers' Arbitration Institution; Vice President of ArbitralWomen.

II. MANDATE OF THE TASK FORCE

In December 2016, ICCA and ASIL joined forces to establish the ICCA-ASIL Task Force on Damages. The Task Force was charged with addressing an issue that, despite its importance, is nevertheless too often overlooked in the field of international arbitration: quantification of damages. The Task Force brings together a blue-ribbon panel of leading legal and economics experts from jurisdictions across the globe to think creatively about how to promote consistency and rigor in the field's approach to damages.

The Task Force consists of the following members:

Co-Chairs:

Catherine Amirfar, Debevoise & Plimpton, United States
Gabrielle Nater-Bass, Homburger, Switzerland

Members:

- Olufunke Adekoya, Aélex, Nigeria
- Sarah Grimmer, Hong Kong International Arbitration Center, Hong Kong
- Hilary Heilbron, Brick Court Chambers, United Kingdom
- Mark Kantor, Independent Arbitrator, United States
- Swee Yen Koh, Wongpartnership LLP, Singapore
- M. Alexis Maniatis, The Brattle Group, United States
- Irmgard Marboe, University of Vienna, Austria
- Chudozie Okongwu, NERA Economic Consulting, United States
- Kathleen Paisley, Amboslaw, Belgium
- Patrick W. Pearsall, Jenner & Block, United States
- Adriana San Román Rivera, Wöss & Partners, United States and Mexico
- Guido Santiago Tawil, M&M Bomchil Abogados, Argentina
- Thierry J. Senechal, Groupe ISD, France
- Jennifer Hall Vanderhart, Analytics Research Group, United States
- Karim A. Youssef, Youssef & Partners, Egypt

The Task Force is assisted by the following Rapporteurs:

- Aasiya Glover, Debevoise & Plimpton, United States
- Azeezah Goodwin, Debevoise & Plimpton, United States
- Stefanie Pfisterer, Homburger, Switzerland
- Christel Y. Tham, PCA, The Netherlands

The Task Force's mandate includes fostering the development of a more robust and uniform approach to damages analyses in international arbitration. To that end, the Task Force have analyzed the legal, economic, and policy issues underpinning damages in the field of international arbitration, with a view not only to achieving consensus on the fundamentals, but also to identifying and disentangling the procedural, legal and financial principles related to damages.

The Task Force is developing an interactive, electronic web app of practical application, to be used by arbitrators and practitioners alike. The web app guides users through the key procedural, legal and quantitative issues implicated by the calculation of damages in international arbitration.

III. THE WEB APPLICATION

1. *Overview of the App*

The intended audience of the web app is broad, but sophisticated. The Task Force has designed the organization and content to speak equally to practitioners putting together a case on damages, to arbitrators deciding questions of damages in cases before them, to law students looking for a deeper dive tutorial on damages subjects, and to experts – financial, economists or otherwise – who want to explore the legal framework underlying damages in international cases.

The web app covers the law on damages in the context of both international investment arbitration and commercial arbitration, and damages topics arising under both international and domestic law. The web app is divided into civil and common law systems, and experts in each system contribute to their respective content.

In terms of function, the web app is fully interactive, permitting users to click through several layers of buttons to reveal an increasingly interrelated network of damages topics. The content for each topic contains links for key words and issues arising in the question of damages, allowing the user to navigate between topics fluidly and to identify the major questions and sources for each topic. The user can therefore explore how topics are networked and related, and how issues arising in each area of the damages phase are often dependent upon each other.

The Task Force hopes the web app drives home the point that damages issues arise from the very outset of cases, throughout the life of the case and should be dealt with proactively and with sophistication in particular about the economic and legal consequences of decisions taken. For example, the treatment of sovereign risk, how such risk is quantified and treated in a damages model goes to basic legal principles about how to compensate and which party should bear the benefit or detriment of future unlawful behavior.

Importantly, the web app is intended to be descriptive, not prescriptive. It is a resource designed to illustrate the landscape of damages in international arbitration and point to the specific locations where that landscape is unsettled or practitioners should take special care to investigate further. If there is a debate on a particular issue – to use the earlier example of the proper calculation of sovereign risk – that debate will be reflected in the underlying discussion reflected in the web app. The idea is to ensure that divergent viewpoints are considered, not necessarily to determine the "right" answer. In some instances, there may exist a common error which the web app will point out and explain. The goal, however, is always to be explicit about the presence of debate or controversy – within the constraints of the web app format, which is most beneficial when balancing usefulness with concise explanation.

2. *Structure of the App*

As mentioned, the web app guides users through the key procedural, legal and quantitative issues implicated by the calculation of damages in international arbitration. It covers the law on damages in the context of both international investment and commercial arbitrations, and damages topics arising under both international and domestic law. Hence, when accessing the web app, the user will first be presented with the primary three topics: "Procedural", "Legal", and "Valuation". Clicking on each topic will reveal the subtopics layered within, demonstrating the avenues each practitioner must pursue when entering the damages phase.

For example, a user interested in learning more about the pertinent legal principles relevant to international investment arbitrations may click the "Legal" button, which opens a new page displaying two alternative options: "International" and "National." Clicking the "International" button provides the user a network of international law legal principles, with the narrower legal concepts nested within the overarching categories until the user clicks on a button to reveal content specific to a certain category. The web app groups the relevant legal principles on international law into seven major categories: Nature of Claim, Legal Standard, Categories of Remedies, Valuation Date, Elements of Claim, Proof Relation to Damages, and Limiting Principles. Each of these groupings includes the primary legal principles or requirements in its set. The Nature of Claim category, for instance, provides detailed information on the damages implications of certain types of international law-based claims, including content on the damages considerations for unlawful and lawful expropriation, as well as other breaches of international law. The Valuation Date category addresses the choice of Date of Breach or Date of Award, in the context of an arbitration governed by international law. The Limiting Principles grouping includes content on the key bases for limiting damages in an arbitration based on international law: Mitigation, Reasonable Certainty, Double Recovery, Contributory Conduct, and Legal Causation.

From there, by clicking on the "Categories of Remedies" button – a user could access the primary remedies available in investment arbitration. These remedies – restitution, compensation, satisfaction, and interest – appear as separate buttons that can be clicked on to reveal more detailed information. For example, the "Restitution" button reveals a final page of content including a general overview of the meaning of the term, a summary of key issues, and selected sources for further reading. Key issues point a user to debates, pitfalls to avoid or important considerations to take into account; in the "Restitution" context, one key issue is that some arbitral tribunals take the position that restitution or specific performance would be an undue interference with a state's sovereignty.

To the extent that the topics arise in national legal systems, the user can click on the "National" button to reveal a decision tree for each of common and civil law, and continue down either path to learn more about "Categories of Remedies" in the context of a commercial arbitration governed by laws under each legal system.

Importantly, the content for each topic also contains intra-site links for key words and issues arising with damages, allowing the user to navigate between topics fluidly and to identify the major questions and sources for each topic. The user can therefore explore how topics are related, and how issues arising in each area of the damages phase are often dependent upon each other.

IV. CONCLUSION

A thorough and nuanced understanding of damages is essential for practitioners in international arbitration. It is a topic that cannot be confined to a "damages phase," left to the end of a case, but rather spills into, and underpins, certain key legal questions as to liability like causation. Even the existence of a dispute may depend on the existence of injury and, therefore, a deep-dive into the valuation of companies or projects. Moreover, this topic – more than the legal and procedural questions – is often a central focus of clients. Yet damages is also an area that too often exists in a silo, sometimes because the procedural steps locate consideration of damages questions towards the end of proceedings. For example, experts may be brought in at a different stage or phase long after jurisdictional questions have been decided, or damages may be pled, briefed, and heard after a final decision on the merits of a claim. However, the various procedural, legal, and quantitative issues arising in a discussion of damages are necessarily interlinked both with the various stages of an arbitration proceeding and with each other. It is necessary, then, for practitioners to engage deeply in the damages issues from the very beginning of a case, with the requisite special consideration given to the procedure early on – an issue which the web app also addresses.

It is the hope of this Task Force that the web app it is creating will contribute to, and serve as a primary resource for, the rigorous and nuanced analysis of damages in international arbitration.

ICCA Sydney Congress List of Participants

Australia

Allsop, James, AO
Federal Court of Australia
184 Phillip St
Sydney, NSW 2000

Ashby, Matthew
Ferrier Hodgson
Level 7, 145 Eagle Street
Brisbane, QLD 4000

Bailey, Ian
Wentworth Chambers
Ground Floor
180 Phillip Street
Sydney NSW 2000

Bajaj, Gitanjali
DLA Piper Australia
Level 22, No 1 Martin Place
Sydney, NSW 2000

Bannon, Frank
Clayton Utz
1 Bligh Street
Sydney, NSW 2000

Bao, Edmund
King & Wood Mallesons
Level 61, Governor Phillip Tower
1 Farrer Place
Sydney, NSW 2000

Barnett, Jonathan
LCM Finance
Level 30, Collins Place
Melbourne, VIC 3000

Barrett-White, Stephen
UGL Pty Limited
Level 8, 40 Miller Street
North Sydney, NSW 2060

Elizabeth Bateman
Isaacs Chambers
555 Lonsdale Street
Melbourne VIC 3000

Bathurst, Thomas, AC
Supreme Court of New South Wales
GPO Box 3
Sydney NSW 2001

Baykitch AM, Alex
King & Wood Mallesons
Level 61, Governor Phillip Tower
1 Farrer Place
Sydney, NSW 2000

Bell, Sarah
Law In Order
Level 3, 123 Pitt Street
Sydney, NSW 2000

Bergin, Paddy
9th Floor, Selborne Chambers
174 Phillip Street
Sydney, NSW 2000

Bernard, Clemence
Australian Centre for
International Commercial Arbitration
Level 16, 1 Castlereagh Street
Sydney, NSW 2000

Blakely, Edward
Greater Sydney Commission
31 Myahgah Rd
Mosman, NSW 2088

Bonnell, Max
White & Case
1 Farrer Place
Sydney, NSW 2000

Brady, Sean
Brady Heywood
Level 7, Christie Centre
320 Adelaide St
Brisbane, QLD 4001

van Brakel, Mark
Allen & Overy
Level 12 Tower/Exchange Tower
2 The Esplanade
Perth, WA 6000

Branford, Dirk
Allen & Overy
Level 12 Tower/Exchange
Tower 2 The Esplanade
Perth, WA 6000

Breach, Natasha
INPEX
Level 22, 100 St Georges Terrace
Perth, WA 6000

Brown, Chester
University of Sydney
Building F10, Eastern Avenue
Sydney, NSW 2006

Butt, Adam
8th Floor Wentworth Chambers
Level 8, 180 Phillip Street
Sydney, NSW 2000

Cairns, Martin
Sapere Forensic
Level 18, 135 King Street
Sydney, NSW 2000

Camenzind, Anne
Business Events Sydney
Level 20, 100 William Street
Sydney, NSW 2011

Cameron, Fiona
Victorian Bar
C/O Young's List
525 Lonsdale Street
Melbourne, VIC 3000

Carroll, Lee
Corrs Chambers Westgarth
Level 25, 567 Collins Street
Melbourne, VIC 3000

Carroll, Monique
King & Wood Mallesons
Level 61, Governor Phillip Tower
1 Farrer Place
Sydney, NSW 2000

Carter, Craig
Third Floor St James' Hall Chambers
Level 3, 169 Phillip Street
Sydney, NSW 2000

Castle, Tim
6 St James Hall
6/169 Phillip Street
Sydney, NSW 2000

Catterwell, Chad
Herbert Smith Freehills
101 Collins Street
Melbourne, VIC 3000

Charrett, Donald
Expert Determination Chambers
Foley's List, 205 William Street
Melbourne, VIC 3150

Chung, Leon
Herbert Smith Freehills
ANZ Tower 161, Castlereagh Street
Sydney, NSW 2000

Clapham, Jason
CPB Contractors Pty Limited
8/177 Pacific Hwy
North Sydney, NSW 2060

Clark, Bryan
Australian Chamber of
Commerce and Industry
24 Brisbane Avenue
Barton, ACT 2600

Colquhoun, Charles
Selborne Wentworth Chambers
Level 10, 174 Phillip Street
Sydney, NSW 2000

Conoulty, Rebecca
Sapere Research Group
Level 18, 135 King Street
Sydney, NSW 2000

Corsaro, Alex
Clayton Utz
1 Bligh Street
Sydney, NSW 2000

Croft, Justice Clyde
Supreme Court of Victoria
210 William Street
Melbourne, VIC 3000

Cubitt, Beth
Clyde & Co

Level 28, 197 St Georges Terrace
Perth, WA 6000

Davidson, Ben
Corrs Chambers Westgarth
Level 25, 567 Collins Street
Melbourne, VIC 3000

Davidson, Ian SC
Eight Selborne
174 Phillip Street
Sydney, NSW 2000

Davis, Simon
Francis Burt Chambers
Allendale Square
77 St George's Terrace
Perth, WA 6011

De Rossi, Helen
Taylor and Francis Publishers
Level 2, Suite 5, 11 Queens Rd,
Melbourne, VIC 3004

DeBoos, Jonathon
CPB Contractors
567 Collins Street
Melbourne, VIC 3000

Delaney, Joachim
Baker McKenzie
100 Barangaroo Avenue
Sydney, NSW 2000

Dempsey SC, Mark
7 Wentworth Selborne Chambers
7th Floor, 180 Phillip Street
Sydney, NSW 2000

Derrington, Sarah
Australian Law Reform Commission
Level 40, MLC Centre, 19 Martin Place
Sydney, NSW 2000

Deveza, Isabela
Pinsent Masons
Level 32, Tower Two
International Towers
200 Barangaroo Avenue
Barangaroo, NSW 2000

Di Pasquale, Andrew
Victorian Bar - List G
Owen Dixon Chambers West,
525 Lonsdale Street
Melbourne, VIC 3000

Douglas, Francis QC
Tenth Floor Chambers
Wentworth Selborne Chambers
180 Phillip Street
Sydney, NSW 2000

Dreosti, Julia
Lipman Karas
Level 23, 25 Grenfell Street
Adelaide, SA 5000

Duffy, Adrian QC
Jeddart Chambers
Level 35, Santos Place
32 Turbot Street
Brisbane, QLD 4000

Earwaker, Michael
Corrs Chambers Westgarth
Level 17, 8 Chifley
8-12 Chifley Square
Sydney, NSW 2000

Einfeld, Alex
Australian Centre for
International Commercial Arbitration
Level 16, 1 Castlereagh Street
Sydney, NSW 2000

Eversgerd, John-Henry
PPB Advisory
Level 21, 181 William Street
Melbourne, VIC 3000

Ewen, Joanne
Victoria University
295 Queen St
Melbourne, VIC 3000

Fairlie, David
Competitive Foods Australia
Pty Limited
Level 13, 100 William Street
East Sydney, NSW 2011

Ganesaratnam, Pavithra
Independent Practitioner
2 Chandos Street
St Leonards, NSW 2065

Gayner, Oliver
IMF Bentham Limited
Level 18, 68 Pitt Street
Sydney, NSW 2000

Gilmour, John
Quayside Chambers
Level 36 Exchange Tower
2 The Esplanade
Perth, WA 6000

Glover, Ashley
Law In Order
Level 3, 123 Pitt Street
Sydney, NSW 2000

Greenham, Phillip
JBM Advisory Pty Ltd
PO Box 24212
Melbourne, VIC 3001

Hales, Mike
MinterEllison
Level 4, 77 St Georges Terrace
Perth, WA 6000

Hayes, Paul QC
The Victorian Bar and
39 Essex Chambers
205 William Street
Melbourne, VIC 3000

Hayward, Benjamin
Department of
Business Law and Taxation
Monash University
900 Dandenong Road
Caulfield East, VIC 3145

Heath, Robert QC
Chancery Chambers
Level 25, 200 Queen Street
Melbourne, VIC 3000

Hepburn, Jarrod
Investment Arbitration Reporter/
University of Melbourne
Santa Monica, USA /
Melbourne, Australia
Melbourne, VIC 3053

Hetherington, Jonathon
Clayton Utz
1 Bligh Street
Sydney, NSW 2000

Hickie, Kieran
Young's List
525 Lonsdale Street, Melbourne
Melbourne, VIC 3000

Hoad, Malcolm
Law In Order
Level 6, 2 Mill Street
Perth, WA 6000

Hockley, John
University of Western Australia
Stirling Highway
Crawley, WA 6009

Hoffmann, Anne
Herbert Smith Freehills
ANZ Tower 161, Castlereagh Street
Sydney, NSW 2000

Holmes, Malcolm
Eleven Wentworth
11/180 Phillip Street
Sydney, NSW 2000

Holmes, Patricia
Department of Foreign Affairs
and Trade
R G Casey Building
John McEwen Crescent
Barton, ACT 0221
Canberra, ACT

Van Homrigh, David
KordaMentha
Level 14, 12 Creek Street
Brisbane, QLD 4000

Horrigan, Brenda
Herbert Smith Freehills
ANZ Tower 161
Castlereagh Street
Sydney, NSW 2000

Huang, Jie (Jeanne)
University of New South Wales
Law Faculty
Law Building, Level 3
Sydney, NSW

Humphrey, Jonathan
Berkley Research Group
Level 32, 1 Market Street
Sydney, NSW 2000

Jaski, Campbell
PPB Advisory
Level 21, 181 William Street
Melbourne, VIC 3000

Jeffries, Andrew
Independent Arbitrator
154 Bundabah Road
Bundabah, NSW 2324

Jenaway, David
Allen & Overy
Level 12 Tower/Exchange Tower 2
The Esplanade
Perth, WA 6000

Jones, Doug
Independent International Arbitrator
1 Bligh Street
Sydney, NSW 2000

Justice, Zoe
King & Wood Mallesons
Level 61, Governor Phillip Tower
1 Farrer Place
Sydney, NSW 2000

Kay Hoyle, Jonathan
11 St James' Hall Chambers
169 Phillip Street
Sydney, NSW 2000

Kennedy, Jesse
New Chambers
Level 34, 126 Phillip Street
Sydney, NSW 2000

Kenny, Caroline QC
Victorian Bar
List B, 525 Lonsdale Street
Melbourne, VIC 3000

Kofman, Marina
Norton Rose Fulbright
Level 18, Grosvenor Place
225 George Street
Sydney, NSW 2000

Kuperholz, Matt
PriceWaterhouse Coopers
2 Riverside Quay
Southbank, VIC 3006

Kwan, Edwina
King & Wood Mallesons
Level 61, Governor Phillip Tower
1 Farrer Place
Sydney, NSW 2000

Landis, Nathan
IMF Bentham Limited
Level 6, 37 St Georges Terrace
Perth, WA 6000

Laughton, Gregory Allan
Greg Laughton SC
Level 13 174 Phillip Street
Sydney, NSW 2000

Le, Cari-Dee
University of Sydney
Unit 208, 302 Crown Street
Darlinghurst, NSW 2010

Lenigas, Harriet
Ashurst
181 William Street
Melbourne, VIC 3000

Lincoln, Bronwyn
Corrs Chambers Westgarth
Level 25, 567 Collins Street
Melbourne, VIC 3000

Lindgren, Kevin
ADR Practitioner
Suite 203, Level 2
8 Help Street,
Chatswood, NSW 2067

Lockhart, Deborah
Australian Disputes Centre
Level 16, 1 Castlereagh St
Sydney, NSW 2000

Longley, Nicholas
HFW Australia
Level 39, Bourke Street
Melbourne, VIC 3000

Luck, Clive
Clayton Utz
Level 27, Qv. 1 Building
250 St Georges Terrace
Perth, WA 6848

Luscombe, Benjamin
Clifford Chance
Level 7, 190 St George's Terrace
Perth, WA 6000

Luttrell, Sam
Clifford Chance
Level 7, 190 St George's Terrace
Perth, WA 6000

Lyons, Peter QC
Level 8, 95 North Quay
Brisbane, QLD 4000

Macknay, Elizabeth
Herbert Smith Freehills
Qv.1 Building, 250 St George's Terrace
Perth, WA 6000

Maguire, Fiona
Business Events Sydney
Level 20, 100 William Street
Sydney, NSW 2011

Maher, Andrew
Allens
101 Collins Street
Melbourne, VIC 3001

Mallett, Daisy
King & Wood Mallesons
Level 61, Governor Phillip Tower
1 Farrer Place
Sydney, NSW 2000

Martignoni, Andrea
Allens
126 Phillip St
Sydney, NSW 2000

Martin AC, Chief Justice Wayne
Supreme Court of WA
David Malcolm Justice Centre, Level 14, 28
Barrack Street
Perth, WA 6000

Maurushat, Alana
University of New South Wales Sydney
Law Building, UNSW
Sydney, NSW 2052

McCormick, Khory
Bartley Cohen Litigation Lawyers
Level 22, 123 Eagle Street
Brisbane, QLD 4000

McGuiness, John
McGrathNicol
20 Martin Place
Sydney, NSW 2000

McIntyre, Kelly
35 West Chambers
Level 35, Santos Place
32 Turbot Street
Brisbane, QLD 4000

McQueen, Peter
University of Queensland
PO Box 2193
Bondi Junction, NSW 1355

Megens, Peter
Outlook Litigation Consulting Pty Ltd
5/41 Carson Street
Kew, VIC 3101

Mehigan, Terry
12 Wentworth Selborne Chambers
12/180 Phillip Street
Sydney, NSW 2000

Meredith, Greg
Ferrier Hodgson
Level 43, Bourke Street
Melbourne, VIC 3000

Miller, Elizabeth
Law In Order
Level 3, 123 Pitt Street
Sydney, NSW 2000

Monichino, Albert
List A Barristers
Owen Dixon Chambers
205 William Street
Melbourne, VIC 3000

Morgan, Richard
Barrister
Level 35 , Santos Place
32 Turbot St
Brisbane, QLD 4000

Morris, Kathleen
Clayton Utz
1 Bligh Street
Sydney, NSW 2000

Morrison, James
Australian Centre for International Commercial Arbitration (ACICA)
Level 16, 1 Castlereagh Street
Sydney NSW 2000

Mullins, Wynand
Ferrier Hodgson
Level 25
One International Towers Sydney
Sydney, NSW 2000

Nasreen, Jahan
Corrs Chambers Westgarth
8 Chifley
8-12 Chifley Square
Sydney NSW 2000

Nell, Gregory SC
New Chambers
Level 34, 126 Phillip Street
Sydney, NSW 2000

Newbold, Beverley
MinterEllison
Governor Macquarie Tower
Level 40, 1 Farrer Place
Sydney, NSW 2000

Ng, Kelvin
Driver Trett
Level 14, Lumley House
309 Kent Street
Sydney, NSW 2000

Nguyen, Anh
KordaMentha
Level 5, Chifley Tower
2 Chifley Square
Sydney, NSW 2000

Nottage, Luke
Sydney Law School
Law School Building (F10)
Eastern Ave
University Of Sydney,
Sydney, NSW

Nygh, Nicola
Resolve Litigation Lawyers
Level 18, 126 Phillip Street
Sydney, NSW 2000

O'Keefe, Catherine
Corrs Chambers Westgarth
Level 25, 567 Collins Street
Melbourne, VIC 3000

O'Sullivan, Patrick QC
Jeffcott Chambers
24 Flinders Street
Adelaide, SA 5000

Owen, Ariane
Allen & Overy LLP
Level 12
Exchange Tower
2 The Esplanade
Perth,

Pacey, Sara
Clayton Utz
1 Bligh Street
Sydney, NSW 2000

Potter, Michael
Axiom Forensics Pty Ltd
Level 6, 44 Market Street
Sydney, NSW 2000

Prescott, Liam
DLA Piper Australia
Level 9, 480 Queen Street
Brisbane, QLD 4000

Priskich, Vicky
Victorian Bar
Owen Dixon Chambers West
525 Lonsdale Street
Melbourne, VIC 3000

Pryles, Michael
ICCA Governing Board Member
Michael Pryles Arbitration and

Mediation
Suite 304, 521 Toorak Road,
Toorak
Melbourne, VIC 3142

Quan-Sing, Jeremy
Allens
250 St Georges Terrace
Perth, WA 6000

Quick, Georgia
Ashurst
5 Martin Place
Sydney, NSW 2000

Rana, Rashda, SC
St James' Hall International
L6, 169 Phillip Street
Sydney, NSW 2000

Reilly, Brendan
Squire Patton Boggs
Level 21, 300 Murray Street
Perth, WA 6005

Robertson, Donald
Herbert Smith Freehills
ANZ Tower 161, Castlereagh Street
Sydney, NSW 2000

Rollnik, Adam
List G Barristers - Victorian Bar
Owen Dixon Chambers West
525 Lonsdale Street
Melbourne, VIC 3000

Ross, Donna
Donna Ross Dispute Resolution
Level 13, 200 Queen Street
Melbourne, VIC 3000

Rudge, Nick
Allens
101 Collins St
Melbourne, VIC 3000

Sadler, Peter
Quinn Emanuel Urquhart & Sullivan
Level 11, 40 St Georges Terrace
Perth, WA 6000

Samuel, Tony
Sapere Forensic
Level 18, 135 King Street
Sydney, NSW 2000

Sedaghati, Navid
Thirteen Wentworth Selborne Chambers
Level 13, 174-180 Phillip Street
Sydney, NSW 2000

Sekula, Geneva
Allens
Level 28, Deutsche Bank Place
126 Phillip Street
Sydney, NSW 2000

Shand, Michael QC
Victorian Bar
205 William Street
Melbourne, VIC 3000

Sharkey AM, John
Professor John Sharkey AM
PO Box 1397, Darling LPO
Darling, VIC 3145

Shelley, Jeremy
Attorney-General's Department
3-5 National Circuit
Barton, ACT 2600

Sindler, Michelle
NCAT
Sydney
Sydney, NSW 2000

Smallbone, David
Frederick Jordan Chambers
53 Martin Place
Sydney, NSW 2000

Smith, Gordon
Gordon Smith Legal
PO Box 797
Claremont, WA 6910

Soars, Julie
Local Court of NSW
232 Johnston St
Annandale, NSW 2038

Sobczyk, Justyna
Deakin University
Gheringhap Street
Geelong, VIC 3220

Spigelman, James QC
One Essex Court
Suite 515 Eastpoint Tower
180 Ocean St, Edgecliff
Sydney, NSW 2027

Stefanidis, William
Clayton Utz
1 Bligh Street
Sydney, NSW 2000

Steinepreis, Greg
Squire Patton Boggs
Level 21, 300 Murray Street
Perth, WA 6005

Stephenson, Andrew
Corrs Chambers Westgarth
Level 25, 567 Collins Street
Melbourne, VIC 3000

Stesin, Vasantha
Stesin Legal
504/365 Little Collins Street
Melbourne, VIC 3000

Stobo, Thomas
Australian Chamber of Commerce and Industry
Commerce House, Level 3
24 Brisbane Avenue
Barton, ACT 2600

Stone, Owain
KordaMentha
Rialto, Level 31, South Tower
525 Collins Street
Melbourne, VIC 3000

Sturzaker, Damian
University of New South Wales
Anzac Parade Kensington
Sydney, NSW 2000

Swartz-Zern, Caroline
Allens
101 Collins St
Melbourne, VIC 3000

Tang, Robert
Allen & Overy
Level 25, 85 Castlereagh St
Sydney, NSW

Tee, Sylvia
Lipman Karas
Level 23, 25 Grenfell Street
Adelaide, SA 5000

Temple-Cole, John
KordaMentha
Level 5, Chifley Tower
2 Chifley Sqaure
Sydney, NSW 2000

Thirgood, Russell
McCullough Robertson
Level 11, 66 Eagle Street
Brisbane, QLD 4000

Thompson, Janine
McGrathNicol
20 Martin Place
Sydney, NSW 2000

Tomkinson, Deborah
Australian Centre for International Commercial Arbitration
Level 16, 1 Castlereagh Street
Sydney, NSW 2000

Totaro, Gianna
Chartered Institute of Arbitrators Australia
5 Tabor Mews
Frankston, Victoria 3199

Trahanas, Christina
Eleven Wentworth
180 Phillip Street
Sydney, NSW 2000

Tseng, I-Ching
Bartley Cohen Litigation Lawyers
Level 22, 123 Eagle Street
Brisbane, QLD 4000

Valcke, Brecht
DLA Piper
No., 22/1 Martin Pl
Sydney, NSW 2000

Voss, Peter
Ashurst
5 Martin Place
Sydney, NSW 2000

Waincymer, Jeffrey
Independent Arbitrator
45 Victoria Road North, Malvern
Melbourne, VIC 3144

Wakefield, John
Holman Webb Lawyers
Level 17, 123 Pitt Street
Sydney, NSW 2000

Wakefield, Samantha
Australian Centre for
International Commercial Arbitration
Level 16, 1 Castlereagh Street
Sydney, NSW 2000

Wee, Natalie
Baker McKenzie
100 Barangaroo Avenue
Sydney, NSW 2000

Williams, Erika
McCullough Robertson
Level 11, 66 Eagle Street
Brisbane, QLD 4000

Wootton, Naomi
Supreme Court of New South Wales
GPO Box 3
Sydney NSW 2001

Wright, Dawna
FTI Consulting
Level 16, 600 Bourke Street
Melbourne, VIC 3000

Xie, Dan
University of New South Wales
UNSW
Sydney, NSW 2052

Xuan, Yan
University of Queensland
Room W258
Level 2, Forgan Smith Building
St Lucia Campus
Brisbane, QLD 4067

Austria

Fremuth-Wolf, Alice
Vienna International Arbitral Centre
Wiedner Hauptstraße 63
1045 Vienna

Karollus-Bruner, Daniela
CMS Reich-Rohrwig
Hainz RAe GmbH
Gauermanngasse 2
1010 Vienna

Klausegger, Christian
Binder Grösswang
Rechtsanwälte GmbH
Sterngasse 13
1010 Vienna

Lindinger, Christoph
Schoenherr Rechtsanwaelte GmbH
Schottenring 19
1010 Vienna

Neil, Amanda
Freshfields Bruckhaus Deringer
Seilergasse 1
1010 Vienna

Wychera, Bernhard
CHSH Cerha Hempel Spiegelfeld
Hlawati Rechtsanwälte GmbH
Parkring 2
1010 Vienna

Bahrain

Ahmed, Salman
Bahrain Chamber for
Dispute Resolution
Park Plaza
(Venture Capital Bank Building)
Suite 701 & 301, Entrance No. 1
Building 247
Road 1704, Block 317,
Diplomatic Area
Manama

Husain, Ahmed
Bahrain Chamber for
Dispute Resolution
Park Plaza
(Venture Capital Bank Building)
Suite 701 & 301, Entrance No. 1
Building 247
Road 1704, Block 317,

Diplomatic Area
Manama

Bangladesh

Hossain, Kamal
Supreme Court of Bangladesh
Dr. Kamal Hossain and Associates,
Chamber Building
122-124 Motijheel C/A
Dhaka

Masum, Abdul Mabud
The Lawyers & Jurists
Aligarh House (5th Floor)
146, Motijheel C/a,
1000 Dhaka

Belgium

van den Berg, Albert Jan
Honorary President of ICCA
Hanotiau & van den Berg
IT Tower, 9th Floor
Avenue Louise 480 B9
1050 Brussels

Hay, Emily
Hanotiau & van den Berg
IT Tower, 9th Floor
Avenue Louise 480 B9
1050 Brussels

van Houtte, Hans
Van Houtte Partners Bvba
A. Smetsplein 3D (Box 402)
3000 Leuven

van Houtte, Vera
ICCA Governing Board Member
Van Houtte Partners BVBA
A. Smetsplein 3D (Box 402)
3000 Leuven

Kohl, Benoit
Universtity of Liège
Boulevard du Rectorat 7
4000 Liège

Paisley, Kathleen
Ambos Law
Rue Neerveld 109
1200 Brussels

Petillion, Flip
Petillion
Oudenakenstraat 19
1600 Sint-Pieters-Leeuw,
Vlaams Brabant

Bermuda

Elkinson, Jeffrey
Conyers Dill and Pearman
Clarendon House, 2 Church Street
HM11 Hamilton

Brazil

Abranches Quintao, Luisa Barbosa
Justen, Pereira, Oliveira e Talamini –
Sociedade de Advogados
Rua Joaquim Floriano, 413, cj. 111
São Paulo, SP 04534-011

Alvares, Samantha
CAM-CCBC
Rua do Rocio 220-cj 122, 12th Floor
São Paulo, SP 04552-000

Braghetta, Adriana
ICCA Governing Board Member
L.O. Baptisa
Av. Paulista, 1294, 8th Floor
São Paulo, SP 01310-100

Coelho, Eleonora
CAM-CCBC
Rua Do Rocio 220-cj 122, 12th Floor
São Paulo, SP 04552-000

Correa, Fabio
Lilla, Huck, Otranto e
Camargo Advogados
Av. Brig. Faria Lima, 1744, 6th Floor
São Paulo, SP 01451-001

Forbes, Carlos
CAM-CCBC
Rua Do Rocio 220-cj 122, 12th Floor
São Paulo, SP 04552-000

Gertel, Cristiane
CAM-CCBC
Rua Do Rocio 220-cj 122, 12th Floor
São Paulo, SP 04552-000

Kobayashi, Patricia
CAM-CCBC
Rua Do Rocio 220-cj 122, 12th Floor
São Paulo, SP 04552-000

Komel, Luiza
CAM-CCBC
Rua Do Rocio 220-cj 122, 12th Floor
São Paulo, SP 04552-000

Macedo Simao, Camila
Finkelstein Advogados
Praça Amadeu Amaral 27
São Paulo, SP 01327-010

Pachikoski, Silvia
Rodrigues Pachikoski and
Staffa Neto Sociedade de Advogados
Alameda Santos, 2395, 4th Floor
São Paulo, SP 01419-101

British Virgin Islands

Lassalle, Francois
BVI International Arbitration Centre
Ashley Ritter Buidling, 3rd Floor,
House, Fleming St
Road Town, Tortola

Leon, Barry
Commercial Division,
Eastern Caribbean Supreme Court
PO Box 227
Road Town, Tortola VG 1110

Smith, Dawn J.
BVI International Arbitration Centre
Ashley Ritter Buidling, 3rd Floor
House, Fleming St
Road Town, Tortola

Brunei Darussalam

Alam, Puteh
PIN & Associates
12 Spg 152-69 kiarong beribi
Bandar Seri Begawan
Brunei and Muara 3186

Canada

Adjei, Ernest Nana
Faculty of Law, University of Ottawa
57 Louis Pasteur Street
Ottawa, Ontario K1N 6N5

Alvarez, Henri
Vancouver Arbitration Chambers
1650 - 885 West Georgia Street
Vancouver, British Columbia V6C 3E8

Chiasson, Craig
Borden Ladner Gervais LLP
1200 - 200 Burrard Street
Vancouver, British Columbia V6C 3E8

Cicchetti, Tina
Vancouver Arbitration Chambers
1650 - 885 West Georgia Street
Vancouver, British Columbia V6C 3E8

Cunningham, Douglas
Arbitration Place
333 Bay Street, Suite 900
Toronto, Ontario M5H 2R2

Deane, Robert
Borden Ladner Gervais LLP
1200 - 200 Burrard Street
Vancouver, British Columbia V3X 1T2

Drymer, Stephen
Woods LLP
2000 McGill College Ave
Montréal, QC H3A 3H3

Eades, Jonathan
Ministry of Attorney General
Government of British Columbia
1001 Douglas Street
Victoria, British Columbia V8W 9J7

Glaholt, Duncan
Glaholt LLP
141 Adelaide Street West
Toronto, Ontario M5H 3L5

Haigh, David QC
Burnet Duckworth & Palmer LLP
2400 525 - 8th Avenue S.W.
Calgary, Alberta T2P 1G1

Harrison, Douglas
Harrison ADR Professional Corporation
120 Adelaide Street West, Suite 420
Toronto, Ontario M5H 1T1

Johannsen, Helmut
Singleton Urquhart LLP
Suite 1200 - 925 West Georgia Street
Vancouver, British Columbia V6C 3L2

Kuttan, Subash
Investor-State LawGuide
1200 Waterfront Centre
200 Burrard Street
Vancouver, British Columbia V6C 3L6

Maguire, Morgan
Investor-State LawGuide
1200 Waterfront Centre
200 Burrard Street
Vancouver, British Columbia V6C 3L6

McArthur, Joe
Blake, Cassels & Graydon LLP
2600-595 Burrard Street
Vancouver, British Columbia V7X 1L3

McDougall, John Lorn
Arbitration Place and
3 Verulam Buildings
333 Bay Street, Suite 900
Toronto, Ontario M5H 2T4

Murphy-Burke, Liam
Investor-State LawGuide
1200 Waterfront Centre
200 Burrard Street
Vancouver, British Columbia V6C 3L6

Reynolds, Helen
Singleton Urquhart Reynolds Vogel LLP
22 Adelaide Street West, East Tower
Toronto, Ontario M5H 4E3

Reynolds, R. Bruce
Singleton Urquhart Reynolds Vogel LLP
150 King Street, Suite 2512
Toronto, Ontario M5H 1J9

Walker, Janet
Arbitration Place
333 Bay Street, Suite 900
Toronto, Ontario M5H 2T4

Chile

Conejero Roos, Cristian
Philippi Prietocarrizosa Ferrero & Uría
Avenida El Golf 40, 20th Floor
Las Condes
Santiago, Región Metropolitana 755-0000

Figueroa, Juan Eduardo
Figueroa, Illanes, Huidobro y Salamanca
Av. Apoquindo N° 3669, 11th Floor
Las Condes
Santiago, Región Metropolitana 755-0190

Jana, Andrés
ICCA Governing Board Member
Bofill Mir & Alvarez Jana
Av. Andrés Bello 2711, 8th Floor
Santiago 755-0611

China PR

Chen, Fuyong
Beijing Arbitration Commission/
Beijing International Arbitration Center
16/F, China Merchants Tower
No.118 Jian Guo Road,
Chaoyang District
Beijing 100022

Cui, Qiang
Commerce & Finance Law Offices
Jianguomen Outer St
Chaoyang
Beijing

Dong, Arthur
AnJie Law Firm
19/f, Tower D1
Liangmaqiao Diplomatic Office Building
No. 19 Dongfangdonglu
Chaoyang District
Beijing 100600

Dou, Peng
Executive Office of

Xi'an Arbitration Commission
Arbitration Building
No. 16 North Gate Street
Lianhu District
Xi'an, Shaanxi Province 710014

Fei, Jia (Jessica)
Herbert Smith Freehills LLP
King & Woods Malleson
28/f Office Tower
Beijing Yintai Centre
2 Jianguomenwai Avenue
Chaoyang District
Beijing 100022

Fei, Ning
Hui Zhong Law Firm
Room 2304, One Indigo
20 Jiuxianqiao Road
Chaoyang District
Beijing 100016

Hew, Kian Heong
Herbert Smith Freehills LLP
28th Floor Office Tower
Beijing Yintai Centre
2 Jianguomenwai Avenue
Chaoyang District
Beijing 100022

Jacomy, Emmanuel
Shearman & Sterling LLP
Unit 3209
China Central Place Tower 2
79 Jianguo Road
Chaoyang
Beijing 100025

Jia, Shen
China International Economic and
Trade Arbitration Commission
6/F, CCOIC Building
2 Huapichang Hutong
Xicheng District
Beijing 100035

Jian, Zhao
China International Economic and
Trade Arbitration Commission
6/F, CCOIC Building,
2 Huapichang Hutong
Xicheng District
Beijing 100035

Jiang, Jane
Allen & Overy
15F, Phase II, Shanghai IFC
8 Century Avenue
Pudong, Shanghai 200120

Jiang, Yujuan (Sylvia)
Zhong Lun Law Firm
31/33/36/37F, SK Tower
6A Jianguomenwai Avenue
Chaoyang District
Beijing 100022

Jin, Denning
Haiwen & Partners
2605 Jing An Kerry Center Tower 1,
1515 Nanjing West Road
Shanghai 200040

Li, Jack (Zhiqiang)
Jin Mao Partners
13F, Hong Kong New World Tower
No.300
Middle Huaihai Road
Shanghai 200021

Li, Qishi
Commerce & Finance Law Offices
Jianguomen Outer St, Chaoyang
Beijing

Liu, Wenpeng
Beijing Arbitration Commission/
Beijing International Arbitration Center
16/F, China Merchants Tower
No.118 Jian Guo Road
Chaoyang District
Beijing 100022

Liu, Yingying
Beijing Arbitration Commission/
Beijing International Arbitration Center
16/F, China Merchants Tower
No.118 Jian Guo Road
Chaoyang District
Beijing, China 100022

Lu, Fei
China International Economic and
Trade Arbitration Commission
6/F, CCOIC Building
2 Huapichang Hutong

Xicheng District
Beijing 100035

Lu, Ye
King & Wood Mallesons
28th Floor, Landmark 4028 Jintian Road
Futian District
Shenzhen, Guangdong 518035

Ma, Arthur
DaHui Lawyers
3720 China World Tower
Beijing 100004

Meng, Tim
GoldenGate Lawyers
Suite 2311-12
The Spaces International Center
No.8 Dongdaqiao Road
Chaoyang District
Beijing 100020

Pan, Junxing
Executive Office of
Xi'an Arbitration Commission
Arbitration Building
No. 16 North Gate Street
Lianhu District
Xi'an, Shaanxi Province 710014

Ping, Zhao
Jincheng Tongda & Neal Shanghai Office
18th Floor, Jinmao Tower
No. 88 Century Avenue
Pudong New District
Shanghai 200120

Shan, Wenhua
Xi'an Jiaotong University
Judicial Case Academy
28 Xianning West Road
Xi'an Shaanxi Province 710049
and
Supreme People's Court, PR China
111 South Fourth Ring Road
Fengtai District
Beijing 100070

Shen, Hongyu
The Supreme People's Court of the
People's Republic of China
No. 6003 Dongjiaominxiang St.
Beijing 100745

Sun, Wei
Beijing Arbitration Commission
16/F, China Merchants Tower
No.118 Jian Guo Road
Chaoyang District
Beijing 100022

Tao, Jingzhou
Dechert LLP
24th Floor, North Tower
Beijing Kerry Centre
1 Guanghua Road
Chaoyang District
Beijing 100020

Wang, Chengjie
China International Economic and
Trade Arbitration Commission
6/F, CCOIC Building
2 Huapichang Hutong
Xicheng District
Beijing 100035

Xu, Jie
Beijing Arbitration Commission/
Beijing International Arbitration Center
16/F, China Merchants Tower
No.118 Jian Guo Road
Chaoyang District
Beijing 100022

Yang, Yang
International Commercial Arbitration
Court of Xi'an Arbitration Commission
Arbitration Building
No. 16 North Gate Street
Lianhu District
Xi'an, Shaanxi Province 710014

Yin, Tong
Beijing Arbitration Commission/
Beijing International Arbitration Center
16/F, China Merchants Tower
No.118 Jian Guo Road
Chaoyang District
Beijing 100022

Zhang, Zhen'an
Co-EFFORT Law Firm LLP
35/f Huaneng Union Tower
958 Lujiazui Ring Rd.
Shanghai 200120

Zhao, Vicky
AnJie Law Firm
19/f, Tower D1
Liangmaqiao Diplomatic Office Building
No. 19 Dongfangdonglu
Chaoyang District
Beijing 100600

Czech Republic

Talašová, Marie
Ministry of Finance of the Czech Republic
Letenská 15
11000 Prague

Ueltzhöffer, Andreas
UEPA advokati s.r.o.
Voctarova 2449/5
18000 Prague 8

Denmark

Lett, Hannah
The Danish Institute of Arbitration
Kronprinsessegade 28, 3rd Floor
1306 Copenhagen

Lett, Jesper
The Danish Institute of Arbitration
Kronprinsessegade 28, 3rd Floor
1306 Copenhagen

Pihlblad, Steffen
The Danish Institute of Arbitration
Kronprinsessegade 28, 3rd Floor
1306 Copenhagen

Egypt

Abdel Wahab, Mohamed
Zulficar & Partners Law Firm
Nile City Building
South Tower, 8th Floor
2005a Cornich El Nil
Ramlet Beaulac.
11221 Cairo

Hussein, Amr Abbas
Matouk Bassiouny Law Firm
12 Mohamed Ali Genah
Garden City
11451 Cairo

Selim, Ismail
The Cairo Regional Centre for International Commercial Arbitration
1 Alsaleh Ayoub Street
Zamalek
11211 Cairo

France

Barsalou, Nicolas
Accuracy
41 rue De Villiers
Neuilly-sur-seine
92523 Paris

Bevilacqua, Thomas
Foley Hoag AARPI
153 rue du Faubourg Saint-Honoré
75008 Paris

Bhushan, Abhinav
International Chamber of Commerce
33-43 Avenue du President Wilson
75116 Paris

Camboulive, Christian
Gide Loyrette Nouel
22 cours Albert 1er
75008 Paris

Castellana, Beatrice
CCA Cabinet Castellane Avocats
14 rue Des Sablons
75116 Paris

Cucinotta, Domenico
White & Case
19 Place Vendôme
75001 Paris

Duprey, Pierre
Linklaters
25 rue de Marignan
75008 Paris

Herbert, James
Shearman & Sterling LLP
7 rue Jacques Bingen
75017 Paris

Honlet, Jean-Christophe
Dentons
5 Boulevard Malesherbes
Paris 75008

Khosla, Sumit
Accuracy
41 rue de Villiers
Neuilly-sur-Seine
92523 Paris

Lehucher, Jérôme
DWF LLP
137-139 rue de l'Université
75007 Paris

Maffei, Antoine
De Pardieu Brocas Maffei
57 Avenue d'Iéna
75773 Paris

Marquardt, Alexander
Kramer Levin Naftalis & Frankel LLP
47 Avenue Hoche
75008 Paris

Mourre, Alexis
ICC International Court of Arbitration
33 - 43 Avenue du Président Wilson
75116 Paris

Nicholson, James
FTI Consulting
22 Place de la Madeleine
75008 Paris

Obamuroh, Tolu
White & Case LLP
19 Place Vendôme
75001 Paris

Ranjeva, Andriamahery
Foley Hoag AARPI
153 rue du Faubourg Saint-Honoré
75008 Paris

Stern, Brigitte
University of Paris
1 Pantheon, Sorbonne
7 rue Pierre Nicole
75005 Paris

Thorp, Peter
Thorp Arbitration
29 Rue Louis Blanc
75010 Paris

Vialard, Chloé
Shearman & Sterling LLP
7 rue Jacques Bingen
75017 Paris

Wetmore, Todd
Three Crowns LLP
104 Avenue Des Champs Elysées
75008 Paris

Yates, George
Yates Avocat
17 Rue Guenegaud
75006 Paris

Younan, Jennifer
Shearman & Sterling LLP
7 rue Jacques Bingen
75017 Paris

Ziade, Roland
Linklaters
25 rue de Marignan
75008 Paris

Georgia

Gvinadze, Nick
Gvinadze & Partners
44 Kote Abkhazi Street
0105 Tbilisi

Germany

Broedermann, Eckart
Broedermann Jahn RA GmbH
ABC-Straße 15
20354 Hamburg

Elsing, Siegfried
Orrick, Herrington & Sutcliffe LLP

Heinrich-Heine-Allee 12
40213 Düsseldorf

Herzberg, Axel Benjamin
Bodenheimer Herzberg
Kurfuerstendamm 194
10707 Berlin

Hirth, Rene-Alexander
Buse Heberer Fromm
Leuschnerstrasse 7
70174 Stuttgart
Baden-Württemberg

Mazza, Francesca
German Arbitration Institute (DIS)
Marienforster Str. 52
53177 Bonn

Pickrahn, Guenter
Baker & McKenzie
Bethmannstrasse 50-54
60311 Frankfurt
Hessen

Reeg, Axel
REEG RAe
Speicher 7
68159 Mannheim
Baden-Wuerttemberg

Risse, Jörg
Baker & McKenzie
Bethmannstrasse 50-54
60311 Frankfurt am Main
Hessen

Sachs, Klaus
ICCA Governing Board Member
CMS Hasche Sigle
Nymphenburger Str. 12
80335 Munich

van de Sande, Carsten
Hengeler Mueller
Bockenheimer Landstraße 24
Frankfurt am Main
60323 Hesse

Ghana

Lithur, Anthony
Lithur Brew & Company
PO Box CT3865
Accra, Greater Accra Region

Hong Kong SAR

Ahuja, Sheila
Allen & Overy
9th Floor, Three Exchange Square
Central

Bao, Chiann
Skadden, Arps, Slate, Meagher & Flom
42nd Floor, Edinburgh Tower
The Landmark
15 Queen's Road
Central

Beechey, John
ICCA Governing Board Member
BeecheyArbitration Ltd
Chinachem-Hollywood Centre
Suite 801
1 Hollywood Road
Central

Chapman, Simon
Herbert Smith Freehills
23rd Floor, Gloucester Tower
15 Queen's Road
Central

Chen, Ada
Department of Justice,
Government of the
Hong Kong Special Administrative Region
2nd Floor, East Wing, Justice Place
18 Lower Albert Road
Central 852

Choong, John
Freshfields Bruckhaus Deringer
55th Floor, One Island East, Taikoo Place
Quarry Bay

Cohen, Julian
Gilt Chambers
8th Floor, Far East Finance Centre
16 Harcourt Road

D'Agostino, Justin
Herbert Smith Freehills LLP
23rd Floor Gloucester Tower
15 Queen's Road
Central

Denton, Gavin
Arbitration Chambers
Chinachem Hollywood Centre
Suite 803
1 Hollywood Road
Central

Dimsey, Mariel
CMS Hasche Sigle, Hong Kong
27th Floor, 8 Queen's Road
Central

Eliasson, Nils
Shearman & Sterling
12th Floor, Gloucester Tower
The Landmark
15 Queen's Road
Central

Gearing, Matthew
Allen & Overy
9th Floor, Three Exchange Square
Central

Grimmer, Sarah
Hong Kong International
Arbitration Centre
38th Floor, Two Exchange Square
8 Connaught Place
Central

Hasofer, Menachem
Mayer Brown JSM
Prince's Building
Central, 10111

Hodgson, Matthew
Allen & Overy
9th Floor, Three Exchange Square
Central, 852

Holloway, David
City University of Hong Kong
Hong Kong

Houghton, Anthony
Des Voeux Chambers
38/F Gloucester Tower
The Landmark
Central

Kaplan, Neil
Arbitration Chambers
Chinachem Hollywood Centre
Suite 803
1 Hollywood Road
Central

Kaplan, Su
Chinachem Centre
Suite 803
1 Hollywood Road
Central

Khong, Cheng-Yee
IMF Bentham
Level 16, Man Yee Building
60-68 Des Voeux Road Central
Central

Kwan, James
Hogan Lovells
11th Floor, One Pacific Place
88 Queensway

Ladharam, Kirti
Hong Kong International Arbitration Centre
38th Floor, Two Exchange Square
8 Connaught Place
Central

Landi, Niccolo
BeecheyArbitration Ltd
Chinachem-Hollywood Centre
Suite 801
1 Hollywood Road
Central

Lee, Anita
Hogan Lovells Lee & Lee
11th Floor, One Pacific Place
88 Queensway
Admiralty

Lee, Sau Kong
Department of Justice
Government of the Hong Kong

Special Administrative Region
5th Floor, Main Wing, Justice Place
18 Lower Albert Road
Central

Leung, William
William KW Leung & Co
1101, Beautiful Group Tower
77 Connaught Road
Central

Lim, Jennifer
Debevoise & Plimpton
21/F AIA Central
1 Connaught Road
Central

McDonald, Damien
Fangda Partners
C/o Peter Yuen & Associates
(in Association With Fangda Partners)
26th Floor, One Exchange Square
8 Connaught Place
Central

McKenzie, James
King & Wood Mallesons
13th Floor Gloucester Tower
The Landmark
15 Queen's Road
Central

Powell, Simon
Latham & Watkins
18th Floor, One Exchange Square
8 Connaught Place
Central

Ragnwaldh, Jakob
Mannheimer Swartling Advokatbyra
Aktiebolag
3313-17, 33rd Floor, Jardine House
1 Connaught Place
Central

Robbins, Tim
Arbitration Chambers
Chinachem Hollywood Centre
Suite 803
1 Hollywood Road
Central

Rooney, Kim
Gilt Chambers, Hong Kong
8th Floor Far East Finance Centre
16 Harcourt Road
Admiralty

Rowell, Jon
FTI Consulting
Level 22, The Center
99 Queen's Road
Central

Sanghera, Kiran
Hong Kong International
Arbitration Centre
38th Floor, Two Exchange Square
8 Connaught Place
Central

Starr, Paul
King & Wood Mallesons
13th Floor Gloucester Tower
The Landmark,
15 Queen's Road
Central

Tan, Karen
Hong Kong International
Arbitration Centre
38th Floor, Two Exchange Square
8 Connaught Place
Central

Teo, Paul
Baker McKenzie
14th Floor, One Taikoo Place
979 King's Road
Quarry Bay

Wang, Brad
China International Economic and
Trade Arbitration Commission
Hong Kong Arbitration Center
4705 Far East Finance Center
16 Harcourt Road
Admiralty 999077

Wang, Jun
Capital Alliance
ADR Advisory Services
Level 12, 1 Peking Road
Tsim Sha Tsui
Kowloon

Wang, Wenying
China International Economic and
Trade Arbitration Commission
Hong Kong Arbitration Center
4705 Far East Finance Centre
16 Harcourt Road
Admiralty 999077

Wiegand, Nicolas
CMS Hasche Sigle, Hong Kong
27th Floor, 8 Queen's Road
Central

Yang, Fan
International Dispute
Resolution Academy
509 Bank of America Tower
12 Harcourt Rd
Central

Yeoh, Friven
Sidley Austin
39th Floor, Two IFC
Central

Yue, Bernard
Department of Justice,
Government of the Hong Kong
Special Administrative Region
5th Floor, East Wing, Justice Place
18 Lower Albert Road
Central

Hungary

Damjanovic, Gabor
Forgó, Damjanovic &
Partners Law Firm
17-19 Alkotas street
1123 Budapest

India

Bakhru, Pallavi
Vedanta Ltd
Dlf Atria, Dlf Phase 2
Jacaranda Marg
DLF City, Gurgaon
Haryana 122008

Bakhru, Vibhu
Delhi High Court
Sher Shah Road
New Delhi 110503

Baya, Madhur
LexArbitri
Suite 206 DBS, 2nd Floor
Mumbai 400021, Maharashtra

Chandrachud, Dhananjaya
Supreme Court of India
Tilak Marg
New Delhi-110201

Chandru, Ganesh
Lakshmikumaran & Sridharan
5 Link Road, Jangpura Extension
New Delhi 110014

Das, Anirudha
Shardul Amarchand
Mangaldas & Co.
Amarchand Towers
216, Okhla Industrial Estate Phase-III
New Delhi 110020

Desai, Vyapak
Nishith Desai Associates
93/ B, Mittal Court, Nariman Point
Mumbai 400021, Maharashtra

Endlaw, Menkka
New Delhi, 110001

Endlaw, Rajiv Sahai
High Court of Delhi
Sher Shah Road
New Delhi 110001

Garg, Shashank
Advani and Company
268 Gf, Masjid Moth
New Delhi 110049

Jain, Sameer
PSL Advocates & Solicitors
A-169, LGF, Defence Colony
New Delhi 110024

Kachwaha, Mamta
Kachwaha and Partners

1/6 Shanti Niketan
New Delhi, 110021

Karia, Tejas
Shardul Amarchand
Mangaldas & Co.
Amarchand Towers,
216, Okhla Industrial Estate
Phase-III
New Delhi 110020

Khanna, Yogesh
Delhi High Court
Sher Shah Road,
New Delhi 110503

Kumar, Sanjeev
Khaitan & Co. LLP Delhi
1105 Ashoka Estate
24 Barakhamba Road
New Delhi 110001

Mayal, Montek
FTI Consulting.
14th Floor, Eros Corporate Tower
Nehru Place
New Delhi 110019

Mody, Zia
ICCA Governing Board Member
AZB & Partners
Azb House
Peninsula Corporate Park,
Ganpatrao Kadam Marg
Lower Parel
Mumbai, Maharashtra 400013

Nirwani, Sanjeev
Nirwani Associates
22, Mausam Vihar
Delhi 110051

Panchmatia, Raj
Khaitan & Co.
One Indiabulls Centre
13 Floor, Tower 1
841 Senapati Bapat Marg
Mumbai, Maharashtra 400013

Shroff, Vismay
Parimal K. Shroff & Co.
Advocates, Solicitors & Notary
29, Veer Nariman Road, 1st Floor
Rustom Building, Fort
Mumbai, Maharashtra 400023

Sikri, Saket
Sikri And Company
C-131 Defence Colony
New Delhi 110024

Singh, Sonal Kumar
A.K. Singh & Co. (Advocates,
Consultants & Solicitors)
Building No. G-16, Second Floor
Saket
New Delhi 110017

Indonesia

Krisnawenda, N.
Badan Arbitrase Nasional Indonesia
(BANI Arbitration Center)
Wahana Graha 1st, 2nd and 4th Floor
Jl. Mampang Prapatan No. 2
Jakarta Selatan 12760

Umar, M. Husseyn
Badan Arbitrase Nasional Indonesia
(BANI Arbitration Center)
Wahana Graha 1st, 2nd and 4th Floor
Jl. Mampang Prapatan No. 2
Jakarta Selatan 12760

Italy

Benedettelli, Massimo
ARBLIT - Radicati di Brozolo
Sabatini Benedettelli
Via Alberto Da Giussano N. 15
20145 Milan

Cicogna, Michelangelo
De Berti Jacchia
Via San Paolo 7
20121 Milan

Concolino, Barbara
BonelliErede
Via Pagliano 31
20149 Milan

Minuto, Giovanni
BonelliErede

Via Michele Barozzi 1
20122 Milan

Paton, Andrew
De Berti Jacchia Franchini Forlani
via S. Paolo 7
20121 Milan

Japan

Greer, Joel
Baker & McKenzie
Ark Hills Sengokuyama Mori Tower
28th Floor
1-9-10 Roppongi, Minato-ku
Tokyo 106-0032

Iseda, Michihito
Kwansei Gakuin University
Rafine 403, Takagihigashi-machi 21-1
Nishinomiya, Hyogo 6638033

Kodama, Masafumi
Kitahama Partners
Osaka Securities Building
1-8-16 Kitahama, Chuo-ku
Osaka 541-0041

Mogi, Teppei
Oh-Ebashi LPC & Partners
27th Floor
2-3-8, Nakanoshima, Kita-ku
Osaka 530-0005

Naito, Junya
Momo-o, Matsuo & Namba
Kojimachi Diamond Building
4-1 Kojimachi, Chiyoda-ku
Tokyo 102-0083

Oghigian, Haig, F.C.I.Arb
Squire Patton Boggs
Ebisu Prime Square Tower
16th Floor
1-1-39 Hiroo, Shibuya-ku
Tokyo 150-0012

Ohara, Yoshimi
ICCA Governing Board Member
Nagashima Ohno & Tsunematsu
JP Tower
2-7-2 Marunouchi, Chiyoda-ku
Tokyo 100-7036

Tada, Shin
Oh-Ebashi LPC & Partners
27th Floor, 2-3-8, Nakanoshima
Kita-ku
Osaka 530-0005

Takara, Mikiko
Ministry of Justice of Japan
1-1-1 Kasumigaseki, Chiyoda-ku
Tokyo 100-8977

Taniguchi, Yasuhei
Advisory Member of ICCA
Matsuo & Kosugi
Fukoku-seimei Bldg., 18th Floor
2-2-2 Uchisaiwai-cho, Chiyoda-ku
Tokyo 100-0011

Tezuka, Hiroyuki
Nishimura & Asahi
Otemon Tower
1-1-2 Otemachi, Chiyoda-ku
Tokyo 1008124

Jordan

Yaghmour, Jawdat
Associated Consulting
Engineers International
Shmeisani, Abdul-Hamid Sharaf St.
Radhi Bishtwi Building 102, Block 96
Amman 11190

Yaghmour, Samer
Associated Consulting
Engineers International
Shmeisani, Abdul Hamid Sharaf St.
Radhi Bishtwi Building 102, Block 96
Amman 11190

Kenya

Muiruri Ngugi, Lawrence
Nairobi Centre for
International Arbitration
Co-operative Bank House
Haile Selassie Avenue
Nairobi 00200

Njogu, Anthony
Coulson Harney LLP
5th Floor, West Wing
ICEA Lion Centre
Nairobi 00100

Nyamasi, Irene
Nairobi Centre for
International Arbitration
Co-operative Bank House
Haile Selassie Avenue
Nairobi 00200

Ohaga, John
TripleOKlaw Advocates LLP
PO Box 43170
Nairobi 00100

Korea, Republic of

Ahn, Taejoon
Yulchon LLP
Parnas Tower, 38th Floor
521 Teheran-ro, Gangnam-gu
Seoul 06164

Baek, Yun Jae
Yulchon LLC
Parnas Tower, 38th Floor
521 Teheran-ro, Gangnam-gu
Seoul 06164

Bang, John P.
Bae, Kim & Lee LLC
133 Teheran-ro, Gangnam-gu
Seoul 06133

Eernisse, Arie
Shin & KIM
State Tower Namsan, 8th Floor
100 Toegye-ro, Jung-gu
Seoul 04631

Kim, David
Lee & Ko
Hanjin Building
63 Namdaemun-ro, Jung-gu
Seoul 04532

Kim, Doo-Sik
Shin & Kim
8th Floor, State Tower Namsan
100 Toegye-ro, Jung-gu
Seoul 04631

Kim, Joongi
Yonsei Law School
50 Yonseriro, Seodaemungu
Seoul 03722

Kim, Kap-you (Kevin)
Advisory Member of ICCA
Bae, Kim & Lee LLC
133 Teheran-ro, Gangnam-gu
Seoul 06133

Kim, Sam
Yoon & Yang LLC
18th Floor, Asem Tower
517 Yeongdong-daero
Seoul 06164

Lee, Junsang
Yoon & Yang LLC
18th Floor Asem Tower
517 Yeongdong-daero
Seoul 06164

Lim, Sean (Sungwoo)
Lee & Ko
Hanjin Building
63 Namdaemun-ro, Jung-gu
Seoul 04532

Oh, Hyun Suk
The Korean Commercial
Arbitration Board
43rd Floor, 511,Yeongdong-daero
(Samseong-dong, Trade Tower)
Gangnam-gu
Seoul 06164

Park, Eun-Young
Kim & Chang
39, Sajik-ro 8-gil, Jongno-gu
Seoul 03170

Shin, Hi-Taek
ICCA Governing Board Member
Seoul IDRC
11 F Seoul Global Center
38, Jongro-gu
Seoul 03188

Wegner, Kay-Jannes
Kim & Chang
39, Sajik-ro 8-gil, Jongno-gu
Seoul 03170

Yoon, Byung-Chol
Kim & Chang
39, Sajik-ro 8-gil, Jongno-gu
Seoul 03170

Lebanon

Comair-Obeid, Nayla
Obeid Law Firm
Stratum Building, Omar Daouk Street
116/2234, Law Courts
Beirut

Obeid, Ziad
Obeid Law Firm
Stratum Building, Omar Daouk Street
116/2234, Law Courts
Beirut

Malaysia

Abraham, Cecil
Advisory Member of ICCA
Cecil Abraham and Partners
Suite 12.01, Level 12, Menara 1MK,
1 Jalan Kiara, Mont' Kiara
50480 Kuala Lumpur

Baskaran, Thayananthan
Baskaran
50-11-7 Wisma UOA Damansara
Jalan Dungun, Damansara Heights
50490 Kuala Lumpur

Lam, Ko Luen
Shook Lin & Bok
20th Floor, Ambank Group Building, No. 55
Jalan Raja Chulan
50200 Kuala Lumpur

Loo, Ivan
Skrine
50-8-1, 8th Floor
Wisma UOA Damansara
Jalan Dungun, Damansara Heights
50490 Kuala Lumpur

Rajoo Nadarajah, Sundra
Sundra Rajoo Arbitration Chambers
No. 28-1, Medan Setia 2
Bukit Damansara
50490 Kuala Lumpur

Selvaratnam, Sitpah
Tommy Thomas
101, Jalan Ara, Bangsar Baru, Bangsar
Kuala Lumpur 59100

Thiyagarajah, Beatrice
Cecil Abraham and Partners
Suite 12.01, Level 12, Menara 1MK
1 Jalan Kiara, Mont' Kiara
Kuala Lumpur, 50480

Mauritius

Gunnoo, Dipna
MCCI Arbitration & Mediation Centre
(MARC)
6 Adolphe de Plevitz Street
Port Louis 11328

Jullienne, Anne-Sophie
PwC Legal (Mauritius) Ltd
PwC Centre
Avenue de Telfair
Telfair 80829
Moka

Khemraz-Chikhuri, Anjana
MCCI Arbitration & Mediation Centre
(MARC)
6 Adolphe de Plevitz Street
Port Louis 11328

Pillay, Barlen
Mauritius Chamber of Commerce &
Industry
6 Adolphe de Plevitz St
Port Louis

Mexico

Brown de Vejar, Kate
DLA Piper
Paseo de los Tamarindos 400 A,
31st Floor

Col. Bosques de las Lomas
Mexico City 05120

Gonzalez De Cossio Guadalajara, Francisco
Gonzalez De Cossio Abogados
Paseo De Los Ahuehuetes Sur 408
Col.lomas De Bezares
Mexico City 11910

Siqueiros, Eduardo
ICCA Treasurer
Arb-Inter, S.C.
Paseo de los Tamarindos 150- P.B.
Bosques de las Lomas
Mexico City 05120

von Wobeser, Claus
Von Wobeser y Sierra, S.C.
Paseo De Los Tamarindos 60, 4th Floor
Bosques De Las Lomas
Mexico City 05120

Montenegro

Božović, Vesko
VMB Law firm
Moskovska 99/ii
Podgorica

Netherlands

Adarghal, Karim
Municipality of The Hague, Netherlands
Spui 70
2511 BT The Hague

van Baren, Willem
Independent Arbitrator
Dijsselhofplantsoen 12
1077BL Amsterdam

Bier, Lyda
dr. L. Bier B.V.
Baroniesingel 32
5262KB Vught

Bingham, Lisa
ICCA/PCA
Peace Palace, Carnegieplein 2
2517 KJ The Hague

Borelli, Silvia
ICCA
Peace Palace, Carnegieplein 2
2517 KJ The Hague

Bosman, Lise
Executive Director of ICCA
Senior Legal Counsel
Permanent Court of Arbitration
Peace Palace, Carnegieplein 2
2517 KJ The Hague

Cervetto Zuffo, Gabriela
Municipality of The Hague, Netherlands
Spui 70
2511 BT The Hague

Di Giacomo Toledo, Tulio
Permanent Court of Arbitration
Peace Palace, Carnegieplein 2
2517 KJ The Hague

Goriatcheva, Evgeniya
Permanent Court of Arbitration
Peace Palace, Carnegieplein 2
2517 KJ The Hague

Groot Koerkamp, Marjolijn
The Hague Business Agency
Prinses Margrietplantsoen 35
2595 AM The Hague

Van Hooijdonk, Maricke
Allen & Overy LLP
Apollolaan 15
1077 AB Amsterdam

Kamau, Ndanga
Ndanga Kamau Law
Kneuterdijk 3B
2514 EM The Hague

Knottenbelt, Dirk
Houthoff
Weena 355
3013 AL Rotterdam

Koppenol-Laforce, Marielle
Houthoff
Weena 355
3013 AL Rotterdam

Kuscher, Matthias L.
De Brauw Blackstone Westbroek
Claude Debussylaan 80
1082 MD Amsterdam

Leijten, Marnix
De Brauw Blackstone Westbroek
Claude Debussylaan 80
1082 MD Amsterdam

Levine, Judith
Permanent Court of Arbitration
Peace Palace, Carnegieplein 2
2517 KJ The Hague

Van Leyenhorst, Max
Legaltree
Rapenburg 83
2311GK Leiden

Marsman, Albert
De Brauw Blackstone Westbroek
Claude Debussylaan 80
1082 MD Amsterdam

Meijer, Gerard
Linklaters LLP
World Trade Centre
Zuidplein 180
1077 XV Amsterdam

Nathwani, Sheena
Wolters Kluwer
Zuidpoolsingel 2
2408 ZE Alphen Aan Den Rijn

Oorthuys, Alexander
Legaltree
Rapenburg 83
2311GK Leiden

Pickard, Duncan
Permanent Court of Arbitration
Peace Palace, Carnegieplein 2
2517 KJ The Hague

Ross, Jonathan
P.R.I.M.E. Finance Stichting
Permanent Court of Arbitration
Peace Palace, Carnegieplein 2
2517 KJ The Hague

Ruff, Jonathan
Loyens & Loeff N.V.
Blaak 31
3011 GA Rotterdam

Schill, Stephan
University of Amsterdam
Nieuwe Achtergracht 166
1018 WV Amsterdam

Siblesz, Hugo
Permanent Court of Arbitration
Peace Palace, Carnegieplein 2
2517 KJ The Hague

Tangkiriphimarn, Amnart
Permanent Court of Arbitration
Peace Palace, Carnegieplein 2
2517 KJ The Hague

Verschoor, Vincent
Wolters Kluwer
Zuidpoolsingel 2
2408 ZE Alphen aan den Rijn

Voges, Lauren
ICCA
Peace Palace, Carnegieplein 2
2517 KJ The Hague

New Zealand

Butler, Petra
Victoria University of Wellington
Faculty of Law
55 Lambton Quay
Wellington 6011

Christie, Graeme
Simpson Grierson
Lumley Centre
88 Shortland Street
Auckland 1010

Foote, Simon
Bankside Chambers
Level 22, 88 Shortland Street
Auckland 1140

Green, Catherine
New Zealand Dispute Resolution
Centre

9 Anzac Street
Takapuna 0622

Green, John
New Zealand International
Arbitration Centre
9 Anzac Street
Takapuna 0622

Hart, Deborah
Arbitrators' and Mediators'
Institute of New Zealand
PO Box 1477
Wellington 6140

Heath, Paul
Paul Heath QC
1101/135 Grafton Road
Auckland 1010

Hindle, Royden
Arbitrators and Mediators
Institute of New Zealand
PO Box 1571
Auckland 1140

Johnston, Derek
Thorndon Chambers
Po Box 1530
Wellington 6140

Kalderimis, Daniel
Chapman Tripp
Maritime Tower
10 Customhouse Quay
Wellington 6011

Kirk, Anna
Sir David Williams QC, Bankside
Chambers
Level 22, 88 Shortland Street
Auckland 1140

Lindsay, Lauren
Bankside Chambers
PO Box 1571, Shortland Street
Auckland, 1140

Lindsay, Timothy
Lindsay LA
Shortland Centre, Level 17
55 Shortland Street
Auckland 1010

McLachlan, Campbell QC
Victoria University of Wellington
Law School
Old Government Buildings
55 Lambton Quay
Wellington 6140

Pope, Polly
Russell McVeagh
Level 30, Vero Centre
48 Shortland Street
Auckland 1140

Smith, Nicole
Nicole Smith Barrister
65 Valley Road
Mount Maunganui 3116

Walker, Campbell
Campbell Walker Chambers
Level 4, 9 High St
Auckland 1010

Williams, Sir David
Advisory Member of ICCA
Bankside Chambers
Level 22, 88 Shortland Street
Auckland 1140

Nigeria

Adekoya, Olufunke
ICCA Governing Board Member
AELEX
7th Floor, Marble House
1 Kingsway Road, Falomo, Ikoyi
Lagos

Egwumba, Emmanuel Success
Chukwuma Chambers
Suite C6, Gateway Building
Plot 208, Zakariyah Maimalari Way
By Central Bank of Nigeria
Central Business District
Abuja

Elias, Gbolahan
G. Elias & Co.
6 Broad Street
Lagos

Ganiyu, Mutiu
Smithworth Partners
3rd Floor, West Wing, City Hall
Catholic Mission Street
Lagos

Okafor, Vitalis Chukwuma
Chukwuma Chambers
Suite C6, Gateway Building
Plot 208, Zakariyah Maimalari Way
By Central Bank of Nigeria
Central Business District
Abuja

Pakistan

Daudpota, Faisal
Daudpota International
401 & 408, Press Center Building
Shahrah-e-Kamal Ataturk
Karachi 74200

Khan, Muhammed Makhdoom Ali
ICCA Governing Board Member
Fazleghani Advocates
F-72/1, Block 8, Kda 5, Clifton
Karachi 75600

Papua New Guinea

Kandakasi, Ambeng
Supreme and National Courts of
Justice of Papua New Guinea
Minihi Ave, Lot 8, Sect 3
Boroko, NCD 0111

Shepherd, Jeffery
Supreme Court of
Papua New Guinea
PO Box 7018
Boroko, NCD 111

Philippines

Arroyo, Laurence Hector
Flaminiano Arroyo & Duenas Law Firm
Unit 1002, One Corporate Centre
Meralco Avenue
Cor. Doña Julia Vargas Avenue
Ortigas Center
Pasig City, Metro Manila 1605

Calderon, Leonardo III
Office of the Solicitor General
134 Amorsolo Street, Legaspi Village
Makati City, Metro Manila 1229

Caluyo, Emmanuel
Office of the Solicitor General
134 Amorsolo Street, Legaspi Village
Pasig City, Manila 1800

Dizon, Maria Antonia Edita
Office of the Solicitor General
134 Amorsolo Street, Legaspi Village
Makati City, Metro Manila 1229

Flores, Sienna
Romulo Mabanta Buenaventura
Sayoc & De Los Angeles
21st Floor Philamlife Tower
8767 Paseo De Roxas
Makati City, Metro Manila 1226

Guzman, Jacqueline
Office of the Solicitor General
134 Amorsolo Street, Legaspi Village
Makati City, Metro Manila 1229

King Kay, Catherine Beatrice Olanka
Romulo Mabanta Buenaventura
Sayoc & De Los Angeles
21st Floor Philamlife Tower
8767 Paseo de Roxas
Makati City, Metro Manila 1226

Lombos, Emmanuel
SyCip Salazar Hernandez & Gatmaitan
105 Paeo De Roxas
Makati City, Metro Manila 1226

Ogsimer, Louie
Romulo Mabanta Buenaventura
Sayoc & De Los Angeles
21st Floor Philamlife Tower
8767 Paseo De Roxas
Makati City, Metro Manila 1226

Prado, Carlos Manuel
Office of the Solicitor General
134 Amorsolo Street, Legaspi Village
Makati City, Metro Manila 1229

Tumangan, Daniel Kendrick
Romulo Mabanta Buenaventura Sayoc &
De Los Angeles
21st Floor Philamlife Tower
8767 Paseo De Roxas
Makati City, Metro Manila 1226

Poland

Gessel-Kalinowska vel Kalisz, Beata
Gessel
ul. Sienna 39
00-121 Warszawa

Portugal

Campos, Ricardo
Gomez Acebo & Pombo Abogados, SLP
Av. Duque De Ávila, no. 46, 6th Floor
Lisbon 1050-083

Pinto Cardoso, Miguel
Vieira de Almeida & Associados
Av. Dom Luis I, No. 28
Lisbon 1200-151

Russia

Khvalei, Vladimir
ICCA Governing Board Member
Baker & McKenzie
9 Lesnaya Street
Moscow 125047

Kroll, Martin
Arbitration Center at the
Institute of Modern Arbitration
Suite 140, 1st Floor,
Ducat Place II Gasheka str. 7
Moscow 123056

Zagonek, Julia
White & Case LLC
4 Romanov Pereulok
Moscow 125009

Zamaziy, Alexander
Arbitration Centre at the
Russian Union of Industrialists
and Entrepreneurs
17, Kotel`nicheskaya Embankment
Moscow 109240

Rwanda

Masengo, Fidele
Kigali International
Arbitration Centre
PO Box 695
Kigali

Saudi Arabia

Al-mogheerah, Abdullah
Saudi Center for Commercial
Arbitration
8th Floor
Council of Saudi Chamber Building
7982 King Fahd Branch Road –
al Mutamarat
Riyadh 12711-4183

Seychelles

MacGregor, Francis
Department of Judiciary
Court of Appeal Seychelles
Palais de Justice
Isle Du Port, Perseverance
Victoria

Singapore

Andre, Yeap Poh Leong
Rajah & Tann Singapore LLP
9 Battery Road #25-01
Singapore 049910

Arora, Chaitanya
FTI Consulting
8 Shenton Way Axa Tower #12-02
Singapore 068811

Bateson, David
39 Essex Chambers
Maxwell Chambers
32 Maxwell Road #02-16
Singapore 069115

Battisson, Andrew
Ocean Financial Centre #40-36
10 Collyer Quay
Singapore 049315

Bull, Cavinder
ICCA Governing Board Member
Drew & Napier LLC
Ocean Financial Centre #10-01
10 Collyer Quay
Singapore 049315

Chan, Hock Keng
WongPartnership LLP
12 Marina Boulevard
Level 28 Marina Bay Financial Centre
Tower 3
Singapore 018982

Chew, Daryl
Shearman & Sterling LLP
6 Battery Road #25-03
Singapore 049909

Chou, Sean Yu
WongPartnership LLP
12 Marina Boulevard
Level 28 Marina Bay Financial Centre
Tower 3
Singapore 018982

Chung, Katie
Norton Rose Fulbright (Asia) LLP
One Raffles Quay
North Tower #34-02
Singapore 048583

Cooke, Timothy
Stephenson Harwood LLP
1 Raffles Place, Tower 2 #18-61
Singapore 048616

Dass, Premjit
Navigant Consulting
PSA Building #22-05
460 Alexandra Road
Singapore 119963

Dearness, Mitchell
Herbert Smith Freehills LLP
50 Raffles Place
Singapore Land Tower #24-01
Singapore 048623

Dewan, Nakul
20 Essex Street Chambers
02-09, Maxwell Chambers
32 Maxwell Road
Singapore 069115

Ellis, Jonathan
Accuracy
One Raffles Place #47-03
Singapore 048616

Fletcher, Karen
Navigant Consulting (APAC) Pte Ltd
PSA Building #22-05
460 Alexandra Road
Singapore 119963

Gill, Judith
ICCA Governing Board Member
Twenty Essex
28 Maxwell Road #02-03
Maxwell Chambers Suit
Singapore 069120

Henderson, Alastair
Herbert Smith Freehills LLP
Singapore Land Tower 24-01
50 Raffles Place
Singapore 048623

Hwang, Michael
Honorary Vice President
and Advisory Member of ICCA
Michael Hwang Chambers LLC
150 Beach Road
Singapore 189720

Jeremiah, Herman
Dentons Rodyk & Davidson LLP
80 Raffles Place
UOB Plaza 1 #33-00
Singapore 048624

Jhangiani, Sapna
Clyde & Co Clasis Singapore Pte Ltd
12 Marina Boulevard
Marina Bay Financial Centre
Tower 3 #30-03
Singapore 018982

Kronenburg, Edmund
Braddell Brothers LLP

11 Beach Road #04-01
Singapore 189675

Lau, Christopher
Christopher Lau
32 Maxwell Road
Maxwell Chambers #02-04
Singapore 069115

Lau, Joanne
Allen & Overy LLP
50 Collyer Quay
OUE Bayfront #09-01
Singapore 049321

Lee, Michael
20 Essex Street Chambers
32 Maxwell Road
Maxwell Chambers #02 09
Singapore 069115

Lee, Michael D.
International Centre for
Dispute Resolution
32 Maxwell Road
Maxwell Chambers #02-06
Singapore 069115

Lees, Amanda
Simmons & Simmons JWS
168 Robinson Road
Capital Tower #11-01
Singapore 068912

Lim, Steven
CMS Cameron McKenna Nabarro
Olswang (Singapore) LLP
7 Straits View
Marina One East Tower #19-01
Singapore 018936

Malintoppi, Loretta
ICCA Governing Board Member
39 Essex Chambers
32 Maxwell Road
Maxwell Chambers #16-02
Singapore, 069115

Mangan, Mark
Dechert (Singapore) Pte Ltd
One George Street #16-03
Singapore 049145

Margetson, Gavin
Berwin Leighton Paisner LLP
9 Raffles Place
Republic Plaza Tower 1 #24-01
Singapore 048619

Menon, Sundaresh
ICCA Governing Board Member
Supreme Court of Singapore
1 Supreme Court Lane
Singapore 178879

Monange, Olivier
DS AVOCATS
Parkview Square #13-06
600 North Bridge Road
Singapore 188778

Moran, Andrew QC
The Arbitration Chambers Singapore
32 Maxwell Rd
Maxwell Chambers
Singapore, Singapore 069115

Morris-Sharma, Natalie Y.
Ministry of Law, Singapore
100 High Street
Singapore 179434

Nai Kin, Chalee
The Chartered Institute of Arbitrators
32 Maxwell Road
Maxwell Chambers #01-07
Singapore 069115

Olbourne, Ben
39 Essex Chambers
32 Maxwell Road
Maxwell Chambers #02-16
Singapore 069115

Ong, Jia Hong
Supreme Court of Singapore
1 Supreme Court Lane
Singapore 178879

Palmer, Rob
Ashurst
12 Marina Boulevard
Marina Bay Financial Centre #24-01
Tower 3
Singapore 018982

Pandjaitan, Jelita
Linklaters
1 George Street
Singapore 049145

Prudhoe, Jon
460 Alexandra Road
PSA Building 22-05
119963 Singapore

Reed, Lucy
Vice-President and
President-Elect of ICCA
National University of Singapore
Centre for International Law
469a Bukit Timah Road
Tower Block #09-01
Singapore, 259770

Shetty, Nish
Clifford Chance Pte Ltd
12 Marina Boulevard, 25th Floor
MBFC Tower 3
Singapore 018982

Singh, Kirindeep
Dentons Rodyk & Davidson LLP
80 Raffles Place
UOB Plaza 1 #33-00
Singapore 048624

Smith, Fedelma
Permanent Court of Arbitration
Singapore Office
Maxwell Suite
28 Maxwell Road #02-07
Singapore 069120

Snadden, Alasdair
Driver Trett
141 Cecil Street #05-01
Tung Ann Association Building
Singapore 069541

Somers, Sandra
Driver Trett
141 Cecil Street #05-01
Tung Ann Association Building,
Singapore 069541

Stackpool-Moore, Ruth
Asia Dispute Funding
50 Raffle Place, Level 19
Singapore 048623

Tan, Richard
Richard Tan Arbitrator
21 Bukit Sedap Road
Singapore 279920

Tan, Karen
Supreme Court Singapore
1 Supreme Court Lane
Singapore 178879

Teh, Lawrence
Dentons Rodyk & Davidson
80 Raffles Place
UOB Plaza 1 #33-00
Singapore 48624

Xavier, Francis
Rajah & Tann Singapore LLP
Battery Road #25-00 9
Singapore 049910

South Africa

Alp, Nick
Webber Wentzel
90 Rivonia Road
Sandton
Johannesburg, Gauteng 2196

Baker, Timothy
Cliffe Dekker Hofmeyr Inc
11 Buitengracht Street,
Cape Town 8001

Feris, Jackwell
Cliffe Dekker Hofmeyr Inc
1 Protea Place
Johannesburg, Gauteng 2001

Movshovich, Vlad
Webber Wentzel
90 Rivonia Road
Sandton
Johannesburg, Gauteng 2196

Ripley Evans, Jonathan
Herbert Smith Freehills South Africa LLP
Rosebank Towers – 4th Floor
15 Biermann Avenue

Rosebank
Johannesburg, 2196

Versfeld, Trevor
Webber Wentzel
90 Rivonia Road
Sandton
Johannesburg, Gauteng 2000

Spain

Gómez-Acebo, Alfonso
Cuatrecasas
Almagro 9
28010 Madrid

McDonnell, Bianca
Armesto & Asociados
Calle Del General Pardiñas, 102
28006 Madrid

Sweden

Ahrel, Ginta
Advokatfirman Lindahl KB
Regeringsgatan 48
PO Box 1065
Stockholm 10139

Dahlquist Cullborg, Joel
Uppsala University
Uppsala 75236

Freij, Annika
Advokatfirman Glimstedt AB
Box 2259
Gothenburg 40314

Kotick, Brian
Mannheimer Swartling Advokatbyrå
Norrlandsgatan 21
Stockholm 11187

Lettius, Carin
Advokatfirman Glimstedt
Stortorget 10
Box 1027
Helsingborg 25110

Lettius, Michael
Advokatfirman Glimstedt
Stortorget 17
Box 1027
Helsingborg 25110

Magnusson, Annette
Arbitration Institute of the
Stockholm Chamber of Commerce
PO Box 16050
Stockholm 10321

Nadar, Aisha
Advokatfirman Runeland AB
Sturegatan 12
Stockholm 11436

Nilsson, Bo
Lindahl
PO Box 1065
Stockholm 10139

Runeland, Per
Advokatfirman Runeland AB
Sturegatan 12
Stockholm 11436

Smedberg, Ulrik
Advokatfirman SJS KB
Kristinehöjdsgatan 16
Gothenburg 411 37

Switzerland

Baertsch, Philippe
Schellenberg Wittmer SA
15bis, rue des Alpes
1211 Geneva

Bangert, Jan
Boeckli Buehler Partners
St. Jakobs-strasse 41
4052 Basel

Boog, Christopher
Schellenberg Wittmer Ltd
Löwenstrasse 19
8021 Zurich

Dasser, Felix
Homburger AG
Hardstrasse 201
PO Box 314
Zurich 8005

Favre-Bulle, Xavier
Lenz & Staehelin
Route de Chêne 30
1211 Geneva

Johnson, Alexandra C.
Bär & Karrer Ltd
12, Quai De La Poste
1204 Geneva

Kaufmann-Kohler, Gabrielle
President of ICCA
Levy Kaufmann-Kohler
3-5 rue du Conseil-Général
1204 Geneva

Lenggenhager, Fadri
Lenz & Staehelin
Brandschenkestrasse 24
8057 Zurich

Mbengue, Makane Moïse
University of Geneva
Faculty of Law
40 Boulevard du Pont d'Arve
(Uni-Mail)
1211 Geneva

McLin, Alex
Swiss Arbitration Association (ASA)
Boulevard du Theatre 4
PO Box 5429
1211 Geneva

Meyer, Bernhard F.
MME Legal Tax Compliance
Zollstrasse 62
8031 Zurich

Moser, Gustavo
Swiss International Law School (SiLS)
Basel, Switzerland
4051 Basel

Nater-Bass, Gabrielle
Homburger
Prime Tower, Hardstrasse 201
8005 Zurich

Radjai, Noradèle
LALIVE
35, Rue De La Mairie
1207 Geneva

Schneider, Michael E.
LALIVE
35, Rue de La Mairie
1207 Geneva

von Segesser, Georg
von Segesser Law Offices
Mühlebachstrasse 173
8008 Zurich

Sester, Peter
University of St. Gallen IFF-HSG
Guisanstrasse 36
9010 St. Gallen

Stutzer, Hansjoerg
Thouvenin Rechtsanwaelte KLG
Klausstrasse 33
8024 Zurich

Tercier, Anne
Bureau Pierre Tercier
Ch. Guillaume-Ritter 5
1700 Fribourg

Tercier, Pierre
Advisory Member of ICCA
Bureau Pierre Tercier
Ch. Guillaume-Ritter 5
1700 Fribourg

Tran Thang, Nhu-Hoang
LALIVE
35, Rue De La Mairie
1207 Geneva

Voser, Nathalie
Schellenberg Wittmer Ltd
Löwenstrasse 19
8021 Zurich,

Wiebecke, Martin
Anwaltsbüro Wiebecke
Kohlrainstrasse 10
8700 Küsnacht/Zurich

Wyatt, Julian
Independent Practitioner
35, Rue de la Mairie
1207 Geneva

Zenhaeusern, Urs
Baker McKenzie Zurich

Holbeinstrasse 30
8008 Zurich

Taiwan

Li, Chien-Fei
Chinese Arbitration Association, Taipei
14th Fl., 376, Sec. 4, Ren-Ai Road
Taipei 10693

Ma, Winnie Jo-Mei
Chinese Arbitration Association, Taipei
14th Fl., 376, Sec. 4, Ren-Ai Road
Taipei 10693

Tanzania

Nyange, Godson
NW Law Associates
House No. 16 Ghuba Road
Oysterbay
Dar Es Salaam

Nyika, Gaspar Asheri
IMMMA Advocates
Immma House, Plot No. 357
United Nations Road, Upanga
Dar Es Salaam

Thailand

Kippen, Jerrold
Duensing Kippen, Lld
1605 Chartered Square
152 North Sathorn Road
Silom, Bangrak
Bangkok 10500

United Arab Emirates

Briggs, Richard
Emirates Maritime Arbitration Centre
PO Box 507333
Dubai 507333

Carver, Jeremy
Crescent Petroleum Company
10th Floor Crescent House
Sharjah 211

Chaykhouni, Jamal
Almarsat Projects Development
Tecom Hessa St. Warsan Bldg.
Office 503
Dubai 357620

Emmerson, Alec
A.E. A.D.R Fze
Rolex Tower
Dubai 31645

Khader, Maali
Emirates Maritime Arbitration Centre
PO Box 507333
Dubai 507333

Lord Hill, Samantha
Freshfields Bruckhaus Deringer
PO Box 506 569
Dubai

Petkovich, Drazen
Crescent Petroleum Company
10th Floor Crescent House
Sharjah 211

Snider, Thomas
Al Tamimi and Company
DIFC Building No. 4 East Level 6
Dubai 9275

United Kingdom

England and Wales

Abrahams, Sidney Anthony George
The Chartered Institute of Arbitrators
12 Bloomsbury Square
London WC1A 2LP

Aglionby, Andrew
Arbitration Chambers
3rd Floor South, Lamb Buildings
Middle Temple Lane, Temple
London EC4Y 7AS

Amsterdam, Robert
Amsterdam & Partners LLP
139 Piccadilly
London W1J 7NU

Arnott, Craig
Burford Capital
24 Cornhill
London EC3V 3ND

Aswani, Ravi
St Philips Stone
4 Field Court, Gray's Inn
London WC1R 5EF

Auchecorne, Taryn
Opus 2 International
5 New Street Square
London EC4A 3BF

Barnes, David
Atkin Chambers
1 Atkin Buildings, Gray's Inn
London WC1R 5AT

Bastin, Lucas
Essex Court Chambers
24 Lincoln's Inn Fields
London WC2A 3EG

Behn, Daniel
University of Liverpool Law School
Room 260, Walnut House,
Mulberry Street
Liverpool, Merseyside L69 7ZY

Bellamy, Jonathan
39 Essex Chambers
81 Chancery Lane
London WC2A 1DD

Bishop, John
Arbitration Chambers
London, Hong Kong
Lamb Building, 3rd Floor South
Temple
London EC4Y 7AS

Bondy, Christophe
Cooley (UK) LLP
Dashwood, 69 Old Broad Street
London EC2M 1QS

Brekoulakis, Stavros
Queen Mary University of London
67-69 Lincoln's Inn Fields
London WC2A 3 JB

Bridgeman, James
The Chartered Institute of Arbitrators
12 Bloomsbury Square
London WC1A 2LP

Capper, Phillip
White & Case LLP
5 Old Broad Street
London EC2N 1DW

Chalk, Gemma
Global Arbitration Review
87 Lancaster Road
London W11 1QQ

Charlotin, Damien
University of Cambridge
10 West Road
Cambridge CB3 9DZ

Clarke, Andrew
ICCA Governing Board Member
ExxonMobil International Limited
Ermyn House, Ermyn Way
Leatherhead, Surrey KT22 8UX

Clarke, Ece
Broomehall Road
1 Broome Hall
Dorking, Surrey RH56HJ

Cohen, Paul
4-5 Gray's Inn Square Chambers
Gray's Inn Rd
London WC1R 5AH

Cordara, Roderick
Essex Court Chambers, London &
New Chambers, Sydney
24 Lincoln's Inn Fields
London WC2A 3EG

Deeley, Caryn
BDO
55 Baker St, Marylebone
London W1U 7EU

Doerries, Chantal-Aimee QC
Atkin Chambers
1 Atkin Buildings, Gray's Inn
London WC1R 5AT

Dymond, Tony
Debevoise & Plimpton LLP
65 Gresham Street
London EC2V 7NQ

Ebere, Solomon
Independent Legal Practitioner
Flat 41 Gainsborough Studios North
1 Poole Street
London N15EB

Facenna, Gerry QC
Monckton Chambers
1 & 2 Raymond Buildings
Gray's Inn
London WC1R 5NR

Farren, Ania
Bryan Cave Leighton Paisner LLP
Adelaide House, London Bridge
London EC4R 9HA

Flannery, Louis
39 Essex Chambers
81 Chancery Lane
London WC2A 1DD

Gal, Daniel
Skadden, Arps, Slate, Meagher & Flom (UK) LLP
40 Bank Street, Canary Wharf
London E14 5DS

Gavaghan, Holly
Keating Chambers
15 Essex St
London WC2R 3AA

Ghaffar, Arshad
XXIV Old Buildings Chambers
24 Old Buildings Chambers
London WC2A 3UP

Giaretta, Benjamin
Mishcon de Reya
Africa House, 70 Kingsway
London WC2B TAH

Goddard, Andrew
Atkin Chambers
1 Atkin Buildings, Gray's Inn,
London WC1R 5AT

Godman, Camilla
The Chartered Institute of Arbitrators
12 Bloomsbury Square
London WCIA 2LP

Golden, Jeffrey
P.R.I.M.E. Finance
35 Elm Bank Gardens, Barnes
London SW13 0NU

Grief, David
Essex Court Chambers
24 Lincoln's Inn Fields
London WC2A 3EG

Griffith, Gavan
Essex Court Chambers
24 Lincoln's Inn Fields
London WC2A 3ED

van Haersolte-van Hof, Jacomijn
LCIA
70 Fleet Street
London
EC4Y 1EU

Halpern, Michaela
Queen Mary University College of London
School of International Arbitration
London WC2A 3JB

Heilbron, Hilary QC
Brick Court Chambers
7-8 Essex Street
London WC2R 3LD

Hiendl, Alex
Allen & Overy LLP
One Bishops Square
London E1 6AD

Hirst, Peter
Clyde & Co LLP
St Botolph Building
138 Houndsditch
London EC3A 7AR

Hodges, Paula QC
Herbert Smith Freehills LLP
Exchange House, Primrose St
London EC2A 2EG

Honey, Damian
HFW
65 Crutched Friars
London EC3N 2AE

Hooper, Katie
Oxford University Press
Great Clarendon Street
Oxford OX2 6DP

Hughes, Adrian QC
39 Essex Chambers
81 Chancery Lane
London WC2A1DD

Hunter, Ian
Essex Court Chambers
24 Lincoln's Inn Fields
London WC2A 3EG

Johnson, Colin
Charles River Associates
8 Finsbury Circus
London EC2M 7EA

Jones, Katie-Beth
Opus 2 International
5 New Street Square
London EC4A 3BF

Jones, Thomas
Global Arbitration Review
87 Lancaster Road
London W11 1QQ

Judge, John
39 Essex Chambers
81 Chancery Lane
London WC2A 1DD

Keane, Lucy
L A Keane Attorney Ltd.
71-75 Shelton Street
London WC2H 9JQ

Kenton, Maurice
Clyde & Co
St Botolph Building,
138 Houndsditch
London EC3A 7AR

Key, Paul
Essex Court Chambers
24 Lincoln's Inn Fields
London WC2A 3EG

Lawrence, Owen
39 Essex Chambers
81 Chancery Lane
London WC2A 1DD

Leaver, Peter
One Essex Court
Temple
London EC4Y 9AR

Lee, Tom
Global Arbitration Review
87 Lancaster Road
London W11 1QQ

Lew, Julian
20 Essex Street
20 Essex Street
London WC2R 3AL

Lidstrom, Tom
Linklaters
One Silk Street
London EC2Y 8HQ

Limond, Katrina
Allen & Overy LLP
One Bishops Square
London, E1 6AD

Marrin, John
Keating Chambers
15 Essex Street
London WC2R 3AA

Martin, Roy QC
Chambers of Steven Hockman QC
6 Pump Court, Temple
London EC4Y 7AR

Martinez, Lucy
Three Crowns LLP
New Fetter Place
8-10 New Fetter Lane
London EC4A 1AZ

Masters, Sara QC
20 Essex Street
20 Essex Street
London WC2R 3AL

Miles, Wendy
Debevoise & Plimpton LLC
65 Gresham Street
London EC2V 7NQ

Mohtashami, Reza
Three Crowns LLP
New Fetter Place
8-10 New Fetter Lane
London EC4 1AZ

Nairn, Karyl QC
Skadden, Arps, Slate, Meagher &
Flom (UK) LLP
40 Bank Street, Canary Wharf
London E14 5DS

Nappert, Sophie
3 Verulam Buildings
Gray's Inn Rd
London WC1R 5NT

Partasides, Constantine QC
ICCA Governing Board Member
Three Crowns LLP
New Fetter Place
8-10 New Fetter Lane
London EC4A 1AZ

Patchett-Joyce, Michael
Chambers
25 Church Row
London NW3 6UP

Patterson, Lindy QC
39 Essex Chambers
81 Chancery Lane
London WC2A 1DD

Pendell, Guy
CMS Law
78 Cannon Street
London EC4N 6AF

Pillai, Rajesh
3 Verulam Buildings
Gray's Inn Rd
London WC1R 5NT

Ramsey, Vivian
Sir Vivian Ramsey
The Old Vicarage, School Lane
Swanley Village, Kent BR8 7PJ

Reichert, Klaus SC
ICCA Governing Board Member
Brick Court Chambers
7-8 Essex Street
London WC2R 3LD

Rix, Bernard
20 Essex Street
20 Essex Street
London WC2R 3AL

Robertson, David
Berwin Leighton Paisner LLP
Adelaide House London Bridge
London EC4R 9HA

Rockall, Max
Squire Patton Boggs (UK) LLP
7 Devonshire Square
London EC2M 4YH

Rogers, Catherine
Oxford University Press
Great Clarendon Street
Oxford OX2 6DP

Saunders, Matthew
Ashurst
Broadwalk House 5 Appold Street
London EC2A 2AG

Schultz, Thomas
King's College London
Strand
London WC2R 2LS

Schwing, Mel
University of Cambridge
10 West Road
Cambridge CB3 9DZ

Selvaratnam, Vasanti QC
St Philips Stone
4 Field Court, Gray's Inn
London WC1R 5EF

Shankar, Ashwin
The Chambers of George A. Rebello
London

Sheppard, Audley QC
Clifford Chance LLP

10 Upper Bank Street
London E14 5JJ

Smith, Henry
One Essex Court
Temple
London EC4Y 9AR

Stanič, Ana
E&A Law Limited
42 Brook Street
London W1K 5DB

Swan, Nicola
Debevoise & Plimpton LLP
65 Gresham Street
London EC2V 7NQ

Taylor, Monty
Arnold & Porter Kaye
Scholer (UK) LLP
International Financial Centre
25 Old Broad St
London EC2N 1HQ

Thomas, David Brynmor
39 Essex Chambers
81 Chancery Lane
London WC2A 1DD

Tyce, Emma
Taylor and Francis
2-4 Park Square, Milton Park
Abingdon OX14 4RN

Weiniger, Matthew
Linklaters
One Silk Street
London EC2Y8HQ

Wolfe, Simon
Amsterdam & Partners LLP
139 Piccadilly
London W1J 7NU

Zaman, Rebecca
3 Verulam Buildings
Gray's Inn
London WC1R 5NT

Scotland

Farndale, Richard
Chartered Institute of Arbitrators
Scotland and
Burness Paull LLP
50 Lothian Road
Edinburgh EH3 9WJ

Jackson, Gordon
Faculty of Advocates
Advocates Library, Parliament House
Edinburgh EH1 1RF

Jardine, Derek
Conference Partners International
5 Semple Street
Edinburgh EH3 8BL

Mackenzie, Andrew
Scottish Arbitration Centre
Level 3, 125 Princes Street
Edinburgh EH2 4AD

MacNeill, Calum
Faculty of Advocates
14 Abercromby Place
Edinburgh EH3 6LB

Malone, Brandon
Scottish Arbitration Centre
Level 3, 125 Princes Street
Edinburgh EH2 4AD

Mulholland, John
Law Society of Scotland
Atria One, 144 Morrison Street
Edinburgh EH3 8EX

Prior, Sarah
Conference Partners International
5 Semple Street
Edinburgh EH3 8BL

Robb, Fiona
Law Society of Scotland
Atria One, 144 Morrison Street
Edinburgh EH3 8EX

United States

Abrahamson, Laura
AECOM
1999 Avenue of the Stars, 26th Floor
Los Angeles, CA 90067

Ahmad, Jawad
Private Law Clerk to
Judge Charles N. Brower
20 Essex Street
University of California, Berkeley
Washington, DC

Alexandrov, Stanimir
ICCA Governing Board Member
Stanimir A. Alexandrov PLLC
1501 K Street NW, Suite C-072
Washington, DC, 20005

Amirfar, Catherine
ICCA Governing Board Member
Debevoise & Plimpton LLP
919 Third Avenue
New York, NY 10022

Barkett, John
Shook, Hardy & Bacon LLP
201 S. Biscayne Boulevard, Suite 3200
Miami, FL 33131

Benton, Gary
Gary Benton Arbitration
228 Hamilton Avenue, 3rd Floor
Palo Alto, CA 94301

Bruno, Paul
Fluor Corporation
6700 Las Colinas Boulevardd
Dallas, TX 75225

Carlson, Hugh
Three Crowns LLP
3000 K. Street NW, Suite 101
Washington, DC 20007

Carska-Sheppard, Andrea
Workplace Options LLC
2912 Highwoods Boulevard
Suite 100
Raleigh, NC 27612

Chang, Eric
Chang Law
4470 West Sunset Boulevard no. 91856
Los Angeles, CA 90027

Clark, Michael
American Arbitration Association
120 Broadway, 21st Floor
New York, NY 10271

Cohen, Stephanie
49 South Elliott Place
Brooklyn, NY 11217

Di Rosa, Paolo
Arnold & Porter Kaye Scholer LLP
601 Massachusetts Avenue NW
Washington, DC, 20001

Donovan, Donald
Honorary President,
Honorary Vice President and
Advisory Member of ICCA
Debevoise & Plimpton LLP
919 Third Avenue
New York, NY 10022

Elul, Hagit Muriel
Hughes Hubbard & Reed LLP
One Battery Park Plaza
New York, NY 10004

Enix-Ross, Deborah
Debevoise & Plimption LLP
919 Third Avenue
New York, NY 10022

Franck, Susan
American University
Washington College of Law
4300 Nebraska Avenue NW
Washington, DC, 20016

Galloway, Patricia
Galloway Arbitration, Inc.
1750 Emerick Road
Cle Elum, WA 98922

González, Daniel
Hogan Lovells
600 Brickell Avenue, Suite 600
Miami, FL 33131

Grove, Rick
Rutter Associates
60 East 42nd Street
New York, NY 10165

Haile, Zewdineh B.
Addis Law Group LLP
1775 I Street NW, Suite 1150
Washington, DC, 20006

Hodgson, Melida
Foley Hoag LLP
1540 Broadway
New York, NY 10036

Hosking, James
Chaffetz Lindsey LLP
1700 Broadway, 33rd Floor
New York, NY 10019

Huebner, David
JAMS
555 W. 5th Street
Los Angeles, CA 90013

Johnson, India
American Arbitration Association
120 Broadway, 21st Floor
New York, NY 10271

Kalicki, Jean
ICCA Governing Board Member
Kalicki Arbitration
201 West 72nd Street, no. 6A
New York, NY 10023

Kantor, Mark
Independent Arbitrator
110 Maryland Avenue NE, Suite 311b
Washington, DC, 20002

Kern, Jackson
Addis Law Group LLP
1775 I Street NW, Suite 1150
Washington, DC, 20006

Kidane, Won
Seattle University
1215 E. Columbia
Seattle, WA 20850

Kinnear, Meg
ICCA Governing Board Member
ICSID
1818 H Street NW
Washington, DC, 20433

Lahlou, Yasmine
Chaffetz Lindsey LLP
1700 Broadway, 33rd Floor
New York, NY 10019

Lake, Jennifer
Independent Diplomat
45 East 20th Street
New York, NY 10003

Lamm, Carolyn
ICCA Governing Board Member
White & Case LLP
701 13th Street NW
Washington, DC, 20005

Maniatis, Alexis
The Brattle Group
1800 M Street NW, Suite 700N
Washington, DC, 20036

Marchili, Silvia
King & Spalding
1100 Louisiana Street
Houston, TX 20006

Micarelli, Carl
Debevoise & Plimpton LLP
919 Third Avenue
New York, NY 10022

Morril, Mark
MorrilADR
413 West 53rd Street
New York, NY 10019

Nelson, Timothy
Skadden, Arps, Slate, Meagher & Flom LLP
Four Times Square
New York, NY 12572

Pearsall, Patrick
Jenner& Block LLP
1099 New York Avenue
Suite 900
Washington, DC, 20001

Pettibone, Peter
Pettibone International ADR LLC
875 Third Avenue, Suite 2409
New York, NY 10022

Popova, Ina
Debevoise & Plimpton LLP
919 Third Avenue
New York, NY 10022

Prager, Dietmar
Debevoise & Plimpton LLP
919 Third Avenue
New York, NY 10022

Rassi, Justin
Debevoise & Plimpton LLP
919 Third Avenue
New York, NY 10022

Reid, Natalie
Debevoise & Plimpton LLP
919 Third Avenue
New York, NY 10022

Rogers, Catherine
Queen Mary, Penn State &
Arbitrator Intelligence
324 Katz Building
State College, PA 16801

Sahani, Victoria
ASU Sandra Day O'Connor
College of Law
MC 9520, 111 E. Taylor Street
Phoenix, AZ 85004-4467

Schill, James
Pegasus Global Holdings, Inc.
1750 Emerick Road
Cle Elum, WA 98922

Silberman, Mallory
Arnold & Porter Kaye Scholer LLP
601 Massachusetts Avenue NW
Washington, DC, 20001

Sinisterra, Laura
Debevoise & Plimpton LLP
919 Third Avenue
New York, NY 10022

Slate, William II
Advisory Member of ICCA
Dispute Resolution Data
PO Box 2034
Mt. Pleasant, SC 29465-2034

Strick, Stephen
Stephen S Strick ADR
501 Madison Avenue, Fourteenth Floor
New York, NY 10022

Strong, S.I.
University of Missouri
216 Hulston Hall
Columbia, MO 65211

Sussman, Edna
SussmanADR LLC
20 Oak Lane
Scarsdale, NY 10583

Tuchmann, Eric
American Arbitration Association
120 Broadway, 21st Floor
New York, NY 10271

Vietnam

Dang, Hop
Allens Hanoi Branch
Suite 401 Hanoi Towers
49 Hai Ba Trung
Hanoi, 10000

Nguyen, Manh Dzung
Dzungsrt & Associates LLC
Unit 1605
Saigon Riverside Office Center
2a-4a Ton Duc Thang Stree,
District 1, Ho Chi Minh City 70000

Zambia

Lumbwe, Bwalya
Incipio
20 Serval Road, Kabulonga
Lusaka 10101

INTERNATIONAL COUNCIL FOR COMMERCIAL ARBITRATION (ICCA)

Correspondence address:
ICCA Bureau
Peace Palace, Carnegieplein 2
Phone: + 31 70 302 2834
E-mail: bureau@arbitration-icca.org

LIST OF ICCA OFFICERS AND GOVERNING BOARD MEMBERS

SEPTEMBER 2019

OFFICERS

President

PROF. DR. GABRIELLE KAUFMANN-KOHLER (Geneva, Switzerland)
Professor Emerita, Geneva University Law School; Partner, Lévy Kaufmann-Kohler; Honorary President, Swiss Arbitration Association (ASA); Founder and Former Director, Geneva LL.M. in International Dispute Settlement (MIDS)

President-Elect

PROF. LUCY REED (Singapore)
Director, Centre for International Law (CIL), National University of Singapore; Member, ICC Governing Body; Member, SIAC Court; Member, LCIA Court; Panel of Arbitrators, ICSID; Former Chair, Institute for Transnational Arbitration; Former President, American Society of International Law

Vice Presidents

DR. JUAN FERNÁNDEZ-ARMESTO (Madrid, Spain)
Arbitrator, Armesto & Asociados; Member, Panel of Arbitrators, ICSID (designated by the Kingdom of Spain); Member, Court of the LCIA and DIAC; Vice-President, Joint Board of Appeal of the European Supervisory Authorities (ESMA, EBA and EIOPA); Chairman, Club Español del Arbitraje; Past President; Spanish Securities and Exchange Commission (CNMV) (1996-2000); past Vice-Chairman, IBA Arbitration Committee (2008-2009); Former Partner, Uría Menéndez (1983-1996); Former Chaired Professor of Commercial Law, Comillas University – ICADE, Madrid (1988-2009)

PROF. LUCY REED (Singapore)
[See details at President-Elect, p. 1141].

Treasurer

MR. EDUARDO SIQUEIROS (Mexico City, Mexico)
Independent Arbitrator; Former Partner, Hogan Lovells BSTL, S.C.; Member, Mexican Arbitration Institute (IMA); Member, Mexican Arbitration Committee (ICC); Panel of Arbitrators, ICSID

Executive Director

MS. LISE BOSMAN (The Hague, The Netherlands)
Senior Legal Counsel, Permanent Court of Arbitration; Executive Editor, ICCA; General Editor, The International Handbook on Commercial Arbitration; Adjunct Professor, University of Cape Town; Fellow, Association of Arbitrators (Southern Africa); Editorial Board, Tijdschrift voor Arbitrage; Series Editor, PCA Award Series

GOVERNING BOARD MEMBERS

DR. MOHAMED ABDEL RAOUF (Cairo, Egypt)
Partner and Head of the International Arbitration Group at Abdel Raouf Law Firm, Cairo-Egypt; Associate Professor at Université Paris 1 Panthéon-Sorbonne; Member of the Board of Trustees and the Advisory Committee of the Cairo Regional Centre for International Commercial Arbitration (CRCICA); Former Member of the Board of the Arbitration Institute of the Stockholm Chamber of Commerce (SCC); Former

Vice President of the International Federation of Commercial Arbitration Institutions (IFCAI); Former Director, CRCICA; CEDR Accredited Mediator; Arbitrator, Court of Arbitration for Sport (CAS); Conciliator designated by the President of the World Bank Group to serve on the Panel of Conciliators maintained by ICSID

MS. OLUFUNKE ADEKOYA, SAN (Lagos, Nigeria)

Head of Dispute Resolution and Litigation, ÆLEX; Fellow and Chartered Arbitrator, Chartered Institute of Arbitrators; Board Member, Lagos Court of Arbitration; Board Member, Cairo Regional Centre for International Commercial Arbitration; Panel Member, Kigali International Arbitration Centre; Advisory Board Member, Africa International Legal Awareness (AILA); Council Member, African Users Council of London Court of International Arbitration; Board Member, Scottish Arbitration Centre; Member, ArbitralWomen; Member, Nigerian National Committee, International Chamber of Commerce; Member, International Bar Association; Member, Business Recovery & Insolvency Practitioners Association of Nigeria; Member, Insolvency International; Member, Nigerian Bar Association

DR. STANIMIR A. ALEXANDROV (Washington, DC, USA)

Arbitrator in numerous cases administered by the International Centre for Settlement of Investment Disputes (ICSID), the International Chamber of Commerce (ICC), the London Court of International Arbitration (LCIA), and the Permanent Court of Arbitration (PCA), as well as ad hoc arbitrations under the UNCITRAL Rules; appointed to the ICSID Panel of Arbitrators; Member of the panel of arbitrators of the Hong Kong International Arbitration Center (HKIAC), the Dubai International Arbitration Centre (DIAC), the Chinese International Economic and Trade Arbitration Commission (CIETAC), and the Arbitration Center at the Institute of Modern Arbitration (Moscow)

MR. MAKHDOOM ALI KHAN (Karachi, Pakistan)

Senior Advocate, Supreme Court of Pakistan; Former Attorney General, Pakistan; Former Member, Court of the London Court of International Arbitration; Former Member of the Board, Dubai International Arbitration Centre; Member of the Board, AAA; Member, Panel of Arbitrators of SIAC and Asian International Arbitration Centre; designated as an arbitrator, ICSID panel

MS. CATHERINE AMIRFAR (New York, USA)

Litigation partner, Co-Chair of the Public International Law Group, and Member of the Management Committee, Debevoise & Plimpton LLP, focusing on public international law, international commercial and treaty arbitration, and international and complex commercial litigation; Former Counselor on International Law to the Legal Adviser at the US Department of State where she received the Superior Honor Award for her service; nominated as President-Elect of the American Society of

International Law; Member of the Council on Foreign Relations, the American Law Institute, and the Advisory Committee on International Law for the US Department of State

MR. JOHN BEECHEY CBE (Hong Kong SAR)

John Beechey has served as chairman, party-appointed arbitrator, or sole arbitrator on international arbitral tribunals in both "ad hoc" (including UNCITRAL) and institutional arbitrations under the Rules of all major arbitral institutions including, inter alia, the European Development Fund (EDF), ICC, ICDR/AAA, ICSID, LCIA, PCA, SIAC and Stockholm Chamber of Commerce

MR. DOAK BISHOP (Houston, USA)

Partner in King & Spalding's Houston office and Co-chair of the firm's International Arbitration Practice Group; listed in Tier 1 by Chambers Global, Chambers Latin America and Chambers USA

MS. ADRIANA BRAGHETTA (São Paulo, Brazil)

Co-Head of the arbitration team at LOBaptista Lawyers – SP; PhD from USP – University of São Paulo, Professor of Arbitration at CEU School of Law, São Paulo; Co-Founding Member and Former President, *Comitê Brasileiro de Arbitragem* – CBAr; Member, ILA International Arbitration Committee; Member, ICC Latin-American Arbitration Commission; Member, ICDR/AAA Board for Latin America; Member, Editorial Council, CBAr Journal, among others

MR. CAVINDER BULL (Singapore)

Chief Executive Officer, Drew & Napier LLC; Vice-President of the SIAC Court of Arbitration; Former Deputy Chairman of SIAC (2010 to 2017); Vice-President of the Asian Pacific Regional Arbitration Group (APRAG)

MS. TERESA CHENG, GBS, SC, JP (Hong Kong SAR)

Secretary of Justice of Hong Kong; Senior Counsel; Chair of the Hong Kong International Arbitration Centre; Past President of the Chartered Institute of Arbitrators; Past Vice-President of the ICC International Court of Arbitration; Visiting Professor of Law School of Tsinghua University, Beijing

MR. ANDREW CLARKE (Leatherhead, Surrey, United Kingdom)

General Counsel, ExxonMobil International Limited; Steering Committee Member and Past Chair, Corporate Counsels' International Arbitration Group; Member, Past Director and Past Court Member, London Court of International Arbitration; Member, Advisory Council to the Centre for Commercial Law Studies at Queen

Mary University of London; Member, Advisory Board for the Turkish Commercial Law Review; Bencher, Middle Temple (London)

JUDITH GILL QC (Singapore)
International arbitrator with extensive experience in matters involving construction, energy contracts, manufacturing, distributorship agreements and other commercial agreements, 20 Essex Street Chambers, Singapore; Former Partner and Former Head of the International Arbitration Group, Allen & Overy; President of the LCIA Court; Second female solicitor-advocate to be appointed QC in England

JUDGE DOMINIQUE HASCHER (Paris, France)
Judge, Supreme Judicial Court (France); International Judge, Supreme Court of Singapore; Past General Counsel and Deputy Secretary General, International Court of Arbitration of the International Chamber of Commerce (ICC); Hon. Bencher of Gray's Inn, London

MS. VERA VAN HOUTTE (Leuven, Belgium)
Independent Arbitrator; Former Partner, Stibbe; Vice-President, ICC Court of Arbitration; ICSID Panel arbitrator; Council Member, American Arbitration Association; Board of Directors Member, CEPANI; Member, Court of the Jerusalem Arbitration Centre; Former Member, Board of Trustees, Dubai International Arbitration Centre; Former Vice Chair of Arbitration Committee, IBA; Former lecturer in the Center for Postgraduate Legal Education of the law faculty of the University of Nijmegen, the Netherlands; Former Vice President, LCIA

ANDRÉS JANA (Santiago, Chile)
Partner, Bofill Mir & Alvarez Jana

MS. JEAN KALICKI (New York, USA)
Vice President, LCIA Court; ICC Commission; Board of Directors of SICANA, Inc. (ICC North America); AAA Council (Former Member, AAA Board of Directors); ICSID Panel of Arbitrators, ICDR/AAA, CPR, BVIIAC, SIAC, HKIAC, KCAB, Asian International Arbitration Centre; Former Adjunct Professor, Georgetown University Law Center; Former Adjunct Professor, American University Washington College of Law; Fellow, Chartered Institute of Arbitrators and College of Commercial Arbitrators; Editorial Boards of the ICSID Review and Global Arbitration Review

MR. VLADIMIR KHVALEI (Moscow, Russia)
Partner and Head of CIS Dispute Resolution Practice Group, Baker & McKenzie; Vice-President, ICC International Court of Arbitration; Member, LCIA; Chairman of the Board, Russian Arbitration Association; Chairman, Arbitration Commission of the Russian National Committee of the ICC; Board Member, International Arbitration Court at the Belarusian Chamber of Commerce and Industry; Board Member, Ukrainian Arbitration Association; Member, Polish Arbitration Association; Member, Austrian Arbitration Association; Former Vice Chair of Arbitration Committee, IBA

MS. MEG KINNEAR (Washington, DC, USA)
Secretary-General, International Centre for Settlement of Investment Disputes (ICSID); Former Senior General Counsel and Director General, Trade Law Bureau of Canada; Former Executive Assistant to the Deputy Minister of Justice of Canada; Counsel, Civil Litigation Section, Department of Justice Canada

MS. CAROLYN LAMM (Washington, DC, USA)
Partner, White & Case LLP; Co-Chair, International Arbitration Americas; Former President of the District of Columbia Bar and the American Bar Association; Chair of the Board of the American-Uzbekistan Chamber of Commerce; Member of the Board, American-Turkish Council and American Indonesian Chamber of Commerce; Member of ICSID Panel of Arbitrators (appointed by Uzbekistan); Member, ICDR International List; Former Member of the American Arbitration Association Executive Committee and Board; US Member of the NAFTA 2022 Committee; Member of the American Law Institute's Council and its Advisory Committee on Restatement on International Arbitration and a Counselor on the ALI Restatement 4th on Public International Law; Counselor to the Executive Board of ASIL; Visiting Professor teaching International Investment Arbitration, University of Miami, School of Law.

MS. MICHELLE MACPHEE (London, United Kingdom)
Managing Counsel, BP Legal's London-based Dispute Resolution Team; Head, BP Legal's International Arbitration Centre of Expertise; Former Counsel, Freshfields Bruckhaus Deringer

MS. LORETTA MALINTOPPI (Singapore)
Arbitrator, 39 Essex Chambers; former Member, ICC International Court of Arbitration; former Vice-President, ICC Court; Member, Council of the ICC Institute of World Business Law

MS. CAROLE MALINVAUD (Paris, France)
Partner and Co-Head of the international arbitration section, Gide in Paris; Chair, Gide Pro Bono Foundation

CHIEF JUSTICE SUNDARESH MENON (Singapore)
Chief Justice, Supreme Court of Singapore; Former Attorney-General, Singapore; Former Judicial Commissioner, Supreme Court of Singapore; Former Dy Chairman, Singapore International Arbitration Centre

MS. ZIA MODY (Mumbai, India)
Founder and Senior Partner, AZB & Partners; Deputy Chairman and a Non-Executive Director, HSBC Asia Pacific Board; Former Member, World Bank Administrative Tribunal; Former Vice-President and Member, LCIA; Arbitrator on the SIAC Panel; Member of various committees of the Confederation of Indian Industry; Member, Godrej Committee on Corporate Governance; Member, Reserve Bank of India Committee on Comprehensive Financial Services for Small Businesses and Low-Income Households

DR. MICHAEL MOSER (Hong Kong SAR)
International arbitrator, 20 Essex Street Chambers; Honorary Past Chairman, Hong Kong International Arbitration Centre; Former Member, LCIA Court; Former Member, SCC Arbitration Institute Board; Board Member, Singapore International Arbitration Centre (SIAC); Board Member, Vienna International Arbitral Centre (VIAC); Commission Member, CIETAC; Chartered Arbitrator and Fellow, Chartered Institute of Arbitrators; Former General Editor, Journal of International Arbitration

JUSTICE ELLEN GRACIE NORTHFLEET (Rio de Janeiro, Brazil)
Attorney in private practice and Arbitrator; Partner, Ellen Gracie Advogados Associados; Former Chief-Justice, Brazilian Federal Supreme Court; Former Presiding Judge, National Justice Council; Vice-President, Ciesp/Fiesp Arbitration Chamber; Board Member, Brazilian Committee of Arbitration (CBAr); Board Member, International Council of Arbitration for Sport; Board Member, World Justice Project; Member, World Bank's Sanctions Board

MS. YOSHIMI OHARA (Tokyo, Japan)
Partner, Nagashima Ohno & Tsunematsu, Tokyo, Japan; Vice-President of the ICC International Court of Arbitration; Board Member, Japan Association of Arbitrators (JAA); Board Member, Swiss Arbitration Association (ASA); Former Vice President, London Court of International Arbitration (LCIA)

CONSTANTINE PARTASIDES QC (London, United Kingdom)
Partner, Three Crowns, LLP; appeared as counsel on some of the largest commercial arbitrations of the last decade, many of which relate to the energy sector; named as one of the "top 20" individuals in the world of arbitration each year since 2011 in "Who's Who" of Commercial Arbitration; co-author of the fourth, fifth and sixth editions of *Redfern and Hunter on International Arbitration*; Solicitor-Advocate (Higher Courts Civil); appointed Queen's Counsel in 2014

PROF. DR. MICHAEL PRYLES AO, PBM (Toorak, Victoria, Australia)
Founder President, SIAC Court of Arbitration; Former Chairman, SIAC Board of Directors; Past President, Australian Centre for International Commercial Arbitration; Former Member, Board of Trustees of the Dubai International Arbitration Centre; Former Chairman, ICC Australia; Foundation President, Asia Pacific Regional Arbitration Group; Former Member, LCIA Court; Former Commissioner, United Nations Compensation Commission

KLAUS REICHERT SC (London, United Kingdom)
Barrister, Bar of England & Wales

PROF. DR. KLAUS SACHS (Munich, Germany)
Senior Partner, CMS Hasche Sigle; Board Member, Swiss Arbitration Association (ASA); Member, Board of Directors, German Institution of Arbitration (DIS); Former Vice-President, ICC International Court of Arbitration; Former Vice-President, London Court of International Arbitration; Member, ICSID Panel of Arbitrators; Honorary Professor on international arbitration law, Ludwig-Maximilian-University of Munich; Co-editor, German Arbitration Journal

DR. ANKE SESSLER (Frankfurt am Main, Germany)
Partner, Skadden, Arps, Slate, Meagher & Flom LLP; Former Chief Counsel Litigation, Siemens AG; Member, DIS Advisory Board; Member, ICC Commission on Arbitration; Member, ICC National Committee for Germany; Member, AAA Board of Directors; Member, ASA Board; Former Member, IBA Arbitration Committee; Former Member, Panel of Conciliators, ICSID

PROF. HI-TAEK SHIN (Seoul, Korea)
Chairman of KCAB INTERNATIONAL, the international arm of Korean Commercial Arbitration Board; teaches the resolution of commercial and investment disputes arising from cross border transactions at Seoul National University since 2007; Former Partner of Kim & Chang; regularly sits as an arbitrator both in international investment treaty arbitrations and international commercial arbitrations; LL.M. and J.S.D, Yale Law School; LL.B. and LL.M, Seoul National University

DR. JIANLONG YU (Beijing, People's Republic of China)
Vice-Chairman and Secretary General, China International Economic and Trade Arbitration Commission (CIETAC); Vice-Chairman, China Maritime Arbitration Commission (CMAC); President, Asia Pacific Regional Arbitration Group; Vice-Chairman, China Academy of Arbitration Law (CAAL)

JUDGE ABDULQAWI AHMED YUSUF (The Hague, The Netherlands)
President, International Court of Justice; Member, ICSID panel of arbitrators; Member, Institute of International Law (*Institut de droit international*); Member, Board of Trustees, PCA Financial Assistance Fund

DR. EDUARDO ZULETA (Bogotá, Colombia)
Vice-President, ICC Court; Past Chair, IBA Arbitration Committee; Vice-Chair, Institute for Transnational Arbitration (ITA); Past Member of the Court of LCIA; Member, ICSID Panel of Arbitrators; Chair, Latin American Arbitration Association (ALARB); Member, ICC Institute of World Business Law

Honorary Presidents

PROF. DR. ALBERT JAN VAN DEN BERG (Brussels, Belgium)
Partner, Hanotiau & van den Berg (Brussels, Belgium); Past President, ICCA; Immediate Past General Editor, ICCA Publications; Past President, Netherlands Arbitration Institute; Professor Emeritus, Erasmus University, Rotterdam; Visiting Professor, Georgetown Law, Washington DC, and Tsinghua University, Beijing; Member, Amsterdam and Brussels Bars

THE HON. GIORGIO BERNINI (Bologna, Italy)
Former Minister of Foreign Trade and Member of Parliament; Former Member, Italian Antitrust Authority; Professor, University of Bologna, Chair of Arbitration and International Commercial Law; President, Association for the Teaching and Study of Arbitration and International Trade Law (AISA); Member, Executive Committee, Italian Arbitration Association; Senior Partner, Studio Bernini e Associati

MR. DONALD FRANCIS DONOVAN (New York, USA)
Co-Head, International Disputes Group, Debevoise & Plimpton LLP; Adjunct Professor, New York University School of Law; Alternate US Member, ICC International Court of Arbitration; Former President, American Society of International Law; Former Chair, Institute for Transnational Arbitration; Former Chair, U.S. National Committee, ICC International Court of Arbitration; Member of the Board of Directors and Chair of the Litigation Committee, Human Rights First

DR. GEROLD HERRMANN (Vienna, Austria)
Former Secretary, United Nations Commission on International Trade Law (UNCITRAL); Honorary Professor, University of Vienna

MR. FALI S. NARIMAN (New Delhi, India)
President Emeritus, Bar Association of India; Honorary Member, International Commission of Jurists; Past President, Law Association for Asia and the Pacific (LAWASIA); Member, Court of the LCIA; Past Vice Chairman, International Court of Arbitration of the International Chamber of Commerce (ICC); Past Co-Chair, Human Rights Institute of the International Bar Association (IBA); Senior Advocate, Supreme Court of India

PROF. JAN PAULSSON (Washington, DC, USA)
Former General Editor, ICCA International Handbook on Commercial Arbitration; Michael Klein Distinguished Scholar Chair, University of Miami School of Law; Partner, Three Crowns LLP; Past Vice-President, ICC Court; Past President, LCIA

Honorary Vice Presidents

MR. MICHAEL HWANG, SC (Singapore)
Former High Court Judge (Fixed Term), Singapore; Senior Counsel, Singapore; Former Member, Permanent Court of Arbitration; Chartered Arbitrator; Former Adjunct Professor, National University of Singapore; Board Member, Swiss Arbitration Association (ASA); Former Vice Chair, Committee D, International Bar Association; Former Member and Vice Chair, ICC International Court of Arbitration; Former Council Member, International Council of Arbitration for Sport (ICAS); Former Member, LCIA; Chief Justice, Dubai International Financial Centre; Former Trustee, Dubai International Arbitration Centre Courts; Member of Advisory Boards, Singapore International Arbitration Centre and Hong Kong International Arbitration Centre; Former President, Law Society of Singapore; Non-Resident Ambassador of Singapore to Switzerland (Former) and Argentina (current)

DDR. WERNER MELIS (Vienna, Austria)
Of Counsel Baier, Attorneys at Law, Vienna; international arbitrator; lecturer on international arbitration, Vienna University; Former President, International Arbitral Centre of the Austrian Federal Economic Chamber (VIAC); Past Vice President, London Court of International Arbitration (LCIA)

MS. TINUADE OYEKUNLE (Lagos, Nigeria)
Barrister and Solicitor, Supreme Court of Nigeria; Arbitrator and Notary Public; Member, Association of Arbitrators of Nigeria; Fellow, Chartered Arbitrator of the Chartered Institute of Arbitrators, London; Member, Arbitration Committee of the Lagos Chamber of Commerce; Member, Panel Membership Group (PMG), Chartered Institute of Arbitrators, London; Former Chairman, Education & Training Committee of the Chartered Institute of Arbitrators, London; Former Member, Board of Management of the Chartered Institute of Arbitrators, London; Regional Representative for Promotion of Arbitration in the West African Region; Past Chairman, Chartered Institute of Arbitrators, Nigeria Branch, and current member of the Executive Committee of the Branch; Former Member, London Court of International Arbitration; Correspondent, UNIDROIT; Member Board of Directors, Kigali International Arbitration Centre

MR. DONALD FRANCIS DONOVAN (New York, USA)
[Honorary President, Honorary Vice-President and Advisory Board Member; see details at p. 1149]

Honorary Secretaries General

MR. ULF FRANKE (Stockholm, Sweden)
Honorary Chairman, Arbitration Institute of the Stockholm Chamber of Commerce (SCC); Past Secretary General, SCC; Past President, International Federation of Commercial Arbitration Institutions (IFCAI)

MR. ANTONIO R. PARRA (Washington, DC, USA)
Past Secretary General, ICCA; Past Deputy Secretary-General and Legal Adviser, International Centre for Settlement of Investment Disputes (ICSID); Fellow, Chartered Institute of Arbitrators; Consultant, World Bank

Advisory Members

MR. CECIL ABRAHAM (Kuala Lumpur, Malaysia)
Fellow, Chartered Institute of Arbitrators; Fellow, Malaysian Institute of Arbitrators; Fellow, Singapore Institute of Arbitrators; Fellow, Australian Centre for International Commercial Arbitration Limited; Member, International Chamber of Commerce (ICC) Commission on Arbitration; Member, Advisory Panel of the Asian International Arbitration Centre; Past Chairman, Chartered Institute of Arbitrators Malaysia Branch; Past Member, LCIA; Past President, Inter-Pacific Bar Association; Past Vice President, Asia Pacific Regional Arbitration Group (APRAG); Past Deputy

President, Malaysian Institute of Arbitrators; Past Vice Chair, Committee D, IBA; Senior Partner, Cecil Abraham and Partners

PROF. PIERO BERNARDINI (Rome, Italy)
Former Member, Court of the London Court of International Arbitration; designated by Italy as an arbitrator, ICSID panel; Member of the Advisory Board, ASA Bulletin; Member Comité Scientifique, Revue de l'arbitrage; past Professor of Arbitration Law, LUISS University, Rome; Former President, Italian Arbitration Association; Past Vice-President, ICC International Court of Arbitration

PROF. DR. KARL-HEINZ BÖCKSTIEGEL (Bergisch-Gladbach, Germany)
Professor Emeritus of International Business Law, University of Cologne; Honorary Chairman and Past Chairman, German Institution of Arbitration (DIS); Past Patron, Chartered Institute of Arbitrators; Past President, International Law Association (ILA); Past President, LCIA; Past President, Iran-United States Claims Tribunal, The Hague; Past Panel Chairman, United Nations Compensation Commission

PROF. DR. NAEL G. BUNNI (Dublin, Ireland)
Past President, Chartered Institute of Arbitrators; Past Member, Board of Trustees and Past Chairman, Executive Committee, Dubai International Arbitration Centre; Past Member, LCIA Board of Directors; Visiting Professor in Construction Law and Contract Administration, Trinity College, Dublin; Chartered Engineer and Chartered Registered Arbitrator

PROF. BERNARDO M. CREMADES (Madrid, Spain)
Professor, Faculty of Law, Madrid University; Fellow, CIArb; Founding Partner, B. Cremades y Asociados; Admitted Madrid, Paris and Brussels Bar Associations; Former President, Spanish Court of Arbitration; Panel of Arbitrators of ICSID by appointment of the Kingdom of Spain; Former Vice President, LCIA; Former President, Institute of Global Arbitration Research; Former President, IBA Committee of International Arbitration

MR. DUSHYANT DAVE (New Delhi, India)
Senior Advocate at the Supreme Court of India; Member of the Board, American Arbitration Association; Former Member, LCIA; Former Vice Chair, Arbitration Committee, IBA; Former Member, National Legal Services Authority of India (NALSA)

M[E] YVES DERAINS (Paris, France)
Partner of Derains & Gharavi, Former Chairman of the Comité Français de l'Arbitrage and Co-Chairman of the ICC Working Group on the reduction of costs and time in international Arbitration; Past Secretary General, ICC International Court of Arbitration; Chairman, ICC Institute of World Business Law; Member of the Paris Bar

PROF. DR. RADOMIR DJUROVIČ (Belgrade, Serbia)
Former President, Arbitration Court of Yugoslavia; Professor of International Commercial Law, Belgrade University

MR. DONALD FRANCIS DONOVAN (New York, USA)
[Honorary President, Honorary Vice-President and Advisory Board Member of ICCA; see details at p. 1149]

THE HONOURABLE L. YVES FORTIER, PC, CC, OQ, QC (Montréal, Canada)
Sole practitioner, Cabinet Yves Fortier, Montréal; Former Chairman Emeritus and Senior Partner, Ogilvy Renault Montréal; Past President, LCIA; Former Ambassador and Permanent Representative of Canada to the United Nations; Former ad hoc Judge, International Court of Justice; Chairman, Sanctions Board of the World Bank; Member, Security and Intelligence Review Committee of Canada; Resident arbitrator, Arbitration Place Toronto; Member, 20 Essex Court Chambers

MR. ULF FRANKE (Stockholm, Sweden)
[Honorary Secretary General of ICCA; see details at p. 1151]

PROF. EMMANUEL GAILLARD (Paris, France)
Visiting Professor of Law, Yale Law School; Chairman, International Arbitration Institute

PROF. BERNARD HANOTIAU (Brussels, Belgium)
Member, Brussels and Paris Bars; Professor Emeritus of International Dispute Resolution, University of Louvain; Vice-Chairman, Board of Trustees of the Dubai International Arbitration Center (DIAC); Member, Court of the Singapore International Arbitration Center (SIAC); Member, Hong Kong International Arbitration Center International Advisory Board (HKIAC); Former Vice President, LCIA; Former Vice-Chairman, Institute of Transnational Arbitration; Former Vice-Chairman, CEPANI (Belgium)

DR. GEROLD HERRMANN (Vienna, Austria)
[Honorary President of ICCA; see details at p. 1150]

PROF. MARTIN HUNTER (London, United Kingdom)
Chartered Arbitrator, Essex Court Chambers, London; Former solicitor and partner, Freshfields (1967-1994); Former Chairman, Dubai International Arbitration Centre (2005-2012); Former member, ICC's International Court of Arbitration; Former member, LCIA Court; Emeritus Professor, Nottingham Trent University

DR. MICHAEL HWANG, SC (Singapore)
[Honorary Vice President of ICCA; see details at p. 1150]

MR. NEIL KAPLAN. CBE, QC, SBS (Hong Kong, SAR)
Former Judge, High Court, Hong Kong; Past Chairman, Hong Kong International Arbitration Centre; Past President, The Chartered Institute of Arbitrators; Member, ICC Court; Honorary Professor, City University of Hong Kong

DR. FATHI KEMICHA (Tunis, Tunisia)
Avocat à la Cour, Member of the Bars of Paris (Honorary) and Tunisia; Former Member, International Law Commission of the United Nations; Former Chair and Member, World Bank Group Sanctions Board; Member, Board of Trustees, Dubai International Arbitration Centre; First appointed Secretary General, Constitutional Court of the Kingdom of Bahrain; Former Vice President, LCIA; Former Vice President, ICC Commission on Arbitration

MR. KAP-YOU (KEVIN) KIM (Seoul, Korea)
Head and founder of Bae, Kim & Lee LLC's International Arbitration & Litigation Practice Group; Vice-President and Court Member of the ICC International Court of Arbitration; Co-chair of Audit Committee of the International Council for Commercial Arbitration (ICCA); Secretary General of ICCA (2010-2014); Chair of the International Arbitration Committee, Korea Commercial Arbitration Board (KCAB); Vice President of the Korean Arbitrators Association; Panel of Arbitrators, ICSID, ICC, LCIA, AAA(ICDR), SIAC, HKIAC, LMAA, BAC, JCAA, UNCITRAL and KCAB

PROF. ALEXANDER S. KOMAROV (Moscow, Russia)
Head of International Private Law Chair, Russian Academy of Foreign Trade; Member of the Presidium, International Commercial Arbitration Court at the Russian Federation Chamber of Commerce and Industry

THE HON. MARC LALONDE, C.P., O.C., C.R. (Montréal, Canada)
Former *ad hoc* Judge, International Court of Justice; Former Minister of Justice and Attorney General; Former Minister of Energy, Mines and Resources; Former Minister of Finance; Former President, LCIA North American Users Committee

DDR. WERNER MELIS (Vienna, Austria)
[Honorary Vice President of ICCA; see details at p.1150]

MR. CARLOS NEHRING NETTO (São Paulo, Brazil)
Founder, Nehring & Associados – Advocacia; Former Member, ICC International Court of Arbitration; Member, London Court of International Arbitration

MS. TINUADE OYEKUNLE (Lagos, Nigeria)
[Honorary Vice President of ICCA; see details at p. 1151]

PROF. WILLIAM W. PARK (Cohasset, USA)
Professor of Law, Boston University; General Editor, Arbitration International; Past President, LCIA; Past Chairman, ABA Committee on International Commercial Dispute Resolution

THE HON. ANDREW JOHN ROGERS, QC (Sydney, Australia)
Former Chief Judge, Commercial Division, Supreme Court of New South Wales; Adjunct Professor, University of Technology, Sydney; Chairman, National Dispute Centre, Sydney

DR. JOSÉ LUIS SIQUEIROS (Mexico City, Mexico)
Past President, Mexican Academy of International Commercial Arbitration; Past President, Inter-American Bar Association; Past Chairman, Inter-American Juridical Committee (OAS)

MR. WILLIAM K. SLATE II (Washington, DC, USA)
Arbitrator and ADR consultant; Senior Visiting Fellow, Duke University Law School; Past President and Chief Executive Officer, American Arbitration Association; Founder, International Centre for Dispute Resolution (ICDR); for fourteen years was an invited member of the UNCITRAL Arbitration Working Group, and a member of the Secretary of State's Advisory Committee on Private International Law; authored forty-two published articles on arbitration, mediation, data, and culture in international conflict management

PROF. HOUZHI TANG (Beijing, People's Republic of China)
Honorary Vice Chairman, CIETAC; Vice Chairman, CCPIT/CCOIC Beijing Conciliation Centre; Professor, Law School of the People's University of China; Visiting Professor, Amoy University School of Law; Arbitration Adviser, UN International Trade Centre; Fellow and Chartered Arbitrator, Chartered Institute of Arbitrators; Former Court Member, LCIA; Honorary Professor, Hong Kong City University School of Law; Former Vice President, IFCAI

PROF. YASUHEI TANIGUCHI (Tokyo, Japan)
Judge of the Singapore International Commercial Court; Former Member, Appellate Body of the World Trade Organization Dispute Settlement Body; Special Advisor, Japan Commercial Arbitration Association; Professor Emeritus, Kyoto University; Former President, Japan Association of Arbitrators; Of Counsel, Matsuo & Kosugi

PROF. DR. GUIDO SANTIAGO TAWIL (Buenos Aires, Argentina)
Professor, University of Buenos Aires School of Law; Former Chairman, Latin American Arbitration Association (ALARB); Former Co-Chair, IBA Arbitration Committee; Former Council Member, IBA Legal Practice Division; Former Court Member, LCIA; Former Member, Institute for Transnational Arbitration Academic Council; Member, ICC Latin American Arbitrators Committee; Member, ICC Institute of World Business Law; Senior Partner, M. & M. Bomchil

PROF. PIERRE TERCIER (Fribourg, Switzerland)
Honorary Chairman, International Court of Arbitration of the International Chamber of Commerce; Professor Emeritus, Law Faculty, University of Fribourg; Former Chairman, Swiss Antitrust Commission; Panel of Arbitrators, ICSID (Chairman list)

MR. V. V. VEEDER, QC (London, United Kingdom)
Arbitrator; Visiting Professor on Investment Arbitration, Dickson Poon School of Law, King's College London

THE HON. S. AMOS WAKO, FCIARB, SC (Nairobi, Kenya)
Former Attorney General, Republic of Kenya; Former Chairman, Arbitration Tribunal, Kenya Chamber of Commerce and Industry; Arbitrator, Vienna Convention on Law of Treaties, Centre for Settlement of Investment Disputes; Former Vice President, LCIA-Africa Region; Former Chairman, Law Society of Kenya; Former Member, International Advisory Committee of the World Intellectual Property Organization (WIPO) Centre for Settlement of Disputes; Former Commission Member, International Commission of Jurists; Former Deputy Secretary General, IBA; Former Secretary General, African Bar Association; Former Senior

Partner, Kaplan & Stratton; Former President, Asian-African Legal Consultative Organisation; Former Member, International Law Commission

DR. SHENGCHANG WANG (Beijing, People's Republic of China)
Past Vice Chairman and past Secretary General, CIETAC; Past Vice Chairman, China Maritime Arbitration Commission (CMAC); Senior Consultant, Beijing Hui Zhong Law Firm, China

SIR DAVID A.R. WILLIAMS KNZM, QC (Auckland, New Zealand)
Barrister, Member of New Zealand and English Bars; Chartered Arbitrator; President of the Cook Islands Court of Appeal; Former Judge of the High Court of New Zealand; Former Chief Justice of the Cook Islands; Former Judge, Court of Dubai International Financial Centre; Past President, Arbitrators and Mediators Institute of New Zealand; Former Member, ICC Court of International Arbitration; Former Member, LCIA; Board of Directors, Former Member, American Arbitration Association; Honorary Professor of Law, University of Auckland, New Zealand

MS. ARIEL YE (Shenzhen, People's Republic of China)
Partner, King & Wood Mallesons Shenzhen office; Member of China Bar Association; Member of the Court of SIAC; Former Member of the Council of LCIA; Arbitrator of CIETAC, HKIAC, SIAC and AAA; Co-chair of Asia Pacific Arbitration Group of IBA